Baseball Prospectus 2005

David Cameron • Will Carroll • James Click
Clay Davenport • Steven Goldman • Gary Huckabay
Rany Jazayerli • Chris Kahrl • Jonah Keri • Dave Pease
Dayn Perry • Joe Sheehan • Nate Silver • Ryan Wilkins
Keith Woolner • Derek Zumsteg

WORKMAN PUBLISHING • NEW YORK

Published simultaneously in Canada by Thomas Allen & Son, Limited.

Library of Congress Cataloging-in-Publication Data is available.

ISBN-13: 978-0-7611-3578-4
ISBN-10: 0-7611-3578-2

Workman books are available at special discounts when purchased in bulk for premiums and sales promotions as well as for fund-raising or educational use. Special editions or book excerpts can also be created to specification. For details, contact the Special Sales Director at the address below.

Design by Barbara Balch
Cover design by Paul Gamarello

Workman Publishing Company, Inc.
708 Broadway
New York, NY 10003-9555
www.workman.com

Printed in the U.S.A.
First printing January 2005

10 9 8 7 6 5 4 3 2 1

Contents

Foreword by *Nate Silver* v

For Rookie Readers of *Baseball Prospectus* by *Dayn Perry* vii

Tools

Statistical Introduction 1
by *Keith Woolner, Clay Davenport, and Nate Silver*

National League

Arizona Diamondbacks 7
Atlanta Braves 23
Chicago Cubs 38
Cincinnati Reds 57
Colorado Rockies 76
Florida Marlins 91
Houston Astros 105
Los Angeles Dodgers 119
Milwaukee Brewers 134
New York Mets 151
Philadelphia Phillies 165
Pittsburgh Pirates 183
St. Louis Cardinals 201
San Diego Padres 218
San Francisco Giants 235
Washington Nationals 252

American League

Anaheim Angels 269
Baltimore Orioles 287
Boston Red Sox 304
Chicago White Sox 322
Cleveland Indians 338
Detroit Tigers 355
Kansas City Royals 372
Minnesota Twins 391
New York Yankees 408
Oakland Athletics 427
Seattle Mariners 444
Tampa Bay Devil Rays 460
Texas Rangers 478
Toronto Blue Jays 495

Fungoes

Station to Station: The Expensive Art of Baserunning by *James Click* 511

An Analytical Framework for Win Expectancy by *Keith Woolner* 520

Life, Death, and Zombies by *Derik Zumsteg* 534

Top 50 Prospects by *Rany Jazayerli and Baseball Prospectus* 539

Team Name Key and Park Factors by *Clay Davenport* 554

Index 559

Biographies 567

Foreword

by Nate Silver

At Baseball Prospectus, we will always remember 2004 for one marvelous victory and one unfathomable loss.

The victory, of course, is that belonging to the Boston Red Sox, who won their first World Championship in 86 years. We aren't alone in celebrating Boston's victory, which was the result, like any championship, of a lot of good fortune and a lot of hard work. But it was also the result of the Red Sox's openness toward new modes of thinking in baseball, their openness toward using the sort of analysis and methodologies that we have been touting in *Baseball Prospectus* since our founding in 1996. The Red Sox, it must be said, are not a "stathead team." We would do certain things differently than they have done, and we have criticized their decision-making many times over, including on matters as fundamental as the Nomar Garciaparra/Orlando Cabrera trade.

What the Red Sox are, rather, are a modern team—a modern business—in an industry that prides itself on its reverence for tradition, and is inherently suspicious of new ideas, whatever their origin. The Red Sox are a modern team because they fully understand that, in the information age, the organization with the best information is going to win, at least more often than not. That information might come from a scout, a manager, an executive, a database, an agent, a newspaper, a business prospectus, a reference book, a computer program, an analyst, a player, or an audio-visual system. It might even come even come from *Baseball Prospectus.* But wherever its source, the Red Sox's emphasis has been taking that information on its own accord, understanding its merits and its limitations, and making a good-faith effort to make the best possible business and baseball decisions as a result. Other major professional sports franchises have been open to accounting for new sources of information. But few of them have done so as creatively or as completely as the Red Sox have, and none of them have won their sport's championship.

This is a book of information. Not just any information, but good information, the sort of information that helps you build a championship-caliber baseball club, whether you're playing in the American League or the office fantasy league. This book relies heavily on our statistical tools, like Keith Woolner's VORP, Clay Davenport's translations, or PECOTA, our state-of-the-art projection system. But in the process of preparing the book, we talk to innumerable scouts, executives, and journalists. And we watch the game. The number of baseball games watched by the 16 people whose names you see on the back cover numbers in the tens of thousands.

We're trying to do exactly what the Red Sox are trying to do—gather as much information as we can find, process it, interpret it, and try to discern its meaning. When we think the conventional wisdom about a certain player is wrong, we'll tell you that. When we have reason to believe that he's been misinterpreted by our statistical tools, we'll tell you that as well. The people who write this book are experts at interpreting information, and have used that ability to do everything from forecasting weather patterns to starting multi-million dollar companies. Since the subject in this case is baseball, we have tremendous fun in doing it, and we hope that you'll have just as much fun reading about it.

We will also always remember 2004 for the day of Friday, May 21. That is the day we learned that Doug Pappas had died. Doug was an author of *Baseball Prospectus,* and this book is worse for his absence. But more importantly, he was a friend to the entire baseball community. Doug's specialty was analyzing the economics and the business of baseball, and he did so with a lawyer's precision, an author's persuasiveness, and a fan's sense of fairness and compassion. He epitomized our belief in taking information and making it useful. I know it's silly, but I would like to think that, in some small way, the players and owners averted a strike in 2002 in part because of the information and writings that Doug made available. This book is dedicated to Doug's memory, and to his loving mother, Carolyn.

We'd like to thank you for purchasing *Baseball Prospectus 2005,* and we trust that your copy will become as dog-eared and coffee-stained as our own. As a result of you, our customers, Baseball Prospectus has become the best-selling book of its kind. We have been able to invest the profits from *Baseball Prospectus* and its companion Web site (http://www.baseballprospectus.com) into developing new technologies and gathering new writing talent, and into getting our products into the hands of even more people. The result is a positive feedback in which the product continues to get better, and the influence of people who think like you do and think like we do continues to grow. Next year will mark our 10th anniversary, and it is surely only a matter of months before we are criticized by some not for being too modern, but for being too traditional. Our job is to make sure we continue to meet and exceed your expectations, even while the entire baseball world is rapidly growing smarter.

We have made a few enemies along the way, but mostly we have made a lot of friends. With that in mind, we'd like to thank some of the people that have made this book possible. You can cue the Oscar music if you like, but the truth is that this list is far too short, and will almost certainly contain some unintentional and embarrassing omissions. Our heartfelt thanks go out to Grady Fuson, Paul DePodesta, Eddie Bane, Ken Forsch, Gary Hughes, Voros McCracken, Dan O'Dowd, Scott Boras, Tyler Pope, Paul Mahler, John Abbamondi, Billy Beane, David Forst, Bryn Alderson, John Sickels, Debbie Gallas, Maria Jacinto, Michael Wolverton, Sherri Nichols, Eddie Epstein, Josh Byrnes, Tod Johnson, Peter Gammons, Alan Schwarz, Ron Antinoja, George Foster (the professor, not the slugger), Scott Davis, Jeff Smith, Randy Hood, Debra Scherber, Greg May, Rob Neyer, Sandy Alderson, Tony Bernazard, Jeff Moorad, Jon Sciambi, Dave Van Horne, Joe Bohringer, Kevin Towers, Luis Garcia, Brad Kullman, Mitch Melnick, Cathy Newton, Shaun Starr, Gabriel Morency, Ryen Russillo, J. P. Ricciardi, Keith Law, Terry Ryan, Dr. Glenn Fleisig, Tom House, Fred Claire, Mark Cuban, Jim McDowell, Joe Borchard, Mike Wilkerson, Craig Counsell, Bill Bavasi, Jon Weisman, Rich Lederer, Jeff Erickson, Tim Schuler, Chris Liss, Scott Pianowski, Michael Salfino, Stan Conte, Jon Daniels, Jamey Newberg, Chris Hand, Scot Hughes, Daniel Valois, Derek Marinos, Scott Nelson, Samatha Newby, Blake Kirkman, Jayson Stark, Theo Epstein, Richard Rosen, Ken Zajac, Ruben Amaro Jr., Jim Hendry, Scott Reifert, Tim Marchman, Mike Woodsworth, Matt Oshinsky, Ivan Dee, Daniel Habib, Mike Smith, Geoff Silver, Josh Orenstein, Chris Antonetti, Tim Purpura, Sydelle Kramer, Sam Stoloff, Chris Gessel, Michael Lewis, Bruce Miles, Aaron Schatz, Stacey Alper, Allen Barra, Gary Gillette, Pete Palmer, Stuart Shea, Peter Workman, Tom Tippett, Zach Manprin, Scott McCauley, Scott Boras, Carlos Lugo, David Schoenfield, Josh Levin, Don Rodgers, Mark Shapiro, Sean Lahman, David Leonhardt, Mark McClusky, Tom Gorman, Jay Jaffe, Christian Ruzich, Alex Belth, Alex Ciepley, Neil deMause, Jim Baker, John Hollinger, Jeff Hildebrand, Greg Spira, Mark Armour, Chaim Bloom, Zack Wolf, Jason Grady, Sean Passainisi, Susan Graham, Austin Johnson, Adam Katz, Cliff Roscow, Dave Kirsch, Jason Karegeannes, Steve Lin, Jeff Barton, William Burke, Bill James, Cory Schwartz, Rob Leibowitz, Kevin Goldstein, Jim Callis, Chris Schofield, Louie Belina, Brian Kenny, and Mark Wolfson.

Nate Silver
Chicago, IL
January 10, 2005

For Rookie Readers of *Baseball Prospectus*

by Dayn Perry

If you're anything like me, you probably cut your statistical teeth by studying whatever you found on the back of a baseball card, on televised games, or what you saw on the scoreboard during trips to the park. In other words, you were probably weaned on batting average, home runs and RBI for hitters and wins, losses and ERA for pitchers (with saves added for relievers). Those metrics have been a part of baseball parlance since time immemorial, so it's hardly surprising that they're still very much with us. But there's a problem. Those reassuring measures are deeply flawed and, in isolation, tell you precious little about how a player is truly performing.

In this book, you'll rarely find batting average mentioned unless it's in the presence of on-base percentage and slugging percentage, two manifestly superior traditional statistics that flesh out the gaps in batting average rather nicely. If you see a pitcher's wins and losses herein, they'll be put through the translation ringer so that they bear little resemblance to his actual record. And it wouldn't surprise me if you can read every word in this tome and find not one non-derisive mention of RBI. After all, we're here to do more than simply provide an alternative to Donruss; we're here to understand the game better. And that means breaking some china from time to time.

In this essay, I'm not going to concern myself with introducing you to our more advanced metrics; rather, I'm going to tell you why you need them in the first place. So here's what's wrong with the statistics most baseball fans are accustomed to seeing and using.

Many of the stats you encounter in mainstream baseball circles are what we call "counting stats." That is, they count things: 23 homers, 107 RBI, six triples, etc. This may sound painfully obvious, but the more a hitter plays in a given season, the higher his counting stats are likely to be. Some counting stats, like RBI and runs scored, are highly team and batting-order dependent. A cleanup hitter logging 600 plate appearances in a potent lineup must work very hard *not* to rack up at least 100 RBI. Whereas a leadoff hitter on an otherwise weak offensive team won't crack the 100-RBI mark no matter how effective he is. If weak hitters surround a superior player, it's entirely possible that he'll cash in on a much greater percentage of his RBI opportunities and still have a lower RBI total than a lesser player in a stronger lineup.

The thing to understand about counting stats is that, absent supporting information, they're really only useful at the margins. That's to say, it's hard to rack up 140 RBI and not be a major contributor to your team's success. Conversely, it's difficult to log a season's worth of plate appearances, total 40 RBI and somehow be any good.

The flip side of this is that it's entirely possible, especially in eras conducive to run scoring, to break the vaunted 100-RBI barrier and still be an ineffective player (see: Carter, Joe; Sierra, Ruben). So counting stats as a species have definite weaknesses, but RBI has its own set of concerns that renders it even less useful.

And then there's batting average. It's a percentage, or rate stat, and not a counting stat, so it has a somewhat different set of concerns. First, it's subject to sample-size errors. To provide an extreme example, a hitter who goes one for three on Opening Day and one who plays the entire season going 196 for 588 (as Will Clark did in 1989) will both be hitting .333 when you check the box scores. Needless to say, it's the latter hitter whose .333 average really means something—a product tested over time, not the residue of a nice day at the office. Sample size is a vital concept to grasp when analyzing baseball statistics.

That's not all that's wrong with batting average. You're no doubt aware that the .300 hitter is one of baseball's sacred cows, but what does that really tell us about a player? It tells us he got a hit of some kind in 30% of his at-bats. We have no idea what kinds of hits he got, and we have no idea how he fared in terms of reaching base by other means. We don't even know how many times he came to the plate.

When dealing with percentage statistics, having at least a rough idea of the number of plate appearances is essential. And as far as batting average goes, you can tell much more about a player if his average (AVG) is presented in tandem with his on-base percentage (OBP) and slugging percentage (SLG). OBP tells you how the hitter reached base by other means, and SLG tells you what kinds of hits he's been getting. Both are essential pieces of information.

On the pitching side of things, we have win-loss records and ERA. Pitcher wins and losses are appallingly useless—despite how often as we try to glean character judgments about whether a certain hurler is a "winner" or not, there's just no getting around the fact that this is a profoundly flawed way to evaluate pitchers. The idea of handing out wins and losses to individual players has always seemed terrifically strange to me, but that's how we do it. Still, know this: pitcher wins and losses have more to do with run support, strength of opposition, and blind luck than they do with unvarnished pitching quality. You should have no use for them when it comes to making performance assessments. And if a certain guy was possessed of the necessary inner cowardice to prevent him from being a "winner" on the mound, chances are he would've been weeded out back in the days when he toiled for Leo's Hardware.

In your fantastic voyage through *BP '05,* you're likely to encounter an infelicitous-sounding acronym by the name of DIPS, which stands for "Defense-Independent Pitching Statistics." DIPS is the progeny of a baseball analyst by the name of Voros McCracken, who's now part of the Boston Red Sox's brain trust. A couple of years ago, McCracken, on the pages of our Web site (BaseballProspectus .com), posited that pitchers have little control over what happens once a ball is put into play, i.e., one batted into fair territory without being a home run. His findings ran counter to almost a century of received baseball wisdom, and, not surprisingly, there were many vocal skeptics. Subsequent research by McCracken himself, Tom Tippett of Diamond Mind Baseball, and our own Clay Davenport made some glancing modifications to the original findings, but the overarching point remained: pitchers' control over what happens to a ball in play appears to range from negligible to surprisingly modest.

The fate of a non-home run ball batted into fair territory is mostly determined by some combination of luck and defense. This isn't to say I could go out there, dial my four-seamer up to 60, and pass muster as a major league pitcher. No, it means when we're evaluating how well a pitcher is doing his job, we'd best focus on those elements of the game over which he exerts the most control. To wit, strikeouts, walks, home runs and groundball-fly ball tendencies (although determination of the latter is also partially up to the batter), which are all facets of the pitching game that, generally speaking, have nothing to do with defensive support. Ergo, they're "defense independent." When you hear us refer to the concept of DIPS, we're talking about these sorts of things. It's not an especially difficult concept to grasp, but it's likely to run up against a few closely held beliefs you have about what makes a good pitcher.

These findings, of course, undermine measures like ERA that, in part, use hit prevention (or the lack thereof) as a basis for their calculation. The "earned" part of ERA is another shortcoming, which dovetails nicely with a brief discussion of defensive statistics. The assigning of errors by major league official scorekeepers is a highly subjective endeavor. What's an error in one park under one set of conditions and circumstances may be a base hit elsewhere. (Personally, I'd like to see the practice of scoring errors go the way of Commodore VIC-20, but that's not likely to happen.) There's another problem with errors. While they do provide a passable thumbnail evaluation of how well a fielder makes the routine plays, they're not informative in the least with regard to range. After all, a defender can't make an error on a ball he didn't even get to. As such, it's entirely possible for a fielder to have a substantially higher error total than one of his counterparts and still be the better glove man. Fielding range is often neglected in mainstream analyses of defense, and the defensive metrics you'll find here try to correct that.

As for how this relates to ERA, consider that ERA is letting pitchers off the hook if they have errors made behind them, but not if they have fielders with poor range behind them, which is much more damaging in terms of run prevention. That's why straight up runs-per-nine, while most assuredly imperfect, is a better measure than ERA—it removes the faulty concept of unearned runs from the calculus.

You'll find us using a couple of acronyms you may not be familiar with. LOOGY, for example, is a term coined by a minor league prospects analyst named John Sickels; it stands for Lefty One-Out Guy, which is a nice bit of shorthand for anyone hoping to make a living in a lefty situational specialist role. A ROOGY is a righthanded version of same, often a right-handed pitcher with a trick delivery that makes life miserable for right-handed hitters. Like a lot of stat-driven analysis, you'll find some alphabet soup going on here, but we try to keep it to a minimum. Again, at the end of the day, the goal here is to understand the game better.

As you've probably noticed, there's a goodly amount of "unlearning" that needs to be done before meaningful analysis is to take place. By removing things like RBI, pitcher wins and losses, and batting average in isolation from your mental inventory, you're well on your way.

If you're interested in other "Baseball Stats 101" articles of this stripe, please visit our "About" page on BaseballProspectus.com (http://www.baseball prospectus.com/about/), where you'll find a whole host of such essays. They're free, and they cover darn near every angle of advanced performance analysis.

Statistical Introduction

by Keith Woolner, Clay Davenport, and Nate Silver

With this year's edition of *Baseball Prospectus,* we continue a tradition of presenting the most advanced sabermetric view of a player available. We use a variety of techniques unique to Baseball Prospectus, and so this section will serve as a brief introduction to those methods for the first time reader, as well as a refresher for our loyal long-time readers.

Each player presented in the book has their stats from every significant stint in the majors, minors, or prominent international leagues (Japanese and Mexican) between 2002 and 2004 shown. An example is shown in table 1.

The first line of the entry contains the player's name and some basic biographical information—batting and throwing hand, birthdate, age, and primary position. The next line shows the headers for the columns of data that follow, where each horizontal line represents one stint of the player's career with some team.

The first few columns of data show time and assignment data—what year, team, and league the player played for, and how old the player was at the time. For "age" we always use the player's effective "baseball age"—that is, age as of July 1 of that year, for the entire season.

The next few columns (AB H 2B 3B HR BB SO SB CS) shows the actual statistical totals the player compiled during this playing stint. The next three columns (AVG, OBP, SLG) show the three most commonly used rate statistics—batting average, on-base percentage, and slugging average—again in raw, unadjusted form.

Baseball Prospectus's unique take on player evaluation comes in the remaining columns. The three columns EQBA, EQOBP, EQSLG are the "translated" rate statistics. Baseball Prospectus's Davenport Translations convert a player's statistics to a common baseline, adjusting for the player's home park, the offensive environment of the league he plays, and, perhaps most importantly, the difficulty of the competition he plays against. Batting .363 against Eastern League competition, as Wright did in 2004 is not the same thing as batting .363 in the majors. The pitchers in the Eastern League are simply not of the same quality, and thus it's easier to hit against them. Similarly, most of the batters in the Eastern League aren't major league quality, so good pitchers will be able to post better ERA's and strikeout numbers than they would if they played in the majors. Most fans intuitively understand this concept. The translation process makes adjustments for the lesser quality of opposition explicit and quantitative, and converts what the player did against the competition he faced to an "equivalent" (hence, the EQ- prefix) major league performance. EQBA, EQOBP, and EQSLG for one player can be directly compared against other players regardless of which league the raw stats were posted in.

This year's DTs have a significant difference from last year's. In previous editions, the player's equivalent batting average was essentially determined by his actual batting average. This year, the player's ability to hit singles was explicitly translated; the translated batting average is simply what you get from having each of the component hits translated separately. This change was especially beneficial to players who had good power in the low minors, particularly if they also had low strikeout totals.

TABLE 1. HITTER STATISTICS EXAMPLE

DAVID WRIGHT **3B** **Bats: R** **Throws: R** Born: 20-Dec-1982 Age: 22

YEAR	TM	LG	AGE	AB	H	2B	3B	HR	BB	SO	SB	CS	AVG	OBP	SLG	MLVR	EQBA	EQOBP	EQSLG	EQMLVR	VORP	DEFENSE
2002	CMB	SAL	19	496	132	30	2	11	76	114	21	5	.266	.367	.401	.132	.228	.307	.354	-.212	-5.1	120-3B -7
2003	SLU	FSL	20	466	126	39	2	15	72	98	19	5	.270	.369	.459	.211	.234	.319	.424	-.089	14.7	130-3B -7
2004	BIN	EAS	21	223	81	27	0	10	39	41	20	6	.363	.467	.619	.600	.320	.409	.542	.308	35.2	56-3B -6
2004	NOR	INT	21	114	34	8	0	8	16	19	2	4	.298	.388	.579	.380	.281	.357	.544	.185	13.6	31-3B 1
2004	NYM	NL	21	263	77	17	1	14	14	40	6	0	.293	.332	.525	.176	.292	.329	.523	.120	21.2	66-3B -3
2005	*NYM*	*NL*	*22*	*422*	*117*	*26*	*2*	*18*	*50*	*83*	*13*	*3*	*.276*	*.358*	*.477*	*.087*	*.280*	*.360*	*.492*	*.111*	*32.4*	*114-3B -4*

Breakout: 21% *Improve: 48%* *Collapse: 23%*

The next steps in understanding the player lines is to focus on the MLVR and EQMLVR columns, which represent Marginal Lineup Value rates of production. With Marginal Lineup Value, we estimate the value of a player by computing the change in expected run scoring between an average team, and a team with 8 average players and the batter in question. If we were to swap one of the 9 average players for the 2004 version of Barry Bonds, we would, naturally, expect them to score more runs. Similarly, if you replaced one such player with Brad Ausmus, expected run scoring would decrease:

	Team A	Team B	Team C
1	Joe Average	Joe Average	Joe Average
2	Joe Average	Joe Average	Joe Average
3	Joe Average	Joe Average	Joe Average
4	Joe Average	Joe Average	Joe Average
5	Joe Average	BARRY BONDS	BRAD AUSMUS
6	Joe Average	Joe Average	Joe Average
7	Joe Average	Joe Average	Joe Average
8	Joe Average	Joe Average	Joe Average
9	Joe Average	Joe Average	Joe Average
Expected runs/game	4.689	5.617	4.501
Difference in runs/game Versus Team A	0	+0.928	−0.188

Since the difference in expected run scoring between Team A and Team B is entirely due to having Barry Bonds in the lineup, we call this difference his Marginal Lineup Value Rate (MLVR). As you can see in the case of Brad Ausmus, who was a below average hitter in 2004, negative MLVR is certainly possible, and actually quite common. A player who was exactly league average would have a MLVR of zero, and anyone below league average would have negative MLVR.

There is a cumulative version of MLVR, simply called Marginal Lineup Value (MLV), that takes into account playing time. If Barry Bonds plays 120 games during the year, then the total impact on his team's lineup can be estimated by taking his MLVR (0.928) and multiplying it by his games played (120).

$$\text{MLV} = 0.928 \times 120 = 111.3 \text{ runs}$$

This means that an average team would have scored about 111 more runs with Bonds in the lineup for 120 games than they would have with a league average player. What if he played all 162 games?

$$\text{MLV} = 0.928 \times 162 = 150.3 \text{ runs}$$

MLVR is a rate of production (how well he did on a per game basis). MLV measure total hitting contribution by including how often he played. MLV itself is not printed in the book, but forms the basis for VORP, which is discussed below, and MLV can be found on the statistical reports on our web site.

What then, is the difference between MLVR and EQMLVR? The answer is simple, but subtle:

MLVR is based on the player's untranslated statistics—it compares a player to the average of the league he played in, after adjusting for a player's home park. It does not translate a player's production to major league level.

EQMLVR is based on a player's translated statistics—it puts the player on an equal footing with players from other leagues (major and minor).

Minor league players will typically have much better MLVR (which compares them to their league competition) than EQMLVR (which compares them to major league-quality competition). Major league players will have less of a gap between MLVR and EQMLVR. Why would there be any gap at all? Well, the translation process converts all leagues, major and minor, across the years, to a single standard. As even the major leagues vary in difficulty and quality over time, there will be slight variations between the "reference league" of the translations and the 2004 National League, for example. The translation process also has some adjustments for differences in rules across league, most notably that some leagues use the designated hitter, and others do not. The translation process tries to even out all of these factors to compare players on as equal and undistorted basis as possible.

The second to last column in Wright's lines above is VORP, which stands for Value Over Replacement Level.

VORP is an estimate of total player value, which builds on MLVR and incorporates what position the player plays, how many games he played, and what "replacement level" is for his position. Replacement level is a concept discussed in great detail in "Understanding and Measuring Replacement Level," an article by Keith Woolner found in *Baseball Prospectus 2002,* so we will only briefly restate it here. Metrics, such as MLVr, that compare a player to league average offense are incomplete by themselves, since they do not properly account for the value of having a player healthy and in the lineup. Losing a starting player typically results in more starts given to a bench player who is significantly below average. By comparing a player's production to the level of a typical bench player or AAAA journeyman (which we dub replacement level), we recognize the value of a player's durability. As defined in *BP2002,* replacement level is: "the expected level of performance a major league team can receive from one or more of the best available players who substitute for a suddenly unavailable starting player at the same position and who can be (or were) obtained with minimal expenditure of team resources." And though we have been discussing it in terms of position players, the concept of VORP equally applies to pitchers.

VORP is available on the BP web site for all players and seasons going back over 30 years, and is updated daily during the season. There are a couple of minor points about how VORP is presented here in BP2005 worth noting:

- Minor league players are rated at their most frequently played position, rather than a weighted average across all positions they appeared at, as is done with major league players. That is, if a minor league player plays 100 games at second base, and 20 at shortstop, he would be considered to be purely a second baseman in calculating his VORP. If a major league player played 100 games at second, and 20 at shortstop, we would his compute the weighted positional average, with second base having 5× the weight of shortstop (100 G@2B / 20 G@SS = 5).
- Most minor leagues typically have shorter seasons than the majors do, and as a result, even excellent translated rates of production may not produce as high a VORP as a player with the benefit of a 162 game schedule.

Although VORP looks at what position a player appears at, it does not directly consider how well he fields that position. Thus we turn to the final column in the batter's lines—Defense—which shows the position, number of games, and fielding rating for the player at one or more positions. Thus "150-SS 3" means 150 games at shortstop, with a defensive performance 3 runs above average for shortstops.

The 2005 year line is the PECOTA projection for the player in the upcoming season. **For more on that, see the discussion of PECOTA to follow.**

Now, let's take a look at a pitcher's entry in table 2.

The first line and the YEAR, TM, LG, and AGE columns are the same as in the hitter's example above, and should be self-explanatory. The next set of columns—G, GS, IP, H, BB, SO, HR—are the actual, unadjusted totals compiled by the pitcher during this stint. The ERA column is the pitcher's actual, unadjusted earned run average.

The next five columns, all starting with "EQ" are the pitcher's rates of production (hits allowed per nine innings, strikeouts per nine innings, etc.) based on his "translated" statistics. As with the hitter example above, a pitcher's raw statistics are adjusted and converted to a neutral-park major league equivalent performance. We present the translated (or equivalent) ERA (EQERA), as well as the per 9 inning rates of hits allowed (EQH9), walks issued (EQBB9), strikeouts recorded (EQSO9), and home runs surrendered (EQHR9). The equivalent league is set up such that an average pitcher allows nine hits, three walks, and one home run per nine innings, while recording six strikeouts. He would have an EQERA and PERA of 4.50

The next column is Peripheral ERA, abbreviated as PERA. PERA is the EqERA a pitcher would be expected to have given his EqH9, EqBB9, EqSO9, and EqHR9. A PERA lower than his actual EqERA may indicate that he was somewhat unlucky, and could be expected to improve his EqERA next season even without substantial change in peripheral rates of production

VORP – Value Over Replacement Player. Based on the translated statistics, a pitcher's VORP is the number of extra runs that a replacement level pitcher would have allowed to score if he pitched the same number of innings as the this pitcher.

The final column is Stuff ratings (STF). Stuff is a shorthand rating of a pitcher's demonstrated skills, relative to his age and level; its primary use is to evaluate prospects, not established major league pitchers. An average major league starter, or a pitcher who has shown the talent to eventually become an average major league starter, will score a 10. Pitchers who score above 20 are excellent prospects; those above 30 belong to the truly elite. The largest single component of STUFF is strikeout rate, but walk rate, home run rate, hit rate, ERA, innings pitched per game, age, and age relative to league all figure in to the final STUFF rating.

As with the hitters, if a 2005 line is present it represents the PECOTA projection for this pitcher in the upcoming season. **For more on that, we can now turn to Nate's discussion of our projection system.**

TABLE 2. PITCHER STATISTICS EXAMPLE

ZACK GREINKE **Bats: R** **Throws: R** Born: 21-Oct-1983 Age: 21

YEAR	TM	LG	AGE	G	GS	IP	H	BB	SO	HR	ERA	EQERA	EQH9	EQBB9	EQSO9	EQHR9	PERA	VORP	STF
2003	WIC	TXS	19	9	9	53.0	58	5	34	5	3.23	4.14	10.3	0.9	4.5	1.3	5.04	3.1	17
2003	WIL	CRL	19	14	14	87.0	56	13	78	5	1.14	2.90	8.0	1.5	6.4	1.0	3.59	17.4	47
2004	KCR	AL	20	24	24	145.0	143	26	100	26	3.97	3.45	8.6	1.5	5.9	1.4	3.83	36.4	22
2004	OMA	PCL	20	6	6	28.7	25	6	23	2	2.51	3.00	8.0	2.0	5.7	0.7	3.33	6.8	24
2005	*KCR*	*AL*	*21*	*24*	*24*	*152.7*	*164*	*36*	*117*	*26*	*4.24*	*3.99*	*9.5*	*1.9*	*6.3*	*1.5*	*4.43*	*33.2*	*14*

Breakout: 23% *Improve: 63%* *Collapse: 0%*

PECOTA

The 2005 line is the PECOTA projection for the player in the upcoming season. Note that the player is projected into the league and park context as indicated by his team abbreviation; Adrian Beltre is now in Seattle, and so forth. The three numbers beneath the player's 2005 line—Breakout, Improve, and Collapse—are also a part of PECOTA, and estimate the likelihood of changes in performance relative to a player's previously-established level of production. PECOTA differs from other projection systems in that it uses historical comparables data to generate a probability distribution for a player's expected performance, rather than just a single forecast line. History might tell us, for example, that an old, slow hitter will manage just fine eighty percent of the time, but will have a disastrous season (collapse) twenty percent of the time that ended his career. Conversely, a young pitcher with a high walk rate might show a sudden and marked improvement (breakout) fifteen percent of the time, while failing to improve much at all in his other seasons. The Breakout, Collapse, and Improve numbers are an attempt to quantify these sorts of performance changes. To be more precise about it:

- **Breakout Rate** is the percent chance that a hitter's equivalent runs produced, or a pitcher's PERA, will improve by at least 20% relative to the weighted average of his performance in his three previous seasons of performance. High breakout rates are indicative of upside risk.
- **Collapse Rate** is the percent chance that a position player's equivalent runs produced will decrease by at least 20% relative to the weighted average of his performance in his three previous seasons of performance, or that a pitcher's PERA will increase by at least 25% relative to his baseline performance in the past three seasons. High collapse rates are indicative of downside risk.
- **Improve Rate** is the percent chance that a hitter's equivalent runs produced or a pitcher's PERA will improve *at all* relative the weighted average of his performance in his three previous seasons of performance. A player who is expected to perform just the same as he has in the past will have an Improve Rate of 50%. Note that Breakout Rate is a subset of Improve Rate; Improve Rate is the chance that a player improves *at all;* Breakout Rate is the chance that he improves *a lot.*

Breakout Rate and Collapse Rate can sometimes be counter-intuitive for players who have already experienced a radical change in their performance levels. Johan Santana, for example, is given a high Breakout Rate this year, but that just means that PECOTA thinks that he'll be able to maintain his fine performance level from 2004, which rates much better than his weighted average performance over the past three seasons. A player's forecast line itself, which describes his projected performance in absolute terms rather than relative to his previous performances, is the first thing that you should look at. Nevertheless, we think that the Breakout, Collapse and Improve numbers provide for some highly interesting information, especially when used to compare players at similar stages of their career paths.

We're also continually performing research and development on PECOTA in order to maintain its status as the industry's state-of-the-art forecasting system. Although some of the resulting improvements are trivial in nature—the sorts of things that might impact one out of one hundred projections, and then only by a small amount—there are three more substantial changes that we've made this year:

- **Minor league comparables for pitchers.** As we've mentioned, PECOTA is based on a system of identifying comparable players. Previously, hitters had been evaluated against a database of major league and translated minor league seasons, whereas pitchers had been evaluated against a database of major league seasons only. This year, minor league comparables have been introduced for pitchers as well, which provides for significantly more robust forecasts for pitching prospects.
- **Groundball-flyball data for minor league pitchers.** Last year, we introduced data on groundballs and flyballs allowed to our pitching projections. Groundball/flyball percentages are very stable over time, and can have a significant impact on a pitcher's forecast line. A pitcher that allowed a lot of flyballs but not very many home runs would be a pretty good bet to see his performance regress in the next season, for example, as some of those warning track shots went over the fence. Last season, our groundball/flyball data covered major league pitchers only, but this year we've gathered it for minor league pitchers as well. It's interesting to know, for example, that Felix Hernandez generated nearly twice as many groundouts as flyouts last season.
- **Park effects are "projected" too.** Previously, we had worked under the assumption that park factors would be the same in the upcoming season as they were in the previous season. This seems like a neutral enough premise, but it ignored the fact that park factors have fluke seasons, just as ballplayers do. This created a problem last season, for example, with the Montreal/San Juan park factor. In 2003, Expos players saw their offensive

numbers boosted by nearly 20 percent by their home parks, a rate that ranks on a par with Coors Field. As a result, we projected a lot of Montreal hitters to have big seasons. But Olympic Stadium hadn't played that way in the past, and the handful of games in Puerto Rico weren't enough to account for the difference all on their own; at least some of the high park factor was a fluke. (Montreal-San Juan, in fact wound up *depressing* run scoring by about five percent last season). In order to avoid a similar complication, we're using park factors that represent our *best guess* of how the park is going to perform in 2005. These estimates are based primarily on longer-term historical averages, with some wiggle room allowed based on changes in dimensions or environmental conditions.

Specifically, the park factors we are using for PECOTA this year are shown in table 3, where 1000 represents league average.

As always, we encourage you to visit our website at http://www.baseballprospectus.com, which has full-fledged PECOTAs available, including charts, graphs, and tables of comparable players, for all of the players covered in this book, as well as a glossary explaining PECOTA's methods and metrics in more detail.

TABLE 3. 2005 PARK FACTORS

Park	PF	Park	PF	Park	PF
Anaheim	980	Detroit	960	Philadelphia	1010
Arizona	1050	Florida	960	Pittsburgh	990
Atlanta	990	Houston	1030	San Diego	920
Baltimore	980	Kansas City	1030	Seattle	930
Boston	1030	Los Angeles	950	San Francisco	970
Chicago (A)	1030	Milwaukee	1010	St. Louis	980
Chicago (N)	1010	Minnesota	1010	Tampa Bay	990
Cincinnati	980	New York (A)	970	Texas	1090
Cleveland	990	New York (N)	970	Toronto	1030
Colorado	1200	Oakland	980	Washington	980

NOTE: PECOTA actually uses a whole series of component park factors for hits, home runs, and so forth; those listed here are the composite, run-scoring park factors, which have the most influence on a player's projection. We will avoid commenting on these specifically, except for the Washington park factor as it is new this year. RFK Stadium played as a pitchers' park more often than not during the Senators' tenure there, and that was at a time when the other parks were larger than they are now. RFK's dimensions profile similarly to Shea Stadium, and while Washington is somewhat warmer than New York, sea level parks along the coastlines generally play favorably for pitchers. We think the 980 number, which implies that RFK will play as a slight pitchers' park, is appropriate.

Arizona Diamondbacks

How long has it been since that little flare landed just a few feet behind Derek Jeter, creating wild celebrations of Snakes on the grass from Bank One Ballpark to Yankee Stadium?

On the field in Phoenix during the 2004 season, the exhilarating World Series victory in 2001 seemed at least 100 years ago, in an entirely different reality. Everything shattered into a million pieces for the Diamondbacks last year. Injuries crippled the team from the beginning, years of poor financial planning came home to roost, and the weaknesses of the club were laid bare for all to witness and opponents to exploit. As a result, there was a strong belief that the window of opportunity in Phoenix had closed and would be difficult to reopen down the road.

For several years, the D-Backs have been something of an old team. While they've had a few young players here and there, the core of the team has been very old. Often very good, but very old. Players like Luis Gonzalez, Steve Finley, Matt Williams, Curt Schilling, and Randy Johnson have been the players the Snakes have built around.

Rather than gambling on young and inexpensive players, the front office borrowed against the future and diluted assets, making cash calls to investors in the late '90s, and borrowing cash for operating expenses at the start of the decade. The D-Backs didn't want to gamble on young and inexpensive players. To an extent, it was a successful strategy. It resulted in a World Series win, due to mid-market players supporting the cast of highly-paid aging stars—all held together by a large number of contracts heavy on deferred payments.

The "pay later" strategy has one simple drawback, be it in baseball or any other endeavor. Eventually, you do have to pay. And pay the Diamondbacks will. In the boardroom, Ken Kendrick has replaced Jerry Colangelo, and he has publicly stated that the club has an additional $250 million in available cash. That should help, although even a number that staggering isn't going to solve the problem. The D-Backs have about $150 million in outstanding deferred salary as an encumbrance against future revenue, along with nearly the same amount in stadium debt.

From a fan's perspective, the financial zigs and zags the franchise needs to make aren't important unless they significantly constrict the club's ability to put a competitive team on the field. Looking ahead to 2005, the evidence strongly suggests that money won't be a problem that should concern fans.

DIAMONDBACKS PROSPECTUS

2004 record: 51–111; Fifth place, NL West

Pythagenport record: 52–110

Runs scored per game: 3.80 (16th in NL)

Runs allowed per game: 5.55 (14th in NL)

Team EqA: .238 (16th in NL)

2004 Batters Age: 29.4 (8th youngest in NL)

2004 Pitchers Age: 30.3 (3rd oldest in NL)

Ballpark: Bank One Ballpark; Severe hitter's park; Park Factor of 1.051

2004: A full-scale collapse in the desert, as everyone from the chairman on down threw in the towel.

2005: Spent money like drunken sailors in the off-season, but they'll still fall comfortably short of the postseason.

General Manager Joe Garagiola Jr. began the hot stove season with two major free-agent signings. After acquiring Troy Glaus for $45 million over four years, he inked Russ Ortiz for $33 million for the same four years (the Yankees will likely feel similar pain after their three-year, $21 million signing of Jaret Wright). You can question the wisdom of the signings—God knows we do—but it is evidence that the ownership team isn't going to let a lack of budget be the factor that prevents the Snakes from winning. That'll be Russ Ortiz's job.

Can't Beat 'Em? Hire 'Em

Pending approval by the commissioner's office, the new CEO of the Diamondbacks is investor and former player agent Jeff Moorad. You may remember Moorad as the chief architect of one of the worst signings of a free agent in history, when he engineered the D-Backs' acquisition of an aging and overrated Matt Williams. Williams was 32 at the start of the contract, his performance and health going downhill faster than a greased Franz Klammer. And yet, largely because of intangible goodies like "community presence," the D-Backs signed him to a five-year deal worth an average of $9 million annually.

So yes, the Diamondback management team knows that Moorad knows how to negotiate. They just have to hope that (a) Moorad has or can develop the other skills that a CEO needs to be successful in baseball, and (b) he can snooker player agents as effectively as he fleeced the Diamondbacks as Williams's agent.

Moorad's placement as CEO hasn't been approved yet by Bud Selig and his staff. The commissioner's office, moving at its usual stately pace, still must finish reviewing Moorad's credentials as an investor in the club, which is a sticking point for his acceptance of the CEO role. Selig was quoted in the *Arizona Republic,* as stating, "I know the Diamondbacks want to move ahead . . . We will do a thorough, adequate check. When you put a major league franchise in someone's control, you want to do the right thing." Of course. It's not as if there's ever been a scoundrel or unqualified party owning or running a club. Considering how fast and how disciplined clubs need to be these days to be profitable and competitive, one would hope the commissioner's office could change its overriding speed from "Glacieresque" to "Ron Hasseyish."

Real Prospects for the Future

One thing that's very different about the 2005 version of the D-Backs compared to past versions is justified optimism about young players. The farm system actually has a number of legitimate prospects, almost all of them outfielders. First among them is Carlos Quentin, a legitimate defensive outfielder who looks like he's going to hit for average and power. Conor Jackson's already demonstrated a potent bat; scouts wonder if he'll be up to the challenge of playing acceptable defense in the majors. The numbers indicate he probably will cover a corner spot acceptably. With his offensive potential, something can be worked out.

Even the next tier down in the D-Back system has some promising bats, specifically Jonathan Zeringue, Josh Kroeger, and catching prospect Chris Snyder. A year or three down the road, the grounds in Phoenix could be stocked with relatively inexpensive, young, homegrown talent, something that really has never been the case in the history of the franchise. Kroeger's brief call-up—he was an emergency patch due to endless injuries on the big club—wasn't particularly pretty, but he had ripped through two levels before looking a little overmatched in Phoenix. While he's a legitimate prospect, if he's not ready it's really nothing to worry about because he's not at the top of the list of potential outfielders—and that's great news for D-Backs fans.

Decision Making Still A Concern

Yes, there's talent coming up in the minors. Real prospects, who are going to be real good major leaguers. But does it really matter, if the front office decision-making processes aren't sound? D-Back fans shouldn't be worried about money, media contracts, or MLB's internal machinations about who should and shouldn't be allowed to invest in or manage major league clubs. Rather, they should worry about how the baseball people are going about the business of making decisions about player personnel. Consider the two major free-agent signings of the off-season made by the Snakes to date.

First, take Troy Glaus at $45 million over four years. If he's healthy, he could be worth the money. But he's missed over 170 games the last two years with serious injuries, including surgery to repair a damaged rotator cuff. Over the last three years, his stat lines have been pretty consistent in BA and OBP, at about .250 and .350 respectively, with only Glaus's shortened 2004 campaign showing any evidence of his prodigious power. So the D-Backs signed on for very significant risk, in the form of both injury risk and performance risk. To get a real return on the money they spent, they need Glaus to be both healthy and effective. If not, it's lots of money down a hole.

But even if Glaus is relatively healthy and performs fairly well, was this really the best use of all that money? One price will be lost playing time for Shea Hillenbrand, a capable backup stretched to help a team either at first or third. That said, without Glaus, the club would enter the 2005 season with Chad Tracy as the starting third baseman. Is Tracy as good as Glaus? No, but he's got a shot to be good, and a better shot than Glaus to stay healthy. Considering the abundance of talent available at a low cost to play first base and Tracy's potential to be a very solid third baseman, $45 million's a lot of money that could have been used elsewhere. Grabbing an elite player for an up-the-middle position, in lieu of, say, Royce Clayton and Luis Terrero, would have been a much wiser move.

As risky a move as Troy Glaus's signing was, it's a Kasparov gambit compared to the signing of Russ Ortiz. Just as the D-Back front office fell into irrational love with Elmer Dessens's one Willie Blair/House of Cards season and parted with Erubiel Durazo, so have they fell in love with Russ Ortiz, and somehow come to the conclusion that it was a good idea to pay him more than $8 million a year. This is an absolutely dismal signing, one that should terrify and anger any Daimondbacks fan.

Here's the seminal problem: Russ Ortiz isn't very good. He's rotation filler, a guy who can give you some innings, but is not a good bet to be all that effective, and a horrible bet to justify the massive dollars thrown his way. Ortiz's entire career to date has been spent in great pitcher's parks, where his performance has been just a tick above average (his career unadjusted ERA has been just 3% better than league average).

Last year, Ortiz posted a 4.13 ERA, but a deeper look should have scared the hell out of clubs looking to sign him. Of his 204 innings, a full 39.2 came against the anemic traveling circus that was the Montreal Expos, whom he held to a .131 batting average and 1.13 earned runs per game. In the second half of the season, his ERA and HR rates ballooned, to the point where he wasn't even going to pitch in the postseason until the injury to John Thomson. He's no Randy Johnson.

In short, Ortiz is a time bomb, and the D-Backs should have known that. That they went ahead and signed him to a big-money contract is indicative of a style of investments and resource allocation that simply isn't good enough to win another World Series. Yes, help is on the way in the form of Quentin, Jackson, and possibly one or two power arms, but no club has enough talent or money to make decisions in such a cavalier fashion and get away with it.

Just before press time, the long-awaited and false-started Randy Johnson deal to the Yankees was finally completed. The deal sent Javier Vazquez, lefty Brad Halsey, catching prospect Dioner Navarro, and about $9 million to the desert, with the Yankees getting their coveted ace. In the long run, it wasn't really a relevant question whether or not Johnson would move. It might make some things financially easier for now if the right deal comes around, but Randy Johnson wasn't going to be part of the D-Backs' next championship team. In many ways, how quickly the front office takes that to heart and focuses on the youthful foundation they've assembled in the minors will be the real test of this regime.

In trading Navarro and pitching prospects William Juarez, Danny Muegge, and Beltran Perez to the Dodgers for Shawn Green, the Diamondbacks showed they're not willing to exercise patience. Green will step into what would have been a questionable right-field situation, no question. But by giving Green a three-year, $32 million contract extension—even with the Dodgers picking up much of Green's '05 salary—the team ensured they'd be blocking the path for their crop of great outfield prospects. Even worse, it's not as if Green is Carlos Beltran, likely to contribute four or five years of MVP-level production. Instead, he's a fading hitter whose 40-homerun power has vanished thanks to a bum shoulder on the wrong side of 30. Building a winner takes a cohesive plan; the Green trade and extension is a big first step toward blowing any semblance of a plan to bits.

Despite their abysmal 2004 showing, the Snakes have enough talent on board to have at least a decent year. But they need to stay focused on making smart moves for the long term. In Ortiz, Glaus, and Green, they're already 0-for-3.

HITTERS

PHIL AVLAS — C — Bats: R — Throws: R — Born: 17-Dec-1982 — Age: 22

YEAR	TM	LG	AGE	AB	H	2B	3B	HR	BB	SO	SB	CS	AVG	OBP	SLG	MLVR	EQBA	EQOBP	EQSLG	EQMLVR	VORP	DEFENSE
2002	MSO	PIO	19	152	42	13	2	0	21	37	3	1	.276	.371	.388	.048	.184	.243	.243	-.515	-29.9	37-C 1
2003	SBN	MDW	20	133	27	7	0	1	16	17	4	1	.203	.283	.278	-.166	.168	.229	.234	-.563	-17.0	45-C 8
2003	YAK	NWN	20	45	15	4	1	0	6	11	0	1	.333	.412	.467	.314	.239	.259	.304	-.370	-5.1	13-C -2
2004	LNC	CLF	21	384	121	22	8	13	29	54	5	4	.315	.359	.516	.137	.239	.280	.389	-.207	-3.8	102-C 4
2005	*ARI*	*NL*	*22*	*240*	*55*	*12*	*1*	*5*	*17*	*47*	*2*	*1*	*.230*	*.283*	*.355*	*-.238*	*.226*	*.277*	*.348*	*-.263*	*-3.9*	*65-C -1*

Breakout: 20% *Improve: 35%* *Collapse: 42%*

Young catcher, who hit well in high-A at the age of 21. We'll have to see how well he makes the jump to Double-A this year, given his low walk rate and dependence on a high average to get on base, and the mitigating aspect of any good season in the Cal League. But right now, there's enough of a base here to build on. If he can consolidate his gains, Avlas will start showing up on prospect lists, particularly because he might actually be able to stay at catcher. He's considered to have above-average receiving and throwing skills. Keep an eye open.

CARLOS BAERGA — PH — Bats: B — Throws: R — Born: 04-Nov-1968 — Age: 36

YEAR	TM	LG	AGE	AB	H	2B	3B	HR	BB	SO	SB	CS	AVG	OBP	SLG	MLVR	EQBA	EQOBP	EQSLG	EQMLVR	VORP	DEFENSE	
2002	BOS	AL	33	182	52	11	0	2	7	20	6	0	.286	.316	.379	-.056	.293	.317	.381	-.108	7.0	13-2B -1	
2003	ARI	NL	34	207	71	13	0	4	18	20	1	1	.343	.396	.464	.196	.337	.380	.449	.145	18.8	14-1B 1	13-2B 0
2004	ARI	NL	35	85	20	2	0	2	6	12	0	0	.235	.309	.329	-.187	.235	.289	.329	-.277	-0.2		
2005	*ARI*	*NL*	*36*	*122*	*33*	*6*	*0*	*2*	*9*	*15*	*1*	*0*	*.269*	*.324*	*.377*	*-.110*	*.264*	*.318*	*.370*	*-.137*	*0.2*	*36-DH*	

Breakout: 8% *Improve: 25%* *Collapse: 48%*

How many times can one be reborn? Baerga's gone from an elite player to being out of baseball, to playing a key role on a club; and now he's in a "busy agent cold-calling clubs" mode. He's pretty much devoid of defensive value, and makes his living as a line-drive hitter. It might be enough for someone to sign him, but there's definitely some scraping going on if a GM's calculus brings him to "Yeah, sign that Baerga kid."

BRIAN BARDEN 3B Bats: R Throws: R Born: 02-Apr-1981 Age: 24

YEAR	TM	LG	AGE	AB	H	2B	3B	HR	BB	SO	SB	CS	AVG	OBP	SLG	MLVR	EQBA	EQOBP	EQSLG	EQMLVR	VORP	DEFENSE	
2002	LNC	CLF	21	269	90	19	1	8	16	63	3	1	.335	.370	.502	.191	.259	.289	.392	-.171	-3.5		
2003	ELP	TXS	22	383	110	24	5	3	29	78	10	4	.287	.348	.399	-.013	.243	.300	.357	-.211	-3.5	100-3B -2	
2004	ELP	TXS	23	195	59	10	6	3	10	48	1	2	.303	.335	.462	.032	.246	.274	.382	-.224	-2.5	42-3B -5	
2004	TUC	PCL	23	332	94	30	5	8	18	83	3	1	.283	.324	.476	-.083	.224	.264	.368	-.278	-9.1	60-3B 5	22-2B 0
2005	*ARI*	*NL*	*24*	*239*	*59*	*14*	*2*	*5*	*12*	*59*	*2*	*1*	*.248*	*.292*	*.385*	*-.170*	*.244*	*.287*	*.377*	*-.196*	*-4.3*	*64-3B -5*	

Breakout: 21% *Improve: 43%* *Collapse: 27%*

Line-drive-hitting third base prospect, plays defense well enough to handle third in the bigs. Gap power to date, but with a fair number of doubles that could convert to homers down the road. He's relatively athletic, and has done a good job of maintaining his production as he moves up. The usual caveats about Diamondbacks hitting prospects apply: He's put up numbers in a series of hitter's parks and leagues (Major League EqA of .215 last year shows he's not ready). He has other issues that affect several D-Back prospects, with a low walk rate and heavy reliance on shiny batting averages. If he consolidates his gains this year, he could make some noise, but he's got work to do.

DANNY BAUTISTA RF Bats: R Throws: R Born: 24-May-1972 Age: 33

YEAR	TM	LG	AGE	AB	H	2B	3B	HR	BB	SO	SB	CS	AVG	OBP	SLG	MLVR	EQBA	EQOBP	EQSLG	EQMLVR	VORP	DEFENSE	
2002	ARI	NL	30	154	50	5	2	6	11	21	4	2	.325	.367	.500	.207	.314	.357	.497	.153	10.9	31-RF -3	
2003	ARI	NL	31	284	78	16	3	4	21	50	3	2	.275	.330	.394	-.053	.265	.319	.385	-.120	2.9	54-RF -5	15-CF -1
2004	ARI	NL	32	539	154	27	1	11	35	66	6	2	.286	.332	.401	-.017	.275	.323	.385	-.105	14.4	134-RF 0	
2005	*TBY*	*AL*	*33*	*380*	*102*	*19*	*2*	*7*	*26*	*55*	*4*	*3*	*.269*	*.319*	*.387*	*-.100*	*.269*	*.321*	*.395*	*-.094*	*2.6*	*99-RF -1*	

Breakout 7% *Improve 31%* *Collapse 44%*

A classic tweener who doesn't hit well enough to help a club from a corner outfield spot, but can't cover center field well enough to play there. He's kind of Mike Devereaux lite, which isn't how you want to be thought of when you're a 33-year-old looking for a free-agent gig. That's right where Bautista finds himself after the D-Backs decided not to offer him arbitration.

JUAN BRITO C Bats: R Throws: R Born: 07-Nov-1979 Age: 25

YEAR	TM	LG	AGE	AB	H	2B	3B	HR	BB	SO	SB	CS	AVG	OBP	SLG	MLVR	EQBA	EQOBP	EQSLG	EQMLVR	VORP	DEFENSE
2002	WIC	TXS	22	302	77	11	0	7	21	46	1	1	.255	.303	.361	-.064	.227	.265	.332	-.325	-13.9	82-C 3
2003	OMA	PCL	23	122	29	2	0	2	3	25	0	2	.238	.262	.303	-.275	.213	.233	.254	-.508	-11.2	36-C 1
2004	TUC	PCL	24	102	32	5	2	3	6	25	1	0	.314	.358	.490	.025	.242	.283	.384	-.207	-1.0	26-C -1
2004	ARI	NL	24	171	35	7	0	3	9	41	1	0	.205	.246	.298	-.367	.194	.233	.276	-.486	-7.9	52-C -4
2005	*ARI*	*NL*	*25*	*236*	*57*	*10*	*1*	*6*	*12*	*52*	*2*	*1*	*.242*	*.283*	*.368*	*-.215*	*.237*	*.277*	*.360*	*-.240*	*-0.9*	*63-C -3*

Breakout: 41% *Improve: 56%* *Collapse: 22%*

A catch-and-throw guy, which is a nicer way of saying that he can't hit. Doesn't hit for average or power, nor does he draw any walks. In terms of doing the stuff that wins ballgames, you have to wonder how guys like this ever get any playing time at all. Let's say he completely shuts down the opponent's running game. Is that really enough, when you actually do the calculations, to justify spending any precious playing time on the guy?

ALEX CINTRON SS Bats: B Throws: R Born: 17-Dec-1978 Age: 26

YEAR	TM	LG	AGE	AB	H	2B	3B	HR	BB	SO	SB	CS	AVG	OBP	SLG	MLVR	EQBA	EQOBP	EQSLG	EQMLVR	VORP	DEFENSE	
2002	TUC	PCL	23	351	113	22	3	4	11	33	9	5	.322	.345	.436	.017	.274	.300	.370	-.171	3.2	47-SS -6	34-2B -2
2002	ARI	NL	23	75	16	6	0	0	12	13	0	0	.213	.322	.293	-.228	.224	.296	.276	-.343	-0.9	12-2B 1	
2003	TUC	PCL	24	107	42	11	2	2	8	6	1	0	.393	.435	.589	.437	.340	.382	.524	.262	14.5	23-SS -2	
2003	ARI	NL	24	448	142	26	6	13	29	33	2	3	.317	.359	.489	.155	.305	.348	.475	.096	38.9	89-SS -8	14-3B -1
2004	ARI	NL	25	564	148	31	7	4	31	59	3	3	.262	.301	.363	-.150	.253	.291	.352	-.229	5.9	123-SS -7	16-2B -2
2005	*ARI*	*NL*	*26*	*504*	*140*	*29*	*4*	*8*	*31*	*50*	*4*	*2*	*.277*	*.320*	*.400*	*-.079*	*.272*	*.314*	*.392*	*-.107*	*14.5*	*129-SS -3*	

Breakout: 5% *Improve: 24%* *Collapse: 40%*

Followed up his dream 2003 with a hard dose of reality in 2004. Didn't hit particularly well, was OK but not great in the field, and just kind of got caught up in the general malaise that the organization suffered through last year. With head-scratching acquisitions Royce Clayton and Craig Counsell on board, he'll start the year as a utility man or on another club. PECOTA thinks Cintron will be the best of the three.

GREG COLBRUNN 1B Bats: R Throws: R Born: 26-Jul-1969 Age: 35

YEAR	TM	LG	AGE	AB	H	2B	3B	HR	BB	SO	SB	CS	AVG	OBP	SLG	MLVR	EQBA	EQOBP	EQSLG	EQMLVR	VORP	DEFENSE
2002	ARI	NL	32	171	57	16	2	10	13	19	0	0	.333	.378	.626	.419	.324	.369	.612	.352	22.7	32-1B -2
2003	SEA	AL	33	58	16	1	1	3	4	16	0	1	.276	.323	.483	.088	.293	.339	.500	.105	2.7	11-1B -1
2004	ARI	NL	34	27	3	0	0	0	1	5	0	0	.111	.143	.111	-.833	.074	.070	.074	-1.144	-4.5	
2005	*TEX*	*AL*	*35*	*117*	*30*	*5*	*0*	*5*	*7*	*23*	*0*	*0*	*.257*	*.301*	*.443*	*-.064*	*.247*	*.293*	*.427*	*-.115*	*1.7*	*34-1B -4*

Breakout: 18% Improve: 37% Collapse: 32%

He who scoffs at studies showing that the platoon righty skill is largely just good fortune has signed with the Rangers, where he's expected to share 550 DH at-bats with David Dellucci. Colbrunn can mash lefties if he's healthy, and won't kill you defensively at first base. For the right club at the right place, he's a reasonable and rational signing.

DOUG DEVORE OF Bats: L Throws: L Born: 14-Dec-1977 Age: 27

YEAR	TM	LG	AGE	AB	H	2B	3B	HR	BB	SO	SB	CS	AVG	OBP	SLG	MLVR	EQBA	EQOBP	EQSLG	EQMLVR	VORP	DEFENSE	
2002	TUC	PCL	24	436	114	20	6	14	27	103	9	6	.261	.311	.431	-.096	.220	.270	.363	-.276	-27.1	104-RF 1	
2003	TUC	PCL	25	462	135	29	7	14	44	95	5	7	.292	.357	.476	.071	.242	.307	.404	-.133	-10.8	64-LF -2	54-RF -4
2004	TUC	PCL	26	234	63	13	0	14	21	67	3	2	.269	.328	.504	-.048	.209	.264	.378	-.274	-14.2	23-RF -3	23-LF -1
2004	ARI	NL	26	107	24	3	2	3	7	31	1	1	.224	.272	.374	-.207	.217	.265	.358	-.295	-2.9	16-LF 0	12-RF 0
2005	*ARI*	*NL*	*27*	*169*	*42*	*9*	*1*	*6*	*14*	*47*	*2*	*1*	*.246*	*.305*	*.419*	*-.104*	*.242*	*.299*	*.410*	*-.131*	*2.2*	*47-RF -2*	

Breakout: 35% Improve: 52% Collapse: 36%

Lefty outfielder, moderate power, doesn't walk, defense won't kill you in a corner. He got a brief look last year as part of the "Might-as-well-audition-people-because-everyone's-injured" marketing campaign. He needs to do something to distinguish himself from the competition, and sooner rather than later. A good 200 PA could make Mr. DeVore a nice chunk of change.

STEPHEN DREW SS Bats: L Throws: R Born: 16-Mar-1983 Age: 22

We haven't seen him play with a wooden bat yet, but based on conversations with the scouts that've seen him and the statheads who focus on college baseball, Drew is the real deal. Observers liken him to a hybrid, crossing Mark Teixeira with Alex Rodriguez. That's possible, and his pedigree is solid, but let's see how he makes the adjustments to pro ball first, before we start anointing him with infused oils. For that matter, let's see if the D-Backs can meet Drew's hefty demands, or we may find him back in the draft come June.

JERRY GIL SS Bats: R Throws: R Born: 14-Oct-1982 Age: 22

YEAR	TM	LG	AGE	AB	H	2B	3B	HR	BB	SO	SB	CS	AVG	OBP	SLG	MLVR	EQBA	EQOBP	EQSLG	EQMLVR	VORP	DEFENSE
2002	YAK	NWN	19	224	56	11	2	2	6	47	14	1	.250	.274	.344	-.059	.211	.222	.298	-.468	-42.2	
2003	SBN	MDW	20	429	111	16	6	4	10	90	19	10	.259	.275	.352	-.051	.226	.241	.325	-.383	-23.2	115-SS -3
2004	TUC	PCL	21	421	117	31	8	11	12	94	12	1	.278	.299	.468	-.144	.221	.244	.366	-.322	-13.7	111-SS -17
2004	ARI	NL	21	86	15	2	1	0	0	33	2	0	.174	.182	.221	-.601	.163	.158	.174	-.798	-7.8	25-SS -2
2005	*ARI*	*NL*	*22*	*445*	*100*	*23*	*3*	*7*	*4*	*110*	*8*	*3*	*.224*	*.235*	*.337*	*-.355*	*.220*	*.230*	*.330*	*-.378*	*-23.1*	*109-SS -11*

Breakout: 16% Improve: 34% Collapse: 51%

Well, he has youth on his side. He's also got a career BB/K ratio of 29/275, which is comparable to Dennis Eckersley's, if you're a creepy optimist who laughs at inopportune times. If you think Gil bears a striking resemblance to various no-hit catchers, you're probably right, but this is the shortstop version; the poor offense still inflates the defensive reputation, because even after all these years, Sherri Nichols still knows more about baseball than we ever will.

LUIS GONZALEZ LF Bats: L Throws: R Born: 03-Sep-1967 Age: 37

YEAR	TM	LG	AGE	AB	H	2B	3B	HR	BB	SO	SB	CS	AVG	OBP	SLG	MLVR	EQBA	EQOBP	EQSLG	EQMLVR	VORP	DEFENSE
2002	ARI	NL	34	524	151	19	3	28	97	76	9	2	.288	.400	.496	.227	.278	.389	.489	.161	46.7	137-LF -2
2003	ARI	NL	35	579	176	46	4	26	94	67	5	3	.304	.402	.532	.265	.291	.391	.515	.212	53.2	154-LF 10
2004	ARI	NL	36	379	98	28	5	17	68	58	2	2	.259	.373	.493	.146	.247	.362	.473	.065	23.7	97-LF -7
2005	*ARI*	*NL*	*37*	*358*	*97*	*20*	*2*	*16*	*56*	*52*	*3*	*1*	*.272*	*.371*	*.476*	*.104*	*.267*	*.364*	*.467*	*.074*	*14.9*	*100-LF -2*

Breakout: 28% Improve: 63% Collapse: 20%

(continued next page)

Luis Gonzalez *(continued)*

Gonzalez's face is a great baseball face. The thing about it is that he always looks like he's in some sort of pain due to soreness, even when he's wearing a big grin. He has the bearing and gait of an independent contractor—perhaps an electrical wiring guy—who played a nine-game softball tournament over the weekend, and shows up to work anyway, his bloodstream laced with borderline dangerous levels of Advil. He's recovering from Tommy John surgery, and should be ready to start next season. He's a fine ballplayer, no matter how much we at BP dislike paying big money for corner outfielders. If he's healthy he'll be productive, probably with some decline, but not an Alvin Davis-level drop-off.

ANDY GREEN **2B/3B** **Bats: R** **Throws: R** Born: 07-Jul-1977 Age: 27

YEAR	TM	LG	AGE	AB	H	2B	3B	HR	BB	SO	SB	CS	AVG	OBP	SLG	MLVR	EQBA	EQOBP	EQSLG	EQMLVR	VORP	DEFENSE	
2002	LNC	CLF	25	401	124	36	4	6	60	59	15	10	.309	.401	.464	.163	.243	.320	.363	-.164	-4.8		
2002	TUC	PCL	25	99	22	8	0	1	9	17	2	1	.222	.294	.333	-.280	.175	.238	.258	-.509	-10.0	23-2B -1	
2003	ELP	TXS	26	490	148	38	2	2	38	51	17	9	.302	.366	.400	.026	.253	.312	.350	-.191	-2.4	59-2B -4	39-SS -5
2004	TUC	PCL	27	309	101	31	3	9	34	45	10	4	.327	.394	.534	.163	.258	.325	.413	-.075	9.7	34-3B -1	29-2B -2
2004	ARI	NL	27	109	22	2	1	1	5	17	1	1	.202	.241	.266	-.425	.200	.238	.255	-.502	-8.6	14-3B -1	
2005	*ARI*	*NL*	*27*	*211*	*54*	*14*	*2*	*3*	*18*	*31*	*4*	*2*	*.257*	*.323*	*.380*	*-.116*	*.252*	*.317*	*.373*	*-.142*	*5.1*	*59-2B -9*	

Breakout: 27% *Improve: 49%* *Collapse: 37%*

He's a better hitter than he showed, but that's not saying very much. Green's got a reasonable bat, and he projects as a utility guy who can actually play all the infield positions. Think of a Craig Counsell-type ballplayer, and you're not far off. He'll have to get lucky to make the roster out of spring training, given the D-Backs have the real McCoy in Counsell, along with Royce Clayton, Alex Cintron, and Matt Kata battling for time. More likely, Green stays in Triple-A until an injury, and bops around the league until he gets the same brand on his butt that Denny Hocking has. We've heard the infielders get some sort of cool Celtic symbol, and the catchers get a smiling caricature of Tom Prince.

SCOTT HAIRSTON **2B?** **Bats: R** **Throws: R** Born: 25-May-1980 Age: 25

YEAR	TM	LG	AGE	AB	H	2B	3B	HR	BB	SO	SB	CS	AVG	OBP	SLG	MLVR	EQBA	EQOBP	EQSLG	EQMLVR	VORP	DEFENSE	
2002	SBN	MDW	22	394	131	35	4	16	58	74	9	3	.332	.426	.563	.464	.279	.353	.478	.084	33.8	95-2B -17	10-3B -1
2002	LNC	CLF	22	79	32	11	1	6	6	16	1	0	.405	.442	.797	.774	.303	.334	.592	.242	8.4		
2003	ELP	TXS	23	337	93	21	7	10	30	80	6	2	.276	.345	.469	.064	.229	.293	.407	-.165	1.0	74-2B -8	
2004	TUC	PCL	24	115	36	8	3	5	11	21	0	3	.313	.375	.565	.160	.245	.310	.436	-.081	3.2	18-2B -4	
2004	ARI	NL	24	339	84	15	6	13	21	88	3	3	.248	.293	.442	-.057	.240	.285	.426	-.145	10.0	79-2B -8	
2005	*ARI*	*NL*	*25*	*387*	*106*	*23*	*3*	*16*	*31*	*87*	*4*	*2*	*.273*	*.335*	*.475*	*.042*	*.268*	*.328*	*.465*	*.012*	*25.7*	*102-2B -6*	

Breakout: 32% *Improve: 65%* *Collapse: 13%*

Is he a great defensive second baseman? No, but he'll hit enough to help a club there anyway. Unfortunately he won't get the chance in 2005 with the D-Backs, who decided they'd be better off playing Counsell and Clayton up the middle. At press time the team looked like it would either crush Hairston's offensive value with a move to right field, or bury with a trade for Shawn Green. The Diamondbacks made far too many moves this off-season that'll net the least possible utility out of their roster.

ROB HAMMOCK **C/UT** **Bats: R** **Throws: R** Born: 13-May-1977 Age: 28

YEAR	TM	LG	AGE	AB	H	2B	3B	HR	BB	SO	SB	CS	AVG	OBP	SLG	MLVR	EQBA	EQOBP	EQSLG	EQMLVR	VORP	DEFENSE	
2002	ELP	TXS	25	441	128	28	4	11	43	68	5	4	.290	.358	.447	.084	.244	.302	.392	-.158	2.1	53-C 0	37-LF -3
2003	TUC	PCL	26	116	31	6	2	2	11	24	1	0	.267	.321	.405	-.099	.228	.283	.360	-.250	-2.6	20-C -2	
2003	ARI	NL	26	195	55	10	2	8	17	44	3	2	.282	.343	.477	.074	.269	.330	.466	.018	11.2	32-C 0	16-3B 3
2004	ARI	NL	27	195	47	16	2	4	13	39	3	3	.241	.287	.405	-.124	.232	.279	.392	-.210	0.9	43-C -2	12-LF -1
2005	*ARI*	*NL*	*28*	*242*	*62*	*15*	*1*	*7*	*20*	*48*	*3*	*2*	*.258*	*.316*	*.421*	*-.074*	*.253*	*.310*	*.412*	*-.101*	*6.5*	*66-C -6*	

Breakout: 26% *Improve: 47%* *Collapse: 33%*

Hammock can hit a little, more than he showed in 2004, and has a reasonable if unspectacular reputation defensively. Given that the D-Backs were used to watching Rod Barajas, it's not surprising they like Hammock. At press time doctors were contemplating a second surgery on his left knee, so he's a long shot to get the starting job out of spring training.

KOYIE HILL C **Bats: B** **Throws: R** Born: 09-Mar-1979 Age: 26

YEAR	TM	LG	AGE	AB	H	2B	3B	HR	BB	SO	SB	CS	AVG	OBP	SLG	MLVR	EQBA	EQOBP	EQSLG	EQMLVR	VORP	DEFENSE
2002	JAX	SOU	23	468	127	25	1	11	76	88	5	3	.271	.368	.400	.115	.252	.333	.391	-.095	12.1	114-C 5
2003	JAX	SOU	24	101	23	7	0	0	6	19	2	1	.228	.271	.297	-.182	.176	.197	.216	-.652	-15.0	23-C 3
2003	LVG	PCL	24	312	98	18	0	3	15	39	5	0	.314	.345	.401	-.000	.259	.289	.331	-.259	-7.8	76-C -7
2004	LVG	PCL	25	350	100	26	0	13	28	69	0	1	.286	.339	.471	-.032	.225	.275	.361	-.266	-9.3	80-C 2
2004	ARI	NL	25	36	9	1	0	1	2	6	1	0	.250	.289	.361	-.177	.250	.256	.361	-.286	0.3	
2005	*ARI*	*NL*	*26*	*172*	*42*	*9*	*1*	*5*	*14*	*33*	*1*	*0*	*.246*	*.303*	*.388*	*-.149*	*.242*	*.297*	*.381*	*-.175*	*3.7*	*48-C -3*

Breakout: 29% *Improve: 45%* *Collapse: 34%*

Did he just pull it all together? Solid defensive catcher, shows occasional flashes of all the tools in previous years; average one year, power the next, plate discipline, then has a pretty good consolidation season at Las Vegas, and gets a taste of the bigs. With Hammock's knee a concern, he'll compete with the more talented but less proven Chris Snyder for the #1 job.

SHEA HILLENBRAND 3B/1B **Bats: R** **Throws: R** Born: 27-Jul-1975 Age: 29

YEAR	TM	LG	AGE	AB	H	2B	3B	HR	BB	SO	SB	CS	AVG	OBP	SLG	MLVR	EQBA	EQOBP	EQSLG	EQMLVR	VORP	DEFENSE	
2002	BOS	AL	26	634	186	43	4	18	25	95	4	2	.293	.330	.459	.084	.298	.336	.469	.060	43.4	150-3B 5	
2003	BOS	AL	27	185	56	17	0	3	7	26	1	0	.303	.335	.443	.035	.306	.330	.443	.019	9.2	26-3B 0	21-1B 1
2003	ARI	NL	27	330	88	18	1	17	17	44	0	0	.267	.302	.482	.017	.257	.292	.471	-.053	12.7	48-1B 3	27-3B 0
2004	ARI	NL	28	562	174	36	3	15	24	49	2	0	.310	.348	.464	.116	.297	.335	.448	.026	34.5	125-1B 7	12-3B 0
2005	*TOR*	*AL*	*29*	*493*	*140*	*30*	*2*	*15*	*26*	*62*	*2*	*1*	*.284*	*.328*	*.445*	*.006*	*.279*	*.326*	*.444*	*-.011*	*13.1*	*126-1B 5*	

Breakout 8% *Improve 31%* *Collapse 34%*

Just doesn't walk, and right off the bat, that means two likely things. One, you're not going to be a great player, and two, you're probably going to be overrated and overpaid. Hillenbrand's been largely crowded out since the acquisition of Troy Glaus, so he may be moved to some team that overrates batting average. As long as he stays at third, he's a .260–.270 EqA guy with some value; otherwise he's a Pedro Feliz type best used as a utility man.

CONOR JACKSON OF **Bats: R** **Throws: R** Born: 07-May-1982 Age: 23

YEAR	TM	LG	AGE	AB	H	2B	3B	HR	BB	SO	SB	CS	AVG	OBP	SLG	MLVR	EQBA	EQOBP	EQSLG	EQMLVR	VORP	DEFENSE
2003	YAK	NWN	21	257	82	35	1	6	36	41	3	0	.319	.410	.533	.386	.248	.314	.420	-.093	-4.1	20-RF -2
2004	ELP	TXS	22	226	68	13	2	6	24	36	3	3	.301	.367	.456	.073	.235	.297	.367	-.209	-11.0	41-LF -3
2004	LNC	CLF	22	258	89	19	2	11	45	36	4	3	.345	.438	.562	.348	.263	.348	.422	-.016	3.2	57-LF -3
2005	*ARI*	*NL*	*23*	*322*	*82*	*19*	*2*	*10*	*33*	*61*	*3*	*1*	*.254*	*.327*	*.415*	*-.064*	*.249*	*.321*	*.407*	*-.092*	*0.4*	*87-LF -7*

Breakout: 19% *Improve: 43%* *Collapse: 27%*

The stathead's choice for a steal in the first round, Jackson's been great, as expected, showing he can hit for average and power, and taking any way possible to get on base. He's going to be ready for the big leagues very quickly, to the point where the D-Backs probably shouldn't be overcrowding the corner OF or 1B spots. A little more power and you're looking at a future star.

MATT KATA INF **Bats: B** **Throws: R** Born: 14-Mar-1978 Age: 27

YEAR	TM	LG	AGE	AB	H	2B	3B	HR	BB	SO	SB	CS	AVG	OBP	SLG	MLVR	EQBA	EQOBP	EQSLG	EQMLVR	VORP	DEFENSE	
2002	ELP	TXS	24	578	172	33	9	11	37	79	12	7	.298	.341	.443	.061	.249	.287	.389	-.187	-2.0	122-2B 3	
2003	TUC	PCL	25	201	58	13	5	3	9	29	2	3	.289	.327	.448	-.017	.245	.284	.393	-.190	-0.8	39-2B -5	
2003	ARI	NL	25	288	74	16	5	7	25	53	3	2	.257	.315	.420	-.063	.247	.305	.410	-.125	8.3	48-2B -3	18-3B 2
2004	ARI	NL	26	162	40	9	2	2	13	29	4	1	.247	.301	.364	-.155	.236	.291	.348	-.246	1.6	38-2B -1	
2005	*ARI*	*NL*	*27*	*317*	*81*	*17*	*3*	*7*	*21*	*53*	*5*	*2*	*.256*	*.306*	*.392*	*-.132*	*.251*	*.300*	*.384*	*-.158*	*4.1*	*83-2B -1*	

Breakout: 16% *Improve: 41%* *Collapse: 32%*

A shoulder separation and the return of Craig Counsell are putting the squeeze on Kata. He could actually be a decent utility guy, but with Cintron, Counsell, Hairston, and the inexplicable Royce Clayton in town, the writing on the wall's pretty clear. If he doesn't light up spring training, he's bus bound.

JOSH KROEGER RF **Bats: L** **Throws: L** Born: 31-Aug-1982 Age: 22

YEAR	TM	LG	AGE	AB	H	2B	3B	HR	BB	SO	SB	CS	AVG	OBP	SLG	MLVR	EQBA	EQOBP	EQSLG	EQMLVR	VORP	DEFENSE
2002	LNC	CLF	19	497	117	20	7	7	23	136	2	4	.235	.274	.346	-.240	.185	.212	.272	-.539	-58.0	
2003	ELP	TXS	20	208	57	9	2	3	10	54	3	5	.274	.315	.380	-.098	.224	.265	.327	-.334	-11.2	27-CF -2 26-RF 0
2003	LNC	CLF	20	305	104	30	6	5	35	58	6	6	.341	.409	.528	.273	.261	.325	.407	-.081	-1.4	58-RF -3 12-CF 0
2004	ARI	NL	21	54	9	3	0	0	1	21	0	1	.167	.182	.222	-.601	.167	.154	.185	-.790	-7.1	
2004	ELP	TXS	21	245	81	28	4	9	21	48	2	1	.331	.393	.588	.313	.272	.326	.490	.047	8.6	57-RF -5
2004	TUC	PCL	21	208	69	23	0	10	15	47	2	1	.332	.376	.587	.212	.251	.290	.442	-.104	-2.3	43-RF -2 11-CF 0
2005	*ARI*	*NL*	*22*	*400*	*100*	*24*	*3*	*12*	*24*	*95*	*3*	*2*	*.251*	*.300*	*.412*	*-.118*	*.246*	*.294*	*.404*	*-.145*	*-1.5*	*103-RF -6*

Breakout: 31% *Improve: 54%* *Collapse: 27%*

Solid prospect with power, ability to hit for average, and a willingness to work on his plate discipline. He got called into emergency service late in the year for the D-Backs, but he'll start the season at Triple-A. Despite a broad set of offensive skills, he needs to keep tweaking that BB/K rate to be a keeper.

QUINTON McCRACKEN OF **Bats: B** **Throws: R** Born: 16-Aug-1970 Age: 34

YEAR	TM	LG	AGE	AB	H	2B	3B	HR	BB	SO	SB	CS	AVG	OBP	SLG	MLVR	EQBA	EQOBP	EQSLG	EQMLVR	VORP	DEFENSE
2002	ARI	NL	31	349	108	27	8	3	32	68	5	4	.309	.367	.458	.119	.300	.357	.453	.075	19.2	61-RF -5 26-CF 2
2003	ARI	NL	32	203	46	5	2	0	15	34	5	1	.227	.276	.271	-.342	.217	.264	.246	-.453	-10.4	20-RF -2 10-CF -1
2004	SEA	AL	33	20	3	0	0	0	2	4	1	1	.150	.227	.150	-.664	.200	.162	.200	-.740	-2.5	
2004	ARI	NL	33	156	45	11	1	2	13	23	2	4	.288	.341	.410	.012	.282	.335	.397	-.060	2.9	18-LF -1
2004	TUC	PCL	33	58	19	5	1	1	3	5	2	2	.328	.361	.500	.058	.255	.293	.400	-.155	-0.5	
2005	*ARI*	*NL*	*34*	*139*	*37*	*8*	*1*	*2*	*11*	*22*	*3*	*1*	*.264*	*.321*	*.380*	*-.114*	*.260*	*.315*	*.373*	*-.141*	*0.5*	*41-LF -1*

Breakout: 23% *Improve: 43%* *Collapse: 30%*

As a fifth outfielder, McCracken's not a bad guy to have around for close to the league minimum. He doesn't have much power, doesn't hit for a huge average, but he can slap some line drives, play acceptable defense, and won't do a lot of moaning about wanting an increased role. Realistically, he's a .265/.335/.375 guy, who plays enough defense to be a caddy for a luggish corner OF slugger. If you need more than that, look elsewhere.

KYLE NICHOLS 1B **Bats: R** **Throws: R** Born: 29-Mar-1978 Age: 27

YEAR	TM	LG	AGE	AB	H	2B	3B	HR	BB	SO	SB	CS	AVG	OBP	SLG	MLVR	EQBA	EQOBP	EQSLG	EQMLVR	VORP	DEFENSE
2002	SBN	MDW	24	453	111	35	0	12	56	101	0	1	.245	.327	.402	.059	.197	.261	.330	-.353	-39.7	69-1B -4
2003	LNC	CLF	25	484	151	34	0	31	51	118	0	0	.312	.378	.574	.263	.229	.288	.422	-.153	-10.1	59-1B -1
2004	ELP	TXS	26	144	42	9	0	7	21	43	0	2	.292	.376	.500	.137	.227	.300	.397	-.167	-4.0	11-1B -1
2004	TUC	PCL	26	167	49	10	0	14	26	64	0	0	.293	.390	.605	.217	.219	.306	.444	-.098	-0.7	21-1B 0
2005	*ARI*	*NL*	*27*	*194*	*45*	*9*	*1*	*9*	*22*	*67*	*0*	*0*	*.232*	*.312*	*.417*	*-.104*	*.228*	*.306*	*.409*	*-.130*	*0.0*	*55-DH*

Breakout: 29% *Improve: 48%* *Collapse: 31%*

Fun player, in the Rob Deer mold. Swings hard, plays first base, sometimes a baseball runs into his bat and soars like John Ashcroft's unshackled eagle. Nichols is old for his level, but teams have worse guys at the end of their benches. It'd be nice to see him get a shot.

TIM OLSON UT **Bats: R** **Throws: R** Born: 01-Aug-1978 Age: 26

YEAR	TM	LG	AGE	AB	H	2B	3B	HR	BB	SO	SB	CS	AVG	OBP	SLG	MLVR	EQBA	EQOBP	EQSLG	EQMLVR	VORP	DEFENSE
2002	ELP	TXS	23	433	118	24	2	10	27	91	9	11	.273	.337	.406	-.010	.225	.276	.354	-.274	-9.2	98-SS -3 11-CF 0
2003	ELP	TXS	24	56	11	2	0	2	5	19	0	2	.196	.258	.339	-.287	.127	.182	.236	-.674	-7.9	12-SS -1
2003	TUC	PCL	24	397	104	22	0	6	31	77	11	2	.262	.323	.363	-.153	.210	.269	.295	-.378	-20.4	96-SS -15
2004	TUC	PCL	25	147	44	11	0	7	16	28	5	1	.299	.373	.517	.077	.220	.286	.369	-.237	-1.5	18-SS -2
2004	ARI	NL	25	97	18	7	0	2	16	18	1	0	.186	.301	.320	-.249	.186	.288	.289	-.360	-2.2	16-3B 0 12-SS -2
2005	*ARI*	*NL*	*26*	*145*	*35*	*7*	*1*	*4*	*13*	*33*	*2*	*1*	*.239*	*.312*	*.388*	*-.138*	*.235*	*.306*	*.380*	*-.164*	*1.7*	*42-SS -6*

Breakout: 49% *Improve: 63%* *Collapse: 23%*

Got a trial by fire last year due to urgent need in Phoenix, and looked pretty overmatched. Olson turns 27 this year, and he's got a very short window in which to shine and earn another opportunity to play in the bigs. Projects as a utility guy if he's going to have a career.

CARLOS QUENTIN RF Bats: R Throws: R Born: 28-Aug-1982 Age: 22

YEAR	TM	LG	AGE	AB	H	2B	3B	HR	BB	SO	SB	CS	AVG	OBP	SLG	MLVR	EQBA	EQOBP	EQSLG	EQMLVR	VORP	DEFENSE
2004	LNC	CLF	21	242	75	14	1	15	25	33	5	1	.310	.428	.562	.297	.230	.319	.416	-.103	-2.8	53-RF 0
2004	ELP	TXS	21	210	75	19	0	6	18	23	0	6	.357	.443	.533	.335	.275	.338	.420	-.028	2.5	54-RF -2
2005	*ARI*	*NL*	*22*	*334*	*90*	*18*	*2*	*13*	*25*	*52*	*1*	*1*	*.269*	*.382*	*.452*	*.087*	*.264*	*.374*	*.443*	*.058*	*28.9*	*96-RF -5*

Breakout: 38% *Improve: 53%* *Collapse: 20%*

Love this guy. Not sure why he hasn't gotten more pub, but he's a better prospect than Conor Jackson at this point, and that's saying something. Lit up the California and Texas Leagues, showing power, solid defense, athleticism, and a great ability to adjust to off-speed pitches. He'll see some time at Triple-A before the year's out, and will be on the Rookie of the Year ballot in '06 or '07. Check that PECOTA: If they let him, he could have a ROY shot right now.

SERGIO SANTOS SS Bats: R Throws: R Born: 04-Jul-1983 Age: 21

YEAR	TM	LG	AGE	AB	H	2B	3B	HR	BB	SO	SB	CS	AVG	OBP	SLG	MLVR	EQBA	EQOBP	EQSLG	EQMLVR	VORP	DEFENSE
2002	MSO	PIO	19	202	55	19	2	9	29	49	6	3	.272	.367	.520	.221	.193	.259	.356	-.324	-14.2	50-SS -10
2003	ELP	TXS	20	137	35	7	1	2	8	25	0	0	.255	.293	.365	-.165	.207	.244	.311	-.408	-8.2	35-SS -4
2003	LNC	CLF	20	341	98	13	2	8	41	64	5	4	.287	.368	.408	.005	.221	.292	.316	-.297	-9.7	84-SS -13
2004	ELP	TXS	21	347	98	19	5	11	24	89	3	2	.282	.332	.461	.012	.227	.274	.375	-.247	-4.7	83-SS -14
2005	*ARI*	*NL*	*21*	*351*	*82*	*18*	*2*	*11*	*26*	*89*	*2*	*1*	*.234*	*.291*	*.386*	*-.181*	*.229*	*.285*	*.379*	*-.207*	*1.3*	*92-SS -11*

Breakout: 36% *Improve: 53%* *Collapse: 26%*

We admit we're not scouts. Having spoken with a number of real scouts, we can say they're good at spotting things. They're trained. They're professionals. We can argue about what role scouting is going to play in an organization, but no one at BP is a scout. And yet unlike Diamondbacks' scouts, it's almost impossible for us to watch Sergio Santos and believe that he's ever going to be able to play a passable shortstop. There's no economy of motion, no instincts. You know how Gabe Kapler looks when he's playing defense? Kind of like Arnold Schwarzenegger in one of the Conan movies, with a kind of hypermechanical, MC Escher quality to his movement. Kapler can get by with that in the outfield, but Santos, in the infield, looks like a complete disaster. But that only goes to his ability to play shortstop. He's got a nice bat, puts a lot of energy into his swing, and held his own in Double-A at the age of 21. He's got a chance to be a good one if he can find somewhere else to play. It's bad enough we have to watch Derek Jeter play shortstop. Lord, save us from Santos.

RICHIE SEXSON 1B Bats: R Throws: R Born: 29-Dec-1974 Age: 30

YEAR	TM	LG	AGE	AB	H	2B	3B	HR	BB	SO	SB	CS	AVG	OBP	SLG	MLVR	EQBA	EQOBP	EQSLG	EQMLVR	VORP	DEFENSE
2002	MIL	NL	27	570	159	37	2	29	70	136	0	0	.279	.363	.504	.207	.279	.361	.513	.147	47.4	150-1B 14
2003	MIL	NL	28	606	165	28	2	45	98	151	2	3	.272	.379	.548	.254	.269	.375	.548	.208	58.7	162-1B 18
2004	ARI	NL	29	90	21	4	0	9	14	21	0	0	.233	.337	.578	.174	.225	.315	.551	.068	7.3	23-1B 3
2005	*SEA*	*AL*	*30*	*371*	*94*	*19*	*1*	*21*	*50*	*88*	*0*	*1*	*.254*	*.347*	*.480*	*.059*	*.261*	*.357*	*.504*	*.103*	*23.6*	*102-1B 2*

Breakout: 21% *Improve: 53%* *Collapse: 14%*

Big, bopping first baseman with mucho power and a very questionable shoulder. Sexson had surgery to repair a torn labrum, which caused his shoulder to basically slip out of place when swinging the bat. Considering the amount of force in Sexson's swing, it's not a lock that he'll be able to play a full season. All things considered, the four-year, $50 million contract the Mariners gave Sexson is probably the worst one doled out all off-season.

CHRIS SNYDER C Bats: R Throws: R Born: 12-Feb-1981 Age: 24

YEAR	TM	LG	AGE	AB	H	2B	3B	HR	BB	SO	SB	CS	AVG	OBP	SLG	MLVR	EQBA	EQOBP	EQSLG	EQMLVR	VORP	DEFENSE
2002	LNC	CLF	21	217	56	16	0	9	25	54	0	0	.258	.337	.456	.018	.194	.255	.343	-.349	-14.6	
2003	LNC	CLF	22	245	77	16	2	10	35	43	0	1	.314	.414	.518	.242	.241	.327	.398	-.104	5.2	56-C -3
2003	ELP	TXS	22	188	38	14	0	4	19	29	0	0	.202	.286	.340	-.236	.155	.227	.267	-.528	-20.2	47-C 2
2004	ELP	TXS	23	346	104	31	0	15	46	57	3	1	.301	.389	.520	.189	.227	.305	.404	-.148	2.9	81-C -3
2004	ARI	NL	23	96	23	6	0	5	13	25	0	0	.240	.327	.458	.020	.232	.307	.432	-.102	5.2	29-C 0
2005	*ARI*	*NL*	*24*	*307*	*76*	*17*	*1*	*12*	*33*	*61*	*1*	*0*	*.248*	*.330*	*.429*	*-.045*	*.244*	*.324*	*.421*	*-.072*	*10.6*	*85-C -5*

Breakout: 42% *Improve: 69%* *Collapse: 16%*

Catching prospect, and a pretty reasonable one. Snyder's got power and projects to gain more of it, he plays credible defense, and can draw some walks. He's going to get a shot to earn a spot and some playing time, and if he gets it, he could develop into a championship-caliber catcher.

LUIS TERRERO CF Bats: R Throws: R Born: 18-May-1980 Age: 25

YEAR	TM	LG	AGE	AB	H	2B	3B	HR	BB	SO	SB	CS	AVG	OBP	SLG	MLVR	EQBA	EQOBP	EQSLG	EQMLVR	VORP	DEFENSE
2002	ELP	TXS	22	360	103	20	6	8	23	89	18	22	.286	.342	.442	.051	.237	.283	.380	-.216	-7.4	99-CF 2
2003	TUC	PCL	23	467	134	20	15	3	31	103	23	19	.287	.345	.413	-.034	.241	.299	.354	-.219	-9.7	111-CF -4
2004	TUC	PCL	24	217	68	9	6	9	17	48	15	3	.313	.374	.535	.116	.249	.304	.416	-.117	1.9	41-CF 1 13-RF -1
2004	ARI	NL	24	229	56	14	0	4	20	78	10	2	.245	.319	.358	-.129	.237	.307	.338	-.228	2.5	55-CF -6
2005	*ARI*	*NL*	*25*	*319*	*83*	*17*	*3*	*8*	*23*	*84*	*10*	*4*	*.262*	*.325*	*.413*	*-.066*	*.257*	*.318*	*.405*	*-.094*	*8.3*	*85-CF -3*

Breakout: 36% *Improve: 58%* *Collapse: 19%*

Fast center fielder who favors a somewhat, um, asymptotic path to the ball. Hits line drives, and seems to have suddenly figured out how to put his speed to good use on the basepaths. Not likely to take a quantum leap forward with the bat, but a little plate discipline could go a long way towards securing his family's financial future.

CHAD TRACY 3B Bats: L Throws: R Born: 22-May-1980 Age: 25

YEAR	TM	LG	AGE	AB	H	2B	3B	HR	BB	SO	SB	CS	AVG	OBP	SLG	MLVR	EQBA	EQOBP	EQSLG	EQMLVR	VORP	DEFENSE
2002	ELP	TXS	22	514	177	39	5	8	38	51	2	3	.344	.389	.486	.225	.289	.329	.428	-.021	24.7	112-3B -10
2003	TUC	PCL	23	522	169	31	4	10	41	52	0	2	.324	.372	.456	.094	.268	.319	.388	-.114	10.2	125-3B 7
2004	ARI	NL	24	481	137	29	3	8	45	60	2	3	.285	.343	.407	.009	.275	.334	.392	-.075	14.8	116-3B 0
2005	*ARI*	*NL*	*25*	*436*	*121*	*26*	*3*	*9*	*37*	*52*	*2*	*1*	*.277*	*.335*	*.415*	*-.033*	*.272*	*.329*	*.407*	*-.061*	*7.2*	*114-3B -1*

Breakout: 14% *Improve: 34%* *Collapse: 33%*

Adjusted nicely in his regular gig in the bigs, continuing his record of adjusting well at every level. He's got that broad skill base we like, he's not particularly old, and he can play defense well enough so that he's not going to slide down the spectrum to DH any time soon. Power remains the one ability that's eluded him, but he's amassed enough doubles to give one hope. With Glaus in town and Tracy entrenched, expect a change of address for Shea Hillenbrand.

JONATHAN ZERINGUE RF Bats: R Throws: R Born: 29-Aug-1983 Age: 21

YEAR	TM	LG	AGE	AB	H	2B	3B	HR	BB	SO	SB	CS	AVG	OBP	SLG	MLVR	EQBA	EQOBP	EQSLG	EQMLVR	VORP	DEFENSE
2004	LNC	CLF	20	230	77	14	3	10	14	53	9	5	.335	.374	.552	.232	.253	.289	.416	-.141	-5.1	35-RF 1
2005	*ARI*	*NL*	*21*	*417*	*99*	*20*	*3*	*13*	*22*	*121*	*9*	*3*	*.237*	*.276*	*.393*	*-.196*	*.233*	*.271*	*.385*	*-.221*	*-10.9*	*106-RF -5*

Breakout: 12% *Improve: 39%* *Collapse: 38%*

Great start to his career, Lancaster bandbox or not. Zeringue has a history of hitting for power and average both at LSU and early in his pro career, and he runs well too. However, there's some concern he may be miscast in the outfield. The Snakes are loaded with hitting prospects, but there's talk Zeringue will start the season in Double-A, and may move up quickly. High ceiling.

PITCHERS

GREG AQUINO Bats: R Throws: R Born: 11-Jan-1978 Age: 27

YEAR	TM	LG	AGE	G	GS	IP	H	BB	SO	HR	ERA	EQERA	EQH9	EQBB9	EQSO9	EQHR9	PERA	VORP	STF
2002	YAK	NWN	24	6	6	35.0	26	17	34	0	2.06	4.50	7.9	5.6	4.8	0.3	3.66	6.9	5
2002	LNC	CLF	24	8	8	49.0	50	18	50	3	3.67	4.21	9.4	3.6	5.4	1.0	4.79	4.2	4
2003	ELP	TXS	25	20	20	106.7	115	38	91	5	3.46	3.88	8.8	3.5	5.7	0.8	4.14	16.9	14
2004	TUC	PCL	26	21	2	29.7	33	18	19	2	6.36	6.52	9.0	5.6	4.3	0.6	4.97	2.0	-21
2004	ARI	NL	26	34	0	35.3	24	17	26	4	3.06	3.55	7.1	4.1	6.3	0.8	3.27	7.4	0
2005	*ARI*	*NL*	*27*	*8*	*3*	*25.0*	*24*	*13*	*18*	*3*	*4.62*	*4.61*	*8.6*	*4.1*	*5.7*	*0.9*	*4.60*	*3.2*	*-3*

Breakout: 19% *Improve: 45%* *Collapse: 25%*

Even on a team as bad as the '04 Diamondbacks, there are multi-million-dollar decisions happening every day. Injuries to Jose Valverde and struggles by Mike Koplove, Brian Bruney, and others opened the door for Aquino to grab the closer's role, and he did a respectable job with it from then on. Aquino's got a history of decent, but not dominant peripherals, so if Valverde's 100% in spring training, he's the more likely bet to get those overrated but lucrative saves, with Aquino settling for a set-up role.

ADAM BASS Bats: R Throws: R Born: 31-Jul-1981 Age: 23

YEAR	TM	LG	AGE	G	GS	IP	H	BB	SO	HR	ERA	EQERA	EQH9	EQBB9	EQSO9	EQHR9	PERA	VORP	STF
2003	YAK	NWN	21	27	0	33.7	26	14	34	2	0.80	3.64	9.4	4.9	5.5	1.8	5.76	-0.5	-17
2004	LNC	CLF	22	28	27	146.7	180	49	117	12	5.03	5.72	10.3	3.6	4.6	1.2	5.78	-2.8	-6
2005	*ARI*	*NL*	*23*	*10*	*9*	*52.0*	*57*	*24*	*33*	*8*	*5.40*	*5.39*	*9.8*	*3.6*	*5.3*	*1.3*	*5.48*	*2.7*	*-3*

Breakout: 12% *Improve: 44%* *Collapse: 19%*

A control guy who didn't pitch particularly well in the Cal League. He'll have to figure out how to keep the ball down a bit more, but he could be helped by improved defense if he gets a shot to move up. Long shot to have a major league career, but that's true of most.

BRIAN BRUNEY Bats: R Throws: R Born: 17-Feb-1982 Age: 23

YEAR	TM	LG	AGE	G	GS	IP	H	BB	SO	HR	ERA	EQERA	EQH9	EQBB9	EQSO9	EQHR9	PERA	VORP	STF
2002	SBN	MDW	20	37	0	48.3	37	17	54	1	1.68	4.67	7.9	4.1	6.3	0.4	3.45	10.6	7
2002	ELP	TXS	20	10	0	12.3	11	4	14	1	2.93	4.63	8.5	3.1	7.7	1.5	4.63	1.3	13
2003	ELP	TXS	21	28	0	31.3	29	13	28	1	2.59	5.04	7.7	4.2	5.9	0.6	3.26	7.9	4
2003	TUC	PCL	21	32	0	32.0	24	18	32	0	2.81	3.60	6.9	5.7	7.8	0.3	3.60	6.7	12
2004	TUC	PCL	22	31	0	38.0	18	20	42	1	1.18	2.06	5.4	5.1	8.0	0.3	2.57	11.8	24
2004	ARI	NL	22	30	0	31.3	20	27	34	2	4.31	4.15	6.5	6.8	8.9	0.6	3.56	3.9	19
2005	*ARI*	*NL*	*23*	*34*	*5*	*66.0*	*46*	*46*	*58*	*8*	*4.21*	*4.20*	*6.1*	*5.4*	*7.3*	*1.0*	*4.02*	*10.6*	*-1*

Breakout: 27% *Improve: 52%* *Collapse: 20%*

Pitched his way up the majors after three years of solid relief work, with good ERAs and peripheral numbers indicative of future success. While not overwhelmed at the major league level, he had a hard time with more patient opponents. He'll contend for a spot in the bullpen, and if he doesn't struggle with his command, he's got good enough stuff to be dominant.

MATT CHICO Bats: L Throws: L Born: 10-Jun-1983 Age: 22

YEAR	TM	LG	AGE	G	GS	IP	H	BB	SO	HR	ERA	EQERA	EQH9	EQBB9	EQSO9	EQHR9	PERA	VORP	STF
2003	YAK	NWN	20	17	13	71.3	75	25	71	4	3.53	5.79	10.9	4.0	5.1	1.7	6.34	-5.4	-9
2004	SBN	MDW	21	14	14	87.7	59	27	89	9	2.57	4.32	8.6	3.7	5.7	2.0	5.26	2.9	0
2004	ELP	TXS	21	14	12	62.3	82	36	59	7	5.78	7.15	10.4	5.5	5.8	1.3	5.98	-2.6	-13
2005	*ARI*	*NL*	*22*	*10*	*9*	*53.0*	*55*	*27*	*39*	*9*	*5.35*	*5.34*	*9.1*	*4.0*	*6.1*	*1.4*	*5.31*	*2.5*	*1*

Breakout: 12% *Improve: 47%* *Collapse: 16%*

Little SoCal lefty pitched well in the Midwest League, but upon arrival in the Texas League, got more pasted than a 21-year old Kennedy watching pole dances. Has problems keeping the ball in the park, often falling behind in the count and then laying cookies down the middle of the plate in search of a strike. Good enough stuff to succeed in a relief role in the majors, especially given his youth, but there's some work to be done before that time arrives.

RANDY CHOATE Bats: L Throws: L Born: 05-Sep-1975 Age: 29

YEAR	TM	LG	AGE	G	GS	IP	H	BB	SO	HR	ERA	EQERA	EQH9	EQBB9	EQSO9	EQHR9	PERA	VORP	STF
2002	COH	INT	26	31	0	36.7	25	15	32	0	1.72	2.62	6.6	4.2	6.8	0.3	2.36	12.3	14
2002	NYY	AL	26	18	0	22.3	18	15	17	1	6.05	6.65	7.5	5.8	6.6	0.4	3.32	-3.2	4
2003	COH	INT	27	54	3	71.3	75	24	56	4	3.91	4.87	9.2	3.4	5.7	0.8	4.61	7.5	-6
2004	TUC	PCL	28	15	0	12.7	10	8	7	1	5.67	4.63	7.7	6.2	3.9	0.8	4.63	1.3	-24
2004	ARI	NL	28	74	0	50.7	52	28	49	1	4.62	4.26	8.3	4.3	7.6	0.2	3.55	6.1	11
2005	*ARI*	*NL*	*29*	*36*	*1*	*50.3*	*50*	*25*	*41*	*4*	*4.23*	*4.22*	*8.8*	*3.9*	*6.8*	*0.6*	*4.45*	*7.8*	*0*

Breakout: 28% *Improve: 51%* *Collapse: 16%*

Choate's that LOOGY floatballer, sporting the telltale 3:2ish ratio of games to innings pitched. In 2004, the left-hander actually was tougher on righties than lefties, to the tune of about 80 points of OPS. He can get people out on his good days, so he'll be around for years to come.

LANCE CORMIER **Bats: R** **Throws: R** Born: 19-Aug-1980 Age: 24

YEAR	TM	LG	AGE	G	GS	IP	H	BB	SO	HR	ERA	EQERA	EQH9	EQBB9	EQSO9	EQHR9	PERA	VORP	STF
2002	SBN	MDW	21	11	3	27.7	29	2	17	1	2.92	4.78	9.6	0.7	3.4	0.7	3.42	6.4	-8
2003	LNC	CLF	22	15	15	94.3	102	16	59	6	3.82	5.60	9.6	1.9	3.6	1.0	4.80	8.0	-3
2003	ELP	TXS	22	9	8	41.3	59	22	26	3	6.10	6.91	10.6	5.2	4.1	1.1	6.05	-2.1	-22
2003	TUC	PCL	22	5	4	27.7	26	5	11	1	2.60	3.46	8.7	1.7	3.1	0.3	3.46	6.2	7
2004	ELP	TXS	23	10	8	63.0	66	17	58	3	2.29	3.23	8.7	2.6	5.7	0.6	3.52	14.2	21
2004	TUC	PCL	23	8	8	50.3	50	17	37	0	2.68	2.94	8.3	3.1	5.1	0.2	3.49	11.5	16
2004	ARI	NL	23	17	5	45.3	62	25	24	13	8.15	7.35	11.3	4.4	4.2	2.2	6.75	-13.1	-26
2005	*ARI*	*NL*	*24*	*17*	*15*	*87.3*	*101*	*35*	*55*	*11*	*5.09*	*5.08*	*10.3*	*3.1*	*5.1*	*1.0*	*5.17*	*6.8*	*0*

Breakout: 13% *Improve: 47%* *Collapse: 28%*

Did OK in the minors but couldn't hold it together in the majors, which is a great recipe to assure spending a lot of your career at Triple-A. Cormier's stuff isn't great, and his performance record isn't one that matches up with a huge career, but he does have a chance to have a long career in long relief if he can keep his control together. Still, he'll want to keep that ERA under 8.00, or perhaps sign on with Colorado or Texas.

CASEY DAIGLE **Bats: R** **Throws: R** Born: 04-Apr-1981 Age: 24

YEAR	TM	LG	AGE	G	GS	IP	H	BB	SO	HR	ERA	EQERA	EQH9	EQBB9	EQSO9	EQHR9	PERA	VORP	STF
2002	LNC	CLF	21	21	21	122.0	137	42	85	19	5.09	6.10	10.7	3.5	3.7	2.3	6.65	-13.4	-17
2002	ELP	TXS	21	7	7	44.3	46	9	29	5	3.25	4.35	10.0	2.0	4.6	1.7	5.23	1.7	5
2003	ELP	TXS	22	29	27	176.3	219	51	115	9	4.59	5.45	9.6	2.8	4.3	0.8	4.42	22.9	1
2004	ARI	NL	23	10	10	49.0	63	27	17	9	7.16	6.70	10.8	4.3	2.8	1.5	5.96	-9.6	-31
2004	TUC	PCL	23	18	15	100.7	154	24	51	21	6.88	6.37	11.5	2.1	3.4	1.7	6.20	-6.8	-24
2005	*ARI*	*NL*	*24*	*17*	*16*	*91.7*	*107*	*36*	*49*	*15*	*5.56*	*5.55*	*10.4*	*3.1*	*4.4*	*1.4*	*5.56*	*2.0*	*-7*

Breakout: 8% *Improve: 43%* *Collapse: 22%*

How do you end up with Casey Daigle making 10 starts for your club? His ERA was north of that magical 7.00 number, and he was giving up 150+ hits in 100 innings at Triple-A, while striking out 51. After each serial battering, did Bob Brenly say "Hey, that Daigle guy just ran into a few bats today; next time, those'll be pop-ups." Daigle's probably filing 2004 under "Just Ignore It," and hoping to try to find the groove he sort of had in 2002 and 2003. Not likely. But hey, how bad can life be when you're married to Jennie Finch?

CASEY FOSSUM **Bats: B** **Throws: L** Born: 06-Jan-1978 Age: 27

YEAR	TM	LG	AGE	G	GS	IP	H	BB	SO	HR	ERA	EQERA	EQH9	EQBB9	EQSO9	EQHR9	PERA	VORP	STF
2002	BOS	AL	24	43	12	106.7	113	30	101	12	3.46	4.36	8.9	2.3	8.1	0.9	4.10	14.9	7
2003	BOS	AL	25	19	14	79.0	82	34	63	9	5.47	5.65	8.7	3.7	7.0	0.9	4.04	-1.6	9
2004	ARI	NL	26	27	27	142.0	171	63	117	31	6.65	6.30	10.0	3.5	6.5	1.7	5.35	-20.1	0
2005	*ARI*	*NL*	*27*	*25*	*21*	*125.3*	*130*	*48*	*106*	*17*	*4.72*	*4.71*	*9.2*	*3.0*	*6.9*	*1.1*	*4.66*	*13.6*	*11*

Breakout: 15% *Improve: 49%* *Collapse: 25%*

For about six weeks, he was a favorite of stathead fans; the next Johan Santana, perhaps? At this point, that looks like more of a pipe dream than substantive and dignified political campaigning. Fossum's 2004 was awful by any measure. He served up bushels of home runs, walked a ton of guys, and was generally just a doppelganger for Charley Kerfeld's less talented cousin. Some rebound is almost inevitable; PECOTA still thinks he can be league-average.

EDGAR GONZALEZ **Bats: R** **Throws: R** Born: 23-Feb-1983 Age: 22

YEAR	TM	LG	AGE	G	GS	IP	H	BB	SO	HR	ERA	EQERA	EQH9	EQBB9	EQSO9	EQHR9	PERA	VORP	STF
2002	LNC	CLF	19	4	4	23.0	24	3	21	1	0.78	3.63	9.3	1.2	4.8	0.4	3.63	4.9	19
2002	SBN	MDW	19	23	23	151.3	141	34	110	4	2.91	5.65	9.0	2.5	4.0	0.6	3.62	31.2	25
2003	ELP	TXS	20	6	6	36.0	40	11	30	1	3.50	4.54	8.6	3.0	5.6	0.3	3.53	8.2	20
2003	ARI	NL	20	9	2	18.3	28	7	14	3	4.92	4.26	11.4	2.8	5.7	1.4	6.16	1.5	23
2003	TUC	PCL	20	20	19	129.7	126	28	69	4	3.75	4.51	8.5	2.2	4.1	0.3	3.27	32.0	38
2004	TUC	PCL	21	15	15	94.0	99	25	66	15	4.88	4.47	9.1	2.5	4.9	1.2	4.47	11.4	27
2004	ARI	NL	21	10	10	46.3	72	18	31	15	9.33	8.37	12.0	3.0	5.1	2.5	7.04	-19.3	8
2005	*ARI*	*NL*	*22*	*18*	*18*	*105.7*	*120*	*37*	*63*	*15*	*5.06*	*5.05*	*10.0*	*2.8*	*4.9*	*1.2*	*5.12*	*7.8*	*1*

Breakout: 5% *Improve: 36%* *Collapse: 27%*

Right-handed control guy. Keeps the ball down, and when he doesn't, it gets pounded. His peripherals aren't indicative of a future filled with Cy Young awards, but he is still young, has had some success, and will have a chance to hone his craft.

ANDREW GOOD **Bats: R** **Throws: R** Born: 19-Sep-1979 Age: 25

YEAR	TM	LG	AGE	G	GS	IP	H	BB	SO	HR	ERA	EQERA	EQH9	EQBB9	EQSO9	EQHR9	PERA	VORP	STF
2002	ELP	TXS	22	28	27	178.0	170	26	127	21	3.54	4.97	9.7	1.5	5.0	2.0	4.97	11.5	8
2003	TUC	PCL	23	11	11	63.0	78	13	45	12	5.00	5.04	10.7	2.1	5.5	2.1	5.79	-1.3	-3
2003	ARI	NL	23	16	10	66.3	74	16	42	15	5.29	5.20	10.0	2.0	5.2	2.0	5.34	-0.1	-5
2004	TUC	PCL	24	5	3	23.7	25	4	17	4	3.04	3.97	9.1	1.6	5.2	1.6	4.37	3.1	6
2004	ARI	NL	24	17	2	40.7	43	13	26	8	5.31	5.03	9.4	2.5	5.3	1.6	4.58	0.8	-5
2005	*DET*	*AL*	*25*	*21*	*9*	*68.7*	*73*	*19*	*45*	*11*	*4.89*	*4.94*	*9.6*	*2.2*	*5.3*	*1.5*	*4.68*	*7.7*	*-3*

Breakout: 20% *Improve: 43%* *Collapse: 24%*

Young version of a prototypical control pitcher. Good survives by keeping the ball down, limiting bases on balls, and relying on the defense. Unfortunately, his season was cut short by bone chips in his elbow, and the Diamondbacks released him in December after they signed Russ Ortiz. For other clubs out there, Good might be a good one to grab, stash in Triple-A while he gets healthy, then see if he can get guys out. At least, that's what the Tigers are probably thinking.

MIKE GOSLING **Bats: L** **Throws: L** Born: 23-Sep-1980 Age: 24

YEAR	TM	LG	AGE	G	GS	IP	H	BB	SO	HR	ERA	EQERA	EQH9	EQBB9	EQSO9	EQHR9	PERA	VORP	STF
2002	ELP	TXS	21	27	27	166.7	149	62	115	7	3.13	4.20	8.5	3.7	4.8	0.6	4.03	27.3	23
2003	TUC	PCL	22	26	26	136.3	190	56	89	13	5.61	6.55	10.7	4.0	4.8	1.0	5.69	-1.4	-14
2004	TUC	PCL	23	24	21	128.3	160	53	67	16	5.82	5.98	10.0	3.8	3.6	1.1	5.41	2.7	-6
2004	ARI	NL	23	6	4	25.3	26	13	14	5	4.62	4.07	9.2	4.1	4.4	1.5	4.81	3.2	-3
2005	*ARI*	*NL*	*24*	*23*	*12*	*82.7*	*93*	*38*	*48*	*12*	*5.28*	*5.27*	*9.9*	*3.7*	*4.7*	*1.2*	*5.44*	*5.4*	*-10*

Breakout: 13% *Improve: 52%* *Collapse: 21%*

Lefty, but not, contrary to what some might believe, a lefty version of Mike Mussina. Gosling's highly regarded by scouts, and there's no shortage of praise out there for him, but does his performance justify it? He gives up a ton of hits, his K rate's absolutely generic, and there's nothing about his performance to date that indicates that he's going to be a particularly successful pitcher in the majors, much less a star. He'll get a look in spring training, with Johnson likely leaving town.

RANDY JOHNSON **Bats: R** **Throws: L** Born: 10-Sep-1963 Age: 41

YEAR	TM	LG	AGE	G	GS	IP	H	BB	SO	HR	ERA	EQERA	EQH9	EQBB9	EQSO9	EQHR9	PERA	VORP	STF
2002	ARI	NL	38	35	35	260.0	197	71	334	26	2.32	2.69	7.1	2.1	10.4	0.9	2.83	80.9	46
2003	ARI	NL	39	18	18	114.0	125	27	125	16	4.26	4.35	8.9	1.8	8.8	1.1	3.96	11.2	32
2004	ARI	NL	40	35	35	245.7	177	44	290	18	2.60	2.98	6.8	1.5	9.7	0.6	2.14	69.3	50
2005	*NYY*	*AL*	*41*	*33*	*33*	*214.3*	*178*	*48*	*232*	*23*	*3.14*	*3.14*	*7.6*	*1.8*	*8.7*	*0.9*	*2.95*	*64.6*	34

Breakout: 34% *Improve: 63%* *Collapse: 19%*

Eventually, you run out of superlatives. Despite pitching for a team that was worse than a 12-episode binge of a Latvian-dubbed "Sex and the City," Johnson was his usual dominant self, showing virtually no negative signs of age or injury. There's nothing in his performance record to suggest that any sort of collapse is imminent, and he'll be a Cy Young candidate in '05, in New York. Enjoy watching him as long as you can—take the day off when he starts if necessary, because it's going to be a long time before we see another pitcher this exciting.

MIKE KOPLOVE **Bats: R** **Throws: R** Born: 30-Aug-1976 Age: 28

YEAR	TM	LG	AGE	G	GS	IP	H	BB	SO	HR	ERA	EQERA	EQH9	EQBB9	EQSO9	EQHR9	PERA	VORP	STF
2002	TUC	PCL	25	23	0	30.7	21	4	31	1	1.17	1.88	6.9	1.3	7.2	0.3	2.51	9.9	18
2002	ARI	NL	25	55	0	61.7	47	23	46	2	3.35	3.38	7.5	2.9	6.1	0.3	2.91	12.8	6
2003	ARI	NL	26	31	0	37.7	31	10	27	3	2.15	2.52	7.8	2.3	6.1	0.8	3.28	12.5	4
2004	ARI	NL	27	76	0	86.7	86	37	55	7	4.05	3.95	8.8	3.4	5.1	0.6	3.84	12.9	-6
2005	*ARI*	*NL*	*28*	*44*	*2*	*65.0*	*67*	*27*	*45*	*6*	*4.21*	*4.21*	*9.2*	*3.2*	*5.6*	*0.7*	*4.43*	*9.7*	*-5*

Breakout: 20% *Improve: 37%* *Collapse: 22%*

(continued next page)

Mike Koplove *(continued)*

His peripheral ERA only went up by about ³/₄th of a run, rather than the nearly two runs of his actual ERA, so he was probably a little lucky in 2003, and a little unlucky in 2004—or hurt, given he had his shoulder scoped after the '03 season. Still a serviceable reliever, someone to soak up some innings and keep the team in the game or come in to face a tough righty. He'll need full health and a halt to that falling strikeout rate to provide real value.

BRANDON LYON Bats: R Throws: R Born: 10-Aug-1979 Age: 25

YEAR	TM	LG	AGE	G	GS	IP	H	BB	SO	HR	ERA	EQERA	EQH9	EQBB9	EQSO9	EQHR9	PERA	VORP	STF
2002	SYR	INT	22	14	14	75.7	99	19	35	4	5.11	6.69	10.7	2.4	3.5	0.6	4.99	5.0	-9
2002	TOR	AL	22	15	10	62.0	78	19	30	14	6.53	6.05	10.6	2.5	4.1	1.8	5.75	-5.8	-20
20200	BOS	AL	23	49	0	59.0	73	19	50	6	4.12	4.50	9.3	2.7	7.2	0.8	4.05	7.1	8
2005	*ARI*	*NL*	*25*	*18*	*6*	*51.0*	*57*	*17*	*32*	*8*	*4.83*	*4.82*	*9.8*	*2.6*	*5.2*	*1.2*	*4.86*	*5.5*	*-5*

Breakout: 27% *Improve: 60%* *17%*

His 15 minutes of fame in Toronto have long since faded. He's now one of the Quadruple-A guys, hoping for the opportunity to show his stuff and make a big league squad. His task isn't going to be made easier by a mysterious elbow injury, which has already caused him to be pulled out of one trade. His stuff is pedestrian; he's going to need a serious break to return to the possibility sets of major league GMs.

MATT MANTEI Bats: R Throws: R Born: 07-Jul-1973 Age: 31

YEAR	TM	LG	AGE	G	GS	IP	H	BB	SO	HR	ERA	EQERA	EQH9	EQBB9	EQSO9	EQHR9	PERA	VORP	STF
2002	ARI	NL	29	31	0	26.7	28	12	26	3	4.72	4.78	8.9	3.4	7.9	1.0	4.44	0.9	4
2003	ARI	NL	30	50	0	55.0	37	18	68	6	2.62	2.56	6.7	2.6	10.3	0.9	2.73	17.3	31
2004	ARI	NL	31	12	0	10.7	17	6	13	5	11.78	11.45	12.3	4.1	9.0	3.3	8.18	-8.2	-4
2005	*BOS*	*AL*	*31*	*22*	*1*	*32.3*	*32*	*13*	*32*	*7*	*5.06*	*4.77*	*8.7*	*3.1*	*8.1*	*1.8*	*4.77*	*5.5*	*4*

Breakout: 29% *Improve: 55%* *Collapse: 27%*

Having seen the Snakes soaked for several pretty pennies over the years, we hope they have learned not to overpay for closers, or at least closers with trick elbows. Nevertheless, picking up Mantei is not a terrible risk for the Red Sox to take. If he's healthy at the right time, he can help them win a few games, but knowing when he'll be available to pitch is the province of the Amazing Kreskin.

SHANE NANCE Bats: L Throws: L Born: 07-Sep-1977 Age: 27

YEAR	TM	LG	AGE	G	GS	IP	H	BB	SO	HR	ERA	EQERA	EQH9	EQBB9	EQSO9	EQHR9	PERA	VORP	STF
2002	LVG	PCL	24	37	0	58.3	58	26	53	5	4.17	4.76	8.4	4.1	6.4	1.0	4.29	8.3	-1
2003	IND	INT	25	35	1	52.3	34	13	53	4	1.38	2.25	7.1	2.6	7.7	0.9	3.19	12.9	14
2003	MIL	NL	25	26	0	24.3	34	10	25	5	4.81	5.76	10.4	3.2	7.9	1.8	6.12	-0.8	0
2004	TUC	PCL	26	46	2	45.3	61	22	48	5	6.36	6.46	10.2	4.3	7.0	1.0	5.48	0.6	-16
2004	ARI	NL	26	19	0	12.3	19	12	9	2	5.85	6.92	11.1	6.9	5.5	1.4	6.92	-3.2	-40
2005	*ARI*	*NL*	*27*	*32*	*0*	*29.0*	*29*	*14*	*24*	*3*	*4.32*	*4.31*	*8.8*	*3.7*	*6.8*	*0.9*	*4.63*	*4.7*	*-2*

Breakout: 24% *Improve: 50%* *Collapse: 24%*

A series of stat lines often tells a really detailed story. For a LOOGY like Nance, it shows a process of specialization, as the average number of innings per outing drops from year to year while he faces fewer and fewer right-handed hitters. Nance has a role carved out—now he's got to perform in it. He didn't do the job in a brief audition in 2004, but there'll be other chances.

DUSTIN NIPPERT Bats: R Throws: R Born: 06-May-1981 Age: 24

YEAR	TM	LG	AGE	G	GS	IP	H	BB	SO	HR	ERA	EQERA	EQH9	EQBB9	EQSO9	EQHR9	PERA	VORP	STF
2002	MSO	PIO	21	17	11	54.7	42	9	77	2	1.65	4.11	8.6	2.0	6.4	0.9	3.58	11.3	16
2003	SBN	MDW	22	17	17	95.7	66	32	96	4	2.82	4.87	8.4	3.9	6.4	1.2	4.45	10.9	18
2004	ELP	TXS	23	14	14	71.7	77	40	73	0	3.64	5.63	8.6	5.4	6.4	0.3	3.97	12.7	19
2005	*ARI*	*NL*	*24*	*21*	*14*	*87.0*	*86*	*43*	*68*	*10*	*4.73*	*4.72*	*8.7*	*3.8*	*6.4*	*1.0*	*4.65*	*9.9*	*4*

Breakout: 13% *Improve: 41%* *Collapse: 25%*

The D-Backs added Nippert to the 40-man roster just before the Rule 5 Draft, so apparently, they're pretty sanguine about the prospects of a full recovery from his elbow troubles. Nippert's numbers in the minors have been mostly excellent—check out those strikeout and home-run rates—and he's got good movement on his pitches. Probably going to be 2006 before he makes any noise in the majors, but he could be a good one.

STEPHEN RANDOLPH Bats: L Throws: L Born: 01-May-1974 Age: 31

YEAR	TM	LG	AGE	G	GS	IP	H	BB	SO	HR	ERA	EQERA	EQH9	EQBB9	EQSO9	EQHR9	PERA	VORP	STF
2002	TUC	PCL	28	28	27	163.3	151	81	129	15	3.47	3.73	8.6	4.8	5.7	1.0	5.02	9.9	13
2003	ARI	NL	29	50	0	60.0	50	43	50	7	4.05	3.86	7.9	5.7	6.8	0.9	4.47	9.5	-4
2004	ARI	NL	30	45	6	81.7	73	76	62	11	5.51	5.51	8.3	7.4	6.1	1.0	5.06	-4.1	-16
2005	*CHC*	*NL*	*31*	*32*	*6*	*66.3*	*64*	*45*	*49*	*9*	*5.50*	*5.70*	*8.7*	*5.3*	*6.0*	*1.1*	*5.58*	*0.9*	*-12*

Breakout: 32% *Improve: 54%* *Collapse: 21%*

Again, most guys never find their control; Randolph's 31 this year, and he still hasn't found his. Since he's left-handed, clubs will give him shot after shot, because if he can control his impressive stuff, he's going to dust lefties. Fought through some shoulder stiffness (how scary are those words?) in the late summer, but he hasn't had any problems since.

SCOTT SERVICE Bats: R Throws: R Born: 26-Feb-1967 Age: 38

YEAR	TM	LG	AGE	G	GS	IP	H	BB	SO	HR	ERA	EQERA	EQH9	EQBB9	EQSO9	EQHR9	PERA	VORP	STF
2002	NAS	PCL	35	47	0	61.7	47	24	70	8	3.35	4.24	8.0	3.8	8.3	1.7	4.40	7.6	12
2003	ARI	NL	36	18	0	18.3	21	2	18	1	4.92	4.42	8.8	1.0	7.9	0.5	3.44	1.4	21
2003	TOR	AL	36	15	0	16.0	17	6	17	3	4.50	3.94	8.4	3.4	9.0	1.7	4.50	2.8	16
2004	TUC	PCL	37	24	0	25.0	28	6	28	2	3.24	3.24	9.0	2.2	7.6	0.7	3.96	4.6	7
2004	ARI	NL	37	21	0	20.3	24	10	17	5	7.09	6.64	9.7	4.0	6.6	1.8	5.31	-4.1	-10
2005	*ARI*	*NL*	*38*	*31*	*0*	*27.3*	*26*	*11*	*22*	*3*	*4.04*	*4.03*	*8.5*	*3.1*	*6.7*	*1.0*	*4.26*	*5.0*	*-1*

Breakout: 22% *Improve: 50%* *Collapse: 18%*

Bullpen filler guy, always has a pretty good K rate and gets an invite or two by teams hit hard by injuries or cash crunches. He's fighting some back spasms, and the D-Backs chose not to offer him arbitration. Look for him at a Central Division spring training camp near you in February of 2005, along with ex-teen Russian perv-pop sensation Tatu.

JESUS SILVA Bats: R Throws: R Born: 24-Dec-1982 Age: 22

YEAR	TM	LG	AGE	G	GS	IP	H	BB	SO	HR	ERA	EQERA	EQH9	EQBB9	EQSO9	EQHR9	PERA	VORP	STF
2002	LNC	CLF	19	34	0	43.3	30	5	51	1	2.08	3.32	7.3	1.1	6.2	0.2	2.43	14.3	28
2002	ELP	TXS	19	21	0	23.3	29	10	22	5	5.02	6.95	11.9	4.1	6.5	2.9	7.77	-5.3	-8
2003	ELP	TXS	20	55	0	66.3	84	20	56	7	5.02	5.79	10.2	2.9	5.6	1.4	5.23	2.7	-5
2004	LNC	CLF	21	28	27	152.0	168	56	126	16	4.38	5.58	10.0	4.1	4.9	1.6	5.95	-5.6	-8
2005	*ARI*	*NL*	*22*	*10*	*9*	*50.3*	*55*	*21*	*35*	*8*	*5.15*	*5.14*	*9.7*	*3.3*	*5.6*	*1.2*	*5.13*	*3.2*	*1*

Breakout: 14% *Improve: 45%* *Collapse: 20%*

Silva went back to A-ball to convert into a starter, and held his own in his first attempt at the job. Peripherals were acceptable but not stellar, and he's got an uphill battle to get a shot in the majors, much less to succeed there. His stuff is OK, but there's room to improve, particularly in terms of developing a change. Will likely start the season at Double-A.

STEVE SPARKS Bats: R Throws: R Born: 02-Jul-1965 Age: 39

YEAR	TM	LG	AGE	G	GS	IP	H	BB	SO	HR	ERA	EQERA	EQH9	EQBB9	EQSO9	EQHR9	PERA	VORP	STF
2002	DET	AL	37	32	30	189.0	238	67	98	23	5.52	6.01	10.1	2.9	4.4	1.0	4.72	-8.4	-1
2003	DET	AL	38	42	0	89.7	95	34	49	11	4.72	5.38	9.3	3.3	4.9	1.0	4.55	3.7	-10
2003	OAK	AL	38	9	0	17.3	19	3	5	2	5.72	4.96	10.5	1.7	2.8	1.1	5.51	0.7	-20
2004	ARI	NL	39	29	18	120.7	139	45	57	18	6.04	5.97	9.9	3.0	3.8	1.1	4.74	-11.8	-12
2005	*SDP*	*NL*	*39*	*32*	*14*	*103.7*	*115*	*38*	*55*	*13*	*5.01*	*5.71*	*10.2*	*2.9*	*4.2*	*1.3*	*5.63*	*0.0*	*-13*

Breakout: 26% *Improve: 43%* *Collapse: 25%*

Knuckleballer. The one thing about them is that they could suddenly become successful and stay that way for years, or they could become the pitching coach in Batavia after three more starts. Sparks will have a chance to pitch if he wants to, be it here or somewhere else after a couple of injuries.

JOSE VALVERDE Bats: R Throws: R Born: 24-Jul-1979 Age: 25

YEAR	TM	LG	AGE	G	GS	IP	H	BB	SO	HR	ERA	EQERA	EQH9	EQBB9	EQSO9	EQHR9	PERA	VORP	STF
2002	TUC	PCL	22	49	0	47.7	45	23	65	8	5.85	5.72	8.7	4.5	9.7	1.6	5.32	1.4	9
2003	TUC	PCL	23	22	0	29.0	26	14	26	1	3.10	3.58	7.8	4.9	6.8	0.3	3.90	5.2	1
2003	ARI	NL	23	54	0	50.3	24	26	71	4	2.15	2.62	5.2	4.1	11.8	0.8	2.44	15.4	38
2004	TUC	PCL	24	10	1	10.7	9	5	5	0	4.21	3.60	8.1	4.5	3.6	0.0	3.60	2.2	-19
2004	ARI	NL	24	29	0	29.7	23	17	38	7	4.24	4.71	7.5	4.7	10.4	1.9	4.40	1.8	15
2005	*ARI*	*NL*	*25*	*26*	*2*	*43.3*	*36*	*23*	*43*	*6*	*4.22*	*4.21*	*7.4*	*4.1*	*8.1*	*1.1*	*4.22*	*7.0*	*7*

Breakout: 18% *Improve: 56%* *Collapse: 23%*

Valverde's got electric stuff, and on occasion, he even has an idea where it's going. Lots of Ks and walks, thanks to lots of movement on his pitches. If he can harness his stuff, he has the potential to be a star. Most guys for whom that's true don't stay in baseball very long. The odds are against him, and stop me if you've heard this before, but if he can dump just one of those walks per nine innings . . .

BRANDON VILLAFUERTE Bats: R Throws: R Born: 17-Dec-1975 Age: 29

YEAR	TM	LG	AGE	G	GS	IP	H	BB	SO	HR	ERA	EQERA	EQH9	EQBB9	EQSO9	EQHR9	PERA	VORP	STF
2002	POR	PCL	26	47	0	58.0	43	22	54	2	2.02	3.21	7.9	3.7	6.9	0.3	3.88	10.2	7
2002	SDP	NL	26	31	0	32.0	29	12	25	2	1.41	1.74	8.1	2.9	6.4	0.6	3.19	14.1	5
2003	POR	PCL	27	37	0	44.0	42	14	40	1	1.84	2.98	8.3	3.2	7.0	0.2	3.40	10.3	6
2003	SDP	NL	27	31	0	40.7	39	26	34	7	4.20	4.54	8.8	5.0	6.8	1.6	4.99	5.4	-9
2004	TUC	PCL	28	23	0	30.7	27	10	23	3	2.64	2.76	8.0	3.1	5.2	0.9	3.68	6.3	0
2004	ARI	NL	28	20	0	20.0	25	14	13	2	4.05	3.54	9.7	5.3	4.9	0.9	5.31	3.7	-14
2005	*SFG*	*NL*	*29*	*22*	*1*	*33.7*	*33*	*16*	*25*	*3*	*3.89*	*4.20*	*8.7*	*3.8*	*6.1*	*0.9*	*4.79*	*5.8*	*-5*

Breakout: 24% *Improve: 53%* *Collapse: 26%*

Not long ago, Villafuerte started the season as the promising closer for the Padres, on the track for fame, fortune, and gaudy save totals. That's no longer the case, but Villafuerte can still get people out. He had a bad run in 2004, but those numbers are strongly against the trend; barring some sort of injury, he's a rebound candidate, more so since he'll be in SBC Park.

OSCAR VILLARREAL Bats: L Throws: R Born: 22-Nov-1981 Age: 23

YEAR	TM	LG	AGE	G	GS	IP	H	BB	SO	HR	ERA	EQERA	EQH9	EQBB9	EQSO9	EQHR9	PERA	VORP	STF
2002	ELP	TXS	20	14	12	84.3	73	26	85	2	3.74	4.48	8.0	3.0	6.8	0.3	3.36	20.0	39
2002	TUC	PCL	20	10	10	64.0	68	22	40	8	4.36	4.43	9.6	3.2	4.4	1.0	5.16	3.0	13
2003	ARI	NL	21	86	1	98.0	80	46	80	6	2.57	3.43	7.6	3.7	6.8	0.5	3.34	21.2	21
2004	ARI	NL	22	17	0	18.0	25	7	17	3	7.00	6.38	10.8	2.9	7.4	1.5	5.40	-2.6	-4
2005	*ARI*	*NL*	*23*	*28*	*4*	*55.0*	*57*	*21*	*44*	*6*	*4.52*	*4.51*	*9.2*	*3.1*	*6.6*	*0.9*	*4.55*	*6.9*	*2*

Breakout: 16% *Improve: 45%* *Collapse: 27%*

After grabbing the fifth starter's spot from John Patterson, Villarreal suffered flexor tendon problems and bone spurs in his elbow. He's the leading candidate for the fifth starter's spot going into spring training, and he's expected to be healthy and ready to go. It might take him a bit to get everything together, but there's a performance record here that indicates a good chance of his being effective.

BRANDON WEBB Bats: R Throws: R Born: 09-May-1979 Age: 26

YEAR	TM	LG	AGE	G	GS	IP	H	BB	SO	HR	ERA	EQERA	EQH9	EQBB9	EQSO9	EQHR9	PERA	VORP	STF
2002	ELP	TXS	23	26	25	152.0	141	59	122	4	3.14	4.48	8.5	3.7	5.5	0.4	3.86	28.0	13
2003	ARI	NL	24	29	28	180.7	140	68	172	12	2.84	3.00	7.3	3.0	7.9	0.6	3.05	49.4	30
2004	ARI	NL	25	35	35	208.0	194	119	164	17	3.59	4.34	8.3	4.6	6.3	0.7	3.90	22.2	12
2005	*ARI*	*NL*	*26*	*29*	*29*	*186.7*	*174*	*86*	*151*	*14*	*3.98*	*3.97*	*8.3*	*3.6*	*6.6*	*0.6*	*3.97*	*31.8*	*15*

Breakout: 23% *Improve: 55%* *Collapse: 9%*

Look out. Yes, he posted a 3.59 ERA, but he was lucky to do it. His peripheral stats weren't outstanding, and it's pretty hard to walk five guys per nine innings and have an ERA that tidy. An excellent candidate for a complete implosion, after tremendous luck holding his numbers steady last year, and a new high in workload in 2004. Yeah, it's not 275 innings, but it is a high number, and those were some pretty interesting innings. Don't be surprised to see an ERA closer to 5.00 than 3.59.

Atlanta Braves

Short of some Teddy Roosevelt/Philander C. Knox–style trust busting, what can be done to stop the Braves from continuing their monopoly on NL-East titles? You strip them of their best starting pitcher, their two best hitters, 104 home runs, and their best lefty reliever... and still, they win 96 games and the division by 10 full games. Not counting strike-shortened 1994, that's a ridiculous 13 consecutive division titles. Cockroach infestations have shown less resolve.

In some ways, Jaret Wright's improbable year was the Braves' year writ small. Although their recent histories bear no similarities, little was expected of both. Once all was said and done, both confounded observers with their successes.

Over much of the past season, Wright's performance was passed off as bracing proof of Leo Mazzone's remarkable faculties as a pitching coach; in reality, Wright may have been Mazzone's masterstroke. Strides like the ones Wright made (laying aside causation for the moment) are manifest rarities under Mazzone (or under anyone, for that matter). What Mazzone does seem to thrive at is divining modest performance gains out of pitchers who are at an age when such gains might not be expected. Whether that's a genuine skill on Mazzone's part or more indicative of John Schuerholz's sense of timing is hard to determine.

Mazzone became the Bobby Cox's pitching coach/philosopher king midway through the 1990 season, when the Braves were in the NL-West and their reign was very much a work in progress. The Mazzone approach, outside of whatever nuanced adjustments he makes on a game-to-game basis, mostly consists of having pitchers throw more on their off days than they would in most programs. It may smack of reductionism, but that's the thrust of his method. Even so, Mazzone, in recent years has been called a genius and has even heard calls for his induction into the Hall of Fame. We're wondering: Is the lavish praise justified?

To peer more closely, we've taken all pitchers who have been Atlanta rotation regulars for at least one season under Mazzone. For comparison's sake, we've separated their Mazzone years from their non-Mazzone years. Included in those non-Mazzone years are whatever seasons they spent in other organizations or with the Braves before Mazzone's first full season.

Our comparative metric will be ERA. However, in this instance the ERA figures you'll see below are adjusted to reflect differences in park and league. Additionally, inning totals are translated to reflect league trends and a 162-game schedule, and the ERA calculation is tied to a replacement-level ERA. In other words, these numbers have been put through the ringer quite a few times to correct for foibles of league, park and era.

Table 1 shows how they stack up.

As you can see, pitchers, by and large, see a substantial improvement under Mazzone. Specifically, their runs-per-game numbers drop 18.9% while on Mazzone's watch.

However, there's some noise in the age numbers. In particular, the mean age is somewhat misleading. For instance, a pitcher could toil for one team at ages 20, 21, and 22 and then again at ages 35, 36, and 37. His average age for that team would be 28.5, but he certainly didn't spend his prime seasons with them.

For that reason, mode is perhaps a more evocative measure for our purposes than mean or median age. That standard shows that these pitchers have been with Mazzone, generally speaking, closer to their prime seasons, making them more likely to succeed.

Table 2 presents the exhaustive list of pitchers within the sample population. In table 2, "Adj. ERA(NM)" is their adjusted non-Mazzone ERA. "Adj. ERA(M)" is their adjusted Mazzone ERA.

Among these pitchers, 14 of 22 performed better while under the aegis of Mazzone. For most of those, regardless of whether you classify them as data points for or against Mazzone, there are mitigating circumstances to

BRAVES PROSPECTUS

2004 record: 96–66; First place, NL East; Lost to Astros in Division Series

Pythagenport record: 95–67

Runs scored per game: 4.96 (5th in NL)

Runs allowed per game: 4.12 (3rd in NL)

Team EqA: .268 (5th in NL)

2004 Batters Age: 29.2 (6th youngest in NL)

2004 Pitchers Age: 30.3 (3rd oldest in NL)

Ballpark: Turner Field; Slight pitcher's park; Park Factor of 0.982

2004: You can't stop them. You can only hope to contain them.

2005: They aren't the strongest team in the division on paper, but we've played that game before and we don't like how it ends.

TABLE 1. PITCHER COMPARISON BEFORE AND DURING MAZZONE

Adj. ERA	Mean Age	Median Age	Mode Age
	Without Mazzone		
3.91	27.6	27	25
	With Mazzone		
3.41	28.8	28	27

TABLE 2. INDIVIDUAL PITCHER PERFORMANCE BEFORE AND DURING MAZZONE

Pitcher	Adj. ERA (NM)	Adj. ERA (M)	%Diff.
Ashby, Andy	4.03	3.45	−14.4
Avery, Steve	4.88	3.87	−20.7
Bielecki, Mike	4.33	3.40	−21.5
Burkett, John	4.12	3.32	−19.4
Byrd, Paul	3.75	4.37	+16.5
Glavine, Tom	3.89	3.22	−17.2
Hampton, Mike	3.81	3.82	+0.26
Leibrandt, Charlie	3.66	3.67	+0.27
Maddux, Greg	3.54	2.82	−20.3
Marquis, Jason	3.67	4.25	+15.8
Mercker, Kent	4.17	3.67	+12.0
Millwood, Kevin	3.98	3.45	−13.3
Moss, Damian	5.07	3.57	−29.6
Neagle, Denny	3.92	3.42	−12.8
Ortiz, Russ	3.84	3.70	−3.6
Perez, Odalis	3.42	4.67	+36.5
Reynolds, Shane	3.83	4.77	+24.5
Schmidt, Jason	3.40	5.85	+72.1
Smith, Pete	4.54	3.95	−13.0
Smoltz, John	3.55	3.27	−7.9
Thomson, John	3.84	3.64	−5.2
Wright, Jaret	4.50	3.24	−28.0

be considered either way. Some pitched for Mazzone at an exceedingly young age (Schmidt) or as the music was swelling on their careers (Reynolds). Some worked a sizeable number of relief innings (which tend to carry with them lower ERAs) while with the Braves (Bielecki). Some left were "rode hard and put away wet" and, thus, left Mazzone and headed out more likely to fail (Avery). Some have posted seemingly aberrant batting averages on balls in play since leaving (Millwood), and some did the same while in the fold (Moss).

If there are indictments to be found, we find them in Marquis and Perez. Marquis had a fairly strong 129.1 innings as a Brave in 2001, but that was surrounded by three seasons in which he posted ERAs of more than 5.00. Traded to the Cardinals as part of the J. D. Drew swap, Marquis pilloried the teachings of Mazzone on the way out and set career-best marks in innings, ERA and strikeout-to-walk ratio. It remains to be seen whether his work in 2004 was anomalous or whether he somehow responded better to the tutelage of Cardinals pitching coach Dave Duncan, who's not exactly known for having a deft touch with young arms.

And then there's Perez. After two seasons and change of disappointment in Atlanta, the Braves shipped him to the Dodgers along with Andy Brown and Brian Jordan in exchange for Gary Sheffield. In L.A., Perez put up dramatically better numbers, and the improvement was such that it can't be explained away by the run-suppression gap between Turner Field and Dodger Stadium. As noted above, Perez saw his R/G improve by more than 50% after leaving Atlanta and Mazzone. Only Schmidt has seen more of a post-Leo performance boost, and no pitcher improved as much under Mazzone as Perez did away from Mazzone. Again, perhaps it was excellent career-curve timing executed by the Dodgers, or perhaps it was that Perez's particular skill set/personality/Rorschach profile didn't dovetail so well with Mazzone's pedagogical chops.

It's worth exploring how much of Mazzone's apparent success is owing to the fact that he's had three Hall of Fame-caliber arms—Glavine, Maddux, and Smoltz—as integral parts of his pitching-coach dossier, a rare blessing for a pitching coach. When Mazzone assumed his role with the Braves, Glavine had been in the majors for four undistinguished seasons, and Smoltz had logged three seasons (one of which was quite strong). Maddux would toil for the Cubs for another two seasons before signing with Atlanta.

Under Mazzone's watch, of course, they would form the most fearsome pitching troika in the annals of the game. Only Glavine saw a marked improvement under Mazzone. Smoltz and Maddux both made gains, but they were already quality hurlers when Mazzone took over. Maddux, in particular, came to Mazzone at an age, 27, when you'd expect a pitcher to make statistical progress, and he left just when he appeared to be knee-deep in his decline phase. Determining whether their Mazzone-era performances were mostly the result of ability or instruction is a nature-nurture debate that's impossible to quantify. Still, how would those aggregate numbers look without the contributions of these three lavishly gifted pitchers?

Adjusted ERA:

With Mazzone	3.75
Without Mazzone	3.95

With Glavine, Maddux, and Smoltz not part of the calculus, Mazzone's charges still fare better. But the gap has narrowed from a 12.8% performance boost to a rather modest 5.1% improvement. That's somewhat notable, but it's not as striking once you calculate around the "Holy Trinity." Whether that's a justifiable exclusion is up for debate.

And then we have Wright, the pitcher who's seen the greatest performance boost under Mazzone. One season isn't an adequate data sample, but under the Braves pitching coach, Wright went from waiver-wide fodder to a hotly coveted free agent who eventually signed a huge deal. Unlike, say, Moss, Wright didn't post a batting average on balls in play that's wildly out of step with the rest of his career (BABIP of .300 in 2004, or just about league average). What he did do was post the best K/BB ratio and home-run rate of his career, which suggests authentic improvement. It's possible that Wright, who has suffered from health and usage issues throughout his career, was acutely responsive to Mazzone's alternative between-start work schedules. Or it could be a fluke. Next year, Wright will be plying his trade with the Yankees, and, suffice it to say, his performance will be telling.

The Braves in 2005 will again face some degree of upheaval in the rotation. Wright and Ortiz are elsewhere. Smoltz will return to a consistent starting role for the first time since 2000. Thomson and Hampton are back, but the remaining two spots are up for grabs. As demonstrated above, pitchers tend to see improvement under Mazzone, but the precise causation is unclear and it's not as extreme as the fawning at large might lead you to believe. Part of it is the front office's penchant for timely acquisitions. Part of it is a historically strong Braves team defense. Part of it is luck. And, to be sure, part of it is probably Mazzone's alchemy. However, mitigations abound in what at first blush looks like a staggering record of success. In reality, it's perhaps as much Schuerholz—one of the best and most underrated minds in the game—and his front-office charges as it is Mazzone.

However you divvy up the plaudits, more of the same is likely on the way. With talents like Andy Marte, Jeff Francoeur, Brian McCann, and Kyle Davies in the organizational queue and with fairly young core players like Marcus Giles already in place, the Braves are poised to continue their dynastic run. The leaders of the organization have proved that they're able to adapt to changing market conditions, and they've won with wildly disparate roster constructions. They'll probably keep it up. That the rest of the division seems so rudderless only helps.

HITTERS

WILSON BETEMIT 3B Bats: B Throws: R Born: 28-Jul-1980 Age: 24

YEAR	TM	LG	AGE	AB	H	2B	3B	HR	BB	SO	SB	CS	AVG	OBP	SLG	MLVR	EQBA	EQOBP	EQSLG	EQMLVR	VORP	DEFENSE
2002	RIC	INT	21	343	84	17	1	8	34	82	8	5	.245	.312	.370	-.068	.230	.301	.359	-.215	-1.3	87-SS -15
2003	RIC	INT	22	478	125	23	13	8	38	115	8	5	.262	.315	.414	.020	.253	.311	.410	-.109	10.6	98-3B -12
2004	RIC	INT	23	356	99	24	2	13	32	99	3	3	.278	.336	.466	.092	.261	.321	.433	-.052	14.3	76-3B -5 15-SS -2
2004	ATL	NL	23	47	8	0	0	0	4	16	0	1	.170	.231	.170	-.562	.191	.194	.191	-.688	-5.2	
2005	*ATL*	*NL*	*24*	*232*	*59*	*13*	*2*	*7*	*23*	*61*	*3*	*1*	*.254*	*.321*	*.415*	*-.077*	*.256*	*.321*	*.420*	*-.071*	*6.8*	*64-3B -3*

Breakout: 30% *Improve: 53%* *Collapse: 27%*

Because of the excessive hype early in his career, he'll always have the patina of disappointment about him. But there's still a strong chance Betemit will develop into a useful contributor at the major league level. He can capably man third, provide some pop and make good contact. His likely destination is probably somewhere in non-Coors Vinny Castilla territory, which has its uses, provided you're not paid like Vinny Castilla and provided you're not trotted out there every day.

GREGOR BLANCO 3B Bats: L Throws: L Born: 12-Dec-1983 Age: 21

YEAR	TM	LG	AGE	AB	H	2B	3B	HR	BB	SO	SB	CS	AVG	OBP	SLG	MLVR	EQBA	EQOBP	EQSLG	EQMLVR	VORP	DEFENSE
2002	MCN	SAL	18	468	127	14	9	7	85	120	40	16	.271	.392	.385	.141	.231	.327	.339	-.191	-22.0	63-LF -7 43-RF -2
2003	MYR	CRL	19	461	125	19	7	5	54	114	34	16	.271	.357	.375	.118	.267	.337	.387	-.082	10.1	110-CF -16 11-RF 0
2004	MYR	CRL	20	435	117	17	9	8	47	114	25	9	.269	.342	.405	.114	.257	.320	.399	-.105	6.1	97-CF -15
2005	*ATL*	*NL*	*21*	*382*	*96*	*18*	*4*	*7*	*41*	*103*	*13*	*5*	*.250*	*.328*	*.378*	*-.114*	*.252*	*.328*	*.383*	*-.109*	*4.2*	*103-CF -12*

Breakout: 17% *Improve: 41%* *Collapse: 31%*

Blanco sports a plus glove in center, but his utter lack of power raises concern that he won't be able to get around on pitches at higher levels. He's posted solid walk rates, but he struggled for the second straight season at High-A Myrtle Beach, even accounting for tough park and league effects. Given his youth, he's still a prospect, especially if he maximizes his already solid on-base skills.

MARK DeROSA — 3B — Bats: R — Throws: R — Born: 02-Feb-1975 — Age: 30

YEAR	TM	LG	AGE	AB	H	2B	3B	HR	BB	SO	SB	CS	AVG	OBP	SLG	MLVR	EQBA	EQOBP	EQSLG	EQMLVR	VORP	DEFENSE	
2002	ATL	NL	27	212	63	9	2	5	12	24	2	3	.297	.339	.429	.085	.299	.339	.439	.022	13.2	28-2B 4	16-SS 2
2003	ATL	NL	28	266	70	14	0	6	16	49	1	0	.263	.316	.383	-.054	.266	.311	.386	-.133	8.6	23-2B 4	20-3B -2
2004	ATL	NL	29	309	74	16	0	3	23	53	1	3	.239	.293	.320	-.222	.244	.291	.318	-.283	-8.8	60-3B -6	
2005	*ATL*	*NL*	*30*	*206*	*52*	*11*	*1*	*4*	*15*	*35*	*1*	*1*	*.252*	*.309*	*.373*	*-.154*	*.254*	*.309*	*.378*	*-.149*	*0.4*	*57-3B 0*	

Breakout: 21% Improve: 38% Collapse: 37%

Most seasons, DeRosa can be a serviceable utility infielder, but, as a regular, he's stretched like Bob Guiney trying to be a troubadour. He opened the 2004 season as the Braves' starting third baseman, but a .223/.276/.317 line as a regular prompted the Braves to move Chipper Jones and his prop-comic glovework back to the hot corner. DeRosa's torn ACL should be fully healed by spring training, but it's too soon to know whether it's cost him any mobility. If he's no longer able to perform spot duty in the middle infield, then he no longer has any business being on a major league roster.

J. D. DREW — RF — Bats: L — Throws: R — Born: 20-Nov-1975 — Age: 29

YEAR	TM	LG	AGE	AB	H	2B	3B	HR	BB	SO	SB	CS	AVG	OBP	SLG	MLVR	EQBA	EQOBP	EQSLG	EQMLVR	VORP	DEFENSE	
2002	STL	NL	26	424	107	19	1	18	57	104	8	2	.252	.349	.429	.065	.255	.348	.444	.008	17.4	99-RF 1	
2003	STL	NL	27	287	83	13	3	15	36	48	2	2	.289	.374	.512	.231	.291	.376	.519	.192	24.6	43-RF 2	19-CF 1
2004	ATL	NL	28	518	158	28	8	31	118	116	12	3	.305	.436	.569	.403	.301	.432	.563	.353	78.7	134-RF 7	
2005	*LAD*	*NL*	*29*	*449*	*126*	*23*	*4*	*24*	*79*	*100*	*7*	*2*	*.282*	*.393*	*.516*	*.197*	*.289*	*.398*	*.531*	*.230*	*44.5*	*127-RF 2*	

Breakout: 18% Improve: 49% Collapse: 16%

Health and performance finally intersected for the erstwhile wunderkind. Even so, because of his chronic, degenerative knee condition, he's no less of a risk for the future. There's a chance this past season was his final full one. With 116 unintentional walks, 67 extra-base hits and the fourth-best OBP in either league, Drew exceeded expectations, but he's a high-risk proposition for the rest of his career. Signed a five-year, $55 million deal with the Dodgers, who are poised to move him back to center. It's somewhat counterintuitive, but that switch may be the best thing for his knee; it's the quick stopping and starting that hurts him the most, and there'll be less of that in center.

MATT ESQUIVEL — RF — Bats: R — Throws: R — Born: 17-Dec-1982 — Age: 22

YEAR	TM	LG	AGE	AB	H	2B	3B	HR	BB	SO	SB	CS	AVG	OBP	SLG	MLVR	EQBA	EQOBP	EQSLG	EQMLVR	VORP	DEFENSE	
2002	DNV	APL	19	227	63	13	2	5	21	67	2	0	.278	.345	.419	.081	.218	.257	.323	-.359	-42.7	55-RF -11	
2003	DNV	APL	20	220	62	10	4	11	20	72	7	4	.282	.352	.514	.295	.239	.286	.434	-.132	2.2	53-CF -4	
2004	ROM	SAL	21	411	117	32	3	16	35	140	14	4	.285	.356	.494	.229	.251	.302	.426	-.105	-5.1	66-RF -6	39-CF -1
2005	*ATL*	*NL*	*22*	*386*	*93*	*21*	*2*	*14*	*26*	*138*	*6*	*2*	*.240*	*.306*	*.416*	*-.110*	*.242*	*.306*	*.422*	*-.104*	*6.4*	*102-RF -4*	

Breakout: 29% Improve: 49% Collapse: 25%

Esquivel was one of the most hotly recruited running backs in Central Texas, and he has some baseball skills to match. Armed with speed and defensive instincts in the outfield that belie his street-corner mailbox build, he also swings a fair bat. In three pro seasons, Esquivel has hit .281/.351/.477. On the downside, he hasn't played above the Sally League, and last season he rang up 140 whiffs in 411 at-bats. Still, 51 extra-base hits in '04 point to his projectable power. Nothing to get excited about just yet, but he's one to monitor.

JOHNNY ESTRADA — C — Bats: B — Throws: R — Born: 27-Jun-1976 — Age: 29

YEAR	TM	LG	AGE	AB	H	2B	3B	HR	BB	SO	SB	CS	AVG	OBP	SLG	MLVR	EQBA	EQOBP	EQSLG	EQMLVR	VORP	DEFENSE
2002	SWB	INT	26	434	121	27	0	11	26	53	1	0	.279	.322	.417	.029	.252	.297	.389	-.166	0.9	112-C 7
2003	RIC	INT	27	354	116	29	0	10	30	30	0	0	.328	.393	.494	.308	.305	.368	.476	.132	33.6	81-C -2
2003	ATL	NL	27	36	11	0	0	0	0	3	0	0	.306	.359	.306	-.052	.378	.297	.378	-.072	1.1	
2004	ATL	NL	28	462	145	36	0	9	39	66	0	0	.314	.378	.450	.165	.315	.372	.446	.106	41.0	118-C -6
2005	*ATL*	*NL*	*29*	*406*	*110*	*24*	*1*	*11*	*35*	*55*	*0*	*0*	*.272*	*.340*	*.419*	*-.023*	*.274*	*.340*	*.425*	*-.017*	*20.5*	*108-C -4*

Breakout: 5% Improve: 14% Collapse: 38%

Estrada before being traded to the Braves: 2338 PA, .274/.322/.332

Estrada after being traded to the Braves: 958 PA, .319/.383/.474

Keep in mind that all of his Braves' plate appearances have come at the Triple-A and major league levels, while his Phillies work was mostly at lower levels. So is it blind luck, or is it possible the Braves knew something we didn't?

PECOTA sees Estrada's recent success, as the result of high batting averages and fluky hits on balls in play rates. Expect significant regression.

JULIO FRANCO **Ageless Wonder** **Bats: R** **Throws: R** Born: 23-Aug-1958 Age: 46

YEAR	TM	LG	AGE	AB	H	2B	3B	HR	BB	SO	SB	CS	AVG	OBP	SLG	MLVR	EQBA	EQOBP	EQSLG	EQMLVR	VORP	DEFENSE
2002	ATL	NL	43	338	96	13	1	6	39	75	5	1	.284	.357	.382	.032	.285	.357	.391	-.025	13.1	81-1B -8
2003	ATL	NL	44	197	58	12	2	5	25	43	0	1	.294	.372	.452	.153	.294	.372	.457	.102	13.3	45-1B -1
2004	ATL	NL	45	320	99	18	3	6	36	68	4	2	.309	.378	.441	.146	.306	.376	.438	.093	22.7	70-1B -4
2005	*ATL*	*NL*	*46*	*294*	*74*	*14*	*1*	*7*	*37*	*69*	*2*	*1*	*.250*	*.333*	*.378*	*-.106*	*.252*	*.333*	*.383*	*-.100*	*0.0*	*66-1B -1*

This likeable old warhorse was pretty effective in spot duty. If he's getting more than 350 plate appearances, as was the case in 2004, it's a source of concern, but his place on the roster has merit. There's no reason to think he can't be a capable reserve for at least another season. It's worth noting that last year he bucked trends and actually hit better against right-handers. Single-season splits are all but meaningless, but a possible decline against lefties is something to monitor.

JEFF FRANCOEUR **RF** **Bats: R** **Throws: R** Born: 08-Jan-1984 Age: 21

YEAR	TM	LG	AGE	AB	H	2B	3B	HR	BB	SO	SB	CS	AVG	OBP	SLG	MLVR	EQBA	EQOBP	EQSLG	EQMLVR	VORP	DEFENSE
2002	DNV	APL	18	147	48	12	1	8	15	34	8	5	.327	.395	.585	.448	.245	.287	.408	-.163	-1.5	36-CF 3
2003	ROM	SAL	19	524	147	26	9	14	30	68	14	6	.281	.325	.445	.174	.250	.281	.406	-.173	-4.2	125-CF -11
2004	MYR	CRL	20	334	98	26	0	15	22	70	10	6	.293	.346	.506	.285	.265	.304	.466	-.032	3.5	82-RF -2
2004	GRN	SOU	20	76	15	2	0	3	0	14	1	0	.197	.208	.342	-.310	.171	.165	.276	-.635	-12.4	15-RF 0
2005	*ATL*	*NL*	*21*	*392*	*99*	*21*	*2*	*14*	*18*	*83*	*6*	*2*	*.251*	*.291*	*.426*	*-.116*	*.253*	*.291*	*.431*	*-.110*	*1.2*	*100-RF -1*

Breakout: 18% *Improve: 49%* *Collapse: 34%*

The Braves have a habit of spending high-round picks on suburban-Atlanta prep talents. Although that sounds like an awfully circumscribed draft strategy, like almost everything else over the last decade-and-a-half, it's worked for them. Francoeur's another success story. The 23rd overall pick of the 2002 draft, he's a raw and toolsy hitter with loads of ability. A move from center to right has dropped his stock a bit (particularly since many feel he was fully capable of handling center at the highest level), but he projects as a Gold Glove-caliber defender at the corners. He lacks plate discipline, but this past season he slugged .508 as a 20-year-old at high-A Myrtle Beach, which is perhaps the toughest hitting environment in the minors. Francoeur struggled badly after a promotion to Double-A Greenville, but it was only an 18-game sample. He doesn't yet merit the stratospheric prospect-ranking others have given him, but he's still got the makings of a fine future.

RAFAEL FURCAL **SS** **Bats: B** **Throws: R** Born: 24-Oct-1977 Age: 27

YEAR	TM	LG	AGE	AB	H	2B	3B	HR	BB	SO	SB	CS	AVG	OBP	SLG	MLVR	EQBA	EQOBP	EQSLG	EQMLVR	VORP	DEFENSE
2002	ATL	NL	24	636	175	31	8	8	43	114	27	15	.275	.323	.387	-.030	.278	.324	.398	-.082	24.4	143-SS 10
2003	ATL	NL	25	664	194	35	10	15	60	76	25	2	.292	.352	.443	.102	.291	.351	.446	.046	57.6	149-SS -13
2004	ATL	NL	26	563	157	24	5	14	58	71	29	6	.279	.344	.414	.027	.276	.342	.412	-.031	38.0	126-SS 1
2005	*ATL*	*NL*	*27*	*540*	*150*	*27*	*5*	*12*	*52*	*71*	*21*	*6*	*.277*	*.341*	*.413*	*-.026*	*.279*	*.341*	*.419*	*-.019*	*28.3*	*141-SS 1*

Breakout: 3% *Improve: 26%* *Collapse: 38%*

The best shortstop in the National League? In terms of WARP3, Here's how Furcal stacks up against Edgar Renteria over the last three seasons:

Player	2002	2003	2004
Furcal	5.9	6.0	5.9
Renteria	5.5	9.4	3.8

Take away Renteria's highly aberrant 2003, and Furcal's been the better player. Considering that he's also more than two years younger, the trend will likely hold—and Renteria's now a Red Sock anyway. If Nomar Garciaparra proves he can stay healthy and still field the position adequately, perhaps we'll revisit the debate.

JESSE GARCIA SS/2B **Bats: R** **Throws: R** Born: 24-Sep-1973 Age: 31

YEAR	TM	LG	AGE	AB	H	2B	3B	HR	BB	SO	SB	CS	AVG	OBP	SLG	MLVR	EQBA	EQOBP	EQSLG	EQMLVR	VORP	DEFENSE	
2002	ATL	NL	28	61	12	1	0	0	0	14	0	1	.197	.197	.213	-.533	.197	.167	.197	-.735	-5.0	13-2B 2	
2002	RIC	INT	28	230	69	12	1	6	16	32	9	5	.300	.349	.439	.127	.287	.339	.426	-.007	11.8	40-2B 0	11-SS -2
2003	RIC	INT	29	425	130	17	3	2	12	50	29	9	.306	.329	.374	.022	.294	.324	.365	-.118	10.6	86-SS 7	
2004	RIC	INT	30	78	17	2	0	0	4	13	0	2	.218	.265	.244	-.392	.169	.201	.169	-.711	-12.6	19-2B 0	
2004	ATL	NL	30	115	29	4	1	1	1	16	1	2	.252	.265	.330	-.257	.250	.262	.336	-.311	-3.0	21-SS 0	
2005	*SDP*	*NL*	*31*	*177*	*44*	*8*	*1*	*1*	*6*	*26*	*3*	*1*	*.246*	*.276*	*.322*	*-.286*	*.255*	*.282*	*.343*	*-.244*	*0.0*	*48-SS -2*	

Breakout: 11% *Improve: 28%* *Collapse: 48%*

An appallingly vanilla utility infielder. He's a capable glove man, but his bat is so anemic that there's no way to regard him as anything other than a frittered away roster spot. You, sir, are no Paul Zuvella.

MARCUS GILES 2B **Bats: R** **Throws: R** Born: 18-May-1978 Age: 27

YEAR	TM	LG	AGE	AB	H	2B	3B	HR	BB	SO	SB	CS	AVG	OBP	SLG	MLVR	EQBA	EQOBP	EQSLG	EQMLVR	VORP	DEFENSE	
2002	RIC	INT	24	115	37	6	0	3	13	15	3	0	.322	.385	.452	.219	.287	.341	.409	-.028	5.4	13-2B 0	13-3B 2
2002	ATL	NL	24	213	49	10	1	8	25	41	1	1	.230	.315	.399	-.050	.234	.317	.411	-.111	7.1	48-2B 4	
2003	ATL	NL	25	551	174	49	2	21	59	80	14	4	.316	.390	.526	.293	.314	.388	.531	.253	69.6	137-2B 16	
2004	ATL	NL	26	379	118	22	2	8	36	70	17	4	.311	.378	.443	.150	.310	.375	.441	.099	35.9	89-2B 10	
2005	*ATL*	*NL*	*27*	*466*	*134*	*28*	*3*	*15*	*51*	*79*	*13*	*3*	*.287*	*.363*	*.457*	*.078*	*.289*	*.363*	*.463*	*.085*	*35.8*	*125-2B 4*	

Breakout: 8% *Improve: 30%* *Collapse: 26%*

Since an ankle injury and the tragic death of his infant daughter undermined his 2002 season, Giles has been one of the best second basemen in the game. In '04, he missed seven weeks with a broken collarbone (the result of a collision with Andruw Jones), but, despite the playing-time deficit, he still wound up as the fifth-best keystoner in the NL. Had he played the full season, his VORP would've been second only to Mark Loretta among all second baseman and tops over a two-year span. Even after he came off the DL his injury dampened his power stroke. He's entering what should be his prime seasons. Don't be stunned if he wins an MVP award within the next three years.

NICK GREEN 2B **Bats: R** **Throws: R** Born: 10-Sep-1978 Age: 26

YEAR	TM	LG	AGE	AB	H	2B	3B	HR	BB	SO	SB	CS	AVG	OBP	SLG	MLVR	EQBA	EQOBP	EQSLG	EQMLVR	VORP	DEFENSE
2002	GRN	SOU	23	355	85	16	2	15	36	92	2	5	.239	.321	.423	.032	.216	.277	.399	-.216	-4.6	75-2B -11
2003	RIC	INT	24	399	99	26	1	11	26	79	7	5	.248	.303	.401	-.028	.233	.292	.390	-.188	-1.5	105-2B -9
2004	RIC	INT	25	77	29	4	1	0	6	9	0	3	.377	.443	.455	.351	.325	.374	.364	-.001	4.1	20-2B 2
2004	ATL	NL	25	264	72	15	3	3	12	63	1	2	.273	.312	.386	-.084	.272	.312	.388	-.124	5.6	63-2B 7
2005	*ATL*	*NL*	*26*	*318*	*81*	*16*	*2*	*9*	*23*	*67*	*2*	*2*	*.254*	*.313*	*.400*	*-.110*	*.256*	*.313*	*.405*	*-.104*	*9.0*	*85-2B -2*

Breakout: 12% *Improve: 34%* *Collapse: 34%*

Last season's plate work is about what you'd expect based on his minor league numbers. Green can play a few positions and provide some vaguely adequate ABs against lefties. There are worse back-of-the-bench types to have hanging on.

MIKE HESSMAN 1B/3B **Bats: R** **Throws: R** Born: 05-Mar-1978 Age: 27

YEAR	TM	LG	AGE	AB	H	2B	3B	HR	BB	SO	SB	CS	AVG	OBP	SLG	MLVR	EQBA	EQOBP	EQSLG	EQMLVR	VORP	DEFENSE	
2002	RIC	INT	24	484	127	28	1	26	34	107	1	5	.262	.321	.486	.113	.242	.302	.457	-.069	16.5	114-3B -5	12-1B 0
2003	ATL	NL	25	21	6	2	0	2	5	6	0	0	.286	.423	.667	.491	.333	.387	.667	.470	3.7		
2003	RIC	INT	25	359	89	15	3	16	24	87	3	1	.248	.296	.440	.014	.234	.287	.426	-.146	-6.9	51-1B -3	19-3B -1
2004	ATL	NL	26	69	9	3	0	2	1	24	0	0	.130	.155	.261	-.617	.130	.143	.246	-.740	-8.1	11-1B -2	
2004	RIC	INT	26	265	76	14	1	19	28	65	4	0	.287	.365	.562	.281	.272	.347	.528	.137	26.7	38-3B 1	21-1B -2
2005	*ATL*	*NL*	*27*	*230*	*59*	*11*	*1*	*12*	*20*	*59*	*1*	*1*	*.254*	*.324*	*.465*	*-.005*	*.256*	*.324*	*.471*	*.002*	*12.2*	*64-3B -6*	

Breakout: 32% *Improve: 53%* *Collapse: 25%*

He's 27 years old. He's also a career .237 hitter in the minors who doesn't draw walks and has struck out once every 3.6 at bats. That said, he does have raw power. His career ISO of .214 is impressive, and he's also smacked 217 extra-base hits over the years. Obviously, we're not looking at a future regular, but he might be "three true outcomes minus one true outcome" quasi-useful bench fauna in the majors.

J. C. HOLT **2B** **Bats: L** **Throws: R** Born: 08-Dec-1982 Age: 22

YEAR	TM	LG	AGE	AB	H	2B	3B	HR	BB	SO	SB	CS	AVG	OBP	SLG	MLVR	EQBA	EQOBP	EQSLG	EQMLVR	VORP	DEFENSE
2004	DNV	APL	21	209	67	15	0	1	18	34	17	5	.321	.377	.407	.203	.261	.294	.322	-.261	-11.5	46-2B -7
2005	*ATL*	*NL*	*22*	*353*	*84*	*15*	*2*	*3*	*19*	*68*	*11*	*4*	*.237*	*.279*	*.316*	*-.293*	*.238*	*.279*	*.320*	*-.289*	*-8.6*	*91-2B -4*

Breakout: 12% *Improve: 29%* *Collapse: 50%*

A third-rounder in 2004 out of LSU, Holt batted .393 his junior year but never showed much in the way of secondary hitting skills. Still, he was the batting champion of the 2003 Cape Cod League, and he hit .321 in the Appy League this past season. If he's going to progress, he'll need to show something besides an ability to ring up base hits.

KELLY JOHNSON **LF/CF** **Bats: L** **Throws: R** Born: 22-Feb-1982 Age: 23

YEAR	TM	LG	AGE	AB	H	2B	3B	HR	BB	SO	SB	CS	AVG	OBP	SLG	MLVR	EQBA	EQOBP	EQSLG	EQMLVR	VORP	DEFENSE
2002	MYR	CRL	20	482	123	21	5	12	51	105	12	15	.255	.325	.394	.083	.238	.298	.378	-.189	2.1	118-SS -1
2003	GRN	SOU	21	334	92	22	5	6	35	81	10	3	.275	.340	.425	.101	.257	.313	.416	-.094	11.8	85-SS 3
2004	GRN	SOU	22	479	135	35	3	16	49	102	9	9	.282	.350	.468	.143	.257	.319	.429	-.064	-1.5	66-LF 0 36-CF -2
2005	*ATL*	*NL*	*23*	*268*	*69*	*15*	*2*	*8*	*24*	*61*	*4*	*2*	*.259*	*.321*	*.421*	*-.064*	*.261*	*.321*	*.426*	*-.058*	*7.3*	*72-LF 3*

Breakout: 24% *Improve: 47%* *Collapse: 22%*

He's not going to meet those "future superstar" expectations that were laid out for him following the 2001 season, but he still might be a quite a player. He's had only one genuinely disappointing season, and in his second look at Double-A Greenville he fared much better. The transition to the outfield was not without its fits and starts, but he'll be a capable corner defender at the highest level. He still has a near-perfect swing, good power numbers, and decent patience. One of these years, he's going to put up big numbers in Atlanta.

ANDRUW JONES **CF** **Bats: R** **Throws: R** Born: 23-Apr-1977 Age: 28

YEAR	TM	LG	AGE	AB	H	2B	3B	HR	BB	SO	SB	CS	AVG	OBP	SLG	MLVR	EQBA	EQOBP	EQSLG	EQMLVR	VORP	DEFENSE
2002	ATL	NL	25	560	148	34	0	35	83	135	8	3	.264	.366	.512	.202	.266	.362	.522	.148	54.2	149-CF 20
2003	ATL	NL	26	595	165	28	2	36	53	125	4	3	.277	.338	.513	.165	.277	.338	.518	.113	46.3	152-CF 14
2004	ATL	NL	27	570	149	34	4	29	71	147	6	6	.261	.345	.488	.116	.260	.344	.488	.065	36.6	150-CF 9
2005	*ATL*	*NL*	*28*	*509*	*138*	*29*	*3*	*30*	*65*	*120*	*5*	*3*	*.271*	*.357*	*.516*	*.131*	*.273*	*.357*	*.522*	*.138*	*39.2*	*137-CF 4*

Breakout: 36% *Improve: 67%* *Collapse: 5%*

The one-time "it girl" of the young-and-talented set is still waiting for that one, true season of pure excellence. That said, he's a 28-year-old center fielder with a staggering defensive reputation and 250 career homers. A dozen Gold Gloves and 400 dingers will gain him admittance to Cooperstown, but he may always have the whiff of unrealized promise about him. Considering how his career figures to shape up, that's patently unfair. Still, his vaunted defensive chops seem to be squarely in decline. This past season was his worst since he became a full-timer in 1998. He's still a good one with the leather, but he's less than a win above average. On the offensive end, only once since taking over for Kenny Lofton has he been outside the top five NL center fielders in VORP. That's not Willie Mays, but it is damn good.

CHIPPER JONES **3B/LF** **Bats: B** **Throws: R** Born: 24-Apr-1972 Age: 33

YEAR	TM	LG	AGE	AB	H	2B	3B	HR	BB	SO	SB	CS	AVG	OBP	SLG	MLVR	EQBA	EQOBP	EQSLG	EQMLVR	VORP	DEFENSE
2002	ATL	NL	30	548	179	35	1	26	107	89	8	2	.327	.435	.536	.396	.325	.432	.546	.356	75.0	144-LF 4
2003	ATL	NL	31	555	169	33	2	27	94	83	2	2	.305	.402	.517	.296	.303	.401	.521	.248	54.9	139-LF -12
2004	ATL	NL	32	472	117	20	1	30	84	96	2	0	.248	.362	.485	.130	.246	.358	.481	.068	32.0	90-3B -7 20-LF 2
2005	*ATL*	*NL*	*33*	*434*	*120*	*24*	*2*	*22*	*73*	*80*	*2*	*0*	*.277*	*.382*	*.490*	*.142*	*.279*	*.382*	*.496*	*.150*	*30.3*	*121-LF -3*

Breakout: 16% *Improve: 63%* *Collapse: 10%*

For the first time since 1997, Jones slugged below .500 and posted an OBP below .400. Much of that was owed to his hitting a career-low .248 on the season, which figures to be aberrant. Also portending rebound is the fact that he hit .278/.391/.548 after the break. As for his defense, make this man a DH, stat. As a third baseman, for his career, Jones is a ghastly −116 runs below average in the field. With his bat in decline, he's squandering much of his value with his shoddy work afield. Since the Braves don't have the DH at their disposal and they have a need for a productive first baseman, Jones should be moved across the diamond. That is, short of making every glove he's ever used a part of the next Viking funeral.

RYAN LANGERHANS

OF **Bats: L** **Throws: L** Born: 20-Feb-1980 Age: 25

YEAR	TM	LG	AGE	AB	H	2B	3B	HR	BB	SO	SB	CS	AVG	OBP	SLG	MLVR	EQBA	EQOBP	EQSLG	EQMLVR	VORP	DEFENSE
2002	GRN	SOU	22	391	98	23	2	9	68	83	10	5	.251	.366	.389	.062	.228	.325	.371	-.154	-0.8	107-CF -1
2003	GRN	SOU	23	336	85	23	2	6	46	85	10	10	.253	.348	.387	.048	.234	.318	.374	-.159	-1.3	87-CF 1
2003	RIC	INT	23	132	37	10	2	4	11	29	2	1	.280	.338	.477	.157	.273	.334	.477	.044	4.5	32-RF 0
2004	RIC	INT	24	456	136	34	3	20	70	113	5	9	.298	.397	.518	.283	.279	.375	.478	.122	40.8	70-CF -2 28-LF 1
2005	*ATL*	*NL*	*25*	*187*	*50*	*12*	*1*	*7*	*25*	*45*	*2*	*1*	*.265*	*.357*	*.456*	*.048*	*.267*	*.357*	*.462*	*.055*	*15.6*	*55-CF -2*

Breakout: 25% *Improve: 56%* *Collapse: 28%*

Langerhans, as you can see, went crazy at Triple-A Richmond in 2004. Fluke or breakout? He's always had a promising collection of tools, but in previous seasons the performance hasn't followed. Some within the organization aren't wild about his swing mechanics, but 70 walks and a .518 slugging in the International League are hard to dispute. Given his raw abilities and recent numbers, he projects at worst as one hell of a fourth outfielder. And maybe better than that.

ADAM LaROCHE

1B **Bats: L** **Throws: L** Born: 06-Nov-1979 Age: 25

YEAR	TM	LG	AGE	AB	H	2B	3B	HR	BB	SO	SB	CS	AVG	OBP	SLG	MLVR	EQBA	EQOBP	EQSLG	EQMLVR	VORP	DEFENSE
2002	MYR	CRL	22	250	84	17	0	9	27	37	0	2	.336	.406	.512	.430	.307	.362	.482	.132	17.5	64-1B -5
2002	GRN	SOU	22	173	50	9	0	4	19	38	1	1	.289	.363	.410	.113	.259	.311	.379	-.148	-3.6	45-1B 2
2003	GRN	SOU	23	219	62	12	1	12	34	53	1	2	.283	.381	.511	.275	.256	.344	.480	.050	9.9	60-1B -1
2003	RIC	INT	23	264	78	21	0	8	27	58	1	2	.295	.360	.466	.189	.275	.340	.449	.017	8.3	71-1B -2
2004	ATL	NL	24	324	90	27	1	13	27	78	0	0	.278	.333	.488	.111	.274	.329	.486	.049	19.1	80-1B -6
2005	*ATL*	*NL*	*25*	*351*	*95*	*20*	*1*	*16*	*36*	*74*	*1*	*0*	*.270*	*.341*	*.474*	*.050*	*.272*	*.341*	*.480*	*.057*	*19.9*	*94-1B -2*

Breakout: 16% *Improve: 50%* *Collapse: 27%*

LaRoche probably provided a bit more power last season than we should expect from him in the future. His career SLG in the minors was .447—a very modest figure for a first baseman. He did slug .512 at Myrtle Beach at the age of 22, but some of that was tied up in his .336 batting average. In terms of usefulness, I expect he'll wind up a little north of Travis Lee, minus the hype. He's a suitable left-handed half of a first-base platoon.

ELI MARRERO

LF/RF **Bats: R** **Throws: R** Born: 17-Nov-1973 Age: 31

YEAR	TM	LG	AGE	AB	H	2B	3B	HR	BB	SO	SB	CS	AVG	OBP	SLG	MLVR	EQBA	EQOBP	EQSLG	EQMLVR	VORP	DEFENSE
2002	STL	NL	28	397	104	19	1	18	40	72	14	2	.262	.327	.451	.063	.264	.328	.464	.007	21.1	32-RF 1 25-C -7
2003	STL	NL	29	107	24	4	2	2	7	18	0	1	.224	.267	.355	-.206	.224	.266	.364	-.280	-3.0	12-RF 0
2004	ATL	NL	30	250	80	18	1	10	23	50	4	1	.320	.374	.520	.260	.315	.368	.518	.203	23.6	43-LF 3 20-RF 1
2005	*KCR*	*AL*	*31*	*251*	*68*	*14*	*2*	*9*	*22*	*47*	*3*	*1*	*.272*	*.330*	*.452*	*.009*	*.267*	*.328*	*.453*	*-.005*	*9.7*	*68-LF 1*

Breakout: 12% *Improve: 34%* *Collapse: 41%*

He's not the paragon of durability, but recent history suggests he can be effective in a limited role when healthy. Last year's numbers (.320/.374/.520) were flukey, but he's been a capable reserve in several seasons. It'd be nice if he'd return catching to his bag of tricks. He's over-deployed as a regular, and will likely fill a utility outfield role after being dealt to the Royals.

ANDY MARTE

3B **Bats: R** **Throws: R** Born: 21-Oct-1983 Age: 21

YEAR	TM	LG	AGE	AB	H	2B	3B	HR	BB	SO	SB	CS	AVG	OBP	SLG	MLVR	EQBA	EQOBP	EQSLG	EQMLVR	VORP	DEFENSE
2002	MCN	SAL	18	488	137	32	4	21	41	114	2	1	.281	.339	.492	.214	.237	.282	.419	-.163	2.8	121-3B 0
2003	MYR	CRL	19	463	132	35	1	16	67	109	5	2	.285	.372	.469	.276	.268	.343	.463	.036	34.2	117-3B -14
2004	GRN	SOU	20	387	104	28	1	23	58	105	1	1	.269	.364	.525	.226	.238	.326	.471	-.009	21.8	102-3B 6
2005	*ATL*	*NL*	*21*	*324*	*85*	*18*	*1*	*16*	*42*	*82*	*1*	*0*	*.263*	*.348*	*.479*	*.062*	*.265*	*.348*	*.486*	*.069*	*19.3*	*89-3B -4*

Breakout: 38% *Improve: 52%* *Collapse: 22%*

The best prospect in baseball and a future superstar. As a 20-year-old toiling in the mostly hitter-unfriendly Southern League, Marte hit .269/.364/.525. In only 387 at-bats, he smacked 52 extra-base hits. He's got monstrous power and a broad base of hitting skills. In his prime, expect a few seasons of Adrian Beltre, circa 2004.

BRIAN McCANN C **Bats: L** **Throws: R** Born: 20-Feb-1984 Age: 21

YEAR	TM	LG	AGE	AB	H	2B	3B	HR	BB	SO	SB	CS	AVG	OBP	SLG	MLVR	EQBA	EQOBP	EQSLG	EQMLVR	VORP	DEFENSE
2003	ROM	SAL	19	424	123	31	3	12	24	73	7	4	.290	.329	.462	.213	.258	.285	.418	-.142	4.2	63-C 2
2004	MYR	CRL	20	385	107	35	0	16	31	54	2	2	.278	.337	.494	.239	.251	.297	.456	-.071	12.6	70-C 4
2005	*ATL*	*NL*	*21*	*342*	*85*	*20*	*2*	*11*	*20*	*64*	*1*	*1*	*.248*	*.291*	*.413*	*-.136*	*.249*	*.291*	*.418*	*-.130*	*2.4*	*89-C -10*

Breakout: 7% *Improve: 35%* *Collapse: 42%*

McCann mans a key position and boasts a light-tower stroke. Normally, we'd be higher on a guy who slugs nearly .500 in Myrtle Beach at age 20, but there's cause for dampened enthusiasm. First, it's highly doubtful he'll stick at catcher; Jarrod Saltalamacchia is ahead of him on the depth charts, and the Braves privately don't care for McCann's defense. Second, his swing is long, his bat is a bit on the slow side, and he has sub-optimal plate discipline. In other words, it'll be surprising if those power numbers hold up at the higher levels.

BILL McCARTHY LF/RF **Bats: R** **Throws: R** Born: 02-Dec-1979 Age: 25

YEAR	TM	LG	AGE	AB	H	2B	3B	HR	BB	SO	SB	CS	AVG	OBP	SLG	MLVR	EQBA	EQOBP	EQSLG	EQMLVR	VORP	DEFENSE
2002	MYR	CRL	22	442	135	26	4	11	38	88	6	5	.305	.386	.457	.297	.287	.346	.448	.037	14.3	89-RF -2
2003	GRN	SOU	23	276	69	19	2	6	41	59	5	1	.250	.355	.399	.071	.230	.323	.387	-.135	-7.4	68-LF 0
2004	GRN	SOU	24	233	70	12	2	9	26	67	1	2	.300	.375	.485	.218	.277	.342	.451	.025	6.7	58-RF -4
2004	RIC	INT	24	178	63	13	1	6	14	32	0	2	.354	.407	.539	.391	.339	.393	.514	.264	17.6	31-LF 1 11-RF 0
2005	*ATL*	*NL*	*25*	*194*	*52*	*11*	*1*	*7*	*18*	*43*	*1*	*1*	*.268*	*.346*	*.445*	*.017*	*.269*	*.346*	*.451*	*.024*	*14.1*	*55-RF -3*

Breakout: 11% *Improve: 37%* *Collapse: 45%*

He's a career .298 hitter with respectable power numbers in the high minors. As a strict corner outfielder in a system stuffed with good hitting prospects, he'll need to ramp up the homer numbers to get a clear path to the majors. There's always a chance he could hone his skills and become a capable supporting actor in Atlanta; PECOTA has him pegged as bench-worthy.

EDDIE PEREZ C **Bats: R** **Throws: R** Born: 04-May-1968 Age: 37

YEAR	TM	LG	AGE	AB	H	2B	3B	HR	BB	SO	SB	CS	AVG	OBP	SLG	MLVR	EQBA	EQOBP	EQSLG	EQMLVR	VORP	DEFENSE
2002	CLE	AL	34	117	25	9	0	0	5	25	0	0	.214	.252	.291	-.372	.224	.247	.276	-.443	-4.4	35-C 0
2003	MIL	NL	35	350	95	17	1	11	17	47	0	1	.271	.304	.420	-.044	.270	.303	.420	-.096	11.0	91-C -12
2004	ATL	NL	36	170	39	12	0	3	11	29	0	0	.229	.286	.353	-.197	.233	.279	.349	-.270	-0.8	44-C 7
2005	*ATL*	*NL*	*37*	*148*	*36*	*8*	*0*	*3*	*9*	*24*	*0*	*0*	*.245*	*.290*	*.370*	*-.196*	*.247*	*.290*	*.375*	*-.191*	*1.2*	*42-C -2*

Breakout: 16% *Improve: 45%* *Collapse: 32%*

Other than a wildly anomalous 1998, Perez has been your garden-variety backup catcher for a decade and, at one time, Greg Maddux's preferred antidote to whatever it was about Javy Lopez that bothered him so much. He's an uninspired addition for most teams, but he's as capable as any number of other caddies. He'll probably be a manager one day.

CHARLES THOMAS CF/LF **Bats: L** **Throws: L** Born: 26-Dec-1978 Age: 26

YEAR	TM	LG	AGE	AB	H	2B	3B	HR	BB	SO	SB	CS	AVG	OBP	SLG	MLVR	EQBA	EQOBP	EQSLG	EQMLVR	VORP	DEFENSE
2002	GRN	SOU	23	229	53	8	0	2	28	43	5	3	.231	.322	.293	-.140	.205	.272	.265	-.416	-26.3	61-RF -1
2003	MYR	CRL	24	207	50	8	1	2	29	54	6	2	.242	.357	.319	.024	.230	.323	.327	-.215	-11.3	40-LF -3 21-RF 0
2003	GRN	SOU	24	176	57	14	4	0	18	25	5	4	.324	.396	.449	.250	.292	.348	.416	-.001	8.3	38-CF 1
2004	RIC	INT	25	215	77	18	4	4	16	40	7	5	.358	.416	.535	.403	.344	.398	.512	.275	28.0	19-CF 0 14-LF 1
2004	ATL	NL	25	236	68	8	4	7	21	45	3	1	.288	.368	.445	.121	.286	.362	.445	.060	12.9	70-LF 6
2005	*OAK*	*AL*	*26*	*289*	*76*	*15*	*3*	*6*	*25*	*60*	*4*	*3*	*.261*	*.335*	*.394*	*-.066*	*.264*	*.339*	*.401*	*-.057*	*6.3*	*79-LF 3*

Breakout: 5% *Improve: 27%* *Collapse: 42%*

A likeable, dirty-uniformed type who can play a capable outfield, Thomas rode a hot late June/July to some respectable 2004 numbers. However, pitchers made adjustments to him later in the season, and it became clear that he doesn't have the hitting skills to be a major league regular. It's possible, if he concentrates on playing good defense and getting on base, that he'll have a long career as a platoon player or fourth outfielder, but the lightning that we saw in mid-summer has been let out of the bottle. Traded to the A's as part of the Tim Hudson swap.

DEWAYNE WISE CF/LF **Bats: L** **Throws: L** Born: 24-Feb-1978 Age: 27

YEAR	TM	LG	AGE	AB	H	2B	3B	HR	BB	SO	SB	CS	AVG	OBP	SLG	MLVR	EQBA	EQOBP	EQSLG	EQMLVR	VORP	DEFENSE
2002	TEN	SOU	24	340	101	21	4	10	29	49	15	8	.297	.350	.471	.158	.262	.303	.434	-.082	6.5	77-CF 1
2002	TOR	AL	24	112	20	4	1	3	4	15	5	0	.179	.207	.312	-.430	.171	.207	.306	-.508	-7.9	26-RF 3
2003	SYR	INT	25	285	62	11	4	10	17	72	11	3	.218	.262	.389	-.155	.201	.251	.370	-.316	-14.6	52-CF -2 21-RF -1
2004	RIC	INT	26	118	37	4	6	5	5	19	5	0	.314	.341	.576	.296	.297	.325	.542	.147	10.4	30-CF -1
2004	ATL	NL	26	162	37	9	4	6	9	28	6	1	.228	.272	.444	-.100	.227	.269	.442	-.162	1.2	22-LF 2
2005	*DET*	*AL*	*27*	*202*	*51*	*10*	*2*	*6*	*12*	*41*	*6*	*2*	*.250*	*.293*	*.417*	*-.117*	*.253*	*.298*	*.435*	*-.092*	*6.0*	*55-CF -2*

Breakout: 24% *Improve: 45%* *Collapse: 38%*

Nothing to see here. Career .256 hitter in the minors, very little plate discipline, only quasi-adequate gap power numbers, already 27. Need we pile on?

PITCHERS

RAY AGUILAR **Bats: B** **Throws: L** Born: 18-Jan-1980 Age: 25

YEAR	TM	LG	AGE	G	GS	IP	H	BB	SO	HR	ERA	EQERA	EQH9	EQBB9	EQSO9	EQHR9	PERA	VORP	STF
2002	MYR	CRL	22	35	6	106.7	82	28	114	1	1.60	3.83	7.8	2.9	6.9	0.2	3.28	25.4	22
2003	GRN	SOU	23	35	7	93.0	81	20	91	8	2.71	4.73	9.2	2.0	6.4	1.6	4.73	8.3	0
2004	MYR	CRL	24	4	4	20.0	15	1	12	0	2.25	3.44	7.9	0.5	3.9	0.5	2.45	6.4	15
2004	GRN	SOU	24	8	7	51.0	35	8	32	7	2.29	3.77	8.3	1.6	4.2	2.0	3.97	8.2	16
2004	RIC	INT	24	9	9	42.0	59	17	31	4	6.21	7.50	10.9	3.6	5.1	0.9	6.00	-1.9	-16
2005	*ATL*	*NL*	*25*	*14*	*11*	*71.0*	*74*	*23*	*48*	*10*	*4.48*	*4.74*	*9.4*	*2.5*	*5.4*	*1.2*	*4.79*	*7.5*	*3*

Breakout: 11% *Improve: 40%* *Collapse: 16%*

He's dominated as a reliever and, last season, proved himself as a starter. Fortunately for the Braves, he's gone unclaimed in two straight Rule 5 drafts. At the very least, he's a capable LOOGY in waiting. No one needs that? Buddy Groom's last contract and C. J. Nitkowski's continued employment say otherwise.

ANTONIO ALFONSECA **Bats: R** **Throws: R** Born: 16-Apr-1972 Age: 33

YEAR	TM	LG	AGE	G	GS	IP	H	BB	SO	HR	ERA	EQERA	EQH9	EQBB9	EQSO9	EQHR9	PERA	VORP	STF
2002	CHC	NL	30	66	0	74.3	73	36	61	5	4.00	4.19	8.6	3.7	6.5	0.6	3.82	10.4	1
2003	CHC	NL	31	60	0	66.3	76	27	51	7	5.84	5.62	9.6	3.2	6.2	1.0	4.66	-1.6	-6
2004	ATL	NL	32	79	0	73.7	71	28	45	5	2.56	3.04	8.7	3.0	4.9	0.5	4.06	22.7	-8
2005	*FLA*	*NL*	*33*	*43*	*0*	*54.3*	*59*	*22*	*34*	*5*	*4.42*	*4.82*	*9.8*	*3.3*	*5.1*	*0.8*	*4.98*	*4.3*	*-11*

Breakout: 16% *Improve: 41%* *Collapse: 35%*

The bane of Inigo Montoya quietly (mostly because he wasn't stamped with the closer's imprimatur) had the best season of his career in '04. Of course, that came on the heels of his worst season, which came on the heels of abject mediocrity. The Braves wisely cut bait on him, and the Marlins, in what's been a piteous attempt to assemble a bullpen by throwing money at guys they've merely heard of, were quick to keep him in clover. Atlanta will miss his quality innings, but history—Darren Holmes, Chris Hammond—suggests they'll turn up a suitable proxy.

BLAINE BOYER **Bats: R** **Throws: R** Born: 11-Jul-1981 Age: 23

YEAR	TM	LG	AGE	G	GS	IP	H	BB	SO	HR	ERA	EQERA	EQH9	EQBB9	EQSO9	EQHR9	PERA	VORP	STF
2002	MCN	SAL	20	43	0	70.3	52	39	73	0	3.07	5.57	8.1	6.4	5.9	0.3	4.43	8.2	-1
2003	ROM	SAL	21	30	26	136.7	146	58	115	5	3.69	6.63	10.2	4.5	4.6	0.8	5.71	-1.6	-5
2004	MYR	CRL	22	28	28	154.0	138	49	95	4	2.98	5.06	8.8	3.4	4.0	0.4	3.98	25.6	5
2005	*ATL*	*NL*	*23*	*15*	*13*	*78.7*	*80*	*37*	*48*	*8*	*4.61*	*4.88*	*9.3*	*3.7*	*4.9*	*0.8*	*4.89*	*6.6*	*-1*

Breakout: 17% *Improve: 48%* *Collapse: 20%*

Another suburban-Atlanta draftee, Boyer, the 100th pick of the 2000 draft, has worked as a starter the last two seasons, but he's stretched in the role. His lack of strong off-speed stuff will probably force him back to the bullpen, but as a reliever he has loads of potential. His fastball sits at 95, and his hammer curve is a plus offering. If the Braves do the right thing and deploy him as a reliever, look out.

PAUL BYRD **Bats: R** **Throws: R** Born: 03-Dec-1970 Age: 34

YEAR	TM	LG	AGE	G	GS	IP	H	BB	SO	HR	ERA	EQERA	EQH9	EQBB9	EQSO9	EQHR9	PERA	VORP	STF
2002	KCR	AL	31	33	33	228.3	224	38	129	36	3.90	3.75	8.9	1.4	5.0	1.3	4.12	40.8	7
2004	ATL	NL	33	19	19	114.3	123	19	79	18	3.94	4.40	9.5	1.4	5.6	1.3	4.49	16.2	10
2005	*ANA*	*AL*	*34*	*24*	*22*	*130.7*	*147*	*27*	*78*	*23*	*4.87*	*4.82*	*10.2*	*1.6*	*4.8*	*1.6*	*4.79*	*17.7*	*2*

Breakout: 17% *Improve: 40%* *Collapse: 28%*

This 2004 was supposed to be his "lost" year, right? Despite coming off reconstructive elbow surgery, Byrd posted a K/BB ratio of better than 4.0 in 19 starts. He's always had homer proclivities, but if the strides he's made in terms of command are genuine, he'll get by. A nifty addition to the Angels' rotation in 2005.

JOSE CAPELLAN **Bats: R** **Throws: R** Born: 13-Jan-1981 Age: 24

YEAR	TM	LG	AGE	G	GS	IP	H	BB	SO	HR	ERA	EQERA	EQH9	EQBB9	EQSO9	EQHR9	PERA	VORP	STF
2003	ROM	SAL	22	14	12	47.3	43	19	32	2	3.81	6.28	9.4	4.4	3.8	1.0	5.44	0.8	-14
2004	MYR	CRL	23	8	8	46.3	27	11	62	0	1.94	3.61	6.6	2.6	8.9	0.2	2.34	15.3	43
2004	GRN	SOU	23	9	8	50.3	53	19	53	1	2.50	3.51	9.2	3.5	6.5	0.2	4.07	8.3	19
2004	RIC	INT	23	7	7	43.0	33	15	37	0	2.51	3.12	7.4	3.3	6.5	0.2	3.35	10.1	25
2004	ATL	NL	23	3	2	8.0	14	5	4	2	11.25	10.80	13.0	4.3	3.2	2.2	8.64	-4.9	-29
2005	*MIL*	*NL*	*24*	*16*	*15*	*89.0*	*91*	*38*	*72*	*11*	*4.76*	*4.93*	*9.2*	*3.4*	*6.6*	*1.1*	*4.90*	*8.9*	*9*

Breakout: 12% *Improve: 36%* *Collapse: 32%*

In most quarters last year, you heard Capellan touted as the Braves' best pitching prospect. Don't buy it: Dan Meyer will be the better major league hurler by a long shot, though now in Oakland. Capellan's probably destined for relief because of his lack of consistent supporting pitches. His fastball—Capellan's lone plus offering—is all velocity and no movement. He'll wind up in the bullpen and probably do a fair Matt Anderson imitation. Shipped to the Brewers in the Dan Kolb swap.

ROMAN COLON **Bats: R** **Throws: R** Born: 13-Aug-1979 Age: 25

YEAR	TM	LG	AGE	G	GS	IP	H	BB	SO	HR	ERA	EQERA	EQH9	EQBB9	EQSO9	EQHR9	PERA	VORP	STF
2002	MYR	CRL	22	26	26	163.0	170	38	94	8	3.53	6.14	10.1	2.6	3.7	1.1	5.19	6.9	-4
2003	GRN	SOU	23	39	12	107.0	104	33	58	9	3.36	4.93	9.9	2.9	3.6	1.6	5.47	1.4	-23
2004	RIC	INT	24	51	0	74.0	72	22	64	4	3.65	4.18	8.6	2.8	6.3	0.5	3.93	13.2	2
2004	ATL	NL	24	18	0	19.0	18	8	15	0	3.32	4.42	8.3	3.4	6.4	0.0	3.44	3.0	0
2005	*ATL*	*NL*	*25*	*22*	*8*	*66.3*	*68*	*23*	*47*	*8*	*4.30*	*4.55*	*9.3*	*2.7*	*5.7*	*1.0*	*4.54*	*7.6*	*0*

Breakout: 23% *Improve: 49%* *Collapse: 17%*

Least likely nickname for Roman (accent, second syllable) Colon, should he become famous enough to merit one: *Bildungsroman.* In any event, this particular novel of education, after some fits and starts, fared well in the low minors as a starter and transitioned deftly to relief work over the last season-and-a-half. Last year, he was named Richmond's pitcher of the year and also pitched well in 19 innings in Atlanta. He's a good bet to win a spot in the Braves' bullpen coming out of spring training.

JUAN CRUZ **Bats: R** **Throws: R** Born: 15-Oct-1978 Age: 26

YEAR	TM	LG	AGE	G	GS	IP	H	BB	SO	HR	ERA	EQERA	EQH9	EQBB9	EQSO9	EQHR9	PERA	VORP	STF
2002	CHC	NL	23	45	9	97.3	84	59	81	11	3.98	5.25	8.2	4.7	6.7	1.0	4.20	2.8	-1
2003	IOW	PCL	24	9	9	50.7	37	11	47	1	1.95	2.83	7.0	2.3	7.2	0.2	2.45	16.7	35
2003	CHC	NL	24	25	6	61.0	66	28	65	7	6.05	6.20	9.0	3.5	8.6	1.0	4.43	-5.6	18
2004	ATL	NL	25	50	0	72.0	59	30	70	7	2.75	2.99	7.7	3.4	7.9	0.8	3.63	21.6	16
2005	*OAK*	*AL*	*26*	*33*	*7*	*74.3*	*67*	*32*	*62*	*10*	*4.17*	*4.13*	*8.2*	*3.4*	*6.7*	*1.1*	*4.15*	*14.3*	*2*

Breakout: 26% *Improve: 51%* *Collapse: 27%*

Cruz put together a very nice season out of the bullpen, albeit in generally low-stress situations. He still needs to cut down on his walks, but 70 whiffs in 72 innings and three runs allowed per nine innings aren't chopped liver. If nothing else, he's earned a chance to work the more fraught innings. Whatever Mazzone does, it seems to work with relievers as well. Cruz now takes his act to Oakland, joining a dynamic pen of young power arms.

DANIEL CURTIS Bats: R Throws: R Born: 03-Nov-1979 Age: 25

YEAR	TM	LG	AGE	G	GS	IP	H	BB	SO	HR	ERA	EQERA	EQH9	EQBB9	EQSO9	EQHR9	PERA	VORP	STF
2002	MYR	CRL	22	17	17	117.3	106	18	99	10	2.53	4.49	9.9	1.8	5.6	1.9	5.25	4.1	0
2002	GRN	SOU	22	10	10	54.3	61	18	29	7	4.81	5.54	11.3	2.9	3.6	2.3	6.79	-6.7	-21
2003	MYR	CRL	23	12	11	64.7	77	23	55	5	4.03	7.15	10.8	3.5	5.5	1.6	5.98	-2.6	-14
2003	GRN	SOU	23	17	12	78.3	72	15	47	4	2.87	4.33	9.2	1.9	4.0	0.9	4.21	11.2	-9
2004	GRN	SOU	24	33	6	95.3	90	35	88	7	3.12	4.42	9.0	3.4	5.8	1.0	4.32	12.8	0
2005	*ATL*	*NL*	*25*	*25*	*11*	*80.3*	*84*	*29*	*58*	*11*	*4.71*	*4.98*	*9.5*	*2.9*	*5.9*	*1.2*	*4.96*	*6.8*	*-1*

Breakout: 22% *Improve: 46%* *Collapse: 25%*

Curtis, who wasn't a bad starter in the lower rungs of the minors, tried his hand at bullpen work last season and wasn't bad there either. In general, he's shown good command and done a fair job of keeping the ball in the park. He's not high in the organizational pitching queue right now, so his chance may come elsewhere.

KYLE DAVIES Bats: R Throws: R Born: 09-Sep-1983 Age: 21

YEAR	TM	LG	AGE	G	GS	IP	H	BB	SO	HR	ERA	EQERA	EQH9	EQBB9	EQSO9	EQHR9	PERA	VORP	STF
2002	DNV	APL	18	14	14	69.3	73	23	62	2	3.51	7.06	10.0	3.7	4.0	0.6	5.12	3.5	0
2003	ROM	SAL	19	27	27	146.3	128	53	148	9	2.89	5.24	9.7	4.0	5.7	1.4	5.58	0.3	10
2004	MYR	CRL	20	14	14	75.3	55	32	95	3	2.63	4.28	7.8	4.5	8.3	0.6	3.89	13.2	34
2004	GRN	SOU	20	11	10	62.0	40	22	73	9	2.32	3.38	7.9	3.5	7.7	1.8	4.18	8.8	37
2005	*ATL*	*NL*	*21*	*22*	*11*	*79.0*	*74*	*39*	*71*	*10*	*4.61*	*4.87*	*8.5*	*3.9*	*7.2*	*1.1*	*4.85*	*7.1*	*6*

Breakout: 11% *Improve: 43%* *Collapse: 21%*

Live arm, good K rates, not much else. His stuff is more marginal than you'd think considering his strikeout numbers. His mechanics have been overhauled several times, and he has trouble repeating his delivery. Davies probably has major surgery somewhere in his tea leaves.

TIM DREW Bats: R Throws: R Born: 31-Aug-1978 Age: 26

YEAR	TM	LG	AGE	G	GS	IP	H	BB	SO	HR	ERA	EQERA	EQH9	EQBB9	EQSO9	EQHR9	PERA	VORP	STF
2002	BUF	INT	23	15	15	96.3	96	23	43	6	3.27	4.60	9.5	2.5	3.5	0.7	4.70	9.0	6
2002	OTT	INT	23	13	13	84.7	77	24	29	5	2.87	3.86	9.5	3.0	2.8	0.7	4.91	5.9	2
2003	EDM	PCL	24	27	15	93.3	128	35	54	10	7.23	8.09	10.8	3.7	4.3	1.4	5.75	-1.5	-31
2004	RIC	INT	25	19	13	81.7	92	24	44	5	3.30	4.00	9.6	2.7	4.0	0.6	4.69	8.0	-15
2004	ATL	NL	25	11	0	16.0	21	5	7	2	4.50	5.74	10.9	2.3	3.4	1.1	5.74	-0.9	-33
2005	*COL*	*NL*	*26*	*20*	*10*	*65.7*	*81*	*25*	*36*	*10*	*5.78*	*5.04*	*10.5*	*3.0*	*4.7*	*1.1*	*5.08*	*5.2*	*-8*

Breakout: 30% *Improve: 53%* *Collapse: 21%*

Drew was once highly regarded, so it would be unfair to lump him in with the Mike Glavine/Pete Rose Jr./John Henry Williams Nepotism All-Star Team. Still, command has never really been his strong suit, and since he's 26, the time to make notable strides has likely passed. There's a chance he could make a passable long man given the right environment, but he's more likely organizational fodder.

KEVIN GRYBOSKI Bats: R Throws: R Born: 15-Nov-1973 Age: 31

YEAR	TM	LG	AGE	G	GS	IP	H	BB	SO	HR	ERA	EQERA	EQH9	EQBB9	EQSO9	EQHR9	PERA	VORP	STF
2002	ATL	NL	28	57	0	51.7	50	37	33	6	3.48	3.62	9.4	5.6	5.3	1.1	5.98	10.9	-23
2003	ATL	NL	29	64	0	44.3	44	23	32	3	3.86	4.57	8.9	4.2	5.8	0.6	4.57	5.7	-8
2004	ATL	NL	30	69	0	50.7	54	23	24	2	2.84	3.83	9.3	3.6	3.8	0.4	4.56	10.1	-16
2005	*ATL*	*NL*	*31*	*40*	*0*	*39.7*	*43*	*20*	*25*	*3*	*4.48*	*4.74*	*9.8*	*4.0*	*5.0*	*0.7*	*5.21*	*3.9*	*-14*

Breakout: 28% *Improve: 51%* *Collapse: 24%*

Normally, you don't expect much from a predominant reliever who posts a strikeout-to-walk ratio of less than 2.0 in the minors, but Gryboski has slowly earned his keep at the highest level. In 146.2 major league relief innings spaced over three seasons, he's posted a 3.38 ERA. Of course, his peripherals (89 strikeouts, 83 walks) are quite weak, so it could be smoke and mirrors. Perhaps Gryboski's the analysis-defying Kirk Rueter of relievers.

MIKE HAMPTON **Bats: R** **Throws: L** Born: 09-Sep-1972 Age: 32

YEAR	TM	LG	AGE	G	GS	IP	H	BB	SO	HR	ERA	EQERA	EQH9	EQBB9	EQSO9	EQHR9	PERA	VORP	STF
2002	COL	NL	29	30	30	178.7	228	91	74	24	6.14	6.00	10.7	3.9	3.3	1.1	5.95	-25.8	-15
2003	ATL	NL	30	31	31	190.0	186	78	110	14	3.84	4.34	9.1	3.3	4.8	0.6	4.24	29.3	6
2004	ATL	NL	31	29	29	172.3	198	65	87	15	4.28	4.43	9.8	3.0	4.1	0.7	4.80	24.4	0
2005	*ATL*	*NL*	*32*	*25*	*24*	*136.3*	*154*	*54*	*72*	*14*	*4.74*	*5.01*	*10.2*	*3.1*	*4.3*	*0.9*	*5.16*	*9.5*	*-3*

Breakout: 17% *Improve: 53%* *Collapse: 23%*

During Hampton's peak seasons of 1998–2000, he posted seasonal groundball-flyball ratios of 2.70, 2.56 and 2.51. Since then, he's broken the 2.00 mark exactly once—last season, with a 2.01 mark. He's made modest strides with his formerly problematic control, but he can't strike anyone out anymore, and he's worked less than 200 innings for three consecutive seasons. In other words, the decline phase has commenced. At least the Marlins are still paying most of his tab. These days, he's a fifth starter with #2 name recognition.

CHUCK JAMES **Bats: L** **Throws: L** Born: 09-Nov-1981 Age: 23

YEAR	TM	LG	AGE	G	GS	IP	H	BB	SO	HR	ERA	EQERA	EQH9	EQBB9	EQSO9	EQHR9	PERA	VORP	STF
2003	DNV	APL	21	11	11	50.3	26	19	68	1	1.25	3.86	6.9	4.7	7.1	0.6	3.45	10.6	25
2004	ROM	SAL	22	26	22	132.7	92	48	156	6	2.24	4.06	7.6	3.8	6.6	0.7	3.39	30.0	31
2005	*ATL*	*NL*	*23*	*16*	*12*	*78.3*	*71*	*35*	*62*	*12*	*4.48*	*4.74*	*8.2*	*3.5*	*6.4*	*1.3*	*4.71*	*9.4*	*5*

Breakout: 11% *Improve: 48%* *Collapse: 22%*

James, to hear those who've been around him tell it, is to a good attitude what Marion Barry is to ascetic restraint. He blew away the Sally League last season, but occasionally had trouble with his control. Despite his semi-gaudy K rate, his stuff is average, and he projects as no better than a back-end starter at the highest level. There's a good chance that he'll one day be on the business end of a highly publicized clubhouse ass-beating. So that's something.

ANTHONY LEREW **Bats: L** **Throws: R** Born: 28-Oct-1982 Age: 22

YEAR	TM	LG	AGE	G	GS	IP	H	BB	SO	HR	ERA	EQERA	EQH9	EQBB9	EQSO9	EQHR9	PERA	VORP	STF
2002	DNV	APL	19	14	14	83.0	60	25	75	2	1.73	4.92	8.2	3.5	4.2	0.5	3.84	14.7	13
2003	ROM	SAL	20	25	25	143.7	112	43	127	7	2.38	4.87	8.9	3.3	5.0	1.2	4.66	13.5	16
2004	MYR	CRL	21	27	27	144.0	145	46	125	12	3.75	6.06	9.9	3.4	5.7	1.5	5.39	3.1	-4
2005	*ATL*	*NL*	*22*	*12*	*10*	*60.7*	*64*	*25*	*42*	*8*	*4.83*	*5.12*	*9.5*	*3.2*	*5.6*	*1.2*	*5.09*	*3.9*	*2*

Breakout: 7% *Improve: 39%* *Collapse: 20%*

Lerew has serious trouble maintaining his velocity from start to start, which makes one wonder whether he's pitching through injuries. His numbers look all right, until you consider he's logged more than one-third of his professional innings at Myrtle Beach and has yet to pitch in the high minors.

TOM MARTIN **Bats: L** **Throws: L** Born: 21-May-1970 Age: 35

YEAR	TM	LG	AGE	G	GS	IP	H	BB	SO	HR	ERA	EQERA	EQH9	EQBB9	EQSO9	EQHR9	PERA	VORP	STF
2003	LAD	NL	33	80	0	51.0	36	24	51	6	3.53	3.91	7.4	3.9	8.4	1.1	3.91	10.8	7
2004	LAD	NL	34	47	0	28.3	32	14	18	3	4.13	4.23	10.1	3.9	5.2	1.0	5.86	5.0	-19
2004	ATL	NL	34	29	0	17.0	17	5	12	4	3.71	3.86	9.4	2.2	5.5	2.2	4.96	3.8	-9
2005	*ATL*	*NL*	*35*	*40*	*0*	*39.3*	*41*	*18*	*30*	*5*	*4.70*	*4.98*	*9.4*	*3.7*	*6.1*	*1.1*	*5.16*	*3.0*	*-8*

Breakout: 19% *Improve: 52%* *Collapse: 22%*

Martin's never worked more than 56 innings in a season, and he has a career ERA that's comfortably worse than the league average over that same span. In other words, despite narrow and carefully crafted deployment, he's still been mostly lousy. Why not Ray Aguilar again?

DAN MEYER

Bats: R Throws: L Born: 03-Jul-1981 Age: 23

YEAR	TM	LG	AGE	G	GS	IP	H	BB	SO	HR	ERA	EQERA	EQH9	EQBB9	EQSO9	EQHR9	PERA	VORP	STF
2002	DNV	APL	21	13	13	65.7	47	18	77	4	2.74	5.37	8.7	3.2	5.5	1.4	4.60	6.5	14
2003	ROM	SAL	22	15	15	81.7	76	15	95	6	2.86	5.91	10.1	2.0	6.5	1.8	5.54	0.5	15
2003	MYR	CRL	22	13	13	78.3	69	17	63	7	2.87	4.79	9.6	2.1	5.6	1.9	4.92	5.4	10
2004	GRN	SOU	23	14	13	65.0	50	12	86	1	2.22	3.23	7.6	1.8	8.2	0.1	2.64	20.2	34
2004	RIC	INT	23	12	11	61.3	62	25	60	6	2.79	3.66	9.0	3.8	7.2	0.9	4.73	5.7	15
2004	ATL	NL	23	2	0	2.0	2	1	1	0	0.00	0.00	9.0	4.5	4.5	0.0	4.50	1.3	-17
2005	*OAK*	*AL*	*23*	*23*	*13*	*91.7*	*91*	*32*	*73*	*14*	*4.49*	*4.45*	*9.0*	*2.7*	*6.4*	*1.3*	*4.45*	*15.3*	*5*

Breakout: 12% *Improve: 35%* *Collapse: 20%*

The most underrated arm in the game? None of his pitches blows scouts away, but he has a deep repertoire and peerless command. The organization loves his poise and intelligence on the mound, and he also earns praise for his ability to set up hitters. For his career, he's fanned more than a batter per inning and posted a sparkling 4.38 strikeout-to-walk ratio. In an organization that has a deft touch with young arms, his ceiling could be somewhere north of Brad Radke. That organization will now be Oakland, who acquired Meyer as the linchpin of the Tim Hudson trade. At press time the A's were debating whether to install him as the fifth starter or sign a vet to fill the role and starting Meyer in Triple-A. He'll crack the big league rotation and succeed soon, either way.

RUSS ORTIZ

Bats: R Throws: R Born: 05-Jun-1974 Age: 31

YEAR	TM	LG	AGE	G	GS	IP	H	BB	SO	HR	ERA	EQERA	EQH9	EQBB9	EQSO9	EQHR9	PERA	VORP	STF
2002	SFG	NL	28	33	33	214.3	191	94	137	15	3.61	4.01	8.7	3.5	5.2	0.7	4.28	42.0	8
2003	ATL	NL	29	34	34	212.3	177	102	149	17	3.82	4.31	8.2	3.9	5.9	0.7	3.96	33.4	11
2004	ATL	NL	30	34	34	204.7	197	112	143	23	4.13	4.27	8.8	4.4	5.7	0.9	4.76	33.1	3
2005	*ARI*	*NL*	*31*	*28*	*26*	*149.0*	*155*	*74*	*104*	*19*	*5.02*	*5.01*	*9.2*	*3.9*	*5.7*	*1.0*	*5.00*	*12.1*	*2*

Breakout: 16% *Improve: 47%* *Collapse: 23%*

He's the quintessence of a tolerable third starter. Ortiz has been blessed with capable teammates throughout his career, which is in part why he sports that comely .632 career winning percentage. In a vacuum, he's a few ticks above average and has never missed a start in his career. That's valuable, but he's not the quasi-ace some see. You'd expect worse from a pitcher who's not noted for his strikeout abilities and also walks a batter every two innings. His groundball-flyball ratio has been down modestly since arriving in Atlanta, and this past season his home run rate finally reflected that. Something to keep in mind as he enters his post-prime seasons. For some reason, the Dbacks saw fit to sign him for $33 million. He'll be critical to their rousing charge for 70 wins.

HORACIO RAMIREZ

Bats: L Throws: L Born: 24-Nov-1979 Age: 25

YEAR	TM	LG	AGE	G	GS	IP	H	BB	SO	HR	ERA	EQERA	EQH9	EQBB9	EQSO9	EQHR9	PERA	VORP	STF
2002	GRN	SOU	22	16	16	92.0	85	32	64	5	3.03	4.83	9.2	3.0	4.7	0.9	4.52	10.3	5
2003	ATL	NL	23	29	29	182.3	181	72	100	21	4.00	4.49	9.3	3.2	4.6	1.0	4.65	24.4	1
2004	ATL	NL	24	10	9	60.3	51	30	31	7	2.39	3.63	8.4	4.1	4.3	0.9	4.42	14.6	-5
2005	*ATL*	*NL*	*25*	*19*	*16*	*93.3*	*102*	*40*	*52*	*11*	*4.69*	*4.96*	*9.9*	*3.4*	*4.5*	*1.0*	*5.18*	*7.4*	*-5*

Breakout: 23% *Improve: 50%* *Collapse: 18%*

Ramirez is the type of pitcher whose stuff is only good enough to get out guys in the minors. He put up passable run-prevention numbers in Atlanta in 2003, but the peripherals didn't justify them. Last season, in 60.1 innings, he struck out 31 against 30 walks for the Braves. The sooner the organization realizes his only hope for an extended stay in the majors is as a reliever, the better off everyone will be.

CHRIS REITSMA

Bats: R Throws: R Born: 31-Dec-1977 Age: 27

YEAR	TM	LG	AGE	G	GS	IP	H	BB	SO	HR	ERA	EQERA	EQH9	EQBB9	EQSO9	EQHR9	PERA	VORP	STF
2002	CIN	NL	24	32	21	138.3	144	45	84	17	3.64	4.66	9.4	2.6	4.9	1.1	4.59	11.3	1
2003	CIN	NL	25	57	3	84.0	92	19	53	14	4.29	4.32	9.6	1.8	5.2	1.4	4.65	11.6	-5
2004	ATL	NL	26	84	0	79.7	89	20	60	9	4.07	4.27	9.5	2.0	6.0	0.9	4.50	12.5	3
2005	*ATL*	*NL*	*27*	*38*	*5*	*74.3*	*78*	*21*	*52*	*8*	*4.09*	*4.33*	*9.5*	*2.3*	*5.6*	*1.0*	*4.47*	*10.6*	*-2*

Breakout: 28% *Improve: 48%* *Collapse: 24%*

There are worse mid-grade middle men out there. Reitsma's been at least league average since going to the bullpen full-time in 2003, and that figures to continue.

JOHN SMOLTZ — **Bats: R** — **Throws: R** — Born: 15-May-1967 Age: 38

YEAR	TM	LG	AGE	G	GS	IP	H	BB	SO	HR	ERA	EQERA	EQH9	EQBB9	EQSO9	EQHR9	PERA	VORP	STF
2002	ATL	NL	35	75	0	80.3	59	24	85	4	3.25	3.43	7.5	2.4	8.8	0.5	3.32	18.0	23
2003	ATL	NL	36	62	0	64.3	48	8	73	2	1.12	1.46	7.0	1.0	9.5	0.3	2.34	31.2	34
2004	ATL	NL	37	73	0	81.7	75	13	85	8	2.75	2.84	8.1	1.2	8.4	0.8	3.29	26.7	21
2005	*ATL*	*NL*	*38*	*50*	*2*	*76.0*	*69*	*18*	*72*	*7*	*2.98*	*3.15*	*8.2*	*1.8*	*7.7*	*0.8*	*3.31*	*20.8*	*15*

Breakout: 23% *Improve: 50%* *Collapse: 30%*

So the closer thing went just fine. Atlanta's decision to move Smoltz back to the rotation, given their needs, is a wise one. Smoltz's health will be worrisome for the rest of his career, but he still has command of a starter's repertoire, and he certainly has the credentials. Since they acceded to Smoltz's wishes to return to starting detail, the Braves wisely used some of that loyalty capital to renegotiate his contract.

JAKE STEVENS — **Bats: L** — **Throws: L** — Born: 15-Mar-1985 Age: 20

YEAR	TM	LG	AGE	G	GS	IP	H	BB	SO	HR	ERA	EQERA	EQH9	EQBB9	EQSO9	EQHR9	PERA	VORP	STF
2004	ROM	SAL	19	27	19	135.0	100	39	140	7	2.27	3.98	7.9	3.0	5.9	0.8	3.40	30.4	39
2005	*ATL*	*NL*	*20*	*16*	*12*	*78.7*	*75*	*30*	*60*	*10*	*4.36*	*4.62*	*8.6*	*3.1*	*6.2*	*1.1*	*4.47*	*10.8*	*7*

Breakout: 12% *Improve: 46%* *Collapse: 22%*

One to watch. Stevens's fastball was touching the mid-90s at age 19, and his breaking ball projects as a plus offering. Strong numbers in the Sally League last season, and with the run-suppressing environs of Myrtle Beach ahead of him, expect some ridiculous numbers in 2005. If his off-speed stuff is properly cultivated, he could be a special prospect.

JOHN THOMSON — **Bats: R** — **Throws: R** — Born: 01-Oct-1973 Age: 31

YEAR	TM	LG	AGE	G	GS	IP	H	BB	SO	HR	ERA	EQERA	EQH9	EQBB9	EQSO9	EQHR9	PERA	VORP	STF
2002	COL	NL	28	21	21	127.3	136	27	76	21	4.88	4.86	9.6	1.7	4.9	1.4	4.78	0.8	1
2002	NYM	NL	28	9	9	54.3	65	17	31	7	4.31	6.62	10.4	2.4	4.6	1.2	5.09	-5.8	0
2003	TEX	AL	29	35	35	217.0	234	49	136	27	4.85	4.46	8.9	1.9	5.5	1.0	3.71	21.7	12
2004	ATL	NL	30	33	33	198.3	210	52	133	20	3.72	4.16	9.2	2.1	5.4	0.8	4.30	34.0	12
2005	*ATL*	*NL*	*31*	*27*	*25*	*149.3*	*159*	*40*	*96*	*19*	*4.46*	*4.73*	*9.7*	*2.1*	*5.2*	*1.1*	*4.59*	*16.3*	*6*

Breakout: 9% *Improve: 45%* *Collapse: 28%*

In most seasons, Thomson's weakness was giving up the homer. That wasn't a glaring problem in 2004, and his supporting numbers were about as strong as they've been in recent seasons. In the right environment, Thomson's a solid and undervalued back-of-the-rotation guy. Credit the Braves for identifying him as such.

JARET WRIGHT — **Bats: R** — **Throws: R** — Born: 29-Dec-1975 Age: 29

YEAR	TM	LG	AGE	G	GS	IP	H	BB	SO	HR	ERA	EQERA	EQH9	EQBB9	EQSO9	EQHR9	PERA	VORP	STF
2002	BUF	INT	26	10	10	55.7	57	24	43	5	3.88	4.96	9.4	4.4	6.0	1.2	5.64	-0.2	-1
2002	CLE	AL	26	8	6	18.3	40	19	12	3	15.74	15.24	13.5	7.4	4.8	1.3	8.71	-21.8	-40
2003	SDP	NL	27	39	0	47.3	69	28	41	9	8.37	8.51	11.3	4.4	6.7	1.7	6.66	-14.4	-16
2003	ATL	NL	27	11	0	9.0	7	3	9	0	2.00	2.08	7.3	3.1	8.3	0.0	3.12	3.6	15
2004	ATL	NL	28	32	32	186.3	168	70	159	11	3.29	3.79	8.1	3.0	6.9	0.5	3.64	40.3	24
2005	*NYY*	*AL*	*29*	*29*	*24*	*144.7*	*151*	*58*	*115*	*17*	*4.69*	*4.69*	*9.5*	*3.2*	*6.4*	*1.0*	*4.61*	*16.5*	*8*

Breakout: 7% *Improve: 52%* *Collapse: 14%*

What's to say? Everything about his record of performance smacks of fluke canoodling with Mazzone legerdemain. And the Yankees ate it up, to the tune of $21 million over three years. If you went to high school with the Yankees, they'd have been the ones touting Hothouse Flowers as the next U2.

Chicago Cubs

CUBS PROSPECTUS

2004 record: 89–73; Third place, NL Central

Pythagenport record: 94–68

Runs scored per game: 4.87 (7th in NL)

Runs allowed per game: 4.10 (2nd in NL)

Team EqA: .265 (6th in NL)

2004 Batters Age: 30.7 (5th oldest in NL)

2004 Pitchers Age: 29.2 (5th youngest in NL)

Ballpark: Wrigley Field; Neutral park; Park Factor of 1.003

2004: A solid season was marred by an epic collapse down the stretch. Snatching defeat from the jaws of victory is unpopular, even among Cubs fans.

2005: The power pitching staff and thumping offense that made them the chic Central favorite last year are still in place.

Sunday, October 3 was an unseasonably cold morning in Chicago. The city woke up to headlines that the Cubs had been defeated 8–6 by the Atlanta Braves, eliminating them from playoff contention in their 161st game of the season. Missing the playoffs had been pretty much a foregone conclusion after the Cubs blew two critical late-season series, losing two out of three games to the Mets and three out of four to the Reds. It would have taken two victories, two Astros losses, two Giants losses, and a win in a three-team tiebreaker just for the Cubs to reach the Divisional Series. Mercifully, both Houston and San Francisco won their games later that day.

Still, there was plenty to add insult to ignominy. The Cubs had been losing close games all season, and they had led 6–2 against the Braves after five innings, only to watch a fatigued Carlos Zambrano, who had been pushed to the brink one too many times, yield three runs in the top of the 6th. An inept Kyle Farnsworth, who was recently off the DL after having applied a karate kick to an electric fan in the clubhouse, gave up three more in the top of the 8th. Meanwhile the headlines were filled with word of a budding confrontation between long-time broadcaster Steve Stone and general manager Jim Hendry; the Cubs didn't appreciate that Stone dared to criticize the team's performance and Dusty Baker's bullpen usage on the air. Word of another crisis would emerge that evening: Apparently, Sammy Sosa had arrived in the clubhouse just 70 minutes before the first pitch, asked himself out of the lineup, and left the premises long before the game was over. It all seemed so . . . so typical—here were the Cubs taking a good opportunity and fumbling it, like so many Bears running backs in the post–Walter Payton era.

In fact, it wasn't so typical at all. People remember the black cat collapse of 1969, Leon Durham's error and the 1984 Padres, and of course Steve Bartman. In each of those seasons, the Cubs had performed unexpectedly well, only to come up a little bit short in the end; the team's playoff-bound seasons of 1984, 1989, 1998, and 2003 had all followed seasons in which the Cubs lost more games than they won, finishing with an average record of 71–91. This was the first time in recent memory in which the Cubs *were expected* to win the pennant. They didn't, and the raised expectations did not make the team's disappointing finish any easier to swallow. In fact 2004 was a qualitatively different sort of failure, one more befitting of the Red Sox—who had always been as competitive as they were cursed—than the Cubs teams that came up a couple tricks short at the end of recent black-magic seasons. The Cubs, it is true, have blown it when they've had a chance, but they've just rarely positioned themselves to have a chance to begin with.

The 2004 Cubs had a chance, and it is thanks in large part to the good works of Hendry and the rest of the Cubs' front office. The 89 games that the team won would have gotten them the division title in 1989 or 2003, and gotten them into a one-game playoff with the Giants in 1998. The team's runs scored and runs allowed figures ordinarily would have been good for 94 wins, and while it's easy enough to blame Farnsworth or LaTroy Hawkins or Dusty Baker, poor performances in close ballgames is mostly a matter of bad luck. Hendry built a 94-win team; sometimes 94-win teams win 94 games, and sometimes they win 100 games, and sometimes they win 89 games and miss the playoffs.

What the Cubs seem to have realized is that their franchise can emulate the Red Sox in more ways than suffering from an ostensible curse. They are not going to be the Yankees, spending dollars as though they're Iraqi dinars. But they can do the things befitting an upper-class club, like adding Greg Maddux in the winter, or Nomar Garciaparra in the summer, or locking up arbitration-eligible players like Kerry Wood with contract extensions. They can be creative, and even slightly shameless, about finding ways to squeeze more revenue out of a small ballpark, whether it's raising ticket prices or adding rotating advertisements behind home plate, or hell, scalping their own tickets. Sure, you can construct an argument that the Cubs are taking a risk by forsaking tradition and fan loyalty, but it isn't a sound one: The Cubs are drawing 40,000 fans to cold-weather, Tuesday-afternoon games against inferior competition like the Reds and Pirates, and they have enough fan loyalty to double ticket prices across the board and still sell out most of their schedule. The Cubs have an exceptionally strong brand, and it is not going to be undermined by, say, adding an LED in center field to replace their rickety old monochrome display, any more than the city of Paris was undermined by accommodating a smattering of Starbuckses.

Sure, the Cubs aren't the most sabermetrically savvy club around, but there is still more to be gained by applying a traditional approach well (think Atlanta), then an analytical approach poorly (think Colorado). That said, the Cubs could gain more than most clubs by stealing a few pages from the sabermetric playbook. Let's take a look at some of those areas in a bit more detail:

Getting guys on base is the most important aspect of offensive performance. The Cubs hit 235 home runs last season. That was the third-best total in baseball, and easily the highest total in franchise history. Wrigley Field helped out a little bit in this regard—the wind was blowing out more than usual in 2004—but it is not quite the home run-haven that it is made out to be, and the Cubs' power is legitimate.

And yet, the Cubs scored only 789 runs as a team, a respectable total, but one which placed them squarely in the middle of the pack. The reason is that a disproportionate number of those home runs—60%, to be exact—were solo shots. Table 1 shows how the 30 teams ranked in terms of *runs scored per home run* in 2004.

TABLE 1. RANKING BY RUNS SCORED PER HOME RUN, 2004

Team	HR	Solo	2R	3R	GS	R on HR	R/HR
Angels	162	76	52	27	7	289	1.78
Dodgers	203	118	52	23	10	331	1.63
Rangers	227	125	68	27	7	370	1.63
Braves	178	99	51	24	4	289	1.62
Marlins	148	83	43	17	5	240	1.62
Devil Rays	145	79	45	19	2	234	1.61
Red Sox	222	129	56	31	6	358	1.61
Yankees	242	143	60	30	9	389	1.61
Blue Jays	145	84	39	17	5	233	1.61
Royals	150	89	38	16	7	241	1.61
Phillies	215	117	68	28	2	345	1.60
Indians	184	113	36	30	5	295	1.60
Brewers	135	77	38	17	3	216	1.60
Reds	194	108	60	22	4	310	1.60
Padres	139	78	40	20	1	222	1.60
A's	189	105	62	16	6	301	1.59
Tigers	201	116	57	22	6	320	1.59
White Sox	242	139	68	31	4	384	1.59
Giants	183	108	49	20	6	290	1.58
Mariners	136	75	45	15	1	214	1.57
D-Backs	135	77	42	14	2	211	1.56
Expos	151	89	44	13	5	236	1.56
Orioles	169	98	50	18	3	264	1.56
Cardinals	214	126	60	24	4	334	1.56
Pirates	142	87	35	16	4	221	1.56
Mets	185	113	46	25	1	284	1.54
Cubs	235	141	68	21	5	360	1.53
Astros	187	118	48	17	4	281	1.50
Rockies	202	118	71	10	3	302	1.50
Twins	191	117	56	16	2	285	1.49
Average							**1.59**

A typical Cub home run scored 1.53 runs last season—only three clubs in the league got less buck for their bang. Had those long balls produced runs at a league-average rate, the Cubs would have scored 14 more runs, which might well have been enough to win them the Wild Card. Power is nice, but in order to have a championship-caliber offense, the Cubs need to find a way to get more men on base.

To be fair, a team doesn't have quite as much flexibility over the composition of its starting lineup as we might make them out to have. The Cubs did well to pick up Aramis Ramirez, a power-oriented player, at the trade deadline last year. Had, say, Sean Burroughs—a player with a nominally higher on-base percentage, but much less power—been available too, the Cubs still would have been considerably better off acquiring Ramirez. If the Cubs had a choice between Ramirez and, say, Hank Blalock, their choice might have been different, but they didn't.

Still, over the long term, a team that places its emphasis on on-base percentage will have the chance to fashion a lineup to reflect that. The Cubs had an opportunity to replace Moises Alou's spot in left field this season with a big-time on-base threat. J. D. Drew, who has a .391 career OBP, would have been a great fit, but he opted for the

Dodgers. Carlos Beltran, still available at press time, would be an all-world fit, for OBP and many other reasons.

Protect your young pitchers' arms. Another staple from the analytical cookbook, this one would seem to have particular relevance for the Cubs. The Cubs' trio of young starters, Mark Prior, Carlos Zambrano, and Kerry Wood, is the team's most important asset. If healthy, they are good enough to form a championship nucleus all by themselves. Yet, in spite of the fact that two of the three were injured for substantial portions of last season, Dusty Baker continued to work his starters as hard as almost any manager in the game. The Cubs placed third in the league in Pitcher Abuse Points, after leading the league by a large margin in 2003. Protecting pitchers' arms is not a matter of machismo. It's about getting the most out of your pitchers for the entire 162-game schedule, and maximizing your return on investment in future seasons when those pitchers are still under your control. This is particularly important for a team like the Cubs that has a reasonable expectation of reaching the playoffs, during which each starting pitcher might be needed to throw an extra 20 innings.

Forget the closer myth; build bullpen depth. It's perhaps no surprise that the Cubs place heavy emphasis on their closer; it was *Tribster* Jerome Holtzman, after all, who invented the save rule. It is also probably the case that analysts do not place as much focus on bullpen support as they ought to. BP's Keith Woolner prepares a relievers report for the Baseball Prospectus Web site (www.baseballprospectus.com). The report accounts both for the performance of relief pitchers, and for the leverage of the situations in which they enter the game—how he pitches in a 3–2 nail-biter will have more of an influence on a pitcher's value than a 9–0 blowout, as well it should. The key figure in this report is wins added, a mathematically rigorous estimate of how many wins a team's bullpen contributed to the bottom line versus a group of replacement-level pitchers. Table 2 shows how the eight playoff teams ranked in that department, as well as the Cubs.

TABLE 2. EFFECT OF BULLPEN DEPTH, 2004

Rank	Team	Wins Added
1	Cardinals	+9.60
2	Dodgers	+8.94
4	Yankees	+8.82
6	Angels	+6.21
8	Red Sox	+4.65
9	Braves	+4.50
12	Twins	+3.45
13	Astros	+3.24
18	Cubs	−0.43

All eight of the playoff teams finished in the top 13 in the majors in bullpen support; the Cardinals' deep bullpen was worth nearly 10 wins all by itself. The Cubs ranked well back of the pack. In fact, we estimate that a team full of replacement-level firemen—is Joe Boever still around?—would have done slightly better.

But the problem was not LaTroy Hawkins, who, in spite of blowing nine saves, was one of the better relievers on the team. The problem, rather, was bullpen depth, as veterans like Farnsworth and Joe Borowski, and youngsters like John Leicester and Francis Beltran, turned in uninspiring performances. The Cubs would be far better off picking up two or three quality arms for their pen than one expensive guy with the "proven closer" tag. It is true that the Cubs have very good organizational pitching depth, and it is nice to be able to use live, cheap arms like Michael Wuertz or Sergio Mitre in long relief spots. But they need someone more reliable than Farnsworth available in key situations in the last three innings. Whether the save opportunities go to Hawkins or someone else is not of much consequence

Create synergies between your bench and your starters. The Cubs are poised to get above-average performance from at least seven out of the eight starting position players. Their bench, on the other hand, is barren. Three of the veterans who have guaranteed contracts for next year—Neifi Perez, Jose Macias, and Henry Blanco—contribute nothing at all with the stick. David Kelton, who is out of options, may also occupy a spot on the bench next season; he's a young player, at least, but he's not the *right* young player, as his struggle to hit Triple-A pitching suggests that he'd be a liability on a major league roster.

The weakness of the team's bench, it seems, reflects at least at one area in which the Cubs' thinking could be improved. That is a tendency to focus on prescribed roles, rather than how the totality of contributed skills fits into the context of the team's strengths and weaknesses. Tom Goodwin, who has mercifully been dispatched to free agency this winter, seems like a perfect fifth outfielder, since he runs well and plays a good center field. But the Cubs would have been far better off with someone like Trenidad Hubbard, who also steals bases, and has posted .405 and .407 OBPs in his last two seasons at Iowa. Hubbard does not have the glove that Goodwin does, but that's not a concern when your center fielder is Corey Patterson. Similarly, Neifi Perez is not a good fit for the starting player that he'll be shadowing. While Nomar Garciaparra does require a defensive replacement—and Perez plays that role well—he is also injury-prone, and having Perez in the starting lineup for a month while Nomar is on the shelf could easily cost the Cubs a couple of wins' worth of run production.

These are not the hardest decisions for a baseball team to make. The most important include finding a way to get quality players in your starting lineup, and figuring out what to do with them as they age, get injured, and have their contracts expire. The Cubs do a very good job of that; their roster contains six or seven star-quality players, and a number of quality secondary contributors like Todd Walker and Michael Barrett. Yes, the Sammy Sosa crisis is going to draw a lot of attention, but it is not especially important to the team's playoff chances: Sosa's best days are behind him, and the Cubs can field an excellent lineup with or without him. As long as the nucleus is intact, the Cubs are going to be competitive, and the team's quality farm system provides some measure of insurance against problematic performances from veterans. The Cubs, like the Red Sox, are going to have some years in which things don't turn out quite as well as planned. They are also, like the Red Sox, going to have some years in which the team is very good, and could compete for the World Series title that has long eluded them. What they won't have, at least in the near future, are the pathetic 69–93 efforts that branded them lovable losers in the past.

The Cubs have a good enough core so that they can begin to focus on the little luxuries that can contribute a few extra wins each season, like intelligent pitcher management, bullpen depth, and bench usage. Lest Jim Hendry think that we're being too picky, we should remind him that these are minor concerns to have; it's a lot harder to go from 79 wins to 89 wins than from 89 wins to 92 wins. As we have seen these last two seasons, those extra two or three wins can make all the difference: Get the little things right, and the bold print in the *Tribune* and the *Sun Times* will be reserved for discussions of whom the Cubs have drawn in the first round of the playoffs, and not some silly squabble between management and WGN's color man.

HITTERS

MOISES ALOU — OF — Bats: R — Throws: R — Born: 03-Jul-1966 — Age: 38

YEAR	TM	LG	AGE	AB	H	2B	3B	HR	BB	SO	SB	CS	AVG	OBP	SLG	MLVR	EQBA	EQOBP	EQSLG	EQMLVR	VORP	DEFENSE
2002	CHC	NL	36	484	133	23	1	15	47	61	8	0	.275	.337	.419	.048	.278	.339	.430	-.009	18.9	109-LF -1
2003	CHC	NL	37	565	158	35	1	22	63	67	3	1	.280	.357	.462	.125	.278	.355	.464	.067	30.5	136-LF -7
2004	CHC	NL	38	601	176	36	3	39	68	80	3	0	.293	.361	.557	.243	.285	.355	.546	.189	51.5	145-LF -3
2005	*SFG*	*NL*	*38*	*466*	*126*	*25*	*2*	*17*	*50*	*66*	*3*	*0*	*.270*	*.342*	*.443*	*.010*	*.274*	*.343*	*.460*	*.035*	*13.7*	*123-LF -5*

Breakout: 9% *Improve: 29%* *Collapse: 19%*

Alou caused something of a stir when he revealed in an interview that his pre-game rituals involve peeing on his own hands to "toughen them up." It is not known whether urine will be on the list of controlled substances that Gene Orza, Bud Selig and the *San Francisco Chronicle* eventually draw up. In any event, Alou has had an unusual career path, with his 39 home runs making our proclamation in last year's book that his power was sapped look awfully silly. Still, there is a pretty wide range on his 2005 forecast, and the market tends to overvalue performance in the previous season; it is probably a sign of progress that the Cubs declined to pick up his option or offer him arbitration. The Giants signed him instead, poising themselves for a big marketing deal with Depends. Alou's middling arm and declining range could be exposed in SBC's right field.

PAUL BAKO — C — Bats: L — Throws: R — Born: 20-Jun-1972 — Age: 33

YEAR	TM	LG	AGE	AB	H	2B	3B	HR	BB	SO	SB	CS	AVG	OBP	SLG	MLVR	EQBA	EQOBP	EQSLG	EQMLVR	VORP	DEFENSE
2002	MIL	NL	30	234	55	8	1	4	20	46	0	2	.235	.295	.329	-.177	.237	.297	.339	-.246	-0.1	65-C -9
2003	CHC	NL	31	188	43	13	3	0	22	47	0	1	.229	.311	.330	-.169	.229	.306	.319	-.261	-0.2	52-C -2
2004	CHC	NL	32	138	28	8	0	1	15	29	1	0	.203	.288	.283	-.305	.203	.282	.261	-.402	-4.3	40-C 3
2005	*LAD*	*NL*	*33*	*161*	*35*	*7*	*1*	*2*	*17*	*35*	*1*	*0*	*.220*	*.299*	*.321*	*-.261*	*.226*	*.303*	*.330*	*-.240*	*-1.0*	*47-C 0*

Breakout: 31% *Improve: 52%* *Collapse: 34%*

Gabor is coasting on his defensive reputation, but over the course of his career, he's caught just under 31% of attempted basestealers, a figure no better than pedestrian. Reputedly he works well with pitchers and helps old ladies cross the street and all that, but there's nothing separating him from 10 or 15 catchers in the International League. None of this is meant to be an endorsement of Henry Blanco, who was brought in to be Bako's replacement, but at least Blanco does his job as advertised.

MICHAEL BARRETT C **Bats: R** **Throws: R** Born: 22-Oct-1976 Age: 28

YEAR	TM	LG	AGE	AB	H	2B	3B	HR	BB	SO	SB	CS	AVG	OBP	SLG	MLVR	EQBA	EQOBP	EQSLG	EQMLVR	VORP	DEFENSE
2002	MON	NL	25	376	99	20	1	12	40	65	6	3	.263	.332	.418	.015	.259	.327	.418	-.063	20.7	106-C -1
2003	MON	NL	26	226	47	9	2	10	21	37	0	0	.208	.280	.398	-.189	.204	.275	.394	-.234	-0.7	61-C -1
2004	CHC	NL	27	456	131	32	6	16	33	64	1	4	.287	.337	.489	.102	.284	.332	.484	.061	31.0	122-C -4
2005	*CHC*	*NL*	*28*	*321*	*81*	*17*	*2*	*12*	*29*	*51*	*2*	*1*	*.253*	*.317*	*.427*	*-.068*	*.253*	*.315*	*.425*	*-.075*	*11.6*	*86-C -2*

Breakout: 10% *Improve: 36%* *Collapse: 34%*

Analysts don't like to give a lot of credence to the notion that a change of scenery ought to produce a marked change in outcomes. But one wonders whether expatriates from the Montreal/San Juan traveling road show warrant an exception, particularly somebody like Barrett, whose minor league numbers always suggested a player who was underachieving his skill set. It surely also helped that Barrett stayed healthy the entire season and was given the comfort of a regular job at a regular position, and it may be that he is one of those players who benefited from getting the good, mentoring half of Dusty Baker. Barrett enters this season just a hair shy of five years of MLB service time, so the Cubs will have two years to determine whether he's a quick fix or a longer-term solution. PECOTA thinks it's the former.

RONNY CEDENO SS **Bats: R** **Throws: R** Born: 02-Feb-1983 Age: 22

YEAR	TM	LG	AGE	AB	H	2B	3B	HR	BB	SO	SB	CS	AVG	OBP	SLG	MLVR	EQBA	EQOBP	EQSLG	EQMLVR	VORP	DEFENSE
2002	BOI	NWN	19	110	24	5	2	0	9	25	8	2	.218	.275	.300	-.151	.159	.192	.204	-.685	-29.7	26-SS 1
2002	LNS	MDW	19	376	80	17	4	2	22	74	14	10	.213	.269	.295	-.184	.179	.219	.256	-.549	-40.1	66-SS -4 31-2B 0
2003	DAY	FSL	20	380	80	18	1	4	21	82	19	6	.211	.257	.295	-.196	.190	.227	.290	-.481	-32.5	77-SS -5 28-2B -3
2004	WTN	SOU	21	384	107	19	5	6	24	74	10	10	.279	.328	.401	.028	.258	.301	.379	-.168	4.2	115-SS 2
2005	*CHC*	*NL*	*22*	*324*	*73*	*17*	*2*	*5*	*15*	*64*	*7*	*3*	*.224*	*.267*	*.334*	*-.301*	*.224*	*.265*	*.333*	*-.308*	*-7.0*	*85-SS -5*

Breakout: 21% *Improve: 38%* *Collapse: 48%*

This was the first season that Cedeno hit anything at all, and even so, his batting average at West Tennessee was pretty empty. It was enough to get him an Arizona Fall League invitation, where the Cubs worked him out at the other infield positions, hoping to groom him as a utility guy. He might well succeed in that role, but still, utility infielders are filler, and it was silly to knock a couple of good arms off the 40-man roster in order to secure a slot for Cedeno.

KEVIN COLLINS LF **Bats: L** **Throws: L** Born: 06-May-1981 Age: 24

YEAR	TM	LG	AGE	AB	H	2B	3B	HR	BB	SO	SB	CS	AVG	OBP	SLG	MLVR	EQBA	EQOBP	EQSLG	EQMLVR	VORP	DEFENSE
2002	BOI	NWN	21	187	64	18	2	13	14	52	0	2	.342	.399	.668	.565	.271	.307	.526	.065	15.4	23-1B -3
2003	LNS	MDW	22	306	69	19	1	14	39	116	1	3	.225	.314	.431	.074	.182	.256	.361	-.330	-25.5	70-1B -11
2004	LNS	MDW	23	397	115	26	2	33	45	126	3	1	.290	.369	.615	.410	.237	.302	.494	-.021	4.1	62-LF -3 10-1B -3
2005	*CHC*	*NL*	*24*	*331*	*80*	*18*	*2*	*18*	*33*	*123*	*1*	*1*	*.242*	*.320*	*.469*	*-.015*	*.242*	*.319*	*.468*	*-.023*	*7.8*	*90-LF -11*

Breakout: 46% *Improve: 67%* *Collapse: 17%*

Collins got some attention last season, mostly for being in the same lineup as Brian Dopirak. Dopirak hit 39 homers for the Lansing Lugnuts, Collins hit 33, and nobody else in the Midwest League hit more than 23. It was an exciting year at Oldsmobile Park, which was also witness to a couple of Mark Prior rehab stints and probably a Neil Diamond concert. Collins is three years older than Dopirak, however, and was repeating the level, so he'll need at least one more season like this before he gets on the prospect radar. The Cubs ought to expedite the process by promoting him directly to Double-A.

MATT CRAIG 3B **Bats: B** **Throws: R** Born: 16-Apr-1981 Age: 24

YEAR	TM	LG	AGE	AB	H	2B	3B	HR	BB	SO	SB	CS	AVG	OBP	SLG	MLVR	EQBA	EQOBP	EQSLG	EQMLVR	VORP	DEFENSE
2002	BOI	NWN	21	140	27	2	0	5	12	28	0	0	.193	.252	.314	-.179	.147	.188	.252	-.632	-35.5	28-3B -6
2003	DAY	FSL	22	442	126	25	2	11	46	87	4	4	.285	.357	.425	.149	.247	.307	.398	-.138	6.1	103-3B -2
2004	WTN	SOU	23	375	103	20	4	20	49	101	3	2	.275	.363	.509	.221	.253	.333	.470	.015	24.7	89-3B -9
2005	*CHC*	*NL*	*24*	*283*	*70*	*14*	*1*	*11*	*28*	*73*	*1*	*1*	*.248*	*.319*	*.430*	*-.063*	*.248*	*.318*	*.429*	*-.070*	*3.5*	*77-3B -6*

Breakout: 26% *Improve: 54%* *Collapse: 20%*

In theory, if Craig can follow through on last year's breakout with a big year at Iowa, there's an opportunity waiting for him in Chicago because Aramis Ramirez will become a free agent at the end of the season. In practice it will need to be a big year indeed. Craig was the Cubs' third-round draft pick in 2002, and while the team regards him a more legitimate prospect than they did, say, Brendan Harris, the organization has always set the bar awfully high for position player prospects. That's especially likely to be the case at a time when the team is fixated on winning a pennant in the here-and-now.

BRIAN DOPIRAK 1B Bats: R Throws: R Born: 20-Dec-1983 Age: 21

YEAR	TM	LG	AGE	AB	H	2B	3B	HR	BB	SO	SB	CS	AVG	OBP	SLG	MLVR	EQBA	EQOBP	EQSLG	EQMLVR	VORP	DEFENSE
2003	BOI	NWN	19	192	46	4	0	13	24	58	0	2	.240	.330	.464	.106	.174	.234	.338	-.409	-37.9	41-1B 1
2003	LNS	MDW	19	78	21	3	0	2	2	22	0	0	.269	.305	.385	.032	.228	.232	.342	-.375	-7.0	13-1B -2
2004	LNS	MDW	20	541	166	38	0	39	48	123	4	3	.307	.363	.593	.395	.253	.299	.482	-.029	8.9	114-1B -23
2005	*CHC*	*NL*	*21*	*351*	*83*	*18*	*1*	*15*	*24*	*99*	*1*	*1*	*.236*	*.287*	*.424*	*-.135*	*.236*	*.286*	*.423*	*-.143*	*-4.1*	*91-1B -10*

Breakout: 21% *Improve: 40%* *Collapse: 34%*

Power is the single most important skill that a positional prospect can possess. Dopriak hit 39 home runs as a 20-year-old in the Midwest League, and he does not have a particularly long swing, so his power should translate very well as he moves up the ladder. Still, there are not too many players who put together major league careers of any consequence based on power alone—Dave Kingman was the exception, not the rule. PECOTA expects some near-term regression as Dopriak strives to improve the other aspects of his game. His athleticism and defense are probably lost causes, so the most obvious choice is his plate discipline; add 20 walks to that stat line and we have a much more attractive prospect.

JASON DUBOIS OF Bats: R Throws: R Born: 26-Mar-1979 Age: 26

YEAR	TM	LG	AGE	AB	H	2B	3B	HR	BB	SO	SB	CS	AVG	OBP	SLG	MLVR	EQBA	EQOBP	EQSLG	EQMLVR	VORP	DEFENSE
2002	DAY	FSL	23	361	116	25	1	20	57	95	6	2	.321	.422	.562	.418	.274	.360	.496	.117	21.6	86-RF -10
2003	WTN	SOU	24	443	119	31	4	15	57	118	2	4	.269	.367	.458	.194	.251	.334	.444	-.021	6.6	104-RF -7 13-1B -1
2004	IOW	PCL	25	385	121	26	1	31	41	97	2	0	.314	.388	.629	.403	.271	.340	.521	.114	19.9	60-LF 0 19-1B -3
2004	CHC	NL	25	23	5	0	1	1	1	7	0	0	.217	.240	.435	-.189	.217	.199	.435	-.309	-0.1	
2005	*CHC*	*NL*	*26*	*212*	*56*	*12*	*1*	*11*	*23*	*60*	*1*	*0*	*.262*	*.344*	*.487*	*.063*	*.262*	*.342*	*.485*	*.055*	*13.2*	*60-RF -4*

Breakout: 16% *Improve: 40%* *Collapse: 32%*

Dubois has never been a favorite of scouts—unfortunately, he's in an organization run by an ex-scout. Still, he's climbed every rung of the ladder successfully and his timing appears to be just right, as he'll go into spring training with some real expectations of playing time, most likely as a platoon partner for Todd Hollandsworth with Moises Alou's left-field slot vacated. Dubois's biggest liability is his awkward defense: He was a little bit better last season playing left field than he had been in right, but that isn't saying very much. Still, he profiles as Jason Bay lite. If he can hit major league pitching like Bay did last season, his defense will be forgiven, especially in one of Wrigley's small corners.

NOMAR GARCIAPARRA SS Bats: R Throws: R Born: 23-Jul-1973 Age: 31

YEAR	TM	LG	AGE	AB	H	2B	3B	HR	BB	SO	SB	CS	AVG	OBP	SLG	MLVR	EQBA	EQOBP	EQSLG	EQMLVR	VORP	DEFENSE
2002	BOS	AL	28	635	197	56	5	24	41	63	5	2	.310	.352	.528	.234	.314	.360	.538	.217	72.3	151-SS -1
2003	BOS	AL	29	658	198	37	13	28	39	61	19	5	.301	.345	.524	.170	.300	.349	.529	.171	67.4	150-SS -7
2004	BOS	AL	30	156	50	7	3	5	8	16	2	0	.321	.367	.500	.159	.320	.368	.503	.186	15.6	32-SS -4
2004	CHC	NL	30	165	49	14	0	4	16	14	2	1	.297	.364	.455	.096	.297	.353	.442	.050	12.6	38-SS -1
2005	*CHC*	*NL*	*31*	*468*	*138*	*29*	*3*	*18*	*36*	*46*	*6*	*2*	*.295*	*.350*	*.486*	*.102*	*.295*	*.348*	*.484*	*.093*	*38.8*	*122-SS -5*

Breakout: 10% *Improve: 34%* *Collapse: 33%*

A good, gutsy acquisition by Jim Hendry. The Cubs were in the midst of a messy playoff race in which an extra run or two a week might have made all the difference, and Garciaparra was a good candidate to provide those runs, especially when the alternative was Ramon Martinez. The deal doesn't shine so brightly based on circumstantial evidence since the Cubs underperformed down the stretch while the Red Sox won it all. But Chicago sports fans are lucky to have a GM who is willing to go for broke like that, and the Cubs sacrificed little in the way in of meaningful prospect talent.

Garciaparra received a warm welcome in Chicago, and there were none of the clubhouse malcontent rumors that helped to hasten his exit from Boston. That being said, the worry about his defense is legitimate, if a bit overblown, as is the concern about his disposition to injury: There is inertia to injuries, in that players who are healthy tend to stay healthy, and players who are hurt tend to stay hurt. Good health is also a strong predictor of a player's aging pattern into his 30s, and Nomar's injury history and declining isolated power suggest that he might be on the outside looking in while the members of the Holy Trinity receive their Hall of Fame plaques. Given these risks, getting him to agree to a one-year contract was a real coup, and presents the possibility of an interesting platoon arrangement, in which Neifi Perez fills in on days when groundballer Carlos Zambrano is pitching, giving Nomar some regular days off in the process.

TOM GOODWIN — CF — Bats: L — Throws: R — Born: 27-Jul-1968 — Age: 36

YEAR	TM	LG	AGE	AB	H	2B	3B	HR	BB	SO	SB	CS	AVG	OBP	SLG	MLVR	EQBA	EQOBP	EQSLG	EQMLVR	VORP	DEFENSE
2002	SFG	NL	33	154	40	5	2	1	14	25	16	2	.260	.321	.338	-.084	.268	.327	.357	-.142	4.7	20-LF -1 15-CF 1
2003	CHC	NL	34	171	49	10	0	1	11	33	19	5	.287	.328	.363	-.059	.292	.324	.357	-.131	5.8	16-CF 0 11-LF 0
2004	CHC	NL	35	105	21	8	0	0	8	22	5	0	.200	.254	.276	-.377	.200	.234	.248	-.520	-4.4	
2005	*CHC*	*NL*	*36*	*91*	*21*	*4*	*1*	*1*	*8*	*19*	*4*	*1*	*.232*	*.296*	*.324*	*-.255*	*.232*	*.294*	*.323*	*-.261*	*-3.4*	*28-CF -4*

Breakout: 20%   Improve: 39%   Collapse: 51%

Fun fact: There are ten active major leaguers who have at least 3,000 at bats and more triples than home runs on their careers. Three of them, including Goodwin, were on the Cubs, roster at some point last season—we'll let you guess at the other two. Goodwin isn't supposed to hit for power, of course, but he needs to maintain some sort of batting average to be worth the roster spot. That didn't happen last year, and as PECOTA suggests, it's going to happen less and less frequently as he ages.

BEN GRIEVE — OF — Bats: L — Throws: R — Born: 04-May-1976 — Age: 29

YEAR	TM	LG	AGE	AB	H	2B	3B	HR	BB	SO	SB	CS	AVG	OBP	SLG	MLVR	EQBA	EQOBP	EQSLG	EQMLVR	VORP	DEFENSE
2002	TBY	AL	26	482	121	30	0	19	69	121	8	2	.251	.353	.432	.039	.258	.359	.444	.030	19.5	114-RF -4
2003	TBY	AL	27	165	38	7	0	4	32	41	0	0	.230	.371	.345	-.055	.238	.371	.354	-.080	4.3	
2004	MIL	NL	28	234	61	15	0	7	39	65	0	0	.261	.364	.415	.065	.258	.355	.403	-.033	12.5	47-RF -2
2004	CHC	NL	28	16	4	2	0	1	0	5	0	0	.250	.316	.562	.154	.250	.229	.500	-.129	1.2	
2005	*CHC*	*NL*	*29*	*150*	*37*	*8*	*1*	*6*	*23*	*39*	*1*	*0*	*.246*	*.351*	*.420*	*-.022*	*.246*	*.350*	*.418*	*-.029*	*6.3*	*45-RF -6*

Breakout: 25%   Improve: 48%   Collapse: 29%

Acquired by the Cubs at the waiver wire deadline for Andy Pratt, Grieve was able to find only 16 at-bats. When you can't win a regular gig with the Brewers, and are losing pinch-hitting at-bats down the stretch to Jose Macias, Tom Goodwin, Darren Baker and Ronnie Woo Woo, it's safe to say that you haven't lived up to expectations. Although it's possible to attribute his disappointing career to any number of factors, he stands as a textbook example of why guys with old players' skills don't tend to age well.

MARK GRUDZIELANEK — 2B — Bats: R — Throws: R — Born: 30-Jun-1970 — Age: 35

YEAR	TM	LG	AGE	AB	H	2B	3B	HR	BB	SO	SB	CS	AVG	OBP	SLG	MLVR	EQBA	EQOBP	EQSLG	EQMLVR	VORP	DEFENSE
2002	LAD	NL	32	536	145	23	0	9	22	89	4	1	.271	.301	.364	-.076	.284	.310	.382	-.127	15.6	133-2B 5
2003	CHC	NL	33	481	151	38	1	3	30	64	6	2	.314	.366	.416	.098	.313	.365	.416	.048	34.6	119-2B -5
2004	CHC	NL	34	257	79	12	1	6	15	32	1	1	.307	.347	.432	.055	.302	.344	.422	.009	15.0	67-2B 0
2005	*STL*	*NL*	*35*	*263*	*72*	*14*	*1*	*4*	*16*	*39*	*1*	*1*	*.274*	*.320*	*.387*	*-.101*	*.277*	*.320*	*.396*	*-.087*	*10.3*	*70-2B 0*

Breakout: 7%   Improve: 17%   Collapse: 53%

It probably wasn't right to give Grudzielanek so many at-bats with Todd Walker also on the roster, but Dusty is as Dusty does, and Grudzielanek held up his end of the bargain by hitting well down the stretch after spending eight weeks on the DL with an Achilles tendon injury. PECOTA, which predicted a collapse for him last year, is stubbornly doing the same this time around, skeptical that a 35-year-old with bad knees can duplicate his batting average.

RYAN HARVEY — RF — Bats: R — Throws: R — Born: 30-Aug-1984 — Age: 20

YEAR	TM	LG	AGE	AB	H	2B	3B	HR	BB	SO	SB	CS	AVG	OBP	SLG	MLVR	EQBA	EQOBP	EQSLG	EQMLVR	VORP	DEFENSE
2004	BOI	NWN	19	231	62	8	0	14	20	77	2	2	.268	.331	.485	.100	.186	.223	.325	-.442	-49.6	37-RF -1
2005	*CHC*	*NL*	*20*	*309*	*60*	*11*	*1*	*10*	*16*	*138*	*2*	*1*	*.194*	*.242*	*.337*	*-.358*	*.194*	*.241*	*.336*	*-.365*	*-19.7*	*80-RF -11*

Breakout: 35%   Improve: 49%   Collapse: 38%

The power was there, inflated as it was by the airy confines of Boise, but Harvey attempted just four stolen bases, failed to hit a triple, and was stuck in an outfield corner. All these were consequences of the nasty knee tear he suffered while in high school. Harvey is a "natural" ballplayer, which means he doesn't do things like defend the strike zone or take good routes in the outfield. The Cubs are very high on him, but at this early stage his upside looks something like Juan Rivera's.

TODD HOLLANDSWORTH OF Bats: L Throws: L Born: 20-Apr-1973 Age: 32

YEAR	TM	LG	AGE	AB	H	2B	3B	HR	BB	SO	SB	CS	AVG	OBP	SLG	MLVR	EQBA	EQOBP	EQSLG	EQMLVR	VORP	DEFENSE
2002	COL	NL	29	298	88	21	1	11	26	71	7	8	.295	.352	.483	.112	.278	.334	.464	.030	13.2	57-LF 1 15-RF 0
2002	TEX	AL	29	132	34	6	0	5	14	27	1	0	.258	.327	.417	-.053	.262	.325	.408	-.079	2.6	17-LF -1 10-CF 0
2003	FLA	NL	30	228	58	23	3	3	22	55	2	3	.254	.317	.421	-.003	.261	.322	.435	-.047	3.9	57-LF 0
2004	CHC	NL	31	148	47	6	2	8	17	26	1	1	.318	.392	.547	.299	.311	.385	.534	.249	16.0	27-RF 2
2005	*CHC*	*NL*	*32*	*178*	*47*	*10*	*1*	*7*	*19*	*38*	*2*	*1*	*.266*	*.338*	*.451*	*.011*	*.266*	*.336*	*.449*	*.003*	*9.3*	*51-LF -2*

Breakout: 12% *Improve: 38%* *Collapse: 40%*

Hollandsworth ranked second in the National League in Bad Hair, trailing only Craig Wilson. He's useful in the fourth-outfielder role, since he tags righties and can man any of the three positions credibly. His absence for much of the summer hurt the Cubs more than you'd think, due mostly to their self-inflicted poverty of useful bench players. The Cubs are good enough elsewhere on the field to get away with using him as a platoon starter. Provided that the team is willing to open up the pursestrings at the trading deadline, as the Tribune Company seems inclined to do, it may well turn out to be prudent to go with Hollandsworth or Jason Dubois in left on Opening Day and preserve their financial flexibility, rather than get locked into a big contract with a sub-premium free agent.

DAVE KELTON OF Bats: R Throws: R Born: 17-Dec-1979 Age: 25

YEAR	TM	LG	AGE	AB	H	2B	3B	HR	BB	SO	SB	CS	AVG	OBP	SLG	MLVR	EQBA	EQOBP	EQSLG	EQMLVR	VORP	DEFENSE
2002	WTN	SOU	22	498	130	28	6	20	52	129	12	6	.261	.332	.462	.141	.244	.300	.446	-.086	-0.4	120-1B -7
2003	IOW	PCL	23	442	119	24	3	16	46	115	8	2	.269	.338	.446	.075	.245	.312	.409	-.115	-6.8	35-RF -2 29-3B -6
2004	IOW	PCL	24	420	104	26	1	19	33	92	7	2	.248	.305	.450	-.083	.215	.270	.378	-.259	-24.2	85-RF -7 16-LF -1
2005	*CHC*	*NL*	*25*	*202*	*50*	*11*	*1*	*8*	*17*	*53*	*3*	*1*	*.247*	*.309*	*.433*	*-.077*	*.247*	*.308*	*.432*	*-.084*	*2.8*	*56-RF -6*

Breakout: 39% *Improve: 60%* *Collapse: 26%*

Kelton needed to have a big year to establish himself a major league–quality player. Instead his plate discipline regressed, his defense proved inadequate even at a corner outfield spot, and he hit .248 as a 24-year-old repeating Triple-A. Options are MLB's bizarre version of social promotion, and since Kelton is out of them, he may well break camp with the big league club this year. Whether he finishes the year there is another matter.

DERREK LEE 1B Bats: R Throws: R Born: 06-Sep-1975 Age: 29

YEAR	TM	LG	AGE	AB	H	2B	3B	HR	BB	SO	SB	CS	AVG	OBP	SLG	MLVR	EQBA	EQOBP	EQSLG	EQMLVR	VORP	DEFENSE
2002	FLA	NL	26	581	157	35	7	27	98	164	19	9	.270	.378	.494	.211	.276	.381	.514	.179	49.4	160-1B 4
2003	FLA	NL	27	539	146	31	2	31	88	131	21	8	.271	.379	.508	.226	.276	.383	.527	.200	51.6	151-1B 5
2004	CHC	NL	28	605	168	39	1	32	68	128	12	5	.278	.356	.504	.148	.273	.350	.498	.101	43.3	158-1B 9
2005	*CHC*	*NL*	*29*	*498*	*139*	*29*	*3*	*28*	*72*	*116*	*11*	*3*	*.279*	*.373*	*.520*	*.169*	*.279*	*.371*	*.518*	*.161*	*37.4*	*136-1B 3*

Breakout: 29% *Improve: 60%* *Collapse: 10%*

Lee was talked about as an MVP candidate in some circles prior to the season, so his year can be viewed as disappointment. But he's a fine player who does a lot of the little things that most slugging first baseman don't, like never getting hurt, running the bases well, and providing value in the field—his big frame makes a nice target for his infielders. Still, two trends merit watching. Lee, a California native who has spent virtually his entire professional career in warm-weather cities, hit poorly in April and September, when it can be downright cold in Chicago and other NL Central cities. More importantly, his walk rate declined by nearly 30%, without any apparent benefit to his isolated power. One hopes that new hitting coach Gene Clines can get Lee back to his walking ways, perhaps with the aid of a couple of nice cardigans.

RICHARD LEWIS 2B Bats: R Throws: R Born: 29-Jun-1980 Age: 25

YEAR	TM	LG	AGE	AB	H	2B	3B	HR	BB	SO	SB	CS	AVG	OBP	SLG	MLVR	EQBA	EQOBP	EQSLG	EQMLVR	VORP	DEFENSE
2002	MYR	CRL	22	484	135	23	4	2	55	80	31	10	.279	.359	.355	.099	.263	.328	.347	-.158	2.7	124-2B 5
2003	GRN	SOU	23	460	110	23	3	6	44	101	19	9	.239	.305	.341	-.085	.223	.280	.334	-.295	-17.7	116-2B -12
2004	WTN	SOU	24	380	125	27	10	10	37	94	7	6	.329	.391	.532	.343	.308	.363	.501	.162	42.0	96-2B 0
2004	IOW	PCL	24	118	29	8	1	3	4	21	4	0	.246	.280	.407	-.199	.216	.248	.336	-.360	-6.2	28-2B 2
2005	*CHC*	*NL*	*25*	*221*	*57*	*13*	*2*	*5*	*17*	*48*	*5*	*2*	*.260*	*.318*	*.400*	*-.096*	*.259*	*.316*	*.399*	*-.104*	*9.1*	*60-2B -2*

Breakout: 13% *Improve: 33%* *Collapse: 34%*

(continued next page)

Richard Lewis *(continued)*

Lewis came over from the Atlanta organization as part of the Juan Cruz trade. While he certainly had a better year than Andy Pratt, winning the Southern League MVP in the process, he was flotsam in a system as deep as the Braves'. PECOTA is wary of his emptyish humble batting average at West Tennessee, and it's not a good sign that his numbers declined as much as they did upon his graduation to Triple-A. The Cubs have talked him up as having a Mark Grudzielanek kind of upside, which apparently is supposed to be a compliment.

JOSE MACIAS — UT — Bats: B — Throws: R — Born: 25-Jan-1972 — Age: 33

YEAR	TM	LG	AGE	AB	H	2B	3B	HR	BB	SO	SB	CS	AVG	OBP	SLG	MLVR	EQBA	EQOBP	EQSLG	EQMLVR	VORP	DEFENSE	
2002	DET	AL	30	107	25	4	0	0	8	13	3	2	.234	.291	.271	-.306	.252	.288	.271	-.352	-3.7	16-2B -1	
2002	MON	NL	30	231	59	17	1	7	13	44	5	6	.255	.294	.429	-.034	.253	.288	.433	-.119	5.9	37-CF 0	19-3B -3
2003	MON	NL	31	272	65	15	2	4	11	45	4	3	.239	.273	.353	-.249	.235	.268	.349	-.290	-8.7	26-LF 2	16-3B 0
2004	CHC	NL	32	194	52	6	3	3	5	38	4	1	.268	.292	.376	-.135	.267	.289	.369	-.199	1.2	10-3B -1	11-RF 1
2005	*CHC*	*NL*	*33*	*129*	*31*	*6*	*1*	*3*	*6*	*24*	*2*	*1*	*.239*	*.278*	*.366*	*-.227*	*.239*	*.276*	*.365*	*-.235*	*-2.3*	*37-3B -3*	

Breakout: 11% *Improve: 31%* *Collapse: 52%*

Macias wears uniform number one, which is one more than the number of things he does well enough to be a major leaguer. You'd expect a guy like this to run the bases well or provide some credible defense at a middle infield position. Macias doesn't.

RAMON MARTINEZ — INF — Bats: R — Throws: R — Born: 10-Oct-1972 — Age: 32

YEAR	TM	LG	AGE	AB	H	2B	3B	HR	BB	SO	SB	CS	AVG	OBP	SLG	MLVR	EQBA	EQOBP	EQSLG	EQMLVR	VORP	DEFENSE	
2002	SFG	NL	29	181	49	10	2	4	14	26	2	0	.271	.335	.414	.050	.279	.340	.432	-.004	11.0	32-SS -3	
2003	CHC	NL	30	293	83	16	1	3	24	50	0	1	.283	.333	.375	-.038	.282	.332	.378	-.093	10.9	30-2B -1	26-3B -2
2004	CHC	NL	31	260	64	15	1	3	26	40	1	0	.246	.313	.346	-.168	.240	.309	.340	-.219	1.5	58-SS 3	15-3B -2
2005	*DET*	*AL*	*32*	*175*	*43*	*8*	*1*	*3*	*15*	*29*	*1*	*1*	*.248*	*.311*	*.357*	*-.166*	*.252*	*.316*	*.373*	*-.144*	*4.3*	*50-SS -4*	

Breakout: 13% *Improve: 29%* *Collapse: 44%*

Martinez is a capable defender across the infield, but his bat has declined to the point where he's a liability if asked to play every day, a fact which played a small part in the decision to acquire both Aramis Ramirez and Nomar Garciaparra. Though a Dusty Baker favorite, Martinez was not likely to return in 2005 with Macias and Neifi Perez both under contract. Thirty-two is a dangerous age for a middle infielder with diminishing power, and PECOTA thinks the end is upon us.

MATT MURTON — OF — Bats: R — Throws: R — Born: 03-Oct-1981 — Age: 23

YEAR	TM	LG	AGE	AB	H	2B	3B	HR	BB	SO	SB	CS	AVG	OBP	SLG	MLVR	EQBA	EQOBP	EQSLG	EQMLVR	VORP	DEFENSE
2003	LOW	NYP	21	189	54	11	2	2	27	39	9	3	.286	.374	.397	.145	.234	.305	.340	-.231	-20.7	47-LF -5
2004	SAR	FSL	22	376	113	16	4	11	42	61	5	4	.301	.372	.452	.207	.268	.328	.417	-.056	-0.2	96-LF 1
2004	DAY	FSL	22	79	20	1	1	2	8	10	2	0	.253	.326	.367	-.039	.212	.269	.325	-.336	-7.9	19-LF -2
2005	*CHC*	*NL*	*23*	*277*	*70*	*14*	*2*	*7*	*26*	*59*	*3*	*1*	*.251*	*.319*	*.395*	*-.107*	*.251*	*.317*	*.394*	*-.115*	*-4.2*	*75-LF -3*

Breakout: 20% *Improve: 52%* *Collapse: 28%*

Murton, the minor leaguer the Cubs nabbed in the Nomar Garciaparra trade, did not finish the year well at Daytona, but he's a legitimate prospect with a nice line-drive swing and an ability to control the strike zone. Murton is said to be a "*Moneyball* type of player," which means he's a college product and not a great athlete. His career path could look something like Bobby Kielty's.

REY ORDONEZ — SS — Bats: R — Throws: R — Born: 11-Jan-1971 — Age: 34

YEAR	TM	LG	AGE	AB	H	2B	3B	HR	BB	SO	SB	CS	AVG	OBP	SLG	MLVR	EQBA	EQOBP	EQSLG	EQMLVR	VORP	DEFENSE
2002	NYM	NL	31	460	117	25	2	1	24	46	2	2	.254	.292	.324	-.168	.265	.299	.342	-.220	1.6	129-SS 6
2003	TBY	AL	32	117	37	11	0	3	2	12	0	2	.316	.328	.487	.119	.328	.329	.491	.112	9.1	34-SS 4
2004	CHC	NL	33	61	10	3	0	1	2	14	0	0	.164	.190	.262	-.554	.175	.186	.238	-.644	-5.5	17-SS -1
2005	*CHC*	*NL*	*34*	*151*	*37*	*8*	*1*	*2*	*6*	*21*	*0*	*0*	*.245*	*.276*	*.353*	*-.245*	*.244*	*.275*	*.352*	*-.252*	*-0.2*	*42-SS 0*

Breakout: 17% *Improve: 34%* *Collapse: 34%*

Ordonez did everything in his power to counteract whatever momentum he might have gained from his 2003 campaign, a hot start fortuitously shortened by injury that some were mistaking for a breakout year. Invited to spring training by the Padres, he missed time due to family issues, then conceded his roster spot in mid-March, leaving camp voluntarily once it became clear that Khalil Greene could play a little bit. It wasn't until May that the Cubs came calling, looking for an emergency replacement for Alex Gonzalez, but Ordonez's bat was even colder than usual, a predictable result for a guy who had played about three weeks of baseball in the previous 12 months. Considering that he's 34, and has fallen out of favor with the one organization that thinks Neifi Perez is nifty, Ordonez's career might be over. That would tragically leave him just one season short of the 10 he needs to qualify for the Hall of Fame.

COREY PATTERSON **CF** **Bats: L** **Throws: R** Born: 13-Aug-1979 Age: 25

YEAR	TM	LG	AGE	AB	H	2B	3B	HR	BB	SO	SB	CS	AVG	OBP	SLG	MLVR	EQBA	EQOBP	EQSLG	EQMLVR	VORP	DEFENSE
2002	CHC	NL	22	592	150	30	5	14	19	142	18	3	.253	.284	.392	-.099	.258	.285	.405	-.161	10.8	139-CF -17
2003	CHC	NL	23	329	98	17	7	13	15	77	16	5	.298	.329	.511	.163	.296	.328	.512	.107	27.0	75-CF -3
2004	CHC	NL	24	631	168	33	6	24	45	168	32	9	.266	.320	.452	.006	.263	.316	.446	-.041	27.9	151-CF 2
2005	*CHC*	*NL*	*25*	*518*	*144*	*29*	*5*	*21*	*37*	*118*	*24*	*7*	*.278*	*.330*	*.475*	*.039*	*.278*	*.328*	*.474*	*.031*	*26.2*	*133-CF -2*

Breakout: 13% *Improve: 48%* *Collapse: 22%*

Patterson drew an unintentional walk in 6.4% of his plate appearances last season, which doesn't sound like much until you consider that his career figure heading into the year was 3.4%. He also began to loft the ball more frequently, using a compact swing to generate power from his small frame. Those are exactly the sorts of trends that you'd like to see from a 24-year-old: The combination of developing power and patience is a potent one. What's more, Patterson appears to have recovered completely from his ACL tear, ably covering Wrigley's small center field and stealing bases with aplomb. He's an excellent breakout candidate, and a good bet to outhit his PECOTA and make several All-Star teams over the course of his career.

NEIFI PEREZ **SS** **Bats: B** **Throws: L** Born: 02-Jun-1973 Age: 32

YEAR	TM	LG	AGE	AB	H	2B	3B	HR	BB	SO	SB	CS	AVG	OBP	SLG	MLVR	EQBA	EQOBP	EQSLG	EQMLVR	VORP	DEFENSE
2002	KCR	AL	29	554	131	20	4	3	20	53	8	9	.236	.260	.303	-.349	.230	.259	.296	-.387	-21.2	135-SS 4
2003	SFG	NL	30	328	84	19	4	1	14	23	3	2	.256	.285	.348	-.194	.259	.289	.352	-.229	-0.7	44-2B 4 44-SS 3
2004	SFG	NL	31	319	74	12	1	2	21	35	0	1	.232	.276	.295	-.314	.230	.275	.289	-.364	-10.3	49-SS 3 36-2B 0
2004	CHC	NL	31	62	23	5	0	2	3	6	1	0	.371	.400	.548	.385	.381	.380	.524	.311	9.3	14-SS 1
2005	*CHC*	*NL*	*32*	*273*	*66*	*12*	*2*	*2*	*13*	*29*	*2*	*1*	*.241*	*.276*	*.322*	*-.289*	*.241*	*.275*	*.321*	*-.296*	*-6.2*	*72-SS 2*

Breakout: 9% *Improve: 23%* *Collapse: 51%*

It's not that Neifi Perez is completely useless. He does have a slick glove, and there are times and places that he makes for an acceptable quick fix. The trouble is that sometimes he does *this.* He hits .371 in a handful of at bats, and the pitchers and announcers drool over his defense, and a team is compelled to re-sign him, as the Cubs did for one year and $1 million. Mercifully, Nomar Garciaparra was brought back too, but there are comparable players like Gookie Dawkins who could have provided the same skill set for the league minimum. There is an important difference between picking up Neifi Perez when you've got a positional emergency on hand, and making a proactive decision to make him a part of your championship-caliber roster.

FELIX PIE **CF** **Bats: L** **Throws: L** Born: 08-Feb-1985 Age: 20

YEAR	TM	LG	AGE	AB	H	2B	3B	HR	BB	SO	SB	CS	AVG	OBP	SLG	MLVR	EQBA	EQOBP	EQSLG	EQMLVR	VORP	DEFENSE
2003	LNS	MDW	18	505	144	22	9	4	41	98	19	13	.285	.346	.388	.104	.248	.295	.357	-.218	-11.5	120-CF -6
2004	DAY	FSL	19	412	123	17	9	8	38	113	31	16	.299	.361	.442	.138	.252	.306	.387	-.151	-0.6	98-CF 0
2005	*CHC*	*NL*	*20*	*380*	*90*	*18*	*4*	*7*	*28*	*99*	*12*	*5*	*.236*	*.294*	*.362*	*-.206*	*.236*	*.293*	*.360*	*-.213*	*-3.9*	*100-CF -6*

Breakout: 17% *Improve: 37%* *Collapse: 37%*

A strange prospect. Pie is ridiculously fast, is developing his strength, and already plays a major league-caliber center field. He also strikes out a ton, runs his team out of rallies on the basepaths, and tends to slap at the ball rather than loft it. He's extremely young for his level, and so he has time to correct those things, but it's going to take some time, and the most likely scenario is that he eventually makes the show as a miscast leadoff hitter, hitting .290/.325/.440 with about 18 triples and 17 times caught stealing.

ARAMIS RAMIREZ 3B **Bats: R** **Throws: R** Born: 25-Jun-1978 Age: 27

YEAR	TM	LG	AGE	AB	H	2B	3B	HR	BB	SO	SB	CS	AVG	OBP	SLG	MLVR	EQBA	EQOBP	EQSLG	EQMLVR	VORP	DEFENSE
2002	PIT	NL	24	522	122	26	0	18	29	95	2	0	.234	.279	.387	-.141	.234	.275	.393	-.215	3.8	118-3B -6
2003	PIT	NL	25	375	105	25	1	12	25	68	1	1	.280	.330	.448	.060	.278	.327	.449	-.004	22.7	94-3B -4
2003	CHC	NL	25	232	60	7	1	15	17	31	1	1	.259	.314	.491	.070	.259	.312	.496	.019	14.7	63-3B -4
2004	CHC	NL	26	547	174	32	1	36	49	62	0	2	.318	.373	.578	.316	.312	.367	.567	.268	59.6	134-3B -10
2005	*CHC*	*NL*	*27*	*523*	*146*	*29*	*1*	*27*	*44*	*78*	*0*	*0*	*.280*	*.339*	*.496*	*.083*	*.280*	*.337*	*.494*	*.075*	*25.9*	*136-3B -4*

Breakout: 13% *Improve: 36%* *Collapse: 27%*

It was Adrian Beltre's breakout season that received the attention, but Ramirez had a huge year, too. The key to Ramirez's development is that he's making contact more frequently—36 home runs to 62 strikeouts is one of the more impressive ratios in all of baseball. He may be the rare player who is better when he attacks early in the at-bat: More than half his home runs came when the count was 0–0, 1–0, or 1–1. Like Beltre, Ramirez is younger than he appears in the rearview mirror, having reached the majors at age 21, so there's good reason to believe that the improvement he's demonstrated is going to stick. PECOTA, which foresaw a breakout for him last year, now seems to think that he's overshot the mark slightly. Still, he's probably the Cubs' most valuable position player heading into next year, in spite of his indifferent defense.

BRANDON SING 1B **Bats: R** **Throws: R** Born: 13-Mar-1981 Age: 24

YEAR	TM	LG	AGE	AB	H	2B	3B	HR	BB	SO	SB	CS	AVG	OBP	SLG	MLVR	EQBA	EQOBP	EQSLG	EQMLVR	VORP	DEFENSE
2002	DAY	FSL	21	440	109	18	5	18	64	96	5	7	.248	.348	.434	.103	.214	.298	.385	-.196	-20.3	63-LF -5 16-RF -2
2003	WTN	SOU	22	139	29	7	0	5	10	39	2	1	.209	.256	.367	-.130	.190	.222	.352	-.404	-14.2	36-1B 2
2003	DAY	FSL	22	136	32	6	0	4	17	29	0	3	.235	.318	.368	-.007	.188	.253	.319	-.389	-14.9	31-LF -5
2004	DAY	FSL	23	408	110	27	0	32	84	101	1	3	.270	.399	.571	.324	.212	.323	.454	-.058	3.9	110-1B -12
2005	*CHC*	*NL*	*24*	*312*	*75*	*16*	*1*	*15*	*40*	*85*	*1*	*1*	*.242*	*.332*	*.449*	*-.021*	*.242*	*.330*	*.448*	*-.028*	*6.4*	*87-1B -5*

Breakout: 46% *Improve: 67%* *Collapse: 15%*

Thirty-two home runs is a lot in the Florida State League. The all-time league record is 33, and Sing might have broken it if not for all those damned hurricanes, which cut the season a few games short. Still, it was his third season at Daytona, and though he has a good excuse for his poor 2003—a long bout with mononucleosis—he was old for the level. The bigger problems, though, are Sing's inability to hit breaking stuff, which has depressed his batting averages, and his lack of a defensive position. His offensive upside resembles Rob Deer's, but people forget that Deer was a heady defender.

SAMMY SOSA RF **Bats: R** **Throws: R** Born: 12-Nov-1968 Age: 36

YEAR	TM	LG	AGE	AB	H	2B	3B	HR	BB	SO	SB	CS	AVG	OBP	SLG	MLVR	EQBA	EQOBP	EQSLG	EQMLVR	VORP	DEFENSE
2002	CHC	NL	33	556	160	19	2	49	103	144	2	0	.288	.399	.594	.381	.289	.398	.605	.342	70.5	139-RF -6
2003	CHC	NL	34	517	144	22	0	40	62	143	0	1	.279	.358	.553	.247	.279	.355	.553	.192	44.5	127-RF -4
2004	CHC	NL	35	478	121	21	0	35	56	133	0	0	.253	.332	.517	.107	.249	.325	.505	.045	27.9	118-RF 8
2005	*CHC*	*NL*	*36*	*385*	*99*	*18*	*1*	*26*	*55*	*106*	*0*	*0*	*.259*	*.351*	*.515*	*.109*	*.258*	*.349*	*.513*	*.101*	*25.3*	*106-RF -3*

Breakout: 28% *Improve 60%* *Collapse: 18%*

We try and avoid commenting on personality issues, but it seems safe to say this: Sosa's anti-social behavior in 2004, which culminated in his going AWOL on the last day of the season after the Cubs had missed the playoffs, was one of the stupidest *marketing* decisions in baseball history. Cubs fans are a forgiving lot, and Sosa, even at 40% of his former self, had the chance to ride off into the sunset gently, chasing Hank Aaron and Barry Bonds in the Wrigley twilight while earning an ill-advised contract extension or two. Instead, he's going to be traded, or fodder for about six Jay Mariotti rants per month.

The strange thing is that Sosa may have done Jim Hendry a favor. Sosa has been a franchise player for a franchise that has always identified itself with franchise players, as well as a franchise that rewards loyalty, both to its players and its fans. Given the public pressures involved, the decision on whether to pick up Sosa's albatross of a team option in 2006 and append years to the contract beyond it would have been much tougher than you'd think. Now that Sosa has managed to disentangle himself from any presumption of sentimentality, the Cubs can treat him purely as a baseball problem. He's not even a particularly important baseball problem, having ranked just eighth on the team in VORP. The Cubs needed, sooner or later, to move beyond Sammy Sosa; this ensures that it will be sooner.

GEOVANY SOTO — C — Bats: R — Throws: R — Born: 20-Jan-1983 — Age: 22

YEAR	TM	LG	AGE	AB	H	2B	3B	HR	BB	SO	SB	CS	AVG	OBP	SLG	MLVR	EQBA	EQOBP	EQSLG	EQMLVR	VORP	DEFENSE
2003	DAY	FSL	20	297	72	12	2	2	31	58	0	0	.242	.312	.316	-.074	.211	.269	.296	-.377	-19.4	76-C -4
2004	WTN	SOU	21	332	90	16	0	9	40	71	1	2	.271	.355	.401	.066	.246	.316	.368	-.163	1.1	100-C 1
2005	*CHC*	*NL*	*22*	*288*	*65*	*12*	*1*	*7*	*25*	*64*	*1*	*0*	*.226*	*.294*	*.345*	*-.235*	*.226*	*.292*	*.344*	*-.242*	*-2.0*	*78-C -4*

Breakout: 17% *Improve: 32%* *Collapse: 46%*

Soto, who has a fine arm and a good defensive reputation, hit just enough at West Tennessee to get himself designated as the team's de jure catcher of the future and added to the 40-man roster. His numbers weren't anything special, but he had a better season than Jeff Goldbach, who hit .233 for the Joliet Jackhammers, or Pat Cline, who was June's Employee of the Month at the Topeka Bed, Bath and Beyond.

TODD WALKER — 2B — Bats: L — Throws: R — Born: 25-May-1973 — Age: 32

YEAR	TM	LG	AGE	AB	H	2B	3B	HR	BB	SO	SB	CS	AVG	OBP	SLG	MLVR	EQBA	EQOBP	EQSLG	EQMLVR	VORP	DEFENSE
2002	CIN	NL	29	612	183	42	3	11	50	81	8	5	.299	.353	.431	.071	.296	.350	.433	.031	40.2	147-2B -6
2003	BOS	AL	30	587	166	38	4	13	48	54	1	1	.283	.333	.428	-.004	.280	.336	.427	-.017	28.2	134-2B -19
2004	CHC	NL	31	372	102	19	4	15	43	52	0	3	.274	.352	.468	.091	.269	.346	.460	.038	25.0	78-2B -1
2005	*CHC*	*NL*	*32*	*344*	*94*	*19*	*2*	*10*	*34*	*44*	*1*	*1*	*.274*	*.340*	*.423*	*-.017*	*.273*	*.338*	*.422*	*-.025*	*17.7*	*92-2B -5*

Breakout: 12% *Improve: 32%* *Collapse: 33%*

One of Jim Hendry's strengths is his flexibility. The Cubs, rightly or wrongly, had determined to give Mark Grudzielanek another go at second base, but when Walker made it known that he was willing to sign cheaply, Hendry did not hesitate to add him to the roster, and let Dusty figure out what to do with both of them. Sure, Walker might have been a gimme signing, but Hendry has a history of buying low, whereas the franchise on the other side of town goes into conniptions when that bastard Omar Vizquel ruins their entire off-season by contracting with the Giants, or Arte Moreno opens up his wallet just a little bit too wide for Bartolo Colon. The market for major league players is not nearly as liquid as we make it out to be: Opportunities and challenges present themselves randomly and irregularly, and the ability to react on the fly distinguishes a winning organization from a losing one.

As for Walker, what you see is what you get: Plus line-drive platoon bat and minus defense, especially when turning the double play. That sums to a worthwhile package. A trio of Ramirez-Garciaparra-Walker won't win any Gold Gloves, but it should produce a ton of runs.

PITCHERS

CHADD BLASKO — Bats: R — Throws: R — Born: 09-Mar-1981 — Age: 24

YEAR	TM	LG	AGE	G	GS	IP	H	BB	SO	HR	ERA	EQERA	EQH9	EQBB9	EQSO9	EQHR9	PERA	VORP	STF
2003	DAY	FSL	22	24	24	136.3	100	43	131	3	1.98	3.67	7.9	3.3	6.3	0.6	3.38	30.8	20
2003	LNS	MDW	22	2	2	11.0	10	5	6	0	1.64	4.50	9.0	5.4	3.6	0.0	4.50	1.2	-11
2004	WTN	SOU	23	13	13	66.7	77	24	65	12	5.67	6.75	11.1	3.4	6.2	2.3	6.75	-8.0	-9
2005	*CHC*	*NL*	*24*	*16*	*10*	*64.7*	*63*	*26*	*52*	*8*	*4.42*	*4.59*	*8.8*	*3.2*	*6.5*	*1.0*	*4.56*	*8.1*	*6*

Breakout: 15% *Improve: 50%* *Collapse: 20%*

Blasko is expected to be out for most of 2005 after undergoing Tommy John surgery. He's got a big fastball and a big (6′ 7″) body, but both his breaking stuff and change-up need work. He keeps the ball down reasonably well, so the lack of a good secondary pitch may have been the cause of his high home-run rate at West Tennessee. Some scouts had pegged him as a reliever coming out of Purdue, and that likely is where he's headed after the injury.

JOE BOROWSKI — Bats: R — Throws: R — Born: 04-May-1971 — Age: 34

YEAR	TM	LG	AGE	G	GS	IP	H	BB	SO	HR	ERA	EQERA	EQH9	EQBB9	EQSO9	EQHR9	PERA	VORP	STF
2002	CHC	NL	31	73	0	95.7	84	29	97	10	2.73	3.11	8.0	2.3	8.2	1.0	3.21	26.1	15
2003	CHC	NL	32	68	0	68.3	53	19	66	5	2.64	3.03	7.4	2.2	8.1	0.7	2.89	19.7	18
2004	CHC	NL	33	22	0	21.3	27	15	17	3	8.03	7.48	10.4	5.4	6.2	1.2	6.23	-5.5	-16
2005	*CHC*	*NL*	*34*	*38*	*0*	*38.0*	*39*	*16*	*29*	*5*	*4.59*	*4.76*	*9.2*	*3.4*	*6.1*	*1.1*	*4.87*	*4.3*	*-7*

Breakout: 19% *Improve: 46%* *Collapse: 27%*

(continued next page)

Joe Borowski *(continued)*

Joe Borowski wasn't Jim Morris, but his 2003 was the stuff that bad Dennis Quaid movies are made of: Minor league Average Joe turned ace closer for the playoff-bound Cubs. Unfortunately, based on his 2004 performance, the movie that Borowski's career would seem to have the most in common with is *Awakenings*. From the start of the season, Borowski's fastball was darting wildly out of the strike zone whenever he attempted to throw more than about 86 miles per hour; he quickly accumulated two blown saves and four losses for the Cubs before being diagnosed with a rotator cuff tear. There was no particular reason to have seen this coming, and there is no particular way to know just how well he is going to recover, but it was evident that he didn't have his velocity back during a late-season rehab stint in Iowa.

BOBBY BROWNLIE Bats: R Throws: R Born: 05-Oct-1980 Age: 24

YEAR	TM	LG	AGE	G	GS	IP	H	BB	SO	HR	ERA	EQERA	EQH9	EQBB9	EQSO9	EQHR9	PERA	VORP	STF
2003	DAY	FSL	22	13	13	66.0	48	24	59	2	3.00	4.95	8.1	3.9	5.8	0.8	3.75	12.3	9
2004	WTN	SOU	23	26	26	147.3	127	36	114	15	3.36	4.60	9.0	2.3	5.0	1.3	4.40	18.0	1
2005	*CHC*	*NL*	*24*	*14*	*11*	*68.0*	*70*	*24*	*44*	*10*	*4.74*	*4.92*	*9.4*	*2.8*	*5.3*	*1.2*	*4.87*	*6.4*	*0*

Breakout: 8% Improve: 32% Collapse: 23%

Brownlie's got less upside than many of the other prospects that you'll read about in this chapter. His fastball has topped out in the low-90s ever since the biceps injury that he suffered in his junior year at Rutgers, he has a tendency to keep the ball up, and neither his overhand curve nor his change-up are considered out pitches. That said, he has a good feel for pitching and excellent command, and is pretty close to being major league-ready. Brownlie could be another Jon Lieber if things break right.

MATT CLEMENT Bats: R Throws: R Born: 12-Aug-1974 Age: 30

YEAR	TM	LG	AGE	G	GS	IP	H	BB	SO	HR	ERA	EQERA	EQH9	EQBB9	EQSO9	EQHR9	PERA	VORP	STF
2002	CHC	NL	27	32	32	205.0	162	85	215	18	3.60	3.82	7.5	3.2	8.5	0.8	3.09	41.3	31
2003	CHC	NL	28	32	32	201.7	169	79	171	22	4.11	4.38	8.0	3.2	7.1	1.0	3.68	27.7	19
2004	CHC	NL	29	30	30	181.0	155	77	190	23	3.68	3.80	7.9	3.4	8.5	1.0	3.90	36.9	25
2005	*BOS*	*AL*	*30*	*28*	*28*	*165.0*	*151*	*65*	*141*	*16*	*3.95*	*3.72*	*8.1*	*3.1*	*7.0*	*0.9*	*3.61*	*38.6*	*18*

Breakout: 21% Improve: 49% Collapse: 20%

Clement has a reputation, not undeserved, for being wildly inconsistent from start to start, but the three seasonal lines that you see above are awfully compatible with one another. He's most effective when he's able to keep the ball down, something he was able to do better in the first half of the year than the second. It's natural to attribute his poor finish to overuse, but Clement hasn't been worked especially hard, and the injuries that were nagging him were to his back and neck, rather than his arm. Signed with the Red Sox; and PECOTA thinks he'll do well in the American League, in part because the current crop of junior-circuit hitters, for whatever reason, are notably less patient than their counterparts.

JON CONNOLLY Bats: R Throws: L Born: 24-Aug-1983 Age: 21

YEAR	TM	LG	AGE	G	GS	IP	H	BB	SO	HR	ERA	EQERA	EQH9	EQBB9	EQSO9	EQHR9	PERA	VORP	STF
2002	ONE	NYP	18	14	14	85.3	102	10	50	7	4.01	6.95	12.5	1.5	3.0	2.3	7.53	-16.7	-20
2003	WMI	MDW	19	25	25	166.0	128	38	104	4	1.41	3.93	8.3	2.6	3.9	0.6	3.58	33.9	34
2004	LAK	FSL	20	4	4	22.0	28	5	8	1	3.68	5.91	11.0	2.1	2.1	0.8	5.48	0.3	-12
2004	DAY	FSL	20	21	21	131.0	123	24	101	9	2.40	4.38	9.4	1.9	4.8	1.2	4.45	15.5	18
2005	*CHC*	*NL*	*21*	*13*	*12*	*70.0*	*79*	*22*	*41*	*11*	*4.93*	*5.11*	*10.2*	*2.4*	*4.7*	*1.3*	*5.21*	*4.4*	*-1*

Breakout: 5% Improve: 34% Collapse: 19%

We are sometimes guilty of treating a club's organizational philosophy as more static than it really is, and the Cubs made a fine deal in picking up Connolly from the Tigers for Double-A lefty Felix Sanchez. Connolly is not a traditional pitching prospect—he's got a chubby body and his fastball does not travel very fast and his slurve does not do much slurving—but he throws strikes, has a good change-up, and has posted outstanding numbers for two seasons running. The key to success for a guy like this is keeping the ball down, and Connolly has done that reasonably well so far. While he faces an uphill battle—even PECOTA is skeptical of soft-tossing pitching prospects—he's certainly better to have around the organization than a generic reliever like Sanchez, who got hurt after the trade to boot.

RYAN DEMPSTER Bats: R Throws: R Born: 03-May-1977 Age: 28

YEAR	TM	LG	AGE	G	GS	IP	H	BB	SO	HR	ERA	EQERA	EQH9	EQBB9	EQSO9	EQHR9	PERA	VORP	STF
2002	FLA	NL	25	18	18	120.3	126	55	87	12	4.79	5.12	9.2	3.5	5.7	0.9	4.51	7.6	7
2002	CIN	NL	25	15	15	88.7	102	38	66	16	6.19	6.00	10.0	3.3	5.9	1.6	5.59	-6.8	-1
2003	CIN	NL	26	22	20	115.7	134	70	84	14	6.53	6.61	9.6	4.7	5.8	1.0	5.21	-15.8	0
2004	IOW	PCL	27	6	4	21.0	19	10	20	1	3.86	4.05	8.1	4.5	6.8	0.4	4.05	3.4	5
2004	CHC	NL	27	23	0	20.7	16	13	18	1	3.91	3.60	7.2	4.9	7.2	0.4	3.60	4.1	0
2005	*CHC*	*NL*	*28*	*19*	*13*	*83.7*	*83*	*38*	*67*	*10*	*4.54*	*4.71*	*8.9*	*3.6*	*6.4*	*0.9*	*4.75*	*8.8*	*6*

Breakout: 28% *Improve: 50%* *Collapse: 21%*

Any time a pitcher returns from Tommy John surgery, it's a good thing. The Cubs seem to have done well for themselves in the deal they signed with Dempster, which included one cheap guaranteed year and a team option, a strategy that paid dividends this year with Jon Lieber and Chris Carpenter. The trouble is that Dempster, when healthy, was not as good a pitcher as Lieber or Carpenter; his resume included just one above-average season (2000), a year in which he still walked 97 hitters and gave up 30 homers in Pro Player Stadium. The usual rap against a pitcher recovering from Tommy John is that his velocity will come back before his command. It's hard to tell if that's the case with Dempster, since his command was never there to begin with. As a power righty out of the bullpen, he might do enough to justify the $2 million that the Cubs are paying him this year, but he's unlikely to do more than that, and he's ill-equipped for a high-leverage role.

KYLE FARNSWORTH Bats: R Throws: R Born: 14-Apr-1976 Age: 29

YEAR	TM	LG	AGE	G	GS	IP	H	BB	SO	HR	ERA	EQERA	EQH9	EQBB9	EQSO9	EQHR9	PERA	VORP	STF
2002	CHC	NL	26	45	0	46.7	53	24	46	9	7.32	8.94	9.7	3.9	7.8	1.7	5.24	-19.1	-3
2003	CHC	NL	27	77	0	76.3	53	36	92	6	3.30	3.67	6.7	3.8	10.0	0.7	2.93	16.7	25
2004	CHC	NL	28	72	0	66.7	67	33	78	10	4.72	5.05	8.6	4.0	9.3	1.2	4.64	3.2	10
2005	*CHC*	*NL*	*29*	*49*	*0*	*61.7*	*55*	*28*	*65*	*7*	*4.24*	*4.40*	*8.1*	*3.6*	*8.5*	*0.9*	*4.20*	*8.2*	*10*

Breakout: 26% *Improve: 50%* *Collapse: 30%*

That's two bad seasons out of three, four out of six. Because he's tall and athletic and can occasionally hit triple digits on the radar gun, there's always been the assumption that Farnsworth is going to turn around one of these days, find himself, and become one of the best relievers in the league. There's plenty of history to suggest the odds are stacked against that, not because of any sort of personality defect, but because pitchers who walk this many hitters and leave too many balls up in the zone are going to have plenty of bad outings whether they're saints, sinners, or somewhere in between. That's not to say that Farnsworth doesn't belong in a major league bullpen, but the Cubs' best hope is to find some team that will overpay for him in trade, vainly hoping their pitching coach can fix the unfixable.

ANGEL GUZMAN Bats: R Throws: R Born: 14-Dec-1981 Age: 23

YEAR	TM	LG	AGE	G	GS	IP	H	BB	SO	HR	ERA	EQERA	EQH9	EQBB9	EQSO9	EQHR9	PERA	VORP	STF
2002	DAY	FSL	20	16	15	94.0	99	33	74	2	2.39	4.34	9.1	3.4	5.0	0.4	3.74	18.9	16
2002	LNS	MDW	20	9	9	62.0	42	16	49	3	1.89	4.45	8.6	3.1	4.6	1.2	4.61	6.0	15
2003	WTN	SOU	21	15	15	89.7	83	26	87	8	2.81	4.07	9.2	2.7	6.3	1.5	4.71	8.3	17
2004	DAY	FSL	22	7	7	30.0	27	0	40	2	4.20	5.53	9.1	0.7	8.5	1.3	3.90	5.2	35
2004	WTN	SOU	22	4	4	17.7	20	4	13	2	5.59	6.48	10.3	2.2	4.9	1.6	5.40	0.4	-4
2005	*CHC*	*NL*	*23*	*21*	*16*	*104.0*	*105*	*31*	*83*	*14*	*4.17*	*4.33*	*9.1*	*2.4*	*6.4*	*1.1*	*4.34*	*15.9*	*11*

Breakout: 16% *Improve: 54%* *Collapse: 18%*

Never mind the unimpressive ERAs; this was a very good season for a pitcher recovering from a torn labrum. There has never been any concern about Guzman's stuff, so the fact that his command was as good as it was—the 40:0 strikeout-to-walk ratio in his Daytona line is not a typo—is highly encouraging. The Cubs have every reason to proceed cautiously with Guzman given the wealth of pitching in the system, but there's good cause to be excited.

LUKE HAGERTY Bats: R Throws: L Born: 01-Apr-1981 Age: 24

YEAR	TM	LG	AGE	G	GS	IP	H	BB	SO	HR	ERA	EQERA	EQH9	EQBB9	EQSO9	EQHR9	PERA	VORP	STF
2002	BOI	NWN	21	10	10	48.0	32	15	50	2	1.12	4.89	8.5	3.6	5.3	1.1	4.46	5.4	9
2005	*FLA*	*NL*	*24*	*15*	*9*	*53.3*	*60*	*38*	*26*	*6*	*6.28*	*6.85*	*10.3*	*5.7*	*4.0*	*1.1*	*6.76*	*-6.7*	*-24*

Breakout: 16% *Improve: 60%* *Collapse: 23%*

(continued next page)

Luke Hagerty *(continued)*

Hagerty threw only 22.7 innings this year after missing all of 2003 because of Tommy John surgery, but nevertheless managed to walk just four fewer hitters (14) than Jon Lieber, who threw 176.2. The concern here is his timetable: Hagerty will turn 24 this year and has yet to pitch higher than the Northwest League. Will Carroll likes Hagerty, and Will knows more about mechanics and pitcher injuries than just about anyone, but it's going to be tough to balance the need to bring him along slowly against his advancing age. The Marlins decided to expedite the process by picking him up in a Rule 5 draft trade; PECOTA thinks he'd be a disaster if asked to pitch in the major leagues at this point, so the Cubs stand a good chance to get him back.

LATROY HAWKINS **Bats: R** **Throws: R** Born: 21-Dec-1972 Age: 32

YEAR	TM	LG	AGE	G	GS	IP	H	BB	SO	HR	ERA	EQERA	EQH9	EQBB9	EQSO9	EQHR9	PERA	VORP	STF
2002	MIN	AL	29	65	0	80.3	63	15	63	5	2.13	2.48	7.5	1.7	7.0	0.5	3.07	30.3	15
2003	MIN	AL	30	74	0	77.3	69	15	75	4	1.86	2.26	7.6	1.7	8.6	0.5	2.85	32.4	25
2004	CHC	NL	31	77	0	82.0	72	14	69	10	2.63	2.88	8.2	1.4	6.9	1.0	3.46	25.0	9
2005	*CHC*	*NL*	*32*	*47*	*2*	*75.0*	*71*	*18*	*62*	*9*	*3.44*	*3.57*	*8.6*	*1.8*	*6.7*	*1.0*	*3.78*	*17.2*	*6*

Breakout: 21% *Improve: 44%* *Collapse: 29%*

Hawkins took a lot of flak for the Cubs' poor record in one-run games, which is bound to happen when you blow nine saves in 34 tries. But did he really pitch all that badly? These were his statistics in save and non-save situations:

	IP	H	R	ER	HR	BB	SO	ERA
Save	33.7	33	13	12	5	6	30	3.21
Non-Save	49.3	40	14	12	5	8	40	2.19

If those lines had come from two different pitchers, it would be tough to see much of a difference between them. They are achieving about the same strikeout rates, walk rates, and home run rates; one had a slightly higher ERA, but that's not a tremendously meaningful difference given the respective sample sizes. In fact, it's pretty darned tough to blow nine saves while pitching this well; the Cubs played a disproportionate number of one-run games under Hawkins's watch, and while it's still his responsibility to get those last three outs, it's not as though he was getting a lot of the three-run gimmes that usually bloat a closer's numbers.

The real problem is that Hawkins came in with a reputation of being just a set-up guy, something which was entrenched by his poor 2001 campaign when he was the Twins' regular closer and posted a 5.96 ERA. Hawkins was a different pitcher back then, yet to really establish his command or his secondary pitches, and it wasn't surprising that he failed. This time around, he just got unlucky. It also doesn't help that Hawkins is relatively soft-spoken, and doesn't have a goatee or a theme song or anything like that: A lot of the closer myth boils down to theatrics, and Hawkins doesn't always act the part. None of this is meant to suggest that Hawkins is on a par with Brad Lidge or Eric Gagne, but he was the best reliever on the staff last year, and he'll be the best reliever on the staff next year. He can certainly be expected to pitch better than someone like Dan Kolb or Ryan Dempster, whom the Cubs have touted at times as potential replacements.

JON LEICESTER **Bats: R** **Throws: R** Born: 07-Feb-1979 Age: 26

YEAR	TM	LG	AGE	G	GS	IP	H	BB	SO	HR	ERA	EQERA	EQH9	EQBB9	EQSO9	EQHR9	PERA	VORP	STF
2002	DAY	FSL	23	20	14	81.7	77	48	57	2	3.97	5.68	8.6	5.8	4.5	0.5	4.17	12.3	-1
2002	WTN	SOU	23	5	4	27.3	24	13	18	1	4.62	6.04	8.9	4.3	4.6	0.7	4.62	2.8	3
2003	WTN	SOU	24	45	9	106.3	89	53	106	7	3.89	5.53	8.5	4.6	6.5	1.2	4.53	11.8	3
2004	IOW	PCL	25	12	12	65.7	61	36	60	3	3.70	4.43	8.1	5.3	6.4	0.4	4.14	10.2	8
2004	CHC	NL	25	32	0	41.7	40	15	35	7	3.88	4.28	8.8	2.9	7.0	1.4	4.50	6.4	-1
2005	*CHC*	*NL*	*26*	*32*	*12*	*91.7*	*87*	*47*	*70*	*11*	*4.62*	*4.79*	*8.6*	*4.1*	*6.2*	*1.0*	*4.79*	*8.9*	*-2*

Breakout: 20% *Improve: 47%* *Collapse: 27%*

Leicester provided some quality relief innings at a time when the Cubs really needed them, but he's always projected as filler at the back end of a pitching staff, and that's how he'll end up without some unanticipated improvement in his command. Leicester also had a lot of trouble retiring left-handed hitters last year; while those things can be fluky, it would be hard to use him in high-leverage situations if the pattern persists.

GREG MADDUX

Bats: R **Throws: R** Born: 14-Apr-1966 Age: 39

YEAR	TM	LG	AGE	G	GS	IP	H	BB	SO	HR	ERA	EQERA	EQH9	EQBB9	EQSO9	EQHR9	PERA	VORP	STF
2002	ATL	NL	36	34	34	199.3	194	45	118	14	2.62	3.15	9.3	1.8	4.9	0.7	4.40	54.8	11
2003	ATL	NL	37	36	36	218.3	225	33	124	24	3.96	4.62	9.5	1.2	4.8	1.0	4.06	26.2	9
2004	CHC	NL	38	33	33	212.7	218	33	151	35	4.02	4.20	9.3	1.3	5.8	1.4	4.33	33.2	10
2005	*CHC*	*NL*	*39*	*31*	*29*	*178.3*	*189*	*34*	*109*	*22*	*4.04*	*4.19*	*9.6*	*1.5*	*5.0*	*1.0*	*4.12*	*28.6*	*8*

Breakout: 12% *Improve: 52%* *Collapse: 20%*

Three factors are responsible for Maddux's 305 major league wins. The first and most important is his uncanny command, which save for a couple of rough cold-weather outings in April, is just as intact as ever. The second is his pitch efficiency, to which he owes his longevity: Maddux had just four outings last year in which he topped the 100-pitch mark, and not because his manager is prone to do his pitchers any arm-saving favors.

The third factor is his capacity to induce groundballs, and that ability appears to be eroding. The movement on Maddux's fastball isn't quite as good as it once was, and the 35 home runs that he allowed in 2004 were a career high, his 1.78 groundball-to-flyball ratio a career low. Without his groundball mojo, Maddux can still be a good pitcher, but he's not going to set the aging curve on its end the way Randy and Roger have.

KENT MERCKER

Bats: L **Throws: L** Born: 01-Feb-1968 Age: 37

YEAR	TM	LG	AGE	G	GS	IP	H	BB	SO	HR	ERA	EQERA	EQH9	EQBB9	EQSO9	EQHR9	PERA	VORP	STF
2002	COL	NL	34	58	0	44.0	55	22	37	12	6.14	5.98	10.7	3.7	6.6	2.3	6.60	-6.7	-17
2003	CIN	NL	35	49	0	38.3	31	25	41	5	2.35	3.13	7.7	5.1	8.7	1.2	4.34	10.9	5
2003	ATL	NL	35	18	0	17.0	15	7	7	1	1.06	1.69	9.0	3.4	3.4	0.6	4.50	7.6	-19
2004	CHC	NL	36	71	0	53.0	39	27	51	4	2.55	2.49	7.3	4.1	7.8	0.7	3.55	18.6	9
2005	*CIN*	*NL*	*37*	*43*	*0*	*42.3*	*42*	*22*	*37*	*6*	*4.35*	*4.65*	*9.2*	*4.1*	*7.0*	*1.2*	*5.43*	*5.8*	*-4*

Breakout: 35% *Improve: 51%* *Collapse: 27%*

ERAs can be deceptive when evaluating situational relief pitchers. Mercker very frequently entered the game with runners on base, runners that wouldn't be charged to his account no matter how badly he pitched. According to our "Reliever Expected Wins Added Report," which accounts for these sorts of situations, Mercker was no more valuable than pitchers like Mike Koplove (4.05 ERA) and Felix Rodriguez (3.29 ERA). That doesn't make him a bad pitcher, but it does mean that he could be overvalued in the market. By handing him a two-year, $2.6 million deal, the Reds overvalued him.

SERGIO MITRE

Bats: R **Throws: R** Born: 16-Feb-1981 Age: 24

YEAR	TM	LG	AGE	G	GS	IP	H	BB	SO	HR	ERA	EQERA	EQH9	EQBB9	EQSO9	EQHR9	PERA	VORP	STF
2002	LNS	MDW	21	27	27	168.7	166	27	96	7	2.83	5.59	10.2	1.8	3.2	1.0	5.18	7.2	-2
2003	WTN	SOU	22	25	24	145.7	162	41	128	6	3.34	5.60	9.6	2.5	5.5	0.7	4.33	19.9	3
2004	IOW	PCL	23	18	15	102.7	97	39	95	9	2.98	3.66	8.4	3.7	6.5	0.8	4.21	15.2	20
2004	CHC	NL	23	12	9	51.7	71	20	37	6	6.62	6.19	10.7	2.9	5.5	0.9	5.33	-4.9	6
2005	*CHC*	*NL*	*24*	*20*	*20*	*113.3*	*118*	*41*	*85*	*11*	*4.27*	*4.43*	*9.4*	*2.8*	*6.1*	*0.8*	*4.55*	*15.2*	*11*

Breakout: 14% *Improve: 46%* *Collapse: 21%*

Mitre did not fare well during his major league trial, but it's a blessing to have this sort of organizational depth in a world in which contending teams routinely make deadline deals for people like Paul Abbott. While he doesn't have the big out pitch he needs to be a star, he does an exceptional job of keeping the ball down, as well as reasonably near the strike zone. PECOTA likes the incremental gains to Mitre's strikeout rate and thinks that he has some sleeper potential.

RICKY NOLASCO

Bats: R **Throws: R** Born: 13-Dec-1982 Age: 22

YEAR	TM	LG	AGE	G	GS	IP	H	BB	SO	HR	ERA	EQERA	EQH9	EQBB9	EQSO9	EQHR9	PERA	VORP	STF
2002	BOI	NWN	19	15	15	90.7	72	25	92	1	2.48	5.20	8.7	3.1	5.1	0.3	4.01	14.7	21
2003	DAY	FSL	20	26	26	149.0	129	48	136	7	2.96	4.94	9.2	3.4	5.9	1.2	4.61	15.0	18
2004	WTN	SOU	21	19	19	107.0	104	37	115	13	3.70	4.95	9.6	3.2	6.8	1.5	5.22	4.2	8
2004	IOW	PCL	21	9	9	40.7	68	16	28	7	9.29	8.64	12.3	3.5	4.5	1.3	6.91	-6.1	-19
2005	*CHC*	*NL*	*22*	*11*	*10*	*59.7*	*61*	*23*	*44*	*8*	*4.67*	*4.85*	*9.2*	*3.1*	*6.0*	*1.1*	*4.88*	*5.7*	*7*

Breakout: 8% *Improve: 40%* *Collapse: 20%*

(continued next page)

Ricky Nolasco *(continued)*

Nolasco was promoted to Iowa in May, got hit hard, and was promptly sent back to West Tennessee. That would be more alarming if he hadn't been promoted so aggressively to begin with—all the way from short-season ball to Triple-A in the span of about 20 months. Nolasco mixes several decent pitches rather than relying on one dominant one, which is not a bad thing, but puts him more in the Brownlie/Mitre class of pitching prospects than the Sisco/Blasko class. Like Mitre, he'll need to keep the ball down to be successful, but his minor league groundball-flyball numbers have been just average.

WILL OHMAN **Bats: L** **Throws: L** Born: 13-Aug-1977 Age: 27

YEAR	TM	LG	AGE	G	GS	IP	H	BB	SO	HR	ERA	EQERA	EQH9	EQBB9	EQSO9	EQHR9	PERA	VORP	STF
2004	IOW	PCL	26	45	1	52.3	53	29	75	6	4.30	4.94	8.8	5.1	9.9	1.1	4.94	3.7	1
2005	*CHC*	*NL*	*27*	*13*	*2*	*24.7*	*21*	*13*	*26*	*2*	*3.88*	*4.02*	*7.8*	*4.0*	*8.6*	*0.8*	*4.11*	*4.7*	*12*

Breakout: 31% *Improve: 53%* *Collapse: 25%*

The notes that you get in the press box include lines of zeroes for players who are on the 60-day DL. Ohman has been a mainstay in that capacity, stashed on various disabled lists without having thrown a pitch in a competitive game during all of 2002 and 2003. His elbow looks to be fine now, and the Cubs apparently felt the need to get something for all the toner that the Wrigley Field copier had expended on his name, adding him to the 40-man roster in October. It was a questionable decision; Ohman can strike people out, but his command has never been very good, and while he can probably be an adequate second or third lefty out of the bullpen, the same can be said for a lot of minor league free agents, none of whom would have cost the Cubs a prospect in the Rule 5 draft.

RENYEL PINTO **Bats: L** **Throws: L** Born: 08-Jul-1982 Age: 22

YEAR	TM	LG	AGE	G	GS	IP	H	BB	SO	HR	ERA	EQERA	EQH9	EQBB9	EQSO9	EQHR9	PERA	VORP	STF
2002	DAY	FSL	19	7	7	32.7	45	11	24	5	5.50	7.18	12.4	3.2	4.6	2.6	7.18	-5.5	-9
2002	LNS	MDW	19	17	16	98.0	79	28	92	9	3.31	5.36	10.2	3.5	5.5	2.2	6.41	-7.7	7
2003	DAY	FSL	20	20	19	114.7	91	45	104	4	3.22	5.14	8.5	4.1	5.9	0.9	4.20	16.3	25
2004	WTN	SOU	21	25	25	141.7	107	72	179	10	2.92	4.04	8.0	4.9	8.1	0.9	4.25	19.7	28
2005	*CHC*	*NL*	*22*	*14*	*13*	*78.7*	*70*	*41*	*70*	*10*	*4.46*	*4.63*	*8.0*	*4.1*	*7.2*	*1.1*	*4.58*	*9.1*	*12*

Breakout: 9% *Improve: 53%* *Collapse: 18%*

Pinto took advantage of a deceptive motion and a fastball with plus movement to post one of the highest strikeout rates in the minor leagues and win the Southern League ERA title. At least one scout has compared him to Dontrelle Willis. Like Willis, Pinto will need to cut down on his walk rate in order to compete with the other good arms that the Cubs have stashed throughout the system.

MARK PRIOR **Bats: R** **Throws: R** Born: 07-Sep-1980 Age: 24

YEAR	TM	LG	AGE	G	GS	IP	H	BB	SO	HR	ERA	EQERA	EQH9	EQBB9	EQSO9	EQHR9	PERA	VORP	STF
2002	CHC	NL	21	19	19	116.7	98	38	147	14	3.32	3.64	7.6	2.5	10.1	1.1	3.17	26.3	45
2003	CHC	NL	22	30	30	211.3	183	50	245	15	2.43	2.88	7.6	1.9	9.5	0.6	2.88	66.8	46
2004	CHC	NL	23	21	21	118.7	112	48	139	14	4.02	3.86	8.2	3.2	9.3	0.9	3.93	24.0	32
2005	*CHC*	*NL*	*24*	*25*	*25*	*157.7*	*134*	*50*	*170*	*18*	*3.32*	*3.44*	*7.7*	*2.5*	*8.7*	*0.9*	*3.55*	*39.9*	*31*

Breakout: 30% *Improve: 50%* *Collapse: 23%*

Chicago is a heavily Catholic city, but if you had asked Chicagoans in April whether they would have preferred a healthy Pope John Paul or a healthy Mark Prior, there's little doubt the pitcher would have gotten their vote. Prior finally returned on June 4, pitching six innings of shutout ball against the Pirates. But he then settled into a long series of stuttering outings in which he was allowing walks and home runs at twice his usual rate, igniting barroom debates about whether he should be left out of the rotation if the Cubs were fortunate enough to reach the post-season. The only noticeable change during Prior's rougher stretches was that the command on his breaking ball was not there—his velocity and mechanics were fine. It may be that the very simplicity of Prior's approach was his undoing. Prior throws fastballs and curveballs, and throws them for strikes, but he doesn't have a third pitch to fall back upon, nor does he have much experience operating in tough situations when he is anything less than 100%.

Fortunately, Prior put most of the questions to rest with an outstanding September in which he posted a 43:7 strikeout-to-walk ratio and a 2.17 ERA in 37.1 innings, numbers that were almost exactly in line with his 2003 performance. Though the Cubs had not rushed him back, it wasn't surprising that a pitcher who had missed spring training took a while to get going. Prior's outlook remains very bright, and he is the odds-on favorite to win the NL Cy Young in 2005; that projection does not account for how well he pitched down the stretch.

MIKE REMLINGER Bats: L Throws: L Born: 23-Mar-1966 Age: 39

YEAR	TM	LG	AGE	G	GS	IP	H	BB	SO	HR	ERA	EQERA	EQH9	EQBB9	EQSO9	EQHR9	PERA	VORP	STF
2002	ATL	NL	36	73	0	68.0	48	28	69	3	1.99	2.38	7.3	3.2	8.4	0.4	3.36	23.6	17
2003	CHC	NL	37	73	0	69.0	54	39	83	11	3.65	3.90	7.5	4.4	9.9	1.3	4.03	13.1	12
2004	CHC	NL	38	48	0	36.7	33	16	35	3	3.43	3.79	8.1	3.5	7.8	0.8	3.79	7.2	7
2005	*CHC*	*NL*	*39*	*45*	*0*	*32.3*	*29*	*15*	*30*	*4*	*4.15*	*4.30*	*8.2*	*3.7*	*7.4*	*0.9*	*4.27*	*5.4*	*2*

Breakout: 25% Improve: 42% Collapse: 22%

Remlinger's season was derailed by two stints on the disabled list, which is what you're going to get when you sign a 37-year-old reliever to a multi-year contract. He was reasonably effective when healthy, but posted a reverse platoon differential for the fourth straight year, allowing an .847 OPS against lefties while holding righties to a .502 figure. That isn't inherently a bad thing, but it does mean that Remlinger needs to be used differently than someone like Scott Eyre. Dusty Baker did not get the memo, and had him face just one or two hitters, almost always lefties, in 14 of his 48 appearances.

GLENDON RUSCH Bats: L Throws: L Born: 07-Nov-1974 Age: 30

YEAR	TM	LG	AGE	G	GS	IP	H	BB	SO	HR	ERA	EQERA	EQH9	EQBB9	EQSO9	EQHR9	PERA	VORP	STF
2002	MIL	NL	27	34	34	210.7	227	76	140	30	4.70	5.03	9.7	2.8	5.3	1.3	4.99	10.8	1
2003	MIL	NL	28	32	19	123.3	171	45	93	11	6.42	6.47	10.4	2.8	5.8	0.7	4.90	-15.1	8
2004	CHC	NL	29	32	16	129.7	127	33	90	10	3.47	3.67	8.8	2.1	5.6	0.6	3.82	27.8	12
2005	*CHC*	*NL*	*30*	*27*	*19*	*120.3*	*127*	*37*	*87*	*14*	*4.19*	*4.34*	*9.5*	*2.4*	*5.8*	*0.9*	*4.47*	*17.8*	*7*

Breakout: 19% Improve: 55% Collapse: 14%

You've probably heard us talk about the Voros McCracken effect. Pitchers have very little influence on whether balls batted into play against them go for hits or outs, and yet this can have an enormous effect on their results. In 2003, 38.7% of balls in play went for hits against Rusch. That's a remarkably high rate; the next highest number among pitchers who threw at least 100 innings belonged to Jeff Weaver, who was at 35.5%. This time around, Rusch yielded hits on balls in play at a rate of 29.5%, a figure very close to league average. Just about everything else about the pitcher was the same—Rusch's walk rate was better in 2004, but only slightly—land yet it was enough to make almost a three-run difference in his ERA. It's important to be able to distinguish between a pitcher like Shawn Estes, who is fundamentally bad, and one like Rusch, who has mostly just been unlucky. Re-signed cheaply for two years, he should provide good value to the Cubs as a swingman.

ANDY SISCO Bats: L Throws: L Born: 13-Jan-1983 Age: 22

YEAR	TM	LG	AGE	G	GS	IP	H	BB	SO	HR	ERA	EQERA	EQH9	EQBB9	EQSO9	EQHR9	PERA	VORP	STF
2002	BOI	NWN	19	14	14	77.7	51	39	101	3	2.43	4.74	8.4	5.9	6.7	1.1	5.14	3.5	17
2003	LNS	MDW	20	19	19	94.0	76	31	99	3	3.54	5.97	8.7	3.8	6.5	0.8	4.19	13.5	17
2004	DAY	FSL	21	26	25	126.0	118	65	134	11	4.21	5.57	9.6	5.4	6.7	1.6	5.96	-4.7	-7
2005	*KCR*	*AL*	*22*	*10*	*8*	*47.3*	*48*	*28*	*37*	*8*	*5.72*	*5.39*	*9.0*	*4.7*	*6.5*	*1.5*	*5.34*	*2.9*	*0*

Breakout: 8% Improve: 37% Collapse: 28%

Sisco is a monster of a guy at 6′9″ and 265 lbs. He's got middling mechanics, gives up a lot of flyballs, doesn't have a good breaking pitch just yet, and both his walk rate and his home-run rate were up at Daytona. In short, he's going to need all his development time, and is about the last guy who might benefit from a premature year on a major league roster. Whether that played into the Cubs' decision to leave him exposed for the Rule 5 draft is hard to say; most clubs are going to take one look at him, think Randy Johnson, and look for the sharpie to sign the contract. Now a Royal.

TODD WELLEMEYER Bats: R Throws: R Born: 30-Aug-1978 Age: 26

YEAR	TM	LG	AGE	G	GS	IP	H	BB	SO	HR	ERA	EQERA	EQH9	EQBB9	EQSO9	EQHR9	PERA	VORP	STF
2002	DAY	FSL	23	14	14	73.7	63	19	87	7	3.79	4.98	8.9	2.6	7.7	1.8	4.33	9.7	17
2002	WTN	SOU	23	8	8	46.0	33	18	37	2	4.70	5.79	7.9	3.4	5.6	0.9	3.86	8.1	12
2003	WTN	SOU	24	4	4	21.3	19	10	34	1	5.49	6.53	8.3	4.4	10.0	0.9	4.35	2.9	26
2003	IOW	PCL	24	13	12	66.0	68	33	56	7	5.18	5.74	9.3	5.0	6.6	1.4	5.60	0.0	-4
2004	IOW	PCL	25	14	4	23.0	24	12	23	2	3.91	4.43	8.9	4.8	6.9	0.8	4.84	1.9	-6
2004	CHC	NL	25	20	0	24.3	27	20	30	1	5.93	5.76	8.6	6.1	9.4	0.4	4.68	-0.6	6
2005	*CHC*	*NL*	*26*	*14*	*6*	*45.0*	*41*	*24*	*40*	*6*	*4.62*	*4.79*	*8.2*	*4.2*	*7.3*	*1.1*	*4.75*	*4.8*	*5*

Breakout: 27% Improve: 44% Collapse: 25%

Wellemeyer has a quiet demeanor and a calm delivery on the mound, one that you'd naturally associate with a command pitcher. Instead, his walk rate has increased sequentially at each step of the ladder, culminating in two poor major

(continued next page)

Todd Wellemeyer *(continued)*

league call-ups in which he walked more than 16% of the batters he faced. One wonders whether Wellemeyer simply needs to be coached to challenge batters more frequently—he's not going to be effective until he does.

KERRY WOOD **Bats: R** **Throws: R** Born: 16-Jun-1977 Age: 28

YEAR	TM	LG	AGE	G	GS	IP	H	BB	SO	HR	ERA	EQERA	EQH9	EQBB9	EQSO9	EQHR9	PERA	VORP	STF
2002	CHC	NL	25	33	33	213.7	169	97	217	22	3.66	4.01	7.5	3.5	8.2	0.9	3.32	38.6	26
2003	CHC	NL	26	32	32	211.0	152	100	266	24	3.20	3.30	7.0	3.8	10.4	1.0	3.22	56.6	38
2004	CHC	NL	27	22	22	140.3	127	51	144	16	3.72	3.83	8.1	2.9	8.3	0.9	3.83	27.9	28
2005	*CHC*	*NL*	*28*	*24*	*24*	*157.3*	*130*	*63*	*159*	*17*	*3.58*	*3.71*	*7.5*	*3.1*	*8.2*	*0.9*	*3.71*	*33.6*	*25*

Breakout: 15% *Improve: 48%* *Collapse: 28%*

The working assumption has always been that Wood is going to wake up one morning and discover that he's Roger Clemens. That's certainly better than waking up to find you've turned into Bobby Witt. But for any metamorphosis to occur, Wood will need to improve on his command. Last year was a step in the right direction, as Wood shaved nearly a full point off his walk rate. It didn't produce better results for him, since his strikeout rate was down too, perhaps the result of his pitching more cautiously with an arm that was tender for much of the season. But the hope is that he'll find the best of both worlds, learning when he can take something off a pitch and when to come at full strength. Will it happen? The odds are always against an established player making a sudden and dramatic improvement, but pitchers don't age in the predictable ways that hitters do; it took Randy Johnson until he was 29 to completely figure things out, and Kevin Brown until he was 31.

MIKE WUERTZ **Bats: R** **Throws: R** Born: 15-Dec-1978 Age: 26

YEAR	TM	LG	AGE	G	GS	IP	H	BB	SO	HR	ERA	EQERA	EQH9	EQBB9	EQSO9	EQHR9	PERA	VORP	STF
2002	IOW	PCL	23	28	27	154.0	185	69	131	24	5.55	6.45	10.3	4.2	6.0	1.6	5.91	-5.1	-11
2003	IOW	PCL	24	43	16	124.0	140	35	92	16	4.57	5.55	10.1	2.9	5.7	1.7	5.55	0.7	-17
2004	IOW	PCL	25	37	0	44.7	30	15	59	4	2.42	3.00	6.9	3.2	9.4	0.9	3.00	12.1	14
2004	CHC	NL	25	31	0	29.0	22	17	30	4	4.34	4.18	7.4	4.8	8.4	1.3	4.18	4.4	0
2005	*CHC*	*NL*	*26*	*17*	*8*	*57.7*	*52*	*24*	*54*	*9*	*4.21*	*4.36*	*8.1*	*3.2*	*7.6*	*1.3*	*4.36*	*10.1*	*10*

Breakout: 35% *Improve: 61%* *Collapse: 12%*

Wuertz has a ton of natural movement on his pitches, which made him tough to hit last year but created problems because his pitches tended to move out of the strike zone. He doesn't have a history of high walk rates in the minors, however, so his propensity to give up the free pass while with the Cubs may have been a blip. Wuertz is more advanced than Todd Wellemeyer or Jon Leicester, and more likely to have a productive major league career.

CARLOS ZAMBRANO **Bats: B** **Throws: R** Born: 01-Jun-1981 Age: 24

YEAR	TM	LG	AGE	G	GS	IP	H	BB	SO	HR	ERA	EQERA	EQH9	EQBB9	EQSO9	EQHR9	PERA	VORP	STF
2002	CHC	NL	21	32	16	108.3	94	63	93	9	3.66	4.53	8.0	4.5	6.9	0.8	3.76	13.0	15
2003	CHC	NL	22	32	32	214.0	188	94	168	9	3.11	3.65	8.0	3.5	6.5	0.3	3.39	47.5	25
2004	CHC	NL	23	31	31	209.7	174	81	188	14	2.75	3.08	7.8	3.1	7.3	0.5	3.44	61.3	28
2005	*CHC*	*NL*	*24*	*28*	*28*	*185.0*	*167*	*75*	*159*	*16*	*3.51*	*3.64*	*8.1*	*3.2*	*7.0*	*0.7*	*3.89*	*39.8*	*19*

Breakout: 30% *Improve: 61%* *Collapse: 14%*

Big Z is one of the more underutilized nicknames in baseball, and Zambrano proved that he had a Bigger Z than Barry Zito by outdueling his arch-nemesis during the Cubs' interleague victory over the A's on June 20. Zambrano was also one of the best pitchers in the league, and when his nasty sinking fastball and hard slider were working together, he was absolutely unhittable. He can be wild at times, but because he generates a lot of double plays and rarely yields extra-base hits, those walks don't harm him as much as they might another pitcher.

Still, one sometimes gets the feeling that Zambrano is a Ming vase teetering on the brink of an unsteady shelf. He has the tendency to overthrow in jams or when he's getting fatigued, sending his mechanics out of whack. While not out of shape, he carries a lot of weight on his frame. He's extremely and demonstrably competitive, so he's about the last guy in the league who is going to beg himself out of a game voluntarily. In spite of all of that, he's been worked more heavily than just about anyone: Zambrano, Jason Schmidt, and Livan Hernandez were the only three starters who averaged more than 110 pitches per start last season, and Big Z was the youngest of that group by six years. We're trying not to be Pitch Count Nazis, but if there's one pitcher who deserves a petition for clemency, it's Zambrano, who is simply too good and too exciting to let go to waste.

Cincinnati Reds

REDS PROSPECTUS

2004 record: 76–86; Fourth place, NL Central

Pythagenport record: 66–96

Runs scored per game: 4.63 (10th in NL)

Runs allowed per game: 5.60 (15th in NL)

Team EqA: .261 (9th in NL)

2004 Batters Age: 28.8 (3rd youngest in NL)

2004 Pitchers Age: 29.0 (4th youngest in NL)

Ballpark: Great American Ballpark; Severe pitcher's park; Park Factor of 0.955

2004: Got out of the gate quickly, but were out of the race by the All-Star break.

2005: With a frightening pitching staff, the offense needs to channel the Big Red Machine, and they aren't up to the task.

The game of baseball is defined as much by myths as fact, by image as much as statistics. Most teams indulge in a certain amount of self-mythologizing: The Yankees are about winning and professionalism, the Red Sox are/were cursed, the Brewers are screwed by the market.

In Cincinnati, the team lives in the constant shadow of the Big Red Machine, a dynasty that was barely extant long enough to be worthy of the title. Its stars still loom large, too large, and even when later Reds' teams have success—as did the 1990 world championship team—they still fail to put so much as a dent in the mythology of the Machine.

In the past five years, the Reds have lacked easy definition, a public persona that could be grasped. As now constituted, they don't have any mythology at all. Their only enduring image is of their last fleeting connection to the Machine, Ken Griffey Jr., laying in agony on the third-base line or on the center-field turf. Perhaps disappointment and missed opportunity define these Reds.

As the team went through one administration and transitioned into another, they did not create a public face. Dan O'Brien can be competent, but hardly stands out. Dave Miley is an organizational soldier, a hard worker who is described as a genuinely nice person. Anecdotes around both men focus on qualities like integrity, work ethic, or competence, but neither evokes qualities of inspiration. Even a player as gregarious as Sean Casey or as accomplished as the now-departed Barry Larkin failed to be the focus of the franchise. Instead, over the past three years the Reds have oddly circled around someone in a role seldom seen, let alone noticed: Dr. Timothy Kremchek, the team physician.

The Reds have developed a reputation as a franchise that's snakebit, injury-prone or worse. But while the medical and training staff should shoulder some of the blame, poor roster construction has been the bigger problem. Massive, unjustified contracts doled out to players like Larkin and Casey have prevented the Reds from upgrading elsewhere on the diamond or assembling the kind of depth they'd need to overcome major injuries.

Moreover, most of the days lost to injury last season belong primarily to three players: Griffey, Larkin, and Austin Kearns—as well as a few scrubs such as John Vander Wal and Jason Romano. No one should be surprised by these events. Kearns has hit a string of bad luck that perhaps only Nick Johnson can match among young, talented big leaguers. The hope is that he'll get through a season without incurring any more freak, unavoidable injuries, then blast off from there. At the other end of the career trail, on the wrong side of 40, Larkin's strained oblique and other injuries were hardly a surprise.

While Griffey, Larkin, and Kearns all missed significant playing time due to injury, only Kearns finished below his PECOTA projection in 2004. Overall, they actually outperformed expectations with the bat. The pitching, on the other hand, fell short. That's saying a lot, given the meager outlook the staff had at the start of last season.

The Jim Bowden Era was based on a plan that never really achieved fruition. The plan hinged on an alchemistic pitching staff forged by Don Gullett. Gullett would spin scrap into gold just enough to keep the Reds competitive until the real gold came through the turnstiles of their new taxpayer-financed stadium.

Gullett did OK in that respect, finding a starter or two a year who did just enough to tantalize, such as Jimmy Haynes in 2002 and Paul Wilson in 2003. But as we discussed last year, Gullett has had his share of failures as well. But Gullett has struggled mightily in his efforts to develop young pitching. Jose Acevedo and Brandon Claussen came into the 2004 season armed with a good minor league track record backed by strong peripherals. Both eventually got a clear shot at a starter's job. Both stunk up the joint.

You can forgive a young pitcher for being slow to come around, and both Acevedo and Claussen are still young and talented enough to put it together. But Gullett has had so much trouble developing young pitching, you wonder if it'll ever happen with the Reds, or at least on Gullett's watch. For a team on a budget, having pitchers come up from the farm and fail to contribute is a huge obstacle to overcome.

Still, Bowden's plan might have been on track once the Great American Ballpark opened in 2003. The team could possible even eschew scrap-heap pickups, and get more conservative in their development of young pitchers, as a fresh stream of revenue flowed in from the new park. Unfortunately, owner Carl Lindner had other ideas. Looking past potential pennant runs, Lindner instead found more dollars to be made by playing it cheap, just as he'd done at the old park. The promised harvest of free-agent acquisitions fell apart, leaving the front office hunting in the couch cushions for talent. Though Bowden had made more than enough mistakes to warrant his dismissal, his fate was sealed only after Lindner smiled down on the citizens of Ohio, pocketed their tax dollars, and slunk off into the sunset.

Then the 2004–2005 off-season rolled around. It's not clear if Dan O'Brien and the rest of the front office got through to Lindner, or if Carlbenezer Scrooge had a visit from the Ghost of Christmas Past, or what. Whatever the case, the Reds suddenly, surprisingly, opened their wallets.

The deals started right after the Winter Meetings. With the lineup mostly set, the Reds inked Joe Randa to a one-year, $2.15 million deal. It was a reasonable short-term venture, in that it ended the foolish talk of moving Austin Kearns to third and ensured top prospect Edwin Encarnacion would get another year of seasoning in the minors. But where the Reds really broke the bank was on pitching. In rapid succession, they snapped up Kent Mercker, Ben Weber, and David Weathers, hoping that money spent equaled quality added to a pen more usually stocked with a few men making the minimum. And although he figured to be non-tendered by the Angels just a few days later, the Reds traded for Ramon Ortiz to make sure they got him. He, too, figures to be well compensated for 2005.

Then came the biggest splurge, notionally their signature signing of the winter. After being pursued by as many as ten teams, Eric Milton signed a free-agent deal with the Reds. The price? Three years, $25.5 million.

The flurry of moves made two things abundantly clear: that the Reds again were willing to spend money, and, unfortunately, they were liable to spend it poorly. Forget Randa and the relievers and focus on the two biggest expenditures, Ortiz and especially Milton. Ortiz turns 32 in March. His career unadjusted ERA is 1% below league average. He was bad enough in the rotation last season for the Angels to demote him to the bullpen. Yes, he fared well there, but well enough to justify the millions of dollars the Reds will now have to pay him? With pitching prospect Dustin Moseley traded away for good measure?

Then there's Milton. What about his record compelled the Reds to throw Fort Knox at him, exactly? Was it a career ERA 1% below league average? The staggering number of home runs he allows every year—including 43 with the Phillies last season—which only figures to be magnified in the Reds' homer-friendly park? The health concerns, including the knee injury that forced him out for almost all of 2003?

At best, the Reds saw multiple holes on their pitching staff, but particularly their lack of an ace. They found their owner finally willing to spend, and figured they could throw money at the hole and make it go away. There's nothing in Milton's performance record that suggests he'll be a good buy. Desperation born of fielding a patchwork rotation every year compelled the Reds to overspend for a guy they could call their ace. The problem is, being the ace of the Reds' pitching staff is like being the smartest Hilton sister—someone has to get the title, but it's not anything worth rewarding.

No organization—be it a Fortune 500 company or a major league baseball team—makes its best decisions out of desperation. While the optimist would argue that signing veteran pitchers lets Gullett work with exactly the kind of pitchers he prefers, the realist sees the Reds' awful track record of developing pitching talent and Gullett's inability to nurture the few that make it down the pike.

The trouble starts on draft day, where the Reds have made a series of colossal misjudgments in recent years. Despite reams of data that overwhelmingly point to their huge failure rates, the Reds continue to favor high-school pitchers. After highly-touted prep and 2002 first-round choice Chris Gruler blew out his arm, you'd think they'd get the message. When 1999 first-rounder Ty Howington struggled with recurring shoulder problems, then had surgery to repair a torn labrum last year, you'd think they'd get the message. But even in a new regime, under a new GM, the Reds reached for high-schooler Homer Bailey in '04, despite an array of lower-risk, better-upside players available on the board. Either the Reds have some serious masochistic fetishes, or they just don't know what they're doing.

Of the few pitchers that made it through the gauntlet of the low minors, none have emerged as impact major leaguers. When the Reds drafted Dustin Moseley as a first-rounder in 2000, they envisioned a tall, lanky body filling out and four or five miles being added to a promising fastball, producing a fireballer and future All-Star. Instead they got a guy whose velocity never grew, who ended up as fodder in a trade for a mediocre pitcher who was about to hit the unemployment line.

Meanwhile Milton's signing could again shine the spotlight on the team's propensity for injuries, putting more pressure on the beleaguered medical staff. After a hot start last season, the team's collapse finally came about the time that Ken Griffey's hamstring gave out, yet again. It was Griffey's third consecutive season scarred by significant injury and ending in surgery. Even younger players like Austin Kearns and Brandon Larson lived up to previously earned reputations as injury-prone. The minor leagues were no different. One after another, top draft picks fell to the wayside, often ending up on the operating table of Dr. Kremchek.

Griffey's sad story over the last few years has mirrored that of the Reds franchise. Since his move from Seattle to Cincinnati, the team has met one disappointment after another, none more painful than that of their superstar. There are concerns that Griffey has tried to coast on natural talent the way he could in his younger days. While Adam Dunn and others will carry the torch for the next few years, you wonder if the Reds would have contended all along with Griffey in peak form, instead of becoming the dull, faceless team it now is.

HITTERS

TONY BLANCO 1B/LF Bats: R Throws: R Born: 10-Nov-1981 Age: 23

YEAR	TM	LG	AGE	AB	H	2B	3B	HR	BB	SO	SB	CS	AVG	OBP	SLG	MLVR	EQBA	EQOBP	EQSLG	EQMLVR	VORP	DEFENSE
2002	SAR	FSL	20	244	54	13	2	6	6	70	2	0	.221	.250	.365	-.134	.199	.220	.341	-.418	-17.6	61-3B -13
2003	POT	CRL	21	241	64	17	2	10	26	62	0	0	.266	.338	.477	.144	.229	.292	.437	-.125	-3.3	15-1B -2
2004	CHT	SOU	22	220	54	8	1	12	15	53	0	0	.245	.300	.455	.017	.226	.273	.421	-.185	-8.5	46-LF -4
2004	POT	CRL	22	216	66	10	0	17	27	66	2	0	.306	.403	.588	.398	.250	.325	.495	.032	7.9	33-1B -4
2005	*WAS*	*NL*	*23*	*312*	*75*	*17*	*1*	*13*	*24*	*90*	*1*	*0*	*.239*	*.308*	*.423*	*-.098*	*.242*	*.309*	*.433*	*-.085*	*2.9*	*84-LF -11*

Breakout: 27% *Improve: 48%* *Collapse: 26%*

Got it together in his third year at high-A ball, whacking 17 homers in 62 games and ramping his average up 40 points. While the Reds have shown a tendency to hold their prospects back too long, Blanco debuted as a raw 17-year-old in the Dominican League and just turned 23 in November, so they could afford to make sure he got it right before advancing to Double-A. There's still plenty of work to be done: Blanco will never play a premium defensive position, and he's going to struggle at higher levels to improve his plate discipline. Given the Reds' lousy recent draft and player development record, Blanco still is one of the best prospects they have. Snagged by the Nationals in the Rule 5 draft, a team whose one area of depth is in the outfield.

DARREN BRAGG PH Bats: L Throws: R Born: 07-Sep-1969 Age: 35

YEAR	TM	LG	AGE	AB	H	2B	3B	HR	BB	SO	SB	CS	AVG	OBP	SLG	MLVR	EQBA	EQOBP	EQSLG	EQMLVR	VORP	DEFENSE
2002	ATL	NL	32	212	57	15	2	3	24	52	5	2	.269	.347	.401	.027	.272	.349	.408	-.026	8.1	27-RF 0 13-CF 1
2003	ATL	NL	33	162	39	5	1	0	13	38	2	1	.241	.305	.284	-.249	.244	.301	.274	-.325	-5.9	15-RF 0 17-LF -1
2004	COH	INT	34	273	77	21	3	8	37	45	7	2	.282	.367	.469	.133	.266	.351	.439	.015	6.0	36-LF -1 13-CF -1
2004	LOU	INT	34	46	11	1	0	2	5	13	1	0	.239	.314	.391	-.135	.200	.255	.356	-.328	-2.9	
2004	CIN	NL	34	94	18	3	1	4	8	29	1	0	.191	.255	.372	-.235	.189	.252	.379	-.309	-2.0	14-CF 1
2005	*CIN*	*NL*	*35*	*116*	*29*	*6*	*1*	*3*	*14*	*27*	*2*	*1*	*.245*	*.326*	*.379*	*-.120*	*.243*	*.323*	*.375*	*-.134*	*0.4*	*36-CF -7*

Breakout: 20% *Improve: 40%* *Collapse: 35%*

Injury woes prompted the Reds to give him 101 at-bats, though even with Griffey and Kearns down, you have to wonder why they'd bother with a known stiff like Bragg as opposed to even a mildly interesting experiment like Kenny Kelly or Rob Stratton. At this stage, Bragg won't help any major league team.

SEAN CASEY 1B Bats: L Throws: R Born: 02-Jul-1974 Age: 30

YEAR	TM	LG	AGE	AB	H	2B	3B	HR	BB	SO	SB	CS	AVG	OBP	SLG	MLVR	EQBA	EQOBP	EQSLG	EQMLVR	VORP	DEFENSE
2002	CIN	NL	28	425	111	25	0	6	43	47	2	1	.261	.334	.362	-.070	.261	.329	.362	-.136	3.0	103-1B -6
2003	CIN	NL	29	573	167	19	3	14	51	58	4	0	.291	.350	.408	.045	.288	.347	.409	-.016	23.3	140-1B -7
2004	CIN	NL	30	571	185	44	2	24	46	36	2	0	.324	.381	.534	.326	.323	.377	.532	.246	66.2	138-1B -5
2005	*CIN*	*NL*	*30*	*508*	*149*	*31*	*2*	*15*	*48*	*46*	*2*	*1*	*.294*	*.358*	*.456*	*.074*	*.292*	*.355*	*.451*	*.058*	*23.5*	*133-1B -5*

Breakout: 5% *Improve: 23%* *Collapse: 32%*

(continued next page)

Sean Casey *(continued)*

Casey's woes of 2002 and 2003 stemmed largely from injuries, notably a serious shoulder injury which raised questions about his ability to keep ripping doubles the way he had. Finally recovered in '04, he started the season with a bang, hitting .414/.458/.667 in April and .377/.422/.623 in May. That would prove to be the apex of his season, but the end result still included a career-high 44 doubles, and 24 homers. Health permitting, Casey's batting eye (46 BB, 36 K in 2004) and line-drive swing should spell several more years of solid production. He'll make $7.8 million this year, plus another $8.5 million in 2006 because the Reds picked up his 2006 this off-season. He'll be 32 at that point, so it'll be interesting to see if the Reds offer another Larkin-like boondoggle deal in the name of misguided loyalty. PECOTA expects a drop-off to '01–'03 levels.

JUAN CASTRO **INF** **Bats: R** **Throws: R** Born: 20-Jun-1972 Age: 33

YEAR	TM	LG	AGE	AB	H	2B	3B	HR	BB	SO	SB	CS	AVG	OBP	SLG	MLVR	EQBA	EQOBP	EQSLG	EQMLVR	VORP	DEFENSE
2002	CIN	NL	30	82	18	3	0	2	7	18	0	0	.220	.278	.329	-.245	.220	.263	.317	-.354	-1.2	12-SS 0
2003	CIN	NL	31	320	81	14	1	9	18	58	2	3	.253	.290	.388	-.134	.252	.290	.391	-.176	2.8	48-2B 3 19-3B 4
2004	CIN	NL	32	299	73	21	2	5	14	51	1	0	.244	.277	.378	-.144	.243	.276	.380	-.225	0.8	39-3B -1 23-SS 2
2005	*MIN*	*AL*	*33*	*241*	*60*	*12*	*1*	*5*	*14*	*43*	*1*	*1*	*.249*	*.291*	*.375*	*-.177*	*.247*	*.291*	*.380*	*-.182*	*0.3*	*65-3B 2*

Breakout: 23% *Improve: 50%* *Collapse: 30%*

You have to figure there are a lot more Frankie Menechino types out there, overlooked players rotting away in the minors or independent leagues who could do a better job than non-productive chaff like Castro. Just because a player's been in the major leagues before doesn't mean he's better major league material than a player putting up higher numbers elsewhere. The Reds didn't repeat the folly of the two-year extension they gave Castro in 2001; the Twins did it instead, pissing away $2.05 million in the process.

JERMAINE CLARK **2B/OF** **Bats: L** **Throws: R** Born: 29-Sep-1976 Age: 28

YEAR	TM	LG	AGE	AB	H	2B	3B	HR	BB	SO	SB	CS	AVG	OBP	SLG	MLVR	EQBA	EQOBP	EQSLG	EQMLVR	VORP	DEFENSE
2002	TAC	PCL	25	368	98	14	4	6	62	59	29	14	.266	.370	.375	.036	.257	.356	.355	-.096	9.8	98-2B -1
2003	OKL	PCL	26	171	38	6	4	6	16	26	11	1	.222	.291	.409	-.072	.209	.278	.390	-.231	-9.1	23-LF -2 10-RF -1
2003	POR	PCL	26	160	40	2	2	4	22	24	14	3	.250	.342	.362	-.028	.230	.316	.342	-.209	-3.1	22-CF -1
2004	LOU	INT	27	398	113	15	5	10	63	54	24	9	.284	.386	.422	.064	.251	.354	.373	-.080	8.7	31-CF -1 24-2B 3
2004	CIN	NL	27	30	4	1	0	0	1	8	1	0	.133	.212	.167	-.615	.161	.176	.194	-.732	-3.5	
2005	*OAK*	*AL*	*28*	*191*	*48*	*9*	*2*	*4*	*24*	*31*	*8*	*3*	*.250*	*.339*	*.380*	*-.086*	*.252*	*.343*	*.387*	*-.078*	*7.7*	*55-2B -7*

Breakout: 34% *Improve: 54%* *Collapse: 30%*

He was never going to be a star, but Clark's deserved more of a chance than he's received, and he can still help any number of teams, including his new employer, the A's. If Mark Ellis struggles to return from injury and Keith Ginter's glove scares Ken Macha, Clark could be as good or better than Marco Scutaro, himself a scrap heap find in Oakland.

JACOB CRUZ **OF/PH** **Bats: L** **Throws: L** Born: 28-Jan-1973 Age: 32

YEAR	TM	LG	AGE	AB	H	2B	3B	HR	BB	SO	SB	CS	AVG	OBP	SLG	MLVR	EQBA	EQOBP	EQSLG	EQMLVR	VORP	DEFENSE
2002	DET	AL	29	88	24	3	1	2	13	20	3	1	.273	.377	.398	.047	.284	.390	.420	.075	4.6	
2003	LOU	INT	30	132	46	8	0	7	14	22	3	0	.348	.409	.568	.406	.313	.369	.527	.215	11.4	25-RF -1
2004	LOU	INT	31	54	17	4	0	3	10	10	0	0	.315	.415	.556	.310	.264	.339	.491	.064	3.4	
2004	CIN	NL	31	147	33	8	0	3	16	43	0	0	.224	.317	.340	-.128	.230	.310	.338	-.226	0.6	17-RF -1
2005	*CIN*	*NL*	*32*	*131*	*34*	*6*	*1*	*5*	*17*	*32*	*1*	*0*	*.260*	*.353*	*.435*	*.010*	*.258*	*.349*	*.431*	*-.005*	*7.3*	*40-RF -5*

Breakout: 27% *Improve: 43%* *Collapse: 39%*

The overall numbers quickly tailed off after a fast start, but Cruz settled into a niche as a decent pinch-hitter, putting up a line of .255/.379/.382 in 66 appearances. Sure, an ace pinch-hitter on a 76-win team is about as useful as a harpsichord player in Jay-Z's posse, but if the Reds ever get back into contention or hip-hop begins experimenting with Baroque-era instruments, watch out!

CHRIS DICKERSON CF Bats: L Throws: L Born: 10-Apr-1982 Age: 23

YEAR	TM	LG	AGE	AB	H	2B	3B	HR	BB	SO	SB	CS	AVG	OBP	SLG	MLVR	EQBA	EQOBP	EQSLG	EQMLVR	VORP	DEFENSE
2003	BIL	PIO	21	201	49	6	4	6	39	66	9	4	.244	.376	.403	.062	.180	.279	.283	-.389	-29.2	56-CF -5
2004	DYT	MDW	22	314	95	15	3	4	51	92	27	14	.303	.410	.408	.155	.244	.332	.334	-.180	-3.4	75-CF 0
2004	POT	CRL	22	45	9	2	0	0	7	14	3	1	.200	.321	.244	-.230	.106	.181	.106	-.853	-10.4	12-CF -1
2005	*CIN*	*NL*	*23*	*335*	*74*	*16*	*2*	*6*	*42*	*120*	*9*	*4*	*.220*	*.320*	*.335*	*-.202*	*.219*	*.317*	*.332*	*-.215*	*-5.4*	*94-CF -6*

Breakout: 26% *Improve: 47%* *Collapse: 28%*

Spent most of the year in the Midwest League, where Dickerson rolled up an impressive .410 OBP and a walk every seven times up. Reminds some in the organization of Adam Dunn, in that Dunn hadn't played a lot of baseball upon being drafted, but showed good instincts and impressive patience when he did arrive, despite a high strikeout total. He's a true center fielder with no platoon split thus far (.301 vs. LH). If he can start producing more power with his 6′4″, 212-lb. frame, the Reds could have themselves a great prospect.

ADAM DUNN LF Bats: L Throws: R Born: 09-Nov-1979 Age: 25

YEAR	TM	LG	AGE	AB	H	2B	3B	HR	BB	SO	SB	CS	AVG	OBP	SLG	MLVR	EQBA	EQOBP	EQSLG	EQMLVR	VORP	DEFENSE
2002	CIN	NL	22	535	133	28	2	26	128	170	19	9	.249	.400	.454	.142	.244	.394	.457	.099	36.1	90-LF -4 40-1B -5
2003	CIN	NL	23	381	82	12	1	27	74	126	8	2	.215	.354	.465	.069	.215	.350	.469	.013	17.4	92-LF -5 10-1B -1
2004	CIN	NL	24	568	151	34	0	46	108	195	6	1	.266	.388	.569	.320	.265	.384	.563	.238	64.8	147-LF -15
2005	*CIN*	*NL*	*25*	*460*	*124*	*25*	*3*	*35*	*90*	*144*	*8*	*2*	*.270*	*.395*	*.562*	*.248*	*.269*	*.391*	*.556*	*.231*	*42.4*	*131-LF -7*

Breakout: 56% *Improve: 87%* *Collapse: 2%*

The *BP2002* cover jinx continued for Dunn, as he set a major league record with 195 strikeouts, embarrassing himself and the org . . . wait, what? He was actually good? Yes, it turns out that striking out a lot is okay, if you've got a well-rounded set of other skills. The Paul Bunyan-like former football star raised his power game to another gear, bashing 46 homers, including a bomb off Jose Lima to dead center that flew out of the stadium, bounced into the Ohio River, and came to rest somewhere in Kentucky—literally. Dunn also cranked 34 doubles, raised his average 51 points and continued to show impressive athleticism for a man his size. The Reds need to forget about nickel-and-diming and get him inked to a long-term deal, because Adam Dunn is The Franchise.

EDWIN ENCARNACION 3B Bats: R Throws: R Born: 07-Jan-1983 Age: 22

YEAR	TM	LG	AGE	AB	H	2B	3B	HR	BB	SO	SB	CS	AVG	OBP	SLG	MLVR	EQBA	EQOBP	EQSLG	EQMLVR	VORP	DEFENSE
2002	DYT	MDW	19	518	146	32	4	17	40	108	25	7	.282	.338	.458	.147	.231	.276	.385	-.226	-15.9	
2003	POT	CRL	20	215	69	15	1	6	24	32	7	1	.321	.387	.484	.263	.281	.340	.456	.032	15.1	56-3B -9
2003	CHT	SOU	20	254	69	13	1	5	22	44	8	3	.272	.331	.390	.034	.249	.301	.381	-.172	0.7	62-3B -3
2004	CHT	SOU	21	469	132	35	1	13	53	79	17	3	.281	.352	.443	.111	.253	.320	.406	-.098	12.0	115-3B -10
2005	*CIN*	*NL*	*22*	*337*	*88*	*19*	*2*	*11*	*30*	*61*	*7*	*2*	*.260*	*.322*	*.424*	*-.058*	*.258*	*.319*	*.419*	*-.073*	*5.2*	*90-3B -10*

Breakout: 25% *Improve: 50%* *Collapse: 21%*

As one of the youngest players in the Southern League, Encarnacion put up a solid line, showing marked improvement in his power. So why were the Reds going the desperate route in having Austin Kearns try to learn how to play third in a matter of weeks, when their best prospect keeps getting better? Because Encarnacion still needs to improve his defense, and you'd like to see more power and overall growth in his game before he competes for the big league job. Still, he could be ready by 2006, if not sooner, so signing Randa to a modest one-year deal keeps Encarnacion's path clear while mercifully ending the Kearns experiment.

RYAN FREEL Super-UT Bats: R Throws: R Born: 08-Mar-1976 Age: 29

YEAR	TM	LG	AGE	AB	H	2B	3B	HR	BB	SO	SB	CS	AVG	OBP	SLG	MLVR	EQBA	EQOBP	EQSLG	EQMLVR	VORP	DEFENSE
2002	DUR	INT	26	448	117	27	4	8	38	51	37	10	.261	.337	.393	-.002	.244	.319	.377	-.146	3.9	55-2B -5 23-RF 0
2003	LOU	INT	27	215	59	11	1	3	21	32	25	6	.274	.336	.377	-.021	.254	.321	.362	-.156	1.2	36-2B 4
2003	CIN	NL	27	137	39	6	1	4	9	13	9	4	.285	.344	.431	.051	.283	.343	.435	.009	7.5	20-CF 0
2004	CIN	NL	28	505	140	21	8	3	67	88	37	10	.277	.375	.368	.038	.278	.375	.370	-.025	26.9	51-3B -1 37-RF -2
2005	*CIN*	*NL*	*29*	*423*	*114*	*22*	*4*	*7*	*45*	*63*	*23*	*8*	*.268*	*.348*	*.385*	*-.058*	*.267*	*.344*	*.381*	*-.072*	*10.1*	*115-3B 0*

Breakout: 11% *Improve: 28%* *Collapse: 31%*

You'd expect a light-hitting backup who'd never started more than a few games at a time to get exposed when thrust into prolonged regular duty. Not so for Freel, who nearly doubled his walk rate, while showing a decent glove and good speed in soaking up playing lost by Brandon Larson, Ken Griffey Jr., and Austin Kearns. With Joe Randa in the fold, Freel will go back to utility duty; which is one reason this team will have better depth than it's had in a while.

KEN GRIFFEY JR. CF Bats: L Throws: L Born: 21-Nov-1969 Age: 35

YEAR	TM	LG	AGE	AB	H	2B	3B	HR	BB	SO	SB	CS	AVG	OBP	SLG	MLVR	EQBA	EQOBP	EQSLG	EQMLVR	VORP	DEFENSE	
2002	CIN	NL	32	197	52	8	0	8	28	39	1	2	.264	.358	.426	.041	.264	.348	.426	-.010	9.4	41-CF -4	
2003	CIN	NL	33	166	41	12	1	13	27	44	1	0	.247	.370	.566	.248	.246	.367	.563	.192	18.9	36-CF -1	
2004	CIN	NL	34	300	76	18	0	20	44	67	1	0	.253	.351	.513	.181	.256	.347	.508	.094	26.4	66-CF 1	
2005	*CIN*	*NL*	*35*	*270*	*72*	*15*	*1*	*16*	*40*	*62*	*1*	*0*	*.265*	*.363*	*.506*	*.122*	*.263*	*.360*	*.500*	*.106*	*21.6*	*77-CF -5*	

Breakout: 36% Improve: 62% Collapse: 18%

They didn't get the Griffey-for-Phil Nevin deal done in '03, and other trade rumors have fallen by the wayside since then. That's a shame, since the Reds could have used the salary and roster room, even if it meant eating much of his contract. Griffey's injury was even more gut-wrenching in '04., He went on a home-run binge in May that made people think he may be back, only to succumb to a torn hamstring yet again. Though some have suggested shifting him to a corner outfield slot to lower his injury risk, Griffey's gone down so often to sudden, violent injuries, that one wonders if there is any way to prevent his body from breaking down over 162 games. His legacy as a Hall of Famer is secure no matter what happens. That's fortunate, since the odds are heavily against his ever again playing a full season.

JESSE GUTIERREZ 1B Bats: R Throws: R Born: 16-Jun-1978 Age: 27

YEAR	TM	LG	AGE	AB	H	2B	3B	HR	BB	SO	SB	CS	AVG	OBP	SLG	MLVR	EQBA	EQOBP	EQSLG	EQMLVR	VORP	DEFENSE	
2002	DYT	MDW	24	458	125	28	1	13	32	78	2	2	.273	.324	.424	.078	.220	.260	.356	-.305	-25.0		
2003	POT	CRL	25	400	111	26	0	16	22	52	1	2	.278	.325	.463	.117	.233	.270	.414	-.195	-2.7	34-C -7	19-1B -2
2003	CHT	SOU	25	107	23	8	1	4	9	16	0	0	.215	.288	.421	-.028	.194	.258	.389	-.280	-6.5	23-1B -1	
2004	CHT	SOU	26	487	142	32	4	17	36	64	0	0	.292	.352	.478	.166	.267	.320	.444	-.033	7.3	123-1B 7	
2005	*CIN*	*NL*	*27*	*179*	*45*	*9*	*1*	*7*	*10*	*28*	*0*	*0*	*.251*	*.302*	*.422*	*-.101*	*.249*	*.300*	*.418*	*-.116*	*2.7*	*50-1B -2*	

Breakout: 25% Improve: 45% Collapse: 41%

Still listed as a catcher in some circles, Gutierrez played all 124 games last year at first, then did the same in the Arizona Fall League. As with Joey Votto, the hope is that his hitting will develop quicker away from the grind of catching. Unlike Votto, Gutierrez is neither reasonably young nor a candidate for future stardom. Having fared pretty well in both Double-A and the AFL, the Reds will hope he cracks the majors by September to see if he can grow into a useful part-timer with pop.

D'ANGELO JIMENEZ 2B Bats: B Throws: R Born: 21-Dec-1977 Age: 27

YEAR	TM	LG	AGE	AB	H	2B	3B	HR	BB	SO	SB	CS	AVG	OBP	SLG	MLVR	EQBA	EQOBP	EQSLG	EQMLVR	VORP	DEFENSE	
2002	SDP	NL	24	321	77	11	4	3	34	63	4	2	.240	.311	.327	-.134	.252	.321	.351	-.173	4.1	53-2B 0	31-3B 1
2002	CHR	INT	24	157	44	11	1	6	24	14	6	2	.280	.372	.478	.188	.259	.350	.449	.021	11.5	42-SS -7	
2002	CWS	AL	24	108	31	4	3	1	16	10	2	1	.287	.384	.407	.073	.290	.391	.411	.069	8.4	16-2B 2	
2003	CWS	AL	25	271	69	11	5	7	32	46	4	3	.255	.332	.410	-.035	.251	.337	.412	-.059	11.6	64-2B -1	
2003	CIN	NL	25	290	84	13	2	7	34	43	7	4	.290	.365	.421	.087	.290	.365	.424	.040	20.0	72-2B 4	
2004	CIN	NL	26	563	152	28	3	12	82	99	13	7	.270	.364	.394	.053	.269	.363	.395	-.021	35.3	141-2B -7	
2005	*CIN*	*NL*	*27*	*487*	*134*	*25*	*3*	*12*	*63*	*78*	*11*	*4*	*.275*	*.359*	*.413*	*.003*	*.274*	*.355*	*.409*	*-.012*	*23.6*	*131-2B 0*	

Breakout: 10% Improve: 42% Collapse: 12%

Fast becoming one of the most predictable players in the league, Jimenez again showed good on-base skills, doubles power and durability. He's well past the broken neck that stalled his career, though his defense remains below-average. Then again, if he was slick with the leather, Jimenez would be a $7-million-a-year hot commodity, instead of the discarded talent the Reds are happy to have. The Reds signed him to a one-year deal, avoiding arbitration.

AUSTIN KEARNS RF Bats: R Throws: R Born: 20-May-1980 Age: 25

YEAR	TM	LG	AGE	AB	H	2B	3B	HR	BB	SO	SB	CS	AVG	OBP	SLG	MLVR	EQBA	EQOBP	EQSLG	EQMLVR	VORP	DEFENSE	
2002	CIN	NL	22	372	117	24	3	13	54	81	6	3	.315	.407	.500	.259	.309	.401	.503	.230	33.7	83-RF 6	12-LF 0
2003	CIN	NL	23	292	77	11	0	15	41	68	5	2	.264	.364	.455	.105	.266	.359	.454	.050	17.5	42-RF 0	40-CF -1
2004	CIN	NL	24	217	50	10	2	9	28	71	2	1	.230	.321	.419	-.009	.230	.323	.415	-.097	6.2	54-RF -3	
2005	*CIN*	*NL*	*25*	*328*	*94*	*19*	*2*	*16*	*50*	*79*	*5*	*2*	*.286*	*.388*	*.500*	*.172*	*.284*	*.384*	*.494*	*.156*	*29.8*	*93-RF 1*	

Breakout: 31% Improve: 64% Collapse: 13%

It's a sad state of affairs when the Reds can take a pleasant dilemma such as having four good hitters in the outfield and turn it into a potential disaster for two of their best young players, Kearns and Edwin Encarnacion. We're all for creative use of roster space if Kearns could somehow morph into a solid-fielding third baseman, stay healthy, and retain his sweet hitting stroke. Happily, the Joe Randa signing scuttles the thought. The worry now is that Kearns won't have a full-time gig, but the Reds are kidding themselves if they think none of their outfielders will get hurt. Opinions differ on whether Kearns himself will go down or finally make it through the year healthy. He's certainly young enough to shake off the injury-prone tag. PECOTA sees a 90-game season ahead, albeit a huge one. We see closer to 120 games played and the first step back toward stardom.

KENNY KELLY **CF** **Bats: R** **Throws: R** Born: 26-Jan-1979 Age: 26

YEAR	TM	LG	AGE	AB	H	2B	3B	HR	BB	SO	SB	CS	AVG	OBP	SLG	MLVR	EQBA	EQOBP	EQSLG	EQMLVR	VORP	DEFENSE
2002	TAC	PCL	23	391	97	13	10	11	26	93	11	3	.248	.296	.417	-.058	.238	.285	.391	-.196	-15.8	68-RF -5 49-CF -3
2003	TAC	PCL	24	341	84	15	5	13	29	79	20	7	.246	.313	.434	.026	.231	.294	.409	-.159	-9.7	82-RF 7
2003	NOR	INT	24	92	24	6	2	4	6	25	5	0	.261	.306	.500	.139	.239	.293	.467	-.073	-0.2	22-RF 0
2004	CHT	SOU	25	191	68	15	3	5	26	46	13	7	.356	.441	.545	.439	.323	.402	.497	.237	23.2	49-CF 2
2004	LOU	INT	25	268	68	15	4	9	24	71	7	4	.254	.320	.440	-.049	.226	.292	.387	-.197	-4.0	53-CF 1 19-RF 0
2005	*CIN*	*NL*	*26*	*172*	*44*	*9*	*2*	*6*	*15*	*45*	*5*	*2*	*.253*	*.319*	*.428*	*-.061*	*.252*	*.316*	*.424*	*-.076*	*6.3*	*49-CF -2*

Breakout: 20% *Improve: 41%* *Collapse: 38%*

Tore up the Southern League with a .356 average in 51 games, then struggled in Triple-A. Kelly remains a scout's favorite, a former quarterback with big-time speed and flashes of greatness. Now 26 and having bounced through several organizations, though, he won't get many more chances. That .260 Major League Equivalent Average and his other skills make him worth a shot as a fifth outfielder with a little upside.

BARRY LARKIN **SS** **Bats: R** **Throws: R** Born: 28-Apr-1964 Age: 41

YEAR	TM	LG	AGE	AB	H	2B	3B	HR	BB	SO	SB	CS	AVG	OBP	SLG	MLVR	EQBA	EQOBP	EQSLG	EQMLVR	VORP	DEFENSE
2002	CIN	NL	38	507	124	37	2	7	44	57	13	4	.245	.305	.367	-.133	.243	.301	.373	-.187	8.7	122-SS -1
2003	CIN	NL	39	241	68	16	1	2	22	32	2	0	.282	.345	.382	-.006	.278	.343	.382	-.069	12.9	53-SS -5
2004	CIN	NL	40	346	100	15	3	8	34	39	2	0	.289	.352	.419	.091	.285	.349	.418	-.002	26.5	73-SS 2
2005	*CIN*	*NL*	*41*	*197*	*53*	*10*	*1*	*3*	*21*	*23*	*2*	*1*	*.270*	*.341*	*.384*	*-.070*	*.269*	*.337*	*.380*	*-.084*	*9.6*	*56-SS 0*

Breakout: 12% *Improve: 44%* *Collapse: 31%*

Let's hope Carl Lindner learned his lesson. Deluded by thinking fans respond better to an aging symbol of past greatness than to a player who wins ballgames, the three-year, $27 million deal the Reds' owner gave Larkin after the 2001 season—over the protests of several front office members—is an error a team like the Reds can ill afford. Lindner needs to stick to writing checks and not negotiating contracts, before Ryan Freel gets his own private jet or something. A free agent, Larkin put up a nice season before his 40-year-old body knocked him down with injuries. He's a deserving Hall of Famer and one of the best shortstops of all time. Whatever he does from here shouldn't diminish what he was at his peak.

BRANDON LARSON **3B** **Bats: R** **Throws: R** Born: 24-May-1976 Age: 29

YEAR	TM	LG	AGE	AB	H	2B	3B	HR	BB	SO	SB	CS	AVG	OBP	SLG	MLVR	EQBA	EQOBP	EQSLG	EQMLVR	VORP	DEFENSE
2002	LOU	INT	26	297	101	20	1	25	24	70	1	1	.340	.393	.667	.517	.305	.362	.610	.314	42.5	64-3B 0
2002	CIN	NL	26	51	14	2	0	4	6	10	1	0	.275	.362	.549	.204	.294	.348	.549	.191	4.8	
2003	LOU	INT	27	282	91	19	2	20	28	70	3	0	.323	.384	.617	.408	.289	.358	.568	.229	35.3	70-3B 7
2003	CIN	NL	27	89	9	1	0	1	13	31	2	2	.101	.212	.146	-.633	.101	.201	.135	-.773	-11.9	22-3B 3
2004	LOU	INT	28	117	33	5	0	9	5	39	0	0	.282	.315	.556	.122	.243	.266	.470	-.114	2.3	29-3B -1
2004	CIN	NL	28	118	25	6	0	3	14	35	1	0	.212	.304	.339	-.162	.220	.298	.331	-.265	-1.1	26-3B -1
2005	*CIN*	*NL*	*29*	*262*	*68*	*13*	*1*	*15*	*25*	*78*	*2*	*0*	*.258*	*.326*	*.481*	*.023*	*.256*	*.323*	*.476*	*.007*	*11.6*	*71-3B -3*

Breakout: 31% *Improve: 54%* *Collapse: 21%*

All the injuries of Austin Kearns, with a lot less talent. Larson's inability to stay healthy and his struggles on the rare occasions he's stayed upright have snuffed out any chance he may have had of claiming the major league third-base job. That's a shame—the 29 homers he socked in 348 at-bats over two levels at age 26 portended more. Now he'll need to catch a break just to stick on a big league bench.

JASON LaRUE — C — Bats: R — Throws: R — Born: 19-Mar-1974 — Age: 31

YEAR	TM	LG	AGE	AB	H	2B	3B	HR	BB	SO	SB	CS	AVG	OBP	SLG	MLVR	EQBA	EQOBP	EQSLG	EQMLVR	VORP	DEFENSE
2002	CIN	NL	28	353	88	17	1	12	27	117	1	2	.249	.324	.405	-.046	.248	.319	.411	-.097	12.9	99-C 7
2003	CIN	NL	29	379	87	23	1	16	33	111	3	3	.230	.321	.422	-.032	.230	.316	.429	-.091	13.8	107-C -5
2004	CIN	NL	30	390	98	24	2	14	26	108	0	2	.251	.334	.431	.037	.253	.330	.435	-.039	21.1	102-C -4
2005	*CIN*	*NL*	*31*	*296*	*73*	*16*	*1*	*12*	*25*	*83*	*1*	*1*	*.247*	*.327*	*.430*	*-.051*	*.245*	*.324*	*.425*	*-.066*	*11.9*	*81-C -4*

Breakout: 24% *Improve: 48%* *Collapse: 29%*

Like a kid holding his nose while gulping down castor oil, you can try to look past the brutal 4:1 strikeout-to-walk ratio and focus on the curative powers of LaRue's 41 extra-base hits. His .337 OBP, modest as it is, was a career high as he improved for the third consecutive year as a regular. LaRue's defense is another matter. He built a reputation for gunning down would-be basestealers by punching out an astounding 61% in 2001 and 45% in 2002, winning Michael Wolverton's Golden Gun award for catchers both seasons. But he's tossed out a more pedestrian 27% and 30% the last two seasons. Add it all up, and you get a player who's not nearly as good as his best moments, nor as bad as his worst. The Reds brought him back for $3 million, at the high end of what they should be willing to pay.

FELIPE LOPEZ — SS — Bats: B — Throws: R — Born: 12-May-1980 — Age: 25

YEAR	TM	LG	AGE	AB	H	2B	3B	HR	BB	SO	SB	CS	AVG	OBP	SLG	MLVR	EQBA	EQOBP	EQSLG	EQMLVR	VORP	DEFENSE
2002	SYR	INT	22	173	55	11	2	3	29	37	13	0	.318	.419	.457	.246	.289	.390	.428	.090	16.0	43-SS -3
2002	TOR	AL	22	282	64	15	3	8	23	90	5	4	.227	.287	.387	-.151	.229	.294	.391	-.185	3.8	72-SS -3
2003	LOU	INT	23	143	40	11	0	2	12	38	2	5	.280	.333	.399	.007	.246	.298	.352	-.220	-0.8	25-SS -3
2003	CIN	NL	23	197	42	7	2	2	28	59	8	5	.213	.313	.299	-.222	.217	.315	.303	-.271	-1.8	45-SS -9
2004	LOU	INT	24	293	80	11	3	9	25	71	2	2	.273	.329	.423	-.041	.242	.301	.374	-.186	1.5	61-SS -7
2004	CIN	NL	24	264	64	18	2	7	25	81	1	1	.242	.314	.405	-.049	.244	.314	.406	-.116	8.0	47-SS -1 24-3B -2
2005	*CIN*	*NL*	*25*	*283*	*72*	*15*	*2*	*8*	*32*	*75*	*5*	*2*	*.255*	*.333*	*.410*	*-.061*	*.253*	*.330*	*.405*	*-.076*	*13.0*	*78-SS -5*

Breakout: 32% *Improve: 58%* *Collapse: 23%*

Starting to see the light. Lopez's pitch recognition remains a work in progress, but he did flash some of the power that first got him noticed in the minors and earned him his major league debut at age 21. People forget that about Lopez: This will be his fifth season getting significant big league playing time, and though it'll be his first clear shot at a full-time job, and he's still not yet 25. If he stalls from here, Lopez has good power for a shortstop and while he is still eratic in the field, he flashes a strong arm. The Reds envision his hitting from the left side improving and the rough edges on his defense smoothing out. Anyway, they have little to lose because he's cheap, he's talented, and he's an upgrade over a 40-something Barry Larkin. Look for a breakout season.

ANDY MACHADO — SS — Bats: B — Throws: R — Born: 25-Jan-1981 — Age: 24

YEAR	TM	LG	AGE	AB	H	2B	3B	HR	BB	SO	SB	CS	AVG	OBP	SLG	MLVR	EQBA	EQOBP	EQSLG	EQMLVR	VORP	DEFENSE
2002	REA	EAS	21	450	113	24	3	12	72	118	40	11	.251	.353	.398	.020	.221	.316	.357	-.194	1.2	122-SS 8
2003	REA	EAS	22	423	83	19	4	5	108	120	49	15	.196	.360	.296	-.134	.171	.320	.264	-.332	-19.3	121-SS -6
2004	SWB	INT	23	295	67	12	5	6	50	73	11	6	.227	.337	.363	-.107	.209	.317	.330	-.235	-3.1	77-SS 1
2004	LOU	INT	23	109	25	5	2	0	10	26	3	2	.229	.295	.312	-.278	.194	.252	.250	-.483	-9.3	31-SS -6
2004	CIN	NL	23	56	15	5	1	0	10	26	3	1	.268	.379	.393	.070	.286	.366	.357	-.055	4.4	14-SS -1
2005	*CIN*	*NL*	*24*	*333*	*79*	*16*	*3*	*6*	*53*	*89*	*14*	*4*	*.237*	*.343*	*.355*	*-.126*	*.235*	*.340*	*.351*	*-.139*	*8.6*	*95-SS -6*

Breakout: 40% *Improve: 62%* *Collapse: 10%*

Acquired from the Phillies in the Todd Jones deal; if you squint long enough, you can make out the faint glimmer of Jackie Rexrode. Actually, Machado's already done the one-time BP favorite one better, making it to the majors, and at age 23 to boot. That gives him some time to grow into something beyond a no-power waterbug who can field, run and draw walks. He could become anything from a souped-up Steve Jeltz to a utility infielder on a championship team. At press time he was battling Lopez for the starting job at short—Lopez will win it.

CORKY MILLER — C — Bats: R — Throws: R — Born: 18-Mar-1976 — Age: 29

YEAR	TM	LG	AGE	AB	H	2B	3B	HR	BB	SO	SB	CS	AVG	OBP	SLG	MLVR	EQBA	EQOBP	EQSLG	EQMLVR	VORP	DEFENSE
2002	LOU	INT	26	134	31	5	0	6	16	21	1	2	.231	.340	.403	-.007	.199	.294	.353	-.256	-3.3	38-C -2
2002	CIN	NL	26	114	29	10	0	3	9	20	0	0	.254	.328	.421	-.002	.261	.318	.417	-.080	5.8	34-C 4
2003	LOU	INT	27	354	88	28	0	11	35	58	0	0	.249	.326	.421	.001	.220	.295	.390	-.191	-1.9	97-C -5
2003	CIN	NL	27	30	8	0	0	0	5	7	0	0	.267	.395	.267	-.069	.367	.334	.367	-.034	1.0	
2004	LOU	INT	28	227	50	14	0	6	25	44	0	0	.220	.316	.361	-.181	.190	.277	.305	-.359	-13.1	52-C 6
2004	CIN	NL	28	39	1	0	0	0	6	12	0	0	.026	.204	.026	-.805	.051	.165	.051	-.965	-7.1	12-C 0
2005	*MIN*	*AL*	*29*	*203*	*46*	*10*	*0*	*6*	*18*	*41*	*0*	*0*	*.227*	*.306*	*.369*	*-.172*	*.226*	*.307*	*.374*	*-.177*	*2.0*	*58-C -3*

Breakout: 40% *Improve: 61%* *Collapse: 25%*

Another one who didn't quite pan out while perennially riding the Louisville-Cincinnati shuttle. Miller sealed his fate with a brutal 1-for-39 season in Cincy. Rany Jazayerli likes to say that any backup catcher with some degree of skill can put up a magical season given 200 or fewer at-bats—the same holds true for a disastrous season, though a .026 average is pushing it. Still, Miller's shown a pulse in the past, and Minnesota should at least get an upgrade over a 67-year-old Pat Borders.

JAVON MORAN — CF — Bats: R — Throws: R — Born: 30-Sep-1982 — Age: 22

YEAR	TM	LG	AGE	AB	H	2B	3B	HR	BB	SO	SB	CS	AVG	OBP	SLG	MLVR	EQBA	EQOBP	EQSLG	EQMLVR	VORP	DEFENSE
2003	BAT	NYP	20	250	71	9	3	1	16	32	27	11	.284	.326	.356	.050	.244	.277	.315	-.315	-23.8	46-CF -2 13-LF -1
2004	LWD	SAL	21	421	120	18	9	2	24	78	41	17	.285	.340	.385	.058	.262	.299	.348	-.213	-8.3	81-CF -5 18-RF -2
2004	DYT	MDW	21	94	36	2	0	0	10	15	11	3	.383	.448	.404	.263	.269	.306	.280	-.293	-4.3	21-CF -1
2005	*CIN*	*NL*	*22*	*358*	*86*	*16*	*3*	*2*	*17*	*67*	*14*	*6*	*.240*	*.285*	*.320*	*-.275*	*.239*	*.283*	*.317*	*-.288*	*-11.9*	*93-CF -6*

Breakout: 7% *Improve: 24%* *Collapse: 50%*

Another acquisition from the Phillies, Moran came over in the Cory Lidle trade and promptly dazzled the Reds' brass with a .383 average and blinding speed over 25 games in Dayton. The one-time Auburn Tiger ran a 6.37-second 60-yard dash last year in spring training and stole 50 bases in just his second professional season. Needs to work on drawing more walks to work his magic on the basepaths, but the Reds already like his developing pitch-recognition skills.

RAINER OLMEDO — SS/2B — Bats: B — Throws: R — Born: 31-May-1981 — Age: 24

YEAR	TM	LG	AGE	AB	H	2B	3B	HR	BB	SO	SB	CS	AVG	OBP	SLG	MLVR	EQBA	EQOBP	EQSLG	EQMLVR	VORP	DEFENSE
2002	CHT	SOU	21	478	118	21	1	3	53	86	15	16	.247	.331	.314	-.090	.224	.291	.298	-.322	-17.8	107-SS 1 21-2B 1
2003	CHT	SOU	22	160	47	11	0	2	14	29	3	3	.294	.349	.400	.089	.268	.308	.378	-.149	2.7	43-SS -3
2003	CIN	NL	22	230	55	6	1	0	13	46	1	1	.239	.280	.274	-.305	.245	.279	.270	-.375	-6.6	43-SS -8 14-2B 0
2004	LOU	INT	23	294	84	13	7	2	23	40	2	3	.286	.342	.398	-.044	.258	.317	.361	-.163	1.1	59-2B 7 23-SS -3
2005	*CIN*	*NL*	*24*	*256*	*64*	*12*	*2*	*3*	*21*	*41*	*2*	*1*	*.249*	*.308*	*.345*	*-.196*	*.247*	*.305*	*.341*	*-.209*	*1.6*	*70-SS -3*

Breakout: 16% *Improve: 36%* *Collapse: 40%*

Major elbow injuries aren't just for pitchers anymore—bad news for Olmedo, great news for Drs. Andrews, Yocum, Jobe, et. al. A mid-season elbow strain presaged a complete tear of his ulnar collateral ligament in the Venezuelan Winter League, and Olmedo got TJ'd in November. With a far shorter recovery time than is typical for pitchers, he could be back just after Opening Day. After making decent strides at the plate in Louisville, Olmedo could be a useful caddy for Felipe Lopez and defensive replacement for D'Angelo Jimenez.

WILY MO PENA — OF — Bats: R — Throws: R — Born: 23-Jan-1982 — Age: 23

YEAR	TM	LG	AGE	AB	H	2B	3B	HR	BB	SO	SB	CS	AVG	OBP	SLG	MLVR	EQBA	EQOBP	EQSLG	EQMLVR	VORP	DEFENSE
2002	CHT	SOU	20	388	99	23	1	11	36	126	8	0	.255	.330	.405	.034	.231	.287	.391	-.197	-16.9	42-LF -3 30-CF -2
2003	LOU	INT	21	51	19	3	0	4	5	13	0	0	.373	.450	.667	.615	.314	.371	.588	.307	7.1	11-CF -2
2003	CIN	NL	21	165	36	6	1	5	12	53	3	2	.218	.283	.358	-.186	.217	.280	.367	-.253	-2.9	22-CF 0 10-RF -1
2004	CIN	NL	22	336	87	10	1	26	22	108	5	2	.259	.316	.527	.145	.258	.315	.528	.069	23.5	34-RF -3 46-CF 4
2005	*CIN*	*NL*	*23*	*340*	*96*	*18*	*2*	*21*	*30*	*99*	*7*	*2*	*.281*	*.351*	*.528*	*.146*	*.279*	*.347*	*.522*	*.129*	*29.3*	*91-CF -4*

Breakout: 53% *Improve: 73%* *Collapse: 15%*

(continued next page)

Wily Mo Pena *(continued)*

Being an inanimate algorithm conceived in the dark recesses of Nate Silver's brain, PECOTA hasn't yet shown the ability to brag. That's too bad, because the forecasting system's 2004 projection for Pena was terrifyingly accurate. Given a chance to play every day due to multiple outfield injuries, Wily Mo amassed a line of .259/.316/.527 over 336 at-bats; his PECOTA projection was .271/.340/.509, in 309 at-bats. Like every forecasting system, PECOTA's going to be wrong often enough—if it weren't, Nate would have long ago bought a small South Pacific island and named it Silvertania. But the system saw a player with precocious power and speed—two of the best markers for success in a prospect—and looked past a litany of warts that included a 177-strikeout season in the Midwest League in 2001. We share PECOTA's call of more of the same, though playing time will be scarce until Griffey goes down again or Kearns gets dealt. If Pena can ever learn to lay off bad pitches . . . well, a certain 574-homer guy with a hop-step home run dance looked pretty similar back when he was young—only when Sammy had his breakout season he was two years older than Wily Mo would be if he had his in 2005.

MIGUEL PEREZ C **Bats: R** **Throws: R** Born: 25-Sep-1983 Age: 21

YEAR	TM	LG	AGE	AB	H	2B	3B	HR	BB	SO	SB	CS	AVG	OBP	SLG	MLVR	EQBA	EQOBP	EQSLG	EQMLVR	VORP	DEFENSE
2003	DYT	MDW	19	58	10	0	0	0	4	19	1	0	.172	.273	.172	-.349	.115	.147	.115	-.915	-13.4	18-C -1
2003	BIL	PIO	19	227	77	11	2	1	18	27	1	1	.339	.410	.419	.222	.262	.311	.324	-.224	-6.3	58-C -2
2004	DYT	MDW	20	249	59	7	0	1	16	62	2	2	.237	.309	.277	-.194	.186	.236	.221	-.559	-29.3	71-C 0
2004	POT	CRL	20	69	16	2	0	0	1	12	1	0	.232	.239	.261	-.336	.162	.150	.176	-.812	-12.6	15-C -3
2005	*CIN*	*NL*	*21*	*256*	*51*	*9*	*1*	*1*	*12*	*61*	*1*	*1*	*.198*	*.264*	*.256*	*-.421*	*.197*	*.262*	*.253*	*-.432*	*-14.7*	*69-C -4*

Breakout: 26% *Improve: 41%* *Collapse: 43%*

Considered the best catching prospect in the system by scouts, but you'd like to see the numbers start to match up. The observational crowd points to his strong 6′3″, 190-pound frame and his projectable swing and sees a future power hitter; we see two homers in his four-year pro career. Of course there are mitigating factors in play, or he wouldn't be in this book: Perez doesn't turn 22 until September, catchers tend to master hitting later, and the Reds rave about his catch-and-throw ability—which would be a lot handier if teams actually tried to steal bases anymore. But remember this is the same team still trying to get over taking Chris Gruler #3 overall in '02, ahead of Zach Greinke, Prince Fielder, Khalil Greene, Scott Kazmir, and many others—maybe they're due for those rose-colored glasses to start paying dividends.

JASON ROMANO UT **Bats: R** **Throws: R** Born: 24-Jun-1979 Age: 26

YEAR	TM	LG	AGE	AB	H	2B	3B	HR	BB	SO	SB	CS	AVG	OBP	SLG	MLVR	EQBA	EQOBP	EQSLG	EQMLVR	VORP	DEFENSE
2002	OKL	PCL	23	196	53	8	1	4	19	41	10	3	.270	.329	.383	-.031	.254	.311	.355	-.186	-2.1	23-CF 0 17-2B -2
2002	TEX	AL	23	54	11	4	0	0	4	13	2	0	.204	.254	.278	-.395	.208	.232	.226	-.552	-2.4	
2002	CSP	PCL	23	129	40	7	2	0	6	27	8	3	.310	.338	.395	-.070	.238	.261	.286	-.393	-9.0	15-CF -1
2003	LVG	PCL	24	216	66	18	4	4	11	32	10	6	.306	.336	.481	.090	.263	.297	.418	-.116	2.0	24-CF 0
2004	LOU	INT	25	163	55	12	4	2	3	24	3	1	.337	.347	.497	.148	.308	.323	.453	.023	7.9	36-CF 0
2004	CIN	NL	25	26	4	0	0	1	2	10	0	0	.154	.214	.269	-.468	.154	.179	.269	-.624	-2.2	
2005	*CIN*	*NL*	*26*	*215*	*55*	*12*	*2*	*4*	*9*	*40*	*5*	*1*	*.255*	*.286*	*.383*	*-.179*	*.254*	*.283*	*.379*	*-.193*	*-2.2*	*57-CF -3*

Breakout: 16% *Improve: 29%* *Collapse: 45%*

Needs to catch a break. A one-time second-base prospect, Romano's become a jack-of-all-trades, able to accomplish none of them in '04 after a slow start and a torn hammy made for a lost season. Not yet 26, he's still young enough to forge a tidy career as an outfield reserve, with gusts up to useful contributions if needed as an injury fill-in a few weeks at a time. After surgery to reattach the top of his right hamstring to the bone (ouch!) and a successful rehab, the Reds re-signed him to a minor league deal.

DANE SARDINHA C **Bats: R** **Throws: R** Born: 08-Apr-1979 Age: 26

YEAR	TM	LG	AGE	AB	H	2B	3B	HR	BB	SO	SB	CS	AVG	OBP	SLG	MLVR	EQBA	EQOBP	EQSLG	EQMLVR	VORP	DEFENSE
2002	CHT	SOU	23	394	81	20	0	4	14	114	0	2	.206	.234	.287	-.303	.183	.197	.268	-.576	-46.1	100-C -1
2003	CHT	SOU	24	246	63	15	0	3	22	61	5	3	.256	.313	.354	-.051	.225	.271	.321	-.330	-12.0	69-C 4
2004	LOU	INT	25	324	85	17	1	9	10	94	0	1	.262	.294	.404	-.137	.234	.268	.359	-.277	-9.7	70-C 2
2005	*CIN*	*NL*	*26*	*172*	*36*	*7*	*1*	*4*	*7*	*49*	*0*	*0*	*.212*	*.246*	*.336*	*-.342*	*.210*	*.244*	*.333*	*-.355*	*-9.2*	*47-C -4*

Breakout: 24% *Improve: 37%* *Collapse: 47%*

A strong defensive catcher with lousy plate discipline and decent pop—sounds like a younger version of Jason LaRue. His decent '04 showing has made things tough on the Reds: Sardinha's too good to be glibly discarded into the Rule 5 dustbin, but not yet good enough to claim a major league starting job. Adding him to the 40-man and letting Sardinha duke it out with Miguel Perez, Ryan Hanigan and Brian Peterson for organizational pecking order behind the plate is the Reds' best bet.

ROB STRATTON RF **Bats: R** **Throws: R** Born: 07-Oct-1977 Age: 27

YEAR	TM	LG	AGE	AB	H	2B	3B	HR	BB	SO	SB	CS	AVG	OBP	SLG	MLVR	EQBA	EQOBP	EQSLG	EQMLVR	VORP	DEFENSE
2002	NOR	INT	24	256	63	8	0	20	18	84	6	3	.246	.305	.512	.128	.230	.284	.479	-.080	-1.2	56-RF -3 14-LF 1
2002	CSP	PCL	24	80	17	2	1	7	6	42	0	1	.212	.308	.525	-.026	.188	.270	.438	-.196	-3.1	18-RF -1
2003	ABQ	PCL	25	372	79	12	2	32	36	175	6	4	.212	.283	.513	-.078	.166	.238	.406	-.314	-27.8	85-RF -3
2004	FRE	PCL	26	109	20	3	0	3	2	54	1	0	.183	.204	.294	-.593	.150	.162	.224	-.724	-19.4	15-RF -1
2004	LOU	INT	26	119	42	10	2	12	9	35	0	1	.353	.392	.773	.623	.310	.355	.681	.413	17.1	14-RF 0
2005	*CIN*	*NL*	*27*	*184*	*42*	*8*	*1*	*12*	*16*	*85*	*2*	*1*	*.229*	*.299*	*.475*	*-.052*	*.227*	*.297*	*.470*	*-.068*	*5.0*	*52-RF -4*

Breakout: 55% *Improve: 69%* *Collapse: 17%*

Stratton has spent his entire career swinging for the moon, often hitting monster homers when he makes contact, whiffing at astounding rates when he doesn't, and not collecting enough walks or other hits to offset his weakness. After joining the Reds in July following his release from the Giants, he widened his stance and began driving the ball up the middle, shocking scouts and fueling a .353 average—with his power well intact—over 34 games in Louisville. Call it a forced epiphany: When you're sitting home unemployed and your livelihood's at stake, there's often no other choice but to change. If he gets a shot with the big club this year he could instantly become the Reds' most dangerous pinch-hitter and a batting-practice treat.

JAVIER VALENTIN C **Bats: B** **Throws: R** Born: 19-Sep-1975 Age: 29

YEAR	TM	LG	AGE	AB	H	2B	3B	HR	BB	SO	SB	CS	AVG	OBP	SLG	MLVR	EQBA	EQOBP	EQSLG	EQMLVR	VORP	DEFENSE
2002	EDM	PCL	26	455	130	33	1	21	41	96	0	1	.286	.346	.501	.165	.259	.317	.454	-.031	19.7	69-C -2
2003	TBY	AL	27	135	30	7	1	3	5	31	0	0	.222	.254	.356	-.267	.224	.259	.366	-.291	-2.3	37-C -1
2004	CIN	NL	28	202	47	10	1	6	17	36	0	0	.233	.293	.381	-.116	.233	.292	.381	-.200	3.1	48-C 1
2005	*CIN*	*NL*	*29*	*208*	*52*	*11*	*1*	*7*	*17*	*43*	*0*	*0*	*.249*	*.310*	*.406*	*-.110*	*.248*	*.307*	*.402*	*-.124*	*3.3*	*57-C -5*

Breakout: 27% *Improve: 51%* *Collapse: 26%*

Got off to a horrendous start and never really recovered. They weren't going to win the Wild Card much less catch the world-beating Cardinals last year, but the 241 at-bats of misery that Valentin and Corky Miller inflicted on the Reds didn't help the club in its unsuccessful quest for .500 either. Of course a lot of the blame goes to Valentin's splits: .109/.146/.109 vs. lefties, .269/.333/.462 vs. righties. Still has enough pop to pull a 15-homer season at some point, if given the playing time.

JOHN VANDER WAL Retired **Bats: L** **Throws: L** Born: 29-Apr-1966 Age: 39

YEAR	TM	LG	AGE	AB	H	2B	3B	HR	BB	SO	SB	CS	AVG	OBP	SLG	MLVR	EQBA	EQOBP	EQSLG	EQMLVR	VORP	DEFENSE
2002	NYY	AL	36	219	57	17	1	6	23	58	1	1	.260	.327	.429	.004	.266	.337	.445	-.002	6.1	40-RF -4
2003	MIL	NL	37	327	84	25	1	14	46	104	1	2	.257	.350	.468	.093	.254	.347	.468	.038	14.8	69-RF -2
2004	CIN	NL	38	51	6	2	0	2	4	20	0	0	.118	.182	.275	-.541	.118	.167	.255	-.683	-4.9	

Today is gonna be the day
That he'll slap a pinch-hit single for you
By now you should've somehow
Wondered how at 34 he slugged .562
I don't believe that anybody
Thought he'd last 14 years except his mom
. . . Because maybe
We tip our caps to his playing
And after all
He was our Vander Wal

JOEY VOTTO 1B **Bats: L** **Throws: R** Born: 10-Sep-1983 Age: 21

YEAR	TM	LG	AGE	AB	H	2B	3B	HR	BB	SO	SB	CS	AVG	OBP	SLG	MLVR	EQBA	EQOBP	EQSLG	EQMLVR	VORP	DEFENSE
2003	DYT	MDW	19	195	45	8	0	1	34	64	2	5	.231	.348	.287	-.078	.175	.268	.220	-.497	-27.5	48-1B -4
2003	BIL	PIO	19	240	76	17	3	6	56	80	4	0	.317	.452	.487	.361	.245	.350	.365	-.102	-2.9	61-1B -8
2004	DYT	MDW	20	391	118	26	2	14	79	110	9	2	.302	.419	.486	.261	.243	.345	.395	-.073	1.4	87-1B -3
2004	POT	CRL	20	84	25	7	0	5	11	21	1	1	.298	.385	.560	.331	.238	.300	.464	-.066	0.5	19-1B 0
2005	*CIN*	*AL*	*21*	*335*	*78*	*16*	*1*	*10*	*43*	*107*	*3*	*1*	*.233*	*.324*	*.375*	*-.128*	*.230*	*.324*	*.373*	*-.143*	*-1.5*	*92-1B -9*

Breakout: 23% *Improve: 42%* *Collapse: 35%*

The Reds' second-round pick out of Toronto in 2002, Votto is the best pure hitter in the organization. Though considered raw due to his limited baseball background, he's already shown a great batting eye, walking 90 times over two levels in '04. He followed four months of terrorizing Midwest League pitching by excelling at Potomac, generating ample power from his 6′3″, 200-pound frame. You could quibble and say the organization gave up on him as a catcher too soon—Votto caught a dozen games as a catcher as a senior in high school and showed decent instincts at the position. But the Reds felt he'd advance quicker and hit better by shifting to first base. At this rate, he'll be Sean Casey's more powerful replacement in 2007.

PITCHERS

JOSE ACEVEDO **Bats: R** **Throws: R** Born: 18-Dec-1977 Age: 27

YEAR	TM	LG	AGE	G	GS	IP	H	BB	SO	HR	ERA	EQERA	EQH9	EQBB9	EQSO9	EQHR9	PERA	VORP	STF
2002	LOU	INT	24	23	23	154.7	146	34	128	16	3.20	4.06	8.8	2.2	6.5	1.3	4.18	23.1	18
2002	CIN	NL	24	6	5	23.7	28	12	14	8	7.22	7.54	11.1	4.0	4.8	3.2	7.54	-6.6	-14
2003	LOU	INT	25	29	3	60.3	56	20	57	5	3.43	4.24	8.5	3.5	6.9	1.1	4.24	8.7	10
2003	CIN	NL	25	5	4	27.0	17	6	23	3	2.67	2.52	6.8	1.8	7.2	1.1	2.88	9.1	33
2004	CIN	NL	26	39	27	157.7	188	45	117	30	5.94	6.03	10.0	2.3	5.9	1.6	4.98	-7.1	2
2005	*CIN*	*NL*	*27*	*24*	*16*	*104.0*	*112*	*33*	*76*	*18*	*5.05*	*5.40*	*9.9*	*2.5*	*5.9*	*1.4*	*5.20*	*5.0*	*2*

Breakout: 16% *Improve: 35%* *Collapse: 34%*

Acevedo	IP	H	HR	BB	K	ERA
As Starter	140.2	181	30	44	107	6.65
As Reliever	17	7	0	1	10	0.00

At first glance you might be inclined to discount those numbers due to small sample size, and 17 innings doesn't tell us everything we'd want to know, especially when they're mostly September innings. But Acevedo also limited hitters to a .254/.287/.361 AVG/OBP/SLG on pitches 1–15 of a game; he got strafed at a .301/.355/.507 rate the rest of the time. Even accounting for some of those 1–15 pitches being thrown in relief, that's still a telling trend; the Reds say Acevedo pared his repertoire after switching to relief, to rave reviews. It's a tough call for the organization: They're starved for quality starting pitching, and Acevedo has maintained strong K/BB rates throughout his major league and minor league career. But while his hit rate will come down (he yielded an abnormally high .318 average on balls in play), Acevedo's shown an inability to keep the ball in the park (1.7 HR/9 IP in 304.1 big league innings) and that's killed his best efforts. Don Gullett and company need to go the extra mile to solve Acevedo's gopheritis—a good reliever is handy to have around, but there's a front-line starter begging to come out here.

HOMER BAILEY **Bats: R** **Throws: R** Born: 03-May-1986 Age: 19

You'd think the Reds' recent history of failures in drafting high school pitchers in the first round—Chris Gruler's only the most recent damning tale—would be enough to sway them toward a different way of thinking in 2004. You'd think all the studies showing the higher success rates of every other stripe of amateur draftee—high school hitter, college hitter, college pitcher—would make them reconsider the move more likely to fail than any other. Instead, they went back to the well. After all, Bailey's a 6′4″, 185-pound specimen from LaGrange. Texas! That's where Josh Beckett comes from! And Roger Clemens! And Nolan Ryan! Bailey's young and talented enough that you can close your eyes and wishcast anything for him. Given the precedents in play, we'll take the under.

MATT BELISLE

Bats: B **Throws: R** Born: 06-Jun-1980 Age: 25

YEAR	TM	LG	AGE	G	GS	IP	H	BB	SO	HR	ERA	EQERA	EQH9	EQBB9	EQSO9	EQHR9	PERA	VORP	STF
2002	GRN	SOU	22	26	26	159.3	162	39	123	18	4.35	5.88	10.5	2.2	5.3	2.0	5.76	-2.6	-8
2003	GRN	SOU	23	21	21	125.3	128	42	94	5	3.52	5.16	9.6	3.1	4.8	0.7	4.78	10.8	1
2003	RIC	INT	23	3	3	20.0	17	0	10	1	2.25	3.44	8.3	0.5	3.9	0.5	2.95	5.4	15
2003	LOU	INT	23	4	4	26.0	31	5	15	2	3.81	5.33	9.9	1.8	4.3	1.1	4.62	2.8	2
2004	LOU	INT	24	28	28	162.7	192	51	106	16	5.26	5.33	9.8	2.9	4.7	1.0	4.88	12.7	-4
2005	*CIN*	*NL*	*25*	*19*	*11*	*73.7*	*81*	*25*	*50*	*10*	*4.75*	*5.08*	*10.1*	*2.7*	*5.4*	*1.1*	*5.11*	*5.4*	*-1*

Breakout: 13% *Improve: 38%* *Collapse: 19%*

Getting Belisle for Kent Mercker in a late-season dump trade with the Braves in 2003 was the kind of move teams like the Reds need to make to help themselves. So far the deal only looks good on paper, after Belisle gave up 1.5 baserunners per inning in Louisville. Whether it's the result of struggling at higher levels or the residual effects of his injury, Belisle has grown more and more mediocre every year since missing all of 2001 due to a ruptured disc in his back. He's still got time to turn it around.

JUNG BONG

Bats: L **Throws: L** Born: 15-Jul-1980 Age: 24

YEAR	TM	LG	AGE	G	GS	IP	H	BB	SO	HR	ERA	EQERA	EQH9	EQBB9	EQSO9	EQHR9	PERA	VORP	STF
2002	GRN	SOU	21	27	17	122.0	136	45	107	6	3.25	5.14	10.0	3.1	5.8	0.8	4.99	8.0	-5
2003	ATL	NL	22	44	0	57.0	56	31	47	8	5.05	5.04	9.1	4.4	6.8	1.1	5.04	3.6	-5
2004	LOU	INT	23	19	19	94.3	118	31	65	13	5.82	5.85	10.3	3.0	5.0	1.3	5.46	1.4	-9
2004	CIN	NL	23	3	3	15.3	17	10	11	3	4.71	7.20	9.6	5.4	6.0	1.8	6.00	-3.2	-11
2005	*CIN*	*NL*	*24*	*31*	*6*	*64.3*	*70*	*26*	*46*	*9*	*4.87*	*5.21*	*10.0*	*3.2*	*5.8*	*1.1*	*5.22*	*3.6*	*-6*

Breakout: 13% *Improve: 47%* *Collapse: 18%*

After a worrisome shoulder injury that portended disaster, Bong made it through with just a relatively routine one-hour arthroscopic procedure to clean out debris surrounding his labrum. It's hoped that the procedure will clear the way for an improved 2005 season—Bong's numbers the last few years don't equal what you'd expect from a legitimate pitching prospect. The Reds still envision Bong harnessing his low-90s fastball and crafty change-up into major league success, though most likely in the bullpen.

BRANDON CLAUSSEN

Bats: L **Throws: L** Born: 01-May-1979 Age: 26

YEAR	TM	LG	AGE	G	GS	IP	H	BB	SO	HR	ERA	EQERA	EQH9	EQBB9	EQSO9	EQHR9	PERA	VORP	STF
2002	COH	INT	23	15	15	93.3	85	46	73	4	3.28	5.04	7.9	4.9	6.0	0.5	3.32	22.6	25
2003	COH	INT	24	11	11	68.7	53	18	39	4	2.75	4.16	8.0	2.9	4.3	0.9	3.73	13.0	18
2003	LOU	INT	24	3	3	15.7	17	6	16	3	7.45	7.36	9.8	4.3	7.4	2.5	6.14	-0.9	5
2004	LOU	INT	25	18	18	100.3	98	47	111	10	4.67	4.72	8.5	4.3	8.0	0.9	4.44	12.5	17
2004	CIN	NL	25	14	14	66.0	80	35	45	9	6.14	6.55	10.0	4.1	5.3	1.1	5.32	-7.7	-5
2005	*CIN*	*NL*	*26*	*20*	*17*	*101.3*	*101*	*50*	*80*	*13*	*4.99*	*5.33*	*9.2*	*3.9*	*6.4*	*1.1*	*5.13*	*4.7*	*5*

Breakout: 15% *Improve: 44%* *Collapse: 29%*

More than a few smart folks had him pegged as a sleeper Rookie of the Year candidate after his excellent '03 campaign, but the Reds' rotational vortex of doom had other ideas. How long will we have to wait before we see another Jose Rijo or Mario Soto? The Reds have started to acquire and develop some promising pitching prospects, to little avail. The fate of Claussen, and down the line Richie Gardner, Thomas Pauly, and others, should ultimately decide Don Gullett's future.

TODD COFFEY

Bats: R **Throws: R** Born: 09-Sep-1980 Age: 24

YEAR	TM	LG	AGE	G	GS	IP	H	BB	SO	HR	ERA	EQERA	EQH9	EQBB9	EQSO9	EQHR9	PERA	VORP	STF
2002	DYT	MDW	21	38	5	80.3	78	25	62	8	3.59	5.50	10.8	3.6	4.4	2.4	6.62	-8.2	-30
2003	DYT	MDW	22	39	0	56.0	61	14	53	1	2.25	4.86	9.7	2.7	5.5	0.5	4.53	6.4	-10
2003	POT	CRL	22	11	0	23.0	16	3	21	0	1.96	3.38	7.2	1.3	6.3	0.4	2.53	7.3	7
2004	CHT	SOU	23	40	0	45.3	36	4	53	3	2.38	3.43	8.4	0.9	7.5	0.9	3.43	10.1	7
2004	LOU	INT	23	15	0	13.7	15	2	11	1	5.26	4.72	9.4	1.4	6.1	0.7	4.05	2.3	0
2005	*CIN*	*NL*	*24*	*38*	*2*	*57.7*	*60*	*15*	*46*	*8*	*4.28*	*4.57*	*9.5*	*2.1*	*6.3*	*1.2*	*4.60*	*8.1*	*0*

Breakout: 16% *Improve: 45%* *Collapse: 26%*

(continued next page)

Todd Coffey *(continued)*

Finally seems to have found his niche as a minor league closer. He turned heads with a 53:4 K:BB rate at Double-A Chattanooga before earning a promotion to Louisville, where he held his own. The Reds liked his performance and stuff—Coffey brews a mid-90s fastball and sharp slider out of the pen—enough to add him to the 40-man roster, send him to the Arizona Fall League and consider him a viable bullpen candidate for 2005. Bonus points for adding velocity while simultaneously shedding 40 pounds last season. Here's hoping he doesn't go all Anna Nicole "Do you like my body?!" on us.

SETH ETHERTON **Bats: R** **Throws: R** Born: 17-Oct-1976 Age: 28

YEAR	TM	LG	AGE	G	GS	IP	H	BB	SO	HR	ERA	EQERA	EQH9	EQBB9	EQSO9	EQHR9	PERA	VORP	STF
2003	LOU	INT	26	21	21	123.3	144	26	69	11	4.31	4.84	9.9	2.1	4.0	1.1	4.76	11.1	0
2003	CIN	NL	26	7	7	30.0	39	15	17	4	6.90	6.60	10.5	3.9	4.5	1.2	5.40	-4.0	-8
2004	CHT	SOU	27	7	7	41.0	31	9	46	2	1.98	3.55	7.8	2.1	7.1	0.7	3.55	8.7	28
2004	LOU	INT	27	19	19	111.7	107	32	110	13	3.46	3.53	8.6	2.7	7.3	1.2	4.12	17.6	22
2005	*OAK*	*AL*	*28*	*23*	*13*	*89.7*	*94*	*29*	*67*	*15*	*4.86*	*4.81*	*9.5*	*2.6*	*6.0*	*1.4*	*4.76*	*11.3*	*3*

Breakout: 9% *Improve: 39%* *Collapse: 18%*

The one-time Angels prospect was another Cincy experiment, with the Redlegs hoping to buck the formidable odds against them and resurrect a pitcher after a torn labrum. The other similarly hopeful comeback was that of the Mariners' Gil Meche; he looked like he might return to his old self for about five minutes. Etherton made a better case for himself, though, hiking his strikeout rate up, keeping his walks down, and showing enough durability to fire off three complete games. The A's took notice. Etherton could be a useful bullpen righty or even a fill-in starter with two of The Big Three gone and rookies a'plenty in their stead.

RICHIE GARDNER **Bats: R** **Throws: R** Born: 01-Feb-1982 Age: 23

YEAR	TM	LG	AGE	G	GS	IP	H	BB	SO	HR	ERA	EQERA	EQH9	EQBB9	EQSO9	EQHR9	PERA	VORP	STF
2004	POT	CRL	22	18	12	86.3	77	13	80	3	2.50	4.33	8.6	1.6	6.0	0.6	3.22	21.4	19
2004	CHT	SOU	22	11	11	70.3	68	13	59	7	2.56	3.86	9.5	1.8	5.4	1.2	4.68	6.7	8
2005	*CIN*	*NL*	*23*	*16*	*13*	*81.3*	*86*	*22*	*58*	*10*	*4.25*	*4.54*	*9.7*	*2.1*	*5.7*	*1.0*	*4.52*	*10.2*	*8*

Breakout: 8% *Improve: 45%* *Collapse: 27%*

Stud. In his first professional season, Gardner fanned 139 and walked just 26 over 156 innings, ending the season at Double-A. The Reds thought so highly of Gardner they didn't bother sending him to instructional league. He's got a good move to first, fields his position well, throws a plus slider, plus change-up and a plus sinking fastball. He's one of the most underrated pitching prospects in the game, and the Reds intend to push him quickly.

This whole feel-good story almost never happened. When the Reds made Gardner their sixth-round pick out of the University of Arizona in 2003, the team wavered on whether or not to sign him. Sure, the big club's starting pitching had been abysmal for years, and the farm system desperately needed an influx of talent. But this was the year the team opted to tighten its belt, with the Reds planning to hold the line on draft bonuses. It took an 11th-hour plea with COO John Allen to convince the club to pay Gardner's bonus . . . all $160,000 of it. Yes, the team that signed a 37-year-old Barry Larkin to a three-year, $27 million deal, that pleaded for years for a palatial new stadium to hike team revenue and afford better talent, almost walked away from signing Gardner because it didn't want to pay the equivalent of half the major league minimum salary for one season. And you wonder why the Reds are in the mess they're in.

DANNY GRAVES **Bats: R** **Throws: R** Born: 07-Aug-1973 Age: 31

YEAR	TM	LG	AGE	G	GS	IP	H	BB	SO	HR	ERA	EQERA	EQH9	EQBB9	EQSO9	EQHR9	PERA	VORP	STF
2002	CIN	NL	28	68	4	98.7	99	25	58	7	3.19	3.41	9.0	2.0	4.7	0.7	3.88	22.2	-1
2003	CIN	NL	29	30	26	169.0	204	41	60	30	5.33	5.51	10.6	1.9	2.9	1.5	5.29	-1.1	-15
2004	CIN	NL	30	68	0	68.3	77	13	40	12	3.95	5.05	9.8	1.5	4.8	1.5	4.64	4.3	-12
2005	*CIN*	*NL*	*31*	*34*	*3*	*58.3*	*67*	*15*	*30*	*8*	*4.88*	*5.22*	*10.5*	*2.0*	*4.1*	*1.2*	*5.07*	*3.7*	*-14*

Breakout: 19% *Improve: 44%* *Collapse: 28%*

Now that the ill-fated move to convert Graves to starting is behind them, the Reds stuck with Graves all year as the team's closer, to phenomenal success . . . or at least that's what you'd think if you looked only at his 41 saves for the year, or his 28 saves through the season's first two months. Looking at our own Reliever Expected Wins Added, we see that Graves finished eighth among relievers—on his own team. The litany of hits and homers allowed by Graves made him barely better than a replacement-level pitcher last year. They're stuck with him at $6.25 million for 2005, plus a mutual option with an escalating buyout for '06. If the Reds were a gambler, they'd be the guy hitting on 17 and parlaying a Devil Rays–Bobcats combo.

CARLOS GUEVARA **Bats: R** **Throws: R** Born: 18-Mar-1982 Age: 23

YEAR	TM	LG	AGE	G	GS	IP	H	BB	SO	HR	ERA	EQERA	EQH9	EQBB9	EQSO9	EQHR9	PERA	VORP	STF
2003	BIL	PIO	21	2	2	11.0	4	3	14	0	0.82	3.72	5.6	3.7	6.5	0.0	1.86	4.0	24
2003	DYT	MDW	21	12	3	39.3	37	14	39	4	3.44	5.35	10.7	4.1	6.1	2.5	6.88	-5.0	-8
2004	DYT	MDW	22	44	0	56.7	47	24	90	6	2.86	4.56	9.5	4.9	8.8	1.9	5.79	-1.1	-6
2005	*CIN*	*NL*	*23*	*11*	*1*	*17.3*	*15*	*9*	*17*	*3*	*4.96*	*5.30*	*8.1*	*4.2*	*7.9*	*1.5*	*5.10*	*1.0*	*0*

Breakout: 13% *Improve: 49%* *Collapse: 22%*

Former Cy Young winner turned kinesiologist and pitching guru Mike Marshall gets shunned by most of mainstream baseball, probably more for his abrasive personality than his unorthodox mound teachings. He may start to get people's attention if Guevara pans out. The skinny righty reliever throws just an average fastball and slider. But the scroogie he learned at St. Mary's University in San Antonio under pitching coach and Marshall disciple John Maley may be more than a trick pitch that baffles bush leaguers; Guevara throws it to lefty and righty hitters and shows great command spotting it in and out of the strike zone. It's hard to get excited about a minor league reliever, but 14.3 K/9 IP and a whatthehellwasthat?! pitch can really get the pulse racing.

JOSH HALL **Bats: R** **Throws: R** Born: 16-Dec-1980 Age: 24

YEAR	TM	LG	AGE	G	GS	IP	H	BB	SO	HR	ERA	EQERA	EQH9	EQBB9	EQSO9	EQHR9	PERA	VORP	STF
2002	STO	CLF	21	7	7	43.7	31	13	51	1	2.27	4.05	8.1	3.2	6.3	0.4	3.83	7.9	22
2002	CHT	SOU	21	22	22	132.0	140	50	116	7	3.75	5.85	9.4	3.2	5.8	0.8	4.37	17.5	12
2003	CHT	SOU	22	26	25	153.0	152	53	114	9	3.47	5.26	9.2	3.2	4.8	1.0	4.33	20.5	7
2003	CIN	NL	22	6	5	24.7	33	15	18	4	6.56	7.56	10.8	4.7	5.8	1.4	6.48	-6.4	-1
2005	*CIN*	*NL*	*24*	*17*	*15*	*85.7*	*92*	*37*	*62*	*11*	*4.92*	*5.26*	*9.8*	*3.5*	*5.8*	*1.1*	*5.30*	*7.1*	*3*

Breakout: 24% *Improve: 48%* *Collapse: 27%*

In the essay of this chapter we spent a good while talking about the frequency of Reds injuries, as well as the weakness of the team's farm system. Josh Hall sits at the intersection of these two boulevards of pain. Considered one of the best pitching prospects in the system, after a great 2001, a good 2002, and a 2003 that saw him make it all the way to the big leagues, Hall was forced to go under the knife to repair a frayed labrum, then had a second surgery to clear out scar tissue. The advantage of drafting college instead of high school pitchers is not just getting to see more years of performance; it's seeing if the pitcher can get through several more years of the injury nexus with his arm intact.

JOSH HANCOCK **Bats: R** **Throws: R** Born: 11-Apr-1978 Age: 27

YEAR	TM	LG	AGE	G	GS	IP	H	BB	SO	HR	ERA	EQERA	EQH9	EQBB9	EQSO9	EQHR9	PERA	VORP	STF
2002	TRN	EAS	24	15	14	84.7	82	18	69	9	3.61	4.93	9.1	2.0	5.7	1.6	4.03	14.0	14
2002	PAW	INT	24	8	8	44.3	39	26	29	2	3.45	4.57	8.3	6.1	5.2	0.7	4.57	4.7	0
2003	SWB	INT	25	28	27	165.7	147	46	122	14	3.86	4.69	8.7	2.9	5.6	1.1	4.22	23.6	9
2004	SWB	INT	26	18	18	107.7	107	21	65	10	4.01	4.34	9.2	1.9	4.5	1.0	4.25	15.3	13
2004	CIN	NL	26	12	9	54.7	60	25	31	14	4.44	5.47	9.9	3.8	4.6	2.2	5.81	1.0	-9
2005	*CIN*	*NL*	*27*	*18*	*14*	*86.0*	*92*	*31*	*54*	*13*	*4.96*	*5.30*	*9.8*	*2.9*	*5.1*	*1.2*	*5.12*	*3.9*	*-2*

Breakout: 19% *Improve: 41%* *Collapse: 26%*

Acquired for Cory Lidle mid-season, Hancock was the front runner for the fifth starter's job until the Reds handed Eric Milton the GDP of Paraguay. We were going to say "at least the Reds didn't flush $6.3 million down the toilet for Cory Lidle," but after one of the worst signings in recent baseball memory, the point's moot.

AARON HARANG **Bats: R** **Throws: R** Born: 09-May-1978 Age: 27

YEAR	TM	LG	AGE	G	GS	IP	H	BB	SO	HR	ERA	EQERA	EQH9	EQBB9	EQSO9	EQHR9	PERA	VORP	STF
2002	SAC	PCL	24	8	8	38.7	41	9	39	1	3.26	4.23	8.5	2.1	6.8	0.2	2.82	11.8	20
2002	OAK	AL	24	16	15	78.3	78	45	64	7	4.83	4.70	8.8	4.8	7.0	0.7	4.81	8.1	6
2003	SAC	PCL	25	12	12	69.7	62	17	60	5	2.71	3.86	8.5	2.5	6.7	1.0	3.99	11.7	14
2003	OAK	AL	25	7	6	30.3	41	9	16	5	5.35	5.10	11.1	2.4	4.5	1.2	6.00	1.5	-10
2003	CIN	NL	25	9	9	46.0	48	10	26	6	5.28	5.28	9.3	1.8	4.7	1.2	4.26	1.1	0
2004	CIN	NL	26	28	28	161.0	177	53	125	26	4.86	4.97	9.4	2.6	6.2	1.3	4.62	13.1	5
2005	*CIN*	*NL*	*27*	*22*	*19*	*116.3*	*123*	*40*	*88*	*16*	*4.81*	*5.14*	*9.8*	*2.7*	*6.1*	*1.1*	*4.95*	*6.1*	*7*

Breakout: 9% *Improve: 31%* *Collapse: 29%*

(continued next page)

Aaron Harang *(continued)*

Check his game log. Harang was miserable through his first 11 starts, tossing up a 5.43 ERA, with ugly peripheral stats. When the Reds diagnosed a sore elbow and placed him on the DL, you had to expect the worst. But then Harang came back strong, yielding just one run in his first three starts back, racking up 21 strikeouts in 18.2 innings and showing vastly improved command. Harang's last few starts were erratic, but the Reds are optimistic that some of his post-injury goodness could carry forward. Even so, he'll need to cure his gopheritis (a homer every 6 IP last year) to succeed.

LUKE HUDSON **Bats: R** **Throws: R** Born: 02-May-1977 Age: 28

YEAR	TM	LG	AGE	G	GS	IP	H	BB	SO	HR	ERA	EQERA	EQH9	EQBB9	EQSO9	EQHR9	PERA	VORP	STF
2002	LOU	INT	25	30	17	117.7	102	57	129	6	4.51	5.29	7.8	4.9	8.4	0.6	4.01	19.8	18
2004	CHT	SOU	27	16	16	86.7	71	25	91	9	3.32	4.41	8.7	2.8	6.8	1.5	4.52	9.6	19
2004	LOU	INT	27	3	3	19.0	15	5	17	2	2.84	3.57	7.6	2.5	6.6	1.0	3.57	4.0	22
2004	CIN	NL	27	9	9	48.3	36	25	38	3	2.42	3.13	7.2	4.3	6.5	0.6	3.33	15.0	17
2005	*CIN*	*NL*	*28*	*19*	*15*	*94.3*	*87*	*41*	*77*	*14*	*4.44*	*4.74*	*8.5*	*3.4*	*6.5*	*1.2*	*4.84*	*11.0*	*7*

Breakout: 14% *Improve: 42%* *Collapse: 25%*

Hudson is another torn labrum casualty, and the Reds didn't expect much from him in 2004. But Tim's baby brother showed flashes of brilliance upon his return, regaining his plus fastball and terrifying curve in nine big league starts. The Reds would do well to keep him on a strict pitch count early in the year as he rebuilds the strength in his shoulder gradually. He's been a favorite of ours since we got a close-up view of his nasty stuff in the Arizona Fall League in 2002, so we're pulling for him.

STEVE KELLY **Bats: R** **Throws: R** Born: 30-Sep-1979 Age: 25

YEAR	TM	LG	AGE	G	GS	IP	H	BB	SO	HR	ERA	EQERA	EQH9	EQBB9	EQSO9	EQHR9	PERA	VORP	STF
2002	DYT	MDW	22	7	7	45.7	42	7	35	1	3.15	4.85	9.1	1.7	4.2	0.4	3.59	9.5	11
2002	STO	CLF	22	19	19	105.7	119	32	80	6	4.09	6.55	10.5	3.0	3.9	0.9	5.65	-0.6	-3
2003	POT	CRL	23	17	17	95.3	105	28	69	3	3.87	5.79	9.6	2.8	4.7	0.6	4.32	13.0	1
2003	CHT	SOU	23	6	6	38.7	34	12	30	0	2.09	3.68	8.1	2.9	4.9	0.2	3.19	9.8	7
2004	CHT	SOU	24	28	28	161.3	156	48	116	12	2.96	4.61	9.4	2.8	4.5	1.0	4.79	13.5	4
2005	*CIN*	*NL*	*25*	*12*	*10*	*60.7*	*67*	*22*	*38*	*8*	*4.72*	*5.04*	*10.2*	*2.8*	*5.0*	*1.0*	*5.19*	*4.7*	*0*

Breakout: 19% *Improve: 40%* *Collapse: 22%*

When the subject of Reds prospects came up in an organizational discussion last year, Kelly's name barely came up. You see, Kelly's velocity is just average, but he's shown plus command of all three of his pitches. Think Don Gullett would like to have a guy like that at the back of the rotation? Kelly parlayed his fastball, curve and change—the last of which dives down and away from lefties—into a solid season at Chattanooga. Sure, he'll need to prove himself at higher levels, but you want to keep arms like these around, lest they get swept away and onto some smart team's 40-man.

DUSTIN MOSELEY **Bats: R** **Throws: R** Born: 26-Dec-1981 Age: 23

YEAR	TM	LG	AGE	G	GS	IP	H	BB	SO	HR	ERA	EQERA	EQH9	EQBB9	EQSO9	EQHR9	PERA	VORP	STF
2002	STO	CLF	20	14	14	88.7	60	21	80	3	2.74	4.24	7.9	2.5	4.9	0.6	3.57	18.2	34
2002	CHT	SOU	20	13	13	80.7	91	37	52	5	4.13	6.00	9.8	3.9	4.3	0.9	4.85	6.5	6
2003	CHT	SOU	21	18	18	112.7	116	28	73	10	3.83	5.35	9.8	2.3	4.2	1.4	4.75	10.0	9
2003	LOU	INT	21	8	8	50.0	46	14	27	5	2.70	3.88	8.9	2.9	4.1	1.2	4.47	5.8	15
2004	CHT	SOU	22	8	8	47.3	33	10	40	4	2.66	3.80	8.0	2.1	5.5	1.1	3.80	8.5	21
2004	LOU	INT	22	12	12	71.7	78	34	48	7	4.64	4.57	9.4	4.4	5.0	0.8	4.96	4.9	5
2005	*ANA*	*AL*	*23*	*22*	*16*	*99.7*	*110*	*40*	*61*	*14*	*5.09*	*5.04*	*10.0*	*3.2*	*5.0*	*1.2*	*5.03*	*8.7*	*-4*

Breakout: 9% *Improve: 44%* *Collapse: 23%*

The Reds and other teams get plenty of flak for picking highly-touted high school pitchers who command top draft choices and flame out due to injury—deservedly so. But there's another downside to taking high school arms: Scouts conjure up images of stardom for tall, projectable preps, envisioning an added four to five miles per hour on the young pitcher's fastball by the time he makes the bigs. All too often that velocity jump never materializes. In the end, you're left with someone like Moseley, whose fastball never got faster, now projected as a back-end starter at best. Traded to the Angels for Ramon Ortiz in the off-season, even though Ortiz was about to be non-tendered.

PHIL NORTON Bats: R Throws: L Born: 01-Feb-1976 Age: 29

YEAR	TM	LG	AGE	G	GS	IP	H	BB	SO	HR	ERA	EQERA	EQH9	EQBB9	EQSO9	EQHR9	PERA	VORP	STF
2003	IOW	PCL	27	48	1	47.7	44	24	43	4	3.77	5.40	8.6	5.2	7.0	1.2	5.00	3.0	-6
2003	CIN	NL	27	17	0	14.7	7	6	7	0	2.45	2.70	6.1	3.4	4.1	0.0	2.03	5.2	-4
2004	CIN	NL	28	69	0	65.7	71	38	48	5	5.07	5.54	9.1	4.6	5.8	0.6	4.57	0.6	-5
2005	*CIN*	*NL*	*29*	*29*	*3*	*47.7*	*51*	*26*	*35*	*5*	*4.97*	*5.31*	*9.8*	*4.3*	*5.9*	*0.8*	*5.37*	*1.9*	*-9*

Breakout: 25% *Improve: 46%* *Collapse: 29%*

A LOOGY by design, Norton didn't get lefties or righties out. Because his mom had the good sense not to insist he eat with his right hand like all the *normals,* he'll get more than his share of chances and a steady stream of $300,000+-a-year jobs. (As always, thanks to John Sickels for one of the better acronyms in the game.)

THOMAS PAULY Bats: R Throws: R Born: 28-Jul-1981 Age: 23

YEAR	TM	LG	AGE	G	GS	IP	H	BB	SO	HR	ERA	EQERA	EQH9	EQBB9	EQSO9	EQHR9	PERA	VORP	STF
2003	DYT	MDW	21	12	12	47.0	45	10	36	5	4.02	6.43	10.9	2.6	4.7	2.8	6.64	-4.9	-15
2004	POT	CRL	22	28	19	121.3	96	26	135	12	2.97	4.55	8.7	2.3	7.4	1.7	4.31	15.9	9
2005	*CIN*	*NL*	*23*	*15*	*8*	*59.0*	*56*	*19*	*51*	*12*	*4.64*	*4.96*	*8.8*	*2.5*	*7.0*	*1.6*	*4.83*	*5.5*	*7*

Breakout: 7% *Improve: 39%* *Collapse: 18%*

Other than that there fancy book learnin', Pauly got the benefit of a moderate workload while pitching at Princeton. The result is a pitcher with a raw, but powerful arm. Pauly's best pitch is an exploding four-seamer that settles in the low 90s. He's making progress with his change and slider. Most importantly, he misses bats: 10 strikeouts and less than two walks per nine frames at Potomac. If he keeps mowing down hitters at Double-A this year, he could come quickly.

JOHN RIEDLING Bats: R Throws: R Born: 29-Aug-1975 Age: 29

YEAR	TM	LG	AGE	G	GS	IP	H	BB	SO	HR	ERA	EQERA	EQH9	EQBB9	EQSO9	EQHR9	PERA	VORP	STF
2002	CIN	NL	26	33	0	46.7	39	26	30	2	2.70	3.02	8.1	4.4	5.2	0.4	3.83	11.9	-8
2003	CIN	NL	27	55	8	101.0	107	47	65	7	4.90	5.26	9.1	3.6	5.3	0.6	4.26	2.4	-5
2004	CIN	NL	28	70	0	77.7	90	40	46	10	5.10	6.10	9.7	4.1	4.7	1.1	5.17	-4.8	-19
2005	*FLO*	*NL*	*29*	*35*	*4*	*61.3*	*66*	*29*	*37*	*5*	*4.62*	*5.04*	*9.8*	*3.7*	*4.8*	*0.8*	*5.26*	*3.6*	*-13*

Breakout: 30% *Improve: 57%* *Collapse: 24%*

We're a long way from the flukish 2.70 ERA he posted in 2002. Riedling's inability to miss bats came home to roost last year, as his already suspect home-run, hit and walk rates all soared, resulting in an ugly season. It's a testament to the Reds' woeful pitching that they kept trotting him out there to get torched, to the tune of 70 appearances. He was briefly touted as a possible closer candidate to replace Danny Graves, but one look at his peripherals should have dispelled that notion right quick. There are dozens of better bullpen options out there for a similar price.

BRIAN ROSE Bats: R Throws: R Born: 13-Feb-1976 Age: 29

YEAR	TM	LG	AGE	G	GS	IP	H	BB	SO	HR	ERA	EQERA	EQH9	EQBB9	EQSO9	EQHR9	PERA	VORP	STF
2003	WIC	TXS	27	7	5	25.0	27	12	11	5	5.40	6.85	11.7	5.2	3.2	4.0	9.27	-9.1	-40
2004	CHT	SOU	28	20	18	106.3	106	17	85	8	3.30	4.42	9.6	1.5	5.1	1.1	4.52	12.0	11
2004	LOU	INT	28	6	6	35.3	39	10	26	2	3.31	3.41	9.2	2.6	5.2	0.5	4.19	5.4	9
2005	*CIN*	*NL*	*29*	*14*	*13*	*78.0*	*84*	*22*	*51*	*13*	*4.86*	*5.19*	*9.9*	*2.2*	*5.2*	*1.4*	*5.14*	*5.1*	*3*

Breakout: 14% *Improve: 46%* *Collapse: 21%*

Yes, that Brian Rose, the one the Red Sox insisted on keeping over future 18-game winner Carl Pavano in the Pedro Martinez trade. That was a zillion years ago, but the one-time top prospect may get another chance soon. A 4:1 K:BB ratio will do that for you, even when you're a 28-year-old facing hitters barely old enough to drink. The Reds gave him a minor league deal with an invite to spring training '05.

BRIAN SHACKELFORD

Bats: L Throws: L Born: 30-Aug-1976 Age: 28

YEAR	TM	LG	AGE	G	GS	IP	H	BB	SO	HR	ERA	EQERA	EQH9	EQBB9	EQSO9	EQHR9	PERA	VORP	STF
2002	WIC	TXS	25	22	0	25.7	23	26	15	1	3.50	5.32	9.1	10.3	4.2	0.8	6.85	-3.3	-43
2003	POT	CRL	26	18	0	27.3	17	8	20	1	1.98	2.92	7.3	2.9	5.1	0.7	3.28	6.4	3
2003	CHT	SOU	26	13	1	20.0	26	14	19	3	6.30	8.84	11.6	6.5	6.1	2.8	8.38	-6.0	-34
2003	LOU	INT	26	12	0	15.7	15	7	10	0	2.29	3.00	8.4	4.8	4.8	0.0	4.20	2.3	-13
2004	LOU	INT	27	59	0	73.0	58	42	63	6	3.58	3.67	7.7	5.5	6.6	0.9	4.33	9.7	4
2005	*CIN*	*NL*	*28*	*16*	*2*	*26.3*	*25*	*17*	*21*	*3*	*4.74*	*5.07*	*8.6*	*5.1*	*6.4*	*0.8*	*5.17*	*1.9*	*-8*

Breakout: 25% *Improve: 52%* *Collapse: 24%*

Close your eyes and think back to 2002. Brooks Kieschnick was a 30-year-old washed-up outfielder finding success in his new role as a two-way player—an effective bullpen arm who could also crush the ball in key pinch-hit situations. Shackelford made the transition at a younger age, and was a 20-homer man as recently as 2001. Armed with a good cut fastball he can throw to righties, he's developing as a pitcher and needs only to tighten his command to earn a shot at a big league job. If he can also keep his batting stroke intact, this could be fun.

JOE VALENTINE

Bats: R Throws: R Born: 24-Dec-1979 Age: 25

YEAR	TM	LG	AGE	G	GS	IP	H	BB	SO	HR	ERA	EQERA	EQH9	EQBB9	EQSO9	EQHR9	PERA	VORP	STF
2002	BIR	SOU	22	55	0	59.3	36	30	63	1	1.97	3.62	6.9	4.4	7.2	0.3	3.13	15.0	14
2003	SAC	PCL	23	40	0	52.3	44	37	53	5	4.82	6.10	8.1	7.4	8.0	1.1	5.36	1.3	-6
2004	LOU	INT	24	30	9	64.7	63	32	61	8	5.01	5.37	8.7	4.6	7.0	1.2	4.79	5.6	-2
2004	CIN	NL	24	24	1	29.3	23	25	29	4	5.22	5.34	7.5	6.9	7.8	1.3	4.71	0.6	-4
2005	*CIN*	*NL*	*25*	*17*	*5*	*45.7*	*42*	*28*	*40*	*6*	*5.14*	*5.50*	*8.5*	*4.8*	*7.0*	*1.1*	*5.29*	*1.8*	*-2*

Breakout: 14% *Improve: 43%* *Collapse: 28%*

Your basic good-stuff, fastball-slider reliever who needs to improve his control to succeed, Valentine consistently walked a batter every other inning or more at every level the last three years. Just 25, he's still young enough to turn it around at any time. Will fight for time as a spare righty with Weber and Weathers now on board.

TODD VAN POPPEL

Bats: R Throws: R Born: 09-Dec-1971 Age: 33

YEAR	TM	LG	AGE	G	GS	IP	H	BB	SO	HR	ERA	EQERA	EQH9	EQBB9	EQSO9	EQHR9	PERA	VORP	STF
2002	TEX	AL	30	50	0	72.7	80	29	85	14	5.45	4.79	8.8	3.2	9.8	1.5	4.66	4.2	13
2003	TEX	AL	31	7	1	12.7	20	9	9	1	8.50	8.78	10.8	5.4	6.1	0.7	6.08	-5.4	-8
2003	CIN	NL	31	9	4	35.7	31	6	25	7	4.54	4.28	8.6	1.3	5.9	1.9	4.01	4.5	15
2004	CIN	NL	32	48	11	115.3	136	32	72	22	6.09	6.07	10.1	2.2	5.0	1.6	5.11	-6.5	-6
2005	*CIN*	*NL*	*33*	*32*	*9*	*83.7*	*91*	*27*	*58*	*14*	*5.04*	*5.39*	*10.0*	*2.5*	*5.6*	*1.4*	*5.26*	*3.5*	*-5*

Breakout: 11% *Improve: 40%* *Collapse: 25%*

Take a cheapskate owner who won't invest in the product, a front office that does a lousy job identifying useful talent, and a pitching coach who gets tons of credit for his occasional salvage jobs but little blame for his repeated failures with prospects and you get HACKING MASS darlings like Van Poppel thrust into regular duty. It's a great way to reward fans who shell out hundreds of millions in public money for palatial new stadiums, and not much less for watered-down ballpark beer. That teams and the media criticize fan loyalty in cities like Cincinnati, Pittsburgh, Milwaukee—and royally shafted Montreal—is a pathetic joke.

RYAN WAGNER

Bats: R Throws: R Born: 15-Jul-1982 Age: 22

YEAR	TM	LG	AGE	G	GS	IP	H	BB	SO	HR	ERA	EQERA	EQH9	EQBB9	EQSO9	EQHR9	PERA	VORP	STF
2003	CIN	NL	20	17	0	21.7	13	12	25	2	1.66	1.74	6.1	4.4	9.6	0.9	3.05	9.5	28
2004	LOU	INT	21	15	0	16.7	13	9	19	0	2.69	2.81	7.3	5.1	8.4	0.0	3.38	3.9	15
2004	CIN	NL	21	49	0	51.7	59	27	37	7	4.70	5.26	9.5	4.0	5.6	1.1	4.91	1.7	-7
2005	*CIN*	*NL*	*22*	*29*	*6*	*62.0*	*62*	*29*	*51*	*7*	*4.50*	*4.81*	*9.2*	*3.7*	*6.6*	*0.9*	*4.85*	*6.0*	*0*

Breakout: 10% *Improve: 37%* *Collapse: 28%*

Score one against the emerging trend of teams drafting dominant college closers and fast-tracking them to the majors. Wagner struggled mightily as a 21-year-old a year out of college in his first extended stint in the bigs. Fellow '03 draftee

David Aardsma also flailed in his 10.2-inning stint with the Giants, though at least he looked good at Triple-A Fresno. Chad Cordero fared well for the Expos, and 2004 draft picks Bill Bray and Huston Street project to play significant roles with Washington and Oakland in the near future. It's an interesting gambit with intriguing upside for contenders looking for a stretch-run boost, but you have to wonder if teams like the Reds wouldn't be better served drafting a high-upside bat or a starter. At the least Wagner should be given every opportunity to master the minor leagues before prematurely starting his service time clock, facing the likes of Berkman and Pujols on a non-contender. He'll get better, but in this case, why the rush?

GABE WHITE **Bats: L** **Throws: L** Born: 20-Nov-1971 Age: 33

YEAR	TM	LG	AGE	G	GS	IP	H	BB	SO	HR	ERA	EQERA	EQH9	EQBB9	EQSO9	EQHR9	PERA	VORP	STF
2002	CIN	NL	30	62	0	54.3	49	10	41	3	2.98	3.12	8.3	1.4	6.2	0.5	3.12	13.5	8
2003	CIN	NL	31	34	0	34.3	36	6	23	5	3.94	3.82	9.3	1.4	5.5	1.4	4.09	6.4	-3
2003	NYY	AL	31	12	0	12.3	8	2	6	2	4.39	4.76	7.1	1.6	4.8	1.6	3.18	1.4	-4
2004	NYY	AL	32	24	0	20.7	33	7	8	2	8.26	7.59	11.8	2.5	3.0	0.8	5.48	-4.6	-25
2004	CIN	NL	32	40	0	39.0	39	5	33	12	6.23	6.08	9.5	1.0	7.1	2.7	4.86	-2.3	-2
2005	*ATL*	*NL*	*33*	*44*	*0*	*48.3*	*50*	*11*	*34*	*9*	*4.56*	*4.82*	*9.4*	*1.7*	*5.6*	*1.6*	*4.75*	*5.3*	*-7*

Breakout: 30% *Improve: 51%* *Collapse: 25%*

Never one to nibble, White succeeds when his pounding of the strike zone results in strikeouts and lazy flies. Owner of one of the lowest groundball/flyball rates in the game (a microscopic 0.45 in '04), he gets into deep doo-doo when the ball sails over the fence, as his 14 homers allowed and 6.94 ERA can attest. It'll be interesting to see if the Mazzone touch makes a difference now that he's a Brave. Given that White made nearly $6 million the last two years thanks mostly to being left-handed, it's no surprise Huckabay's got his kid doing lefty Tinkertoy exercises three times a day.

PAUL WILSON **Bats: R** **Throws: R** Born: 28-Mar-1973 Age: 32

YEAR	TM	LG	AGE	G	GS	IP	H	BB	SO	HR	ERA	EQERA	EQH9	EQBB9	EQSO9	EQHR9	PERA	VORP	STF
2002	TBY	AL	29	30	30	193.7	219	67	111	29	4.83	4.85	9.7	2.9	4.9	1.2	4.90	15.7	0
2003	CIN	NL	30	28	28	166.7	190	50	93	24	4.64	5.03	9.8	2.4	4.5	1.2	4.76	8.5	0
2004	CIN	NL	31	29	29	183.7	192	63	117	26	4.36	4.50	9.2	2.8	5.2	1.2	4.45	24.6	3
2005	*CIN*	*NL*	*32*	*25*	*24*	*138.7*	*155*	*45*	*84*	*22*	*5.01*	*5.35*	*10.3*	*2.6*	*4.9*	*1.3*	*5.38*	*5.4*	*0*

Breakout: 8% *Improve: 41%* *Collapse: 26%*

Wilson yielded too many hits and too many homers, but still kicked in a couple wins above replacement level, thanks largely to his durability; his 2.34 May ERA smoothed over an otherwise erratic year. He's a good story considering how far he's come from one-time phenom to Dallas Green-induced burnout. Though he's unlikely to get significantly better at this stage of his career, the two-year, $8.2 million deal given to Wilson now looks like a decent deal, compared to the insane money doled out to Russ Ortiz, Jaret Wright, and the Reds' own Eric Milton.

Colorado Rockies

ROCKIES PROSPECTUS

2004 record: 68–94; Fourth place, NL West

Pythagenport record: 73–89

Runs scored per game: 5.14 (4th in NL)

Runs allowed per game: 5.70 (16th in NL)

Team EqA: .259 (11th in NL)

2004 Batters Age: 31.0 (4th oldest in NL)

2004 Pitchers Age: 29.4 (6th youngest in NL)

Ballpark: Coors Field; Severe hitter's park; Park Factor of 1.116

2004: Hit a little better, pitched a little worse, and finished an uninspiring fourth or below for the seventh straight year.

2005: It's a shame they're made to play baseball—this organization treads water like a crack synchronized swimming squad.

We're bloody sick of discussing the Colorado Rockies and listening to people talk about the altitude. "It takes time to learn how to win at altitude." "We've commissioned studies, and pitchers that rely on changing speeds perform better than other pitchers in extreme environments." "It's harder to win at Coors because the pitchers have to throw more pitches." "You need hitters that don't strike out in Coors."

Hey, here's an idea . . . why not get some really good hitters and pitchers, without any regard for altitude whatsoever?

Assessment and confidence are at the core of decision making. You can't go out and get quality players if you don't know what a quality player does. Throughout its entire history, the Rockies front office has done an abysmal job of assessing player performance. They either can't distinguish a player's performance from that of other players, or they've chosen not to. Either way, it's a situation that has to change if this organization's going to find its way out of the woods. The Rockies find themselves today in a position where they're in real trouble. The spiral's gaining momentum, and not in a good way.

Dan O'Dowd's been in place since 1999, and is beginning his sixth full season as general manager. At this point, he's pretty much out of excuses, and out of time. It's admirable that the ownership of the Rockies has given him sufficient time to actually build a team on and off the field, make an assessment of the club's state, put together a plan, and execute it.

But while consistency can be a good thing, that's only true if it doesn't lapse into unresponsiveness. The Rockies' on-field performance under O'Dowd's leadership has been poor, and the bottom line's suffering significantly. If the Rockies don't demonstrate some progress in the near future, there will be changes in the front office.

The Rockies had a historic opportunity when the franchise began in 1993, and got an extension on that opportunity when one of the best bullpens in history dragged an overrated offense kicking and screaming to success in 1995. The introduction of one of baseball's most beautiful fields added to the confluence of events that gave the Rockies a chance to etch themselves into the psyche of a region and generation that most clubs never get. Unfortunately, they were unable to take advantage of that opportunity, and now find themselves precipitously close to being yet another flyover club, indistinguishable from the bland and unsuccessful teams that dot baseball's competitive landscape.

With the proper team and proper marketing, the Rockies might have been able to build something like the Cubs have built in Chicago. The Cubs have one of the lower "attendance elasticities" in the league; people flock to Wrigley Field for the experience. Sure, winning would be nice, but it's not a place loaded with fair-weather fans, who'll come out when the team wins, and religiously stay away when the team isn't successful. Cub fans seem to take a sort of perverse pride in overpaying for bad beer and watching indifferent baseball, and it's a tradition that's passed from dysfunctional generation to dysfunctional generation. From a business standpoint, it's a great thing, as it leads to lots of revenue, and lots of revenue means lots of resources when it's time to figure out what kind of players you can get for the club. The Rockies can still put together something like that, but now they're starting closer to everyone else than if they'd done it successfully 10 years ago.

Let's take a quick look in table 1 at Rockies' attendance.

You don't have to be a statistician to make out the trend here. (Causality for the trend is another issue, with lots of intervening variables.) Attendance has steadily been heading in one direction—down. Part of that defi-

TABLE 1. ROCKIES' AVERAGE ANNUAL ATTENDANCE, 1993–2004

Year	Winning Percent	Average Attendance
1993	.414	55,350
1994	.453	57,570
1995	.535	47,084
1996	.512	48,037
1997	.512	48,006
1998	.475	46,823
1999	.444	42,976
2000	.506	40,681
2001	.450	39,097
2002	.450	33,800
2003	.457	28,816
2004	.420	28,865

nitely has to do with the increased price of tickets and concessions, but that winning percentage column certainly tells a lot of the story. This has been a dull, mediocre club. It's hard to put together a compelling story if everyone knows you're a .450 ballclub. If you crater, a la the 2003 Tigers, there's a rebuilding story that can take place. The team can put together a new foundation, based on some specific plan or team attribute, and build excitement as they climb from .300 to .480 over a couple of years. The Rockies have no interesting story. Even their best player, Todd Helton, is as vanilla as it gets. He's productive, but not to the heights of some of the very best; he plays first base, not something flashy like shortstop; and he's not cutting a bad alt-rock album, voicing inane political views in public, or doing local A.M. television with his new celebrity girlfriend.

The easiest way to avoid being boring is to become positively wretched. When Pepto-Bismol runs an ad with a team jersey as a source of indigestion to sell its product, you know you're following the Warhol strategy of getting airtime.

The best way to get some attention that'll last is to start winning a whole bunch of games. The media will find something interesting to focus on; worry about the baseball, and everything else will mostly take care of itself.

Dan O'Dowd and the Rockies deserve some credit for trying to figure out how to win. There is a large number of baseball people who believe that winning at altitude is a qualitatively different thing than winning at sea level. That may be the case; not to sound flippant, but we've seen few clubs be successful club at altitude so far. We do know that significantly more runs will be scored, and we know that because of that, teams in Coors Field are going to have more wear and tear on their pitchers. So there is at least that one specific issue that the Rockies front office will have to address.

So the Rockies have tried a number of different things to win a mile high. They tried going after pitchers who rely on changing speeds rather than breaking pitches, the theory being (in part) that since curveballs curve less at altitude, pitchers that rely on them won't be able to avoid getting crushed. Maybe that was a good strategy, but the execution was questionable.

And that's kind of the whole story of Dan O'Dowd's tenure as GM. O'Dowd's been willing to embrace several different approaches, for which he deserves some credit. But it's not really a strategy if you change it every time you hit a bump. That's a reflex. And if you're making personnel decisions reflexively, you're letting the game play you, rather than vice versa. The nature of decision-making is that it's harder to execute in critical circumstances. If you're constantly responding to perceived crises, like "Our pitching sucks again, and we've got to do something or this coming year, we're going to get our butts kicked," you're going to make bad decisions. And in baseball's current environment, one really bad decision can hamstring a club for years to come, leading to more bad decisions down the road, and creating a spiral of low performance that can cripple an organization.

The Rockies' decisions have been made in precisely that fashion, and the result has been predictably painful. The twin pitching signings of Denny Neagle and Mike Hampton were awful. This isn't 20/20 hindsight; no serious analyst believed those signings were anything short of abysmal at the time, either in terms of performance or money. Even the Todd Helton contract was excessive, both in terms of length and dollars. Where is the upside for the club? Long-term contracts are really more like venture capital agreements than sports contracts at that level, and the club really should do something to make it possible to get a big return on what is a very risky investment, even for the very best players. Injuries and performance drop-offs happen, and clubs systematically underestimate those risks, overestimate the marginal revenue gain created by a single player (actually, almost no teams even make that calculation), and end up overpaying as a result. Without a strategy, it's an easy trap to fall in, and the Rockies find themselves climbing out of that trap right now.

The bright side? It's twofold. First, the farm system, although somewhat thin, has some fantastic prospects in it. What it lacks in depth, it makes up for in top-tier prospects. Jeff Francis is one of the very best prospects in baseball, loved by tools hounds, scouts, statheads, and even the growing medhead crowd. Ian Stewart might be an even better prospect, and the Rockies might have the good fortune to see him blocked at third base by Garrett Atkins. Somewhat overlooked because of his age, Atkins has the potential to be a plus-two- to plus-four-win player down the road, with some truly eye-popping raw numbers in the minors. Brad Hawpe's going to have a major league bat of quality; the question is whether he'll be enough of a hitter to start, or will he be a role player instead. The pitchers in the system aren't up to the caliber of the hitters, but there are a few relief prospects who have good stuff and good numbers, and no team needs a deep, effective bullpen more than the Rockies.

The Rockies have an organizational and cultural problem that a lot of clubs don't really have to deal with: Because of the memories of fans and people in the front office, it's hard to put together a plan. The Rockies had success under Don Baylor on the field, and the general perception is that when the team was successful in the past, it was because of sluggers like Andres Galarraga, Dante Bichette, and Vinny Castilla, when the reality is that the one really successful Rockies club was built around a tremendous bullpen. It takes a lot of courage to make a plan and stick to it, especially when the local press and public has such a dissonant perception of what makes a successful team compared to what really does.

Where's the club heading? The talented new blood's going to get a chance to play, with Atkins, Hawpe, Francis, and J. D. Closser likely to have big roles from the get-go. The rotation's not going to be overhauled in the short term, and that's kind of a problem, as only Francis and Joe Kennedy have notable upsides. The bullpen's being done on the cheap, which can be a good thing, and some of the gambles being made on young relievers with great K rates are very good ones. That's a considerably better idea than spending a fortune on a closer because everyone remembers close games lost in the late innings, and no one remembers blowouts lost in the second inning because you don't have good starting pitching or an offense with comeback capability.

The Rockies are heading in the right direction for the most part, putting themselves in a position where the passage of time will make the team better rather than worse. That may sound like a simple thing, but it's an accomplishment that requires a semblance of strategic vision, and courage of convictions. That Dan O'Dowd is demonstrating both, rather than competing with frantic GMs to sign an overrated pitcher who'll be a bad contract four months down the road is a very good sign for Rockies fans.

HITTERS

GARRETT ATKINS — 3B — Bats: R — Throws: R — Born: 12-Dec-1979 — Age: 25

YEAR	TM	LG	AGE	AB	H	2B	3B	HR	BB	SO	SB	CS	AVG	OBP	SLG	MLVR	EQBA	EQOBP	EQSLG	EQMLVR	VORP	DEFENSE
2002	CAR	SOU	22	510	138	27	3	12	59	77	6	6	.271	.345	.406	.067	.247	.307	.391	-.148	5.2	119-3B -8
2003	CSP	PCL	23	439	140	30	1	13	45	52	2	4	.319	.382	.481	.148	.262	.328	.407	-.075	14.2	110-3B -6
2003	COL	NL	23	69	11	2	0	0	3	14	0	0	.159	.205	.188	-.606	.132	.167	.132	-.845	-7.2	14-3B -3
2004	CSP	PCL	24	445	163	43	3	15	57	45	0	0	.366	.434	.578	.347	.298	.366	.461	.101	38.3	104-3B -3
2004	COL	NL	24	28	10	2	0	1	4	3	0	0	.357	.424	.536	.337	.370	.377	.481	.225	3.5	
2005	*COL*	*NL*	*25*	*233*	*67*	*15*	*1*	*7*	*23*	*28*	*0*	*0*	*.287*	*.354*	*.461*	*.069*	*.266*	*.332*	*.416*	*-.048*	*7.1*	*64-3B -4*

Breakout: 11% *Improve: 35%* *Collapse: 39%*

He's 25, he's inexpensive, and he'll rightfully start the season as the primary third baseman in Denver. Atkins's defense is acceptable at third, and he'll hit. He's not a Grade-A prospect, but he's going to put up some pretty reasonable numbers and potentially provide one of the building blocks for the next good Rockies team. Think of a slightly better version of Joe Randa, with more offense and less defense, and you won't be far off.

JEFF BAKER — 3B — Bats: R — Throws: R — Born: 21-Jun-1981 — Age: 24

YEAR	TM	LG	AGE	AB	H	2B	3B	HR	BB	SO	SB	CS	AVG	OBP	SLG	MLVR	EQBA	EQOBP	EQSLG	EQMLVR	VORP	DEFENSE
2003	ASH	SAL	22	263	76	17	0	11	30	79	4	2	.289	.377	.479	.185	.216	.278	.369	-.255	-6.1	61-3B -8
2004	VIS	CLF	23	267	88	23	1	11	47	70	1	0	.330	.439	.547	.383	.262	.358	.430	.012	16.2	68-3B -5
2004	TUL	TXS	23	91	27	5	1	4	7	22	1	0	.297	.343	.505	.203	.278	.320	.467	.010	5.4	20-3B 2
2005	*COL*	*NL*	*24*	*306*	*80*	*17*	*2*	*13*	*33*	*95*	*1*	*1*	*.262*	*.344*	*.461*	*.031*	*.242*	*.323*	*.416*	*-.081*	*4.6*	*84-3B -7*

Breakout: 23% *Improve: 49%* *Collapse: 23%*

Another third base prospect, one year younger than Atkins, and about two levels behind him. Has some plate discipline issues, but did bully the California League pretty effectively last year. He'll spend this season in Double-A, working to cut down on his strikeouts and improve his defense. High potential for being trade bait if someone else's scouts catch him on a good day.

CLINT BARMES SS **Bats: R** **Throws: R** Born: 06-Mar-1979 Age: 26

YEAR	TM	LG	AGE	AB	H	2B	3B	HR	BB	SO	SB	CS	AVG	OBP	SLG	MLVR	EQBA	EQOBP	EQSLG	EQMLVR	VORP	DEFENSE
2002	CAR	SOU	23	438	119	23	2	15	31	72	15	11	.272	.329	.436	.086	.245	.286	.417	-.152	6.7	101-SS -12
2003	CSP	PCL	24	493	136	35	1	7	22	63	12	7	.276	.316	.394	-.110	.227	.270	.335	-.311	-15.5	122-SS -10
2004	CSP	PCL	25	533	175	42	2	16	28	61	20	8	.328	.376	.505	.104	.262	.307	.398	-.127	11.6	117-SS 4
2004	COL	NL	25	71	20	3	1	2	3	10	0	1	.282	.320	.437	-.042	.268	.305	.408	-.111	2.0	
2005	*COL*	*NL*	*26*	*318*	*87*	*18*	*2*	*8*	*14*	*43*	*6*	*3*	*.272*	*.315*	*.424*	*-.061*	*.251*	*.295*	*.382*	*-.169*	*5.6*	*83-SS -2*

Breakout: 16% *Improve: 42%* *Collapse: 37%*

He hit OK but not great at Colorado Springs, and even those numbers were significantly above his established track record. But Barmes is at an age where those kind of jumps can be meaningful, and he looked OK for a few weeks in Denver to boot. With Royce Clayton gone to Arizona, Barmes will get a shot to show what he can do at shortstop. If he can play acceptable defense there, the Rockies will be pretty happy with .280/.330/.440, which Barmes is fully capable of doing in Coors. It's a pretty good experiment for everyone involved.

JEROMY BURNITZ OF **Bats: L** **Throws: R** Born: 14-Apr-1969 Age: 36

YEAR	TM	LG	AGE	AB	H	2B	3B	HR	BB	SO	SB	CS	AVG	OBP	SLG	MLVR	EQBA	EQOBP	EQSLG	EQMLVR	VORP	DEFENSE
2002	NYM	NL	33	479	103	15	0	19	58	135	10	7	.215	.311	.365	-.094	.225	.315	.386	-.155	-4.0	119-RF 0
2003	NYM	NL	34	234	64	18	0	18	21	55	1	4	.274	.344	.581	.257	.281	.344	.591	.230	19.7	38-RF -2 16-CF 1
2003	LAD	NL	34	230	47	4	0	13	14	57	4	0	.204	.252	.391	-.190	.212	.253	.403	-.258	-4.6	50-LF -3
2004	COL	NL	35	540	153	30	4	37	58	124	5	6	.283	.356	.559	.179	.264	.339	.520	.104	40.2	58-RF 3 51-CF -3
2005	*COL*	*NL*	*36*	*400*	*110*	*21*	*2*	*26*	*43*	*90*	*5*	*2*	*.276*	*.349*	*.536*	*.149*	*.255*	*.327*	*.483*	*.024*	*15.9*	*107-RF -3*

Breakout: 40% *Improve: 74%* *Collapse: 12%*

A better defender than perceived, and precisely the hitter that people think he is. He's a swing from the heels bomber who's not as good as he looked last year in Colorado, and certainly isn't worth an enormous sum. That said, he's a legitimate 30-homer guy who plays pretty reasonable outfield defense, and those don't grow on trees. A free agent, he's spoken to several teams and will likely sign soon after press time.

VINNY CASTILLA 3B **Bats: R** **Throws: R** Born: 04-Jul-1967 Age: 37

YEAR	TM	LG	AGE	AB	H	2B	3B	HR	BB	SO	SB	CS	AVG	OBP	SLG	MLVR	EQBA	EQOBP	EQSLG	EQMLVR	VORP	DEFENSE
2002	ATL	NL	35	543	126	23	2	12	22	69	4	1	.232	.268	.348	-.198	.237	.270	.360	-.269	-3.8	136-3B -12
2003	ATL	NL	36	542	150	28	3	22	26	86	1	2	.277	.310	.461	.047	.277	.310	.465	-.012	29.1	140-3B -9
2004	COL	NL	37	583	158	43	3	35	51	113	0	0	.271	.332	.535	.097	.251	.313	.498	.016	31.7	146-3B 11
2005	*WAS*	*NL*	*37*	*424*	*104*	*23*	*2*	*15*	*29*	*76*	*0*	*0*	*.245*	*.297*	*.411*	*-.129*	*.247*	*.297*	*.421*	*-.116*	*0.1*	*110-3B -1*

Breakout: 7% *Improve: 41%* *Collapse: 29%*

Led the league in RBI, which says more about RBI than it does about Castilla. For all the talk about his great season, this is still the same guy who gobbles up outs, and does all the things that make him expensive without being enormously productive—away from Coors, he hit .218/.281/.493. One of Jim Bowden's first actions as the GM of the Nationals/Expos/Las Vegas Lucky Sevens was to sign Castilla to a two-year deal for $6.2 million, which is great news for Castilla and his family, bad news for fans of the club, and another action which compels one to ask, once again, "What is Jim Bowden thinking?"

ROYCE CLAYTON SS **Bats: R** **Throws: R** Born: 02-Jan-1970 Age: 35

YEAR	TM	LG	AGE	AB	H	2B	3B	HR	BB	SO	SB	CS	AVG	OBP	SLG	MLVR	EQBA	EQOBP	EQSLG	EQMLVR	VORP	DEFENSE
2002	CWS	AL	32	342	86	14	2	7	20	67	5	1	.251	.295	.365	-.169	.251	.300	.369	-.189	5.2	99-SS 10
2003	MIL	NL	33	483	110	16	1	11	49	92	5	2	.228	.301	.333	-.191	.227	.300	.335	-.252	1.9	135-SS 4
2004	COL	NL	34	574	160	36	4	8	48	125	10	5	.279	.338	.397	-.084	.260	.320	.369	-.144	17.3	138-SS -9
2005	*ARI*	*NL*	*35*	*427*	*109*	*21*	*2*	*9*	*35*	*85*	*6*	*3*	*.255*	*.313*	*.374*	*-.144*	*.250*	*.307*	*.367*	*-.170*	*6.0*	*113-SS -3*

Breakout: 16% *Improve: 40%* *Collapse: 25%*

An aging defensive specialist hits .279/.338/.397 in Coors Field, and his defense deteriorates due to age in front of the eyes of a dwindling fan base. The obvious thing to do? Let him go. The Rockies nailed this one, letting Clayton leave for grayer pastures in Arizona, where he signed a one-year deal for $1.35 million. You know what he'll do.

J. D. CLOSSER — C — Bats: B — Throws: R — Born: 15-Jan-1980 — Age: 25

YEAR	TM	LG	AGE	AB	H	2B	3B	HR	BB	SO	SB	CS	AVG	OBP	SLG	MLVR	EQBA	EQOBP	EQSLG	EQMLVR	VORP	DEFENSE	
2002	CAR	SOU	22	315	89	27	1	13	44	69	9	3	.283	.369	.498	.233	.249	.323	.461	-.019	15.5	64-C -6	
2003	TUL	TXS	23	410	116	28	5	13	47	79	3	2	.283	.359	.471	.185	.261	.330	.449	-.013	20.9	94-C 2	
2004	CSP	PCL	24	298	89	19	1	7	41	47	0	2	.299	.384	.440	.000	.240	.322	.347	-.184	-1.0	76-C -4	
2004	COL	NL	24	113	36	6	0	1	6	22	0	0	.319	.364	.398	.005	.310	.339	.363	-.080	5.3	31-C 1	
2005	*COL*	*NL*	*25*	*274*	*78*	*18*	*2*	*10*	*30*	*52*	*2*	*1*	*.283*	*.357*	*.473*	*.085*	*.262*	*.335*	*.427*	*-.033*	*15.6*	*76-C -3*	

Breakout: 19% *Improve: 48%* *Collapse: 22%*

The guy scouts keep comparing him to is Terry Steinbach, and that may be a fair comparison. Closser doesn't blow you away with any one facet of his game, but he's been consistent and successful at each level, his defense is well-regarded, and he's done everything that's asked of him. He should have a successful major league career, and could be a championship-caliber catcher. Closser could improve in any one of five or six areas and become a three- to four-win player.

CHOO FREEMAN — OF — Bats: R — Throws: R — Born: 20-Oct-1979 — Age: 25

YEAR	TM	LG	AGE	AB	H	2B	3B	HR	BB	SO	SB	CS	AVG	OBP	SLG	MLVR	EQBA	EQOBP	EQSLG	EQMLVR	VORP	DEFENSE	
2002	CAR	SOU	22	430	125	18	6	12	64	101	15	13	.291	.400	.444	.210	.264	.353	.424	-.003	19.9	116-CF -4	
2003	CSP	PCL	23	327	83	9	4	7	23	71	2	8	.254	.315	.370	-.157	.211	.271	.313	-.349	-19.6	64-CF -7	19-LF -1
2004	CSP	PCL	24	360	107	21	7	10	26	84	7	3	.297	.350	.478	-.009	.239	.290	.374	-.210	-6.5	100-CF -4	
2004	COL	NL	24	90	17	3	2	1	14	21	1	1	.189	.298	.300	-.297	.169	.282	.270	-.404	-3.4	29-CF -1	
2005	*COL*	*NL*	*25*	*192*	*52*	*10*	*2*	*7*	*17*	*45*	*2*	*1*	*.272*	*.345*	*.452*	*.028*	*.251*	*.323*	*.408*	*-.085*	*8.8*	*55-CF -4*	

Breakout: 44% *Improve: 59%* *Collapse: 20%*

Hit .297 at Colorado Springs, which along with lousy plate discipline and only moderate power numbers, is evidence that you are, in fact, not doing all that much. He's a long shot to develop into a player that you want to build around, or even keep around for the short term. Not enough walks, not enough power, and defensively, he's iffy to cover that outfield in Coors.

LUIS GONZALEZ — UT — Bats: R — Throws: R — Born: 26-Jun-1979 — Age: 26

YEAR	TM	LG	AGE	AB	H	2B	3B	HR	BB	SO	SB	CS	AVG	OBP	SLG	MLVR	EQBA	EQOBP	EQSLG	EQMLVR	VORP	DEFENSE	
2002	AKR	EAS	23	263	70	10	3	6	12	37	4	0	.266	.304	.395	-.041	.238	.270	.362	-.266	-6.9	31-2B 1	11-3B -3
2003	AKR	EAS	24	431	137	22	4	7	46	41	1	0	.318	.385	.436	.161	.282	.344	.403	-.035	6.5	43-1B 1	30-2B -3
2004	COL	NL	25	322	94	17	2	12	15	67	1	5	.292	.330	.469	.018	.273	.313	.441	-.045	11.2	33-2B 1	11-LF 0
2005	*COL*	*NL*	*26*	*335*	*93*	*18*	*2*	*9*	*22*	*51*	*2*	*2*	*.278*	*.329*	*.428*	*-.026*	*.257*	*.308*	*.387*	*-.136*	*2.7*	*89-2B -7*	

Breakout: 13% *Improve: 28%* *Collapse: 52%*

Versatility Guy at the start of his career. He's not perfect, but he can play defense around the field without killing you, and can hit a little. Young enough to take a step forward in either plate discipline or power; if that happens, you've got someone that can really help a club. What he hit last year is fully doable again.

TODD GREENE — C — Bats: R — Throws: R — Born: 08-May-1971 — Age: 34

YEAR	TM	LG	AGE	AB	H	2B	3B	HR	BB	SO	SB	CS	AVG	OBP	SLG	MLVR	EQBA	EQOBP	EQSLG	EQMLVR	VORP	DEFENSE	
2002	LVG	PCL	31	125	44	12	0	11	3	21	0	0	.352	.373	.712	.498	.295	.303	.598	.193	12.5	24-C 0	
2002	OKL	PCL	31	152	46	9	0	6	9	27	2	0	.303	.339	.480	.159	.278	.307	.430	-.067	4.4	23-C -5	
2002	TEX	AL	31	112	30	5	0	10	2	23	0	0	.268	.282	.580	.096	.270	.278	.577	.091	7.4	12-1B 0	13-C -1
2003	TEX	AL	32	205	47	10	1	10	2	47	0	0	.229	.243	.434	-.199	.223	.242	.421	-.245	0.2	47-C -2	
2004	COL	NL	33	195	55	14	0	10	13	38	0	0	.282	.325	.508	.055	.266	.303	.469	-.029	11.3	43-C -6	
2005	*COL*	*NL*	*34*	*218*	*61*	*13*	*1*	*13*	*13*	*45*	*0*	*0*	*.279*	*.323*	*.527*	*.100*	*.258*	*.303*	*.476*	*-.025*	*12.7*	*59-C -7*	

Breakout: 34% *Improve: 50%* *Collapse: 19%*

OK, we're prepared to admit that he's probably not going to be a 40-homer catcher for the Angels. Still, as a backup catcher there's a lot to like, and it's all in Greene's power. With Closser around, Greene's been offered arbitration, and will likely sign on as a backup. It's really just a question of how expediently Charles Johnson can be shipped off.

BRAD HAWPE OF **Bats: L** **Throws: L** Born: 22-Jun-1979 Age: 26

YEAR	TM	LG	AGE	AB	H	2B	3B	HR	BB	SO	SB	CS	AVG	OBP	SLG	MLVR	EQBA	EQOBP	EQSLG	EQMLVR	VORP	DEFENSE
2002	SLM	CRL	23	450	156	38	2	22	81	84	1	1	.347	.447	.587	.528	.298	.388	.521	.222	45.6	120-1B 10
2003	TUL	TXS	24	346	96	27	0	17	31	84	1	3	.277	.338	.503	.193	.244	.299	.459	-.069	-0.4	48-RF -2 17-1B -3
2004	CSP	PCL	25	345	111	19	1	31	36	91	3	2	.322	.384	.652	.320	.257	.319	.502	.038	10.7	76-RF 4 10-LF 1
2004	COL	NL	25	105	26	3	2	3	11	34	1	1	.248	.322	.400	-.098	.223	.300	.369	-.208	0.3	27-RF 1
2005	*COL*	*NL*	*26*	*262*	*76*	*16*	*2*	*16*	*29*	*67*	*2*	*1*	*.289*	*.360*	*.550*	*.197*	*.267*	*.337*	*.496*	*.067*	*18.2*	*72-RF 1*

Breakout: 33% *Improve: 60%* *Collapse: 25%*

Lefty flail-and-mash guy who's been learning how to play the outfield since he's been in the system. He has improved, and looks pretty decent in the field compared to many others who've tried that conversion. Offensively, he's shown all the skills except stealing bases, so it's reasonable to assume that he's going to be able to consolidate some or all of them. Barring a surprise trade or signing, he'll start in RF for the Rockies this year.

TODD HELTON 1B **Bats: L** **Throws: L** Born: 20-Aug-1973 Age: 31

YEAR	TM	LG	AGE	AB	H	2B	3B	HR	BB	SO	SB	CS	AVG	OBP	SLG	MLVR	EQBA	EQOBP	EQSLG	EQMLVR	VORP	DEFENSE
2002	COL	NL	28	553	182	39	4	30	99	91	5	1	.329	.429	.577	.362	.306	.407	.548	.298	73.1	153-1B 16
2003	COL	NL	29	583	209	49	5	33	111	72	0	4	.358	.458	.630	.523	.336	.439	.598	.450	99.9	155-1B 21
2004	COL	NL	30	547	190	49	2	32	127	72	3	0	.347	.469	.620	.477	.321	.447	.572	.409	94.8	149-1B 18
2005	*COL*	*NL*	*31*	*516*	*171*	*39*	*2*	*29*	*98*	*71*	*2*	*0*	*.331*	*.437*	*.584*	*.401*	*.306*	*.410*	*.527*	*.260*	*52.7*	*146-1B 10*

Breakout: 12% *Improve: 47%* *Collapse: 17%*

A steady, consistent performer at a high level. Helton's really more of an average hitter than a power hitter, and just plain does a great job of putting a great swing on the ball and hitting line drives. He's not just a product of Coors Field; he's a .310/.422/.517 hitter on the road. Is he a masher? No, he's kind of like Rusty Greer's best two months ever (those two when he wasn't hurt), day in and day out, for an entire career. That's a hell of a ballplayer.

MATT HOLLIDAY LF **Bats: R** **Throws: R** Born: 15-Jan-1980 Age: 25

YEAR	TM	LG	AGE	AB	H	2B	3B	HR	BB	SO	SB	CS	AVG	OBP	SLG	MLVR	EQBA	EQOBP	EQSLG	EQMLVR	VORP	DEFENSE
2002	CAR	SOU	22	463	128	19	2	10	67	102	16	2	.276	.375	.391	.096	.252	.334	.377	-.112	-8.5	113-LF -10
2003	TUL	TXS	23	522	132	28	5	12	43	74	15	9	.253	.313	.395	-.016	.234	.290	.379	-.206	-24.5	121-LF -5
2004	COL	NL	24	400	116	31	3	14	31	86	3	3	.290	.349	.487	.078	.271	.331	.458	.010	15.2	99-LF 0
2005	*COL*	*NL*	*25*	*408*	*119*	*27*	*3*	*18*	*38*	*74*	*6*	*2*	*.292*	*.360*	*.504*	*.141*	*.270*	*.338*	*.455*	*.017*	*13.7*	*109-LF -1*

Breakout: 31% *Improve: 63%* *Collapse: 17%*

Holliday performed way above what could have been reasonably expected of him given his minor league numbers. He hit .253 in Tulsa in 2003, then .290 in Colorado in 2004. He hit for more power, played better defense, and pretty much just played about 2/3 of a season of lights-out baseball before hurting his elbow. Gotta love that. (The lights-out ball, not the elbow injury.) Is he likely to keep it up? It's possible. Twenty-year-olds have been known to take a big step forward and actually hang onto their gains. He's expected to be healthy, so hopefully he'll continue to progress.

CHARLES JOHNSON C **Bats: R** **Throws: R** Born: 20-Jul-1971 Age: 33

YEAR	TM	LG	AGE	AB	H	2B	3B	HR	BB	SO	SB	CS	AVG	OBP	SLG	MLVR	EQBA	EQOBP	EQSLG	EQMLVR	VORP	DEFENSE
2002	FLA	NL	30	244	53	19	0	6	31	61	0	0	.217	.301	.369	-.118	.224	.300	.382	-.189	5.0	69-C 2
2003	COL	NL	31	356	82	20	0	20	49	84	1	3	.230	.320	.455	-.028	.214	.302	.426	-.133	12.7	101-C 3
2004	COL	NL	32	305	72	20	0	13	49	91	2	1	.236	.350	.430	-.034	.219	.328	.394	-.123	12.1	86-C -5
2005	*COL*	*NL*	*33*	*188*	*48*	*11*	*1*	*10*	*28*	*48*	*1*	*0*	*.256*	*.354*	*.472*	*.056*	*.236*	*.332*	*.426*	*-.057*	*9.0*	*55-C -2*

Breakout: 50% *Improve: 69%* *Collapse: 21%*

Johnson's been maddeningly ineffective on the field since coming to Colorado. The Rockies are trying to move him anywhere they possibly can, but his contract has a $1-million-poison-pill provision, Johnson's not that desirable a commodity based on his lousy on-field performance, and his prickly reputation doesn't help. They'll probably find a taker eventually, but they'll have to eat some money to do it.

AARON MILES 2B Bats: B Throws: R Born: 15-Dec-1976 Age: 28

YEAR	TM	LG	AGE	AB	H	2B	3B	HR	BB	SO	SB	CS	AVG	OBP	SLG	MLVR	EQBA	EQOBP	EQSLG	EQMLVR	VORP	DEFENSE	
2002	BIR	SOU	25	531	171	39	1	9	40	45	25	16	.322	.369	.450	.246	.304	.338	.445	.034	34.7	125-2B -17	
2003	CHR	INT	26	546	166	34	5	11	40	52	8	9	.304	.351	.445	.146	.291	.343	.440	.024	33.2	120-2B 2	
2004	COL	NL	27	522	153	15	3	6	29	53	12	7	.293	.329	.368	-.117	.275	.311	.346	-.184	7.9	116-2B -3	
2005	*COL*	*NL*	*28*	*508*	*149*	*28*	*3*	*9*	*33*	*48*	*9*	*4*	*.292*	*.335*	*.414*	*-.023*	*.270*	*.315*	*.373*	*-.133*	*7.3*	*130-2B -2*	

Breakout: 7% *Improve: 21%* *Collapse: 41%*

This is not a player who helps a good club. He's a slap hitter who hasn't held onto his gains as he's advanced, and a full-time player in Coors who hits an empty .293 had better be +20 runs with the glove, which Miles isn't. He could hang onto his job due to inertia and the dissonance created by that .293 number, no matter how little else is actually there. If his hand injury's healed, and he gets any sleep after the birth of his child, his offense might perk up, but it's not a good bet.

TONY MILLER CF Bats: R Throws: R Born: 18-Aug-1980 Age: 24

YEAR	TM	LG	AGE	AB	H	2B	3B	HR	BB	SO	SB	CS	AVG	OBP	SLG	MLVR	EQBA	EQOBP	EQSLG	EQMLVR	VORP	DEFENSE	
2002	ASH	SAL	21	501	142	23	4	17	88	129	50	19	.283	.396	.447	.156	.216	.309	.352	-.218	-11.7	127-CF -15	
2003	VIS	CLF	22	266	66	14	5	4	40	58	11	7	.248	.349	.383	-.030	.202	.289	.311	-.320	-14.7	63-CF -2	
2004	TUL	TXS	23	414	113	17	2	11	68	99	20	12	.273	.385	.403	.107	.245	.342	.365	-.118	4.1	83-CF -1	21-LF 1
2005	*COL*	*NL*	*24*	*226*	*60*	*11*	*2*	*7*	*28*	*55*	*8*	*3*	*.265*	*.353*	*.423*	*-.002*	*.245*	*.331*	*.382*	*-.110*	*3.7*	*64-CF -4*	

Breakout: 35% *Improve: 55%* *Collapse: 25%*

Love this guy. Just 5′9″, 180 lbs., Miller draws a lot of walks, has some pop, can catch the ball, and is unbelievably fast. He'll play this coming season at Triple-A, and if he can add 10 singles a year and steal bases more efficiently, he could end up as an outstanding major leaguer a couple years down the road. There's no reason he can't be a more complete version of Juan Pierre.

JAYSON NIX 2B Bats: R Throws: R Born: 26-Aug-1982 Age: 22

YEAR	TM	LG	AGE	AB	H	2B	3B	HR	BB	SO	SB	CS	AVG	OBP	SLG	MLVR	EQBA	EQOBP	EQSLG	EQMLVR	VORP	DEFENSE	
2002	ASH	SAL	19	487	120	29	2	14	62	105	14	5	.246	.340	.400	.002	.189	.261	.318	-.374	-30.8	128-2B -22	
2003	VIS	CLF	20	562	158	46	0	21	54	131	24	8	.281	.351	.475	.122	.217	.275	.369	-.260	-14.6	135-2B 14	
2004	TUL	TXS	21	456	97	17	1	14	40	101	14	3	.213	.292	.346	-.173	.190	.256	.312	-.392	-30.9	118-2B 8	
2005	*COL*	*NL*	*22*	*264*	*66*	*15*	*1*	*9*	*22*	*62*	*4*	*2*	*.249*	*.319*	*.416*	*-.081*	*.230*	*.299*	*.376*	*-.184*	*1.4*	*72-2B -3*	

Breakout: 52% *Improve: 68%* *Collapse: 20%*

Took a step back as one of the youngest players in the Texas League, hitting .213 after a great '03 season at Visalia. Nix runs well, hits for power, and could be a solid second baseman, but his batting eye may limit him for a while. There's talk of moving him to Triple-A this year, but you'd like to see him fare well in the Texas League first. Either way, one bad season doesn't wreck a prospect, so keep him on your radar screen.

KIT PELLOW OF Bats: R Throws: R Born: 28-Aug-1973 Age: 31

YEAR	TM	LG	AGE	AB	H	2B	3B	HR	BB	SO	SB	CS	AVG	OBP	SLG	MLVR	EQBA	EQOBP	EQSLG	EQMLVR	VORP	DEFENSE	
2002	OMA	PCL	28	402	116	25	2	27	21	82	4	2	.289	.350	.562	.270	.270	.324	.516	.079	29.9	79-3B -6	22-1B -2
2002	KCR	AL	28	63	15	1	0	1	9	21	1	1	.238	.342	.302	-.189	.242	.323	.306	-.237	-0.6	11-3B -1	
2003	CSP	PCL	29	320	93	15	1	19	25	75	2	1	.291	.363	.522	.148	.236	.307	.433	-.098	-1.4	51-1B -2	21-C -1
2004	CSP	PCL	30	42	15	4	0	3	4	7	0	0	.357	.417	.667	.436	.250	.276	.450	-.119	0.1		
2004	COL	NL	30	121	29	5	1	2	8	43	1	0	.240	.308	.347	-.218	.225	.292	.317	-.294	-2.7	12-RF 1	
2005	*COL*	*NL*	*31*	*163*	*45*	*10*	*1*	*8*	*13*	*43*	*1*	*0*	*.277*	*.352*	*.496*	*.102*	*.256*	*.330*	*.448*	*-.018*	*8.1*	*47-RF -2*	

Breakout: 39% *Improve: 55%* *Collapse: 30%*

The Service Time Quest continues. Pellow does what he does. Got a corner spot you need filled for a reasonable price by someone with some right-handed pop? Kit's available, and can be there quickly. If someone gives him 500 AB, well, he would certainly take them. Still has a shot at a career as a pinch-hitter/bench guy; has absolutely demonstrated perseverance.

JORGE PIEDRA — OF — Bats: L — Throws: L — Born: 17-Apr-1979 — Age: 26

YEAR	TM	LG	AGE	AB	H	2B	3B	HR	BB	SO	SB	CS	AVG	OBP	SLG	MLVR	EQBA	EQOBP	EQSLG	EQMLVR	VORP	DEFENSE
2002	SLM	CRL	23	392	118	37	12	13	37	55	10	2	.301	.366	.556	.346	.262	.318	.493	.028	10.0	58-LF 1 41-RF -1
2002	WTN	SOU	23	60	10	3	1	0	3	11	2	0	.167	.219	.250	-.379	.131	.154	.197	-.784	-12.9	14-LF 0
2003	TUL	TXS	24	357	98	17	7	18	31	50	5	2	.275	.342	.513	.209	.249	.310	.478	-.019	5.2	62-RF 1 14-LF 0
2004	CSP	PCL	25	377	126	29	5	15	23	56	4	3	.334	.372	.557	.179	.271	.308	.442	-.054	0.1	70-LF 1 20-RF 0
2004	COL	NL	25	91	27	8	0	3	5	19	0	1	.297	.340	.484	.061	.289	.316	.444	-.021	3.6	13-CF 0
2005	*COL*	*NL*	*26*	*252*	*72*	*17*	*3*	*11*	*18*	*41*	*2*	*1*	*.286*	*.340*	*.506*	*.105*	*.265*	*.319*	*.456*	*-.018*	*9.1*	*68-LF 1*

Breakout: 19% *Improve: 50%* *Collapse: 30%*

Decent outfielder who wasn't overmatched in his first go at the majors. Piedra's not going to be a superstar, but he could earn a starting job with just mild improvement in his offensive game. He'll probably get at least a platoon shot this season, perhaps more than that if he performs well and Preston Wilson gets dealt or comes back slowly from injury.

JEFF SALAZAR — CF — Bats: L — Throws: L — Born: 24-Nov-1980 — Age: 24

YEAR	TM	LG	AGE	AB	H	2B	3B	HR	BB	SO	SB	CS	AVG	OBP	SLG	MLVR	EQBA	EQOBP	EQSLG	EQMLVR	VORP	DEFENSE
2002	TRI	NWN	21	268	63	5	4	4	47	43	10	6	.235	.351	.328	.070	.217	.302	.304	-.296	-24.4	71-CF -2
2003	ASH	SAL	22	486	138	23	4	29	77	74	28	14	.284	.387	.527	.250	.216	.299	.404	-.167	-3.1	126-CF 6
2004	VIS	CLF	23	314	109	18	9	13	38	33	17	2	.347	.419	.586	.429	.278	.342	.458	.036	17.2	71-CF 2
2004	TUL	TXS	23	224	50	13	2	1	35	31	10	3	.223	.331	.312	-.141	.207	.300	.291	-.322	-13.0	46-CF 0 16-LF 0
2005	*COL*	*NL*	*24*	*229*	*65*	*13*	*3*	*8*	*26*	*33*	*6*	*2*	*.286*	*.361*	*.475*	*.097*	*.264*	*.339*	*.429*	*-.022*	*10.0*	*65-CF 0*

Breakout: 43% *Improve: 68%* *Collapse: 14%*

Frequently pops up on prospect lists, for the same reasons that Choo Freeman and Matt Holliday did, and with just as much reason. Aided by friendly parks and leagues in A-ball, assuming he can regroup and master Double-A in time to have a career, he's a solid enough center fielder to handle the position. More likely to aspire to the wanderings of fourth outfielderdom.

RYAN SHEALY — 1B — Bats: R — Throws: R — Born: 29-Aug-1979 — Age: 25

YEAR	TM	LG	AGE	AB	H	2B	3B	HR	BB	SO	SB	CS	AVG	OBP	SLG	MLVR	EQBA	EQOBP	EQSLG	EQMLVR	VORP	DEFENSE
2002	CAS	PIO	22	231	85	21	1	19	50	52	0	0	.368	.497	.714	.714	.250	.345	.466	.028	15.6	65-1B 3
2003	VIS	CLF	23	341	102	31	1	14	42	72	0	0	.299	.391	.519	.260	.234	.311	.406	-.129	-4.8	76-1B -5
2004	TUL	TXS	24	469	149	32	3	29	61	123	1	1	.318	.411	.584	.434	.280	.360	.514	.147	35.1	125-1B -11
2005	*COL*	*NL*	*25*	*263*	*76*	*17*	*2*	*15*	*30*	*70*	*0*	*0*	*.289*	*.382*	*.536*	*.213*	*.267*	*.358*	*.484*	*.085*	*19.7*	*75-1B -3*

Breakout: 31% *Improve: 47%* *Collapse: 28%*

A born DH, Shealy's hit at every stop along the way, often to the extent where you say "How come they're leaving this dude in the Cal League? Do they want to destroy the confidence of opposing pitchers, or do they just want to dent the fences of some field in the Inland Empire?" Shealy's something of an ox-boy, but he plays the role well, swinging at pitches in the strike zone with seriously bad intentions. He draws his walks, gets his hits, and yes, strikes out a lot. Definitely has the masher look; when he creams the ball, he looks like a right-handed Travis Hafner.

IAN STEWART — 3B — Bats: L — Throws: R — Born: 05-Apr-1985 — Age: 20

YEAR	TM	LG	AGE	AB	H	2B	3B	HR	BB	SO	SB	CS	AVG	OBP	SLG	MLVR	EQBA	EQOBP	EQSLG	EQMLVR	VORP	DEFENSE
2003	CAS	PIO	18	224	71	14	5	10	29	54	4	1	.317	.401	.558	.323	.224	.291	.379	-.211	-3.9	51-3B -7
2004	ASH	SAL	19	505	161	31	9	30	66	112	19	9	.319	.398	.594	.328	.245	.314	.449	-.055	20.2	115-3B 13
2005	*COL*	*NL*	*20*	*409*	*110*	*24*	*4*	*17*	*42*	*101*	*7*	*3*	*.270*	*.340*	*.476*	*.051*	*.249*	*.319*	*.430*	*-.065*	*6.3*	*109-3B -3*

Breakout: 34% *Improve: 56%* *Collapse: 23%*

Definitely the most Scottish-sounding name in the NL West, with the possible exception of Angus MacBondsgunnghaggh in the San Diego system. A third-base prospect with serious power, he's young enough to develop into a star if he continues his current trajectory at High-A or Double-A this season. Eighteen months younger than Andy Marte, he's on the same development path, and could claim Marte's lofty place on the prospect hierarchy, and make the big league roster by 2006.

MARK SWEENEY PH **Bats: L** **Throws: L** Born: 26-Oct-1969 Age: 35

YEAR	TM	LG	AGE	AB	H	2B	3B	HR	BB	SO	SB	CS	AVG	OBP	SLG	MLVR	EQBA	EQOBP	EQSLG	EQMLVR	VORP	DEFENSE
2002	SDP	NL	32	65	11	3	0	1	4	19	0	0	.169	.217	.262	-.430	.185	.216	.262	-.545	-4.7	
2003	CSP	PCL	33	165	49	10	1	5	34	32	1	4	.297	.407	.461	.143	.249	.357	.396	-.045	1.1	23-RF -1
2003	COL	NL	33	97	25	9	0	2	9	27	0	1	.258	.321	.412	-.045	.247	.297	.381	-.181	1.7	
2004	COL	NL	34	177	47	12	2	9	32	51	1	0	.266	.377	.508	.136	.243	.356	.469	.046	14.0	16-RF 1
2005	*COL*	*NL*	*35*	*125*	*32*	*7*	*1*	*5*	*18*	*33*	*0*	*0*	*.256*	*.352*	*.454*	*.029*	*.237*	*.330*	*.410*	*-.082*	*2.5*	*38-RF -6*

Breakout: 28% *Improve: 42%* *Collapse: 26%*

It's gratifying to see Sweeney do well enough to provide long term for his family. He never really got the playing time that many have felt he earned. He's productive off the bench, can fill in for a while as a starter and keep a good team going while doing it. Defensively, he's exposed in the outfield, but not so much as the likes of Pete Incaviglia. Landed in San Diego, where he'll be a good fourth outfielder and potent bat off the Padres' much-improved bench. A class act, and we'll be rooting for him.

ANDY TRACY 1B/3B **Bats: L** **Throws: R** Born: 11-Dec-1973 Age: 31

YEAR	TM	LG	AGE	AB	H	2B	3B	HR	BB	SO	SB	CS	AVG	OBP	SLG	MLVR	EQBA	EQOBP	EQSLG	EQMLVR	VORP	DEFENSE	
2002	NOR	INT	28	432	86	16	1	20	56	123	4	1	.199	.295	.380	-.097	.189	.285	.366	-.262	-11.2	66-3B -5	39-1B 0
2003	TUL	TXS	29	384	115	24	1	25	41	116	3	3	.299	.371	.562	.346	.266	.333	.516	.090	32.9	74-3B -1	21-1B -2
2004	COL	NL	30	16	3	1	0	0	1	8	0	0	.188	.235	.250	-.501	.187	.148	.250	-.700	-1.2		
2004	CSP	PCL	30	464	146	42	3	33	58	115	4	2	.315	.390	.631	.292	.252	.327	.488	.028	15.7	96-1B -7	14-3B 0
2005	*COL*	*NL*	*31*	*110*	*29*	*6*	*1*	*6*	*13*	*34*	*1*	*0*	*.264*	*.346*	*.508*	*.096*	*.244*	*.324*	*.458*	*-.023*	*5.3*	*34-1B -2*	

Breakout: 40% *Improve: 53%* *Collapse: 30%*

Is he good enough to be a Ken Phelps All-Star? Tracy's better than some starting third basemen, and the Rockies have signed him to hang around and possibly replace Mark Sweeney. If he gets the playing time, he could put up some big numbers in XBH and Ks, so you know we love him. Something in the .275/.350/.500 range is probably a pretty good guess in Coors, though small sample size caveats apply.

PRESTON WILSON CF **Bats: R** **Throws: R** Born: 19-Jul-1974 Age: 30

YEAR	TM	LG	AGE	AB	H	2B	3B	HR	BB	SO	SB	CS	AVG	OBP	SLG	MLVR	EQBA	EQOBP	EQSLG	EQMLVR	VORP	DEFENSE
2002	FLA	NL	27	510	124	22	2	23	58	140	20	11	.243	.329	.429	.026	.250	.332	.452	-.015	22.9	128-CF -13
2003	COL	NL	28	600	169	43	1	36	54	139	14	7	.282	.343	.537	.160	.264	.327	.508	.067	46.8	151-CF -13
2004	COL	NL	29	202	50	11	0	6	17	49	2	1	.248	.315	.391	-.131	.231	.293	.357	-.233	0.6	52-CF -3
2005	*COL*	*NL*	*30*	*288*	*78*	*17*	*1*	*15*	*30*	*65*	*6*	*2*	*.273*	*.347*	*.497*	*.091*	*.252*	*.326*	*.448*	*-.028*	*11.9*	*79-CF -6*

Breakout: 36% *Improve: 62%* *Collapse: 21%*

A nagging knee injury cost him most of the season, depressing endless roto owners who have an inflated idea of Wilson's real value because of his combination of speed and power and his home park. When it comes to real baseball, Wilson's dramatically overrated: He's fast, but doesn't steal bases efficiently, doesn't hit particularly well for average or draw walks, and plays visible but ineffective defense, a la Ken Griffey Jr. early in his career. The Rockies are trying to move him, but his injury and prohibitive salary have thwarted all attempts to date.

PITCHERS

ADAM BERNERO **Bats: R** **Throws: R** Born: 28-Nov-1976 Age: 28

YEAR	TM	LG	AGE	G	GS	IP	H	BB	SO	HR	ERA	EQERA	EQH9	EQBB9	EQSO9	EQHR9	PERA	VORP	STF
2002	TOL	INT	25	9	9	57.0	46	13	49	2	1.58	2.68	7.7	2.3	6.7	0.5	3.19	14.4	24
2002	DET	AL	25	28	11	101.7	128	31	69	17	6.19	6.20	10.1	2.5	5.8	1.4	4.87	-6.5	-3
2003	DET	AL	26	18	17	100.7	104	41	54	14	6.08	5.64	9.2	3.5	4.8	1.2	4.72	0.0	-3
2003	COL	NL	26	31	0	32.7	33	13	26	5	5.23	5.34	8.7	3.1	6.5	1.1	4.22	-1.6	-2
2004	CSP	PCL	27	9	8	48.3	57	10	48	0	3.17	3.91	9.1	1.9	6.7	0.2	3.54	11.1	16
2004	COL	NL	27	16	2	32.3	36	17	21	7	5.57	4.78	9.6	4.2	5.1	1.7	5.62	0.6	-23
2005	*ATL*	*NL*	*28*	*24*	*13*	*89.7*	*92*	*32*	*65*	*12*	*4.63*	*4.90*	*9.3*	*2.8*	*5.8*	*1.2*	*4.83*	*8.8*	*1*

Breakout: 22% *Improve: 47%* *Collapse: 20%*

Acquired from Detroit as part of the Ben Petrick trade, Bernero always has been a borderline prospect with a little potential to surprise. He had some reasonable numbers in the minors, and occasionally showed a glimpse of that potential in the bigs, even as he was generally getting whacked around the yard. He's now clearly established as a fringe pitcher in the John Wasdin phylum, and was outrighted. He'll have his agent on the phone trying to wrangle a spring training invite somewhere.

SHAWN CHACON Bats: R Throws: R Born: 23-Dec-1977 Age: 27

YEAR	TM	LG	AGE	G	GS	IP	H	BB	SO	HR	ERA	EQERA	EQH9	EQBB9	EQSO9	EQHR9	PERA	VORP	STF
2002	COL	NL	24	21	21	119.3	122	60	67	25	5.73	5.57	9.6	3.9	4.6	1.8	5.65	-11.1	-13
2003	COL	NL	25	23	23	137.0	124	58	93	12	4.60	4.21	8.1	3.4	5.6	0.7	3.80	13.7	13
2004	COL	NL	26	66	0	63.3	71	52	52	12	7.11	6.36	9.3	6.4	6.4	1.4	5.94	-11.9	-19
2005	*COL*	*NL*	*27*	*22*	*5*	*48.0*	*53*	*28*	*35*	*9*	*6.17*	*5.39*	*9.3*	*4.4*	*6.2*	*1.3*	*5.26*	*3.0*	*-8*

Breakout: 20% *Improve: 44%* *Collapse: 32%*

It's kind of hard to pick nits about what role a guy should play when he's pitching this badly. His 7+ ERA last season was not just an artifice of Coors Field; his road ERA was above 6.00. Right-handers hit him about how Bobby Abreu hits against the league; left-handers didn't fare much worse. Chacon has to bounce back somewhat; no one's this bad. And credit Colorado GM Dan O'Dowd for chutzpah, because after Chacon's 2004 debacle, he spent the off-season attempting to trade him to Texas for Ian Kinsler. "Gosh, really? Wait by the phone, Dan. We'll get back to you."

AARON COOK Bats: R Throws: R Born: 08-Feb-1979 Age: 26

YEAR	TM	LG	AGE	G	GS	IP	H	BB	SO	HR	ERA	EQERA	EQH9	EQBB9	EQSO9	EQHR9	PERA	VORP	STF
2002	CAR	SOU	23	14	14	95.0	73	19	58	4	1.42	3.31	8.2	1.8	4.2	0.7	2.90	26.1	11
2002	CSP	PCL	23	10	10	64.3	67	18	32	6	3.78	5.05	8.7	2.6	3.5	0.9	3.47	14.7	14
2002	COL	NL	23	9	5	35.7	41	13	14	4	4.54	4.15	10.1	2.9	3.1	1.0	5.19	3.7	0
2003	COL	NL	24	43	16	124.0	160	57	43	8	6.02	5.57	10.2	3.5	2.8	0.5	5.07	-10.8	-12
2004	CSP	PCL	25	7	7	46.0	34	8	25	1	2.74	2.93	7.1	1.7	4.0	0.2	2.51	14.8	17
2004	COL	NL	25	16	16	96.7	112	39	40	7	4.28	3.78	9.5	3.2	3.3	0.6	4.53	14.9	3
2005	*COL*	*NL*	*26*	*21*	*18*	*102.7*	*128*	*40*	*50*	*13*	*5.28*	*4.61*	*10.6*	*3.0*	*4.1*	*0.9*	*4.94*	*11.8*	*-5*

Breakout: 22% *Improve: 44%* *Collapse: 24%*

He's never put up the big strikeout numbers you like to see, but he did have a fairly nice year, all things considered. A 4.28 ERA in roughly half a season's worth of work in Coors is worth a handshake and a pat on the back. Is he likely to keep it up? Well, he didn't have tremendous control, but he did prevent opponents from hitting the ball over the fence, which is certainly a good thing. Still, the numbers look more like David Fleming than David Wells. He's out until at least the beginning of June after surgery to remove a rib that was impairing his circulation.

MIKE ESPOSITO Bats: R Throws: R Born: 27-Sep-1981 Age: 23

YEAR	TM	LG	AGE	G	GS	IP	H	BB	SO	HR	ERA	EQERA	EQH9	EQBB9	EQSO9	EQHR9	PERA	VORP	STF
2003	VIS	CLF	21	27	27	161.0	173	55	116	14	3.75	5.50	10.0	3.9	4.2	1.5	5.97	-6.2	-8
2004	TUL	TXS	22	24	24	143.3	138	35	90	12	3.33	4.44	9.8	2.5	4.2	1.2	5.33	4.0	0
2005	*COL*	*NL*	*23*	*17*	*10*	*64.3*	*81*	*27*	*37*	*12*	*6.11*	*5.34*	*10.7*	*3.2*	*4.9*	*1.3*	*5.39*	*3.1*	*-8*

Breakout: 6% *Improve: 44%* *Collapse: 20%*

Pitched pretty well in Tulsa after earning a promotion from Visalia, where good control kept his ERA down. He throws to spots with a broad repertoire, without any one pitch that can make batters miss. If everything breaks right for him, he could become Justin Duchscherer lite.

SHAWN ESTES Bats: R Throws: L Born: 18-Feb-1973 Age: 32

YEAR	TM	LG	AGE	G	GS	IP	H	BB	SO	HR	ERA	EQERA	EQH9	EQBB9	EQSO9	EQHR9	PERA	VORP	STF
2002	NYM	NL	29	23	23	132.7	133	66	92	12	4.54	4.95	9.1	3.8	5.6	0.8	4.53	11.1	5
2002	CIN	NL	29	6	6	28.0	38	17	17	1	7.71	7.53	10.4	4.4	4.7	0.3	5.34	-6.9	-7
2003	CHC	NL	30	29	28	152.3	182	83	103	20	5.73	6.42	10.1	4.2	5.4	1.1	5.41	-16.6	-4
2004	COL	NL	31	34	34	202.0	223	105	117	30	5.84	5.10	9.3	4.1	4.6	1.1	5.06	-3.6	-5
2005	*ARI*	*NL*	*32*	*27*	*26*	*146.7*	*161*	*70*	*91*	*18*	*5.05*	*5.04*	*9.7*	*3.7*	*5.1*	*1.0*	*5.11*	*9.7*	*-1*

Breakout 18% *Improve 51%* *Collapse 17%*

(continued next page)

Shawn Estes *(continued)*

One thing you need to get used to if you're going to make business decisions in extreme environments is distorted numbers. Estes's ERA for the year was 5.84, which would be absolutely horrible just about anywhere else. But the Equivalent ERA is only 5.10, so Estes wasn't absolutely abysmal, merely lousy. It's an important distinction. Aside from poor walk, strikeout, hit, and home run numbers, everything else about Estes screams "Cy Young Candidate."

JEFF FRANCIS Bats: L Throws: L Born: 08-Jan-1981 Age: 24

YEAR	TM	LG	AGE	G	GS	IP	H	BB	SO	HR	ERA	EQERA	EQH9	EQBB9	EQSO9	EQHR9	PERA	VORP	STF
2003	VIS	CLF	22	27	27	160.7	135	45	153	8	3.47	4.71	8.4	3.2	5.6	0.8	4.23	22.7	12
2004	TUL	TXS	23	17	17	113.7	73	22	147	9	1.98	3.05	7.7	2.0	8.7	1.2	3.66	22.3	32
2004	CSP	PCL	23	7	7	41.0	35	7	49	3	2.85	3.40	7.5	1.6	8.4	0.7	2.95	11.7	37
2004	COL	NL	23	7	7	36.7	42	13	32	8	5.15	4.71	9.4	2.7	6.9	1.7	4.95	1.5	12
2005	*COL*	*NL*	*24*	*19*	*18*	*106.7*	*114*	*38*	*90*	*18*	*5.04*	*4.40*	*9.0*	*2.7*	*7.1*	*1.2*	*4.31*	*17.0*	*16*

Breakout: 7% Improve: 21% Collapse: 30%

Highly touted, Grade A prospect. Francis throws hard, has good command and control, big K rates, nothing not to like. He had a couple of rough outings in his call-up, but even then, his peripheral numbers were very good. He's ready to be a #1 starter larva in the bigs, but he is facing a serious mountain climb because of the organization he's in. Looking through the history of the Rockies, one is not exactly overwhelmed with their ability to draft and develop pitchers that lead rotations. Still, Francis was handled well until last year, when the Rockies should have cut him off before 30 starts (over three levels). It's not as if Francis was the difference between the wild card and an early end to the season.

BRIAN FUENTES Bats: L Throws: L Born: 09-Aug-1975 Age: 29

YEAR	TM	LG	AGE	G	GS	IP	H	BB	SO	HR	ERA	EQERA	EQH9	EQBB9	EQSO9	EQHR9	PERA	VORP	STF
2002	CSP	PCL	26	41	0	48.7	44	32	61	0	3.70	4.34	7.4	6.2	8.7	0.2	3.40	11.7	8
2002	COL	NL	26	31	0	26.7	25	13	38	4	4.72	4.05	8.1	3.7	11.1	1.4	4.39	1.9	22
2003	COL	NL	27	75	0	75.3	64	34	82	7	2.75	2.55	7.4	3.5	8.9	0.7	3.41	23.0	16
2004	COL	NL	28	47	0	44.7	46	19	48	5	5.64	5.24	8.3	3.4	8.5	0.8	4.03	-1.7	13
2005	*COL*	*NL*	*29*	*41*	*1*	*57.0*	*56*	*29*	*58*	*8*	*4.74*	*4.14*	*8.4*	*3.9*	*8.7*	*1.0*	*4.36*	*10.4*	*10*

Breakout: 17% Improve: 42% Collapse: 34%

He doubled his ERA from 2003 to 2004, but that's more a function of luck switching from good to bad than his underlying performance changing much. A strained back muscle that knocked him out for several weeks didn't help, and the Rockies will monitor his condition closely this season. It'll be interesting to see if the real Fuentes is the specialist who fared 258 OPS points better against lefties than righties in '04 or the balanced pitcher of '03.

CHRIS GISSELL Bats: R Throws: R Born: 04-Jan-1978 Age: 27

YEAR	TM	LG	AGE	G	GS	IP	H	BB	SO	HR	ERA	EQERA	EQH9	EQBB9	EQSO9	EQHR9	PERA	VORP	STF
2002	IOW	PCL	24	28	27	154.3	177	61	133	19	6.12	6.37	9.9	3.7	6.0	1.3	5.29	5.2	-8
2003	CSP	PCL	25	38	10	109.0	96	35	82	8	3.55	4.47	8.2	3.3	5.9	0.9	3.68	21.9	-9
2004	CSP	PCL	26	24	8	90.7	80	17	74	11	3.67	3.87	8.2	1.8	5.8	1.2	3.56	19.5	22
2004	COL	NL	26	5	1	8.7	20	3	11	4	14.48	12.10	14.9	2.8	9.3	2.8	9.31	-8.5	11
2005	*STL*	*NL*	*27*	*22*	*10*	*77.0*	*71*	*26*	*58*	*10*	*4.03*	*4.31*	*8.4*	*2.7*	*6.1*	*1.2*	*4.33*	*12.0*	*4*

Breakout: 29% Improve: 49% Collapse: 28%

He's bounced around some, and got beaten up in a short stint in the bigs in 2004, but Gissell wouldn't be a bad flyer for a team looking to fill out a roster. He's had some success in the minors, can make batters swing and miss with some pretty good stuff, and his control's gotten better over the years. For the league minimum, some club could take a reasonable gamble. He's not going to be Roger Clemens, but he could be Kenny Rogers's younger brother for a few years if he gets a shot.

TIM HARIKKALA Bats: R Throws: R Born: 15-Jul-1971 Age: 33

YEAR	TM	LG	AGE	G	GS	IP	H	BB	SO	HR	ERA	EQERA	EQH9	EQBB9	EQSO9	EQHR9	PERA	VORP	STF
2002	IND	INT	30	31	20	162.0	172	23	90	8	3.50	4.55	9.6	1.5	4.3	0.6	4.20	24.0	11
2003	OAX	MEX	31	12	12	79.7	98	17	50	5	4.63	5.73	9.2	1.8	5.5	0.8	4.09	7.4	25
2003	OTT	INT	31	20	3	44.3	27	7	29	0	0.81	1.58	7.0	1.8	4.9	0.2	2.47	13.9	20
2004	COL	NL	32	55	0	62.7	55	23	30	10	4.74	4.25	8.3	3.0	3.9	1.2	4.10	5.7	-17
2005	*OAK*	*AL*	*33*	*32*	*2*	*51.0*	*56*	*16*	*28*	*7*	*4.60*	*4.55*	*10.0*	*2.6*	*4.5*	*1.1*	*4.64*	*8.4*	*-12*

Breakout: 24% *Improve: 56%* *Collapse: 21%*

Journeyman who managed to get in nearly an entire season in the bigs, and pitched pretty well. Considering his lengthy career itinerary, it's nice to see him catch on somewhere and earn some more service time. He got picked up by Oakland in October, and since then, the A's have added Juan Cruz, Kiko Calero, Jairo Garcia, and Huston Street to the pen, for all intents and purposes. You think it's going to take him long to pack, or do you think Tim's got that pretty well down?

JASON JENNINGS Bats: L Throws: R Born: 17-Jul-1978 Age: 26

YEAR	TM	LG	AGE	G	GS	IP	H	BB	SO	HR	ERA	EQERA	EQH9	EQBB9	EQSO9	EQHR9	PERA	VORP	STF
2002	COL	NL	23	32	32	185.3	201	70	127	26	4.52	4.38	9.5	2.9	5.5	1.2	4.92	11.3	3
2003	COL	NL	24	32	32	181.3	212	88	119	20	5.11	4.96	9.5	3.8	5.3	0.9	4.91	-0.2	2
2004	COL	NL	25	33	33	201.0	241	101	133	27	5.51	4.78	9.6	3.9	5.2	1.0	5.10	3.7	0
2005	*COL*	*NL*	*26*	*27*	*27*	*153.7*	*185*	*71*	*102*	*22*	*5.66*	*4.94*	*10.2*	*3.6*	*5.6*	*1.0*	*5.03*	*12.6*	*4*

Breakout: 9% *Improve: 42%* *Collapse: 18%*

Jennings hasn't been as bad as his raw numbers, and it's hard to appreciate his value given his surroundings. He's been pretty much a league neutralish pitcher, throwing a bunch of innings for a team that needs more than that. On another club, he might be perceived as a solid workhorse. What you see with Jennings is what you get; a mild bounceback is a reasonable expectation.

JOE KENNEDY Bats: R Throws: L Born: 24-May-1979 Age: 26

YEAR	TM	LG	AGE	G	GS	IP	H	BB	SO	HR	ERA	EQERA	EQH9	EQBB9	EQSO9	EQHR9	PERA	VORP	STF
2002	TBY	AL	23	30	30	196.7	204	55	109	23	4.53	4.82	9.2	2.4	4.8	1.0	4.21	16.7	6
2003	TBY	AL	24	32	22	133.7	167	47	77	19	6.13	6.24	10.6	3.0	5.1	1.2	5.76	-10.6	-7
2004	COL	NL	25	27	27	162.3	163	67	117	17	3.66	3.28	8.5	3.3	5.8	0.8	4.07	36.0	11
2005	*COL*	*NL*	*26*	*27*	*25*	*143.3*	*169*	*55*	*99*	*23*	*5.46*	*4.77*	*10.0*	*3.0*	*5.9*	*1.1*	*4.85*	*14.3*	*6*

Breakout: 11% *Improve: 42%* *Collapse: 18%*

Not long ago, he was one of the hottest prospects in baseball after posting a 0.19 ERA over 47 Double-A innings in the Tampa Bay system. The Rays overworked him, his velocity vanished, and he was moved to Colorado, another knot in the "Chuck LaMar as GM" dreamcatcher. Kennedy, who's always had a rep for being a smart pitcher, got some of his velocity back, and starting dusting hitters again. He missed some time with shoulder inflammation in mid-season, but came back and pitched very well. Overall, he was a bargain, and the Rockies likely will try to sign him to a long-term deal. If he's healthy, he's a good gamble—though PECOTA's bearish.

JAVIER LOPEZ Bats: L Throws: L Born: 11-Jul-1977 Age: 27

YEAR	TM	LG	AGE	G	GS	IP	H	BB	SO	HR	ERA	EQERA	EQH9	EQBB9	EQSO9	EQHR9	PERA	VORP	STF
2002	ELP	TXS	24	61	0	46.3	34	16	47	3	2.72	3.80	7.8	3.4	7.2	1.1	3.80	8.5	6
2003	COL	NL	25	75	0	58.3	58	12	40	5	3.70	3.34	8.6	1.6	5.6	0.6	3.49	11.4	8
2004	COL	NL	26	64	0	40.7	45	26	20	1	7.52	6.42	9.1	5.1	3.8	0.2	4.65	-8.2	-21
2005	*COL*	*NL*	*27*	*45*	*0*	*50.3*	*61*	*24*	*31*	*6*	*5.54*	*4.84*	*10.2*	*3.7*	*5.2*	*0.9*	*4.95*	*4.5*	*-12*

Breakout: 16% *Improve: 42%* *Collapse: 26%*

It's pretty hard to rack up 64 appearances and post a 7.52 ERA. If someone does that, you can be pretty sure that he's (a) left-handed, and (b) not on a particularly good team. Like Fuentes, Lopez's numbers just ballooned after a strong 2003. Unlike Fuentes, the spike was supported by a breakdown in his peripherals. He could rebound at a new address, and the Rockies looked to be shopping him as of this writing.

LUIS MARTINEZ **Bats: L** **Throws: L** Born: 20-Jan-1980 Age: 25

YEAR	TM	LG	AGE	G	GS	IP	H	BB	SO	HR	ERA	EQERA	EQH9	EQBB9	EQSO9	EQHR9	PERA	VORP	STF
2002	HUN	SOU	22	29	18	109.0	114	65	106	6	5.20	6.60	9.6	5.1	6.4	0.9	5.49	1.3	-13
2003	HUN	SOU	23	20	20	115.0	93	54	116	4	2.58	4.63	8.4	4.4	6.6	0.6	4.46	13.6	2
2003	IND	INT	23	7	7	45.7	37	19	46	0	0.98	1.67	7.5	4.4	7.5	0.2	3.35	10.8	25
2003	MIL	NL	23	4	4	16.3	25	15	10	3	9.94	9.53	11.6	6.9	4.8	1.6	7.94	-7.7	-26
2004	TEN	SOU	24	16	16	94.3	96	36	77	7	4.10	5.36	9.5	3.5	5.2	1.0	4.96	6.3	0
2004	MEM	PCL	24	7	7	42.7	53	23	35	7	5.06	5.57	10.3	4.9	5.6	1.5	6.43	-3.9	-11
2004	CSP	PCL	24	5	4	27.7	34	16	21	4	6.82	6.26	9.9	5.3	5.3	1.3	5.93	-1.0	-11
2005	*COL*	*NL*	*25*	*20*	*12*	*75.0*	*86*	*40*	*56*	*11*	*5.83*	*5.09*	*9.7*	*4.1*	*6.3*	*1.0*	*5.06*	*5.1*	*0*

Breakout: 11% *Improve: 40%* *Collapse: 23%*

Has a live arm, with a curve that makes scouts drool, and his early-career performance records were promising. But 2004 was one of those years for Martinez, who pitched badly everywhere except the Southern League, where he was undistinguished, and ended up getting outrighted. He may well re-sign with the Rockies, but he could also end up somewhere else.

JIM MILLER **Bats: R** **Throws: R** Born: 28-Apr-1982 Age: 23

YEAR	TM	LG	AGE	G	GS	IP	H	BB	SO	HR	ERA	EQERA	EQH9	EQBB9	EQSO9	EQHR9	PERA	VORP	STF
2004	TRI	NWN	22	34	0	37.0	21	11	65	1	0.97	4.13	7.7	3.9	8.5	0.6	3.58	7.3	12
2005	*COL*	*NL*	*23*	*26*	*2*	*43.3*	*44*	*20*	*41*	*5*	*4.75*	*4.15*	*8.6*	*3.5*	*8.1*	*0.9*	*4.16*	*7.1*	*10*

Breakout: 11% *Improve: 34%* *Collapse: 31%*

Drafted in the eighth round, Miller was sent to the Tri-City Dust Devils and went all Eric Gagne on the league: Hitters came up to the plate, and returned the dugout in shriveled despair. Miller struck out 65 in 37 innings, allowing a mere 21 hits. With his stuff, he'll have the opportunity to move up quickly. Don't be surprised to see him in Colorado very shortly.

CHRIS NARVESON **Bats: L** **Throws: L** Born: 20-Dec-1981 Age: 23

YEAR	TM	LG	AGE	G	GS	IP	H	BB	SO	HR	ERA	EQERA	EQH9	EQBB9	EQSO9	EQHR9	PERA	VORP	STF
2002	PEO	MDW	20	9	9	42.3	49	8	36	5	4.47	7.04	12.4	2.1	4.9	3.1	7.98	-10.1	-18
2003	PMB	FSL	21	15	14	91.3	83	19	65	4	2.86	4.93	9.3	2.1	4.6	1.2	4.29	12.2	10
2003	TEN	SOU	21	10	10	57.0	56	26	34	6	3.00	4.13	10.3	4.3	4.0	1.7	6.54	-5.5	-9
2004	TEN	SOU	22	23	23	127.7	114	51	121	11	4.16	5.07	8.9	3.8	6.0	1.1	4.76	11.1	8
2004	TUL	TXS	22	4	4	20.0	16	13	14	1	3.15	7.00	8.5	7.0	5.0	1.0	6.00	-0.8	-13
2005	*COL*	*NL*	*23*	*12*	*11*	*60.0*	*71*	*29*	*42*	*12*	*6.19*	*5.41*	*10.1*	*3.8*	*6.0*	*1.4*	*5.44*	*3.0*	*0*

Breakout: 14% *Improve: 47%* *Collapse: 16%*

Part of the tribute for Larry Walker, Narveson kind of stalled out in 2004. That wasn't really that surprising given that his ERA had been below what his peripherals told us to expect at pretty much every stop he's ever made. Reality had to kick in eventually. He's a Grade C prospect, with the potential to move up as he moves another year further from his Tommy John surgery.

VLADIMIR NUNEZ **Bats: R** **Throws: R** Born: 15-Mar-1975 Age: 30

YEAR	TM	LG	AGE	G	GS	IP	H	BB	SO	HR	ERA	EQERA	EQH9	EQBB9	EQSO9	EQHR9	PERA	VORP	STF
2002	FLA	NL	27	77	0	97.7	80	37	73	8	3.41	3.77	7.9	3.0	6.1	0.8	3.39	20.3	2
2003	FLA	NL	28	14	0	10.7	21	7	10	7	15.98	17.47	15.1	4.8	7.1	5.6	11.91	-14.3	-26
2003	ABQ	PCL	28	46	3	68.0	67	20	54	13	4.76	4.52	9.5	3.0	6.2	2.5	5.65	-0.4	-6
2004	COL	NL	29	22	0	25.7	26	14	22	6	7.00	6.75	8.9	4.3	6.8	1.8	5.33	-5.7	-10
2004	CSP	PCL	29	23	8	63.3	76	22	60	7	5.69	5.43	9.6	3.1	6.4	1.1	4.86	5.2	-2
2005	*TEX*	*AL*	*30*	*38*	*0*	*39.3*	*44*	*17*	*30*	*7*	*5.85*	*5.21*	*9.8*	*3.3*	*6.3*	*1.5*	*5.01*	*3.7*	*-8*

Breakout: 20% *Improve: 44%* *Collapse: 26%*

Once a toolsy prospect who had a couple of nice years with the Marlins, Nunez has never developed the command he needs to succeed consistently. So what happens when he's off? Well, he throws a few nasty pitches that never have a prayer of reaching the strike zone, then he takes something off to get the 3–1 pitch over. Major league hitters kind of know that story, and greet him with a barrage of ash and maple. Just speculation, but this guy might need a dash of Leo Mazzone. After signing a minor league deal with Texas, he'll get a pinch of Orel Hershiser instead.

STEVE REED Bats: R Throws: R Born: 11-Mar-1965 Age: 40

YEAR	TM	LG	AGE	G	GS	IP	H	BB	SO	HR	ERA	EQERA	EQH9	EQBB9	EQSO9	EQHR9	PERA	VORP	STF
2002	SDP	NL	37	40	0	41.0	33	10	36	2	1.98	2.29	7.3	1.8	7.1	0.5	2.29	15.5	14
2002	NYM	NL	37	24	0	26.0	23	4	14	0	2.08	2.22	8.5	1.1	4.4	0.4	3.33	9.5	-1
2003	COL	NL	38	67	0	63.3	59	26	39	9	3.27	2.95	8.6	3.2	5.2	1.2	4.28	15.5	-11
2004	COL	NL	39	65	0	66.0	72	17	38	7	3.68	3.48	9.0	2.1	4.6	0.8	4.04	12.8	-7
2005	*BAL*	*AL*	*40*	*60*	*0*	*56.7*	*58*	*18*	*40*	*7*	*4.11*	*4.07*	*9.3*	*2.5*	*5.7*	*1.1*	*4.47*	*12.7*	*-5*

Breakout: 28% *Improve: 48%* *Collapse: 27%*

Is he the greatest Rockie pitcher ever? Back in the one year when the Rockies were good, people think it was because of big hitters like Dante Bichette and Andres Galarraga, but the real heroes were in the pen, which was deep, effective, and anchored by Steve Reed. He's played in Denver for seven full seasons, allowed 201 earned runs in 499 innings, for an ERA of 3.63. If you run into Steve on the street, salute him, buy him a beer, pummel those who refuse to genuflect in his presence. Whatever feels right.

ALLAN SIMPSON Bats: R Throws: R Born: 26-Aug-1977 Age: 27

YEAR	TM	LG	AGE	G	GS	IP	H	BB	SO	HR	ERA	EQERA	EQH9	EQBB9	EQSO9	EQHR9	PERA	VORP	STF
2002	SAN	TXS	24	56	0	82.3	53	50	99	4	3.06	4.92	7.4	6.1	8.5	1.0	4.44	9.7	8
2003	TAC	PCL	25	43	0	62.7	60	42	69	7	4.16	5.03	9.0	6.9	8.5	1.5	5.95	-2.3	-2
2004	CSP	PCL	26	27	0	35.3	30	10	43	1	2.80	3.41	7.3	2.6	8.4	0.3	2.88	10.4	19
2004	COL	NL	26	32	0	39.0	44	20	46	4	5.08	5.22	8.6	3.9	9.1	0.7	4.31	-1.3	13
2005	*COL*	*NL*	*27*	*31*	*0*	*31.7*	*31*	*16*	*30*	*4*	*4.72*	*4.12*	*8.3*	*3.9*	*8.2*	*1.0*	*4.30*	*5.7*	*6*

Breakout: 23% *Improve: 46%* *Collapse: 28%*

Relief prospect who could end up producing fairly quickly. Good stuff, and control that's apparently improved dramatically during the last 18 months. Held his own but didn't dominate in 32 games with the big club. He'll be in the running for a bullpen spot, and if he can hang onto his newly found control, he's a good bet to be successful.

RYAN SPEIER Bats: R Throws: R Born: 24-Jul-1979 Age: 25

YEAR	TM	LG	AGE	G	GS	IP	H	BB	SO	HR	ERA	EQERA	EQH9	EQBB9	EQSO9	EQHR9	PERA	VORP	STF
2002	ASH	SAL	22	28	0	36.7	32	13	39	3	3.92	6.21	9.2	4.1	5.9	1.9	5.40	0.7	-11
2002	SLM	CRL	22	24	0	32.0	35	11	33	0	3.94	7.34	9.7	3.8	6.5	0.3	4.70	3.1	1
2003	VIS	CLF	23	56	0	58.7	50	17	73	2	1.53	3.44	8.3	3.3	7.4	0.7	4.09	9.2	4
2004	TUL	TXS	24	61	0	61.7	33	25	70	3	2.04	3.09	6.8	4.2	7.8	0.8	3.58	12.4	16
2005	*COL*	*NL*	*25*	*50*	*0*	*55.7*	*55*	*26*	*48*	*8*	*4.82*	*4.21*	*8.4*	*3.6*	*7.3*	*1.0*	*4.16*	*8.6*	*3*

Breakout: 19% *Improve: 40%* *Collapse: 19%*

Another potentially very good relief prospect. Speier's got a live arm in terms of his movement on the ball, and he can definitely make batters miss. After an obscene season at Tulsa (33 hits allowed in 61.2 IP), he'll start the year at Triple-A. Could be up to the big club very quickly depending on injuries and his performance in the minors, which beats overpaying for veteran chaff any day.

DENNY STARK Bats: R Throws: R Born: 27-Oct-1974 Age: 30

YEAR	TM	LG	AGE	G	GS	IP	H	BB	SO	HR	ERA	EQERA	EQH9	EQBB9	EQSO9	EQHR9	PERA	VORP	STF
2002	COL	NL	27	32	20	128.3	108	64	64	25	4.00	4.34	8.8	4.0	4.1	1.7	5.09	9.2	-15
2003	COL	NL	28	17	13	78.7	98	33	30	12	5.83	5.65	10.3	3.2	3.1	1.3	5.54	-7.3	-16
2004	COL	NL	29	6	6	26.0	53	18	10	9	11.42	12.54	14.1	5.1	2.9	2.6	9.32	-26.3	-23
2004	CSP	PCL	29	14	13	79.7	73	26	51	9	3.50	3.82	8.4	3.1	4.5	1.2	4.18	11.9	19
2005	*CLE*	*AL*	*30*	*27*	*12*	*85.3*	*99*	*38*	*44*	*13*	*5.63*	*5.52*	*10.4*	*3.5*	*4.2*	*1.3*	*5.45*	*3.5*	*-15*

Breakout: 20% *Improve: 46%* *Collapse: 23%*

After three years of shuttling between Colorado Springs and Denver, you'd think Stark would be ready for a change of scenery, even if the scenery looked like, oh, Brainerd, Minnesota in January. Stark was nothing short of horrendous in his short stint with the big club in 2004, posting an ERA with too many digits in it, and allowing more than two baserunners per inning. The Rockies outrighted Stark, who's been snapped up by the Indians.

CHIN-HUI TSAO Bats: R Throws: R Born: 02-Jun-1981 Age: 24

YEAR	TM	LG	AGE	G	GS	IP	H	BB	SO	HR	ERA	EQERA	EQH9	EQBB9	EQSO9	EQHR9	PERA	VORP	STF
2002	SLM	CRL	21	9	9	47.3	34	12	45	3	2.09	4.01	8.2	3.0	6.3	1.3	4.01	7.5	19
2003	TUL	TXS	22	18	18	113.3	88	26	125	7	2.46	3.59	7.9	2.4	7.8	1.0	3.67	22.6	32
2003	COL	NL	22	9	8	43.3	48	20	29	11	6.03	5.31	9.8	3.6	5.5	2.1	5.95	-2.6	-1
2004	TUL	TXS	23	2	2	13.0	12	2	10	1	2.77	3.75	9.8	1.5	5.2	1.5	5.25	0.5	7
2004	CSP	PCL	23	4	4	12.7	22	5	14	5	8.50	6.92	13.2	3.5	6.9	3.5	9.00	-4.9	-16
2004	COL	NL	23	10	0	9.3	7	1	11	2	3.87	3.00	7.0	1.0	10.0	2.0	3.00	1.9	25
2005	*COL*	*NL*	*24*	*17*	*11*	*69.3*	*75*	*23*	*56*	*12*	*4.80*	*4.20*	*9.2*	*2.6*	*6.8*	*1.3*	*4.34*	*12.1*	*10*

Breakout: 22% *Improve: 53%* *Collapse: 20%*

There were several philosophical discussions about the nature of a Colorado pitching prospect that started around Tsao. He missed significant time in 2004 because of external obligations, shoulder soreness, and blister problems. The Rockies see Tsao as a future closer, which is what every team heading for 65 wins needs most, rather than a starting pitcher, right?

JAMEY WRIGHT Bats: R Throws: R Born: 24-Dec-1974 Age: 30

YEAR	TM	LG	AGE	G	GS	IP	H	BB	SO	HR	ERA	EQERA	EQH9	EQBB9	EQSO9	EQHR9	PERA	VORP	STF
2002	MIL	NL	27	19	19	114.3	115	63	69	15	5.35	5.63	9.4	4.3	4.9	1.1	5.14	-2.1	-4
2002	STL	NL	27	4	3	15.0	15	12	8	2	4.80	5.02	10.0	6.3	4.4	1.3	6.28	1.2	-22
2003	IND	INT	28	7	4	22.0	32	10	17	5	7.36	8.44	12.2	4.6	5.5	3.0	8.44	-6.7	-28
2003	OKL	PCL	28	7	7	39.3	38	21	40	1	4.12	4.74	8.1	5.4	7.8	0.5	4.26	5.7	15
2003	OMA	PCL	28	13	12	76.7	70	38	65	10	3.64	4.71	9.2	5.2	6.8	1.9	5.99	-3.1	3
2003	KCR	AL	28	4	4	25.3	23	11	19	1	4.27	4.38	8.0	3.6	6.6	0.4	3.65	3.1	24
2004	OMA	PCL	29	18	18	104.7	111	35	70	13	4.21	5.11	9.3	3.2	4.7	1.3	4.93	7.5	8
2004	COL	NL	29	14	14	78.7	82	45	41	8	4.12	3.84	9.0	4.5	4.2	0.8	4.77	11.4	7
2005	*COL*	*NL*	*30*	*20*	*19*	*103.3*	*122*	*52*	*68*	*17*	*5.89*	*5.14*	*10.0*	*3.9*	*5.6*	*1.2*	*5.24*	*6.9*	*0*

Breakout: 9% *Improve: 33%* *Collapse: 21%*

Winner of the Grover Cleveland Award for non-consecutive terms of service in the Rockies rotation. Hey, he's done the gig, can handle the pressures, doesn't get his uniform dirty from all that wallowing in self-pity. . . . When you're the Rockies, you like these things in a guy. All things considered, he'll be an asset, at least in that he'll take his turns, pitch with a reliable mediocrity, and generally keep Colorado in games for five or six innings. Sometimes, you get rich doing that, and sometimes, you don't have time for a mortgage.

JASON YOUNG Bats: R Throws: R Born: 28-Sep-1979 Age: 25

YEAR	TM	LG	AGE	G	GS	IP	H	BB	SO	HR	ERA	EQERA	EQH9	EQBB9	EQSO9	EQHR9	PERA	VORP	STF
2002	CAR	SOU	22	14	14	88.7	71	30	76	1	2.64	4.00	7.9	2.9	5.8	0.2	2.81	25.8	28
2002	CSP	PCL	22	13	13	79.7	87	38	74	10	4.97	5.29	8.8	4.5	6.4	1.1	4.25	11.7	18
2003	CSP	PCL	23	23	21	116.3	128	37	99	10	3.95	4.86	9.2	3.2	6.5	1.0	4.38	15.3	9
2004	CSP	PCL	24	7	7	40.0	54	12	20	6	4.72	5.22	10.7	2.7	3.4	1.4	5.67	-0.3	-13
2004	COL	NL	24	2	2	8.3	15	5	7	3	13.01	11.00	13.0	4.0	6.0	3.0	9.00	-6.7	-19
2005	*COL*	*NL*	*25*	*19*	*15*	*88.3*	*105*	*35*	*62*	*14*	*5.84*	*5.09*	*10.1*	*3.1*	*6.0*	*1.1*	*4.91*	*6.1*	*4*

Breakout: 14% *Improve: 47%* *Collapse: 16%*

A broken rib, following some questionable communication between Young and the club, ended his season after just a few innings. He was once considered a top prospect by the organization, but his star's dimmed, and he'll have to pitch lights-out in order to start getting attention again. Well, either that, or the big club would have to have most of the pitching staff collapse. Of course, that would never happen.

Florida Marlins

MARLINS PROSPECTUS

2004 record: 83–79; Third place, NL East

Pythagenport record: 82–80

Runs scored per game: 4.43 (11th in NL)

Runs allowed per game: 4.32 (6th in NL)

Team EqA: .261 (9th in NL)

2004 Batters Age: 29.1 (5th youngest in NL)

2004 Pitchers Age: 27.8 (3rd youngest in NL)

Ballpark: Pro Player Stadium; Severe pitcher's park; Park Factor of 0.941

2004: Hurricanes and hitting problems aside, the defending champions hung around the playoff race until September.

2005: There's talent on the roster, but they'll again fight an uphill battle against the Braves and Phillies.

The history of the Florida Marlins is as strange as that of any team in the annals of professional sports. They've been in existence for a dozen seasons, ending two of those as the champions of baseball. Those titles, in 1997 and 2003, have given them two more World Championships than they have division crowns. The Marlins are the only NL team to win a World Series from the Wild Card slot, and they've done it twice. Neither title team is part of a success cycle; in fact, 2004 was the first time outside of those two years in which the Marlins finished over .500.

Three .500 seasons, two world championships, no division titles. That's an unusual track record in any league.

One of the reasons the Marlins' successes are islands unto themselves is that, almost from the day they started playing, their owners have been focused more on getting a baseball-only ballpark built than on building a baseball team. Time after time, Wayne Huizenga, John Henry, and Jeffrey Loria have taken their case to the politicians and the public in South Florida, and every time, they've been rebuffed.

The Marlins play in Pro Player Stadium, itself less than 20 years old, built in the mid-1980s to be the home of the Miami Dolphins. The Stadium was originally named after the Dolphins' popular owner and the man who got the stadium built, Joe Robbie, before Huizenga sold the naming rights in 1996, wiping out Robbie's name in favor of the underwear ad. Like the Marlins' various owners, Robbie wasn't able to convince taxpayers to fund a stadium for his team. Unlike them, however, he went ahead and financed the stadium privately. It is, in a nutshell, the difference between being a businessman and a leech. No wonder Huizenga wanted his name off the ballpark.

To a certain extent, you can understand the frustration. As relatively new a facility as Underwear Park is, it is a dual-purpose stadium that lacks a certain flair. Robbie actually had it designed to accommodate a baseball team, one he expected Miami to eventually get. The Marlins came into existence just as Camden Yards kicked off the retro-park era, and teams from coast to coast were clamoring for their own taxpayer-funded Oriole Park knockoffs as a means of generating risk-free revenue. The relationship between new parks and on-field success is tenuous at best, but new parks are about money, and from Baltimore to Cleveland to Philadelphia to San Diego, new ballparks have been a boon for baseball owners.

Huizenga tore down the first title team after the '97 season to spite the city that wouldn't grant him hundreds of millions of taxpayer dollars, then sold it to Henry soon afterwards. But Huizenga continues reap the benefits of a usurious lease that funnels baseball-related revenue to him, as the owner of the stadium. Henry presided over years of drift on the field, lobbying throughout his tenure as owner for a new park while doing everything short of booby-trapping random seats as a means of keeping fans away.

Now, it's Loria's team, and the former owner of the Expos has had no more success than his predecessors in getting public money for his private venture. Worse yet, he's found that the previous owners screwed things up so thoroughly that not only is a publicly-funded stadium unlikely, but the Marlins may not be able to succeed no matter how much on-field success they have.

Consider 2004. It's a fact of baseball life that championship teams garner the financial fruits of their labor in the season after a title. The success drives ticket sales, usually at higher prices, and the revenue generated in parking lots, souvenir shops and concession stands go up. Yet, despite two championships in seven years, the Marlins were 14th

TABLE 1. POST-CHAMPIONSHIP ATTENDANCE

Year	Champion	Next Year Attendance	Gain/Loss
2003	Marlins	1,723,105	+419,890
2002	Angels	3,061,094	+755,547
2001	Diamondbacks	3,198,977	+462,526
2000	Yankees	3,264,907	+350,283
1999	Yankees	2,914,624	−378,112
1998	Yankees	3,292,736	+712,411
1997	Marlins	1,730,384	−16,383

in the National League in attendance last year, with the lowest post-title attendance of any team playing a full schedule since the 1980 Pirates drew just 1.6 million fans—and that was at least good for sixth in the league. (See table 1.)

On a percentage basis, the Marlins actually did fairly well, bumping attendance by 32%, and their raw gain is consistent with what the Diamondbacks and Yankees got after 2001 and 2000. The problem is that it's an inadequate total. If a team can't get two million people to come out in the wake of a championship season, it's time to throw in the towel in that city. The Brewers haven't been competitive since 1992, their new-park smell has worn off and it frankly was never that special, and they still drew 2.06 million. The Rockies don't have a new park or a good team, and they drew 2.34 million.

The Marlins' problems in 1998 can be traced to the teardown of the championship team, and Wayne Huizenga's very public stance that he wouldn't be putting a winning team on the field. Last year, though, they had essentially the same attendance as they did in '98, this after re-signing some of the team's best players, coming off a title, and staying in the Wild Card race deep into September. On September 7, they took the field two games out of a playoff spot. Attendance: 14,308.

The people have spoken. The two things that drive attendance, always and forever, are winning and a brand new park. There isn't going to be a new ballpark here, and the upside of winning appears to be 1.7 million tickets sold. If that's the case, it's time to go. The history of major league baseball in Miami would no doubt be different had Wayne Huizenga not been such a horse's ass in November of 1997, but he was, and he permanently poisoned the well not only for a new park, but for baseball.

It's that reality that has the Marlins playing footsie with Las Vegas. Marlins executives met with Vegas officials in December, as much to fire a warning shot to Miami as anything else. (It inspired quick action; landlord Huizenga threatened to evict the Fish when their lease expires in 2009.) MLB does few things as well as it plays cities without baseball against ones that do, and they've been dancing with Portland and Las Vegas for years now, trying to extract the best possible deal. Vegas' growth and its apparent eagerness to have a team of its own are attractive to MLB, and certainly to Loria, who has been fighting ballpark battles for the better part of a decade, going back to his time with the Expos.

The main problem is that Vegas combines the worst features of Kansas City and San Diego: It's a small market by itself and it has no access to secondary markets, so its media revenue would be small for the foreseeable future.

Of course, Las Vegas is nothing like Kansas City or San Diego. The city's core industry is gambling, and there is no topic that makes baseball more uncomfortable. The shadow of the 1919 World Series hangs over the game, as near as the latest mention of Pete Rose and his ineligibility. This original sin, rather than any practical concerns, is the biggest barrier to being the first league to put a team in Las Vegas. Realistically, baseball would be in no more danger of a gambling scandal with a team in Las Vegas than it is now. Sports betting is, more and more, the province of offshore, quasi-legal sports books, rather than the Vegas casinos. If anything, the hyperawareness of the Vegas books makes it less likely that a Vegas team could be at the center of a scandal. MLB isn't going to get a blanket ban on gambling on MLB games in Vegas, and they don't need one.

Vegas presents other problems. Obviously, any new park would have to have a roof, most likely a retractable one, because no one is going to sit outside for three hours in a Las Vegas summer unless it's next to a pool. That adds cost. There's no Fox Sports Nevada to cover the team's games, and no short-term chance of another pro team becoming available to help create an attractive package around which to build a network. As a 24-hour city, a larger percentage of its residents have schedules that will preclude attending baseball games, no matter when you schedule them. While supporters of Vegas baseball are counting heavily on the biggest industry in town to provide a revenue base through the purchase of suites and stadium signage, all those big hotels didn't get there because their owners made bad bets.

The least credible argument for a team is that it will serve as a tourist attraction. Certainly there will be a few people who come to the city and catch a ballgame, but that's not why people go to Vegas. They go to Vegas to do the things they can't do at home. Tourist attendance would be no more, and could very well be less, than other teams see.

The key issue for the Marlins is that the landscape has changed. With the Expos' relocation to Washington, D.C., the biggest argument against a franchise move—that baseball simply doesn't do that—is gone. After the Braves moved from Boston to Milwaukee in 1953, there were eight more franchise shifts in the next 20 years. Some team is going to move to Las Vegas before the decade ends, and since it looks like the Marlins' upside has been reached in Miami, it might as well be them.

For any other franchise, becoming the first major pro sports team in Las Vegas would be the peak of strangeness. For the Marlins, though, the move not only makes sense, but also fits perfectly their weird, colorful history.

HITTERS

CHRIS AGUILA   OF   Bats: R   Throws: R   Born: 23-Feb-1979   Age: 26

YEAR	TM	LG	AGE	AB	H	2B	3B	HR	BB	SO	SB	CS	AVG	OBP	SLG	MLVR	EQBA	EQOBP	EQSLG	EQMLVR	VORP	DEFENSE
2002	PME	EAS	23	429	126	28	4	6	48	101	14	8	.294	.369	.420	.089	.257	.325	.374	-.130	-10.6	64-LF 0 49-CF 0
2003	CAR	SOU	24	337	108	21	3	11	36	67	6	2	.320	.384	.499	.302	.298	.355	.485	.116	18.2	43-LF 1 25-RF 1
2004	ABQ	PCL	25	330	103	23	2	11	37	82	8	3	.312	.380	.494	.058	.247	.315	.383	-.144	0.4	45-CF -1 25-RF 0
2004	FLA	NL	25	45	10	2	1	3	2	12	0	0	.222	.255	.511	-.036	.217	.250	.522	-.092	1.0	
2005	*FLA*	*NL*	*26*	*147*	*37*	*8*	*1*	*4*	*13*	*38*	*2*	*1*	*.252*	*.315*	*.411*	*-.093*	*.257*	*.318*	*.426*	*-.067*	*4.8*	*42-CF -5*

Breakout: 17%   *Improve: 37%*   *Collapse: 34%*

Aguila has developed so slowly—he was drafted in 1997—that he's lost his prospect status even while having the best two seasons of his pro career. He showed no ill effects from a broken wrist that cut his '03 season short, almost matching his Double-A stat line at Albuquerque. The difference between Aguila and Juan Encarnacion is virtually nil, save for the money guaranteed to the veteran.

CHIP AMBRES   OF   Bats: R   Throws: R   Born: 19-Dec-1979   Age: 25

YEAR	TM	LG	AGE	AB	H	2B	3B	HR	BB	SO	SB	CS	AVG	OBP	SLG	MLVR	EQBA	EQOBP	EQSLG	EQMLVR	VORP	DEFENSE
2002	JUP	FSL	22	509	120	25	7	9	57	98	23	8	.236	.323	.365	.015	.222	.291	.358	-.241	-14.9	122-CF -12
2003	CAR	SOU	23	380	98	23	8	10	72	81	9	6	.258	.376	.439	.162	.240	.344	.425	-.037	14.3	106-CF -4
2004	CAR	SOU	24	452	109	28	3	20	76	117	26	9	.241	.352	.449	.102	.217	.319	.406	-.126	3.3	75-CF -5 42-RF 0
2005	*BOS*	*AL*	*25*	*188*	*49*	*11*	*1*	*7*	*23*	*42*	*6*	*2*	*.263*	*.349*	*.441*	*.019*	*.259*	*.346*	*.444*	*.008*	*11.1*	*54-CF -5*

Breakout: 43%   *Improve: 61%*   *Collapse: 21%*

It's one thing to make a reasoned decision on when to give up on a failed first-round draft pick. It's another to lose him because you need to make space on the 40-man roster for a panic move. The Marlins designated Ambres for assignment in early September because they wanted to pull Logan Kensing out of A-ball for a start against the Cubs. Kensing was pounded, and Ambres cleared waivers and became a free agent. He's just 25, with a decent mix of offensive skills, and the Red Sox did well to snatch him up.

MIGUEL CABRERA   OF   Bats: R   Throws: R   Born: 18-Apr-1983   Age: 22

YEAR	TM	LG	AGE	AB	H	2B	3B	HR	BB	SO	SB	CS	AVG	OBP	SLG	MLVR	EQBA	EQOBP	EQSLG	EQMLVR	VORP	DEFENSE
2002	JUP	FSL	19	489	134	43	1	9	38	85	10	1	.274	.333	.421	.130	.251	.297	.403	-.147	5.0	87-3B -2
2003	CAR	SOU	20	266	97	29	3	10	31	49	9	4	.365	.429	.609	.553	.341	.397	.589	.382	47.8	64-3B 9
2003	FLA	NL	20	314	84	21	3	12	25	84	0	2	.268	.325	.468	.074	.271	.329	.479	.036	13.9	53-LF 0 27-3B 0
2004	FLA	NL	21	603	177	31	1	33	68	148	5	2	.294	.366	.512	.231	.297	.368	.521	.188	54.4	90-RF -5 51-LF 5
2005	*FLA*	*NL*	*22*	*548*	*160*	*35*	*3*	*28*	*51*	*117*	*7*	*2*	*.291*	*.356*	*.519*	*.152*	*.297*	*.359*	*.538*	*.185*	*43.0*	*143-RF 0*

Breakout: 8%   *Improve: 60%*   *Collapse: 16%*

Cabrera continued to improve in his first full major league season, adapting to the outfield, working on his plate discipline and showing excellent durability by playing in 160 games. He's not fast for his age, a factor that may cause him to develop less like statistical comps Hank Aaron and Mickey Mantle and more like, say, Juan Gonzalez, where power ends up as the primary tool. That sounds like a drop-off, but Gonzalez was a terrific player through age 29—that's seven years away for Cabrera.

LUIS CASTILLO 2B Bats: B Throws: R Born: 12-Sep-1975 Age: 29

YEAR	TM	LG	AGE	AB	H	2B	3B	HR	BB	SO	SB	CS	AVG	OBP	SLG	MLVR	EQBA	EQOBP	EQSLG	EQMLVR	VORP	DEFENSE
2002	FLA	NL	26	606	185	18	5	2	55	76	48	15	.305	.364	.361	.039	.314	.371	.375	.001	40.7	140-2B -6
2003	FLA	NL	27	595	187	19	6	6	63	60	21	19	.314	.381	.397	.103	.323	.390	.409	.092	39.0	150-2B 4
2004	FLA	NL	28	564	164	12	7	2	75	68	21	4	.291	.373	.348	.011	.295	.376	.353	-.035	33.5	143-2B 7
2005	*FLA*	*NL*	*29*	*516*	*142*	*21*	*4*	*4*	*58*	*60*	*19*	*6*	*.274*	*.349*	*.354*	*-.093*	*.279*	*.352*	*.367*	*-.068*	*20.3*	*138-2B 1*

Breakout: 0% Improve: 16% Collapse: 46%

His lack of power is drifting into historical range. Since the strike zone returned to normal in 1969, just 24 other players have come to bat 600 times and had 21 or fewer extra-base hits. Castillo's total was the sixth-lowest in the game since 1980. He's just outside of the bottom 25 since World War II in terms of isolated power. He's a close to normal from the right side, but when he bats left-handed, he just slaps the ball and runs. Second basemen of middling value often hit the wall between 29 and 31, and Castillo's loss of speed marks him as someone edging toward the cliff. Beware.

RAMON CASTRO C Bats: R Throws: R Born: 01-Mar-1976 Age: 29

YEAR	TM	LG	AGE	AB	H	2B	3B	HR	BB	SO	SB	CS	AVG	OBP	SLG	MLVR	EQBA	EQOBP	EQSLG	EQMLVR	VORP	DEFENSE
2002	FLA	NL	26	101	24	4	0	6	14	24	0	0	.238	.322	.455	.035	.245	.313	.471	-.027	6.3	23-C -4
2003	FLA	NL	27	53	15	2	0	5	4	11	0	0	.283	.333	.604	.291	.302	.323	.623	.270	6.5	
2004	FLA	NL	28	96	13	3	0	3	11	30	0	0	.135	.231	.260	-.454	.146	.236	.271	-.508	-7.0	27-C 1
2005	*NYM*	*NL*	*29*	*210*	*47*	*9*	*0*	*11*	*22*	*58*	*0*	*0*	*.222*	*.298*	*.422*	*-.129*	*.225*	*.300*	*.436*	*-.109*	*6.1*	*59-C -1*

Breakout: 36% Improve: 67% Collapse: 25%

Sexual assault charges stemming from a 2003 incident followed Castro all year long until a plea agreement ended the issue in November. Whether it was the charges, an early-season slump or an injured toe that did it, 2004 was a lost year. The Mets signed him to a minor league deal; he'd make a fine backup for Mike Piazza in New York, but he has to beat out Jason Phillips, or be part of a three-catcher roster.

JEFF CONINE 1B/LF Bats: R Throws: R Born: 27-Jun-1966 Age: 39

YEAR	TM	LG	AGE	AB	H	2B	3B	HR	BB	SO	SB	CS	AVG	OBP	SLG	MLVR	EQBA	EQOBP	EQSLG	EQMLVR	VORP	DEFENSE
2002	BAL	AL	36	451	123	26	4	15	25	66	8	0	.273	.307	.448	.007	.282	.320	.464	.009	17.5	103-1B -10
2003	BAL	AL	37	493	143	33	3	15	37	60	5	0	.290	.338	.460	.094	.293	.346	.471	.075	29.7	118-1B -1
2003	FLA	NL	37	84	20	3	0	5	13	10	0	0	.238	.337	.452	.050	.247	.326	.459	-.018	3.5	24-LF 1
2004	FLA	NL	38	521	146	35	1	14	48	78	5	5	.280	.340	.432	.062	.284	.343	.441	.019	20.1	83-LF 11 55-1B 3
2005	*FLA*	*NL*	*39*	*384*	*103*	*21*	*2*	*11*	*32*	*59*	*4*	*1*	*.269*	*.327*	*.422*	*-.046*	*.274*	*.329*	*.437*	*-.018*	*9.8*	*101-1B 2*

Breakout: 14% Improve: 25% Collapse: 29%

Durable, popular and hopelessly average, Conine keeps grinding out serviceable seasons deep into his 30s. It's a shame he's spent so much time at first base, because his bat has rarely been enough for the spot, and statistically, it's his worst defensive position. He's actually a good left fielder and an adequate third baseman. He'll likely be the Marlins' everyday first baseman in '05, when he'll slip well below average.

WIL CORDERO 1B Bats: R Throws: R Born: 03-Oct-1971 Age: 33

YEAR	TM	LG	AGE	AB	H	2B	3B	HR	BB	SO	SB	CS	AVG	OBP	SLG	MLVR	EQBA	EQOBP	EQSLG	EQMLVR	VORP	DEFENSE
2002	MON	NL	30	143	39	9	0	6	17	26	2	0	.273	.349	.462	.113	.273	.333	.462	.021	9.0	20-LF -1
2003	MON	NL	31	436	121	27	0	16	49	90	1	1	.278	.354	.450	.048	.270	.344	.441	.009	17.8	114-1B 3
2004	FLA	NL	32	66	13	3	0	1	3	19	1	0	.197	.250	.288	-.362	.197	.240	.273	-.474	-3.8	12-1B 0
2005	*WAS*	*NL*	*33*	*178*	*45*	*9*	*1*	*6*	*18*	*39*	*1*	*0*	*.253*	*.326*	*.407*	*-.077*	*.256*	*.327*	*.417*	*-.064*	*3.4*	*51-1B -1*

Breakout: 23% Improve: 46% Collapse: 33%

Baseball is strange. Cordero, who's been a marginal power threat with no defensive value since his infield career ended, missed almost all of '04 with a matching set of knee surgeries. Despite all that, Jim Bowden gave him a guaranteed contract for $700,000 in November, while sending Val Pascucci—same type of player, cheaper, more upside—to Japan. You have to really love "experience" to make that kind of decision.

JOE DILLON — 3B/2B — Bats: R — Throws: R — Born: 02-Aug-1975 — Age: 29

YEAR	TM	LG	AGE	AB	H	2B	3B	HR	BB	SO	SB	CS	AVG	OBP	SLG	MLVR	EQBA	EQOBP	EQSLG	EQMLVR	VORP	DEFENSE	
2002	NBR	EAS	26	344	90	20	2	9	54	62	3	1	.262	.368	.410	.088	.241	.334	.382	-.113	7.7	75-3B -8	
2004	CAR	SOU	28	117	40	13	0	9	14	29	3	2	.342	.426	.684	.607	.303	.367	.597	.300	18.1	33-3B 5	
2004	ABQ	PCL	28	403	131	33	7	30	46	85	12	3	.325	.400	.665	.340	.254	.327	.503	.050	27.6	59-3B -1	22-2B -5
2005	*FLA*	*NL*	*29*	*169*	*44*	*10*	*1*	*7*	*19*	*41*	*3*	*1*	*.263*	*.346*	*.465*	*.039*	*.267*	*.349*	*.482*	*.068*	*13.3*	*49-3B -2*	

Breakout: 26% *Improve: 47%* *Collapse: 31%*

The return of Dillon was one of the best baseball stories of 2004. Forced out of organized baseball after 2002 due to back problems, Dillon spent 2003 coaching at Texas Tech. He was a good hitter before injuries sapped his power, and while his '04 performance was over his head, the basic skills—good power and average, reasonable plate discipline—are real. There's no spot for him in the Marlins' infield, and an experiment in left field didn't take, so he's fighting an uphill battle for a job. Root for him.

DAMION EASLEY — 2B/3B — Bats: R — Throws: R — Born: 11-Nov-1969 — Age: 35

YEAR	TM	LG	AGE	AB	H	2B	3B	HR	BB	SO	SB	CS	AVG	OBP	SLG	MLVR	EQBA	EQOBP	EQSLG	EQMLVR	VORP	DEFENSE	
2002	DET	AL	32	304	68	14	1	8	27	43	1	3	.224	.307	.355	-.145	.236	.318	.377	-.154	4.7	84-2B -3	
2003	TBY	AL	33	107	20	3	1	1	2	18	0	0	.187	.202	.262	-.517	.189	.211	.264	-.550	-8.2	18-3B 0	
2004	FLA	NL	34	223	53	20	1	9	24	36	4	1	.238	.331	.457	.050	.240	.331	.467	-.004	13.1	18-2B 0	14-1B 0
2005	*FLA*	*NL*	*35*	*143*	*32*	*7*	*1*	*4*	*13*	*26*	*1*	*1*	*.227*	*.303*	*.365*	*-.191*	*.231*	*.306*	*.379*	*-.168*	*0.2*	*42-2B -7*	

Breakout: 31% *Improve: 49%* *Collapse: 31%*

Kind of a poor man's, Motor City version of Jason Kendall, Easley is a useful player whose godawful contract—four years, $26.5 million, ending last year—made it hard to evaluate him as anything but a bust. He slots in now as a good fifth infielder and a pinch-hitter at either end of an inning.

JUAN ENCARNACION — RF — Bats: R — Throws: R — Born: 08-Mar-1976 — Age: 29

YEAR	TM	LG	AGE	AB	H	2B	3B	HR	BB	SO	SB	CS	AVG	OBP	SLG	MLVR	EQBA	EQOBP	EQSLG	EQMLVR	VORP	DEFENSE	
2002	CIN	NL	26	321	89	11	2	16	26	63	9	4	.277	.330	.474	.080	.273	.326	.475	.027	15.6	59-CF -3	28-RF 2
2002	FLA	NL	26	263	69	11	3	8	20	50	12	5	.262	.317	.418	.012	.268	.320	.438	-.041	8.5	51-RF -1	11-CF -1
2003	FLA	NL	27	601	162	37	6	19	37	82	19	8	.270	.313	.446	.030	.274	.318	.460	-.008	17.7	150-RF 3	
2004	LAD	NL	28	324	76	18	1	13	21	53	3	3	.235	.289	.417	-.095	.237	.291	.425	-.138	0.6	75-RF -2	
2004	FLA	NL	28	160	38	12	1	3	17	33	2	1	.237	.320	.381	-.070	.241	.320	.395	-.122	1.9	48-RF -2	
2005	*FLA*	*NL*	*29*	*448*	*117*	*25*	*3*	*15*	*36*	*78*	*8*	*3*	*.262*	*.320*	*.433*	*-.046*	*.267*	*.323*	*.450*	*-.019*	*12.7*	*117-RF -2*	

Breakout: 26% *Improve: 51%* *Collapse: 12%*

The Marlins made a good decision to let him go in the fall of '03, watching as Dan Evans signed him to a silly two-year deal. Then they relieved Paul DePodesta of the burden at the trade deadline, one of the many reasons the popular opinion of the trade—that the Marlins got the best of it—was wrong. Encarnacion looks good in a uniform, plays right field well, and occasionally hits a mistake a long way. He's also one of the worst regular right fielders in baseball.

ALEX GONZALEZ — SS — Bats: R — Throws: R — Born: 15-Feb-1977 — Age: 28

YEAR	TM	LG	AGE	AB	H	2B	3B	HR	BB	SO	SB	CS	AVG	OBP	SLG	MLVR	EQBA	EQOBP	EQSLG	EQMLVR	VORP	DEFENSE
2002	FLA	NL	25	151	34	7	1	2	12	32	3	1	.225	.296	.325	-.193	.234	.300	.344	-.235	0.1	40-SS 0
2003	FLA	NL	26	528	135	33	6	18	33	106	0	4	.256	.313	.443	.016	.261	.315	.460	-.025	27.7	149-SS 6
2004	FLA	NL	27	561	130	30	3	23	27	126	3	1	.232	.270	.419	-.122	.235	.272	.428	-.170	11.3	151-SS -1
2005	*FLA*	*NL*	*28*	*433*	*107*	*24*	*3*	*14*	*29*	*93*	*3*	*2*	*.247*	*.302*	*.410*	*-.120*	*.252*	*.304*	*.426*	*-.094*	*14.7*	*112-SS 0*

Breakout: 14% *Improve: 43%* *Collapse: 26%*

Dropped back from his peak '04 season to be a huge part of the Marlins' offensive problem—too many outs from too many lineup spots. More than a third of his walks the past two seasons were intentionals, and it's virtually impossible to be a good hitter with a 6-to-1 strikeout-to-walk ratio. His power is real, though, and will keep his counting stats high enough to earn him a generous contract after 2005.

LENNY HARRIS PH Bats: L Throws: R Born: 28-Oct-1964 Age: 40

YEAR	TM	LG	AGE	AB	H	2B	3B	HR	BB	SO	SB	CS	AVG	OBP	SLG	MLVR	EQBA	EQOBP	EQSLG	EQMLVR	VORP	DEFENSE
2002	MIL	NL	37	197	60	8	2	3	14	17	4	1	.305	.355	.411	.090	.308	.357	.419	.033	12.6	13-LF 1
2003	CHC	NL	38	131	24	3	0	1	13	20	1	0	.183	.255	.229	-.423	.191	.253	.221	-.522	-8.0	24-3B -2
2003	FLA	NL	38	14	4	0	0	0	3	1	0	0	.286	.412	.286	.015	.500	.312	.500	.366	0.8	
2004	FLA	NL	39	95	20	5	0	1	3	8	0	0	.211	.232	.295	-.362	.221	.230	.284	-.467	-4.8	
2005	*FLA*	*NL*	*40*	*77*	*18*	*3*	*0*	*1*	*5*	*9*	*0*	*0*	*.235*	*.281*	*.319*	*-.287*	*.239*	*.284*	*.331*	*-.267*	*-3.3*	*25-3B -5*

Breakout: 38% *Improve: 51%* *Collapse: 36%*

Back-to-back bad years can be the kiss of death at Harris's age. If he's not hitting, he's not helping, and the Fish—he'll go to camp with them—have a bunch of guys coming through the system fighting for bench jobs. Mike Mordecai, another unproductive member of the '04 bench, retired to take a minor league managing job. Doesn't that sound like fun, Lenny?

JEREMY HERMIDA RF Bats: L Throws: R Born: 30-Jan-1984 Age: 21

YEAR	TM	LG	AGE	AB	H	2B	3B	HR	BB	SO	SB	CS	AVG	OBP	SLG	MLVR	EQBA	EQOBP	EQSLG	EQMLVR	VORP	DEFENSE
2003	GRB	SAL	19	468	133	23	5	6	80	100	28	2	.284	.387	.393	.165	.246	.328	.349	-.166	-16.6	123-RF -17
2004	JUP	FSL	20	340	101	17	1	10	42	73	10	3	.297	.377	.441	.214	.265	.333	.412	-.056	1.1	76-RF -9
2005	*FLA*	*NL*	*21*	*401*	*99*	*21*	*3*	*8*	*43*	*99*	*8*	*2*	*.247*	*.322*	*.372*	*-.135*	*.252*	*.325*	*.386*	*-.111*	*2.4*	*107-RF -7*

Breakout: 16% *Improve: 38%* *Collapse: 32%*

For all the outfield prospects they've had, from Nigel Wilson and Carl Everett through Chip Ambres and Abraham Nunez, the Marlins haven't developed any of them for themselves in their dozen years (Miguel Cabrera is a converted third baseman) of existence. Hermida, a left-handed hitter with a line-drive stroke, should be the first. A hamstring pull cut into his speed and his playing time last year, but shouldn't be a problem in '05. Be patient, and think Paul O'Neill.

PAUL Lo DUCA C Bats: R Throws: R Born: 12-Apr-1972 Age: 33

YEAR	TM	LG	AGE	AB	H	2B	3B	HR	BB	SO	SB	CS	AVG	OBP	SLG	MLVR	EQBA	EQOBP	EQSLG	EQMLVR	VORP	DEFENSE
2002	LAD	NL	30	580	163	38	1	10	34	31	3	1	.281	.330	.402	.033	.293	.338	.425	-.005	33.6	132-C -2
2003	LAD	NL	31	568	155	34	2	7	44	54	0	2	.273	.335	.377	-.021	.281	.342	.391	-.056	20.3	123-C 10 18-1B -3
2004	LAD	NL	32	349	105	18	1	10	22	27	2	4	.301	.351	.444	.101	.304	.353	.452	.070	22.5	77-C -1
2004	FLA	NL	32	186	48	11	1	3	14	22	2	1	.258	.314	.376	-.088	.263	.315	.389	-.124	4.2	47-C -1
2005	*FLA*	*NL*	*33*	*427*	*116*	*24*	*1*	*7*	*31*	*41*	*2*	*1*	*.272*	*.329*	*.387*	*-.085*	*.277*	*.332*	*.401*	*-.060*	*16.3*	*112-C -1*

Breakout: 5% *Improve: 33%* *Collapse: 39%*

That 690 OPS as a Marlin includes a hot first week in teal. Just as he'd done in '02 and '03, he fell apart in August and September. Lo Duca's ability to stay in the lineup and hit for decent averages will earn him a pretty penny in arbitration, far more than he's likely to be worth on the field. The Dodgers got the best years of his career for less than $8 million, or near what Lo Duca will make in 2005 alone.

MIKE LOWELL 3B Bats: R Throws: R Born: 24-Feb-1974 Age: 31

YEAR	TM	LG	AGE	AB	H	2B	3B	HR	BB	SO	SB	CS	AVG	OBP	SLG	MLVR	EQBA	EQOBP	EQSLG	EQMLVR	VORP	DEFENSE
2002	FLA	NL	28	597	165	44	0	24	65	92	4	3	.276	.346	.471	.135	.283	.347	.488	.092	46.8	154-3B 13
2003	FLA	NL	29	492	136	27	1	32	56	78	3	1	.276	.350	.530	.215	.281	.354	.545	.181	52.0	127-3B 2
2004	FLA	NL	30	598	175	44	1	27	64	77	5	1	.293	.365	.505	.217	.296	.367	.510	.169	53.9	146-3B 10
2005	*FLA*	*NL*	*31*	*509*	*141*	*32*	*2*	*24*	*55*	*77*	*4*	*1*	*.277*	*.350*	*.488*	*.088*	*.282*	*.353*	*.506*	*.119*	*33.0*	*134-3B 2*

Breakout: 13% *Improve: 43%* *Collapse: 23%*

He exercised his "stadium option" in October, then agreed to stay in Florida for the next three years, being guaranteed $25.5 million over that time. His deal looks like a bargain when you consider what Corey Koskie—inferior, fragile—and Troy Glaus—comparable, fragile—signed for over the winter. Other than the fluke injury in '03, Lowell has been durable. He'll settle in at a level just below his '03–'04 peak and be a championship-caliber player for a team less than that.

JUAN PIERRE CF Bats: L Throws: L Born: 14-Aug-1977 Age: 27

YEAR	TM	LG	AGE	AB	H	2B	3B	HR	BB	SO	SB	CS	AVG	OBP	SLG	MLVR	EQBA	EQOBP	EQSLG	EQMLVR	VORP	DEFENSE
2002	COL	NL	24	592	170	20	5	1	31	52	47	12	.287	.332	.343	-.123	.273	.317	.329	-.198	10.7	137-CF 8
2003	FLA	NL	25	668	204	28	7	1	55	35	65	20	.305	.361	.373	.030	.314	.369	.384	.010	38.4	160-CF -11
2004	FLA	NL	26	678	221	22	12	3	45	35	45	24	.326	.374	.407	.114	.336	.382	.420	.105	44.6	162-CF -7
2005	*FLA*	*NL*	*27*	*614*	*177*	*27*	*7*	*3*	*42*	*38*	*39*	*12*	*.288*	*.338*	*.370*	*-.081*	*.293*	*.341*	*.384*	*-.056*	*19.9*	*157-CF -2*

Breakout: 0% *Improve: 12%* *Collapse: 47%*

Pierre has turned out to be a much better player than he looked like as a Rockie, largely because his ability to hit for average wasn't left behind at altitude. His post-Colorado performance bolsters the argument that using global park factors to adjust performance lines doesn't work for everyone, that you have to consider individual skill sets rather than merely run environment. As a player who doesn't hit many fly balls or have much power, Pierre theoretically doesn't benefit from thin air as much as others. He's a good player, overrated for his steals and perceived defense, likely to be a very expensive arbitration case after this season.

MIKE REDMOND C Bats: R Throws: R Born: 05-May-1971 Age: 34

YEAR	TM	LG	AGE	AB	H	2B	3B	HR	BB	SO	SB	CS	AVG	OBP	SLG	MLVR	EQBA	EQOBP	EQSLG	EQMLVR	VORP	DEFENSE
2002	FLA	NL	31	256	78	15	0	2	21	34	0	2	.305	.372	.387	.084	.315	.371	.400	.037	17.6	70-C 5
2003	FLA	NL	32	125	30	7	1	0	7	16	0	0	.240	.302	.312	-.201	.252	.296	.315	-.273	-0.6	27-C -4
2004	FLA	NL	33	246	63	15	0	2	14	28	1	0	.256	.315	.341	-.128	.268	.316	.348	-.176	3.7	68-C -4
2005	*MIN*	*AL*	*34*	*179*	*46*	*10*	*0*	*2*	*11*	*26*	*1*	*0*	*.254*	*.317*	*.351*	*-.161*	*.252*	*.317*	*.355*	*-.165*	*3.2*	*51-C -2*

Breakout: 12% *Improve: 30%* *Collapse: 44%*

The moderately useful backup catcher went to the Twins after the season on the first multi-year deal of his career. He'll make a good backup to Joe Mauer if Mauer catches, and a decent half-time player if Mauer has to play elsewhere. The on-field difference between Redmond and Lo Duca, similar players in type, certainly isn't the $6-million-a-year difference in their salaries.

ERIC REED CF Bats: L Throws: L Born: 02-Dec-1980 Age: 24

YEAR	TM	LG	AGE	AB	H	2B	3B	HR	BB	SO	SB	CS	AVG	OBP	SLG	MLVR	EQBA	EQOBP	EQSLG	EQMLVR	VORP	DEFENSE
2002	JAM	NYP	21	250	77	5	1	0	17	30	19	10	.308	.348	.336	.039	.227	.258	.243	-.466	-43.6	60-CF -4
2002	KNC	MDW	21	50	18	1	0	0	3	11	7	1	.360	.396	.380	.234	.255	.238	.255	-.476	-5.0	11-CF -2
2003	JUP	FSL	22	514	154	15	8	0	52	83	53	18	.300	.367	.360	.131	.272	.325	.338	-.170	-4.0	125-CF 9
2004	CAR	SOU	23	222	68	9	6	3	14	55	24	5	.306	.345	.441	.133	.287	.321	.422	-.046	6.9	47-CF -4
2005	*FLA*	*NL*	*24*	*277*	*70*	*13*	*3*	*2*	*16*	*55*	*13*	*4*	*.251*	*.293*	*.342*	*-.226*	*.256*	*.295*	*.355*	*-.203*	*-3.4*	*73-CF -4*

Breakout: 8% *Improve: 20%* *Collapse: 60%*

Think Juan Pierre without the pan-European name. Reed is a legitimate burner and a true center fielder. He has more power than Pierre, and took a big step forward in that department last year before breaking his wrist. Whether he ends up as an extra outfielder or Pierre's successor largely depends on whether he can display the plate discipline he showed in 2003. His AFL stint, with one walk in 49 at-bats, wasn't encouraging.

JASON STOKES 1B Bats: R Throws: R Born: 23-Jan-1982 Age: 23

YEAR	TM	LG	AGE	AB	H	2B	3B	HR	BB	SO	SB	CS	AVG	OBP	SLG	MLVR	EQBA	EQOBP	EQSLG	EQMLVR	VORP	DEFENSE
2002	KNC	MDW	20	349	119	25	0	27	47	96	1	1	.341	.421	.645	.602	.281	.344	.525	.137	25.1	86-1B 4
2003	JUP	FSL	21	462	119	31	3	17	36	135	6	4	.258	.312	.448	.143	.233	.279	.428	-.159	-11.3	100-1B -9
2004	CAR	SOU	22	394	107	26	0	23	42	121	5	0	.272	.345	.513	.198	.241	.306	.460	-.058	3.2	103-1B 4
2005	*FLA*	*NL*	*23*	*356*	*89*	*19*	*1*	*17*	*36*	*107*	*3*	*1*	*.249*	*.322*	*.451*	*-.029*	*.254*	*.325*	*.468*	*-.001*	*11.5*	*95-1B -2*

Breakout: 37% *Improve: 53%* *Collapse: 15%*

Surgery on his left hamate bone in 2002 is the most obvious reason for his stagnation, but keep in mind that Stokes's strikeout rate and strikeout-to-walk ratios have remained unacceptably high, even as his power returned. Striking out in 30% of your at-bats in Double-A is a big negative, and that figure is going up as he advances. It's in his favor that he's still very young and his power is real. He could put up huge power numbers at Albuquerque, but his contact rate will be the key stat.

LARRY SUTTON

1B | Bats: L | Throws: L | Born: 14-May-1970 | Age: 35

YEAR	TM	LG	AGE	AB	H	2B	3B	HR	BB	SO	SB	CS	AVG	OBP	SLG	MLVR	EQBA	EQOBP	EQSLG	EQMLVR	VORP	DEFENSE
2002	SAC	PCL	32	431	126	40	2	12	93	108	2	0	.292	.417	.478	.253	.269	.389	.435	.081	22.4	44-1B 0 25-LF -2
2004	ABQ	PCL	34	308	114	31	1	21	59	61	3	1	.370	.472	.682	.526	.286	.390	.514	.204	28.0	69-1B -1
2005	*FLA*	*NL*	*35*	*108*	*27*	*6*	*1*	*4*	*21*	*28*	*0*	*0*	*.250*	*.373*	*.422*	*.020*	*.254*	*.376*	*.438*	*.047*	*7.5*	*35-1B -4*

Breakout: 25% *Improve: 40%* *Collapse: 35%*

His ridiculous year at Albuquerque was likely the last gasp of a dying career, one already interrupted in 2003 by knee surgery. Then again, if you're the Marlins and you start six right-handed hitters and you're not getting much from first base, why not stick him in the lineup and try to catch lightning in a bottle? As badly as this team needed lefty pop and OBP after the Choi trade, they missed this opportunity. The playoffs, too.

DEREK WATHAN

UT | Bats: B | Throws: R | Born: 13-Dec-1976 | Age: 28

YEAR	TM	LG	AGE	AB	H	2B	3B	HR	BB	SO	SB	CS	AVG	OBP	SLG	MLVR	EQBA	EQOBP	EQSLG	EQMLVR	VORP	DEFENSE
2002	CLG	PCL	25	329	92	18	7	5	23	44	7	11	.280	.330	.422	-.071	.234	.287	.352	-.250	-4.8	61-SS -1
2003	ABQ	PCL	26	409	121	24	7	4	34	56	21	8	.296	.350	.418	-.031	.242	.300	.350	-.222	-16.8	45-1B -4 17-SS 1
2004	ABQ	PCL	27	414	125	26	5	10	33	74	15	10	.302	.354	.461	-.042	.239	.292	.358	-.228	-6.3	37-2B -4 24-CF -1
2005	*FLA*	*NL*	*28*	*146*	*35*	*7*	*2*	*2*	*11*	*27*	*3*	*2*	*.242*	*.297*	*.361*	*-.198*	*.247*	*.299*	*.375*	*-.176*	*2.6*	*42-2B -6*

Breakout: 28% *Improve: 44%* *Collapse: 34%*

John's younger son doesn't have much prospect sheen left, but the Fish saw enough in his third year at Albuquerque to add him to their 40-man roster. He made 10 or more appearances at four different positions last season, and when you add in his ability to hit singles and run, it makes for a nice bench package, especially in the NL. His dad arrived late too, peaking in the majors from ages 30–33.

JOSH WILLINGHAM

C/1B | Bats: R | Throws: R | Born: 17-Feb-1979 | Age: 26

YEAR	TM	LG	AGE	AB	H	2B	3B	HR	BB	SO	SB	CS	AVG	OBP	SLG	MLVR	EQBA	EQOBP	EQSLG	EQMLVR	VORP	DEFENSE
2002	JUP	FSL	23	376	103	21	4	17	63	88	18	5	.274	.394	.487	.299	.253	.348	.459	.026	13.5	30-1B -3 20-3B -1
2003	JUP	FSL	24	193	51	17	1	12	46	42	9	2	.264	.422	.549	.407	.224	.357	.493	.063	17.1	35-C -6
2003	CAR	SOU	24	67	20	2	1	5	13	20	0	0	.299	.434	.582	.447	.290	.402	.580	.316	10.1	
2004	CAR	SOU	25	338	95	24	0	24	91	87	6	3	.281	.449	.565	.416	.246	.396	.497	.155	40.5	78-C 0 17-1B 1
2004	FLA	NL	25	25	5	0	0	1	4	8	0	0	.200	.310	.320	-.184	.240	.256	.360	-.294	-0.3	
2005	*FLA*	*NL*	*26*	*214*	*57*	*12*	*2*	*11*	*41*	*55*	*3*	*1*	*.264*	*.399*	*.486*	*.154*	*.269*	*.402*	*.504*	*.184*	*29.1*	*65-C -12*

Breakout: 30% *Improve: 55%* *Collapse: 28%*

Willingham would be enormously valuable if there was more confidence that he'll be a catcher. He's played behind the plate for just two years, and his defense is a work in progress at best. As well as he's hit at Carolina, and as much as PECOTA likes him, he's 26 and has just 25 at-bats above Double-A, and all of his good hitting has come in leagues where he's been among the oldest players. He has to do something at Triple-A or the majors to justify the buzz.

JOSH WILSON

SS | Bats: R | Throws: R | Born: 26-Mar-1981 | Age: 24

YEAR	TM	LG	AGE	AB	H	2B	3B	HR	BB	SO	SB	CS	AVG	OBP	SLG	MLVR	EQBA	EQOBP	EQSLG	EQMLVR	VORP	DEFENSE
2002	JUP	FSL	21	398	102	17	1	11	28	67	7	10	.256	.318	.387	.050	.238	.284	.373	-.223	-2.4	103-SS 4
2003	CAR	SOU	22	434	110	30	6	3	27	70	6	5	.253	.294	.371	-.050	.239	.272	.368	-.253	-6.6	110-SS -12
2004	CAR	SOU	23	311	98	21	1	10	42	50	8	4	.315	.396	.486	.276	.289	.363	.451	.073	27.9	73-SS -2
2004	ABQ	PCL	23	240	67	12	2	5	19	51	6	1	.279	.337	.408	-.164	.220	.274	.315	-.335	-9.1	56-SS 2
2005	*FLA*	*NL*	*24*	*217*	*54*	*12*	*1*	*4*	*16*	*40*	*3*	*1*	*.250*	*.305*	*.377*	*-.158*	*.254*	*.308*	*.391*	*-.134*	*5.8*	*59-SS -3*

Breakout: 21% *Improve: 40%* *Collapse: 25%*

The heir apparent to Gonzalez, Wilson was named the best defensive shortstop in the Southern League in *Baseball America*'s poll, and is probably ready to handle the position at the major league level right now. His bat, however, has needed time to adjust to each new level, and his plate discipline fell apart after a midseason promotion, so another year at Triple-A won't hurt him. He should be the Opening Day shortstop in 2006.

PITCHERS

JEFF ALLISON Bats: R Throws: R Born: 27-Nov-1984 Age: 20

The Marlins' #1 pick in 2003 has fought substance-abuse problems, most notably an addiction to Oxycontin. He has made just three professional appearances, none last year. We list him here largely as a reminder that he's still under Marlins' control, and a warning to those who evaluate potential draftees to take the notion of "makeup" with a grain of salt. It's largely guesswork.

YORMAN BAZARDO Bats: R Throws: R Born: 11-Jul-1984 Age: 20

YEAR	TM	LG	AGE	G	GS	IP	H	BB	SO	HR	ERA	EQERA	EQH9	EQBB9	EQSO9	EQHR9	PERA	VORP	STF
2002	JAM	NYP	17	25	0	36.3	39	6	26	0	2.73	4.89	9.0	2.1	3.6	0.3	2.83	10.8	2
2003	GRB	SAL	18	21	21	130.0	132	26	70	8	3.12	5.69	10.5	2.2	3.0	1.3	5.38	2.9	7
2004	JUP	FSL	19	25	25	154.3	161	30	95	3	3.27	5.88	9.4	2.0	3.7	0.3	3.73	30.5	22
2005	*FLA*	*NL*	*20*	*14*	*14*	*82.3*	*92*	*26*	*42*	*11*	*4.66*	*5.09*	*10.1*	*2.5*	*4.1*	*1.2*	*5.25*	*4.6*	*-3*

Breakout: 5% *Improve: 27%* *Collapse: 17%*

The convention of using a July 1 cutoff to determine player age mislabels Bazardo, who's an "old" 20. Scouts love him for his mid-90s fastball and slider. The low strikeout rate is a definite concern, although it's mitigated by his great control and insanely low home-run rate. The real concern is his arm; by no means has Bazardo been abused, but the attrition rate is high for guys this young and this advanced.

JOSH BECKETT Bats: R Throws: R Born: 15-May-1980 Age: 25

YEAR	TM	LG	AGE	G	GS	IP	H	BB	SO	HR	ERA	EQERA	EQH9	EQBB9	EQSO9	EQHR9	PERA	VORP	STF
2002	FLA	NL	22	23	21	107.7	93	44	113	13	4.09	4.92	8.0	3.2	8.5	1.1	3.71	9.8	23
2003	FLA	NL	23	24	23	142.0	132	56	152	9	3.04	3.59	8.0	3.1	8.7	0.6	3.40	35.9	34
2004	FLA	NL	24	26	26	156.7	137	54	152	16	3.79	4.23	8.1	2.8	7.9	0.9	3.70	28.3	26
2005	*FLA*	*NL*	*25*	*27*	*26*	*160.3*	*142*	*54*	*149*	*15*	*3.51*	*3.83*	*8.0*	*2.7*	*7.5*	*0.9*	*3.77*	*32.3*	*22*

Breakout: 24% *Improve: 51%* *Collapse: 19%*

As aggravating as Beckett's blister problems have been for the right-hander and his team, they may end up as a long-term benefit, as they've kept his workload down during a critical period for a young pitcher. His performance hasn't varied much in three seasons, and he's at an age where he can be expected to add innings and show improvement. The hero of the 2003 World Series could have the kind of big-step-forward performance that another right-hander, Ben Sheets, had in his fourth season.

ARMANDO BENITEZ Bats: R Throws: R Born: 03-Nov-1972 Age: 32

YEAR	TM	LG	AGE	G	GS	IP	H	BB	SO	HR	ERA	EQERA	EQH9	EQBB9	EQSO9	EQHR9	PERA	VORP	STF
2002	NYM	NL	29	62	0	67.3	46	25	79	8	2.27	2.95	7.0	3.0	9.6	1.1	3.09	20.2	21
2003	NYM	NL	30	45	0	49.3	41	24	50	5	3.10	3.38	7.7	3.9	8.2	0.9	3.75	12.8	10
2003	NYY	AL	30	9	0	9.3	8	6	10	0	1.94	3.86	6.8	5.8	9.6	0.0	2.89	2.3	14
2003	SEA	AL	30	15	0	14.3	10	11	15	1	3.15	3.29	7.2	6.6	9.2	0.7	3.95	4.7	7
2004	FLA	NL	31	64	0	69.7	36	21	62	6	1.29	1.69	6.2	2.5	7.6	0.7	2.39	33.1	15
2005	*SFG*	*NL*	*32*	*45*	*1*	*66.0*	*52*	*25*	*52*	*9*	*3.30*	*3.57*	*7.0*	*3.0*	*6.4*	*1.4*	*3.82*	*16.1*	*-1*

Breakout: 24% *Improve: 46%* *Collapse: 21%*

His ridiculously low 1.29 ERA was largely the result of a ridiculously low .178 batting average allowed on balls in play. Last season was the first year in which he struck out less than a man per inning, which may just be the effect of the great defense behind him. Everything else in his line was typical post-peak Benitez. The Giants gave him a three-year deal for $21 million, which seemed like too much at first, but really there are few relievers with Benitez's track record. The guy is just never bad.

ADAM BOSTICK **Bats: L** **Throws: L** Born: 17-Mar-1983 Age: 22

YEAR	TM	LG	AGE	G	GS	IP	H	BB	SO	HR	ERA	EQERA	EQH9	EQBB9	EQSO9	EQHR9	PERA	VORP	STF
2003	JAM	NYP	20	15	15	77.3	77	39	76	9	5.12	7.32	11.6	6.1	5.5	3.9	8.25	-19.9	-32
2003	GRB	SAL	20	7	1	14.3	12	12	15	1	3.78	5.68	9.9	9.2	6.4	1.4	7.11	-2.1	-23
2004	GRB	SAL	21	23	22	114.0	100	58	163	10	3.79	5.42	8.9	5.3	8.0	1.4	4.91	8.1	10
2005	*FLA*	*NL*	*22*	*12*	*9*	*57.0*	*52*	*33*	*54*	*9*	*5.15*	*5.63*	*8.3*	*4.6*	*7.6*	*1.5*	*5.52*	*1.3*	*5*

Breakout: 14% *Improve: 44%* *Collapse: 20%*

Call us crazy, but we think if you lead your league in strikeouts, and do so at a rate of nearly 13 per nine innings, you have to be one of the top 20 prospects in the circuit. Yet *Baseball America* left Bostick off their Sally League list. Conceding that BP and BA run at things a bit differently, I don't see how that kind of performance doesn't make you a prospect until you prove otherwise. Bostick throws a big deuce—cause of the strikeouts and, by extension, BA's apathy—and a reasonable fastball, and should be watched at Jupiter this year.

NATE BUMP **Bats: R** **Throws: R** Born: 24-Jul-1976 Age: 28

YEAR	TM	LG	AGE	G	GS	IP	H	BB	SO	HR	ERA	EQERA	EQH9	EQBB9	EQSO9	EQHR9	PERA	VORP	STF
2002	PME	EAS	25	20	20	127.7	110	29	81	5	3.38	4.40	8.6	2.2	4.6	0.6	3.72	24.8	23
2003	ABQ	PCL	26	15	15	85.3	89	24	52	4	4.43	4.83	8.9	2.9	4.6	0.5	3.95	15.0	12
2003	FLA	NL	26	32	0	36.3	34	20	17	3	4.71	5.40	8.7	4.4	3.9	0.8	4.37	1.7	-15
2004	FLA	NL	27	50	2	73.7	86	32	44	7	5.01	5.60	10.0	3.5	4.7	0.7	4.98	0.7	-8
2005	*FLA*	*NL*	*28*	*28*	*8*	*70.7*	*76*	*27*	*44*	*6*	*4.34*	*4.74*	*9.8*	*3.0*	*5.0*	*0.8*	*4.93*	*6.9*	*-7*

Breakout: 25% *Improve: 42%* *Collapse: 27%*

Bump is replacement-level staff filler who provides a good example of why it's often best to use pitching prospects to trade for established major league pitching. The Giants' #1 pick in 1998, he was swapped along with Jason Grilli for Livan Hernandez during the '99 division race. Bump and Grilli haven't amounted to much, while Hernandez was part of two division titles and a pennant. When it comes to pitchers and pennant races, certainty can often trump potential.

A. J. BURNETT **Bats: R** **Throws: R** Born: 03-Jan-1977 Age: 28

YEAR	TM	LG	AGE	G	GS	IP	H	BB	SO	HR	ERA	EQERA	EQH9	EQBB9	EQSO9	EQHR9	PERA	VORP	STF
2002	FLA	NL	25	31	29	204.3	153	90	203	12	3.30	3.94	7.2	3.4	8.1	0.5	3.02	40.9	31
2003	FLA	NL	26	4	4	23.0	18	18	21	2	4.70	5.24	7.7	6.0	7.7	0.8	4.43	1.6	9
2004	FLA	NL	27	20	19	120.0	102	38	113	9	3.67	3.90	7.9	2.6	7.7	0.6	3.36	26.8	27
2005	*FLA*	*NL*	*28*	*23*	*22*	*134.3*	*117*	*50*	*122*	*13*	*3.76*	*4.10*	*7.9*	*2.9*	*7.3*	*0.9*	*3.91*	*23.3*	*19*

Breakout: 22% *Improve: 48%* *Collapse: 30%*

Burnett came back from Tommy John surgery in just over 13 months to post the best strikeout-to-walk ratio of his career, and he was devastating for much of the second half. The bad news is that inflammation in the repaired elbow shut him down in early September. No damage was found, and he made a token relief appearance on the last weekend of the season, so he has a green light. He could be a top-10 starter in 2005.

CHAD FOX **Bats: R** **Throws: R** Born: 03-Sep-1970 Age: 34

YEAR	TM	LG	AGE	G	GS	IP	H	BB	SO	HR	ERA	EQERA	EQH9	EQBB9	EQSO9	EQHR9	PERA	VORP	STF
2003	BOS	AL	32	17	0	18.0	19	17	19	2	4.50	4.42	8.3	7.9	8.8	1.0	4.91	2.2	-4
2003	FLA	NL	32	21	0	25.3	16	14	27	1	2.13	2.22	6.3	4.4	8.9	0.4	2.96	9.8	15
2004	FLA	NL	33	12	0	10.7	9	8	17	1	6.73	6.75	7.6	5.9	12.7	0.8	4.22	-1.2	25
2005	*CHC*	*NL*	*34*	*19*	*2*	*34.3*	*28*	*21*	*39*	*5*	*4.10*	*4.25*	*7.4*	*4.7*	*9.2*	*1.2*	*4.79*	*5.9*	*10*

Breakout 39% *Improve 64%* *Collapse 9%*

Fox just can't stay healthy long enough to become wealthy. Despite a career strikeout rate of more than 10 per nine innings, he has just three full seasons under his belt since making his major league debut in 1997. He's had two Tommy John surgeries and might well have had a third last year after being shut down with another elbow injury in April. A free agent on a rehab program this winter, he'll either be effective or unavailable in 2005.

BEN HOWARD **Bats: R** **Throws: R** Born: 15-Jan-1979 Age: 26

YEAR	TM	LG	AGE	G	GS	IP	H	BB	SO	HR	ERA	EQERA	EQH9	EQBB9	EQSO9	EQHR9	PERA	VORP	STF
2002	MOB	SOU	23	6	6	33.0	26	16	30	2	2.18	3.52	8.2	4.4	6.2	1.2	4.40	4.1	6
2002	POR	PCL	23	11	7	45.0	47	15	25	10	6.20	7.02	11.0	3.3	4.2	2.4	7.24	-7.5	-20
2003	POR	PCL	24	22	22	130.7	118	49	68	17	4.54	5.35	9.3	4.0	4.1	1.8	5.28	4.2	3
2003	SDP	NL	24	6	6	34.7	31	15	24	10	3.63	4.73	9.2	3.6	5.8	2.8	5.57	4.9	19
2004	ABQ	PCL	25	23	0	34.3	29	22	28	3	3.67	3.90	7.8	6.1	5.8	0.8	4.73	3.1	8
2004	FLA	NL	25	31	0	37.7	37	21	33	6	5.49	5.65	8.8	4.4	7.1	1.2	4.91	0.9	18
2005	*FLA*	*NL*	*26*	*14*	*6*	*45.3*	*44*	*24*	*33*	*8*	*5.04*	*5.50*	*8.7*	*4.2*	*5.9*	*1.5*	*5.58*	*2.0*	*-8*

Breakout: 24% *Improve: 42%* *Collapse: 21%*

Darkhorse closer candidate who came over from the Padres in exchange for the guy who had been a darkhorse closer candidate, Blaine Neal. Howard gets into the mid-90s with his fastball, and also throws a slider and change-up, but none of them for strikes consistently. He's been better as a reliever, just not enough to have an impact. Like Bump, he'll be fighting for a job now that Antonio Alfonseca and Todd Jones are around.

TREVOR HUTCHINSON **Bats: R** **Throws: R** Born: 08-Oct-1979 Age: 25

YEAR	TM	LG	AGE	G	GS	IP	H	BB	SO	HR	ERA	EQERA	EQH9	EQBB9	EQSO9	EQHR9	PERA	VORP	STF
2003	CAR	SOU	23	8	6	35.0	32	13	18	1	3.86	6.40	9.2	3.6	3.3	0.6	4.73	3.1	-6
2003	JUP	FSL	23	14	13	84.3	77	16	58	3	2.78	4.87	9.4	2.0	4.4	1.0	4.40	10.4	9
2004	CAR	SOU	24	24	24	123.3	133	38	86	11	4.23	5.86	9.9	2.9	4.3	1.2	5.09	6.6	-5
2005	*FLA*	*NL*	*25*	*13*	*10*	*61.3*	*65*	*20*	*36*	*8*	*4.63*	*5.06*	*9.7*	*2.6*	*4.7*	*1.2*	*5.04*	*4.9*	*-2*

Breakout: 13% *Improve: 47%* *Collapse: 23%*

Hutchinson played his senior year in college, then held out after being drafted in '02. Now, he's 25 and has just 242 professional innings under his belt. His stuff belies his 6′5″ frame; he's a sinker/slider pitcher, not a hard thrower, and his strikeout rates reflect that. He missed time last year with elbow and shoulder discomfort, the latter ending his AFL stint quickly. Not much upside, but his size, command and low-use arm could make him a nice cheap guy at the back of the rotation come 2006.

LOGAN KENSING **Bats: R** **Throws: R** Born: 03-Jul-1982 Age: 22

YEAR	TM	LG	AGE	G	GS	IP	H	BB	SO	HR	ERA	EQERA	EQH9	EQBB9	EQSO9	EQHR9	PERA	VORP	STF
2003	JAM	NYP	21	8	6	33.0	48	6	20	1	5.73	7.91	11.2	1.9	3.0	0.8	4.64	3.5	-9
2003	GRB	SAL	21	4	4	20.0	18	5	11	2	4.50	6.11	10.7	3.1	3.1	2.5	6.62	-2.0	-12
2004	JUP	FSL	22	23	23	127.7	120	35	100	5	2.96	5.05	9.1	2.9	4.8	0.8	4.15	19.2	11
2004	FLA	NL	22	5	3	13.7	19	9	7	5	9.85	9.45	12.2	5.4	4.1	3.4	8.78	-6.3	-29
2005	*FLA*	*NL*	*22*	*15*	*12*	*74.7*	*81*	*27*	*47*	*9*	*4.66*	*5.08*	*9.9*	*2.9*	*5.0*	*1.1*	*5.20*	*4.7*	*-1*

Breakout: 14% *Improve: 50%* *Collapse: 16%*

The Marlins' #2 pick in the '03 draft is best known for being yanked out of the Florida State League to make a start against the Cubs in the middle of the Wild Card race. Kensing throws a good sinking fastball, and as polished as he is, had no business pitching in the majors last year. Check back in 2006.

BILLY KOCH **Bats: R** **Throws: R** Born: 14-Dec-1974 Age: 30

YEAR	TM	LG	AGE	G	GS	IP	H	BB	SO	HR	ERA	EQERA	EQH9	EQBB9	EQSO9	EQHR9	PERA	VORP	STF
2002	OAK	AL	27	84	0	93.7	73	46	93	7	3.27	3.39	7.4	4.2	8.7	0.6	3.69	24.2	15
2003	CWS	AL	28	55	0	53.0	59	28	42	10	5.77	5.54	9.7	4.5	6.9	1.6	5.88	-0.1	-12
2004	CWS	AL	29	24	0	23.3	24	16	25	3	5.41	5.01	8.5	5.4	8.9	1.2	5.01	1.3	2
2004	FLA	NL	29	23	0	25.7	21	20	25	3	3.50	3.60	7.9	6.1	7.9	1.1	4.68	6.3	-4
2005	*TOR*	*AL*	*30*	*45*	*0*	*43.0*	*43*	*26*	*40*	*6*	*5.12*	*4.82*	*8.9*	*4.8*	*7.5*	*1.1*	*4.94*	*5.4*	*-3*

Breakout: 26% *Improve: 46%* *Collapse: 28%*

If you're going to be an effective short reliever relying largely on your fastball, you have to throw strikes. Koch doesn't, and despite the 30-save seasons, he's only been a very good pitcher in two years, 2000 and 2002—and he's been terrible the past two seasons. The fastball and the closer label will keep him employed for the next five years, although no one seems to be in a hurry to sign him this winter.

GUILLERMO MOTA Bats: R Throws: R Born: 25-Jul-1973 Age: 31

YEAR	TM	LG	AGE	G	GS	IP	H	BB	SO	HR	ERA	EQERA	EQH9	EQBB9	EQSO9	EQHR9	PERA	VORP	STF
2002	LVG	PCL	28	20	0	36.7	34	8	38	1	2.94	3.28	7.8	2.0	7.3	0.3	3.03	10.2	17
2002	LAD	NL	28	43	0	60.7	45	27	49	4	4.15	4.89	7.9	3.6	6.6	0.6	3.79	6.2	6
2003	LAD	NL	29	76	0	105.0	78	26	99	7	1.97	2.18	7.5	2.0	8.0	0.6	3.00	42.6	23
2004	LAD	NL	30	52	0	63.0	51	27	52	4	2.14	2.40	7.9	3.5	6.8	0.6	3.75	24.9	7
2004	FLA	NL	30	26	0	33.7	24	10	33	4	4.81	4.83	7.4	2.6	8.2	1.1	3.41	3.3	16
2005	*FLA*	*NL*	*31*	*44*	*4*	*78.3*	*73*	*28*	*65*	*8*	*3.59*	*3.92*	*8.4*	*2.8*	*6.7*	*0.9*	*4.13*	*14.8*	*4*

Breakout: 25% *Improve: 51%* *Collapse: 26%*

Like Lo Duca, Mota was a bit of a disappointment after being acquired, although that was largely due to pitching in bad luck; his 4.81 ERA belied his improved post-trade peripherals. Mota is not likely to match his 2002–03 run again, but he'll have more fantasy value in 2005, as Jack McKeon has named him the closer. Think Octavio Dotel coming off of '01–'02, or maybe Duane Ward circa 1992. He's not young.

SCOTT OLSEN Bats: L Throws: L Born: 12-Jan-1984 Age: 21

YEAR	TM	LG	AGE	G	GS	IP	H	BB	SO	HR	ERA	EQERA	EQH9	EQBB9	EQSO9	EQHR9	PERA	VORP	STF
2003	GRB	SAL	19	25	24	128.3	101	59	129	4	2.81	5.43	8.8	5.0	5.7	0.7	4.73	11.2	18
2004	JUP	FSL	20	25	25	136.3	127	54	158	8	2.97	5.09	9.3	4.1	7.1	1.1	4.88	10.2	14
2005	*FLA*	*NL*	*21*	*13*	*12*	*73.7*	*69*	*35*	*61*	*8*	*4.34*	*4.73*	*8.5*	*3.8*	*6.6*	*1.1*	*4.79*	*7.6*	*9*

Breakout: 11% *Improve: 51%* *Collapse: 14%*

Olsen was drafted out of high school, the Marlins' #6 pick in 2002. He's a tall left-hander who throws a low-90s fastball and a slider, and he hasn't been anything but successful as a pro. His performance record sparkles; his being a slider-throwing pro at ages 19–21 doesn't. Even though he's the best pitching prospect in the system, beware.

CARL PAVANO Bats: R Throws: R Born: 08-Jan-1976 Age: 29

YEAR	TM	LG	AGE	G	GS	IP	H	BB	SO	HR	ERA	EQERA	EQH9	EQBB9	EQSO9	EQHR9	PERA	VORP	STF
2002	MON	NL	26	15	14	74.3	98	31	51	14	6.30	6.42	10.8	3.1	5.3	1.6	6.05	-9.6	-9
2002	FLA	NL	26	22	8	61.7	76	14	41	5	3.79	5.02	10.0	1.8	5.3	0.7	4.43	4.4	0
2003	FLA	NL	27	33	32	201.0	204	49	133	19	4.30	4.53	9.0	1.9	5.5	0.8	3.79	28.2	13
2004	FLA	NL	28	31	31	222.3	212	49	139	16	3.00	3.40	8.8	1.8	5.1	0.6	3.69	62.4	15
2005	*NYY*	*AL*	*29*	*28*	*28*	*174.7*	*199*	*42*	*109*	*23*	*4.64*	*4.64*	*10.4*	*1.9*	*5.0*	*1.1*	*4.63*	*21.3*	*7*

Breakout: 12% *Improve: 47%* *Collapse: 20%*

Here's the problem with Pavano's new wealth: The four-year, $39 million contract he signed with the Yankees is for twice as many full seasons as he has on his résumé. Pavano isn't a top-tier, dominant starter so much as he's a guy who managed to stay in the rotation in front of a good defense for a team in a pitcher's park. His strikeout rate is below average, and while he has good command and gets his share of ground balls, strikeout rate is the key indicator for pitchers. His low ERA last year was about the Marlins' defense, not his performance. Pavano will chew up innings and be average, which means the Yankees are going to be disappointed. At least it's a forgiving organization.

MATT PERISHO Bats: L Throws: L Born: 08-Jun-1975 Age: 30

YEAR	TM	LG	AGE	G	GS	IP	H	BB	SO	HR	ERA	EQERA	EQH9	EQBB9	EQSO9	EQHR9	PERA	VORP	STF
2002	TOL	INT	27	51	2	66.0	62	19	44	4	2.45	3.34	8.9	2.9	5.2	0.9	4.21	9.6	-1
2003	DUR	INT	28	34	0	38.7	43	12	41	5	6.51	6.81	10.0	3.2	7.8	1.7	5.84	-1.0	-6
2003	CSP	PCL	28	8	4	23.7	25	14	15	1	3.42	5.96	8.7	6.0	4.8	0.4	4.76	2.1	-13
2004	FLA	NL	29	66	0	47.0	45	26	42	6	4.40	4.53	8.7	4.5	7.3	1.0	4.73	6.8	-3
2005	*FLA*	*NL*	*30*	*29*	*1*	*39.7*	*40*	*20*	*33*	*5*	*4.52*	*4.93*	*9.1*	*3.9*	*6.6*	*1.1*	*5.23*	*3.8*	*-5*

Breakout: 27% *Improve: 50%* *Collapse: 24%*

It's just fun when a guy who'd been left behind in the previous century comes out of nowhere to win a job in spring training. Perisho held lefties to a .207 average and was effective enough against righties that he could pitch complete innings when necessary. The difference in value between a guy like that and, say, Mike Myers, is significant.

TOMMY PHELPS

Bats: L **Throws: L** Born: 04-Mar-1974 Age: 31

YEAR	TM	LG	AGE	G	GS	IP	H	BB	SO	HR	ERA	EQERA	EQH9	EQBB9	EQSO9	EQHR9	PERA	VORP	STF
2002	CLG	PCL	28	51	0	74.3	76	21	62	8	3.15	3.15	9.1	2.6	5.9	1.1	4.54	8.4	0
2003	FLA	NL	29	27	7	63.0	70	23	43	3	4.00	4.62	9.2	2.9	5.5	0.4	4.04	7.6	2
2004	FLA	NL	30	19	4	34.0	34	12	28	6	4.76	5.23	9.1	2.8	6.6	1.4	4.68	1.7	0
2005	*MIL*	*NL*	*31*	*26*	*4*	*52.0*	*54*	*19*	*41*	*6*	*4.49*	*4.66*	*9.4*	*2.9*	*6.3*	*1.0*	*4.63*	*5.9*	*0*

Breakout: 23% *Improve: 45%* *Collapse: 31%*

He'd be having a nice little career if the Marlins would stop slapping him into the rotation. Phelps has a 2.42 career ERA as a reliever, but 5.85 in 11 career starts, and when he pitches poorly as a starter, they get frustrated and demote him. After getting sent out again in June, Phelps complained of elbow soreness and underwent surgery to remove bone spurs, effectively ending his season. Hopefully the Brewers will make better use of him, because he can be a minor asset.

RUDY SEANEZ

Bats: R **Throws: R** Born: 20-Oct-1968 Age: 36

YEAR	TM	LG	AGE	G	GS	IP	H	BB	SO	HR	ERA	EQERA	EQH9	EQBB9	EQSO9	EQHR9	PERA	VORP	STF
2002	TEX	AL	33	33	0	33.0	28	24	40	5	5.73	6.06	7.4	6.1	10.5	1.1	4.41	-3.1	11
2003	PAW	INT	34	17	0	20.7	20	10	24	5	6.09	6.63	9.9	5.2	9.0	3.8	7.58	-4.2	-9
2004	OMA	PCL	35	24	0	34.3	19	12	41	3	1.57	2.56	6.3	3.4	8.8	1.1	2.84	9.7	25
2004	KCR	AL	35	16	0	23.0	21	11	21	0	3.91	3.52	7.4	3.9	7.8	0.0	3.13	6.1	20
2004	FLA	NL	35	23	0	23.0	18	8	25	3	2.74	2.86	7.8	2.9	9.0	1.2	3.68	7.6	25
2005	*SDP*	*NL*	*36*	*27*	*3*	*45.3*	*40*	*22*	*46*	*6*	*4.08*	*4.65*	*8.1*	*3.9*	*8.1*	*1.3*	*4.82*	*6.1*	*5*

Breakout: 32% *Improve: 44%* *Collapse: 26%*

The guy Chad Fox aspires to be, Seanez not only carted himself to the mound enough times to make a roster, he actually managed to pick up some trade value, getting swapped to Florida at midseason. He's had a 13-year career with a peak of 53 $^2/_3$ innings in a single season, thanks mostly to a body that keeps betraying him. He throws hard stuff down, which makes him difficult to hit, as the numbers above show. He'll be in his third tour of duty with the Padres in '05.

TAYLOR TANKERSLEY

Bats: L **Throws: L** Born: 07-Mar-1983 Age: 22

YEAR	TM	LG	AGE	G	GS	IP	H	BB	SO	HR	ERA	EQERA	EQH9	EQBB9	EQSO9	EQHR9	PERA	VORP	STF
2004	JAM	NYP	21	6	6	26.7	21	8	32	2	3.37	6.00	9.0	3.8	6.4	1.9	4.88	1.9	6
2005	*FLA*	*NL*	*22*	*16*	*8*	*58.3*	*53*	*27*	*47*	*10*	*4.79*	*5.23*	*8.3*	*3.7*	*6.5*	*1.6*	*5.04*	*3.6*	*-1*

Breakout: 10% *Improve: 45%* *Collapse: 13%*

The Marlins' #1 pick out of Alabama, Tankersley already has one of the best sliders in the organization. The Marlins have had some success with pushing guys such as Burnett and Beckett quickly through the system, and that's the path Tankersley could be on. His fastball is just average, and its development will determine whether he's a #1 starter or a mid-rotation guy.

ISMAEL VALDEZ

Bats: R **Throws: R** Born: 21-Aug-1973 Age: 31

YEAR	TM	LG	AGE	G	GS	IP	H	BB	SO	HR	ERA	EQERA	EQH9	EQBB9	EQSO9	EQHR9	PERA	VORP	STF
2002	SEA	AL	28	8	8	49.3	59	11	27	7	4.93	5.25	10.3	1.9	4.7	1.1	5.06	3.8	2
2002	TEX	AL	28	23	23	146.7	135	36	75	19	3.93	3.54	8.6	2.1	4.5	1.1	4.00	32.5	4
2003	TEX	AL	29	22	22	115.0	148	29	47	23	6.10	5.59	10.4	2.1	3.5	1.6	5.12	-5.3	-11
2004	SDP	NL	30	23	20	114.0	141	31	37	21	5.53	6.14	10.9	2.2	2.6	1.6	5.65	-2.0	-19
2004	FLA	NL	30	11	11	56.0	61	18	30	12	4.50	4.89	10.1	2.7	4.4	1.9	5.57	5.9	-7
2005	*FLA*	*NL*	*31*	*26*	*20*	*125.3*	*145*	*34*	*55*	*20*	*5.05*	*5.52*	*10.5*	*2.2*	*3.5*	*1.5*	*5.50*	*4.7*	*-11*

Breakout: 15% *Improve: 43%* *Collapse: 28%*

How weird would it be to find out you'd been misspelling your name your entire life? Valdez learned last winter that his surname is properly spelled with a "z" rather than an "s." Does this mean his old autographs go up in value? How long do you think it took him to start signing his checks correctly? All of this is much more interesting than his pitching, which is properly spelled with a "p" and a "u." Just 31, he's probably done.

JUSTIN WAYNE

Bats: R **Throws: R** Born: 16-Apr-1979 Age: 26

YEAR	TM	LG	AGE	G	GS	IP	H	BB	SO	HR	ERA	EQERA	EQH9	EQBB9	EQSO9	EQHR9	PERA	VORP	STF
2002	HAR	EAS	23	17	17	98.7	74	32	47	7	2.37	4.35	8.4	3.2	3.5	1.0	4.35	12.4	-5
2002	PME	EAS	23	7	7	42.7	43	13	30	3	4.85	5.80	9.6	2.9	4.9	0.9	4.69	4.1	3
2002	FLA	NL	23	5	5	23.7	22	13	16	3	5.32	6.35	8.7	4.4	5.6	1.2	4.76	-1.5	2
2003	ABQ	PCL	24	23	23	136.0	138	40	82	10	4.24	5.07	8.9	3.0	4.7	0.9	4.16	20.8	11
2004	ABQ	PCL	25	13	13	65.7	82	34	43	11	6.58	6.02	10.2	4.9	4.5	1.5	6.44	-6.0	-18
2004	FLA	NL	25	19	1	32.7	35	18	20	6	5.78	6.54	9.7	4.5	4.8	1.4	5.68	-3.3	-19
2005	*FLA*	*NL*	*26*	*18*	*9*	*61.0*	*62*	*27*	*40*	*7*	*4.74*	*5.18*	*9.2*	*3.5*	*5.2*	*1.1*	*5.10*	*3.4*	*-6*

Breakout: 25% *Improve: 51%* *Collapse: 23%*

Strong command got Wayne through college ball and the low minors, but you need more at the upper levels. He doesn't have it. His ERA at Triple-A and in the majors is 5.32, and he's not showing any improvement.

DAVE WEATHERS

Bats: R **Throws: R** Born: 25-Sep-1969 Age: 35

YEAR	TM	LG	AGE	G	GS	IP	H	BB	SO	HR	ERA	EQERA	EQH9	EQBB9	EQSO9	EQHR9	PERA	VORP	STF
2002	NYM	NL	32	71	0	77.3	69	36	61	6	2.91	3.74	8.3	3.6	6.4	0.7	3.86	16.2	0
2003	NYM	NL	33	77	0	87.7	87	40	75	6	3.08	3.44	8.5	3.5	7.0	0.6	4.07	21.7	4
2004	NYM	NL	34	32	0	33.7	41	15	25	5	4.27	4.86	10.3	3.5	5.9	1.1	5.40	2.3	-11
2004	HOU	NL	34	26	0	32.0	31	13	26	5	4.78	5.23	8.7	3.2	6.7	1.2	4.35	0.3	-2
2004	FLA	NL	34	8	2	16.7	13	7	10	2	2.69	2.87	8.0	3.4	5.2	1.1	4.02	5.6	-7
2005	*CIN*	*NL*	*35*	*44*	*2*	*63.3*	*64*	*28*	*49*	*8*	*4.47*	*4.78*	*9.3*	*3.4*	*6.3*	*1.0*	*4.94*	*6.0*	*-4*

Breakout 16% *Improve 48%* *Collapse 30%*

He rode the knife-edge of viability the last couple of seasons, surviving his increased walk rate by not giving up home runs. But when that ended, he crossed the line from "useful" to something less, someone who would be thrown into a dump trade and released in the course of one summer. He still throws enough ground balls to be effective, which could make him a decent fit for Great American Ball Park.

DONTRELLE WILLIS

Bats: L **Throws: L** Born: 12-Jan-1982 Age: 23

YEAR	TM	LG	AGE	G	GS	IP	H	BB	SO	HR	ERA	EQERA	EQH9	EQBB9	EQSO9	EQHR9	PERA	VORP	STF
2002	KNC	MDW	20	19	19	127.7	91	21	101	3	1.83	4.05	8.1	1.9	4.5	0.6	3.11	32.0	34
2003	CAR	SOU	21	6	6	36.3	24	9	32	2	1.49	2.48	8.0	2.5	6.1	0.8	3.86	6.3	24
2003	FLA	NL	21	27	27	160.7	148	58	142	13	3.30	3.57	8.2	2.9	7.3	0.7	3.45	40.7	32
2004	FLA	NL	22	32	32	197.0	210	61	139	20	4.02	4.61	9.4	2.5	5.7	0.8	4.37	27.2	16
2005	*FLA*	*NL*	*23*	*28*	*28*	*177.3*	*175*	*54*	*135*	*18*	*3.76*	*4.10*	*8.9*	*2.4*	*6.1*	*0.9*	*4.24*	*31.2*	*14*

Breakout: 25% *Improve: 60%* *Collapse: 16%*

If you evaluate him not as a star, but as a young pitcher rushed to the majors, his 2004 season is perfectly fine. It was a regression from his rookie season, but remember that 2003 was a tremendous start followed by considerable backsliding. Willis's complicated mechanics get out of whack on occasion, making his bad starts look very bad. With those mechanics, the heavy workload at 21 and 22, and a good but not great, strikeout rate, he's not the safest bet over the next year or two.

Houston Astros

ASTROS PROSPECTUS

2004 record: 92–70; Second place, NL Central; Lost to Cardinals in Championship Series

Pythagenport record: 91–71

Runs scored per game: 4.96 (5th in NL)

Runs allowed per game: 4.31 (5th in NL)

Team EqA: .265 (6th in NL)

2004 Batters Age: 32.4 (Oldest in NL)

2004 Pitchers Age: 30.6 (2nd oldest in NL)

Ballpark: Minute Maid Park; Slight hitter's park; Park Factor of 1.015

2004: Leapfrogged an astounding eight teams with a huge second-half effort before giving the Cards a scare in the LCS.

2005: Still a quality team, but they're heavily dependent on some graying talent. When it comes, the collapse won't be pretty, and it isn't far off.

Every season, good or bad, has a turning point, a moment when one direction is established and everything from that point forward goes that way. For some teams, that point can occur as early as Opening Day, when a 6–1 loss puts the lack of a #1 starter and the presence of a poor offense on display. For others, it can happen as late as the middle of October, such as when Kevin Millar draws a walk off Mariano Rivera to spark a game-tying rally that helps push a playoff series to a fifth game.

When the Astros added Carlos Beltran on June 24, dealing away closer Octavio Dotel and catching prospect John Buck to pick up the center fielder, they surely felt it would be their turning point. They were 38–34 at the time, trundling along near the back of the Wild Card pack and unable to even see the Cardinals, who were running away with the NL Central. Beltran's presence wasn't a salve, though; the Astros went 6–10 with him leading up to the All-Star break, dropping to .500 and falling further from the pack.

During the All-Star break, they fired manager Jimy Williams. In two seasons in Houston, Williams had not only failed to meet expectations, but his decisions had been repeatedly questioned by analysts and fans. His folksy personality seemed to mesh well with the veterans in the clubhouse, a group that never quite warmed to Larry Dierker, but the results paled in comparison to what the team had accomplished with the cerebral Dierker at the helm. In context, Williams's performance looks like one of the worst managerial jobs in recent memory. (See table 1.)

With Williams out and Garner in, the Astros no doubt hoped they'd created a turning point for their season. Not quite. The team dropped their first two games after the break, and wouldn't get over .500 again until July 28. By that time, not only was the division race over, but the Wild Card seemed out of reach. Speculation was that the Astros, rather than play out the season with Beltran, would flip him to another contender in an effort to get some return on their investment. Jeff Kent was rumored to be on his way out as well, and even Roger Clemens found himself the topic of trade rumors. The deadline passed without incident, however.

By August 14, the Astros were 56–60, 18–26 since Beltran arrived, and 12–16 under Garner. They appeared to be playing out the string, buried behind a half-dozen teams in the Wild Card chase, closer to last place than to first in the division. With an aging roster, a rotation that had fallen apart due to injury and a number of impending free agents, the season—and perhaps the Biggio/Bagwell era—looked to be over. Trade rumors once again spread; in fact, it was only Athletics' owner Steve Schott's unwillingness to add payroll that kept Jeff Kent in Houston.

And then they reached their turning point.

Down 4–2 to the Expos in Montreal, on their way to their fifth loss in a row, the Astros rallied for three runs in the ninth to eke out a 5–4 win. It was the first time they'd won all season after trailing in the ninth inning, and although no one knew it at the time, they were on their way to the most successful season in franchise history. Starting that night, the Astros would win 36 of their last 46 games and overtake the Cubs and Giants in the last week of the season to win the Wild Card. They'd then go on to beat the Braves in the Division Series and push the Cardinals to seven games in the NLCS before their run ended.

Now, the Astros are at another turning point. As exhilarating as the 2004 run was, the challenges they face now are much the same as they've faced for the past few off-seasons. It's more complicated than it's been, though. They'll likely go forward without their best player—Beltran—and their

TABLE 1. ASTROS' PERFORMANCE UNDER LAST THREE MANAGERS

Manager	Years	Record	Division Titles	Playoffs
Larry Dierker	5	448–362	4	4
Jimy Williams	2.5	215–197	0	0
Phil Garner	.5	48–26	0	1

best pitcher—Clemens—from '04. At least at the start of the year, they'll be without their best hitter. Lance Berkman. The Astros project as clearly inferior to the Cubs and Cardinals going into 2005, with a dysfunctional, aging roster and funneling far too much money to players who won't be productive enough.

One of the hardest things to do in sports is to let go of the success you've had in the past in order to ensure more success in the future. Each year, we see teams become too attached to the players who were responsible for a good season, compensating them richly for their contributions without taking a critical look at what they can expect for the investment. The '02 Angels brought back virtually everyone from their championship team and fell quickly back to the pack in the AL. The late-'90s Yankees went too long with the declining veterans who helped them win multiple World Series, and have been reaching for the right mix ever since 2001, although they have continued to win division titles in that time.

The Astros have one of the worst structural problems you can have in baseball: Their "stars" are consuming huge amounts of the payroll while not playing at a level commensurate with their compensation. Meanwhile, their farm system isn't strong, and the paths of the players it *has* produced have been blocked by expensive veterans with ties to the teams' past success. Jason Lane is a better baseball player than Craig Biggio, but hasn't been able to force his way into a job the past two years. There's been no effort made to replace Brad Ausmus, who as a ballplayer is, as they say in Texas, all hat and no cattle.

There is almost no chance that the Astros can repeat their '04 success in 2005. Only Berkman and Morgan Ensberg are good bets to be above-average hitters at their positions and Berkman could miss as much as the first month of the season. The Astros may have no above-average defenders on Opening Day, although center-field prospect Willy Taveras provides some hope for the future. With Clemens not likely to return and Wade Miller definitely not doing so, the Astros will be leaning heavily on Andy Pettitte's unstable elbow to boost a rotation that includes little certainty beyond the greatness of Roy Oswalt. Even the bullpen, so dominant in September, is largely a great back-end reliever in Brad Lidge carrying and the group of mediocre pitchers in front of him.

This isn't a contending team. The question is whether new GM Tim Purpura can get his hands around that fact early enough to salvage positives from the season. The turning point for the 2005 Astros is as likely to be a 6–1 loss on Opening Day as anything else, what with all their flaws. But if they can use the year to get Chris Burke established at second base and add some talent to the system's upper levels through trades, and then have a strong draft that replenishes the lower levels, they can lessen the time it takes for them to be a factor again.

Most important, the Astros have to change their identity. The Killer Bs aren't killing anyone any longer, only Drayton McLane's checkbook. Craig Biggio and Jeff Bagwell are going to go into the Hall of Fame, quite possibly together, and the memory of their time as the Astros' greatest players ever will stay with Houston baseball fans long after that. This year, though, has to be the year in which Biggio's role is reduced, creating space for Lane. It has to be the year in which Bagwell becomes a secondary member of the offense, a role befitting his diminished performance. There's nothing Purpura can do about the money Bagwell is owed, but he can build his team in a way that shifts the focus from him to Berkman, to Oswalt, to the guys who form the championship core of the team, not its history.

The hardest thing to do in sports is let go of your success. We'll know very quickly whether Purpura, who's been a big part of that success as Gerry Hunsicker's right-hand man, is up to the task.

HITTERS

JASON ALFARO **INF** **Bats: R** **Throws: R** Born: 29-Nov-1977 Age: 27

YEAR	TM	LG	AGE	AB	H	2B	3B	HR	BB	SO	SB	CS	AVG	OBP	SLG	MLVR	EQBA	EQOBP	EQSLG	EQMLVR	VORP	DEFENSE			
2002	ROU	TXS	24	455	143	36	2	16	50	75	11	9	.314	.393	.508	.317	.283	.349	.471	.071	35.7	113-3B	7		
2003	ROU	TXS	25	81	12	3	0	0	5	20	0	1	.148	.198	.185	-.564	.099	.126	.111	-.968	-19.2	21-3B	-1		
2003	NWO	PCL	25	361	107	20	4	9	30	53	2	3	.296	.354	.449	.199	.294	.348	.448	.047	24.6	40-3B	3	43-SS	-4
2004	NWO	PCL	26	465	151	32	0	13	26	58	3	6	.325	.363	.477	.222	.306	.339	.430	.015	29.6	49-SS	-6	41-3B	2
2005	*TOR*	*AL*	*27*	*147*	*40*	*8*	*0*	*4*	*9*	*25*	*1*	*1*	*.273*	*.322*	*.418*	*-.050*	*.269*	*.320*	*.416*	*-.067*	*6.2*	*42-3B*	*0*		

Breakout: 17% *Improve: 30%* *Collapse: 49%*

New Orleans is a good pitcher's park, so Alfaro's doubles power in two years there can be taken seriously. He's signed with the Blue Jays, who'll deploy him as a utilityman. He's pretty much where Keith Ginter was when the Astros let him go, and has a good chance to be as good a player for the next couple of seasons.

JOSH ANDERSON CF Bats: L Throws: R Born: 10-Aug-1982 Age: 22

YEAR	TM	LG	AGE	AB	H	2B	3B	HR	BB	SO	SB	CS	AVG	OBP	SLG	MLVR	EQBA	EQOBP	EQSLG	EQMLVR	VORP	DEFENSE
2003	TCV	NYP	20	297	85	11	4	3	16	53	26	9	.286	.339	.380	.098	.245	.282	.343	-.265	-19.7	71-CF -4
2004	LEX	SAL	21	298	97	12	3	4	33	47	48	9	.326	.403	.426	.166	.266	.329	.347	-.154	-0.6	72-CF -8
2004	SLM	CRL	21	280	75	13	6	2	13	53	31	4	.268	.314	.379	-.009	.246	.284	.366	-.228	-6.9	66-CF 0
2005	*HOU*	*NL*	*22*	*378*	*94*	*18*	*4*	*4*	*21*	*76*	*18*	*6*	*.249*	*.301*	*.353*	*-.196*	*.247*	*.297*	*.349*	*-.213*	*-4.8*	*99-CF -6*

Breakout: 12% *Improve: 37%* *Collapse: 29%*

The Astros have a thin system, and the top hitting prospects in it are almost all old for their leagues. Anderson, their #4 pick in 2003 out of Eastern Kentucky, is emblematic of the problem, putting up good performances while being a level or two below where you'd want him to be. He applies his speed well—79-for-92 on the bases last year—but the collapse in his walk rate after his promotion is disturbing.

BRAD AUSMUS C Bats: R Throws: R Born: 14-Apr-1969 Age: 36

YEAR	TM	LG	AGE	AB	H	2B	3B	HR	BB	SO	SB	CS	AVG	OBP	SLG	MLVR	EQBA	EQOBP	EQSLG	EQMLVR	VORP	DEFENSE
2002	HOU	NL	33	447	115	19	3	6	38	71	2	3	.257	.322	.353	-.100	.254	.316	.355	-.176	9.8	120-C 13
2003	HOU	NL	34	450	103	12	2	4	46	66	5	3	.229	.303	.291	-.246	.227	.299	.289	-.317	-8.6	131-C 13
2004	HOU	NL	35	403	100	14	1	5	33	56	2	2	.248	.306	.325	-.188	.244	.302	.321	-.257	-1.5	114-C 1
2005	*HOU*	*NL*	*36*	*245*	*59*	*10*	*1*	*3*	*21*	*38*	*1*	*1*	*.239*	*.303*	*.324*	*-.237*	*.237*	*.299*	*.320*	*-.253*	*-4.3*	*67-C 1*

Breakout: 15% *Improve: 37%* *Collapse: 35%*

The ongoing organizational commitment to Ausmus costs the Astros a little more each season, as he slips from average to replacement level. He's been a .220 EqA hitter since 2000, and his once-vaunted arm gets a little bit worse each year: He allowed the most steals and highest success rate of his career in 2004. With John Buck out of the way and a $3 million salary in '05, he'll be the starter again, but Ausmus may be the worst regular in baseball.

JEFF BAGWELL 1B Bats: R Throws: R Born: 27-May-1968 Age: 37

YEAR	TM	LG	AGE	AB	H	2B	3B	HR	BB	SO	SB	CS	AVG	OBP	SLG	MLVR	EQBA	EQOBP	EQSLG	EQMLVR	VORP	DEFENSE
2002	HOU	NL	34	571	166	33	2	31	101	130	7	3	.291	.401	.518	.267	.283	.392	.515	.205	58.7	151-1B 3
2003	HOU	NL	35	605	168	28	2	39	88	119	11	4	.278	.373	.524	.211	.271	.367	.517	.154	52.0	153-1B -13
2004	HOU	NL	36	572	152	29	2	27	96	131	6	4	.266	.377	.465	.143	.260	.371	.454	.067	41.0	145-1B -6
2005	*HOU*	*NL*	*37*	*474*	*128*	*23*	*2*	*26*	*72*	*103*	*4*	*1*	*.271*	*.370*	*.493*	*.122*	*.269*	*.365*	*.487*	*.103*	*27.8*	*130-1B -9*

Breakout: 32% *Improve: 64%* *Collapse: 9%*

There's just no getting around this contract. Bagwell is owed $15 million this year, $17 million in '06 and a $7 million buyout of an '07 option. He's 37 and has been in a slow decline at the plate since 1999, one accelerated over the last two years by an arthritic right shoulder that has also turned him into a disaster in the field. Neither problem—the investment or the bum shoulder—is going away, leaving the Astros with an average first baseman who'll be one of the then highest-paid players in the game.

CARLOS BELTRAN CF Bats: B Throws: R Born: 24-Apr-1977 Age: 28

YEAR	TM	LG	AGE	AB	H	2B	3B	HR	BB	SO	SB	CS	AVG	OBP	SLG	MLVR	EQBA	EQOBP	EQSLG	EQMLVR	VORP	DEFENSE
2002	KCR	AL	25	637	174	44	7	29	71	135	35	7	.273	.346	.501	.080	.267	.346	.494	.083	49.3	146-CF 6
2003	KCR	AL	26	521	160	14	10	26	72	81	41	4	.307	.389	.522	.214	.299	.387	.513	.210	64.1	130-CF 3
2004	KCR	AL	27	266	74	19	2	15	37	44	14	3	.278	.367	.534	.207	.277	.371	.535	.192	30.7	69-CF 3
2004	HOU	NL	27	333	86	17	7	23	55	57	28	0	.258	.368	.559	.239	.249	.358	.538	.146	43.8	89-CF 1
2005	*NYM*	*NL*	*28*	*527*	*148*	*31*	*6*	*26*	*80*	*92*	*30*	*6*	*.280*	*.377*	*.508*	*.161*	*.284*	*.378*	*.525*	*.187*	*51.6*	*144-CF 1*

Breakout: 18% *Improve: 52%* *Collapse: 14%*

His amazing October clued America in to what hardcore baseball fans already knew: Beltran is one of the best players in baseball. Like Alex Rodriguez, Beltran contributes in virtually every area of play, putting up big numbers at the plate, stealing bases at a historically high success rate, and playing Gold Glove-caliber defense. Look for the recent trend of increased home-run power to continue; Beltran might hit 50 homers in the right park. Bagwell's contract is a big reason why it likely won't be Minute Maid.

LANCE BERKMAN OF **Bats: B** **Throws: L** Born: 10-Feb-1976 Age: 29

YEAR	TM	LG	AGE	AB	H	2B	3B	HR	BB	SO	SB	CS	AVG	OBP	SLG	MLVR	EQBA	EQOBP	EQSLG	EQMLVR	VORP	DEFENSE			
2002	HOU	NL	26	578	169	35	2	42	107	118	8	4	.292	.405	.578	.348	.283	.396	.571	.287	76.9	96-CF	-12	50-LF	1
2003	HOU	NL	27	538	155	35	6	25	107	108	5	3	.288	.412	.515	.267	.280	.405	.506	.213	51.3	147-LF	6		
2004	HOU	NL	28	544	172	40	3	30	127	101	9	7	.316	.450	.566	.433	.308	.441	.555	.364	83.7	83-RF	6	59-LF	-4
2005	*HOU*	*NL*	*29*	*500*	*146*	*31*	*4*	*29*	*96*	*98*	*6*	*2*	*.291*	*.409*	*.539*	*.260*	*.288*	*.404*	*.533*	*.240*	*46.5*	*142-LF*	*-2*		

Breakout: 20% *Improve: 53%* *Collapse: 13%*

Life without Beltran looks potentially that much worse after Berkman blew out his right knee playing flag football in November. He'll miss at least the first month of the season, during which Jason Lane will probably get his last chance to win a job in Houston. Although Berkman didn't have much speed to lose, he may devolve from here into a Chili Davis–type player, eventually becoming a liability in the field and then a full-time DH. He still doesn't hit for power from the right side, but he remains useful there, putting up a decent average and good walk rates.

CRAIG BIGGIO Stump **Bats: R** **Throws: R** Born: 14-Dec-1965 Age: 39

YEAR	TM	LG	AGE	AB	H	2B	3B	HR	BB	SO	SB	CS	AVG	OBP	SLG	MLVR	EQBA	EQOBP	EQSLG	EQMLVR	VORP	DEFENSE			
2002	HOU	NL	36	577	146	36	3	15	50	111	16	2	.253	.330	.404	-.030	.249	.322	.407	-.096	27.6	139-2B	-5		
2003	HOU	NL	37	628	166	44	2	15	57	116	8	4	.264	.350	.412	.018	.260	.343	.413	-.040	27.0	150-CF	-1		
2004	HOU	NL	38	633	178	47	0	24	40	94	7	2	.281	.337	.469	.089	.276	.328	.460	.012	33.1	77-LF	-8	61-CF	-1
2005	*HOU*	*NL*	*39*	*480*	*126*	*29*	*3*	*16*	*39*	*87*	*5*	*2*	*.262*	*.330*	*.432*	*-.031*	*.259*	*.326*	*.427*	*-.049*	*11.5*	*128-CF*	*-8*		

Breakout: 10% *Improve: 27%* *Collapse: 20%*

The unheralded benefit of the Beltran pickup was getting Biggio out of center field. He's an enormous liability out there, the worst defensive center fielder to hold the job across multiple seasons in recent memory. Add in that he posted the lowest walk rate and OBP of his career, and it's clear that his continued employment by the Astros is a sinecure, rather than a good baseball decision. If Beltran doesn't return, the Astros need Willy Taveras to win the center-field job and allow Biggio to stay in left field, minimizing the damage he does.

ERIC BRUNTLETT SS **Bats: R** **Throws: R** Born: 29-Mar-1978 Age: 27

YEAR	TM	LG	AGE	AB	H	2B	3B	HR	BB	SO	SB	CS	AVG	OBP	SLG	MLVR	EQBA	EQOBP	EQSLG	EQMLVR	VORP	DEFENSE			
2002	ROU	TXS	24	464	123	21	2	2	56	61	35	12	.265	.351	.332	-.021	.242	.315	.310	-.248	-6.6	83-SS	-5	33-2B	1
2002	NWO	PCL	24	68	14	3	0	0	10	10	1	1	.206	.308	.250	-.259	.174	.239	.188	-.602	-8.6	16-SS	2		
2003	NWO	PCL	25	324	84	10	0	2	35	51	9	4	.259	.332	.309	-.075	.253	.317	.299	-.253	-5.0	47-SS	-2	26-2B	1
2003	HOU	NL	25	54	14	3	0	1	0	10	0	0	.259	.255	.370	-.210	.259	.229	.333	-.374	-0.2				
2004	NWO	PCL	26	332	83	12	4	6	35	72	14	4	.250	.331	.364	-.095	.242	.314	.338	-.211	-0.9	64-SS	0	18-CF	-2
2004	HOU	NL	26	52	13	2	0	4	7	13	4	0	.250	.328	.519	.122	.250	.302	.500	-.001	5.7	11-SS	0		
2005	*HOU*	*NL*	*27*	*128*	*31*	*6*	*1*	*2*	*12*	*26*	*3*	*1*	*.246*	*.319*	*.358*	*-.159*	*.244*	*.315*	*.354*	*-.175*	*3.2*	*38-SS*	*-4*		

Breakout: 24% *Improve: 43%* *Collapse: 45%*

Any chance Bruntlett had for a meaningful career most likely ended when the Astros went with Jose Vizcaino instead of him after Adam Everett's broken hand wiped out the starting shortstop's season. Bruntlett never has hit as a pro, advancing on his glove and the momentum of getting older every year. Alfaro, with less pedigree and less defense, is a better prospect. With Vizcaino re-signed, Bruntlett should start the year in New Orleans.

CHRIS BURKE 2B **Bats: R** **Throws: R** Born: 11-Mar-1980 Age: 25

YEAR	TM	LG	AGE	AB	H	2B	3B	HR	BB	SO	SB	CS	AVG	OBP	SLG	MLVR	EQBA	EQOBP	EQSLG	EQMLVR	VORP	DEFENSE			
2002	ROU	TXS	22	481	127	19	8	3	39	61	16	15	.264	.330	.356	-.025	.243	.297	.335	-.248	-10.7	94-2B	4	42-SS	-6
2003	ROU	TXS	23	549	165	23	8	3	57	57	34	10	.301	.379	.388	.109	.277	.348	.371	-.076	16.9	93-2B	5	42-SS	-6
2004	NWO	PCL	24	483	152	33	6	16	55	76	37	14	.315	.396	.507	.314	.300	.372	.460	.112	42.6	121-2B	-3		
2005	*HOU*	*NL*	*25*	*203*	*55*	*11*	*2*	*3*	*19*	*30*	*8*	*3*	*.270*	*.344*	*.396*	*-.050*	*.268*	*.339*	*.391*	*-.067*	*12.9*	*58-2B*	*0*		

Breakout: 13% *Improve: 33%* *Collapse: 40%*

Baseball America named Burke the best defensive second baseman in the PCL in his first season in which he didn't also play shortstop. The Astros' #1 pick in 2001 out of Tennessee also had a big power spike in his first exposure to Triple-A, fixing what has been his biggest problem as a pro. Considering opportunity and established skills, Burke is an excellent bet for NL Rookie of the Year. He'll never be a Biggio-level star, but will be an across-the-board contributor for the next six years. Note PECOTA's pessimism.

RAUL CHAVEZ C **Bats: R** **Throws: R** Born: 18-Mar-1973 Age: 32

YEAR	TM	LG	AGE	AB	H	2B	3B	HR	BB	SO	SB	CS	AVG	OBP	SLG	MLVR	EQBA	EQOBP	EQSLG	EQMLVR	VORP	DEFENSE
2002	NWO	PCL	29	373	85	10	0	3	21	50	3	4	.228	.278	.279	-.268	.226	.269	.269	-.407	-25.3	105-C 14
2003	NWO	PCL	30	355	97	28	1	6	13	43	0	2	.273	.315	.408	.050	.270	.310	.407	-.102	7.3	55-C 0 38-3B 3
2003	HOU	NL	30	37	10	1	1	1	1	6	0	0	.270	.289	.432	-.052	.270	.289	.432	-.104	1.1	
2004	HOU	NL	31	162	34	8	0	0	10	38	0	1	.210	.256	.259	-.391	.209	.245	.239	-.506	-9.2	48-C 3
2005	*HOU*	*NL*	*32*	*164*	*37*	*8*	*1*	*2*	*8*	*30*	*0*	*0*	*.228*	*.270*	*.320*	*-.311*	*.226*	*.267*	*.316*	*-.326*	*-7.6*	*46-C 0*

Breakout: 12% *Improve: 29%* *Collapse: 45%*

Chavez didn't hit enough to force the Astros into addressing the Ausmus problem, and spent the year as a virtually empty roster spot. His presence is less about not exploiting the free-talent market than it is the organization's obsession with catch-and-throw guys.

BROOKS CONRAD 2B **Bats: B** **Throws: R** Born: 16-Jan-1980 Age: 25

YEAR	TM	LG	AGE	AB	H	2B	3B	HR	BB	SO	SB	CS	AVG	OBP	SLG	MLVR	EQBA	EQOBP	EQSLG	EQMLVR	VORP	DEFENSE
2002	MIC	MDW	22	499	143	25	14	14	62	102	18	8	.287	.368	.477	.234	.238	.304	.402	-.145	4.9	118-2B -13
2003	LEX	SAL	23	140	26	5	2	3	17	25	7	1	.186	.287	.314	-.151	.153	.229	.264	-.529	-16.2	38-2B 0
2003	SLM	CRL	23	345	98	24	3	11	42	60	4	2	.284	.369	.467	.224	.260	.332	.446	-.015	18.3	95-2B 0
2004	ROU	TXS	24	480	139	39	6	13	63	105	8	7	.290	.365	.477	.182	.257	.326	.422	-.061	17.2	124-2B -2
2005	*HOU*	*NL*	*25*	*194*	*51*	*11*	*2*	*6*	*21*	*44*	*3*	*1*	*.261*	*.336*	*.432*	*-.022*	*.258*	*.332*	*.427*	*-.040*	*14.2*	*55-2B -2*

Breakout: 30% *Improve: 54%* *Collapse: 30%*

It's worth mentioning that PECOTA sees better things in 2005 for Conrad than it does for Burke, with the former's power and walks carrying the day. They're the same age, both taken out of college in the 2001 draft. Conrad has trailed Burke largely because he started in the New York–Penn League, while Burke debuted in the Midwest. Conrad is good trade bait, someone who could end up starting for your team in September.

MITCH EINERTSON CF **Bats: R** **Throws: R** Born: 04-Apr-1986 Age: 19

YEAR	TM	LG	AGE	AB	H	2B	3B	HR	BB	SO	SB	CS	AVG	OBP	SLG	MLVR	EQBA	EQOBP	EQSLG	EQMLVR	VORP	DEFENSE
2004	GRV	APL	18	227	70	15	0	24	32	70	4	4	.308	.415	.692	.618	.244	.310	.513	.025	23.7	
2005	*HOU*	*NL*	*19*	*372*	*96*	*21*	*1*	*24*	*43*	*127*	*1*	*1*	*.259*	*.355*	*.514*	*.114*	*.256*	*.351*	*.508*	*.095*	*25.3*	*103-DH*

Breakout: 45% *Improve: 56%* *Collapse: 19%*

There aren't a dozen guys in this book who got there for their work in the Appalachian League. Einertson, the Astros' fifth-round pick out of a Southern California high school, was player of the year in the Appy as a center fielder. Along with Hunter Pence and Ben Zobrist, Einertson is part of a 2004 draft class that played well in its pro debut, but didn't contain a lot of high-impact prospects. The Astros project him as a second baseman. Einerston won't come anywhere near the majors this season, of course, but if he keeps his power up, that PECOTA bodes well for the future.

MORGAN ENSBERG 3B **Bats: R** **Throws: R** Born: 26-Aug-1975 Age: 29

YEAR	TM	LG	AGE	AB	H	2B	3B	HR	BB	SO	SB	CS	AVG	OBP	SLG	MLVR	EQBA	EQOBP	EQSLG	EQMLVR	VORP	DEFENSE
2002	NWO	PCL	26	292	84	12	3	7	50	56	9	5	.288	.401	.421	.218	.291	.392	.416	.079	24.4	77-3B -7
2002	HOU	NL	26	132	32	7	2	3	18	25	2	0	.242	.346	.394	-.018	.235	.338	.394	-.093	5.9	38-3B 0
2003	HOU	NL	27	385	112	15	1	25	48	60	7	2	.291	.377	.530	.235	.284	.371	.521	.179	43.2	98-3B 6
2004	HOU	NL	28	411	113	20	3	10	36	46	6	4	.275	.330	.411	-.005	.268	.325	.404	-.080	11.4	95-3B -9
2005	*HOU*	*NL*	*29*	*346*	*98*	*19*	*2*	*13*	*40*	*51*	*6*	*2*	*.284*	*.361*	*.463*	*.078*	*.281*	*.356*	*.457*	*.059*	*18.6*	*95-3B -3*

Breakout: 21% *Improve: 52%* *Collapse: 19%*

One of the most disappointing players in baseball last year, Ensberg wasn't helped by Jimy Williams's eagerness to get Mike Lamb into the lineup, or Lamb's hot start. He's not young, so you can't realistically expect another 2003 from him. The .299/.349/.477 line he put up after Williams was fired seems like a more reasonable expectation. His defense should fall in between his '03 and '04 performances.

ADAM EVERETT SS **Bats: R** **Throws: R** Born: 05-Feb-1977 Age: 28

YEAR	TM	LG	AGE	AB	H	2B	3B	HR	BB	SO	SB	CS	AVG	OBP	SLG	MLVR	EQBA	EQOBP	EQSLG	EQMLVR	VORP	DEFENSE
2002	NWO	PCL	25	345	95	16	7	2	24	59	12	3	.275	.331	.380	.018	.282	.332	.382	-.087	11.7	84-SS 12
2002	HOU	NL	25	88	17	3	0	0	12	19	3	0	.193	.297	.227	-.354	.202	.276	.225	-.463	-3.1	30-SS -1
2003	NWO	PCL	26	100	25	6	1	1	7	16	3	1	.250	.306	.360	-.058	.257	.310	.376	-.156	1.4	21-SS -2
2003	HOU	NL	26	387	99	18	3	8	28	66	8	1	.256	.320	.380	-.095	.251	.315	.376	-.151	12.5	115-SS 1
2004	HOU	NL	27	384	105	15	2	8	17	56	13	2	.273	.317	.385	-.088	.268	.310	.380	-.142	13.9	98-SS 3
2005	*HOU*	*NL*	*28*	*411*	*108*	*21*	*3*	*7*	*28*	*65*	*11*	*3*	*.262*	*.319*	*.381*	*-.118*	*.260*	*.315*	*.377*	*-.135*	*12.4*	*110-SS 3*

Breakout: 7% *Improve: 24%* *Collapse: 41%*

Unlike Ausmus, Everett takes enough runs off the board with his glove to warrant a lineup spot. His walk rate is abysmal, but he has a little pop, keeps his average above .250 and is 25-for-28 lifetime as a base thief. Taking a Claudio Vargas fastball off his left wrist August 6 effectively ended Everett's season, but he pinch-ran in the playoffs and is expected to be back at full strength in the spring. Think Kevin Elster with more defense.

CHARLTON JIMERSON OF **Bats: R** **Throws: R** Born: 22-Sep-1979 Age: 25

YEAR	TM	LG	AGE	AB	H	2B	3B	HR	BB	SO	SB	CS	AVG	OBP	SLG	MLVR	EQBA	EQOBP	EQSLG	EQMLVR	VORP	DEFENSE
2002	LEX	SAL	22	439	100	22	4	14	36	168	34	9	.228	.295	.392	-.033	.189	.240	.333	-.396	-32.9	116-CF 3
2003	SLM	CRL	23	336	89	19	3	12	25	109	27	4	.265	.317	.446	.111	.241	.286	.426	-.142	0.5	84-CF -11
2004	ROU	TXS	24	488	116	22	5	18	31	163	39	6	.238	.290	.414	-.073	.209	.253	.368	-.309	-35.2	91-RF 3 30-CF 0
2005	*HOU*	*NL*	*25*	*225*	*50*	*11*	*1*	*7*	*15*	*86*	*9*	*2*	*.224*	*.278*	*.385*	*-.210*	*.222*	*.275*	*.381*	*-.227*	*-7.0*	*61-RF 1*

Breakout: 30% *Improve: 52%* *Collapse: 28%*

The NL Central's version of Reggie Abercrombie, Jimerson is a tools goof with a career .240 batting average and a nearly 5-to-1 strikeout-to-walk ratio as a pro. It's tempting to cut that with a mention of how fast and strong he is, and to reference how players of this type do sometimes become major leaguers. Jimerson, though, is 26 and has yet to master Double-A. He's not a prospect, just another in a long line of ath-a-letes who couldn't play the game.

JEFF KENT 2B **Bats: R** **Throws: R** Born: 07-Mar-1968 Age: 37

YEAR	TM	LG	AGE	AB	H	2B	3B	HR	BB	SO	SB	CS	AVG	OBP	SLG	MLVR	EQBA	EQOBP	EQSLG	EQMLVR	VORP	DEFENSE
2002	SFG	NL	34	623	195	42	2	37	52	101	5	1	.313	.368	.565	.352	.317	.370	.586	.306	85.4	143-2B 12
2003	HOU	NL	35	505	150	39	1	22	39	85	6	2	.297	.351	.509	.181	.290	.344	.503	.115	45.7	125-2B 1
2004	HOU	NL	36	540	156	34	8	27	49	96	7	3	.289	.348	.531	.208	.281	.341	.520	.125	55.2	132-2B 14
2005	*LAD*	*NL*	*37*	*469*	*129*	*27*	*2*	*24*	*44*	*84*	*4*	*2*	*.276*	*.341*	*.498*	*.086*	*.283*	*.345*	*.512*	*.117*	*38.7*	*123-2B 0*

Breakout: 14% *Improve: 42%* *Collapse: 13%*

Kent can still hit any fastball, any time, anywhere, something Jason Isringhausen will not soon forget. His decline—mostly batting average and walk rate—has been masked a bit by the move from San Francisco to Houston, so his raw numbers could take a big hit as he moves to Chavez Ravine. He's long been better defensively than he gets credit for being. Is he a Hall of Famer? He can boast fantastic raw numbers thanks to his era, but his career value is on the low end for a Hall of Fame second baseman, and very low for a BBWAA pick. The next two years will be critical for him.

MIKE LAMB 3B **Bats: L** **Throws: R** Born: 09-Aug-1975 Age: 29

YEAR	TM	LG	AGE	AB	H	2B	3B	HR	BB	SO	SB	CS	AVG	OBP	SLG	MLVR	EQBA	EQOBP	EQSLG	EQMLVR	VORP	DEFENSE
2002	TEX	AL	26	314	89	13	0	9	33	48	0	0	.283	.354	.411	-.000	.284	.353	.406	-.012	11.7	42-1B -1 13-3B -3
2003	OKL	PCL	27	274	79	19	4	9	42	45	1	1	.288	.383	.485	.248	.268	.359	.453	.050	20.2	65-3B -7
2004	HOU	NL	28	278	80	14	3	14	31	63	1	1	.288	.356	.511	.191	.279	.350	.493	.100	22.9	57-3B -7
2005	*HOU*	*NL*	*29*	*251*	*66*	*13*	*2*	*10*	*31*	*53*	*1*	*0*	*.262*	*.344*	*.447*	*.011*	*.260*	*.339*	*.442*	*-.007*	*12.1*	*70-3B -5*

Breakout: 13% *Improve: 37%* *Collapse: 36%*

Lamb had his best season after being traded by the Yankees in spring training. He's a useful hitter and a decent third baseman, the kind of player a good team gets three or four wins from a year. It's not his fault the Astros should have been playing Ensberg. Throw out the lost 2003 season; Lamb hits .280 with walks and some pop, and will probably do so for another five years.

JASON LANE OF Bats: R Throws: L Born: 22-Dec-1976 Age: 28

YEAR	TM	LG	AGE	AB	H	2B	3B	HR	BB	SO	SB	CS	AVG	OBP	SLG	MLVR	EQBA	EQOBP	EQSLG	EQMLVR	VORP	DEFENSE	
2002	NWO	PCL	25	426	116	36	2	15	31	90	13	3	.272	.328	.472	.147	.264	.315	.451	-.035	14.1	84-CF 2	
2002	HOU	NL	25	69	20	3	1	4	10	12	1	1	.290	.375	.536	.265	.275	.362	.536	.176	6.9	17-RF 1	
2003	NWO	PCL	26	248	74	17	0	7	30	26	2	1	.298	.374	.452	.240	.287	.354	.434	.031	7.4	27-RF -3	15-CF 0
2003	HOU	NL	26	27	8	2	0	4	0	2	0	0	.296	.296	.815	.512	.296	.242	.815	.442	4.1		
2004	HOU	NL	27	136	37	10	2	4	16	33	1	0	.272	.348	.463	.096	.265	.341	.449	.010	8.7	16-LF -1	15-RF 1
2005	*HOU*	*NL*	*28*	*155*	*41*	*9*	*1*	*6*	*15*	*31*	*2*	*0*	*.265*	*.334*	*.451*	*.003*	*.263*	*.330*	*.446*	*-.015*	*7.5*	*45-RF 1*	

Breakout: 10% *Improve: 33%* *Collapse: 42%*

Career: .280/.351/.526 in 263 plate appearances. He's been a better baseball player than Craig Biggio for three years now, which hasn't done him a whole lot of good in his effort to get more playing time. Berkman's injury opens one more door for him; he'll likely be dueling with Willy Taveras to see who keeps a job once Berkman returns. Lane can rake, and would put up All-Star numbers if left alone to play. His career from here will look like Matt Stairs's or Geronimo Berroa's.

ORLANDO PALMEIRO OF Bats: L Throws: R Born: 19-Jan-1969 Age: 36

YEAR	TM	LG	AGE	AB	H	2B	3B	HR	BB	SO	SB	CS	AVG	OBP	SLG	MLVR	EQBA	EQOBP	EQSLG	EQMLVR	VORP	DEFENSE	
2002	ANA	AL	33	263	79	12	1	0	30	22	7	2	.300	.368	.354	.000	.310	.378	.352	-.022	8.6	37-RF 0	25-LF 1
2003	STL	NL	34	317	86	13	1	3	32	31	3	3	.271	.336	.347	-.077	.275	.339	.356	-.116	1.3	38-RF 2	25-LF 0
2004	HOU	NL	35	133	32	5	0	3	18	19	2	1	.241	.344	.346	-.094	.239	.329	.336	-.186	1.9	11-LF -1	
2005	*HOU*	*NL*	*36*	*80*	*20*	*4*	*0*	*1*	*9*	*11*	*1*	*0*	*.249*	*.327*	*.336*	*-.171*	*.247*	*.323*	*.332*	*-.187*	*-1.4*	*26-RF -2*	

Breakout: 9% *Improve: 24%* *Collapse: 52%*

While Palmeiro's raw numbers weren't good, he was essentially the same player he's always been. On an NL team carrying Ausmus and Everett, an early-inning pinch-hitter with on-base skills and some speed has tremendous tactical value, especially when he can also serve as a defensive replacement for a guy like Biggio. Lamb, Lane, Palmeiro . . . the Astros' bench last year was among the strongest for recent playoff teams.

LUKE SCOTT OF Bats: L Throws: R Born: 25-Jun-1978 Age: 27

YEAR	TM	LG	AGE	AB	H	2B	3B	HR	BB	SO	SB	CS	AVG	OBP	SLG	MLVR	EQBA	EQOBP	EQSLG	EQMLVR	VORP	DEFENSE	
2002	CGA	SAL	24	171	44	15	4	7	21	58	9	1	.257	.345	.515	.232	.211	.280	.423	-.180	-7.0	24-LF -3	
2002	KIN	CRL	24	163	39	7	1	8	16	47	2	1	.239	.326	.442	.103	.214	.284	.405	-.195	-6.6	17-RF 0	
2003	KIN	CRL	25	241	67	12	1	13	27	62	6	3	.278	.360	.498	.258	.252	.319	.476	-.003	5.0	18-RF 0	16-LF 0
2003	AKR	EAS	25	183	50	13	1	7	11	37	0	1	.273	.317	.470	.065	.240	.281	.426	-.152	-5.3	17-LF 0	
2004	SLM	CRL	26	241	67	20	1	8	41	58	6	1	.278	.376	.469	.213	.246	.335	.422	-.053	1.0	39-RF -2	25-CF -1
2004	ROU	TXS	26	208	62	17	0	19	33	43	0	2	.298	.401	.654	.483	.249	.336	.536	.106	11.5	22-RF 0	21-LF -2
2005	*HOU*	*NL*	*27*	*195*	*51*	*11*	*1*	*10*	*21*	*54*	*1*	*1*	*.260*	*.340*	*.482*	*.049*	*.257*	*.336*	*.476*	*.030*	*11.2*	*56-RF -5*	

Breakout: 35% *Collapse: 61%* *Collapse: 22%*

A throw-in in the Willy Taveras trade, Scott gets in here because of his big half-season at Round Rock. He's shown this kind of power before, both in the Indians' system and at Oklahoma State, so that wasn't a huge surprise. His big step up in walk rate and walk-to-strikeout ratio was more interesting. He doesn't bring much else to the table other than his bat, so his future lies largely in the numbers he puts up at Triple-A.

TODD SELF 1B Bats: L Throws: R Born: 09-Nov-1978 Age: 26

YEAR	TM	LG	AGE	AB	H	2B	3B	HR	BB	SO	SB	CS	AVG	OBP	SLG	MLVR	EQBA	EQOBP	EQSLG	EQMLVR	VORP	DEFENSE	
2002	MIC	MDW	23	491	152	36	5	12	65	104	10	1	.310	.394	.477	.287	.261	.327	.413	-.069	-0.6	65-RF 3	52-1B -1
2003	SLM	CRL	24	431	137	27	2	6	87	93	2	1	.318	.433	.432	.292	.291	.393	.415	.079	24.7	89-1B -5	21-RF -1
2004	ROU	TXS	25	476	150	34	1	11	89	95	8	0	.315	.420	.460	.268	.276	.373	.409	.022	16.6	127-1B -7	
2005	*HOU*	*NL*	*26*	*218*	*57*	*13*	*1*	*5*	*31*	*53*	*2*	*1*	*.264*	*.359*	*.409*	*-.010*	*.261*	*.355*	*.404*	*-.027*	*8.5*	*63-1B -3*	

Breakout: 14% *Improve: 36%* *Collapse: 37%*

Self is just a marginal prospect—not hitting in the AFL didn't help him—but it's worth noting that the Astros are going to pay Jeff Bagwell a billion jillion dollars for not much more performance than they'd get by handing Self the job. His plate discipline is real and he could be good for 40 doubles and 15 homers, maybe a bit more, through his peak. A Mark Grace/Wally Joyner hitter with average defense will let you spend money elsewhere. You could even platoon Self with Royce Huffman, a comparable player who bats right-handed and has been stuck at New Orleans for two years.

WILLY TAVERAS CF Bats: R Throws: R Born: 25-Dec-1981 Age: 23

YEAR	TM	LG	AGE	AB	H	2B	3B	HR	BB	SO	SB	CS	AVG	OBP	SLG	MLVR	EQBA	EQOBP	EQSLG	EQMLVR	VORP	DEFENSE	
2002	CGA	SAL	20	313	83	14	1	4	45	68	54	12	.265	.385	.355	.092	.226	.312	.317	-.253	-11.0	81-CF -11	
2003	KIN	CRL	21	397	112	9	6	2	52	68	57	12	.282	.381	.350	.097	.261	.343	.341	-.138	1.2	104-CF -1	
2004	ROU	TXS	22	409	137	13	1	2	38	76	55	11	.335	.402	.386	.154	.297	.355	.343	-.088	7.3	88-CF -2	11-LF -1
2005	*HOU*	*NL*	*23*	*303*	*77*	*13*	*2*	*2*	*28*	*63*	*19*	*5*	*.252*	*.330*	*.334*	*-.166*	*.250*	*.326*	*.330*	*-.182*	*1.9*	*83-CF -5*	

Breakout: 7% *Improve: 19%* *Collapse: 59%*

Taken in the 2003 Rule 5 Draft from the Indians, the Astros sent Jeriome Robertson to Cleveland for Taveras's rights, one of many excellent moves Gerry Hunsicker made in his last year. Taveras is one of the fastest players in the game, and while his '04 has been hailed as a breakthrough, it was almost entirely a batting average thing: He didn't hit for more power and his strike-zone judgment regressed. He wasn't putting the ball in play any more (slightly less, in fact). Thirty-eight walks and 16 extra-base hits in 460-odd plate appearances at Double-A are negatives, no matter how fast you are or how much scouts like you. He needs time at Triple-A almost as much as the Astros need him to push Biggio aside.

JOSE VIZCAINO INF Bats: B Throws: R Born: 26-Mar-1968 Age: 37

YEAR	TM	LG	AGE	AB	H	2B	3B	HR	BB	SO	SB	CS	AVG	OBP	SLG	MLVR	EQBA	EQOBP	EQSLG	EQMLVR	VORP	DEFENSE	
2002	HOU	NL	34	406	123	19	2	5	24	40	3	5	.303	.342	.397	.018	.297	.336	.396	-.048	18.3	47-SS -2	22-3B 2
2003	HOU	NL	35	189	47	7	3	3	8	22	0	1	.249	.281	.365	-.186	.247	.279	.363	-.241	-0.2	18-SS -1	16-2B 0
2004	HOU	NL	36	358	98	21	3	3	20	39	1	1	.274	.311	.374	-.094	.267	.304	.368	-.171	7.8	51-SS 2	20-2B 3
2005	*HOU*	*NL*	*37*	*182*	*48*	*9*	*1*	*3*	*12*	*22*	*1*	*0*	*.263*	*.308*	*.370*	*-.153*	*.260*	*.304*	*.365*	*-.170*	*2.3*	*50-SS -3*	

Breakout: 7% *Improve: 27%* *Collapse: 48%*

Pushed into a starting role after Everett's injury, Vizcaino was, predictably, an inadequate solution. He hit .268/.297/.377 from August 7 through the end of the year, including a 548 OPS in September. His defense was passable, good on the double play and on catching what he reached, but with unimpressive range. He'll return in 2005 as the backup to Everett and Burke up the middle. Can you believe that he has a good chance to reach 1,500 hits in his career?

TOMMY WHITEMAN SS Bats: R Throws: R Born: 14-Jul-1979 Age: 25

YEAR	TM	LG	AGE	AB	H	2B	3B	HR	BB	SO	SB	CS	AVG	OBP	SLG	MLVR	EQBA	EQOBP	EQSLG	EQMLVR	VORP	DEFENSE	
2002	LEX	SAL	22	350	106	29	2	10	36	66	6	6	.303	.374	.483	.246	.251	.306	.408	-.123	8.6	83-SS 3	
2002	ROU	TXS	22	56	10	2	1	0	4	17	1	1	.179	.246	.250	-.354	.123	.161	.140	-.849	-10.9	14-SS -4	
2003	ROU	TXS	23	532	139	18	2	13	35	102	3	8	.261	.310	.376	-.049	.238	.284	.358	-.244	-6.7	98-SS -16	33-3B 1
2004	ROU	TXS	24	277	93	14	0	8	20	45	5	3	.336	.381	.473	.246	.293	.328	.414	-.039	13.5	68-SS 5	
2004	NWO	PCL	24	98	27	6	0	0	8	21	2	2	.276	.336	.337	-.105	.235	.265	.265	-.416	-6.3	24-SS -3	
2005	*HOU*	*NL*	*25*	*145*	*36*	*7*	*1*	*4*	*10*	*30*	*1*	*1*	*.252*	*.304*	*.386*	*-.145*	*.249*	*.301*	*.382*	*-.162*	*3.7*	*41-SS -4*	

Breakout: 21% *Improve: 43%* *Collapse: 43%*

Finally escaping the loving embrace of Alvin, Texas had to feel good for Whiteman, who reached Triple-A after two years spread over three seasons at Round Rock. Had it not been for a broken thumb he suffered in July, he might well have been the Astros' shortstop in September. Whiteman showed no lingering ill effects while hitting .333/.439/.458 in the AFL, but with Everett well-established, he'll be a fixture at New Orleans, hoping for an injury or trade.

PITCHERS

EZEQUIEL ASTACIO Bats: R Throws: R Born: 04-Nov-1979 Age: 25

YEAR	TM	LG	AGE	G	GS	IP	H	BB	SO	HR	ERA	EQERA	EQH9	EQBB9	EQSO9	EQHR9	PERA	VORP	STF
2002	LWD	SAL	22	25	25	152.3	159	46	100	9	3.31	5.52	10.7	3.4	3.6	1.4	6.30	-10.8	-18
2003	CLR	FSL	23	25	22	147.7	140	29	83	9	3.29	5.23	10.0	2.1	3.7	1.7	5.29	4.6	-1
2004	ROU	TXS	24	28	28	176.0	155	56	185	12	3.89	5.35	8.6	3.2	6.9	1.0	4.25	24.8	18
2005	*HOU*	*NL*	*25*	*13*	*13*	*77.0*	*81*	*29*	*57*	*11*	*4.82*	*4.90*	*9.4*	*2.9*	*6.0*	*1.2*	*4.89*	*7.1*	*8*

Breakout: 7% *Improve: 44%* *Collapse: 23%*

One of three pitchers acquired for Billy Wagner, Astacio led the Texas League in strikeouts thanks to a low-90s fastball, hard curve and change-up. His strikeout rate nearly doubled compared to 2003 with a comparable improvement in his strike-out-to-walk ratio. Astacio wasn't worked hard from 19–22, so his arm is in good shape. His streak of four straight years at one level each is about to end; he'll be in Houston before the year is over, and could have a big role in their bullpen.

BRANDON BACKE **Bats: R** **Throws: R** Born: 05-Apr-1978 Age: 27

YEAR	TM	LG	AGE	G	GS	IP	H	BB	SO	HR	ERA	EQERA	EQH9	EQBB9	EQSO9	EQHR9	PERA	VORP	STF
2002	ORL	SOU	24	20	14	92.3	91	37	45	9	4.68	6.46	10.1	3.6	3.4	1.8	5.82	-2.1	-13
2003	DUR	INT	25	16	2	33.0	33	13	27	1	4.64	5.74	8.9	4.0	6.0	0.3	4.60	3.5	7
2003	TBY	AL	25	28	0	44.7	40	25	36	6	5.44	5.23	8.4	4.8	7.3	1.0	4.81	2.3	7
2004	NWO	PCL	26	19	9	64.3	57	26	74	7	2.80	4.13	8.4	3.8	8.1	1.2	4.28	8.9	12
2004	HOU	NL	26	33	9	67.0	75	27	54	10	4.30	4.21	9.4	3.1	6.4	1.2	4.88	9.8	-1
2005	*HOU*	*NL*	*27*	*24*	*12*	*86.0*	*87*	*37*	*71*	*12*	*4.63*	*4.71*	*9.0*	*3.4*	*6.7*	*1.2*	*4.85*	*10.3*	*4*

Breakout: 23% *Improve: 45%* *Collapse: 28%*

Swapping non-tender bait like Geoff Blum for a live arm like Backe is the kind of low-profile move that adds wins. The Astros had as much free and almost-free talent as any team in baseball last year, and it was largely Hunsicker's doing. Backe was much more effective as a starter than out of the pen, coming back from a mid-season demotion to solidify the rotation down the stretch and then make two good starts in the postseason. He's still a fastball/slider guy, and his future success as a starter will hinge on how effective his change-up is against left-handed hitters. A converted outfielder, he's a good hitter to boot.

TAYLOR BUCHHOLZ **Bats: R** **Throws: R** Born: 13-Oct-1981 Age: 23

YEAR	TM	LG	AGE	G	GS	IP	H	BB	SO	HR	ERA	EQERA	EQH9	EQBB9	EQSO9	EQHR9	PERA	VORP	STF
2002	CLR	FSL	20	23	23	158.7	140	51	129	11	3.29	4.80	9.3	3.3	5.4	1.3	5.04	9.1	15
2002	REA	EAS	20	4	4	23.0	29	6	17	5	7.43	7.48	12.0	2.5	5.4	2.5	7.48	-4.5	-1
2003	REA	EAS	21	25	24	144.7	136	33	114	14	3.55	4.41	9.2	2.3	5.9	1.4	4.75	12.7	18
2004	NWO	PCL	22	20	17	98.0	107	29	74	16	5.23	5.88	9.9	2.8	5.3	1.4	5.01	6.1	5
2005	*HOU*	*NL*	*23*	*23*	*15*	*95.0*	*102*	*34*	*67*	*14*	*4.85*	*4.93*	*9.6*	*2.8*	*5.8*	*1.2*	*4.91*	*8.6*	*2*

Breakout: 12% *Improve: 45%* *Collapse: 19%*

Pitcher #2 in the Wagner trade adjusted poorly to Triple-A, not entirely a surprise for a 22-year-old who doesn't pack a great fastball. His curve is major league ready, and his command was voted best in the Pacific Coast League, so there are positives. If his change-up comes around, he has a nice future as a starter; if it doesn't, he'll make a nice set-up man. Either way, 2005 is going to be a much better year for him.

ROGER CLEMENS **Bats: R** **Throws: R** Born: 04-Aug-1962 Age: 42

YEAR	TM	LG	AGE	G	GS	IP	H	BB	SO	HR	ERA	EQERA	EQH9	EQBB9	EQSO9	EQHR9	PERA	VORP	STF
2002	NYY	AL	39	29	29	180.0	172	63	192	18	4.35	4.49	8.0	2.9	9.1	0.8	3.38	25.6	35
2003	NYY	AL	40	33	33	211.7	199	58	190	24	3.91	4.07	8.0	2.3	7.9	1.0	3.25	44.1	28
2004	HOU	NL	41	33	33	214.3	169	79	218	15	2.98	3.13	7.3	3.0	8.3	0.6	3.04	61.3	34
2005	*HOU*	*NL*	*42*	*30*	*30*	*191.3*	*173*	*63*	*174*	*21*	*3.79*	*3.85*	*8.1*	*2.6*	*7.4*	*0.9*	*3.69*	*36.6*	*22*

Breakout: 8% *Improve: 26%* *Collapse: 15%*

There's been virtually no degradation in his skills set or his performance since he last won a Cy Young Award, with the Yankees in 2001. Last year, in fact, featured his best ERA, adjusted ERA and home-run rate since 1998. He could retire, or he could keep pitching as one of the twenty best starters in the game. If this is his last time in the book, let's not let it pass: Roger, it's been a privilege to watch you.

BRANDON DUCKWORTH **Bats: R** **Throws: R** Born: 23-Jan-1976 Age: 29

YEAR	TM	LG	AGE	G	GS	IP	H	BB	SO	HR	ERA	EQERA	EQH9	EQBB9	EQSO9	EQHR9	PERA	VORP	STF
2002	PHI	NL	26	30	29	163.0	167	69	167	26	5.41	5.87	9.2	3.3	8.2	1.5	4.91	-3.4	13
2003	PHI	NL	27	24	18	93.0	98	44	68	12	4.94	5.66	9.4	3.8	6.0	1.1	4.96	0.8	-1
2003	SWB	INT	27	3	3	18.7	21	4	14	3	3.37	5.60	10.7	2.0	5.6	2.0	6.11	-1.0	1
2004	HOU	NL	28	19	6	39.3	55	13	23	11	6.87	6.41	11.2	2.5	4.6	2.3	6.64	-4.9	-24
2004	NWO	PCL	28	14	13	70.0	81	28	63	10	5.53	5.99	10.0	3.7	6.3	1.6	5.59	0.1	-4
2005	*HOU*	*NL*	*29*	*23*	*12*	*82.3*	*84*	*32*	*63*	*13*	*4.80*	*4.88*	*9.2*	*3.0*	*6.2*	*1.2*	*4.87*	*8.6*	*2*

Breakout: 26% *Improve: 50%* *Collapse: 23%*

His impressive 2002 campaign looks more and more like a fluke. That year, he struck out 167 men in 163 innings for the Phillies. Since then, he's been around seven strikeouts per nine, and he hasn't been able to get his longball problems

(continued next page)

Brandon Duckworth *(continued)*

under control. You can't blame Williams for this one; no manager is going to stick with a pitcher giving up a homer every four innings. Duckworth still has enough raw stuff that he could accidentally put up an ERA in the 2.00s, but at 29, it's most likely that it'll happen at the back of someone's bullpen.

RODRIGO ESCOBAR Bats: R Throws: R Born: 11-Feb-1983 Age: 22

YEAR	TM	LG	AGE	G	GS	IP	H	BB	SO	HR	ERA	EQERA	EQH9	EQBB9	EQSO9	EQHR9	PERA	VORP	STF
2002	MAR	APL	19	16	10	78.0	71	18	64	7	3.12	5.89	10.1	2.7	3.8	1.9	5.89	-2.3	-9
2003	LEX	SAL	20	25	0	46.3	49	22	41	9	5.64	7.71	13.4	5.4	5.2	4.8	10.66	-22.3	-47
2003	TCV	NYP	20	15	1	36.3	35	8	38	1	2.98	5.40	10.0	2.7	5.7	0.8	5.13	1.7	0
2004	TCV	NYP	21	25	2	54.3	38	16	62	2	1.33	3.38	8.8	3.8	6.0	0.9	5.06	2.9	0
2005	*HOU*	*NL*	*22*	*21*	*3*	*41.3*	*43*	*18*	*30*	*7*	*5.14*	*5.22*	*9.2*	*3.3*	*5.8*	*1.4*	*5.17*	*2.6*	*-8*

Breakout: 17% *Improve: 50%* *Collapse: 20%*

Escobar's a small righty signed out of Colombia way back in 1999. He had a strong second season at Tri-City, displaying power stuff that makes him the top closer prospect in the system. Teammate Ronnie Martinez had comparable numbers and made the league All-Star team, but he doesn't have Escobar's upside.

MIKE GALLO Bats: L Throws: L Born: 02-Apr-1977 Age: 28

YEAR	TM	LG	AGE	G	GS	IP	H	BB	SO	HR	ERA	EQERA	EQH9	EQBB9	EQSO9	EQHR9	PERA	VORP	STF
2002	LEX	SAL	25	42	2	88.3	69	26	93	6	1.83	4.71	9.4	3.4	6.0	1.7	5.63	-0.3	-6
2003	ROU	TXS	26	17	0	19.7	17	6	22	1	1.37	2.41	8.2	2.9	7.7	1.0	3.38	4.6	9
2003	NWO	PCL	26	16	0	17.3	13	3	11	0	2.08	2.81	7.9	1.7	5.1	0.0	2.81	5.0	1
2003	HOU	NL	26	32	0	30.0	28	10	16	3	3.00	2.86	9.2	2.9	4.4	1.0	4.76	8.7	-11
2004	HOU	NL	27	69	0	49.3	55	20	34	12	4.75	4.69	9.8	3.2	5.6	2.1	5.62	4.3	-16
2005	*HOU*	*NL*	*28*	*26*	*1*	*38.7*	*40*	*16*	*26*	*6*	*4.67*	*4.75*	*9.3*	*3.3*	*5.6*	*1.2*	*5.00*	*4.3*	*-9*

Breakout: 16% *Improve: 40%* *Collapse: 32%*

A lefty specialist who can't get out lefties is completely worthless. Gallo, who had the Astros' LOOGY job because... well, because he was the only lefty in the room, faced nearly 60% left-handed batters, and those lucky guys hit .286/.367/.518 off him. Not having someone effective versus tough lefty batters was a key element in Houston's NLCS loss to the Cardinals. Gallo will be back in the same role in 2005, to the Astros' detriment. Purpura should keep an eye on the waiver wire throughout March.

JARED GOTHREAUX Bats: R Throws: R Born: 27-Jan-1980 Age: 25

YEAR	TM	LG	AGE	G	GS	IP	H	BB	SO	HR	ERA	EQERA	EQH9	EQBB9	EQSO9	EQHR9	PERA	VORP	STF
2002	TCV	NYP	22	28	0	46.3	55	12	53	3	2.72	6.49	11.7	3.1	5.9	2.1	6.91	-6.3	-27
2003	SLM	CRL	23	29	22	146.7	144	26	85	4	2.82	4.57	9.1	1.8	3.8	0.6	3.78	27.9	11
2004	ROU	TXS	24	27	24	157.0	172	35	110	16	3.96	5.46	10.1	2.2	4.6	1.5	5.34	4.3	-4
2005	*HOU*	*NL*	*25*	*11*	*9*	*53.7*	*62*	*16*	*32*	*7*	*4.80*	*4.88*	*10.3*	*2.4*	*4.9*	*1.1*	*4.96*	*5.0*	*1*

Breakout: 11% *Improve: 39%* *Collapse: 18%*

After a terrible start to his season, Gothreaux pitched well enough to be yet another effective member of the Round Rock rotation. He has a decent fastball and a good slider, and like any number of Astros prospects, good command. Although his upside is limited, especially in this organization, he has a strong track record and a name worth remembering.

JEREMY GRIFFITHS Bats: R Throws: R Born: 22-Mar-1978 Age: 27

YEAR	TM	LG	AGE	G	GS	IP	H	BB	SO	HR	ERA	EQERA	EQH9	EQBB9	EQSO9	EQHR9	PERA	VORP	STF
2002	BIN	EAS	24	27	26	152.7	157	54	126	12	3.89	4.84	9.6	3.4	5.8	1.1	5.03	9.2	0
2003	NOR	INT	25	21	19	115.0	94	26	78	6	2.74	4.05	8.0	2.4	5.1	0.7	3.38	26.3	8
2003	NYM	NL	25	9	6	41.0	57	19	25	5	7.02	7.34	10.8	3.5	4.8	1.1	5.83	-8.1	-12
2004	NOR	INT	26	13	13	70.0	63	29	31	6	3.47	4.15	8.9	4.0	3.3	1.0	4.43	8.4	2
2004	NWO	PCL	26	15	14	80.0	95	26	58	9	5.85	6.49	10.1	3.0	5.0	1.2	5.10	4.3	-6
2005	*HOU*	*NL*	*27*	*19*	*9*	*63.0*	*68*	*26*	*39*	*10*	*5.22*	*5.31*	*9.6*	*3.3*	*5.0*	*1.2*	*5.22*	*3.5*	*-8*

Breakout: 15% *Improve: 44%* *Collapse: 29%*

Picked up in exchange for the Mets' willingness to pay some of Richard Hidalgo's contract, Griffiths got one chance to impress his new team and blew it, getting pounded in a spot start on July 3. He was never a great prospect, and his strikeout rate has faded badly over the past couple of years at Triple-A and in the majors. The Astros will be looking for pitchers to win jobs this spring, so he'll have a chance.

CHAD HARVILLE Bats: R Throws: R Born: 16-Sep-1976 Age: 28

YEAR	TM	LG	AGE	G	GS	IP	H	BB	SO	HR	ERA	EQERA	EQH9	EQBB9	EQSO9	EQHR9	PERA	VORP	STF
2002	SAC	PCL	25	24	0	30.0	32	13	26	5	5.40	5.90	9.3	4.0	6.2	1.9	5.28	1.0	-14
2003	SAC	PCL	26	48	0	57.0	42	21	57	5	2.05	3.25	7.7	3.9	7.9	1.2	3.93	9.8	11
2003	OAK	AL	26	21	0	21.7	25	17	18	3	5.81	5.82	9.6	6.6	7.1	1.2	6.65	-0.3	-9
2004	HOU	NL	27	56	0	53.0	54	26	46	8	4.75	5.54	8.8	4.0	6.9	1.2	4.67	-1.4	-2
2005	*HOU*	*NL*	*28*	*30*	*4*	*54.3*	*52*	*27*	*43*	*6*	*4.41*	*4.48*	*8.6*	*3.9*	*6.5*	*0.9*	*4.54*	*6.5*	*-2*

Breakout: 20% Improve: 50% Collapse: 20%

In another of Hunsicker's one-for-one deals, Harville came over from Oakland in exchange for Kirk Saarloos in a swap of guys about to be lost on waivers. While he still throws hard, his command hasn't improved since he was the A's future closer back in the late '90s, limiting his value. Like a lot of pitchers, he could find it at any time and put up a really low ERA for a season.

CARLOS HERNANDEZ Bats: B Throws: L Born: 22-Apr-1980 Age: 25

YEAR	TM	LG	AGE	G	GS	IP	H	BB	SO	HR	ERA	EQERA	EQH9	EQBB9	EQSO9	EQHR9	PERA	VORP	STF
2002	HOU	NL	22	23	21	111.0	112	61	93	11	4.38	4.35	8.8	4.2	6.6	0.8	4.43	11.8	11
2004	NWO	PCL	24	23	23	127.7	115	46	81	9	3.59	4.35	8.6	3.5	4.5	0.8	3.97	21.7	14
2004	HOU	NL	24	9	9	42.0	50	23	26	11	6.43	6.31	10.2	4.4	5.0	2.2	6.31	-4.1	-2
2005	*HOU*	*NL*	*25*	*18*	*16*	*94.3*	*99*	*44*	*61*	*13*	*4.93*	*5.02*	*9.4*	*3.6*	*5.2*	*1.1*	*5.14*	*7.6*	*-1*

Breakout: 13% Improve: 44% Collapse: 20%

Rotator-cuff surgery wiped out his '03 and put its stamp on his '04, as he struggled to find the big-time fastball he'd had during his charge through the system. He wasn't ready to join the major league rotation in August, but the Astros simply had no good choices and landed on this particular bad one. He'll continue to improve at a slow pace, on his way to being a good pitcher again in 2006.

D. J. HOULTON Bats: R Throws: R Born: 12-Aug-1979 Age: 25

YEAR	TM	LG	AGE	G	GS	IP	H	BB	SO	HR	ERA	EQERA	EQH9	EQBB9	EQSO9	EQHR9	PERA	VORP	STF
2002	MIC	MDW	22	35	16	140.7	120	30	138	12	3.13	5.46	10.2	2.5	5.7	2.2	6.10	-7.0	-10
2003	ROU	TXS	23	18	18	109.0	93	28	101	11	3.47	4.35	8.5	2.7	6.5	1.7	4.00	18.0	12
2003	NWO	PCL	23	11	11	61.7	70	19	48	12	5.40	6.59	11.1	3.1	6.1	2.5	7.22	-10.3	-11
2004	ROU	TXS	24	28	28	159.0	141	47	159	14	2.94	4.25	8.8	3.0	6.6	1.3	4.55	17.3	14
2005	*LAD*	*NL*	*25*	*19*	*8*	*64*	*61*	*24*	*52*	*11*	*4.71*	*5.19*	*8.8*	*3.0*	*6.5*	*1.5*	*5.02*	*3.8*	*1*

Breakout: 13% Improve: 30% Collapse: 24%

Houlton is a command guy who throws a lot of off-speed stuff that puts balls in the air. He reached Triple-A in 2003 and could have been there last season but for a glut of arms at New Orleans. The Dodgers, who have just the park for a guy like this, took Houlton in the Rule 5 Draft. Remember the name; he's good enough to be a league-average starter, and the Dodgers have a lot of question marks at the back of their rotation.

BRAD LIDGE Bats: R Throws: R Born: 23-Dec-1976 Age: 28

YEAR	TM	LG	AGE	G	GS	IP	H	BB	SO	HR	ERA	EQERA	EQH9	EQBB9	EQSO9	EQHR9	PERA	VORP	STF
2002	NWO	PCL	25	24	19	111.7	83	47	110	9	3.38	4.40	8.1	4.2	7.3	1.0	4.57	11.7	9
2003	HOU	NL	26	78	0	85.0	60	42	97	6	3.60	3.64	7.1	4.0	9.5	0.6	3.42	17.1	19
2004	HOU	NL	27	80	0	94.7	57	30	157	8	1.90	2.05	5.8	2.5	13.4	0.7	2.25	39.0	51
2005	*HOU*	*NL*	*28*	*57*	*2*	*90.0*	*58*	*36*	*123*	*8*	*2.43*	*2.48*	*5.7*	*3.1*	*11.2*	*0.7*	*2.57*	*32.6*	*34*

Breakout: 36% Improve: 51% Collapse: 25%

Lidge was important to the Astros not just for the quality of his pitching, but also because his performance enabled the team to trade Octavio Dotel for Carlos Beltran, a deal that fell just short of putting them in the World Series. He's not young; remember that he basically lost three years to arm problems, making just 19 appearances from 1999 through 2001. If recent history is a guide, he'll pitch another three months at his 2004 level, then regress just a bit.

DAN MICELI Bats: R Throws: R Born: 09-Sep-1970 Age: 34

YEAR	TM	LG	AGE	G	GS	IP	H	BB	SO	HR	ERA	EQERA	EQH9	EQBB9	EQSO9	EQHR9	PERA	VORP	STF
2003	COL	NL	32	14	0	20.7	24	9	18	7	5.65	4.87	10.2	3.5	7.1	2.7	6.64	-0.1	-10
2003	CLE	AL	32	13	0	15.0	9	6	19	1	1.20	2.51	5.7	3.8	11.3	0.6	2.51	6.2	34
2003	HOU	NL	32	23	0	30.0	22	7	20	3	2.10	1.95	7.8	2.0	5.9	1.0	3.58	11.7	1
2004	HOU	NL	33	74	0	77.7	74	27	83	10	3.59	3.77	8.3	2.7	8.5	1.1	3.89	15.2	12
2005	*HOU*	*NL*	*34*	*42*	*5*	*77.0*	*72*	*27*	*72*	*11*	*4.02*	*4.09*	*8.4*	*2.7*	*7.6*	*1.1*	*4.14*	*13.6*	*8*

Breakout: 25% *Improve: 46%* *Collapse: 24%*

We really need a pithy name for guys like Miceli, right-handed relievers who bounces around, often gets dealt at the trade deadline, usually posts ERAs between 3.50 and 4.50, picks up few saves, and rarely play on more than a one-year deal. Todd Jones now lives in this zone; Mike Timlin is in the upper bound of it, Mike Fetters the low end. Miceli signed a one-year, $1.7 million deal with the Yomiuri Giants, where he'll bask in Tuffy Rhodes's warm glow.

WADE MILLER Bats: R Throws: R Born: 13-Sep-1976 Age: 28

YEAR	TM	LG	AGE	G	GS	IP	H	BB	SO	HR	ERA	EQERA	EQH9	EQBB9	EQSO9	EQHR9	PERA	VORP	STF
2002	HOU	NL	25	26	26	164.7	151	62	144	14	3.28	3.37	8.2	2.9	7.0	0.7	3.65	37.7	22
2003	HOU	NL	26	33	33	187.3	168	77	161	17	4.13	4.34	8.4	3.3	7.1	0.8	4.19	22.6	18
2004	HOU	NL	27	15	15	88.7	76	44	74	11	3.35	3.48	8.0	4.0	6.9	1.1	4.01	21.8	12
2005	*BOS*	*AL*	*28*	*21*	*19*	*113.7*	*116*	*47*	*86*	*14*	*4.55*	*4.29*	*8.9*	*3.2*	*6.2*	*1.1*	*4.33*	*20.2*	*9*

Breakout: 14% *Improve: 49%* *Collapse: 27%*

Miller was forced to the sidelines with shoulder pain in June, and never returned. Diagnosed with a frayed rotator cuff, he tried rest, rehab and a cortisone shot, but not surgery. The Astros non-tendered him rather than risk paying $4 million or more to a pitcher who can't take the mound. The Red Sox called his agent at 12:01 A.M. on deadline night, and soon after signed him to a one-year deal for $1.5 million plus incentives. It's a good gamble; the most likely result is Miller makes 10–15 effective starts, and that's worth the money.

PETER MUNRO Bats: R Throws: R Born: 14-Jun-1975 Age: 30

YEAR	TM	LG	AGE	G	GS	IP	H	BB	SO	HR	ERA	EQERA	EQH9	EQBB9	EQSO9	EQHR9	PERA	VORP	STF
2002	NWO	PCL	27	19	13	94.3	68	15	73	3	2.39	3.54	7.8	1.6	5.7	0.4	3.34	21.7	32
2002	HOU	NL	27	19	14	80.7	89	23	45	5	3.57	3.99	9.3	2.2	4.4	0.6	3.99	12.2	15
2003	HOU	NL	28	40	2	54.0	63	26	27	7	4.67	4.78	10.3	3.8	4.1	1.0	5.64	3.8	-25
2004	ROC	INT	29	10	10	51.0	51	11	34	6	3.88	4.99	9.1	2.0	5.0	1.3	4.25	7.3	10
2004	HOU	NL	29	21	19	99.7	120	26	63	12	5.15	5.03	9.9	2.1	5.0	1.0	4.58	4.8	10
2005	*HOU*	*NL*	*30*	*24*	*15*	*99.0*	*108*	*30*	*61*	*11*	*4.23*	*4.31*	*9.8*	*2.4*	*5.0*	*0.9*	*4.57*	*14.6*	*1*

Breakout: 22% *Improve: 51%* *Collapse: 20%*

It's a funny game. One minute, you're being released by the Twins because they'd rather do that than call you up and stick you in their bullpen. The next, you're starting Game Two of the National League Championship Series. In between, Munro made 19 unimpressive starts for an Astros team that might well have put Ashlee Simpson on the mound had she shown up with a glove. He's staff filler.

FERNANDO NIEVE Bats: R Throws: R Born: 15-Jul-1982 Age: 22

YEAR	TM	LG	AGE	G	GS	IP	H	BB	SO	HR	ERA	EQERA	EQH9	EQBB9	EQSO9	EQHR9	PERA	VORP	STF
2002	MAR	APL	19	13	13	67.7	46	27	60	5	2.39	5.31	8.6	4.7	4.2	1.7	5.31	1.9	-4
2003	LEX	SAL	20	28	28	150.3	133	65	144	10	3.65	5.75	10.0	4.8	5.5	1.5	6.28	-10.2	-9
2004	SLM	CRL	21	24	24	149.0	136	40	117	9	2.96	4.27	8.8	2.8	5.1	1.0	4.14	22.5	18
2004	ROU	TXS	21	3	3	17.3	12	8	17	0	1.56	3.38	7.3	4.5	6.8	0.0	3.38	3.9	18
2005	*HOU*	*NL*	*22*	*14*	*14*	*79.3*	*83*	*33*	*55*	*13*	*5.16*	*5.25*	*9.4*	*3.3*	*5.7*	*1.3*	*5.13*	*4.6*	*3*

Breakout: 11% *Improve: 40%* *Collapse: 20%*

Nieve is a Venezuelan righty whose money pitch is a low-90s fastball that he keeps down in the zone. His three good starts at Round Rock help mitigate the concern over the drop in his strikeout rate at Salem, which may be more about him getting groundball outs than a real dip. Astacio's live arm gets more play, but Nieve's future could be just as bright.

DARREN OLIVER Bats: R Throws: L Born: 06-Oct-1970 Age: 34

YEAR	TM	LG	AGE	G	GS	IP	H	BB	SO	HR	ERA	EQERA	EQH9	EQBB9	EQSO9	EQHR9	PERA	VORP	STF
2002	BOS	AL	31	14	9	58.0	70	27	32	7	4.66	4.26	10.3	3.9	4.7	0.9	5.53	8.5	-8
2003	COL	NL	32	33	32	180.3	201	61	88	21	5.04	4.69	9.4	2.6	4.0	0.9	4.53	6.1	-1
2004	FLA	NL	33	18	8	58.7	75	17	33	13	6.44	6.75	11.0	2.4	4.6	1.9	6.12	-6.6	-15
2004	HOU	NL	33	9	2	14.0	12	4	13	1	3.86	3.95	7.9	2.0	7.2	0.7	3.29	2.9	13
2005	*COL*	*NL*	*34*	*23*	*8*	*62.3*	*80*	*24*	*38*	*10*	*6.04*	*5.27*	*10.9*	*3.0*	*5.2*	*1.2*	*5.33*	*3.5*	*-8*

Breakout 15% *Improve 39%* *Collapse 29%*

If you think we're exaggerating the Astros' lack of left-handed relief and starting pitching last summer, consider that they traded for Oliver in July, and were actually dismayed when a sore shoulder pushed him to the DL for the balance of the year. He's 34 now and isn't going to be Jamie Moyer, so it's just a matter of how many ERAs in the 5.00s it takes to push him out of the league.

ROY OSWALT Bats: R Throws: R Born: 29-Aug-1977 Age: 27

YEAR	TM	LG	AGE	G	GS	IP	H	BB	SO	HR	ERA	EQERA	EQH9	EQBB9	EQSO9	EQHR9	PERA	VORP	STF
2002	HOU	NL	24	35	34	233.0	215	62	208	17	3.01	3.30	8.2	2.1	7.2	0.6	3.34	56.4	28
2003	HOU	NL	25	21	21	127.3	116	29	108	15	2.97	3.25	8.6	1.8	7.1	1.0	3.99	32.6	22
2004	HOU	NL	26	36	35	237.0	233	62	206	17	3.49	3.65	8.4	2.1	7.0	0.6	3.42	51.8	27
2005	*HOU*	*NL*	*27*	*29*	*29*	*197.3*	*195*	*53*	*161*	*22*	*3.73*	*3.80*	*8.8*	*2.1*	*6.6*	*0.9*	*3.90*	*40.9*	*19*

Breakout: 17% *Improve: 49%* *Collapse: 19%*

The groin problems that plagued him in 2003 were just a memory last year, as he tied for the NL lead in starts and finished third in innings pitched. Through four seasons, his career is a virtual match for Mike Mussina's, except Mussina never took that step forward, staying at his established level for ten more years. Oswalt could; he has everything it takes to make the same leap Greg Maddux did in 1992 that allowed him to become the best pitcher of the '00s.

ANDY PETTITTE Bats: L Throws: L Born: 15-Jun-1972 Age: 33

YEAR	TM	LG	AGE	G	GS	IP	H	BB	SO	HR	ERA	EQERA	EQH9	EQBB9	EQSO9	EQHR9	PERA	VORP	STF
2002	NYY	AL	30	22	22	134.7	144	32	97	6	3.27	3.79	8.8	2.0	6.2	0.3	3.32	31.5	27
2003	NYY	AL	31	33	33	208.3	227	50	180	21	4.02	4.50	8.7	2.0	7.5	0.8	3.50	31.8	28
2004	HOU	NL	32	15	15	83.0	71	31	79	8	3.90	3.81	7.7	3.0	7.7	0.8	3.36	16.2	27
2005	*HOU*	*NL*	*33*	*22*	*17*	*108.3*	*108*	*38*	*90*	*9*	*3.85*	*3.91*	*8.9*	*2.8*	*6.8*	*0.7*	*3.98*	*20.7*	*15*

Breakout: 16% *Improve: 44%* *Collapse: 37%*

The wonky elbow that contributed to the Yankees' less-than-enthusiastic effort to keep Pettitte cut short his season. Surgery to repair a flexor tendon was deemed successful, and he's expected to be back in the rotation this spring. When on the mound, he was basically the same pitcher he's been since 1995. The Astros need him to be healthy and effective, because his heavily backloaded contract—he'll make $17.5 million in 2006—is untradeable.

CHAD QUALLS Bats: R Throws: R Born: 17-Aug-1978 Age: 26

YEAR	TM	LG	AGE	G	GS	IP	H	BB	SO	HR	ERA	EQERA	EQH9	EQBB9	EQSO9	EQHR9	PERA	VORP	STF
2002	ROU	TXS	23	29	29	163.0	174	67	142	9	4.36	6.07	9.7	4.0	5.9	0.9	4.97	10.9	4
2003	ROU	TXS	24	28	28	175.3	174	61	132	12	3.85	4.97	8.9	3.5	5.2	1.1	4.16	26.7	12
2004	NWO	PCL	25	32	14	106.7	134	30	72	8	5.57	6.17	10.2	2.6	4.6	0.8	4.71	10.4	11
2004	HOU	NL	25	25	0	33.0	34	8	24	3	3.55	3.38	9.0	2.0	5.9	0.8	3.94	7.9	18
2005	*HOU*	*NL*	*26*	*17*	*9*	*61.7*	*67*	*23*	*42*	*7*	*4.49*	*4.57*	*9.7*	*2.9*	*5.5*	*0.9*	*4.77*	*7.4*	*0*

Breakout: 17% *Improve: 45%* *Collapse: 24%*

Qualls made his first 97 pro appearances as a starter before moving to the Zephyrs' bullpen in June. He was effective out of the pen for New Orleans, then took over the set-up job in Houston in August and was a big part of the Astros' Wild Card run down the stretch. His sinker/slider/strikes mix should work well at Minute Maid Park, giving the Astros yet another cheap, effective reliever.

TIM REDDING **Bats: R** **Throws: R** Born: 12-Feb-1978 Age: 27

YEAR	TM	LG	AGE	G	GS	IP	H	BB	SO	HR	ERA	EQERA	EQH9	EQBB9	EQSO9	EQHR9	PERA	VORP	STF
2002	NWO	PCL	24	11	7	38.0	32	13	50	6	5.21	5.86	8.9	3.3	9.7	1.8	5.09	2.0	15
2002	HOU	NL	24	18	14	73.3	78	35	63	10	5.40	5.72	9.2	3.6	6.8	1.1	4.85	-4.3	2
2003	HOU	NL	25	33	32	176.0	179	65	116	16	3.68	4.14	9.3	3.0	5.5	0.8	4.67	26.4	5
2004	NWO	PCL	26	5	5	28.3	30	12	26	2	6.04	6.91	9.2	4.0	6.3	0.7	4.61	3.0	6
2004	HOU	NL	26	27	17	100.7	125	43	56	15	5.72	6.14	10.2	3.3	4.4	1.2	5.33	-8.6	-14
2005	*HOU*	*NL*	*27*	*21*	*14*	*87.7*	*96*	*35*	*56*	*12*	*5.07*	*5.16*	*9.8*	*3.1*	*5.2*	*1.2*	*5.10*	*5.9*	*-3*

Breakout: 14% *Improve: 40%* *Collapse: 23%*

The Astros did well to keep the long-time BP favorite in the rotation following a season in which he pitched well but received terrible run support. He didn't reward that faith, losing his rotation spot in July and pitching poorly out of the bullpen. At 26, with a career ERA of 4.75 and a dwindling strikeout rate, it may be time to recant our endorsement and recognize that he's roster filler. He'll fight for a job in March.

DAN WHEELER **Bats: R** **Throws: R** Born: 10-Dec-1977 Age: 27

YEAR	TM	LG	AGE	G	GS	IP	H	BB	SO	HR	ERA	EQERA	EQH9	EQBB9	EQSO9	EQHR9	PERA	VORP	STF
2002	RIC	INT	24	27	25	155.0	163	42	110	23	4.65	5.55	9.9	2.8	5.5	1.8	5.55	0.8	-4
2003	NOR	INT	25	22	5	45.7	48	16	44	4	3.94	4.53	9.3	3.5	7.0	1.2	4.95	3.2	2
2003	NYM	NL	25	35	0	51.0	49	17	35	6	3.71	4.04	8.8	2.8	5.7	1.1	4.22	8.8	0
2004	NYM	NL	26	32	1	50.7	65	17	46	9	4.79	4.97	10.5	2.7	7.1	1.4	5.51	3.1	-3
2004	HOU	NL	26	14	0	14.3	11	3	9	1	2.52	2.70	7.4	2.0	5.4	0.7	2.70	5.1	0
2005	*HOU*	*NL*	*27*	*31*	*6*	*69.0*	*70*	*23*	*54*	*10*	*4.30*	*4.37*	*9.0*	*2.7*	*6.4*	*1.2*	*4.54*	*10.6*	*1*

Breakout: 32% *Improve: 54%* *Collapse: 24%*

Wheeler nearly out-Lidged Brad Lidge in the NLCS, throwing seven shutout innings with nine strikeouts and no walks against the Cardinals. Not bad for a guy who spent most of his year throwing mop-up relief for the Mets. He's tough on righties, which is particularly useful in a division with lots of righty-heavy lineups.

Los Angeles Dodgers

Sound the alarm. Dance around naked. The Dodgers have a talent base on the field, a talent base in the front office, and a resource base from which to draw cash. They're about to embark on a run similar to that decade enjoyed by Atlanta since the early 90s, and the rest of the division is going to have to come up with a perfect plan and execute it well if they want to keep up.

No matter what happens in the minds of Brian Sabean, Dan O'Dowd, Kevin Towers, or Joe Garagiola Jr., the potential values of the local broadcast rights for the Giants, Rockies, Padres, and Diamondbacks are going to be highly disparate. It's possible that the rest of the NL West was extremely lucky when the Dodgers signed a new local broadcast deal with KCAL in Los Angeles for approximately $10 million annually through 2013 in December. If the Dodgers were coming off a long string of successful seasons, it's entirely possible the contract could have been much larger. The effects of geography on local revenue may be diminishing because of more league-wide deals like the new pact with XM Radio, but there's still a significant and undeniable benefit to just being in a big market. More eyeballs equals more money for everyone.

One nice little advantage is that the Dodgers just plain have a protected monopoly in a major media market. Consider the size of each NL West team's home market as shown in table 1.

Of the teams in these cities, the Dodgers have not only the greatest population but the best ability to take advantage of their opportunities over the next decade or so. At the heart of the organization is baseball's most overqualified general manager, Paul DePodesta. He learned his craft under Billy Beane in Oakland, and several insiders believe that the real man behind the curtain in Oakland was DePodesta, not Beane. In his brief tenure as GM in Los Angeles, DePodesta's managed the roster, the budget, and the people with equal dexterity, building consensus in an organization that was supposed to have tremendous inertia and resistance to a brash outsider. DePodesta arrived and behaved in a respectful fashion, wisely listening to counsel from a variety of sources, rather than just a few with whom he agreed. He's done something that many general managers never do—he's led.

DePodesta still had some issues at hand. Like many GMs new to their jobs, he inherited a few serious dog-food contracts. Darren Dreifort and Kevin Brown, the two most damning relics of past regimes, are finally off the books.

DODGERS PROSPECTUS

2004 record: 93–69; First place, NL West; Lost to Cardinals in Division Series

Pythagenport record: 89–73

Runs scored per game: 4.70 (9th in NL)

Runs allowed per game: 4.22 (4th in NL)

Team EqA: .265 (6th in NL)

2004 Batters Age: 29.2 (6th youngest in NL)

2004 Pitchers Age: 30.0 (5th oldest in NL)

Ballpark: Dodger Stadium; Severe pitcher's park; Park Factor of 0.950

2004: The new front office wasted no time, heavily revising the roster and giving LA their first division title since 1995.

2005: Not all of the offseason turnover was for the better, but DePodesta and company should have this team in the thick of it.

One albatross remained: Shawn Green's deal, which mercifully had only one year left on it, at a tidy $16 million. Green's production at the time the contract was signed was considerably more palatable to the club, but that's the nature of bad contracts. At this point, Green's last 1,200 plate appearances pretty clearly indicate that he's a .360/.450 hitter. That's a good player, particularly in Dodger Stadium, but it's not a great player, and for that price, you'd better be a great player to justify that kind of money. Green plays an easy corner, and he doesn't play it like he used to; at first base, even Keith Hernandez-level defense wouldn't make up for the offensive letdown, and Green is no Hernandez with the leather.

DePodesta spent much of the off-season trying to trade Green. With the pitching staff sporting several big question marks, DePodesta hoped to unload Green, freeing up cash to add pitching. First, the Dodgers conducted an elaborate dance with the Diamondbacks and Yankees, as a proposed three-way deal figured to send Randy Johnson and Javier Vazquez and a slew of other players scampering between the three teams. But after protracted negotiations, DePodesta pulled out of the deal. He didn't like parting with Brad Penny or young power reliever Yhency

TABLE 1. NL WEST TEAM HOME MARKETS

NL West City	Population (SMSA)
Los Angeles	16,000,000
San Francisco	6,900,000
Phoenix	3,000,000
San Diego	2,800,000
Denver	2,400,000

Brazoban, and felt he could find a way to unload Green more effectively.

He got pummeled for pulling out. The New York media in particular, eager to pillory the 32-year-old statistically-minded outsider and hungry for a juicy story, lapped up quotes from pissed-off Yankee execs at light speed. Though the Yankees feature their own pretty good General Manager in Brian Cashman, the dysfunctional, two-tiered front office decided it needed to intervene, with George Steinbrenner's Tampa minions taking the podium. When it looked like their efforts to get Randy Johnson might be short-circuited, Yankee President Randy Levine ratcheted up the sulk factor: "We'll have to think long and hard before ever doing business with the Dodgers again."

Though we rarely discuss it, a GM's ability to handle the politics of the media, fans, and other teams is one of the toughest aspects of the job. The best GMs politely nod to the masses—and then largely ignore them. Theo Epstein has done this with aplomb in Boston, making several unpopular moves in the face of rampant criticism, and winning a World Series for his efforts.

DePodesta showed similar resolve. After a second aborted trade—this time one sans the Yankees—the Dodgers finally shipped Green to the desert. In exchange for Green and $10 million, the Dodgers got young catcher Dioner Navarro and pitching prospects William Juarez, Beltran Perez, and Danny Muegge, after the Yankees traded Navarro to Arizona in getting Johnson directly from the D-Backs. The deal provided much needed payroll flexibility, and added a catcher the Dodgers hope will fill the major league void by 2006.

The team still needed to parlay the savings from the Green deal into a trade or signing, ideally of a solid starter. A few days earlier, the club had re-signed Odalis Perez to a three-year, $24 million deal, accomplishing part of that goal. By inking the best remaining pitcher on the market, the Dodgers addressed their biggest concern heading into 2005. Penny's health concerns, Kaz Ishii's plummeting peripherals and Edwin Jackson's rough 2004—which suggested he may not be ready to succeed in '05—all remain question marks.

The way the Perez signing came together spoke to a key trait of DePodesta's: His ability to draw up and execute a sensible plan, something many teams never get around to. Trading Green cleared exactly $8 million off the books. Just days after the league approved the deal, the Dodgers nabbed Perez—while paying him an average of exactly $8 million a year.

The Dodgers' plan extends to all points on the diamond. Critics bemoan Hee Seop Choi's struggles with lefties, his purported inability to hit inside pitches, and the lousy tip he left that time the Dodgers stopped at Denny's in Milwaukee. But DePodesta sees a young hitter with a proven track record of performance, both in the minor leagues and during the first half of last season with the Marlins. The difference between Choi at first and a Jayson Werth/Ricky Ledee/Jason Grabowski time-share at a corner-outfield spot compared to Green and less playing time for those three players figures to be minimal, and is certainly worth the $8 million saved. Critics renewed their complaints when the second Green deal was announced, but DePodesta's banking on performance—not high-pitched cries for experience and team chemistry—to inform his decisions.

Signing Derek Lowe on the heels of the Green trade should help further fortify the rotation. But while Lowe's a clear upgrade over, say, Ishii, is he worth the four years, $36 million the Dodgers gave him? It's hard to see how. Here are the Equivalent ERAs—park-neutral ERAs, with a 4.50 league average—for Lowe, as projected by *BP*'s PECOTA system for the next four years:

Year	Projected EqERA
2005	4.43
2006	4.83
2007	4.92
2008	5.19

These are the numbers of a league-average pitcher—or worse—not the kind of top-line starter worth $36 million and four years. Lowe does have his strengths. He's durable, which means even those pedestrian EqERAs project to be worth 3.4, 2.0, 1.5 and 1.0 wins above replacement level from '05 to '08. He also does a good job of keeping the ball in the park, which should be magnified by the move to Dodger Stadium from Fenway Park. But Lowe's only had one truly stellar season as a starter in his career: In 2002 he parlayed one of the lowest, and luckiest, hits-allowed-on-balls-in-play rates in recent memory (.238) into a Cy Young–caliber year. Owner of one of the most extreme groundball rates in baseball, Lowe depends heavily on his defense, even more so given his soft strikeout rates. Is Lowe any worse a signing than Jaret Wright, Kris Benson, Russ Ortiz, or Carl Pavano? Probably not. But just because several other teams overpaid for pitching doesn't make it right. Call the Lowe deal a case of DePodesta using the resources available to him in Los Angeles. Just don't call it an optimal use of resources.

DePodesta's busy off-season continued his work from last season. The whirlwind of deals that saw the Dodgers ship off popular catcher Paul Lo Duca, set-up man Guillermo Mota, and others similarly raised Angelenos' ire. Not all of that anger was misplaced. The trades didn't work out perfectly: Notably, David Ross and Brent Mayne proved hapless in taking over catching duties from Lo Duca, and Brad Penny's arm gave out after just one start following his arrival from the Marlins.

But the carousel of deadline deals allowed the Dodgers to land Steve Finley, who helped carry the team into the playoffs, even hitting a division-clinching grand slam against the Giants in the season's final weekend. It also shaved several million more off the payroll: The Marlins are now likely to pay Lo Duca about $8 million in 2005 to be a good but not great catcher, and Brazoban projects to match Mota's projection for considerably less money. Though Choi did little to help the Dodgers' cause last year, he made Green even more expendable this off-season, and should start gaining believers in 2005. Looking at the pieces in that sequence, you see DePodesta's plan at work.

The Dodgers' 2004 season had a fair number of performances that might be described as one-year wonders. Specifically in the cases of Alex Cora and Beltre, it's reasonable to expect some sort of reversion to established levels of performance, even at their respective ages. Beltre in particular is something of a bitter pill for the Dodgers, and kind of a Faustian bargain. The Dodgers brought him up early, and his performance was pretty flat (with a notable exception or two) during those years when a team can get that performance at a low price. Then he goes and finally puts together the year the team's been waiting for, and becomes one of the most expensive properties in baseball. It's tough to kiss a performance like Beltre's 2004 effort goodbye, but that's exactly what DePodesta did. It's always possible that Beltre established a new level of performance; the Dodgers simply followed the odds and bet against it.

DePodesta stayed busy with other deals during the off-season, working to shore up the weaknesses in the club, particularly on the offensive side. Noted truck-detailing enthusiast Jeff Kent was brought in to play second base and hit the ball hard. J. D. Drew, who's an amazing player when he can take the field, will patrol the outfield along with Milton Bradley and Werth. Drew's a true offensive superstar, but he'll need to take the field 130–150 times a year for the Dodgers to see some return on his five-year, $55 million deal. The new acquisitions should offensively cover for some of the real talent and flukish single years the Dodgers lost.

Perhaps most encouraging, the Dodger farm system is stacked. Where most organizations would kill to have a single Grade A Prospect™, the Dodgers have several, and also have a few guys who don't rate as highly but have tremendous upside. Think about this from a strategic perspective. You've got a club in a big media market, with significant financial resources. Then you add a bunch of very good prospects—more than one guy who has superstar potential. That frees up financial resources to use to patch holes elsewhere, and that can be a nightmare for competitors, much like the Yankees of the late '90s. Instead of names like Jeter, Posada, and Rivera, the names will be Guzman and Billingsley.

A big advantage the Dodgers figure to have in the NL West is the state of the competition. While the Dodgers were out signing Kent and Drew, the Giants have thrown the car into reverse, acquiring and retaining a bunch of very old players who are neither particularly great nor particularly cheap. It's a team of Barry Bonds, Jason Schmidt, and warm bodies who are cooling fast. The Giants might compete in 2005; beyond that, it could get ugly fast.The Diamondbacks have a long climb back from the depths of loss and despair, and could improve by 30 games and be a .500 team. They also owe nearly $150 million in deferred salary alone. The Rockies have some interesting young talent, but it's going to be a couple years before they're ready to compete. That leaves Tommy Lasorda's favorite club in direct competition with their neighbors to the south for the next few years. But while the Padres have two young stars in Jake Peavy and Khalil Greene, a new stadium and some good complementary players, they're also shackled with several aging beer leaguers. More important, they lack the Dodgers' ability to dig deep into the war chest and spend for premium talent, Petco Park or no.

Add it all up and the Dodgers find themselves in a very favorable competitive position: They get to roll downhill for the next few years, with a great driver behind the wheel.

HITTERS

WILLY AYBAR 2B **Bats: B** **Throws: R** Born: 09-Mar-1983 Age: 22

YEAR	TM	LG	AGE	AB	H	2B	3B	HR	BB	SO	SB	CS	AVG	OBP	SLG	MLVR	EQBA	EQOBP	EQSLG	EQMLVR	VORP	DEFENSE
2002	VRO	FSL	19	372	80	18	2	11	69	54	15	8	.215	.339	.363	-.032	.184	.291	.321	-.312	-17.8	107-3B 3
2003	VRO	FSL	20	445	122	29	3	11	41	70	9	9	.274	.336	.427	.105	.236	.289	.396	-.183	-0.3	108-3B 8
2004	JAX	SOU	21	482	133	27	0	15	50	77	8	10	.276	.346	.425	.103	.257	.318	.400	-.107	10.6	122-2B 11
2005	*LAD*	*NL*	*22*	*274*	*65*	*14*	*1*	*8*	*27*	*46*	*3*	*1*	*.238*	*.309*	*.385*	*-.146*	*.244*	*.314*	*.396*	*-.122*	*3.5*	*75-2B -3*

Breakout: 29% *Improve: 48%* *Collapse: 28%*

Young infielder with a broad set of offensive and defensive skills. Aybar's shown some gap power, shown some plate discipline, and has done enough with the bat to warrant his promotions. In the field, he's looked pretty good at both second and third base, and might hit enough to have a career at either spot, without depending on the potential "Utility Guy" label. He'll play this season at 22 in Triple-A, perhaps with a few weeks in Double-A for some seasoning.

ADRIAN BELTRE 3B **Bats: R** **Throws: R** Born: 07-Apr-1979 Age: 26

YEAR	TM	LG	AGE	AB	H	2B	3B	HR	BB	SO	SB	CS	AVG	OBP	SLG	MLVR	EQBA	EQOBP	EQSLG	EQMLVR	VORP	DEFENSE
2002	LAD	NL	23	587	151	26	5	21	37	96	7	5	.257	.303	.426	.003	.268	.310	.451	-.040	24.4	151-3B -18
2003	LAD	NL	24	559	134	30	2	23	37	103	2	2	.240	.290	.424	-.056	.246	.295	.441	-.100	17.7	152-3B 1
2004	LAD	NL	25	598	200	32	0	48	53	87	7	2	.334	.388	.629	.459	.338	.388	.634	.431	89.1	149-3B 14
2005	*SEA*	*AL*	*26*	*529*	*147*	*29*	*2*	*26*	*45*	*86*	*4*	*2*	*.279*	*.337*	*.486*	*.071*	*.287*	*.346*	*.509*	*.117*	*30.9*	*137-3B 2*

Breakout: 8% *Improve: 26%* *Collapse: 26%*

Exhibit A for the folks who believe in the Salary Drive. After several years of unfulfilled promise and somewhat aimless wandering, Beltre finally put it all together and had a season worthy of a Most Valuable Mortal Player award. Of course, fat lot of good it does the Dodgers, who suffered through some miserable seasons waiting for Beltre to gel and provide some serious bang for the buck. The Mariners signed him to a five-year, $65 million deal. His 2005 season will land somewhere between that extremely conservative PECOTA and a 2004 season he'll never again replicate.

MILTON BRADLEY CF **Bats: B** **Throws: R** Born: 15-Apr-1978 Age: 27

YEAR	TM	LG	AGE	AB	H	2B	3B	HR	BB	SO	SB	CS	AVG	OBP	SLG	MLVR	EQBA	EQOBP	EQSLG	EQMLVR	VORP	DEFENSE
2002	CLE	AL	24	325	81	18	3	9	32	58	6	3	.249	.317	.406	-.072	.252	.325	.413	-.080	8.9	91-CF -10
2003	CLE	AL	25	377	121	34	2	10	64	73	17	7	.321	.421	.501	.316	.332	.433	.524	.335	52.6	93-CF 0
2004	LAD	NL	26	516	138	24	0	19	71	123	15	11	.267	.362	.424	.066	.274	.364	.434	.038	25.2	88-CF 6 31-RF 0
2005	*LAD*	*NL*	*27*	*432*	*118*	*24*	*2*	*14*	*60*	*95*	*13*	*5*	*.274*	*.365*	*.441*	*.050*	*.281*	*.370*	*.454*	*.079*	*27.1*	*118-CF 0*

Breakout: 19% *Improve: 43%* *Collapse: 22%*

Paul DePodesta immediately demonstrated that his disutility function for cranky behavior was considerably smaller than Cleveland's, and picked up a very good player at a bargain price. Bradley's got a rep, is demonstrative with his displeasure, but most importantly, he's a hell of a player. Plays solid defense, and produces at the plate. Gets pissed when someone throws something at him, which somehow makes him different from us perfect fans. His acquisition is another data point in support of the Dodger front office's understanding what's of critical importance, and also understanding what isn't. Bradley's not Ron Artest.

HEE CHOI 1B **Bats: L** **Throws: L** Born: 16-Mar-1979 Age: 26

YEAR	TM	LG	AGE	AB	H	2B	3B	HR	BB	SO	SB	CS	AVG	OBP	SLG	MLVR	EQBA	EQOBP	EQSLG	EQMLVR	VORP	DEFENSE
2002	IOW	PCL	23	478	137	24	3	26	95	119	3	2	.287	.406	.513	.281	.266	.380	.468	.106	29.7	127-1B -8
2002	CHC	NL	23	50	9	1	0	2	7	15	0	0	.180	.281	.320	-.242	.200	.274	.340	-.312	-1.9	14-1B -1
2003	IOW	PCL	24	66	17	4	1	6	9	19	0	1	.258	.351	.621	.322	.242	.327	.561	.118	4.3	16-1B 0
2003	CHC	NL	24	202	44	17	0	8	37	71	1	1	.218	.350	.421	.011	.222	.346	.419	-.054	6.5	60-1B 0
2004	FLA	NL	25	281	76	16	1	15	52	78	1	0	.270	.388	.495	.216	.275	.391	.500	.176	27.5	81-1B 0
2004	LAD	NL	25	62	10	5	0	0	11	18	0	0	.161	.289	.242	-.341	.177	.265	.226	-.495	-3.9	18-1B -1
2005	*LAD*	*NL*	*26*	*329*	*85*	*19*	*2*	*18*	*57*	*93*	*2*	*1*	*.258*	*.374*	*.493*	*.118*	*.265*	*.379*	*.508*	*.148*	*29.2*	*95-1B -1*

Breakout: 45% *Improve: 72%* *Collapse: 16%*

Primary bounty for shipping Lo Duca and Mota to Florida. Choi's the hitter he's always been, despite a rough showing in his brief stint with the Dodgers late in the season. He can still hit for average, power, and draw walks, but there's concern that he may end up as a platoon player. It looked like he might be involved in a trade, but the Dodgers shipped Shawn Green and his giant 2005 salary out instead, and got to keep Odalis Perez as a result. Choi's a good bet to outperform Green this season, which would make the millions saved by trading Green mighty tasty.

ALEX CORA — 2B — Bats: L — Throws: R — Born: 18-Oct-1975 — Age: 29

YEAR	TM	LG	AGE	AB	H	2B	3B	HR	BB	SO	SB	CS	AVG	OBP	SLG	MLVR	EQBA	EQOBP	EQSLG	EQMLVR	VORP	DEFENSE
2002	LAD	NL	26	258	75	14	4	5	26	38	7	2	.291	.371	.434	.154	.303	.379	.458	.124	24.7	50-SS -2 19-2B 0
2003	LAD	NL	27	477	119	24	3	4	16	59	4	2	.249	.287	.338	-.181	.260	.295	.355	-.212	-0.7	125-2B 7
2004	LAD	NL	28	405	107	9	4	10	47	41	3	4	.264	.364	.380	.003	.270	.366	.388	-.024	19.4	121-2B 8
2005	*LAD*	*NL*	*29*	*362*	*94*	*17*	*3*	*7*	*32*	*46*	*4*	*2*	*.261*	*.336*	*.378*	*-.093*	*.268*	*.341*	*.389*	*-.068*	*15.8*	*99-2B 3*

Breakout: 10% *Improve: 30%* *Collapse: 31%*

Bounced back after a rough 2003. He's worth at least a win with the glove, so a season like 2004 makes him a valuable player. Still, he probably played a bit over his head—his 18 HBPs added a lot to his on-base percentage and likely won't be replicated—and the Dodgers non-tendered him after signing the more potent Jeff Kent. Even at a half-step below his '04 output, Cora will make a decent signing, for the right price.

CORY DUNLAP — 1B — Bats: L — Throws: L — Born: 13-Apr-1984 — Age: 21

YEAR	TM	LG	AGE	AB	H	2B	3B	HR	BB	SO	SB	CS	AVG	OBP	SLG	MLVR	EQBA	EQOBP	EQSLG	EQMLVR	VORP	DEFENSE
2004	OGD	PIO	20	245	86	18	1	7	68	40	0	0	.351	.492	.518	.366	.224	.326	.306	-.241	-24.5	50-1B -8
2005	*LAD*	*NL*	*21*	*317*	*69*	*14*	*1*	*4*	*44*	*77*	*0*	*0*	*.217*	*.315*	*.308*	*-.247*	*.223*	*.320*	*.317*	*-.226*	*-8.5*	*88-1B -6*

Breakout: 25% *Improve: 40%* *Collapse: 33%*

Yes, it was Ogden. Yes, it's the Pioneer League. Yes, many of the pitchers in it were flipping burgers a few months before and think the current cast of SNL is actually funny. But Dunlap just dismantled opposing pitchers. He hit for average, hit for power, showed great selectivity and patience. He faces the potential Travis Hafner problem in the long term; some work on his defense is going to be part of his daily routine if he wants to have a big league career.

STEVE FINLEY — CF — Bats: L — Throws: L — Born: 12-Mar-1965 — Age: 40

YEAR	TM	LG	AGE	AB	H	2B	3B	HR	BB	SO	SB	CS	AVG	OBP	SLG	MLVR	EQBA	EQOBP	EQSLG	EQMLVR	VORP	DEFENSE
2002	ARI	NL	37	505	145	24	4	25	65	73	16	4	.287	.370	.499	.183	.278	.361	.493	.118	46.5	128-CF 7
2003	ARI	NL	38	516	148	24	10	22	57	94	15	8	.287	.363	.500	.150	.277	.353	.488	.096	39.9	128-CF -5
2004	ARI	NL	39	404	111	16	1	23	40	52	8	4	.275	.338	.490	.095	.263	.327	.471	.014	25.8	99-CF -9
2004	LAD	NL	39	224	59	12	0	13	21	30	1	3	.263	.324	.491	.093	.270	.325	.491	.045	12.2	54-CF 4
2005	*ANA*	*AL*	*40*	*503*	*131*	*26*	*3*	*21*	*54*	*81*	*9*	*5*	*.260*	*.333*	*.447*	*-.001*	*.262*	*.337*	*.458*	*.013*	*20.9*	*134-CF -2*

Breakout: 28% *Improve: 41%* *Collapse: 18%*

Changed SoCal addresses by moving to Anaheim, where he'll patrol CF for the next two years for too much money. He's a fantastic guy, a hard worker, and a hard baseball guy, but he's 40 years old this year, and it wouldn't be shocking to see him (a) fall off the face of the Earth in terms of production, or (b) miss a bunch of games due to nagging injuries. Probably better to spend $15 million a year on Carlos Beltran and a well-placed scrap-heaper than on Finley and Orlando Cabrera.

JASON GRABOWSKI — UT — Bats: L — Throws: R — Born: 24-May-1976 — Age: 29

YEAR	TM	LG	AGE	AB	H	2B	3B	HR	BB	SO	SB	CS	AVG	OBP	SLG	MLVR	EQBA	EQOBP	EQSLG	EQMLVR	VORP	DEFENSE
2002	SAC	PCL	26	265	78	22	3	12	39	56	6	4	.294	.387	.536	.285	.271	.363	.485	.104	13.4	20-RF -3 14-C -6
2003	SAC	PCL	27	250	73	13	2	9	31	46	7	2	.292	.364	.468	.169	.273	.344	.442	.013	5.8	45-RF -5
2004	LAD	NL	28	173	38	7	0	7	19	50	0	0	.220	.297	.382	-.126	.224	.293	.385	-.199	0.1	21-LF 0
2005	*LAD*	*NL*	*29*	*130*	*31*	*6*	*1*	*5*	*16*	*34*	*1*	*0*	*.241*	*.323*	*.411*	*-.087*	*.247*	*.327*	*.423*	*-.061*	*3.4*	*39-LF -3*

Breakout: 26% *Improve: 51%* *Collapse: 33%*

One of the Tammany Hall faithful from Oakland. Grabowski's a useful player, one of the Type II utility guys who can hit the occasional home run, and won't kill your offense if he gets pressed into service for a few weeks due to injury. He's kind of screwed by circumstance, as Jayson Werth can pretty much do everything Grabowski can except play third base, and do it all a little bit better.

SHAWN GREEN RF/1B **Bats: L** **Throws: L** Born: 10-Nov-1972 Age: 32

YEAR	TM	LG	AGE	AB	H	2B	3B	HR	BB	SO	SB	CS	AVG	OBP	SLG	MLVR	EQBA	EQOBP	EQSLG	EQMLVR	VORP	DEFENSE
2002	LAD	NL	29	582	166	31	1	42	93	112	8	5	.285	.385	.558	.338	.294	.391	.589	.316	65.5	154-RF 10
2003	LAD	NL	30	611	171	49	2	19	68	112	6	2	.280	.355	.460	.137	.286	.358	.477	.098	36.6	157-RF 9
2004	LAD	NL	31	590	157	28	1	28	71	114	5	2	.266	.352	.459	.101	.269	.354	.465	.059	34.7	100-1B -9 43-RF -2
2005	*ARI*	*NL*	*32*	*504*	*140*	*30*	*2*	*23*	*64*	*98*	*5*	*1*	*.278*	*.363*	*.486*	*.107*	*.273*	*.356*	*.476*	*.076*	*26.7*	*135-RF -4*

Breakout: 15% *Improve: 57%* *Collapse: 15%*

Green's health and offensive production have been slipping for three straight years, from borderline MVP candidate to "solid but unspectacular." If DePodesta knows anything, it's how to find acceptable to very good offensive talent for the corners at a low price; Green's production can be approximately matched at a considerable discount, and that money can be put to better use elsewhere. DePo looked in his own cupboard, saw Hee Seop Choi sitting there, and flipped Green to Arizona for Dioner Navarro and three pitching prospects at the end of the Great Randy Johnson Caper.

JOEL GUZMAN SS **Bats: R** **Throws: R** Born: 24-Nov-1984 Age: 20

YEAR	TM	LG	AGE	AB	H	2B	3B	HR	BB	SO	SB	CS	AVG	OBP	SLG	MLVR	EQBA	EQOBP	EQSLG	EQMLVR	VORP	DEFENSE
2002	GRF	PIO	17	151	38	8	2	3	18	54	5	3	.252	.331	.391	-.008	.193	.248	.293	-.432	-19.8	42-SS -1
2003	SGA	SAL	18	217	51	13	0	8	9	62	4	4	.235	.263	.406	-.020	.196	.211	.338	-.442	-16.0	57-SS -5
2003	VRO	FSL	18	240	59	13	1	5	11	60	0	4	.246	.279	.371	-.060	.212	.240	.349	-.359	-12.2	57-SS -9
2004	VRO	FSL	19	329	101	22	8	14	21	78	8	5	.307	.347	.550	.282	.261	.297	.474	-.037	17.5	86-SS 4
2004	JAX	SOU	19	182	51	11	3	9	13	44	1	2	.280	.325	.522	.206	.262	.304	.486	-.006	11.2	42-SS -4
2005	*LAD*	*NL*	*20*	*404*	*98*	*23*	*2*	*15*	*22*	*110*	*4*	*2*	*.242*	*.281*	*.418*	*-.149*	*.248*	*.285*	*.431*	*-.125*	*10.5*	*103-SS -6*

Breakout: 28% *Improve: 49%* *Collapse: 30%*

Guzman's a solid prospect who looks a lot like Alfonso Soriano. He's got the ability to hit pretty much any pitch thrown near the plate with authority. He also has the ability to miss any pitch thrown over the plate with even greater authority. It's not clear he's going to be able to play an acceptable defensive shortstop at the big league level, but he'll certainly swing hard once he gets there. Good power, plate discipline more of a theoretical concept in his worldview than anything substantive. He might get a September cup of coffee this season, but 2006 is probably his first chance at significant playing time.

JOSE HERNANDEZ INF **Bats: R** **Throws: R** Born: 14-Jul-1969 Age: 35

YEAR	TM	LG	AGE	AB	H	2B	3B	HR	BB	SO	SB	CS	AVG	OBP	SLG	MLVR	EQBA	EQOBP	EQSLG	EQMLVR	VORP	DEFENSE
2002	MIL	NL	32	525	151	24	2	24	52	188	3	5	.288	.356	.478	.169	.287	.354	.488	.107	47.6	147-SS 17
2003	COL	NL	33	257	61	6	1	8	27	95	1	1	.237	.308	.362	-.156	.221	.294	.340	-.261	2.0	61-SS 2
2003	CHC	NL	33	69	13	3	1	2	3	26	0	0	.188	.222	.348	-.315	.188	.222	.362	-.391	-2.1	12-3B 0
2003	PIT	NL	33	193	43	9	1	3	16	56	1	0	.223	.282	.326	-.223	.219	.280	.328	-.306	-1.2	54-3B 3
2004	LAD	NL	34	211	61	12	1	13	26	61	3	1	.289	.370	.540	.256	.288	.370	.542	.211	24.3	39-2B 2
2005	*CLE*	*AL*	*35*	*154*	*37*	*7*	*1*	*5*	*15*	*50*	*1*	*1*	*.243*	*.313*	*.400*	*-.110*	*.243*	*.315*	*.410*	*-.103*	*5.1*	*44-SS -3*

Breakout: 10% *Improve: 27%* *Collapse: 43%*

Hernandez does certain things very well. Defensively, he can play any of the infield spots acceptably well, but he does have a propensity for the highly visible defensive misplay. (see also ERROR) At the plate, he makes lots of highly visible but not particularly damaging outs, usually with a grand flail for strike three. What he does well is hit the ball, particularly against lefties. (Yes, there is some evidence to suggest that the ability to lefty-bash is largely illusory, but Hernandez has been doing so fairly well for the last three seasons, so he's earned the slack.) Hernandez is a valuable player, particularly for a contending team looking for a stopgap solution and some flexibility. Signed with the Indians.

CHIN-LUNG HU SS **Bats: R** **Throws: R** Born: 02-Feb-1984 Age: 21

YEAR	TM	LG	AGE	AB	H	2B	3B	HR	BB	SO	SB	CS	AVG	OBP	SLG	MLVR	EQBA	EQOBP	EQSLG	EQMLVR	VORP	DEFENSE
2003	OGD	PIO	19	220	67	9	5	3	14	33	5	4	.305	.343	.432	.036	.221	.254	.305	-.389	-22.3	53-SS 0
2004	CGA	SAL	20	332	99	15	4	6	20	50	17	7	.298	.342	.422	.097	.260	.293	.365	-.202	0.1	84-SS 6
2004	VRO	FSL	20	75	23	4	1	0	5	6	3	1	.307	.350	.387	.066	.237	.259	.276	-.412	-5.0	18-SS 2
2005	*LAD*	*NL*	*21*	*396*	*90*	*17*	*2*	*4*	*17*	*65*	*8*	*4*	*.227*	*.262*	*.309*	*-.341*	*.233*	*.266*	*.318*	*-.321*	*-11.7*	*102-SS -2*

Breakout: 3% *Improve: 15%* *Collapse: 57%*

Hu's strong season at Columbus earned him a promotion to Vero Beach and a spot on the radar of prospect mavens. He's only 20, is "projectable" at the plate, and according to scouts, has the ability to actually stay at shortstop as he moves up through the system. With Hu and Guzman, the Dodgers have two of the top shortstop prospects in baseball, giving them an embarrassment of riches compared to most other clubs in that department. Of course, when we started writing Baseball Prospectus annuals some time back, the same could be said of Seattle with Desi Relaford and Arquimedez Pozo, so perhaps a little perspective is a good thing.

CESAR IZTURIS SS **Bats: B** **Throws: R** Born: 10-Feb-1980 Age: 25

YEAR	TM	LG	AGE	AB	H	2B	3B	HR	BB	SO	SB	CS	AVG	OBP	SLG	MLVR	EQBA	EQOBP	EQSLG	EQMLVR	VORP	DEFENSE
2002	LAD	NL	22	439	102	24	2	1	14	39	7	7	.232	.253	.303	-.281	.248	.268	.329	-.311	-12.5	110-SS -6
2003	LAD	NL	23	558	140	21	6	1	25	70	10	5	.251	.282	.315	-.219	.259	.291	.329	-.258	-2.2	151-SS 13
2004	LAD	NL	24	670	193	32	9	4	43	70	25	9	.288	.330	.381	-.036	.292	.334	.388	-.067	29.7	153-SS 4
2005	*LAD*	*NL*	*25*	*582*	*152*	*27*	*5*	*6*	*36*	*64*	*16*	*6*	*.261*	*.304*	*.353*	*-.185*	*.267*	*.308*	*.364*	*-.161*	*9.5*	*148-SS 2*

Breakout: 0% *Improve: 9%* *Collapse: 51%*

If he can hit like he did last year, and play outstanding defense, he's probably worth having as a starter. Offensively, he took a big step forward in 2004, posting his highest OBP by nearly 50 points, and showing enough gap power to keep opposing outfielders mildly honest. It's not likely that he'll hang onto all that improvement, but if he can keep posting a .330 OBP in Dodger Stadium, that's probably enough. Defensively, he's not far from building the kind of defensive reputation that can serve you well long after you no longer deserve it, a la Omar Vizquel.

MATT KEMP RF **Bats: R** **Throws: R** Born: 23-Sep-1984 Age: 20

YEAR	TM	LG	AGE	AB	H	2B	3B	HR	BB	SO	SB	CS	AVG	OBP	SLG	MLVR	EQBA	EQOBP	EQSLG	EQMLVR	VORP	DEFENSE
2004	CGA	SAL	19	423	122	22	8	17	24	100	8	7	.288	.330	.499	.179	.251	.282	.421	-.149	-10.9	101-RF -2
2004	VRO	FSL	19	37	13	5	0	1	4	12	2	1	.351	.405	.568	.421	.270	.284	.459	-.073	-0.1	12-RF -1
2005	*LAD*	*NL*	*20*	*380*	*89*	*18*	*3*	*11*	*17*	*106*	*4*	*2*	*.235*	*.272*	*.386*	*-.214*	*.241*	*.276*	*.397*	*-.191*	*-6.2*	*97-RF -4*

Breakout: 9% *Improve: 29%* *Collapse: 44%*

Hit for power in the Sally League, enough to earn a few ABs at Vero Beach, where he had 40 or so good plate appearances. He'll begin the season in High-A, but could end up being promoted if he wallops the ball early in the season. Kemp's ability to improve his plate discipline will ultimately decide his fate.

ANDY LaROCHE 3B **Bats: R** **Throws: R** Born: 13-Sep-1983 Age: 21

YEAR	TM	LG	AGE	AB	H	2B	3B	HR	BB	SO	SB	CS	AVG	OBP	SLG	MLVR	EQBA	EQOBP	EQSLG	EQMLVR	VORP	DEFENSE
2004	CGA	SAL	20	244	69	20	0	13	29	30	12	5	.283	.375	.525	.272	.229	.295	.414	-.151	2.3	61-3B -3
2004	VRO	FSL	20	219	51	13	0	10	17	42	2	3	.233	.290	.429	-.016	.186	.230	.348	-.396	-15.3	54-3B -9
2005	*LAD*	*NL*	*21*	*335*	*72*	*15*	*1*	*11*	*23*	*65*	*3*	*2*	*.216*	*.277*	*.364*	*-.247*	*.222*	*.281*	*.374*	*-.226*	*-10.6*	*89-3B -8*

Breakout: 25% *Improve: 50%* *Collapse: 27%*

Earned some time in Vero Beach based on hitting pretty well in the Pioneer League, and the Dodgers wanting to get him playing time. Could start the year either in high-A or, less likely, Double-A. No one knows yet whether or not he'll be able to handle third base defensively as he moves up.

JAMES LONEY 1B **Bats: L** **Throws: L** Born: 07-May-1984 Age: 21

YEAR	TM	LG	AGE	AB	H	2B	3B	HR	BB	SO	SB	CS	AVG	OBP	SLG	MLVR	EQBA	EQOBP	EQSLG	EQMLVR	VORP	DEFENSE
2002	GRF	PIO	18	170	63	22	3	5	25	18	5	4	.371	.457	.624	.630	.283	.345	.464	.054	13.6	41-1B -5
2002	VRO	FSL	18	67	20	6	0	0	6	10	0	0	.299	.356	.388	.072	.209	.232	.254	-.512	-9.6	12-1B 0
2003	VRO	FSL	19	468	129	31	3	7	43	80	9	4	.276	.337	.400	.073	.239	.292	.376	-.203	-19.0	106-1B -3
2004	JAX	SOU	20	395	94	19	2	4	42	75	6	5	.238	.314	.327	-.106	.225	.292	.312	-.301	-27.9	101-1B -6
2005	*LAD*	*NL*	*21*	*360*	*87*	*20*	*2*	*7*	*29*	*66*	*4*	*1*	*.242*	*.301*	*.363*	*-.188*	*.248*	*.305*	*.374*	*-.165*	*-4.7*	*95-1B -5*

Breakout: 29% *Improve: 53%* *Collapse: 25%*

Well, at least he's still young, and serves as a nice cautionary tale regarding Cory Dunlap. Loney had a very nice season in the Pioneer League right out of high school, and has pretty much been in a tailspin since. He was largely uncomfortable, even overmatched, by the pitching in the Southern League. He's young enough so that he can take a couple of shots at a given league, perhaps twice, and still have a very nice career. But we've now got 170 AB that say he's something of a prospect, and about 800 that say he's not. The Dodgers hope Loney's struggles are the result of the broken wrist and broken finger he's suffered the last couple years, but he'll have to prove himself either way.

RUSSELL MARTIN C Bats: R Throws: R Born: 15-Feb-1983 Age: 22

YEAR	TM	LG	AGE	AB	H	2B	3B	HR	BB	SO	SB	CS	AVG	OBP	SLG	MLVR	EQBA	EQOBP	EQSLG	EQMLVR	VORP	DEFENSE
2003	OGD	PIO	20	188	51	13	0	6	26	26	3	1	.271	.368	.436	.056	.182	.251	.283	-.445	-29.8	49-C -4
2003	SGA	SAL	20	98	28	4	1	3	9	11	5	2	.286	.343	.439	.170	.240	.287	.380	-.206	-1.0	14-C -6
2004	VRO	FSL	21	416	104	24	1	15	72	54	9	5	.250	.366	.421	.094	.209	.310	.362	-.207	-4.9	101-C 3
2005	*LAD*	*NL*	*22*	*262*	*58*	*12*	*1*	*8*	*27*	*43*	*2*	*1*	*.223*	*.306*	*.363*	*-.190*	*.228*	*.311*	*.374*	*-.167*	*3.5*	*73-C -7*

Breakout: 30% *Improve: 49%* *Collapse: 27%*

A power/patience catcher who held his own at Vero Beach. So far during his career, he's walked more than he's struck out, a rare, attractive feat. He's had a surprisingly low average for a guy who's struck out so rarely, and he's actually shown some speed on the field, which makes you wonder how long he'll have either (a) the speed, or (b) any time actually catching, rather than moving to another position. Defensively, the jury's out, but he's done well enough to keep getting penciled in there, and he's young enough to learn the craft.

BRENT MAYNE C Bats: L Throws: R Born: 19-Apr-1968 Age: 37

YEAR	TM	LG	AGE	AB	H	2B	3B	HR	BB	SO	SB	CS	AVG	OBP	SLG	MLVR	EQBA	EQOBP	EQSLG	EQMLVR	VORP	DEFENSE
2002	KCR	AL	34	326	77	8	2	4	34	54	4	4	.236	.309	.310	-.255	.227	.307	.302	-.283	-3.9	94-C 3
2003	KCR	AL	35	372	91	17	1	6	32	59	0	2	.245	.307	.344	-.210	.238	.306	.336	-.232	-1.8	106-C 1
2004	ARI	NL	36	94	24	6	1	0	13	17	1	0	.255	.343	.340	-.120	.245	.324	.298	-.245	1.9	26-C 1
2004	LAD	NL	36	96	18	0	0	0	14	24	0	0	.188	.286	.188	-.419	.206	.265	.206	-.511	-6.3	32-C 0
2005	*LAD*	*NL*	*37*	*141*	*31*	*5*	*0*	*2*	*16*	*27*	*0*	*0*	*.216*	*.297*	*.296*	*-.298*	*.222*	*.301*	*.304*	*-.279*	*-2.7*	*42-C -3*

Breakout: 25% *Improve: 38%* *Collapse: 34%*

Mayne makes his living by being a known quantity. He's no longer an acceptable player for longer than short periods of time and has no business being on a contender at this stage. Few reasons to hire Mayne rather than say, a Tom Wilson at a lower cost.

ANTONIO PEREZ 2B Bats: R Throws: R Born: 26-Jan-1980 Age: 25

YEAR	TM	LG	AGE	AB	H	2B	3B	HR	BB	SO	SB	CS	AVG	OBP	SLG	MLVR	EQBA	EQOBP	EQSLG	EQMLVR	VORP	DEFENSE
2002	SAN	TXS	22	240	62	8	2	2	11	64	15	9	.258	.312	.333	-.039	.254	.293	.335	-.249	-5.3	58-2B -5
2003	DUR	INT	23	134	38	12	2	6	10	38	3	1	.284	.345	.537	.202	.261	.325	.500	.049	9.1	33-2B -2
2003	TBY	AL	23	125	31	6	1	2	18	34	4	1	.248	.345	.360	-.092	.250	.351	.371	-.089	4.2	23-2B -3
2004	LVG	PCL	24	476	141	24	6	22	61	87	23	12	.296	.379	.511	.105	.243	.323	.403	-.104	14.2	71-SS -9 44-2B -1
2004	LAD	NL	24	13	3	1	0	0	0	5	1	0	.231	.286	.308	-.251	.308	.195	.385	-.316	0.1	
2005	*LAD*	*NL*	*25*	*240*	*60*	*12*	*2*	*7*	*24*	*56*	*8*	*3*	*.250*	*.330*	*.399*	*-.084*	*.257*	*.334*	*.411*	*-.058*	*15.3*	*67-2B -4*

Breakout: 23% *Improve: 49%* *Collapse: 28%*

Not all such gambles work out so well, but getting a one-time top prospect for a player as forgettable as Jason Romano is the kind of move befitting a sharp organization like the Dodgers—and made possible by a dull one like the Devil Rays. Perez consolidated his tools into a solid season at Triple-A, hitting for power and average while hiking his walk rate dramatically. Of course it's Vegas, so you take the grain of salt, throw it over your shoulder, and pray for the straight flush. Jeff Kent's blocking his path to a starting job, but the Dodgers now have a semi-revived prospect they can use off the bench while fishing for another deal like the rumored Hudson-Jackson/Perez off-season swap that never panned out.

DAVE ROSS C Bats: R Throws: R Born: 19-Mar-1977 Age: 28

YEAR	TM	LG	AGE	AB	H	2B	3B	HR	BB	SO	SB	CS	AVG	OBP	SLG	MLVR	EQBA	EQOBP	EQSLG	EQMLVR	VORP	DEFENSE
2002	LVG	PCL	25	293	87	16	2	15	35	86	1	1	.297	.384	.519	.183	.259	.342	.448	.005	15.6	87-C 6
2003	LVG	PCL	26	86	19	4	0	5	11	27	0	2	.221	.313	.442	-.069	.176	.260	.353	-.336	-4.4	24-C 4
2003	LAD	NL	26	124	32	7	0	10	13	42	0	0	.258	.336	.556	.210	.272	.334	.576	.183	13.1	32-C 0
2004	LAD	NL	27	165	28	3	1	5	15	62	0	0	.170	.253	.291	-.357	.175	.253	.307	-.412	-7.9	51-C -2
2005	*LAD*	*NL*	*28*	*173*	*39*	*7*	*1*	*8*	*19*	*59*	*0*	*0*	*.227*	*.317*	*.420*	*-.095*	*.233*	*.322*	*.432*	*-.070*	*10.4*	*50-C -4*

Breakout: 53% *Improve: 64%* *Collapse: 22%*

Ouchie. There's no way to polish last season. Ross was awful; there was no part of his game that was a positive for the Dodgers. Even in Chavez Ravine, you have to hit more than .170, and striking out in over a third of your at bats isn't good, either. Ross will have to step it up to guarantee himself a roster spot that comes with major league meal money. He's got enough pop to do it, and can be useful if he can ever top .240.

OLMEDO SAENZ PH Bats: R Throws: R Born: 08-Oct-1970 Age: 34

YEAR	TM	LG	AGE	AB	H	2B	3B	HR	BB	SO	SB	CS	AVG	OBP	SLG	MLVR	EQBA	EQOBP	EQSLG	EQMLVR	VORP	DEFENSE	
2002	OAK	AL	31	156	43	10	1	6	13	31	1	1	.276	.354	.468	.097	.282	.359	.487	.110	10.0	20-1B 2	15-3B -2
2004	LAD	NL	33	111	31	1	0	8	12	33	0	0	.279	.352	.505	.167	.288	.348	.495	.108	9.5	16-1B -2	
2005	*LAD*	*NL*	*34*	*124*	*30*	*5*	*0*	*6*	*13*	*35*	*0*	*0*	*.244*	*.337*	*.424*	*-.044*	*.250*	*.341*	*.437*	*-.018*	*8.7*	*38-1B -3*	

Breakout: 21% *Improve: 40%* *Collapse: 46%*

This guy can still hit searing line drives. He was a Ken Phelps All-Star until Billy Beane grabbed him and stuck him in the lineup in Oakland, and he's been either injured or raking since then. He's still a solid bat and can handle a slightly bigger role than lefty masher off the bench, but from a tactical standpoint, he's a good guy to have in that role. He appears to have recovered pretty well from a tendon injury, so don't be surprised to see Saenz get 250 PA and hit pretty well in 2005, especially if the Dodgers move slowly with Choi.

JOE THURSTON 2B Bats: L Throws: R Born: 29-Sep-1979 Age: 25

YEAR	TM	LG	AGE	AB	H	2B	3B	HR	BB	SO	SB	CS	AVG	OBP	SLG	MLVR	EQBA	EQOBP	EQSLG	EQMLVR	VORP	DEFENSE	
2002	LVG	PCL	22	587	196	39	13	12	25	60	22	9	.334	.372	.506	.182	.291	.328	.443	.001	28.7	118-2B 10	17-SS 0
2003	LVG	PCL	23	538	156	27	6	7	31	48	1	12	.290	.345	.401	-.019	.250	.304	.353	-.205	-4.7	124-2B 10	
2004	LVG	PCL	24	317	90	17	3	4	20	46	7	2	.284	.356	.394	-.111	.232	.296	.316	-.283	-9.7	81-2B -4	
2004	LAD	NL	24	17	3	1	1	0	0	5	0	0	.176	.167	.353	-.437	.176	.124	.353	-.602	-1.0		
2005	*LAD*	*NL*	*25*	*165*	*41*	*8*	*2*	*2*	*8*	*22*	*2*	*1*	*.246*	*.306*	*.352*	*-.191*	*.252*	*.310*	*.362*	*-.168*	*4.6*	*47-2B -2*	

Breakout: 21% *Improve: 43%* *Collapse: 35%*

Here's what happens when players get pegged as prospects based on high batting averages in offense-crazy ballparks. Thurston was tabbed as a potential star after hitting .334 in Las Vegas in '02. Sent back to Triple-A the next season, his lousy plate discipline caught up with him and his numbers cratered. His upside is utility infielder/pinch-runner, and nothing more.

ROBIN VENTURA Retired Bats: L Throws: R Born: 14-Jul-1967 Age: 37

YEAR	TM	LG	AGE	AB	H	2B	3B	HR	BB	SO	SB	CS	AVG	OBP	SLG	MLVR	EQBA	EQOBP	EQSLG	EQMLVR	VORP	DEFENSE
2002	NYY	AL	34	465	115	17	0	27	90	101	3	1	.247	.368	.458	.103	.258	.379	.474	.106	38.1	128-3B 0
2003	NYY	AL	35	283	71	13	0	9	40	62	0	0	.251	.344	.392	-.030	.256	.350	.402	-.045	11.9	70-3B 6
2003	LAD	NL	35	109	24	5	1	5	18	25	0	0	.220	.331	.422	.011	.227	.336	.436	-.047	5.3	28-1B -4
2004	LAD	NL	36	152	37	3	0	5	22	31	0	0	.243	.337	.362	-.066	.248	.331	.359	-.145	3.1	25-1B -2

Take a bow, Robin. Ventura retired shortly after the season, capping a nice career. Played great defense, and played in some very tough hitters' parks; if he'd toiled somewhere more neutral, somebody would make a Hall of Fame argument for him. His single moment of ignominy has probably been forgotten by most—that unfortunate incident when he charged elder statesman Nolan Ryan, only to find himself on the business end of a power-noogie.

JAYSON WERTH OF Bats: R Throws: R Born: 20-May-1979 Age: 26

YEAR	TM	LG	AGE	AB	H	2B	3B	HR	BB	SO	SB	CS	AVG	OBP	SLG	MLVR	EQBA	EQOBP	EQSLG	EQMLVR	VORP	DEFENSE	
2002	SYR	INT	23	443	114	25	2	18	67	125	24	7	.257	.354	.445	.082	.233	.330	.411	-.087	-4.5	93-LF -1	21-C -6
2002	TOR	AL	23	46	12	2	1	0	6	11	1	0	.261	.340	.348	-.081	.267	.328	.311	-.206	0.6	10-RF 1	
2003	SYR	INT	24	236	56	19	1	9	15	68	11	1	.237	.285	.441	-.037	.217	.271	.417	-.201	-3.9	33-CF -1	16-RF -1
2003	TOR	AL	24	48	10	4	0	2	3	22	1	0	.208	.255	.417	-.211	.213	.250	.383	-.291	-0.8	14-RF -1	
2004	LAD	NL	25	290	76	11	3	16	30	85	4	1	.262	.338	.486	.106	.264	.340	.490	.064	15.4	64-LF 2	10-RF 0
2005	*LAD*	*NL*	*26*	*347*	*88*	*19*	*2*	*17*	*41*	*102*	*8*	*2*	*.253*	*.335*	*.469*	*.019*	*.260*	*.340*	*.483*	*.047*	*17.2*	*94-LF 1*	

Breakout: 20% *Improve: 59%* *Collapse: 17%*

One time Oriole catching prospect, now a super-utility man who can swing the power bat while nominally occupying a left-spectrum defensive position. Fully capable of putting up a big offensive season that would make him a very rich man. Given how tough it is to find 162-game players, a guy like Werth who can be worked into a rotation can be very valuable, particularly with the DH spot coming up a few times a year in interleague play. He'll likely see a time-share with Grabowski and Ricky Ledee, but Werth's good enough to be a bopping outfielder on a number of teams.

TOM WILSON C Bats: R Throws: R Born: 19-Dec-1970 Age: 34

YEAR	TM	LG	AGE	AB	H	2B	3B	HR	BB	SO	SB	CS	AVG	OBP	SLG	MLVR	EQBA	EQOBP	EQSLG	EQMLVR	VORP	DEFENSE
2002	TOR	AL	31	265	68	10	0	8	28	79	0	0	.257	.334	.385	-.046	.262	.337	.384	-.090	10.7	53-C -7
2003	TOR	AL	32	256	66	19	0	5	28	80	0	0	.258	.331	.391	-.071	.254	.327	.385	-.113	8.5	62-C -6
2004	NOR	INT	33	115	37	10	0	7	25	24	0	1	.322	.443	.591	.506	.296	.403	.539	.269	17.7	19-C -4
2004	SAC	PCL	33	42	10	2	0	1	15	13	0	0	.238	.439	.357	.053	.195	.356	.293	-.211	-1.2	
2004	LVG	PCL	33	38	16	2	0	4	4	10	0	0	.421	.476	.789	.819	.333	.341	.639	.364	5.5	
2005	*LAD*	*NL*	*34*	*154*	*37*	*7*	*0*	*6*	*25*	*50*	*0*	*0*	*.239*	*.348*	*.399*	*-.060*	*.245*	*.353*	*.411*	*-.034*	*9.6*	*46-C -11*

Breakout: 19% *Improve: 40%* *Collapse: 38%*

The stathead GM's favorite backup. Draws walks, hits for power, has been bouncing around the baseball world looking for a regular gig since Janet Reno roamed the earth. Wilson's going to end up getting a 150-PA job somewhere once a catcher goes down with some sort of injury near the beginning of the season. Very capable of helping a contending club.

DELWYN YOUNG 2B Bats: B Throws: R Born: 30-Jun-1982 Age: 23

YEAR	TM	LG	AGE	AB	H	2B	3B	HR	BB	SO	SB	CS	AVG	OBP	SLG	MLVR	EQBA	EQOBP	EQSLG	EQMLVR	VORP	DEFENSE
2002	GRF	PIO	20	240	72	18	1	10	27	60	4	2	.300	.380	.508	.279	.227	.279	.378	-.233	-7.9	42-2B -6
2003	SGA	SAL	21	443	143	38	7	15	36	87	5	2	.323	.381	.542	.388	.278	.321	.472	.019	27.5	110-2B -12
2004	VRO	FSL	22	470	132	36	3	22	57	134	11	4	.281	.364	.511	.227	.233	.304	.437	-.100	11.9	114-2B -22
2005	*LAD*	*NL*	*23*	*289*	*70*	*16*	*1*	*10*	*24*	*86*	*3*	*1*	*.243*	*.310*	*.414*	*-.104*	*.249*	*.315*	*.426*	*-.078*	*11.1*	*78-2B -13*

Breakout: 24% *Improve: 44%* *Collapse: 28%*

Flailing, slugging middle infielder who's about to embark on a magical journey down the defensive spectrum. Young's got power to burn, can hit for average, and has occasionally worked the strike zone pretty well. What he can't do is field. Think Julio Franco at second base; not back when he was 25 and could play there without the team instantly forfeiting, but rather eight or nine years from today. Perhaps after hip-replacement surgery.

PITCHERS

WILSON ALVAREZ Bats: L Throws: L Born: 24-Mar-1970 Age: 35

YEAR	TM	LG	AGE	G	GS	IP	H	BB	SO	HR	ERA	EQERA	EQH9	EQBB9	EQSO9	EQHR9	PERA	VORP	STF
2002	TBY	AL	32	23	10	75.0	80	36	56	13	5.28	5.25	9.3	4.0	6.5	1.5	5.13	2.8	-3
2003	LVG	PCL	33	8	8	47.0	36	6	33	1	1.34	2.25	7.4	1.2	5.5	0.2	2.45	15.4	33
2003	LAD	NL	33	21	12	95.0	80	23	82	5	2.37	2.78	8.0	2.0	7.2	0.5	3.28	32.9	37
2004	LAD	NL	34	40	15	120.7	109	31	102	12	4.03	4.23	8.5	2.1	7.0	0.9	3.99	21.0	23
2005	*LAD*	*NL*	*35*	*25*	*12*	*90.3*	*82*	*25*	*75*	*12*	*3.68*	*4.06*	*8.4*	*2.2*	*6.6*	*1.1*	*4.02*	*16.9*	*10*

Breakout: 27% *Improve: 46%* *Collapse: 25%*

Occupied a role that more teams should utilize, the hybrid starter/reliever, making 15 starts and 25 relief appearances. Alvarez pitched OK, showing very good control throughout the year, and doing what he was asked for the team. This role may be perfect for him, as he tired as a pure starter. He's still got very good stuff from time to time, and if he's in the right environment, he could be effective for a few more years. The Dodgers wisely brought him back, and he'll see his share of starts with Edwin Jackson and Kaz Ishii both question marks at the back of the rotation.

CHAD BILLINGSLEY Bats: R Throws: R Born: 29-Jul-1984 Age: 20

YEAR	TM	LG	AGE	G	GS	IP	H	BB	SO	HR	ERA	EQERA	EQH9	EQBB9	EQSO9	EQHR9	PERA	VORP	STF
2003	OGD	PIO	18	11	11	54.0	49	15	62	0	2.83	5.51	8.3	3.7	5.2	0.4	3.38	12.5	22
2004	VRO	FSL	19	18	18	92.0	68	49	111	6	2.35	4.30	8.3	5.7	7.6	1.1	4.95	6.0	30
2004	JAX	SOU	19	8	8	42.3	32	22	47	1	2.98	4.31	7.5	5.0	7.0	0.2	3.63	8.7	33
2005	*LAD*	*NL*	*20*	*15*	*14*	*83.0*	*69*	*47*	*71*	*9*	*4.05*	*4.47*	*7.6*	*4.5*	*6.9*	*0.9*	*4.50*	*11.6*	*10*

Breakout: 19% *Improve: 48%* *Collapse: 15%*

The Dodger system is absolutely loaded with arms. You want velocity? It's there. K Rates worthy of Johan Santana? Yup. Got some of those. Lefties? Yep. Righties? You betcha. Billingsley (depending on health) is the class of the bunch. Billingsley's got plus stuff, struck out 158 in 134 innings, showed good command, and his only injury history involves his ankle rather than a shoulder or elbow. He's got to face the injury nexus, but there's nothing not to like about the 2003 first-rounder.

YHENCY BRAZOBAN **Bats: R** **Throws: R** Born: 11-Jun-1980 Age: 25

YEAR	TM	LG	AGE	G	GS	IP	H	BB	SO	HR	ERA	EQERA	EQH9	EQBB9	EQSO9	EQHR9	PERA	VORP	STF
2003	TAM	FSL	23	24	0	28.7	27	12	34	0	2.82	5.67	9.0	4.3	7.3	0.3	4.33	3.8	-1
2003	TRN	EAS	23	20	0	27.7	33	14	19	5	7.80	8.20	10.9	4.8	5.1	2.7	7.18	-4.6	-36
2004	JAX	SOU	24	37	0	51.0	38	22	61	4	2.65	3.99	7.8	4.2	7.6	1.1	3.99	8.5	7
2004	LAD	NL	24	31	0	32.7	25	15	27	2	2.48	2.61	7.8	3.8	7.0	0.6	4.06	11.7	0
2004	LVG	PCL	24	10	0	12.3	14	1	17	1	2.20	2.19	8.8	0.7	9.5	0.7	3.65	2.7	21
2005	*LAD*	*NL*	*25*	*27*	*7*	*65.0*	*57*	*30*	*59*	*8*	*4.14*	*4.57*	*8.2*	*3.6*	*7.2*	*1.1*	*4.59*	*8.3*	*4*

Breakout: 14% *Improve: 39%* *Collapse: 29%*

Was good enough that he made Guillermo Mota expendable. He pitched exceptionally well until a single outing against the Giants raised his ERA into the "minuscule" range from the "microscopic" range. Great stuff, can reasonably be expected to be part of a lights-out 8th and 9th inning many, many times this year.

JONATHAN BROXTON **Bats: R** **Throws: R** Born: 16-Jun-1984 Age: 21

YEAR	TM	LG	AGE	G	GS	IP	H	BB	SO	HR	ERA	EQERA	EQH9	EQBB9	EQSO9	EQHR9	PERA	VORP	STF
2002	GRF	PIO	18	11	6	29.3	22	16	33	0	2.76	4.78	8.2	6.5	5.5	0.3	4.78	2.4	3
2003	SGA	SAL	19	9	8	37.3	27	22	30	1	3.14	5.61	8.0	6.4	4.5	0.5	4.01	6.0	5
2004	VRO	FSL	20	23	23	128.3	110	43	144	7	3.23	4.61	8.8	3.5	7.0	1.0	4.54	14.0	22
2005	*LAD*	*NL*	*21*	*15*	*14*	*85.7*	*76*	*42*	*68*	*11*	*4.20*	*4.63*	*8.2*	*3.9*	*6.3*	*1.1*	*4.70*	*10.5*	*8*

Breakout: 11% *Improve: 46%* *Collapse: 14%*

Burly starter on a Vero Beach team chock full o' prospects. Broxton's mechanics are solid, and he performed well, with a K rate high enough to make him a real prospect. He's behind Billingsley, but not by much, and would be the best prospect in a number of organizations. There is talk that his future may be in the bullpen rather than the rotation, but such rumblings are out there for most pitching prospects.

GIOVANNI CARRARA **Bats: R** **Throws: R** Born: 04-Mar-1968 Age: 37

YEAR	TM	LG	AGE	G	GS	IP	H	BB	SO	HR	ERA	EQERA	EQH9	EQBB9	EQSO9	EQHR9	PERA	VORP	STF
2002	LAD	NL	34	63	1	90.7	83	32	56	14	3.27	3.72	9.5	2.9	5.1	1.5	5.21	20.2	-15
2003	SEA	AL	35	23	0	29.0	40	14	13	6	6.83	6.67	11.8	4.1	3.8	1.6	7.31	-2.4	-32
2003	TAC	PCL	35	18	0	27.7	28	9	27	2	4.22	5.13	9.2	3.4	7.5	1.0	4.78	2.4	2
2004	IOW	PCL	36	20	0	28.3	29	8	23	3	3.82	3.95	8.9	2.6	5.6	1.3	4.28	4.0	-2
2004	LAD	NL	36	42	0	53.7	46	20	48	1	2.18	2.61	8.0	3.0	7.3	0.2	3.48	19.0	15
2005	*LAD*	*NL*	*37*	*31*	*3*	*54.0*	*55*	*20*	*42*	*7*	*3.99*	*4.40*	*9.4*	*3.0*	*6.1*	*1.1*	*5.00*	*8.8*	*-3*

Breakout: 43% *Improve: 61%* *Collapse: 26%*

He's found a home for that Vicente Padilla pitch that he throws better than Vicente Padilla. Keeps the ball down, can make batters miss, has good durability. He will allow more homers than he did in '04; some regression is almost inevitable.

MARCOS CARVAJAL **Bats: R** **Throws: R** Born: 19-Aug-1984 Age: 20

YEAR	TM	LG	AGE	G	GS	IP	H	BB	SO	HR	ERA	EQERA	EQH9	EQBB9	EQSO9	EQHR9	PERA	VORP	STF
2003	OGD	PIO	18	23	0	38.0	32	22	50	1	3.08	5.56	8.2	8.2	6.4	0.5	5.03	2.2	0
2004	CGA	SAL	19	36	0	72.0	50	35	72	2	1.88	3.56	7.5	5.2	5.8	0.4	3.84	12.8	17
2005	*MIL*	*NL*	*20*	*17*	*7*	*50.3*	*45*	*31*	*37*	*6*	*4.59*	*4.76*	*8.0*	*4.8*	*6.0*	*0.9*	*4.86*	*5.3*	*-5*

Breakout: 16% *Improve: 48%* *Collapse: 18%*

Dominated the Sally League with very live stuff at the age of 19. He'll start the year at high-A, but he's got a long way to go, especially as he battles the injury concerns so prevalent with precocious arms. He throws hard, which is why the Brewers picked him up in the Rule 5 Draft, and sold him to the Rockies. So you might well get a chance to see him doing mop-up duties at Coors Field. And with the Rockies, that could be 350 innings of work.

ELMER DESSENS **Bats: R** **Throws: R** Born: 13-Jan-1972 Age: 33

YEAR	TM	LG	AGE	G	GS	IP	H	BB	SO	HR	ERA	EQERA	EQH9	EQBB9	EQSO9	EQHR9	PERA	VORP	STF
2002	CIN	NL	30	30	30	178.0	173	49	93	24	3.03	3.52	9.2	2.2	4.3	1.2	4.43	38.8	0
2003	ARI	NL	31	34	30	175.7	212	57	113	22	5.07	4.97	10.0	2.5	5.2	1.0	4.86	4.1	2
2004	ARI	NL	32	38	9	85.3	107	23	55	11	4.75	5.08	10.1	2.1	5.1	1.0	4.45	0.3	-4
2004	LAD	NL	32	12	1	19.7	16	8	18	4	3.20	3.38	8.2	3.4	7.7	1.9	4.82	5.5	2
2005	*LAD*	*NL*	*33*	*28*	*10*	*83.3*	*86*	*26*	*53*	*10*	*4.24*	*4.68*	*9.6*	*2.5*	*5.1*	*1.0*	*4.64*	*9.4*	*-4*

Breakout: 18% *Improve: 44%* *Collapse: 28%*

The D-Backs are probably feeling pretty good about that Durazo deal about now, yes? Dessens was picked up when Dodger starters kept getting knocked out by various injuries. The 3.20 ERA he posted as a reliever in L.A. is more of an indictment of using ERA to measure reliever effectiveness than it is an indicator that Dessens pitched well. He didn't, allowing 4 homers in just under 20 innings of work—and he's still, well, Elmer Dessens. Doesn't throw hard, gives up more than his share of hits, and doesn't have the big strikeout numbers, but he survives on guile. What you saw in 2003 and 2004 is what ye shall have going forward.

DARREN DREIFORT **Bats: R** **Throws: R** Born: 03-May-1972 Age: 33

YEAR	TM	LG	AGE	G	GS	IP	H	BB	SO	HR	ERA	EQERA	EQH9	EQBB9	EQSO9	EQHR9	PERA	VORP	STF
2003	LAD	NL	31	10	10	60.3	58	25	67	6	4.03	4.42	8.5	3.2	9.0	0.9	4.27	9.2	29
2004	LAD	NL	32	60	0	50.7	43	36	63	5	4.44	4.53	7.8	5.6	10.0	0.9	4.53	7.1	11

Hey, *there's* a nice contract, huh? Dreifort signed a five-year deal, at a tidy average of eight figures per season, in December of 2000. Since then, he's pretty much physically exploded, with limbs flying all over the field, his head exploding in that regrettable game against the Astros in '02, and the unfortunate hip and knee problems that will make him unavailable for the start of the season and possibly all of '05. Hopefully, he'll rehab well and come back and pitch. You never want to see anyone go down so many times, get back up again and again, and just keep getting beaten down by freak injuries.

ERIC GAGNE **Bats: R** **Throws: R** Born: 07-Jan-1976 Age: 29

YEAR	TM	LG	AGE	G	GS	IP	H	BB	SO	HR	ERA	EQERA	EQH9	EQBB9	EQSO9	EQHR9	PERA	VORP	STF
2002	LAD	NL	26	77	0	82.3	55	16	114	6	1.97	2.30	6.8	1.5	11.4	0.7	2.53	31.2	42
2003	LAD	NL	27	77	0	82.3	37	20	137	2	1.20	1.60	4.9	1.9	13.8	0.2	1.60	39.4	63
2004	LAD	NL	28	70	0	82.3	53	22	114	5	2.19	2.75	6.4	2.2	11.3	0.6	2.52	28.2	42
2005	*LAD*	*NL*	*29*	*58*	*0*	*79.7*	*46*	*24*	*97*	*7*	*1.90*	*2.09*	*5.4*	*2.4*	*9.7*	*0.8*	*2.08*	*32.5*	*27*

Breakout: 46% *Improve: 67%* *Collapse: 26%*

One AL scouting director calls Gagne "a bargain at $15 million," which must be music to the ears of Gagne and Scott Boras. An absolutely devastating pitcher with no real comparable in recent history. One of a very few men that can exorcise the stoicism out of Dodger Stadium and make it just plain rock. He's thrown exactly 82.1 innings in each of the last three years, which is at least pretty cool, if not particularly important. In those 247 innings of work, he's allowed 145 hits, 58 walks, and struck out 365. That's more than pretty good.

JOEL HANRAHAN **Bats: R** **Throws: R** Born: 06-Oct-1981 Age: 23

YEAR	TM	LG	AGE	G	GS	IP	H	BB	SO	HR	ERA	EQERA	EQH9	EQBB9	EQSO9	EQHR9	PERA	VORP	STF
2002	VRO	FSL	20	25	25	143.7	129	51	139	11	4.20	5.40	9.3	3.6	6.4	1.4	5.06	8.0	15
2002	JAX	SOU	20	3	3	11.0	15	7	10	2	10.64	12.19	13.1	5.2	6.1	2.6	9.58	-4.6	-16
2003	JAX	SOU	21	23	23	133.3	117	53	130	5	2.43	4.08	8.5	3.7	6.3	0.6	4.01	22.2	22
2003	LVG	PCL	21	5	5	25.0	36	20	13	2	10.08	9.49	10.9	7.7	4.0	0.7	6.93	-3.7	-26
2004	LVG	PCL	22	25	22	119.3	128	75	97	22	5.05	5.31	9.2	5.9	5.6	1.5	5.70	-1.3	3
2005	*LAD*	*NL*	*23*	*13*	*8*	*49.7*	*48*	*26*	*37*	*7*	*4.87*	*5.38*	*8.9*	*4.2*	*5.9*	*1.2*	*5.40*	*2.0*	*-4*

Breakout: 10% *Improve: 43%* *Collapse: 24%*

Hanrahan's control deserted him in 2004, and he ended up getting hit pretty hard as a result. He was once highly touted, but his performance record is going in the wrong direction pretty fast. He needs to do everything right this year if he wants to have a shot at a serious major league career. That means making batters miss, and not working into bad counts that result in walks or cookie service.

KAZUHISA ISHII **Bats: L** **Throws: L** Born: 09-Sep-1973 Age: 31

YEAR	TM	LG	AGE	G	GS	IP	H	BB	SO	HR	ERA	EQERA	EQH9	EQBB9	EQSO9	EQHR9	PERA	VORP	STF
2002	LAD	NL	28	28	28	154.0	137	106	143	20	4.27	5.15	8.8	5.4	7.5	1.2	5.33	12.1	5
2003	LAD	NL	29	27	27	147.0	129	101	140	16	3.86	4.54	8.4	5.5	7.8	0.9	4.86	21.1	11
2004	LAD	NL	30	31	31	172.0	155	98	99	21	4.71	5.09	9.0	4.7	4.8	1.1	5.15	13.2	-6
2005	*LAD*	*NL*	*31*	*27*	*20*	*123.3*	*121*	*70*	*88*	*17*	*5.04*	*5.56*	*9.1*	*4.5*	*5.7*	*1.2*	*5.66*	*2.7*	*-5*

Breakout: 9% *Improve: 51%* *Collapse: 15%*

Serious collapse potential. Ishii posted a translated ERA above 5.00 in a season in which he was extremely hit-lucky, yielding hits on just 26% of balls hit in play—well below league average. A mainstay on the leader board for most walks allowed, Ishii's also been fortunate to have Dodger Stadium around to help him prevent all those runners from scoring. Still, with his strikeout rate having suddenly plunged into oblivion, he officially has no useful peripherals. Though the Dodgers found themselves thin in starting pitching in the off-season, you could scarcely blame them for shopping Ishii harder than a pair of Mighty Ducks season tickets.

EDWIN JACKSON **Bats: R** **Throws: R** Born: 09-Sep-1983 Age: 21

YEAR	TM	LG	AGE	G	GS	IP	H	BB	SO	HR	ERA	EQERA	EQH9	EQBB9	EQSO9	EQHR9	PERA	VORP	STF
2002	SGA	SAL	18	19	19	104.7	79	33	85	2	1.98	4.96	8.3	3.6	4.6	0.4	3.63	20.6	36
2003	JAX	SOU	19	27	27	148.3	121	53	157	9	3.70	5.22	8.5	3.3	6.9	0.9	4.04	23.9	42
2003	LAD	NL	19	4	3	22.0	17	11	19	2	2.45	2.57	7.7	3.9	7.3	0.9	3.86	7.9	48
2004	LVG	PCL	20	19	19	90.7	90	55	70	4	5.85	5.73	8.3	5.7	5.3	0.3	4.19	13.8	23
2004	LAD	NL	20	8	5	24.7	31	11	16	7	7.29	7.12	11.2	3.8	5.2	2.2	7.12	-4.2	4
2005	*LAD*	*NL*	*21*	*21*	*11*	*77.0*	*73*	*41*	*57*	*10*	*4.64*	*5.11*	*8.8*	*4.2*	*5.9*	*1.1*	*5.21*	*4.6*	*-3*

Breakout: 11% *Improve: 42%* *Collapse: 21%*

Back spasms limited his effectiveness for part of the year, but he didn't really do himself any favors either. The Brad Penny injury and the Jose Lima experience forced Jackson into the Dodger rotation briefly, where he looked overmatched against big league hitters. Needs to regain the control that appears to have departed him for warmer climes and could use at least half a season in Triple-A. If the Dodgers don't sign another starter, they might want to consider D. J. Houlton—a shrewd Rule 5 pick from Houston—as an early-season option while Jackson hones his craft in Vegas.

JOSE LIMA **Bats: R** **Throws: R** Born: 30-Sep-1972 Age: 32

YEAR	TM	LG	AGE	G	GS	IP	H	BB	SO	HR	ERA	EQERA	EQH9	EQBB9	EQSO9	EQHR9	PERA	VORP	STF
2002	DET	AL	29	20	12	68.3	86	21	33	12	7.77	7.32	10.4	2.5	4.1	1.5	5.05	-14.6	-14
2003	KCR	AL	30	14	14	73.3	80	26	32	7	4.91	4.29	9.5	3.0	3.9	0.8	4.67	9.6	-3
2004	LAD	NL	31	36	24	170.3	178	34	93	33	4.07	4.37	10.0	1.7	4.5	1.7	5.32	28.0	-8
2005	*KCR*	*AL*	*32*	*27*	*18*	*115.3*	*139*	*29*	*58*	*19*	*5.37*	*5.06*	*10.7*	*2.0*	*4.1*	*1.4*	*4.95*	*10.2*	*-7*

Breakout: 16% *Improve: 41%* *Collapse: 22%*

One NL GM says that "Lima will always be able to succeed, under the right circumstances." Well, if you define those circumstances as "in a tremendous pitcher's park," "in front of a great defense," and "with a 40 mph headwind," then yes, he can succeed. Signed with the Royals, who should now assume their fifth-starter slot will be a rough patch all year long.

MIKE MEGREW **Bats: L** **Throws: L** Born: 29-Jan-1984 Age: 21

YEAR	TM	LG	AGE	G	GS	IP	H	BB	SO	HR	ERA	EQERA	EQH9	EQBB9	EQSO9	EQHR9	PERA	VORP	STF
2003	OGD	PIO	19	14	14	76.7	64	24	99	6	3.40	6.13	9.1	4.3	6.1	1.8	5.22	2.9	7
2004	VRO	FSL	20	22	22	105.7	84	43	125	7	3.41	4.93	8.7	4.3	7.4	1.2	4.84	8.2	21
2005	*LAD*	*NL*	*21*	*13*	*11*	*69.0*	*60*	*35*	*60*	*12*	*4.74*	*5.23*	*8.1*	*4.1*	*7.0*	*1.5*	*5.13*	*4.4*	*6*

Breakout: 14% *Improve: 37%* *Collapse: 25%*

Lefty, obviously pitched pretty well at Vero Beach. Gotta like the peripherals, gotta like the left-handedness, which at the very least improves his perceived value should he need to be traded. He'll start the season at Double-A, which is kind of the testing ground for prospects. If his K rate stays north of one per inning, you've probably got your garden-variety top prospect.

GREG MILLER

Bats: L **Throws: L** Born: 03-Nov-1984 Age: 20

YEAR	TM	LG	AGE	G	GS	IP	H	BB	SO	HR	ERA	EQERA	EQH9	EQBB9	EQSO9	EQHR9	PERA	VORP	STF
2002	GRF	PIO	17	11	7	38.0	27	13	37	1	2.37	5.24	8.1	4.2	4.7	0.5	4.19	5.4	12
2003	JAX	SOU	18	4	4	26.7	15	7	40	1	1.01	2.92	6.6	2.6	9.9	0.7	2.55	8.4	66
2003	VRO	FSL	18	21	21	115.7	103	41	111	5	2.49	4.49	9.4	3.7	6.2	0.9	4.99	7.2	30
2005	*LAD*	*NL*	*20*	*9*	*9*	*57.3*	*53*	*26*	*45*	*7*	*4.19*	*4.63*	*8.5*	*3.5*	*6.3*	*1.0*	*4.58*	*6.8*	*10*

Breakout: 13% *Improve: 41%* *Collapse: 20%*

Miller's season was completely scratched because of shoulder surgery in March. The surgery was fairly unusual for a ballplayer, because it didn't involve either the rotator cuff or the labrum, but rather the removal of a bursa sac. He was expected to pitch last year, but the rehab process stalled. Miller had electric stuff before the surgery, and if he can avoid the degradation that comes with labrum and cuff problems, he could be back to the top of prospect lists by year's end.

BRAD PENNY

Bats: R **Throws: R** Born: 24-May-1978 Age: 27

YEAR	TM	LG	AGE	G	GS	IP	H	BB	SO	HR	ERA	EQERA	EQH9	EQBB9	EQSO9	EQHR9	PERA	VORP	STF
2002	FLA	NL	24	24	24	129.3	148	50	93	18	4.66	5.46	9.9	3.0	5.7	1.3	4.96	3.1	2
2003	FLA	NL	25	32	32	196.3	195	56	138	21	4.13	4.50	8.9	2.3	5.8	0.9	3.93	28.3	13
2004	FLA	NL	26	21	21	131.3	124	39	105	10	3.15	3.55	8.5	2.4	6.5	0.6	3.69	34.1	22
2004	LAD	NL	26	3	3	11.7	6	6	6	2	3.08	4.35	7.0	4.4	4.4	1.7	4.35	2.5	-9
2005	*LAD*	*NL*	*27*	*24*	*21*	*128.3*	*127*	*42*	*97*	*16*	*4.14*	*4.57*	*9.1*	*2.6*	*6.0*	*1.1*	*4.55*	*15.4*	*9*

Breakout: 18% *Improve: 43%* *Collapse: 21%*

Viewed by most as the centerpiece to last year's Marlins deadline deal, Penny briefly silenced Dodger fans who'd mourned over Paul Lo Duca's departure and lamented not getting Randy Johnson, spinning eight shutout innings and yielding just two infield hits in his first L.A. start. "I think it's safe to say Brad Penny walked in here and lived up to his billing," manager Jim Tracy beamed after the outing. The very next start, Penny suffered a biceps injury, knocking him out for six weeks. He returned against the Padres in late September, only to re-injure his pitching arm. Long suspected of having a serious injury—the Phantom MRI debacle when it looked like Penny might get dealt to the Reds a while back still lingers—Penny's being counted on to produce 200 innings of #2 quality starter stuff in 2005. He's talented enough to thrive if healthy, but that's a big if. The Dodgers' pitching staff remains questionable even after Odalis Perez's re-signing; Hee Seop Choi will prove to be the gem of last year's trade.

ODALIS PEREZ

Bats: L **Throws: L** Born: 11-Jun-1977 Age: 28

YEAR	TM	LG	AGE	G	GS	IP	H	BB	SO	HR	ERA	EQERA	EQH9	EQBB9	EQSO9	EQHR9	PERA	VORP	STF
2002	LAD	NL	25	32	32	222.3	182	38	155	21	3.00	3.45	8.5	1.4	5.8	0.9	3.71	59.9	18
2003	LAD	NL	26	30	30	185.3	191	46	141	28	4.52	4.86	9.5	2.0	6.3	1.4	4.76	19.3	10
2004	LAD	NL	27	31	31	196.3	180	44	128	26	3.26	3.61	9.0	1.9	5.5	1.2	4.39	49.7	9
2005	*LAD*	*NL*	*28*	*28*	*27*	*166.7*	*169*	*41*	*112*	*20*	*3.89*	*4.29*	*9.4*	*1.9*	*5.4*	*1.0*	*4.28*	*24.9*	*10*

Breakout: 13% *Improve: 45%* *Collapse: 21%*

A very good pitcher with tremendous control. His 3.26 ERA was dampened somewhat by Dodger Stadium, and his PERA was higher still. Still, Perez is durable, and he's been healthy, effective and fairly inexpensive. One of those things changed, as Perez re-signed for three years, at $24 million. Given the horrid contracts signed elsewhere and how little talent was left by the time the Dodgers re-upped him, it's a reasonable deal price for an arm they desperately needed.

JULIO PIMENTEL

Bats: R **Throws: R** Born: 14-Dec-1985 Age: 19

YEAR	TM	LG	AGE	G	GS	IP	H	BB	SO	HR	ERA	EQERA	EQH9	EQBB9	EQSO9	EQHR9	PERA	VORP	STF
2004	CGA	SAL	18	23	23	111.3	106	47	102	14	3.48	5.47	10.0	4.5	5.2	1.8	6.00	-4.5	12
2005	*LAD*	*NL*	*19*	*9*	*8*	*46.7*	*47*	*22*	*34*	*7*	*4.96*	*5.47*	*9.3*	*3.8*	*5.7*	*1.4*	*5.54*	*1.4*	*-1*

Breakout: 14% *Improve: 44%* *Collapse: 20%*

Pitched pretty well for Columbus, with a K rate of nearly one per inning, good control and good results. He'll move up the ladder this year, and if he can sustain the K rate (which few can), he could start showing up on prospect lists by the end of next summer. Not blessed with a single amazing pitch; Pimentel will have to work his entire repertoire to be successful, so there may be hiccups along the way.

DUANER SANCHEZ | Bats: R | Throws: R | Born: 14-Oct-1979 | Age: 25

YEAR	TM	LG	AGE	G	GS	IP	H	BB	SO	HR	ERA	EQERA	EQH9	EQBB9	EQSO9	EQHR9	PERA	VORP	STF
2002	ELP	TXS	22	31	0	35.7	31	13	37	1	3.03	4.50	7.9	3.4	7.1	0.5	3.71	7.1	5
2002	NAS	PCL	22	20	0	22.7	23	11	20	2	4.76	5.40	9.1	4.6	6.2	0.8	4.98	1.5	-7
2003	NAS	PCL	23	41	1	61.0	63	27	34	3	3.69	4.99	9.4	4.5	4.4	0.6	4.68	5.9	-15
2004	LAD	NL	24	67	0	80.0	81	27	44	9	3.38	3.91	9.6	2.7	4.5	0.9	4.86	16.7	-11
2005	*LAD*	*NL*	*25*	*32*	*7*	*72.0*	*72*	*26*	*46*	*8*	*4.10*	*4.52*	*9.2*	*2.9*	*5.1*	*1.0*	*4.71*	*9.0*	*-7*

Breakout: 26% *Improve: 51%* *Collapse: 18%*

Yeah, the 3.38 ERA is kind of shiny, but you don't want your relievers giving up that many hits or home runs. With a K rate in that area, but a home-run rate likely to come down a bit, expect a modest climb for his ERA.

CHUCK TIFFANY | Bats: L | Throws: L | Born: 25-Jan-1985 | Age: 20

YEAR	TM	LG	AGE	G	GS	IP	H	BB	SO	HR	ERA	EQERA	EQH9	EQBB9	EQSO9	EQHR9	PERA	VORP	STF
2004	CGA	SAL	19	22	22	99.7	76	40	141	11	3.70	4.86	8.8	4.3	8.0	1.6	5.06	5.4	24
2005	*LAD*	*NL*	*20*	*13*	*10*	*64.7*	*51*	*31*	*62*	*9*	*4.07*	*4.49*	*7.3*	*3.8*	*7.7*	*1.2*	*4.46*	*9.1*	*13*

Breakout: 14% *Improve: 50%* *Collapse: 13%*

Statheads, begin your drooling. Tiffany was one of two "first-round arms," along with Billingsley, that the Dodgers picked up in the 2003 draft. He pitched well his first time in pro ball in Columbus, allowing only 76 hits in 100 innings, while striking out 141. He's going to be watched carefully for both his performance and his health. Fifteen starts from now, there could be an enormous prospect buzz around him. If he gets past the injury nexus, he's going to be a good one.

MIKE VENAFRO | Bats: L | Throws: L | Born: 02-Aug-1973 | Age: 31

YEAR	TM	LG	AGE	G	GS	IP	H	BB	SO	HR	ERA	EQERA	EQH9	EQBB9	EQSO9	EQHR9	PERA	VORP	STF
2002	OAK	AL	28	47	0	37.0	45	14	16	5	4.62	5.00	10.5	3.2	3.8	1.0	5.75	2.6	-25
2003	NWO	PCL	29	23	0	28.0	35	5	11	0	3.54	4.33	10.7	1.7	3.0	0.3	5.00	1.8	-21
2003	TBY	AL	29	24	0	19.0	24	3	9	1	4.74	4.34	10.6	1.4	4.3	0.5	4.82	2.9	-14
2004	OMA	PCL	30	35	0	57.7	70	19	41	8	4.37	4.95	10.1	3.0	5.0	1.4	5.43	1.1	-15
2004	LAD	NL	30	17	0	9.0	11	3	6	1	4.00	5.00	10.0	3.0	5.0	1.0	5.00	0.7	-9
2005	*LAD*	*NL*	*31*	*12*	*2*	*22.3*	*23*	*7*	*14*	*2*	*4.15*	*4.58*	*9.8*	*2.6*	*5.0*	*0.9*	*4.82*	*2.3*	*-8*

Breakout: 22% *Improve: 45%* *Collapse: 17%*

Junkballing lefty, indistinguishable from hundreds of others. Keeps his job as a lefty specialist from year to year by doing what he's supposed to, retiring lefty hitters and neutralizing the running game when needed. He's still got a few years of bouncing around to do; for guys in his niche, the Holy Grail is the Buddy Groom Contract.

JEFF WEAVER | Bats: R | Throws: R | Born: 22-Aug-1976 | Age: 28

YEAR	TM	LG	AGE	G	GS	IP	H	BB	SO	HR	ERA	EQERA	EQH9	EQBB9	EQSO9	EQHR9	PERA	VORP	STF
2002	DET	AL	25	17	17	121.7	112	33	75	4	3.18	3.58	8.1	2.3	5.3	0.3	2.90	30.9	21
2002	NYY	AL	25	15	8	78.0	81	15	57	12	4.04	4.26	9.0	1.7	6.4	1.3	3.91	13.8	13
2003	NYY	AL	26	32	24	159.3	211	47	93	16	5.99	6.02	10.1	2.5	5.0	0.8	4.52	-5.3	3
2004	LAD	NL	27	34	34	220.0	219	67	153	19	4.01	4.31	9.2	2.5	5.7	0.7	4.40	37.9	13
2005	*LAD*	*NL*	*28*	*29*	*29*	*178.0*	*181*	*49*	*124*	*19*	*4.07*	*4.49*	*9.4*	*2.2*	*5.6*	*0.9*	*4.46*	*21.7*	*10*

Breakout: 11% *Improve: 52%* *Collapse: 12%*

One of the least popular pitchers ever to call Yankee Stadium his home moved to Chavez Ravine and was pretty much rotation filler. An ERA of 4.00 while playing half your games in Dodger Stadium is nothing to write home about, but most clubs could use someone to just take the ball every fifth day and give the club a good chance to win, especially one with as many question marks as the Dodgers. They'll need more of the same—or slightly better—as he enters the final year of his contract in 2005.

Milwaukee Brewers

We've been writing the *Baseball Prospectus* annual for a long time now—this is our 10th year in print—so we end up repeating ourselves now and then. We don't mean to do it most of the time; it's just that, when it comes to organizations that seem to have stood in place over the entire period, it's tough to invent fresh, new descriptions for old problems. Repeating "There's no such thing as a pitching prospect" and "It's a bad move to overpay for replacement-level talent" can only take you so far before you begin to sound like a Chatty Cathy doll.

Other than moving to the National League, no team in baseball has changed less than the Brewers in the last decade. It might as well be 1995 for fans in Milwaukee; that year, they won 65 games, last year 67. The on-field problems this organization is dealing with today are more or less the same problems they've been dealing with since Bill Clinton was in his first term and the Crash Test Dummies were at the top of the charts.

The reason *why* the Brewers are experiencing a real-life Groundhog Day is a bit more interesting. What could cause a team to stagnate in the way Milwaukee has over the past decade? Sure, they've gone through periods of increased optimism, where the farm system seemed ready to bear fruit, and the front office had locked up homegrown talent for the foreseeable future. But by and large, this has been an organization that no reasonable person could have pegged for a winning record in any given year of the last ten. So what has kept them running in place for so long?

The first reason the Brew Crew hasn't come close to legitimately competing is that they've lacked direction—the blame for that falls on the front office, which hasn't been able to decide if it would rather compete today or compete tomorrow. Because of this lack of decisiveness, the organization has achieved nothing either way. And that's a huge problem in and of itself: The concept of a "success cycle" appears to be about as foreign to the Brewers as your uncle's mail-order bride, and it's reflected in every move the team has made, and almost as importantly, every move the team hasn't made.

At best, the current front office regime has conducted a shell game at the major league level, shaking up the roster by turning to a collection of journeymen whose chief recommendation was that they weren't the same old collection of Brewers. It wasn't all to the good that they elevated the essentially cosmetic changes of 2003 into a symbol of progress. Guys like Scott Podsednik, Wes Helms, and Brady Clark might be good enough to play in the major leagues, but they're not building blocks. That was amply demonstrated in 2004, when the offense collapsed, in no small part because of the limitations of such players.

BREWERS PROSPECTUS

2004 record: 67–94; Sixth place, NL Central

Pythagenport record: 67–95

Runs scored per game: 3.94 (14th in NL)

Runs allowed per game: 4.70 (10th in NL)

Team EqA: .248 (14th in NL)

2004 Batters Age: 29.0 (4th youngest in NL)

2004 Pitchers Age: 27.8 (3rd youngest in NL)

Ballpark: Miller Park; Neutral park; Park Factor of 1.002

2004: Stayed in contention through early July before fading, while the farm system continued to provide hope.

2005: Ownership change is a good sign, and so are the team's winter moves, but they'll struggle to finish in the top half of the division.

General Manager Doug Melvin continued to take similar little steps, making transitional deals like the one that sent Richie Sexson's contract to Arizona for a handful of useful parts. Lyle Overbay and Junior Spivey are useful for the time being, and Chris Capuano could turn out nicely. Happily, Melvin also has been willing to take flyers on free talent like Russ Branyan and Doug Davis. He's then had the good sense to make improvements, not getting too comfortable with the guys he's retreaded, played, and then talked up. Parlaying Dan Kolb's fluky first half for a live arm like Jose Capellan from the Braves could end up looking like a stroke of genius. Flipping Podsednik's much-lauded hustle to the White Sox to get a peak-age season or two from Carlos Lee is a major upgrade in an offense that needed the help, while also potentially giving the Brewers a slugger who could bring them serious goodies if they deal him at the deadline. Granted, what Milwaukee needs if it is to contend is a complete overhaul, but this is at least movement in the right direction.

Beyond the nuts and bolts of player personnel decisions, the real issue behind the Brewers' persistent track record of failure over the past decade is more closely related to basic economic concerns. Among the most obvious of these issues is the significant reduction in operating costs that the front office imposed at the end of 2003, leading into 2004, which eventually resulted in the trade of Sexson and a 31% reduction in Opening Day payroll. At the time, management claimed that these cuts were needed to "create an economic structure so that the Brewers have the financial resources to consistently field competitive teams, which will maximize attendance and the economic benefits to the city, county and state." But can the Milwaukee front office—a business that was run by the Selig family for six years after Bud was named commissioner—be trusted?

According to some calculations done by the late and sorely missed Doug Pappas, this appears not to be the case. Based on projections derived from MLB's 2001 financial disclosures, the Brewers were still low-balling their budget in late 2003, setting themselves up for as much as $25 million in profit per season (represented by the unexplained gap between the franchise's stated budget for 2004, 2005, 2006, and conservative revenue estimates, which include revenue-sharing incurrence). Since when is an extra $25 million in the pocket not the "financial resources to consistently field a competitive team"? Answer: When it's all lip service from a team that hasn't truly cared about winning in a decade.

Forgive us if we're being a bit cynical. Maybe the Brewers *have* cut operating costs because they're a failing business after all. (It's not like we can ever know for sure, given the fact that MLB refuses to open its books to the public.) It wouldn't be terribly surprising, given the inherent constraints the franchise encounters by making its home in Milwaukee.

That's because there's an argument to be made that Milwaukee is too small a market to support a professional sports franchise that doesn't have the benefit of industry-wide revenue sharing. According to market research conducted by Mike Jones during the last labor conflict, Milwaukee—not former contraction candidate Minnesota, not Tampa Bay, not barren Montreal—is the second-smallest market in all of baseball, and the smallest in the National League. In creating something he called Market Score, based on publicly available Nielsen TV ratings, Jones scored Milwaukee just barely above the smallest market in baseball, Kansas City, only slightly ahead of minor league markets like Nashville and Salt Lake City, and *below* markets like Birmingham, Norfolk, New Orleans, and Greensboro/Winston-Salem/High Point.

Competent and dedicated management could overcome all of this to put a winner on the field, even in the industry as it's structured today. But no matter how you slice it, the less money you have to work with, the fewer mistakes you're allowed to make and the tougher the climb to the top of the standings. Instead of trying to let management of their on-field product solve their problems, however, the Brewers placed these economic issues front and center, figuring that Miller Park would prove to be the formulaic antidote to waning attendance and revenue that Bud Selig prescribes for any struggling team. Needless to say, the Stadium Myth is one that has largely been debunked by evidence. But in the interest of further examination, let's look at a recent group of teams (including the Brewers) to enter a new stadium with a losing record, and how that place of business has affected attendance, influenced payroll, and done absolutely nothing for on-field success (see table 1).

Make no mistake, whether we look at the before or after periods, these are bad ballclubs. There's not a single winning season in the 19 under examination, and the teams' aggregate winning percentage in this chart is .418, equivalent to a 68–94 record (or rather, 19 different 68–94 seasons).

Averaging the seasons together, we begin to see some trends emerge. Entertaining delusions of grandeur, these teams boosted their payroll by a whopping 54% upon moving to a new park. Attendance shot up almost as dramatically (40%). But in that new stadium, the teams were roughly three games worse overall. The second year in the

TABLE 1. UNDER-.500 TEAMS, BEFORE AND AFTER GETTING A NEW STADIUM

Team	Old	New 1	New 2	New 3	New 4	New 5
Detroit	1999	2000	2001	2002	2003	2004
Payroll	$35.0	$61.7	$49.4	$55.0	$49.2	$46.8
Attendance	2.03	2.44	1.92	1.50	1.36	1.91
Win %	.426	.487	.407	.339	.266	.444
Milwaukee	2000	2001	2002	2003	2004	
Payroll	$35.8	$45.1	$50.3	$40.6	$27.5	
Attendance	1.57	2.81	1.97	1.70	2.06	
Win %	.451	.420	.346	.407	.416	
Pittsburgh	2000	2001	2002	2003	2004	
Payroll	$29.6	$57.8	$42.3	$54.8	$32.2	
Attendance	1.75	2.46	1.78	1.64	1.58	
Win %	.426	.383	.444	.463	.444	
Cincinnati	2002	2003	2004			
Payroll	$45.1	$59.4	$46.6			
Attendance	1.86	2.36	2.28			
Win %	.481	.426	.469			

NOTE: Payroll and Attendance figures in millions, "Old" is the last year in the old stadium, "New" is the season in the new park.

new park, we see payrolls reduced by 16%, reduced success on the field by four full games, and a 25% drop in attendance after the novelty's worn off. In year three, payroll increased ever so slightly, but the on-field product stagnated, and attendance sagged another 15%. As Rob Neyer wrote in his *Big Book of Baseball Lineups,* "People will come to the ballpark for two things, and two things only: free stuff, and baseball. Winning baseball." Granted, it's a small sample, but these recent cases lend some notable credence to that theory. A loser in a pretty, publicly-funded park is still a loser. The Brewers are learning this first-hand.

All that being said, the pertinent question seems to be: Where does the franchise go from here?

The NL Central is a tough piece of turf, with a number of teams drawing well and spending the requisite cash to contend. With the Brewers' budget sitting where it is, it's doubtful that the franchise will be able to compete in the pen and pocketbook department any time in the foreseeable future. The current commitment to player development makes sense, but the organization must continue drafting well, and perhaps lean more toward a scouty bias than is normally advocated by the performance-analysis crowd. If they're going to go that route, however, they need to do it right. A consistent, organization-wide approach like the kind practiced by the Braves and Twins could do wonders toward building a winning club.

Admittedly, the immediate payoffs and overall return on investment might not be as high with the selection of high school players or signing foreign kids, but what the Brewers need is to continue to develop high-impact individual players. First baseman Prince Fielder, second baseman Rickie Weeks, and shortstop J. J. Hardy already form a decent group with some upside. Certainly, they represent a better collection of talent than the team can afford shopping on the free-agent market. Playing in Milwaukee requires that they develop more top-tier players to add to that little group of prospects over the next three seasons. Keep in mind, within the division, the Astros, Cardinals, and Reds have pretty miserable farm systems, and the Pirates might be in even worse shape than the Brewers because, whatever they might have in terms of depth in their organization, they're not as fortunate as the Brewers when it comes to blue-chip talent in their system. The second half of the decade is Milwaukee's window of opportunity.

Above all else, the Brewers need to see their performance on the field and in the front office within the context of a long-term plan. In a general sense, they need some goals. Whether those goals are "Win 85 games in a season by 2008," or "Develop two starting pitchers who will be major league ready by 2007," or more easily achieved benchmarks than those, it's up to them. But what is important is that they stop acting like the decisions made in the front office are independent from the team's on-field success, and just as importantly, the number of fans paying to get into the ballpark. To borrow from David O. Russell's messy film, *I (Heart) Huckabees,* "It's all connected."

HITTERS

GARY BENNETT — **C** — **Bats: R** — **Throws: R** — Born: 17-Apr-1972 — Age: 33

YEAR	TM	LG	AGE	AB	H	2B	3B	HR	BB	SO	SB	CS	AVG	OBP	SLG	MLVR	EQBA	EQOBP	EQSLG	EQMLVR	VORP	DEFENSE
2002	COL	NL	30	291	77	10	2	4	15	45	1	3	.265	.314	.354	-.147	.252	.298	.341	-.232	2.0	79-C -2
2003	SDP	NL	31	307	73	15	0	2	24	48	3	0	.238	.296	.306	-.204	.251	.301	.318	-.259	-1.3	78-C -7
2004	MIL	NL	32	219	49	14	0	3	22	32	1	0	.224	.297	.329	-.190	.220	.289	.317	-.303	-0.3	58-C -2
2005	*WAS*	*NL*	*33*	*203*	*47*	*10*	*1*	*3*	*18*	*32*	*1*	*0*	*.232*	*.300*	*.326*	*-.245*	*.235*	*.301*	*.333*	*-.234*	*-1.4*	*57-C -3*

Breakout: 20% *Improve: 50%* *Collapse: 35%*

Bennett broke into the majors in 1995 with Philadelphia, and has since carried the torch for journeyman backup catchers everywhere. He has nine years of major league experience, and in that time, compiled a .247/.310/.335 line in 390 games. The Brewers gave him $600,000 in 2004 for the security of having a proven out-maker to back up their inexperienced out-making starter, Chad Moeller. He performed the task so well, Jim Bowden gave him a raise, so he'll make $750,000 for Washington in 2005 for, apparently, being a nice guy who doesn't mind sitting on the bench.

RUSS BRANYAN 1B/3B/OF **Bats: L** **Throws: R** Born: 19-Dec-1975 Age: 29

YEAR	TM	LG	AGE	AB	H	2B	3B	HR	BB	SO	SB	CS	AVG	OBP	SLG	MLVR	EQBA	EQOBP	EQSLG	EQMLVR	VORP	DEFENSE	
2002	CLE	AL	26	161	33	4	0	8	17	65	1	2	.205	.278	.379	-.200	.213	.281	.381	-.235	-3.8	35-LF -1	
2002	CIN	NL	26	217	53	9	1	16	34	86	3	1	.244	.349	.516	.136	.240	.344	.516	.085	14.7	20-LF -1	18-1B 0
2003	CIN	NL	27	176	38	12	0	9	27	69	0	0	.216	.322	.438	-.012	.216	.313	.438	-.095	6.0	20-3B 4	13-LF 0
2004	BUF	INT	28	313	90	16	2	25	42	102	5	2	.288	.374	.591	.334	.266	.352	.542	.158	23.0	33-1B 4	29-3B -1
2004	MIL	NL	28	158	37	11	1	11	20	68	1	0	.234	.324	.525	.127	.228	.317	.519	.031	10.8	44-3B -2	
2005	*MIL*	*NL*	*29*	*200*	*50*	*10*	*1*	*13*	*33*	*73*	*2*	*1*	*.252*	*.361*	*.502*	*.102*	*.252*	*.358*	*.502*	*.096*	*17.2*	*59-3B -4*	

Breakout: 37% *Improve: 65%* *Collapse: 24%*

All hail the Three True Outcomes™. Branyan stepped to the big league plate 182 times in 2004. In 99 of those plate appearances (54%), the men wearing gloves were irrelevant, as Branyan walked to first, struck out, or launched a souvenir over the outfield wall. In the past 30 years, only Mark McGwire, Jack Clark, and Rob Deer have posted higher TTO percentages in a season with at least 182 plate appearances. As is usually the case with TTO players, Branyan produced a solid season despite a miserable .224 average. In a perfect world, he would go to spring training as the favorite for the third base job, but Milwaukee is nobody's idea of paradise.

BRADY CLARK OF **Bats: R** **Throws: R** Born: 18-Apr-1973 Age: 32

YEAR	TM	LG	AGE	AB	H	2B	3B	HR	BB	SO	SB	CS	AVG	OBP	SLG	MLVR	EQBA	EQOBP	EQSLG	EQMLVR	VORP	DEFENSE	
2002	LOU	INT	29	109	33	7	0	1	3	9	0	2	.303	.328	.394	.012	.269	.286	.352	-.228	-5.2	22-LF 0	
2002	CIN	NL	29	66	10	3	0	0	6	9	1	2	.152	.233	.197	-.520	.164	.213	.194	-.653	-7.5		
2003	MIL	NL	30	315	86	21	1	6	21	40	13	2	.273	.330	.403	-.019	.272	.324	.405	-.077	9.1	56-RF -3	16-LF -1
2004	MIL	NL	31	353	99	18	1	7	53	48	15	8	.280	.385	.397	.094	.280	.382	.395	.023	22.0	93-RF 0	
2005	*MIL*	*NL*	*32*	*279*	*71*	*14*	*1*	*5*	*28*	*37*	*7*	*3*	*.256*	*.331*	*.366*	*-.122*	*.255*	*.329*	*.365*	*-.128*	*1.5*	*77-RF 0*	

Breakout: 11% *Improve: 31%* *Collapse: 48%*

After spending the prime of his career in the minors rather than helping a major league team as a versatile bench player, Clark is finally getting his opportunity to show that he was a quality player several years ago. Now heading into his Age-32 season, his skills have diminished a bit, but he's still somewhat useful, especially at the plate. His .280/.385/.397 line received little notice, but is a valuable performance for any club. He plays all three outfield positions, though is primarily a right fielder. With the trade of Scott Podsednik, Clark will head to spring training competing for the first everyday job of his career, though playing him in center field regularly might be a stretch.

CRAIG COUNSELL SS/2B **Bats: L** **Throws: R** Born: 21-Aug-1970 Age: 34

YEAR	TM	LG	AGE	AB	H	2B	3B	HR	BB	SO	SB	CS	AVG	OBP	SLG	MLVR	EQBA	EQOBP	EQSLG	EQMLVR	VORP	DEFENSE	
2002	ARI	NL	31	436	123	22	1	2	45	52	7	5	.282	.348	.351	-.056	.278	.343	.346	-.120	12.0	94-3B 11	16-SS -1
2003	ARI	NL	32	303	71	6	3	3	41	32	11	4	.234	.328	.304	-.199	.225	.319	.295	-.269	-0.2	49-3B 5	21-SS -1
2004	MIL	NL	33	473	114	19	5	2	59	88	17	4	.241	.330	.315	-.150	.238	.325	.312	-.227	8.7	122-SS 13	
2005	*ARI*	*NL*	*34*	*274*	*68*	*11*	*2*	*3*	*31*	*42*	*7*	*3*	*.249*	*.328*	*.337*	*-.167*	*.245*	*.322*	*.331*	*-.192*	*2.9*	*76-SS 2*	

Breakout: 21% *Improve: 42%* *Collapse: 33%*

Counsell has managed to carve out quite a career for himself as the White Hustling Utility Fan Favorite despite an underwhelming set of skills. Part of the package the Brewers received in the Richie Sexson trade, his performance defensively at shortstop was one of the biggest surprises of the 2004 season. After only playing 117 games at short in the previous eight seasons, he spent 129 on the left side of the bag and was, by most accounts and Clay Davenport's fielding rankings, terrific with the glove. It isn't often that a player can hit .241/.330/.315 and still be a productive player, but Counsell managed to pull it off. He returns to Arizona for 2005 with a spiffy new two-year contract in hand.

CALLIX CRABBE 2B **Bats: B** **Throws: R** Born: 14-Feb-1983 Age: 22

YEAR	TM	LG	AGE	AB	H	2B	3B	HR	BB	SO	SB	CS	AVG	OBP	SLG	MLVR	EQBA	EQOBP	EQSLG	EQMLVR	VORP	DEFENSE
2002	OGD	PIO	19	250	82	16	4	4	29	34	22	9	.328	.407	.472	.234	.245	.297	.355	-.219	-6.2	63-2B -6
2003	BLT	MDW	20	465	121	25	6	1	68	52	25	9	.260	.356	.346	.030	.225	.303	.314	-.276	-15.6	112-2B -7
2004	HDS	CLF	21	540	157	26	11	7	59	64	37	11	.291	.366	.419	-.015	.218	.283	.315	-.318	-23.4	132-2B -19
2005	*MIL*	*NL*	*22*	*342*	*80*	*17*	*2*	*3*	*31*	*47*	*9*	*3*	*.233*	*.301*	*.323*	*-.246*	*.233*	*.299*	*.323*	*-.252*	*-4.4*	*92-2B -11*

Breakout: 17% *Improve: 43%* *Collapse: 33%*

(continued next page)

Callix Crabbe *(continued)*

Crabbe is a moderately intriguing prospect beyond the entertaining name. Generously listed at 5′8″ and 190 pounds: If Luis Castillo shrunk in the wash, you'd have a nice approximation of Crabbe's physique and style. He managed to hit seven home runs at High Desert, which is something like hitting none at sea level. Since he handles the bat well and knows the strike zone, he has a chance to succeed despite non-existent power. And, thanks to the indispensable Brewer Fan.net, one of the best team-specific references on the web, we also know that he strides to the plate to the tunes of Sean Paul's "Like Glue."

ENRIQUE CRUZ **SS/3B** **Bats: R** **Throws: R** Born: 21-Nov-1981 Age: 23

YEAR	TM	LG	AGE	AB	H	2B	3B	HR	BB	SO	SB	CS	AVG	OBP	SLG	MLVR	EQBA	EQOBP	EQSLG	EQMLVR	VORP	DEFENSE
2002	SLU	FSL	20	467	136	21	2	6	32	76	33	16	.291	.336	.383	.066	.261	.299	.355	-.204	-3.3	103-3B -1 21-SS -4
2003	MIL	NL	21	71	6	1	0	0	4	30	0	0	.085	.145	.099	-.835	.085	.126	.085	-1.005	-11.1	
2004	HUN	SOU	22	101	19	3	1	2	14	37	2	1	.188	.284	.297	-.235	.175	.259	.282	-.433	-7.8	29-SS -3
2004	HDS	CLF	22	360	102	19	0	17	36	82	12	7	.283	.347	.478	.029	.206	.262	.349	-.320	-12.7	94-SS -11
2005	*MIL*	*NL*	*23*	*248*	*55*	*11*	*1*	*5*	*20*	*68*	*4*	*1*	*.221*	*.281*	*.337*	*-.271*	*.221*	*.279*	*.337*	*-.277*	*-5.7*	*67-SS -8*

Breakout: 53% *Improve: 66%* *Collapse: 22%*

Taken with the first pick in the 2002 Rule 5 Draft, Cruz hasn't turned into the player the Brewers hoped they were getting. The offensive potential he flashed in the Mets organization didn't make the move north with him. After spending 2003 on the Brewers bench, he flailed at Double-A and found himself demoted back to A-ball. Defensively, he's best at third base, though a move to second isn't out of the question. However, if he doesn't rediscover his stroke soon, his best major league position will be spectator.

MATT ERICKSON **3B/2B** **Bats: L** **Throws: R** Born: 30-Jul-1975 Age: 29

YEAR	TM	LG	AGE	AB	H	2B	3B	HR	BB	SO	SB	CS	AVG	OBP	SLG	MLVR	EQBA	EQOBP	EQSLG	EQMLVR	VORP	DEFENSE
2002	CLG	PCL	26	379	109	30	2	1	31	63	15	4	.288	.359	.385	-.064	.244	.310	.327	-.233	-6.9	57-2B 0 29-3B 2
2003	ABQ	PCL	27	298	102	22	4	2	43	42	14	9	.342	.442	.463	.206	.278	.374	.385	-.007	16.2	41-3B 1 31-2B -6
2004	IND	INT	28	400	108	27	1	2	45	69	12	10	.270	.359	.357	-.060	.244	.329	.322	-.202	-3.4	63-2B -7 33-3B 2
2005	*MIL*	*NL*	*29*	*107*	*28*	*6*	*1*	*1*	*11*	*19*	*2*	*1*	*.258*	*.343*	*.359*	*-.108*	*.258*	*.341*	*.359*	*-.113*	*4.0*	*33-2B -5*

Breakout: 28% *Improve: 40%* *Collapse: 39%*

An infielder in the David Eckstein mold, his window for getting a shot in the majors is closing. Milwaukee signed him as a minor league free agent after a monster 2003 season in the Pacific Coast League, but the power didn't carry over. He lacks the physical tools to catch anyone's eye, but has become a good enough fielder that he deserves a look as some team's backup. If the hometown Brewers won't give him that shot, however, it's unlikely he'll ever see any real time in the majors.

PRINCE FIELDER **1B** **Bats: L** **Throws: R** Born: 09-May-1984 Age: 21

YEAR	TM	LG	AGE	AB	H	2B	3B	HR	BB	SO	SB	CS	AVG	OBP	SLG	MLVR	EQBA	EQOBP	EQSLG	EQMLVR	VORP	DEFENSE
2002	BLT	MDW	18	112	27	7	0	3	10	27	0	0	.241	.320	.384	.003	.193	.245	.325	-.394	-10.9	30-1B -6
2002	OGD	PIO	18	146	57	12	0	10	37	27	3	4	.390	.531	.678	.733	.273	.373	.455	.082	15.5	35-1B -5
2003	BLT	MDW	19	502	157	22	2	27	71	80	2	1	.313	.409	.526	.358	.258	.336	.450	-.003	13.2	125-1B -14
2004	HUN	SOU	20	497	135	29	1	23	65	93	11	7	.272	.366	.473	.173	.244	.329	.431	-.054	4.9	132-1B -11
2005	*MIL*	*NL*	*21*	*347*	*93*	*20*	*2*	*16*	*42*	*67*	*4*	*1*	*.268*	*.357*	*.470*	*.067*	*.268*	*.355*	*.469*	*.061*	*18.9*	*96-1B -9*

Breakout: 36% *Improve: 53%* *Collapse: 22%*

After terrorizing Midwest League pitching in 2003, the organization pushed him up to Double-A Huntsville, an aggressive challenge for the 20-year-old. He held his own, a fine performance for a player with his limited experience, even if he wasn't the monster he's been at lower levels. Prince's power is still prodigious, and his knowledge of the strike zone should make him an offensive force for years to come. While still not svelte, Fielder has improved his agility and is a competent first baseman. With a ticket to Triple-A for 2005, he'll be putting pressure on Overbay for the foreseeable future.

KEITH GINTER 2B/3B Bats: R Throws: R Born: 05-May-1976 Age: 29

YEAR	TM	LG	AGE	AB	H	2B	3B	HR	BB	SO	SB	CS	AVG	OBP	SLG	MLVR	EQBA	EQOBP	EQSLG	EQMLVR	VORP	DEFENSE
2002	NWO	PCL	26	435	115	28	1	12	56	97	3	4	.264	.362	.416	.121	.259	.349	.402	-.045	17.6	56-2B -2 53-3B -1
2002	MIL	NL	26	76	18	8	0	1	15	14	0	0	.237	.363	.382	.015	.250	.354	.368	-.087	3.9	20-3B -3
2003	MIL	NL	27	358	92	15	2	14	37	87	1	1	.257	.352	.427	.044	.256	.346	.433	-.010	21.0	47-2B -2 30-3B -4
2004	MIL	NL	28	386	101	23	2	19	37	100	8	1	.262	.333	.479	.101	.256	.327	.468	.004	27.7	50-2B -8 40-3B -1
2005	*OAK*	*AL*	*29*	*389*	*101*	*21*	*1*	*16*	*42*	*93*	*5*	*2*	*.260*	*.341*	*.442*	*.005*	*.262*	*.346*	*.450*	*.016*	*19.6*	*106-2B -8*

Breakout: 22% *Improve: 52%* *Collapse: 14%*

While not a Three True Outcomes hero like Branyan, Ginter has taken a bad rap for his inability to make consistent contact with the ball. His high strikeout totals and mediocre defense have caused both the Astros and now the Brewers to overlook the fact that Ginter is a productive player. Power is his best asset, but he gets on base adequately and isn't a disaster in the field. Sensing an opportunity to find another Mark Bellhorn, Billy Beane acquired Ginter from the Brewers, and will give him a shot at the A's second base job.

ANTHONY GWYNN CF Bats: L Throws: R Born: 04-Oct-1982 Age: 22

YEAR	TM	LG	AGE	AB	H	2B	3B	HR	BB	SO	SB	CS	AVG	OBP	SLG	MLVR	EQBA	EQOBP	EQSLG	EQMLVR	VORP	DEFENSE
2003	BLT	MDW	20	236	66	8	0	1	32	31	14	2	.280	.364	.326	.026	.219	.288	.256	-.389	-18.8	61-CF 0
2004	HUN	SOU	21	534	130	20	5	2	53	95	35	16	.243	.318	.311	-.132	.227	.293	.292	-.325	-30.8	134-CF -11
2005	*MIL*	*NL*	*22*	*328*	*74*	*13*	*2*	*2*	*28*	*57*	*13*	*4*	*.226*	*.291*	*.296*	*-.304*	*.226*	*.289*	*.296*	*-.310*	*-13.2*	*88-CF -5*

Breakout: 22% *Improve: 54%* *Collapse: 24%*

Ozzie Canseco. Craig Griffey. Mike Glavine. Matt Boone. Jim Campanis. Pete Rose Jr. In that vein, Anthony Gwynn continues the lineage of players who were given a shot because they were related to someone who was pretty good. While Gwynn Sr. made an All-Star career out of slapping singles, Junior doesn't have the same knack. There isn't enough life in his bat to carry him to the Show, but he'll continue to get chances because of the letters on the back of his jersey.

BILL HALL 2B/SS Bats: R Throws: R Born: 28-Dec-1979 Age: 25

YEAR	TM	LG	AGE	AB	H	2B	3B	HR	BB	SO	SB	CS	AVG	OBP	SLG	MLVR	EQBA	EQOBP	EQSLG	EQMLVR	VORP	DEFENSE
2002	IND	INT	22	465	106	20	1	4	25	105	17	10	.228	.272	.301	-.261	.203	.252	.275	-.444	-33.6	125-SS -19
2003	IND	INT	23	354	100	25	2	5	27	79	10	11	.282	.335	.407	.030	.260	.319	.387	-.121	5.9	51-2B -3 36-SS -3
2003	MIL	NL	23	142	37	9	2	5	7	28	1	2	.261	.298	.458	-.019	.257	.293	.465	-.060	5.3	18-SS 0 18-2B -2
2004	MIL	NL	24	390	93	20	3	9	20	119	12	6	.238	.276	.374	-.158	.236	.273	.374	-.244	2.5	47-2B -8 37-SS 4
2005	*MIL*	*NL*	*25*	*326*	*82*	*16*	*2*	*8*	*22*	*79*	*9*	*4*	*.251*	*.301*	*.389*	*-.148*	*.251*	*.299*	*.389*	*-.154*	*6.5*	*86-2B -2*

Breakout: 30% *Improve: 57%* *Collapse: 21%*

Formerly the shortstop of the future, Hall's offense hasn't really progressed over the last three seasons. He makes highlight reel plays defensively and has a military grade weapon for a right arm, but it is hard to look past the fact that he cannot hit major league pitching. It's likely he'll keep his job as the backup at short until J. J. Hardy pushes him off of the roster.

J. J. HARDY SS Bats: R Throws: R Born: 19-Aug-1982 Age: 22

YEAR	TM	LG	AGE	AB	H	2B	3B	HR	BB	SO	SB	CS	AVG	OBP	SLG	MLVR	EQBA	EQOBP	EQSLG	EQMLVR	VORP	DEFENSE
2002	HDS	CLF	19	335	98	19	1	6	19	38	9	3	.293	.327	.409	-.039	.224	.253	.315	-.375	-16.7	80-SS 11
2002	HUN	SOU	19	145	33	7	0	1	9	19	1	2	.228	.269	.297	-.213	.203	.224	.270	-.508	-13.6	37-SS 1
2003	HUN	SOU	20	416	116	26	0	12	58	54	6	4	.279	.368	.428	.152	.254	.329	.409	-.076	17.3	106-SS 10
2004	IND	INT	21	101	28	10	0	4	9	8	0	0	.277	.330	.495	.080	.232	.279	.424	-.165	1.2	23-SS 2
2005	*MIL*	*NL*	*22*	*323*	*87*	*19*	*1*	*11*	*29*	*34*	*2*	*1*	*.268*	*.328*	*.437*	*-.022*	*.268*	*.326*	*.437*	*-.029*	*19.3*	*87-SS -2*

Breakout: 39% *Improve: 53%* *Collapse: 21%*

Hardy's career has been one of ups and down. After some mediocre performances in the lower minors, he broke out with a terrific season in 2003, but a torn labrum interrupted his season in 2004. He performed well after his return, however, and the Brewers remain enamored with his defense. Now healthy, he is going to camp with the big club in March, and even if he does not win the starting job in spring training, the organization is expecting him to force his way onto the roster in the early going. If his bat continues to progress and he gets the normal power spike as he ages, Hardy could be a perennial contender for the Brewers token All-Star slot.

COREY HART — OF — Bats: R — Throws: R — Born: 24-Mar-1982 — Age: 23

YEAR	TM	LG	AGE	AB	H	2B	3B	HR	BB	SO	SB	CS	AVG	OBP	SLG	MLVR	EQBA	EQOBP	EQSLG	EQMLVR	VORP	DEFENSE
2002	HDS	CLF	20	393	113	26	10	22	37	101	24	11	.288	.356	.573	.214	.219	.275	.428	-.177	0.4	47-3B -9 43-1B -1
2002	HUN	SOU	20	94	25	3	0	2	7	16	3	2	.266	.340	.362	.009	.229	.269	.312	-.344	-4.8	19-3B -2
2003	HUN	SOU	21	493	149	40	1	13	28	101	25	8	.302	.340	.467	.185	.275	.308	.450	-.039	21.3	114-3B -11
2004	IND	INT	22	440	124	29	8	15	42	92	17	7	.282	.344	.486	.095	.253	.318	.438	-.057	1.1	90-RF -5
2005	*MIL*	*NL*	*23*	*331*	*86*	*19*	*2*	*11*	*26*	*74*	*10*	*3*	*.260*	*.318*	*.435*	*-.049*	*.260*	*.317*	*.435*	*-.055*	*6.3*	*88-RF -6*

Breakout: 24%   Improve: 48%   Collapse: 30%

If scouts could create an athlete from scratch, Specimen A might look strikingly similar to Hart. A lean 6′6″, he runs extremely well for his size and has tools to spare. Light-tower power? Check. Cannon Arm? Check. Speed on the bases? Check. Knowledge of the strike zone? Him, not so much. Hart's aggressive approach at the plate makes him a relatively easy out, and his long swing leaves him susceptible to pitches on the inner half of the plate. After experiments at first and third base, he's settled into right field. The acquisition of Carlos Lee makes it likely he'll be patrolling the grass in Nashville for most of 2004.

WES HELMS — 3B/1B — Bats: R — Throws: R — Born: 12-May-1976 — Age: 29

YEAR	TM	LG	AGE	AB	H	2B	3B	HR	BB	SO	SB	CS	AVG	OBP	SLG	MLVR	EQBA	EQOBP	EQSLG	EQMLVR	VORP	DEFENSE
2002	ATL	NL	26	210	51	16	0	6	11	57	1	1	.243	.283	.405	-.097	.251	.279	.412	-.167	0.9	32-1B -2 14-3B -2
2003	MIL	NL	27	476	124	21	0	23	43	131	0	1	.261	.330	.450	.040	.261	.324	.452	-.020	26.9	130-3B -14
2004	MIL	NL	28	274	72	13	1	4	24	60	0	1	.263	.331	.361	-.064	.259	.328	.354	-.151	3.4	59-3B -8
2005	*MIL*	*NL*	*29*	*253*	*65*	*14*	*1*	*9*	*21*	*62*	*0*	*0*	*.256*	*.322*	*.422*	*-.063*	*.256*	*.320*	*.422*	*-.069*	*6.0*	*69-3B -6*

Breakout: 21%   Improve: 43%   Collapse: 24%

The least interesting of several options at third base, he nonetheless has become the favorite of Ned Yost. What he lacks in actual production, he makes up for with personality, so Mr. Congeniality was given 274 at-bats when he was healthy enough to play in 2004. With a few underappreciated players as his main competition, expect Helms to continue to provide heaps of near-adequacy.

HERNAN IRIBARREN — 2B — Bats: L — Throws: R — Born: 29-Jun-1984 — Age: 21

YEAR	TM	LG	AGE	AB	H	2B	3B	HR	BB	SO	SB	CS	AVG	OBP	SLG	MLVR	EQBA	EQOBP	EQSLG	EQMLVR	VORP	DEFENSE
2004	BLT	MDW	20	67	25	6	5	1	5	16	1	0	.373	.411	.657	.580	.328	.362	.567	.280	9.5	14-2B 1

If it weren't for Callix Crabbe, he'd have the best name in the organization. With a name that conjures up images of conquering warlords, Iribarren isn't the intimidating presence you might expect, but he had few problems claiming the Arizona League as his personal kingdom. Complex Leagues have been known to create prospects out of suspects thanks to a low level of competition, but Iribarren is better than the Chris Tritle types. He has solid skills across the board and superior bat control, making him a perfect fit at the top of a batting order. The Brewers will promote him aggressively, and if all goes well, he could finish the season in Double-A. By far the best hitting prospect in the lower levels of the system.

GEOFF JENKINS — RF — Bats: L — Throws: R — Born: 21-Jul-1974 — Age: 30

YEAR	TM	LG	AGE	AB	H	2B	3B	HR	BB	SO	SB	CS	AVG	OBP	SLG	MLVR	EQBA	EQOBP	EQSLG	EQMLVR	VORP	DEFENSE
2002	MIL	NL	27	243	59	17	1	10	22	60	1	2	.243	.320	.444	.038	.246	.320	.455	-.035	7.0	63-LF 5
2003	MIL	NL	28	487	144	30	2	28	58	120	0	0	.296	.375	.538	.257	.294	.372	.538	.215	42.6	122-LF -2
2004	MIL	NL	29	617	163	36	6	27	46	152	3	1	.264	.325	.473	.083	.259	.318	.467	-.011	26.1	152-LF -1
2005	*MIL*	*NL*	*30*	*480*	*128*	*27*	*3*	*23*	*47*	*117*	*2*	*1*	*.267*	*.341*	*.480*	*.055*	*.267*	*.339*	*.480*	*.048*	*16.2*	*127-LF -2*

Breakout: 19%   Improve: 55%   Collapse: 21%

His 2003 resurgence brought hope that he was returning to his previous levels of success, but 2004 was a disappointment. The notoriously injury-prone outfielder set a career high with 157 games played, but in this case, quantity did not equal quality. He still possesses the serious power that got him to the majors, but as a player who struggles to make contact and doesn't walk, he reaches first base about as often as Bill Gates did in high school. Thanks to the generous contract extension he received last March, Jenkins is now a very expensive average player who will consistently be mentioned in trade rumors for the next 18 months. To accommodate Carlos Lee, he'll move to right field.

MARK JOHNSON C Bats: L Throws: R Born: 12-Sep-1975 Age: 29

YEAR	TM	LG	AGE	AB	H	2B	3B	HR	BB	SO	SB	CS	AVG	OBP	SLG	MLVR	EQBA	EQOBP	EQSLG	EQMLVR	VORP	DEFENSE
2002	CWS	AL	26	263	55	8	1	4	30	52	0	0	.209	.297	.293	-.286	.211	.303	.295	-.309	-4.4	79-C 7
2003	OAK	AL	27	27	3	1	0	0	3	4	0	0	.111	.219	.148	-.656	.111	.162	.111	-.888	-3.5	
2003	SAC	PCL	27	162	37	11	1	3	35	23	0	1	.228	.369	.364	-.007	.207	.339	.329	-.194	-1.1	49-C -6
2004	IND	INT	28	281	72	18	0	5	43	44	3	2	.256	.355	.374	-.055	.227	.323	.327	-.217	-4.0	64-C -8
2005	*MIL*	*NL*	*29*	*148*	*35*	*7*	*1*	*3*	*22*	*26*	*1*	*0*	*.234*	*.333*	*.353*	*-.147*	*.234*	*.331*	*.353*	*-.153*	*3.5*	*45-C -7*

Breakout: 38% *Improve: 53%* *Collapse: 28%*

There's no question that we are big fans of plate discipline and players that can draw walks. However, there's more to offensive production than convincing yourself to keep the bat on your shoulder, and Johnson simply lacks the requisite skills to actually hit a baseball. His .217 career batting average isn't a fluke; if you throw him strikes, you can get him out. Re-signed to a minor league deal, Johnson should head to Nashville and play Crash Davis for the pitching staff.

DAVID KRYNZEL CF Bats: L Throws: L Born: 07-Nov-1981 Age: 23

YEAR	TM	LG	AGE	AB	H	2B	3B	HR	BB	SO	SB	CS	AVG	OBP	SLG	MLVR	EQBA	EQOBP	EQSLG	EQMLVR	VORP	DEFENSE
2002	HDS	CLF	20	365	98	13	12	11	64	100	29	17	.268	.391	.460	.107	.208	.308	.347	-.231	-9.8	93-CF 0
2002	HUN	SOU	20	129	31	2	3	2	4	30	13	5	.240	.269	.349	-.134	.223	.238	.354	-.349	-7.8	30-CF -2
2003	HUN	SOU	21	457	122	13	11	2	60	119	43	21	.267	.357	.357	.037	.248	.327	.345	-.172	-3.7	115-CF 2
2004	IND	INT	22	258	70	10	4	6	20	63	10	8	.271	.327	.411	-.044	.244	.300	.368	-.195	-3.8	62-CF 0
2004	MIL	NL	22	41	9	1	0	0	3	15	0	0	.220	.319	.244	-.255	.244	.274	.268	-.389	-1.4	
2005	*MIL*	*NL*	*23*	*285*	*69*	*13*	*3*	*5*	*26*	*73*	*9*	*4*	*.244*	*.316*	*.367*	*-.154*	*.243*	*.314*	*.367*	*-.160*	*0.1*	*78-CF -2*

Breakout: 20% *Improve: 42%* *Collapse: 27%*

If we're going to call J. J. Hardy's career up-and-down, there might not be words to describe the inconsistency Dave Krynzel has had. Projected as a Johnny Damon type when selected in the first round of the 2000 draft, Krynzel has managed to hit for average, run up his walk totals, hit for power, and show speed, if not efficiency, on the bases. Unfortunately, he's never come close to doing all of these things at the same time. Despite the questions still surrounding his productivity at the plate, most agree that his range in center field will cover a multitude of offensive sins. He covers a lot of ground, and could find himself in Milwaukee sooner rather than later as a flycatcher. The trade of Scott Podsednik opens the door for Krynzel to at least finish the 2005 season in Milwaukee, though he likely will break camp with Triple-A Nashville.

CHRIS MAGRUDER OF Bats: B Throws: R Born: 26-Apr-1977 Age: 28

YEAR	TM	LG	AGE	AB	H	2B	3B	HR	BB	SO	SB	CS	AVG	OBP	SLG	MLVR	EQBA	EQOBP	EQSLG	EQMLVR	VORP	DEFENSE	
2002	BUF	INT	25	191	51	10	2	5	26	34	3	2	.267	.364	.419	.090	.254	.349	.409	-.039	6.5	23-CF 0	13-RF 1
2002	CLE	AL	25	258	56	15	1	6	15	55	2	0	.217	.261	.353	-.264	.223	.271	.359	-.278	-9.0	34-LF -2	19-RF -1
2003	BUF	INT	26	137	45	7	2	3	15	27	5	1	.328	.391	.474	.272	.314	.382	.467	.152	12.9	14-CF 0	12-RF 0
2004	IND	INT	27	305	83	17	4	6	21	55	7	4	.272	.337	.413	-.023	.251	.313	.383	-.145	-8.3	68-LF -1	
2004	MIL	NL	27	89	21	6	1	2	8	21	0	1	.236	.310	.393	-.082	.225	.304	.382	-.181	0.6		
2005	*MIL*	*NL*	*28*	*193*	*50*	*11*	*2*	*5*	*16*	*41*	*3*	*1*	*.258*	*.325*	*.417*	*-.064*	*.257*	*.323*	*.417*	*-.070*	*5.1*	*54-LF -1*	

Breakout: 19% *Improve: 34%* *Collapse: 35%*

The well-traveled Magruder fits the mold of a fifth outfielder; can play center field capably though is best suited for a corner, has enough punch to play sparingly, is an above average runner, and gets along well with his coaches. Though not a huge asset, he's capable of playing a role if used properly and contributing to a team. The Brewers ran out of room for him, however, and designated him for assignment to create space on the 40-man-roster.

CHAD MOELLER C Bats: R Throws: R Born: 18-Feb-1975 Age: 30

YEAR	TM	LG	AGE	AB	H	2B	3B	HR	BB	SO	SB	CS	AVG	OBP	SLG	MLVR	EQBA	EQOBP	EQSLG	EQMLVR	VORP	DEFENSE
2002	TUC	PCL	27	211	67	8	2	10	29	46	1	0	.318	.401	.517	.213	.271	.352	.440	.023	13.0	59-C 1
2002	ARI	NL	27	105	30	11	1	2	17	23	0	1	.286	.385	.467	.159	.276	.377	.457	.095	9.4	35-C -1
2003	ARI	NL	28	239	64	17	1	7	23	59	1	2	.268	.335	.435	-.001	.256	.326	.424	-.059	10.1	64-C -3
2004	MIL	NL	29	317	66	13	1	5	21	74	0	1	.208	.265	.303	-.303	.209	.264	.303	-.378	-10.7	100-C 1
2005	*MIL*	*NL*	*30*	*265*	*64*	*13*	*1*	*7*	*24*	*61*	*1*	*1*	*.243*	*.311*	*.381*	*-.146*	*.242*	*.309*	*.381*	*-.152*	*4.0*	*73-C 1*

Breakout: 31% *Improve: 55%* *Collapse: 21%*

(continued next page)

Chad Moeller *(continued)*

Moeller was statistically the worst regular catcher in the National League in 2004, with an ugly −10.7 VORP. He hit significantly better as a backup in Arizona, but was overexposed as an everyday player. The signing of Damian Miller to a three-year contract insures that the Brewers won't be challenging him with 349 at-bats again anytime soon.

BRAD NELSON LF/1B **Bats: L** **Throws: R** Born: 23-Dec-1982 Age: 22

YEAR	TM	LG	AGE	AB	H	2B	3B	HR	BB	SO	SB	CS	AVG	OBP	SLG	MLVR	EQBA	EQOBP	EQSLG	EQMLVR	VORP	DEFENSE
2002	BLT	MDW	19	417	124	38	2	17	34	86	4	1	.297	.353	.520	.262	.238	.283	.425	-.152	-8.9	103-1B -13
2002	HDS	CLF	19	102	26	11	0	3	12	28	0	0	.255	.333	.451	-.001	.208	.261	.366	-.297	-6.7	26-1B 0
2003	HDS	CLF	20	167	52	9	1	1	12	22	2	2	.311	.363	.395	-.011	.241	.287	.309	-.306	-11.1	30-1B -1
2003	HUN	SOU	20	143	30	12	0	1	11	34	2	2	.210	.274	.315	-.180	.193	.238	.297	-.447	-17.5	25-LF -2
2004	HUN	SOU	21	500	127	31	1	19	47	146	11	10	.254	.321	.434	.040	.228	.289	.397	-.187	-21.4	103-LF -5 28-RF 0
2005	*MIL*	*NL*	*22*	*363*	*88*	*21*	*1*	*13*	*29*	*93*	*5*	*2*	*.242*	*.303*	*.413*	*-.119*	*.242*	*.301*	*.413*	*-.125*	*-2.1*	*96-LF -8*

Breakout: 49% *Improve: 66%* *Collapse: 14%*

After a solid 2002 at Beloit, Nelson appeared to be one of the better power-hitting prospects in the game, but his progress has stagnated the past two seasons after a hamate injury. His pitch recognition is not where it needs to be, and he won't hit for enough of an average to be a star without also walking. If we're being kind, we can call his defense a work-in-progress, but we'll admit it's pretty lousy if pressed. There's still some potential here, but it's untapped at the moment, and he's closer to being next in the long line of what-could-have-beens than he is to Miller Park.

LYLE OVERBAY 1B **Bats: L** **Throws: L** Born: 28-Jan-1977 Age: 28

YEAR	TM	LG	AGE	AB	H	2B	3B	HR	BB	SO	SB	CS	AVG	OBP	SLG	MLVR	EQBA	EQOBP	EQSLG	EQMLVR	VORP	DEFENSE
2002	TUC	PCL	25	525	180	40	0	19	42	86	0	0	.343	.396	.528	.245	.284	.336	.441	.006	14.1	123-1B 4
2003	ARI	NL	26	254	70	20	0	4	35	67	1	0	.276	.365	.402	.016	.270	.353	.385	-.052	8.7	71-1B 8
2003	TUC	PCL	26	119	34	11	0	4	28	19	0	0	.286	.419	.479	.167	.224	.347	.371	-.114	-1.2	33-1B 1
2004	MIL	NL	27	579	174	53	1	16	81	128	2	1	.301	.385	.478	.222	.295	.379	.470	.133	53.5	152-1B 12
2005	*MIL*	*NL*	*28*	*467*	*126*	*28*	*2*	*17*	*62*	*100*	*1*	*1*	*.269*	*.356*	*.442*	*.031*	*.268*	*.354*	*.442*	*.025*	*18.9*	*126-1B 5*

Breakout: 10% *Improve: 38%* *Collapse: 24%*

Arizona fell in love with Richie Sexson's power and was willing to give up Overbay and the Seven Dwarves in order to acquire him last winter. While Sexson's shoulder gave out and Arizona got little for its trouble, Milwaukee saw Overbay blossom into an All-Star hitter in the first half before cooling off down the stretch. Despite hitting for average throughout the minors, his home run totals had never been up to the levels expected from a first baseman, so his power spike was a bit unexpected. His development was one of the pleasant surprises of 2004, although Overbay may not have won himself any job security despite his breakthrough. With Prince Fielder on his heels, he's going to have to keep hitting to keep his job, so he may end up moving to another club in the not-too-distant future.

LOU PALMISANO C **Bats: R** **Throws: R** Born: 16-Sep-1982 Age: 22

YEAR	TM	LG	AGE	AB	H	2B	3B	HR	BB	SO	SB	CS	AVG	OBP	SLG	MLVR	EQBA	EQOBP	EQSLG	EQMLVR	VORP	DEFENSE
2003	HEL	PIO	20	174	68	13	2	6	18	29	13	2	.391	.458	.592	.632	.308	.359	.453	.086	25.1	37-C 1
2004	BLT	MDW	21	409	120	22	3	7	43	93	3	2	.293	.371	.413	.127	.246	.309	.352	-.199	-3.4	82-C -4
2005	*MIL*	*NL*	*22*	*279*	*68*	*14*	*2*	*6*	*23*	*69*	*3*	*1*	*.243*	*.317*	*.370*	*-.149*	*.242*	*.315*	*.370*	*-.155*	*7.6*	*76-C -9*

Breakout: 15% *Improve: 29%* *Collapse: 53%*

A third round pick in the 2002 draft, Palmisano made a nice splash in his debut and earned raves for his abilities with the bat in his hands. However, a troubling 2004 season has lowered his stock. He was suspended for 20 games for using a banned substance, though he is adamant that he did not realize it was outlawed. On the field, he didn't perform as hoped, and his defense, never a strong suit, continued to raise concerns. Palmisano will be looking to rebound in 2005 and reclaim his role as catcher of the future. Of officials polled, however, most expect him to spend most of his major league service time at first base, which hampers his prospects.

SCOTT PODSEDNIK CF Bats: L Throws: L Born: 18-Mar-1976 Age: 29

YEAR	TM	LG	AGE	AB	H	2B	3B	HR	BB	SO	SB	CS	AVG	OBP	SLG	MLVR	EQBA	EQOBP	EQSLG	EQMLVR	VORP	DEFENSE
2002	TAC	PCL	26	438	122	25	6	9	43	70	35	13	.279	.347	.425	.073	.269	.333	.405	-.063	11.8	91-CF -7 30-LF -2
2003	MIL	NL	27	558	175	29	8	9	56	91	43	10	.314	.379	.443	.140	.310	.376	.444	.105	48.0	119-CF -1 13-RF 0
2004	MIL	NL	28	640	156	27	7	12	58	105	70	13	.244	.313	.364	-.106	.240	.309	.358	-.195	19.3	151-CF -6
2005	*CWS*	*AL*	*29*	*564*	*157*	*29*	*6*	*13*	*50*	*90*	*41*	*13*	*.278*	*.342*	*.416*	*-.013*	*.275*	*.341*	*.409*	*-.035*	*17.7*	*147-CF -4*

Breakout: 10% *Improve: 37%* *Collapse: 23%*

Podzilla's 2003 season was so far out of line with his career performances that one could only expect a serious collapse in 2004. After a hot start, that crash materialized and Podsednik went from the toast of Milwaukee to being shipped off to Chicago in the Carlos Lee trade. His calling card is his speed, and he did steal 70 bases while getting caught only 13 times. However, he lacks power, and doesn't reach base often enough to justify a regular spot in the lineup, especially since his defense is erratic at best. Despite his speed, he takes poor routes to the ball and has reactions that would make Starr Jones look swift. If utilized properly, he could be a nice bench player, but as the White Sox starting left-fielder, he's going to do quite well in helping Minnesota win another AL Central crown.

JUNIOR SPIVEY 2B Bats: R Throws: R Born: 28-Jan-1975 Age: 30

YEAR	TM	LG	AGE	AB	H	2B	3B	HR	BB	SO	SB	CS	AVG	OBP	SLG	MLVR	EQBA	EQOBP	EQSLG	EQMLVR	VORP	DEFENSE
2002	ARI	NL	27	538	162	34	6	16	65	100	11	6	.301	.389	.476	.192	.292	.378	.473	.133	54.6	139-2B 2
2003	ARI	NL	28	365	93	22	2	13	33	95	4	3	.255	.326	.433	-.026	.245	.315	.424	-.088	13.5	89-2B -3
2004	MIL	NL	29	228	62	13	0	7	25	48	5	3	.272	.359	.421	.068	.275	.351	.415	-.011	15.1	58-2B -3
2005	*MIL*	*NL*	*30*	*342*	*90*	*20*	*2*	*11*	*35*	*72*	*5*	*2*	*.264*	*.343*	*.432*	*-.008*	*.264*	*.341*	*.432*	*-.014*	*20.0*	*93-2B -1*

Breakout: 16% *Improve: 48%* *Collapse: 24%*

Yes, another player from the Sexson haul. Spivey's 2002 season with Arizona has earned him several years of job stability, though his recent performances don't merit the financial windfall he's going to get as an arbitration-eligible player. His skillset makes him a nice fit as a useful role player, but he's miscast as an everyday second baseman. However, the trade of Keith Ginter nearly guarantees that he'll be keeping second base warm until Rickie Weeks is ready.

RICKIE WEEKS 2B Bats: R Throws: R Born: 13-Sep-1982 Age: 22

YEAR	TM	LG	AGE	AB	H	2B	3B	HR	BB	SO	SB	CS	AVG	OBP	SLG	MLVR	EQBA	EQOBP	EQSLG	EQMLVR	VORP	DEFENSE
2003	BLT	MDW	20	63	22	8	1	1	15	9	2	0	.349	.494	.556	.520	.294	.409	.471	.186	8.1	17-2B -2
2004	HUN	SOU	21	479	124	35	6	8	55	107	11	12	.259	.366	.407	.081	.242	.332	.386	-.111	10.2	128-2B -15
2005	*MIL*	*NL*	*22*	*280*	*72*	*18*	*3*	*7*	*30*	*63*	*5*	*2*	*.256*	*.356*	*.409*	*-.020*	*.255*	*.354*	*.409*	*-.026*	*20.7*	*80-2B -8*

Breakout: 25% *Improve: 46%* *Collapse: 27%*

The second pick in the 2002 draft, Weeks is the object of lofty expectations. His performance at Double-A in his first full season of professional baseball was solid, particularly the 55 walks and 49 extra base hits, but it was well short of the dominance that was expected of him. Viewing him as a disappointment this early is rash, however. His season highlights the improvements he must make, particularly with the glove, but the Brewers remain optimistic. While he may not be ready for the Show as quickly as imagined, there are still few better prospects in the game at the position. Weeks could be challenging for the second base job in Milwaukee by 2006.

PITCHERS

MIKE ADAMS Bats: R Throws: R Born: 29-Jul-1978 Age: 26

YEAR	TM	LG	AGE	G	GS	IP	H	BB	SO	HR	ERA	EQERA	EQH9	EQBB9	EQSO9	EQHR9	PERA	VORP	STF
2002	BLT	MDW	23	11	0	15.3	13	2	21	1	2.94	5.02	8.8	1.3	7.5	1.9	4.40	1.9	7
2002	HDS	CLF	23	10	0	14.0	9	7	23	2	2.57	4.26	8.5	5.0	9.2	2.1	5.68	-0.1	1
2002	HUN	SOU	23	13	0	18.7	14	12	17	3	3.37	5.94	9.2	5.9	6.5	2.7	6.48	-1.6	-19
2003	HUN	SOU	24	45	2	74.3	58	33	83	6	3.15	4.63	8.7	4.2	7.4	1.5	5.16	3.3	-1
2004	IND	INT	25	10	2	31.0	23	4	37	3	2.61	3.07	7.1	1.2	8.9	0.9	2.76	9.2	34
2004	MIL	NL	25	46	0	53.0	50	14	39	5	3.40	3.53	8.5	2.1	6.0	0.7	3.53	12.6	6
2005	*MIL*	*NL*	*26*	*30*	*7*	*70.3*	*66*	*24*	*57*	*10*	*4.11*	*4.26*	*8.5*	*2.7*	*6.6*	*1.2*	*4.29*	*11.6*	*3*

Breakout: 20% *Improve: 41%* *Collapse: 29%*

(continued next page)

Mike Adams *(continued)*

After he spent a significant portion of his college career playing basketball at Texas A&M-Kingville, the Brewers signed him as an undrafted free agent in 2001. Since then, Adams has used a 90–93 MPH fastball and a sharp-breaking slider to move through the system with few problems, before becoming one of Milwaukee's better relievers during the second half of 2004. After the trades of Dan Kolb and Luis Vizcaino, Adams is penciled in as the Brewers closer for 2005. His minor league track record backs up his stuff, and Adams has a chance to be a very good reliever.

JEFF BENNETT **Bats: R** **Throws: R** Born: 10-Jun-1980 Age: 25

YEAR	TM	LG	AGE	G	GS	IP	H	BB	SO	HR	ERA	EQERA	EQH9	EQBB9	EQSO9	EQHR9	PERA	VORP	STF
2002	LYN	CRL	22	24	20	124.3	137	30	90	7	3.62	5.86	10.3	2.6	4.6	1.1	5.40	2.6	-2
2003	ALT	EAS	23	33	2	59.7	45	23	62	2	2.71	4.20	7.6	3.9	7.8	0.5	3.72	11.6	11
2003	NAS	PCL	23	9	5	23.3	26	12	16	4	6.57	8.72	10.8	5.4	5.4	2.1	7.06	-3.5	-23
2004	MIL	NL	24	60	0	71.3	78	26	45	12	4.80	5.06	9.6	3.0	5.1	1.4	4.80	2.2	-13
2005	*MIL*	*NL*	*25*	*30*	*8*	*75.7*	*80*	*28*	*56*	*11*	*4.82*	*5.00*	*9.6*	*2.9*	*6.0*	*1.2*	*4.92*	*6.6*	*-2*

Breakout: 18% *Improve: 49%* *Collapse: 25%*

Bennett pitched well enough in 2004 to justify the Rule 5 pick that the Brewers made to acquire him from Pittsburgh, but probably not well enough to guarantee himself a spot on the 2005 staff. He still lacks a true out pitch, having just an average fastball and a mediocre slider, but his command is better than most pitchers his age. He has enough usefulness to stick around as a cheap middle reliever, but there isn't a compelling reason to keep him once he reaches arbitration eligibility.

CHRIS CAPUANO **Bats: L** **Throws: L** Born: 19-Aug-1978 Age: 26

YEAR	TM	LG	AGE	G	GS	IP	H	BB	SO	HR	ERA	EQERA	EQH9	EQBB9	EQSO9	EQHR9	PERA	VORP	STF
2002	TUC	PCL	23	6	6	36.3	30	11	29	1	2.73	3.15	7.9	2.9	5.8	0.3	3.41	8.3	20
2003	TUC	PCL	24	23	23	142.7	133	43	108	9	3.34	4.18	8.4	3.1	5.8	0.8	3.78	27.4	21
2003	ARI	NL	24	9	5	33.0	27	11	23	3	4.64	4.60	8.0	2.6	5.7	0.9	3.45	1.8	18
2004	MIL	NL	25	17	17	88.3	91	37	80	18	4.99	5.23	9.2	3.3	7.3	1.7	4.92	1.6	4
2005	*MIL*	*NL*	*26*	*25*	*19*	*121.3*	*116*	*49*	*101*	*15*	*4.37*	*4.53*	*8.6*	*3.2*	*6.7*	*1.0*	*4.44*	*14.7*	*10*

Breakout: 23% *Improve: 53%* *Collapse: 21%*

Before Tommy John surgery in 2002, Capuano featured a low-90's fastball and struck out more than a batter per inning, making him a nifty little prospect for the Diamondbacks. After returning from surgery, his velocity and strikeout rates both dropped, and the Brewers got him in—surprise!—the Richie Sexson deal. Capuano showed some flashes during the season, and his K rate is encouraging. If his stuff ever gets back to where it was in 2001, there would be reason for even more optimism. Of course, one could say the same thing about Chan Ho Park and Joe Mays.

DOUG DAVIS **Bats: R** **Throws: L** Born: 21-Sep-1975 Age: 29

YEAR	TM	LG	AGE	G	GS	IP	H	BB	SO	HR	ERA	EQERA	EQH9	EQBB9	EQSO9	EQHR9	PERA	VORP	STF
2002	TEX	AL	26	10	10	59.7	67	22	28	7	4.97	4.78	9.6	3.1	4.0	0.9	4.78	3.7	-2
2002	OKL	PCL	26	9	9	61.3	70	11	48	7	4.99	5.88	9.7	1.7	5.4	1.4	4.22	9.2	8
2003	TOR	AL	27	12	11	54.0	70	26	25	6	5.00	4.97	10.3	4.0	4.0	0.8	5.30	3.5	-9
2003	MIL	NL	27	8	8	52.3	49	21	35	8	2.58	3.04	8.6	3.2	5.5	1.3	4.11	15.1	8
2004	MIL	NL	28	34	34	207.3	192	79	166	14	3.39	3.50	8.3	3.1	6.5	0.5	3.54	48.8	22
2005	*MIL*	*NL*	*29*	*26*	*26*	*152.0*	*158*	*56*	*111*	*18*	*4.35*	*4.52*	*9.3*	*2.9*	*5.9*	*1.0*	*4.62*	*18.6*	*10*

Breakout: 8% *Improve: 44%* *Collapse: 17%*

Measuring by VORP, Davis was the 19th best pitcher in baseball last year. In that sense, he was essentially the equal of Tim Hudson, Pedro Martinez, Mark Buehrle, or Roy Oswalt. Since being signed to a minor league contract in July 2003, Davis has thrown 259 innings for the Brewers with a 2.81 ERA. Not bad for a guy with average stuff who had plowed his way through two organizations that needed pitching. Regardless of whether Davis can continue to pitch well, he's the best free talent acquisition any team has made in the past two years.

JORGE DE LA ROSA Bats: L Throws: L Born: 05-Apr-1981 Age: 24

YEAR	TM	LG	AGE	G	GS	IP	H	BB	SO	HR	ERA	EQERA	EQH9	EQBB9	EQSO9	EQHR9	PERA	VORP	STF
2002	SAR	FSL	21	23	23	120.7	105	52	95	10	3.65	4.98	9.5	4.4	5.3	1.6	5.47	1.6	0
2002	TRN	EAS	21	4	4	18.0	17	9	15	0	5.50	6.23	8.3	4.7	5.7	0.0	3.12	4.8	8
2003	PME	EAS	22	22	20	99.7	87	36	102	6	2.80	4.02	8.3	3.5	7.6	1.0	4.12	15.5	17
2003	PAW	INT	22	5	5	24.0	27	12	17	0	3.75	5.87	9.4	5.1	5.1	0.4	5.09	1.3	-5
2004	IND	INT	23	20	20	85.7	80	36	86	9	4.52	4.59	8.3	3.9	7.4	1.0	4.15	13.3	17
2004	MIL	NL	23	5	5	22.7	29	14	5	1	6.34	7.25	10.5	4.8	1.6	0.4	5.24	-5.5	-21
2005	*MIL*	*NL*	*24*	*21*	*12*	*78.0*	*78*	*37*	*61*	*10*	*4.89*	*5.07*	*9.0*	*3.7*	*6.4*	*1.1*	*4.94*	*6.4*	*1*

Breakout: 15% *Improve: 43%* *Collapse: 31%*

He was once labeled the "Mexican John Rocker" by former Red Sox GM Dan Duquette, who had signed de la Rosa out of the Mexican League at age 19. He was one of the main pieces in the Curt Schilling and Richie Sexson trades. His bad boy persona has faded the past two seasons as he focused on getting his mid-90s fastball to the major leagues. He spent the majority of 2004 pitching at Triple-A, posting a solid strikeout rate but a mediocre ERA, thanks to inconsistent control and a propensity to give up the long ball. He managed to get a big league call-up, but the 14 walks and only five strikeouts wasn't the first impression he was hoping for. The Brewers still like his arm, and he'll be given a chance to win a spot in the bullpen during spring training.

DANA EVELAND Bats: L Throws: L Born: 29-Oct-1983 Age: 21

YEAR	TM	LG	AGE	G	GS	IP	H	BB	SO	HR	ERA	EQERA	EQH9	EQBB9	EQSO9	EQHR9	PERA	VORP	STF
2003	HEL	PIO	19	19	0	26.0	30	8	41	1	2.08	5.18	11.1	4.1	7.0	0.7	6.29	-1.9	3
2004	BLT	MDW	20	22	16	117.3	108	24	119	8	2.84	5.02	9.8	2.3	5.5	1.3	5.10	6.0	4
2004	HUN	SOU	20	4	4	23.7	23	4	14	0	2.28	4.03	8.9	1.6	3.6	0.0	3.22	5.9	13
2005	*MIL*	*NL*	*21*	*14*	*12*	*72.7*	*79*	*24*	*52*	*8*	*4.43*	*4.60*	*9.8*	*2.6*	*5.8*	*1.0*	*4.74*	*8.4*	*8*

Breakout: 9% *Improve: 42%* *Collapse: 16%*

After using the 469th overall pick in the 2002 draft to select Eveland, the Brewers signed him in 2003 as a draft-and-follow, and he's paid early dividends. He pounded the Midwest League with his "strikes only" mentality, posting a sparkling 24–119 walk-strikeout ratio in 117 innings. He continued throwing strikes in a late promotion to Double-A, and didn't let the two-level jump affect him. Eveland doesn't have a dominating pitch, but his command is well above average. Conditioning will have to become a more regular part of his routine, however, as he can be referred to, generously, as rotund.

BEN FORD Bats: R Throws: R Born: 15-Aug-1975 Age: 29

YEAR	TM	LG	AGE	G	GS	IP	H	BB	SO	HR	ERA	EQERA	EQH9	EQBB9	EQSO9	EQHR9	PERA	VORP	STF
2002	IOW	PCL	26	32	23	142.0	157	73	84	13	4.88	5.88	9.6	4.9	4.2	1.1	5.35	3.8	-11
2003	IND	INT	27	26	9	84.0	80	18	72	8	3.00	3.86	8.8	2.3	6.4	1.4	4.31	11.4	10
2004	IND	INT	28	32	1	42.7	53	21	36	2	4.85	5.06	9.5	4.4	5.9	0.4	4.85	3.6	-12
2004	MIL	NL	28	19	0	24.0	25	10	13	4	6.38	5.87	9.4	3.5	4.3	1.6	4.70	-1.8	-21
2005	*MIL*	*NL*	*29*	*20*	*4*	*40.7*	*42*	*19*	*29*	*5*	*4.62*	*4.80*	*9.2*	*3.6*	*5.8*	*1.0*	*5.03*	*4.6*	*-6*

Breakout: 33% *Improve: 59%* *Collapse: 21%*

At the end of the last century, Ford was a fairly significant prospect in the Yankees system, before injuries derailed his career. He's spent most of this century as a minor league free agent attempting to work his way back, and finally got himself to the majors after a four-year absence. He has become a sinkerball pitcher who succeeds by keeping the ball down in the zone. He did give up four taters in just 24 innings at the major league level, however, including number 661 to Barry Bonds. After not being re-signed as a minor league free agent, it is likely that his link to home run history will be the most memorable moment of his career.

BEN HENDRICKSON

Bats: R **Throws: R** Born: 04-Feb-1981 Age: 24

YEAR	TM	LG	AGE	G	GS	IP	H	BB	SO	HR	ERA	EQERA	EQH9	EQBB9	EQSO9	EQHR9	PERA	VORP	STF
2002	HDS	CLF	21	14	14	81.3	61	41	70	3	2.55	4.06	7.6	5.3	4.7	0.6	3.70	15.9	19
2002	HUN	SOU	21	13	13	69.7	57	35	50	2	2.97	4.96	8.1	4.4	4.8	0.4	3.86	12.6	15
2003	HUN	SOU	22	17	16	78.3	82	28	56	6	3.45	5.03	10.2	3.3	4.7	1.3	5.77	-1.4	-13
2004	IND	INT	23	21	21	125.0	114	26	93	6	2.02	2.48	8.0	2.0	5.5	0.5	3.08	33.5	34
2004	MIL	NL	23	10	9	46.3	58	20	29	6	6.22	6.07	10.4	3.3	4.9	1.0	5.28	-3.3	10
2005	*MIL*	*NL*	*24*	*19*	*19*	*109.3*	*114*	*42*	*76*	*12*	*4.47*	*4.63*	*9.4*	*3.0*	*5.6*	*0.9*	*4.62*	*12.8*	*7*

Breakout: 13% *Improve: 46%* *Collapse: 24%*

Hendrickson's potential has been a source of disagreement as he has climbed up the organizational ladder. His curveball was often lauded as one of the best in the minor leagues and his ERAs have been among the best in his league at nearly every stop, but he has never missed bats in the way that you might expect from a top prospect. With a low-90s fastball and a 12-to-6 curve that generates comparisons to Aaron Sele, he has a repertoire that should produce strikeouts, but his approach is to throw strikes regardless of the count. He's continued to hone his command to the point where it is now the strength of his game after being a question mark two years ago. His major league debut was rough, but he's going to go to spring training with a legitimate chance to break camp as the team's 4th or 5th starter.

JEFF HOUSMAN

Bats: L **Throws: L** Born: 04-Aug-1981 Age: 23

YEAR	TM	LG	AGE	G	GS	IP	H	BB	SO	HR	ERA	EQERA	EQH9	EQBB9	EQSO9	EQHR9	PERA	VORP	STF
2002	OGD	PIO	20	16	5	32.3	55	12	23	5	8.08	10.52	14.2	4.3	3.1	3.7	9.95	-15.3	-54
2003	BLT	MDW	21	20	15	89.3	79	26	50	5	1.81	5.67	9.4	3.3	3.4	1.4	4.89	6.4	-21
2003	HUN	SOU	21	8	8	46.3	49	17	26	4	3.30	5.02	10.5	3.3	3.8	1.5	6.07	-2.2	-8
2004	HUN	SOU	22	23	20	112.0	108	38	121	10	3.13	5.04	9.3	3.2	6.8	1.2	4.78	9.6	2
2004	IND	INT	22	5	3	18.7	31	13	13	3	7.70	6.98	12.1	6.1	4.7	1.4	7.45	-4.0	-27
2005	*MIL*	*NL*	*23*	*11*	*8*	*49.7*	*52*	*23*	*36*	*8*	*5.24*	*5.43*	*9.5*	*3.6*	*5.9*	*1.4*	*5.48*	*1.5*	*-1*

Breakout: 13% *Improve: 31%* *Collapse: 15%*

Here's an interesting career: a 33rd round pick on ability in 2002, he was torched in rookie ball after signing, but posted a 1.81 ERA for Beloit in 2003 and made a successful jump to Double-A Huntsville to end the season. Despite keeping runs off the board, his peripherals were, well, lousy, and his raw stuff has never gotten anyone excited. Sent back to Double-A for 2004, his K/9 jumped, but all his other numbers stayed virtually the same, including his ERA. Despite nearly doubling his strikeouts by improving the location on his changeup, he allowed hits, walks, and runs at the same rates as in previous years. His gaudy strikeout totals opened some eyes, however, and he'll now be given a second look that other pitchers with his modest stuff might not otherwise get. He'll head to Triple-A for 2005, but could be among the first in line for a call-up if Milwaukee needs an arm.

MIKE JONES

Bats: R **Throws: R** Born: 23-Apr-1983 Age: 22

YEAR	TM	LG	AGE	G	GS	IP	H	BB	SO	HR	ERA	EQERA	EQH9	EQBB9	EQSO9	EQHR9	PERA	VORP	STF
2002	BLT	MDW	19	27	27	138.7	135	62	132	3	3.11	5.72	8.9	5.0	5.2	0.5	4.27	19.3	15
2003	HUN	SOU	20	17	17	97.7	87	47	63	4	2.40	4.28	9.1	4.6	4.3	0.7	5.08	5.2	14
2004	HUN	SOU	21	6	6	23.7	22	13	16	0	4.18	6.04	8.9	5.2	4.4	0.4	4.43	2.9	-7
2005	*MIL*	*NL*	*22*	*17*	*12*	*75.0*	*80*	*43*	*47*	*11*	*5.43*	*5.63*	*9.6*	*4.5*	*5.1*	*1.2*	*5.78*	*0.3*	*-10*

Breakout: 6% *Improve: 38%* *Collapse: 29%*

Selected 12th overall in 2001, Jones has taken the path frequently traveled by high school pitching prospects. He showed strong promise in 2002, then struggled in 2003 and was finally diagnosed with an injury, in his case a torn labrum, in 2004. He had surgery in October and will miss the entire 2005 season. The Brewers will have to decide whether to use a 40-man roster spot on him next fall. Labrum surgery hasn't proven kind, and Jones may be simply the next in a long line of pitchers who couldn't survive the injury nexus.

BROOKS KIESCHNICK Bats: L Throws: R Born: 06-Jun-1972 Age: 33

YEAR	TM	LG	AGE	G	GS	IP	H	BB	SO	HR	ERA	EQERA	EQH9	EQBB9	EQSO9	EQHR9	PERA	VORP	STF
2002	CHR	INT	30	25	0	31.3	30	10	30	1	2.59	3.26	8.3	3.3	7.4	0.3	3.56	6.9	7
2003	IND	INT	31	8	0	13.7	17	10	14	3	8.54	9.69	11.1	7.6	7.6	3.5	9.00	-4.9	-28
2003	MIL	NL	31	42	0	53.0	66	13	39	5	5.26	5.23	9.8	1.9	5.9	0.8	4.22	1.1	0
2004	MIL	NL	32	32	0	43.0	44	13	28	6	3.77	3.92	9.1	2.4	5.2	1.1	4.14	8.2	-5
2005	*MIL*	*NL*	*33*	*30*	*2*	*47.7*	*52*	*17*	*32*	*6*	*4.66*	*4.84*	*9.8*	*2.7*	*5.4*	*1.0*	*4.89*	*4.4*	*-7*

Breakout: 16% *Improve: 37%* *Collapse: 32%*

And at the plate:

YEAR	TM	LG	AGE	AB	H	2B	3B	HR	BB	SO	SB	CS	AVG	OBP	SLG	MLVR	EQBA	EQOBP	EQSLG	EQMLVR	VORP	DEFENSE
2002	CHR	INT	30	189	52	11	0	13	14	46	0	0	.275	.320	.540	.188	.250	.294	.495	-.022	6.0	
2003	MIL	NL	31	70	21	1	0	7	6	13	0	0	.300	.355	.614	.338	.314	.346	.614	.307	11.5	
2004	MIL	NL	32	63	17	3	0	1	5	16	0	0	.270	.324	.365	-.059	.270	.301	.349	-.203	4.9	
2005	*MIL*	*NL*	*33*	*64*	*15*	*3*	*0*	*3*	*7*	*16*	*0*	*0*	*.238*	*.310*	*.415*	*-.106*	*.237*	*.309*	*.415*	*-.112*	*2.8*	

Breakout: 12% *Improve: 24%* *Collapse: 43%*

Kieschnick has now done the two-way thing for two seasons and has been a pretty nifty player for the Brewers. In 2003, he was very good at the plate but strictly a mop-up man on the mound, while 2004 found the inverse to be true; he ended the year as the Brewers fourth best reliever but didn't hit particularly well. The samples are small enough to discount any firm conclusions drawn from the swing, but it is pretty clear that the Brewers have a competitive advantage over everyone else in the 25th man department. Now if they could only do something about the other 24 spots.

DAN KOLB Bats: R Throws: R Born: 29-Mar-1975 Age: 30

YEAR	TM	LG	AGE	G	GS	IP	H	BB	SO	HR	ERA	EQERA	EQH9	EQBB9	EQSO9	EQHR9	PERA	VORP	STF
2002	TEX	AL	27	34	0	32.0	27	22	20	1	4.22	4.35	7.8	5.8	5.5	0.3	4.06	4.2	-12
2003	IND	INT	28	26	0	39.3	26	13	46	1	1.37	2.70	6.6	3.4	8.8	0.2	2.70	11.8	25
2003	MIL	NL	28	37	0	41.3	34	19	39	2	1.96	2.23	7.4	3.6	7.8	0.4	2.90	15.8	17
2004	MIL	NL	29	64	0	57.3	50	15	21	3	2.98	3.35	8.6	2.2	3.0	0.5	3.35	14.3	-7
2005	*ATL*	*NL*	*30*	*35*	*1*	*49.7*	*52*	*20*	*30*	*5*	*4.25*	*4.49*	*9.5*	*3.2*	*4.9*	*0.8*	*4.68*	*6.0*	*-10*

Breakout: 16% *Improve: 46%* *Collapse: 29%*

How unusual was Dan Kolb in 2004? He made the All-Star team despite posting a higher groundball-to-flyball ratio (3.33) than strikeouts-per-nine-innings rate (3.30). He allowed three runs in the first three months of the season while striking out just ten batters. The clock struck midnight in the second half, as his post-All-Star break ERA was 4.88. Kolb's ability to keep the ball on the ground helps him survive his inability to get people out at the plate, but he's not the dominant run-preventing force that he appeared to be in the first half. The Brewers wisely sent him and his newfound "proven closer" label to Atlanta for youngster Jose Capellan, who simply gets hitters out the old fashioned way: 100 MPH fastballs.

PEDRO LIRIANO Bats: R Throws: R Born: 23-Oct-1980 Age: 24

YEAR	TM	LG	AGE	G	GS	IP	H	BB	SO	HR	ERA	EQERA	EQH9	EQBB9	EQSO9	EQHR9	PERA	VORP	STF
2002	RCU	CLF	21	28	28	167.3	129	74	176	14	3.60	5.52	8.5	4.6	5.7	1.4	4.40	20.4	17
2003	HUN	SOU	22	27	26	142.7	138	62	116	12	3.78	5.78	9.9	4.1	5.3	1.5	5.92	-4.7	-10
2004	IND	INT	23	29	21	126.3	149	50	97	21	5.20	5.49	10.0	3.7	5.6	1.5	5.49	1.5	-6
2004	MIL	NL	23	11	0	15.7	15	3	10	3	4.01	5.52	9.2	1.8	5.5	1.8	4.91	-0.1	-3
2005	*PHI*	*NL*	*24*	*24*	*10*	*74.7*	*76*	*34*	*54*	*12*	*5.16*	*5.35*	*9.2*	*3.6*	*5.8*	*1.3*	*5.20*	*3.4*	*-5*

Breakout: 13% *Improve: 36%* *Collapse: 26%*

Liriano is a sinkerball pitcher who relies on keeping the ball down but doesn't have the command to make it work consistently. When he gets on top of the pitch and puts it at the knees, he induces a fair share of groundballs and can be reasonably effective. However, it flattens out and can turn too many outings into batting practice. The Brewers put him on waivers to clear a spot on the 40-man roster, so now the Phillies will try to get him to keep the ball away from the hitter's wheelhouse.

WES OBERMUELLER

Bats: R **Throws: R** Born: 22-Dec-1976 Age: 28

YEAR	TM	LG	AGE	G	GS	IP	H	BB	SO	HR	ERA	EQERA	EQH9	EQBB9	EQSO9	EQHR9	PERA	VORP	STF
2002	WIC	TXS	25	17	17	105.7	98	40	65	6	2.89	4.44	9.4	3.8	4.3	1.1	5.18	4.5	2
2002	WIL	CRL	25	8	4	45.7	38	14	44	1	2.76	4.29	8.4	3.4	6.2	0.4	4.07	7.1	15
2003	OMA	PCL	26	17	17	106.3	108	42	62	11	4.40	5.73	9.7	4.1	4.6	1.5	5.64	-0.4	-4
2003	MIL	NL	26	12	11	65.7	81	25	34	10	5.07	5.26	10.2	2.9	4.2	1.2	5.26	1.5	-1
2004	IND	INT	27	4	4	26.0	30	7	17	3	5.19	5.33	9.6	2.5	4.6	1.1	4.62	2.8	4
2004	MIL	NL	27	25	20	118.0	138	42	59	15	5.80	5.71	10.0	2.9	4.0	1.0	4.85	-4.5	-6
2005	*MIL*	*NL*	*28*	*20*	*16*	*96.3*	*110*	*37*	*54*	*13*	*5.21*	*5.41*	*10.3*	*3.0*	*4.5*	*1.1*	*5.31*	*3.8*	*-5*

Breakout: 14% *Improve: 40%* *Collapse: 25%*

By now, you know that Brooks Kieschnick has established himself as a legitimate two-way player for the Brewers. Interestingly enough, though, Kieschnick wasn't even the best hitting pitcher on the staff. Wes Obermueller went 15 for 39 with three extra base hits and five walks, good for a .385/.400/.462 line. His VORP of 10.0 in just 42 plate appearances helped cancel out the fact that he contributed a −4.5 VORP on the mound. We'll go out on a limb and say that Obermueller isn't really a .385 hitter, so it will be hard to overlook the fact that, as a pitcher, he makes a nice pinch-hitter.

MANNY PARRA

Bats: L **Throws: L** Born: 30-Oct-1982 Age: 22

YEAR	TM	LG	AGE	G	GS	IP	H	BB	SO	HR	ERA	EQERA	EQH9	EQBB9	EQSO9	EQHR9	PERA	VORP	STF
2002	OGD	PIO	19	11	10	47.7	59	10	51	3	3.21	6.80	10.9	2.3	4.7	1.6	5.63	-0.2	0
2003	BLT	MDW	20	23	23	138.7	127	24	117	9	2.73	4.95	9.7	2.0	5.2	1.6	4.74	12.2	10
2004	HDS	CLF	21	13	12	67.3	76	19	64	3	3.48	5.56	9.0	3.0	5.3	0.7	3.53	15.2	11
2005	*MIL*	*NL*	*22*	*19*	*12*	*79.7*	*88*	*26*	*54*	*11*	*4.78*	*4.96*	*10.0*	*2.6*	*5.5*	*1.1*	*4.98*	*6.6*	*1*

Breakout: 5% *Improve: 38%* *Collapse: 23%*

Parra signed for $1.55 million as one of the most compensated draft-and-follows in history during the spring of 2002. While opposing hitters haven't proven a challenge to Parra as a professional, he has had a series of health problems that have kept him off of the mound. He managed just 73 innings in 2004, thanks to "shoulder soreness," but no injury was ever diagnosed. Parra has the best stuff of anyone in the organization not named Ben Sheets, but he has to stay healthy, something he hasn't yet shown he can accomplish.

LUIS PENA

Bats: R **Throws: R** Born: 10-Jan-1983 Age: 22

YEAR	TM	LG	AGE	G	GS	IP	H	BB	SO	HR	ERA	EQERA	EQH9	EQBB9	EQSO9	EQHR9	PERA	VORP	STF
2003	BLT	MDW	20	23	18	90.0	92	46	53	6	3.90	6.59	10.3	5.9	3.6	1.8	6.48	-8.0	-23
2004	BLT	MDW	21	21	16	98.7	101	35	76	7	3.92	5.76	10.3	4.1	4.2	1.3	6.06	-4.6	-9

The Brewers added Pena to the 40-man roster to protect him from the Rule 5 Draft, which struck some as a curious decision. Pena signed in 1999, made his debut in the U.S. in 2001, and has yet to throw an inning above low-A Beloit, where his performances have been mediocre. However, the Brewers feel the 22-year-old is on the verge of a breakthrough and they love his projectable body. Right now, he's simply a young arm who may or may not throw in the mid-90s eventually. Not the best use of a 40-man roster spot.

DAN REICHERT

Bats: R **Throws: R** Born: 12-Jul-1976 Age: 28

YEAR	TM	LG	AGE	G	GS	IP	H	BB	SO	HR	ERA	EQERA	EQH9	EQBB9	EQSO9	EQHR9	PERA	VORP	STF
2002	KCR	AL	25	30	6	66.0	77	25	36	10	5.32	5.54	9.8	3.2	4.7	1.2	5.12	-4.2	-18
2003	SYR	INT	26	41	0	58.0	55	35	60	2	3.57	4.39	8.3	6.2	7.6	0.5	4.39	7.4	-2
2003	TOR	AL	26	15	0	16.3	28	8	13	2	6.07	5.60	11.2	4.1	6.1	1.0	6.11	-0.9	-12
2004	IND	INT	27	49	0	86.7	89	38	73	6	3.74	4.48	8.6	4.1	6.1	0.7	4.27	12.5	1
2005	*SEA*	*AL*	*28*	*42*	*0*	*50.3*	*51*	*24*	*37*	*5*	*4.46*	*4.65*	*9.5*	*3.7*	*5.9*	*0.9*	*4.83*	*6.8*	*-8*

Breakout: 23% *Improve: 43%* *Collapse: 27%*

Picked seventh overall by the Royals in the 1997 draft, Reichert hasn't panned out quite like anybody hoped. Toronto gave him a shot and passed after an uninspiring performance in 2003, and the Brewers never bothered to call him up in 2004 despite pitching moderately well for Indianapolis. Still just 28 years old, there are worse ways to spend a minor league contract and an invite to spring training than to give them to Reichert.

MARK ROGERS **Bats: R** **Throws: R** Born: 30-Jan-1986 Age: 19

When you use your first round pick on a high school pitcher from the baseball hotbed that is Orr's Island, Maine, odds are he must have a pretty special arm. Rogers lights up radar guns with a mid-90s fastball and has two usable breaking balls, unusual for a player with his experience. As Mike Jones shows, however, a great arm doesn't guarantee success. Along with Yovani Gallardo and Robbie Wooley, Rogers represents the top tier of pitching prospects in the lower levels of the Brewers system.

VICTOR SANTOS **Bats: R** **Throws: R** Born: 02-Oct-1976 Age: 28

YEAR	TM	LG	AGE	G	GS	IP	H	BB	SO	HR	ERA	EQERA	EQH9	EQBB9	EQSO9	EQHR9	PERA	VORP	STF
2002	CSP	PCL	25	21	21	118.0	147	43	134	17	5.72	5.52	9.5	3.3	7.6	1.4	4.61	13.1	11
2002	COL	NL	25	24	2	26.0	41	22	25	3	10.38	9.11	11.4	5.9	7.2	1.0	6.83	-14.4	-15
2003	OKL	PCL	26	20	16	108.3	112	35	65	6	3.41	5.14	9.1	3.3	4.6	0.8	4.35	14.3	7
2003	TEX	AL	26	8	4	25.7	29	16	15	5	7.00	6.39	9.6	5.3	5.0	1.4	5.33	-3.6	-10
2004	MIL	NL	27	31	28	154.0	169	57	115	18	4.97	5.25	9.4	3.0	6.0	1.0	4.41	3.6	6
2005	*MIL*	*NL*	*28*	*24*	*20*	*120.3*	*131*	*45*	*86*	*16*	*5.06*	*5.25*	*9.8*	*3.0*	*5.8*	*1.1*	*5.10*	*6.3*	*4*

Breakout: 9% *Improve: 43%* *Collapse: 27%*

Despite just turning 28, Santos is already a journeyman, having been through four organizations in the past three seasons. His success in the first half (4.08 ERA) of the season was a revelation for the Brewers, but the wheels came flying off after the All-Star break (5.97 ERA). From that point on, he allowed 13 home runs in 72 innings, accounting for his collapse. He will go to spring training penciled in as a member of the rotation, but don't expect him to stay there for the entire season.

DENNIS SARFATE **Bats: R** **Throws: R** Born: 09-Apr-1981 Age: 24

YEAR	TM	LG	AGE	G	GS	IP	H	BB	SO	HR	ERA	EQERA	EQH9	EQBB9	EQSO9	EQHR9	PERA	VORP	STF
2003	BLT	MDW	22	26	26	139.7	114	66	140	11	2.83	4.92	9.4	5.6	6.3	2.2	6.08	-6.6	-3
2004	HUN	SOU	23	28	25	129.0	128	78	113	12	3.98	5.58	9.6	5.7	5.5	1.2	5.80	-2.7	0
2005	*MIL*	*NL*	*24*	*15*	*6*	*44.0*	*45*	*27*	*34*	*8*	*5.78*	*6.00*	*9.2*	*4.9*	*6.3*	*1.5*	*5.98*	*-0.7*	*-9*

Breakout: 16% *Improve: 51%* *Collapse: 16%*

Sarfate throws a powerful fastball and slider that he can blow hitters away with, but his command leaves a lot to be desired. After walking 78 men in 129 innings for Huntsville, he'll find himself in Triple-A, probably coming out of the bullpen, where he can attempt to harness his control. A future in the rotation is just a slim possibility.

BEN SHEETS **Bats: R** **Throws: R** Born: 18-Jul-1978 Age: 26

YEAR	TM	LG	AGE	G	GS	IP	H	BB	SO	HR	ERA	EQERA	EQH9	EQBB9	EQSO9	EQHR9	PERA	VORP	STF
2002	MIL	NL	23	34	34	216.7	237	70	170	21	4.15	4.37	9.4	2.5	6.2	0.8	4.41	27.4	15
2003	MIL	NL	24	34	34	220.7	232	43	157	29	4.44	4.78	9.1	1.6	5.8	1.1	3.98	17.7	13
2004	MIL	NL	25	34	34	237.0	201	32	264	25	2.70	3.15	7.7	1.1	9.1	0.9	2.80	66.8	41
2005	*MIL*	*NL*	*26*	*30*	*30*	*214.7*	*196*	*42*	*215*	*23*	*3.22*	*3.34*	*8.2*	*1.5*	*8.1*	*0.9*	*3.32*	*54.7*	*31*

Breakout: 29% *Improve: 58%* *Collapse: 10%*

Sheets made the leap from innings eater to All-Star in 2004, improving every way he could across the board. Particularly notable was jumping his strikeout rate from 6.4 to 10.0 per nine innings while trimming his walk total down to 32 despite throwing 237 innings. For being one of the dominant pitchers in baseball, his team came up short in their support of him, producing 12 wins. Most writers didn't notice, so he was named on just two of the 32 Cy Young ballots, garnering one second and one third-place vote, a ridiculously low total. While huge spikes in performance like Sheets's are hard to sustain, all indicators point to him being a perennial All-Star, as long as he can keep his right arm away from Dr. Andrews.

LUIS VIZCAINO **Bats: R** **Throws: R** Born: 06-Aug-1974 Age: 30

YEAR	TM	LG	AGE	G	GS	IP	H	BB	SO	HR	ERA	EQERA	EQH9	EQBB9	EQSO9	EQHR9	PERA	VORP	STF
2002	MIL	NL	27	76	0	81.3	55	30	79	6	2.99	3.16	7.0	2.9	7.9	0.7	3.04	21.6	15
2003	MIL	NL	28	75	0	62.0	64	25	61	16	6.39	6.23	9.2	3.1	8.0	2.2	5.19	-6.3	-4
2004	MIL	NL	29	73	0	72.0	61	24	63	12	3.75	4.19	8.1	2.8	7.2	1.4	3.93	10.6	1
2005	*CWS*	*AL*	*30*	*50*	*0*	*60.7*	*58*	*22*	*50*	*12*	*4.91*	*4.62*	*8.7*	*2.9*	*6.7*	*1.5*	*4.46*	*10.0*	*-3*

Breakout: 29% *Improve: 49%* *Collapse: 24%*

Vizcaino spent three years with the Brewers after being acquired from Texas. He was terrific in 2002, awful in 2003, and about average in 2004. He simply gives up too many home runs to be a great reliever, and Doug Melvin did a nice job of selling high and moving Vizcaino to the White Sox in the Carlos Lee trade. Milwaukee had picked up Pena for practically nothing initially, but after getting three years of use out of him, they sensibly moved him once he was eligible for a real payday. His tenure and exit from Milwaukee is a feather in the cap of the Brewers front office.

MATT WISE **Bats: R** **Throws: R** Born: 18-Nov-1975 Age: 29

YEAR	TM	LG	AGE	G	GS	IP	H	BB	SO	HR	ERA	EQERA	EQH9	EQBB9	EQSO9	EQHR9	PERA	VORP	STF
2002	SLC	PCL	26	16	16	78.0	102	15	76	12	5.42	5.45	10.5	1.7	6.6	1.6	5.45	1.3	-6
2004	MIL	NL	28	30	3	52.7	51	15	30	3	4.44	4.44	8.7	2.3	4.6	0.5	3.55	6.4	4
2005	*MIL*	*NL*	*29*	*26*	*6*	*58.7*	*61*	*19*	*41*	*8*	*4.43*	*4.60*	*9.4*	*2.5*	*5.6*	*1.1*	*4.68*	*7.9*	*-3*

Breakout: 24% *Improve: 45%* *Collapse: 29%*

If you like changeups, Matt Wise is your guy. A true junkballer, you'll never see him crack 90 on the radar gun, but his command and ability to change speeds are effective enough weapons to succeed in relief. Barring a catastrophe in spring training, Wise will be one of the Brewers middle relievers in 2005.

GLENN WOOLARD **Bats: R** **Throws: R** Born: 18-Apr-1981 Age: 24

YEAR	TM	LG	AGE	G	GS	IP	H	BB	SO	HR	ERA	EQERA	EQH9	EQBB9	EQSO9	EQHR9	PERA	VORP	STF
2002	SLO	NWN	21	17	11	67.0	51	32	75	3	2.96	5.43	9.1	5.6	5.7	1.2	5.58	0.1	-4
2003	HAG	SAL	22	26	25	144.0	126	43	135	10	3.44	5.62	10.3	3.3	5.4	1.7	6.26	-9.4	-11
2004	HDS	CLF	23	12	2	48.0	58	21	46	2	4.69	5.89	9.3	4.6	5.3	0.6	4.18	7.5	-4
2004	HUN	SOU	23	23	11	82.3	61	35	67	2	2.73	3.93	7.7	4.0	5.2	0.4	3.57	17.1	2
2005	*MIL*	*NL*	*24*	*17*	*8*	*57.7*	*60*	*28*	*41*	*7*	*4.91*	*5.09*	*9.3*	*3.8*	*5.8*	*1.0*	*5.09*	*3.9*	*-4*

Breakout: 17% *Improve: 49%* *Collapse: 25%*

The Giants selected Woolard in the tenth round of the 2002 draft, then sent him (with Carlos Villanueva) to Milwaukee for Wayne Franklin and Leo Estrella. Woolard pitched well for Huntsville in 2004, mixing three average pitches to retire hitters, but he lacks a true out pitch. He was left unprotected in the Rule 5 Draft and went unselected, as most teams have several pitchers like Woolard in their own organizations. If he continues to pitch well, he'll get a shot in Milwaukee, perhaps in the second half of 2005.

New York Mets

How to Make a First Impression, by Omar Minaya:

1. Sign the second-best free agent on the market;
2. Celebrate holidays;
3. Sign the best free agent on the market.

After three years at the helm of the MLB Expos, running a team on a shoestring budget for players and just about everything else, Minaya moved to New York in September and made himself a local hero by January. Taking over his hometown's National League franchise, one that had been drifting since winning the pennant in 2000, Minaya quickly re-established the Mets as a premier team by signing Pedro Martinez and Carlos Beltran. With the approval of owner Fred Wilpon, Minaya leveraged the Mets' half of the biggest market in the game into one of the best off-seasons in recent memory.

The signings were a salve for the Mets, who endured a 2004 season in which they once again finished under .500, far from contention. Worse, they tossed away some of their most prized prospects for little return in an attempt to chase a Wild Card spot they had little chance of grabbing. To the north, the ongoing success of the Yankees, and that team's considerable star power, had relegated the Mets to something less than second-class status. At any given time, New York is either a Mets or Yankees town, the rivalry played out on back pages and front stoops throughout the city. It's been a Yankees town for more than a decade now.

What's striking about the pursuits of Martinez and Beltran was how much they called to mind the strategy the Yankees had been making prior to this off-season. The Yankees have spent years focusing on the very top of the free-agent market. They re-signed Bernie Williams after 1998, in the midst of his peak, for top-tier money; they signed Mike Mussina in the winter of 2000 and Jason Giambi a year later, each on the short list of top prizes in the market that year, Giambi's recent health issues aside.

In pursuing the cream of the crop, the Yankees acted as if they understood a key principle of the market for baseball players: Free-agent signings tend to be worth it at the top and bottom of the spectrum. The best free-agent signings in history—Barry Bonds and Greg Maddux in 1992, Randy Johnson in 1999—have been elite players earning large contracts and major awards while playing them out.

METS PROSPECTUS

2004 record: 71–91; Fourth place, NL East

Pythagenport record: 75–87

Runs scored per game: 4.22 (13th in NL)

Runs allowed per game: 4.51 (8th in NL)

Team EqA: .255 (12th in NL)

2004 Batters Age: 30.1 (6th oldest in NL)

2004 Pitchers Age: 33.1 (Oldest in NL)

Ballpark: Shea Stadium; Moderate pitcher's park; Park Factor of 0.968

2004: The most interesting baseball-related goings-on in Flushing were in the Mets' chaotic front office.

2005: Almost everyone's past expiration, but a commitment to free-agency quick fixes makes this the most transparent attempt in years to buy instead of build a contender.

At the other end, there's little risk involved in the kind of one-year deals many relievers and bench players sign.

It's the middle class, back with a vengeance this past winter, where the bad deals happen. And over the past few years, it was the middle class where the Mets did most of their business. Since trading for Mike Piazza in 1999 and signing him to a long contract extension, the Mets had paid too much for second-tier talent, and been stuck with high payrolls and disappointing results. Roger Cedeno and Pedro Astacio and Kevin Appier and Cliff Floyd are all on the list of Mets fans' recent least favorite names. The player—or rather, the contract—the Mets acquired in exchange for Appier, Mo Vaughn, is symbolic of the entire post-2000 period for them. Vaughn made $46 million over three years while playing in just 166 games and hitting .250 with 29 home runs.

Signing Martinez and Beltran is a huge step away from that history. Beltran turns 28 in April, and is one of the ten best players in baseball and smack in the middle of his prime. He's a complete player, possessing all five tools and, more important, the skills associated with them. As with Bonds in '92 and Alex Rodriguez in '00, there's little doubt that Beltran is going to be a fantastic player for the duration of the contract. The shape of his contributions may change—he'll probably run less with age, while the steady increase in power he's shown will more than make up for that—but he's as sure a property as there is in the game. The premium the Mets paid over what the other top free-agent hitters received this off-season is based on that certainty.

Martinez comes to New York with more caveats. The condition of his shoulder had Bostonians holding their breaths for the past three seasons. Despite that, he made 92 starts and threw 603 innings in that time, posting a 2.84 ERA. His peripheral stats, while down from his 1999–2000 peak, mark him as among the best pitchers in the game. Certainly, the Mets have assumed risk here, but the gamble is between Martinez being effective and being unavailable. Contrast that with some of the other free-agent signings this winter; Russ Ortiz, Carl Pavano, and Jaret Wright all come with questions, one of which, for all of them, is, "Will this guy's ERA look like a gymnastics score at some point?"

Martinez was the best pitcher and Beltran the best everyday player available on the market this winter. They're actually both among the elite in the game, period. It's rare that any team pulls in that kind of exacta in any off-season, as much because it takes a synergy of player availability and team willingness to make it happen. Minaya has made the Mets a real contender, perhaps even the best team in the NL East, with two moves. This isn't a reiteration of the Bobby Bonilla Mets; this is the addition of two players who should, combined, be worth 10 to 15 wins above replacement a year for the next couple of years.

It's hard to not notice the stark contrast of just who is negotiating the two biggest contracts of the winter. Minaya was hamstrung during his three seasons in Montreal, forced to deal off Javier Vazquez, Orlando Cabrera, and Bartolo Colon while watching Vladimir Guerrero leave via free agency. He wasn't able to elbow his way into the market for big-ticket free agents, and MLB's heavy-handed budgeting affected the team's drafts enough that future Nationals teams will not owe their success to a Montreal core. Not even knowing if the team would exist after the 2002 season, his first, Minaya mortgaged much of the team's future to bolster a run at contending. When contraction was shelved, his gamble looked worse, but at the time it was a bold decision.

Because of the Expos' unique situation, it's difficult to evaluate Minaya based on his three years there. Certainly, he has a demonstrated preference for athletic players, and he's not someone with a lot of performance-analysis experience. That said, he's shown a willingness to learn, and he inherited a staff in New York who can do the heavy quantitative lifting. If the best front offices use both approaches, there's a chance that the Mets could do so in much the same way the Dodgers, Red Sox, and A's have done. Surely, signing Martinez and Beltran are moves that both traditional baseball people and performance analysts can celebrate.

Even with Martinez and Beltran, the Mets face some challenges. How they address them will add information to the dossier on Minaya and, for that matter, new manager Willie Randolph. First and foremost, the Mets have to reverse the error they made in the development of Jose Reyes. The team's top prospect two years ago, Reyes was rushed to the majors. After an encouraging half-season with the big club in '03, injuries and inexperience short-circuited his '04 campaign. With a number of qualified fill-ins for second base, the Mets have to let Reyes get himself on track at Norfolk. A half-season of Jeff Keppinger or Danny Garcia won't hurt them much if the other half is the player some hope Reyes can be, a .290/.350/.440 version, with lots of speed and a good glove at shortstop. Kazuo Matsui can wait three months to move to second base full-time in deference to Reyes; how well he makes that transition will reflect on new manager Willie Randolph, one of the smoother second basemen of his day.

The Mets' investment in Martinez will have to be protected. Extra days between starts would be most helpful, although that may be difficult. Fortunately, the Mets have a number of swingman candidates. "Pedro's Extra Day" might be the role that lets Aaron Heilman get established in the majors. If not Heilman, perhaps Tyler Yates, or maybe another chance for Jae Seo.

When he's on the mound, Martinez's pitch counts have to be monitored, and given his established splits, a hard count of 100 pitches per start may be necessary—he's just not the same pitcher past that point. The Mets can lean on a reservoir of no-profile right-handed relievers who miss bats and get outs and fill the gap between Martinez and Braden Looper. The team could have an Angels-style bullpen in 2005, thanks to people like Heath Bell, Bartolome Fortunato, and Orber Moreno.

The sport-coat side of the Mets' new brain trust has made a terrific first impression. It's now Randolph's turn to take a team that finally does have enough talent to win and show that it's ready for its close-up.

HITTERS

AAROM BALDIRIS — 3B — Bats: R — Throws: R — Born: 05-Jan-1983 — Age: 22

YEAR	TM	LG	AGE	AB	H	2B	3B	HR	BB	SO	SB	CS	AVG	OBP	SLG	MLVR	EQBA	EQOBP	EQSLG	EQMLVR	VORP	DEFENSE	
2002	KNG	APL	19	217	71	9	1	3	14	24	9	5	.327	.390	.419	.183	.253	.283	.323	-.287	-14.5	55-3B 2	
2003	BRO	NYP	20	88	32	5	2	0	14	13	2	2	.364	.451	.466	.416	.286	.340	.352	-.112	3.9	25-3B 0	
2003	CMB	SAL	20	393	123	19	4	6	51	55	13	5	.313	.396	.427	.246	.271	.334	.382	-.092	11.8	81-3B 2	11-1B -1
2004	SLU	FSL	21	406	124	15	5	4	46	64	6	6	.305	.384	.397	.143	.265	.331	.354	-.141	5.6	104-3B 8	
2004	BIN	EAS	21	81	19	3	1	0	6	13	0	0	.235	.284	.296	-.237	.185	.226	.210	-.596	-9.9	21-3B -2	
2005	*NYM*	*NL*	*22*	*289*	*70*	*14*	*2*	*3*	*22*	*48*	*3*	*1*	*.243*	*.310*	*.342*	*-.198*	*.247*	*.312*	*.353*	*-.180*	*-2.3*	*78-3B -2*	

Breakout: 12% *Improve: 30%* *Collapse: 50%*

As a Venezuelan third baseman with a good glove in the Mets system, the comps to Edgardo Alfonzo are everywhere. Of course, at 21, Alfonzo was in his first year with the Mets, playing unimpressively, but in the majors. There's considerable doubt about prospects with good walk rates but little power because as they advance, they tend to lose walks because they get challenged much more often. Baldiris has to drive the ball more, or he'll stall in Double-A as a .260/.330/.350 guy with good defense.

IAN BLADERGROEN — 1B — Bats: L — Throws: L — Born: 23-Feb-1983 — Age: 22

YEAR	TM	LG	AGE	AB	H	2B	3B	HR	BB	SO	SB	CS	AVG	OBP	SLG	MLVR	EQBA	EQOBP	EQSLG	EQMLVR	VORP	DEFENSE
2003	BRO	NYP	20	274	78	12	3	6	21	51	0	2	.285	.354	.416	.172	.247	.295	.382	-.183	-16.2	70-1B -12
2004	CMB	SAL	21	269	92	23	3	13	25	55	1	1	.342	.397	.595	.450	.293	.336	.496	.094	15.0	42-1B -3
2005	*NYM*	*NL*	*22*	*391*	*100*	*21*	*3*	*12*	*26*	*88*	*0*	*1*	*.255*	*.318*	*.418*	*-.077*	*.259*	*.319*	*.431*	*-.056*	*11.4*	*103-1B -6*

Breakout: 21% *Improve: 38%* *Collapse: 29%*

The 2002 draft-and-follow was having a monster year at Cap City when he tore a ligament in his left wrist, ending his season and putting another big red flag next to his name. The first? His age; as good as his year was, 21 is not young in the Sally League. With a good chance that the wrist injury will sap his power for a while, Bladergroen probably will end up as an overaged minor league slugger and not reach the majors until he's 25 or 26, if at all.

CRAIG BRAZELL — 1B — Bats: L — Throws: R — Born: 10-May-1980 — Age: 25

YEAR	TM	LG	AGE	AB	H	2B	3B	HR	BB	SO	SB	CS	AVG	OBP	SLG	MLVR	EQBA	EQOBP	EQSLG	EQMLVR	VORP	DEFENSE	
2002	SLU	FSL	22	402	107	25	3	16	13	78	2	1	.266	.292	.463	.092	.238	.257	.428	-.195	-13.2	100-1B 3	
2002	BIN	EAS	22	130	40	8	0	6	1	28	0	2	.308	.343	.508	.190	.262	.275	.431	-.138	-2.0	28-1B -3	
2003	BIN	EAS	23	432	126	23	2	17	23	97	2	1	.292	.331	.472	.120	.259	.295	.434	-.100	-2.2	108-1B -6	
2004	NOR	INT	24	475	126	22	2	23	21	99	1	2	.265	.300	.465	.040	.257	.294	.445	-.087	-0.6	92-1B -8	13-LF -2
2004	NYM	NL	24	34	9	2	0	1	1	7	0	0	.265	.286	.412	-.086	.294	.275	.382	-.184	0.5		
2005	*NYM*	*NL*	*25*	*315*	*79*	*17*	*1*	*11*	*11*	*68*	*0*	*0*	*.252*	*.284*	*.421*	*-.133*	*.255*	*.285*	*.435*	*-.112*	*-0.5*	*81-1B -4*	

Breakout: 18% *Improve: 42%* *Collapse: 34%*

Brazell has played some left field, which would matter if his bat was really something you wanted to get into the lineup. It's not. Brazell's career strikeout-to-walk ratio is 520:99, and if he had an MLB job, he'd hit a bit like Vinny Castilla does at sea level. The Mets need to stop acting like he's a prospect.

BRIAN BUCHANAN — OF — Bats: R — Throws: R — Born: 21-Jul-1973 — Age: 31

YEAR	TM	LG	AGE	AB	H	2B	3B	HR	BB	SO	SB	CS	AVG	OBP	SLG	MLVR	EQBA	EQOBP	EQSLG	EQMLVR	VORP	DEFENSE	
2002	MIN	AL	28	135	34	5	1	5	6	33	2	1	.252	.294	.415	-.086	.254	.299	.425	-.109	1.3	21-RF 1	
2002	SDP	NL	28	92	27	5	0	6	9	26	0	1	.293	.363	.543	.299	.309	.357	.574	.259	9.0	10-RF -1	
2003	SDP	NL	29	198	52	10	2	8	24	51	6	2	.263	.346	.455	.102	.275	.354	.480	.085	12.2	18-RF -1	16-1B 0
2004	SDP	NL	30	60	12	2	0	2	6	19	0	0	.200	.279	.333	-.223	.217	.282	.350	-.273	-1.7		
2005	*TBY*	*AL*	*31*	*144*	*36*	*8*	*1*	*6*	*16*	*36*	*1*	*0*	*.252*	*.333*	*.439*	*-.018*	*.253*	*.336*	*.448*	*-.010*	*7.1*	*42-1B 0*	

Breakout: 23% *Improve: 45%* *Collapse: 33%*

A strained oblique ruined Buchanan's season. Once he got healthy, the Padres released him to alleviate a late-season roster crunch. The Mets claimed him, gave him three at-bats, and designated him for assignment. The basic skills are still there, but they're common ones, which means Buchanan always will be a step away from the minors. The Rays have a better, much younger version of this player in Johnny Gomes, so Buchanan will be in a tough spot this spring.

MIKE CAMERON CF Bats: R Throws: R Born: 08-Jan-1973 Age: 32

YEAR	TM	LG	AGE	AB	H	2B	3B	HR	BB	SO	SB	CS	AVG	OBP	SLG	MLVR	EQBA	EQOBP	EQSLG	EQMLVR	VORP	DEFENSE
2002	SEA	AL	29	545	130	26	5	25	79	176	31	8	.239	.340	.442	.037	.253	.356	.473	.059	35.7	146-CF 6
2003	SEA	AL	30	534	135	31	5	18	70	137	17	7	.253	.344	.431	.025	.263	.357	.455	.045	29.1	144-CF 24
2004	NYM	NL	31	493	114	30	1	30	57	143	22	6	.231	.319	.479	.039	.232	.319	.481	-.013	27.0	134-CF 3
2005	*NYM*	*NL*	*32*	*384*	*97*	*21*	*2*	*18*	*53*	*112*	*15*	*5*	*.253*	*.348*	*.461*	*.029*	*.257*	*.349*	*.476*	*.052*	*24.4*	*105-CF 3*

Breakout: 31% Improve: 67% Collapse: 17%

He didn't take well to Shea Stadium with the bat or, oddly, the glove. Cameron's strikeout rate was the same at Shea and on the road, so if it was a visibility thing, it didn't manifest itself that way. Damaged cartilage in his left wrist required off-season surgery and will keep him off the field until late April. Wrist injuries can affect power, which is about all Cameron has going for him at the plate these days, so beware. Ticketed for right field on Opening Day with Beltran in center, assuming that Cameron hasn't been traded by then.

AMBIORIX CONCEPCION RF Bats: R Throws: R Born: 15-Oct-1983 Age: 21

YEAR	TM	LG	AGE	AB	H	2B	3B	HR	BB	SO	SB	CS	AVG	OBP	SLG	MLVR	EQBA	EQOBP	EQSLG	EQMLVR	VORP	DEFENSE
2004	BRO	NYP	20	259	79	14	3	8	13	54	28	11	.305	.338	.475	.229	.261	.290	.414	-.136	-10.5	60-RF 1
2005	*NYM*	*NL*	*21*	*412*	*98*	*21*	*3*	*9*	*16*	*104*	*17*	*6*	*.237*	*.268*	*.370*	*-.241*	*.241*	*.269*	*.382*	*-.223*	*-12.3*	*104-RF -3*

Breakout: 10% Improve: 26% Collapse: 48%

The former Roberto Solano was named the best prospect in the New York–Penn circuit. His season wasn't particularly good, mostly some extra pop, nothing you wouldn't expect from maturing. His plate discipline is bad and didn't change much. He'll be old in the Sally League; even if he hits, his prospect status will be shaky until he plays well in a league where he's not among the oldest players. It may never happen.

WILSON DELGADO INF Bats: B Throws: R Born: 15-Jul-1972 Age: 32

YEAR	TM	LG	AGE	AB	H	2B	3B	HR	BB	SO	SB	CS	AVG	OBP	SLG	MLVR	EQBA	EQOBP	EQSLG	EQMLVR	VORP	DEFENSE
2002	MEM	PCL	29	365	95	19	2	7	23	54	2	5	.260	.309	.381	-.064	.252	.299	.362	-.200	0.3	94-SS 6
2003	MEM	PCL	30	86	20	2	0	2	10	15	2	1	.233	.312	.326	-.136	.221	.280	.314	-.324	-3.3	25-SS 1
2003	STL	NL	30	77	13	3	0	0	3	10	0	0	.169	.207	.208	-.544	.182	.194	.195	-.686	-6.5	
2003	ANA	AL	30	50	16	0	0	0	8	8	0	0	.320	.414	.320	.076	.388	.384	.388	.110	4.1	
2004	NOR	INT	31	352	92	18	5	3	27	73	1	6	.261	.317	.366	-.074	.258	.314	.357	-.174	3.1	98-SS 8
2004	NYM	NL	31	130	38	4	1	2	15	29	1	0	.292	.366	.385	.030	.290	.363	.389	-.013	8.2	37-SS 0
2005	*FLA*	*NL*	*32*	*175*	*41*	*8*	*1*	*2*	*14*	*36*	*1*	*1*	*.233*	*.292*	*.331*	*-.252*	*.237*	*.295*	*.344*	*-.231*	*0.4*	*49-SS -2*

Breakout: 15% Improve: 31% Collapse: 41%

He has now established himself as a major league utility infielder, and the comparison to Tom Prince in last year's book holds. The walk spike in New York wasn't real; he drew all of 15, including three intentionals, hitting ahead of the pitcher. He had no walks and seven strikeouts in 19 at-bats other than in the #8 hole. He'll fight a number of better, younger players with no service time for a bench spot in Florida.

VICTOR DIAZ RF Bats: R Throws: R Born: 10-Dec-1981 Age: 23

YEAR	TM	LG	AGE	AB	H	2B	3B	HR	BB	SO	SB	CS	AVG	OBP	SLG	MLVR	EQBA	EQOBP	EQSLG	EQMLVR	VORP	DEFENSE
2002	SGA	SAL	20	349	122	26	2	10	27	69	20	6	.350	.407	.521	.449	.310	.350	.475	.105	31.2	62-3B -8 11-2B 0
2002	JAX	SOU	20	152	32	7	0	4	7	42	7	5	.211	.258	.336	-.181	.195	.221	.318	-.451	-16.6	26-1B 0
2003	JAX	SOU	21	316	92	20	2	10	27	60	8	10	.291	.353	.462	.209	.276	.327	.458	.007	18.4	77-2B -10
2003	BIN	EAS	21	175	62	11	0	6	8	32	7	5	.354	.382	.520	.326	.306	.324	.462	.036	11.2	43-2B -7
2004	NOR	INT	22	528	154	31	1	24	31	133	6	8	.292	.332	.491	.157	.280	.322	.468	.017	13.0	125-RF 2
2004	NYM	NL	22	51	15	3	0	3	1	15	0	0	.294	.321	.529	.175	.314	.308	.549	.150	3.6	14-RF -1
2005	*NYM*	*NL*	*23*	*324*	*87*	*18*	*2*	*13*	*21*	*75*	*5*	*2*	*.269*	*.320*	*.454*	*-.013*	*.272*	*.322*	*.469*	*.010*	*17.3*	*86-RF -1*

Breakout: 14% Improve: 42% Collapse: 28%

Jim Duquette can't point to many accomplishments in his time as interim GM with the Mets, but picking up Diaz and Kole Strayhorn from the Dodgers for Jeromy Burnitz was a good deal. Never a scouts' favorite, Diaz and his bad body moved off of second base last year. The bad body is forgivable, but the decaying plate discipline isn't. Diaz's power is real, and he's young enough to improve his strike zone judgment, ideally in Norfolk this year.

CLIFF FLOYD LF **Bats: L** **Throws: R** Born: 05-Dec-1972 Age: 32

YEAR	TM	LG	AGE	AB	H	2B	3B	HR	BB	SO	SB	CS	AVG	OBP	SLG	MLVR	EQBA	EQOBP	EQSLG	EQMLVR	VORP	DEFENSE
2002	FLA	NL	29	296	85	20	0	18	58	68	10	5	.287	.414	.537	.333	.297	.414	.557	.312	35.0	60-RF 0 20-LF 1
2002	MON	NL	29	53	11	2	0	3	3	10	1	0	.208	.263	.415	-.133	.208	.240	.396	-.296	-0.4	
2002	BOS	AL	29	171	54	21	0	7	15	28	4	0	.316	.374	.561	.312	.329	.378	.571	.312	19.6	18-LF -1
2003	NYM	NL	30	365	106	25	2	18	51	66	3	0	.290	.376	.518	.238	.292	.378	.527	.207	33.3	79-LF -2
2004	NYM	NL	31	396	103	26	0	18	47	103	11	4	.260	.352	.462	.097	.264	.350	.465	.047	20.0	93-LF -2
2005	*NYM*	*NL*	*32*	*381*	*103*	*23*	*2*	*17*	*50*	*87*	*8*	*3*	*.270*	*.363*	*.476*	*.088*	*.274*	*.364*	*.492*	*.113*	*23.1*	*105-LF -3*

Breakout: 13% *Improve: 59%* *Collapse: 16%*

Floyd's salary, $6.5 million, seems reasonable for a hitter of his caliber until you realize that he plays only two-thirds of every season. At his level, that takes him from being a four- or five-win player to closer to three, at which point he's not worth it. He hits left-handers about as well as any non-Bonds left-handed hitter in baseball. Floyd would make a good DH for a team willing to keep him off the field. The Blue Jays, perhaps?

DANNY GARCIA 2B **Bats: R** **Throws: R** Born: 12-Apr-1980 Age: 25

YEAR	TM	LG	AGE	AB	H	2B	3B	HR	BB	SO	SB	CS	AVG	OBP	SLG	MLVR	EQBA	EQOBP	EQSLG	EQMLVR	VORP	DEFENSE
2002	SLU	FSL	22	432	118	34	5	4	53	77	13	6	.273	.369	.403	.125	.251	.326	.383	-.120	7.6	105-2B -16 17-SS -4
2003	BIN	EAS	23	117	39	12	1	3	10	20	2	2	.333	.391	.530	.329	.299	.351	.487	.113	10.6	28-2B -7
2003	NOR	INT	23	388	102	23	3	4	22	60	11	1	.263	.313	.369	-.028	.258	.311	.371	-.160	1.7	97-2B -13
2003	NYM	NL	23	56	12	2	0	2	2	11	0	0	.214	.274	.357	-.221	.228	.258	.368	-.287	-0.7	16-2B -3
2004	NOR	INT	24	242	63	14	1	2	15	35	9	5	.260	.322	.351	-.087	.258	.316	.344	-.189	-1.0	38-2B -4 13-SS -2
2004	NYM	NL	24	138	32	7	1	3	22	34	3	0	.232	.371	.362	-.041	.234	.368	.369	-.069	6.7	38-2B -4
2005	*NYM*	*NL*	*25*	*265*	*70*	*16*	*2*	*5*	*21*	*46*	*6*	*2*	*.262*	*.335*	*.388*	*-.081*	*.266*	*.336*	*.401*	*-.061*	*15.1*	*74-2B -7*

Breakout: 25% *Improve: 52%* *Collapse: 20%*

Scrappy non-hitter who plays some second base. His walk spike with the Mets last year was out of line with his career, but what's interesting is that it wasn't just a #8 hitter thing: He had the same walk rate batting second or eighth, in small samples of each. That doesn't mean it's something he'll sustain; it just rules out one possible reason for the jump. Jeff Keppinger has passed him for the job of waiting for Jose Reyes to get hurt, and David Bacani is about to as well.

RICHARD HIDALGO RF **Bats: R** **Throws: R** Born: 02-Jul-1975 Age: 29

YEAR	TM	LG	AGE	AB	H	2B	3B	HR	BB	SO	SB	CS	AVG	OBP	SLG	MLVR	EQBA	EQOBP	EQSLG	EQMLVR	VORP	DEFENSE
2002	HOU	NL	27	388	91	17	4	15	43	85	6	2	.235	.319	.415	-.043	.229	.311	.418	-.116	3.3	103-RF 8
2003	HOU	NL	28	514	159	43	4	28	58	104	9	7	.309	.385	.572	.321	.303	.377	.566	.272	52.5	134-RF 15
2004	HOU	NL	29	199	51	15	2	4	17	53	1	2	.256	.309	.412	-.047	.253	.305	.404	-.129	2.6	56-RF 4
2004	NYM	NL	29	324	74	11	1	21	27	76	3	2	.228	.296	.463	-.024	.231	.296	.468	-.073	7.4	76-RF -1
2005	*TEX*	*AL*	*29*	*471*	*130*	*28*	*3*	*24*	*47*	*104*	*6*	*3*	*.277*	*.347*	*.503*	*.108*	*.266*	*.339*	*.485*	*.054*	*20.4*	*124-RF 3*

Breakout: 27% *Improve: 54%* *Collapse: 12%*

In what was a decent gamble, as the Mets snagged Hidalgo for a Grade C pitching prospect and the willingness to pay a chunk of Hidalgo's salary and buyout. After a hot first two weeks as a Met, including homers in five straight games, Hidalgo was basically useless: He had a 664 OPS after the break. In the off-season the Rangers rolled the dice on a cheap one-year deal. Whatever he does—and PECOTA aside, he's proven he can be either really good or sub-par—it'll look better thanks to playing in Texas.

MIKE JACOBS C **Bats: L** **Throws: R** Born: 30-Oct-1980 Age: 24

YEAR	TM	LG	AGE	AB	H	2B	3B	HR	BB	SO	SB	CS	AVG	OBP	SLG	MLVR	EQBA	EQOBP	EQSLG	EQMLVR	VORP	DEFENSE
2002	SLU	FSL	21	467	117	26	1	11	25	95	2	3	.251	.291	.381	-.029	.221	.253	.355	-.320	-20.4	56-C -5
2003	BIN	EAS	22	407	134	36	1	17	28	87	0	3	.329	.376	.548	.329	.285	.328	.493	.068	30.4	64-C -7
2004	NOR	INT	23	96	17	3	0	2	9	30	0	0	.177	.245	.271	-.398	.167	.225	.250	-.550	-11.3	16-C -1
2005	*NYM*	*NL*	*24*	*262*	*62*	*14*	*1*	*9*	*17*	*66*	*0*	*0*	*.238*	*.289*	*.399*	*-.164*	*.241*	*.291*	*.413*	*-.144*	*1.7*	*70-C -12*

Breakout: 29% *Improve: 49%* *Collapse: 29%*

The organizational player of the year in 2003 had his '04 ruined by a torn right labrum and a nerve problem in the same shoulder. Even healthy, he's not a great prospect; he's had a consistent 3-to-1 strikeout-to-walk ratio coming through the

(continued next page)

Mike Jacobs *(continued)*

system. His '03 campaign featured a big batting average spike along with a drop in contact rate, indicating it wouldn't be sustained. With Justin Huber gone, Jacobs is the nominal catching prospect in this system, at least until Jesus Flores reaches the full-season leagues.

JEFF KEPPINGER — 2B — Bats: R — Throws: R — Born: 21-Apr-1980 — Age: 25

YEAR	TM	LG	AGE	AB	H	2B	3B	HR	BB	SO	SB	CS	AVG	OBP	SLG	MLVR	EQBA	EQOBP	EQSLG	EQMLVR	VORP	DEFENSE
2002	HIC	SAL	22	478	132	23	4	10	47	33	6	2	.276	.344	.404	.069	.228	.280	.348	-.273	-14.6	110-2B 6
2003	LYN	CRL	23	342	111	21	2	3	23	28	3	2	.325	.365	.424	.164	.291	.326	.401	-.064	12.3	87-2B -13
2004	ALT	EAS	24	315	106	17	2	1	27	15	10	5	.337	.387	.413	.188	.317	.364	.387	.007	17.9	74-2B 2
2004	BIN	EAS	24	47	17	3	1	0	6	2	2	1	.362	.426	.468	.337	.277	.311	.319	-.222	-1.4	
2004	NYM	NL	24	116	33	2	0	3	6	7	2	1	.284	.317	.379	-.055	.293	.312	.388	-.107	3.7	29-2B 1
2005	*NYM*	*NL*	*25*	*324*	*87*	*17*	*2*	*3*	*24*	*21*	*4*	*2*	*.269*	*.321*	*.364*	*-.133*	*.273*	*.322*	*.376*	*-.114*	*9.3*	*86-2B -1*

Breakout: 7% *Improve: 30%* *Collapse: 43%*

Keppinger is trying to ride the Joe McEwing career path, hitting for high averages as a second baseman and hoping no one notices how little else he does. The Mets ended up with him as part of the Kris Benson ménage à trois, somehow giving Justin Huber to the Royals for the privilege. The high average and scrappiness will play well in a job fight, but he needs the Mets to find a taker for him; or Kazuo Matsui to create an opportunity.

KAZUO MATSUI — SS/2B — Bats: B — Throws: R — Born: 23-Oct-1975 — Age: 29

YEAR	TM	LG	AGE	AB	H	2B	3B	HR	BB	SO	SB	CS	AVG	OBP	SLG	MLVR	EQBA	EQOBP	EQSLG	EQMLVR	VORP	DEFENSE
2002	SEI	JPL	26	582	193	46	6	36	53	112	33	0	.332	.391	.617	.447	.326	.394	.518	.257	68.7	
2003	SEI	JPL	27	587	179	36	4	33	55	4	13	104	.305	.364	.549	.000	.290	.353	.438	.038	29.2	
2004	NYM	NL	28	460	125	32	2	7	40	97	14	3	.272	.331	.396	-.020	.272	.332	.395	-.076	23.7	105-SS -6
2005	*NYM*	*NL*	*29*	*488*	*131*	*28*	*4*	*10*	*47*	*100*	*15*	*4*	*.268*	*.334*	*.405*	*-.056*	*.272*	*.336*	*.418*	*-.035*	*25.9*	*128-SS -3*

Breakout: 9% *Improve: 27%* *Collapse: 29%*

Perhaps the biggest disappointment in baseball last year after being a Barry Larkin clone in Japan, Matsui was a slightly below-average player in his first Stateside season. It might have turned out differently had a bad back not sidelined him for much of the second half, because his bat was coming around in July and early August. He's moving to second base this season to accommodate Jose Reyes, reversing the controversial decision of last spring. Look for him to emulate another Matsui and hit a lot more like his old self in his sophomore year.

JOE McEWING — UT — Bats: R — Throws: R — Born: 19-Oct-1972 — Age: 32

YEAR	TM	LG	AGE	AB	H	2B	3B	HR	BB	SO	SB	CS	AVG	OBP	SLG	MLVR	EQBA	EQOBP	EQSLG	EQMLVR	VORP	DEFENSE
2002	NYM	NL	29	196	39	8	1	3	9	50	4	4	.199	.242	.296	-.330	.216	.252	.322	-.372	-10.2	16-RF 0 13-SS -1
2003	NYM	NL	30	278	67	11	0	1	25	57	3	0	.241	.309	.291	-.224	.248	.311	.298	-.269	-2.5	41-2B -3 30-SS 4
2004	NYM	NL	31	138	35	3	1	1	9	32	4	1	.254	.297	.312	-.238	.255	.298	.319	-.261	-1.5	20-2B -1 11-SS 0
2005	*NYM*	*NL*	*32*	*95*	*22*	*4*	*1*	*1*	*7*	*22*	*2*	*1*	*.227*	*.286*	*.318*	*-.283*	*.230*	*.287*	*.329*	*-.268*	*-0.8*	*30-2B -3*

Breakout: 9% *Improve: 29%* *Collapse: 53%*

He's willing to play a lot of positions. He's popular. He has nothing to do with reality television. It's not much, but it keeps him employed. McEwing doesn't do enough with the bat, glove or legs to help a team win, and is an extreme example of the preference for familiar mediocrity within the baseball industry. Just 32, he'll be around for a while.

LASTINGS MILLEDGE — CF — Bats: R — Throws: R — Born: 05-Apr-1985 — Age: 20

YEAR	TM	LG	AGE	AB	H	2B	3B	HR	BB	SO	SB	CS	AVG	OBP	SLG	MLVR	EQBA	EQOBP	EQSLG	EQMLVR	VORP	DEFENSE
2003	KNG	APL	18	26	6	2	0	0	3	4	5	1	.231	.323	.308	-.083	.111	.134	.111	-.949	-15.5	
2004	CMB	SAL	19	262	89	22	1	13	17	53	23	6	.340	.399	.580	.429	.284	.325	.477	.039	14.9	54-CF -9
2004	SLU	FSL	19	81	19	6	2	2	9	21	3	2	.235	.319	.432	.044	.217	.282	.398	-.207	-1.7	21-CF 2
2005	*NYM*	*NL*	*20*	*402*	*98*	*24*	*3*	*10*	*27*	*90*	*16*	*5*	*.245*	*.309*	*.395*	*-.130*	*.248*	*.310*	*.408*	*-.110*	*9.3*	*106-CF -7*

Breakout: 18% *Improve: 39%* *Collapse: 34%*

The Mets' #1 pick in the 2003 draft got a late start after breaking his finger in spring training, then tore apart the Sally League for three months. He's a big-time tools guy who can actually apply his power and speed. Milledge has so little pro experience that you can excuse his lack of patience at the plate so far, especially since his strikeout rate wasn't out of hand in Capital City. We'll learn a lot this year. Aside: There are a lot of great names in this system, names that top anything Dickens could come up with.

JASON PHILLIPS C **Bats: R** **Throws: R** Born: 27-Sep-1976 Age: 28

YEAR	TM	LG	AGE	AB	H	2B	3B	HR	BB	SO	SB	CS	AVG	OBP	SLG	MLVR	EQBA	EQOBP	EQSLG	EQMLVR	VORP	DEFENSE			
2002	NOR	INT	25	323	91	22	1	13	24	29	1	0	.282	.327	.477	.148	.266	.316	.458	-.021	14.9	80-C	-5		
2003	NYM	NL	26	403	120	25	0	11	39	50	0	1	.298	.373	.442	.142	.303	.372	.451	.102	28.3	78-1B	-6	26-C	-4
2004	NYM	NL	27	362	79	18	0	7	35	42	0	1	.218	.298	.326	-.209	.223	.296	.324	-.277	-5.3	74-C	5	28-1B	0
2005	*NYM*	*NL*	*28*	*300*	*78*	*17*	*1*	*8*	*30*	*38*	*0*	*0*	*.260*	*.336*	*.399*	*-.066*	*.264*	*.337*	*.413*	*-.046*	*11.7*	*82-C*	*-8*		

Breakout: 20% *Improve: 49%* *Collapse: 25%*

His 2003 line was batting average-driven, and that it pushed the Mets into the Piazza-to-first mess that was a big contribution to 2004's lost season. When Phillips's average collapsed, it took the rest of his offense with him. He's qualified to be a Mike Redmond-level backup catcher, with a little more pop than that. He's not Brian Harper, and even if he were, nothing would have justified messing around with the Mets' best player.

MIKE PIAZZA C, Just C **Bats: R** **Throws: R** Born: 04-Sep-1968 Age: 36

YEAR	TM	LG	AGE	AB	H	2B	3B	HR	BB	SO	SB	CS	AVG	OBP	SLG	MLVR	EQBA	EQOBP	EQSLG	EQMLVR	VORP	DEFENSE			
2002	NYM	NL	33	478	134	23	2	33	57	82	0	3	.280	.359	.544	.269	.286	.361	.565	.226	56.8	113-C	-29		
2003	NYM	NL	34	234	67	13	0	11	35	40	0	0	.286	.377	.483	.188	.294	.375	.489	.152	24.0	61-C	-7		
2004	NYM	NL	35	455	121	21	0	20	68	78	0	0	.266	.362	.444	.098	.265	.358	.445	.035	29.9	55-1B	-2	43-C	-8
2005	*NYM*	*NL*	*36*	*342*	*90*	*18*	*1*	*16*	*47*	*61*	*0*	*0*	*.264*	*.353*	*.461*	*.047*	*.267*	*.355*	*.476*	*.070*	*24.2*	*94-C*	*-15*		

Breakout: 26% *Improve: 51%* *Collapse: 19%*

Injuries and the failed transition to first base contributed to Piazza's worst year as a pro. This is his decline phase, and it hasn't been pretty, but injuries and discomfort with his status haven't helped. His underlying indicators have largely remained stable, with a dip in power that could well be just the leg injuries he played through. With Piazza in the last year of his contract, the Mets should ride him for all he's worth.

PRENTICE REDMAN RF **Bats: R** **Throws: R** Born: 23-Aug-1979 Age: 25

YEAR	TM	LG	AGE	AB	H	2B	3B	HR	BB	SO	SB	CS	AVG	OBP	SLG	MLVR	EQBA	EQOBP	EQSLG	EQMLVR	VORP	DEFENSE			
2002	BIN	EAS	22	491	139	35	2	11	59	112	43	9	.283	.367	.430	.099	.249	.325	.387	-.118	-8.2	57-RF	-7	38-LF	0
2003	NOR	INT	23	433	110	29	2	11	40	96	24	8	.254	.326	.406	.040	.245	.320	.406	-.104	-6.6	52-LF	-1	50-RF	-1
2004	BIN	EAS	24	245	70	29	1	13	28	68	9	4	.286	.367	.571	.313	.247	.321	.490	.016	6.1	50-RF	-2		
2004	NOR	INT	24	213	54	17	2	4	17	57	9	3	.254	.308	.408	-.038	.249	.303	.399	-.142	-5.8	33-LF	-4	18-CF	0
2005	*NYM*	*NL*	*25*	*175*	*44*	*11*	*1*	*6*	*17*	*45*	*6*	*2*	*.253*	*.327*	*.430*	*-.047*	*.257*	*.328*	*.444*	*-.025*	*9.0*	*50-RF*	*-2*		

Breakout: 30% *Improve: 50%* *Collapse: 30%*

On the surface, it looks like he found his stroke back at Double-A. Really, though, he just grew some additional power. His strikeout rate jumped to an unacceptable level, and when he was pushed back to Triple-A, once again, he didn't hit. The Mets weren't fooled, even lopping him off the 40-man roster in September, just to make room for waiver-bait Brian Buchanan.

JOSE REYES SS, Just SS **Bats: B** **Throws: R** Born: 11-Jun-1983 Age: 22

YEAR	TM	LG	AGE	AB	H	2B	3B	HR	BB	SO	SB	CS	AVG	OBP	SLG	MLVR	EQBA	EQOBP	EQSLG	EQMLVR	VORP	DEFENSE	
2002	SLU	FSL	19	288	83	10	11	6	30	35	31	13	.288	.353	.462	.191	.257	.313	.425	-.081	10.9	69-SS	-2
2002	BIN	EAS	19	275	79	16	8	2	16	42	27	11	.287	.331	.425	.041	.260	.299	.392	-.152	4.2	63-SS	-3
2003	NOR	INT	20	160	43	6	4	0	15	25	26	5	.269	.333	.356	-.005	.259	.318	.340	-.190	0.6	37-SS	-1
2003	NYM	NL	20	274	84	12	4	5	13	36	13	3	.307	.334	.434	.073	.309	.338	.444	.037	21.6	67-SS	9
2004	NYM	NL	21	220	56	16	2	2	5	31	19	2	.255	.271	.373	-.171	.252	.272	.374	-.235	5.2	38-2B	1
2005	*NYM*	*NL*	*22*	*418*	*110*	*23*	*3*	*6*	*25*	*57*	*29*	*7*	*.262*	*.304*	*.374*	*-.154*	*.266*	*.305*	*.387*	*-.135*	*12.7*	*108-SS*	*0*

Breakout: 9% *Improve: 25%* *Collapse: 54%*

(continued next page)

Jose Reyes *(continued)*

It's easy to point to Reyes's hamstring injuries as the reason for his lousy 2004, but the fact is that he's been rushed by the Mets. He isn't ready to hit at the major league level, and his power and batting eye both need serious work. With so many stop-gap middle-infield candidates, the Mets should let Reyes go to Norfolk for at least half a season so that he can continue developing as a hitter. He can still be a star.

SHANE SPENCER **OF** **Bats: R** **Throws: R** Born: 20-Feb-1972 Age: 33

YEAR	TM	LG	AGE	AB	H	2B	3B	HR	BB	SO	SB	CS	AVG	OBP	SLG	MLVR	EQBA	EQOBP	EQSLG	EQMLVR	VORP	DEFENSE	
2002	NYY	AL	30	288	71	15	2	6	31	62	0	3	.247	.324	.375	-.091	.254	.336	.387	-.093	-0.8	47-RF -3	30-LF 2
2003	CLE	AL	31	210	57	10	0	8	18	52	2	0	.271	.328	.433	.022	.279	.333	.438	-.008	7.7	27-RF -1	13-LF 1
2003	TEX	AL	31	185	42	10	0	4	27	40	0	0	.227	.329	.346	-.165	.221	.323	.326	-.222	-2.8	41-LF -4	12-RF 1
2004	NYM	NL	32	185	52	10	1	4	13	37	6	0	.281	.332	.411	.007	.280	.332	.403	-.059	7.3	32-LF -1	17-RF 0
2005	*NYM*	*NL*	*33*	*163*	*40*	*8*	*1*	*4*	*17*	*36*	*2*	*1*	*.248*	*.324*	*.377*	*-.125*	*.251*	*.326*	*.389*	*-.105*	*0.4*	*47-LF -2*	

Breakout: 12% *Improve: 34%* *Collapse: 42%*

The rules are different when you're a marginal player. Spencer, whose rope-the-lefty act made him a decent living in the majors since 1998, was arrested twice last year on alcohol-related charges. The second arrest, a DUI incident while he was on the DL in July, pushed the Mets to release him two weeks later. Now, he's off to Japan. Suffice to say that the level of disdain baseball's front offices have for this type of thing is inversely proportional to a player's VORP.

ERIC VALENT **OF/1B** **Bats: L** **Throws: L** Born: 04-Apr-1977 Age: 28

YEAR	TM	LG	AGE	AB	H	2B	3B	HR	BB	SO	SB	CS	AVG	OBP	SLG	MLVR	EQBA	EQOBP	EQSLG	EQMLVR	VORP	DEFENSE	
2002	SWB	INT	25	546	137	34	2	9	49	94	0	2	.251	.311	.370	-.073	.235	.299	.355	-.221	-25.0	111-RF 10	21-1B -2
2003	SWB	INT	26	450	98	27	2	12	60	102	0	0	.218	.308	.367	-.100	.202	.295	.350	-.256	-27.3	107-RF -3	20-CF 0
2003	CIN	NL	26	42	9	0	0	0	2	9	0	0	.214	.250	.214	-.434	.238	.203	.238	-.582	-3.4		
2004	NYM	NL	27	270	72	15	2	13	28	61	0	1	.267	.337	.481	.103	.266	.335	.483	.048	14.9	22-LF 0	23-1B 1
2005	*NYM*	*NL*	*28*	*188*	*45*	*10*	*1*	*6*	*19*	*43*	*0*	*0*	*.241*	*.312*	*.408*	*-.110*	*.244*	*.314*	*.421*	*-.090*	*3.0*	*53-RF -1*	

Breakout: 23% *Improve: 45%* *Collapse: 28%*

We're used to seeing pleasant surprises emerge from the major league phase of the Rule 5 Draft. Valent, however, came to the Mets in the Triple-A portion. When injuries and incompetence wiped out the Mets' corners in the second half, Valent provided a little bit of pop and good outfield defense. He won't be much better than this; given his low-contact rate and the previous two years, there's a good chance he can't even do this again.

GERALD WILLIAMS **OF** **Bats: R** **Throws: R** Born: 10-Aug-1966 Age: 38

YEAR	TM	LG	AGE	AB	H	2B	3B	HR	BB	SO	SB	CS	AVG	OBP	SLG	MLVR	EQBA	EQOBP	EQSLG	EQMLVR	VORP	DEFENSE	
2002	LOU	INT	35	205	54	10	3	2	11	36	6	4	.263	.307	.371	-.082	.245	.292	.353	-.231	-4.9	47-CF -2	
2003	ABQ	PCL	36	327	99	22	5	14	24	45	15	11	.303	.356	.529	.128	.242	.297	.434	-.110	3.6	69-CF 3	
2004	NOR	INT	37	246	75	10	3	7	9	35	6	9	.305	.335	.455	.124	.300	.330	.445	.016	5.1	33-LF 0	12-CF 1
2004	NYM	NL	37	129	30	8	2	4	8	26	2	1	.233	.277	.419	-.120	.231	.275	.423	-.175	0.4	15-CF 0	
2005	*NYM*	*NL*	*38*	*148*	*34*	*7*	*1*	*3*	*8*	*28*	*2*	*1*	*.231*	*.272*	*.364*	*-.246*	*.234*	*.273*	*.376*	*-.228*	*0.0*	*42-CF -9*	

Breakout: 9% *Improve: 36%* *Collapse: 46%*

The Mets have a handful of players who are underqualified for the extra outfielder job. Esix Snead and Jeff Duncan and now Ron Calloway are all in the organization, but Williams is the only one old enough to be a dad to the Mets' rookie-ball prospects. It's long past due for Ice to be put on ice.

VANCE WILSON **C** **Bats: R** **Throws: R** Born: 17-Mar-1973 Age: 32

YEAR	TM	LG	AGE	AB	H	2B	3B	HR	BB	SO	SB	CS	AVG	OBP	SLG	MLVR	EQBA	EQOBP	EQSLG	EQMLVR	VORP	DEFENSE
2002	NYM	NL	29	163	40	7	0	5	5	32	0	1	.245	.301	.380	-.074	.259	.301	.398	-.140	4.4	44-C 13
2003	NYM	NL	30	268	65	9	1	8	15	56	1	2	.243	.293	.373	-.132	.248	.298	.381	-.178	2.9	75-C 5
2004	NYM	NL	31	157	43	10	1	4	11	24	1	0	.274	.335	.427	.025	.272	.330	.430	-.031	8.8	41-C 2
2005	*DET*	*AL*	*32*	*121*	*30*	*6*	*0*	*3*	*7*	*22*	*0*	*0*	*.249*	*.307*	*.391*	*-.129*	*.253*	*.312*	*.408*	*-.105*	*4.2*	*36-C 1*

Breakout: 14% *Improve: 34%* *Collapse: 44%*

Decent backup catcher with a little more pop than most. The Mets got themselves in trouble by thinking they had three starting catchers and could move one to first base. What they actually had was one starter and two good backups in Phillips and Wilson. With Piazza likely to be back behind the plate and Ramon Castro now in the system, the Mets were free to trade Wilson to the Tigers. There, he'll back up another Hall of Famer.

DAVID WRIGHT 3B **Bats: R** **Throws: R** Born: 20-Dec-1982 Age: 22

YEAR	TM	LG	AGE	AB	H	2B	3B	HR	BB	SO	SB	CS	AVG	OBP	SLG	MLVR	EQBA	EQOBP	EQSLG	EQMLVR	VORP	DEFENSE
2002	CMB	SAL	19	496	132	30	2	11	76	114	21	5	.266	.367	.401	.132	.228	.307	.354	-.212	-5.1	120-3B -7
2003	SLU	FSL	20	466	126	39	2	15	72	98	19	5	.270	.369	.459	.211	.234	.319	.424	-.089	14.7	130-3B -7
2004	BIN	EAS	21	223	81	27	0	10	39	41	20	6	.363	.467	.619	.600	.320	.409	.542	.308	35.2	56-3B -6
2004	NOR	INT	21	114	34	8	0	8	16	19	2	4	.298	.388	.579	.380	.281	.357	.544	.185	13.6	31-3B 1
2004	NYM	NL	21	263	77	17	1	14	14	40	6	0	.293	.332	.525	.176	.292	.329	.523	.120	21.2	66-3B -3
2005	*NYM*	*NL*	*22*	*422*	*117*	*26*	*2*	*18*	*50*	*83*	*13*	*3*	*.276*	*.358*	*.477*	*.087*	*.280*	*.360*	*.492*	*.111*	*32.4*	*114-3B -4*

Breakout: 21% *Improve: 48%* *Collapse: 23%*

He took much the same path Reyes did, getting pushed through the system as the Mets tried to distract the fans from the lousy season they were having. Unlike Reyes, though, he played very well at Triple-A and in the majors, with just some degradation in his walk rate along the way. His defense is good, too, so he's staying at third base. He's right where Scott Rolen was at 22, and should continue to match the All-Star's career path.

TODD ZEILE 1B/3B **Bats: R** **Throws: R** Born: 09-Sep-1965 Age: 39

YEAR	TM	LG	AGE	AB	H	2B	3B	HR	BB	SO	SB	CS	AVG	OBP	SLG	MLVR	EQBA	EQOBP	EQSLG	EQMLVR	VORP	DEFENSE
2002	COL	NL	36	506	138	23	0	18	66	92	1	1	.273	.353	.425	.014	.257	.334	.409	-.064	24.3	134-3B -15
2003	MON	NL	37	113	29	2	2	5	10	18	1	0	.257	.331	.442	-.061	.248	.319	.442	-.054	3.3	32-3B 0
2003	NYY	AL	37	186	39	8	0	6	24	36	0	0	.210	.294	.349	-.197	.217	.301	.353	-.231	-0.5	26-3B 2 21-1B 0
2004	NYM	NL	38	348	81	16	0	9	44	83	0	0	.233	.319	.356	-.122	.235	.316	.355	-.188	0.4	43-1B 0 41-3B -4

It was a feel-good last season for Zeile, who picked up his 2,000th hit and 250th homer along the way, and even got to go back behind the plate a couple of times; whether out of sympathy or fear, no one tried to steal on him. He's one of the best players to ever play on ten major league teams.

PITCHERS

BRIAN BANNISTER **Bats: R** **Throws: R** Born: 28-Feb-1981 Age: 24

YEAR	TM	LG	AGE	G	GS	IP	H	BB	SO	HR	ERA	EQERA	EQH9	EQBB9	EQSO9	EQHR9	PERA	VORP	STF
2003	BRO	NYP	22	12	9	46.0	27	18	42	0	2.15	4.46	7.6	4.7	5.1	0.2	4.02	7.1	6
2004	SLU	FSL	23	20	20	110.3	111	27	106	6	4.24	6.23	9.6	2.5	5.9	1.0	4.59	11.7	3
2004	BIN	EAS	23	8	8	44.3	45	17	28	2	4.06	5.14	9.4	3.6	4.3	0.6	4.71	4.2	-7
2005	*NYM*	*NL*	*24*	*14*	*12*	*73.0*	*75*	*28*	*51*	*8*	*4.37*	*4.72*	*9.2*	*3.1*	*5.7*	*1.0*	*4.78*	*8.8*	*5*

Breakout: 13% *Improve: 40%* *Collapse: 31%*

Floyd's son is a command guy who throws a four-pitch assortment for strikes and has the usual adjectives—savvy, gutsy, etc.—floating around him. It's all air until he proves he can get older hitters out, and his stint at Double-A wasn't encouraging. Eventually he could be a back-end starter, but the development path is going to be long. Bannister is one of two scions who played at St. Lucie last year; first baseman Brett Harper hits a bit like his dad, the one-time Twins' catcher.

HEATH BELL **Bats: R** **Throws: R** Born: 29-Sep-1977 Age: 27

YEAR	TM	LG	AGE	G	GS	IP	H	BB	SO	HR	ERA	EQERA	EQH9	EQBB9	EQSO9	EQHR9	PERA	VORP	STF
2002	BIN	EAS	24	24	0	38.0	22	6	49	0	1.18	2.29	6.4	1.5	9.2	0.3	2.04	14.0	34
2002	NOR	INT	24	22	0	31.7	38	9	28	2	4.26	4.88	9.5	2.9	6.6	0.9	4.60	3.5	-4
2003	NOR	INT	25	40	0	49.7	54	8	54	4	4.71	5.40	9.3	1.7	7.8	1.1	4.28	7.1	5
2004	NOR	INT	26	45	0	55.7	42	24	69	4	3.23	3.76	7.3	4.1	9.2	0.9	3.59	11.8	18
2004	NYM	NL	26	17	0	24.3	22	6	27	5	3.33	3.47	8.5	1.9	9.3	1.5	4.24	6.4	19
2005	*NYM*	*NL*	*27*	*23*	*4*	*49.3*	*45*	*17*	*49*	*6*	*3.55*	*3.84*	*8.2*	*2.7*	*8.0*	*1.0*	*4.05*	*10.3*	*12*

Breakout: 16% *Improve: 46%* *Collapse: 32%*

(continued next page)

Heath Bell *(continued)*

This minor league closer is the rare case whose peripherals have been better than his ERAs for three years running, in part because Bell has given up just one unearned run in three years. As Michael Wolverton suggests, we should ignore the difference between earned and unearned runs anyway, focusing on all runs allowed. Roughly comparable to the Rangers' Carlos Almanzar, Bell should be the Mets' top set-up man by the end of the year.

KRIS BENSON Bats: R Throws: R Born: 07-Nov-1974 Age: 30

YEAR	TM	LG	AGE	G	GS	IP	H	BB	SO	HR	ERA	EQERA	EQH9	EQBB9	EQSO9	EQHR9	PERA	VORP	STF
2002	PIT	NL	27	25	25	130.3	152	50	79	18	4.70	5.16	10.2	3.0	4.8	1.2	5.37	3.7	-2
2003	PIT	NL	28	18	18	105.0	127	36	68	14	4.97	5.54	10.0	2.7	5.2	1.1	5.02	-0.5	5
2004	PIT	NL	29	20	20	132.3	137	44	83	7	4.22	4.53	8.9	2.7	5.0	0.4	3.70	15.8	17
2004	NYM	NL	29	11	11	68.0	65	17	51	8	4.50	4.85	8.9	2.1	6.1	1.0	4.02	6.6	19
2005	*NYM*	*NL*	*30*	*26*	*26*	*152.3*	*159*	*51*	*102*	*18*	*4.50*	*4.86*	*9.4*	*2.7*	*5.4*	*1.1*	*4.77*	*13.6*	*6*

Breakout: 11% *Improve: 47%* *Collapse: 23%*

Benson is one of the ten most overrated players in baseball, largely based on his status as the #1 overall pick in 1996. Last year was his first as a league-average pitcher since 2000, and the season was just that—average. His peripherals are just okay, and the idea that he's a high-upside guy is wrong. He's 30, for crying out loud. The three-year, $22 million contract he signed in November kicked off the silly off-season for pitchers, and like so many other free agents this winter, Benson is likely going to be a disappointment for the life of the deal.

P. J. BEVIS Bats: R Throws: R Born: 28-Jul-1980 Age: 24

YEAR	TM	LG	AGE	G	GS	IP	H	BB	SO	HR	ERA	EQERA	EQH9	EQBB9	EQSO9	EQHR9	PERA	VORP	STF
2002	ELP	TXS	21	49	0	63.7	50	29	62	3	2.83	3.79	7.9	4.6	6.8	0.8	3.94	10.9	10
2003	BIN	EAS	22	46	0	71.0	55	30	100	4	4.18	5.21	7.5	4.1	10.3	0.9	3.61	14.9	22
2004	NOR	INT	23	22	0	26.7	28	23	16	3	5.06	8.17	9.6	8.2	4.6	1.1	6.39	-2.2	-34
2004	BIN	EAS	23	27	0	32.3	26	8	32	3	3.07	3.90	8.4	2.4	6.9	1.2	3.90	5.7	7
2005	*NYM*	*NL*	*24*	*18*	*2*	*28.7*	*27*	*15*	*25*	*4*	*4.77*	*5.15*	*8.4*	*4.2*	*7.0*	*1.3*	*5.09*	*2.3*	*-3*

Breakout: 9% *Improve: 34%* *Collapse: 34%*

Bevis's command, long his nemesis, deserted him again at Norfolk, forcing the Mets to send him back down. In another organization, his mid-90s heat would mark him as more of a prospect, but the Mets have so many right-handed relievers in their system that they can be picky. Another hard thrower, Matt Lindstrom, touched 100 this season but is old and didn't do much at St. Lucie.

RICKY BOTTALICO Bats: L Throws: R Born: 26-Aug-1969 Age: 35

YEAR	TM	LG	AGE	G	GS	IP	H	BB	SO	HR	ERA	EQERA	EQH9	EQBB9	EQSO9	EQHR9	PERA	VORP	STF
2002	PHI	NL	32	30	0	27.3	33	13	24	3	4.62	5.60	10.2	3.6	6.9	1.0	5.27	0.3	-4
2003	TUC	PCL	33	31	0	39.3	39	16	28	4	3.66	5.30	8.9	4.1	5.5	1.4	5.06	2.2	-9
2004	NYM	NL	34	60	0	69.3	54	34	61	3	3.38	3.93	7.5	4.1	7.2	0.4	3.39	13.9	8
2005	*MIL*	*NL*	*35*	*35*	*4*	*61.0*	*59*	*30*	*52*	*7*	*4.62*	*4.79*	*8.7*	*3.9*	*6.9*	*1.0*	*4.85*	*6.6*	*-1*

Breakout: 24% *Improve: 52%* *Collapse: 25%*

One thing the Mets do a better job of than their cross-town rivals is filling the bottom of the roster. Bottalico provided good low-leverage relief after spending most of 2003 in the minors, and even moved into a set-up role in the second half. His year was a bit fluky in that he had a very low home-run rate for a flyball pitcher, so expecting a repeat of that ERA is optimistic. He's a free agent.

MIKE DeJEAN Bats: R Throws: R Born: 28-Sep-1970 Age: 34

YEAR	TM	LG	AGE	G	GS	IP	H	BB	SO	HR	ERA	EQERA	EQH9	EQBB9	EQSO9	EQHR9	PERA	VORP	STF
2002	MIL	NL	31	68	0	75.0	66	39	65	7	3.12	3.47	8.3	4.1	6.9	0.9	4.21	16.8	0
2003	MIL	NL	32	58	0	64.7	69	27	58	12	4.87	5.09	9.2	3.3	7.2	1.6	4.81	2.4	-3
2003	STL	NL	32	18	0	18.0	17	12	13	1	4.00	4.08	8.7	5.1	6.1	0.5	4.58	3.2	-11
2004	BAL	AL	33	37	0	39.7	49	28	36	2	6.12	5.71	9.4	5.5	7.5	0.4	5.05	-1.3	-3
2004	NYM	NL	33	17	0	21.3	21	5	24	0	1.69	2.14	8.1	1.7	9.0	0.0	3.00	8.5	24
2005	*NYM*	*NL*	*34*	*45*	*1*	*59.7*	*57*	*29*	*53*	*5*	*3.97*	*4.29*	*8.7*	*3.8*	*7.2*	*0.7*	*4.59*	*9.1*	*3*

Breakout: 30% *Improve: 45%* *Collapse: 24%*

DeJean made three appearances after a line drive fractured his right tibia on August 19, one of the better tough-guy stories of the season. Up until the injury, he'd been very good in his two months with the Mets, who picked him up for Karim Garcia after the Orioles lost interest. He's expected to be healthy in 2005, and will be the Mets' top set-up man, getting ground balls and walking a few too many guys to be really good.

PEDRO FELICIANO Bats: L Throws: L Born: 25-Aug-1976 Age: 28

YEAR	TM	LG	AGE	G	GS	IP	H	BB	SO	HR	ERA	EQERA	EQH9	EQBB9	EQSO9	EQHR9	PERA	VORP	STF
2002	CHT	SOU	25	28	0	38.7	33	11	26	1	2.56	4.21	8.2	2.5	4.5	0.5	3.22	9.6	0
2002	LOU	INT	25	20	0	26.7	35	4	19	3	3.03	3.76	10.6	1.4	5.5	1.4	5.13	1.4	0
2003	NOR	INT	26	15	0	22.7	20	6	18	3	3.96	4.71	9.0	3.0	6.0	1.7	4.71	2.1	-3
2003	NYM	NL	26	23	0	48.3	52	21	43	5	3.35	3.94	9.0	3.4	7.1	0.9	4.50	9.2	8
2004	NOR	INT	27	32	0	35.7	35	15	25	4	5.29	6.42	9.1	4.0	5.3	1.3	5.08	1.9	-12
2004	NYM	NL	27	22	0	18.3	14	12	14	2	5.41	5.71	7.8	5.2	6.2	1.0	4.15	-0.4	-5
2005	*NYM*	*NL*	*28*	*21*	*2*	*37.3*	*37*	*16*	*28*	*4*	*4.29*	*4.64*	*9.0*	*3.4*	*6.0*	*1.0*	*4.81*	*4.6*	*-4*

Breakout: 25% *Improve: 52%* *Collapse: 27%*

If he's going to have a career, now is the time. The Mets have traded Mike Stanton, leaving Feliciano to beat Felix Heredia for the lefty set-up job. He's not dominant, just a guy who keeps the ball in the park and changes speeds. Needs to throw more strikes.

BARTOLOME FORTUNATO Bats: R Throws: R Born: 24-Aug-1974 Age: 30

YEAR	TM	LG	AGE	G	GS	IP	H	BB	SO	HR	ERA	EQERA	EQH9	EQBB9	EQSO9	EQHR9	PERA	VORP	STF
2002	BAK	CLF	27	25	5	60.7	58	25	85	3	4.00	5.55	8.8	4.2	7.3	0.8	4.17	9.3	4
2002	ORL	SOU	27	10	2	25.7	16	11	34	2	2.10	3.42	7.2	3.8	9.1	1.5	3.80	4.7	20
2003	ORL	SOU	28	35	1	53.0	48	20	63	4	3.06	5.26	9.2	3.4	7.8	1.4	4.89	3.9	0
2003	DUR	INT	28	5	4	21.7	15	11	20	3	3.32	4.66	7.9	5.6	7.4	1.9	5.59	0.0	4
2004	DUR	INT	29	34	0	44.7	28	21	54	4	2.42	2.81	6.7	4.5	9.1	1.1	3.46	9.9	22
2004	NYM	NL	29	15	0	18.7	14	13	20	2	3.85	4.00	7.5	5.5	8.5	1.0	4.00	3.8	6
2005	*NYM*	*NL*	*30*	*42*	*0*	*46.7*	*40*	*24*	*45*	*6*	*4.09*	*4.42*	*7.8*	*4.0*	*7.8*	*1.1*	*4.48*	*7.0*	*3*

Breakout: 30% *Improve: 53%* *Collapse: 22%*

Here's a scary thought: Fortunato may end up being the best pitcher the Mets got for Scott Kazmir, what with Victor Zambrano's well-worn arm. That's not entirely a bad thing. A fastball/slider guy, Fortunato hasn't pitched badly since 2001 in the New York–Penn League, and was effective in short major league stints on both sides of the trade. The Mets are loaded from the right side of the pen.

JOHN FRANCO Bats: L Throws: L Born: 17-Sep-1960 Age: 44

YEAR	TM	LG	AGE	G	GS	IP	H	BB	SO	HR	ERA	EQERA	EQH9	EQBB9	EQSO9	EQHR9	PERA	VORP	STF
2003	NYM	NL	42	38	0	34.3	35	13	16	5	2.62	3.00	9.5	3.0	3.8	1.4	4.91	10.4	-20
2004	NYM	NL	43	52	0	46.0	46	24	36	6	5.28	5.44	9.1	4.2	6.2	1.0	4.84	1.1	-8
2005	*HOU*	*NL*	*44*	*22*	*1*	*31.7*	*35*	*15*	*23*	*5*	*4.87*	*4.96*	*9.9*	*3.8*	*6.0*	*1.2*	*5.48*	*3.5*	*-9*

Breakout: 29% *Improve: 44%* *Collapse: 22%*

He should retire, although he hadn't officially done so as of early January. Franco has nothing to be ashamed of: a career ERA of 2.84, a five-year run with the Reds in which he was one of the best relievers in baseball, and a stretch twice that long of effective, if not dominant, short relief. He's not a Hall of Famer, which shouldn't be the insult so many people take it to be.

MATT GINTER Bats: R Throws: R Born: 24-Dec-1977 Age: 27

YEAR	TM	LG	AGE	G	GS	IP	H	BB	SO	HR	ERA	EQERA	EQH9	EQBB9	EQSO9	EQHR9	PERA	VORP	STF
2002	CWS	AL	24	33	0	54.3	59	21	37	6	4.48	5.09	9.5	3.2	5.9	0.8	4.92	2.1	-5
2003	CHR	INT	25	49	0	68.3	66	22	52	2	3.03	4.15	8.6	3.3	5.5	0.4	3.88	12.4	-1
2004	NOR	INT	26	11	11	64.0	55	8	49	4	2.95	4.03	8.2	1.2	5.8	0.7	3.28	15.5	26
2004	NYM	NL	26	15	14	69.3	82	20	38	8	4.55	5.19	10.1	2.3	4.4	0.9	4.92	3.4	3
2005	*NYM*	*NL*	*27*	*21*	*14*	*90.0*	*95*	*29*	*58*	*11*	*4.57*	*4.94*	*9.5*	*2.6*	*5.2*	*1.1*	*4.83*	*7.2*	*-1*

Breakout: 14% *Improve: 39%* *Collapse: 27%*

(continued next page)

Matt Ginter *(continued)*

Acquired in the spring for Timo Perez, the Mets put Ginter back into the rotation, a role he hadn't had since mid-2001. He pitched so well at Norfolk that they called him up to patch a hole in May. He fell apart soon afterwards, and his season eventually ended early due to bone chips in his ankle. With the rebuilt rotation, a lot of things will have to go wrong for him to get 14 major league starts again.

TOM GLAVINE **Bats: L** **Throws: L** Born: 25-Mar-1966 Age: 39

YEAR	TM	LG	AGE	G	GS	IP	H	BB	SO	HR	ERA	EQERA	EQH9	EQBB9	EQSO9	EQHR9	PERA	VORP	STF
2002	ATL	NL	36	36	36	224.7	210	78	127	21	2.96	3.53	9.3	2.8	4.7	0.9	4.81	52.3	3
2003	NYM	NL	37	32	32	183.3	205	66	82	21	4.52	4.60	9.8	2.9	3.7	1.0	4.90	22.1	-5
2004	NYM	NL	38	33	33	212.3	204	70	109	20	3.60	3.97	9.1	2.7	4.2	0.8	4.28	42.0	3
2005	*NYM*	*NL*	*39*	*30*	*28*	*163.3*	*178*	*59*	*84*	*20*	*4.62*	*4.99*	*9.8*	*2.9*	*4.1*	*1.1*	*5.07*	*12.2*	*-5*

Breakout: 6% *Improve: 45%* *Collapse: 25%*

Glavine continued his slow fade in '04, although he's still an effective mid-rotation guy. You wonder if the decision to leave Atlanta might have cost him his shot at 300 wins. A peek at Glavine's translated line shows that the Mets' lack of support has cost him 11 wins over the past two seasons (projected record: 31–23, actual 20–28). He's at 262, and the difference between that and 273 is a season, huge for a guy who won't have many seasons left. He's a Hall of Famer, regardless.

AARON HEILMAN **Bats: R** **Throws: R** Born: 12-Nov-1978 Age: 26

YEAR	TM	LG	AGE	G	GS	IP	H	BB	SO	HR	ERA	EQERA	EQH9	EQBB9	EQSO9	EQHR9	PERA	VORP	STF
2002	BIN	EAS	23	17	17	96.7	85	28	97	7	3.82	4.45	8.6	2.8	7.0	1.0	4.15	14.7	17
2002	NOR	INT	23	10	7	49.3	42	16	35	3	3.29	4.08	8.2	3.3	5.6	0.8	3.88	8.8	15
2003	NOR	INT	24	16	16	94.3	99	32	71	5	3.24	4.18	9.1	3.5	5.5	0.7	4.38	12.2	5
2003	NYM	NL	24	14	13	65.3	79	41	51	13	6.75	7.16	10.2	4.8	6.2	1.7	6.20	-11.7	-12
2004	NOR	INT	25	26	26	151.7	156	66	123	15	4.33	5.39	9.2	4.1	6.0	1.1	4.83	12.4	2
2004	NYM	NL	25	5	5	28.0	27	13	22	4	5.46	5.33	9.0	3.7	6.3	1.3	5.00	0.9	3
2005	*NYM*	*NL*	*26*	*23*	*11*	*78.7*	*77*	*36*	*59*	*9*	*4.68*	*5.06*	*8.9*	*3.6*	*6.1*	*1.0*	*4.88*	*4.5*	*-1*

Breakout: 12% *Improve: 36%* *Collapse: 27%*

Ginter's success gave the Mets an excuse to leave Heilman in Triple-A most of the year. He didn't improve, strengthening the case for simply ignoring anything a college pitcher does before he gets to Triple-A. Heilman's strikeout rate dropped 20% from Double-A to Triple-A, and has never really come back. He'll be waiting for at least one pitcher, maybe two, to get hurt.

BOB KEPPEL **Bats: R** **Throws: R** Born: 11-Jun-1982 Age: 23

YEAR	TM	LG	AGE	G	GS	IP	H	BB	SO	HR	ERA	EQERA	EQH9	EQBB9	EQSO9	EQHR9	PERA	VORP	STF
2002	SLU	FSL	20	27	26	152.0	162	43	109	13	4.32	5.93	10.4	2.8	4.7	1.5	5.43	2.7	-1
2003	BIN	EAS	21	18	17	94.7	92	27	46	6	3.04	4.08	9.2	2.9	3.7	0.9	4.18	13.9	11
2004	NOR	INT	22	17	16	93.7	111	22	42	8	4.71	5.08	10.2	2.2	3.3	0.8	4.68	9.2	1
2005	*NYM*	*NL*	*23*	*23*	*14*	*91.7*	*102*	*31*	*48*	*13*	*4.83*	*5.21*	*10.1*	*2.7*	*4.3*	*1.3*	*5.34*	*5.1*	*-9*

Breakout: 8% *Improve: 39%* *Collapse: 28%*

Pick your problem: Keppel, the Mets' #1 pick in 2000, has been shut down the past two seasons with shoulder soreness. When on the mound, he's posted awful strikeout rates at the top two minor league levels. You can make a good case that the Mets had no business pushing him to Norfolk last year. Until Keppel shows he can be both healthy and effective, he's properly considered a first-round bust.

AL LEITER **Bats: L** **Throws: L** Born: 23-Oct-1965 Age: 39

YEAR	TM	LG	AGE	G	GS	IP	H	BB	SO	HR	ERA	EQERA	EQH9	EQBB9	EQSO9	EQHR9	PERA	VORP	STF
2002	NYM	NL	36	33	33	204.3	194	69	172	23	3.48	4.61	8.7	2.6	6.8	1.1	4.07	25.9	16
2003	NYM	NL	37	30	30	180.7	176	94	139	15	3.98	4.17	8.6	4.1	6.3	0.7	4.32	31.4	12
2004	NYM	NL	38	30	30	173.7	138	97	117	16	3.21	3.40	8.0	4.6	5.6	0.8	4.16	46.2	5
2005	*FLA*	*NL*	*39*	*30*	*24*	*148.3*	*141*	*69*	*113*	*16*	*4.25*	*4.64*	*8.6*	*3.7*	*6.1*	*1.0*	*4.83*	*14.9*	*5*

Breakout: 9% *Improve: 49%* *Collapse: 8%*

Like Mariano Rivera, Leiter has become basically a one-pitch pitcher, building everything around a cut fastball that he busts in on right-handed hitters. He works off the plate so much that his ratios have fallen apart; his low ERA had more to do with a .244 batting average allowed on balls in play, not a number he can expect to sustain. The Marlins' good defense may help him stave off the descent a bit, but expect his ERA to go up a run in 2005 and get worse from there.

BRADEN LOOPER **Bats: R** **Throws: R** Born: 28-Oct-1974 Age: 30

YEAR	TM	LG	AGE	G	GS	IP	H	BB	SO	HR	ERA	EQERA	EQH9	EQBB9	EQSO9	EQHR9	PERA	VORP	STF
2002	FLA	NL	27	78	0	86.0	73	28	55	8	3.14	3.43	8.3	2.5	5.3	0.9	3.54	20.4	-3
2003	FLA	NL	28	74	0	80.7	82	29	56	4	3.68	3.99	8.8	2.8	5.7	0.5	3.76	16.4	1
2004	NYM	NL	29	71	0	83.3	86	16	60	5	2.70	3.12	9.0	1.6	5.8	0.4	3.68	24.8	6
2005	*NYM*	*NL*	*30*	*52*	*2*	*74.7*	*76*	*22*	*52*	*6*	*3.48*	*3.76*	*9.2*	*2.4*	*5.6*	*0.8*	*4.15*	*14.9*	*-1*

Breakout: 29% *Improve: 59%* *Collapse: 18%*

It's amazing how many happy things occur when you just flat stop walking people. Looper, a closer prospect seemingly since *Baseball Prospectus 1955,* had his best season by halving his walk rate while continuing to keep the ball down. He's improved in four straight seasons, and is on the brink of becoming a very wealthy man. He's no hothouse flower, either: Looper had the second-highest average of innings per appearance of any 20-save man in baseball.

ORBER MORENO **Bats: R** **Throws: R** Born: 27-Apr-1977 Age: 28

YEAR	TM	LG	AGE	G	GS	IP	H	BB	SO	HR	ERA	EQERA	EQH9	EQBB9	EQSO9	EQHR9	PERA	VORP	STF
2003	NOR	INT	26	38	0	52.0	36	17	58	1	1.90	2.59	6.8	3.3	8.3	0.2	2.77	15.3	23
2003	NYM	NL	26	7	0	8.0	10	3	5	1	7.88	7.88	10.1	3.4	4.5	1.1	5.62	-2.0	-9
2004	NYM	NL	27	33	0	34.7	29	11	29	0	3.37	4.36	7.9	2.7	6.8	0.3	3.27	5.0	7
2005	*NYM*	*NL*	*28*	*18*	*1*	*26.7*	*26*	*10*	*21*	*2*	*3.90*	*4.21*	*8.7*	*2.9*	*6.3*	*0.7*	*4.11*	*4.3*	*1*

Breakout: 16% *Improve: 36%* *Collapse: 31%*

Finally healthy for a little while, the erstwhile closer prospect got back to the majors and pitched well. Then he got unhealthy again, straining his heretofore sound right shoulder in June and eventually undergoing season-ending surgery. There are so many reasons to like him—in addition to what you see above, he had a 2-to-1 GB:FB ratio—but he's kind of the 21st-century version of Steve Ontiveros.

YUSMEIRO PETIT **Bats: R** **Throws: R** Born: 22-Nov-1984 Age: 20

YEAR	TM	LG	AGE	G	GS	IP	H	BB	SO	HR	ERA	EQERA	EQH9	EQBB9	EQSO9	EQHR9	PERA	VORP	STF
2003	KNG	APL	18	12	12	62.0	47	8	65	2	2.32	4.74	8.4	1.6	5.2	0.9	3.16	15.5	31
2004	CMB	SAL	19	15	15	83.0	47	22	122	8	2.39	4.22	7.4	2.9	8.6	1.4	3.38	18.4	51
2004	SLU	FSL	19	9	9	44.3	27	14	62	0	1.22	3.10	6.9	3.3	8.9	0.2	2.66	13.3	49
2004	BIN	EAS	19	2	2	12.0	10	5	16	0	4.50	4.76	7.9	4.0	8.7	0.0	3.18	3.0	43
2005	*NYM*	*NL*	*20*	*18*	*15*	*99.0*	*81*	*35*	*96*	*11*	*3.44*	*3.72*	*7.4*	*2.8*	*7.8*	*1.0*	*3.67*	*22.3*	*22*

Breakout: 16% *Improve: 50%* *Collapse: 17%*

Petit features a fastball, slider and otherworldly command for a teenager. His age is clearly a concern, with his control and efficiency (good) working against his repertoire (the slider) in the battle for the condition of his right arm. That he showed no hiccups in a brief Double-A stint is encouraging. The Mets' free-agent signings this winter should keep them from rushing Petit; he'll be in the rotation mix in '06, however.

JAE SEO **Bats: R** **Throws: R** Born: 24-May-1977 Age: 28

YEAR	TM	LG	AGE	G	GS	IP	H	BB	SO	HR	ERA	EQERA	EQH9	EQBB9	EQSO9	EQHR9	PERA	VORP	STF
2002	NOR	INT	25	26	24	128.7	145	22	87	14	3.99	5.30	9.8	1.7	5.2	1.4	4.72	12.1	0
2003	NYM	NL	26	32	31	188.3	193	46	110	18	3.82	4.51	9.1	1.9	4.9	0.8	4.06	25.2	9
2004	NOR	INT	27	4	4	22.3	22	8	20	1	2.83	3.32	8.7	3.3	6.6	0.4	4.15	3.5	13
2004	NYM	NL	27	24	21	117.7	133	50	54	17	4.89	5.07	10.1	3.4	3.7	1.2	5.38	8.3	-14
2005	*NYM*	*NL*	*28*	*20*	*16*	*98.7*	*109*	*34*	*54*	*13*	*4.84*	*5.22*	*10.0*	*2.8*	*4.4*	*1.2*	*5.24*	*6.4*	*-5*

Breakout: 16% *Improve: 48%* *Collapse: 29%*

Seo's inability to be better than replacement level indirectly led to the Benson and Zambrano trades. He needs to give up as few walks as possible to succeed, and last year, the command wasn't there. Like Ginter and Heilman, Seo awaits word on Zambrano's health to determine his '05 role. A change of scenery would help.

MIKE STANTON

Bats: L **Throws: L** Born: 02-Jun-1967 Age: 38

YEAR	TM	LG	AGE	G	GS	IP	H	BB	SO	HR	ERA	EQERA	EQH9	EQBB9	EQSO9	EQHR9	PERA	VORP	STF
2002	NYY	AL	35	79	0	78.0	73	28	44	4	3.00	3.35	8.4	3.0	4.9	0.5	3.46	22.8	-3
2003	NYM	NL	36	50	0	45.3	37	19	34	6	4.57	5.02	8.2	3.3	6.3	1.3	4.19	3.3	-7
2004	NYM	NL	37	83	0	77.0	70	33	58	6	3.16	3.77	8.4	3.5	6.2	0.6	3.89	16.8	-3
2005	*NYY*	*AL*	*38*	*48*	*0*	*49.3*	*55*	*19*	*33*	*5*	*4.43*	*4.43*	*10.2*	*3.1*	*5.3*	*0.9*	*4.95*	*8.9*	*-10*

Breakout: 36% *Improve: 58%* *Collapse: 16%*

The Yankees have gotten nothing in the way of quality left-handed relief since Stanton was let go as a free agent, so their trading for him two years later is an apparent admission of remorse. The thing is, Stanton wasn't that good in exile; he slipped after 2001 and hasn't had the same power or command since then. Stanton is miscast as a specialist—he's effective against right-handed hitters and doesn't destroy lefties. He should be used for complete innings, even multiple innings, rather than as a LOOGY.

STEVE TRACHSEL

Bats: R **Throws: R** Born: 31-Oct-1970 Age: 34

YEAR	TM	LG	AGE	G	GS	IP	H	BB	SO	HR	ERA	EQERA	EQH9	EQBB9	EQSO9	EQHR9	PERA	VORP	STF
2002	NYM	NL	31	30	30	173.7	170	69	105	16	3.37	4.37	9.1	3.1	4.9	0.9	4.32	26.2	5
2003	NYM	NL	32	33	33	204.7	204	65	111	26	3.78	3.99	9.2	2.6	4.5	1.1	4.50	39.6	1
2004	NYM	NL	33	33	33	202.7	203	83	117	25	4.00	4.55	9.3	3.3	4.7	1.0	4.73	25.8	0
2005	*NYM*	*NL*	*34*	*26*	*26*	*152.0*	*163*	*58*	*85*	*20*	*4.74*	*5.12*	*9.7*	*3.0*	*4.5*	*1.2*	*5.16*	*9.7*	*-2*

Breakout: 10% *Improve: 45%* *Collapse: 22%*

The top three starters in the Mets' rotation last season combined to strike out 343 hitters and walk 250 (223 unintentionally). The ERAs and the innings totals look good, but that's a shaky foundation on which to build a home. Once a much better pitcher than now, Trachsel is just barely getting by, leaning heavily on the big park and the Mets' defense. He doesn't have great command any longer, and he never had really great stuff. He's the starter most likely to make 15 relief appearances this year.

TYLER YATES

Bats: R **Throws: R** Born: 07-Aug-1977 Age: 27

YEAR	TM	LG	AGE	G	GS	IP	H	BB	SO	HR	ERA	EQERA	EQH9	EQBB9	EQSO9	EQHR9	PERA	VORP	STF
2002	NOR	INT	24	24	0	34.0	29	13	34	1	1.32	3.31	7.4	3.9	7.7	0.3	3.31	8.3	10
2003	SLU	FSL	25	14	11	48.0	41	24	49	5	4.31	6.80	10.6	5.5	6.8	3.2	7.65	-9.6	-19
2003	BIN	EAS	25	8	8	39.3	33	17	36	4	4.35	5.45	8.7	4.5	6.9	1.7	4.95	2.6	8
2003	NOR	INT	25	4	4	20.0	22	9	15	1	4.05	4.66	9.3	4.7	5.6	0.5	4.66	2.0	4
2004	NOR	INT	26	30	1	39.7	28	22	43	2	3.17	4.34	7.0	5.3	8.2	0.5	3.62	8.2	10
2004	NYM	NL	26	21	7	46.7	61	25	35	6	6.36	6.70	10.5	4.2	5.9	1.0	5.74	-6.2	-6
2005	*NYM*	*NL*	*27*	*20*	*6*	*50.7*	*50*	*26*	*41*	*6*	*4.63*	*5.00*	*9.0*	*4.0*	*6.5*	*1.0*	*5.07*	*4.4*	*-2*

Breakout: 21% *Improve: 43%* *Collapse: 35%*

Since coming back from Tommy John surgery in '02, Yates has been tried as both a starter and a reliever. He's a big guy who seems to have the build to carry a lot of innings, but he's done his best work out of the bullpen, both before and after the surgery. He washed out of the early-season rotation pretty quickly, then pitched well out of the pen at Norfolk and in September with the Mets. If he shows up to start in Shea this year, though, bad things have happened.

VICTOR ZAMBRANO

Bats: R **Throws: R** Born: 06-Aug-1975 Age: 29

YEAR	TM	LG	AGE	G	GS	IP	H	BB	SO	HR	ERA	EQERA	EQH9	EQBB9	EQSO9	EQHR9	PERA	VORP	STF
2002	TBY	AL	26	42	11	114.0	120	68	73	15	5.53	5.56	9.2	5.0	5.6	1.1	5.16	-1.3	-9
2003	TBY	AL	27	34	28	188.3	165	106	132	21	4.21	4.32	8.4	5.0	6.4	1.0	4.82	30.3	4
2004	TBY	AL	28	23	22	128.0	107	96	109	13	4.43	4.33	7.9	6.1	7.4	0.8	4.62	20.6	8
2004	NYM	NL	28	3	3	14.0	12	6	14	0	3.86	5.93	7.9	3.3	7.9	0.0	3.29	0.0	21
2005	*NYM*	*NL*	*29*	*21*	*17*	*100.7*	*94*	*63*	*83*	*11*	*4.84*	*5.23*	*8.4*	*4.9*	*6.7*	*1.0*	*5.24*	*4.7*	*3*

Breakout: 10% *Improve: 42%* *Collapse: 31%*

He tied for the AL lead in walks despite being sent to the NL at the trade deadline, which is just an amazing feat. A strained flexor muscle ended his season after three starts with the Mets; he's expected to be healthy in the spring. The Mets traded Kazmir to get Zambrano in large part because of Rick Peterson's convictions. How Zambrano develops from here will go a long way to either cementing or ruining Peterson's reputation. Given Zambrano's age, workload and control, Peterson had better be a miracle worker.

Philadelphia Phillies

Every season that doesn't result in a championship is an opportunity lost. We didn't view this season as a staging ground for the next step. We viewed this season as one that presented us with an opportunity to get to the finish line. We didn't do it, so it's an opportunity lost. What we have to do is figure out a way not to let these opportunities slip by.

PHILLIES GM ED WADE, TO MLB.COM'S KEVIN MANDEL, OCT. 3, 2004.

Ed Wade is savvy enough to blame himself for his team's disappointing finish in 2004. That's certainly better than blaming his players, his departed manager, his new ballpark, or the Phillie Phanatic for his organization's troubles. But read between the lines and you can identify what the Phillies believe was the real cause of their trouble: plain old bad luck.

The Phillies have spent the past two winters putting together what looked to be a championship-caliber nucleus. Certainly, there is room to question individual decisions, most notably the trades for expensive pitchers like Eric Milton, Billy Wagner, and Kevin Millwood. But the end result was what appeared to be a 90–95-win team that likely would sweep through a rebuilding division. Of the twelve *Baseball Prospectus* authors who guessed the final standings prior to last season, ten picked the Phillies to win the NL East, and five picked them to be the senior circuit's representative in the World Series.

So what exactly went wrong? Should we have foreseen the Phillies' problems ahead of time? Should Ed Wade have?

As is usually the case, figuring out what went wrong is the easiest part of the problem, and the answer can be summed up in two words: starting pitching. Table 1 presents the innings pitched, ERA and VORP for the Phillies' starting rotation as PECOTA forecast them immediately prior to the start of the season. PECOTA, it should be noted, is fairly conservative when it comes to addressing pitcher performances. Table 2 describes the performance that the Phillies actually obtained from their starters, and the difference between projected and actual VORP for each player.

All told, the Phillies starters allowed about 82 more runs than predicted, a deficit which translates to eight or nine wins over the course of a full season. The Phillies offense performed almost exactly as we'd expected, as did the team's bullpen. Add those eight starting pitching wins to the Phillies' record, and they would have finished at 94–68 and made the post-season, right in line with our expectation.

PHILLIES PROSPECTUS

2004 record: 86–76; Second place, NL East

Pythagenport record: 86–76

Runs scored per game: 5.19 (3rd in NL)

Runs allowed per game: 4.82 (13th in NL)

Team EqA: .273 (2nd in NL)

2004 Batters Age: 29.7 (8th oldest in NL)

2004 Pitchers Age: 29.7 (7th youngest in NL)

Ballpark: Citizen's Bank Park; Neutral park; Park Factor of 1.009

2004: Another disappointing Phillies campaign left the team home for the playoffs and finally sealed Larry Bowa's fate.

2005: The whole's got to add up to the sum of the parts sometime, right?

Usually, when you see a team-wide pitching performance that is out of line with the projections, it is the result of one or two catastrophic performances—say the first starter blows out his labrum in May, and the second starter loses his splitter in July. The Phillies' problems were much more widespread. All five of the top starters finished with an ERA at least 40 points higher than PECOTA projected, and three of the five were injured for some meaningful portion of the season. Individually, each of the performances is readily explicable: Eric Milton's troubles with home runs were compounded in a power-friendly ballpark; Randy Wolf's left arm finally suffered the consequences of years of heavy usage; Kevin Millwood allowed an uncharacteristically high percentage of hits on balls in play, and so forth. The Phillies bogeyed five holes in a row; Vijay Singh sometimes has days like that too. Those sorts of things happen all the time to pitchers—they're unpredictable creatures. But they usuallyy happen to only

TABLE 1. PHILLIES' STARTING ROTATION PERFORMANCE, PROJECTED

Pitcher	IP	ERA	VORP
Kevin Millwood	210	4.06	30.5
Randy Wolf	200	3.82	35.9
Vicente Padilla	190	4.10	27.1
Eric Milton	170	4.25	23.5
Brett Myers	180	4.22	22.8
Josh Hancock	30	4.44	2.9
Total	**980**	**4.09**	**142.7**

TABLE 2. PHILLIES' STARTING ROTATION PERFORMANCE, ACTUAL

Pitcher	IP	ERA	VORP	Difference
Kevin Millwood	141	4.85	10.1	-20.4
Randy Wolf	136.7	4.28	15.3	-20.6
Vicente Padilla	115.3	4.53	11.5	-15.6
Eric Milton	201	4.75	19.8	-3.7
Brett Myers	175	5.50	1.2	-21.6
Josh Hancock	7	11.57	-4.4	-7.3
Cory Lidle	62.3	3.90	12.2	+12.2
Paul Abbott	49	6.24	-5.2	-5.2
Gavin Floyd	21.3	3.80	4.8	+4.8
Brian Powell	13	4.15	1.4	+1.4
Ryan Madson	0.7	81.00	-5.5	-5.5
Total	**922.3**	**4.91**	**61.2**	**-81.5**

FIGURE 1. SEASON-OVER-SEASON RUNS SCORED PER GAME, MLB TEAMS SINCE 1946

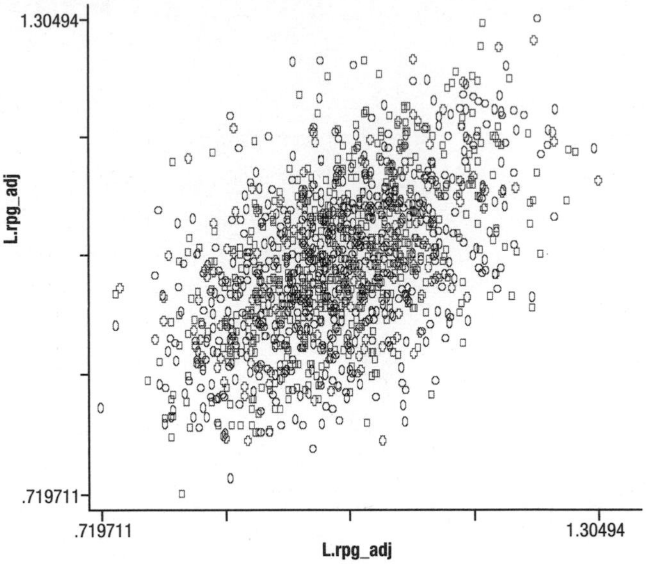

FIGURE 2. SEASON-OVER-SEASON RUNS ALLOWED PER GAME, MLB TEAMS SINCE 1946

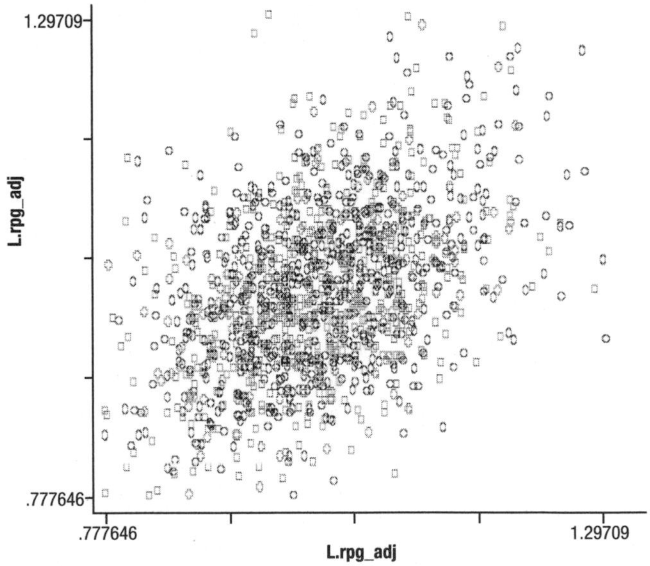

one or two of the pitchers on the staff, and often there are pitchers who outperform expectations elsewhere on the staff who make up the difference.

And so, rather than looking at the individual examples, perhaps it's more worthwhile to step back and look at the big picture. Figures 1 and 2 detail the performances of each major league team's position players and pitching staffs from 1946 until last year, as measured by park-adjusted runs scored and runs allowed per game relative to league average. A team is evaluated based on how its performance changes from season to season.

It should be apparent that the points in figure 1—which describes offensive performance from season to season—are bunched together a bit more closely than the points in figure 2—which describes defensive performances from season-to-season. Mathematically speaking, the correlations between team-wide offensive and defensive performances in consecutive seasons are .52 and .43, respectively. Offense is more consistent than defense. That is, it is more consistent than pitching.

This shouldn't come as any great surprise. It's been acknowledged for a long time that position players, as individuals, turn in more consistent performances from year to year than do pitchers; the same holds true for team-wide performance. And yet, as well established as this principle might seem to be, baseball teams aren't doing a very good job of adapting to it. Overall, about 41% of MLB opening day payrolls last season were expended on pitchers. At first glance, that might not seem too out of line. Roughly speaking, about 40% of success in baseball is attributable to pitching, as compared to 50% to offense and 10% to position defense.

But there isn't any hedging built in to account for the fact that pitchers are less consistent from year to year. Compare, for example, the experience in a typical rotisserie baseball league. While rotisserie baseball is not a good approximation of the real article for any number of reasons, one of its convenient properties is that offense and pitching account for exactly 50% of a team's success apiece. A 4×4 roto league, for example, uses four offensive categories and four pitching categories, each of which is given exactly equal weight. And yet, rotisserie managers routinely allocate two-thirds of their budgets or more to offensive players. It is not because rotisserie managers believe that offensive players are more valuable than pitchers—they aren't. Rather, it is because rotisserie managers recognize, quite correctly, that offensive players are more *consistent* than pitchers. Creating a winning fantasy baseball team involves, almost invariably, investing in an outstanding offensive core and perhaps one or two truly great pitchers, then filling out the rest of the staff with live arms with some upside. It doesn't involve blowing 15% of your payroll on Russ Ortiz. We are not suggesting that major league front offices ought to be running their ballclubs like fantasy teams, but by apportioning such a large percentage of their budgets to their pitching staffs, they aren't optimizing bang for their buck.

What does any of this have to do with the Phillies? As you might have guessed, they've been one of the worst offenders when it comes to overspending on pitching. Table 3 lists the percentage of 2004 opening day payroll that was spent on pitchers for each of the 30 major league clubs.

TABLE 3. FRACTION OF OPENING DAY PAYROLL SPENT ON PITCHERS, 2004

Rangers	61.9%	Cubs	40.5%
Dodgers	55.9%	Expos	39.9%
Braves	52.7%	White Sox	39.1%
Phillies	49.2%	Reds	38.5%
Mets	47.7%	Marlins	38.3%
Pirates	46.1%	Astros	35.4%
Diamondbacks	45.6%	Twins	33.8%
Indians	45.4%	Giants	33.0%
Red Sox	45.1%	Brewers	28.3%
A's	44.3%	Orioles	28.0%
Angels	44.0%	Devil Rays	27.4%
Cardinals	43.6%	Royals	26.5%
Blue Jays	43.2%	Padres	25.2%
Mariners	42.1%	Tigers	22.9%
Yankees	40.9%	Rockies	13.1%
		Average	**40.7%**

Only three teams—the Rangers, Dodgers, and Braves—spent a higher fraction of their payroll on pitching than the Phillies did. The Rangers and Dodgers have the contracts of Chan Ho Park and Darren Dreifort, respectively, still on their books, both of which were signed by ousted management teams, while the Braves, under our accounting system, are credited with the entirety of Mike Hampton's contract, when in fact the Marlins are picking up most of it. Remove the Park, Dreifort, and Hampton contracts from the books, and the Phillies would rank atop the table.

So if the Phillies had allocated, say, the $9 million dollars they gave to Eric Milton to a center fielder instead, would they have won the pennant? It isn't quite that simple. Real baseball teams face one significant constraint that a typical fantasy player doesn't: guaranteed multi-year contracts. These guaranteed deals perpetuate the systematic overpayment of starting pitchers in at least two important ways. First, they establish a market value for pitchers that will remain more or less consistent from season to season. If a starting pitcher who came off a year in which he pitched 200 innings of 4.25 ERA ball signed a deal for three years and $24 million last winter, that forms a benchmark that arbitrators, agents and executives are going to use to determine the value of a free agent with similar statistics the next time around.

The second problem is a little bit more subtle, and it has to do with the substitutability of pitchers versus position players. The ordering of the five men who make up the starting rotation is arbitrary and interchangeable. Pretty much any team could pick up a starter with a league-average ERA and make good use of him. He'd be the second starter for some teams and the fifth starter for others, but either way they'd be able to realize the entirety of his value.

This isn't the case for offensive players, who must also play a position in the field. If the Yankees wanted to sign a catcher, for example, they'd have to find something to do with Jorge Posada, and either trading him or moving him to a new position would be attendant with transaction costs and inefficiencies. In other words, there almost always will be an abundance of teams willing to bid on a pitcher, whereas the market for position players will be limited to those clubs that have an opening at that particular place in the field.

These inefficiencies are deeply embedded within baseball's economic system, and they're difficult ones to work around. An "enlightened" team might try and buck the trend by refusing to pay prevailing market prices for pitchers, but that could shut them out of the pitching racket entirely, which is not an acceptable result for a team that, like the Phillies, is looking to win a pennant.

The best available solution is to turn the problem of pitcher inconsistency on its head by emphasizing depth. Just as pitchers are more likely than position players to foil expectations, they are also more likely to exceed them. Go into the year with seven or eight guys who might be acceptable major league starting pitchers and select the five of them that have the best seasons. While it costs something to separate the haves from the have-nots, that will produce an acceptable result more often than not. Having learned from last year's disasters with break-glass-in-case-of-fire pitchers like Paul Abbott, the Phillies are well positioned to do this. If things go well with Gavin Floyd and Brett Myers, then Cory Lidle will be the Phillies' swingman. If the young pitchers aren't ready, Lidle will be their fourth starter. Either way, he'll provide the team with some flexibility.

It's not signing elite pitchers like Pedro Martinez that dooms a team to disappointing seasons, nor inking relatively cheap alternatives like Cory Lidle. Rather, it's getting caught up in the rat race for overrated pitchers like Milton, Jaret Wright, and Kris Benson. A team can enhance its position by focusing on pitchers' key peripheral numbers like walk, strikeout and groundball rates, rather than their ERAs, which can fluctuate wildly from season to season. The Phillies picked up Jon Lieber this winter, who was dumped by the Yankees in favor of Carl Pavano. Pavano had the better ERA last season, but they are essentially identical pitchers with essentially identical peripheral numbers: Our projection system thinks that Lieber will put up a 4.55 EqERA, and Pavano a 4.64 EqERA. While Lieber won't be a great bargain at $7 million a year, he'll come nearly 50% cheaper than Pavano. Lidle, for that matter, projects out at a 4.80 EqERA—barely worse than Pavano, at a fraction of the price.

The Phillies haven't tried to force anything this winter. That is to their credit, because it's usually those teams that fail to meet expectations that are most inclined to push the panic button; compare the Phillies, for example, to the White Sox's last three seasons under Kenny Williams. The Phillies will have a new manager, but the firing of Larry Bowa was long overdue, and the hiring of Charlie Manuel, a low-key guy, was handled in a low-key way, rather than being presented as some sort of magic bullet. The Phillies have made a questionable trade for Kenny Lofton, and crossed their arbitration signals with Placido Polanco, but neither of these things will cost a huge amount of money, and they may enhance the team's flexibility.

Ed Wade, for his part, seems at least a little bit closer to finding the truth that all great stock traders and poker players understand intuitively: Blaming your troubles on bad luck accomplishes nothing, but comprehending the role that luck plays is essential. Wade is correct to recognize the Phillies still do have the nucleus of a championship-caliber club; he's correct to recognize that moves that enhance a team's depth without compromising their financial flexibility too greatly are the right ones for such a club.

The Phillies will enter 2005 in the same position that they entered 2004, as the odds-on favorite to take the NL East. Better luck to them this time around.

HITTERS

BOB ABREU **RF** **Bats: L** **Throws: R** Born: 11-Mar-1974 Age: 31

YEAR	TM	LG	AGE	AB	H	2B	3B	HR	BB	SO	SB	CS	AVG	OBP	SLG	MLVR	EQBA	EQOBP	EQSLG	EQMLVR	VORP	DEFENSE	
2002	PHI	NL	28	572	176	50	6	20	104	117	31	12	.308	.413	.521	.359	.315	.417	.543	.317	70.4	138-RF -10	17-CF 1
2003	PHI	NL	29	577	173	35	1	20	109	126	22	9	.300	.409	.468	.247	.305	.412	.481	.214	53.3	154-RF 0	
2004	PHI	NL	30	574	173	47	1	30	127	116	40	5	.301	.428	.544	.349	.300	.425	.542	.313	83.8	151-RF 5	
2005	*PHI*	*NL*	*31*	*521*	*157*	*35*	*3*	*25*	*100*	*109*	*24*	*6*	*.301*	*.414*	*.527*	*.263*	*.301*	*.412*	*.526*	*.255*	*54.8*	*147-RF 0*	

Breakout: 29% *Improve: 57%* *Collapse: 8%*

Back when *BP* was a fledgling publication with a circulation the size of the waiting list at your neighborhood Outback Steakhouse, we had a favorite one-word sentence that would get thrown around in a few player comments each year: "Ballplayer." We used it so often that it became a cliché, and hence was retired, but if there were ever a guy who deserves the tag, it is Abreu, who does just about everything that you'd want a ballplayer to do, and does it exceedingly well. It's amazing that Abreu made his first All-Star team this year. If he ages well—and players with this type of skill set usually do—he'll have a viable case for the Hall of Fame come 2018 or so.

DAVID BELL 3B Bats: R Throws: R Born: 14-Sep-1972 Age: 32

YEAR	TM	LG	AGE	AB	H	2B	3B	HR	BB	SO	SB	CS	AVG	OBP	SLG	MLVR	EQBA	EQOBP	EQSLG	EQMLVR	VORP	DEFENSE	
2002	SFG	NL	29	552	144	29	2	20	54	80	1	2	.261	.333	.429	.053	.268	.336	.448	.002	31.0	126-3B 0	11-2B 0
2003	PHI	NL	30	297	58	14	0	4	41	40	0	0	.195	.296	.283	-.257	.205	.297	.299	-.319	-6.2	80-3B 5	
2004	PHI	NL	31	533	155	33	1	18	57	75	1	1	.291	.363	.458	.122	.290	.361	.456	.077	32.2	135-3B 8	
2005	*PHI*	*NL*	*32*	*369*	*92*	*19*	*1*	*12*	*41*	*56*	*0*	*0*	*.250*	*.331*	*.403*	*-.076*	*.250*	*.330*	*.401*	*-.084*	*4.9*	*100-3B 2*	

Breakout: 11% *Improve: 36%* *Collapse: 29%*

It's easy to confound injury and underperformance. Bell, the ink still trying on a four-year, $17 million contract, had a horrible 2003, his swing impeded by hip and back injuries. Healthy in 2004, he turned in a performance that was slightly stronger than the 2002 season that earned him the big contract to begin with. That doesn't mean that injuries are to be ignored—staying healthy is a skill. But analysts need to be careful not to punish a player twice over for playing hurt and playing badly when they have one and the same cause.

JAKE BLALOCK LF Bats: R Throws: R Born: 06-Aug-1983 Age: 21

YEAR	TM	LG	AGE	AB	H	2B	3B	HR	BB	SO	SB	CS	AVG	OBP	SLG	MLVR	EQBA	EQOBP	EQSLG	EQMLVR	VORP	DEFENSE	
2003	BAT	NYP	19	261	64	23	7	5	30	81	9	4	.245	.323	.444	.132	.204	.266	.379	-.272	-32.1	26-RF 0	27-LF -2
2004	LWD	SAL	20	517	140	40	2	16	61	126	4	3	.271	.350	.449	.151	.239	.302	.389	-.166	-18.2	123-LF -4	
2005	*PHI*	*NL*	*21*	*371*	*86*	*21*	*2*	*12*	*34*	*106*	*3*	*1*	*.231*	*.299*	*.391*	*-.163*	*.231*	*.297*	*.390*	*-.170*	*-7.8*	*99-LF -6*	

Breakout: 26% *Improve: 53%* *Collapse: 29%*

Blalock made the book last year based on having a famous older brother, but he's done it on his own merits this time around. The most important number from his stat line at Lakewood this year is the "40" in the doubles column; that is a sign of budding home-run power. Jake has not demonstrated Hank's ability to make contact, however, and there are already concerns about his defense, so it's far too early to tell whether the upside here is the Waners, the Giambis, or the Cansecos.

MICHAEL BOURN CF Bats: L Throws: R Born: 27-Dec-1982 Age: 22

YEAR	TM	LG	AGE	AB	H	2B	3B	HR	BB	SO	SB	CS	AVG	OBP	SLG	MLVR	EQBA	EQOBP	EQSLG	EQMLVR	VORP	DEFENSE	
2003	BAT	NYP	20	125	35	0	1	0	23	28	23	5	.280	.404	.296	.082	.212	.288	.212	-.452	-31.4	18-LF -1	15-CF 0
2004	LWD	SAL	21	413	130	20	14	5	85	88	58	6	.315	.431	.467	.340	.283	.381	.411	.045	27.2	55-CF -2	50-RF -5
2005	*PHI*	*NL*	*22*	*365*	*89*	*15*	*5*	*4*	*46*	*84*	*22*	*6*	*.244*	*.333*	*.343*	*-.154*	*.244*	*.331*	*.342*	*-.161*	*-1.9*	*100-CF -9*	

Breakout: 2% *Improve: 21%* *Collapse: 50%*

A couple of years ago, we might have gotten very, very excited about a player who posted a .379 translated OBP as a 21-year-old. Now we're only very excited about him. Bourn's plate discipline is outstanding, and it helps that he's a little bit undersized at 5′11″, reducing the size of his strike zone. His stolen-base ability rates just about as high as it can: He not only has tremendous speed, but also instinctive technique on the basepaths, which led to perhaps the most impressive SB:CS ratio in minor league baseball. While he's not a natural center fielder, he certainly has the speed to handle the position, and should improve his routes over time.

The reservation that we have—the reservation that PECOTA has—is that much of Bourn's potential is tied up in his walks, and minor league walk rates sometimes evaporate as a player moves up the ladder. This is most often the case for a player who takes a lot of pitches but has little power, someone like Esteban German or Jackie Rexrode. If the hitter is not capable of doing threatening things with the ball when he makes contact, the better pitchers will simply throw him a ton of strikes. Bourn's coaches are working to make him less of a slap hitter, but the jury is still out on whether he will be able to break through the Rexrode Threshold.

PAT BURRELL LF Bats: R Throws: R Born: 10-Oct-1976 Age: 28

YEAR	TM	LG	AGE	AB	H	2B	3B	HR	BB	SO	SB	CS	AVG	OBP	SLG	MLVR	EQBA	EQOBP	EQSLG	EQMLVR	VORP	DEFENSE
2002	PHI	NL	25	586	165	39	2	37	89	153	1	0	.282	.376	.544	.309	.287	.378	.564	.253	61.7	149-LF 0
2003	PHI	NL	26	522	109	31	4	21	72	142	0	0	.209	.309	.404	-.074	.212	.312	.416	-.129	0.1	133-LF 3
2004	PHI	NL	27	448	115	17	0	24	78	130	2	0	.257	.365	.455	.096	.258	.362	.452	.046	21.8	118-LF 5
2005	*PHI*	*NL*	*28*	*413*	*107*	*22*	*2*	*24*	*63*	*113*	*1*	*0*	*.258*	*.357*	*.498*	*.097*	*.258*	*.355*	*.497*	*.089*	*19.7*	*114-LF 0*

Breakout: 36% *Improve: 68%* *Collapse: 7%*

(continued next page)

Pat Burrell *(continued)*

Was this a step back or a step forward? Burrell split the difference between his two previous campaigns, improving his batting average and walk rate, but not recovering his isolated power. It seems clear that Burrell will avoid the infamy of the Kevin Maas/Cory Snyder career path. But slow corner outfielders who come into their age-28 season fresh off an .820 OPS and a wrist injury are not generally bound for superstardom. The Phillies are hopeful that he'll work better under Charlie Manuel, both in the dugout and in the batting cage, and PECOTA remains optimistic, citing the examples of other strikeout-prone hitters like Jay Buhner who took time to consolidate their skill sets.

MARLON BYRD CF **Bats: R** **Throws: R** Born: 30-Aug-1977 Age: 27

YEAR	TM	LG	AGE	AB	H	2B	3B	HR	BB	SO	SB	CS	AVG	OBP	SLG	MLVR	EQBA	EQOBP	EQSLG	EQMLVR	VORP	DEFENSE
2002	SWB	INT	24	538	160	37	7	15	46	98	15	1	.297	.362	.476	.186	.278	.342	.455	.032	28.2	134-CF -12
2002	PHI	NL	24	35	8	2	0	1	1	8	0	2	.229	.250	.371	-.172	.257	.244	.371	-.289	-1.5	
2003	PHI	NL	25	495	150	28	4	7	44	94	11	1	.303	.366	.418	.107	.308	.369	.428	.068	34.9	129-CF -1
2004	SWB	INT	26	152	40	11	1	2	10	18	2	3	.263	.323	.388	-.075	.245	.301	.364	-.198	-2.3	37-CF -2
2004	PHI	NL	26	346	79	13	2	5	22	68	2	2	.228	.287	.321	-.239	.230	.288	.325	-.288	-8.7	77-CF 0
2005	*PHI*	*NL*	*27*	*345*	*95*	*19*	*3*	*8*	*26*	*63*	*4*	*2*	*.274*	*.334*	*.422*	*-.029*	*.274*	*.332*	*.420*	*-.037*	*14.0*	*91-CF -3*

Breakout: 21% *Improve: 37%* *Collapse: 31%*

When a player suffers such an across-the-board decline—Byrd's numbers were down in every department, right down to his speed metrics—it is natural to go seeking out causes. The Philly press corps was quick to blame Byrd's conditioning, perhaps because he's always had a somewhat chubby appearance, but there is no evidence of that. It is equally easy to speculate that Byrd has been suffering from some sort of undiagnosed injury, but there is no evidence of that, either. In any event, the organization has soured on him, which is understandable: Byrd's minor league numbers projected him as a solid regular, but not a star, and insofar as collateral damage goes for an organization that is gunning to win a championship in the here and now, he's expendable. He'd be a better fit for a team like Detroit, which has less to lose by seeing what he does in his next 400 major league plate appearances.

JOHN CASTELLANO C/UT **Bats: R** **Throws: R** Born: 08-Sep-77 Age: 27

YEAR	TM	LG	AGE	AB	H	2B	3B	HR	BB	SO	SB	CS	AVG	OBP	SLG	MLVR	EQBA	EQOBP	EQSLG	EQMLVR	VORP	DEFENSE
2002	SBR	CLF	24	239	80	18	0	3	23	25	6	3	.335	.392	.448	.261	.287	.333	.392	-.067	1.2	25-1B 0 26-C -4
2002	SAN	TXS	24	194	51	10	0	1	10	30	3	3	.263	.295	.330	-.070	.251	.281	.318	-.299	-13.5	16-RF -2
2003	SBR	CLF	25	461	141	34	2	12	32	50	11	3	.306	.354	.466	.188	.263	.306	.404	-.119	-4.9	86-1B -3
2004	CLR	FSL	26	91	22	4	1	3	11	10	0	0	.242	.337	.407	.059	.215	.292	.387	-.204	-2.4	
2004	REA	EAS	26	368	125	25	1	18	32	55	0	3	.340	.395	.560	.349	.296	.347	.488	.104	18.2	45-LF -2 13-C -3
2005	*PHI*	*NL*	*27*	*134*	*35*	*7*	*1*	*4*	*9*	*20*	*1*	*0*	*.260*	*.311*	*.406*	*-.100*	*.260*	*.309*	*.404*	*-.108*	*1.7*	

Breakout: 16% *Improve: 33%* *Collapse: 53%*

While the Phillies have a couple of top-tier prospects like Gavin Floyd and Ryan Howard, their system is not very deep. (One of the players they sent to the Arizona Fall League was Buzz Hannahan, a 29-year-old utility infielder who slugged .355 in Scranton this year.) Castellano is one of the more interesting pseudo-prospects in the system, if only because he has some pop in his bat and the ability to catch a couple of times a week. Befitting the Crash Davis stereotype, he's pudgy and not very athletic, but his pitchers have given him reasonable marks for his arm and game-calling skills. Castellano is not going to get much better, but he'd probably make for an above-average major league backup right now.

LOU COLLIER UT **Bats: R** **Throws: R** Born: 21-Aug-1973 Age: 31

YEAR	TM	LG	AGE	AB	H	2B	3B	HR	BB	SO	SB	CS	AVG	OBP	SLG	MLVR	EQBA	EQOBP	EQSLG	EQMLVR	VORP	DEFENSE
2002	OTT	INT	28	307	97	26	6	6	37	69	5	2	.316	.394	.498	.287	.301	.378	.485	.158	20.9	23-LF 0 17-3B 0
2003	PAW	INT	29	392	115	19	4	14	32	94	8	7	.293	.354	.469	.179	.279	.341	.459	.036	10.9	71-LF 3 19-SS 1
2004	SWB	INT	30	387	126	26	3	14	34	82	14	3	.326	.383	.517	.259	.301	.360	.476	.114	19.8	46-LF -1 41-3B -8
2004	PHI	NL	30	36	10	1	0	1	5	10	1	0	.278	.381	.389	.067	.306	.359	.417	.032	2.2	
2005	*PHI*	*NL*	*31*	*129*	*34*	*7*	*1*	*4*	*12*	*32*	*2*	*1*	*.268*	*.338*	*.433*	*-.012*	*.268*	*.336*	*.432*	*-.020*	*6.1*	*38-LF -1*

Breakout: 11% *Improve: 28%* *Collapse: 48%*

Collier has been serving as a de facto 27th or 28th man for the past couple of seasons, and an organization puts those sorts of guys where it damned well pleases, so the fact that he's most frequently played left field during his tour of the International League should not be taken to mean that he can no longer handle the infield positions. The question, given a sustained late-career offensive surge, is why Collier hasn't been a 23rd or a 24th man instead. After the Phillies non-tendered him, he's out there for the taking.

DOUG GLANVILLE CF **Bats: R** **Throws: R** Born: 25-Aug-1970 Age: 34

YEAR	TM	LG	AGE	AB	H	2B	3B	HR	BB	SO	SB	CS	AVG	OBP	SLG	MLVR	EQBA	EQOBP	EQSLG	EQMLVR	VORP	DEFENSE			
2002	PHI	NL	31	422	105	16	3	6	25	57	19	2	.249	.292	.344	-.140	.259	.300	.361	-.195	4.8	99-CF	4		
2003	TEX	AL	32	195	53	5	0	4	6	25	4	0	.272	.294	.359	-.188	.266	.284	.344	-.246	0.6	44-CF	-2		
2003	CHC	NL	32	51	12	0	0	1	2	4	0	1	.235	.259	.294	-.381	.255	.234	.255	-.484	-3.6	13-CF	0		
2004	PHI	NL	33	162	34	1	1	2	8	21	8	0	.210	.244	.265	-.407	.209	.247	.264	-.467	-8.6	35-CF	0	11-LF	1
2005	*PHI*	*NL*	*34*	*105*	*25*	*4*	*1*	*1*	*6*	*14*	*3*	*1*	*.243*	*.285*	*.335*	*-.253*	*.243*	*.284*	*.334*	*-.260*	*-3.2*	*31-CF*	*-1*		

Breakout: 26% *Improve: 46%* *Collapse: 29%*

The term "baseball intelligence" gets thrown around from time to time, usually with a wink or an asterisk, but nevertheless with the implication that guys who draw more walks or make fewer errors would have a fighting chance against Ken Jennings in the *Jeopardy! Tournament of Champions.* Why then does Doug Glanville, who has an Ivy League degree and is one of the most articulate ballplayers in recent memory, take about three walks per season, while a rube like Will Clark finishes his career with a .384 OBP? Come to think of it, the rubes in this case are in the Phillies front office, which brought back a player whose inadequacies should have been obvious by now.

GREG GOLSON CF **Bats:R** **Throws: R** Born: 17-Sep-85 Age: 19

The Phillies' first-round pick as a high schooler out of Austin, Tex., Golson signed quickly, and had a decidedly toolsy debut in Rookie ball, where he posted a .295/.345/.410 untranslated line, with lots of stolen bases and triples. It was just enough of a season to keep the scouts abuzz, but Golson's plate discipline was poor, and opinions about the quality of his swing are mixed.

MICHEL HERNANDEZ C **Bats: R** **Throws: R** Born: 12-Aug-1978 Age: 26

YEAR	TM	LG	AGE	AB	H	2B	3B	HR	BB	SO	SB	CS	AVG	OBP	SLG	MLVR	EQBA	EQOBP	EQSLG	EQMLVR	VORP	DEFENSE	
2002	NRW	EAS	23	61	19	6	0	1	5	6	0	1	.311	.358	.459	.196	.262	.282	.377	-.204	-1.5		
2002	COH	INT	23	121	34	5	1	1	8	13	1	3	.281	.336	.364	-.027	.264	.318	.347	-.177	-0.1	31-C	-7
2003	COH	INT	24	282	79	14	0	4	37	35	0	2	.280	.367	.372	.048	.254	.340	.346	-.142	2.7	82-C	1
2004	SWB	INT	25	231	59	9	0	6	25	24	0	1	.255	.328	.372	-.093	.235	.300	.339	-.242	-4.9	67-C	-3
2005	*PHI*	*NL*	*26*	*136*	*34*	*6*	*0*	*3*	*14*	*16*	*0*	*0*	*.248*	*.324*	*.369*	*-.134*	*.248*	*.322*	*.368*	*-.141*	*3.2*	*40-C*	*-2*

Breakout: 29% *Improve: 46%* *Collapse: 31%*

A catch-and-throw prospect in the Yankees system, Hernandez was claimed off waivers, and became a catch-and-throw prospect in the Phillies system. Hernandez can take an occasional walk, but otherwise has little to recommend him; his arm is good but not outstanding. The Phillies closed the circle by non-tendering him, so he'll return to Triple-A somewhere and hope for someone to get hurt.

BRIAN HITCHCOX 2B-3B **Bats: L** **Throws: R** Born: 21-Jul-1978 Age: 26

YEAR	TM	LG	AGE	AB	H	2B	3B	HR	BB	SO	SB	CS	AVG	OBP	SLG	MLVR	EQBA	EQOBP	EQSLG	EQMLVR	VORP	DEFENSE	
2002	CLR	FSL	23	121	30	4	0	1	12	17	4	3	.248	.324	.306	-.078	.203	.257	.244	-.477	-12.0	29-2B	0
2002	REA	EAS	23	297	79	18	2	6	16	30	4	5	.266	.313	.401	-.031	.236	.276	.364	-.253	-6.9	74-2B	10
2003	REA	EAS	24	304	76	13	4	5	41	54	8	5	.250	.351	.368	-.031	.219	.308	.337	-.238	-6.1	87-2B	1
2003	SWB	INT	24	45	10	1	0	1	0	3	0	1	.222	.222	.311	-.320	.205	.196	.295	-.528	-4.5	12-2B	3
2004	REA	EAS	25	140	36	4	1	7	22	25	4	1	.257	.377	.450	.104	.227	.335	.390	-.110	3.0	41-2B	-1
2004	SWB	INT	25	136	32	10	1	1	18	16	3	0	.235	.346	.346	-.108	.221	.326	.324	-.219	-1.6	27-3B	-3
2005	*PHI*	*NL*	*26*	*123*	*30*	*6*	*1*	*3*	*13*	*20*	*2*	*1*	*.243*	*.325*	*.368*	*-.138*	*.243*	*.323*	*.367*	*-.145*	*2.8*	*37-2B*	*-2*

Breakout: 31% *Improve: 53%* *Collapse: 33%*

Another of the organizational players that might be mistaken for a prospect in the Phillies system, Hitchcox can best be described as a minor league version of Craig Counsell, a scrub with just a smattering of plate discipline and doubles power and the ability to handle a couple of infield positions without making a lot of errors. Scouts have concerns about his arm, and whatever chance he has at a major league career will depend on his ability to adjust to Triple-A successfully, which he has yet to do in two brief trials.

RYAN HOWARD 1B Bats: L Throws: L Born: 19-Nov-1979 Age: 25

YEAR	TM	LG	AGE	AB	H	2B	3B	HR	BB	SO	SB	CS	AVG	OBP	SLG	MLVR	EQBA	EQOBP	EQSLG	EQMLVR	VORP	DEFENSE
2002	LWD	SAL	22	493	138	20	6	19	66	145	5	4	.280	.367	.460	.242	.243	.312	.405	-.122	-6.3	118-1B -9
2003	CLR	FSL	23	490	149	32	1	23	50	151	0	0	.304	.374	.514	.328	.265	.323	.480	.021	17.2	114-1B 4
2004	REA	EAS	24	374	111	18	1	37	46	129	1	2	.297	.386	.647	.405	.259	.337	.552	.140	26.8	97-1B -7
2004	SWB	INT	24	111	30	10	0	9	14	37	0	0	.270	.362	.604	.285	.227	.309	.509	.003	3.0	29-1B -2
2004	PHI	NL	24	39	11	5	0	2	2	13	0	0	.282	.333	.564	.237	.308	.317	.538	.141	3.5	
2005	*PHI*	*NL*	*25*	*288*	*75*	*15*	*1*	*18*	*31*	*100*	*0*	*0*	*.259*	*.341*	*.508*	*.086*	*.259*	*.339*	*.507*	*.078*	*19.4*	*79-1B -3*

Breakout: 30% *Improve: 61%* *Collapse: 26%*

You can read the stat lines as well as we can—Howard has big league power and then some. The problem is that he has nowhere to play: While Howard worked with Milt Thompson on his corner outfield skills in Arizona, he's going to wind up at first base, and Jim Thome isn't about to go anywhere. He could stand a half season at Scranton to improve his pitch selection—his walk rate is not that high for someone who gets pitched around so much—but he's as close to being good as he's going to get, and if he languishes in the International League for two more years, it isn't going to do wonders for his trade value. We usually criticize organizations for moving good prospects prematurely, but if the Phillies find themselves in a pennant race and get an attractive offer for Howard, it would behoove them to bite.

Howard's PECOTA comparables list is interesting. The list is headlined by some unflattering names, Sam Horn, Daryle Ward, and Franklin Stubbs to name a few. But just a bit further down are encouraging comparisons like Carlos Delgado and Derrek Lee, players who improved their walk rates and became very dangerous hitters. It's a potent mixture of one shot boom and two shots bust.

MIKE LIEBERTHAL C Bats: R Throws: R Born: 18-Jan-1972 Age: 33

YEAR	TM	LG	AGE	AB	H	2B	3B	HR	BB	SO	SB	CS	AVG	OBP	SLG	MLVR	EQBA	EQOBP	EQSLG	EQMLVR	VORP	DEFENSE
2002	PHI	NL	30	476	133	29	2	15	38	58	0	1	.279	.349	.443	.128	.286	.351	.465	.069	38.6	123-C 5
2003	PHI	NL	31	508	159	30	1	13	38	59	0	0	.313	.373	.453	.182	.318	.375	.463	.138	46.2	128-C -7
2004	PHI	NL	32	476	129	31	1	17	37	69	1	1	.271	.335	.447	.047	.270	.333	.448	-.001	26.8	123-C -4
2005	*PHI*	*NL*	*33*	*400*	*112*	*23*	*1*	*13*	*33*	*55*	*1*	*0*	*.281*	*.346*	*.441*	*.023*	*.281*	*.344*	*.440*	*.015*	*22.8*	*106-C -3*

Breakout: 9% *Improve: 40%* *Collapse: 34%*

Lieberthal has given the Phillies a lot of value over the years, but he's a 33-year-old catcher who doesn't handle the running game well, and the modest decline that his stats underwent last year is likely the start of a downtrend. This is the last year of Lieberthal's contract, and the Phillies should survive it fine, but they'll need to turn outside the organization for a replacement because their motley crew of catching prospects all project as backups. Who'd have thought they'd miss Johnny Estrada?

JASON MICHAELS OF Bats: R Throws: R Born: 04-May-1976 Age: 29

YEAR	TM	LG	AGE	AB	H	2B	3B	HR	BB	SO	SB	CS	AVG	OBP	SLG	MLVR	EQBA	EQOBP	EQSLG	EQMLVR	VORP	DEFENSE	
2002	PHI	NL	26	105	28	10	3	2	13	33	1	1	.267	.347	.476	.151	.274	.351	.491	.094	8.2		
2003	PHI	NL	27	109	36	11	0	5	15	22	0	0	.330	.416	.569	.423	.345	.411	.573	.385	15.9		
2004	PHI	NL	28	299	82	12	0	10	42	80	2	2	.274	.364	.415	.059	.277	.360	.417	.010	13.7	37-CF -1	27-LF 2
2005	*PHI*	*NL*	*29*	*264*	*70*	*15*	*2*	*10*	*35*	*66*	*2*	*1*	*.265*	*.355*	*.443*	*.027*	*.265*	*.353*	*.441*	*.020*	*13.4*	*74-CF -5*	

Breakout: 13% *Improve: 38%* *Collapse: 27%*

Michaels has accumulated about a full season's worth of big league playing since his debut, to the tune of a .283/.370/.457 batting line. That's reasonable for a corner outfielder and excellent for a center fielder. But in spite of his acceptable glovework in center in the waning months of the season, the Phillies regard Michaels as a tweener, and a career backup. That's a shame, because Michaels would give the Phillies a lot more value than Kenny Lofton, but organizational perceptions about a player's role can be hard-wired.

TOMAS PEREZ INF Bats: B Throws: R Born: 29-Dec-1973 Age: 31

YEAR	TM	LG	AGE	AB	H	2B	3B	HR	BB	SO	SB	CS	AVG	OBP	SLG	MLVR	EQBA	EQOBP	EQSLG	EQMLVR	VORP	DEFENSE	
2002	PHI	NL	28	212	53	13	1	5	21	40	1	0	.250	.319	.392	-.019	.256	.323	.409	-.086	9.2	31-2B -3	11-3B 0
2003	PHI	NL	29	298	79	18	1	5	23	54	0	1	.265	.316	.383	-.059	.270	.322	.390	-.104	8.5	44-3B 2	20-2B 0
2004	PHI	NL	30	176	38	13	2	6	9	44	0	0	.216	.257	.415	-.181	.219	.258	.416	-.225	-0.9	12-3B 0	11-2B 1
2005	*PHI*	*NL*	*31*	*164*	*42*	*9*	*1*	*5*	*13*	*35*	*0*	*0*	*.254*	*.310*	*.413*	*-.097*	*.254*	*.308*	*.412*	*-.105*	*5.6*	*46-3B -1*	

Breakout: 24% *Improve: 42%* *Collapse: 42%*

Utility infielders tend to engender the sort of irrational brand loyalty usually reserved for cigarette brands; the Phillies re-signed Perez and his .257 OBP to a two-year extension following the season. Sure, the organization lacks middle-infield depth, but Camels give you cancer just the same as Wal-Mart Golds.

PLACIDO POLANCO **2B** **Bats: R** **Throws: R** Born: 10-Oct-1975 Age: 29

YEAR	TM	LG	AGE	AB	H	2B	3B	HR	BB	SO	SB	CS	AVG	OBP	SLG	MLVR	EQBA	EQOBP	EQSLG	EQMLVR	VORP	DEFENSE
2002	STL	NL	26	342	97	19	1	5	12	27	3	1	.284	.316	.389	-.024	.289	.318	.404	-.076	12.6	66-3B 9 10-SS -1
2002	PHI	NL	26	206	61	13	1	4	14	14	2	2	.296	.353	.427	.125	.305	.358	.443	.067	14.7	53-3B 9
2003	PHI	NL	27	492	142	30	3	14	42	38	14	2	.289	.352	.447	.105	.291	.353	.458	.067	37.8	96-2B 7 17-3B 2
2004	PHI	NL	28	503	150	21	0	17	27	39	7	4	.298	.345	.441	.077	.301	.342	.441	.032	31.5	108-2B 13 13-3B 2
2005	*PHI*	*NL*	*29*	*521*	*149*	*29*	*2*	*14*	*38*	*44*	*8*	*2*	*.287*	*.343*	*.430*	*.007*	*.287*	*.341*	*.429*	*.000*	*24.8*	*136-2B 5*

Breakout: 3% *Improve: 24%* *Collapse: 35%*

Polanco has turned in an admirable performance since joining the Phillies, providing good batting averages, excellent defense, and occasional home-run power. The Phillies were planning on breaking their relationship with him, preferring young stud Chase Utley instead, but Polanco surprised them by accepting arbitration. It was, indeed, an awfully risk-averse decision on Polanco's part; even with the modest regression that PECOTA is projecting, he figures to provide production comparable to that of Edgar Renteria or Orlando Cabrera for the next couple of seasons, and those guys had no trouble commanding top dollar on the market. If Utley bogarts his playing time as expected, the move could cost Polanco millions down the road.

TODD PRATT **C** **Bats: R** **Throws: R** Born: 09-Feb-1967 Age: 38

YEAR	TM	LG	AGE	AB	H	2B	3B	HR	BB	SO	SB	CS	AVG	OBP	SLG	MLVR	EQBA	EQOBP	EQSLG	EQMLVR	VORP	DEFENSE
2002	PHI	NL	35	106	33	11	0	3	24	28	2	0	.311	.449	.500	.397	.333	.445	.537	.373	18.8	33-C -2
2003	PHI	NL	36	125	34	10	1	4	22	38	0	0	.272	.400	.464	.193	.276	.396	.480	.159	13.0	33-C -3
2004	PHI	NL	37	128	33	5	0	3	18	38	0	0	.258	.351	.367	-.044	.264	.343	.364	-.105	4.6	36-C -5
2005	*PHI*	*NL*	*38*	*86*	*21*	*6*	*0*	*3*	*13*	*24*	*0*	*0*	*.246*	*.351*	*.416*	*-.028*	*.246*	*.349*	*.415*	*-.035*	*7.0*	*29-C -3*

Breakout: 22% *Improve: 34%* *Collapse: 49%*

To the extent that you can glean anything from 150 plate appearances, it wasn't Todd Pratt's best season, but why hasn't this guy ever had a starting job in the bigs? He's outhit most third basemen—let alone most catchers—and by all accounts he's a defensive asset and a pleasure in the clubhouse. He'd be an interesting fit for a team like the Dodgers, who might just be crazy enough to see what the 38-year-old does with 100 games behind the plate; alas, the Phillies re-signed him to caddy for Lieberthal instead.

CHRIS ROBERSON **CF** **Bats: R** **Throws: R** Born: 23-Aug-1979 Age: 25

YEAR	TM	LG	AGE	AB	H	2B	3B	HR	BB	SO	SB	CS	AVG	OBP	SLG	MLVR	EQBA	EQOBP	EQSLG	EQMLVR	VORP	DEFENSE
2002	BAT	NYP	22	214	59	8	3	2	26	51	17	8	.276	.377	.369	.107	.220	.294	.305	-.309	-20.1	30-CF 2 20-RF 1
2003	LWD	SAL	23	470	110	19	5	2	57	108	59	16	.234	.331	.309	-.021	.215	.285	.293	-.346	-32.7	101-CF -1 31-RF -2
2004	CLR	FSL	24	313	96	13	6	9	27	71	16	12	.307	.371	.473	.246	.271	.324	.432	-.039	11.2	78-CF -6
2005	*PHI*	*NL*	*25*	*171*	*42*	*9*	*2*	*4*	*14*	*43*	*5*	*2*	*.247*	*.318*	*.381*	*-.131*	*.246*	*.316*	*.380*	*-.138*	*3.2*	*49-CF -3*

Breakout: 24% *Improve: 44%* *Collapse: 33%*

Roberson was in the midst of a breakout season of sorts at Clearwater when he broke his leg. Although he's expected to recover fully, his timing couldn't have been worse, as he was old for his league and will quickly be lapped by Michael Bourn. Roberson routinely receives raves (say that five times fast) for his fine range in center, but unless the extra pop in his bat was for real, the best he projects to become is Brian L. Hunter.

JIMMY ROLLINS **SS** **Bats: B** **Throws: R** Born: 27-Nov-1978 Age: 26

YEAR	TM	LG	AGE	AB	H	2B	3B	HR	BB	SO	SB	CS	AVG	OBP	SLG	MLVR	EQBA	EQOBP	EQSLG	EQMLVR	VORP	DEFENSE
2002	PHI	NL	23	637	156	33	10	11	54	103	31	13	.245	.306	.380	-.060	.254	.312	.402	-.118	22.1	148-SS 5
2003	PHI	NL	24	628	165	42	6	8	54	113	20	12	.263	.320	.387	-.043	.267	.326	.399	-.086	24.3	154-SS 4
2004	PHI	NL	25	657	190	43	12	14	57	73	30	9	.289	.348	.455	.090	.289	.348	.457	.055	50.9	152-SS -9
2005	*PHI*	*NL*	*26*	*601*	*172*	*35*	*7*	*14*	*56*	*82*	*26*	*9*	*.286*	*.347*	*.437*	*.022*	*.285*	*.345*	*.435*	*.015*	*34.9*	*156-SS -2*

Breakout: 11% *Improve: 36%* *Collapse: 16%*

(continued next page)

Jimmy Rollins *(continued)*

Rollins has always run well and been extremely durable, and the fact that he cut his strikeouts by nearly 40% while mashing 69 extra-base hits suggests that he's on the verge of several All-Star appearances. PECOTA doesn't expect too much more improvement, but at the very least Rollins looks a safe bet for a Ray Durham–career path, which is pretty darn good.

CARLOS RUIZ **C** **Bats: R** **Throws: R** Born: 22-Jan-1979 Age: 26

YEAR	TM	LG	AGE	AB	H	2B	3B	HR	BB	SO	SB	CS	AVG	OBP	SLG	MLVR	EQBA	EQOBP	EQSLG	EQMLVR	VORP	DEFENSE
2002	CLR	FSL	23	342	73	18	3	5	18	30	3	1	.213	.264	.327	-.160	.196	.233	.314	-.432	-27.8	57-C 0
2003	CLR	FSL	24	54	17	0	0	2	2	5	2	2	.315	.339	.426	.178	.241	.227	.352	-.361	-3.2	10-C 0
2003	REA	EAS	24	169	45	6	0	2	12	15	1	1	.266	.321	.337	-.113	.219	.263	.278	-.410	-12.1	45-C 1
2004	REA	EAS	25	349	99	15	2	17	22	37	8	4	.284	.338	.484	.108	.249	.295	.427	-.118	5.9	86-C 5
2005	*PHI*	*NL*	*26*	*148*	*36*	*7*	*1*	*4*	*7*	*16*	*1*	*1*	*.243*	*.285*	*.382*	*-.190*	*.243*	*.284*	*.381*	*-.198*	*1.4*	*42-C -4*

Breakout: 24% *Improve: 39%* *Collapse: 40%*

Ordinarily, it would be safe to ignore a 25-year-old who suddenly started hitting at Double-A, but Ruiz has a good excuse for being a late-bloomer: The high school that he went to in Panama did not sponsor baseball, and unlike the vast majority of Latin American prospects who get signed to contracts in their teens, Ruiz's first year in American professional ball came at age 20. Though he had never played catcher at the time of his signing, Ruiz's arm and overall defense are considered to be assets. He was added to the 40-man roster in November, and has a good chance to be a major league-caliber backup.

JIM THOME **1B** **Bats: L** **Throws: R** Born: 27-Aug-1970 Age: 34

YEAR	TM	LG	AGE	AB	H	2B	3B	HR	BB	SO	SB	CS	AVG	OBP	SLG	MLVR	EQBA	EQOBP	EQSLG	EQMLVR	VORP	DEFENSE
2002	CLE	AL	31	480	146	19	2	52	122	139	1	2	.304	.445	.677	.532	.311	.455	.700	.576	95.4	123-1B 0
2003	PHI	NL	32	578	154	30	3	47	111	182	0	3	.266	.385	.573	.316	.269	.387	.585	.277	65.8	152-1B -5
2004	PHI	NL	33	508	139	28	1	42	104	144	0	2	.274	.396	.581	.320	.271	.395	.576	.279	60.3	129-1B -11
2005	*PHI*	*NL*	*34*	*439*	*120*	*23*	*2*	*36*	*87*	*131*	*0*	*0*	*.274*	*.395*	*.582*	*.277*	*.274*	*.393*	*.580*	*.269*	*47.2*	*126-1B -6*

Breakout: 35% *Improve: 58%* *Collapse: 8%*

One thing that analysts don't talk about a lot is what happens when a great player devolves into being a merely very good player. There are all the usual signs that Thome is entering his decline phase, with his batting average having settled in the .270 range, his defense eroding to the point where it's become a real problem, and his injury problems becoming more frequent. Jim Thome is still a very good player, and should continue to be so for the foreseeable future, but the loss in expected productivity will still need to be accounted for, just as if it had come from a scrubby second baseman who was coming off a career year.

CHASE UTLEY **2B** **Bats: L** **Throws: R** Born: 17-Dec-1978 Age: 26

YEAR	TM	LG	AGE	AB	H	2B	3B	HR	BB	SO	SB	CS	AVG	OBP	SLG	MLVR	EQBA	EQOBP	EQSLG	EQMLVR	VORP	DEFENSE
2002	SWB	INT	23	464	122	39	1	17	46	89	8	3	.263	.352	.461	.123	.238	.324	.433	-.065	15.9	123-3B -20
2003	SWB	INT	24	431	139	26	2	18	41	75	10	4	.323	.390	.517	.305	.301	.371	.500	.167	45.3	113-2B 6
2003	PHI	NL	24	134	32	10	1	2	11	22	2	0	.239	.322	.373	-.072	.244	.326	.385	-.122	4.2	33-2B 4
2004	SWB	INT	25	123	35	8	1	6	18	29	4	2	.285	.368	.512	.187	.262	.346	.475	.052	8.9	33-2B 0
2004	PHI	NL	25	267	71	11	2	13	15	40	4	1	.266	.308	.468	.018	.265	.306	.470	-.023	12.9	43-2B 4 12-1B -1
2005	*PHI*	*NL*	*26*	*309*	*83*	*18*	*2*	*12*	*31*	*58*	*6*	*2*	*.270*	*.348*	*.456*	*.037*	*.270*	*.346*	*.455*	*.029*	*21.9*	*85-2B -2*

Breakout: 14% *Improve: 44%* *Collapse: 22%*

The Phillies are believers in Utley, citing his improved defense at second base and the ungodly number of RBI that he accumulated in the big leagues (57 in 267 at-bats, a rate that exceeded Thome's). We're believers too, though we could care less about the RBI and would like to see Utley refine his pitch selection. Utley is not going to be a star, but second base is a thin position and his extra-base power should provide the Phillies with a competitive advantage. Polanco's unexpected return might cripple Utley's fantasy value, but it's not the disaster that it may seem to be; Utley should still get the lion's share of at bats against right-handed pitchers, and he's posted a pretty big platoon split in his brief time in the bigs.

SHAWN WOOTEN 1B/C/3B Bats: R Throws: R Born: 24-Jul-1972 Age: 32

YEAR	TM	LG	AGE	AB	H	2B	3B	HR	BB	SO	SB	CS	AVG	OBP	SLG	MLVR	EQBA	EQOBP	EQSLG	EQMLVR	VORP	DEFENSE
2002	ANA	AL	29	113	33	8	0	3	6	24	2	0	.292	.331	.442	.051	.304	.332	.455	.038	6.2	
2003	ANA	AL	30	272	66	8	0	7	24	45	0	4	.243	.303	.349	-.152	.252	.311	.359	-.181	-1.4	26-1B 0 13-C -5
2004	SWB	INT	31	225	66	22	0	4	24	29	0	1	.293	.370	.444	.107	.260	.331	.390	-.094	6.0	47-3B -5
2004	PHI	NL	31	53	9	3	0	0	2	9	0	0	.170	.228	.226	-.498	.189	.205	.208	-.642	-4.6	
2005	*PHI*	*NL*	*32*	*174*	*43*	*9*	*1*	*4*	*16*	*30*	*0*	*0*	*.246*	*.316*	*.375*	*-.143*	*.246*	*.314*	*.374*	*-.150*	*0.4*	*49-3B -9*

Breakout: 22% *Improve: 46%* *Collapse: 34%*

Wooten's most useful gimmick is his ability to catch a few times a month, and so he was an odd fit for the Phillies, who had good pinch-hitting and catching backups. Even odder was that they tried him at third base in Scranton, a position for which his slow feet and chubby frame do not leave him particularly well suited. It was a bit like training an underworked CPA in sales, then turning around two weeks later and downsizing him.

PITCHERS

PAUL ABBOTT Bats: R Throws: R Born: 15-Sep-1967 Age: 37

YEAR	TM	LG	AGE	G	GS	IP	H	BB	SO	HR	ERA	EQERA	EQH9	EQBB9	EQSO9	EQHR9	PERA	VORP	STF
2002	SEA	AL	34	7	5	26.3	40	20	22	5	11.98	11.85	11.5	5.9	6.9	1.6	7.24	-18.5	-13
2003	KCR	AL	35	10	8	47.7	47	26	32	8	5.28	4.66	8.7	4.7	6.0	1.4	5.05	3.2	-4
2004	TBY	AL	36	10	9	47.0	49	27	25	8	6.70	6.70	9.7	4.7	4.5	1.4	5.72	-6.4	-9
2004	PHI	NL	36	10	10	49.0	57	31	21	14	6.24	6.70	10.9	5.2	3.4	2.5	7.28	-5.6	-28
2005	*PHI*	*NL*	*37*	*21*	*13*	*78.7*	*89*	*45*	*48*	*12*	*5.73*	*5.95*	*10.2*	*4.5*	*4.9*	*1.2*	*6.17*	*-0.1*	*-13*

Breakout: 32% *Improve: 55%* *Collapse: 25%*

He's still living off the rotting carcass of the 17–4 record that he managed with the Mariners in 2001, a feat that was only slightly luckier than Robert Varkonyi winning the World Series of Poker, or The Tony Danza Show making it past the pilot. There's no indication at this point that he's a competent big league pitcher.

KEITH BUCKTROT Bats: L Throws: R Born: 27-Nov-1980 Age: 24

YEAR	TM	LG	AGE	G	GS	IP	H	BB	SO	HR	ERA	EQERA	EQH9	EQBB9	EQSO9	EQHR9	PERA	VORP	STF
2002	CLR	FSL	21	27	24	160.3	167	78	84	10	4.88	6.55	10.2	4.9	3.4	1.2	6.01	-6.8	-15
2003	CLR	FSL	22	19	17	110.7	104	29	68	8	3.33	5.67	10.3	2.8	4.1	2.0	5.94	-3.8	-16
2003	REA	EAS	22	7	7	45.7	34	15	30	3	2.56	3.89	8.0	3.2	5.0	1.1	3.89	7.9	15
2004	REA	EAS	23	20	20	105.3	140	39	60	16	4.87	5.72	11.4	3.4	3.8	1.8	6.77	-13.3	-14
2005	*PHI*	*NL*	*24*	*22*	*13*	*82.3*	*92*	*36*	*46*	*15*	*5.61*	*5.82*	*10.1*	*3.5*	*4.6*	*1.5*	*5.83*	*0.0*	*-12*

Breakout: 10% *Improve: 43%* *Collapse: 20%*

This was supposed to be a breakthrough year for Bucktrot, but instead he staggered at Reading, missing a month with a shoulder injury and failing to strike batters out at an acceptable rate. While he can throw as hard as 95 mph, his fastball doesn't have the movement to miss opposing bats, and he has yet to develop an acceptable secondary pitch, experimenting at times with a curve, slider and cutter. He's no better than a C+ prospect at this stage.

DAVE COGGIN Bats: R Throws: R Born: 30-Oct-1976 Age: 28

YEAR	TM	LG	AGE	G	GS	IP	H	BB	SO	HR	ERA	EQERA	EQH9	EQBB9	EQSO9	EQHR9	PERA	VORP	STF
2002	PHI	NL	25	38	7	77.0	65	51	64	4	4.68	5.06	8.1	5.2	6.6	0.5	4.10	4.4	1
2004	SWB	INT	27	16	8	53.3	50	18	39	9	4.73	4.89	9.2	3.3	5.6	1.8	5.44	0.9	-1
2005	*PHI*	*NL*	*28*	*27*	*7*	*65.0*	*63*	*29*	*44*	*8*	*4.61*	*4.79*	*8.7*	*3.6*	*5.5*	*1.0*	*4.63*	*6.4*	*-6*

Breakout: 17% *Improve: 41%* *Collapse: 20%*

Recovering from a torn labrum that cost him virtually all of 2003, Coggin appears to be well back on the road to mediocrity. He was not protected on the 40-man roster, and the Phillies have a deep bullpen to begin with, so a major league opportunity will have to come somewhere else.

RHEAL CORMIER | **Bats: L** | **Throws: L** | Born: 23-Apr-1967 | Age: 38

YEAR	TM	LG	AGE	G	GS	IP	H	BB	SO	HR	ERA	EQERA	EQH9	EQBB9	EQSO9	EQHR9	PERA	VORP	STF
2002	PHI	NL	35	54	0	60.0	61	32	49	6	5.25	5.83	9.2	4.1	6.4	0.9	4.91	-2.2	-5
2003	PHI	NL	36	65	0	84.7	54	25	67	4	1.70	2.16	6.8	2.4	6.7	0.5	2.62	34.9	14
2004	PHI	NL	37	84	0	81.0	70	26	46	7	3.56	3.66	8.5	2.7	4.7	0.7	3.89	19.3	-6
2005	*PHI*	*NL*	*38*	*42*	*0*	*42.0*	*44*	*16*	*28*	*4*	*4.04*	*4.19*	*9.6*	*3.0*	*5.4*	*0.8*	*4.68*	*7.1*	*-7*

Breakout: 24% *Improve: 35%* *Collapse: 22%*

Timing is everything when it comes to contract extensions, and the Phillies pulled the trigger on Cormier's $3 million option—the legacy of an irrationally exuberant deal signed in November 2000—after he posted a stellar 2003 ERA that was out of line with both his past performances and his peripheral stats. They were probably disappointed with his performance, but it was right in line with what our projection system expected. Cormier, who has won more big league games than any other native of Moncton, New Brunswick, keeps the ball down often enough to contribute for another couple seasons, but the Phillies' two-year, $5.25 million contract extension was too much.

GAVIN FLOYD | **Bats: R** | **Throws: R** | Born: 27-Jan-1983 | Age: 22

YEAR	TM	LG	AGE	G	GS	IP	H	BB	SO	HR	ERA	EQERA	EQH9	EQBB9	EQSO9	EQHR9	PERA	VORP	STF
2002	LWD	SAL	19	27	27	166.0	119	64	140	13	2.77	5.14	9.3	4.6	4.9	1.8	5.95	-5.6	16
2003	CLR	FSL	20	24	20	138.0	128	45	115	9	3.00	5.59	10.0	3.4	5.4	1.6	5.66	-0.8	5
2004	REA	EAS	21	20	20	119.0	93	46	94	5	2.57	3.49	7.9	3.7	5.4	0.5	3.73	23.1	33
2004	SWB	INT	21	5	5	30.7	39	9	18	4	4.98	5.76	10.9	2.7	4.2	1.2	5.76	-0.5	0
2004	PHI	NL	21	6	4	28.3	25	16	24	1	3.50	3.58	8.1	4.6	6.8	0.3	3.90	7.1	15
2005	*PHI*	*NL*	*22*	*17*	*16*	*92.7*	*93*	*44*	*67*	*13*	*4.84*	*5.02*	*9.0*	*3.7*	*5.9*	*1.2*	*5.05*	*6.9*	*4*

Breakout: 10% *Improve: 41%* *Collapse: 26%*

The Phillies allowed Floyd to throw his curveball this year, after discouraging him from using it in the past in an effort to get him to concentrate on his change-up. Determining just how much difference the full arsenal made depends on which statistic you look at. Floyd's strikeout rate barely moved, which is discouraging since the curve is supposed to be his out pitch. Where the curve might have helped Floyd is in limiting the longball, as he halved his translated homers allowed rate. While you might think of Bert Blyleven and assume that curveball artists are flyball pitchers, it depends on exactly what sort of curveball we're talking about. Floyd's is a hard curve that has a lot of downward movement—it functions almost like a splitter, usually ending up south of the strike zone and inducing a lot of groundballs. Still, striking batters out is the most important skill a pitcher can have, and Floyd's track record in that department is just average. While Floyd is plenty young and will have the opportunity to improve the finer points of his pitching—his curve might induce more strikeouts, for example, if he learns how to set it up better—there's also the chance that he winds up like Jon Garland, a merely competent pitcher who is perennially on the verge of a breakout that never comes.

GEOFF GEARY | **Bats: R** | **Throws: R** | Born: 26-Aug-1976 | Age: 28

YEAR	TM	LG	AGE	G	GS	IP	H	BB	SO	HR	ERA	EQERA	EQH9	EQBB9	EQSO9	EQHR9	PERA	VORP	STF
2002	SWB	INT	25	38	8	101.0	108	32	82	9	3.03	4.69	9.8	3.2	6.3	1.1	5.34	2.8	-3
2003	SWB	INT	26	46	3	87.7	73	13	80	3	2.16	3.27	7.9	1.5	6.8	0.4	2.83	25.5	21
2004	SWB	INT	27	21	0	23.3	20	13	23	1	2.32	2.82	8.1	5.2	7.3	0.4	4.03	3.9	0
2004	PHI	NL	27	33	0	44.7	52	16	30	8	5.44	5.77	10.1	2.9	5.4	1.4	5.36	-0.7	-11
2005	*PHI*	*NL*	*28*	*23*	*5*	*52.7*	*54*	*20*	*41*	*7*	*4.44*	*4.60*	*9.2*	*3.0*	*6.3*	*1.1*	*4.71*	*6.6*	*0*

Breakout: 21% *Improve: 45%* *Collapse: 27%*

Because he's small of stature and has just a middling fastball, Geary has not received many favors, and he did not help his cause with a marginal big league debut in which he was just as hittable as the scouts had feared. Protected on the 40-man roster, but he'll need a good spring training to avoid getting shipped to Scranton or placed on the waiver wire.

DAN GIESE — **Bats: R** — **Throws: R** — Born: 19-May-1977 Age: 28

YEAR	TM	LG	AGE	G	GS	IP	H	BB	SO	HR	ERA	EQERA	EQH9	EQBB9	EQSO9	EQHR9	PERA	VORP	STF
2002	MOB	SOU	25	32	0	52.7	56	13	51	3	2.90	4.80	9.6	2.1	6.4	1.1	4.62	5.5	-2
2002	TRN	EAS	25	23	0	49.3	53	9	39	6	3.83	4.94	9.7	1.7	5.5	1.7	4.56	5.5	-3
2003	SWB	INT	26	34	0	48.3	37	10	49	8	3.17	4.09	8.6	2.2	7.8	2.2	4.70	4.4	9
2004	SWB	INT	27	54	0	83.3	63	18	54	8	2.81	3.07	8.0	2.1	5.0	1.1	3.66	16.4	15
2005	*PHI*	*NL*	*28*	*39*	*0*	*43.0*	*42*	*13*	*31*	*8*	*4.46*	*4.63*	*8.7*	*2.4*	*5.7*	*1.5*	*4.58*	*5.5*	*-7*

Breakout: 25% *Improve: 47%* *Collapse: 23%*

Giese was a 34th-round draft choice six years ago as a closer out of the University of San Diego. He has since spent time in three organizations, always as a reliever, and always with a terrific propensity to throw strikes. Giese doesn't have tremendous stuff in spite of some decent strikeout rates, as is manifest in the high number of home runs that he allows. He's deserving of a major league trial, however. The Phillies might seem like the right team to give it to him, having dispatched Giese to the AFL for two seasons running. But it's hard to take the organization's commitment to him seriously when they traded for Todd Jones rather than recalling Giese from Scranton.

COLE HAMELS — **Bats: L** — **Throws: L** — Born: 27-Dec-1983 Age: 21

YEAR	TM	LG	AGE	G	GS	IP	H	BB	SO	HR	ERA	EQERA	EQH9	EQBB9	EQSO9	EQHR9	PERA	VORP	STF
2003	CLR	FSL	19	5	5	26.3	29	14	32	0	2.74	4.62	9.6	5.3	7.5	0.4	4.97	1.8	18
2003	LWD	SAL	19	13	13	74.7	32	25	115	0	0.84	2.98	6.2	3.8	8.8	0.3	2.58	22.2	59
2004	CLR	FSL	20	4	4	16.0	10	4	24	0	1.12	2.45	7.4	2.5	9.2	0.0	2.45	5.1	42
2005	*PHI*	*NL*	*21*	*21*	*16*	*103.3*	*87*	*41*	*105*	*7*	*3.25*	*3.37*	*7.6*	*3.1*	*8.2*	*0.5*	*3.38*	*25.4*	*26*

Breakout: 23% *Improve: 48%* *Collapse: 15%*

Asking anyone who might know better for straight information about Cole Hamels's left elbow is about as useful as asking Karen Hughes for her take on W.'s performance in the Presidential Debates, so let's just report the facts as we know them:

- Cole Hamels's left elbow was born in San Diego, California Dec. 27, 1983.
- While playing in a pickup football game during his sophomore year of high school, Hamels slammed into a parked pickup while attempting to catch a pass. The arm was moderately sore, but the extent of the injury was unclear, and Hamels continued pitching with it. Three weeks later, his arm snapped while he was throwing a fastball, and Hamels found that he had broken his left humerus bone. He skipped his junior season, but pitched exceptionally well in his senior year, prompting the Phillies to take him in the first round of the 2002 draft.
- The Phillies cancelled plans for Hamels to try out for the US Olympic team in October 2003 after he suffered back spasms during his instructional league stint. There were no reported complications with his arm.
- Hamels appeared in three games during spring training this year, and was highly impressive, striking out nine batters in seven innings. Hamels was optioned to minor league camp, as was expected, on March 19.
- On April 7, the Phillies announced that Hamels had undergone an MRI on his elbow and was going to miss the first month of the minor league season. The announcement referred to the injury as "mild soreness" and did not disclose precisely what the MRI had found, but its results were negative. The injury was later reported to be tendonitis.
- Hamels was assigned to Clearwater from extended spring training May 17. He made four starts between May 20 and June 4 and was very effective, striking out 24 batters and compiling a 1.13 ERA.
- Hamels missed his next turn in the rotation for Clearwater with what was described as an inflamed left elbow. According to *The Philadelphia Inquirer,* the injury was separate and distinct from his tendonitis. He was initially shut down for seven to 10 days and later placed on the minor league DL. Reports in July said that Hamels was not feeling any discomfort, but put his timetable several weeks away. He did not return to action before Clearwater's season ended September 2.
- Hamels was assigned to the Florida Instructional League in October, and was reportedly throwing well.

There—that's what we know. All of that stuff is available publicly, though it takes a bit of digging to get it. We're not going to try and spin it or interpret it. Obviously health is the key issue here, and obviously people have a disposition toward panic when it comes to valuable baseball players, especially prized pitching prospects. We're the sort of people who react to fear by attempting to collect as much information about a situation as possible, and in the absence of complete information, it's at least worthwhile to attempt to prevent misinformation, even if it takes half a page to do it.

TODD JONES **Bats: R** **Throws: R** Born: 24-Apr-1968 Age: 37

YEAR	TM	LG	AGE	G	GS	IP	H	BB	SO	HR	ERA	EQERA	EQH9	EQBB9	EQSO9	EQHR9	PERA	VORP	STF
2002	COL	NL	34	79	0	82.3	84	28	73	10	4.70	4.13	8.9	2.6	7.0	1.0	4.35	6.2	3
2003	COL	NL	35	33	1	39.3	61	18	28	8	8.24	7.68	11.4	3.3	5.5	1.5	6.37	-14.4	-18
2003	BOS	AL	35	26	0	29.3	32	13	31	2	5.53	5.16	8.5	3.6	9.1	0.6	3.64	0.9	15
2004	CIN	NL	36	51	0	57.0	49	25	37	4	3.79	3.95	8.1	3.6	5.3	0.7	3.62	11.1	-5
2004	PHI	NL	36	27	0	25.3	35	8	22	3	4.98	4.91	10.9	2.5	6.7	1.1	5.61	2.0	-3
2005	*FLA*	*NL*	*37*	*47*	*0*	*61.0*	*63*	*22*	*47*	*6*	*4.05*	*4.42*	*9.3*	*2.9*	*6.3*	*0.9*	*4.72*	*8.3*	*-2*

Breakout: 31% *Improve: 55%* *Collapse: 17%*

Another element in the Phillies' master plan to counteract the injuries to their starting pitchers by acquiring as many washed-up middle relievers as possible, Jones pitched just well enough to extend his major league career by a season or two. The homophobia thing is old news now, but it was doubly ironic coming from someone whose mustache comes straight from central casting on a Chi Chi LaRue soundstage.

CORY LIDLE **Bats: R** **Throws: R** Born: 22-Mar-1972 Age: 33

YEAR	TM	LG	AGE	G	GS	IP	H	BB	SO	HR	ERA	EQERA	EQH9	EQBB9	EQSO9	EQHR9	PERA	VORP	STF
2002	OAK	AL	30	31	30	192.0	191	39	111	17	3.89	3.91	9.0	1.8	5.1	0.7	4.06	37.6	14
2003	TOR	AL	31	31	31	192.7	216	60	112	24	5.74	5.50	9.3	2.7	5.1	1.0	4.37	-2.8	5
2004	CIN	NL	32	24	24	149.0	170	44	93	24	5.32	5.62	9.8	2.3	5.0	1.3	4.70	0.4	0
2004	PHI	NL	32	10	10	62.3	54	17	33	3	3.90	3.99	8.4	2.3	4.4	0.5	3.68	11.9	9
2005	*PHI*	*NL*	*33*	*28*	*26*	*157.3*	*169*	*46*	*91*	*20*	*4.62*	*4.80*	*9.7*	*2.3*	*4.7*	*1.0*	*4.59*	*13.8*	*3*

Breakout: 12% *Improve: 44%* *Collapse: 21%*

Lidle is durable and keeps the ball down, which makes him a reasonable back-of-the-rotation fit for a team with a power-friendly ballpark and an offense good enough to win games on its own. The Phillies re-signed him for two years and $6.3 million. That's not a terrible price compared to some recent doozies, but pitchers with this sort of strikeout rate don't tend to age well.

RYAN MADSON **Bats: L** **Throws: R** Born: 28-Aug-1980 Age: 24

YEAR	TM	LG	AGE	G	GS	IP	H	BB	SO	HR	ERA	EQERA	EQH9	EQBB9	EQSO9	EQHR9	PERA	VORP	STF
2002	REA	EAS	21	26	26	171.3	150	53	132	11	3.20	4.14	8.9	3.1	5.5	0.9	4.59	17.8	19
2003	SWB	INT	22	26	26	157.0	157	42	138	9	3.50	4.45	9.0	2.8	6.4	0.7	4.03	26.1	22
2004	PHI	NL	23	52	1	77.0	68	19	55	6	2.34	2.84	8.4	2.1	5.9	0.6	3.58	25.8	8
2005	*PHI*	*NL*	*24*	*34*	*11*	*93.0*	*91*	*29*	*72*	*10*	*3.86*	*4.00*	*8.9*	*2.5*	*6.3*	*0.9*	*4.17*	*17.0*	*5*

Breakout: 15% *Improve: 45%* *Collapse: 23%*

Madson's season was not quite as good as it looks on the surface—note the difference between his ERA and his PERA. Nevertheless, the guy can pitch, facing hitters with one nasty change-up after another, and it was surprising that he made just one start for the Phillies given their injury problems. He'll likely get that chance in the future as he bulks up and refines his breaking pitch, though one wonders whether his success in the bullpen will doom him to it.

SCOTT MATHIESON **Bats: R** **Throws: R** Born: 27-Feb-1984 Age: 21

YEAR	TM	LG	AGE	G	GS	IP	H	BB	SO	HR	ERA	EQERA	EQH9	EQBB9	EQSO9	EQHR9	PERA	VORP	STF
2004	LWD	SAL	20	25	25	131.3	130	50	112	7	4.32	6.06	9.4	3.9	4.7	0.8	4.67	12.7	2
2005	*PHI*	*NL*	*21*	*13*	*11*	*66.3*	*66*	*29*	*43*	*10*	*4.82*	*5.00*	*9.0*	*3.4*	*5.2*	*1.3*	*5.06*	*5.7*	*-1*

Breakout: 11% *Improve: 46%* *Collapse: 14%*

Mathieson is nicknamed "The Goose" due to his Canadian ancestry, which is a hell of a lot better than being nicknamed "The Loonie." He's better liked by the organization than you'd gather from his stats because he throws as hard as 94 and pitched continually better as the season wore on. He needs to put in some significant work on his command and his secondary pitches, as most 21-year-old pitchers do.

KEVIN MILLWOOD **Bats: R** **Throws: R** Born: 24-Dec-1974 Age: 30

YEAR	TM	LG	AGE	G	GS	IP	H	BB	SO	HR	ERA	EQERA	EQH9	EQBB9	EQSO9	EQHR9	PERA	VORP	STF
2002	ATL	NL	27	35	34	217.0	186	65	178	16	3.24	3.55	8.5	2.4	6.8	0.7	3.99	49.6	22
2003	PHI	NL	28	35	35	222.0	210	68	169	19	4.01	4.30	8.7	2.4	6.3	0.8	3.88	37.6	18
2004	PHI	NL	29	25	25	141.0	155	51	125	14	4.85	5.12	9.3	2.8	7.1	0.8	4.53	9.3	17
2005	*CLE*	*AL*	*30*	*28*	*25*	*151.3*	*162*	*50*	*115*	*17*	*4.45*	*4.36*	*9.6*	*2.6*	*6.2*	*1.0*	*4.37*	*23.5*	*11*

Breakout: 11% *Improve: 49%* *Collapse: 10%*

Millwood is a high-fastball pitcher and the new ballpark in Philadelphia was not the ballpark for him.

— Scott Boras, agent for Kevin Millwood, quoted in *New York Times*, November 26, 2004

Boras is a smart guy, but let's consider some of the problems with this statement:

1. Millwood, though he throws a good four-seamer, has never been overly dependent on the pitch;
2. Millwood has consistently given up fewer homers than league average throughout his career, and he gave up fewer homers than league average last season;
3. Millwood's problems, such as they were, were not confined to pitching at Citizens Bank Park: His ERA was 4.95 at home, 4.77 on the road;
4. It is too early to come to any definitive conclusions about Citizens Bank Park. Its home-run park factor last season was 106, which is not statistically significant given just one year's worth of data.

What's interesting is that Millwood really does have a good excuse for his poor performance last season; he gave up hits on nearly 34% of batted balls in play, a rate far higher than the normal range and enough to have increased his ERA by approximately a full point. That's something largely outside of Millwood's control, and it means that he's likely to bounce back next season. But park effects sell in a way that Voros McCracken doesn't, in part because Citizens yielded a lot of home runs early last season, when there was a lot of attention focused on the Phillies and their new digs.

Millwood is likely to be one of the relatively better buys on the free-agent market, so the Indians were smart to sign him up. But one wonders just how he and Boras feel about turning down a big contract extension prior to the start of last season. Gambling on a breakout season might seem the obvious choice given the way that the market tends to overvalue big one-year performances (see also: Carl Pavano). But our projection system, PECOTA, figured that there was only about a 25% chance that Millwood would exceed the 37.6 VORP that he posted in 2003. There are more things that can go wrong for a pitcher than can go right; the things that undermined Millwood's season—modest injury problems and poor hit-luck—are the sorts of things that happen to pitchers all the time. While they won't necessarily impact Millwood's future, they did impact his market value, and substantially so. All else being equal, a pitcher should take reasonable guaranteed money when he can get it.

ERIC MILTON **Bats: L** **Throws: L** Born: 04-Aug-1975 Age: 29

YEAR	TM	LG	AGE	G	GS	IP	H	BB	SO	HR	ERA	EQERA	EQH9	EQBB9	EQSO9	EQHR9	PERA	VORP	STF
2002	MIN	AL	26	29	29	171.0	173	30	121	24	4.84	4.64	9.1	1.5	6.2	1.1	4.20	17.7	14
2003	MIN	AL	27	3	3	17.0	15	1	7	2	2.65	2.25	8.4	0.6	3.9	1.1	3.38	6.5	7
2004	PHI	NL	28	34	34	201.0	196	75	161	43	4.75	4.87	9.2	3.0	6.6	1.8	5.15	18.7	2
2005	*CIN*	*NL*	*29*	*28*	*27*	*163.7*	*169*	*54*	*122*	*29*	*4.80*	*5.13*	*9.5*	*2.6*	*6.0*	*1.4*	*5.10*	*10.9*	*7*

Breakout: 4% *Improve: 44%* *Collapse: 17%*

Now, if there's a guy who you'd think should be adversely affected by Citizens Bank Park, it is Milton, a pronounced flyball pitcher whose problems with the longball have long been his Achilles' heel. Milton did, in fact, yield a league-high 43 bombs, but a majority of those were on the road: Opponents slugged .451 against him at Citizens, and .539 in away games. It is this disposition to giving up home runs that keeps Milton from being the pitcher that a lot of analysts want him to be. Groundball/flyball ratios are extremely stable for most pitchers, and so long as opponents are hitting the ball skyward more than 60% of the time against Milton, he's going to give up a lot of homers. He's one of the most overrated pitchers around, and Great American Ball Park, which enhances home runs but depresses the other aspects of offensive performance, is about the worst possible home for him.

BRETT MYERS **Bats: R** **Throws: R** Born: 17-Aug-1980 Age: 24

YEAR	TM	LG	AGE	G	GS	IP	H	BB	SO	HR	ERA	EQERA	EQH9	EQBB9	EQSO9	EQHR9	PERA	VORP	STF
2002	SWB	INT	21	19	19	128.0	121	20	97	9	3.59	4.41	9.0	1.6	5.9	0.7	4.11	19.9	32
2002	PHI	NL	21	12	12	72.0	73	29	34	11	4.25	5.00	9.7	3.2	3.8	1.4	5.27	6.0	5
2003	PHI	NL	22	32	32	193.0	205	76	143	20	4.43	4.68	9.4	3.1	6.1	0.9	4.64	23.2	18
2004	PHI	NL	23	32	31	176.0	196	62	116	31	5.52	5.71	9.9	2.9	5.3	1.5	5.39	-0.3	4
2005	*PHI*	*NL*	*24*	*26*	*24*	*145.0*	*152*	*51*	*102*	*18*	*4.40*	*4.56*	*9.5*	*2.8*	*5.7*	*1.0*	*4.65*	*17.3*	*7*

Breakout: 15% *Improve: 52%* *Collapse: 18%*

Sticking with a theme, here's another Phillie whose season was ruined by a high home-run rate. Unlike Milton, Myers is a groundball pitcher, which makes it more likely that he's going to bounce back to at least the level of performance he established in 2003. If there's a silver lining here, it's that Myers's habit of giving up big innings last season got him pulled early from a lot of games, keeping his workload down.

VICENTE PADILLA **Bats: R** **Throws: R** Born: 27-Sep-1977 Age: 27

YEAR	TM	LG	AGE	G	GS	IP	H	BB	SO	HR	ERA	EQERA	EQH9	EQBB9	EQSO9	EQHR9	PERA	VORP	STF
2002	PHI	NL	24	32	32	206.0	198	53	128	16	3.28	3.86	9.0	2.0	5.1	0.7	3.95	42.9	12
2003	PHI	NL	25	32	32	208.7	196	62	133	22	3.62	4.17	8.9	2.4	5.3	1.0	4.12	38.1	9
2004	PHI	NL	26	20	20	115.3	119	36	82	16	4.53	4.85	9.3	2.5	5.8	1.1	4.61	10.9	6
2005	*PHI*	*NL*	*27*	*23*	*21*	*125.3*	*128*	*40*	*87*	*15*	*4.18*	*4.34*	*9.2*	*2.5*	*5.6*	*0.9*	*4.44*	*17.6*	*8*

Breakout: 18% *Improve: 50%* *Collapse: 11%*

This shouldn't be considered all that surprising. Though Padilla pitched fine after returning from the DL in August, there have always been questions about his stamina, and he had notably overachieved his peripheral numbers in both 2002 and 2003. In the long run, he might be best suited to a swingman role.

BRIAN POWELL **Bats: R** **Throws: R** Born: 10-Oct-1973 Age: 31

YEAR	TM	LG	AGE	G	GS	IP	H	BB	SO	HR	ERA	EQERA	EQH9	EQBB9	EQSO9	EQHR9	PERA	VORP	STF
2002	TOL	INT	28	20	20	119.3	127	26	82	8	3.92	4.57	9.4	2.2	5.3	0.9	4.41	15.1	11
2002	DET	AL	28	13	9	57.7	64	21	30	11	4.84	4.98	9.6	3.1	4.5	1.6	4.98	4.3	-8
2003	FRE	PCL	29	23	15	101.0	118	32	59	10	4.19	5.34	9.9	3.1	4.4	1.4	4.98	6.7	-3
2003	SWB	INT	29	8	7	52.7	57	12	36	1	4.61	6.04	9.2	2.3	5.0	0.4	3.91	9.5	11
2004	SWB	INT	30	8	8	44.3	27	6	29	2	1.63	2.45	6.9	1.3	5.1	0.4	2.68	13.1	31
2004	PHI	NL	30	17	2	39.3	39	16	24	5	5.04	5.26	9.1	3.3	5.0	1.0	4.54	2.0	5
2005	*PHI*	*NL*	*31*	*17*	*10*	*65.7*	*71*	*22*	*40*	*10*	*4.91*	*5.09*	*9.7*	*2.6*	*4.9*	*1.2*	*4.88*	*6.0*	*-4*

Breakout: 16% *Improve: 46%* *Collapse: 28%*

Powell has stuck around long enough to earn major league service time during the course of five different seasons. He hasn't pitched well during any of those big league trials, but that's what you'd expect from his middling minor league numbers. For you *Scoresheet Baseball* fans, this is Pitcher, AAA.

FELIX RODRIGUEZ **Bats: R** **Throws: R** Born: 09-Sep-1972 Age: 32

YEAR	TM	LG	AGE	G	GS	IP	H	BB	SO	HR	ERA	EQERA	EQH9	EQBB9	EQSO9	EQHR9	PERA	VORP	STF
2002	SFG	NL	29	71	0	69.0	53	29	58	5	4.17	4.55	7.9	3.3	6.9	0.7	3.72	8.2	4
2003	SFG	NL	30	68	0	61.0	59	29	46	5	3.10	3.20	9.0	3.8	6.3	0.8	4.88	17.1	-5
2004	SFG	NL	31	53	0	44.7	43	19	31	7	3.42	3.56	9.0	3.6	5.7	1.3	4.81	10.3	-11
2004	PHI	NL	31	23	0	21.0	18	10	28	1	3.00	3.05	7.4	3.9	10.5	0.4	3.48	6.3	25
2005	*NYY*	*AL*	*32*	*45*	*0*	*55.0*	*55*	*23*	*44*	*8*	*4.48*	*4.48*	*9.2*	*3.3*	*6.5*	*1.2*	*4.77*	*9.1*	*-4*

Breakout: 26% *Improve: 51%* *Collapse: 24%*

Rodriguez is not a bad reliever, but he hasn't worn the "closer of the future" tag well since 2001, following seasons in which he worked in 76 and 80 games for Dusty Baker. Analysts haven't spent a lot of time studying the differential effects of innings versus appearances when it comes to the longer-term effects on a reliever's arm. But there are right-handers who cross the 80-appearance barrier and run into trouble: Scott Sullivan, Billy Koch, and Paul Quantrill are three good examples. Traded to the Yankees for Kenny Lofton; both teams will be disappointed.

BUD SMITH Bats: L Throws: L Born: 23-Oct-1979 Age: 25

YEAR	TM	LG	AGE	G	GS	IP	H	BB	SO	HR	ERA	EQERA	EQH9	EQBB9	EQSO9	EQHR9	PERA	VORP	STF
2002	STL	NL	22	11	10	48.0	67	22	22	4	6.94	7.31	11.4	3.4	3.6	0.8	6.19	-9.7	-16
2002	MEM	PCL	22	6	6	38.0	33	13	34	1	2.13	3.00	8.2	3.2	6.5	0.2	3.75	7.4	22
2002	SWB	INT	22	3	3	17.3	21	6	11	0	4.16	4.76	10.1	3.2	4.8	0.0	5.29	0.6	0
2003	CLR	FSL	23	4	2	18.3	10	4	12	0	1.48	3.31	6.6	2.2	4.4	0.0	2.20	6.2	13
2003	REA	EAS	23	8	8	37.0	40	15	24	6	5.35	6.03	10.7	3.9	5.0	2.6	6.82	-4.6	-13
2004	CLR	FSL	24	5	5	13.7	13	5	12	0	3.94	5.54	9.0	3.5	5.5	0.0	4.15	2.1	-5
2005	*PHI*	*NL*	*25*	*16*	*10*	*64.7*	*72*	*27*	*41*	*9*	*5.13*	*5.32*	*10.0*	*3.3*	*5.1*	*1.1*	*5.32*	*2.9*	*-5*

Breakout: 22% *Improve: 49%* *Collapse: 24%*

Smith is sometimes held up as a lesson in why soft-tossers do not make good pitching prospects, but that is not quite the issue here. Smith's shoulder began bothering him in 2002, his problems compounding as he attempted to pitch his way through the pain. By December of that year, Dr. Lewis Yocum was operating on his torn labrum, and Smith hasn't been the same since, losing most of this season due to recurrent problems with the injury.

The lesson, rather, is that you can't be too careful when trading for a young pitcher who is dealing with an injury problem. It's not as though the Phillies can claim they were completely taken by surprise. Smith was pitching terribly at the time they acquired him in the Scott Rolen package, and had spent three weeks on the DL earlier that season. Major league teams have certain protocols when it comes to sharing medical information about a player who might be included in a trade, but even a good-faith effort to provide access to a player's medical records and make him available for a physical is no substitute for having had your doctors examine a player regularly for months and years. You shouldn't just err on the side of caution when acquiring an injured pitcher; you should err on the side of being anal retentive.

AMAURY TELEMACO Bats: R Throws: R Born: 19-Jan-1974 Age: 31

YEAR	TM	LG	AGE	G	GS	IP	H	BB	SO	HR	ERA	EQERA	EQH9	EQBB9	EQSO9	EQHR9	PERA	VORP	STF
2003	SWB	INT	29	25	24	155.3	125	22	116	15	3.25	3.91	8.4	1.5	5.7	1.5	3.79	28.7	33
2003	PHI	NL	29	8	8	45.3	41	11	29	5	3.97	4.40	8.8	1.9	5.4	1.0	3.98	6.7	42
2004	PHI	NL	30	42	0	54.3	51	19	32	12	4.31	4.41	9.4	3.0	4.9	1.9	5.29	7.4	-18
2005	*PHI*	*NL*	*31*	*28*	*4*	*54.0*	*55*	*18*	*36*	*8*	*4.53*	*4.70*	*9.2*	*2.6*	*5.4*	*1.2*	*4.62*	*6.4*	*-6*

Breakout: 22% *Improve: 46%* *Collapse: 24%*

Contrary to rumors, Telemaco did not disappear into the Springfield Mystery Spot along with Ozzie Smith and Jeff Pico. He's been in the Phillies organization since 1999, but missed virtually all of the 2002 season due to shoulder surgery. Telemaco has been a much better pitcher since the surgery, although in '04 he did not exhibit the stellar command that characterized his 2003 campaign. Useful swingman to have around.

BILLY WAGNER Bats: L Throws: L Born: 25-Jul-1971 Age: 33

YEAR	TM	LG	AGE	G	GS	IP	H	BB	SO	HR	ERA	EQERA	EQH9	EQBB9	EQSO9	EQHR9	PERA	VORP	STF
2002	HOU	NL	30	70	0	75.0	51	22	88	7	2.52	2.51	6.7	2.3	9.5	0.9	2.76	23.8	26
2003	HOU	NL	31	78	0	86.0	52	23	105	8	1.78	1.88	6.4	2.2	10.3	0.8	2.66	35.7	32
2004	PHI	NL	32	45	0	48.3	31	6	59	5	2.42	3.15	6.5	1.0	10.1	0.8	2.17	14.6	35
2005	*PHI*	*NL*	*33*	*63*	*0*	*50.7*	*39*	*12*	*51*	*5*	*2.54*	*2.64*	*7.0*	*1.9*	*8.1*	*0.8*	*2.79*	*17.1*	*16*

Breakout: 39% *Improve: 42%* *Collapse: 35%*

Wagner cost the Phillies exactly $165,517.24 per inning pitched. OK, so perhaps that's unfair. There's little doubt that closers are overpaid as a group, but there are only four or five pitchers in the league who can attain the elite levels that a healthy Wagner can. If we adopt the Economics 101 notion of value being determined by scarcity, then Wagner's contract is a lot more justifiable than say, Richie Sexson's.

It's the injury troubles, of course, which are cause for concern. There are conflicting reports about whether there is structural damage to Wagner's rotator cuff. The Phillies insist that there isn't, and they're willing to put their money where their mouth is, having picked up his $9 million option. Interestingly, the Phillies also believe that Wagner is still maturing as a pitcher, learning when he can take a little bit off and throw "just" 97 mph. If Wagner can learn when and where to let up, then both his walk rate, which he cut in half last season, and his shoulder should benefit.

RANDY WOLF **Bats: L** **Throws: L** Born: 22-Aug-1976 Age: 28

YEAR	TM	LG	AGE	G	GS	IP	H	BB	SO	HR	ERA	EQERA	EQH9	EQBB9	EQSO9	EQHR9	PERA	VORP	STF
2002	PHI	NL	25	31	31	210.7	172	63	172	23	3.20	3.53	8.2	2.4	6.8	1.0	3.76	51.8	19
2003	PHI	NL	26	33	33	200.0	176	78	177	27	4.23	4.65	8.4	3.1	7.4	1.2	4.23	25.6	17
2004	PHI	NL	27	23	23	136.7	145	36	89	20	4.28	4.80	9.5	2.1	5.3	1.2	4.73	14.5	4
2005	*PHI*	*NL*	*28*	*24*	*23*	*140.3*	*141*	*41*	*99*	*19*	*4.21*	*4.37*	*9.1*	*2.3*	*5.7*	*1.1*	*4.42*	*20.9*	*10*

Breakout: 21% *Improve: 57%* *Collapse: 14%*

The injuries that the Philadelphia pitching staff suffered last season weren't catastrophic events like torn labrums or rotator cuffs. They were closer to the shoulder tendonitis that caused Randy Wolf to miss seven weeks between two DL stints. The Phillies' feeling is that the former kind of injury is more preventable than the latter, but both types have the same underlying cause, which is the accumulated strain from the wholly unnatural act of repeatedly throwing a small spheroid faster than a speeding vehicle. Sometimes the San Andreas Fault will lay dormant for a while then go off for a big one; at other times it will content itself with a series of localized quakes, which are barely noticed by anyone but seismologists. Wolf's injury measured only about 5.2 on the Saunders Scale, and his doctors insist his arm is fine, though it's a troubling sign that his strikeout rate dropped as much as it did.

TIM WORRELL **Bats: R** **Throws: R** Born: 05-Jul-1967 Age: 37

YEAR	TM	LG	AGE	G	GS	IP	H	BB	SO	HR	ERA	EQERA	EQH9	EQBB9	EQSO9	EQHR9	PERA	VORP	STF
2002	SFG	NL	35	80	0	72.0	55	30	55	3	2.25	2.91	7.8	3.3	6.4	0.4	3.57	22.0	3
2003	SFG	NL	36	76	0	78.3	74	28	65	5	2.87	4.04	8.7	2.9	6.9	0.6	4.16	13.9	6
2004	PHI	NL	37	77	0	78.3	75	21	64	10	3.68	4.18	8.7	2.2	6.7	1.1	4.18	13.6	2
2005	*PHI*	*NL*	*37*	*49*	*0*	*61.3*	*62*	*20*	*45*	*6*	*3.69*	*3.82*	*9.1*	*2.5*	*6.0*	*0.9*	*4.23*	*12.9*	*-1*

Breakout: 37% *Improve: 57%* *Collapse: 22%*

This is becoming redundant, but of all the things that sabermetricians have discovered, the one that has the potential to save teams the most money is the idea that past ERA is not a particularly good predictor of future ERA. The peripheral numbers tell a much better story, and Worrell's peripheral numbers suggested that he was a pitcher pretty much like what we saw last season: PECOTA had him pegged for a 3.75 ERA after accounting for the change in home ballparks. The Phillies, though, were expecting more than that for their $2.75 million.

ED YARNALL **Bats: L** **Throws: L** Born: 04-Dec-1975 Age: 29

YEAR	TM	LG	AGE	G	GS	IP	H	BB	SO	HR	ERA	EQERA	EQH9	EQBB9	EQSO9	EQHR9	PERA	VORP	STF
2002	ORX	JPL	26	25	1	164.3	149	62	120	13	0.00	4.31	8.7	3.9	5.6	0.7	4.31	21.8	8
2003	SAC	PCL	27	18	13	64.7	72	30	46	6	3.76	4.52	9.8	4.7	5.4	1.3	5.69	-0.6	-13
2004	SWB	INT	28	24	23	118.0	103	56	93	12	3.97	4.15	8.5	4.6	5.9	1.1	4.72	10.8	14
2005	*PHI*	*NL*	*29*	*24*	*14*	*95.0*	*93*	*47*	*70*	*14*	*4.74*	*4.91*	*8.9*	*3.9*	*6.0*	*1.2*	*5.12*	*9.3*	*-2*

Breakout: 31% *Improve: 49%* *Collapse: 15%*

You'd like to be able to pinpoint the precise moment at which Ed Yarnall's career jumped the shark. While seeing him don an Orix Blue Wave uniform might seem to be the obvious candidate, the truth is that there really isn't one. Here's what we wrote about him in *BP 2000:*

> He's going to be special. Yarnall throws four pitches for strikes, hides the ball well and has a major league fastball. Like many young left-handers, his control can be a problem, but that's the only negative here. He even has a good health record and hasn't been worked that hard. Yarnall could be the best left-hander in the league by 2002.

Most of the substance of that comment still holds today; it's the spin that would be different. Yarnall's control has never been major league-caliber. That might be the only negative, but it's a really big, flashing-red negative, and it's not one that he's going to be able to overcome. You can take a 23-year-old hitting prospect who hits 40 doubles and 15 homers when he's 23 and project with some reasonable certainty what he's going to do when he's 27; you can't do that with a pitching prospect. Pitchers aren't subject to a smooth, gentle aging curve so much as they are a scary, probabilistic step function. A certain percentage of them improve, but they do so suddenly and dramatically, while others like Yarnall flatline for years at a time.

Pittsburgh Pirates

If ever you wondered whether "and then they lived happily ever after" was just a way of saying "we'd really rather skip the mundane afterward," ponder life in Steeltown, USA.

Beautiful ballpark, their first Rookie of the Year in franchise history, young talent on the roster and in the system, expensive veterans dealt for packages of goodies... In its outline, it's what you'd think are all the symptoms of a franchise that's in the initial stages of an organization-wide renaissance, powered by a publicly-financed stadium. They're the sorts of things fans willing to buckle up for the long-term return ride towards respectability ought to get excited about, and they're also the sorts of things that normally draw favorable commentary in *Baseball Prospectus.* But as ever, happiness in the "ever after" portion of the program can be relative.

As much as you might think that the Pirates have turned it around, they haven't. They're stuck, not because they're a bad organization, but because they're at a point where they have to decide what sort of organization they really want to grow up to be, and how realistic that ambition might be with the limited resources at their disposal. There are a series of interlocking reasons for why it's hard to determine whether the Pirates are really going in the right direction for the duration. Are they financially even weaker than is readily acknowledged? Can they cope with that problem and nevertheless execute a plan to achieve some near- or long-term success? Do they know what they're doing?

That last question is one that fuels one of the ongoing debates within the analysis community about the merits of Dave Littlefield as a general manager. Yes, it's a real debate, because whatever some may say about groupthink among the analytically minded, consensus is the product of convincing arguments, and some pretty good arguments about Littlefield's virtues and shortcomings alike can be put forward. And even then, special consideration needs to be given to the circumstances in which Littlefield has to operate.

Consider the ways that the so-called smart set builds teams these days. You know, the stuff that gets frothing old-timers like Tracy Ringolsby into full-foamed dudgeon.

1. They pick up big league or big league-ready talent on the cheap.
2. They generally prefer people who put runs on the board over guys who do the little things.
3. They know that finding adequate relievers isn't always that hard or expensive.
4. They prefer the lower risks, investments, and returns involved with drafting certain pockets of collegiate talent to the higher prices and possibilities for success and failure with top-rated high-school talent.

PIRATES PROSPECTUS

2004 record: 72–89; Fifth place, NL Central

Pythagenport record: 74–88

Runs scored per game: 4.22 (12th in NL)

Runs allowed per game: 4.62 (9th in NL)

Team EqA: .251 (13th in NL)

2004 Batters Age: 27.4 (Youngest in NL)

2004 Pitchers Age: 27.5 (2nd youngest in NL)

Ballpark: PNC Park; Slight pitcher's park; Park Factor of 0.982

2004: The roster got younger, but the results didn't get any better as the Pirates again finished in the bottom of the division.

2005: A solid bet to play 162 baseball games that count in the standings this year—no more, and no less.

In picking up the pieces left behind by the aimless Bonifay regime, Littlefield resembles a GM who has incorporated elements of all of these points into what he's supposed to be doing in a rebuilding project. He's signed low-end free agents, generally avoiding multi-year mistake contracts. He's dealt expensive veterans for polished prospects, including landing the front four of the current rotation. Through past deals, the lineup can now boast young sluggers like Jason Bay and Craig Wilson and a useful hitter at shortstop in Jack Wilson. Rather than indulge in any of the expensive bullpen shopping that characterizes Pennsylvania's other ballclub, Littlefield has filled out his pen with inexpensive retreads, getting good enough work out of Jose Mesa and Salomon Torres last year, and guys like Julian Tavarez in years past. Down on the farm, he has largely picked college talent in the amateur draft.

Sounds like he should be called a genius, right? Maybe. But how many of Littlefield's moves have been by design, and how many were just his going through the motions or were forced on him by economic circumstance?

Consider the first point. One of the frequent choices in the Littlefield management menu is accommodating the desperate veteran. By having big league jobs to offer, Littlefield has been able to entice veteran players at relatively modest rates when, all their other plans having failed, the players reason that any gig's better than not working. So guys like Jeff Suppan, Reggie Sanders, Matt Stairs, or Kenny Lofton cycle through town. Unfortunately, so too do Raul Mondesi or Chris Stynes, not to mention less celebrated signings, like what was left of Henry Rodriguez and Rick Reed last year. Rentals such as these can make sense as long as you're landing useful placeholders for big league jobs pending the arrival of players with real promise. More important, they give you cheap veterans who might come in handy for some needy contender towards the trading deadline; ideally, you can turn a crummy early February spring invite into four months' employment and a prospect by August 1.

Unfortunately, that isn't really what Littlefield is doing. When he has to move an overpaid star or flip one of his short-term Rent-a-Vets, his track record has been less hit than miss. In 2004, the package acquired from the Mets for Kris Benson was execrable: Ty Wigginton, a modestly useful utility infielder at his highest market value (courtesy of an early July hot streak), Matt Peterson, a young pitcher with command issues and a low ceiling, and third baseman Jose Bautista, one of the infamous Rule 5 fivesome lost in the previous December's draft. To swing that glorified salary dump on the Mets, the Pirates had to toss in a big league-ready farmhand, second baseman Jeff Keppinger. That's not exactly brilliant leveraging. If anything, the move was all too similar to the previous summer's trade of Aramis Ramirez and Kenny Lofton to the Cubs at the end of '03. In the Cubbies' moment of need, all Littlefield netted was Bobby Hill, who at best appears to have wandered onto the Keith Lockhart career path. The double deals with the Red Sox at the end of '03 that shipped off Suppan were no less appalling, at most landing them yet another second baseman with modest offensive skills, Freddy Sanchez. Why Littlefield felt the need to pick up both Hill and Sanchez defies explanation. It says something that neither wound up being the team's second baseman in 2004.

Now, to be fair to Littlefield, keep in mind that one of the downsides of renting vets is that if you don't deal them, you get nothing for them after the year, unless you make the mistake of offering them arbitration. Offering somebody like Reggie Sanders or Matt Stairs arbitration is a great way to get stuck with an unwanted budget handicap or two, since they're the sorts of players who can generally expect to do better in front of an arbitration panel than they can on the free market. So you do have to move them—or else non-tender them at season's end. More often than not these days, the other GMs know that. That can mean that after four months of Kenny Lofton, for your troubles you get little more in return than the memories of four months with Kenny Lofton. The model suddenly doesn't work so well because of your obvious financial weakness: The other guy knows Littlefield loses by keeping the rental.

In Littlefield's defense, there is the Brian Giles trade. But even that deal was a scrambled by-product of a larger original salary dump involving Jason Kendall as well. Still, in landing Bay and Oliver Perez—who looks likes a front-like pitcher if he can stay healthy—it's now the trade with which Littlefield hopes to maintain a reputation that transcends any active memory of those numerous other, less happy deals.

The problem with examining Littlefield is that even the most generous interpretation of his activities may not really help the Pirates transcend the shallow—or at least unwilling—pockets of Kid McClatchy. Although the woeful state of the Nationals has made them the poster child for basket-case franchises, the Pirates have given everyone reason to believe that their financial problems are significant enough to leave them seriously handicapped to do much more than exist. When they axed 11 front office employees at the same time that Littlefield pulled the trigger on the big Brian Giles deal at the end of the 2003 season, it illustrated how this team can find itself in a cash crunch. They also stopped picking up health care premiums on recently retired employees. Some speculate that the Pirates' Rule 5 imbroglio at the 2003 Winter Meetings had everything to do with their trying to get some cash, which hardly bodes well.

These sorts of problems also help to explain why the Pirates passed on picking top college talents like Stephen Drew or Jered Weaver in last summer's amateur draft. While a Littlefield defender can point out that such an approach is defensible if no single pick is going to save a team, nevertheless, it sort of undermines the virtue of the idea that you can mitigate risk and rebuild with college talent. College juniors and seniors don't have a lot of leverage, barring another Varitek-style standoff; yet even then, the Pirates apparently have to settle for less. So beyond having problems with a rent-and-flip approach when your pockets aren't deep, the draft is a second area of player acquisition handicapped by financial limitations. Littlefield isn't merely acceding to McClatchy's oft-stated preference for college talent or following a *Moneyball*–minded script; he has to worm his way down to signability-inspired choices.

If Pirates drafts have been lacking in star power, at least the farm system is well stocked. The problem is that it's well stocked with middling to good prospects, but few blue-chippers likely to turn into really good ballplayers. In particular, the Pirates have a lot of promising pitching in the system, and as always, lots of pitchers make for great package deals. Most of them flame out, and some of them burn you, but ideally, you know your own guys well enough to identify the keepers. Again, in the abstract, that would make for an opportunity for Littlefield to try to exploit bad organizations who need to move a useful star player; that, more than anything else, is what the current crop of sharper GMs have tried to do. When Walt Jocketty was nabbing former Oakland stars, or Billy Beane was pillaging the Royals, their series of deals owed as much to having first piled up a supply of adequate farmhands as they did to any particular brand of genius.

But if you can't dip into an accumulated reservoir of adequate talent, what then? There are upsides, but only if you like Indian summers. Every beat writer who fancies himself a defender of the old way of doing things from within loves to mention the Twins; though they generally skip over mentioning the Twins' false start in the mid '90s, when they turned to a generation of merely adequate homegrown players. Guys like Marty Cordova, Rich Becker, and Denny Hocking—even Scott Stahoviak—could play in the majors, but they weren't the building blocks with which the Twins improved themselves. With those players as the team's new core, the Twins got all the way up to 78 wins in 1996, their high-water mark before another collapse. A better crop of farmhands would emerge a few years later, leading to the Twins' current, winning incarnation.

With that in mind, are the Pirates any better off with the cast at hand? With the exception of Bay and Perez, most of this team's other players are at an age where they figure to plateau or fall off; younger names like Jose Castillo simply don't project to be all that good.

Swapping out Jason Kendall for low-upside, older players like Mark Redman and Arthur Rhodes—while adding others like Matt Lawton and Benito Santiago—doesn't help either. In sum, the Pirates lose just a little more ground while throwing away one of their best commodities. If anything, it's sort of ominous that the team that felt it was helping itself by getting one of those mid '90s Twins, Pat Meares, in his heyday now feels the same way about Lawton, one of that team's last survivors.

So for the time being, sadly, the Pirates more closely resemble a bit of performance art on the nature of entropy. Every trade has resembled progress in some way or another. Every move, however sickly, resembles the sorts of things a healthy organization does. The real dilemma is that Littlefield's roster shell game has no visible relationship to eventual Bucco success. Since he isn't drafting stars, he's going to start hunting for them, and if he can't afford to sign them through their arbitration years, he won't bother.

The odds are that Jason Bay's career will wind up being a lot like Brian Giles's; after being acquired in trade, he'll settle for stardom in a sea of adequacy. If he's lucky, he'll eventually get dealt to a team where winning 80 games isn't unrealistic.

HITTERS

TONY ALVAREZ **OF** **Bats: R** **Throws: R** Born: 10-May-78 Age: 27

YEAR	TM	LG	AGE	AB	H	2B	3B	HR	BB	SO	SB	CS	AVG	OBP	SLG	MLVR	EQBA	EQOBP	EQSLG	EQMLVR	VORP	DEFENSE			
2002	ALT	EAS	24	507	161	37	1	15	27	71	29	18	.318	.361	.483	.243	.291	.327	.450	.010	24.0	109-CF	-11	13-LF	0
2002	PIT	NL	24	26	8	2	0	1	3	5	1	0	.308	.379	.500	.209	.333	.343	.481	.126	2.8				
2003	NAS	PCL	25	349	104	27	3	9	28	69	22	9	.298	.361	.470	.221	.288	.347	.456	.051	11.3	47-LF	-2	25-CF	-1
2004	NAS	PCL	26	335	97	12	1	14	35	63	19	12	.290	.365	.457	.115	.270	.338	.409	-.047	0.8	56-LF	-5	11-RF	0
2004	PIT	NL	26	38	8	2	0	1	4	7	0	0	.211	.289	.342	-.186	.237	.276	.316	-.320	-0.6				
2005	*CWS*	*AL*	*27*	*142*	*37*	*8*	*1*	*5*	*11*	*29*	*5*	*2*	*.263*	*.327*	*.430*	*-.033*	*.260*	*.326*	*.422*	*-.055*	*7.1*	*41-LF*	*-2*		

Breakout: 17% *Improve: 33%* *Collapse: 43%*

Classic tweeners generally run the risk of suffering the classic tweener fate, which is not being enough of something to make it, whether it's hitting or fielding or running or picking the right donuts or whatever. In Alvarez's case, there was some off-field trouble, and the Pirates outrighted him off the 40-man in December. He's still young enough to be handy, and he's never failed to hit well enough to make a fine fourth outfielder.

JOSE BAUTISTA 3B Bats: R Throws: R Born: 19-Oct-80 Age: 24

YEAR	TM	LG	AGE	AB	H	2B	3B	HR	BB	SO	SB	CS	AVG	OBP	SLG	MLVR	EQBA	EQOBP	EQSLG	EQMLVR	VORP	DEFENSE
2002	HIC	SAL	21	438	132	26	3	14	67	104	3	2	.301	.402	.470	.248	.247	.328	.397	-.100	11.6	118-3B -16
2003	LYN	CRL	22	165	40	14	2	4	27	48	1	5	.242	.359	.424	.095	.214	.315	.393	-.153	1.6	44-3B 3
2004	BAL	AL	23	11	3	0	0	0	1	3	0	0	.273	.333	.273	-.250	.455	.222	.455	.050	-0.2	
2004	KCR	AL	23	25	5	1	0	0	1	12	0	0	.200	.231	.240	-.489	.200	.167	.200	-.729	-2.0	
2004	TBY	AL	23	12	2	0	0	0	3	7	0	1	.167	.333	.167	-.410	.333	.233	.333	-.310	-0.9	
2004	PIT	NL	23	40	8	2	0	0	2	18	0	0	.200	.238	.250	-.432	.200	.208	.250	-.571	-3.1	
2005	*PIT*	*NL*	*24*	*144*	*35*	*8*	*1*	*4*	*17*	*47*	*1*	*1*	*.242*	*.329*	*.394*	*-.097*	*.243*	*.329*	*.402*	*-.088*	*3.3*	*43-3B -1*

Breakout: 58% Improve: 73% Collapse: 16%

Bautista will probably have to spend a year in Double-A to regain the development time lost to the screwup of exposing him to the Rule 5 Draft, but he should still be able to reclaim a career. In this, he might be like Eddie Williams, who lost part of his career to roster shenanigans, but who finally did OK when he got an opportunity. But that's two years of playing time that he's lost to injury and organizational oversight, and that's a dent in anybody's career.

JASON BAY LF Bats: R Throws: R Born: 20-Sep-78 Age: 26

YEAR	TM	LG	AGE	AB	H	2B	3B	HR	BB	SO	SB	CS	AVG	OBP	SLG	MLVR	EQBA	EQOBP	EQSLG	EQMLVR	VORP	DEFENSE
2002	SLU	FSL	23	261	71	12	2	9	34	54	22	2	.272	.363	.437	.159	.247	.322	.412	-.090	-3.0	45-LF -3 10-RF 0
2002	BIN	EAS	23	107	31	4	2	4	15	23	13	3	.290	.383	.477	.190	.259	.340	.435	-.016	1.7	18-RF -2
2002	MOB	SOU	23	81	25	5	2	4	13	22	4	2	.309	.411	.568	.394	.268	.352	.524	.136	7.0	
2003	POR	PCL	24	307	93	11	1	20	55	71	23	4	.303	.410	.541	.375	.282	.384	.502	.173	31.7	47-CF -1 37-RF -2
2003	PIT	NL	24	79	23	6	1	3	18	28	3	1	.291	.423	.506	.304	.291	.423	.506	.253	9.1	17-LF -1
2004	PIT	NL	25	411	116	24	4	26	41	129	4	6	.282	.358	.550	.249	.283	.356	.548	.191	34.6	113-LF 0
2005	*PIT*	*NL*	*26*	*442*	*121*	*25*	*3*	*24*	*61*	*124*	*10*	*4*	*.274*	*.370*	*.507*	*.142*	*.275*	*.369*	*.517*	*.153*	*32.0*	*122-LF 0*

Breakout: 17% Improve: 52% Collapse: 13%

As expected, last year's pre-season shoulder surgery meant a late start, but Bay was everything his proponents expected him to be, even hitting for more power than projected. Getting traded for Lou Collier (by Omar Minaya in Montreal) and Steve Reed (by Steve Phillips in New York) isn't the kind of thing you normally find on the résumé of an All-Star caliber player, but it's nice to see some latter-day Bob Sykes or Ricky Rincon deals, and Bay's plugged in for a starring role in left for the next five years. There's some talk of putting him in center if the Pirates don't deal Craig Wilson, which would make for a stronger offense, and wouldn't mean a huge defensive hit.

ADAM BOEVE OF Bats: R Throws: R Born: 20-Jun-80 Age: 25

YEAR	TM	LG	AGE	AB	H	2B	3B	HR	BB	SO	SB	CS	AVG	OBP	SLG	MLVR	EQBA	EQOBP	EQSLG	EQMLVR	VORP	DEFENSE
2003	WPT	NYP	23	132	33	9	1	3	15	39	6	1	.250	.353	.402	.159	.220	.290	.376	-.220	-12.1	15-RF 0
2004	HIC	SAL	24	459	133	25	2	28	61	112	10	2	.290	.385	.536	.266	.236	.312	.429	-.094	-5.7	80-LF -4 27-RF 0
2005	*PIT*	*NL*	*25*	*222*	*57*	*12*	*2*	*9*	*22*	*61*	*2*	*1*	*.259*	*.341*	*.445*	*.003*	*.260*	*.341*	*.454*	*.013*	*9.3*	*63-LF -2*

Breakout: 49% Improve: 63% Collapse: 19%

FYI, Boeve rhymes with groovy; he was picked out of the University of Northern Iowa after winning the Player of the Year award for the Missouri Valley Conference. Considered by some as the organization's top power prospect, but when you're an old man at the lowest full-season rung of the chain, that and a buck will buy you a bag of chips. He's toolsy, and there's hope that he's making progress in terms of making contact and hitting to all fields. He's going to have to get into Double-A this year to have a career.

JOSE CASTILLO 2B Bats: R Throws: R Born: 19-Mar-81 Age: 24

YEAR	TM	LG	AGE	AB	H	2B	3B	HR	BB	SO	SB	CS	AVG	OBP	SLG	MLVR	EQBA	EQOBP	EQSLG	EQMLVR	VORP	DEFENSE
2002	LYN	CRL	21	503	151	25	2	16	49	95	27	14	.300	.370	.453	.183	.252	.312	.402	-.119	13.0	129-SS 11
2003	ALT	EAS	22	498	143	24	6	5	40	81	19	10	.287	.339	.390	.051	.271	.319	.378	-.126	7.5	71-2B 1 52-SS -3
2004	PIT	NL	23	383	98	15	2	8	23	92	3	2	.256	.298	.368	-.128	.255	.298	.369	-.190	5.0	103-2B 5
2005	*PIT*	*NL*	*24*	*373*	*93*	*20*	*2*	*8*	*29*	*77*	*6*	*2*	*.251*	*.308*	*.383*	*-.143*	*.252*	*.308*	*.391*	*-.135*	*8.3*	*98-2B 2*

Breakout: 14% Improve: 29% Collapse: 29%

It's actually a bit refreshing when an actual dark horse can slip into camp, have a great March, earn a job, and then basically keep it all year. He's relatively young, has more power than you'd expect, and the team basically preferred his skill set to Bobby Hill's appearance of immobility. He'll have to fend off Freddy Sanchez this year, but possession counts for something, and he hasn't already exasperated the organization. He could stick for a few years with an upside like Pokey Reese's better years.

JORGE CORTES OF **Bats: L** **Throws: L** Born: 17-Oct-80 Age: 24

YEAR	TM	LG	AGE	AB	H	2B	3B	HR	BB	SO	SB	CS	AVG	OBP	SLG	MLVR	EQBA	EQOBP	EQSLG	EQMLVR	VORP	DEFENSE
2002	WPT	NYP	21	253	83	14	4	1	44	20	7	7	.328	.426	.427	.340	.289	.366	.387	-.011	8.3	46-RF -1 20-LF 1
2003	HIC	SAL	22	345	112	24	2	8	56	47	9	5	.325	.427	.475	.318	.267	.348	.402	-.040	1.7	57-LF 1 23-CF -1
2003	LYN	CRL	22	129	34	6	0	1	11	25	1	1	.264	.315	.333	-.072	.221	.258	.282	-.413	-11.3	15-CF -1 11-RF -1
2004	LYN	CRL	23	260	76	20	1	5	37	48	1	2	.292	.385	.435	.169	.257	.338	.398	-.072	-1.5	56-LF -3
2004	ALT	EAS	23	139	40	8	1	6	13	24	0	1	.288	.344	.489	.182	.271	.324	.450	-.014	1.8	31-LF 0
2005	*PIT*	*NL*	*24*	*220*	*58*	*13*	*2*	*5*	*23*	*39*	*1*	*1*	*.261*	*.335*	*.404*	*-.061*	*.262*	*.335*	*.412*	*-.052*	*3.2*	*62-LF -1*

Breakout: 23% *Improve: 43%* *Collapse: 30%*

The stealth candidate among the Pirates' various outfield options. Before this year, Cortes was a slow-blooming free agent out of Colombia entering his seventh year in the organization. But after hitting in '03, he kept hitting in '04, making himself a prospect. He has the most offensive upside of any of the Pirates' gaggle of young outfielders, and if he has another two-level jump season to follow the last two, he might skip past the organizational herd and cut to the front of the line for a big league job.

HUMBERTO COTA C **Bats: R** **Throws: R** Born: 07-Feb-79 Age: 26

YEAR	TM	LG	AGE	AB	H	2B	3B	HR	BB	SO	SB	CS	AVG	OBP	SLG	MLVR	EQBA	EQOBP	EQSLG	EQMLVR	VORP	DEFENSE
2002	NAS	PCL	23	404	108	27	1	9	31	106	5	8	.267	.321	.406	.011	.257	.308	.389	-.141	3.9	82-C -9
2003	NAS	PCL	24	200	41	9	0	8	20	59	2	0	.205	.284	.370	-.135	.194	.262	.353	-.322	-9.3	57-C -3
2004	PIT	NL	25	66	15	1	1	5	3	20	0	0	.227	.271	.500	-.013	.227	.270	.500	-.079	2.8	15-C -1
2005	*PIT*	*NL*	*26*	*137*	*33*	*7*	*1*	*5*	*10*	*39*	*0*	*0*	*.239*	*.300*	*.416*	*-.122*	*.240*	*.300*	*.424*	*-.113*	*6.7*	*40-C -4*

Breakout: 26% *Improve: 47%* *Collapse: 30%*

Cota is ready to step into a more regular role. Unfortunately, he'll initially be stuck behind Benito Santiago, with no reasonable expectation that this represents an improvement. So instead, Cota will have to outshine J. R. House to stick and be in a position to stake a claim to the starter's job by July; with Paulino and Doumit both on the way up, it won't pay to lose that fight. Cota's problem is that his future is now, so his shot at being a regular depends on getting a break in 2005.

J. J. DAVIS OF **Bats: R** **Throws: R** Born: 25-Oct-78 Age: 26

YEAR	TM	LG	AGE	AB	H	2B	3B	HR	BB	SO	SB	CS	AVG	OBP	SLG	MLVR	EQBA	EQOBP	EQSLG	EQMLVR	VORP	DEFENSE
2002	ALT	EAS	23	348	100	17	3	20	33	101	7	4	.287	.351	.526	.258	.263	.320	.483	.019	9.2	98-RF -1
2003	NAS	PCL	24	426	121	29	4	26	35	85	23	6	.284	.342	.554	.298	.270	.326	.523	.092	20.6	105-RF -5
2004	NAS	PCL	25	84	21	6	1	8	3	28	3	0	.250	.270	.631	.162	.217	.239	.518	-.117	-1.3	10-RF 0
2004	PIT	NL	25	35	5	1	0	0	4	10	2	0	.143	.225	.171	-.571	.143	.180	.171	-.761	-4.0	
2005	*WAS*	*NL*	*26*	*172*	*45*	*9*	*1*	*9*	*14*	*50*	*4*	*2*	*.263*	*.323*	*.492*	*.038*	*.266*	*.324*	*.503*	*.054*	*11.3*	*48-RF -2*

Breakout: 36% *Improve: 64%* *Collapse: 18%*

The strong-armed former pitcher got a semi-break, in that he earned the right to be ignored on the bottom of the bench when he wasn't hurt, and get a year's worth of service time for his trouble. Now that he's been dumped on the Nationals, you might harbor Kieschnickian wishes for him, but it's more a case of Jim Bowden's inevitable yen for strong arms and power and no real sense of what to do with either. Marooned, and probably destined for stardom abroad.

RAJAI DAVIS CF **Bats: B** **Throws: R** Born: 19-Oct-80 Age: 24

YEAR	TM	LG	AGE	AB	H	2B	3B	HR	BB	SO	SB	CS	AVG	OBP	SLG	MLVR	EQBA	EQOBP	EQSLG	EQMLVR	VORP	DEFENSE
2003	HIC	SAL	22	478	146	21	7	6	55	65	40	13	.305	.383	.416	.174	.254	.312	.358	-.179	-5.2	102-CF -4 14-LF 0
2004	LYN	CRL	23	509	160	27	7	5	59	60	57	15	.314	.388	.424	.178	.275	.339	.384	-.076	11.7	116-CF -7
2005	*PIT*	*NL*	*24*	*257*	*69*	*13*	*3*	*3*	*24*	*37*	*14*	*5*	*.269*	*.334*	*.382*	*-.086*	*.270*	*.334*	*.390*	*-.077*	*9.0*	*70-CF -4*

Breakout: 23% *Improve: 43%* *Collapse: 31%*

You have to start liking this guy's chances. Davis was a 38th rounder who started off pretty raw but has slowly put together a good game. He has his limitations in center, particularly his arm, but he won the Carolina League batting title, and let's face it, Tike Redman is still the center fielder. If Davis thrives in the jump to Double-A, economics and talent might create opportunity in 2006.

RYAN DOUMIT C? Bats: B Throws: R Born: 03-Apr-81 Age: 24

YEAR	TM	LG	AGE	AB	H	2B	3B	HR	BB	SO	SB	CS	AVG	OBP	SLG	MLVR	EQBA	EQOBP	EQSLG	EQMLVR	VORP	DEFENSE
2002	HIC	SAL	21	258	83	14	1	6	18	40	3	5	.322	.377	.453	.212	.261	.302	.383	-.158	1.2	28-C -7
2003	LYN	CRL	22	458	126	38	1	11	45	79	4	0	.275	.351	.434	.120	.242	.306	.410	-.127	7.1	82-C -3
2004	ALT	EAS	23	221	58	20	0	10	21	49	0	1	.262	.343	.489	.155	.231	.294	.431	-.128	3.1	24-C -6
2005	*PIT*	*NL*	*24*	*258*	*64*	*15*	*1*	*8*	*20*	*54*	*0*	*0*	*.250*	*.319*	*.416*	*-.080*	*.251*	*.319*	*.425*	*-.071*	*8.9*	*71-DH*

Breakout: 23% *Improve: 49%* *Collapse: 29%*

The snake-bit wonder among the Pirates clutch of interesting catchers in the system. This year, it was mono at season's start and a bum elbow that limited him to DH once he could play. He might still learn how to catch, and at only 24, it's way too early to give up on clothing him in the tools of ignorance. He had a nifty AFL, but so did just about everybody with a bat. If he doesn't log a second healthy season to go with 2003, his prospectdom's going to stall in the "maybe" category. Still enough offensive upside to get excited.

CHRIS DUFFY CF Bats: L Throws: L Born: 20-Apr-80 Age: 25

YEAR	TM	LG	AGE	AB	H	2B	3B	HR	BB	SO	SB	CS	AVG	OBP	SLG	MLVR	EQBA	EQOBP	EQSLG	EQMLVR	VORP	DEFENSE
2002	LYN	CRL	22	539	162	27	5	10	33	101	22	7	.301	.353	.425	.123	.257	.301	.385	-.160	-2.1	126-CF -10
2003	ALT	EAS	23	494	135	23	6	1	44	78	34	12	.273	.355	.350	.012	.260	.327	.344	-.166	-2.9	134-CF -3
2004	ALT	EAS	24	453	140	23	6	8	33	77	32	8	.309	.378	.439	.186	.291	.348	.411	-.009	19.3	109-CF 5
2005	*PIT*	*NL*	*25*	*224*	*59*	*12*	*2*	*3*	*14*	*41*	*7*	*2*	*.263*	*.324*	*.375*	*-.117*	*.265*	*.324*	*.383*	*-.108*	*4.5*	*62-CF -2*

Breakout: 9% *Improve: 26%* *Collapse: 45%*

Another one of the Bucs' legion of merely OK outfield farmhands, and the one who's in danger of being passed by Cortes, McLouth, and Rajai Davis. Duffy can hit a little, but not well enough to merit being a regular. He's about to turn 25 but hasn't cracked Triple-A yet, and an injured wrist kept him out of the AFL; he's probably slipped behind McLouth in terms of in-house regard. Could still turn into a Mike Kingery type, and become a top fourth outfielder, if that isn't an oxymoron.

BRAD ELDRED 1B Bats: R Throws: R Born: 12-Jul-80 Age: 24

YEAR	TM	LG	AGE	AB	H	2B	3B	HR	BB	SO	SB	CS	AVG	OBP	SLG	MLVR	EQBA	EQOBP	EQSLG	EQMLVR	VORP	DEFENSE
2002	WPT	NYP	21	276	78	22	3	10	18	74	10	1	.283	.338	.493	.278	.246	.286	.433	-.128	-6.8	56-1B -4
2003	HIC	SAL	22	420	105	22	0	28	38	142	7	1	.250	.326	.502	.167	.198	.250	.400	-.278	-26.8	104-1B -17
2004	LYN	CRL	23	335	104	22	1	21	35	97	5	2	.310	.397	.570	.380	.265	.336	.497	.068	16.3	88-1B -7
2004	ALT	EAS	23	147	41	9	0	17	6	51	0	0	.279	.329	.687	.427	.236	.271	.581	.047	5.7	38-1B 2
2005	*PIT*	*NL*	*24*	*364*	*93*	*21*	*2*	*20*	*27*	*127*	*2*	*1*	*.256*	*.326*	*.485*	*.028*	*.258*	*.326*	*.495*	*.039*	*15.9*	*97-1B -4*

Breakout: 45% *Improve: 71%* *Collapse: 14%*

A hulkster at 6′6″ and almost enough weight to play offensive tackle in the NFL, Eldred was the biggest of the breakouts in the minor leagues from among a group of high-strikeout thumpers. For him, it shouldn't have been that much of a surprise: He led NCAA Division I in home runs in 2002 at Florida International. Despite leading the minors in RBI in 2004, the organization remains concerned about the strikeouts. Eldred will mash, but will he mash enough, or pick up some plate judgment? He could wind up anywhere from Joey Meyer to Dave Kingman to Bob Watson, but in today's game, non-walking slugs have problems getting multiple opportunities.

JAVIER GUZMAN SS Bats: R Throws: R Born: 04-May-84 Age: 21

YEAR	TM	LG	AGE	AB	H	2B	3B	HR	BB	SO	SB	CS	AVG	OBP	SLG	MLVR	EQBA	EQOBP	EQSLG	EQMLVR	VORP	DEFENSE
2003	WPT	NYP	19	173	42	9	2	2	10	26	4	3	.243	.283	.353	-.004	.219	.252	.331	-.357	-15.1	40-SS -8
2004	HIC	SAL	20	470	144	20	12	2	20	78	31	14	.306	.334	.413	.040	.256	.278	.342	-.267	-8.8	124-SS -9
2005	*PIT*	*NL*	*21*	*376*	*88*	*18*	*3*	*3*	*11*	*65*	*9*	*4*	*.233*	*.255*	*.319*	*-.336*	*.235*	*.255*	*.326*	*-.330*	*-10.8*	*95-SS -7*

Breakout: 5% *Improve: 22%* *Collapse: 52%*

Although Jack Wilson will keep him down on the farm for the next couple of seasons, Guzman's someone to watch. This was the Dominican's first year in a full-season league, and he showed the ability to hit with some authority, as well as the speed and defensive tools that had scouts excited in the first place. He's still inconsistent defensively, but the Pirates can afford to go slowly here.

BOBBY HILL 2B Bats: B Throws: R Born: 03-Apr-78 Age: 27

YEAR	TM	LG	AGE	AB	H	2B	3B	HR	BB	SO	SB	CS	AVG	OBP	SLG	MLVR	EQBA	EQOBP	EQSLG	EQMLVR	VORP	DEFENSE
2002	IOW	PCL	24	354	99	23	3	8	49	66	29	5	.280	.382	.429	.123	.262	.356	.397	-.036	15.3	88-2B 0
2002	CHC	NL	24	190	48	7	2	4	17	42	6	1	.253	.327	.374	-.055	.259	.330	.389	-.098	7.9	45-2B 3
2003	IOW	PCL	25	361	104	23	4	6	37	65	8	7	.288	.365	.424	.106	.269	.341	.402	-.052	13.8	83-2B -11
2003	NAS	PCL	25	66	11	2	1	1	8	8	1	2	.167	.257	.273	-.342	.164	.243	.269	-.489	-6.6	16-2B -1
2004	PIT	NL	26	233	62	7	2	2	20	39	0	3	.266	.353	.339	-.054	.268	.352	.340	-.118	5.2	31-2B 1 14-3B -1
2005	*PIT*	*NL*	*27*	*205*	*53*	*10*	*2*	*4*	*19*	*37*	*3*	*1*	*.257*	*.338*	*.373*	*-.099*	*.258*	*.337*	*.381*	*-.090*	*8.4*	*58-2B -4*

Breakout: 15% Improve: 44% Collapse: 38%

When the blush leaves a rose, does it get pasty? The bloom is definitely off Hill, and now, given his age and the perception that he can't handle second, he's been shunted into a pinch-hitting role that's a lot less than what was expected of him during his celebrated foray into the indy leagues. The criticisms of his defense seem overstated, like a truth that only becomes true because it gets repeated so many times that people start believing it. He still could be a useful regular, but it won't happen here, and he won't grow up to be Mark Bellhorn.

J. R. HOUSE C/OF Bats: R Throws: R Born: 11-Nov-79 Age: 25

YEAR	TM	LG	AGE	AB	H	2B	3B	HR	BB	SO	SB	CS	AVG	OBP	SLG	MLVR	EQBA	EQOBP	EQSLG	EQMLVR	VORP	DEFENSE
2002	ALT	EAS	22	91	24	6	0	2	13	21	0	0	.264	.349	.396	.056	.228	.291	.337	-.266	-2.8	20-C -2
2003	ALT	EAS	23	63	21	6	0	2	5	11	0	0	.333	.382	.524	.356	.274	.306	.435	-.065	1.2	
2004	NAS	PCL	24	309	89	21	1	15	23	72	1	1	.288	.344	.508	.152	.260	.311	.442	-.058	10.7	58-C -8 14-1B -2
2005	*PIT*	*NL*	*25*	*164*	*41*	*8*	*1*	*6*	*12*	*40*	*0*	*0*	*.249*	*.305*	*.417*	*-.103*	*.250*	*.305*	*.426*	*-.094*	*6.4*	*46-C -10*

Breakout: 15% Improve: 34% Collapse: 42%

The Pirates had him play some outfield and first base, so any thought that he's the catcher of the future has faded. He might eventually be slotted for Craig Wilson's job should Littlefield feel he can't afford Wilson down the road. Like Jayson Werth, House is athletic enough to have value in the role, but like Wilson, he's not much of a catcher, and unlike either of them, he's not loaded with offensive upside. He's on his last option, so it's likely that he'll start the season at Triple-A.

JASON KENDALL C Bats: R Throws: R Born: 26-Jun-74 Age: 31

YEAR	TM	LG	AGE	AB	H	2B	3B	HR	BB	SO	SB	CS	AVG	OBP	SLG	MLVR	EQBA	EQOBP	EQSLG	EQMLVR	VORP	DEFENSE
2002	PIT	NL	28	545	154	25	3	3	49	29	15	8	.283	.350	.356	-.031	.283	.348	.360	-.087	23.4	134-C -1
2003	PIT	NL	29	587	191	29	3	6	49	40	8	7	.325	.399	.416	.168	.327	.396	.421	.123	51.1	143-C -8
2004	PIT	NL	30	574	183	32	0	3	60	41	11	8	.319	.399	.390	.135	.321	.395	.390	.072	47.5	142-C 11
2005	*OAK*	*AL*	*31*	*512*	*150*	*28*	*2*	*6*	*45*	*42*	*8*	*5*	*.293*	*.362*	*.390*	*-.003*	*.296*	*.366*	*.397*	*.008*	*26.5*	*135-C 0*

Breakout: 5% Improve: 22% Collapse: 43%

So a big sigh of relief, he's no longer the big contract Littlefield inherited, and Kendall can get on with playing somewhere consequential in the standings. With Oakland, it won't matter if he bats first or second; neither he nor Kotsay run enough to create distractions for the other, so Ken Macha can play platoon percentages or fuss about having Kotsay having the "hole" to take advantage of with Kendall on base. He should profit from seeing his catching workload decrease to 120 games behind the plate while soaking up some DH at-bats, which might prolong his career to the point where he'll be a serious Hall of Fame candidate.

ROB MACKOWIAK UT Bats: L Throws: R Born: 20-Jun-76 Age: 29

YEAR	TM	LG	AGE	AB	H	2B	3B	HR	BB	SO	SB	CS	AVG	OBP	SLG	MLVR	EQBA	EQOBP	EQSLG	EQMLVR	VORP	DEFENSE
2002	PIT	NL	26	385	94	22	0	16	42	120	9	3	.244	.328	.426	-.011	.245	.321	.433	-.065	12.6	47-RF 3 30-CF -2
2003	NAS	PCL	27	217	50	11	1	2	18	51	7	3	.230	.286	.318	-.188	.226	.282	.313	-.319	-15.7	41-1B 1 13-3B -1
2003	PIT	NL	27	174	47	4	4	6	15	53	6	0	.270	.342	.443	.073	.264	.338	.443	-.004	12.0	12-3B 0
2004	PIT	NL	28	491	121	22	6	17	50	114	13	4	.246	.319	.420	-.021	.246	.317	.419	-.091	14.2	46-RF -2 49-3B 1
2005	*PIT*	*NL*	*29*	*311*	*78*	*15*	*3*	*10*	*33*	*78*	*7*	*3*	*.252*	*.328*	*.418*	*-.060*	*.253*	*.328*	*.427*	*-.051*	*8.1*	*85-RF 1*

Breakout: 24% Improve: 52% Collapse: 18%

An easy favorite in Steeltown, in that he can play six positions and makes for a nifty spare part. There might be a bit of a rush to compare to him to John Lowenstein, another infielder who turned into a platoon masher with an uppercut stroke. It's more probable that Mackowiak just had a career year, courtesy of a great May spiked with a trip to Coors Field. He deserves a crack at the job at third, but if the Pirates feel they have to show something for Kris Benson, he'll have to settle for staying in the supersub role.

NATE McLOUTH OF Bats: L Throws: R Born: 28-Oct-81 Age: 23

YEAR	TM	LG	AGE	AB	H	2B	3B	HR	BB	SO	SB	CS	AVG	OBP	SLG	MLVR	EQBA	EQOBP	EQSLG	EQMLVR	VORP	DEFENSE
2002	LYN	CRL	20	393	96	23	4	9	41	48	20	7	.244	.324	.392	.001	.209	.276	.352	-.287	-28.3	62-LF -7 27-RF 0
2003	LYN	CRL	21	440	132	27	2	6	55	68	40	4	.300	.386	.411	.156	.268	.341	.394	-.064	-1.4	59-LF -2 48-CF -3
2004	ALT	EAS	22	515	166	40	4	8	48	62	31	7	.322	.384	.462	.241	.302	.355	.430	.040	17.1	98-RF -12 23-CF 0
2005	*PIT*	*NL*	*23*	*251*	*69*	*15*	*2*	*5*	*22*	*34*	*8*	*2*	*.273*	*.338*	*.409*	*-.041*	*.274*	*.337*	*.417*	*-.032*	*10.7*	*70-RF -4*

Breakout: 12% Improve: 33% Collapse: 34%

Some optimistically compare McLouth to Lenny Dykstra, but that's code for a white guy who can run and get dirty. It's expected that he can play center field, and with his line-drive hitting skills, he fits a lot of people's idea of a fine fourth outfielder. As long as Tike Redman's in center, that means he's got a shot at a regular job. He's young enough to keep picking up power, and within the system, he's the guy with the best shot of winding up in center or right by 2006.

ABRAHAM NUNEZ INF Bats: B Throws: R Born: 16-Mar-76 Age: 29

YEAR	TM	LG	AGE	AB	H	2B	3B	HR	BB	SO	SB	CS	AVG	OBP	SLG	MLVR	EQBA	EQOBP	EQSLG	EQMLVR	VORP	DEFENSE
2002	PIT	NL	26	253	59	14	1	2	27	44	3	4	.233	.311	.320	-.188	.235	.312	.325	-.237	-1.4	39-2B 5 17-SS 0
2003	PIT	NL	27	311	77	8	7	4	26	53	9	3	.248	.310	.357	-.133	.248	.310	.362	-.182	5.0	58-2B 2 16-SS -1
2004	PIT	NL	28	182	43	9	0	2	10	36	1	3	.236	.275	.319	-.251	.240	.271	.317	-.327	-4.7	26-2B 2
2005	*PIT*	*NL*	*29*	*129*	*32*	*6*	*1*	*2*	*11*	*25*	*2*	*1*	*.245*	*.304*	*.348*	*-.201*	*.246*	*.304*	*.356*	*-.193*	*0.9*	*38-2B -1*

Breakout: 25% Improve: 44% Collapse: 35%

This is what happens when you let Sammy Khalifa get tenure. One of the artifacts of fandom is that you wind up with certain guys you can talk about with your fellow loyal rooters. If you have been growing up a Pirates fan in the present, you might already have permanently low expectations for your utility infielders in the future. Nunez is an adequate reserve, but keeping him around for much more than the minimum is the sort of mistake the Pirates shouldn't afford.

RONNY PAULINO C Bats: R Throws: R Born: 21-Apr-81 Age: 24

YEAR	TM	LG	AGE	AB	H	2B	3B	HR	BB	SO	SB	CS	AVG	OBP	SLG	MLVR	EQBA	EQOBP	EQSLG	EQMLVR	VORP	DEFENSE
2002	LYN	CRL	21	442	116	26	2	12	39	87	2	1	.262	.321	.412	.034	.223	.278	.368	-.252	-10.6	111-C 13
2003	LYN	CRL	22	81	19	3	0	1	8	8	1	0	.235	.308	.309	-.130	.171	.226	.220	-.587	-11.1	14-C -1
2003	ALT	EAS	22	159	36	6	1	6	12	35	0	2	.226	.283	.390	-.087	.206	.259	.363	-.307	-6.5	43-C 7
2004	ALT	EAS	23	365	104	23	2	15	32	61	3	2	.285	.345	.482	.171	.267	.320	.444	-.033	16.0	80-C 3
2005	*PIT*	*NL*	*24*	*243*	*59*	*13*	*1*	*8*	*18*	*48*	*1*	*1*	*.244*	*.299*	*.400*	*-.141*	*.245*	*.299*	*.408*	*-.132*	*4.4*	*66-C -1*

Breakout: 21% Improve: 42% Collapse: 33%

The Eastern league's All-Star catcher hasn't had an easy path, having lost time in 2003 to the Rule 5 Draft (yes, it was a problem in previous years too), and injuries plagued him in 2002 and 2003. However, he finally put in a healthy season, and played his way onto the 40-man roster. His future depends on two things: If Cota fails to claim the job from Santiago some time this year, and if Doumit keeps getting hurt. He lacks Doumit's offensive potential, but he's not too dissimilar from Cota, including the plus defensive rep.

TIKE REDMAN CF Bats: L Throws: L Born: 10-Mar-77 Age: 28

YEAR	TM	LG	AGE	AB	H	2B	3B	HR	BB	SO	SB	CS	AVG	OBP	SLG	MLVR	EQBA	EQOBP	EQSLG	EQMLVR	VORP	DEFENSE
2002	NAS	PCL	25	311	84	9	4	2	21	24	16	7	.270	.315	.344	-.089	.268	.313	.335	-.201	-5.0	72-CF -4
2003	NAS	PCL	26	360	106	12	7	4	36	32	42	9	.294	.357	.400	.109	.288	.348	.393	-.037	12.4	87-CF -5
2003	PIT	NL	26	230	76	16	5	3	14	18	7	3	.330	.374	.483	.201	.329	.372	.485	.176	20.2	50-CF 1
2004	PIT	NL	27	546	153	19	4	8	23	52	18	6	.280	.310	.374	-.076	.281	.310	.376	-.138	11.0	139-CF -4
2005	*PIT*	*NL*	*28*	*447*	*122*	*20*	*5*	*5*	*29*	*43*	*16*	*5*	*.274*	*.319*	*.372*	*-.122*	*.275*	*.318*	*.380*	*-.114*	*6.7*	*115-CF -1*

Breakout: 4% Improve: 15% Collapse: 47%

The curse of Marvell Wynne is that you have to be Marvell Wynne, and sometimes, you can be OK with that. If your team is smart enough to want to replace you, you're still playing in the meantime. Redman fended off one of Marvell's other incarnations (Chris Singleton) in camp. Like the original, he'll get opportunities if not stardom, which means a career.

CARLOS RIVERA **1B** **Bats: L** **Throws: L** Born: 10-Jun-78 Age: 27

YEAR	TM	LG	AGE	AB	H	2B	3B	HR	BB	SO	SB	CS	AVG	OBP	SLG	MLVR	EQBA	EQOBP	EQSLG	EQMLVR	VORP	DEFENSE			
2002	ALT	EAS	24	494	149	28	2	22	27	75	1	1	.302	.345	.500	.228	.278	.315	.466	-.001	12.3	112-1B	2		
2003	NAS	PCL	25	262	69	18	0	9	13	38	3	1	.263	.300	.435	.033	.249	.280	.410	-.170	-6.7	68-1B	5		
2003	PIT	NL	25	95	21	5	0	3	8	28	0	0	.221	.283	.368	-.180	.232	.277	.358	-.262	-1.2	24-1B	-3		
2004	NAS	PCL	26	312	91	19	0	17	24	54	6	7	.292	.348	.516	.176	.258	.308	.435	-.075	0.8	68-1B	-9	11-LF	-1
2005	*PIT*	*NL*	*27*	*213*	*55*	*11*	*1*	*7*	*13*	*42*	*2*	*1*	*.256*	*.303*	*.421*	*-.097*	*.257*	*.303*	*.430*	*-.088*	*2.9*	*57-1B*	*-4*		

Breakout: 28% *Improve: 45%* *Collapse: 35%*

A bad idea kept on the 40-man after 2003 at the same time that they were intending to sign Randall Simon, made especially redundant once they added Ward with a NRI deal. One lesson they learned is that guys like Ward are always out there—another lesson was that a spot on the roster is too precious a commodity to waste on a light-hitting defensive sub at first base, Rivera has been excused from the 40-man.

RAY SADLER **OF** **Bats: R** **Throws: R** Born: 19-Sep-80 Age: 24

YEAR	TM	LG	AGE	AB	H	2B	3B	HR	BB	SO	SB	CS	AVG	OBP	SLG	MLVR	EQBA	EQOBP	EQSLG	EQMLVR	VORP	DEFENSE			
2002	DAY	FSL	21	462	132	31	1	11	27	91	30	12	.286	.333	.429	.103	.247	.283	.391	-.193	-6.4	105-CF	-13		
2003	WTN	SOU	22	412	120	31	5	6	33	81	17	7	.291	.352	.434	.160	.281	.331	.438	-.010	18.2	102-CF	-8		
2003	ALT	EAS	22	53	14	5	0	1	3	16	0	0	.264	.310	.415	.022	.226	.250	.358	-.318	-3.1				
2004	ALT	EAS	23	428	114	24	1	20	23	89	16	6	.266	.306	.467	.071	.245	.279	.429	-.148	-12.1	74-LF	-1	30-RF	-3
2005	*PIT*	*NL*	*24*	*220*	*58*	*13*	*2*	*7*	*11*	*48*	*5*	*2*	*.262*	*.305*	*.428*	*-.079*	*.263*	*.305*	*.437*	*-.070*	*4.7*	*59-LF*	*-1*		

Breakout: 21% *Improve: 50%* *Collapse: 25%*

The prize acquired from the Cubs for Randall Simon in 2003. In the same way that most of the Pirates outfielders with limited futures can boast tools and limitations, Sadler has his uses and his issues. He has a little bit of power, but not a lot, and runs well enough to let him run. But he doesn't play center and doesn't get on base well, so he's not a prospect. If the Pirates decide they need a fifth outfielder with right-handed sock who can also pinch-run, Sadler might be that guy.

FREDDY SANCHEZ **2B/SS** **Bats: R** **Throws: R** Born: 21-Dec-77 Age: 27

YEAR	TM	LG	AGE	AB	H	2B	3B	HR	BB	SO	SB	CS	AVG	OBP	SLG	MLVR	EQBA	EQOBP	EQSLG	EQMLVR	VORP	DEFENSE			
2002	TRN	EAS	24	311	102	23	1	3	37	45	19	3	.328	.403	.437	.227	.294	.363	.396	-.000	19.8	68-SS	-9	11-2B	-1
2002	PAW	INT	24	183	55	10	1	4	12	21	5	3	.301	.350	.432	.120	.288	.339	.418	-.018	10.0	35-SS	0	11-2B	-1
2003	PAW	INT	25	211	72	17	0	5	31	36	8	0	.341	.430	.493	.369	.318	.399	.472	.192	27.1	34-SS	3	20-2B	-1
2004	NAS	PCL	26	125	33	7	1	1	11	17	4	1	.264	.326	.360	-.131	.242	.300	.323	-.260	-3.2	19-2B	0		
2005	*PIT*	*NL*	*27*	*190*	*50*	*10*	*1*	*3*	*17*	*30*	*4*	*1*	*.262*	*.327*	*.377*	*-.109*	*.263*	*.327*	*.385*	*-.101*	*8.9*	*54-SS*	*-5*		

Breakout: 16% *Improve: 36%* *Collapse: 45%*

The expected Opening Day starter at second, but preseason ankle surgery, the discovery that he's club-footed, and a subsequent quad strain pretty much derailed his season. You have to wonder how the club foot was missed, but keep in mind that the Red Sox were also surprised to find that Tim Naehring had one leg shorter than the other. Anyway, Sanchez had a good AFL and played short there, but his opportunity is at second. The Pirates want to believe he'll be a run-producing middle infielder, and if he's still a guy who might lace a few doubles and hit for a solid average, even if he won't be a star.

CHRIS STYNES **3B** **Bats: R** **Throws: R** Born: 19-Jan-73 Age: 32

YEAR	TM	LG	AGE	AB	H	2B	3B	HR	BB	SO	SB	CS	AVG	OBP	SLG	MLVR	EQBA	EQOBP	EQSLG	EQMLVR	VORP	DEFENSE			
2002	CHC	NL	29	195	47	9	1	5	21	29	1	1	.241	.314	.374	-.098	.247	.317	.389	-.131	3.8	28-3B	-3	12-2B	2
2003	COL	NL	30	443	113	31	3	11	48	76	3	1	.255	.335	.413	-.037	.237	.319	.390	-.133	17.0	109-3B	-5		
2004	PIT	NL	31	162	35	10	0	1	9	23	0	0	.216	.266	.296	-.314	.221	.261	.288	-.399	-8.1	45-3B	1		
2005	*BAL*	*AL*	*32*	*152*	*36*	*7*	*1*	*3*	*13*	*26*	*1*	*1*	*.236*	*.300*	*.354*	*-.197*	*.238*	*.304*	*.361*	*-.191*	*-2.6*	*44-3B*	*1*		

Breakout 32% *Improve 46%* *Collapse 38%*

Pink keisters are all well and good in theory, and you'll find plenty of people in the game who will tell you that Stynes is a fiery gamer you want to have around. Those people are usually the ones who've never employed him, or the ones who have him at the moment; it isn't coincidence that he's been on five teams in five years, and hasn't been dealt (or dealable) in any of the last four. Since his Age-27 season in Cincinnati in 2000, he's disappointed everyone who's picked him up. At some point, you expect that the disappointments will mean a future in the Atlantic League. Or substitute teaching. Maybe even an appearance in a Roger Corman flick as Irritable Victim #2.

RICH THOMPSON CF Bats: L Throws: R Born: 23-Apr-79 Age: 26

YEAR	TM	LG	AGE	AB	H	2B	3B	HR	BB	SO	SB	CS	AVG	OBP	SLG	MLVR	EQBA	EQOBP	EQSLG	EQMLVR	VORP	DEFENSE			
2002	TEN	SOU	23	554	155	13	4	2	50	86	45	13	.280	.361	.329	-.027	.242	.303	.295	-.293	-39.2	95-LF	-5	29-CF	1
2003	NHV	EAS	24	182	57	5	1	0	10	24	15	3	.313	.373	.352	.074	.277	.317	.304	-.232	-9.3	23-LF	0		
2003	SYR	INT	24	112	33	2	1	0	9	10	11	1	.295	.373	.330	.003	.248	.316	.257	-.316	-5.9	25-CF	1		
2003	NAS	PCL	24	109	28	3	2	0	9	21	22	3	.257	.333	.321	-.075	.236	.295	.282	-.330	-6.1	17-CF	-1		
2004	NAS	PCL	25	411	118	7	13	5	26	62	41	15	.287	.348	.404	.000	.267	.320	.362	-.149	-0.3	101-CF	-8		
2005	*PIT*	*NL*	*26*	*228*	*58*	*10*	*3*	*1*	*13*	*37*	*12*	*4*	*.253*	*.313*	*.335*	*-.197*	*.254*	*.313*	*.342*	*-.190*	*0.0*	*63-CF*	*-7*		

Breakout: 13% *Improve: 31%* *Collapse: 44%*

Officially, the Pirates like to claim that the Rule 5 debacle of December 2003 didn't hurt them. Of the five guys picked, they're quick to mention that they got three back. Except of course that they didn't, not quite like that; Bautista had to be reacquired in trade and lose a year of his career to their mistake, Frank Brooks is gone again, and who wants Rich Thompson? Meanwhile, Chris Shelton and Jeff Bennett look pretty useful, and the Bucs get to brag about how smart it was to sign Chris Stynes, Raul Mondesi, and Randall Simon with the three roster spots they left open.

CHRIS TRUBY 3B Bats: R Throws: R Born: 09-Dec-73 Age: 31

YEAR	TM	LG	AGE	AB	H	2B	3B	HR	BB	SO	SB	CS	AVG	OBP	SLG	MLVR	EQBA	EQOBP	EQSLG	EQMLVR	VORP	DEFENSE			
2002	MON	NL	28	105	27	5	2	2	5	27	1	1	.257	.297	.400	-.073	.255	.287	.415	-.145	2.1	24-3B	-3		
2002	DET	AL	28	277	55	13	2	2	5	71	1	1	.199	.215	.282	-.436	.207	.227	.297	-.462	-17.6	87-3B	9		
2003	DUR	INT	29	430	113	27	0	16	44	77	4	6	.263	.339	.437	.048	.229	.306	.397	-.154	3.5	66-3B	6	25-1B	0
2003	TBY	AL	29	43	12	3	0	0	5	13	0	0	.279	.354	.349	-.067	.310	.328	.357	-.110	1.6	13-3B	2		
2004	NAS	PCL	30	466	140	41	2	25	47	96	11	2	.300	.367	.558	.284	.271	.334	.483	.051	33.3	70-3B	6	30-2B	1
2005	*KCR*	*AL*	*31*	*185*	*46*	*11*	*1*	*6*	*15*	*41*	*2*	*1*	*.251*	*.312*	*.415*	*-.087*	*.247*	*.310*	*.416*	*-.101*	*4.3*	*52-3B*	*0*		

Breakout: 20% *Improve: 40%* *Collapse: 36%*

Truby has nothing to do with the Pirates, and you might otherwise think he's as over as Barbara Dare's cinematic career. But after getting guaranteed money from the Royals, he's in the book because he's Mark Teahen's veteran competition for the starting job at third in Kansas City. Sort of like the observation about how Wallis Simpson wound up little better than a sweaty sailor, there was nevertheless once a time when Truby was considered hot stuff. That time is long over.

DARYLE WARD 1B Bats: L Throws: L Born: 27-Jun-75 Age: 30

YEAR	TM	LG	AGE	AB	H	2B	3B	HR	BB	SO	SB	CS	AVG	OBP	SLG	MLVR	EQBA	EQOBP	EQSLG	EQMLVR	VORP	DEFENSE	
2002	HOU	NL	27	453	125	31	0	12	33	82	1	3	.276	.324	.424	.010	.272	.315	.423	-.068	9.5	84-LF	4
2003	LAD	NL	28	109	20	1	0	0	3	19	0	0	.183	.211	.193	-.550	.193	.207	.193	-.657	-11.9	12-1B	-1
2003	LVG	PCL	28	128	38	9	0	4	10	22	0	0	.297	.343	.461	.064	.232	.275	.368	-.252	-6.5	28-1B	1
2004	NAS	PCL	29	96	27	7	0	7	5	16	0	0	.281	.317	.573	.195	.245	.269	.468	-.110	-0.8	20-1B	-2
2004	PIT	NL	29	293	73	17	2	15	22	45	0	0	.249	.305	.474	.022	.249	.304	.471	-.039	10.8	63-1B	-7
2005	*PIT*	*NL*	*30*	*264*	*65*	*15*	*1*	*9*	*19*	*49*	*0*	*0*	*.247*	*.299*	*.411*	*-.123*	*.248*	*.299*	*.419*	*-.115*	*0.9*	*70-1B*	*-3*

Breakout: 20% *Improve: 41%* *Collapse: 29%*

It was nice to see Ward reclaim some small portion of his former promise; at least the new edition of the team's Randall Simon fetish didn't cost them talent to acquire. Now that he's inked for 2005, he's more of a signature Pirate than Bay is: Neither young nor old, not especially great or especially bad, and worth a pizza and beer for anyone who's hard up for a veteran bat at the deadline. He's the fill-in at first should they deal Craig Wilson, and until or if Brad Eldred ever arrives.

TY WIGGINTON 3B Bats: R Throws: R Born: 11-Oct-77 Age: 27

YEAR	TM	LG	AGE	AB	H	2B	3B	HR	BB	SO	SB	CS	AVG	OBP	SLG	MLVR	EQBA	EQOBP	EQSLG	EQMLVR	VORP	DEFENSE			
2002	NOR	INT	24	383	115	26	3	6	43	50	5	3	.300	.366	.431	.163	.294	.359	.429	.039	26.3	46-3B	-8	31-2B	-2
2002	NYM	NL	24	116	35	8	0	6	8	19	2	1	.302	.354	.526	.270	.316	.352	.538	.207	12.7	10-3B	0	12-2B	-1
2003	NYM	NL	25	573	146	36	6	11	46	124	12	2	.255	.318	.396	-.049	.259	.320	.406	-.093	22.3	151-3B	0		
2004	NYM	NL	26	312	89	23	2	12	23	48	6	1	.285	.334	.487	.125	.284	.333	.489	.070	21.3	55-3B	-4	20-2B	1
2004	PIT	NL	26	182	40	7	0	5	22	34	1	0	.220	.306	.341	-.159	.220	.298	.335	-.260	-1.3	50-3B	-2		
2005	*PIT*	*NL*	*27*	*434*	*116*	*26*	*3*	*13*	*42*	*78*	*6*	*2*	*.266*	*.334*	*.430*	*-.024*	*.268*	*.333*	*.439*	*-.015*	*14.7*	*115-3B*	*-2*		

Breakout: 18% *Improve: 48%* *Collapse: 27%*

The prize of a terrible deal with the Mets, one of the added benefits of having to address McClendon's Benson-inspired fits of pique. Wigginton elevated his value with a good run in July (on 7/1, he was at .261/.306/.436; at the All-Star break, he'd gotten that up to .275/.317/.500). Had he turned a corner? Only the Pirates seemed to think so. Not a great defender in his best moments, he deserves nothing more than a job-sharing arrangement with Mackowiak, but because he's "the guy" from the Benson deal, he'll get left out there until Bautista's ready.

CRAIG WILSON 1B/RF **Bats: R** **Throws: R** Born: 30-Nov-76 Age: 28

YEAR	TM	LG	AGE	AB	H	2B	3B	HR	BB	SO	SB	CS	AVG	OBP	SLG	MLVR	EQBA	EQOBP	EQSLG	EQMLVR	VORP	DEFENSE			
2002	PIT	NL	25	368	97	16	1	16	32	116	2	3	.264	.355	.443	.074	.264	.350	.450	.027	14.9	58-RF	4	29-1B	0
2003	PIT	NL	26	309	81	15	4	18	35	89	3	1	.262	.360	.511	.181	.260	.354	.518	.123	24.6	38-RF	0	25-1B	-1
2004	PIT	NL	27	561	148	35	5	29	50	169	2	2	.264	.354	.499	.158	.264	.349	.501	.095	41.0	76-RF	-4	54-1B	-6
2005	*PIT*	*NL*	*28*	*440*	*117*	*25*	*2*	*23*	*45*	*128*	*4*	*2*	*.267*	*.355*	*.489*	*.090*	*.268*	*.355*	*.500*	*.101*	*26.9*	*119-RF*	*-6*		

Breakout: 17% *Improve: 53%* *Collapse: 14%*

This was a season where at least one Pirate player became an identifiable fan fave, but some markets are uniquely poised to appreciate the talents of Mulletman. Even with Ward re-signed, now that Matt Lawton's plugged into the job in right, Wilson is the starter at first unless he's dealt, which remains the $64,000 question in Pittsburgh at the end of December. Although you can understand that there will be some gnashing of teeth if arbitration forces a move, he did just have his Age-27 season, and his value will never be higher. It's a pity he didn't hit a 30th homerun to join Don Baylor as baseball's only 30-30 men: 30 home runs, 30 HBPs.

JACK WILSON SS **Bats: R** **Throws: R** Born: 29-Dec-77 Age: 27

YEAR	TM	LG	AGE	AB	H	2B	3B	HR	BB	SO	SB	CS	AVG	OBP	SLG	MLVR	EQBA	EQOBP	EQSLG	EQMLVR	VORP	DEFENSE	
2002	PIT	NL	24	527	133	22	4	4	37	74	5	2	.252	.306	.332	-.175	.256	.307	.340	-.213	2.0	134-SS	6
2003	PIT	NL	25	558	143	21	3	9	36	74	5	5	.256	.303	.353	-.142	.256	.302	.358	-.197	7.3	146-SS	0
2004	PIT	NL	26	652	201	41	12	11	26	71	8	4	.308	.335	.459	.109	.305	.333	.456	.042	50.6	154-SS	17
2005	*PIT*	*NL*	*27*	*564*	*153*	*29*	*5*	*10*	*33*	*69*	*7*	*3*	*.272*	*.315*	*.398*	*-.095*	*.274*	*.315*	*.406*	*-.086*	*18.5*	*143-SS*	*7*

Breakout: 4% *Improve: 20%* *Collapse: 44%*

Walt Jocketty gets a lot of credit for moves that worked, but dealing Wilson in the package that brought Jason Christiansen to St. Louis won't be remembered as one of his finest moments. Whether you want to compare his development to Jay Bell's, or credit Wilson's exceptionally quick wrists, or praise hitting coach Gerald Perry's advice that he exploit those wrists and learn to wait on pitches, Wilson finally took the huge step forward at the plate we'd been waiting for. There's no element to his game where he hasn't improved, and with the star shortstops generally congregating in the AL, his first All-Star appearance in 2004 won't be his last.

PITCHERS

BRIAN BOEHRINGER **Bats: B** **Throws: R** Born: 08-Jan-70 Age: 35

YEAR	TM	LG	AGE	G	GS	IP	H	BB	SO	HR	ERA	EQERA	EQH9	EQBB9	EQSO9	EQHR9	PERA	VORP	STF
2002	PIT	NL	32	70	0	79.7	65	33	65	5	3.39	3.42	7.9	3.3	6.6	0.6	3.66	17.6	5
2003	PIT	NL	33	62	0	62.3	64	30	47	11	5.49	5.49	9.2	3.9	6.2	1.5	5.19	-0.1	-12
2004	PIT	NL	34	21	0	25.3	27	17	20	2	4.62	4.97	8.9	5.3	6.0	0.7	4.97	2.0	-10
2005	*COL*	*NL*	*35*	*26*	*0*	*29.3*	*33*	*17*	*24*	*6*	*5.87*	*5.12*	*9.4*	*4.6*	*7.1*	*1.3*	*5.48*	*3.2*	*-6*

Breakout: 28% *Improve: 46%* *Collapse: 28%*

Jose Mesa's personal ghost of Christmases yet to come. He is also a solid example of why when you invest in recycling as a major portion of your player-acquisition strategy, you don't stop once you get your first few nickels back. You might have hoped that Littlefield learned that paying seven figures to this sort of guy doesn't work, but he re-upped both Mesa and Torres for bigger money after their '04 contributions, so he apparently didn't. Meanwhile, Boehringer's rumored to be headed for Colorado.

BOBBY BRADLEY Bats: R Throws: R Born: 15-Dec-80 Age: 24

YEAR	TM	LG	AGE	G	GS	IP	H	BB	SO	HR	ERA	EQERA	EQH9	EQBB9	EQSO9	EQHR9	PERA	VORP	STF
2003	LYN	CRL	22	12	12	50.3	43	28	36	1	3.40	4.79	8.2	5.6	4.8	0.4	4.02	8.3	-4
2004	ALT	EAS	23	19	19	101.3	85	41	78	8	3.11	4.48	8.6	3.9	5.2	1.0	4.39	12.7	1
2005	*PIT*	*NL*	*24*	*16*	*13*	*77.0*	*78*	*38*	*53*	*8*	*4.77*	*5.05*	*9.1*	*3.9*	*5.6*	*1.0*	*5.01*	*5.5*	*0*

Breakout: 15% *Improve: 39%* *Collapse: 28%*

After his enduring multiple shoulder surgeries and a Tommy John surgery, you can be forgiven if you'd begun to wonder if Bradley was ever going to amount to anything. Despite losing seven weeks to a strained shoulder last year, Bradley finally flashed some of the talent people are willing to wait for, mowing hitters down with a classic bender. You might think the durability issues would inspire a move to the pen, but Bradley left his velocity on the surgeon's table. He's going to have to tighten up his control to really earn a shot, and even then, he has to be healthy for more than three months at a time.

FRANK BROOKS Bats: L Throws: L Born: 06-Sep-78 Age: 26

YEAR	TM	LG	AGE	G	GS	IP	H	BB	SO	HR	ERA	EQERA	EQH9	EQBB9	EQSO9	EQHR9	PERA	VORP	STF
2002	CLR	FSL	23	35	0	39.0	34	27	33	2	3.46	5.25	9.0	7.0	5.8	1.0	5.75	-0.6	-23
2002	REA	EAS	23	17	1	29.0	29	12	23	1	3.10	3.90	9.1	3.9	5.5	0.3	4.55	3.2	-5
2003	NAS	PCL	24	16	0	28.3	22	11	22	2	2.54	3.81	8.0	4.2	6.2	1.0	4.15	4.2	0
2003	REA	EAS	24	34	0	58.7	40	13	71	5	2.30	3.17	7.5	2.2	9.2	1.3	3.50	12.6	25
2004	NAS	PCL	25	42	8	83.3	81	22	55	13	4.11	4.81	9.0	2.5	4.7	1.6	4.58	8.9	-11
2004	PIT	NL	25	11	1	17.3	13	9	18	5	4.68	4.96	7.7	4.4	8.8	2.2	4.96	0.0	7
2005	*LAD*	*NL*	*26*	*15*	*4*	*36.7*	*34*	*15*	*28*	*6*	*4.35*	*4.80*	*8.5*	*3.2*	*6.0*	*1.3*	*4.76*	*3.9*	*-4*

Breakout: 29% *Improve: 50%* *Collapse: 19%*

In Brooks's case, as one of the Rule 5 December '03 claims, there's plenty of blame to go around—to the Pirates for not protecting him, but also to statheads for overstating his value. Can he grow up to be a useful situational lefty? Absolutely. Does that make him a worthwhile Rule 5 pickup? Yes. Is he absolutely worth a 40-man roster spot? Not necessarily, it depends on who else you've got hanging around. Signed by the Dodgers upon being outrighted after the '04 season, he'll help the pen.

BRYAN BULLINGTON Bats: R Throws: R Born: 30-Sep-80 Age: 24

YEAR	TM	LG	AGE	G	GS	IP	H	BB	SO	HR	ERA	EQERA	EQH9	EQBB9	EQSO9	EQHR9	PERA	VORP	STF
2003	HIC	SAL	22	8	7	45.3	25	11	46	3	1.39	3.89	8.0	2.7	5.9	1.6	4.35	5.5	19
2003	LYN	CRL	22	17	17	97.3	101	27	67	5	3.05	4.71	9.7	2.7	4.6	1.0	4.61	10.1	11
2004	ALT	EAS	23	26	26	145.0	160	47	100	18	4.10	5.43	10.3	3.1	4.6	1.5	5.62	-0.3	-2
2005	*PIT*	*NL*	*24*	*11*	*10*	*60.7*	*65*	*22*	*39*	*8*	*4.82*	*5.11*	*9.6*	*2.9*	*5.3*	*1.2*	*5.13*	*4.1*	*1*

Breakout: 12% *Improve: 43%* *Collapse: 18%*

Although he's cursed with being the guy the Pirates picked instead of B. J. Upton in the first round of '02, the former Ball State star is on track to reach the majors at the tail end of this year. He might not grow up to be a dominant starter, but he has the assortment to be a useful rotation regular. He's gotten his velocity up into the low 90s, and he can throw four pitches for strikes. The problem is that a pitcher with his modest potential illustrates the peril of making safe choices when there's no breakout potential anywhere in the organization, and no money to acquire it anywhere except in the draft.

SEAN BURNETT Bats: L Throws: L Born: 17-Sep-1982 Age: 22

YEAR	TM	LG	AGE	G	GS	IP	H	BB	SO	HR	ERA	EQERA	EQH9	EQBB9	EQSO9	EQHR9	PERA	VORP	STF
2002	LYN	CRL	19	26	26	155.3	118	33	96	4	1.80	4.03	8.2	2.4	4.1	0.4	3.52	32.5	40
2003	ALT	EAS	20	27	27	159.7	158	29	86	2	3.21	4.28	8.9	1.8	4.0	0.2	3.69	32.1	26
2004	NAS	PCL	21	10	10	47.0	58	17	25	5	5.36	5.67	10.0	3.3	3.7	0.8	4.89	3.6	-2
2004	PIT	NL	21	13	13	71.7	86	28	30	9	5.02	4.99	10.1	3.1	3.3	1.0	4.99	4.9	-1

There's no projection because he won't be pitching in 2005. His elbow was scragged, and the surgery revealed the need for more than the usual reconstruction, so his recovery time might be more than the normal 11–12 months. His quick ascent did make it clear that there are opportunities for the young and talented grown in-house, and not just for the guys picked up in barter. Check back next year.

MIKE CONNOLLY Bats: L Throws: L Born: 02-Jun-82 Age: 23

YEAR	TM	LG	AGE	G	GS	IP	H	BB	SO	HR	ERA	EQERA	EQH9	EQBB9	EQSO9	EQHR9	PERA	VORP	STF
2002	LYN	CRL	20	29	19	122.3	111	46	100	5	2.94	4.65	9.1	4.2	5.3	0.8	4.81	9.9	8
2003	ALT	EAS	21	25	23	127.3	123	38	90	10	3.39	4.78	9.4	3.0	5.3	1.2	4.93	8.8	9
2004	ALT	EAS	22	20	20	110.7	118	39	102	10	4.39	5.35	9.8	3.3	6.1	1.1	5.18	4.9	-3
2005	*PIT*	*NL*	*23*	*19*	*11*	*73.0*	*74*	*31*	*56*	*10*	*4.75*	*5.02*	*9.0*	*3.4*	*6.2*	*1.2*	*4.98*	*6.0*	*1*

Breakout: 13% *Improve: 44%* *Collapse: 19%*

An underrated and popular organizational soldier, Connolly gutted out a 2004 campaign with bone chips that were removed after the season; he's supposed to be ready in time for camp. He's not a flamethrower, but he's survived so far without having a really bad year, and that can lead to a big league gig at the back of a rotation. It's the Jimmy Anderson career path.

ZACH DUKE Bats: L Throws: L Born: 19-Apr-83 Age: 22

YEAR	TM	LG	AGE	G	GS	IP	H	BB	SO	HR	ERA	EQERA	EQH9	EQBB9	EQSO9	EQHR9	PERA	VORP	STF
2003	HIC	SAL	20	26	26	141.7	124	46	113	7	3.11	5.85	9.7	3.6	4.5	1.1	5.29	4.4	0
2004	ALT	EAS	21	9	9	51.3	41	10	36	2	1.58	2.83	8.1	1.9	4.9	0.4	3.21	12.7	23
2004	LYN	CRL	21	17	17	97.0	73	20	106	3	1.39	3.30	7.8	2.2	7.2	0.5	3.20	24.0	36
2005	*PIT*	*NL*	*22*	*25*	*15*	*101.0*	*103*	*33*	*75*	*12*	*4.18*	*4.43*	*9.1*	*2.5*	*6.1*	*1.0*	*4.45*	*13.6*	*6*

Breakout: 7% *Improve: 36%* *Collapse: 15%*

That projection might seem pretty modest, but keep in mind Duke's age and lack of experience above A-ball. It's also pretty hard to break out or improve on a season when you were the ERA leader for the entire minors. He's got exceptional mechanics and outstanding control, but this year he really started learning to be economical with his pitches. He needed to, because when you're rail-thin, everyone's going to fuss about whether or not you've got the stamina to start. Still, he can dial up heat into the low 90s, he's mastering a change, and he's got plus breaking stuff. If there's a prospect in this chapter with an upside you want a piece of, it's Duke.

NELSON FIGUEROA Bats: B Throws: R Born: 18-May-74 Age: 31

YEAR	TM	LG	AGE	G	GS	IP	H	BB	SO	HR	ERA	EQERA	EQH9	EQBB9	EQSO9	EQHR9	PERA	VORP	STF
2002	IND	INT	28	6	6	39.7	39	13	25	2	3.63	4.34	9.2	3.4	4.8	0.7	4.34	5.2	6
2002	MIL	NL	28	30	11	93.0	96	37	51	18	5.03	5.68	9.8	3.1	4.5	1.7	5.48	-2.6	-17
2003	NAS	PCL	29	23	23	151.3	144	37	121	11	2.97	4.10	8.9	2.5	6.2	1.1	4.10	23.8	20
2003	PIT	NL	29	12	3	35.3	28	13	23	8	3.31	3.27	8.5	3.0	5.5	1.9	4.64	9.2	4
2004	NAS	PCL	30	25	23	152.3	168	36	129	20	4.20	4.93	9.4	2.2	5.8	1.5	4.56	17.1	14
2004	PIT	NL	30	10	3	28.3	32	11	10	4	5.72	5.60	9.9	3.3	3.0	1.3	5.27	0.0	-9
2005	*PIT*	*NL*	*31*	*25*	*11*	*82.0*	*85*	*26*	*53*	*11*	*4.44*	*4.69*	*9.3*	*2.5*	*5.3*	*1.2*	*4.73*	*9.4*	*-3*

Breakout: 20% *Improve: 52%* *Collapse: 25%*

Has arm, will travel. For every Rick Reed, there are a dozen guys like Figueroa, where a lack of velocity is the sort of handicap that will never generate any breaks. There are considerably worse choices to have around as your fifth starter, so any near-contender short on options in the fifth spot or hoping to stash somebody in Triple-A can do better than resurrecting Scott Erickson and just pick up a guy like this.

JOSH FOGG Bats: R Throws: R Born: 13-Dec-76 Age: 28

YEAR	TM	LG	AGE	G	GS	IP	H	BB	SO	HR	ERA	EQERA	EQH9	EQBB9	EQSO9	EQHR9	PERA	VORP	STF
2002	PIT	NL	25	33	33	194.3	199	69	113	28	4.35	4.65	9.5	2.8	4.7	1.3	4.98	16.8	-2
2003	PIT	NL	26	26	26	142.0	166	40	71	22	5.26	5.48	10.2	2.2	4.1	1.3	5.09	-0.1	-7
2004	PIT	NL	27	32	32	178.3	193	66	82	17	4.64	4.79	9.5	3.0	3.7	0.8	4.42	16.2	-3
2005	*PIT*	*NL*	*28*	*24*	*20*	*120.7*	*137*	*43*	*64*	*15*	*4.91*	*5.19*	*10.2*	*2.8*	*4.3*	*1.1*	*5.27*	*6.9*	*-5*

Breakout: 16% *Improve: 49%* *Collapse: 21%*

Fogg is a fun pitcher if not a great one. He'll scrap, he'll take his turn on the mound, and he probably has the best right-handed pickoff move in baseball. Although he had a big performance split before and after the All-Star Break (5.97 ERA vs. 3.32), Fogg drew a lot of weak opponents in the second half, so he's not about to become something more. As the other guy in the Ritchie trade behind Kip Wells, he's done his bit, but he's not a building block. With the assortment of pitchers in the system rising while Fogg's beginning to get expensive, he may well get dealt this year or non-tendered next winter.

MIKE GONZALEZ

Bats: R   Throws: L   Born: 23-May-78   Age: 27

YEAR	TM	LG	AGE	G	GS	IP	H	BB	SO	HR	ERA	EQERA	EQH9	EQBB9	EQSO9	EQHR9	PERA	VORP	STF
2002	ALT	EAS	24	16	16	85.3	77	47	82	4	3.80	4.80	8.6	5.4	6.7	0.7	4.80	7.2	7
2003	NAS	PCL	25	7	0	10.0	9	4	10	0	4.50	5.59	8.4	3.7	7.4	0.0	3.72	2.0	7
2003	PIT	NL	25	16	0	8.3	7	6	6	4	7.59	7.04	9.4	5.9	5.9	4.7	8.22	-1.8	-29
2004	NAS	PCL	26	14	0	20.0	12	7	35	0	0.90	1.89	6.2	3.3	12.3	0.0	2.37	6.8	41
2004	PIT	NL	26	47	0	43.3	32	6	55	2	1.25	1.50	6.6	1.1	10.3	0.4	2.14	20.5	37
2005	*PIT*	*NL*	*27*	*33*	*5*	*65.7*	*52*	*25*	*71*	*5*	*2.71*	*2.87*	*7.1*	*3.0*	*8.7*	*0.7*	*3.25*	*19.7*	*20*

Breakout: 33%   Improve: 53%   Collapse: 22%

Happily salvaged out of the messy double-deals with the Red Sox in '03, Gonzalez is not just your basic situational reliever. With pure 90s heat, Gonzalez can basically smoke anybody at the plate. If there's a guy to step into the closer's role once Mesa craters, it's Gonzalez, not Torres—the problem being whether or not the Pirates want to risk accelerating his earnings potential through arbitration. Either way, he's got the stuff.

TOM GORZELANNY

Bats: B   Throws: L   Born: 12-Jul-82   Age: 22

YEAR	TM	LG	AGE	G	GS	IP	H	BB	SO	HR	ERA	EQERA	EQH9	EQBB9	EQSO9	EQHR9	PERA	VORP	STF
2003	WPT	NYP	20	8	8	30.3	23	10	22	1	1.78	4.10	9.6	4.1	4.1	1.0	5.81	-0.6	-10
2004	HIC	SAL	21	16	15	93.0	63	34	106	9	2.23	3.87	8.2	4.0	6.6	1.5	4.73	8.1	9
2004	LYN	CRL	21	10	10	55.7	54	19	61	6	4.85	5.92	9.8	3.7	7.1	1.9	5.75	-0.9	6
2005	*PIT*	*NL*	*22*	*11*	*10*	*60.7*	*58*	*29*	*47*	*9*	*4.76*	*5.04*	*8.5*	*3.7*	*6.3*	*1.3*	*4.91*	*4.6*	*5*

Breakout: 8%   Improve: 47%   Collapse: 19%

Lefties who cook with open flame tend to rise faster than other mortals, so Gorzelanny could come quickly, despite being a 2003 pick with no experience above A-ball. A product of Triton's powerhouse juco program, Gorzelanny has mid-90s heat, power breaking stuff, and a good change. He got a taste of Double-A with Altoona in the playoffs, but that won't be the only level he pitches at in '05. The best breakout candidate in the system.

JOHN GRABOW

Bats: L   Throws: L   Born: 04-Nov-78   Age: 26

YEAR	TM	LG	AGE	G	GS	IP	H	BB	SO	HR	ERA	EQERA	EQH9	EQBB9	EQSO9	EQHR9	PERA	VORP	STF
2002	ALT	EAS	23	28	27	146.3	181	47	97	10	5.48	6.45	10.5	3.0	4.5	0.9	5.50	1.6	-4
2003	ALT	EAS	24	24	9	83.0	87	19	73	9	3.36	4.50	9.9	2.3	6.6	1.8	5.54	0.5	-6
2003	NAS	PCL	24	17	0	24.7	31	7	26	0	4.74	6.93	9.9	2.9	7.7	0.4	4.38	3.3	0
2004	PIT	NL	25	68	0	61.7	81	28	64	8	5.11	5.54	9.9	3.4	8.0	1.0	4.97	0.1	-5
2005	*PIT*	*NL*	*26*	*32*	*4*	*58.7*	*62*	*23*	*50*	*6*	*4.22*	*4.47*	*9.5*	*3.1*	*6.9*	*0.9*	*4.75*	*8.0*	*3*

Breakout: 28%   Improve: 53%   Collapse: 22%

Officially, Grabow's place in history is secure: He's the Beimel eraser. Otherwise, his future's a little less certain. He didn't thrive in a situational role, as lefties slugged nearly .500 against him. Grabow does do a good job of keeping the ball on the ground, and more hits dropped against him than you'd expect, so it's reasonable to expect some improvement. But if he doesn't start beating lefties, his career as a second bullpen southpaw will be short and involve a lot of annual migrations.

MIKE JOHNSTON

Bats: L   Throws: L   Born: 30-Mar-79   Age: 26

YEAR	TM	LG	AGE	G	GS	IP	H	BB	SO	HR	ERA	EQERA	EQH9	EQBB9	EQSO9	EQHR9	PERA	VORP	STF
2002	LYN	CRL	23	15	10	57.0	50	26	50	2	3.63	5.85	8.8	5.2	5.7	0.7	4.82	4.5	-3
2003	ALT	EAS	24	46	0	72.3	49	27	65	4	2.12	3.14	7.5	3.8	6.8	1.0	3.82	13.1	14
2004	NAS	PCL	25	19	0	15.0	19	13	6	3	8.40	8.16	10.7	8.2	2.5	1.9	7.53	-3.1	-42
2004	PIT	NL	25	24	0	22.7	29	15	18	2	4.36	6.26	10.2	5.1	6.3	0.8	5.87	-1.6	-2
2005	*PIT*	*NL*	*26*	*8*	*1*	*14.0*	*14*	*8*	*10*	*1*	*4.70*	*4.98*	*8.9*	*4.5*	*5.9*	*0.9*	*5.17*	*1.3*	*-9*

Breakout: 22%   Improve: 51%   Collapse: 23%

Although he might seem a bit old to be called a prospect, Johnston is a special case. He lost time on the mound to his living with Tourette's Syndrome, which led his parents to pull him out of high school. He got back into the game through American Legion ball, got noticed and picked by the Pirates. He was still very raw, and the Pirates took their time sorting out what to do with him. After finally cracking the Show in '04, elbow soreness cost him time, but in the AFL, he was flashing his mid-90s velocity again. He'll have every opportunity to win a job out of camp.

PAUL MAHOLM **Bats: L** **Throws: L** Born: 25-Jun-82 Age: 23

YEAR	TM	LG	AGE	G	GS	IP	H	BB	SO	HR	ERA	EQERA	EQH9	EQBB9	EQSO9	EQHR9	PERA	VORP	STF
2003	WPT	NYP	21	8	8	34.3	25	10	32	1	1.84	5.10	9.3	3.6	5.1	1.2	5.40	0.7	0
2004	LYN	CRL	22	8	8	44.0	39	15	28	2	1.84	3.35	8.9	3.6	4.2	0.9	4.46	5.1	-4
2005	*PIT*	*NL*	*23*	*13*	*9*	*57.0*	*61*	*30*	*37*	*7*	*5.13*	*5.43*	*9.5*	*4.1*	*5.3*	*1.1*	*5.42*	*1.5*	*-5*

Breakout: 9% *Improve: 47%* *Collapse: 26%*

Although Bullington's selection over B. J. Upton doesn't look so good, picking Maholm over Jeff Allison the following season doesn't look so bad. Unfortunately, Maholm had his skull and nose cracked by a line drive that ended his year early and kept him out of both the instructional league and the AFL. He does still have the tools that made him a top prospect out of Mississippi State, and everybody likes lefties who can reach 90 and throw a good curve. Here's hoping for a complete recovery.

BRIAN MEADOWS **Bats: R** **Throws: R** Born: 21-Nov-75 Age: 29

YEAR	TM	LG	AGE	G	GS	IP	H	BB	SO	HR	ERA	EQERA	EQH9	EQBB9	EQSO9	EQHR9	PERA	VORP	STF
2002	NAS	PCL	26	23	22	126.3	132	26	98	15	4.28	5.32	9.6	2.0	5.6	1.4	4.65	12.7	5
2002	PIT	NL	26	11	11	62.7	62	14	31	7	3.88	4.10	9.3	1.8	4.1	1.1	4.40	9.3	3
2003	NAS	PCL	27	9	8	51.0	32	0	40	2	1.41	2.93	6.8	0.6	6.5	0.6	1.96	18.6	41
2003	PIT	NL	27	34	7	76.3	91	11	38	8	4.72	5.09	10.0	1.1	4.1	0.8	4.24	2.9	6
2004	PIT	NL	28	68	0	78.0	76	19	46	7	3.58	4.44	8.8	2.0	4.8	0.7	3.72	9.4	8
2005	*PIT*	*NL*	*29*	*29*	*5*	*63.3*	*67*	*15*	*38*	*7*	*4.27*	*4.52*	*9.6*	*1.9*	*4.9*	*1.1*	*4.36*	*8.0*	*-5*

Breakout: 21% *Improve: 50%* *Collapse: 22%*

Although something of a utility pitcher because of his durability, Meadows is more a middle reliever who can spot start than someone you really want in the rotation. Even the hope that he could be a good setup man is a bit unrealistic: See him often enough, and his various flavors of junk don't surprise any more. Expect an ERA a full run higher in '05. There are worse 11th men on a staff, but by tendering him, the Pirates will end up overpaying.

JOSE MESA **Bats: R** **Throws: R** Born: 22-May-66 Age: 39

YEAR	TM	LG	AGE	G	GS	IP	H	BB	SO	HR	ERA	EQERA	EQH9	EQBB9	EQSO9	EQHR9	PERA	VORP	STF
2002	PHI	NL	36	74	0	75.7	65	39	64	5	2.97	3.33	8.3	4.1	6.8	0.6	4.07	19.2	1
2003	PHI	NL	37	61	0	58.0	71	31	45	7	6.52	6.83	10.1	4.2	6.2	1.1	5.59	-7.8	-11
2004	PIT	NL	38	70	0	69.3	78	20	37	6	3.25	3.33	9.6	2.3	4.3	0.7	4.26	17.9	-10
2005	*PIT*	*NL*	*39*	*40*	*0*	*36.3*	*41*	*16*	*23*	*4*	*5.07*	*5.37*	*10.2*	*3.4*	*5.1*	*1.1*	*5.42*	*1.3*	*-14*

Breakout: 16% *Improve: 46%* *Collapse: 25%*

Senor Smokeless has been pretty fun, all things considered. No, he's not a great closer, but you have to credit him with persistence and occasional usefulness in his career. He'll have especially bad stretches, and he's almost always pitching his way into trouble, but if you're paying him cheaply and hoping to peddle him to a suitably desperate contender at the deadline, he's handy. Signing him to a one-year deal plus an option that won't be picked up was about right, but Littlefield needs to deal him for the first useful offer, should one come.

JEFF MILLER **Bats: R** **Throws: R** Born: 01-Feb-80 Age: 25

YEAR	TM	LG	AGE	G	GS	IP	H	BB	SO	HR	ERA	EQERA	EQH9	EQBB9	EQSO9	EQHR9	PERA	VORP	STF
2002	HIC	SAL	22	31	15	103.3	100	28	75	11	3.75	5.48	10.9	3.1	4.1	2.4	6.95	-13.8	-26
2003	LYN	CRL	23	27	7	75.7	89	25	59	4	4.87	7.06	10.3	3.2	5.1	1.0	5.08	4.2	-17
2004	ALT	EAS	24	52	0	68.0	48	28	79	8	2.91	4.02	7.9	4.0	8.0	1.6	4.45	8.0	9
2005	*PIT*	*NL*	*25*	*35*	*4*	*61.3*	*57*	*26*	*54*	*8*	*4.39*	*4.65*	*8.4*	*3.3*	*7.1*	*1.2*	*4.66*	*7.7*	*1*

Breakout: 22% *Improve: 56%* *Collapse: 12%*

Miller's a favored organization soldier, because he stepped out of relative obscurity, took over the closer's role at Altoona in July and rattled off 18 saves in two months, and followed that up with a good AFL stint. With a heater in the low 90s, if he continues to thrive as a full-time reliever, he'll enter the big league picture shortly.

LEO NUNEZ Bats: R Throws: R Born: 14-Aug-83 Age: 21

YEAR	TM	LG	AGE	G	GS	IP	H	BB	SO	HR	ERA	EQERA	EQH9	EQBB9	EQSO9	EQHR9	PERA	VORP	STF
2003	HIC	SAL	19	13	7	48.3	59	14	37	6	5.59	7.77	12.7	3.1	4.3	2.7	8.18	-12.6	-25
2003	WPT	NYP	19	8	8	38.3	31	12	41	0	3.05	5.71	9.1	3.6	5.7	0.3	4.67	3.6	12
2004	HIC	SAL	20	27	20	144.0	121	46	140	16	3.12	4.26	9.2	3.4	5.6	1.7	5.43	2.5	9
2005	*KCR*	*AL*	*21*	*12*	*10*	*60.0*	*67*	*23*	*41*	*11*	*5.48*	*5.16*	*9.8*	*3.1*	*5.6*	*1.6*	*5.20*	*4.8*	*0*

Breakout: 13% *Improve: 45%* *Collapse: 16%*

A Dominican string bean with mid-90s heat still learning his craft, Nunez was nevertheless the ace of a good Hickory team. Naturally, at his age and with his lack of a classic pitcher's body, there are concerns about his durability after elbow problems cropped up in 2003. Still, as maybes go, an outstanding pickup for Benito Santiago by Allard Baird.

OLIVER PEREZ Bats: L Throws: L Born: 15-Aug-81 Age: 23

YEAR	TM	LG	AGE	G	GS	IP	H	BB	SO	HR	ERA	EQERA	EQH9	EQBB9	EQSO9	EQHR9	PERA	VORP	STF
2002	LEL	CLF	20	9	8	48.7	36	24	66	0	1.85	3.60	8.0	5.2	7.2	0.2	4.00	8.0	24
2002	MOB	SOU	20	4	4	23.0	11	16	34	1	1.17	2.11	5.9	6.3	10.1	0.8	3.38	5.3	44
2002	SDP	NL	20	16	15	90.0	71	48	94	13	3.50	4.03	7.6	4.1	8.4	1.3	3.72	18.0	32
2003	POR	PCL	21	8	8	47.7	44	12	48	6	3.02	4.40	8.8	2.6	7.8	1.4	4.20	7.0	31
2003	SDP	NL	21	19	19	103.7	103	65	117	20	5.38	5.80	8.9	4.9	9.1	1.7	5.19	0.6	22
2003	PIT	NL	21	5	5	23.0	26	12	24	2	5.87	5.79	9.3	3.9	8.1	0.8	4.63	-0.4	27
2004	PIT	NL	22	30	30	196.0	145	81	239	22	2.98	3.27	7.0	3.3	9.9	0.9	3.13	54.5	43
2005	*PIT*	*NL*	*23*	*23*	*23*	*150.0*	*129*	*65*	*147*	*19*	*3.97*	*4.20*	*7.7*	*3.4*	*8.0*	*1.1*	*4.18*	*24.6*	*21*

Breakout: 15% *Improve: 40%* *Collapse: 26%*

Downright Langstonesque, in that like Mark Langston, Perez can dominate, and like Langston, he's a tremendous talent starting off with a lousy team. Unlike Langston, Perez isn't blessed with tremendous durability. For now Perez's closest PECOTA comparables are guys like Juan Pizarro, Pete Falcone, and a little lower down, Frank Tanana. McClendon did a good job of watching Perez's workload, which is encouraging. Near-term, you can expect more of the same; the NL Central isn't quite the slaughterhouse for lefty pitching it used to be when McGwire and Sosa and the Killer B's ruled the roost. There are still concerns about his delivery, making Littlefield's unwillingness to give Perez a multi-year deal this winter prudent, but prudence with a potentially huge price tag if Perez has another year like '04.

MATT PETERSON Bats: R Throws: R Born: 11-Feb-82 Age: 23

YEAR	TM	LG	AGE	G	GS	IP	H	BB	SO	HR	ERA	EQERA	EQH9	EQBB9	EQSO9	EQHR9	PERA	VORP	STF
2002	CMB	SAL	20	26	26	137.7	109	61	153	13	3.86	6.23	9.5	5.2	6.4	2.2	6.08	-6.5	0
2003	SLU	FSL	21	15	15	84.0	65	24	73	2	1.71	4.11	8.5	3.1	5.6	0.6	3.87	14.7	19
2003	BIN	EAS	21	6	6	31.3	29	20	23	2	3.45	5.52	8.9	6.4	5.5	0.9	4.91	2.2	0
2004	BIN	EAS	22	19	18	104.7	97	45	90	11	3.27	4.42	9.3	4.1	5.9	1.3	5.16	4.8	0
2004	ALT	EAS	22	7	7	36.0	36	22	29	7	6.25	6.75	10.3	5.9	5.7	2.4	7.02	-5.3	-14
2005	*PIT*	*NL*	*23*	*11*	*10*	*55.3*	*56*	*29*	*43*	*8*	*5.13*	*5.43*	*9.1*	*4.1*	*6.2*	*1.3*	*5.38*	*2.0*	*2*

Breakout: 11% *Improve: 44%* *Collapse: 21%*

Notionally the best prospect in the Benson deal, since Wigginton's just a ham 'n egger at third, and Bautista was the correction of a previous error. Peterson comes over with the moxie rep, and he's got that big build scouts like. However, he's not a flamethrower, instead relying on spotting his breaking stuff. His mechanics fell apart in time for the Mets (and presumably Rick Peterson) to give him up or give up on him, depending on your point of view, so he's sort of like Scott Kazmir, without the huge upside and with even more doubt.

IAN SNELL Bats: R Throws: R Born: 30-Oct-81 Age: 23

YEAR	TM	LG	AGE	G	GS	IP	H	BB	SO	HR	ERA	EQERA	EQH9	EQBB9	EQSO9	EQHR9	PERA	VORP	STF
2002	HIC	SAL	20	24	22	139.7	127	45	149	8	2.71	4.82	9.7	3.7	6.0	1.3	5.46	2.0	2
2003	ALT	EAS	21	6	6	36.7	36	10	23	2	1.96	4.19	9.2	2.6	4.7	0.8	4.46	4.3	9
2003	LYN	CRL	21	20	20	116.3	105	33	122	3	3.33	4.65	8.5	2.8	6.9	0.5	3.51	25.6	24
2004	ALT	EAS	22	26	26	151.0	147	40	142	16	3.16	3.97	9.4	2.5	6.4	1.3	4.78	13.0	7
2004	PIT	NL	22	3	1	12.0	14	9	9	2	7.50	7.50	9.8	6.0	6.0	1.5	6.00	-2.4	-13
2005	*PIT*	*NL*	*23*	*14*	*12*	*74.3*	*77*	*28*	*59*	*10*	*4.53*	*4.80*	*9.2*	*2.9*	*6.5*	*1.2*	*4.80*	*8.1*	*9*

Breakout: 13% *Improve: 41%* *Collapse: 17%*

A short, slight righty, and so a victim of the usual biases against the type, but Snell's a comer. First, he had a brilliant season at Altoona, posting the best year of any starter in the Eastern League. Perhaps more importantly for some, his velocity picked up a couple of ticks, moving more consistently into the low- to mid-90s range. There's already talk of his having a shot at a utility pitcher or relief role in camp this year, but that could turn into more if he stays healthy while guys like Vogelsong fizzle out.

CORY STEWART **Bats: L** **Throws: L** Born: 14-Nov-79 Age: 25

YEAR	TM	LG	AGE	G	GS	IP	H	BB	SO	HR	ERA	EQERA	EQH9	EQBB9	EQSO9	EQHR9	PERA	VORP	STF
2002	FTW	MDW	22	17	11	64.0	46	18	86	4	2.39	4.87	8.8	3.3	7.7	1.6	4.55	6.7	12
2002	LEL	CLF	22	12	12	64.7	60	29	69	3	3.20	5.19	9.0	4.6	5.6	0.7	4.75	5.7	6
2003	MOB	SOU	23	24	24	125.7	104	50	133	10	3.72	5.20	8.9	3.8	7.0	1.4	4.81	10.2	8
2004	NAS	PCL	24	18	18	93.0	112	47	53	11	5.13	5.86	9.9	4.8	3.9	1.2	5.46	1.4	-15
2005	*PIT*	*NL*	*25*	*22*	*11*	*74.0*	*79*	*38*	*51*	*11*	*5.34*	*5.65*	*9.6*	*4.0*	*5.6*	*1.4*	*5.71*	*0.6*	*-9*

Breakout: 5% *Improve: 49%* *Collapse: 22%*

Credit the Padres for their devoted attention to the indy leagues; Stewart was released by the Reds after losing a year to shoulder surgery, and managed to resurrect his career by pitching in the Texas-Louisiana League. For their scouting troubles, Stewart then got to be the third man the Pads tossed into the Giles trade, but with lefty heat that cracks 90 and a big bender, he's not your average throw-in. After a hot start, he lost the better part of six weeks to a strained ribcage, but his arm isn't a source of concern. If he has a good first half, he'll start getting consideration for the jobs of guys like Vogelsong or Williams.

SALOMON TORRES **Bats: R** **Throws: R** Born: 11-Mar-72 Age: 33

YEAR	TM	LG	AGE	G	GS	IP	H	BB	SO	HR	ERA	EQERA	EQH9	EQBB9	EQSO9	EQHR9	PERA	VORP	STF
2002	NAS	PCL	30	26	24	162.3	169	39	136	12	3.83	4.80	9.3	2.3	5.9	0.9	4.22	23.9	15
2002	PIT	NL	30	5	5	30.0	28	13	12	2	2.70	3.18	8.9	3.5	3.2	0.6	4.13	8.3	-1
2003	PIT	NL	31	41	16	121.0	128	42	84	19	4.76	4.68	9.4	2.8	5.7	1.4	4.76	11.3	-3
2004	PIT	NL	32	84	0	92.0	87	22	62	6	2.64	3.25	8.4	1.9	5.5	0.5	3.35	25.3	5
2005	*PIT*	*NL*	*33*	*37*	*5*	*70.3*	*73*	*22*	*48*	*7*	*3.93*	*4.16*	*9.3*	*2.5*	*5.5*	*0.9*	*4.41*	*11.3*	*-3*

Breakout: 23% *Improve: 51%* *Collapse: 24%*

One of the more inspired retreadings that Littlefield and company can really take credit for. Instead of merely being a formerly famous guy down on his luck, Torres is a right-handed version of Mike Remlinger, a former prospect who melted down, and then actually came back to have a career. Torres will probably get first crack at the closer's job once Mesa turns back into a pumpkin, and he'd do a creditable job. If the fate of short right-handers not gifted with Pedro's stuff is to make money in the pen, that isn't all bad for them.

JOHN VANBENSCHOTEN **Bats: R** **Throws: R** Born: 14-Apr-80 Age: 25

YEAR	TM	LG	AGE	G	GS	IP	H	BB	SO	HR	ERA	EQERA	EQH9	EQBB9	EQSO9	EQHR9	PERA	VORP	STF
2002	HIC	SAL	22	27	27	148.0	119	62	145	6	2.80	5.13	8.8	4.8	5.5	0.9	5.13	7.0	6
2003	LYN	CRL	23	9	9	48.7	33	18	49	1	2.22	3.80	7.2	3.6	6.8	0.4	3.00	13.0	26
2003	ALT	EAS	23	17	17	90.3	95	34	78	5	3.69	5.42	9.4	3.6	6.3	0.8	5.00	5.8	14
2004	NAS	PCL	24	23	23	131.7	135	49	101	16	4.72	5.34	9.0	3.6	5.3	1.2	4.56	14.6	7
2004	PIT	NL	24	6	5	28.7	33	19	18	3	6.90	8.16	9.4	5.3	5.0	0.9	5.34	-8.7	0
2005	*PIT*	*NL*	*25*	*15*	*15*	*92.7*	*96*	*42*	*67*	*11*	*4.98*	*5.27*	*9.3*	*3.6*	*5.9*	*1.0*	*5.02*	*4.9*	*6*

Breakout: 14% *Improve: 44%* *Collapse: 29%*

Since being the Pirates' top pick in the '01 draft, people have been asking if they made the right choice in making him a full-time pitcher. You have to wonder about the scout who complained his arms were like Michael Jordan's, "too long" to allow him to hit. Comparing a high school baseball washout to the guy who led the NCAA Division I in home runs seems like some sort of latter-day Lamarckian farfel to support a decision already made. It's sort of moot to fret about now; he could still be like former Bucs Don Robinson or Rick Rhoden, and be one of the best-hitting pitchers in the league.

The real problem is that VanBenschoten didn't make that much progress in the last two years above A-ball, and there are times when it's clear that he's still not picking up a lot of the finer points of pitching. His control isn't terrible, but his command within the strike zone is still a bit spotty, and holding runners isn't considered a strong suit. He's got a good fastball, but all of his breaking and off-speed stuff needs work. He could figure it all out, but he's nowhere close to a finished product. That could mean lots of good stuff once he is, but if the organization gets any more impatient, it might not happen here, if at all.

RYAN VOGELSONG

Bats: R Throws: R Born: 22-Jul-77 Age: 27

YEAR	TM	LG	AGE	G	GS	IP	H	BB	SO	HR	ERA	EQERA	EQH9	EQBB9	EQSO9	EQHR9	PERA	VORP	STF
2002	LYN	CRL	24	4	4	15.7	19	7	20	0	8.03	8.80	10.0	4.7	7.6	0.0	4.70	1.5	4
2002	ALT	EAS	24	8	8	43.7	47	10	35	5	5.56	6.31	10.0	2.2	5.7	1.7	5.44	0.7	1
2003	NAS	PCL	25	26	26	149.0	142	54	146	12	4.29	5.36	8.8	3.7	7.6	1.1	4.40	18.8	15
2003	PIT	NL	25	6	5	22.0	30	9	15	1	6.55	7.25	10.5	3.2	5.2	0.4	5.24	-5.1	-3
2004	PIT	NL	26	31	26	133.0	148	67	92	22	6.50	6.27	9.6	4.0	5.5	1.4	5.23	-10.9	-8
2005	*PIT*	*NL*	*27*	*21*	*15*	*93.7*	*98*	*42*	*67*	*13*	*5.11*	*5.41*	*9.4*	*3.5*	*5.8*	*1.3*	*5.35*	*4.0*	*-1*

Breakout: 17% *Improve: 43%* *Collapse: 27%*

At this point, Vogelsong isn't one of the organization's brighter lights. Although he did beat out both Rick Reed and Sean Burnett in camp for the last spot in the rotation, he didn't really earn his keep. Still technically in the rotation, Vogelsong will have to have a great camp if he's really going to keep his job. His only good stretch during the year was when he moved into the pen; it's a place where he might have a good future.

KIP WELLS

Bats: R Throws: R Born: 21-Apr-77 Age: 28

YEAR	TM	LG	AGE	G	GS	IP	H	BB	SO	HR	ERA	EQERA	EQH9	EQBB9	EQSO9	EQHR9	PERA	VORP	STF
2002	PIT	NL	25	33	33	198.3	197	71	134	21	3.59	4.15	9.1	2.8	5.5	0.9	4.48	29.2	8
2003	PIT	NL	26	31	31	197.3	171	76	147	24	3.28	3.48	8.3	3.1	6.2	1.0	3.96	47.9	12
2004	PIT	NL	27	24	24	138.3	145	66	116	14	4.56	4.48	8.9	3.8	6.7	0.8	4.28	17.6	13
2005	*PIT*	*NL*	*28*	*23*	*22*	*130.7*	*129*	*53*	*101*	*13*	*4.14*	*4.38*	*8.8*	*3.2*	*6.3*	*0.9*	*4.46*	*17.9*	*11*

Breakout: 17% *Improve: 53%* *Collapse: 19%*

Wells had something of a lost season. Although he remained hard to hit, command of his pitches became a problem as his fingers started bothering him. Surgery to repair carpal-tunnel syndrome appears to have left him none the worse for wear, and might even earn him some sympathy among the fourth estate. He'll be back in full form, giving the Pirates a good front pair with Perez.

DAVE WILLIAMS

Bats: L Throws: L Born: 12-Mar-79 Age: 26

YEAR	TM	LG	AGE	G	GS	IP	H	BB	SO	HR	ERA	EQERA	EQH9	EQBB9	EQSO9	EQHR9	PERA	VORP	STF
2002	PIT	NL	23	9	9	43.3	38	24	33	9	4.99	5.23	8.7	4.4	6.3	2.0	5.23	0.5	-2
2003	NAS	PCL	24	16	16	77.3	78	30	56	7	4.19	5.94	9.4	4.0	5.7	1.2	4.95	5.3	-3
2004	NAS	PCL	25	21	21	116.7	113	33	103	10	3.47	4.33	8.5	2.7	6.2	0.9	3.77	22.8	13
2004	PIT	NL	25	10	6	38.7	31	13	33	4	4.42	4.86	7.5	2.7	7.1	1.0	3.41	3.7	14
2005	*PIT*	*NL*	*26*	*20*	*14*	*91.3*	*88*	*36*	*69*	*11*	*4.48*	*4.74*	*8.6*	*3.2*	*6.2*	*1.1*	*4.53*	*9.1*	*6*

Breakout: 16% *Improve: 42%* *Collapse: 25%*

A survivor. After earning a slot in the rotation at the end of 2001, Williams lost more than two years to shoulder surgery the following July. It had to be frustrating to lose an extra month or so to a ribcage strained by a violent sneeze, but Williams finally did make it back. His velocity occasionally gets back into the upper 80s but remains a source of concern; he does seem to have improved command of his curve. He'll get a shot at winning a rotation spot in camp.

St. Louis Cardinals

The Cardinals plowed their way to 105 wins in 2004 by dint of a very good bullpen, a rotation that was good enough, and a legendary heart of the order. En route to those 105 wins and an NL championship, St. Louis racked up a total team VORP of 672.3, which was tops in all of baseball. What's also noteworthy is that of that VORP total, 368.4 (or 54.8 %) runs were contributed by players acquired by general manager Walt Jocketty in trade.

At its heart, every culminated negotiation is an act of arrogance on the part of the decision-makers. It's the case with trades, too. As such, it's perhaps surprising that Jocketty's head doesn't have its own set of moons in orbit around it. That's to say, if "Trader Jock" were the type to gloat, he'd have plenty of reasons to. Not only was the foundation of last year's record-setting Cardinals team put in place via trade, but Jocketty's also been doing this sort of thing for years. Jocketty's penchant for the headline-grabbing deal was thrown into bright relief again this past winter when he acquired Mark Mulder from Oakland for Daric Barton, Kiko Calero, and Dan Haren. It's how he's built this team, and also how he's kept them in contention for the last half decade.

With that in mind, let's evaluate the major deals Jocketty has been a part of since he became the Cards' GM in the winter of 1994.

CARDINALS PROSPECTUS

2004 record: 105–57; First place, NL Central; Lost to Red Sox in World Series

Pythagenport record: 100–62

Runs scored per game: 5.28 (1st in NL)

Runs allowed per game: 4.07 (1st in NL)

Team EqA: .277 (1st in NL)

2004 Batters Age: 31.3 (3rd oldest in NL)

2004 Pitchers Age: 30.6 (2nd oldest in NL)

Ballpark: Busch Stadium; Severe pitcher's park; Park Factor of 0.959

2004: Rode one of the best hitting quartets in history to the Series, not to mention the best NL regular season enjoyed by any team since 1998.

2005: They're a proven organization, and they return the most intimidating defending champion the league's seen in years.

1/9/96 – Traded OF Allen Battle and Ps Carl Dale and Jay Witasick to the A's for P Todd Stottlemyre.

Battle would play only 108 games in the majors, and Dale would log four career big league innings. Witasick never developed into a solid major league pitcher for the A's, but once the Padres made him a full-time reliever for the 2001 season, he had a run of effectiveness.

Stottlemyre had two and two-thirds quality seasons in St. Louis, including 1996, when the Cards won the division. That year, Stottlemyre finished in the top 15 among NL starting pitchers in VORP.

Advantage: Jocketty.

1/22/96 – Traded OF Bernard Gilkey to the Mets for Ps Erik Hiljus and Eric Ludwick, and OF Yudith Ororio.

Gilkey, in what was a rare career-curve misread by Jocketty, and would see his performance spike after leaving the Cardinals. Prior to the trade, Gilkey had hit .282/.354/.431 in parts of six major league seasons. His first year in New York, in a tougher environment for hitters, Gilkey hit .317/.393/.562. In terms of VORP, that placed him among the top 25 hitters in the game that season. Gilkey was about 40 runs better than Ron Gant, the Cards' regular left fielder that year, but Gilkey never again approached that level of production.

Ozorio would never make the majors, and Hiljus and Ludwick would both spend four undistinguished seasons in the Show.

Advantage: Mets

7/31/97 – Traded Ps Eric Ludwick, T. J. Mathews, and Blake Stein to the A's for 1B Mark McGwire.

Certainly, the Cardinals had to make a significant financial outlay, paying McGwire more than $40 million for his four-and-a-half years in St. Louis, but there's no comparison in terms of on-field value:

Player	VORP after trade
McGwire	300.5
Ludwick + Mathews + Stein	32.1

Still, this is one of several Jocketty deals in which he leveraged an advantage in terms of payroll flexibility to extract talent from poorer teams. Jocketty and the Cardinals have had the "buyer's latitude," which allows them to make trades that are patently uneven in terms of the talent exchanged. Even so, he certainly has an eye for who might make these kind of deals.

Advantage: Jocketty

11/10/97 – Traded 1B/OF Dmitri Young to the Reds for P Jeff Brantley.

Brantley's career was effectively over by the time he reached St. Louis. In Young's brief time as a Cardinal, he slugged .354. He was also only 23; since being traded, he's slugged .494. Considering the difficulties the Cards have had filling both outfield corners in the intervening years (Eric Davis/Darren Bragg/Willie McGee in '99, spotting for J. D. Drew's injuries in other seasons), Young could have been useful.

Advantage: Reds

7/31/98 – Traded SS Royce Clayton and P Todd Stottlemyre to the Rangers for 3B Fernando Tatis, P Darren Oliver, and OF Mark Little.

Over a season-and-a-half, Oliver gave the Cards more than 250 innings of roughly league-average pitching. That has value. Little was a fringe type who had a nice pinch-hitting run with the Rockies in 2001 but did little else. Tatis gave the Cards the rough equivalent of two seasons of outstanding production at third (more on him below).

As for the Rangers, Stottlemyre was heading into his walk year, and gave the Rangers 60 respectalbe innings for their stretch drive. Clayton hit at a decent clip for a season-and-a-half before getting back to the business of being Royce Clayton in 2000. Considering that Clayton and Stottlemyre contributed roughly two wins to the Rangers in a season in which they made the playoffs by only three games, you can make a case that this was an essential deal for Texas. Still, the return package was better.

Advantage: Jocketty, narrowly.

11/19/98 – Traded LF Ron Gant, and Ps Jeff Brantley and Cliff Politte to the Phillies for Ps Ricky Bottalico and Garrett Stephenson.

Gant, somewhat passable. Brantley, *Con Air* bad. Politte, quite effective for most of his stay in Philly. Bottalico, below average, but better than Brantley. Stephenson, overrated but pitched in a slew of league-average innings. It's a less important trade than the names might lead you to believe.

Advantage: Draw

12/14/98 – Traded Ps Armando Almanza and Braden Looper, and INF Pablo Ozuna to the Marlins for SS Edgar Renteria.

Save for 15.2 innings in 1999, Almanza hasn't cut it in the majors. Once a ballyhooed middle-infield prospect, Ozuna was one of Agegate's biggest disappointments. He's now 30, has logged only 65 games in the bigs, and spent all of 2004 in the minors. Looper has been fairly effective in seven major league seasons, but he's now a Met, having left the Marlins via free agency prior to the 2004 season.

Renteria is generally regarded as the best shortstop in the NL over the last few seasons. That sounds more impressive than it really is, given the concentration of shortstop talent in the junior circuit. His defense has been overrated, but his 2003 season was MVP caliber. However, this is another trade made possible by the team's willingness to take on a player headed for his high-salary years. The Marlins were in their post-championship tear-down on Wayne Huizenga's orders, and Dave Dombrowski had to make a deal, any deal.

Advantage: Jocketty

11/11/99 – Traded C Alberto Castillo and Ps Matt DeWitt and Lance Painter to the Blue Jays for Ps Pat Hentgen and Paul Spoljaric.

Despite the 15 wins, Hentgen was actually a tick below average in his lone season for the Cards, although he did chew up almost 195 frames. The team released Spoljaric just prior to Opening Day. On the Jays' side of the equation, Castillo is a backup catcher of little note, but with an Andy Rooney–style knack for staying in clover despite there being countless others who could do the job better. DeWitt threw 40 innings in the majors, and Painter was merely decent in his lone full season in Toronto.

Advantage: Jocketty

11/16/99 – Traded Ps Manuel Aybar, Rich Croushore, and Jose Jimenez and INF Brent Butler to the Rockies for Ps Darryl Kile, Dave Veres, and Luther Hackman.

Back in the days when we didn't really know what would become of a formerly effective starting pitcher who'd been shelled in Coors Field. Jocketty was willing to see Kile as someone who still had something, and in his two full seasons with the Cardinals, Kile ranked 20th and eighth among all major league starters in Support-Neutral Value-Added. In 2000, Dave Veres logged the seventh-highest VORP of any NL reliever, and Luther Hackman even contributed some sufferable mop-up innings in 2002. As for the Rockies, Jimenez was a highly effective reliever for three seasons, but none of the others achieved anything of consequence.

Advantage: Jocketty

12/20/99 – Traded Ps Juan Acevedo and Matt Parker, and C Eliezer Alfonzo to the Brewers for 2B Fernando Vina.

Acevedo's a board-certified live arm who's been short on performance but long on organizations who thought they could fix him; at least his second-best season did come as a Brewer. Alfonzo and Parker never made the bigs. Vina gave the Cards three full seasons of on-base sufficiency and excellent-to-good defense at the keystone.

Advantage: Jocketty

3/23/00 – Traded P Kent Bottenfield and 2B Adam Kennedy to the Angels for CF Jim Edmonds.

Bottenfield would spend four grossly ineffective months with the Angels before being shipped to the Phillies for Ron Gant. Kennedy has, to date, given Anaheim five seasons as their starting second baseman, three of which were solid to good. He also nabbed the MVP award for the 2002 ALCS. It still doesn't equal what they lost in Edmonds. In five seasons to date as a Cardinal, Edmonds has won five Gold Gloves and ranked sixth, 26th, 13th, 21st, and 23rd in all of baseball in VORP. It is, however, another case of the Cardinals being willing and able to pursue the high-dollar talent of another team.

Advantage: Jocketty

7/29/00 – Traded SS Jack Wilson to the Pirates for P Jason Christiansen.

The Cardinals were already better off with Renteria as their shortstop, but this turned out to be a poor return on the dollar for Jocketty. Wilson was a no-hit, good-glove starting shortstop for the Bucs from 2001–2003, but he broke out in 2004, arguably becoming the best at his position in the NL. Even if that doesn't last, Wilson's been far more valuable than a vanilla lefty reliever like Christiansen, without noting he's had only one effective season since leaving Pittsburgh.

Advantage: Pirates

7/31/00 – Traded 3B/1B Jose Leon to the Orioles for 1B Will Clark and cash.

Leon is a corner defender/DH-type who, at 28 years of age, has logged 209 at bats and slugged .321 in the majors. Clark spent only 51 games in a Cardinal uniform, but while spotting for the crumbling Mark McGwire down the stretch in 2000, he hit .345/.426/.655 after the trade. Among first basemen acquired at or near the deadline by playoff-bound teams since 1980, only Fred McGriff of the '93 Braves posted a higher VORP with his new team. Yet again, team ownership allowed Jocketty to add payroll for the stretch drive, and yet again he made the most of it.

Advantage: Jocketty

12/14/00 – Traded P Britt Reames and 3B Fernando Tatis to the Expos for Ps Dustin Hermanson and Steve Kline.

In baseball terms, is there a better example of market timing than Jocketty's acquisition of and subsequent defenestration of Fernando Tatis? Consider Tatis career breakdowns:

	Games	AVG/OBP/SLG
Before Cardinals	155	.264/.301/.378
With Cardinals	300	.282/.389/.525
After Cardinals	208	.225/.305/.357

Someone alert Eliot Spitzer. The sense of knowing the very moment to take action is striking. It's as if the lovely and talented Ms. Sheffield, while on a Sunday drive with the family, changes the radio station moments before a brazenly recognizable R. Kelly song comes on. Mentioning that the Cardinals got one tolerable tour of duty out of Hermanson and two good-to-great years out of Kline is piling on at this point.

Advantage: Jocketty

8/2/01 – Traded OF Ray Lankford and cash to the Padres for P Woody Williams.

What often gets overlooked when hashing this frequently rehashed swap is that Lankford was pretty darn good immediately following the swap. In 40 games after the trade to San Diego, Lankford hit .288/.386/.480. Of course, he was awful the following season and out of baseball altogether in 2003. As for Williams, in 75 homestretch innings in 2001, he posted a 2.28 ERA, and the Cards went 8–3 when he started. Over the next three seasons, Williams would log more than 500 innings and allow less than four runs per game.

Advantage: Jocketty

7/19/02 – Traded OF Coco Crisp and 1B Luis Garcia to the Indians for P Chuck Finley.

In 2001, Finley was 38 years of age, posted a 5.54 ERA and went on the DL twice because of a strained neck muscle. That doesn't sound like the makings of a great deadline addition, but Finley's improved first half the following season prompted Jocketty to make a play for him. After the deal, Finley worked 85.1 innings with a 3.80 ERA. He pitched quite well in his start against the Diamondbacks in the Division Series, but was then lit up by the Giants in the NLCS. The Cards won the division by 13 games, swept the NLDS, and were handily beaten by the Giants in the LCS. In other words, Finley didn't make much difference to the team's prevailing fortunes. Flags do indeed fly forever, but the Cards would've won—and lost—the very same flags with or without Finley.

As for the return package, Garcia is coming off a potential breakout season, but it was at Las Vegas, and he's now 26 and a Dodger farmhand. In his first full-time season in the majors, Crisp was a useful member of the Indians, and at worst figures to be an effective fourth outfielder in the years to come. He's not a percolating superstar by any means, but the word "useful" comes to mind.

Advantage: Indians

7/29/02 – Traded INF Placido Polanco and Ps Bud Smith and Mike Timlin to the Phillies for 3B Scott Rolen, P Doug Nickle, and cash.

Polanco has been a very effective infield regular since becoming a Phillie. Smith, once a highly promising young arm, is in grave disrepair and may never overcome his injuries, and Timlin has long since moved on after two decent months in Philadelphia.

Health permitting, Rolen is a future Hall of Famer waist-deep in his prime seasons. The Cards signed him to a long-term deal that probably will extend beyond the point of his being really good, but he'll more than earn his keep for the time being.

This time, Jocketty leveraged a different sort of advantage—Cardinal atmospherics. Philadelphia certainly had the wherewithal to re-sign Rolen, but Rolen wanted no part of it. Jocketty stepped in and used his city and his team, with an adoring fan base, as a marketing point to eventually lock up Rolen for good.

Advantage: Jocketty

12/13/03 – Traded OF J. D. Drew and C/UT Eli Marrero to the Braves for Ps Ray King, Jason Marquis and Adam Wainwright.

In 2004, King had a fine season (62 innings, 2.61 ERA), and Marquis was the Cards' second-best starter. Despite having his season truncated by an elbow problem, Wainwright likely remains the Cards' best farmhand (which is, in part, damning with faint praise).

For the Braves, Drew was both potent and healthy for the first time in his career. Drew's line is what Cardinal fans had waited for with bated breath: 145 games, 31 homers, 118 walks, .305/.436/.569. Not only did Drew fail to become the greatest post-punk Cardinal, but he also cobbled together his best season on someone else's watch. And let's not forget Marrero, who hit .320/.374/.520 in 280 plate appearances. With Wainwright still gestating and Marquis still only 26 years of age, it's too early to call it definitively. At the first turn, however, it's squarely advantage Braves. Depending on how the younger components develop, that could change.

Advantage: Braves

8/7/04 – Traded Ps Jason Burch and Chris Narveson and 1B John Gall for OF Larry Walker.

Walker hit .280/.393/.560 after the trade, raked like a house afire in the postseason, and even prompted me to mix metaphors. He's signed through 2005, and barring injury or precipitous decline (neither strains credulity in Walker's case) he should be productive yet again. The Rockies seem to always be in the process of shedding burdensome contracts, a phenomenon made possible by their perpetual willingness to grant burdensome contracts. Yet again, Jocketty was willing to take on such a contract, but only after identifying the player in question as a potent contributor.

As for the package of prospects that went Colorado's way, only Narveson has any upside to speak of, but the Coors Field pitching wood-chipper will likely take care of that. In other words, they'll probably wind up being to prospects what Good Charlotte is to ass-beating rock music.

Advantage: Jocketty

That's 19 trades that can be classified as "major," not including the recent Mulder deal. Indulging in the zero-sum approach for a moment, by our count Trader Jock has rung up a 13–5–1 record in major deals. Jocketty's touch isn't nearly as deft on the free-agent scene, and the Cardinal farm system has generally been Mary Kate-thin on his watch, but when it comes to leveraging the trade market, he's the peerless leader. It's also why the Cardinals have been perennial contenders for the second half of his tenure. If not for his trading chops, Cardinal Nation certainly wouldn't have been graced with the historic 2004 season.

As for 2005, it's unreasonable to expect another 105 wins, but the team should still be in contention. Albert Pujols should continue being Albert Pujols, but an aging and at times fragile outfield should be a source of concern. The Cardinals' fourth outfielder could wind up logging in excess of 300 plate appearances, which means they'd do well to have someone reasonably productive in that role. The core of the offensive talent base—Pujols, Jim Edmonds, Scott Rolen, and Larry Walker—is back and will be productive if healthy.

Jocketty wisely read the market for Edgar Renteria as being over-inflated and passed on him. Less wise was the decision to sign the non-tendered David Eckstein to a three-year deal. That Womack took his late-career quasi-fluke season and went elsewhere is also fortunate for St. Louis. As for the rotation, they badly need Mark Mulder to return to 2003 form, for Chris Carpenter to remain healthy, and for Marquis not to regress. The '05 model won't be a great one, but it can be good enough to win a division devoid of great teams.

HITTERS

MARLON ANDERSON 2B/LF **Bats: L** **Throws: R** Born: 06-Jan-1974 Age: 31

YEAR	TM	LG	AGE	AB	H	2B	3B	HR	BB	SO	SB	CS	AVG	OBP	SLG	MLVR	EQBA	EQOBP	EQSLG	EQMLVR	VORP	DEFENSE	
2002	PHI	NL	28	539	139	30	6	8	42	71	5	1	.258	.315	.380	-.034	.266	.320	.398	-.099	21.9	130-2B -17	
2003	TBY	AL	29	482	130	27	3	6	41	60	19	3	.270	.328	.376	-.079	.273	.336	.382	-.086	19.0	124-2B -15	
2004	STL	NL	30	253	60	12	0	8	12	38	6	2	.237	.269	.379	-.171	.241	.267	.383	-.239	-0.9	25-2B -4	20-LF 2
2005	*NYM*	*NL*	*31*	*224*	*57*	*12*	*2*	*4*	*17*	*32*	*5*	*1*	*.254*	*.308*	*.379*	*-.146*	*.258*	*.310*	*.391*	*-.127*	*5.6*	*61-2B -5*	

Breakout: 19% *Improve: 38%* *Collapse: 36%*

Here we have the "unskilled worker" of the '04 Cardinals. Anderson didn't hit and didn't field any of his various and sundry defensive positions particularly well. That Tony La Russal viewed him as his best DH option in the World Series is a joke that's not particularly funny. Clue: When your DH is batting ninth, it's a sign you've tabbed the wrong guy.

DARIC BARTON C/1B? **Bats: L** **Throws: R** Born: 16-Aug-1985 Age: 19

YEAR	TM	LG	AGE	AB	H	2B	3B	HR	BB	SO	SB	CS	AVG	OBP	SLG	MLVR	EQBA	EQOBP	EQSLG	EQMLVR	VORP	DEFENSE
2003	JCY	APL	17	170	50	10	0	4	37	48	0	3	.294	.420	.424	.229	.229	.319	.337	-.211	-4.8	35-C -5
2004	PEO	MDW	18	313	98	23	0	13	69	44	4	4	.313	.445	.511	.399	.262	.369	.425	.026	21.0	51-C -4
2005	*OAK*	*AL*	*19*	*369*	*94*	*19*	*1*	*12*	*55*	*74*	*2*	*1*	*.255*	*.361*	*.408*	*-.008*	*.257*	*.365*	*.415*	*.002*	*19.9*	*104-C -13*

Breakout: 33% *Improve: 48%* *Collapse: 26%*

Tyler Johnson was snagged by the A's in the Rule 5, and Blake Hawksworth's shoulder is in tatters. This leads us to the concept of TINSTAACP. It doesn't roll off the tongue like "TINSTAAPP," but "There is no such thing as a Cardinals prospect" is an idea with legs. Now that Barton's gone west in the Mark Mulder deal, that's even more the case. He's a tremendous natural hitter whose bat will carry him. That he's a catcher is a temporary situation; it's doubtful he'll ever catch a game in the majors. At some point soon, he'll begin a transition to first or an outfield corner, but it may be that he eventually replaces Erubiel Durazo as the A's DH. Wherever he winds up, he'll hit for average, draw walks by the bushel and hit for gap power.

SHAUN BOYD OF **Bats: R** **Throws: R** Born: 15-Aug-1981 Age: 23

YEAR	TM	LG	AGE	AB	H	2B	3B	HR	BB	SO	SB	CS	AVG	OBP	SLG	MLVR	EQBA	EQOBP	EQSLG	EQMLVR	VORP	DEFENSE	
2002	PEO	MDW	20	520	163	36	5	12	54	78	32	7	.313	.379	.471	.291	.272	.325	.418	-.057	19.2	127-2B -17	
2003	PMB	FSL	21	416	107	17	2	5	54	70	28	14	.257	.343	.344	.046	.238	.309	.340	-.221	-10.1	50-CF -4	42-2B -11
2003	TEN	SOU	21	88	24	6	0	0	4	12	2	2	.273	.305	.341	-.082	.211	.215	.256	-.543	-10.6	26-CF -1	
2004	PMB	FSL	22	157	54	12	1	4	11	22	7	6	.344	.390	.510	.378	.314	.352	.484	.125	13.9	16-CF 1	14-LF -1
2004	TEN	SOU	22	158	30	5	1	0	13	40	9	5	.190	.256	.234	-.380	.151	.203	.170	-.711	-32.0	28-LF -2	
2005	*STL*	*NL*	*23*	*245*	*62*	*13*	*2*	*4*	*19*	*46*	*8*	*2*	*.254*	*.310*	*.375*	*-.148*	*.257*	*.311*	*.384*	*-.135*	*1.0*	*66-CF -7*	

Breakout: 30% *Improve: 52%* *Collapse: 18%*

Boyd hit in the Midwest League in 2002 and the FSL last season. On the downside, he was inconsistent in the low minors. and has twice failed to handle Double-A pitching. Since he'll be confined to a corner outfield spot in the majors, the bar for offensive production there looks beyond his grasp.

ROGER CEDENO OF **Bats: B** **Throws: R** Born: 16-Aug-1974 Age: 30

YEAR	TM	LG	AGE	AB	H	2B	3B	HR	BB	SO	SB	CS	AVG	OBP	SLG	MLVR	EQBA	EQOBP	EQSLG	EQMLVR	VORP	DEFENSE	
2002	NYM	NL	27	511	133	19	2	7	42	92	25	4	.260	.318	.346	-.083	.270	.325	.363	-.136	5.1	114-LF -7	
2003	NYM	NL	28	484	129	25	4	7	38	86	14	9	.267	.320	.378	-.064	.272	.325	.387	-.101	2.5	96-RF -7	12-CF 1
2004	STL	NL	29	200	53	9	2	3	19	41	5	1	.265	.327	.375	-.059	.267	.329	.376	-.112	4.0	18-RF -1	11-LF 1
2005	*STL*	*NL*	*30*	*209*	*53*	*10*	*2*	*4*	*19*	*41*	*5*	*2*	*.254*	*.317*	*.373*	*-.139*	*.256*	*.317*	*.382*	*-.127*	*1.1*	*58-RF -1*	

Breakout: 12% *Improve: 38%* *Collapse: 36%*

The Mets' decision to sign Roger Cedeno to a four-year, $18 million deal in December of 2001 was one of the worst contract decisions of recent memory. The fact that even the Mets came to realize this is even more of an indictment against the original decision. When the Mets traded Cedeno to the Cards last April, he had nearly $10 million remaining on his contract. The Mets agreed to pay almost $9 million of that balance. Outside of a fluke season-and-a-half five years ago, Cedeno's been a cipher his entire career.

CHRIS DUNCAN 1B/RF Bats: L Throws: R Born: 05-May-1981 Age: 24

YEAR	TM	LG	AGE	AB	H	2B	3B	HR	BB	SO	SB	CS	AVG	OBP	SLG	MLVR	EQBA	EQOBP	EQSLG	EQMLVR	VORP	DEFENSE	
2002	PEO	MDW	21	487	132	25	4	16	44	118	5	5	.271	.337	.437	.155	.234	.286	.385	-.205	-18.3	114-1B -10	
2003	PMB	FSL	22	425	108	20	0	2	44	115	4	4	.254	.322	.315	-.023	.228	.282	.297	-.340	-35.4	113-1B -11	
2004	TEN	SOU	23	387	112	23	0	16	64	94	8	4	.289	.393	.473	.202	.251	.344	.415	-.042	5.3	78-1B -6	16-RF 0
2005	*STL*	*NL*	*24*	*330*	*78*	*16*	*1*	*9*	*35*	*88*	*2*	*1*	*.237*	*.314*	*.375*	*-.152*	*.239*	*.314*	*.384*	*-.140*	*-1.8*	*89-1B -6*	

Breakout: 22% *Improve: 48%* *Collapse: 24%*

Coming into last season, Duncan hadn't shown much power above the low-A Midwest League, but he broke out in '04 at Double-A Tennessee. The power is still sub-optimal by first base standards, but the 64 walks are praiseworthy. He'll need to consolidate the gains he made last season and find a power spike somewhere along the way if he's ever to be a regular at the highest level.

JIM EDMONDS CF Bats: L Throws: L Born: 27-Jun-1970 Age: 35

YEAR	TM	LG	AGE	AB	H	2B	3B	HR	BB	SO	SB	CS	AVG	OBP	SLG	MLVR	EQBA	EQOBP	EQSLG	EQMLVR	VORP	DEFENSE
2002	STL	NL	32	476	148	31	2	28	86	134	4	3	.311	.420	.561	.405	.312	.419	.575	.360	73.7	127-CF 15
2003	STL	NL	33	447	123	32	2	39	77	127	1	3	.275	.385	.617	.374	.278	.387	.629	.345	60.7	118-CF 8
2004	STL	NL	34	498	150	38	3	42	101	150	8	3	.301	.418	.643	.480	.301	.416	.647	.440	88.9	142-CF 9
2005	*STL*	*NL*	*35*	*398*	*114*	*25*	*2*	*31*	*69*	*118*	*3*	*1*	*.287*	*.395*	*.592*	*.303*	*.290*	*.396*	*.606*	*.323*	*54.0*	*112-CF 3*

Breakout: 20% *Improve: 59%* *Collapse: 5%*

Let's compare Edmonds's Cardinal years to the best five-year spans of some other great center fielders. Using cumulative WARP3s:

Player (Years)	Total WARP3
W. Mays (1954–58)	64.7
M. Mantle (1955–59)	62.8
J. DiMaggio (1937–41)	60.0
T. Cobb (1909–13)	56.5
K. Griffey Jr. (1996–2000)	52.6
D. Snider (1952–56)	51.0
J. Edmonds (2000–04)	50.8

In terms of offense alone, over the last five seasons Edmonds has been roughly as good as Duke Snider in his prime. Throw Edmonds's superior glove work into the mix, and he's been more valuable over that span than both Snider and Ken Griffey Jr. in their best seasons. In other words, he's had one of the greatest peaks of any center fielder in baseball history, short of the Mays-Mantle clash of titans.

REID GORECKI CF Bats: R Throws: R Born: 22-Dec-1980 Age: 24

YEAR	TM	LG	AGE	AB	H	2B	3B	HR	BB	SO	SB	CS	AVG	OBP	SLG	MLVR	EQBA	EQOBP	EQSLG	EQMLVR	VORP	DEFENSE
2002	NWJ	NYP	21	274	77	8	13	8	20	57	22	11	.281	.327	.493	.245	.231	.268	.406	-.212	-10.3	69-CF 3
2003	PEO	MDW	22	480	128	19	8	15	51	90	23	11	.267	.338	.433	.153	.230	.288	.388	-.200	-8.3	127-CF -8
2004	PMB	FSL	23	440	122	23	3	8	46	80	23	9	.277	.343	.398	.098	.253	.307	.376	-.164	-2.5	111-CF 3
2005	*STL*	*NL*	*24*	*232*	*60*	*12*	*2*	*6*	*18*	*49*	*6*	*2*	*.259*	*.312*	*.410*	*-.093*	*.261*	*.313*	*.420*	*-.080*	*5.9*	*63-CF 0*

Breakout: 36% *Improve: 60%* *Collapse: 16%*

Gorecki profiled as a leadoff type, but that's more an indictment of his power numbers than lofty praise for his on-base skills. He's reasonably speedy, but he hasn't shown noteworthy power above the NY-Penn League, and his career OBP is only .338. Unless he makes gains in 2005, he profiles as a fifth outfielder, and that's with luck.

CODY HAERTHER LF Bats: L Throws: R Born: 14-Jul-1983 Age: 21

YEAR	TM	LG	AGE	AB	H	2B	3B	HR	BB	SO	SB	CS	AVG	OBP	SLG	MLVR	EQBA	EQOBP	EQSLG	EQMLVR	VORP	DEFENSE
2003	JCY	APL	19	226	75	12	6	3	22	30	2	1	.332	.390	.478	.292	.271	.316	.404	-.094	-6.1	41-LF -3 10-3B -1
2004	PEO	MDW	20	326	103	20	2	5	32	59	7	3	.316	.383	.436	.221	.275	.330	.384	-.093	-3.8	51-LF -3
2005	*STL*	*NL*	*21*	*385*	*95*	*21*	*3*	*7*	*29*	*77*	*3*	*1*	*.248*	*.304*	*.368*	*-.173*	*.250*	*.305*	*.376*	*-.161*	*-5.6*	*101-LF -6*

Breakout: 7% *Improve: 22%* *Collapse: 45%*

The secondary skills are somewhat lacking, but Haerther has a good line-drive swing and makes good contact. He's not a great defender in either outfield corner, but in this organization his bat will carry him. He's worth following as he climbs up the rungs of the system.

DEE HAYNES OF Bats: R Throws: R Born: 22-Feb-1978 Age: 27

YEAR	TM	LG	AGE	AB	H	2B	3B	HR	BB	SO	SB	CS	AVG	OBP	SLG	MLVR	EQBA	EQOBP	EQSLG	EQMLVR	VORP	DEFENSE
2002	NHV	EAS	24	504	157	29	4	21	25	67	3	2	.312	.355	.510	.272	.292	.327	.483	.059	16.9	117-LF -5
2003	MEM	PCL	25	441	111	24	3	18	15	50	3	1	.252	.279	.442	-.017	.237	.267	.418	-.192	-17.7	107-LF 1
2004	TEN	SOU	26	103	25	2	0	3	8	18	0	0	.243	.328	.350	-.087	.212	.276	.317	-.333	-8.5	15-RF 0
2004	MEM	PCL	26	182	61	5	0	14	7	25	1	0	.335	.359	.593	.368	.299	.317	.508	.086	7.8	24-RF 1 15-LF -1
2005	*STL*	*NL*	*27*	*133*	*34*	*6*	*1*	*5*	*6*	*21*	*0*	*0*	*.257*	*.293*	*.421*	*-.113*	*.259*	*.294*	*.431*	*-.100*	*1.6*	*38-LF -2*

Breakout: 14% *Improve: 32%* *Collapse: 45%*

Somebody to get excited about? Doubtful. Haynes showed flashes of power two years ago in the high minors, and this past season flashed some power at Memphis. Still, he's already 27 years of age, and his sense of restraint at the plate is worse than Dom DeLuise's. Eventually, he'll get a look as a pinch hitter, but he'll probably never be more than that.

RAY LANKFORD LF Bats: L Throws: L Born: 05-Jun-1967 Age: 38

YEAR	TM	LG	AGE	AB	H	2B	3B	HR	BB	SO	SB	CS	AVG	OBP	SLG	MLVR	EQBA	EQOBP	EQSLG	EQMLVR	VORP	DEFENSE
2002	SDP	NL	35	205	46	7	1	6	30	61	2	2	.224	.326	.356	-.070	.236	.334	.385	-.112	0.7	50-LF -4
2004	STL	NL	37	200	51	14	1	6	29	55	2	2	.255	.349	.425	.043	.259	.350	.433	-.000	6.9	44-LF 2
2005	*STL*	*NL*	*38*	*118*	*27*	*6*	*0*	*4*	*16*	*34*	*1*	*0*	*.227*	*.323*	*.376*	*-.142*	*.229*	*.323*	*.384*	*-.130*	*-0.7*	*36-LF -2*

Breakout: 19% *Improve: 39%* *Collapse: 38%*

In all likelihood, the curtain has dropped on a highly underrated career. He was the best center fielder in the National League in 1997 and '98, and he gave his employers a decade of strong plate production and capable defense. Heck, he even hit like a house afire this past April when no one expected anything from him. Lankford merited better from the St. Louis front office during the latter part of his career, and he deserves to be remembered as one of the best of the "has no prayer at the Hall of Fame" sub-stratum of greatness.

HECTOR LUNA SS/2B Bats: R Throws: R Born: 01-Feb-1980 Age: 25

YEAR	TM	LG	AGE	AB	H	2B	3B	HR	BB	SO	SB	CS	AVG	OBP	SLG	MLVR	EQBA	EQOBP	EQSLG	EQMLVR	VORP	DEFENSE
2002	KIN	CRL	22	468	129	15	6	11	39	79	32	11	.276	.334	.404	.093	.248	.300	.383	-.171	4.5	122-SS -6
2003	AKR	EAS	23	462	137	19	2	2	48	64	17	5	.297	.368	.359	.013	.259	.323	.324	-.202	0.0	125-SS -13
2004	STL	NL	24	173	43	7	2	3	13	37	6	3	.249	.304	.364	-.128	.253	.306	.374	-.169	2.3	20-SS -3 11-2B -1
2005	*STL*	*NL*	*25*	*238*	*61*	*11*	*2*	*4*	*19*	*44*	*7*	*2*	*.254*	*.314*	*.368*	*-.150*	*.256*	*.315*	*.377*	*-.137*	*8.3*	*65-SS -3*

Breakout: 21% *Improve: 47%* *Collapse: 29%*

Luna is a 2003 Rule 5 selection who managed to stick on the roster all season. His footwork on defense needs work, but he should be able to handle the shortstop position in the big leagues. He's a strong hitter, but his swing's mechanics don't lend themselves to power numbers. At least his on-base skills are passable by middle-infield standards. He's not a future star, but he could be an adequate regular for a few seasons. More likely, he'll be an adequate utility man.

JOHN MABRY — OF/1B — Bats: L — Throws: R — Born: 17-Oct-1970 — Age: 34

YEAR	TM	LG	AGE	AB	H	2B	3B	HR	BB	SO	SB	CS	AVG	OBP	SLG	MLVR	EQBA	EQOBP	EQSLG	EQMLVR	VORP	DEFENSE
2002	OAK	AL	31	193	53	13	1	11	14	37	1	1	.275	.322	.523	.115	.277	.331	.534	.124	11.2	15-1B 1 27-LF 1
2003	SEA	AL	32	104	22	6	0	3	15	21	0	0	.212	.328	.356	-.133	.231	.333	.365	-.144	0.3	
2004	MEM	PCL	33	136	46	7	0	12	17	29	0	0	.338	.406	.654	.540	.299	.349	.545	.193	11.6	19-1B -2
2004	STL	NL	33	240	71	11	0	13	26	63	0	1	.296	.363	.504	.191	.296	.358	.502	.143	18.2	25-LF 2 12-RF -1
2005	*STL*	*NL*	*34*	*197*	*51*	*9*	*1*	*9*	*24*	*47*	*0*	*0*	*.257*	*.340*	*.450*	*.005*	*.260*	*.341*	*.460*	*.020*	*10.4*	*56-LF -4*

Breakout: 15% *Improve: 42%* *Collapse: 37%*

In two of the last three seasons, Mabry's been a highly capable reserve. He's not a regular, particularly on a team like the Cardinals who are well stocked at the corner slots. Still, a worthy guy to have for pinch-hitting detail or spot-starting for Reggie Sanders.

MIKE MATHENY — C — Bats: R — Throws: R — Born: 22-Sep-1970 — Age: 34

YEAR	TM	LG	AGE	AB	H	2B	3B	HR	BB	SO	SB	CS	AVG	OBP	SLG	MLVR	EQBA	EQOBP	EQSLG	EQMLVR	VORP	DEFENSE
2002	STL	NL	31	315	77	12	1	3	32	49	1	3	.244	.313	.317	-.158	.253	.318	.331	-.206	1.6	88-C 9
2003	STL	NL	32	441	111	18	2	8	44	81	1	1	.252	.320	.356	-.103	.254	.324	.364	-.148	7.9	124-C 1
2004	STL	NL	33	385	95	22	1	5	23	83	0	2	.247	.292	.348	-.171	.250	.296	.351	-.223	-0.4	111-C 8
2005	*SFG*	*NL*	*34*	*248*	*59*	*11*	*1*	*4*	*21*	*53*	*0*	*1*	*.236*	*.299*	*.342*	*-.224*	*.239*	*.300*	*.355*	*-.204*	*0.5*	*68-C 3*

Breakout: 13% *Improve: 28%* *Collapse: 43%*

Pat Hentgen's good luck charm had a five-year run in St. Louis. His reputation with the glove is warranted; in terms of defense alone, he's been almost a win-and-a-half better than Pudge Rodriguez over the last half-decade. But the man cannot hit. At age 34, he certainly didn't warrant a three-year, $10.5 million contract from the Giants. On balance, the Cardinals will get the same level of production/run prevention from the infinitely cheaper Yadier Molina.

CODY McKAY — C — Bats: L — Throws: R — Born: 11-Jan-1974 — Age: 31

YEAR	TM	LG	AGE	AB	H	2B	3B	HR	BB	SO	SB	CS	AVG	OBP	SLG	MLVR	EQBA	EQOBP	EQSLG	EQMLVR	VORP	DEFENSE
2002	SAC	PCL	28	378	109	16	1	13	21	59	2	1	.288	.337	.439	.061	.268	.313	.408	-.096	8.0	71-C 2
2003	IND	INT	29	371	86	15	1	6	26	50	2	2	.232	.294	.326	-.177	.213	.278	.310	-.338	-18.7	92-C -10
2004	STL	NL	30	74	17	2	0	0	2	14	0	0	.230	.269	.257	-.354	.253	.256	.280	-.403	-3.1	12-C 3
2004	MEM	PCL	30	90	25	4	1	3	4	15	0	0	.278	.323	.444	-.002	.256	.290	.389	-.176	-0.1	16-C -4
2005	*STL*	*NL*	*31*	*133*	*30*	*6*	*1*	*2*	*7*	*23*	*0*	*0*	*.229*	*.281*	*.334*	*-.272*	*.232*	*.281*	*.342*	*-.261*	*-2.6*	*38-C -5*

Breakout: 16% *Improve: 34%* *Collapse: 43%*

In a long minor league career, McKay has displayed passable on-base skills for a catcher, but the power's not there. He's 31 without an impressive record of performance, so he can set his sights on earning a pension, perhaps becoming a poor man's Steve Lake. There are certainly worse fates, like finding something incisive to say about Cody McKay.

YADIER MOLINA — C — Bats: R — Throws: R — Born: 13-Jul-1982 — Age: 22

YEAR	TM	LG	AGE	AB	H	2B	3B	HR	BB	SO	SB	CS	AVG	OBP	SLG	MLVR	EQBA	EQOBP	EQSLG	EQMLVR	VORP	DEFENSE
2002	PEO	MDW	19	393	110	20	0	7	21	36	2	7	.280	.331	.384	.083	.236	.269	.333	-.310	-16.1	105-C 10
2003	TEN	SOU	20	364	100	13	1	2	25	45	0	1	.275	.327	.332	-.059	.245	.290	.311	-.295	-13.7	100-C 9
2004	MEM	PCL	21	129	39	6	0	1	17	14	0	0	.302	.387	.372	.038	.260	.329	.299	-.225	-2.1	36-C 6
2004	STL	NL	21	135	36	6	0	2	13	20	0	1	.267	.329	.356	-.086	.272	.322	.353	-.155	2.7	39-C 2
2005	*STL*	*NL*	*22*	*335*	*81*	*15*	*1*	*5*	*24*	*42*	*0*	*1*	*.243*	*.302*	*.336*	*-.221*	*.245*	*.303*	*.344*	*-.210*	*-0.9*	*89-C 2*

Breakout: 16% *Improve: 37%* *Collapse: 45%*

He's every bit a Molina, like his brothers in Anaheim: admirable defensive skills, inadequate bat. However, his age is such that you can hope for improvement. Expect Matheny levels of production with maybe a handful more homers, and at much lower cost. He's best suited to a backup role, but this organization seems to be seeking some sort of methadone to battle their Matheny addiction. They've found it.

JOHN NELSON SS Bats: R Throws: R Born: 03-Mar-1979 Age: 26

YEAR	TM	LG	AGE	AB	H	2B	3B	HR	BB	SO	SB	CS	AVG	OBP	SLG	MLVR	EQBA	EQOBP	EQSLG	EQMLVR	VORP	DEFENSE
2002	PEO	MDW	23	481	132	28	5	16	54	123	16	3	.274	.349	.453	.194	.235	.295	.395	-.173	4.4	129-SS -3
2003	TEN	SOU	24	506	120	22	1	5	44	117	10	5	.237	.301	.314	-.143	.210	.267	.292	-.387	-29.3	131-SS 5
2004	TEN	SOU	25	206	62	16	3	8	31	56	6	2	.301	.396	.524	.281	.264	.354	.462	.050	17.1	54-SS 4
2005	*STL*	*NL*	*26*	*173*	*42*	*9*	*1*	*4*	*17*	*46*	*3*	*1*	*.239*	*.309*	*.380*	*-.153*	*.242*	*.310*	*.389*	*-.140*	*6.8*	*49-SS -1*

Breakout: 22% *Improve: 43%* *Collapse: 33%*

An eighth-round pick in 2001 out of the University of Kansas, Nelson did little as a pro prior to last season. However, he broke out at Double-A Tennessee last year, showing good plate discipline and excellent power. After he missed time with a broken hand in the AFL at the end of '03, it's encouraging that his power stroke recovered to such a degree. While he has average range, his arm is excellent, and he figures to stick at the position. In isolation, his numbers from last season look aberrant, but the hitting tools always have been there. He's old for a prospect, but he has a future. Whether that's as a regular or as an elite utility player remains to be seen.

ALBERT PUJOLS 1B Bats: R Throws: R Born: 16-Jan-1980 Age: 25

YEAR	TM	LG	AGE	AB	H	2B	3B	HR	BB	SO	SB	CS	AVG	OBP	SLG	MLVR	EQBA	EQOBP	EQSLG	EQMLVR	VORP	DEFENSE
2002	STL	NL	22	590	185	40	2	34	72	69	2	4	.314	.394	.561	.369	.316	.393	.575	.325	72.6	89-LF -3 33-3B 2
2003	STL	NL	23	591	212	51	1	43	79	65	5	1	.359	.439	.667	.612	.360	.438	.677	.592	108.2	98-LF -2 41-1B 3
2004	STL	NL	24	592	196	51	2	46	84	52	5	5	.331	.415	.657	.535	.333	.415	.661	.500	103.5	150-1B 10
2005	*STL*	*NL*	*25*	*546*	*182*	*41*	*2*	*39*	*76*	*59*	*4*	*1*	*.334*	*.419*	*.633*	*.443*	*.337*	*.420*	*.648*	*.466*	*83.7*	*149-1B 5*

Breakout: 16% *Improve: 48%* *Collapse: 15%*

I suppose writing the Barry Bonds comment would be more taxing in terms of the use of superlatives, but what do you say about this guy? In terms of career numbers compiled before age 25, Pujols ranks eighth in home runs, ninth in doubles and sixth in extra-base hits. Additionally, among those who logged at least 2,000 plate appearances before age 25, Pujols places third in SLG and ninth in OBP. In other words, stay tuned: he's a luminary in the making.

EDGAR RENTERIA SS Bats: R Throws: R Born: 07-Aug-1975 Age: 29

YEAR	TM	LG	AGE	AB	H	2B	3B	HR	BB	SO	SB	CS	AVG	OBP	SLG	MLVR	EQBA	EQOBP	EQSLG	EQMLVR	VORP	DEFENSE
2002	STL	NL	26	544	166	36	2	11	49	57	22	7	.305	.364	.439	.143	.309	.364	.452	.095	49.4	145-SS -14
2003	STL	NL	27	587	194	47	1	13	65	54	34	7	.330	.394	.480	.260	.332	.395	.488	.222	75.3	152-SS 0
2004	STL	NL	28	586	168	37	0	10	39	78	17	11	.287	.327	.401	-.005	.293	.329	.407	-.048	27.3	142-SS -8
2005	*BOS*	*AL*	*29*	*546*	*165*	*34*	*2*	*12*	*46*	*67*	*19*	*6*	*.302*	*.356*	*.440*	*.061*	*.296*	*.354*	*.443*	*.049*	*37.7*	*142-SS -4*

Breakout: 10% *Improve: 33%* *Collapse: 28%*

His platoon issues are overstated, but so is his defensive prowess. The Red Sox inked him for four years and $40 million. If that was the going rate, the Cardinals were wise to pass on him. Renteria's had his moments of brilliance, but his lone MVP-caliber season, in 2003, is beginning to look more and more aberrant. Someone like Julio Lugo will provide infinitely more value on the dollar.

SCOTT ROLEN 3B Bats: R Throws: R Born: 04-Apr-1975 Age: 30

YEAR	TM	LG	AGE	AB	H	2B	3B	HR	BB	SO	SB	CS	AVG	OBP	SLG	MLVR	EQBA	EQOBP	EQSLG	EQMLVR	VORP	DEFENSE
2002	PHI	NL	27	375	97	21	4	17	52	68	5	2	.259	.358	.472	.160	.264	.360	.493	.103	32.9	96-3B 9
2002	STL	NL	27	205	57	8	4	14	20	34	3	2	.278	.354	.561	.263	.280	.354	.575	.222	22.6	55-3B 10
2003	STL	NL	28	559	160	49	1	28	82	104	13	3	.286	.382	.528	.265	.289	.383	.537	.226	68.0	150-3B 8
2004	STL	NL	29	500	157	32	4	34	72	92	4	3	.314	.409	.598	.425	.315	.408	.601	.383	73.7	139-3B 19
2005	*STL*	*NL*	*30*	*471*	*138*	*30*	*3*	*27*	*66*	*89*	*6*	*1*	*.293*	*.386*	*.545*	*.237*	*.296*	*.387*	*.558*	*.255*	*50.4*	*129-3B 7*

Breakout: 15% *Improve: 53%* *Collapse: 9%*

Scott Rolen is a genuinely great player. He now boasts a career batting line of .286/.378/.520, and his defensive reputation squares with statistical realities. He's under a contract that will probably extend beyond the point of his peak performance years, but it'll certainly be fun getting there. Provided injuries don't derail him, he's bound for Cooperstown.

BRENDAN RYAN SS Bats: R Throws: R Born: 26-Mar-1982 Age: 23

YEAR	TM	LG	AGE	AB	H	2B	3B	HR	BB	SO	SB	CS	AVG	OBP	SLG	MLVR	EQBA	EQOBP	EQSLG	EQMLVR	VORP	DEFENSE
2003	NWJ	NYP	21	193	60	14	4	0	14	25	11	3	.311	.363	.425	.211	.268	.297	.374	-.175	3.1	30-SS -6
2004	PEO	MDW	22	426	137	21	4	2	24	42	30	7	.322	.356	.404	.145	.276	.306	.350	-.187	1.9	104-SS -11
2005	*STL*	*NL*	*23*	*334*	*85*	*18*	*3*	*2*	*14*	*41*	*9*	*3*	*.254*	*.289*	*.342*	*-.231*	*.257*	*.290*	*.350*	*-.220*	*1.2*	*87-SS -9*

Breakout: 8% *Improve: 24%* *Collapse: 51%*

A seventh-round choice in 2003 out of a small college in Idaho, Ryan is athletic with good defensive instincts at short. He hasn't played above low-A Peoria yet, but if he's to pass muster higher up in the system, despite his .322 career average, he'll need to improve his plate discipline and show at least a semblance of gap power.

REGGIE SANDERS OF Bats: R Throws: R Born: 01-Dec-1967 Age: 37

YEAR	TM	LG	AGE	AB	H	2B	3B	HR	BB	SO	SB	CS	AVG	OBP	SLG	MLVR	EQBA	EQOBP	EQSLG	EQMLVR	VORP	DEFENSE
2002	SFG	NL	34	505	126	23	6	23	47	121	18	6	.250	.324	.455	.070	.257	.328	.476	.017	20.1	127-RF 4
2003	PIT	NL	35	453	129	27	4	31	38	110	15	5	.285	.345	.567	.253	.283	.343	.570	.201	39.9	77-RF 0 34-LF -1
2004	STL	NL	36	446	116	27	3	22	33	118	21	5	.260	.315	.482	.067	.261	.316	.487	.015	23.0	78-RF -4 35-LF 3
2005	*STL*	*NL*	*37*	*336*	*88*	*17*	*3*	*17*	*31*	*82*	*13*	*4*	*.262*	*.330*	*.484*	*.038*	*.265*	*.331*	*.496*	*.053*	*18.1*	*90-RF -1*

Breakout: 13% *Improve: 51%* *Collapse: 20%*

He's not a potent hitter against same-side pitching, but he handles lefties quite well, and he's a good glove in either outfield corner. He actually showed reverse platoon numbers last year, but that's likely a single-season fluke, and given age-related decline, it's probable he'll be a net liability against right-handed pitching next season. But he'll still have value. It's easy to pull for Sanders, one of the game's genuine good guys.

SKIP SCHUMAKER CF Bats: L Throws: R Born: 03-Feb-1980 Age: 25

YEAR	TM	LG	AGE	AB	H	2B	3B	HR	BB	SO	SB	CS	AVG	OBP	SLG	MLVR	EQBA	EQOBP	EQSLG	EQMLVR	VORP	DEFENSE
2002	POT	CRL	22	551	158	22	4	2	45	84	26	16	.287	.342	.352	-.003	.241	.291	.308	-.299	-39.9	123-RF -13 10-CF -1
2003	TEN	SOU	23	342	86	20	3	2	37	54	6	6	.251	.330	.345	-.052	.228	.297	.327	-.268	-13.3	82-CF -2
2004	TEN	SOU	24	516	163	29	6	4	60	61	19	14	.316	.389	.419	.147	.284	.352	.380	-.051	15.8	117-CF -3 10-RF 1
2005	*STL*	*NL*	*25*	*217*	*55*	*12*	*2*	*2*	*21*	*31*	*4*	*2*	*.253*	*.320*	*.353*	*-.161*	*.256*	*.321*	*.361*	*-.149*	*1.3*	*60-CF -5*

Breakout: 15% *Improve: 39%* *Collapse: 31%*

Lest you get too excited about Schumaker's season at Double-A Tennessee last season, let's add some perspective. First, Tennessee is a pretty fair park for hitters. Second, at 24, he wasn't that young for the level, and he was repeating it. Third, his numbers were radically different from the rest of his career. Fourth, he showed little in the way of secondary skills. In other words, find something besides Skip Schumaker to get you excited.

SCOTT SEABOL INF Bats: R Throws: R Born: 17-May-1975 Age: 30

YEAR	TM	LG	AGE	AB	H	2B	3B	HR	BB	SO	SB	CS	AVG	OBP	SLG	MLVR	EQBA	EQOBP	EQSLG	EQMLVR	VORP	DEFENSE
2002	COH	INT	27	428	111	29	1	15	29	89	3	3	.259	.309	.437	.011	.232	.286	.404	-.180	-12.4	86-1B 3 12-SS -2
2003	MEM	PCL	28	307	92	22	1	16	32	64	2	0	.300	.376	.534	.323	.278	.349	.498	.104	27.2	78-3B 4
2004	MEM	PCL	29	514	156	26	1	31	37	93	6	3	.304	.356	.539	.232	.274	.322	.468	.011	28.9	91-3B -5 36-2B -1
2005	*STL*	*NL*	*30*	*103*	*26*	*6*	*1*	*4*	*8*	*24*	*1*	*0*	*.255*	*.311*	*.428*	*-.075*	*.257*	*.312*	*.438*	*-.061*	*5.3*	*31-3B -3*

Breakout: 16% *Improve: 38%* *Collapse: 35%*

Give him a shot, already. He spent all of last season squirreled away in Memphis, but he's a career .480 slugger in the minors. As long as you're going to lose a talent like Tyler Johnson in Rule 5 for the sake of keeping Seabol on the 40-man, you might as well get some mileage out of him. He'd certainly be a better use of active-roster space than Roger Cedeno.

SO TAGUCHI OF **Bats: R** **Throws: R** Born: 02-Jul-1969 Age: 35

YEAR	TM	LG	AGE	AB	H	2B	3B	HR	BB	SO	SB	CS	AVG	OBP	SLG	MLVR	EQBA	EQOBP	EQSLG	EQMLVR	VORP	DEFENSE
2002	MEM	PCL	33	304	75	17	0	5	13	44	6	3	.247	.286	.352	-.159	.232	.266	.324	-.332	-16.8	82-CF 2
2002	NHV	EAS	33	107	33	10	0	1	9	15	3	1	.308	.375	.430	.185	.278	.321	.389	-.101	1.5	26-CF 1
2003	MEM	PCL	34	258	66	8	2	2	22	36	14	5	.256	.318	.326	-.111	.247	.308	.317	-.249	-8.0	60-CF -2
2003	STL	NL	34	54	14	3	1	3	4	11	0	0	.259	.310	.519	.108	.255	.305	.527	.047	3.2	
2004	STL	NL	35	179	52	10	2	3	12	23	6	3	.291	.337	.419	.012	.293	.340	.424	-.003	6.3	21-LF 1 18-CF 1
2005	*STL*	*NL*	*35*	*138*	*34*	*7*	*1*	*2*	*8*	*24*	*3*	*1*	*.244*	*.293*	*.352*	*-.217*	*.247*	*.293*	*.360*	*-.205*	*0.4*	*40-CF -4*

Breakout: 5% *Improve: 22%* *Collapse: 52%*

Taguchi's a better player than he gets credit for in stathead circles. He's a reasonably strong defender at all three outfield positions, and his career batting line of .290/.339/.440 is just fine for a reserve (although, to be fair, he's logged only 284 plate appearances in the U.S. major leagues). Still, the Cardinals' starting outfield in 2005 will be comprised of two fragile regulars and one with platoon issues. What they badly need is a fourth outfielder who bats lefty, can play all three positions and can rake by bench player standards. Ricky Ledee would've been an ideal fit. Taguchi will be capable in the role, but St. Louis missed an opportunity to upgrade.

LARRY WALKER RF **Bats: L** **Throws: R** Born: 01-Dec-1966 Age: 38

YEAR	TM	LG	AGE	AB	H	2B	3B	HR	BB	SO	SB	CS	AVG	OBP	SLG	MLVR	EQBA	EQOBP	EQSLG	EQMLVR	VORP	DEFENSE
2002	COL	NL	35	477	161	40	4	26	65	73	6	5	.338	.421	.602	.393	.316	.400	.576	.337	59.7	116-RF 5
2003	COL	NL	36	454	129	25	7	16	98	87	7	4	.284	.422	.476	.204	.265	.405	.448	.124	37.0	123-RF -4
2004	COL	NL	37	108	35	9	3	6	25	23	2	0	.324	.464	.630	.447	.302	.441	.575	.383	18.6	34-RF 3
2004	STL	NL	37	150	42	7	1	11	24	34	4	0	.280	.393	.560	.318	.278	.392	.563	.265	19.2	34-RF -2
2005	*STL*	*NL*	*38*	*272*	*73*	*15*	*2*	*12*	*43*	*53*	*3*	*1*	*.270*	*.378*	*.478*	*.116*	*.273*	*.379*	*.489*	*.132*	*23.6*	*78-RF -3*

Breakout: 12% *Improve: 53%* *Collapse: 27%*

He's not the fielder he once was, but when healthy, Walker can still take and rake. He's 38 and perpetually at risk for breaking down, but if he can answer the bell for 135 games next season he'll be a tremendous boon to the Cardinals. His acquisition was sound, and proved that the Cardinals understand that runs are runs are runs. Some argued they should've bolstered the rotation at the deadline, but implicit in that complaint, in light of the Walker acquisition anyway, is the idea that there's somehow a way to score too many runs. There's not. Trust us.

TONY WOMACK 2B **Bats: L** **Throws: R** Born: 25-Sep-1969 Age: 35

YEAR	TM	LG	AGE	AB	H	2B	3B	HR	BB	SO	SB	CS	AVG	OBP	SLG	MLVR	EQBA	EQOBP	EQSLG	EQMLVR	VORP	DEFENSE
2002	ARI	NL	32	590	160	23	5	5	46	80	29	12	.271	.325	.353	-.099	.267	.319	.350	-.168	14.7	139-SS -13
2003	ARI	NL	33	219	52	10	3	2	8	27	8	3	.237	.270	.338	-.263	.229	.261	.330	-.335	-2.9	49-SS -6
2003	CHC	NL	33	51	12	2	1	0	1	11	2	1	.235	.250	.314	-.311	.235	.228	.275	-.477	-1.4	
2003	COL	NL	33	79	15	2	0	0	0	9	3	1	.190	.200	.215	-.563	.165	.152	.190	-.787	-6.6	10-SS 0
2004	STL	NL	34	553	170	22	3	5	36	60	26	5	.307	.349	.385	.024	.310	.352	.387	-.020	33.8	123-2B -13
2005	*NYY*	*AL*	*35*	*391*	*102*	*16*	*3*	*5*	*22*	*50*	*14*	*5*	*.261*	*.303*	*.353*	*-.178*	*.264*	*.308*	*.362*	*-.165*	*5.6*	*101-2B -7*

Breakout: 3% *Improve: 19%* *Collapse: 49%*

In terms of VORP, he was the tenth-best second baseman in baseball last season, but it was a year out of step with the rest of his statistical record.

Womack in 2004: .307/.345/.385, 606 plate appearances
Womack before 2004: .270/.315/.359, 4,352 plate appearances.

It's remotely conceivable that, at age 35, Womack has established a new level of ability, but it's not bloody likely. Expect the Yankees to be disappointed by their new second baseman.

PITCHERS

RICK ANKIEL

Bats: L | Throws: L | Born: 19-Jul-1979 | Age: 25

YEAR	TM	LG	AGE	G	GS	IP	H	BB	SO	HR	ERA	EQERA	EQH9	EQBB9	EQSO9	EQHR9	PERA	VORP	STF
2003	TEN	SOU	23	20	10	54.3	45	49	64	5	6.30	7.51	9.1	8.6	7.7	1.6	6.79	-6.7	-18
2004	STL	NL	24	5	0	10.0	10	1	9	2	5.40	5.59	9.3	0.9	7.4	1.9	4.66	0.3	14
2005	*STL*	*NL*	*25*	*8*	*3*	*26.0*	*22*	*10*	*23*	*3*	*3.79*	*4.05*	*7.8*	*3.1*	*7.0*	*1.0*	*3.93*	*4.5*	*10*

Breakout: 17% *Improve: 40%* *Collapse: 24%*

Are better days ahead? It's possible his grievous control problems of yore were at least in part of a physical origin. In his first season back from Tommy John surgery, in 33.2 innings spread across four different levels, Ankiel struck out 32 and walked only three. In tandem with an excellent performance in the Puerto Rican winter leagues, it points to his being back on track. In all likelihood, he'll work exclusively out of the bullpen in 2005, but if all goes well, he could be in the St. Louis rotation the following season.

KIKO CALERO

Bats: R | Throws: R | Born: 09-Jan-1975 | Age: 30

YEAR	TM	LG	AGE	G	GS	IP	H	BB	SO	HR	ERA	EQERA	EQH9	EQBB9	EQSO9	EQHR9	PERA	VORP	STF
2002	OMA	PCL	27	20	18	125.7	112	35	109	11	3.44	4.11	8.5	2.7	6.2	1.1	4.03	20.6	24
2002	WIC	TXS	27	5	2	16.0	10	5	15	2	2.25	3.86	8.4	3.2	7.1	2.6	5.14	0.7	5
2003	STL	NL	28	26	1	38.3	29	20	51	5	2.82	2.89	7.2	4.1	10.8	1.2	3.86	12.0	36
2004	MEM	PCL	29	12	3	25.3	20	11	33	3	2.49	3.38	7.5	4.1	9.4	1.5	4.12	3.9	16
2004	STL	NL	29	41	0	45.3	27	10	47	5	2.78	3.00	6.6	1.9	8.8	1.1	3.00	14.7	24
2005	*OAK*	*AL*	*30*	*29*	*5*	*62.3*	*55*	*24*	*57*	*10*	*3.85*	*3.81*	*8.0*	*3.1*	*7.4*	*1.3*	*4.02*	*15.9*	*6*

Breakout: 26% *Improve: 42%* *Collapse: 23%*

Two years ago, Calero was a six-year minor league free agent—the quintessence of "freely available talent." In fact, at that time we featured him as one of the best freely available arms on the market. Since then, Calero has pitched 83.2 innings in the majors, recorded a 2.80 ERA and struck out 98 against 27 unintentional walks. In short, he's been one of the best scrapheap finds around. He deserves a higher-leverage role in the bullpen, and he's likely to get that in 2005 now that he's in Oakland.

CARMEN CALI

Bats: L | Throws: L | Born: 02-Nov-1978 | Age: 26

YEAR	TM	LG	AGE	G	GS	IP	H	BB	SO	HR	ERA	EQERA	EQH9	EQBB9	EQSO9	EQHR9	PERA	VORP	STF
2002	PEO	MDW	23	24	0	35.3	36	14	27	0	1.78	6.27	9.8	4.4	4.1	0.3	5.18	1.5	-22
2002	POT	CRL	23	29	0	35.0	31	21	24	1	4.11	5.62	8.7	6.8	4.5	0.6	5.06	1.9	-23
2003	PMB	FSL	24	62	0	70.3	72	32	70	2	4.99	7.83	9.5	4.6	6.2	0.8	5.00	4.4	-15
2004	MEM	PCL	25	17	0	20.0	17	4	20	4	2.70	3.38	8.7	1.9	7.2	1.9	4.34	2.6	3
2004	TEN	SOU	25	38	0	46.3	43	19	47	3	2.92	4.33	8.9	3.9	6.4	0.8	4.53	5.2	-4
2005	*STL*	*NL*	*26*	*13*	*2*	*25.3*	*25*	*12*	*19*	*3*	*4.17*	*4.46*	*8.8*	*3.7*	*6.2*	*0.9*	*4.69*	*3.5*	*-3*

Breakout: 22% *Improve: 52%* *Collapse: 27%*

Cali is a generic lefty reliever with good strikeout potential but prone to bouts of wildness. He's undersized, but his fastball touches the mid-90s on occasion. The organization likes him, and he'll likely get a shot in 2006 to stick on the major league roster as a LOOGY.

CHRIS CARPENTER

Bats: R | Throws: R | Born: 27-Apr-1975 | Age: 30

YEAR	TM	LG	AGE	G	GS	IP	H	BB	SO	HR	ERA	EQERA	EQH9	EQBB9	EQSO9	EQHR9	PERA	VORP	STF
2002	TOR	AL	27	13	13	73.3	89	27	45	11	5.28	4.95	10.0	3.1	5.2	1.2	5.33	3.7	-1
2004	STL	NL	29	28	28	182.0	169	38	152	24	3.46	3.80	8.8	1.7	6.9	1.1	4.21	41.6	18
2005	*STL*	*NL*	*30*	*27*	*27*	*163.7*	*164*	*45*	*119*	*19*	*3.91*	*4.18*	*9.0*	*2.2*	*5.9*	*1.0*	*4.20*	*25.1*	*13*

Breakout: 5% *Improve: 36%* *Collapse: 12%*

Coming off a pair of shoulder surgeries, Carpenter was one of the game's most pleasant surprises in 2004. Despite finishing with the fewest innings of any Cardinal rotation member, Carpenter led the staff in VORP, and also ranked fifth in the NL in K/BB ratio. His health concerns aren't going anywhere (nerve irritation in his arm snuffed out the last month-and-a-half of his season), but he still figures to be a bargain in 2005.

BRANDON DeJAYNES Bats: R Throws: R Born: 10-Sep-1980 Age: 24

YEAR	TM	LG	AGE	G	GS	IP	H	BB	SO	HR	ERA	EQERA	EQH9	EQBB9	EQSO9	EQHR9	PERA	VORP	STF
2003	JCY	APL	22	25	0	32.7	24	13	27	0	1.10	4.25	7.9	4.9	4.2	0.3	3.64	6.5	-9
2004	PEO	MDW	23	49	1	71.3	38	57	106	6	4.29	6.34	7.7	9.9	8.6	1.8	6.20	-4.1	-11
2005	*STL*	*NL*	*24*	*7*	*2*	*15.3*	*11*	*12*	*13*	*2*	*4.97*	*5.31*	*6.7*	*6.2*	*6.6*	*1.4*	*5.15*	*1.1*	*-12*

Breakout: 19% *Improve: 39%* *Collapse: 19%*

The Cards signed DeJaynes in 2003 as an undrafted free agent. By glancing at his numbers, you'd think he was a Nuke LaLoosh type. However, his fastball rarely touches 90, and it's his curveball he relies upon. It can be a devastating pitch at times, but he struggles with his command. Fathom that relief line last season at low-A Peoria: obviously, without drastically improved control, he'll never advance, but he does have the ability to miss bats.

CAL ELDRED Bats: R Throws: R Born: 24-Nov-1967 Age: 37

YEAR	TM	LG	AGE	G	GS	IP	H	BB	SO	HR	ERA	EQERA	EQH9	EQBB9	EQSO9	EQHR9	PERA	VORP	STF
2003	STL	NL	35	62	0	67.3	62	31	67	9	3.74	4.39	8.4	3.7	8.1	1.2	4.52	10.0	5
2004	STL	NL	36	52	0	67.0	71	17	54	11	3.76	4.20	9.7	2.1	6.6	1.4	4.90	11.4	-1
2005	*STL*	*NL*	*37*	*37*	*3*	*61.7*	*61*	*19*	*49*	*8*	*3.88*	*4.15*	*8.9*	*2.5*	*6.4*	*1.1*	*4.39*	*11.1*	*1*

Breakout: 32% *Improve: 54%* *Collapse: 29%*

Presumably, at this stage of his career, his arm is attached at the joints by school glue and cargo hooks. Nevertheless, Eldred has turned in a nice pair of years as a Cardinal reliever. The organization thought enough of his work to re-up him for '05. The pattern down the stretch was to give the more critical innings to other right-handers, but there are worse guys to have as the fourth option out of the pen.

DANNY HAREN Bats: R Throws: R Born: 17-Sep-1980 Age: 24

YEAR	TM	LG	AGE	G	GS	IP	H	BB	SO	HR	ERA	EQERA	EQH9	EQBB9	EQSO9	EQHR9	PERA	VORP	STF
2002	PEO	MDW	21	14	14	101.7	89	12	89	6	1.95	4.79	9.9	1.4	5.0	1.5	4.99	6.2	5
2002	POT	CRL	21	14	14	92.0	90	19	82	8	3.62	5.29	9.8	2.3	5.7	1.7	5.08	4.9	4
2003	MEM	PCL	22	8	8	45.7	50	8	35	6	4.92	5.65	10.3	1.9	6.1	1.5	5.65	-0.2	8
2003	STL	NL	22	14	14	72.7	84	22	43	9	5.08	5.45	10.0	2.4	4.8	1.1	5.07	2.0	2
2003	TEN	SOU	22	8	8	55.0	36	6	49	2	0.82	2.34	7.6	1.1	5.9	0.7	3.06	14.1	33
2004	MEM	PCL	23	21	21	128.0	137	33	150	19	4.15	4.55	9.2	2.5	8.1	1.4	4.69	12.6	16
2004	STL	NL	23	14	5	46.0	45	17	32	4	4.50	4.50	9.2	3.1	5.7	0.8	4.70	6.3	-3
2005	*OAK*	*AL*	*24*	*27*	*15*	*104.0*	*107*	*32*	*82*	*14*	*4.45*	*4.41*	*9.4*	*2.4*	*6.3*	*1.1*	*4.32*	*17.7*	*7*

Breakout: 14% *Improve: 40%* *Collapse: 24%*

He's suffered some fits and starts during his call-ups, but this is a pitcher who deserves an extended look in the major league rotation. Haren's a "four-pitch guy" without a truly dominant offering, which means it's possible he might not make the transition to the majors. But, by golly, let him prove it first. You don't post a career 5.37 strikeout-to-walk ratio in the minors by accident. For what it's worth, he looked much better during his 2004 major league look-see than he did in '03. Now that he's in Oakland, Haren will have every opportunity to stick in the rotation on a long-term basis. Don't be shocked if he roughly approximates the quality of Mark Mulder v.2004.

BLAKE HAWKSWORTH Bats: R Throws: R Born: 01-Mar-1983 Age: 22

YEAR	TM	LG	AGE	G	GS	IP	H	BB	SO	HR	ERA	EQERA	EQH9	EQBB9	EQSO9	EQHR9	PERA	VORP	STF
2002	JCY	APL	19	13	12	66.0	58	18	61	8	3.14	6.22	10.0	3.2	4.4	2.6	5.92	-2.1	-9
2003	PEO	MDW	20	10	10	54.7	37	12	57	0	2.30	4.50	7.6	2.5	6.5	0.2	3.06	14.1	32
2003	PMB	FSL	20	6	6	32.0	28	11	32	2	3.94	5.52	9.5	3.7	6.4	1.5	4.91	2.2	14
2005	*STL*	*NL*	*22*	*9*	*8*	*48.7*	*46*	*17*	*37*	*8*	*4.55*	*4.86*	*8.5*	*2.8*	*6.2*	*1.5*	*4.69*	*5.3*	*6*

Breakout: 14% *Improve: 41%* *Collapse: 25%*

Loads of potential and easily the coolest name since Dack Rambo. The problem, however, is that Hawksworth is trying to fight his way through a serious and confounding shoulder malady. He was shut down early in the season because of poor circulation in his shoulder. At this juncture, his future is quite uncertain. What is certain is that even if he does manage to return to form one of these days, he'll have a permanent red flag attached.

JASON ISRINGHAUSEN

Bats: R **Throws: R** Born: 07-Sep-1972 Age: 32

YEAR	TM	LG	AGE	G	GS	IP	H	BB	SO	HR	ERA	EQERA	EQH9	EQBB9	EQSO9	EQHR9	PERA	VORP	STF
2002	STL	NL	29	60	0	65.3	46	18	68	0	2.48	3.21	7.2	2.2	8.6	0.1	2.77	17.0	25
2003	STL	NL	30	40	0	42.0	31	18	41	2	2.36	3.12	7.1	3.3	8.0	0.4	3.12	12.2	14
2004	STL	NL	31	74	0	75.3	55	23	71	5	2.87	3.30	7.5	2.5	7.9	0.6	3.30	20.7	15
2005	*STL*	*NL*	*32*	*43*	*0*	*56.7*	*50*	*20*	*51*	*5*	*3.47*	*3.71*	*8.0*	*2.7*	*7.2*	*0.8*	*3.71*	*11.9*	*7*

Breakout: 19% *Improve: 41%* *Collapse: 31%*

He'll never be the picture of durability, but he has been a heck of a reliever since coming to the Cardinals. He'll be entering the final year of his contract this season (although the Cards do hold an option on him for 2006). While name-value closers rarely provide value on the dollar, he's been quite good. He underwent major hip surgery, this off-season so his health and mechanics will be worth monitoring in the early going. Still, his peripherals point to continued success.

TYLER JOHNSON

Bats: B **Throws: L** Born: 07-Jun-1981 Age: 24

YEAR	TM	LG	AGE	G	GS	IP	H	BB	SO	HR	ERA	EQERA	EQH9	EQBB9	EQSO9	EQHR9	PERA	VORP	STF
2002	PEO	MDW	21	22	18	121.3	96	42	132	7	2.00	4.57	9.3	4.1	6.2	1.5	5.48	1.4	2
2003	PMB	FSL	22	22	10	79.0	79	38	81	2	3.08	4.94	9.3	4.8	6.5	0.7	4.70	7.5	2
2003	TEN	SOU	22	20	0	27.3	16	15	39	1	1.65	3.20	6.8	5.3	9.2	0.7	3.91	4.8	16
2004	TEN	SOU	23	53	0	56.3	48	37	77	4	4.80	5.60	8.5	6.1	8.7	0.8	4.92	4.0	0
2005	*OAK*	*AL*	*24*	*24*	*7*	*62.0*	*58*	*36*	*52*	*8*	*4.86*	*4.82*	*8.5*	*4.6*	*6.7*	*1.1*	*4.75*	*7.3*	*-2*

Breakout: 12% *Improve: 44%* *Collapse: 28%*

When your system is as thin as the Cardinals', why do you leave a talent like Johnson unprotected in the Rule 5 Draft? Johnson makes his hay with a nasty 12-6 curve, which he sets up with a low-90s fastball. His control could stand improvement, but he's whiffed 402 batters in 338 career innings. It's hardly surprising that the A's scooped him up; he'll be a force in the bullpen one day.

JIMMY JOURNELL

Bats: R **Throws: R** Born: 29-Dec-1977 Age: 27

YEAR	TM	LG	AGE	G	GS	IP	H	BB	SO	HR	ERA	EQERA	EQH9	EQBB9	EQSO9	EQHR9	PERA	VORP	STF
2002	MEM	PCL	24	7	7	36.7	38	18	32	3	3.68	4.37	9.3	4.6	6.2	1.0	5.40	0.8	-1
2002	NHV	EAS	24	10	10	66.7	50	18	66	3	2.70	3.92	7.7	2.6	7.1	0.7	3.34	15.6	30
2003	MEM	PCL	25	40	7	78.0	80	32	70	3	3.92	5.06	8.9	4.1	6.9	0.5	4.58	8.5	0
2005	*STL*	*NL*	*27*	*17*	*10*	*68.0*	*63*	*31*	*66*	*6*	*3.94*	*4.21*	*8.4*	*3.6*	*7.8*	*0.8*	*4.42*	*11.6*	*14*

Breakout: 23% *Improve: 45%* *Collapse: 30%*

Once a prospect, but no more. Journell endured a slew of shoulder injuries before finally undergoing surgery last May to repair a torn labrum. These stories rarely end well. Symptomatically, Journell's control failed him in recent seasons before his wing finally gave out. It'll be surprising if he's ever anything of consequence at the highest level.

RAY KING

Bats: L **Throws: L** Born: 15-Jan-1974 Age: 31

YEAR	TM	LG	AGE	G	GS	IP	H	BB	SO	HR	ERA	EQERA	EQH9	EQBB9	EQSO9	EQHR9	PERA	VORP	STF
2002	MIL	NL	28	76	0	65.0	61	24	50	5	3.05	3.45	8.6	2.9	6.2	0.7	3.88	14.8	0
2003	ATL	NL	29	80	0	59.0	46	27	43	3	3.51	4.50	7.7	3.7	6.1	0.5	3.54	6.8	0
2004	STL	NL	30	86	0	62.0	43	24	40	1	2.61	2.97	7.5	3.3	5.5	0.2	3.28	20.3	0
2005	*STL*	*NL*	*31*	*54*	*0*	*49.3*	*46*	*21*	*34*	*3*	*3.70*	*3.95*	*8.4*	*3.4*	*5.5*	*0.6*	*4.13*	*9.0*	*-6*

Breakout: 33% *Improve: 50%* *Collapse: 24%*

He has the build to erase memories of Terry Forster, but, my, he put together a nice season. King's peripherals didn't really justify the low ERA, but he's always had a knack for keeping runs off the board. The 2004 season was likely his career year, but, barring injury, he should remain effective and in clover for at least a few more seasons.

STEVE KLINE **Bats: B** **Throws: L** Born: 22-Aug-1972 Age: 32

YEAR	TM	LG	AGE	G	GS	IP	H	BB	SO	HR	ERA	EQERA	EQH9	EQBB9	EQSO9	EQHR9	PERA	VORP	STF
2002	STL	NL	29	66	0	58.3	54	21	41	3	3.40	3.72	8.7	2.9	5.8	0.5	4.04	11.8	0
2003	STL	NL	30	78	0	63.7	56	30	31	5	3.81	4.18	8.7	3.9	4.0	0.7	4.48	10.8	-15
2004	STL	NL	31	67	0	50.3	37	17	35	3	1.79	2.30	7.7	2.9	5.9	0.6	3.45	19.9	1
2005	*BAL*	*AL*	*32*	*51*	*0*	*41.0*	*44*	*16*	*25*	*4*	*4.38*	*4.33*	*9.8*	*3.1*	*5.0*	*0.9*	*4.61*	*7.2*	*-11*

Breakout: 25% *Improve: 47%* *Collapse: 26%*

Never possessed of tremendous peripheral numbers, Kline nevertheless posted sub-2.00 ERAs in two of his four seasons in St. Louis. You know the deal: he has a dirty hat, he talks about his gut, he flips off his manager. He's also been quite a reliever since his awful rookie season in '97. He's now overpaid and replaceable, but in St. Louis, he'll be missed. Landed in Baltimore, where he'll replace Buddy Groom as the franchise's must-have "veteran lefty signed to an onerous contract."

JASON MARQUIS **Bats: L** **Throws: R** Born: 21-Aug-1978 Age: 26

YEAR	TM	LG	AGE	G	GS	IP	H	BB	SO	HR	ERA	EQERA	EQH9	EQBB9	EQSO9	EQHR9	PERA	VORP	STF
2002	ATL	NL	23	22	22	114.3	127	49	84	19	5.04	5.22	10.3	3.3	6.0	1.5	6.04	3.9	-4
2003	ATL	NL	24	21	2	40.7	43	18	19	3	5.53	5.95	9.6	3.4	3.9	0.7	4.81	-1.5	-16
2003	RIC	INT	24	15	15	94.0	93	34	75	5	3.35	4.43	8.8	3.7	5.8	0.7	4.23	13.6	10
2004	STL	NL	25	32	32	201.3	215	70	138	26	3.71	4.13	9.7	2.8	5.6	1.1	5.06	39.0	4
2005	*STL*	*NL*	*26*	*26*	*26*	*165.0*	*173*	*60*	*111*	*18*	*4.38*	*4.68*	*9.5*	*2.9*	*5.4*	*1.0*	*4.76*	*16.6*	*6*

Breakout: 5% *Improve: 40%* *Collapse: 17%*

Along with Odalis Perez, we have a rare counterexample to the ballyhooed "Mazzone Factor." Marquis struggled during most of his time in Atlanta and, just after being sent to St. Louis in the J. D. Drew trade, harrumphed about never learning a cotton-pickin' thing from Leo Mazzone. Whether that's true or just an indignant parting gift, Marquis did cobble together a strong season on Dave Duncan's watch. It remains to be seen whether that's repeatable.

MATT MORRIS **Bats: R** **Throws: R** Born: 09-Aug-1974 Age: 30

YEAR	TM	LG	AGE	G	GS	IP	H	BB	SO	HR	ERA	EQERA	EQH9	EQBB9	EQSO9	EQHR9	PERA	VORP	STF
2002	STL	NL	27	32	32	210.3	210	64	171	16	3.42	3.86	9.1	2.4	6.6	0.7	4.26	42.6	19
2003	STL	NL	28	27	27	172.3	164	39	120	20	3.76	4.04	8.8	1.8	5.8	1.0	4.04	33.1	13
2004	STL	NL	29	32	32	202.0	205	56	131	35	4.72	5.21	9.6	2.3	5.4	1.5	5.12	13.4	1
2005	*STL*	*NL*	*30*	*28*	*28*	*170.3*	*177*	*48*	*112*	*20*	*4.21*	*4.50*	*9.4*	*2.2*	*5.3*	*1.1*	*4.42*	*20.7*	*8*

Breakout: 9% *Improve: 43%* *Collapse: 20%*

For the first time in his seven-year career, Morris posted an ERA worse than the league average. Additionally, he logged the worst K/9 and K/BB since his post–Tommy John season of 2000, and he also posted the worst HR/9 mark of his career. The organization believes he's in a transition period from semi-power pitcher to finesse hurler. Regardless, the Morris of yore seems to be gone, and whether he's able to refashion himself remains to be seen. The bet here is that he's a league-average innings guy until his decline phase.

STUART POMERANZ **Bats: R** **Throws: R** Born: 17-Dec-1984 Age: 20

YEAR	TM	LG	AGE	G	GS	IP	H	BB	SO	HR	ERA	EQERA	EQH9	EQBB9	EQSO9	EQHR9	PERA	VORP	STF
2003	JCY	APL	18	4	3	14.7	13	4	14	2	6.12	7.82	11.4	3.6	5.0	4.3	8.53	-4.1	-4
2004	PEO	MDW	19	17	17	101.3	95	25	88	10	3.55	6.68	10.2	2.8	4.7	1.8	5.60	0.0	7
2005	*STL*	*NL*	*20*	*13*	*12*	*70.0*	*69*	*26*	*49*	*10*	*4.55*	*4.87*	*8.9*	*2.9*	*5.7*	*1.3*	*4.91*	*5.9*	*4*

Breakout: 20% *Improve: 53%* *Collapse: 5%*

A big-bodied right-hander who certainly looks as though he can bring it. Except he can't. He's shown great command thus far, but his average stuff raises concerns about how he'll adapt to the higher levels. Still, he merits following in a system this thin.

AL REYES

Bats: R **Throws: R** Born: 10-Apr-1970 Age: 35

YEAR	TM	LG	AGE	G	GS	IP	H	BB	SO	HR	ERA	EQERA	EQH9	EQBB9	EQSO9	EQHR9	PERA	VORP	STF
2002	NAS	PCL	32	43	0	66.7	40	22	90	5	2.70	3.48	6.5	3.2	9.9	1.0	2.90	18.6	35
2002	PIT	NL	32	15	0	17.0	9	7	21	1	2.65	2.81	5.6	3.4	10.1	0.6	2.25	5.2	40
2003	COH	INT	33	15	0	17.0	16	5	21	1	3.71	4.41	8.3	2.8	8.8	1.1	3.86	3.2	14
2003	NYY	AL	33	13	0	17.0	13	9	9	1	3.18	3.38	7.3	4.5	5.1	0.6	2.81	4.5	-10
2004	DUR	INT	34	20	0	22.0	22	5	22	0	2.45	2.53	8.4	2.1	7.2	0.4	3.38	5.3	10
2004	MEM	PCL	34	37	0	39.7	32	14	47	7	2.95	3.38	8.0	3.4	8.4	1.9	4.34	5.2	11
2004	STL	NL	34	12	2	12.0	3	2	11	0	0.75	0.84	4.2	1.7	8.4	0.0	0.84	6.6	34
2005	*STL*	*NL*	*35*	*55*	*0*	*39.7*	*30*	*15*	*36*	*5*	*3.39*	*3.63*	*6.9*	*2.9*	*7.4*	*1.2*	*3.68*	*9.7*	*4*

Breakout: 25% *Improve: 47%* *Collapse: 16%*

He's averaged less than 30 league innings per season in his peripatetic decade-long career. Reyes has been ferried back and forth from Triple-A to the majors for his entire career, but he's been occasionally effective when called upon. Certainly, he gave the Cards a nifty 12 innings last year. He's a capable option, but a better guy to stow away on the Triple-A roster, in case of emergency in the big league pen.

ANTHONY REYES

Bats: R **Throws: R** Born: 16-Oct-1981 Age: 23

YEAR	TM	LG	AGE	G	GS	IP	H	BB	SO	HR	ERA	EQERA	EQH9	EQBB9	EQSO9	EQHR9	PERA	VORP	STF
2004	PMB	FSL	22	6	6	30.7	32	7	36	3	4.40	6.35	10.8	2.5	7.3	1.9	6.35	-2.4	9
2004	TEN	SOU	22	12	12	74.3	62	13	102	3	3.03	3.97	8.2	1.7	8.6	0.5	3.20	18.7	33
2005	*STL*	*NL*	*23*	*17*	*17*	*102.7*	*94*	*27*	*94*	*12*	*3.60*	*3.85*	*8.2*	*2.1*	*7.4*	*1.0*	*3.80*	*22.0*	*23*

Breakout: 12% *Improve: 37%* *Collapse: 30%*

Here's one to keep an eye on. Reyes fought through a number of elbow problems while pitching at USC, so those concerns will forever loom. Still, the numbers from his first pro season were incredible. Pitching between Palm Beach and Double-A Tennessee, in 111 innings Reyes struck out 140 and walked only 20, a 7:1 strikeout to walk ratio. Even with those peripherals, his hit rates were somewhat elevated, but there's no ignoring that kind of command indicator. He boasts a tough slider and low-90s fastball, and at this juncture looks like a future difference maker.

JASON SIMONTACCHI

Bats: R **Throws: R** Born: 13-Nov-1973 Age: 31

YEAR	TM	LG	AGE	G	GS	IP	H	BB	SO	HR	ERA	EQERA	EQH9	EQBB9	EQSO9	EQHR9	PERA	VORP	STF
2002	MEM	PCL	28	6	6	42.3	44	5	28	2	2.34	3.12	9.4	1.1	4.7	0.7	4.24	6.1	12
2002	STL	NL	28	24	24	143.3	134	54	72	18	4.02	4.41	9.4	3.0	4.1	1.2	4.95	19.6	-3
2003	STL	NL	29	46	16	126.3	153	41	74	21	5.56	5.82	10.4	2.5	4.8	1.5	5.60	-2.4	-13
2004	MEM	PCL	30	33	8	81.0	101	12	55	8	4.33	5.06	10.0	1.4	4.6	1.0	4.72	7.8	-5
2004	STL	NL	30	13	0	15.3	17	7	3	5	5.29	5.65	11.3	3.8	1.9	3.1	7.53	-0.3	-46
2005	*STL*	*NL*	*31*	*21*	*7*	*59.3*	*64*	*17*	*32*	*9*	*4.74*	*5.07*	*9.8*	*2.3*	*4.4*	*1.3*	*5.00*	*5.3*	*-10*

Breakout: 21% *Improve: 48%* *Collapse: 28%*

He certainly got some mileage out of that initial 11–5 season. Paying too much attention (read: any attention at all) to win-loss records can lead you by the hand to some faulty decisions. He may be an adequate swingman, but he's not worth it if he makes anything north of the league minimum. Simontacchi's foundering in the majors is often what becomes of "command guys" who get by with middling stuff. Invest well, Jason.

JEFF SUPPAN

Bats: R **Throws: R** Born: 02-Jan-1975 Age: 30

YEAR	TM	LG	AGE	G	GS	IP	H	BB	SO	HR	ERA	EQERA	EQH9	EQBB9	EQSO9	EQHR9	PERA	VORP	STF
2002	KCR	AL	27	33	33	208.0	229	68	109	32	5.32	4.94	9.6	2.8	4.5	1.2	4.89	4.2	-1
2003	BOS	AL	28	11	10	63.0	70	20	32	12	5.57	5.28	9.5	2.8	4.5	1.6	4.84	1.6	-4
2003	PIT	NL	28	21	21	141.0	147	31	78	11	3.57	3.57	9.2	1.8	4.6	0.7	3.90	32.3	10
2004	STL	NL	29	31	31	188.0	192	65	110	25	4.16	4.73	9.6	2.8	4.8	1.2	5.03	22.4	0
2005	*STL*	*NL*	*30*	*27*	*25*	*151.7*	*157*	*49*	*92*	*19*	*4.28*	*4.58*	*9.3*	*2.6*	*4.9*	*1.1*	*4.65*	*17.5*	*3*

Breakout: 15% *Improve: 51%* *Collapse: 16%*

Suppan is pretty much the ultimate example of the league-average starter. He'll give you 180-plus innings and an ERA around the league mean. That's got value, but he's not necessarily the guy you want to trot out for Game Three of the World Series. He's performed at this level pretty much since being given a full season's work for the first time in 1999. Not a bad guy to have around if your rotation's back end doesn't call to mind Vida Guerra's.

JULIAN TAVAREZ Bats: L Throws: R Born: 22-May-1973 Age: 32

YEAR	TM	LG	AGE	G	GS	IP	H	BB	SO	HR	ERA	EQERA	EQH9	EQBB9	EQSO9	EQHR9	PERA	VORP	STF
2002	FLA	NL	29	29	27	153.7	188	74	67	9	5.39	6.03	10.2	3.7	3.4	0.5	4.90	-6.1	-6
2003	PIT	NL	30	64	0	83.7	75	27	39	1	3.66	3.95	8.4	2.6	4.0	0.1	3.28	15.2	-3
2004	STL	NL	31	77	0	64.3	57	19	48	1	2.38	3.08	8.4	2.5	6.2	0.1	3.52	19.8	6
2005	*STL*	*NL*	*32*	*42*	*1*	*58.0*	*60*	*21*	*35*	*4*	*4.07*	*4.35*	*9.4*	*2.8*	*4.9*	*0.6*	*4.43*	*7.6*	*-7*

Breakout: 20% *Improve: 42%* *Collapse: 16%*

The psycho reliever du jour put together the best season of his career since '95. What's most impressive is that Tavarez has coughed up exactly two home runs in his last 148 innings. If you're that stingy with dingers, there's that much room for error. There's no reason he can't be an effective, if mercurial, middle man for the next few seasons.

BRAD THOMPSON Bats: R Throws: R Born: 31-Jan-1982 Age: 23

YEAR	TM	LG	AGE	G	GS	IP	H	BB	SO	HR	ERA	EQERA	EQH9	EQBB9	EQSO9	EQHR9	PERA	VORP	STF
2003	PEO	MDW	21	30	4	65.0	70	10	43	2	2.91	4.99	10.1	1.8	4.0	0.7	4.70	6.1	-8
2004	TEN	SOU	22	13	12	72.3	56	11	57	6	2.37	3.14	8.3	1.5	5.0	1.1	3.55	15.0	23
2004	MEM	PCL	22	3	3	14.7	20	3	10	3	5.51	6.28	11.3	1.9	4.4	1.9	6.28	-1.1	-4
2005	*STL*	*NL*	*23*	*18*	*13*	*83.0*	*84*	*22*	*53*	*9*	*3.98*	*4.25*	*9.1*	*2.1*	*5.1*	*1.0*	*4.32*	*12.7*	*4*

Breakout: 8% *Improve: 44%* *Collapse: 23%*

Thompson made headlines for his record-setting scoreless innings streak last season at Double-A Tennessee. He's long on command, but short on projectable stuff. There's much to like about him from a statistical standpoint, but he's one of those deep-repertoire pitchers without a true out pitch. At this point, he looks like Dan Haren Lite.

ADAM WAINWRIGHT Bats: R Throws: R Born: 30-Aug-1981 Age: 23

YEAR	TM	LG	AGE	G	GS	IP	H	BB	SO	HR	ERA	EQERA	EQH9	EQBB9	EQSO9	EQHR9	PERA	VORP	STF
2002	MYR	CRL	20	28	28	163.3	149	66	167	7	3.31	5.39	9.2	4.5	6.6	0.8	4.97	10.5	13
2003	GRN	SOU	21	27	27	149.7	133	37	128	9	3.37	4.53	9.1	2.3	5.6	1.0	4.40	18.5	18
2004	MEM	PCL	22	12	12	63.7	68	28	64	12	5.37	6.60	9.5	4.1	7.0	1.6	5.72	-0.8	8
2005	*STL*	*NL*	*23*	*21*	*16*	*101.7*	*96*	*44*	*84*	*13*	*4.40*	*4.70*	*8.6*	*3.5*	*6.7*	*1.1*	*4.73*	*11.9*	*8*

Breakout: 15% *Improve: 40%* *Collapse: 23%*

Nominally the Cards' best prospect coming into last season, Wainwright missed much of the year with elbow problems. He managed to avoid surgery, and was able to pitch in the Arizona Fall League. He didn't pitch well, mind you, but he did make four starts. The organization hoped to have him in the big league rotation by '05; instead, he'll be in Triple-A and treated with kid gloves for much of the season. Barring further health problems or poor performance, he'll be in St. Louis for good starting in September.

WOODY WILLIAMS Bats: R Throws: R Born: 19-Aug-1966 Age: 38

YEAR	TM	LG	AGE	G	GS	IP	H	BB	SO	HR	ERA	EQERA	EQH9	EQBB9	EQSO9	EQHR9	PERA	VORP	STF
2002	STL	NL	35	17	17	103.3	84	25	76	10	2.53	2.89	8.3	2.0	6.1	0.9	3.82	33.2	19
2003	STL	NL	36	34	33	220.7	220	55	153	20	3.87	4.18	8.9	2.0	5.7	0.8	4.01	38.7	16
2004	STL	NL	37	31	31	189.7	193	58	131	20	4.18	4.46	9.4	2.5	5.6	0.9	4.61	28.5	11
2005	*SDP*	*NL*	*38*	*27*	*25*	*155.0*	*153*	*47*	*103*	*17*	*4.01*	*4.57*	*9.0*	*2.4*	*5.3*	*1.1*	*4.57*	*18.0*	*6*

Breakout: 17% *Improve: 31%* *Collapse: 16%*

That was certainly a nice run. Williams looked like a thoroughly forgettable acquisition when the Cards traded Ray Lankford for him midway through the 2001 season, but he wound up giving them almost 600 innings that ranged in quality from exceptional to average. He'll be missed; the peripherals were still reasonably strong last season, and the comfy environs of Petco should help his numbers in '05.

San Diego Padres

PADRES PROSPECTUS

2004 record: 87–75; Third place, NL West

Pythagenport record: 87–75

Runs scored per game: 4.74 (8th in NL)

Runs allowed per game: 4.34 (7th in NL)

Team EqA: .270 (4th in NL)

2004 Batters Age: 30.1 (6th oldest in NL)

2004 Pitchers Age: 30.1 (4th oldest in NL)

Ballpark: Petco Park; Severe pitcher's park; Park Factor of 0.917

2004: Enjoyed a big rebound, but got little help at the trading deadline and fell short in a surprisingly competitive division.

2005: The Friars return a solid all-around squad, but pitching depth and age-related decline are concerns.

"Play Downtown." That was the Padres' slogan for Year One of the Great Petco Park Adventure. Moving to Petco, the team figured, would rid the Padres of multi-purpose Qualcomm Stadium, tap into the booming popularity of the nearby Gaslamp District, and offer a first-class facility that would give the fans a fun, new place to watch a game.

The on-field effects of the new park were more unknown. Yes, the added revenue generated by the new park figured to give John Moores a better profit cushion and Kevin Towers more money to pursue free agents and beneficial trades. Sure, if everything broke right, players deciding on Padre-offered contracts could count the new park as a worthwhile perk. No doubt, removed from the dual-tenant set-up of Qualcomm Stadium, the Padres could design the new park to their specifications and reap all of its benefits.

But how would Petco play? It took a year to find out. That time spent may have cost the Padres a shot at the pennant.

The Padres knew they could control certain elements. The outfield dimensions would play longer than most parks, notably in right-center. Playing closer to the ocean meant the heavy sea air could further suppress offense. In short, they banked on a pitcher's park.

They got one. But the results weren't as extreme as you'd expect, as seen in table 1.

For all the hype Petco received as a death zone for offense, it was actually slightly *more* generous to hitters than its Qualcomm predecessor was in three of the prior four years. More than the broad numbers, though, the shape of Petco's effects and how it affected individual players' worth proved most enlightening.

No player's worth was more muted than Ryan Klesko's. Klesko came into 2004 having topped 20 homers in eight of the previous nine seasons. After a down year in '03, a modified Mumford procedure in the off-season was supposed to restore his power and make him good as new for '04. Didn't happen. Klesko turned into a player who got on base but offered woefully inadequate power.

Petco magnified Klesko's shortcomings. Although his ailing shoulder cut into his power, the Yellowstone-like dimensions in right-center and marine layer hanging over the ballpark turned potential homers into harmless fly-outs. The early power struggles grew so bad that Klesko and Phil Nevin were seen berating Kevin Towers after one game, wailing over the painfully unfair effects of the new ballpark.

Compounding the problem was Klesko's horrendous defense. Figuring the quirky bends in right and the big alley in right-center would be a tougher assignment, the Padres made Brian Giles the right fielder and played Klesko in left. The decision hardly helped. Moving to his right, Klesko struggled. Moving to his left, Klesko struggled. Moving back on balls or in on balls, Klesko struggled. In all, he proved a major disappointment.

With Andruw Jones in center, the Padres could've lived with Klesko's struggles. Jay Payton is no Andruw Jones. Signed to a two-year, $5.5 million deal in January 2004, Payton was seen as a cheap, adequate center-field option while Freddy Guzman grew into the job for another year or two in the minors. Payton actually wasn't awful defensively. But not awful doesn't cut it when you hit like Rey Sanchez. Between Payton and Klesko, the Padres fielded two players who fell cripplingly short of expectations. Given how close the team came to making the playoffs, one could argue that upgrading those two spots alone would've delivered post-season baseball to San Diego.

As the season went on, that fact became ever more obvious. In a talk given to some 100 BP guests before a

TABLE 1. BATTER'S PARK FACTORS, PETCO 2004 VS. QUALCOM 2000–2003

Year	Team	Batter's Park Factor
2000	San Diego	91
2001	San Diego	91
2002	San Diego	92
2003	San Diego	91
2004	San Diego	92

mid-June game against the Blue Jays, Kevin Towers answered questions about the club's strengths and weaknesses. The subject turned to the Padres' outfield. Towers shook his head, recalling the just-completed series against the visiting Devil Rays, a series swept by Tampa Bay.

Referring to the D-Rays' young, speedy tandem of Rocco Baldelli and Carl Crawford, Towers said: "For a park like ours, you'd love to have two guys like that out there for you." The yearning in his voice was plain to the entire audience.

Things improved slightly as the year went on. Klesko regained at least part of his lost power and became a big on-base weapon. The club's right-handed hitters started coming alive, as the Pads realized yanking the ball down the left-field line could net plenty of doubles as well as homers off the tantalizing Western Metals building. Nevin enjoyed a particularly solid turnaround.

But the damage in the standings had already been done. Needing a stirring rally to come back and catch the front-running Dodgers and Giants, the Padres came up short. They tried to get Steve Finley at the trade deadline, only to see something worse than not getting him occur instead—Finley landed with the arch-rival Dodgers, playing a big role down the stretch and even hitting the division-clinching homer in the season's final weekend against the Giants.

The Finley situation was just one of several unsuccessful attempts by Towers and company to upgrade the outfield. After trading Mark Kotsay as part of a deal for Ramon Hernandez, the Padres made a run at Mike Cameron to fill the vacant center-field slot. When the Mets signed Cameron instead to a three-year, $19.5 million deal, the Padres were forced to settle for Payton—mediocre skill set, Coors-inflated 2003 numbers and all. Pads fans could be forgiven for wondering if it was merely another case of the Padres crying poor and settling for second-best.

Indeed, as we noted last year, teams getting a new stadium this late into the construction cycle are merely playing catch-up to other clubs, some of whom have already gone through the revenue-spiking honeymoon period and are now playing in just another gigantic taxpayer boondoggle that gets spun as intimate and old-timey. While Padres management persevered through lawsuit threats and miles of red tape to finally get Petco built, the promise was always that the team would do business in a new, more aggressive way. Instead of settling for leftovers, fans could gorge themselves on the baseball equivalent of prime rib.

Unfortunately, that hasn't been the case. Over the last 15 months, the Padres have targeted outfielders ranging from Cameron and Finley to an '04 deadline sniff at Carlos Beltran. They've flirted with Greg Maddux and other "name" pitchers to shore up their pitching staff. Yet time and again they've come up short, apparently beholden to most of the same payroll barriers they've always had, even if their threshold is somewhat higher today than in the days of Friars Road futility.

So how have the team's taste for Plan B options panned out this winter? Not too badly, for the most part. Payton was a bust in lieu of the Cameron signing Towers craved. But realizing he needed to upgrade the position, the Padres GM did so cheaply in the off-season, landing Dave Roberts from the Red Sox for Payton, utility man Ramon Vazquez, pitching prospect David Pauley, and cash. Roberts has his faults—he lacks power and turns 33 in May, for starters. But he's also a solid on-base threat vs. righties, one of the best base-stealers in the game and the rare waterbug who can cover Petco's wide center-field expanse.

With concern still stirring over Sean Burroughs's slow development—he stubbornly refuses to alter his hitting style and learn to drive the ball—the Pads weren't going to get Adrian Beltre or even Corey Koskie. But they did pick up Eric Young to give their bench some flexibility. David Wells proved a terrific Plan B when the Padres couldn't land Maddux before the '04 season. He bolts to Boston? Please welcome Woody Williams and Darrell May, two good control pitchers whose one major, common weakness—the home-run ball—could be concealed in Petco.

What the Padres can't afford to do is make major personnel errors. Late in the '03 season, they nabbed Brian Giles from the Pirates in exchange for two young players. This was the kind of deal that would normally have the Padres getting the no-name young guys, trading the star player. Giles enters his mid-30s more likely to decline than improve, but remains a solid middle-of-the-order hitter. Unfortunately the price paid for Giles—fire-balling young lefty Oliver Perez and thumping outfielder Jason Bay—is exactly the sort of cheap, productive talent the Padres desperately need now to go from fringe contenders to playoff hosts. Then where the #1 overall pick in the 2004 amateur draft figured to be a boon, the early returns on Matt Bush scream bust—and point to another case of the Padres letting budget, not the best available talent, rule their decisions.

The no-trade clauses embedded in the fat contracts of Phil Nevin and Ryan Klesko make it difficult to impossible to deal either one, compounding the team's problems. Nevin still has two years left on a four-year, $34 million contract. He's one of the team's best power threats, but he's not getting any younger and plays the position on the diamond where it's easiest to find a cheap, effective replacement. Klesko starts year one of a two-year, $16.5 million extension in 2005; his problems have already been documented at length. Is either Nevin or Klesko a bad player? No. Are they both sub-optimal uses of precious funds for a team hungry for both payroll and positional flexibility? You bet your fish tacos they are.

Still, they've made their bed, and the Padres are prepared to lay in it. Towers has made it known that rookies and untested commodities won't be given key roles the next couple years. With Klesko, Nevin, Giles, and Loretta signed through '06 and an army of young veterans due to get expensive soon, the team feels that now is the time to make a run at it. Young center fielder Freddy Guzman will get all the time he needs to mature in Triple-A. Top pitching prospect Tim Stauffer won't be rushed; neither will line-drive machine Josh Barfield. The Padres' plan closely resembles Brian Sabean's Win-With-Barry-Now! blueprint in San Francisco . . . only without an all-world player like Bonds, or the stupefying sums thrown at dreck like Mike Matheny.

Major league teams tend to trust veterans most when the stakes are highest; for the Padres, they've never been higher than they are right now. With Arizona and Colorado down, the Dodgers going through major roster reconstruction and the Giants relying heavily on old and increasingly limited players, the Padres have a chance to seize control of the NL West. A couple seasons of winning baseball could cement Petco as the place to be on a warm summer's night, sandwiched between happy-hour and late-night celebrations a few blocks away downtown. If they're in it, the Padres need to loosen their belts and take aggressive risks, knowing that flags fly forever.

At the same time, they need to remain realistic about their chances and aware of their talent at all times. If the ship starts to sink, they need to trade veterans for help down the road without hemming and hawing. With Jake Peavy on the brink of stardom and Adam Eaton, Justin Germano, and Tim Stauffer on the rise, the team has the core of a pitching staff that can compete for years to come. In Khalil Greene it has another centerpiece player to build around, with Josh Barfield, George Kottaras, (hopefully) Sean Burroughs, and others on board to play future supporting roles. A few well-placed deals and the team could quickly gear up for another run.

The worst-case scenario: a mediocre pair of seasons, coupled with inertia. Whatever the Padres decide to do, they need to do it decisively. No honeymoon lasts forever.

HITTERS

RICH AURILIA SS **Bats: R** **Throws: R** Born: 02-Sep-1971 Age: 33

YEAR	TM	LG	AGE	AB	H	2B	3B	HR	BB	SO	SB	CS	AVG	OBP	SLG	MLVR	EQBA	EQOBP	EQSLG	EQMLVR	VORP	DEFENSE
2002	SFG	NL	30	538	138	35	2	15	37	90	1	2	.257	.305	.413	-.011	.263	.310	.431	-.073	23.2	127-SS -6
2003	SFG	NL	31	505	140	26	1	13	36	82	2	2	.277	.325	.410	-.002	.277	.325	.414	-.058	25.0	112-SS 1
2004	SEA	AL	32	261	63	13	0	4	22	43	1	0	.241	.304	.337	-.205	.255	.315	.347	-.188	1.0	72-SS -3
2004	SDP	NL	32	138	35	8	2	2	15	28	0	0	.254	.331	.384	-.038	.264	.338	.393	-.074	5.1	24-3B -2
2005	*CIN*	*NL*	*33*	*298*	*77*	*15*	*1*	*8*	*25*	*51*	*1*	*0*	*.257*	*.317*	*.395*	*-.108*	*.255*	*.314*	*.391*	*-.122*	*9.3*	*80-SS -4*

Breakout: 16% *Improve: 38%* *Collapse: 38%*

The Padres snagged Aurilia from the Mariners for table scraps in July, in the process successfully buying low on a useful veteran who did a decent job subbing for the erratic and banged-up Sean Burroughs at third. Right move, just not enough. It's the kind of deal a pennant winner looks back on as the nifty little side move on top of grabbing Randy Johnson or Steve Finley. The Pads never landed the big fish, though. Aurilia's now a free agent looking to sign on somewhere as a regular.

JOSH BARFIELD 2B? **Bats: R** **Throws: R** Born: 17-Dec-1982 Age: 22

YEAR	TM	LG	AGE	AB	H	2B	3B	HR	BB	SO	SB	CS	AVG	OBP	SLG	MLVR	EQBA	EQOBP	EQSLG	EQMLVR	VORP	DEFENSE
2002	FTW	MDW	19	536	164	22	3	8	26	105	26	8	.306	.340	.403	.144	.269	.295	.363	-.194	-3.2	128-2B -3
2003	LEL	CLF	20	549	185	46	6	16	50	122	16	4	.337	.389	.530	.353	.287	.335	.448	.017	31.1	130-2B 3
2004	MOB	SOU	21	521	129	28	3	18	48	119	4	2	.248	.313	.417	-.001	.229	.288	.389	-.199	-4.0	136-2B 3
2005	*SDP*	*NL*	*22*	*290*	*71*	*16*	*2*	*7*	*22*	*67*	*4*	*1*	*.243*	*.299*	*.376*	*-.172*	*.252*	*.306*	*.401*	*-.124*	*8.4*	*77-2B -4*

Breakout: 23% *Improve: 41%* *Collapse: 40%*

Barfield impresses scouts with his all-field gap power and smooth athleticism, and impresses statheads with his run-creating prowess. You'd think both sides would fret over his 2004 season, which saw his batting average plummet nearly 100 points while his ability to make contact remained shaky. In recent years both sides have come to realize the importance of age and park factors in evaluating a player's future; Barfield held his own as one of the youngest everyday players in the Southern League, a run-scoring wasteland compared to Barfield's previous stop, the California League. The knock on Barfield is his erratic defense and unwillingness to work harder to improve afield. Meanwhile PECOTA frets that much of his value is tied up in batting average, an erratic, unpredictable skill. He needs to stick at second to really make an impact.

TAGG BOZIED **1B** **Bats: R** **Throws: R** Born: 24-Jul-1979 Age: 25

YEAR	TM	LG	AGE	AB	H	2B	3B	HR	BB	SO	SB	CS	AVG	OBP	SLG	MLVR	EQBA	EQOBP	EQSLG	EQMLVR	VORP	DEFENSE
2002	LEL	CLF	22	282	84	23	1	15	35	60	3	4	.298	.377	.546	.337	.253	.317	.453	-.038	3.9	64-1B -1
2002	MOB	SOU	22	234	50	14	0	9	16	43	1	0	.214	.268	.389	-.114	.191	.227	.360	-.382	-21.3	57-1B -8
2003	POR	PCL	23	450	123	25	2	14	38	80	1	0	.273	.331	.431	.066	.257	.314	.411	-.099	-2.1	107-1B 3
2004	POR	PCL	24	213	67	17	1	16	18	29	0	0	.315	.374	.629	.396	.273	.329	.526	.105	11.8	52-1B 1
2005	*SDP*	*NL*	*25*	*224*	*55*	*13*	*1*	*8*	*17*	*41*	*0*	*0*	*.247*	*.308*	*.428*	*-.087*	*.256*	*.314*	*.456*	*-.034*	*9.5*	*61-1B 0*

Breakout: 13% *Improve: 39%* *Collapse: 39%*

Was in the midst of a breakout season at Triple-A before a knee injury felled him for the year. That's a shame, as Bozied had hiked his contact rate and power numbers in his second go-round at Portland. Still, he's ready for the bigs, and the Pads hope to use him as a super-utility player with their infield and outfield corner positions spoken for. He'd have been even more intriguing if he'd panned out as a catcher in instructional league the way the Padres originally intended, but the ruptured patella tendon Bozied sustained celebrating a game-winning grand slam in July scuttled those plans. That's not as humiliating as tearing your ACL doing on-field jazzercise after booting a game-winning field goal, but when you're being judged against a Gramatica, nobody wins.

SEAN BURROUGHS **3B** **Bats: L** **Throws: R** Born: 12-Sep-1980 Age: 24

YEAR	TM	LG	AGE	AB	H	2B	3B	HR	BB	SO	SB	CS	AVG	OBP	SLG	MLVR	EQBA	EQOBP	EQSLG	EQMLVR	VORP	DEFENSE
2002	POR	PCL	21	179	54	16	2	2	21	16	1	0	.302	.380	.447	.193	.296	.369	.436	.069	14.0	29-2B 1 14-3B 0
2002	SDP	NL	21	192	52	5	1	1	12	30	2	0	.271	.317	.323	-.106	.287	.331	.344	-.140	3.8	37-3B -2
2003	SDP	NL	22	517	148	27	6	7	44	75	7	2	.286	.352	.402	.065	.296	.360	.420	.030	34.0	129-3B 4
2004	SDP	NL	23	523	156	23	3	2	31	52	5	4	.298	.348	.365	.003	.308	.356	.375	-.032	14.6	125-3B -6
2005	*SDP*	*NL*	*24*	*485*	*132*	*26*	*4*	*6*	*41*	*59*	*6*	*3*	*.272*	*.336*	*.380*	*-.083*	*.281*	*.343*	*.405*	*-.032*	*12.4*	*127-3B 0*

Breakout: 2% *Improve: 24%* *Collapse: 46%*

Burroughs is far too stubborn for his own good—he's been a top talent his whole life, his dad is a former major-league MVP, and Tony Gwynn became a legend in San Diego using the same shoot-the-ball-to-all-fields approach. Still, the Padres are frustrated with his refusal to alter his swing, and let his hips fire, so he can pull the ball into Petco's massive right-center-field gap for doubles and triples. Without more walks or extra-base hits, Burroughs is only a moderately useful player, and nowhere near the star many expected. The trade rumors floated at the deadline and in the off-season were real: The team feels Xavier Nady can play third base every day, and Burroughs won't have leading off as an excuse for his mediocrity anymore with Dave Roberts in tow. Check that out that Breakout/Collapse split above. If he doesn't produce, he'll be playing elsewhere by 2006.

JEFF CIRILLO **Cooked** **Bats: R** **Throws: R** Born: 23-Sep-1969 Age: 35

YEAR	TM	LG	AGE	AB	H	2B	3B	HR	BB	SO	SB	CS	AVG	OBP	SLG	MLVR	EQBA	EQOBP	EQSLG	EQMLVR	VORP	DEFENSE
2002	SEA	AL	32	485	121	20	0	6	31	67	8	4	.249	.301	.328	-.184	.267	.318	.348	-.173	0.9	126-3B 10
2003	SEA	AL	33	258	53	11	0	2	24	32	1	1	.205	.284	.271	-.334	.218	.295	.280	-.342	-8.9	74-3B 0
2004	SDP	NL	34	75	16	3	0	1	5	14	0	0	.213	.259	.293	-.311	.227	.255	.293	-.401	-3.3	
2005	*SDP*	*NL*	*35*	*144*	*33*	*7*	*0*	*2*	*13*	*22*	*1*	*0*	*.230*	*.297*	*.315*	*-.265*	*.239*	*.304*	*.336*	*-.224*	*-3.9*	*42-3B -3*

Breakout: 27% *Improve: 50%* *Collapse: 37%*

Nightly plagues of locusts descending on Petco Park wouldn't sap as much cash from the franchise as Cirillo will by the end of the '05 season. In trying to rid themselves of Kevin Jarvis, Ben Davis and their salaries, the Padres absorbed Cirillo's $6.6 million 2004 and $6.9 million 2005 salaries, with a $1.25 million buyout thrown in for bad measure. Once a .300-hitting, slick-fielding machine, Cirillo's legacy will more likely be as the single biggest albatross in Padres history.

ROBERT FICK — 1B — Bats: L — Throws: R — Born: 15-Mar-1974 — Age: 31

YEAR	TM	LG	AGE	AB	H	2B	3B	HR	BB	SO	SB	CS	AVG	OBP	SLG	MLVR	EQBA	EQOBP	EQSLG	EQMLVR	VORP	DEFENSE
2002	DET	AL	28	556	150	36	2	17	46	90	0	1	.270	.331	.433	.036	.279	.343	.452	.030	19.5	135-RF -6
2003	ATL	NL	29	409	110	26	1	11	42	47	1	0	.269	.335	.418	.026	.267	.333	.422	-.040	14.3	102-1B -8
2004	TBY	AL	30	214	43	5	2	6	20	32	0	0	.201	.273	.327	-.305	.208	.281	.335	-.301	-8.0	
2004	SDP	NL	30	12	2	0	0	0	2	4	0	0	.167	.333	.167	-.360	.333	.229	.333	-.317	-0.8	
2005	*SDP*	*NL*	*31*	*200*	*48*	*9*	*1*	*5*	*20*	*34*	*0*	*0*	*.239*	*.310*	*.369*	*-.166*	*.247*	*.317*	*.393*	*-.119*	*2.6*	*56-1B -2*

Breakout: 21% *Improve: 44%* *Collapse: 35%*

Once a highly-touted catching prospect with a potent bat, Fick has proven he can't catch, and lately, that he can't hit either. He could still prove to be a decent left-handed pinch-hitter for some needy team, with the hope that he strikes Vander Walian gold somewhere down the line.

J. J. FURMANIAK — SS — Bats: R — Throws: R — Born: 31-Jul-1979 — Age: 25

YEAR	TM	LG	AGE	AB	H	2B	3B	HR	BB	SO	SB	CS	AVG	OBP	SLG	MLVR	EQBA	EQOBP	EQSLG	EQMLVR	VORP	DEFENSE
2002	LEL	CLF	22	381	98	16	6	7	26	100	11	9	.257	.311	.386	-.026	.229	.269	.338	-.308	-14.0	69-3B -2 21-SS -4
2003	LEL	CLF	23	309	97	22	8	9	36	55	10	4	.314	.397	.524	.330	.265	.334	.440	-.015	17.5	76-SS -4
2003	MOB	SOU	23	103	27	4	1	3	8	27	0	0	.262	.336	.408	.060	.236	.291	.396	-.179	0.8	31-SS -4
2004	POR	PCL	24	425	124	24	4	17	33	86	8	5	.292	.346	.487	.104	.261	.311	.419	-.090	14.0	117-SS -9
2005	*SDP*	*NL*	*25*	*162*	*40*	*9*	*1*	*4*	*12*	*37*	*2*	*1*	*.246*	*.308*	*.388*	*-.139*	*.255*	*.314*	*.414*	*-.090*	*10.9*	*46-SS -6*

Breakout: 23% *Improve: 46%* *Collapse: 33%*

The last man added to the 40-man roster this off-season, Furmaniak shows good power for a player who won't embarrass himself on either side of second base, or over at third. Ramon Vazquez had been entrenched as the primary utility guy, but with his and Aurilia's departure, Furmaniak can hope to nail down one of their roster spots. Petco favors right-handed pull hitters, so he could prove useful if the Pads give him a chance in '05.

JAKE GAUTREAU — 3B/2B — Bats: L — Throws: R — Born: 14-Nov-1979 — Age: 25

YEAR	TM	LG	AGE	AB	H	2B	3B	HR	BB	SO	SB	CS	AVG	OBP	SLG	MLVR	EQBA	EQOBP	EQSLG	EQMLVR	VORP	DEFENSE
2002	LEL	CLF	22	371	106	20	1	10	42	86	2	3	.286	.358	.426	.130	.249	.309	.367	-.176	-0.1	87-2B 1
2003	MOB	SOU	23	438	106	24	0	14	50	131	1	4	.242	.324	.393	.009	.214	.283	.367	-.249	-10.4	109-2B -10
2004	MOB	SOU	24	212	55	13	0	10	31	52	1	1	.259	.351	.462	.126	.229	.309	.407	-.135	3.2	61-3B 0
2004	POR	PCL	24	168	46	9	1	9	14	37	1	0	.274	.333	.500	.081	.242	.300	.424	-.118	3.1	35-3B 2
2005	*SDP*	*NL*	*25*	*166*	*39*	*8*	*1*	*5*	*17*	*43*	*1*	*0*	*.236*	*.309*	*.385*	*-.148*	*.244*	*.316*	*.411*	*-.100*	*3.8*	*48-3B 0*

Breakout: 31% *Improve: 54%* *Collapse: 28%*

Part of last year's Brad Fullmer deadline deal that got nixed by Fullmer's injuries, Gautreau has played his way out of the Padres' favor. He's still got a useful bat, and he responded to Kevin Towers's gambit that a Triple-A promotion would help his confidence and production. Unfortunately, Gautreau's a miserable fielder anywhere on the diamond, and it's going to take some fearless club willing to absorb some brutal infield play for him to get a shot at regular playing time. Gautreau, Tagg Bozied, and Xavier Nady tracking Bermuda Triangle pop-ups in the 2002 Arizona Fall League remains one of the funniest flailings in recent baseball memory.

BRIAN GILES — RF — Bats: L — Throws: L — Born: 20-Jan-1971 — Age: 34

YEAR	TM	LG	AGE	AB	H	2B	3B	HR	BB	SO	SB	CS	AVG	OBP	SLG	MLVR	EQBA	EQOBP	EQSLG	EQMLVR	VORP	DEFENSE
2002	PIT	NL	31	497	148	37	5	38	135	74	15	6	.298	.450	.622	.465	.293	.444	.624	.441	85.4	140-LF 7
2003	PIT	NL	32	388	116	30	4	16	85	48	0	3	.299	.430	.521	.325	.296	.428	.521	.286	43.2	94-LF 0 16-CF 1
2003	SDP	NL	32	104	31	4	2	4	20	10	4	0	.298	.414	.490	.291	.305	.420	.514	.272	12.3	29-LF -1
2004	SDP	NL	33	609	173	33	7	23	89	80	10	3	.284	.374	.475	.186	.291	.379	.488	.154	50.8	157-RF -9
2005	*SDP*	*NL*	*34*	*487*	*137*	*28*	*4*	*21*	*86*	*69*	*7*	*2*	*.282*	*.392*	*.486*	*.158*	*.292*	*.400*	*.518*	*.219*	*45.6*	*137-RF -3*

Breakout: 23% *Improve: 64%* *Collapse: 9%*

Just a year after the big trade for Oliver Perez and Jason Bay, the Giles acquisition looks like a bust. But there are some caveats in play here—Perez's biggest fan wouldn't have figured he'd be this good, this fast. More importantly from the

Padres' perspective, Giles's 2004 numbers need to be taken with a lump of salt. Sean Burroughs's lousy season kept Giles's run-cashing chances down, and Petco Park hurt his numbers. Giles's .298 Equivalent Average ranked a decent 8th among major league outfielders with 600 or more plate appearances. Still, the Padres underestimated the impact Petco's heavy air and cavernous dimensions would have on lefty hitters. Now that he's 34, with one year left on his contract, they'd do well to let Giles walk after this season, or trade him at the deadline for an impact young bat if they're out of the race.

ALEX GONZALEZ SS **Bats: R** **Throws: R** Born: 08-Apr-1973 Age: 32

YEAR	TM	LG	AGE	AB	H	2B	3B	HR	BB	SO	SB	CS	AVG	OBP	SLG	MLVR	EQBA	EQOBP	EQSLG	EQMLVR	VORP	DEFENSE
2002	CHC	NL	29	513	127	27	5	18	46	136	5	3	.248	.312	.425	-.014	.251	.313	.438	-.068	22.6	140-SS 0
2003	CHC	NL	30	536	122	37	0	20	47	123	3	3	.228	.295	.409	-.099	.228	.294	.412	-.157	13.9	136-SS 18
2004	CHC	NL	31	129	28	10	0	3	4	26	1	1	.217	.241	.364	-.280	.215	.230	.354	-.370	-2.9	35-SS -1
2004	MON	NL	31	133	32	7	0	4	8	32	1	1	.241	.289	.383	-.145	.239	.276	.373	-.238	1.5	33-SS -3
2004	SDP	NL	31	23	4	1	1	0	2	6	0	0	.174	.240	.304	-.365	.217	.233	.348	-.371	-1.0	
2005	*TBY*	*AL*	*32*	*308*	*77*	*17*	*1*	*10*	*24*	*74*	*2*	*2*	*.250*	*.307*	*.409*	*-.104*	*.250*	*.309*	*.417*	*-.098*	*12.4*	*82-SS 1*

Breakout: 39% *Improve: 60%* *Collapse: 18%*

A low-cost pickup made with two weeks left in the season, to fill in for the injured Khalil Greene, Gonzalez ended 2004 the way he'd played it all year: horribly. Once a highly-touted prospect with a tantalizing blend of power and speed, he now blends deplorable on-base skills with a whifftastic swing that could cool off Death Valley in July.

KHALIL GREENE SS **Bats: R** **Throws: R** Born: 21-Oct-1979 Age: 25

YEAR	TM	LG	AGE	AB	H	2B	3B	HR	BB	SO	SB	CS	AVG	OBP	SLG	MLVR	EQBA	EQOBP	EQSLG	EQMLVR	VORP	DEFENSE
2002	LEL	CLF	22	183	58	9	1	9	12	33	0	0	.317	.368	.525	.316	.283	.320	.462	.007	11.1	37-SS -6
2003	MOB	SOU	23	229	63	17	2	3	16	55	2	3	.275	.327	.406	.053	.260	.302	.407	-.125	5.5	47-SS -2
2003	POR	PCL	23	319	92	19	0	10	20	52	5	4	.288	.346	.442	.121	.262	.312	.409	-.102	9.4	76-SS -7
2003	SDP	NL	23	65	14	4	1	2	4	19	0	1	.215	.271	.400	-.134	.227	.280	.424	-.167	0.5	19-SS -2
2004	SDP	NL	24	484	132	31	4	15	53	94	4	2	.273	.349	.446	.095	.280	.354	.460	.062	37.6	136-SS -3
2005	*SDP*	*NL*	*25*	*467*	*121*	*26*	*2*	*15*	*39*	*92*	*3*	*2*	*.260*	*.327*	*.424*	*-.048*	*.269*	*.334*	*.452*	*.005*	*28.9*	*123-SS -3*

Breakout: 19% *Improve: 42%* *Collapse: 29%*

With an old core that includes a punchless Ryan Klesko, a disappointing Brian Giles, and an overpaid and aging Phil Nevin, here's your franchise player. Greene is the soft-spoken, blonde locks-sporting urchin who takes you into the weight room and has you gasping as he lifts Mo Vaughn–like weights with ease, and then dazzles you on the field with his whip-like swing and emerging power. And that's before we discuss his defense. Oh, that defense. Rookie of the Year voters must have missed late-night SportsCenter highlights, because anyone watching the blitzkrieg of jaw-dropping Greene Web Gems all year would've stood up and applauded their High-Defs, let alone Khalil'd their ballots. Jason Bay's no Pat Listach or Joe Charbonneau; he's also no Khalil Greene.

FREDDY GUZMAN CF **Bats: B** **Throws: R** Born: 20-Jan-1981 Age: 24

YEAR	TM	LG	AGE	AB	H	2B	3B	HR	BB	SO	SB	CS	AVG	OBP	SLG	MLVR	EQBA	EQOBP	EQSLG	EQMLVR	VORP	DEFENSE
2002	FTW	MDW	21	190	53	7	5	0	18	37	39	7	.279	.341	.368	.080	.232	.277	.304	-.338	-11.6	38-CF -3
2003	LEL	CLF	22	281	80	12	3	2	40	60	49	10	.285	.375	.370	.054	.238	.315	.310	-.250	-8.9	48-CF -5
2003	MOB	SOU	22	177	48	5	2	1	26	34	38	7	.271	.368	.339	.025	.250	.334	.328	-.181	-1.9	45-CF -2
2004	MOB	SOU	23	138	39	5	2	1	16	28	17	5	.283	.359	.370	.036	.264	.332	.350	-.145	0.1	33-CF 3
2004	POR	PCL	23	264	77	12	4	1	30	46	48	5	.292	.365	.379	-.021	.269	.336	.342	-.145	0.2	67-CF 1
2005	*SDP*	*NL*	*24*	*338*	*83*	*14*	*3*	*2*	*30*	*67*	*34*	*7*	*.244*	*.309*	*.326*	*-.221*	*.253*	*.315*	*.348*	*-.178*	*4.4*	*90-CF -3*

Breakout: 22% *Improve: 44%* *Collapse: 32%*

On paper, Guzman seems the perfect candidate to man center field for the Padres for the next ten years. Then you dig into his credentials. He's got blazing speed, but takes lousy routes to the ball, a fault the Padres hope gets better with experience. He's shown decent plate discipline in the past, but looked totally overmatched in his Padre audition. There's clearly a need for the Padres to develop a few fleet outfielders to cover the wide expanses of Petco. Guzman's too raw to be given center field on a pennant contender, so he'll work on his game in Portland while the Pads play Dave Roberts in center.

DAVE HANSEN — PH — Bats: L — Throws: R — Born: 24-Nov-1968 — Age: 36

YEAR	TM	LG	AGE	AB	H	2B	3B	HR	BB	SO	SB	CS	AVG	OBP	SLG	MLVR	EQBA	EQOBP	EQSLG	EQMLVR	VORP	DEFENSE
2002	LAD	NL	33	120	35	6	0	2	14	22	1	0	.292	.363	.392	.089	.311	.366	.402	.028	8.1	
2003	SDP	NL	34	135	33	4	1	2	23	25	1	0	.244	.358	.333	-.055	.255	.366	.350	-.085	4.4	13-1B 1
2004	SEA	AL	35	78	22	5	0	2	18	16	0	0	.282	.412	.423	.157	.312	.421	.429	.166	7.8	
2004	SDP	NL	35	28	4	0	0	0	3	5	0	0	.143	.226	.143	-.603	.179	.174	.179	-.752	-3.2	
2005	*SDP*	*NL*	*36*	*81*	*19*	*3*	*0*	*1*	*15*	*18*	*0*	*0*	*.236*	*.353*	*.328*	*-.140*	*.244*	*.361*	*.350*	*-.096*	*4.3*	*27-1B -1*

Breakout: 13% *Improve: 34%* *Collapse: 37%*

Dave Magadan's illegitimate little brother proved a dangerous pinch-hitting weapon for the cellar-dwelling Mariners, and then a non-entity for the contending Padres. Kevin Towers made improving the bench one of his top winter priorities, so the Pads hunted down former Pad Mark Sweeney to be their top lefty bat off the pine in '05, leaving Hansen looking for work. There are plenty of teams smart enough to recognize that Hansen's significantly better than Lenny Harris, and sign him up.

RAMON HERNANDEZ — C — Bats: R — Throws: R — Born: 20-May-1976 — Age: 29

YEAR	TM	LG	AGE	AB	H	2B	3B	HR	BB	SO	SB	CS	AVG	OBP	SLG	MLVR	EQBA	EQOBP	EQSLG	EQMLVR	VORP	DEFENSE
2002	OAK	AL	26	403	94	20	0	7	43	64	0	0	.233	.313	.335	-.183	.237	.317	.340	-.206	4.3	120-C 12
2003	OAK	AL	27	483	132	24	1	21	33	79	0	0	.273	.331	.458	.068	.276	.337	.466	.036	34.4	133-C 7
2004	SDP	NL	28	384	106	23	0	18	35	45	1	0	.276	.341	.477	.121	.285	.342	.490	.088	30.3	106-C 1
2005	*SDP*	*NL*	*29*	*349*	*89*	*19*	*1*	*11*	*34*	*53*	*0*	*0*	*.254*	*.325*	*.409*	*-.076*	*.263*	*.332*	*.436*	*-.025*	*17.6*	*94-C 1*

Breakout: 7% *Improve: 34%* *Collapse: 37%*

Keeps getting better. Hernandez hiked his walk rate and power numbers slightly from an already solid 2003; throw in the adjustment from a good pitcher's park in Oakland to a great one in San Diego and the gains look even more impressive. The dramatic spike in his contact rate points to further gains in his future. He's still an above-average defensive catcher, and at $4.1 million, the Padres have themselves a relative bargain. Here comes a career year.

BEN JOHNSON — RF — Bats: R — Throws: R — Born: 18-Jun-1981 — Age: 24

YEAR	TM	LG	AGE	AB	H	2B	3B	HR	BB	SO	SB	CS	AVG	OBP	SLG	MLVR	EQBA	EQOBP	EQSLG	EQMLVR	VORP	DEFENSE
2002	MOB	SOU	21	456	110	23	4	10	65	127	11	9	.241	.337	.375	-.010	.219	.299	.358	-.227	-24.0	122-RF -13
2003	LEL	CLF	22	184	49	9	0	8	20	49	6	1	.266	.354	.446	.107	.222	.285	.373	-.232	-9.2	26-RF 0 16-CF -1
2003	MOB	SOU	22	127	23	5	0	1	10	36	0	1	.181	.252	.244	-.324	.155	.210	.209	-.642	-22.7	29-RF -4
2004	MOB	SOU	23	475	119	28	6	23	55	136	5	6	.251	.335	.480	.118	.226	.302	.436	-.110	-7.0	88-RF -3 32-LF -3
2005	*SDP*	*NL*	*24*	*253*	*57*	*12*	*2*	*8*	*25*	*76*	*2*	*1*	*.226*	*.304*	*.382*	*-.168*	*.235*	*.310*	*.407*	*-.122*	*1.2*	*70-RF -5*

Breakout: 35% *Improve: 62%* *Collapse: 16%*

It was July 2000 and Kevin Towers was talking to one of his closest friends in the game, Cardinals GM Walt Jocketty, about a deadline deal. The Cards settled on getting catcher Carlos Hernandez and infielder Nate Tebbs. The Padres would take Heathcliff Slocumb in the deal, plus a minor leaguer. Towers asked for one of two low-minors hitters: Ben Johnson . . . or Albert Pujols. Jocketty thought it over, then said he'd rather keep Pujols. The rest is history. Johnson's a decent hitter and defender who could be a solid fourth outfielder or even a fringe starter for a few years in the bigs. Still, you think about all the near-misses in this game sometimes and wonder . . . what might have been?

MIKE JOHNSON — 1B — Bats: L — Throws: R — Born: 25-Jun-1980 — Age: 25

YEAR	TM	LG	AGE	AB	H	2B	3B	HR	BB	SO	SB	CS	AVG	OBP	SLG	MLVR	EQBA	EQOBP	EQSLG	EQMLVR	VORP	DEFENSE
2003	LEL	CLF	23	178	49	17	1	5	17	48	0	1	.275	.343	.466	.126	.232	.290	.384	-.200	-6.2	33-1B -8
2004	LEL	CLF	24	331	84	23	2	15	52	106	0	0	.254	.353	.471	.102	.202	.289	.366	-.247	-17.1	67-1B -7
2005	*SDP*	*NL*	*25*	*306*	*66*	*16*	*2*	*9*	*35*	*113*	*0*	*0*	*.215*	*.298*	*.367*	*-.204*	*.223*	*.305*	*.391*	*-.159*	*-3.9*	*84-1B -6*

Breakout: 43% *Improve: 59%* *Collapse: 22%*

More from the "what might have been?" file: A teammate of Khalil Greene's at Clemson, Johnson put up a pedestrian '04 season, given he was a 24-year-old first baseman in the offense-happy Cal League. You wonder where he'd be if he didn't hold out after being drafted in '02, missed that whole summer and gone back to school as a fifth-year senior. Johnson's got a shot, but he needs to improve in a hurry and make the big leagues by '06 to have a realistic shot at a productive career. He's already doomed to toil in his ex-teammate's shadow, at best.

RYAN KLESKO "LF" **Bats: L** **Throws: L** Born: 12-Jun-1971 Age: 34

YEAR	TM	LG	AGE	AB	H	2B	3B	HR	BB	SO	SB	CS	AVG	OBP	SLG	MLVR	EQBA	EQOBP	EQSLG	EQMLVR	VORP	DEFENSE
2002	SDP	NL	31	540	162	39	1	29	76	86	6	2	.300	.388	.537	.322	.310	.395	.566	.308	61.4	109-1B -9 21-RF -2
2003	SDP	NL	32	397	100	18	0	21	65	83	2	5	.252	.354	.456	.116	.265	.360	.477	.082	22.3	102-1B 4
2004	SDP	NL	33	402	117	32	2	9	73	67	3	2	.291	.399	.448	.197	.300	.406	.459	.170	31.3	75-LF -4 17-1B 0
2005	*SDP*	*NL*	*34*	*349*	*95*	*20*	*2*	*13*	*54*	*64*	*2*	*1*	*.272*	*.369*	*.455*	*.072*	*.281*	*.377*	*.484*	*.129*	*22.6*	*97-LF -6*

Breakout: 26% *Improve: 54%* *Collapse: 15%*

Whether it was the Mumford procedure done on his ailing shoulder after the '03 season or the impossibly distant wall in right-center at Petco, Klesko's power went from fading in 2003 to neutered in '04. Klesko is also a huge defensive liability in a corner outfield spot, where he must play with Nevin locked in at first—the Padres are already calling him a six-inning player for 2005. His batting eye's clearly still intact, even with little power to scare pitchers, but Klesko looks a lot more like a lousy-fielding J. T. Snow than a true power threat for as long as he remains a Padre.

JON KNOTT LF **Bats: R** **Throws: R** Born: 04-Aug-1978 Age: 26

YEAR	TM	LG	AGE	AB	H	2B	3B	HR	BB	SO	SB	CS	AVG	OBP	SLG	MLVR	EQBA	EQOBP	EQSLG	EQMLVR	VORP	DEFENSE
2002	FTW	MDW	23	126	42	12	3	3	17	33	2	1	.333	.411	.548	.455	.292	.355	.477	.098	6.8	19-RF -2
2002	LEL	CLF	23	367	125	33	8	8	46	68	5	4	.341	.414	.540	.428	.304	.363	.472	.117	22.4	43-1B -1 41-RF -1
2003	MOB	SOU	24	432	109	32	0	27	82	117	5	3	.252	.387	.514	.256	.218	.334	.465	-.019	6.8	65-RF -9 50-1B 2
2004	POR	PCL	25	435	126	22	3	26	58	110	5	3	.290	.376	.533	.225	.259	.340	.453	.009	8.5	101-LF -6
2005	*SDP*	*NL*	*26*	*201*	*51*	*12*	*1*	*8*	*24*	*56*	*1*	*1*	*.253*	*.342*	*.441*	*-.005*	*.262*	*.350*	*.470*	*.049*	*11.2*	*57-LF -6*

Breakout: 24% *Improve: 51%* *Collapse: 19%*

The Pads have as little wiggle room on the corners as any team in baseball, between no-trade cases Nevin and Klesko, star player Giles, and young guns in Burroughs and Nady. As a result, the Padres find themselves with an interesting dilemma. Between Tagg Bozied, Jake Gautreau, Greg Sain, and Knott, the Pads have a group of decent power hitters in the high minors without obvious defensive positions. If two or three of these guys net one legit center field prospect or a good, young arm in trade, mazel tov. Tip o' the cap to the Padres just for getting this far with Knott; signed out of an open tryout camp, he defied the odds for years, smoked Triple-A pitching in '04, and made the Show for good measure. An AL team looking to save money on a productive part-time bat could do a lot worse.

CHRISTOPHER KOLKHORST CF **Bats: L** **Throws: R** Born: 07-Mar-1982 Age: 23

YEAR	TM	LG	AGE	AB	H	2B	3B	HR	BB	SO	SB	CS	AVG	OBP	SLG	MLVR	EQBA	EQOBP	EQSLG	EQMLVR	VORP	DEFENSE
2004	EUG	NWN	22	91	32	5	1	0	22	17	6	1	.352	.496	.429	.382	.263	.349	.316	-.160	-0.7	18-CF -1
2004	FTW	MDW	22	47	16	4	1	1	5	7	1	1	.340	.429	.532	.455	.300	.362	.460	.094	2.2	13-LF -1
2005	*SDP*	*NL*	*23*	*281*	*70*	*13*	*3*	*2*	*33*	*61*	*5*	*2*	*.247*	*.353*	*.336*	*-.125*	*.256*	*.361*	*.358*	*-.079*	*9.1*	*81-CF -7*

Breakout: 15% *Improve: 31%* *Collapse: 36%*

Kolkhorst is another product of the Rice University assembly line with some upside. The 10th-round pick showed the plate discipline of fellow Rice alum Lance Berkman, both in college and in his first half-season of pro ball (35 BB, 27 K). He's got the defensive chops to play center in the Show to boot. Keep an eye on him: He's a future Top 50 candidate if he can add a little pop.

GEORGE KOTTARAS C **Bats: L** **Throws: R** Born: 16-May-1983 Age: 22

YEAR	TM	LG	AGE	AB	H	2B	3B	HR	BB	SO	SB	CS	AVG	OBP	SLG	MLVR	EQBA	EQOBP	EQSLG	EQMLVR	VORP	DEFENSE
2003	IDA	PIO	20	143	37	8	1	7	19	36	1	1	.259	.348	.476	.053	.177	.247	.305	-.426	-21.2	25-C 1
2004	FTW	MDW	21	271	84	18	1	7	51	41	0	0	.310	.415	.461	.316	.272	.363	.409	.001	15.8	48-C -10
2005	*SDP*	*NL*	*22*	*310*	*72*	*16*	*1*	*7*	*37*	*68*	*0*	*0*	*.234*	*.315*	*.363*	*-.168*	*.242*	*.321*	*.387*	*-.122*	*5.7*	*85-C -14*

Breakout: 24% *Improve: 33%* *Collapse: 45%*

With apologies to Josh Barfield, here's the best prospect in the system. A native Canadian grabbed out of junior college as a 20th-round pick as a draft-and-follow, Kottaras showed a precocious batting eye, intriguing doubles power and great defensive instincts behind the plate. The Padres compare him to a young Brad Ausmus with the glove, Jorge Posada with the bat. If you're in a deep dynasty league, feign ignorance, grab him, and you'll be gloating four years from now.

TERRENCE LONG LF **Bats: L** **Throws: L** Born: 29-Feb-1976 Age: 29

YEAR	TM	LG	AGE	AB	H	2B	3B	HR	BB	SO	SB	CS	AVG	OBP	SLG	MLVR	EQBA	EQOBP	EQSLG	EQMLVR	VORP	DEFENSE
2002	OAK	AL	26	587	141	32	4	16	48	96	3	6	.240	.298	.390	-.129	.244	.307	.397	-.141	4.2	158-CF 1
2003	OAK	AL	27	486	119	22	2	14	31	67	4	1	.245	.293	.385	-.124	.245	.299	.391	-.164	-2.0	63-LF 2 70-RF 3
2004	SDP	NL	28	288	85	19	4	3	19	51	3	2	.295	.335	.420	.052	.303	.342	.434	.024	12.1	46-LF -3 18-CF 2
2005	*KCR*	*AL*	*29*	*225*	*60*	*12*	*2*	*6*	*17*	*37*	*2*	*1*	*.266*	*.319*	*.410*	*-.069*	*.262*	*.318*	*.411*	*-.083*	*4.0*	*61-LF 1*

Breakout: 18% *Improve: 35%* *Collapse: 39%*

A couple years ago this guy I worked with was helping me buy a new car stereo, so we went around to some local places—one was called Car Stereo Plus. My friend looks over the inventory with disdain, can't find anything worth buying, and as we walk out, he shakes his head and says "Car Stereo Plus? More like Car Stereo Minus." Having long since worn out his prospect status, the Padres' Car Stereo Minus actually had a decent year subbing for the execrable Jay Payton. Kevin Towers promptly shopped him, shipping TShort to Kansas City before anyone realized they'd been had.

MARK LORETTA 2B **Bats: R** **Throws: R** Born: 14-Aug-1971 Age: 33

YEAR	TM	LG	AGE	AB	H	2B	3B	HR	BB	SO	SB	CS	AVG	OBP	SLG	MLVR	EQBA	EQOBP	EQSLG	EQMLVR	VORP	DEFENSE
2002	MIL	NL	30	217	58	14	0	2	23	32	0	0	.267	.350	.359	-.031	.276	.347	.362	-.091	8.4	44-3B -4
2002	HOU	NL	30	66	28	4	0	2	9	5	1	1	.424	.481	.576	.631	.431	.455	.569	.562	14.1	
2003	SDP	NL	31	589	185	28	4	13	54	62	5	4	.314	.372	.441	.175	.325	.381	.459	.150	52.3	140-2B 0
2004	SDP	NL	32	620	208	47	2	16	58	45	5	3	.335	.391	.495	.286	.342	.396	.508	.264	76.2	150-2B 19
2005	*SDP*	*NL*	*33*	*526*	*152*	*31*	*2*	*11*	*50*	*52*	*3*	*1*	*.290*	*.355*	*.418*	*.014*	*.300*	*.362*	*.446*	*.070*	*37.4*	*139-2B 3*

Breakout: 0% *Improve: 14%* *Collapse: 49%*

Toward the end of the season, Jonah Keri wrote an article for the BP website looking at Loretta's breakout in 2003 at age 32, followed by his borderline MVP-caliber season in '04 at age 33. What made his emergence doubly sweet for the Padres was the way they acquired him: The team wanted to sign a middle infielder after the 2002 season to play alongside Ramon Vazquez. The finalists were Loretta and Royce Clayton. Being a shortstop, and with Vazquez better suited for playing second, Clayton was the first choice. The Pads got lucky, and they now have the best second baseman in the league signed cheaply through 2006. Still, there's a lesson to be learned: Loretta's worst OBP in any season with over 350 plate appearances was .346. Clayton's *best* was .348—and that in hitter-happy Arlington. When in doubt, take the guy who gets on base.

PAUL McANULTY 1B **Bats: L** **Throws: R** Born: 24-Feb-1981 Age: 24

YEAR	TM	LG	AGE	AB	H	2B	3B	HR	BB	SO	SB	CS	AVG	OBP	SLG	MLVR	EQBA	EQOBP	EQSLG	EQMLVR	VORP	DEFENSE
2002	IDA	PIO	21	235	89	29	0	8	49	43	7	2	.379	.488	.604	.590	.266	.345	.419	-.023	14.6	
2003	FTW	MDW	22	455	124	27	0	7	67	82	5	3	.273	.370	.378	.138	.236	.312	.348	-.205	-18.7	118-1B -15
2004	LEL	CLF	23	495	147	36	3	23	88	106	3	1	.297	.404	.521	.297	.244	.337	.417	-.058	-0.5	56-LF -2 26-1B -2
2005	*SDP*	*NL*	*24*	*304*	*73*	*17*	*2*	*9*	*39*	*74*	*1*	*0*	*.240*	*.333*	*.391*	*-.096*	*.249*	*.340*	*.417*	*-.047*	*5.8*	*85-1B -6*

Breakout: 24% *Improve: 56%* *Collapse: 20%*

McAnulty played above the herd at Lake Elsinore, taking pitchers deep into counts, smoking fat pitches for extra bases and taking free passes when he didn't get them. Still, playing as a 23-year-old out of Long Beach State, you'd expect him to dominate in the hitter-friendly Cal League. If he can show the same on-base ability and power at Mobile, he'll be a contender for the first base or left-field job just as Nevin and Klesko come off the books.

XAVIER NADY RF **Bats: R** **Throws: R** Born: 14-Nov-1978 Age: 26

YEAR	TM	LG	AGE	AB	H	2B	3B	HR	BB	SO	SB	CS	AVG	OBP	SLG	MLVR	EQBA	EQOBP	EQSLG	EQMLVR	VORP	DEFENSE
2002	LEL	CLF	23	169	47	6	3	13	28	40	2	0	.278	.382	.580	.368	.234	.322	.468	-.024	5.4	
2002	POR	PCL	23	315	89	12	1	10	20	60	0	1	.283	.329	.422	.050	.278	.323	.409	-.068	-1.3	55-LF -1
2003	POR	PCL	24	136	36	7	0	7	12	28	0	0	.265	.329	.471	.111	.235	.291	.412	-.157	-3.7	32-RF -3
2003	SDP	NL	24	371	99	17	1	9	24	74	6	2	.267	.321	.391	-.025	.277	.329	.407	-.061	5.8	94-RF -5
2004	POR	PCL	25	291	97	19	1	22	22	42	3	0	.333	.394	.632	.459	.292	.347	.535	.168	19.7	39-RF -3 17-CF -1
2004	SDP	NL	25	77	19	4	0	3	5	13	0	0	.247	.301	.416	-.081	.256	.291	.423	-.125	0.5	10-LF -1
2005	*SDP*	*NL*	*26*	*250*	*66*	*14*	*1*	*9*	*19*	*49*	*2*	*0*	*.262*	*.322*	*.437*	*-.038*	*.271*	*.329*	*.466*	*.017*	*13.8*	*68-RF -5*

Breakout: 18% *Improve: 37%* *Collapse: 39%*

Having played some third base at Cal, the Padres had Nady man the hot corner this off-season at instructional league, hoping to find ways to get more use out of him. In a park that favors right-handed pull hitters, Nady could be a much cheaper replacement for Klesko in left, minus some OBP, plus ample defense and power. But the no-trade clauses handed Klesko and Nevin keep tripping up the Padres, and will continue to do so through '06. With the Padres in desperate need of better outfield speed and defense and Nady and other hitters blocked, the situation's a bit painful.

PHIL NEVIN 1B **Bats: R** **Throws: R** Born: 19-Jan-1971 Age: 34

YEAR	TM	LG	AGE	AB	H	2B	3B	HR	BB	SO	SB	CS	AVG	OBP	SLG	MLVR	EQBA	EQOBP	EQSLG	EQMLVR	VORP	DEFENSE
2002	SDP	NL	31	407	116	16	0	12	38	87	4	0	.285	.344	.413	.079	.299	.352	.434	.038	24.6	66-3B -1 32-1B -3
2003	SDP	NL	32	226	63	8	0	13	21	44	2	0	.279	.339	.487	.155	.289	.341	.504	.110	14.9	28-1B 2 25-RF -2
2004	SDP	NL	33	547	158	31	1	26	66	121	0	0	.289	.368	.492	.206	.295	.372	.505	.170	46.9	133-1B -5
2005	*SDP*	*NL*	*34*	*380*	*100*	*19*	*1*	*15*	*42*	*83*	*1*	*0*	*.263*	*.337*	*.437*	*-.012*	*.272*	*.344*	*.466*	*.043*	*17.9*	*102-1B -3*

Breakout: 8% *Improve: 34%* *Collapse: 35%*

A nice bounceback season, as Nevin stayed healthy enough to rack up some solid numbers. Still, he's a perpetual health risk who drifts further and further from the .306/.395/.588 career year he had in 2000 as he gets into his mid-30s. It's worth asking whether any first baseman over 30 is worth signing to a long-term contract of three years or more, *ever.* For every Jim Thome success story (so far—call me in 2007), you'll find a Jason Giambi or Mo Vaughn horror show, massive men with big swings and old player skills who age poorly and cripple a team's payroll for years. Even with players like Nevin, you get a hitter who remains productive, though nowhere near as good as he was when he posted the career year that earned him huge cash. Meanwhile younger, cheaper options get left untapped. It'll be interesting to see if teams make the right moves when the league's David Ortizes come due, or if they're doomed to repeat the money-wasting habits of the past.

MIGUEL OJEDA C **Bats: R** **Throws: R** Born: 29-Jan-1975 Age: 30

YEAR	TM	LG	AGE	AB	H	2B	3B	HR	BB	SO	SB	CS	AVG	OBP	SLG	MLVR	EQBA	EQOBP	EQSLG	EQMLVR	VORP	DEFENSE
2002	MCD	MEX	27	341	120	22	1	19	66	49	8	5	.352	.458	.589	.339	.255	.357	.440	.019	19.7	
2003	MCD	MEX	28	159	52	14	2	10	24	23	4	1	.327	.422	.629	.313	.248	.334	.490	.039	10.4	
2003	SDP	NL	28	141	33	6	0	4	18	26	1	1	.234	.331	.362	-.057	.252	.333	.378	-.113	4.3	41-C -5
2004	SDP	NL	29	156	40	3	0	8	15	34	0	0	.256	.322	.429	.011	.268	.321	.439	-.037	7.7	36-C 2
2005	*SDP*	*NL*	*30*	*216*	*53*	*11*	*1*	*8*	*26*	*48*	*1*	*0*	*.245*	*.329*	*.414*	*-.070*	*.254*	*.336*	*.441*	*-.018*	*13.2*	*61-C -2*

Breakout: 17% *Improve: 45%* *Collapse: 26%*

He's no Erubiel Durazo, but this Mexican Leagues veteran crafted a nifty little season, doing a good job spelling Ramon Hernandez during injury downtime. Still, when crunch time came in September, the Pads rode Hernandez for 21 straight games before falling out of contention. With his outrageous .351/.432/.757 split vs. lefties, Strat-O-Matic players are already planning elaborate robberies using 20-sided dice as a weapon to get this guy.

JAY PAYTON CF/LF **Bats: R** **Throws: R** Born: 22-Nov-1972 Age: 32

YEAR	TM	LG	AGE	AB	H	2B	3B	HR	BB	SO	SB	CS	AVG	OBP	SLG	MLVR	EQBA	EQOBP	EQSLG	EQMLVR	VORP	DEFENSE
2002	NYM	NL	29	275	78	6	3	8	21	34	4	1	.284	.336	.415	.058	.291	.342	.432	.010	14.1	67-CF 1
2002	COL	NL	29	170	57	14	4	8	8	20	3	3	.335	.376	.606	.340	.315	.356	.577	.269	19.4	26-LF 1 13-CF 1
2003	COL	NL	30	600	181	32	5	28	43	77	6	4	.302	.354	.512	.158	.283	.337	.486	.071	35.3	142-LF 14
2004	SDP	NL	31	458	119	17	4	8	43	56	2	0	.260	.326	.367	-.065	.268	.333	.378	-.101	9.5	120-CF 12
2005	*BOS*	*AL*	*32*	*366*	*100*	*19*	*2*	*9*	*29*	*50*	*3*	*2*	*.274*	*.331*	*.414*	*-.037*	*.270*	*.329*	*.417*	*-.049*	*9.0*	*97-CF 0*

Breakout: 10% *Improve: 28%* *Collapse: 32%*

This is what happens when you're not willing to go that extra buck. The Padres were hot after Mike Cameron following the 2003 season, envisioning a graceful center fielder who could cover Petco Park's vast expanses and rope line drives off the Western Metal building in left. When the Mets beat them out with an affordable three-year, $19.5 million deal, the Pads settled for Payton. Ignore Payton's defensive numbers, a function largely of covering for Ryan Klesko in left; Payton's an average defensive center fielder at best who was so bad at bat Terrence Long became the more palatable alternative. Part of the package traded to Boston for Dave Roberts.

HUMBERTO QUINTERO C Bats: R Throws: R Born: 02-Aug-1979 Age: 25

YEAR	TM	LG	AGE	AB	H	2B	3B	HR	BB	SO	SB	CS	AVG	OBP	SLG	MLVR	EQBA	EQOBP	EQSLG	EQMLVR	VORP	DEFENSE
2002	WNS	CRL	22	160	31	1	1	0	8	23	2	3	.194	.247	.212	-.357	.158	.198	.176	-.711	-26.2	51-C 17
2002	MOB	SOU	22	125	30	8	0	1	5	12	0	3	.240	.286	.328	-.152	.205	.225	.283	-.487	-11.6	32-C 6
2003	MOB	SOU	23	386	115	26	0	3	19	41	0	0	.298	.343	.389	.070	.268	.301	.365	-.181	-0.9	106-C 13
2004	POR	PCL	24	259	82	25	0	5	8	18	0	0	.317	.348	.471	.110	.277	.301	.399	-.124	3.5	65-C 11
2004	SDP	NL	24	72	18	3	0	2	5	16	0	2	.250	.295	.375	-.110	.264	.289	.375	-.192	0.0	19-C 0
2005	*SDP*	*NL*	*25*	*259*	*61*	*12*	*1*	*4*	*8*	*31*	*0*	*0*	*.236*	*.273*	*.335*	*-.280*	*.244*	*.279*	*.357*	*-.237*	*-1.9*	*68-C 5*

Breakout: 10% *Improve: 25%* *Collapse: 49%*

In spring training last year Quintero picked off two unsuspecting baserunners and threw out another would-be basestealer with David Wells on the mound. Asked after the game what he thought of his battery mate, Wells played the role of campaign manager: "It's stupid; he's showing me up. He's throwing 110 (mph) down to first and I'm only pitching 88 to home plate. I'm retiring if they don't take him with us." Wells reneged on his vow after Quintero started the year in Triple-A, but at least the young backstop finally hit better in addition to terrorizing baserunners. He profiles as a low-strikeout, low-walk hitter with modest pop, but the Pads are wishcasting for some .290 seasons with doubles power. With Ramon Hernandez's contract up at year's end, they may give Quintero his shot sooner than expected.

KERRY ROBINSON OF Bats: L Throws: L Born: 03-Oct-1973 Age: 31

YEAR	TM	LG	AGE	AB	H	2B	3B	HR	BB	SO	SB	CS	AVG	OBP	SLG	MLVR	EQBA	EQOBP	EQSLG	EQMLVR	VORP	DEFENSE
2002	STL	NL	28	181	47	7	4	1	11	29	7	4	.260	.301	.359	-.102	.262	.302	.372	-.173	0.7	27-LF -1
2003	STL	NL	29	208	52	6	3	1	8	27	6	1	.250	.281	.322	-.224	.252	.286	.329	-.273	-4.2	22-RF 1
2004	POR	PCL	30	170	52	6	3	2	19	15	25	1	.306	.383	.412	.077	.286	.357	.375	-.047	0.9	16-RF -1 14-CF 0
2004	SDP	NL	30	92	27	4	0	0	5	8	11	4	.293	.330	.337	-.077	.323	.323	.344	-.129	2.4	18-LF -1
2005	*NYM*	*NL*	*31*	*164*	*42*	*7*	*2*	*1*	*10*	*20*	*10*	*3*	*.256*	*.303*	*.342*	*-.204*	*.259*	*.304*	*.353*	*-.186*	*0.2*	*46-LF 2*

Breakout: 8% *Improve: 19%* *Collapse: 48%*

With as empty a .293 average as you'll ever find, Robinson proved that even when everything breaks right, he's still a punchless waste of roster space. Sure, the Pads used him as a defensive upgrade over Klesko in the late innings, but geez, Rick Majerus in a tutu could've done that, and been far more entertaining to boot.

GREG SAIN 3B Bats: R Throws: R Born: 26-Dec-1979 Age: 25

YEAR	TM	LG	AGE	AB	H	2B	3B	HR	BB	SO	SB	CS	AVG	OBP	SLG	MLVR	EQBA	EQOBP	EQSLG	EQMLVR	VORP	DEFENSE
2002	FTW	MDW	22	387	95	29	0	13	35	77	2	0	.245	.323	.421	.099	.203	.257	.355	-.323	-17.6	55-3B 0 15-1B -2
2003	LEL	CLF	23	467	128	35	0	19	43	119	3	1	.274	.336	.471	.121	.220	.272	.378	-.251	-9.8	94-3B -8 13-C -1
2004	MOB	SOU	24	456	107	22	0	28	66	140	1	0	.235	.338	.467	.092	.207	.299	.415	-.158	-11.5	111-1B -12
2005	*SDP*	*NL*	*25*	*238*	*54*	*11*	*1*	*9*	*24*	*67*	*0*	*0*	*.228*	*.308*	*.401*	*-.134*	*.237*	*.314*	*.428*	*-.086*	*2.5*	*66-1B -4*

Breakout: 44% *Improve: 63%* *Collapse: 21%*

Showed decent progress, improving his walk rate and isolated power as he made the tough transition from High-A hitter's paradise at Lake Elsinore to the tougher challenge of Double-A Mobile. Still, Sain's another Padres farmhand without an obvious defensive position at the big league level, only with a lower contact rate and less offensive ability than the Gautreaus, Bozieds, and Knotts of the system. You'll know the Padres contended in 2005 if most of these guys are toiling in other organizations a year from now.

RAMON VAZQUEZ SS Bats: L Throws: R Born: 21-Aug-1976 Age: 28

YEAR	TM	LG	AGE	AB	H	2B	3B	HR	BB	SO	SB	CS	AVG	OBP	SLG	MLVR	EQBA	EQOBP	EQSLG	EQMLVR	VORP	DEFENSE
2002	SDP	NL	25	423	116	21	5	2	45	79	7	2	.274	.344	.362	-.013	.288	.355	.384	-.037	20.2	62-2B 1 31-SS 1
2003	SDP	NL	26	422	110	17	4	3	52	88	10	3	.261	.342	.341	-.062	.273	.353	.360	-.085	17.1	100-SS -10
2004	POR	PCL	27	184	55	21	1	8	33	28	2	0	.299	.402	.554	.311	.258	.354	.467	.052	13.4	43-2B -5
2004	SDP	NL	27	115	27	3	2	1	11	24	1	1	.235	.297	.322	-.203	.239	.305	.333	-.238	-1.1	14-SS -1
2005	*BOS*	*AL*	*28*	*190*	*51*	*11*	*2*	*4*	*22*	*35*	*2*	*2*	*.269*	*.345*	*.398*	*-.039*	*.264*	*.343*	*.401*	*-.051*	*11.3*	*55-SS -5*

Breakout: 15% *Improve: 40%* *Collapse: 39%*

A decent little stopgap at short when they had no better options, Vazquez stepped aside for Khalil Greene in 2004, and should now function as a workable utility man for the next couple years. He's a better player than he showed in '04, and a much better bargain than the contracts doled out to the likes of Neifi Perez and Juan Castro the last couple years. He'll be a useful utility guy for the Red Sox.

PITCHERS

BRAD BAKER

Bats: R Throws: R Born: 06-Nov-1980 Age: 24

YEAR	TM	LG	AGE	G	GS	IP	H	BB	SO	HR	ERA	EQERA	EQH9	EQBB9	EQSO9	EQHR9	PERA	VORP	STF
2002	MOB	SOU	21	12	12	64.3	47	45	57	5	4.48	5.31	8.2	6.2	6.1	1.2	5.01	3.9	11
2002	SAR	FSL	21	12	12	61.3	53	25	65	4	2.79	4.26	9.0	4.1	6.9	1.3	4.89	4.5	10
2003	LEL	CLF	22	27	4	44.7	31	14	69	2	2.01	3.92	7.4	3.5	9.1	0.9	3.27	10.7	31
2003	MOB	SOU	22	17	9	50.7	50	36	53	3	5.68	6.75	9.6	6.6	6.8	1.1	5.81	-1.1	-14
2004	MOB	SOU	23	55	0	57.3	37	24	68	2	1.57	2.56	7.2	4.1	7.7	0.5	3.42	12.8	3
2005	*SDP*	*NL*	*24*	*29*	*6*	*63.7*	*54*	*35*	*60*	*7*	*4.23*	*4.81*	*7.7*	*4.4*	*7.6*	*1.1*	*4.80*	*5.8*	*2*

Breakout: 16% *Improve: 40%* *Collapse: 26%*

With a devastating change-up that baffles opposing hitters, Baker's drawn comparisons to Keith Foulke and the Padres' own Trevor Hoffman. A starter at the beginning of his pro career, Baker's gone from serviceable to nearly unhittable, as his employers have figured out how tough he is to handle one time through the order and kept him shackled to the pen. Kevin Towers still talks wistfully about the period around the 2002 trade deadline; you would too if you got Baker and Jason Bay for a couple middle relievers.

TRAVIS CHICK

Bats: R Throws: R Born: 10-Jun-1984 Age: 21

YEAR	TM	LG	AGE	G	GS	IP	H	BB	SO	HR	ERA	EQERA	EQH9	EQBB9	EQSO9	EQHR9	PERA	VORP	STF
2003	JAM	NYP	19	13	10	52.0	63	26	48	3	5.71	8.63	10.8	5.7	4.8	1.8	6.24	-3.5	-16
2004	FTW	MDW	20	7	7	42.3	32	9	55	4	2.13	4.23	8.9	2.6	7.0	1.9	4.46	4.9	25
2004	GRB	SAL	20	28	11	91.3	79	27	112	11	4.04	5.85	9.0	3.1	6.9	1.8	4.57	9.7	9
2005	*SDP*	*NL*	*21*	*13*	*9*	*58.3*	*52*	*24*	*51*	*9*	*4.30*	*4.89*	*8.2*	*3.2*	*7.0*	*1.5*	*4.83*	*5.5*	*7*

Breakout: 17% *Improve: 49%* *Collapse: 12%*

One of the most comical occurrences of the Padres' 2004 season was the grief the team took for trading Ismael Valdez at the deadline. Valdez had pieced together a shiny 9–6 record in San Diego, and the media raked the team over the coals for weakening their shot at a playoff spot by shipping its fifth starter to Florida for some unknown kid pitcher. Of course few took the time to dig a little deeper. If they had, they'd have found three things to be true. First, that Valdez got huge run support—6.3 runs per game—with the Padres, thus overcoming his ugly 5.53 ERA. Second, Dennis Tankersley, Justin Germano, and Brian Sweeney got a collective 1.9 runs per start in run support in the #5 hole, a far bigger reason for their 0–9 record than any inferiority to Valdez. Finally, in Chick, the Pads got a big, strong, talented pitcher who scouts compare to Curt Schilling and statheads adore for his 4.6:1 K:BB ratio last season. Years from now, Chick will be blowing big league hitters away with his devastating slider. Meanwhile Valdez will be selling insurance, and the talking heads who blasted the Padres will be railing against some other supposed blunder.

ADAM EATON

Bats: R Throws: R Born: 23-Nov-1977 Age: 27

YEAR	TM	LG	AGE	G	GS	IP	H	BB	SO	HR	ERA	EQERA	EQH9	EQBB9	EQSO9	EQHR9	PERA	VORP	STF
2002	SDP	NL	24	6	6	33.3	28	17	25	5	5.41	5.62	8.2	3.9	6.2	1.4	4.22	0.4	9
2003	SDP	NL	25	31	31	183.0	173	68	146	20	4.08	4.69	8.7	3.0	6.6	1.0	4.02	24.9	17
2004	SDP	NL	26	33	33	199.3	204	52	153	28	4.61	5.33	9.1	2.1	6.2	1.2	4.25	14.7	14
2005	*SDP*	*NL*	*27*	*28*	*26*	*157.0*	*154*	*49*	*116*	*19*	*4.18*	*4.76*	*9.0*	*2.5*	*5.9*	*1.2*	*4.62*	*16.2*	*9*

Breakout: 13% *Improve: 42%* *Collapse: 22%*

As maddening as any player on the roster, and maybe any pitcher in the league. Example: Pitching against Jeff Weaver and the Dodgers June 25 at Petco, Eaton dominated, yielding just one hit and two walks in seven innings. Five days later, at still-pitcher-friendly Dodger Stadium, again against Weaver, Eaton got waxed for seven runs on nine hits in 3.2 IP. With a mid-90s fastball and a good assortment of breaking pitches, Eaton's got the stuff to be a lights-out #2 man behind Jake Peavy in San Diego. Two big bugaboos remain: Eaton's gopheritis and his propensity for racking up hefty pitch counts early in games. He can solve both problems if he can learn to throw low strikes early in the count, thereby inducing more quick outs, and fewer dangerous fly balls. If Darren Balsley does nothing else beyond helping Eaton take that next step, he'll have earned a big raise.

JUSTIN GERMANO

Bats: R Throws: R Born: 06-Aug-1982 Age: 22

YEAR	TM	LG	AGE	G	GS	IP	H	BB	SO	HR	ERA	EQERA	EQH9	EQBB9	EQSO9	EQHR9	PERA	VORP	STF
2002	FTW	MDW	19	24	24	155.7	166	19	119	14	3.18	5.59	11.1	1.4	4.3	2.1	5.78	-2.9	-1
2003	LEL	CLF	20	19	19	110.7	127	25	78	4	4.23	6.04	9.6	2.4	4.0	0.6	4.11	17.8	10
2003	MOB	SOU	20	9	9	58.0	60	13	44	6	4.34	6.04	10.4	2.2	5.0	1.7	5.37	1.4	9
2004	MOB	SOU	21	5	5	32.3	31	7	20	3	2.51	3.94	9.7	2.1	3.9	1.2	5.16	1.5	3
2004	POR	PCL	21	20	20	122.7	113	25	98	12	3.37	3.89	8.7	1.9	5.7	0.9	3.97	21.0	35
2004	SDP	NL	21	7	5	21.3	31	14	16	2	8.87	10.23	11.0	4.9	5.7	0.8	6.14	-10.3	11
2005	*SDP*	*NL*	*22*	*15*	*14*	*83.7*	*91*	*25*	*54*	*10*	*4.57*	*5.20*	*9.9*	*2.4*	*5.1*	*1.1*	*5.04*	*4.9*	*3*

Breakout: 8% *Improve: 46%* *Collapse: 25%*

The Padres could do a lot worse than make Germano their #5 starter this season, foregoing expensive external options. Instead, they'll take the known commodity approach, giving Germano more seasoning at Triple-A. No harm there: Germano's just 22, shows excellent control and a good fastball-curve-change arsenal that elicits plenty of ground balls. Without a true out pitch he'll need to stay precise at all times to forge a successful career, something he's been able to do so far. Intriguing sleeper.

TREVOR HOFFMAN

Bats: R Throws: R Born: 13-Oct-1967 Age: 37

YEAR	TM	LG	AGE	G	GS	IP	H	BB	SO	HR	ERA	EQERA	EQH9	EQBB9	EQSO9	EQHR9	PERA	VORP	STF
2002	SDP	NL	34	61	0	59.3	52	18	69	2	2.73	3.38	7.4	2.3	9.2	0.3	2.45	15.4	27
2003	SDP	NL	35	9	0	9.0	7	3	11	1	2.00	2.08	7.3	3.1	10.4	1.0	3.12	3.6	26
2004	SDP	NL	36	55	0	54.7	42	8	53	5	2.30	2.61	7.5	1.2	8.0	0.9	2.96	20.6	20
2005	*SDP*	*NL*	*37*	*37*	*0*	*36.3*	*32*	*9*	*33*	*4*	*3.01*	*3.43*	*8.1*	*1.9*	*7.3*	*1.0*	*3.59*	*9.1*	*8*

Breakout: 33% *Improve: 46%* *Collapse: 40%*

A successful return from shoulder surgery, and then some. Hoffman yielded less than a baserunner an inning, picking up where he left off in his nine-inning comeback stint in late 2003 despite his fastball being a distant memory. He was a bargain at $2.5 million (plus incentives) last season, though his $6 million option was as much a nod to his status as heir to the Tony Gwynn Lifetime Padre mantle. Watching Hoffman trot in for the ninth inning with Hell's Bells blaring, then strike out the side with his dainty 75 mph change-up, remains one of the biggest treats in all of baseball.

BRIAN LAWRENCE

Bats: R Throws: R Born: 14-May-1976 Age: 29

YEAR	TM	LG	AGE	G	GS	IP	H	BB	SO	HR	ERA	EQERA	EQH9	EQBB9	EQSO9	EQHR9	PERA	VORP	STF
2002	SDP	NL	26	35	31	210.0	230	52	149	16	3.69	4.53	9.1	1.9	5.6	0.7	3.53	31.3	17
2003	SDP	NL	27	33	33	210.7	206	57	116	27	4.19	4.76	9.2	2.2	4.6	1.2	4.22	27.4	2
2004	SDP	NL	28	34	34	203.0	226	55	121	26	4.12	4.71	9.7	2.2	4.9	1.1	4.62	29.0	3
2005	*SDP*	*NL*	*29*	*28*	*27*	*163.3*	*173*	*43*	*101*	*17*	*3.98*	*4.54*	*9.7*	*2.1*	*4.9*	*1.0*	*4.69*	*19.2*	*5*

Breakout: 22% *Improve: 55%* *Collapse: 19%*

A rough April led some to wonder if the staff's resident junkballer could continue to get hitters out. Lawrence righted his ship thereafter, proving his usual effective self, at least against righties, although lefties continued to hit him hard, to the tune of .301/.354/.486. Though he's added a tailing sidearm fastball the last couple years as a way to deal with lefties, the pitch only works in spurts, and a hanging Lawrence slider is a recipe for disaster when an Adam Dunn or Jim Thome digs in. He'll make $5.75 million the next two years as part of the four-year deal he signed in 2003, after which Germano, Chick and company should replace him.

SCOTT LINEBRINK

Bats: R Throws: R Born: 04-Aug-1976 Age: 28

YEAR	TM	LG	AGE	G	GS	IP	H	BB	SO	HR	ERA	EQERA	EQH9	EQBB9	EQSO9	EQHR9	PERA	VORP	STF
2002	HOU	NL	25	22	0	24.3	31	13	24	2	7.04	7.20	9.7	4.0	7.6	0.7	5.04	-6.5	0
2003	HOU	NL	26	9	6	31.7	38	14	17	4	4.26	4.06	10.5	3.5	4.4	1.2	5.81	5.0	-11
2003	SDP	NL	26	43	0	60.7	55	22	51	5	2.82	3.53	8.3	2.9	6.9	0.8	3.68	15.9	8
2004	SDP	NL	27	73	0	84.0	61	26	83	8	2.14	2.60	7.2	2.6	8.1	0.8	2.94	31.2	18
2005	*SDP*	*NL*	*28*	*38*	*6*	*78.7*	*72*	*30*	*71*	*9*	*3.72*	*4.24*	*8.4*	*3.0*	*7.2*	*1.1*	*4.55*	*12.6*	*6*

Breakout: 17% *Improve: 43%* *Collapse: 24%*

In Trevor Hoffman, Aki Otsuka, and Linebrink, the Padres fielded three of the top 20 relievers in baseball according to *BP*'s brand spankin' new "Reliever Expected Wins Added Report" (Keith Woolner has more on our new pitching reports toward the end of this book). The Padres are banking on making every game a six-inning affair, after which they turn it over to the bullpen's three amigos and call it a night. Given Hoffman's age and Linebrink's short history of success, they did well to add Rudy Seanez, and to have Brad Baker standing by just in case. Linebrink will have a good 2005, but simple regression to the mean suggests he'll never again duplicate his '04 performance, especially his ridiculous numbers vs. lefties (.178/.277/.281).

NATANAEL MATEO **Bats: R** **Throws: R** Born: 24-Dec-1980 Age: 24

YEAR	TM	LG	AGE	G	GS	IP	H	BB	SO	HR	ERA	EQERA	EQH9	EQBB9	EQSO9	EQHR9	PERA	VORP	STF
2004	LEL	CLF	23	39	0	51.7	46	11	59	2	2.79	4.47	8.6	2.4	6.7	0.6	3.54	11.1	5
2005	*SDP*	*NL*	*24*	*25*	*5*	*54.7*	*52*	*17*	*44*	*5*	*3.71*	*4.23*	*8.7*	*2.5*	*6.5*	*1.0*	*4.37*	*8.7*	*4*

Breakout: 18% *Improve: 42%* *Collapse: 25%*

The Padres managed to slip Mateo under the radar by not adding him to the 40-man roster and sneaking him through the Rule 5 Draft. Good thing. While we're rarely high on minor league relievers, this rangy Dominican brings a live fastball and a slider that's a powerful weapon as an out pitch. He keeps the ball in the park, he's got an Everyday Eddie rubber arm, and by 2006 he could be a cheap, effective member of the pen. Heck, PECOTA thinks he's good to go right now, projected for a better '05 ERA than Linebrink.

BLAINE NEAL **Bats: L** **Throws: R** Born: 06-Apr-1978 Age: 27

YEAR	TM	LG	AGE	G	GS	IP	H	BB	SO	HR	ERA	EQERA	EQH9	EQBB9	EQSO9	EQHR9	PERA	VORP	STF
2002	CLG	PCL	24	29	0	31.0	27	15	26	2	2.90	3.07	8.0	4.6	6.1	0.6	3.99	5.2	-5
2002	FLA	NL	24	32	0	33.0	32	14	33	1	2.73	3.58	8.3	3.3	8.0	0.3	3.31	7.7	14
2003	ABQ	PCL	25	40	0	46.3	55	16	32	1	2.33	4.14	9.3	3.4	5.1	0.2	4.14	7.4	-4
2003	FLA	NL	25	18	0	21.0	38	9	10	2	8.14	8.46	12.5	3.2	3.6	0.8	6.04	-6.9	-22
2004	POR	PCL	26	27	0	38.7	32	12	38	0	1.86	2.95	7.9	2.9	6.9	0.2	3.44	8.8	9
2004	SDP	NL	26	40	0	42.0	49	11	36	6	4.07	4.35	9.8	2.2	6.8	1.3	4.79	7.6	1
2005	*SDP*	*NL*	*27*	*26*	*6*	*60.7*	*60*	*21*	*48*	*5*	*3.78*	*4.30*	*9.1*	*2.8*	*6.4*	*0.9*	*4.61*	*9.1*	*3*

Breakout: 24% *Improve: 46%* *Collapse: 23%*

A run-of-the-mill reliever with great velocity and lukewarm results, Neal will likely play out his career fighting for the last spot on pitching staffs, usually doing just enough to stay on the roster.

ANTONIO OSUNA **Bats: R** **Throws: R** Born: 12-Apr-1973 Age: 32

YEAR	TM	LG	AGE	G	GS	IP	H	BB	SO	HR	ERA	EQERA	EQH9	EQBB9	EQSO9	EQHR9	PERA	VORP	STF
2002	CWS	AL	29	59	0	67.7	64	28	66	1	3.86	3.92	8.1	3.4	8.4	0.1	3.51	12.9	18
2003	NYY	AL	30	48	0	50.7	58	20	47	3	3.73	3.86	8.8	3.3	7.9	0.5	3.68	12.3	12
2004	SDP	NL	31	31	0	36.7	32	11	36	3	2.45	3.06	7.9	2.5	7.9	0.8	3.31	12.2	16
2005	*WAS*	*NL*	*32*	*47*	*0*	*46.7*	*42*	*16*	*43*	*5*	*3.47*	*3.71*	*8.2*	*2.7*	*7.4*	*0.9*	*3.97*	*10.1*	*7*

Breakout: 27% *Improve: 49%* *Collapse: 28%*

The Padres went with an all-righty pen throughout the '04 season, and everyone was cool with that. Carrying a mediocre lefty on the staff can cause a manager to make dumb decisions, such as spotting said lefty against Barry Bonds. Osuna is no great shakes, but considering the desperate hunger for Tony Fossas clones shown by most other teams, he was still a better option than most spot lefties.

AKINORI OTSUKA **Bats: R** **Throws: R** Born: 13-Jan-1972 Age: 33

YEAR	TM	LG	AGE	G	GS	IP	H	BB	SO	HR	ERA	EQERA	EQH9	EQBB9	EQSO9	EQHR9	PERA	VORP	STF
2002	OSA	JPL	30	41	1	42.3	22	3	54	4	0.00	2.09	6.1	0.7	9.8	0.9	2.09	15.1	34
2003	CHU	JCL	31	51	0	43.0	31	5	56	4	0.00	2.45	7.1	1.3	9.4	0.7	2.68	13.1	27
2004	SDP	NL	32	73	0	77.3	56	26	87	6	1.75	2.19	7.1	2.8	9.2	0.7	2.92	33.0	23
2005	*SDP*	*NL*	*33*	*48*	*2*	*74.7*	*59*	*24*	*73*	*6*	*2.61*	*2.97*	*7.3*	*2.6*	*7.8*	*0.8*	*3.35*	*22.9*	*13*

Breakout: 33% *Improve: 48%* *Collapse: 33%*

For all the relative hype given not only the Matsuis but also stiffs like Tsuyoshi Shinjo, Otsuka has been the best bargain to emerge out of Japan. The once-dominating closer settled in as a seventh- and eighth-inning assassin, confounding hitters with his funky hesitation delivery. Though cynics said major league hitters would figure out his motion and start belting him, Otsuka's slider-splitter combo fooled all comers from April to October. Though an Ichiro in his prime will always be the prize all teams shoot for, the big years Otsuka and Shingo Takatsu put up for rock-bottom prices will trigger far greater demand the next time a 30-something Japanese stopper comes up for bid.

CHRIS OXSPRING **Bats: L** **Throws: R** Born: 13-May-1977 Age: 28

YEAR	TM	LG	AGE	G	GS	IP	H	BB	SO	HR	ERA	EQERA	EQH9	EQBB9	EQSO9	EQHR9	PERA	VORP	STF
2002	LEL	CLF	25	15	1	26.3	24	8	30	2	4.79	6.57	9.5	3.3	6.2	1.5	5.11	1.3	-6
2002	MOB	SOU	25	6	1	14.3	13	8	21	0	1.26	2.57	8.4	4.5	9.6	0.0	3.86	2.7	15
2003	MOB	SOU	26	40	18	135.7	106	62	129	6	2.92	4.08	8.2	4.3	6.2	0.9	4.15	20.3	13
2004	POR	PCL	27	17	17	85.7	82	44	81	7	3.99	4.85	8.7	5.0	6.6	0.9	4.85	6.8	6
2005	*SDP*	*NL*	*28*	*21*	*7*	*60.0*	*58*	*29*	*46*	*6*	*4.49*	*5.11*	*8.8*	*3.8*	*6.1*	*1.0*	*5.07*	*4.6*	*-3*

Breakout: 19% *Improve: 44%* *Collapse: 28%*

The Pads took a calculated risk protecting Oxspring and leaving A-ball firebreathers Natanael Mateo and Wilmer Villatoro exposed to the Rule 5 Draft. They got away with it, and Oxspring will now offer bullpen depth when the inevitable Rudy Seanez injury occurs or if Hoffman's shoulder flares up. Though he's been a half-decent starter in the minors, if the Padres get so low on the depth chart they need to resort to Oxspring, you can safely assume they're already planning for 2006.

JAKE PEAVY **Bats: R** **Throws: R** Born: 31-May-1981 Age: 24

YEAR	TM	LG	AGE	G	GS	IP	H	BB	SO	HR	ERA	EQERA	EQH9	EQBB9	EQSO9	EQHR9	PERA	VORP	STF
2002	MOB	SOU	21	14	14	80.3	65	30	89	4	2.80	3.81	8.1	3.2	7.5	0.8	3.93	14.0	30
2002	SDP	NL	21	17	17	97.7	106	33	90	11	4.51	5.38	9.0	2.6	7.2	1.0	3.90	5.7	27
2003	SDP	NL	22	32	32	194.7	173	82	156	33	4.11	4.55	8.6	3.4	6.7	1.5	4.50	29.2	10
2004	SDP	NL	23	27	27	166.3	146	53	173	13	2.27	2.96	7.9	2.6	8.4	0.7	3.29	57.5	37
2005	*SDP*	*NL*	*24*	*24*	*24*	*157.7*	*142*	*53*	*147*	*17*	*3.54*	*4.03*	*8.3*	*2.7*	*7.5*	*1.1*	*4.19*	*28.8*	*21*

Breakout: 22% *Improve: 44%* *Collapse: 18%*

An inflamed forearm ligament knocked him out for a month-and-a-half, otherwise Peavy's name would have showed up on plenty of Cy Young ballots. Otherwise, it all came together in '04, as Peavy hiked his strikeout rate to more than one per inning, took a hatchet to his walk rate, and allowed far fewer home runs, exploiting the forgiveness of Petco's huge power alleys. He's not even eligible for arbitration until after the '05 season, though the Pads were discussing a two-year deal at press time. There's not a team in baseball that wouldn't kill to have Peavy, but San Diegans get to keep him all to themselves for the foreseeable future.

TIM STAUFFER **Bats: R** **Throws: R** Born: 02-Jun-1982 Age: 23

YEAR	TM	LG	AGE	G	GS	IP	H	BB	SO	HR	ERA	EQERA	EQH9	EQBB9	EQSO9	EQHR9	PERA	VORP	STF
2004	LEL	CLF	22	6	6	35.3	28	9	30	0	1.78	3.86	8.0	2.8	5.0	0.3	3.31	8.3	13
2004	MOB	SOU	22	8	8	51.3	56	13	33	3	2.63	3.72	10.1	2.4	4.1	0.7	5.03	3.1	-2
2004	POR	PCL	22	14	14	81.3	83	26	50	15	3.54	5.21	9.8	3.1	4.4	1.7	5.57	0.3	5
2005	*SDP*	*NL*	*23*	*13*	*13*	*75.7*	*82*	*27*	*44*	*9*	*4.62*	*5.27*	*9.9*	*2.8*	*4.6*	*1.2*	*5.27*	*4.2*	*-1*

Breakout: 9% *Improve: 45%* *Collapse: 30%*

In his first year of pro ball after rehabbing a shoulder injury in 2003, Stauffer started to show his potential. He wielded good command of three above-average pitches, including a smooth, over-the-top curve and a high-80s fastball. We like Justin Germano, but management has hinted that between Germano and Stauffer for an in-season promotion and fifth-starter assignment, they may favor Stauffer. Still, there are holes: too many homers, especially at Portland, and limited experience. You'd like to see him get more than a year in the minors, especially after playing through three levels last year. Should settle in as an effective back-of-the-rotation guy by '06, with room for growth.

RICKY STONE **Bats: R** **Throws: R** Born: 28-Feb-1975 Age: 30

YEAR	TM	LG	AGE	G	GS	IP	H	BB	SO	HR	ERA	EQERA	EQH9	EQBB9	EQSO9	EQHR9	PERA	VORP	STF
2002	HOU	NL	27	78	0	77.3	78	34	63	9	3.61	4.04	8.8	3.3	6.5	1.0	4.40	10.2	-2
2003	HOU	NL	28	65	0	83.0	76	31	47	11	3.69	3.68	9.1	3.1	4.8	1.1	4.83	15.8	-13
2004	HOU	NL	29	16	0	19.0	26	7	16	5	5.68	5.21	10.9	2.8	6.6	1.9	6.16	0.0	-9
2004	SDP	NL	29	27	0	32.7	40	9	22	6	6.88	7.59	10.4	2.2	5.3	1.7	5.62	-6.3	-12
2005	*CIN*	*NL*	*30*	*35*	*0*	*45.7*	*48*	*16*	*32*	*6*	*4.30*	*4.60*	*9.6*	*2.7*	*5.6*	*1.1*	*4.91*	*5.9*	*-7*

Breakout: 36% *Improve: 54%* *Collapse: 23%*

Plucked off waivers by San Diego at midseason, the Padres relegated Stone to mop-up work, knowing Linebrink, Otsuka, and Hoffman had most close games well in hand. Signed a minor league deal with the Reds, where he may be forced to play a bigger role given Cincy's lack of viable arms. Expect many screaming line drives.

BRIAN SWEENEY

Bats: R **Throws: R** Born: 13-Jun-1974 Age: 31

YEAR	TM	LG	AGE	G	GS	IP	H	BB	SO	HR	ERA	EQERA	EQH9	EQBB9	EQSO9	EQHR9	PERA	VORP	STF
2002	TAC	PCL	28	30	23	142.0	157	28	113	16	3.80	4.60	9.7	1.9	5.6	1.3	4.60	15.2	5
2003	TAC	PCL	29	29	21	141.0	165	32	115	17	4.28	5.79	10.3	2.3	6.3	1.7	5.59	0.2	-6
2004	POR	PCL	30	24	23	138.7	130	42	110	16	3.83	4.41	8.9	3.0	5.6	1.3	4.68	13.4	17
2004	SDP	NL	30	7	2	14.3	20	2	10	1	5.66	5.65	10.7	1.3	5.7	0.6	5.02	0.1	17
2005	*TBY*	*AL*	*31*	*21*	*9*	*69.7*	*75*	*21*	*47*	*10*	*4.65*	*4.56*	*9.7*	*2.4*	*5.5*	*1.3*	*4.54*	*10.8*	*-1*

Breakout: 22% *Improve: 50%* *Collapse: 26%*

Two starts all year, both against Randy Johnson, and he goes 1–0 with a no-decision. How 'bout them apples?! OK, so Sweeney got smoked in his second tilt with the Unit. But he'll be 31 in June, he'll never be more than a fringe major leaguer, and his name will soon be forgotten by most of the few who know it now. If you were Sweeney, wouldn't you perch your grandkids on your lap 40 years from now, and regale them with your David vs. Goliath tale, the night you shoved a 5.1-4-1-1-0-1-5 line in Randy Johnson's face? Kudos, Brian. Somewhere, Moonlight Graham smiles down on you.

DENNIS TANKERSLEY

Bats: R **Throws: R** Born: 24-Feb-1979 Age: 26

YEAR	TM	LG	AGE	G	GS	IP	H	BB	SO	HR	ERA	EQERA	EQH9	EQBB9	EQSO9	EQHR9	PERA	VORP	STF
2002	MOB	SOU	23	10	10	50.7	47	21	56	1	3.02	4.41	8.4	3.5	7.3	0.4	3.86	9.5	19
2002	POR	PCL	23	9	9	51.0	43	30	51	6	3.88	5.36	8.8	5.9	7.3	1.3	5.74	-0.7	5
2002	SDP	NL	23	17	9	51.3	59	40	39	10	8.07	8.42	9.8	5.8	6.0	1.8	5.96	-14.8	-16
2003	POR	PCL	24	27	27	151.0	149	67	148	15	4.65	5.51	8.9	4.5	7.6	1.3	4.89	11.3	5
2004	POR	PCL	25	19	19	120.0	114	37	86	10	3.15	4.21	8.9	3.0	5.1	0.9	4.45	14.5	2
2004	SDP	NL	25	9	6	35.0	35	17	29	3	5.14	6.55	8.7	3.9	6.6	0.8	4.46	-2.6	1
2005	*KCR*	*AL*	*26*	*25*	*12*	*84.3*	*91*	*39*	*60*	*11*	*5.34*	*5.03*	*9.6*	*3.6*	*5.8*	*1.2*	*4.84*	*6.5*	*-3*

Breakout: 15% *Improve: 42%* *Collapse: 26%*

From his uneven off-field demeanor to his periodic battles on the mound, Tankersley never panned out as the 1A pitcher who'd slot in alongside Jake Peavy and lead the San Diego rotation into the next decade. More than just inner demons, Tankersley struggled even harder to gain command of his fastball, and get back the velocity on his slider that had slipped from where it was two or three years ago. Traded to Kansas City with Terrence Long for Darrell May and Ryan Bukvich, Tankersley gets the fresh start he needed in Kansas City.

DALE THAYER

Bats: R **Throws: R** Born: 17-Dec-1980 Age: 24

YEAR	TM	LG	AGE	G	GS	IP	H	BB	SO	HR	ERA	EQERA	EQH9	EQBB9	EQSO9	EQHR9	PERA	VORP	STF
2003	FTW	MDW	22	45	0	48.0	31	15	72	2	2.06	4.78	7.9	3.5	9.3	1.2	3.95	7.9	15
2004	LEL	CLF	23	50	0	55.3	36	11	54	1	1.63	3.20	7.1	2.3	5.9	0.4	2.49	17.5	16
2005	*SDP*	*NL*	*24*	*31*	*3*	*55.0*	*51*	*20*	*44*	*7*	*3.84*	*4.38*	*8.4*	*2.8*	*6.4*	*1.2*	*4.47*	*7.6*	*0*

Breakout: 14% *Improve: 37%* *Collapse: 26%*

Originally drafted by the Cubs in '99, Thayer went to Chico State instead, and then hooked on with the Padres a few years later out of a SoCal tryout camp. Thus far, he's overpowered hitters out of the pen with a fastball/slider combo, but his violent delivery raises injury concerns. He's got the goods to make the show inside of two years, but he'll start this season in Mobile.

SEAN THOMPSON

Bats: L **Throws: L** Born: 13-Oct-1982 Age: 22

YEAR	TM	LG	AGE	G	GS	IP	H	BB	SO	HR	ERA	EQERA	EQH9	EQBB9	EQSO9	EQHR9	PERA	VORP	STF
2002	IDA	PIO	19	13	11	56.3	51	38	69	4	3.84	6.75	9.6	8.2	5.9	1.8	6.39	-4.5	-10
2003	EUG	NWN	20	15	15	80.0	58	39	97	5	2.48	5.40	9.4	5.8	6.4	1.9	6.30	-5.4	-2
2004	FTW	MDW	21	27	27	148.0	125	57	157	15	3.10	5.21	9.4	4.5	5.9	2.0	5.48	1.8	-7
2005	*SDP*	*NL*	*22*	*10*	*7*	*46.0*	*40*	*27*	*36*	*8*	*5.02*	*5.72*	*8.0*	*4.6*	*6.2*	*1.7*	*5.53*	*0.8*	*-5*

Breakout: 12% *Improve: 44%* *Collapse: 20%*

Check out those strikeout rates and you'll see why the Padres hope this little lefty can mature into Mike Hampton in his prime. Though his fastball only tops out a tick above 90, he locates well and throws an overhand curve and change-up with aplomb. They added him to the 40-man, with good reason.

STEVE WATKINS Bats: R Throws: R Born: 19-Jul-1978 Age: 26

YEAR	TM	LG	AGE	G	GS	IP	H	BB	SO	HR	ERA	EQERA	EQH9	EQBB9	EQSO9	EQHR9	PERA	VORP	STF
2002	MOB	SOU	23	37	15	116.7	124	49	88	8	3.78	5.74	9.8	3.6	5.0	1.1	5.25	4.3	-11
2003	MOB	SOU	24	18	18	101.3	100	34	75	8	4.18	5.34	9.8	3.1	4.9	1.4	5.15	4.7	-3
2003	POR	PCL	24	14	0	26.3	20	12	23	1	3.08	4.38	7.3	4.7	6.9	0.4	3.65	5.4	4
2004	MOB	SOU	25	10	10	59.3	50	15	57	6	3.64	4.97	8.9	2.5	6.1	1.5	4.64	5.8	15
2004	POR	PCL	25	22	6	55.7	53	19	58	3	3.07	3.54	8.6	3.2	7.3	0.5	4.05	9.2	15
2004	SDP	NL	25	11	0	14.3	17	4	7	3	6.29	6.59	10.5	2.0	4.0	2.0	5.93	-0.9	-15
2005	*CLE*	*AL*	*26*	*17*	*10*	*65.3*	*71*	*25*	*46*	*8*	*4.82*	*4.73*	*9.7*	*3.0*	*5.7*	*1.1*	*4.69*	*8.3*	*0*

Breakout: 23% *Improve: 44%* *Collapse: 22%*

Fared poorly in his brief stint in the majors, but his strikeout-an-inning performance in Mobile and Portland earned him a minor league deal with the Indians. I'm pretty sure this isn't the same Steve Watkins I worked with for several years, the scrappy Midwesterner with the pleasant demeanor, kick-ass Wisconsin accent and reliable infielder's glove on the softball diamond. But hey, if it is, nice going, Steve! Think you can buy your old buddy a beer, Mr. Big Shot?

DAVID WELLS Bats: L Throws: L Born: 20-May-1963 Age: 42

YEAR	TM	LG	AGE	G	GS	IP	H	BB	SO	HR	ERA	EQERA	EQH9	EQBB9	EQSO9	EQHR9	PERA	VORP	STF
2002	NYY	AL	39	31	31	206.3	210	45	137	21	3.75	4.22	8.8	1.8	5.8	0.9	3.63	37.1	16
2003	NYY	AL	40	31	30	213.0	242	20	101	24	4.14	4.10	9.5	0.8	4.2	1.0	3.72	43.0	8
2004	SDP	NL	41	31	31	195.7	203	20	101	23	3.73	4.15	9.4	0.8	4.3	1.0	3.91	40.3	7
2005	*BOS*	*AL*	*42*	*23*	*20*	*118.7*	*146*	*26*	*56*	*17*	*4.97*	*4.68*	*10.8*	*1.7*	*3.8*	*1.3*	*4.80*	*15.6*	*-4*

Breakout: 13% *Improve: 30%* *Collapse: 33%*

He ambles around the mound, his belly bulging under his baggy uniform, jersey flapping behind him, untucked and disheveled. As he wipes the sweat from his brow and squints in at the sign, he looks like he'd rather throw down beers than throw to a big league hitter. But when David Wells delivers his sweeping curve or darting fastball, he does so with a surgeon's precision. The Padres did well to patch the rotation with Woody Williams and Darrell May, but they'll still miss Boomer now that he's a Red Sock. His age and health aside, Wells's success in Boston will depend largely on his ability the keep the ball on the ground: His 1.51 GB/FB rate last year was a career high, and either a sign of Wells making a valuable adjustment or a fluke that portends more flyballs in '05, many of them over the Monster.

JAY WITASICK Bats: R Throws: R Born: 28-Aug-1972 Age: 32

YEAR	TM	LG	AGE	G	GS	IP	H	BB	SO	HR	ERA	EQERA	EQH9	EQBB9	EQSO9	EQHR9	PERA	VORP	STF
2002	SFG	NL	29	44	0	68.3	58	21	54	3	2.37	2.77	8.2	2.5	6.5	0.4	3.46	21.8	10
2003	SDP	NL	30	46	0	45.7	42	25	42	6	4.53	4.87	8.5	4.3	7.5	1.2	4.47	4.5	0
2004	SDP	NL	31	44	0	61.7	57	26	57	8	3.21	4.37	8.4	3.5	7.5	1.1	4.22	11.1	4
2005	*BAL*	*AL*	*32*	*38*	*2*	*58*	*60*	*24*	*47*	*8*	*4.51*	*4.47*	*9.4*	*3.3*	*6.5*	*1.1*	*4.69*	*9.1*	*-2*

Breakout: 17% *Improve: 39%* *Collapse: 25%*

Teams pondering hefty contract offers to veteran relief pitchers should consider the case of Jay Witasick. After seven awful seasons in which he never posted an ERA below 4.50, Witasick suddenly caught fire, putting up big years in 2001 and 2002, prompting the Padres to sign him to a two-year, $2.75 million deal. He then re-lost his control in 2003, before putting up a competent but unremarkable '04 campaign. Teams need to learn this simple lesson: If you're able to pull a reliever off the scrap heap and get 60 great innings from him, odds are you can do it again with somebody else. A free agent at press time.

San Francisco Giants

When people talk about making history, they usually mean in a positive way. When the Red Sox won their first World Series in 86 years last fall, for instance, observers raved at length about the team that made history in New England.

But sometimes the connotation is far more sour. In the Giants' case, it's potentially devastating and humiliating: They're one step closer to wasting the greatest stretch of hitting in the history of baseball, by the greatest hitter in the history of baseball.

That fact has weighed on Brian Sabean's mind for years. Barry Bonds continues to put up numbers that used to exist only in video games, the Giants GM knows his star player turns 41 this year, knows his back and legs and stamina are nowhere near what they used to be. Sooner or later, Barry Bonds will stop being Barry Bonds. And, more than anything, Sabean wants to win a World Series before that happens.

To that end, Sabean and the rest of the organization spent the off-season acting as if a gun were pointed squarely at its temple. The Giants loaded up on well-known veterans, paying significant sums to do so. The hope was to surround Bonds with the kind of experienced players who can be trusted to perform well enough during the home stretch of Bonds's career to get the Giants back into the playoffs and hopefully to a championship.

This strategy makes a lot of sense, if done correctly. The Giants' best players consist not only of over-40 Bonds, but also 30-somethings Jason Schmidt and Ray Durham. With that kind of core, plus a nearly barren farm system, a win-now philosophy is the right move . . . *if* you use your resources properly and find the right players.

Unfortunately, the Giants didn't do that. In fact, each of their four major free-agent signings of the off-season provides a different reason for Giants fans to frown:

Moises Alou: As recently as 2003, Alou was a run-of-the-mill 20-homer corner outfielder, the kind who could be had on the open market cheaply. A year before that, he was an old, injury-prone flop, with fading power and an ugly future outlook. Then Alou put up his 2004, a .293/.361/.557 season, with 39 homers and 36 doubles.

Do the Giants really believe that's what they should expect as Alou enters his Age-39 and Age-40 seasons? How else can we explain paying him nearly $7 million a year for the next two years? They'll soon learn that Bonds's career path is impossible to duplicate, as Alou reverts back to 2003 form. The team's outfield defense, with Alou, Grissom, and Bonds patrolling the wide expanse, will be a nightmare.

Armando Benitez: This one made sense at first glance. Pundits weighing in on the deal trotted out the Giants' 28 saves blown in 74 chances last year, second-highest behind only the Reds. Ignoring misleading stats such as blown saves, any team relying on the likes of Jim Brower, Tyler Walker, and Matt Herges as shutdown arms clearly needs to upgrade its pen.

But throwing a big wad of cash at the available closer who had the best 2004 wasn't the best use of resources, not when gaping holes existed in center field, at catcher, and other much tough-to-fill positions. Giving Benitez $21.5 million over three years meant overpaying for the Capital C on his Closer resume. Did the Giants learn nothing from the success of Dustin Hermanson and Tim Worrell in the closer role the last two years? Benitez adds an excellent power arm to the bullpen, no question. But a solid reliever or two without a closer's pedigree could have been had for millions less, improving the pen while freeing up money for other problems.

GIANTS PROSPECTUS

2004 record: 91–71; Second place, NL West

Pythagenport record: 88–74

Runs scored per game: 5.25 (2nd in NL)

Runs allowed per game: 4.75 (12th in NL)

Team EqA: .272 (3rd in NL)

2004 Batters Age: 32.2 (2nd oldest in NL)

2004 Pitchers Age: 30.1 (4th oldest in NL)

Ballpark: SBC Park; Neutral park; Park Factor of 1.006

2004: Despite some acute pitching problems, the Giants were *thisclose* to a third consecutive postseason appearance.

2005: They've girded themselves for one more pennant drive in the Barry Bonds era, and should be contenders again.

Mike Matheny: Though signed at what may seem like a modest rate of $10.5 million over three years, Matheny is easily the worst of the Giants' off-season moves. Letting A. J. Pierzynski go rather than pay him $5+ million wasn't a bad idea; tabbing Matheny as his replacement was. Regarded by reputation as one of the best defensive catchers in baseball, the numbers back up the claim: According to BP's defensive metrics, Matheny was 11 Fielding Runs Above Average (FRAA) last season, ranking among the game's elite for the fourth time in the last five years. But catching defense only takes you so far: Teams employ the running game to less effect these days, and, besides, Matheny only threw out a pedestrian 30% of attempted basestealers. While the Giants talked up Matheny's ability to handle a pitching staff, research by Baseball Prospectus's Keith Woolner has shown that catchers by and large have no significant effect on pitchers' ERA.

That's the *good* part of Matheny's game. At the plate, instead of behind it, Matheny has been one of the most useless offensive players in baseball. He's topped a .240 Equivalent Average just once, and sports a horrific career EqA of .221. Put another way, while Matheny netted 11 runs FRAA last season, he cost his team 16 batting runs compared to the average catcher. Already 34, he's most likely to get even worse over the next three years, and will struggle just to equal replacement level for the life of the contract. While we've heard so much about the big-dollar contracts doled out to undeserving players, Matheny ranks among the worst signings of the off-season.

Omar Vizquel: One of the better deals of the four, but that's not saying much. Once an elite defender, Vizquel's range has declined with age to merely average. That's a problem because he's not likely to contribute much with the bat; his production depends heavily on his batting average, a stat that fluctuates and isn't likely to improve as his speed ebbs. His surprising 2002 spike aside, Vizquel has little power potential and doesn't walk enough to be more than an adequate on-base threat. He'll be a modest upgrade over Deivi Cruz, but not one worth more precious coin that could have been funneled into pursuing elite talent at the position.

The Giants' mounting desperation amid the grim prospect of Bonds retiring without winning the big one brings to mind the Red Sox's plight from an earlier era, with Ted Williams. The one hitter in baseball history who most closely resembles Bonds—for his unreal ability to control the strike zone, hit for power, and seemingly do anything he wanted with any pitch—Williams also put up huge numbers as his career wound to a close.

As the Giants have done with Bonds, the Red Sox also aggressively acquired name players past their primes, albeit much earlier in Williams's career: Jimmie Foxx, Lefty Grove, and Joe Cronin were among those whose stars were dimming as Williams rose to prominence.

Boston's glory years came from 1946 to 1951. The team sported a .605 winning percentage, and never finished lower than third during that span. Bad luck played a big role in their near misses: The team lost the '46 World Series in seven games; in '47 virtually the entire pitching staff got hurt; in '48 they lost a one-game playoff to Cleveland; in '49 they went into the last weekend of the season needing to win just one of two from the Yankees, but lost both.

The Giants can relate. Since 1997, San Francisco has finished first or second every year, winning three division titles and four playoff berths. In 2002, they were nine outs away from winning their first World Series in 48 years, before blowing a five-run lead. As the Marlins and other teams of recent vintage have shown, any team can win three short playoff series, and the best team doesn't always win. A few breaks here and there and we'd be talking about the Giants' dynasty, not their disappointment.

You could almost forgive the Giants for bringing in all that new old blood to try and change the team's luck. But the advantage of getting known commodities when signing old players is far outweighed by their likely declines over the life of their contracts, even in year one. Given all we know about players' development curves, the Giants have little reason to expect players like Matheny, Vizquel, and Alou to replicate their most recent seasons' output, let alone what they did in their primes. While teams often label such deals as low-risk, the fact is, they carry huge risks; players entering their mid to late 30s are more likely to decline, more likely to get injured, and more likely to get useless before the end of their contracts.

Minor league statistics, when adjusted for age, park and league effects, do an excellent job of predicting a player's major league output. The Giants have made it clear they don't believe that concept to be true. They're loath to pick hitters in the high rounds of the amateur draft. They promote their hitting prospects more slowly than almost any other team. So complete is management's mistrust of prospects—especially young hitters—that the Giants have begun an interesting experiment: They purposely sign players early in the free-agent cycle to ensure they'll owe teams compensatory draft picks and hence avoid the signing bonuses doled out to top selections.

Making an all-out run at a pennant by signing veterans and avoiding the minefield of risks posed by the high rounds of the amateur can pay off. The problem, of course, lies in execution.

If you're going to pursue a veteran player, target one with solid skills, closer to 30 than 35. It'll cost more, but you can mine the non-tender and minor league free-agent markets to find the kind of supporting players you'll need to win.

If you're going to sacrifice high draft picks for free-agent signings, go after elite players who'll make a big difference to your team. Is money spent on Michael Tucker instead of comparable, cheaper talent really worth a well-researched draft pick to boot? Not bloody likely.

For all the perplexing moves made by management, the Giants still stand an excellent chance of returning to the playoffs. Bonds as 80% the player he was in 2004 would still be the envy of 29 other clubs. Jason Schmidt remains one of the hardest-worked, but also one of the very best pitchers in the game. Moises Alou, Ray Durham, J. T. Snow, and others all have faults, but all also bring varying degrees of offensive utility.

The pitching staff could improve, as the Giants have done a much better job developing young pitchers than they have hitters. Jesse Foppert will start to show flashes of his huge ability as he moves further away from his Tommy John surgery. Jerome Williams and Noah Lowry can build on promising '04 campaigns.

Most promising of all, if the Giants are in the race, Brian Sabean can rely on his greatest skill: engineering knockout trades at the deadline to get his teams into the playoffs. The Jason Schmidt deal of 2001 alone was a career-maker, and the Giants have pulled some excellent, smaller trades as well. With a solid stable of B-level pitching prospects on the farm, Sabean will have a chance to add that last bat or arm he'll need to claim what is again a very winnable NL West.

If they get that far, it'll be anyone's ballgame. And then the quick-strike nature of the playoffs means anyone can be a hero. Yes, even Mike Matheny. But if it's another year where they fall short, as we've seen, the flaws are in their offseason investments, and the future isn't just ignored, it doesn't exist.

HITTERS

EDGARDO ALFONZO — 3B — Bats: R — Throws: R — Born: 08-Nov-1973 — Age: 31

YEAR	TM	LG	AGE	AB	H	2B	3B	HR	BB	SO	SB	CS	AVG	OBP	SLG	MLVR	EQBA	EQOBP	EQSLG	EQMLVR	VORP	DEFENSE
2002	NYM	NL	28	490	151	26	0	16	62	55	6	0	.308	.391	.459	.232	.317	.393	.476	.187	54.3	130-3B 10
2003	SFG	NL	29	514	133	25	2	13	58	41	5	2	.259	.334	.391	-.031	.260	.335	.396	-.078	20.7	121-3B -5
2004	SFG	NL	30	519	150	26	1	11	46	40	1	1	.289	.350	.407	.021	.283	.344	.401	-.037	17.9	117-3B 4
2005	*SFG*	*NL*	*31*	*446*	*121*	*24*	*1*	*9*	*45*	*42*	*2*	*1*	*.272*	*.342*	*.396*	*-.051*	*.275*	*.343*	*.412*	*-.028*	*12.1*	*119-3B -1*

Breakout: 8% *Improve: 31%* *Collapse: 30%*

Hiked his average 30 points, but so what? For the second straight year, Alfonzo showed himself for what he's sadly become: a slap hitter with little power and eroding plate discipline. Back injuries and age have robbed him of the electric bat that made him a star in 1999. The Giants now find themselves staring at a run-of-the-mill third baseman making star-level cash at $13.5 million over the next two years. Considering the Alfonzo deal was regarded in many circles as wholly reasonable in the Chan Ho Park–for-$65-million era, we applaud teams' new efforts to sign middle-class free agents to shorter deals for a little more money per year.

BARRY BONDS — LF — Bats: L — Throws: L — Born: 24-Jul-1964 — Age: 40

YEAR	TM	LG	AGE	AB	H	2B	3B	HR	BB	SO	SB	CS	AVG	OBP	SLG	MLVR	EQBA	EQOBP	EQSLG	EQMLVR	VORP	DEFENSE
2002	SFG	NL	37	403	149	31	2	46	198	47	9	2	.370	.582	.799	.946	.373	.582	.821	.951	147.4	119-LF -6
2003	SFG	NL	38	390	133	22	1	45	148	58	7	0	.341	.529	.749	.785	.338	.526	.751	.763	112.6	112-LF 10
2004	SFG	NL	39	373	135	27	3	45	232	41	6	1	.362	.609	.812	.928	.349	.600	.785	.893	142.0	122-LF 1
2005	*SFG*	*NL*	*40*	*330*	*112*	*24*	*1*	*29*	*135*	*43*	*2*	*0*	*.339*	*.532*	*.687*	*.656*	*.344*	*.534*	*.713*	*.694*	*88.1*	*112-LF -3*

Breakout: 32% *Improve: 51%* *Collapse: 15%*

Do steroids, all things considered, improve a baseball player's performance? For all the hand-wringing, moralizing, and high-horsing the issue has triggered, the net effect of steroids on baseball players remains unknown. Can they help a player get stronger and thus hit the ball further? Maybe. Do they increase the chance of injury, ranging from hamstring pulls to the sad case of Jason Giambi? Possibly. Do the potential benefits outweigh the potential negatives? No one knows for sure. As performance analysts, we're far more interested in the on-field effects than anything else. Given the obvious difficulties in setting up control groups of major league players using and not using, it's unlikely we'll find anything conclusive any time soon.

In the meantime, Barry Bonds remains implicated in one of the biggest scandals in sports history, having never tested positive for any banned substance but admitting he unwittingly used them for a brief period of time. At the end of the day Bonds remains the best hitter in baseball. He posted the best on-base percentage of all-time and one of the highest slugging averages ever in '04, well after the first steroids rumblings were supposed to send baseball's sluggers back down to Earth. Bonds will remain the best hitter in the game in '05, though injuries and age will start cutting into his production. We'll leave the moral outrage to someone else.

MIKE CERVENAK — 3B — Bats: R — Throws: R — Born: 17-Aug-1976 — Age: 28

YEAR	TM	LG	AGE	AB	H	2B	3B	HR	BB	SO	SB	CS	AVG	OBP	SLG	MLVR	EQBA	EQOBP	EQSLG	EQMLVR	VORP	DEFENSE
2002	NRW	EAS	25	492	136	34	1	21	30	78	5	2	.276	.330	.478	.145	.251	.296	.438	-.099	4.1	
2003	NRW	EAS	26	511	138	26	1	20	36	80	2	1	.270	.329	.442	.085	.246	.298	.418	-.127	8.5	81-3B -2 47-1B -7
2004	NRW	EAS	27	410	138	36	1	21	52	53	6	1	.337	.414	.583	.461	.303	.374	.522	.205	50.0	92-3B 4 13-1B -2
2004	FRE	PCL	27	44	11	1	0	5	0	7	0	0	.250	.267	.614	.055	.186	.175	.419	-.402	-3.2	
2005	*SFG*	*NL*	*28*	*192*	*50*	*11*	*1*	*7*	*15*	*33*	*1*	*0*	*.258*	*.322*	*.428*	*-.053*	*.262*	*.323*	*.445*	*-.029*	*8.0*	*53-3B -5*

Breakout: 11% *Improve: 31%* *Collapse: 36%*

When a player like Adrian Beltre puts up an MVP-level season way out of character with the rest of his career, teams must decide whether that represents a new standard of performance worth tens of millions of dollars, or an anomaly not worth paying for. Considering Cervenak was nearly three years older than Beltre and put up his numbers in Double-A, there's a lot less at stake. But on a team sorely lacking good bats, he merits a spring training invite and a shot at a big league job. They already installed him as a starter in the Arizona Fall League, so there's hope.

DEIVI CRUZ — SS — Bats: R — Throws: R — Born: 06-Nov-1972 — Age: 32

YEAR	TM	LG	AGE	AB	H	2B	3B	HR	BB	SO	SB	CS	AVG	OBP	SLG	MLVR	EQBA	EQOBP	EQSLG	EQMLVR	VORP	DEFENSE
2002	SDP	NL	29	514	135	28	2	7	22	58	2	3	.263	.294	.366	-.098	.276	.305	.390	-.131	10.3	130-SS -1
2003	BAL	AL	30	548	137	24	2	14	13	49	1	2	.250	.269	.378	-.184	.252	.277	.385	-.209	5.3	144-SS -2
2004	SFG	NL	31	397	116	30	2	7	17	32	1	3	.292	.322	.431	.002	.290	.318	.428	-.040	17.9	86-SS 5
2005	*SFG*	*NL*	*32*	*310*	*80*	*16*	*1*	*5*	*14*	*31*	*1*	*1*	*.258*	*.292*	*.370*	*-.184*	*.262*	*.293*	*.385*	*-.162*	*5.4*	*81-SS -1*

Breakout: 13% *Improve: 22%* *Collapse: 46%.*

Cheers to the Giants for seeing Cruz's surprising 2004 season for what it was—an outlier not likely to repeat itself. Jeers to the Giants for trying to solve the problem by signing 37-year-old Omar Vizquel for too many years and too much money, burning a draft pick for good measure. Cruz will be a decent backup and could see significant playing time given the elevated risk of injury and ineffectiveness for a player Vizquel's age.

BRIAN DALLIMORE — UT — Bats: R — Throws: R — Born: 15-Nov-1973 — Age: 31

YEAR	TM	LG	AGE	AB	H	2B	3B	HR	BB	SO	SB	CS	AVG	OBP	SLG	MLVR	EQBA	EQOBP	EQSLG	EQMLVR	VORP	DEFENSE
2002	TUC	PCL	28	419	123	26	2	6	28	72	13	4	.294	.346	.408	-.042	.248	.300	.345	-.225	-5.5	85-3B 0 13-2B -2
2003	FRE	PCL	29	330	116	16	2	4	37	37	6	4	.352	.427	.448	.266	.312	.385	.403	.065	24.6	67-2B -5 20-3B -1
2004	FRE	PCL	30	432	140	21	4	8	40	53	9	2	.324	.396	.447	.119	.282	.347	.379	-.063	14.0	45-2B -1 34-3B 0
2004	SFG	NL	30	43	12	2	0	1	4	7	0	1	.279	.347	.395	.003	.279	.312	.372	-.142	1.2	
2005	*SFG*	*NL*	*31*	*178*	*46*	*9*	*1*	*2*	*14*	*26*	*2*	*1*	*.258*	*.327*	*.348*	*-.151*	*.261*	*.328*	*.362*	*-.131*	*5.4*	*51-2B -3*

Breakout: 9% *Improve: 26%* *Collapse: 52%*

Just another minor league journeyman who can hit in Fresno, Dallimore's a long shot given all the infield bodies in the mix this spring. But hey, you never know: He's 31, so maybe the Giants will mistake him for a grizzled major league veteran and give him a three-year deal.

RAY DURHAM — 2B — Bats: B — Throws: R — Born: 30-Nov-1971 — Age: 33

YEAR	TM	LG	AGE	AB	H	2B	3B	HR	BB	SO	SB	CS	AVG	OBP	SLG	MLVR	EQBA	EQOBP	EQSLG	EQMLVR	VORP	DEFENSE
2002	CWS	AL	30	345	103	20	2	9	49	59	20	5	.299	.390	.446	.137	.304	.397	.456	.153	35.1	90-2B 1
2002	OAK	AL	30	219	60	14	4	6	24	34	6	2	.274	.350	.457	.063	.276	.357	.465	.070	15.4	11-2B 0
2003	SFG	NL	31	410	117	30	5	8	50	82	7	7	.285	.366	.441	.119	.286	.366	.449	.073	30.0	95-2B 10
2004	SFG	NL	32	471	133	28	8	17	57	60	10	4	.282	.364	.484	.143	.278	.358	.475	.088	40.3	108-2B -8
2005	*SFG*	*NL*	*33*	*426*	*119*	*25*	*4*	*12*	*53*	*66*	*9*	*3*	*.278*	*.362*	*.439*	*.045*	*.282*	*.364*	*.457*	*.071*	*34.1*	*116-2B -3*

Breakout: 16% *Improve: 41%* *Collapse: 26%*

Though injuries forced him to miss significant playing time for the second straight year, Durham has shown only mild signs of wear when he plays, his speed and defense gently fading while his power game blossoms; Durham's .202 isolated slugging was the best of his career. A heady player and consistent on-base threat, it's easy to envision Durham hanging around for several more years. For now, he's a worthy leadoff hitter and a good running mate for Bonds on a team sorely lacking in offensive talent.

JASON ELLISON CF **Bats: R** **Throws: R** Born: 04-Apr-1978 Age: 27

YEAR	TM	LG	AGE	AB	H	2B	3B	HR	BB	SO	SB	CS	AVG	OBP	SLG	MLVR	EQBA	EQOBP	EQSLG	EQMLVR	VORP	DEFENSE			
2002	SJO	CLF	24	322	87	13	0	5	25	37	9	9	.270	.325	.357	-.026	.237	.274	.308	-.335	-18.3	79-CF	2		
2002	FRE	PCL	24	196	61	8	1	3	21	28	16	3	.311	.389	.408	.087	.275	.350	.358	-.092	3.4	48-CF	2		
2003	FRE	PCL	25	461	136	22	4	6	39	52	21	13	.295	.356	.399	.033	.267	.327	.365	-.132	2.2	113-CF	-3		
2004	FRE	PCL	26	505	159	32	7	9	40	66	27	12	.315	.368	.459	.077	.271	.322	.386	-.109	5.6	118-CF	3		
2005	*SFG*	*NL*	*27*	*126*	*32*	*6*	*1*	*2*	*10*	*18*	*3*	*2*	*.255*	*.313*	*.363*	*-.158*	*.258*	*.314*	*.377*	*-.137*	*2.8*	*37-CF*	*1*		

Breakout: 24% *Improve: 45%* *Collapse: 39%*

Fifth outfielder material at best, Ellison's best asset in his speed, and even then he's highly unreliable as a basestealer with only a 66% success rate the last two years. With zero-upside, Ellison-types waiting in the wings, you can almost see the logic in signing below-average players to multi-million-dollar free-agent deals. Almost.

PEDRO FELIZ 1B/3B **Bats: R** **Throws: R** Born: 27-Apr-1975 Age: 30

YEAR	TM	LG	AGE	AB	H	2B	3B	HR	BB	SO	SB	CS	AVG	OBP	SLG	MLVR	EQBA	EQOBP	EQSLG	EQMLVR	VORP	DEFENSE			
2002	SFG	NL	27	146	37	4	1	2	6	27	0	0	.253	.281	.336	-.157	.259	.285	.354	-.234	0.5	34-3B	0		
2003	SFG	NL	28	235	58	9	3	16	10	53	2	2	.247	.278	.515	.029	.247	.280	.519	-.015	9.8	40-3B	0	11-LF	0
2004	SFG	NL	29	503	139	33	3	22	23	85	5	2	.276	.305	.485	.040	.271	.300	.479	-.015	20.6	59-1B	-1	40-3B	2
2005	*SFG*	*NL*	*30*	*374*	*97*	*20*	*3*	*15*	*21*	*73*	*3*	*1*	*.260*	*.300*	*.450*	*-.059*	*.263*	*.301*	*.468*	*-.033*	*10.6*	*96-1B*	*6*		

Breakout: 11% *Improve: 34%* *Collapse: 27%*

In a year that started with the Giants crowing about their next star offensive player, Feliz finished the season with the same incomplete skill set and lukewarm production that make him the new Tony Batista. For all his prodigious power, Feliz shows no interest in improving his strike-zone judgment and lacks the offensive game to be an everyday first baseman. He's a useful super-utility man who's blocked from his best defensive position by Alfonzo. There are few teams in baseball more poorly constructed than the Giants; if Bonds weren't around, they'd have blown this whole thing up years ago.

MARQUIS GRISSOM CF **Bats: R** **Throws: R** Born: 17-Apr-1967 Age: 38

YEAR	TM	LG	AGE	AB	H	2B	3B	HR	BB	SO	SB	CS	AVG	OBP	SLG	MLVR	EQBA	EQOBP	EQSLG	EQMLVR	VORP	DEFENSE			
2002	LAD	NL	35	343	95	21	4	17	22	68	5	1	.277	.321	.510	.165	.285	.327	.539	.133	26.8	53-CF	-1	26-LF	1
2003	SFG	NL	36	587	176	33	3	20	20	82	11	3	.300	.322	.468	.088	.299	.322	.474	.044	35.2	136-CF	-9		
2004	SFG	NL	37	562	157	26	2	22	37	83	3	1	.279	.323	.450	.027	.273	.317	.442	-.036	23.5	132-CF	-4		
2005	*SFG*	*NL*	*38*	*438*	*118*	*25*	*2*	*14*	*27*	*70*	*4*	*1*	*.270*	*.312*	*.430*	*-.058*	*.273*	*.314*	*.447*	*-.033*	*14.3*	*112-CF*	*-6*		

Breakout: 6% *Improve: 31%* *Collapse: 33%*

The Giants smartly targeted Steve Finley and Dave Roberts as lefty-swinging on-base threats to pair with Grissom's lefty-mashing stick, but struck out on both counts at last year's deadline. Grip's been a useful part the last few years, but his speed is nearly gone (a career-low three steals and a career-high 22 GIDPs in '04), and his poor defense makes people forget his incredible range as a young gazelle with the mid-90s Expos. Still, as PECOTA often tells us, fast players tend to age better than those with old-player skills; Grissom has used a late-career power spike to age fairly gracefully, enough that he could be an excellent part-time player at age 38 if the Giants can find him a platoon partner. With Moises Alou signed, a Tucker/Grissom platoon would be a nightmare defensively, but works in the lineup.

JEFFREY HAMMONDS OF **Bats: R** **Throws: R** Born: 05-Mar-1971 Age: 34

YEAR	TM	LG	AGE	AB	H	2B	3B	HR	BB	SO	SB	CS	AVG	OBP	SLG	MLVR	EQBA	EQOBP	EQSLG	EQMLVR	VORP	DEFENSE			
2002	MIL	NL	31	448	115	26	5	9	52	86	4	5	.257	.332	.397	-.001	.258	.330	.409	-.071	12.1	61-CF	0	42-RF	-2
2003	SFG	NL	32	94	26	10	0	3	13	21	1	0	.277	.370	.479	.132	.287	.367	.468	.102	6.3	10-CF	0		
2004	SFG	NL	33	95	20	5	0	3	15	22	1	0	.211	.336	.358	-.111	.211	.319	.347	-.208	0.5	18-RF	0		
2005	*WAS*	*NL*	*34*	*151*	*37*	*8*	*1*	*4*	*20*	*33*	*2*	*0*	*.248*	*.340*	*.396*	*-.072*	*.250*	*.340*	*.406*	*-.059*	*6.0*	*45-RF*	*0*		

Breakout: 39% *Improve: 57%* *Collapse: 27%*

It's a shame that Jeffrey Hammonds's legacy will be the three-year, $21.75 million Brewers deal that battled Pat Meares's four-year Pirates for the worst debacle in the annals of WTF?!-contract history. His career line of .272/.339/.451 is nothing to sneeze at, and Hammonds could have been more useful if he'd stayed healthy. We won't weep too much for a man set for life if he invested wisely, but baseball can be a cruel game. Actually, considering what awaits Hammonds on the horror-show Nationals, pass the Kleenex.

TRAVIS ISHIKAWA 1B Bats: L Throws: L Born: 24-Sep-1983 Age: 21

YEAR	TM	LG	AGE	AB	H	2B	3B	HR	BB	SO	SB	CS	AVG	OBP	SLG	MLVR	EQBA	EQOBP	EQSLG	EQMLVR	VORP	DEFENSE
2002	SLO	NWN	18	88	27	2	1	1	5	22	1	1	.307	.347	.386	.109	.244	.270	.311	-.335	-11.7	21-1B -3
2003	SLO	NWN	19	248	63	17	4	3	44	77	0	0	.254	.376	.391	.102	.200	.288	.314	-.319	-34.3	66-1B -3
2003	HAG	SAL	19	194	40	5	0	3	33	69	3	4	.206	.329	.278	-.114	.159	.250	.214	-.549	-31.6	57-1B -3
2004	HAG	SAL	20	358	92	19	2	15	45	110	10	5	.257	.357	.447	.089	.215	.291	.366	-.235	-17.6	95-1B 3
2004	SJO	CLF	20	56	13	7	0	1	10	16	0	0	.232	.353	.411	.031	.175	.259	.316	-.388	-5.5	16-1B 1
2005	SFG	NL	21	337	73	16	1	8	33	109	3	1	.215	.299	.339	-.238	.218	.300	.353	-.220	-7.3	92-1B -5

Breakout: 32% Improve: 51% Collapse: 22%

We covered his back-story last year: 21st-round pick with high-round talent given nearly a million bucks to sign and skip college. Ishikawa can now be viewed as simply an intriguing prospect. Showed good sock for a 20-year-old in his first year in the Sally League, and didn't embarrass himself in 16 games at high-A at season's end. Between Ishikawa and Brad Vericker, the Giants could have nice options at first base in a few years, if ever they get over their disdain for rookies.

JUSTIN KNOEDLER C Bats: R Throws: R Born: 17-Jul-1980 Age: 24

YEAR	TM	LG	AGE	AB	H	2B	3B	HR	BB	SO	SB	CS	AVG	OBP	SLG	MLVR	EQBA	EQOBP	EQSLG	EQMLVR	VORP	DEFENSE
2002	HAG	SAL	21	280	72	16	2	5	37	56	6	5	.257	.349	.382	.054	.217	.288	.332	-.286	-10.2	81-C -28
2003	SJO	CLF	22	354	91	25	2	10	35	78	13	3	.257	.326	.424	.039	.217	.275	.358	-.275	-11.3	96-C 2
2004	NRW	EAS	23	409	112	28	3	9	32	98	5	3	.274	.335	.423	.058	.255	.306	.391	-.144	3.7	102-C -2
2005	SFG	NL	24	168	40	9	1	4	12	41	2	1	.238	.297	.369	-.189	.241	.299	.383	-.168	2.1	47-C -3

Breakout: 24% Improve: 39% Collapse: 38%

Not a bad season, as Knoedler experienced his first full season at Double-A. It was also year three of the switch-back experiment, with Knoedler having gone from college catcher to dominant rookie-ball reliever in 2001, and then back to catcher. He's shown emerging power, so it's unlikely he'll switch back. If everything breaks right, in a couple years he'll be a candidate for a big league backup job, probably just before the Giants give Einar Diaz a four-year deal.

RICKY LEDEE CF Bats: L Throws: L Born: 22-Nov-1973 Age: 31

YEAR	TM	LG	AGE	AB	H	2B	3B	HR	BB	SO	SB	CS	AVG	OBP	SLG	MLVR	EQBA	EQOBP	EQSLG	EQMLVR	VORP	DEFENSE
2002	PHI	NL	28	203	46	13	1	8	35	50	1	2	.227	.342	.419	.046	.234	.347	.434	-.024	9.8	33-CF 1
2003	PHI	NL	29	255	63	15	2	13	34	59	0	0	.247	.334	.475	.094	.250	.339	.484	.042	15.4	30-CF 0 20-LF 1
2004	PHI	NL	30	123	35	7	0	7	22	27	2	0	.285	.393	.512	.235	.293	.387	.520	.214	12.9	13-CF 2
2004	SFG	NL	30	53	6	2	0	0	5	20	1	0	.113	.200	.151	-.669	.113	.169	.151	-.819	-6.9	
2005	LAD	NL	31	114	26	5	1	5	16	30	1	0	.229	.326	.408	-.094	.235	.330	.420	-.069	4.4	35-CF -6

Breakout: 27% Improve: 49% Collapse: 34%

After a monster first four months as a part-timer in Philly, Ledee faded off the face of the Earth after being dealt to San Francisco for Felix Rodriguez, "hitting" .113/.151/.200 as a Giant. Still, his slump was a fluke, and Brian Sabean deftly got Alfredo Simon thrown into the deal. Ledee doesn't have the game to play every day, but the Dodgers have both the personnel and the savvy manager in Jim Tracy to get the most out of him for the next two years.

FRED LEWIS CF Bats: L Throws: R Born: 09-Dec-1980 Age: 24

YEAR	TM	LG	AGE	AB	H	2B	3B	HR	BB	SO	SB	CS	AVG	OBP	SLG	MLVR	EQBA	EQOBP	EQSLG	EQMLVR	VORP	DEFENSE
2002	SLO	NWN	21	239	77	9	3	1	26	58	9	6	.322	.396	.397	.196	.258	.312	.324	-.225	-10.2	40-CF -5
2003	HAG	SAL	22	420	105	17	8	1	68	112	30	15	.250	.361	.336	.023	.216	.302	.297	-.306	-23.1	107-CF -9
2004	SJO	CLF	23	439	132	20	11	8	84	109	33	14	.301	.424	.451	.269	.262	.364	.386	-.036	15.8	112-CF -6
2005	SFG	NL	24	271	67	13	3	4	32	76	9	3	.246	.334	.358	-.133	.249	.336	.372	-.112	4.5	76-CF -5

Breakout: 21% Improve: 42% Collapse: 31%

A breakout year, as Lewis drew 84 walks, stole 33 bases, hiked his power and played an excellent center field. The Giants skipped him all the way up to Triple-A, where he looked good in a brief six-game audition, but their history of moving prospects slowly suggests he'll start the year at Double-A. He'll need at least one more season before he's ready, and it's an open question if he'll make it before the Giants ship him off for another help-Barry-now veteran. Still, he's a rare jewel in a system where players have more trouble getting to first base than Nathan Lane on the Isle of Lesbos.

TODD LINDEN OF **Bats: B** **Throws: R** Born: 30-Jun-1980 Age: 25

YEAR	TM	LG	AGE	AB	H	2B	3B	HR	BB	SO	SB	CS	AVG	OBP	SLG	MLVR	EQBA	EQOBP	EQSLG	EQMLVR	VORP	DEFENSE
2002	SHV	TXS	22	392	123	26	2	12	61	101	9	5	.314	.419	.482	.334	.290	.378	.458	.110	23.5	110-RF -3
2002	FRE	PCL	22	100	25	2	1	3	20	35	2	0	.250	.380	.380	-.010	.222	.345	.333	-.168	-3.9	21-LF -1
2003	FRE	PCL	23	471	131	24	3	11	40	105	14	4	.278	.356	.412	.038	.252	.324	.380	-.127	-8.8	106-RF -13 11-CF 0
2004	FRE	PCL	24	489	127	28	2	23	63	149	8	6	.260	.349	.466	.001	.221	.305	.379	-.186	-17.7	105-RF -4 14-LF 1
2004	SFG	NL	24	32	5	1	0	0	5	7	0	0	.156	.289	.188	-.475	.182	.242	.212	-.560	-3.4	
2005	*SFG*	*NL*	*25*	*242*	*62*	*13*	*1*	*7*	*28*	*70*	*3*	*1*	*.256*	*.344*	*.413*	*-.037*	*.259*	*.346*	*.429*	*-.013*	*9.1*	*69-RF -4*

Breakout: 42% *Improve: 62%* *Collapse: 19%*

In 1647 Friedrich Wilhelm I planted a line of majestic linden trees stretching from the electoral palace to the gates of the city of Berlin. The path grew to become Germany's greatest boulevard, a hub of pedestrian, carriage, and, later, automobile traffic. To this day, it remains a signature element of a nation's history. *Todd* Linden hiked his walk rate and doubled his home run total in his second go-round in Fresno, and might even turn into a decent fourth outfielder. But he'll never generate anything like that kind of passion.

EDDY MARTINEZ-ESTEVE LF **Bats: R** **Throws: R** Born: 14-Jul-1983 Age: 21

YEAR	TM	LG	AGE	AB	H	2B	3B	HR	BB	SO	SB	CS	AVG	OBP	SLG	MLVR	EQBA	EQOBP	EQSLG	EQMLVR	VORP	DEFENSE
2004	HAG	SAL	20	46	10	1	1	1	8	8	1	1	.217	.339	.348	-.089	.170	.265	.255	-.459	-5.2	
2004	SJO	CLF	20	69	29	7	2	0	4	9	0	1	.420	.446	.580	.649	.328	.330	.418	.002	1.1	12-LF -1
2005	*SFG*	*NL*	*21*	*391*	*94*	*21*	*4*	*4*	*32*	*85*	*1*	*2*	*.239*	*.304*	*.341*	*-.214*	*.242*	*.305*	*.354*	*-.195*	*-9.9*	*103-LF -4*

Breakout: 8% *Improve: 23%* *Collapse: 46%*

The Giants' highest '04 draft pick, Martinez-Esteve finished the season with a flourish in San Jose, albeit in a small sample size. He's got the big-college pedigree (Florida State) and the bat to move up quickly, especially since Fred Lewis is the only outfielder in the organization likely to be starting in San Francisco by 2007, assuming Bonds has called it quits by then.

DAMON MINOR 1B **Bats: L** **Throws: L** Born: 05-Jan-1974 Age: 31

YEAR	TM	LG	AGE	AB	H	2B	3B	HR	BB	SO	SB	CS	AVG	OBP	SLG	MLVR	EQBA	EQOBP	EQSLG	EQMLVR	VORP	DEFENSE
2002	SFG	NL	28	173	41	6	0	10	24	34	0	0	.237	.333	.445	.055	.251	.332	.463	.001	7.0	37-1B -1
2003	FRE	PCL	29	141	33	2	1	8	6	29	0	0	.234	.278	.433	-.101	.207	.249	.386	-.293	-8.6	20-1B 4
2003	SWB	INT	29	328	76	17	1	16	27	60	1	2	.232	.305	.436	-.008	.213	.287	.413	-.180	-9.6	39-1B -4
2004	FRE	PCL	30	338	102	23	3	17	50	78	0	0	.302	.399	.538	.233	.258	.349	.444	.012	9.8	58-1B -3
2004	SFG	NL	30	58	14	2	0	0	12	18	0	0	.241	.405	.276	-.085	.259	.364	.276	-.186	0.7	15-1B 0
2005	*SFG*	*NL*	*31*	*171*	*42*	*9*	*1*	*6*	*19*	*42*	*0*	*0*	*.244*	*.329*	*.415*	*-.068*	*.247*	*.330*	*.432*	*-.045*	*6.2*	*50-1B -5*

Breakout: 29% *Improve: 52%* *Collapse: 26%*

Some teams have found moderate success with low-cost cast-offs, so why not take a flyer here? At some point you wonder if that team will ever develop enough young impact players to contend again, but as long as guys like Minor don't block anyone good, no worries. The 1-in-100 chance he gets a job, swats 15 bombs and gets dealt for a decent prospect is the upside here.

DUSTAN MOHR OF **Bats: R** **Throws: R** Born: 19-Jun-1976 Age: 29

YEAR	TM	LG	AGE	AB	H	2B	3B	HR	BB	SO	SB	CS	AVG	OBP	SLG	MLVR	EQBA	EQOBP	EQSLG	EQMLVR	VORP	DEFENSE
2002	MIN	AL	26	383	103	23	2	12	31	86	6	3	.269	.325	.433	.014	.269	.331	.438	-.020	11.3	82-RF 3 21-LF 2
2003	MIN	AL	27	348	87	22	0	10	33	106	5	2	.250	.314	.399	-.090	.251	.318	.397	-.116	2.1	70-RF 1 24-LF -1
2004	SFG	NL	28	263	72	20	1	7	46	64	0	3	.274	.394	.437	.110	.268	.385	.430	.066	14.4	41-RF 0 30-LF 1
2005	*COL*	*NL*	*29*	*201*	*56*	*12*	*1*	*8*	*26*	*49*	*2*	*1*	*.277*	*.365*	*.475*	*.096*	*.256*	*.342*	*.429*	*-.022*	*8.4*	*58-RF 0*

Breakout: 21% *Improve: 48%* *Collapse: 25%*

An impressive season, which makes you wonder why the Giants needed to forfeit a high draft pick for two years of Michael Tucker. Yes, we've established that they purposely forfeited the pick, figuring the risk to not be worth the cost of a signing bonus. But is the small degree of likelihood that Tucker's mediocrity will hold up against a younger outfielder with a shorter track record but equal or better ability really worth giving up the upside of a well-drafted prep or collegian? If the Giants hit one out of ten picks right, it's a bad proposition, and even a blindfolded Syd Thrift could hit .100. He's arbitration-eligible, and the Giants' concerns over his biceps injury and the dubious odds of a repeat '04 earned him a non-tender. The Rockies scooped him up, which instantly makes him a roto sleeper.

LANCE NIEKRO 1B Bats: R Throws: R Born: 29-Jan-1979 Age: 26

YEAR	TM	LG	AGE	AB	H	2B	3B	HR	BB	SO	SB	CS	AVG	OBP	SLG	MLVR	EQBA	EQOBP	EQSLG	EQMLVR	VORP	DEFENSE
2002	SHV	TXS	23	297	92	20	1	4	7	32	0	2	.310	.327	.424	.117	.284	.298	.399	-.124	-3.7	48-1B -3 26-3B -2
2003	FRE	PCL	24	381	115	15	2	4	19	39	3	3	.302	.334	.383	-.021	.267	.301	.341	-.216	-4.0	71-3B -8 16-1B 0
2004	FRE	PCL	25	242	72	21	4	12	14	32	1	1	.298	.337	.566	.162	.255	.292	.472	-.054	2.0	34-1B -1 20-3B 0
2005	*SFG*	*NL*	*26*	*234*	*59*	*13*	*1*	*4*	*8*	*31*	*1*	*0*	*.253*	*.280*	*.374*	*-.204*	*.256*	*.281*	*.389*	*-.183*	*-4.7*	*61-1B -1*

Breakout: 11% *Improve: 28%* *Collapse: 49%*

Like Linden, Niekro had a nice breakout in his second tour of duty at Fresno. Probably more likely to hit for average than Linden given his put-everything-in-play approach, but his overall upside is more limited, as he swings at good and bad pitches alike. He's trade bait waiting for when the Giants go shopping come July 31. The beauty of Sabean making those deadline deals is knowing there's very little chance any of the guys he's trading away will amount to anything.

DAN ORTMEIER RF Bats: B Throws: L Born: 11-May-1981 Age: 24

YEAR	TM	LG	AGE	AB	H	2B	3B	HR	BB	SO	SB	CS	AVG	OBP	SLG	MLVR	EQBA	EQOBP	EQSLG	EQMLVR	VORP	DEFENSE
2002	SLO	NWN	21	195	57	9	1	5	18	37	3	0	.292	.352	.426	.154	.242	.288	.364	-.225	-18.1	27-LF -2
2003	SJO	CLF	22	408	124	32	6	8	39	89	13	6	.304	.378	.471	.236	.264	.323	.408	-.081	-2.0	71-RF -6
2004	NRW	EAS	23	377	95	23	6	10	47	110	18	2	.252	.353	.424	.073	.235	.321	.394	-.126	-7.2	98-RF 3
2005	*SFG*	*NL*	*24*	*322*	*80*	*19*	*3*	*7*	*31*	*91*	*7*	*2*	*.250*	*.329*	*.394*	*-.091*	*.253*	*.330*	*.410*	*-.069*	*6.1*	*87-RF -4*

Breakout: 23% *Improve: 57%* *Collapse: 22%*

A disappointing season on the surface, but Ortmeier actually improved his walk rate and isolated power slightly on the jump to Double-A, in a tougher hitter's league to boot. Batting average is the most variable of the major offensive stats, and Ortmeier's '04 mark of .252 looks like the outlier in his career-to-date, so we're forecasting a nice rebound for '05. At 6′4″, 225 lbs, he often looks lost in the outfield, but he runs the bases well. Needs a consolidation year and an added power spike to take the next step, but he's on the right track.

A. J. PIERZYNSKI C Bats: L Throws: R Born: 30-Dec-1976 Age: 28

YEAR	TM	LG	AGE	AB	H	2B	3B	HR	BB	SO	SB	CS	AVG	OBP	SLG	MLVR	EQBA	EQOBP	EQSLG	EQMLVR	VORP	DEFENSE
2002	MIN	AL	25	440	132	31	6	6	13	61	1	2	.300	.334	.439	.059	.304	.339	.447	.039	30.1	115-C 6
2003	MIN	AL	26	487	152	35	3	11	24	55	3	1	.312	.360	.464	.130	.315	.363	.470	.125	41.4	130-C 10
2004	SFG	NL	27	471	128	28	2	11	19	27	0	1	.272	.319	.410	-.042	.268	.312	.406	-.101	15.2	111-C 1
2005	*CWS*	*AL*	*28*	*403*	*112*	*23*	*2*	*12*	*21*	*44*	*1*	*1*	*.277*	*.327*	*.430*	*-.021*	*.274*	*.327*	*.422*	*-.044*	*16.3*	*105-C 1*

Breakout: 5% *Improve: 23%* *Collapse: 40%*

Two unfair but true rules of baseball: (1) What you do in April gets scrutinized a lot more than what you do in June or July; (2) hard-nosed players who produce are called gamers—hard-nose players who don't are thrown under the bus. After a brutal April in which he hit .246/.267/.250, one teammate said: "He's the cancer in here. The pitchers aren't happy with him. If they can trade him, that would be fine with me." Pierzynski played at his career norms the rest of the season, but when an arbitration decision came due at season's end, the Giants decided they didn't need his personality anymore. You could forgive the Giants for not wanting to pay the $5 million or so it would have cost to retain him. Pierzynski's a better player than half the starting catchers in baseball, and he's a great short-term fix for the White Sox's continual catching problems. Meanwhile the Giants will pay $10.5 million over three years to a more genial and helpless Mike Matheny.

CODY RANSOM SS Bats: R Throws: R Born: 17-Feb-1976 Age: 29

YEAR	TM	LG	AGE	AB	H	2B	3B	HR	BB	SO	SB	CS	AVG	OBP	SLG	MLVR	EQBA	EQOBP	EQSLG	EQMLVR	VORP	DEFENSE
2002	FRE	PCL	26	449	93	18	4	13	47	151	6	4	.207	.283	.352	-.252	.181	.256	.304	-.407	-29.1	132-SS 0
2003	FRE	PCL	27	396	100	16	4	12	45	91	14	4	.253	.331	.404	-.035	.226	.302	.365	-.208	-0.6	109-SS -11
2004	FRE	PCL	28	136	42	6	2	10	19	30	8	0	.309	.397	.603	.330	.258	.345	.485	.061	9.7	24-2B 0
2004	SFG	NL	28	68	17	6	0	1	6	20	2	2	.250	.320	.382	-.123	.261	.316	.362	-.161	0.6	12-SS 0
2005	*SFG*	*NL*	*29*	*102*	*24*	*5*	*1*	*3*	*11*	*30*	*2*	*1*	*.233*	*.308*	*.381*	*-.157*	*.236*	*.310*	*.396*	*-.136*	*3.7*	*32-SS -4*

Breakout: 33% *Improve: 52%* *Collapse: 34%*

Realizing he may have to spend the rest of his life in Fresno, Ransom mashed for 36 games, earned a call-up and had a few flashes of usefulness with the big club. Looked like he'd be back for a fifth season of Triple-A baseball and sweet, sweet raisins, but the Giants non-tendered him. He'll get a spring-training invite somewhere, at least.

NATE SCHIERHOLTZ 3B/OF **Bats: L** **Throws: R** Born: 15-Feb-1984 Age: 21

YEAR	TM	LG	AGE	AB	H	2B	3B	HR	BB	SO	SB	CS	AVG	OBP	SLG	MLVR	EQBA	EQOBP	EQSLG	EQMLVR	VORP	DEFENSE	
2003	SLO	NWN	19	124	38	6	2	3	12	15	0	1	.306	.382	.460	.236	.244	.293	.378	-.195	-1.0	31-3B -3	
2004	HAG	SAL	20	235	70	22	0	15	19	52	1	0	.298	.356	.583	.305	.234	.273	.451	-.136	3.2	54-3B -3	
2004	SJO	CLF	20	258	76	18	9	3	15	41	3	1	.295	.338	.469	.145	.262	.297	.410	-.128	3.9	35-3B -1	17-RF -1
2005	*SFG*	*NL*	*21*	*398*	*97*	*23*	*4*	*9*	*22*	*84*	*1*	*1*	*.244*	*.293*	*.393*	*-.162*	*.247*	*.294*	*.408*	*-.140*	*-1.1*	*103-3B -7*	

Breakout: 12% *Improve: 38%* *Collapse: 31%*

The '03 draftee showed some good signs, cracking a homer for every 17 trips at Hagerstown and building on his impressive first year. His power took a step back at San Jose, and his plate discipline remains spotty, but still, Schierholtz is one of the best hitting prospects in the system. The Giants had him stumbling in the outfield instead, convinced that he can't handle the hot corner. Given his Lonnie Smith-like adventures upon the switch, the hope is the Giants give him a chance to go back to the infield. Young enough and talented enough to amount to something.

J. T. SNOW 1B **Bats: B** **Throws: L** Born: 26-Feb-1968 Age: 37

YEAR	TM	LG	AGE	AB	H	2B	3B	HR	BB	SO	SB	CS	AVG	OBP	SLG	MLVR	EQBA	EQOBP	EQSLG	EQMLVR	VORP	DEFENSE
2002	SFG	NL	34	422	104	26	2	6	59	90	0	0	.246	.344	.360	-.020	.254	.348	.378	-.083	8.9	113-1B 0
2003	SFG	NL	35	330	90	18	3	8	55	55	1	2	.273	.387	.418	.109	.274	.387	.425	.068	18.9	94-1B 2
2004	SFG	NL	36	346	113	32	1	12	58	61	4	0	.327	.429	.529	.347	.318	.420	.517	.289	45.1	89-1B -3
2005	*SFG*	*NL*	*37*	*273*	*74*	*16*	*1*	*8*	*40*	*51*	*1*	*0*	*.271*	*.370*	*.427*	*.036*	*.274*	*.371*	*.444*	*.061*	*14.2*	*78-1B -2*

Breakout: 14% *Improve: 40%* *Collapse: 30%*

Had a sudden, dramatic, late-career spike in production, which can only mean one thing: Wheaties. Doomed to remain nothing but an overmatched slap hitter as long as he stuck to Apple Jacks and Corn Pops, Snow is clearly involved with the Breakfast of Champions Organization (BOCO). Plus, have you seen the size of his cereal bowl lately? Compared to the bowls from his days as an Angel, or even earlier in his Giants career, it's much bigger. Or so we hear.

We feel 100% confident—despite having nothing concrete to prove it and a dozen viable alternate explanations—that he's now eating those nasty Wheaties. He's setting a bad example for kids, whose parents are completely absolved from helping them make informed decisions about their lives. J. T. Snow should be held solely responsible for any bad choices the children of America make, and by eating Wheaties, he's the lowest form of scum imaginable. Hopefully Congress will intervene.

TONY TORCATO Bust **Bats: L** **Throws: R** Born: 25-Oct-1979 Age: 25

YEAR	TM	LG	AGE	AB	H	2B	3B	HR	BB	SO	SB	CS	AVG	OBP	SLG	MLVR	EQBA	EQOBP	EQSLG	EQMLVR	VORP	DEFENSE	
2002	FRE	PCL	22	490	142	23	3	13	29	65	4	6	.290	.330	.429	-.006	.256	.298	.376	-.179	-18.6	66-LF -2	55-RF -5
2003	FRE	PCL	23	423	125	18	2	3	6	33	4	0	.296	.304	.369	-.100	.262	.276	.329	-.286	-24.3	58-1B 2	34-LF -2
2004	FRE	PCL	24	395	114	22	0	3	11	35	4	1	.289	.314	.367	-.188	.244	.266	.301	-.357	-32.6	42-LF 1	19-1B -1
2005	*SFG*	*NL*	*25*	*220*	*53*	*11*	*1*	*2*	*5*	*23*	*1*	*0*	*.240*	*.262*	*.323*	*-.313*	*.243*	*.264*	*.336*	*-.295*	*-13.2*	*58-LF -6*	

Breakout: 12% *Improve: 27%* *Collapse: 42%*

This is why the Giants are eager to unload their early-round draft choices every year. Torcato was the 19th overall pick in 1998, and showed some promise early in his career, including hitting .324 at San Jose as a 20-year-old. But it's been downhill since, with Torcato's projected power never materializing, and his walk rate regressing to comically bad levels. If the Giants can get any kind of decent value in trade for him, they should jump on it.

YORVIT TORREALBA C **Bats: R** **Throws: R** Born: 19-Jul-1978 Age: 26

YEAR	TM	LG	AGE	AB	H	2B	3B	HR	BB	SO	SB	CS	AVG	OBP	SLG	MLVR	EQBA	EQOBP	EQSLG	EQMLVR	VORP	DEFENSE
2002	SFG	NL	23	136	38	10	0	2	14	20	0	0	.279	.355	.397	.058	.295	.355	.403	-.004	9.1	42-C 1
2003	SFG	NL	24	200	52	10	2	4	14	39	1	0	.260	.312	.390	-.073	.259	.312	.398	-.119	5.6	56-C 12
2004	SFG	NL	25	172	39	7	3	6	17	31	2	0	.227	.302	.407	-.116	.224	.298	.402	-.166	3.4	51-C 2
2005	*SFG*	*NL*	*26*	*183*	*46*	*10*	*1*	*5*	*17*	*33*	*1*	*0*	*.252*	*.321*	*.404*	*-.091*	*.255*	*.322*	*.420*	*-.068*	*9.4*	*53-C 3*

Breakout: 24% *Improve: 43%* *Collapse: 29%*

When Brian Sabean traded Joe Nathan, Boof Bonser, and Francisco Liriano for A. J. Pierzynski, many Giants fans wondered why they didn't simply play Torrealba instead. Now the Pierzynski deal looks even worse, while Torrealba remains a somewhat flawed but cheap, serviceable option. He won't play much with Matheny on board for the next three years.

MIKE TUCKER OF Bats: L Throws: R Born: 25-Jun-1971 Age: 34

YEAR	TM	LG	AGE	AB	H	2B	3B	HR	BB	SO	SB	CS	AVG	OBP	SLG	MLVR	EQBA	EQOBP	EQSLG	EQMLVR	VORP	DEFENSE	
2002	KCR	AL	31	475	118	27	6	12	56	105	23	9	.248	.330	.406	-.090	.242	.330	.396	-.101	4.9	62-RF 3	31-LF -2
2003	KCR	AL	32	389	102	20	5	13	39	88	8	10	.262	.331	.440	-.037	.257	.331	.435	-.034	6.0		
2004	SFG	NL	33	464	119	21	6	13	70	106	5	2	.256	.353	.412	.004	.252	.349	.402	-.050	16.0	93-RF -2	22-CF -1
2005	*SFG*	*NL*	*34*	*331*	*83*	*17*	*3*	*9*	*42*	*74*	*6*	*3*	*.250*	*.337*	*.404*	*-.064*	*.253*	*.338*	*.420*	*-.041*	*9.5*	*92-RF -2*	

Breakout: 26.4% *Improve: 52.4%* *Collapse: 19.3%*

The career high in walks was nice, but he remains below average for a corner outfielder and more likely to get worse than better at his age. The only difference between Tucker and 100 guys in Triple-A is Tucker's been in the majors and thus makes GMs feel safer. In an industry where not embarrassing yourself can be enough to ensure job security, mediocrities will always find good-paying jobs. He'll see less playing time after Moises Alou signed for the next two years.

BRAD VERICKER 1B Bats: L Throws: L Born: 08-May-1981 Age: 24

YEAR	TM	LG	AGE	AB	H	2B	3B	HR	BB	SO	SB	CS	AVG	OBP	SLG	MLVR	EQBA	EQOBP	EQSLG	EQMLVR	VORP	DEFENSE	
2003	SLO	NWN	22	243	69	19	0	15	48	58	0	1	.284	.404	.547	.354	.204	.289	.392	-.210	-22.6	19-LF -3	10-1B -1
2004	SJO	CLF	23	358	99	29	3	14	60	83	0	2	.277	.375	.492	.221	.231	.316	.397	-.134	-5.7	73-1B 1	
2004	NRW	EAS	23	52	10	3	0	0	10	20	0	0	.192	.317	.250	-.249	.132	.209	.151	-.728	-10.5		
2005	*SFG*	*NL*	*24*	*316*	*71*	*17*	*1*	*9*	*40*	*94*	*0*	*0*	*.225*	*.313*	*.376*	*-.160*	*.227*	*.315*	*.391*	*-.139*	*-1.0*	*87-1B -6*	

Breakout: 26% *Improve: 52%* *Collapse: 23%*

Signed as an undrafted free agent out of Point Loma Nazarene University in 2003, Vericker's had that non-prospect perception hanging over his head from the get-go. He's shrugged that tag off so far, flashing power and patience at Salem in '03 and San Jose last year. There are concerns about his defense at first base, but as Michael Wolverton noted in his midseason look at San Jose on baseballprospectus.com, Vericker has looked smoother afield, playing first more and DH less. He's not young so he'll need to make quick strides, but he's got a shot.

PITCHERS

DAVID AARDSMA Bats: R Throws: R Born: 27-Dec-1981 Age: 23

YEAR	TM	LG	AGE	G	GS	IP	H	BB	SO	HR	ERA	EQERA	EQH9	EQBB9	EQSO9	EQHR9	PERA	VORP	STF
2003	SJO	CLF	21	18	0	18.3	14	7	28	2	1.97	3.24	8.6	4.3	9.2	2.2	5.40	0.4	8
2004	FRE	PCL	22	44	0	55.3	46	30	53	2	3.09	3.59	7.5	5.1	6.7	0.3	3.93	9.8	8
2004	SFG	NL	22	11	0	10.7	20	10	5	1	6.73	6.17	13.1	6.9	3.1	0.8	8.49	-1.2	-37
2005	*SFG*	*NL*	*23*	*19*	*3*	*37.7*	*35*	*21*	*31*	*4*	*4.11*	*4.44*	*8.3*	*4.3*	*6.6*	*0.9*	*4.89*	*5.7*	*-3*

Breakout: 15% *Improve: 44%* *Collapse: 26%*

Didn't have the instant success that fellow fast-track college closer Chad Cordero had in Montreal, but Aardsma logged a fine season at Triple-A, fanning nearly a batter per inning and keeping the ball in the park. He posted similar numbers in the Arizona Fall League, though he looked wild for stretches. He's expected to win a bullpen job in '05, and he's got the arsenal for a high-leverage or closer job.

JIM BROWER Bats: R Throws: R Born: 29-Dec-1972 Age: 32

YEAR	TM	LG	AGE	G	GS	IP	H	BB	SO	HR	ERA	EQERA	EQH9	EQBB9	EQSO9	EQHR9	PERA	VORP	STF
2002	CIN	NL	29	22	0	39.3	38	10	24	2	3.89	4.06	8.8	1.9	5.0	0.5	3.58	5.5	0
2002	MON	NL	29	30	0	41.0	39	22	33	5	4.83	4.72	8.6	4.1	6.5	1.1	4.50	2.5	-5
2003	SFG	NL	30	51	5	100.0	90	39	65	8	3.96	4.26	8.7	3.1	5.5	0.8	4.36	14.7	-1
2004	SFG	NL	31	89	0	93.0	90	36	63	6	3.29	3.90	8.7	3.1	5.5	0.5	3.90	16.9	-1
2005	*SFG*	*NL*	*32*	*43*	*4*	*73.0*	*74*	*27*	*47*	*6*	*3.99*	*4.31*	*9.1*	*2.9*	*5.3*	*0.8*	*4.47*	*9.9*	*-6*

Breakout: 23% *Improve: 47%* *Collapse: 21%*

A ROOGY if ever there was one, Brower helped the Giants by soaking up 93 mostly middle innings (after tossing 100 in '03) and holding righty batters to a microscopic .213/.267/.282. But he continued to show he lacks a pitch to neutralize lefties, as they made a .333/.411/.508 piñata out of him. Tightness and fatigue in his throwing bothered him late in the year, so the Giants have two good reasons to limit his workload in '05.

DAVE BURBA Bats: R Throws: R Born: 07-Jul-1966 Age: 38

YEAR	TM	LG	AGE	G	GS	IP	H	BB	SO	HR	ERA	EQERA	EQH9	EQBB9	EQSO9	EQHR9	PERA	VORP	STF
2002	CLE	AL	36	12	3	34.0	30	17	25	3	4.50	4.91	7.9	4.1	6.3	0.8	3.55	2.6	5
2002	TEX	AL	36	23	18	111.3	125	40	70	13	5.42	5.07	9.3	2.9	5.4	0.9	4.50	3.0	5
2003	MIL	NL	37	17	2	43.3	42	19	35	5	3.53	3.83	8.5	3.4	6.6	1.1	4.04	8.1	1
2004	MIL	NL	38	45	0	70.7	63	24	47	6	4.07	4.41	8.4	2.8	5.5	0.7	3.61	8.8	-2
2004	SFG	NL	38	6	0	6.3	7	2	3	1	5.71	6.00	10.5	3.0	4.5	1.5	6.00	0.0	-23
2005	*HOU*	*NL*	*38*	*34*	*4*	*61*	*66*	*27*	*39*	*9*	*5.33*	*5.42*	*9.6*	*3.4*	*5.3*	*1.2*	*5.23*	*1.9*	*-11*

Breakout 12% *Improve 39%* *Collapse 29%*

Decent little late-career season for a pitcher who'll get unfairly pegged as "that guy that cost the Indians Sean Casey," and not the solid innings eater he was in his prime. Somewhere Doyle Alexander and Larry Andersen are saving a spot in their support group. Non-tendered, but he could be back with the Giants May 1.

BRIAN BURRES Bats: L Throws: L Born: 08-Apr-1981 Age: 24

YEAR	TM	LG	AGE	G	GS	IP	H	BB	SO	HR	ERA	EQERA	EQH9	EQBB9	EQSO9	EQHR9	PERA	VORP	STF
2002	HAG	SAL	21	32	16	119.3	114	53	119	15	4.75	7.39	10.8	5.2	5.7	2.9	7.05	-17.1	-32
2003	SJO	CLF	22	39	0	60.7	55	36	64	4	3.86	5.95	8.7	6.8	6.3	1.3	5.30	1.9	-17
2004	SJO	CLF	23	36	15	123.7	115	30	114	10	2.84	4.80	9.4	2.8	5.5	1.4	5.04	7.1	-1
2005	*SFG*	*NL*	*24*	*35*	*6*	*72.3*	*68*	*33*	*50*	*9*	*4.40*	*4.75*	*8.4*	*3.6*	*5.6*	*1.2*	*4.80*	*7.1*	*-8*

Breakout: 20% *Improve: 49%* *Collapse: 21%*

Given a chance to start, the 31st-round community-college pick opened some eyes, slashing his walk rate from 5.3 to 2.2 while keeping his strong K and HR rates intact. On the mound he doesn't look like anything more than a skinny lefty junkballer, but few in the system can match those '04 results. After two seasons in San Jose, we'll know more after his '05 promotion to Double-A.

MATT CAIN Bats: R Throws: R Born: 01-Oct-1984 Age: 20

YEAR	TM	LG	AGE	G	GS	IP	H	BB	SO	HR	ERA	EQERA	EQH9	EQBB9	EQSO9	EQHR9	PERA	VORP	STF
2003	HAG	SAL	18	14	14	74.0	57	24	90	5	2.55	4.68	9.6	3.7	7.0	1.4	5.65	-0.4	24
2004	SJO	CLF	19	13	13	72.7	58	17	89	5	1.86	4.32	8.5	2.7	7.4	1.1	4.18	10.5	37
2004	NRW	EAS	19	15	15	86.0	73	40	72	7	3.35	5.18	8.8	4.5	5.7	0.8	4.84	6.8	28
2005	*SFG*	*NL*	*20*	*14*	*14*	*82.7*	*74*	*35*	*71*	*10*	*4.13*	*4.47*	*8.1*	*3.4*	*7.0*	*1.2*	*4.43*	*11.4*	*13*

Breakout: 15% *Improve: 50%* *Collapse: 12%*

While Tony Torcato makes a case for the Giants' strategy of sacrificing first-round picks, Cain makes that tack look terrible. The 25th-overall pick in 2002 has zoomed past Merkin Valdez to claim top-prospect status in the Giants' system. He destroyed Cal League batters as one of the youngest pitchers in the circuit, then held his own as a 19-year-old in Double-A, a startling feat. His fastball blazes at 95 and moves to both sides of the plate, and he can throw his huge, sweeping curve for knee-buckling strikes on any count. His circle-change needs work, and we'll want to see the Giants monitor his workload after an elbow stress fracture cost him half of '03. Still, Cain's developed a more fluid delivery that has observers bullish about him staying healthy. Granting TINSTAAPP, you're looking at one of the five best pitching prospects in baseball.

JASON CHRISTIANSEN Bats: R Throws: L Born: 21-Sep-1969 Age: 35

YEAR	TM	LG	AGE	G	GS	IP	H	BB	SO	HR	ERA	EQERA	EQH9	EQBB9	EQSO9	EQHR9	PERA	VORP	STF
2003	SFG	NL	33	40	0	26.0	25	11	22	3	5.19	5.04	9.0	3.2	7.2	1.1	5.04	1.2	-1
2004	SFG	NL	34	60	0	36.0	34	26	22	3	4.50	4.89	8.7	5.9	4.9	0.8	4.89	2.8	-20
2005	*SFG*	*NL*	*35*	*21*	*0*	*20.0*	*21*	*12*	*14*	*3*	*5.32*	*5.75*	*9.3*	*4.7*	*5.5*	*1.2*	*5.79*	*0.3*	*-18*

Breakout: 20% *Improve: 46%* *Collapse: 33%*

Two years after Tommy John surgery, Christiansen walked more batters than he struck out. He hasn't been a truly solid pitcher since his late 20s, and has struggled with his control even then. Nevertheless, the Giants signed him for $1.5 million plus an option for '06, obviously because the three-year, $6.8 million deal they gave him a few years ago wasn't enough wasted money. Memo to Brian Sabean: Just because you want to get guys who can help Bonds reach the promised land right now doesn't mean they need to be AARP-eligible and average at best.

KEVIN CORREIA

Bats: R Throws: R Born: 24-Aug-1980 Age: 24

YEAR	TM	LG	AGE	G	GS	IP	H	BB	SO	HR	ERA	EQERA	EQH9	EQBB9	EQSO9	EQHR9	PERA	VORP	STF
2002	SLO	NWN	21	10	8	37.7	37	14	31	1	4.54	6.49	9.9	4.2	4.2	0.8	5.45	0.6	-13
2003	NRW	EAS	22	16	14	86.3	80	30	73	3	3.65	4.70	8.3	3.4	6.2	0.5	3.50	19.2	19
2003	FRE	PCL	22	3	3	19.0	16	2	23	3	2.84	4.00	8.0	1.0	9.5	2.0	4.00	3.2	41
2003	SFG	NL	22	10	7	39.3	41	18	28	6	3.66	3.79	9.7	3.6	5.9	1.4	5.45	8.9	1
2004	FRE	PCL	23	29	16	105.3	118	35	70	12	4.53	5.03	9.5	3.2	4.6	1.1	4.94	7.5	-1
2004	SFG	NL	23	12	1	19.0	25	10	14	3	8.05	9.00	10.4	4.3	5.7	1.4	6.16	-7.9	-7
2005	*SFG*	*NL*	*24*	*18*	*9*	*62.3*	*64*	*25*	*44*	*7*	*4.55*	*4.92*	*9.2*	*3.2*	*5.7*	*1.1*	*4.95*	*6.4*	*-2*

Breakout: 16% *Improve: 48%* *Collapse: 28%*

The first player from the 2002 draft to reach the major leagues, due more to fluky circumstances than great ability or boffo results. Correia's a soft-tosser who can benefit from SBC Park's generous dimensions; he'd make a reasonable fifth starter. More likely he'll shuttle between Fresno and San Francisco for the next few years, until he's dealt or outrighted.

SCOTT EYRE

Bats: L Throws: L Born: 30-May-1972 Age: 33

YEAR	TM	LG	AGE	G	GS	IP	H	BB	SO	HR	ERA	EQERA	EQH9	EQBB9	EQSO9	EQHR9	PERA	VORP	STF
2002	TOR	AL	30	49	3	63.3	69	29	51	4	4.98	4.71	8.9	3.7	6.9	0.6	4.29	5.0	2
2002	SFG	NL	30	21	0	11.3	11	7	7	0	1.59	3.27	9.0	4.9	4.9	0.0	4.09	2.8	-15
2003	SFG	NL	31	74	0	57.0	60	26	35	4	3.32	3.58	9.4	3.6	5.0	0.7	5.04	12.6	-12
2004	SFG	NL	32	83	0	52.7	43	27	49	8	4.10	4.29	7.9	4.1	7.7	1.3	4.11	7.4	0
2005	*SFG*	*NL*	*33*	*50*	*0*	*43.0*	*41*	*20*	*34*	*4*	*4.09*	*4.42*	*8.6*	*3.7*	*6.4*	*0.9*	*4.64*	*6.0*	*-5*

Breakout: 24% *Improve: 53%* *Collapse: 22%*

A LOOGY well suited for the role, Eyre has held lefties to a .219/.281/.327 line the last three years; righties have teed off at a .293/.380/.423 clip. Eyre and Brower were sixth and first in the NL in appearances, respectively, a function more of Felipe Alou's heavy reliever usage and their lopsided, get-them-out-of-there-fast profiles than any innate ability.

JESSE FOPPERT

Bats: R Throws: R Born: 10-Jul-1980 Age: 24

YEAR	TM	LG	AGE	G	GS	IP	H	BB	SO	HR	ERA	EQERA	EQH9	EQBB9	EQSO9	EQHR9	PERA	VORP	STF
2002	SHV	TXS	21	11	11	61.3	44	21	74	3	2.79	4.26	7.6	3.5	8.4	0.8	3.32	14.4	37
2002	FRE	PCL	21	14	14	79.0	71	35	109	12	3.99	4.18	8.5	4.3	9.8	1.3	4.78	6.9	34
2003	SFG	NL	22	23	21	111.0	103	69	101	16	5.03	5.52	8.8	4.9	7.5	1.3	5.27	1.2	6
2004	FRE	PCL	23	4	4	14.7	14	9	13	2	3.67	6.43	8.4	5.8	6.4	1.3	5.14	0.7	-5
2005	*SFG*	*NL*	*24*	*19*	*13*	*86.0*	*77*	*42*	*80*	*10*	*4.29*	*4.63*	*8.1*	*3.9*	*7.5*	*1.1*	*4.65*	*10.5*	*11*

Breakout: 26% *Improve: 46%* *Collapse: 20%*

The recovery rates for ulnar collateral ligament replacement surgery have increased in the 30+ years since Dr. Frank Jobe first jury-rigged Tommy John's elbow. Foppert is one of the surgery's latest success stories, having returned to pitching less than a year after going under the knife. Next for both the procedure and Foppert is seeing how fast a promising pitcher can return to full strength; Foppert gained top-prospect status by fanning 183 in 140.1 combined Double- and Triple-A innings at age 21. That ability's still there, if the Giants use him judiciously. Expect a decent 2005, then a big breakout in '06.

WAYNE FRANKLIN

Bats: L Throws: L Born: 09-Mar-1974 Age: 31

YEAR	TM	LG	AGE	G	GS	IP	H	BB	SO	HR	ERA	EQERA	EQH9	EQBB9	EQSO9	EQHR9	PERA	VORP	STF
2002	NWO	PCL	28	29	27	179.0	153	59	141	14	3.12	4.09	8.9	3.3	5.8	1.0	4.80	14.7	15
2002	MIL	NL	28	4	4	24.0	16	17	17	1	2.62	3.18	7.1	5.6	6.0	0.4	3.57	6.7	20
2003	MIL	NL	29	36	34	194.7	201	94	116	36	5.50	5.68	9.3	3.9	4.9	1.6	5.15	-5.8	-2
2004	SFG	NL	30	43	2	50.7	55	22	40	11	6.39	6.20	9.7	3.5	6.4	1.8	5.47	-4.9	-10
2005	*SFG*	*NL*	*31*	*28*	*7*	*65.0*	*62*	*28*	*49*	*8*	*4.42*	*4.78*	*8.5*	*3.4*	*6.1*	*1.1*	*4.69*	*6.4*	*-3*

Breakout: 23% *Improve: 58%* *Collapse: 23%*

The cavalcade of forgettable relievers rolls on! After yielding an insane 36 homers in 194.2 innings in '03, Franklin gave up cookies at an ever higher rate last year, surrendering 11 in 50.2 frames. You see enough balls land near the giant Coke bottle, and you'd start thinking about $21 million for Armando Benitez too. Non-tendered, then re-signed.

JAMES GARCIA **Bats: R** **Throws: R** Born: 03-Feb-1980 Age: 25

YEAR	TM	LG	AGE	G	GS	IP	H	BB	SO	HR	ERA	EQERA	EQH9	EQBB9	EQSO9	EQHR9	PERA	VORP	STF
2002	SLO	NWN	22	14	0	17.3	9	6	24	2	2.08	4.91	9.2	4.3	7.4	3.7	6.75	-1.9	-8
2003	SJO	CLF	23	33	3	71.3	67	35	105	4	4.17	5.78	8.9	5.5	8.6	1.1	4.84	5.7	-2
2003	FRE	PCL	23	7	4	23.7	23	12	22	3	4.18	4.84	8.9	5.2	7.3	1.6	4.84	1.9	1
2004	SJO	CLF	24	43	1	70.3	57	24	84	5	2.94	4.62	8.5	3.9	7.3	1.3	4.76	6.0	1
2004	FRE	PCL	24	8	7	34.7	35	16	34	7	5.19	4.91	9.3	4.4	6.8	1.9	5.73	-0.5	0
2005	*SFG*	*NL*	*25*	*13*	*5*	*40.7*	*36*	*18*	*35*	*5*	*4.15*	*4.48*	*7.9*	*3.6*	*6.9*	*1.1*	*4.38*	*5.3*	*5*

Breakout: 21% *Improve: 49%* *Collapse: 19%*

After watching him dominate the Cal League in 2003, the Giants inexplicably sent Garcia back to San Jose, where he . . . dominated again. He finished the season in Triple-A for the second straight season, and needs to start moving quickly to have a shot. We'll be especially interested to see how his slider fares at higher levels—Garcia owes much of his stratospheric K rates to the hitters' inability to hit his out pitch. We'd also like to see what he can do as a full-time starter, especially after the Giants gave him seven starts at Triple-A, after keeping him mostly chained in the pen. He'll be a viable option for the big league bullpen by year's end.

JOSH HABEL **Bats: L** **Throws: L** Born: 10-Sep-1980 Age: 24

YEAR	TM	LG	AGE	G	GS	IP	H	BB	SO	HR	ERA	EQERA	EQH9	EQBB9	EQSO9	EQHR9	PERA	VORP	STF
2002	SLO	NWN	21	16	7	48.0	57	24	33	2	6.00	8.26	11.3	5.6	3.4	1.0	6.85	-6.2	-36
2003	HAG	SAL	22	37	16	122.0	90	35	127	9	2.36	4.47	9.6	3.3	6.1	1.9	5.91	-3.7	-6
2004	NRW	EAS	23	27	25	136.3	130	50	123	21	4.36	5.54	9.8	3.6	6.2	1.9	5.90	-4.2	-4
2005	*SFG*	*NL*	*24*	*10*	*7*	*44.0*	*44*	*20*	*32*	*6*	*4.83*	*5.22*	*9.0*	*3.5*	*5.9*	*1.3*	*5.14*	*2.7*	*0*

Breakout: 16% *Improve: 44%* *Collapse: 23%*

After a big '03 season in the Sally League, the Giants took a rare aggressive approach and promoted Habel straight to Double-A Norwich. The Iowa-born southpaw kept his strikeout and walk rates mostly intact, but saw his home-run rate swell more then twofold. The hope here is that Habel's a late bloomer, given the shorter baseball season in the Midwest—he's already improved on his college numbers. With a solid change, good command and a crafty pick-off move, Habel could soon be a cheaper alternative to the Eyre-Christiansen brigade.

BRAD HENNESSEY **Bats: R** **Throws: R** Born: 07-Feb-1980 Age: 25

YEAR	TM	LG	AGE	G	GS	IP	H	BB	SO	HR	ERA	EQERA	EQH9	EQBB9	EQSO9	EQHR9	PERA	VORP	STF
2003	HAG	SAL	23	15	15	79.3	81	27	44	6	4.20	7.13	11.3	3.8	3.2	1.9	7.26	-13.0	-28
2004	NRW	EAS	24	18	18	101.0	106	34	55	8	3.56	4.34	9.9	3.2	3.7	1.0	5.38	2.3	-7
2004	FRE	PCL	24	5	5	35.7	26	15	16	2	2.02	2.48	7.4	4.1	3.3	0.6	3.58	7.3	6
2004	SFG	NL	24	7	7	34.3	42	15	25	2	4.99	6.03	9.7	3.4	5.8	0.5	4.72	-2.0	16
2005	*SFG*	*NL*	*25*	*14*	*13*	*73.3*	*83*	*32*	*40*	*9*	*5.13*	*5.54*	*10.1*	*3.4*	*4.5*	*1.2*	*5.57*	*1.6*	*-7*

Breakout: 11% *Improve: 40%* *Collapse: 21%*

His meteoric rise looked a lot like Kevin Correia's in 2003. The 2001 first-rounder out of Youngstown State started the year in Double-A after spending all of '03 in the Sally League. By year's end he'd made it all the way to the big leagues, starting a few games when the Giants were short-handed. What's odd is Hennessey hasn't shown the peripherals worthy of a top-tier prospect at any level, yet they're now penciling in as a fifth-starter. His recovery after the removal of multiple tumors in 2002 is a great story, but Hennessey's going to get rocked in the rotation.

MATT HERGES **Bats: L** **Throws: R** Born: 01-Apr-1970 Age: 35

YEAR	TM	LG	AGE	G	GS	IP	H	BB	SO	HR	ERA	EQERA	EQH9	EQBB9	EQSO9	EQHR9	PERA	VORP	STF
2002	MON	NL	32	62	0	64.7	80	26	50	10	4.03	4.45	10.2	3.1	6.0	1.3	5.29	5.6	-10
2003	SDP	NL	33	40	0	44.0	40	20	40	2	2.86	3.56	8.2	3.6	7.3	0.4	3.56	11.5	10
2003	SFG	NL	33	27	0	35.0	28	9	28	1	2.31	2.97	7.8	2.2	6.8	0.3	3.24	10.9	13
2004	SFG	NL	34	70	0	65.3	90	21	39	8	5.24	5.76	10.8	2.5	4.7	1.0	5.35	-2.6	-12
2005	*SFG*	*NL*	*35*	*43*	*0*	*49.7*	*55*	*17*	*33*	*5*	*4.42*	*4.77*	*10.0*	*2.8*	*5.4*	*1.0*	*5.04*	*5.0*	*-8*

Breakout: 18% *Improve: 44%* *Collapse: 32%*

Stunk up the joint, leading the Giants to conclude he didn't have the intestinal fortitude to be a closer. Of course, only two years earlier fans in Montreal just thought he sucked. Speaking of the Expos, between Herges, Brower, and Hermanson, it's a wonder the Giants didn't go with a full array of forgettable ex-'Spos. Was Bryan Eversgerd unavailable?

DUSTIN HERMANSON

Bats: R **Throws: R** Born: 21-Dec-1972 Age: 32

YEAR	TM	LG	AGE	G	GS	IP	H	BB	SO	HR	ERA	EQERA	EQH9	EQBB9	EQSO9	EQHR9	PERA	VORP	STF
2002	BOS	AL	29	12	1	22.0	35	7	13	3	7.77	7.15	11.9	2.4	4.8	1.2	6.35	-4.4	-12
2003	STL	NL	30	23	0	29.7	35	14	12	4	5.45	5.59	10.2	3.7	3.4	1.2	5.59	0.5	-25
2003	SFG	NL	30	9	6	39.0	35	10	27	5	3.00	3.19	8.8	2.2	5.9	1.2	4.42	10.6	9
2004	SFG	NL	31	47	18	131.0	132	46	102	15	4.53	4.66	8.9	2.8	6.3	0.9	4.17	12.7	6
2005	*CWS*	*AL*	*32*	*31*	*16*	*109.7*	*122*	*37*	*71*	*18*	*5.09*	*4.79*	*10.1*	*2.6*	*5.3*	*1.2*	*4.80*	*12.7*	*-3*

Breakout: 19% *Improve: 44%* *Collapse: 22%*

Having never regained the promise he showed as a young starter in his first tour of duty with Felipe Alou, Hermanson returned to the short reliever role he'd held as a flame-throwing minor leaguer and former #3 overall draft pick. In the process he hiked his strikeout rate, sliced his homers-allowed rate and cemented his reputation as a Proven Closer™. The White Sox gave him a two-year, $5.5 million to be double insurance, either for Shingo Takatsu or in case their historic fifth starter problems goes another year.

RYAN JENSEN

Bats: R **Throws: R** Born: 17-Sep-1975 Age: 29

YEAR	TM	LG	AGE	G	GS	IP	H	BB	SO	HR	ERA	EQERA	EQH9	EQBB9	EQSO9	EQHR9	PERA	VORP	STF
2002	SFG	NL	26	32	30	171.7	183	66	105	21	4.51	5.12	9.8	3.0	5.0	1.1	5.12	11.8	-1
2003	FRE	PCL	27	27	18	103.7	114	36	50	14	5.29	6.24	9.9	3.6	3.8	1.8	5.42	2.0	-9
2004	FRE	PCL	28	30	26	169.7	178	81	127	23	5.36	5.30	9.2	4.5	5.2	1.4	5.41	3.4	4
2005	*KCR*	*AL*	*29*	*25*	*12*	*84.0*	*97*	*38*	*51*	*16*	*6.02*	*5.67*	*10.3*	*3.6*	*5.0*	*1.6*	*5.59*	*2.8*	*-12*

Breakout: 14% *Improve: 41%* *Collapse: 17%*

Had a lousy season in Fresno and struggled in two starts with the big club. However, Jensen is in the process of transforming into a full-fledged knuckleballer, and reports have him throwing it with increasing success. There's no way to know how such experiments will go, but Jensen had no shot at a career otherwise, and if he masters the pitch he could remain gainfully employed for the next ten years. As Craig Wright once asked, how much harm would it do for teams to push a few fringe prospects to try the knuckler? It's the kind of low-risk, moderate-reward move teams should be attempting.

NOAH LOWRY

Bats: L **Throws: L** Born: 10-Oct-1980 Age: 24

YEAR	TM	LG	AGE	G	GS	IP	H	BB	SO	HR	ERA	EQERA	EQH9	EQBB9	EQSO9	EQHR9	PERA	VORP	STF
2002	SJO	CLF	21	15	12	58.7	38	20	62	4	2.15	4.44	8.0	3.6	5.8	1.2	4.44	6.8	13
2003	NRW	EAS	22	23	23	118.3	127	47	97	7	4.72	5.68	9.2	3.9	5.9	0.9	4.50	13.9	1
2003	FRE	PCL	22	4	4	19.0	15	6	13	0	2.37	3.06	7.6	3.1	5.6	0.0	3.06	5.0	13
2004	FRE	PCL	23	17	17	89.3	98	28	73	9	4.13	5.07	9.2	2.9	5.6	0.9	4.55	10.2	8
2004	SFG	NL	23	16	14	92.0	91	28	72	10	3.82	3.84	8.8	2.4	6.4	0.9	4.04	17.9	18
2005	*SFG*	*NL*	*24*	*22*	*22*	*130.0*	*126*	*46*	*95*	*15*	*4.02*	*4.35*	*8.7*	*2.8*	*5.9*	*1.1*	*4.40*	*19.5*	*10*

Breakout: 16% *Improve: 50%* *Collapse: 21%*

One of the most pleasant surprises of 2004. Lowry had all the makings of a crafty lefty who could settle into a bullpen spot in a few years, giving up far too many hits to be a viable starting candidate. But when the big league rotation collapsed after several injuries, they chucked Lowry into a trial by fire, to great results. His K, BB, and HR rates clung to his historically solid levels, as Lowry added a curve to his fastball-changeup repertoire to become an effective three-pitch starter. Looks like a keeper, even with that reverse split (931 OPS allowed vs. LH, 681 vs. RH).

PAT MISCH

Bats: R **Throws: L** Born: 18-Aug-1981 Age: 23

YEAR	TM	LG	AGE	G	GS	IP	H	BB	SO	HR	ERA	EQERA	EQH9	EQBB9	EQSO9	EQHR9	PERA	VORP	STF
2003	SLO	NWN	21	14	14	86.7	78	20	61	3	2.18	5.56	9.4	2.6	3.6	1.0	4.88	6.3	6
2004	NRW	EAS	22	26	26	159.0	138	35	123	13	3.00	4.14	8.9	2.1	5.3	1.0	4.33	20.8	16
2005	*SFG*	*NL*	*23*	*15*	*12*	*76.7*	*79*	*25*	*49*	*10*	*4.39*	*4.74*	*9.2*	*2.6*	*5.2*	*1.3*	*4.76*	*8.1*	*2*

Breakout: 7% *Improve: 31%* *Collapse: 23%*

Yet another effective lefty in a system full of pitching sleepers. The Giants made him a seventh-rounder in the '03 draft once the Astros failed to sign him in '02, and Misch has made a swift climb since. Another guy who uses his change as his best pitch, Misch also relies on an average fastball he throws for strikes and a slider-curve combo he can alternate to handle hitters from both sides. He's a relative unknown, but keep him on your radar.

ROBB NEN

Bats: R **Throws: R** Born: 28-Nov-1969 Age: 35

YEAR	TM	LG	AGE	G	GS	IP	H	BB	SO	HR	ERA	EQERA	EQH9	EQBB9	EQSO9	EQHR9	PERA	VORP	STF
2002	SFG	NL	32	68	0	73.7	64	20	81	2	2.20	2.64	7.8	2.1	8.8	0.3	3.14	25.0	26
2005	*SFG*	*NL*	*35*	*28*	*3*	*54.0*	*48*	*16*	*56*	*4*	*2.93*	*3.17*	*8.0*	*2.3*	*8.4*	*0.7*	*3.45*	*14.7*	*19*

Breakout: 31% *Improve: 48%* *Collapse: 23%*

Non-tendered, marking a sad end to a great Giants career derailed by a torn rotator cuff. The Rockies had expressed interest at press time, but Coors Field is a scary proposition for a pitcher trying to come back from two years lost to injury, and Giants trainer Stan Conte was pessimistic about any kind of return. Still, work is work, and here's hoping Nen makes it back, even if he'll never be the Nen of old. It'd be cool to see him trot out from the pen to the strains of *I Palindrome I.*

KIRK RUETER

Bats: L **Throws: L** Born: 01-Dec-1970 Age: 34

YEAR	TM	LG	AGE	G	GS	IP	H	BB	SO	HR	ERA	EQERA	EQH9	EQBB9	EQSO9	EQHR9	PERA	VORP	STF
2002	SFG	NL	31	33	33	203.7	204	54	76	22	3.23	3.95	9.7	2.1	3.1	1.0	4.80	41.5	-5
2003	SFG	NL	32	27	27	147.0	170	47	41	14	4.53	4.67	10.6	2.6	2.3	0.8	5.50	16.1	-12
2004	SFG	NL	33	33	33	190.3	225	66	56	21	4.73	4.89	10.3	2.8	2.4	0.9	5.09	13.9	-11
2005	*SFG*	*NL*	*34*	*26*	*22*	*132.3*	*156*	*42*	*47*	*15*	*4.78*	*5.16*	*10.5*	*2.5*	*2.9*	*1.1*	*5.30*	*6.9*	*-13*

Breakout: 13% *Improve: 51%* *Collapse: 11%*

Owns one of the more underrated bad contracts in the game today, with $6 million more due in '05 as he closes out his two-year deal. Rueter is barely above replacement level at this stage, and the Giants have enough good, young arms that they don't need to get by with his meager contributions any longer. If he makes it through the whole year in the rotation, he'll have done it on managerial stubbornness, not for on-field results.

JASON SCHMIDT

Bats: R **Throws: R** Born: 29-Jan-1973 Age: 32

YEAR	TM	LG	AGE	G	GS	IP	H	BB	SO	HR	ERA	EQERA	EQH9	EQBB9	EQSO9	EQHR9	PERA	VORP	STF
2002	SFG	NL	29	29	29	185.3	148	73	196	15	3.45	4.04	7.7	3.1	8.6	0.8	3.59	35.3	31
2003	SFG	NL	30	29	29	207.7	152	46	208	14	2.34	2.57	7.3	1.8	8.4	0.6	3.03	75.5	38
2004	SFG	NL	31	32	32	225.0	165	77	251	18	3.20	3.30	7.1	2.8	9.1	0.7	2.92	60.1	39
2005	*SFG*	*NL*	*32*	*30*	*30*	*212.7*	*170*	*66*	*212*	*19*	*2.98*	*3.22*	*7.2*	*2.5*	*8.1*	*0.9*	*3.18*	*56.8*	*28*

Breakout: 17% *Improve: 60%* *Collapse: 10%*

As much flak as Brian Sabean gets for his veteran fetish and bizarre signing tactics, he deserves every bit of the credit for Schmidt. Getting the ace (and John Vander Wal) for Ryan Vogelsong and Armando Rios at the 2001 deadline ranks as one of the biggest heists of the last decade. The four-year, $30 million contract they gave him after the '01 season is also grand larceny, and at this rate Schmidt's $10 million team option in '06 looks like a lock. Injuries remain a concern, but Schmidt overcame elbow tendon surgery last off-season, exceeded expectations yet again, and keeps getting better as his innings totals mount. Giants fans can only hope he's got the Livan Hernandez–like ability to shoulder the load and avoid injury; Bonds gets hailed as The Franchise, but they'd be lost without Schmidt.

ALFREDO SIMON

Bats: R **Throws: R** Born: 08-May-1981 Age: 24

YEAR	TM	LG	AGE	G	GS	IP	H	BB	SO	HR	ERA	EQERA	EQH9	EQBB9	EQSO9	EQHR9	PERA	VORP	STF
2003	LWD	SAL	22	14	7	71.3	59	25	66	4	3.79	6.05	9.4	3.9	5.2	1.4	5.06	3.8	0
2004	CLR	FSL	23	22	21	134.7	121	38	107	13	3.27	5.16	9.8	3.0	5.1	2.0	5.75	-2.0	0
2004	SJO	CLF	23	6	6	31.7	44	12	21	7	5.68	7.67	13.2	4.3	4.0	4.0	9.82	-13.7	-39
2005	*SFG*	*NL*	*24*	*8*	*7*	*42.0*	*43*	*17*	*28*	*6*	*4.73*	*5.11*	*9.1*	*3.2*	*5.4*	*1.4*	*5.06*	*2.8*	*-1*

Breakout: 8% *Improve: 38%* *Collapse: 13%*

Shipped to the Giants in the Felix Rodriguez trade, Simon got a bit of a shock in San Jose, dealing with much tougher parks in a much tougher league than he did while at Clearwater. Still, he's got the stuff and command on his résumé to bounce back. With a bottleneck of pitching prospects emerging at the upper levels, he'll get all the time he needs.

BRETT TOMKO

Bats: R **Throws: R** Born: 07-Apr-1973 Age: 32

YEAR	TM	LG	AGE	G	GS	IP	H	BB	SO	HR	ERA	EQERA	EQH9	EQBB9	EQSO9	EQHR9	PERA	VORP	STF
2002	SDP	NL	29	32	32	204.3	212	60	126	31	4.49	5.06	9.3	2.3	5.0	1.4	4.20	17.9	1
2003	STL	NL	30	33	32	202.7	252	57	114	35	5.28	5.62	10.6	2.2	4.6	1.5	5.62	2.3	-5
2004	SFG	NL	31	32	31	194.0	196	64	108	19	4.04	4.40	9.1	2.7	4.5	0.8	4.25	26.2	6
2005	*SFG*	*NL*	*32*	*26*	*24*	*146.0*	*160*	*44*	*80*	*20*	*4.67*	*5.05*	*9.8*	*2.4*	*4.4*	*1.3*	*5.02*	*10.1*	*-2*

Breakout: 6% *Improve: 41%* *Collapse: 24%*

Improbably emerged as the staff ace down the stretch, posting a 1.43 ERA in his last eight starts and keeping the Giants in it down to the wire. That was enough for the Giants to pick up his $2.5 million option for '05, so Tomko will be back at the end of the rotation. Big finish or not, Tomko's ugly .294/.362/.450 season line vs. lefties and borderline strikeout rate bode ill for the year. SBC will mask the damage, but look for an EqERA in the 5.00s.

MERKIN VALDEZ

Bats: R **Throws: R** Born: 10-Nov-1981 Age: 23

YEAR	TM	LG	AGE	G	GS	IP	H	BB	SO	HR	ERA	EQERA	EQH9	EQBB9	EQSO9	EQHR9	PERA	VORP	STF
2003	HAG	SAL	21	26	26	156.0	119	49	166	11	2.25	4.20	9.7	3.5	6.2	1.7	5.91	-4.7	1
2004	SJO	CLF	22	7	7	35.7	30	5	44	4	2.52	4.41	9.1	1.7	7.4	1.9	4.96	2.3	17
2004	NRW	EAS	22	10	7	41.7	35	15	31	3	4.32	5.12	8.6	3.5	5.1	0.9	4.42	5.1	3
2005	*SFG*	*NL*	*23*	*15*	*9*	*62.0*	*59*	*25*	*49*	*8*	*4.30*	*4.64*	*8.5*	*3.2*	*6.4*	*1.2*	*4.55*	*6.9*	*5*

Breakout: 17% *Improve: 52%* *Collapse: 15%*

Since being acquired from the Braves in the Russ Ortiz trade, Valdez has breezed through four levels, making it all the way to the majors by year's end. He spent both of his big league outings as a reliever, and there lies the rub. Hitters either swing and miss at his unhittable mid-90s sinking fastball or bang it harmlessly into the turf. His hard slider is coming along, though it still needs work. Unfortunately, Randy Johnson has been the only starter in recent memory to be successful in the majors with just two pitches. The old Earl Weaver approach seems prudent here: let Valdez start the season in a high-leverage, multi-inning bullpen role out of spring training. If all goes well, it would spare his arm mileage, while giving him time to perfect a change-up, and he'd start when needed. As long as they don't get carried away: As great as it would be to have a Brad Lidge on their hands, it's worth finding out if they've got a right-handed Johan Santana.

KEVIN WALKER

Bats: L **Throws: L** Born: 20-Sep-1976 Age: 28

YEAR	TM	LG	AGE	G	GS	IP	H	BB	SO	HR	ERA	EQERA	EQH9	EQBB9	EQSO9	EQHR9	PERA	VORP	STF
2003	POR	PCL	26	34	1	46.3	53	10	43	5	4.08	5.20	9.8	2.2	7.0	1.4	4.80	4.0	-4
2004	FRE	PCL	27	48	1	69.7	79	35	63	8	4.26	4.21	9.4	4.7	6.2	1.2	5.40	1.5	-13
2005	*CWS*	*AL*	*28*	*8*	*2*	*17.0*	*18*	*9*	*13*	*3*	*5.24*	*4.94*	*9.7*	*4.0*	*6.4*	*1.3*	*5.11*	*2.0*	*-5*

Breakout: 20% *Improve: 47%* *Collapse: 24%*

Walker saw little action with the Giants after a lousy season at Fresno, then inked a one-year, $525,000 deal with the White Sox for '05. With Damaso Marte rumored in several possible deals, the Sox want to have lefty options available just in case. They'll get a rude awakening if they think Walker can be even half as good as Marte.

TYLER WALKER

Bats: R **Throws: R** Born: 15-May-1976 Age: 29

YEAR	TM	LG	AGE	G	GS	IP	H	BB	SO	HR	ERA	EQERA	EQH9	EQBB9	EQSO9	EQHR9	PERA	VORP	STF
2002	NOR	INT	26	28	25	142.0	152	38	109	13	3.99	4.81	9.3	2.7	5.9	1.2	4.54	16.1	5
2003	TOL	INT	27	26	22	131.3	139	47	117	13	4.46	5.41	9.6	3.7	6.6	1.4	5.34	3.6	-1
2004	FRE	PCL	28	9	1	15.7	16	2	15	1	1.72	2.93	8.8	1.2	6.5	0.6	3.52	3.5	9
2004	SFG	NL	28	52	0	63.7	69	24	48	8	4.24	4.19	9.4	3.0	6.1	1.0	4.62	9.3	-4
2005	*SFG*	*NL*	*29*	*29*	*7*	*71.3*	*69*	*25*	*56*	*8*	*3.89*	*4.20*	*8.7*	*2.8*	*6.3*	*1.1*	*4.40*	*11.6*	*2*

Breakout: 21% *Improve: 53%* *Collapse: 17%*

Finally got his first extended shot at the bigs in his eighth professional season. Result? He ate innings, but didn't do much to help his team win. A mountain of a man, Walker may be worth keeping as an 11th pitcher just for enforcer duty in a brawl. Top five guys you'd least want to face in a brawl, 1980-present:

5. Tyler Walker: Huge, but Cal grad, so potential for "Hey duuude, take a hit and relaaax . . ."

4. David Eckstein: Would flit around like a hummingbird; right height for easy low blows.

3. Mo Vaughn: If he sits on you, it's all over.
2. George Bell: How many former MVPs are likely to karate-kick you in the middle of a scrum? The Rick Tocchet of baseball.
1. Kevin Gross: No one would go near him whenever a fight erupted. So scary, he could stare you down and end it right there.

CRAIG WHITAKER **Bats: R** **Throws: R** Born: 19-Nov-1984 Age: 20

YEAR	TM	LG	AGE	G	GS	IP	H	BB	SO	HR	ERA	EQERA	EQH9	EQBB9	EQSO9	EQHR9	PERA	VORP	STF
2004	SLO	NWN	19	15	15	70.7	58	43	77	4	3.44	6.14	8.9	7.7	5.3	1.1	5.71	-0.8	0
2005	*SFG*	*NL*	*20*	*12*	*10*	*58.0*	*55*	*38*	*39*	*9*	*5.39*	*5.82*	*8.5*	*5.2*	*5.4*	*1.5*	*5.86*	*-0.3*	*-9*

Breakout: 17% *Improve: 44%* *Collapse: 13%*

Tall Texan high-schooler, the kind that makes scouts drool. Statheads won't mind the 77 Ks in 70 innings in his short-season debut either. The 2003 first-round pick's biggest obstacle is his control—he's got juice on his fastball, but 43 walks, 14 wild pitches and six hit batsmen scream Rick Vaughn more than Josh Beckett. Still, he's one to watch.

JEROME WILLIAMS **Bats: R** **Throws: R** Born: 04-Dec-1981 Age: 23

YEAR	TM	LG	AGE	G	GS	IP	H	BB	SO	HR	ERA	EQERA	EQH9	EQBB9	EQSO9	EQHR9	PERA	VORP	STF
2002	FRE	PCL	20	28	28	160.7	140	50	130	16	3.58	4.24	8.4	3.0	5.9	0.9	4.18	23.8	39
2003	FRE	PCL	21	10	10	57.0	52	16	40	3	2.68	3.50	8.2	2.8	5.5	0.5	3.33	13.6	27
2003	SFG	NL	21	21	21	131.0	116	49	88	10	3.30	3.76	8.6	3.0	5.6	0.7	4.20	28.9	25
2004	SFG	NL	22	22	22	129.3	123	44	80	14	4.25	4.58	8.8	2.8	5.1	0.9	4.08	13.8	18
2005	*SFG*	*NL*	*23*	*23*	*23*	*136.3*	*133*	*47*	*98*	*13*	*4.00*	*4.32*	*8.7*	*2.7*	*5.8*	*0.9*	*4.32*	*20.4*	*10*

Breakout: 18% *Improve: 49%* *Collapse: 24%*

Sometimes compared to Greg Maddux in his prime for his poise and command, Williams has a long way to get even a whiff of that level of excellence. Pros: His GB/FB rate is on the rise, his already solid walk rates are falling further as he adjusts to the majors, he bounced back quickly from in-season elbow surgery, and a forgiving park will help. Cons: His strikeout rates are going the wrong way, and he remains an injury risk, particularly considering his age. There's plenty to like here, but he may need a while to put it all together. Foppert may be the better long-term bet.

Washington Nationals

There have been compromised teams before. However, even when John McGraw's Orioles were being looted to supply the Brooklyn Superbas, at least those responsible had a sense of embarrassment about it. Some good players were left behind for McGraw to build a decent team around, even when those players would have been upgrades for the Brooklyn team.

The shame baseball felt over these kinds of episodes eventually led to the implementation of limitations on what kind of ownership interest any one party could have in two teams. In post-war baseball, there's only been one blatant violation of those rules: The long, drawn out Expos saga. It started with John Henry and Jeffrey Loria doing a complicated tango that technically violated rules about who could own what when, and included Major League Baseball loaning Loria money so that he could hire thugs to loot the Expos and haul the booty to Florida.

That complicated transaction helped reduce the franchise to a state so moribund as to be beyond belief. With 29 owners each owning a little over 3% of the Expos while MLB stalled and bungled finding the franchise a new home, there was no chance the team would be anything more than a placeholder. They could have gone out with all-white uniforms with "Your City Team Name Here" and at least it would have assured the co-owners that something was being done. With no foreseeable end to the situation, all they could hope for was minimizing their losses.

Omar Minaya struggled to make the team competitive, to fight against the impossible odds. While it's evident now that he did more harm than good, it's hard to criticize anyone who takes up a helpless, righteous struggle and fails, even if he wasn't that good at it.

When contraction threatened the 2002 Expos team, Minaya was reduced to going-out-of-business sales, even if it would later turn out that he wasn't really going out of business. "Today, I announce the final clearance bonanza. Our landlord is forcing us to deal any and all players before the next pay period is due. We've lost our lease! We're not going to be around next year, and the boss says everything must go. The continued mismanagement of this franchise is your good fortune, as we must, must, must get rid of quality players at and below cost. Everything must go, as new owners will . . . what's that, Mr. Selig? We're going to be here for another year? Oh. No, no, it's no problem, I just started so . . . Never mind, folks." He ended up a bored cashier at a 7-Eleven, staring at the "Need a penny, take a penny, have a penny, give a penny" dish on the counter, and waiting for his shift to end.

NATIONALS PROSPECTUS

2004 record: 67–95; Fifth place, NL East

Pythagenport record: 66–96

Runs scored per game: 3.91 (15th in NL)

Runs allowed per game: 4.75 (11th in NL)

Team EqA: .245 (15th in NL)

2004 Batters Age: 28.1 (2nd youngest in NL)

2004 Pitchers Age: 27.0 (Youngest in NL)

Ballpark: RFK Stadium (New—sort of—for 2005)

2004: The franchise finally has a new home, although in typical MLB style, the process was harder than it had to be.

2005: A depleted talent base and questionable off-season player moves will send the Nats' inaugural season back to subcommittee.

So he sat there for three years, spending money on impulse buys when permitted, taking on other people's turkey contracts when asked. Then after enduring that wait—while fluffing up his reputation among as many media members as possible, even appearing on the cover of *Inc.* magazine—he found greener pastures. The current general manager of a baseball franchise was hired to immediately run another team—*before the end of the season.* After the last home game against Florida (attendance 31,395), Minaya was named Executive Vice President of Baseball Operations and General Manager of the Mets. The same Mets the Expos were about to face in the last series of the season.

It's hard to put words to how appalling this was. After years of having their best talent poached, the Expos suffered the ultimate indignity. The man supposedly in charge of keeping them respectable was taken to immediately run the franchise they were facing for the last games of their existence.

I'm not going to argue that Minaya was a great prize, or that his leaving the team early was a dramatically greater blow than having him quit after the last game on October 3. But it's as if baseball, having treated the fans in

Montreal so badly for so long, wanted to slap them one last time while they had the chance.

There were many reasons the team was in such sad shape, from the very start of MLB's take-over. When Loria swapped franchises, leaving Montreal for Florida, he took everyone he could and everything that wasn't nailed down with him. Then, unsatisfied, he came back with a claw-hammer. The few baseball operations people who remained behind fought valiantly, but there's almost no recovering from that without being well funded and strongly led, and they weren't. Whether motivated by MLB's puppet strings or simply bad decision making, bad moves were rampant. For instance, offering Vlad Guerrero arbitration would have netted the team a first-round draft pick at no risk, but they didn't do it. And for their one hefty long-term contract, they chose Jose Vidro, a good but not great second baseman with durability issues.

On the plus side, Minaya's strength as Expos GM was that he was willing to participate in almost any deal if he felt it would help the team—even if it often didn't. Many of the worthwhile prospects in the system came as part of some random trade. There are almost no future superstars, but there are players who could provide solid, cheap contributions to the team, and that's exactly what the Expos were after.

Minaya's weakness was his inability to concentrate, to, say, figure his way out of a problem if he went to the winter meetings with Plan A and Plan A fell apart. Or to think more than a couple of months ahead. Or to set aside his scouting-minded, old-school baseball philosophy and learn something from the low-budget success of Oakland or the better-honed, scouting-focused approach of the Twins. He was good enough at keeping busy and playing the great man, but the team he left is in worse shape than when he found it. Despite the difficulties he faced, Minaya is responsible for that.

Enter Jim Bowden. How far can the Boy Wonder fly this new Washington Nationals team? As pilots like to joke, all the way to the crash site.

Bowden's time in Cincinnati wasn't a total disaster, but all of his transactions and roster moves were a lot of sound and fury, and they usually ended up signifying nothing. The team hunted through bargain bins not knowing what they really needed, and bought whatever looked interesting, like a bored teenager with money wandering through thrift stores.

More important, Bowden ticked everyone off. Players who signed below-market deals to get closer to their homes were traded. One by one, he alienated other teams, often to the point where they wouldn't talk trade with the Reds as long as he was there. His conduct during the Ken Griffey Jr. trade, for instance, nearly put Pat Gillick on a plane from Seattle to Cincinnati with a length of piano wire to strangle Bowden. Given a star player who wanted to come to the Reds, Bowden didn't try to strike a reasonably fair deal to accommodate the uncomfortable situation—which in an industry as small as baseball, is how people try to get along. No, instead he acted like the jerk of a fantasy league, unwilling to make a trade that did not clearly screw over the other side just so he could brag about it to his buddies.

The universe, thankfully, apportioned karma appropriately.

Bowden is here to be fired. A likeable, competent general manager could be trouble. He might figure out some way to get the team to respectability. Then the new owners come in, they want their own guy, but the city's already attached to someone . . . that's a difficult situation. For instance, Pat Gillick lobbied publicly for the job (and boy, how it must have hacked him off to see Bowden hired instead). But it's hard to fire Pat Gillick and his reputation, as the Mariners ownership group will tell you.

But nobody cares if you fire Bowden. His goal in the next year, or less, is to make enough moves so that this item on his resume causes someone to remember him, and helps him get the next job he hadn't gotten after he was axed by the Reds. As if to make our point, Bowden immediately set out to provide reasons to fire him: Vinny Castilla, two years, $6.2 million. Cristian Guzman, four years, $16.8 million.

These are bad signings on first examination, and the more you know about the team's organizational strengths, the worse they get. The position players the Expos had ready to contribute for the big team were infielders, and on the Nationals there was no good place for them. Beyond the money, they cost the Nats draft picks the organization badly needs to put talent into the farm system. They will add nothing to the team's offense, and they'll do nothing significant to improve the team's defense. They're supposed to provide gritty veteran leadership, and you'll see how many wins that'll put on the board.

That might not have been enough, so Bowden then traded young outfielder Juan Rivera to the Angels for more famous outfielder Jose Guillen. Juan Rivera *is* Jose Guillen without the service time, and Bowden traded him for the much more expensive version. Bowden can't even fall back on the veteran leadership excuse here, as Guillen has repeatedly shown himself to be a troublemaker.

This is a start without hope or promise. The first year of this franchise is already regarded as a write-off, a freebie. Bowden's attempt to make a splash, to see what attention he can attract (perhaps really only towards himself), does the team no good if he's only degrading the on-field product with each move. It may have the opposite effect.

At this rate, by the time the season is over the Nationals may have demonstrated how quickly and thoroughly interest in baseball can be snuffed out. The hugely expensive stadium plan could start to tumble, taken down by countless angry citizen actions like Gulliver being pulled down by Lilliputians. At that point, having kept the franchise for themselves if they don't sell soon, Bob DuPuy might be leading the conga line to the next city.

HITTERS

TONY BATISTA 3B Bats: R Throws: R Born: 09-Dec-1973 Age: 31

YEAR	TM	LG	AGE	AB	H	2B	3B	HR	BB	SO	SB	CS	AVG	OBP	SLG	MLVR	EQBA	EQOBP	EQSLG	EQMLVR	VORP	DEFENSE
2002	BAL	AL	28	615	150	36	1	31	50	107	5	4	.244	.309	.457	-.001	.252	.320	.477	.000	30.3	153-3B 16
2003	BAL	AL	29	631	148	20	1	26	28	102	4	3	.235	.270	.393	-.168	.237	.278	.403	-.193	5.4	152-3B 10
2004	MON	NL	30	606	146	30	2	32	26	78	14	6	.241	.272	.455	-.054	.236	.268	.448	-.148	10.3	145-3B 11
2005	*WAS*	*NL*	*31*	*484*	*122*	*25*	*2*	*18*	*31*	*76*	*8*	*4*	*.253*	*.301*	*.428*	*-.092*	*.256*	*.302*	*.438*	*-.079*	*4.5*	*124-3B 3*

Breakout: 35% *Improve: 66%* *Collapse: 13%*

The power's nice and he's good with the glove, but even giving him generous credit for both, he's still below-average for his position. In the right situation, for a suitably low salary, he could . . . not hurt a team badly. For the Nats, what was the point? The Fukuoka Hawks of Japan gave him $15 million over two years, an offer too good to refuse.

ROGEARVIN BERNADINA CF Bats: L Throws: L Born: 12-Jun-1984 Age: 21

YEAR	TM	LG	AGE	AB	H	2B	3B	HR	BB	SO	SB	CS	AVG	OBP	SLG	MLVR	EQBA	EQOBP	EQSLG	EQMLVR	VORP	DEFENSE	
2003	SAV	SAL	19	278	66	12	3	4	19	53	11	4	.237	.292	.345	-.055	.207	.246	.312	-.403	-31.4	28-LF -5	21-CF -4
2004	SAV	SAL	20	450	107	24	7	7	60	113	24	2	.238	.338	.369	-.021	.211	.289	.325	-.297	-22.5	72-CF -3	39-RF -3
2005	*WAS*	*NL*	*21*	*342*	*76*	*16*	*3*	*5*	*28*	*88*	*8*	*3*	*.222*	*.291*	*.329*	*-.264*	*.224*	*.291*	*.337*	*-.254*	*-9.7*	*91-CF -10*	

Breakout: 28% *Improve: 53%* *Collapse: 23%*

Rogearvin supposedly has the potential to be a five-tool player. But he doesn't have five tools now: Low average, with lots of strikeouts. Power? Look at the doubles long enough, and you might start seeing them as a good sign. Defensively, he's, uh, he's fast. He can steal bases. He's young, and there is potential. But like with a suspiciously lucrative mail-in rebate, don't get excited about the great deal you got until you cash the check, because there's a lot that can go wrong between potential and realization.

LARRY BROADWAY 1B Bats: L Throws: L Born: 17-Dec-1980 Age: 24

YEAR	TM	LG	AGE	AB	H	2B	3B	HR	BB	SO	SB	CS	AVG	OBP	SLG	MLVR	EQBA	EQOBP	EQSLG	EQMLVR	VORP	DEFENSE
2002	VER	NYP	21	127	40	3	0	4	13	33	0	0	.315	.379	.433	.256	.256	.299	.372	-.183	-7.4	32-1B -2
2003	SAV	SAL	22	290	89	25	4	14	44	70	3	4	.307	.400	.566	.425	.258	.331	.475	.022	10.7	80-1B 5
2003	BRV	FSL	22	76	17	7	1	1	18	20	0	1	.224	.367	.382	.119	.225	.342	.387	-.102	-0.5	20-1B 2
2003	HAR	EAS	22	78	25	3	0	5	7	15	0	0	.321	.371	.551	.317	.269	.300	.462	-.041	1.0	19-1B 0
2004	HAR	EAS	23	473	128	20	0	22	68	102	2	3	.271	.362	.452	.113	.238	.318	.396	-.126	-6.6	121-1B 0
2005	*WAS*	*NL*	*24*	*318*	*79*	*16*	*2*	*12*	*38*	*80*	*0*	*0*	*.248*	*.330*	*.424*	*-.052*	*.251*	*.331*	*.434*	*-.038*	*5.9*	*87-1B -1*

Breakout: 22% *Improve: 58%* *Collapse: 16%*

Returning to Harrisburg, Broadway got off to a terrible start but rebounded to finish with that respectable line. For a 23-year old in his first full year of competition at this level, it's entirely possible that the organization's right, and he did adjust and adapt. Broadway's development makes the team's corner outfielder/first-base dilemma even tougher, and it's likely Bowden will trade Broadway somewhere for some shiny object, or he'll get a flat and move him for a four-tool tire technician who scores at least a 60 on the 20–80 scale for tire changing, tire balancing, flat repairs, and rotation service.

RON CALLOWAY OF Bats: L Throws: L Born: 04-Sep-1976 Age: 28

YEAR	TM	LG	AGE	AB	H	2B	3B	HR	BB	SO	SB	CS	AVG	OBP	SLG	MLVR	EQBA	EQOBP	EQSLG	EQMLVR	VORP	DEFENSE	
2002	OTT	INT	25	447	118	21	5	14	44	89	16	12	.264	.335	.427	.055	.246	.317	.406	-.109	-6.1	121-RF 10	
2003	MON	NL	26	340	81	17	1	9	20	80	9	2	.238	.282	.374	-.200	.229	.275	.368	-.254	-8.4	46-LF 4	35-RF -2
2004	EDM	PCL	27	223	63	17	1	5	34	39	13	5	.283	.385	.435	.103	.259	.351	.386	-.063	0.2	32-RF -1	24-LF 1
2004	MON	NL	27	84	14	2	0	1	5	22	2	0	.167	.211	.226	-.527	.167	.200	.202	-.668	-8.0	11-RF 1	
2005	*WAS*	*NL*	*28*	*157*	*39*	*8*	*1*	*4*	*16*	*36*	*4*	*2*	*.246*	*.320*	*.397*	*-.108*	*.249*	*.320*	*.406*	*-.095*	*2.9*	*46-RF 0*	

Breakout: 35% *Improve: 56%* *Collapse: 31%*

2004 was his Age-27 year, and Calloway hit in Edmonton, though not for power, and hit in Montreal, though not often or well. Calloway's future is as a Triple-A floater. He might, through chance or injuries to others, bob up and get small chunks of playing time and many portions of fine, easily available Annies who don't understand career-worth projection.

JAMEY CARROLL INF Bats: R Throws: R Born: 18-Feb-1974 Age: 31

YEAR	TM	LG	AGE	AB	H	2B	3B	HR	BB	SO	SB	CS	AVG	OBP	SLG	MLVR	EQBA	EQOBP	EQSLG	EQMLVR	VORP	DEFENSE
2002	OTT	INT	28	421	118	19	2	8	37	39	6	10	.280	.342	.392	.032	.263	.326	.374	-.124	7.4	81-3B 11 27-2B 3
2002	MON	NL	28	71	22	5	3	1	4	12	1	0	.310	.347	.507	.191	.301	.338	.507	.122	6.9	13-3B -2
2003	MON	NL	29	227	59	10	1	1	19	39	5	2	.260	.323	.326	-.203	.257	.320	.322	-.212	-0.9	55-3B 1
2004	MON	NL	30	218	63	14	2	0	32	21	5	1	.289	.378	.372	.051	.284	.366	.353	-.062	14.6	39-2B -5 12-3B 0
2005	*WAS*	*NL*	*31*	*199*	*50*	*10*	*1*	*2*	*19*	*24*	*3*	*1*	*.253*	*.320*	*.343*	*-.173*	*.255*	*.321*	*.351*	*-.161*	*3.0*	*56-2B -2*

Breakout: 3% *Improve: 24%* *Collapse: 49%*

As an injury-replacement guy off the bench who can play around the infield, Carroll's okay. He's not a good glove anywhere, there's no power, and he can't steal a base. But his single-and-walk-based .378 OBP was the highest on-base percentage by any Expo with more than three plate appearances. Sadly, that says more about that Expos team than Jamey Carroll. He'll regress back to career norms this year.

MATT CEPICKY LF Bats: L Throws: R Born: 10-Nov-1977 Age: 27

YEAR	TM	LG	AGE	AB	H	2B	3B	HR	BB	SO	SB	CS	AVG	OBP	SLG	MLVR	EQBA	EQOBP	EQSLG	EQMLVR	VORP	DEFENSE
2002	HAR	EAS	24	419	116	25	2	16	33	94	7	1	.277	.327	.461	.083	.246	.292	.416	-.141	-10.8	79-LF -2
2002	MON	NL	24	74	16	3	0	3	4	21	0	0	.216	.256	.378	-.186	.216	.241	.365	-.332	-1.4	11-LF 0
2003	EDM	PCL	25	442	133	23	4	7	31	82	7	2	.301	.349	.419	.096	.282	.330	.395	-.072	-2.3	89-LF -9
2004	EDM	PCL	26	312	84	15	3	15	18	75	2	1	.269	.305	.481	.004	.245	.279	.418	-.163	-9.7	73-LF 3
2004	MON	NL	26	60	13	4	0	1	1	18	1	0	.217	.230	.333	-.311	.217	.212	.300	-.482	-2.4	
2005	*WAS*	*NL*	*27*	*151*	*37*	*8*	*1*	*4*	*9*	*38*	*1*	*0*	*.247*	*.290*	*.393*	*-.164*	*.249*	*.291*	*.402*	*-.152*	*-0.4*	*42-LF -3*

Breakout: 18% *Improve: 34%* *Collapse: 44%*

He was once touted for a sweet swing, but Cepicky is just Ron Calloway except with a bit more power. Also like Calloway, the Nationals don't have any place for Cepicky to play and no pressing reason to create one for him.

ENDY CHAVEZ CF Bats: L Throws: L Born: 07-Feb-1978 Age: 27

YEAR	TM	LG	AGE	AB	H	2B	3B	HR	BB	SO	SB	CS	AVG	OBP	SLG	MLVR	EQBA	EQOBP	EQSLG	EQMLVR	VORP	DEFENSE
2002	OTT	INT	24	405	139	28	5	4	33	37	21	13	.343	.392	.467	.267	.325	.378	.448	.128	34.5	93-CF 6
2002	MON	NL	24	125	37	8	5	1	5	16	3	5	.296	.321	.464	.078	.289	.313	.469	.011	5.2	35-CF 2
2003	MON	NL	25	483	121	25	5	5	31	59	18	7	.251	.294	.354	-.207	.244	.289	.349	-.243	-6.4	119-CF 0
2004	MON	NL	26	502	139	20	6	5	30	40	32	7	.277	.318	.371	-.073	.271	.313	.362	-.160	14.5	121-CF -6
2005	*WAS*	*NL*	*27*	*455*	*124*	*24*	*5*	*6*	*33*	*46*	*20*	*6*	*.272*	*.321*	*.382*	*-.108*	*.274*	*.322*	*.391*	*-.095*	*10.5*	*118-CF 0*

Breakout: 10% *Improve: 37%* *Collapse: 35%*

This is a dangerous player. His batting average is high enough so that he looks like a good enough hitter. He'll steal enough bases so that you'll want him for that. His range and speed are good enough that sometimes he'll come in a long way to catch a shallow fly and look like a solid defender. Managers bite on these kinds of players, and suddenly they're at the top of the lineup every day. As a result, guys like Chavez have the potential to wreak havoc on their teams far out of proportion to how much their modest talents can benefit them. Compared to Jim Bowden, that's small potatoes.

RYAN CHURCH RF Bats: L Throws: L Born: 14-Oct-1978 Age: 26

YEAR	TM	LG	AGE	AB	H	2B	3B	HR	BB	SO	SB	CS	AVG	OBP	SLG	MLVR	EQBA	EQOBP	EQSLG	EQMLVR	VORP	DEFENSE
2002	KIN	CRL	23	181	59	12	1	10	31	51	4	4	.326	.433	.569	.485	.285	.377	.505	.168	14.1	33-RF -1 11-CF -2
2002	AKR	EAS	23	291	86	17	4	12	12	58	1	0	.296	.325	.505	.169	.263	.290	.453	-.078	5.8	37-CF 0 31-RF 2
2003	AKR	EAS	24	371	97	17	3	13	32	64	4	3	.261	.325	.429	.013	.226	.285	.383	-.215	-17.0	82-RF 3 16-CF -1
2004	EDM	PCL	25	347	120	29	8	17	51	62	0	1	.346	.430	.622	.530	.313	.393	.537	.268	35.9	74-RF -3
2004	MON	NL	25	63	11	1	0	1	7	16	0	0	.175	.257	.238	-.426	.175	.240	.238	-.532	-5.3	
2005	*WAS*	*NL*	*26*	*202*	*53*	*12*	*2*	*7*	*21*	*46*	*1*	*1*	*.263*	*.335*	*.444*	*-.006*	*.265*	*.336*	*.454*	*.009*	*11.3*	*57-RF 2*

Breakout: 22% *Improve: 38%* *Collapse: 32%*

Another of the Nationals' minor league outfielders who got some playing time and looked bad in a brief trial. Church's advantage over Cepicky and Calloway is that he's a little younger and has a minor league track record that bodes well. His problem is that he has trouble staying healthy. The crowded outfield situation means he'll see only bench duty for the Nats in '05, which is like being told you don't get to be shift leader at Cold Stone Creamery, choosing which insufferable song the team will break into next as you contemplate whether the extra 15 cents an hour will add up to enough over the next pay period to buy yourself an ice cream.

EINAR DIAZ — C — Bats: R — Throws: R — Born: 28-Dec-1972 — Age: 32

YEAR	TM	LG	AGE	AB	H	2B	3B	HR	BB	SO	SB	CS	AVG	OBP	SLG	MLVR	EQBA	EQOBP	EQSLG	EQMLVR	VORP	DEFENSE
2002	CLE	AL	29	320	66	19	0	2	17	27	0	1	.206	.258	.284	-.371	.213	.263	.288	-.399	-12.9	96-C -3
2003	TEX	AL	30	334	86	14	1	4	9	32	3	1	.257	.294	.341	-.224	.252	.291	.333	-.257	-1.4	99-C -1
2004	MON	NL	31	139	31	6	1	1	11	10	2	0	.223	.293	.302	-.240	.221	.287	.300	-.329	-1.7	40-C -4
2005	*STL*	*NL*	*32*	*146*	*35*	*7*	*1*	*1*	*9*	*13*	*1*	*0*	*.236*	*.291*	*.316*	*-.272*	*.238*	*.292*	*.323*	*-.262*	*-3.4*	*42-C 0*

Breakout: 33% *Improve: 46%* *Collapse: 39%*

It's hard to spot the good defensive catcher who could hit well enough to contribute—the guy who played for Cleveland four or five years ago. Diaz's defensive skills have eroded and he hasn't hit at all in years. Without a contribution to make either way around the plate, he's a poor choice in any role. Diaz should have warranted a spring training invite at most, but the Cards' Matheny fetish led them to form a Yadier Molina/Einar Diaz time-share.

BRENDAN HARRIS — 2B/3B — Bats: R — Throws: R — Born: 26-Aug-1980 — Age: 24

YEAR	TM	LG	AGE	AB	H	2B	3B	HR	BB	SO	SB	CS	AVG	OBP	SLG	MLVR	EQBA	EQOBP	EQSLG	EQMLVR	VORP	DEFENSE
2002	DAY	FSL	21	425	140	35	6	13	43	57	16	4	.329	.395	.532	.356	.289	.344	.483	.085	35.4	59-3B 3 54-2B 1
2002	WTN	SOU	21	53	17	4	1	2	2	5	1	1	.321	.345	.547	.341	.302	.315	.528	.116	3.7	
2003	WTN	SOU	22	435	122	34	7	5	51	72	6	7	.280	.364	.425	.157	.269	.341	.424	-.021	23.0	94-3B -11 15-2B -1
2004	IOW	PCL	23	254	79	21	1	11	16	40	0	2	.311	.353	.531	.195	.270	.313	.444	-.043	9.8	49-2B 6
2004	EDM	PCL	23	130	35	6	0	6	10	21	0	0	.269	.317	.454	-.015	.242	.278	.383	-.218	-1.4	34-3B -5
2004	MON	NL	23	50	8	2	0	1	2	11	0	0	.160	.208	.260	-.486	.160	.187	.220	-.673	-4.1	
2005	*WAS*	*NL*	*24*	*268*	*73*	*18*	*1*	*8*	*21*	*44*	*2*	*1*	*.271*	*.329*	*.435*	*-.022*	*.274*	*.330*	*.445*	*-.007*	*15.4*	*72-3B -1*

Breakout: 19% *Improve: 47%* *Collapse: 21%*

Part of the Orlando Cabrera trade, Harris came to the Expos with an impressive minor league resume, having shown the ability to hit for average, take walks, and hit for decent power. Like everyone else that got called up, he stunk in his short major league audition, but look at those lines at 23 in Triple-A, which show the bigger picture; that's pretty nice. So the Nationals signed Castilla to play third, and Guzman to play short. Combined with Vidro's contract, Harris now has no chance to play. Meanwhile, the team gets equal or less performance for far more money.

MAICER IZTURIS — SS — Bats: B — Throws: R — Born: 12-Sep-1980 — Age: 24

YEAR	TM	LG	AGE	AB	H	2B	3B	HR	BB	SO	SB	CS	AVG	OBP	SLG	MLVR	EQBA	EQOBP	EQSLG	EQMLVR	VORP	DEFENSE
2002	KIN	CRL	21	233	61	13	1	1	24	26	24	6	.262	.332	.339	-.005	.241	.303	.325	-.251	-5.6	53-2B -4
2002	AKR	EAS	21	253	70	12	7	0	17	28	8	4	.277	.326	.379	-.019	.244	.283	.335	-.275	-7.4	64-2B -1
2003	AKR	EAS	22	218	61	11	5	1	24	23	14	6	.280	.351	.390	.016	.252	.320	.362	-.160	1.0	41-2B -4
2003	BUF	INT	22	301	79	16	4	2	24	28	14	6	.262	.317	.362	-.051	.254	.313	.356	-.180	2.1	66-SS 5 20-2B 3
2004	EDM	PCL	23	376	127	19	2	3	57	30	14	12	.338	.428	.423	.220	.314	.397	.382	.059	30.7	84-SS -7
2004	MON	NL	23	107	22	5	2	1	10	20	4	0	.206	.286	.318	-.247	.204	.281	.315	-.330	-0.4	23-SS -2
2005	*WAS*	*NL*	*24*	*323*	*85*	*16*	*3*	*2*	*33*	*35*	*10*	*4*	*.263*	*.334*	*.353*	*-.127*	*.266*	*.335*	*.362*	*-.115*	*12.4*	*88-SS -5*

Breakout: 17% *Improve: 35%* *Collapse: 35%*

A .400+ OBP from a 24-year-old shortstop, even in the Pacific Coast League, is a great thing to have. Of course—stop us if you've heard this before—Izturis flopped in his trial with the big club. Big deal. Even if he only puts up a high, power-void OBP, he'd be a second-tier shortstop for almost no money at all, which is what the Nationals need. So they blocked him with Guzman. During spring training, Izturis was at risk of being driven out to a remote Florida swamp, tied up and left for the crocodiles, because nothing hopeful is allowed to live in this organization. But he was liberated through a deal to the Dodgers, where he might earn a utility role.

NICK JOHNSON 1B Bats: L Throws: L Born: 19-Sep-1978 Age: 26

YEAR	TM	LG	AGE	AB	H	2B	3B	HR	BB	SO	SB	CS	AVG	OBP	SLG	MLVR	EQBA	EQOBP	EQSLG	EQMLVR	VORP	DEFENSE
2002	NYY	AL	23	378	92	15	0	15	48	98	1	3	.243	.347	.402	-.010	.254	.354	.418	-.017	10.7	62-1B 5
2003	NYY	AL	24	324	92	19	0	14	70	57	5	2	.284	.422	.472	.235	.295	.429	.491	.247	34.7	59-1B 0
2004	MON	NL	25	251	63	16	0	7	40	58	6	3	.251	.359	.398	.034	.248	.350	.388	-.070	10.8	68-1B 5
2005	*WAS*	*NL*	*26*	*328*	*88*	*18*	*1*	*13*	*55*	*74*	*5*	*2*	*.267*	*.381*	*.446*	*.077*	*.270*	*.382*	*.456*	*.093*	*22.9*	*94-1B -1*

Breakout: 29% *Improve: 61%* *Collapse: 16%*

The ball jumps off his bat. He has amazing control of the strike zone. He's still potentially one of the best hitters in all of baseball. He plays first well enough that when he can be penciled onto a lineup card, he can be a huge asset to his team. But Johnson can't stay healthy. He's Elijah Price, he attracts injuries of all kinds. Last year he had a sore knee and trouble with his back, which was aggravated by the turf at Olympic Stadium; and a ground ball jumped up and broke his cheekbone, ending his season. To continue the litany of complaints about the franchise, the Expos didn't pay for video, so preparation freaks like Johnson couldn't study opposing pitchers. It's as if the team wouldn't pay to turn on the lights early in Olympic Stadium, forcing the Expos to take batting practice in the dark.

JOSH LABANDEIRA SS Bats: R Throws: R Born: 25-Feb-1979 Age: 26

YEAR	TM	LG	AGE	AB	H	2B	3B	HR	BB	SO	SB	CS	AVG	OBP	SLG	MLVR	EQBA	EQOBP	EQSLG	EQMLVR	VORP	DEFENSE
2002	CLN	MDW	23	493	141	27	3	8	45	73	15	12	.286	.350	.402	.102	.236	.285	.341	-.268	-22.6	
2003	BRV	FSL	24	238	77	13	4	0	24	35	6	5	.324	.386	.412	.254	.298	.345	.392	-.036	13.8	55-SS -9
2003	HAR	EAS	24	238	57	18	2	2	20	38	0	2	.239	.298	.357	-.132	.218	.269	.335	-.319	-8.4	60-SS 4
2004	HAR	EAS	25	510	138	21	4	9	52	90	9	5	.271	.356	.380	.009	.245	.319	.344	-.191	1.8	127-SS 0
2005	*WAS*	*NL*	*26*	*164*	*40*	*8*	*1*	*2*	*12*	*29*	*2*	*1*	*.244*	*.307*	*.352*	*-.191*	*.246*	*.308*	*.360*	*-.179*	*2.8*	*47-SS -9*

Breakout: 22% *Improve: 42%* *Collapse: 34%*

The hits just keep coming. Not that Labandeira was worth much. In Harrisburg, he was too old for the level to be a serious prospect, but he had an okay season. So he got the call, didn't get much playing time and didn't hit at all—no really, 14 at-bats, no hits. Bowden outrighted him off of the 40-man to make space for his projects, but Labandeira made it through the Rule 5 Draft unclaimed. He'll start the year at the team's new Triple-A affiliate in New Orleans.

ALEJANDRO MACHADO 2B Bats: B Throws: R Born: 26-Apr-1982 Age: 23

YEAR	TM	LG	AGE	AB	H	2B	3B	HR	BB	SO	SB	CS	AVG	OBP	SLG	MLVR	EQBA	EQOBP	EQSLG	EQMLVR	VORP	DEFENSE
2002	WIL	CRL	20	325	102	9	1	2	27	43	20	6	.314	.381	.366	.134	.275	.329	.328	-.175	2.8	90-SS -4
2003	HUN	SOU	21	155	35	4	1	0	15	24	11	1	.226	.302	.265	-.191	.194	.248	.219	-.534	-17.6	38-2B 1
2003	WIC	TXS	21	289	83	13	5	1	34	45	19	9	.287	.368	.377	.075	.268	.342	.361	-.108	6.1	75-2B 7
2004	BRV	FSL	22	186	66	10	2	1	22	27	11	6	.355	.424	.446	.348	.325	.383	.414	.088	19.7	38-SS -6
2004	HAR	EAS	22	346	97	5	4	4	41	39	19	9	.280	.365	.353	-.007	.254	.330	.320	-.197	-2.4	77-2B 6 11-SS 2
2005	*WAS*	*NL*	*23*	*318*	*82*	*16*	*3*	*2*	*30*	*45*	*10*	*3*	*.257*	*.329*	*.338*	*-.162*	*.260*	*.329*	*.346*	*-.150*	*7.7*	*87-2B -1*

Breakout: 13% *Improve: 36%* *Collapse: 33%*

"Son, it's been fun having you in the Braves organization, but we're shipping you to Kansas City."

"Nooooooooooooooooooo!"

Later...

"Kid, we've got news. We've traded you."

"Oh, thank God."

"To Montreal."

"Nooooooooooooooooooo!"

No power, decent batting eye, fair defender. Machado has some foot speed but needs to learn how to steal bases successfully with it. Young enough to develop into a useful utilityman.

HENRY MATEO 2B Bats: B Throws: R Born: 14-Oct-1976 Age: 28

YEAR	TM	LG	AGE	AB	H	2B	3B	HR	BB	SO	SB	CS	AVG	OBP	SLG	MLVR	EQBA	EQOBP	EQSLG	EQMLVR	VORP	DEFENSE			
2002	OTT	INT	25	285	73	10	6	5	18	53	15	6	.256	.306	.386	-.053	.241	.295	.374	-.199	-2.0	53-2B	5	22-SS	-4
2003	MON	NL	26	154	37	3	1	0	11	38	11	1	.240	.304	.273	-.291	.240	.292	.253	-.375	-2.6	29-2B	-2		
2004	EDM	PCL	27	119	36	8	3	0	8	16	10	1	.303	.354	.420	.038	.248	.285	.316	-.296	-4.2	25-2B	-2		
2004	MON	NL	27	44	12	2	0	0	1	9	2	3	.273	.289	.318	-.212	.295	.255	.318	-.321	-0.9				
2005	*WAS*	*NL*	*28*	*172*	*42*	*8*	*2*	*1*	*11*	*33*	*8*	*3*	*.245*	*.296*	*.340*	*-.227*	*.248*	*.296*	*.348*	*-.216*	*2.2*	*48-2B*	*-2*		

Breakout: 13% *Improve: 30%* *Collapse: 46%*

A minor league infielder without upside, Mateo distinguished himself from the other guys who got some playing time by hitting a modest .273. Better than nothing, but he failed to make the big impression he needed. He tore the labrum in his throwing shoulder, but is expected to be healthy for spring training. Still, if you forget about him entirely, the Nationals may have already beaten you to it.

SHAWN NORRIS 3B Bats: L Throws: R Born: 01-Aug-1980 Age: 24

YEAR	TM	LG	AGE	AB	H	2B	3B	HR	BB	SO	SB	CS	AVG	OBP	SLG	MLVR	EQBA	EQOBP	EQSLG	EQMLVR	VORP	DEFENSE			
2002	VER	NYP	21	157	45	5	2	4	22	23	2	0	.287	.376	.420	.213	.247	.319	.370	-.154	2.5	40-3B	-5		
2003	SAV	SAL	22	223	64	19	2	2	31	42	4	2	.287	.375	.417	.187	.252	.319	.378	-.139	3.2	63-3B	-8		
2003	BRV	FSL	22	194	38	9	1	2	37	49	1	2	.196	.331	.284	-.068	.187	.295	.291	-.342	-12.2	29-2B	-2	20-3B	0
2004	BRV	FSL	23	351	96	15	8	2	59	80	5	2	.274	.379	.379	.128	.254	.343	.362	-.114	8.9	42-3B	1	30-SS	-4
2004	HAR	EAS	23	124	39	10	2	3	25	37	1	1	.315	.429	.500	.315	.288	.396	.440	.116	12.6	37-3B	-2		
2005	*WAS*	*NL*	*24*	*200*	*49*	*11*	*2*	*3*	*26*	*49*	*2*	*1*	*.243*	*.332*	*.367*	*-.126*	*.245*	*.333*	*.375*	*-.114*	*3.9*	*58-3B*	*-3*		

Breakout: 19% *Improve: 42%* *Collapse: 36%*

A versatile glove around the infield, as a Manatee (no really) he split time between second, short, and third, though he played third exclusively at Double-A. Norris has shown enough bat control and plate discipline to warrant more promotions. He needs to turn on the power to become a legit prospect; PECOTA doesn't see it happening.

JERRY OWENS LF Bats: L Throws: L Born: 16-Feb-1981 Age: 24

YEAR	TM	LG	AGE	AB	H	2B	3B	HR	BB	SO	SB	CS	AVG	OBP	SLG	MLVR	EQBA	EQOBP	EQSLG	EQMLVR	VORP	DEFENSE			
2004	SAV	SAL	23	418	122	17	2	1	46	59	30	13	.292	.365	.349	.034	.257	.315	.307	-.243	-25.9	46-LF	-5	17-CF	-2
2005	*WAS*	*NL*	*24*	*324*	*76*	*14*	*3*	*1*	*23*	*54*	*13*	*4*	*.233*	*.286*	*.297*	*-.308*	*.235*	*.287*	*.304*	*-.299*	*-16.6*	*85-LF*	*-8*		

Breakout: 19% *Improve: 36%* *Collapse: 45%*

The Nationals really like Owens. He can slap a single, take a walk, steal a base. Still, he was old for the Sally League at 23, and that lack of power is worrisome. Owens didn't hit well at all in the Arizona Fall League, either. If you can't even look good in an institutional dog show for hitting prospects, why should anyone pay attention to you?

VAL PASCUCCI RF Bats: R Throws: R Born: 17-Nov-1978 Age: 26

YEAR	TM	LG	AGE	AB	H	2B	3B	HR	BB	SO	SB	CS	AVG	OBP	SLG	MLVR	EQBA	EQOBP	EQSLG	EQMLVR	VORP	DEFENSE			
2002	HAR	EAS	23	459	108	14	1	27	93	115	2	0	.235	.374	.447	.106	.206	.330	.393	-.129	-9.7	102-RF	-3	17-1B	-2
2003	EDM	PCL	24	459	129	29	1	15	101	132	3	2	.281	.419	.447	.235	.257	.386	.417	.043	16.8	105-RF	0	27-1B	-2
2004	EDM	PCL	25	393	117	32	1	25	78	96	9	2	.298	.422	.575	.384	.261	.377	.481	.114	25.2	75-1B	0	28-RF	-1
2004	MON	NL	25	62	11	1	0	2	10	22	1	0	.177	.297	.290	-.260	.177	.277	.274	-.406	-2.1	11-RF	1		
2005	*WAS*	*NL*	*26*	*216*	*54*	*11*	*1*	*9*	*37*	*65*	*2*	*1*	*.250*	*.371*	*.432*	*.029*	*.253*	*.372*	*.442*	*.043*	*12.1*	*64-RF*	*-5*		

Breakout: 18% *Improve: 43%* *Collapse: 20%*

When even the most interesting of the Expos prospects flailed around miserably in their call-ups, it got sad. Watching the minor leagues last year was like the *Peanuts Halloween Special,* when they go trick-or-treating, with the Expos Charlie Brown. What came out of your farm system this year, guys?

Pirates: I got Rookie of the Year Jason Bay, who the Expos traded in 2002.

Padres: I have a defensive whiz of a shortstop!

Dodgers: I have five pieces of candy!

Expos: I got a rock.

Early Peanuts was so bleak, sad, and depressing it was funny. Being an Expos fan must have been like that, so awful you had to laugh to keep from crying. Pascucci was sold to Japan to finance Bowden's $8,000-a-day veteran habit. He could help a major league team if he's back a year from now.

JUAN RIVERA RF Bats: R Throws: R Born: 03-Jul-1978 Age: 26

YEAR	TM	LG	AGE	AB	H	2B	3B	HR	BB	SO	SB	CS	AVG	OBP	SLG	MLVR	EQBA	EQOBP	EQSLG	EQMLVR	VORP	DEFENSE
2002	COH	INT	24	265	86	21	1	8	13	39	5	1	.325	.355	.502	.228	.297	.333	.471	.056	9.5	64-RF -8
2002	NYY	AL	24	83	22	5	0	1	6	10	1	1	.265	.311	.361	-.107	.289	.316	.361	-.143	-0.4	14-RF -1 13-LF 1
2003	COH	INT	25	308	100	21	0	7	26	37	1	3	.325	.374	.461	.211	.300	.348	.436	.035	9.1	54-RF -1 24-LF 0
2003	NYY	AL	25	173	46	14	0	7	10	27	0	0	.266	.304	.468	.025	.275	.312	.474	.003	5.5	32-LF -3 14-RF 0
2004	MON	NL	26	391	120	24	1	12	34	45	6	2	.307	.364	.465	.173	.301	.360	.455	.084	30.2	75-RF 6
2005	*ANA*	*AL*	*26*	*379*	*106*	*22*	*1*	*11*	*29*	*52*	*4*	*2*	*.279*	*.331*	*.434*	*-.008*	*.281*	*.334*	*.445*	*.005*	*13.5*	*99-RF 0*

Breakout: 10% *Improve: 27%* *Collapse: 37%*

Rivera was heralded as the next great Yankee prospect so long ago it's strange to think he's only 26 and that this was the first season in which he got serious playing time. Rivera's a contact hitter who still gets his walks, and has good power. That makes him an average right fielder without consideration of his great arm, and at something around the league minimum, that's a great deal. His minor league performances are solid, so there's reason to think that this kind of production is sustainable. Naturally, the Nationals traded him to the Angels for a better-paid Juan Rivera-equivalent with personality issues. Bowden's treating this team like a spouse who's not allowed to have nice things: Even something modestly cool like Juan Rivera is too good for this team, and must be removed to prove a greater point about who's in charge.

BRIAN SCHNEIDER C Bats: L Throws: R Born: 26-Nov-1976 Age: 28

YEAR	TM	LG	AGE	AB	H	2B	3B	HR	BB	SO	SB	CS	AVG	OBP	SLG	MLVR	EQBA	EQOBP	EQSLG	EQMLVR	VORP	DEFENSE
2002	MON	NL	25	207	57	19	2	5	21	41	1	2	.275	.339	.459	.097	.274	.334	.462	.024	14.9	56-C 9
2003	MON	NL	26	335	77	26	1	9	37	75	0	2	.230	.309	.394	-.139	.225	.303	.389	-.174	2.0	98-C 15
2004	MON	NL	27	436	112	20	3	12	42	63	0	1	.257	.325	.399	-.031	.249	.319	.391	-.123	16.6	123-C 14
2005	*WAS*	*NL*	*28*	*283*	*69*	*16*	*1*	*7*	*29*	*50*	*0*	*1*	*.243*	*.316*	*.388*	*-.127*	*.246*	*.317*	*.397*	*-.115*	*7.3*	*77-C 6*

Breakout: 23% *Improve: 46%* *Collapse: 27%*

For the second season in a row, Schneider almost eliminated the stolen base from other teams' offensive games. He threw out half the base runners who dared take off against him. He committed only four passed balls, so it's not as if they were able to make up for it by advancing on his poor defense catching the ball, either. Few other catchers can match Schneider's +38 fielding rating over the last three years. Combined with some decent power and patience, and you have a bargain at $2 million for 2005 who's flat-out fun to watch.

TERRMEL SLEDGE LF Bats: L Throws: L Born: 18-Mar-1977 Age: 28

YEAR	TM	LG	AGE	AB	H	2B	3B	HR	BB	SO	SB	CS	AVG	OBP	SLG	MLVR	EQBA	EQOBP	EQSLG	EQMLVR	VORP	DEFENSE
2002	HAR	EAS	25	396	119	18	6	8	55	70	11	8	.301	.401	.437	.184	.270	.357	.398	-.027	15.0	70-CF 1 16-LF 0
2002	OTT	INT	25	80	21	5	2	1	11	15	1	1	.263	.359	.412	.074	.262	.357	.425	.004	1.5	13-LF 0
2003	EDM	PCL	26	497	161	26	9	22	61	93	13	5	.324	.397	.545	.378	.300	.371	.506	.175	49.8	46-CF -2 43-LF -3
2004	MON	NL	27	398	107	20	6	15	40	66	3	3	.269	.336	.462	.082	.263	.332	.451	-.005	18.1	68-LF 1 34-RF 2
2005	*WAS*	*NL*	*28*	*382*	*103*	*22*	*4*	*13*	*44*	*73*	*4*	*3*	*.271*	*.349*	*.448*	*.029*	*.273*	*.350*	*.458*	*.044*	*17.2*	*104-LF 1*

Breakout: 16% *Improve: 40%* *Collapse: 20%*

Sledge isn't the problem. At the league-minimum salary last year, he played a decent left field and started hitting after a terrible April. Still, his overall stats were dragged down by a nasty platoon split: He hit .241/.275/.368 against lefties, .277/.352/.489 against righties. At his salary, you can afford a platoon partner to make him look good. Unfortunately, they ditched Pascucci, the most obvious in-house candidate.

JOSE VIDRO 2B Bats: B Throws: R Born: 27-Aug-1974 Age: 30

YEAR	TM	LG	AGE	AB	H	2B	3B	HR	BB	SO	SB	CS	AVG	OBP	SLG	MLVR	EQBA	EQOBP	EQSLG	EQMLVR	VORP	DEFENSE
2002	MON	NL	27	604	190	43	3	19	60	70	2	1	.315	.378	.490	.227	.308	.370	.490	.158	65.9	148-2B 9
2003	MON	NL	28	509	158	36	0	15	69	50	3	2	.310	.397	.470	.161	.304	.386	.462	.142	47.0	127-2B -5
2004	MON	NL	29	412	121	24	0	14	49	43	3	1	.294	.367	.454	.149	.289	.359	.442	.053	36.9	97-2B -11
2005	*WAS*	*NL*	*30*	*415*	*118*	*26*	*2*	*12*	*49*	*47*	*2*	*1*	*.284*	*.360*	*.440*	*.048*	*.287*	*.361*	*.450*	*.063*	*30.0*	*112-2B -7*

Breakout: 12% *Improve: 37%* *Collapse: 24%*

Vidro's past his prime, a good hitter who doesn't figure to get any better. His range has dropped off sharply, so he's not making the plays. Then you have to cope with four years and $30 million—it's not the worst deal in the majors, but what motivation is there when money is tight, to spend so much of it on Vidro? And beyond that, when there are others you'd be much better off spending the money on, more productive players who could have been locked up to longer, cheaper deals? Did the organization feel that they owed something to Vidro for his past contributions, that they were obligated to reward him? If so, why Vidro over other Expos who toiled for major league minimum? Did he give an impassioned speech about how much he loved the organization and how much he'd hate to leave that moved Minaya so much that they gave him what he wanted before they could come to their senses?

Vidro had successful surgery to relieve tendonitis in his knee in September, and is expected to be ready in time for spring training. Here's hoping Bowden's non-stop drive to wheel and deal prompts him to trade Vidro to a contender with no second baseman and money to burn.

BRANDON WATSON **CF** **Bats: L** **Throws: R** Born: 30-Sep-1981 Age: 23

YEAR	TM	LG	AGE	AB	H	2B	3B	HR	BB	SO	SB	CS	AVG	OBP	SLG	MLVR	EQBA	EQOBP	EQSLG	EQMLVR	VORP	DEFENSE
2002	BRV	FSL	20	424	113	16	2	0	27	53	22	13	.267	.314	.314	-.046	.243	.278	.285	-.357	-28.6	106-CF 4
2003	HAR	EAS	21	565	180	17	6	1	38	60	18	17	.319	.362	.375	.055	.285	.326	.343	-.153	-0.9	138-CF -1
2004	EDM	PCL	22	526	154	17	3	2	31	68	22	10	.293	.332	.348	-.126	.273	.312	.318	-.224	-11.6	118-CF -9
2005	*WAS*	*NL*	*23*	*287*	*70*	*12*	*2*	*0*	*15*	*37*	*7*	*3*	*.244*	*.282*	*.305*	*-.299*	*.246*	*.283*	*.312*	*-.289*	*-10.7*	*75-CF -5*

Breakout: 9% *Improve: 19%* *Collapse: 61%*

He sucks, but he's fast. Obviously, the Expos have no choice but to keep him around, while letting other useful or interesting players go. It'd be sad, except they're now in other organizations, while Watson is a National. This chapter is like tasting entries in the annual chili cook-off in Edinburgh, Scotland. Yes, this one isn't too spicy. The overboiling did make the beans too mushy on this one, but it also made the ground intestinal lining easier to chew on. This is good—is that beef? Wait, no, don't tell me.

BRAD WILKERSON **1B/OF** **Bats: L** **Throws: L** Born: 01-Jun-1977 Age: 28

YEAR	TM	LG	AGE	AB	H	2B	3B	HR	BB	SO	SB	CS	AVG	OBP	SLG	MLVR	EQBA	EQOBP	EQSLG	EQMLVR	VORP	DEFENSE
2002	MON	NL	25	507	135	27	8	20	81	161	7	8	.266	.370	.469	.150	.261	.365	.468	.076	35.1	56-CF 0 54-LF -1
2003	MON	NL	26	504	135	34	4	19	89	155	13	10	.268	.380	.464	.098	.261	.373	.458	.076	25.7	82-LF 7 30-CF 0
2004	MON	NL	27	572	146	39	2	32	106	152	13	6	.255	.374	.498	.184	.249	.368	.487	.096	48.2	79-1B 7 50-LF 1
2005	*WAS*	*NL*	*28*	*468*	*119*	*26*	*3*	*22*	*78*	*127*	*8*	*4*	*.254*	*.362*	*.462*	*.055*	*.256*	*.363*	*.473*	*.070*	*23.5*	*130-1B 7*

Breakout: 29% *Improve: 61%* *Collapse: 9%*

Wilkerson was the bright light of the franchise this year, hitting for great power and creating further offense with bushels of walks. Even while afflicted with a sore knee and a tight hamstring, his power took a step up. His health is a continuing concern, as every year seems to bring a couple things that ail him. And yet he hits like crazy.

Wilkerson went on the All-Star tour in Japan as an Expo, even as MLB was moving the team. He wore the Expo colors in the Tokyo Dome, a week before the team's new uniforms were held out and waved like capes as if the presenters were matadors. Above their nervous smiles, eyes darted around the room, scanning the crowd for the angry, wounded Expos fan who might charge with the next flash of fabric. Given Wilkerson's contributions in the final years of this once-proud franchise, there was no better choice to be the last Expo.

PITCHERS

TONY ARMAS **Bats: R** **Throws: R** Born: 29-Apr-1978 Age: 27

YEAR	TM	LG	AGE	G	GS	IP	H	BB	SO	HR	ERA	EQERA	EQH9	EQBB9	EQSO9	EQHR9	PERA	VORP	STF
2002	MON	NL	24	29	29	164.3	149	78	131	22	4.44	4.65	8.5	3.7	6.4	1.2	4.37	13.5	7
2003	MON	NL	25	5	5	31.0	25	8	23	4	2.61	2.45	8.0	2.1	6.1	1.2	3.68	10.6	16
2004	MON	NL	26	16	16	72.0	66	45	54	13	4.88	4.80	8.7	5.1	6.1	1.4	5.32	5.1	-7
2005	*WAS*	*NL*	*27*	*19*	*16*	*96.3*	*94*	*48*	*71*	*14*	*4.89*	*5.22*	*8.8*	*4.0*	*5.9*	*1.3*	*5.25*	*6.6*	*0*

Breakout: 15% *Improve: 37%* *Collapse: 32%*

Rushed back from injury, shoulder soreness dogged him and eventually ended his season. The shoulder was examined repeatedly, though they found nothing. Since he tore his labrum the previous year, you'd think they'd be pretty paranoid about it. Expect more injuries for Armas, cinching the failure to have realized any real gains from having dealt Pedro Martinez once upon a time.

LUIS AYALA **Bats: R** **Throws: R** Born: 12-Jan-1978 Age: 27

YEAR	TM	LG	AGE	G	GS	IP	H	BB	SO	HR	ERA	EQERA	EQH9	EQBB9	EQSO9	EQHR9	PERA	VORP	STF
2003	MON	NL	25	65	0	71.0	65	13	46	8	2.92	3.21	8.7	1.5	5.5	0.9	3.88	17.3	0
2004	MON	NL	26	81	0	90.3	92	15	63	6	2.69	2.89	9.0	1.3	5.7	0.5	3.71	27.2	6
2005	*WAS*	*NL*	*27*	*43*	*6*	*84.3*	*84*	*21*	*58*	*8*	*3.47*	*3.71*	*9.0*	*2.0*	*5.6*	*0.9*	*4.06*	*18.4*	*0*

Breakout: 29% *Improve: 46%* *Collapse: 30%*

See, you can get good things in the Rule 5 Draft. You can get quality bullpen arms like Ayala here, who was the second-best pitcher on the team last year. Ayala had a little trouble with elbow stiffness, and this was a big jump in innings pitched for him, after he went from throwing 60 innings in two years to more than 70 in 2003 to 90+ in '04. Temper your expectations.

FRANCIS BELTRAN **Bats: R** **Throws: R** Born: 29-Nov-1979 Age: 25

YEAR	TM	LG	AGE	G	GS	IP	H	BB	SO	HR	ERA	EQERA	EQH9	EQBB9	EQSO9	EQHR9	PERA	VORP	STF
2002	WTN	SOU	22	39	0	41.7	28	19	43	2	2.59	3.99	7.7	4.0	7.0	0.9	3.99	6.9	6
2002	CHC	NL	22	11	0	12.0	14	16	11	2	7.50	8.03	9.5	9.5	7.3	1.5	7.30	-3.8	-23
2003	IOW	PCL	23	31	2	48.7	46	19	33	2	2.96	3.72	8.6	3.9	5.3	0.6	4.11	7.6	-3
2004	CHC	NL	24	34	0	35.0	27	22	40	8	4.63	4.81	7.8	5.1	9.4	1.9	4.81	3.2	5
2004	MON	NL	24	11	0	14.3	20	5	8	3	7.55	6.91	11.3	2.5	4.4	1.9	6.28	-2.9	-19
2005	*WAS*	*NL*	*25*	*27*	*7*	*64.3*	*62*	*30*	*53*	*7*	*4.44*	*4.74*	*8.7*	*3.7*	*6.7*	*1.0*	*4.68*	*5.9*	*1*

Breakout: 18% *Improve: 43%* *Collapse: 23%*

The 2004 Caribbean World Series MVP, Beltran is still young, but even with plus heat, he lacks the control to make him a big future contributor. As a relief prospect his potential contributions are limited as is. He's an option for cheap innings at close to league average, but without improvement, he'll become a wanderer as soon as he hits arbitration eligibility.

CHAD BENTZ **Bats: L** **Throws: L** Born: 05-May-1980 Age: 25

YEAR	TM	LG	AGE	G	GS	IP	H	BB	SO	HR	ERA	EQERA	EQH9	EQBB9	EQSO9	EQHR9	PERA	VORP	STF
2002	BRV	FSL	22	23	0	29.7	30	14	34	1	3.64	5.40	9.5	4.4	7.3	0.6	5.08	1.6	-1
2003	HAR	EAS	23	52	0	84.7	72	39	56	4	2.55	4.02	8.5	4.6	4.9	0.8	4.60	8.7	-12
2004	MON	NL	24	36	0	27.7	23	23	18	5	5.85	5.81	8.5	6.8	5.5	1.4	5.47	-0.5	-24
2005	*FLO*	*NL*	*25*	*7*	*1*	*12.7*	*13*	*8*	*8*	*1*	*5.52*	*6.02*	*9.4*	*5.1*	*5.3*	*1.0*	*5.79*	*0.1*	*-17*

Breakout: 20% *Improve: 39%* *Collapse: 29%*

We'd say he has a future as a LOOGY, but the thing about bringing in a guy to face one or more tough left-handers is that you want to get them out. Until Bentz can throw a strike reliably, he's not going to serve well in even that limited role. Released, and signed by the Marlins.

ROCKY BIDDLE **Bats: R** **Throws: R** Born: 21-May-1976 Age: 29

YEAR	TM	LG	AGE	G	GS	IP	H	BB	SO	HR	ERA	EQERA	EQH9	EQBB9	EQSO9	EQHR9	PERA	VORP	STF
2002	CWS	AL	26	44	7	77.7	72	39	64	13	4.05	4.46	8.7	4.3	7.2	1.4	5.06	9.6	-3
2003	MON	NL	27	73	0	71.7	71	40	54	10	4.64	5.01	9.0	4.4	6.2	1.2	5.01	1.7	-10
2004	MON	NL	28	47	9	78.0	98	31	51	15	6.92	7.36	10.5	3.2	5.1	1.5	5.96	-19.3	-17
2005	*WAS*	*NL*	*29*	*33*	*5*	*65.3*	*63*	*28*	*48*	*7*	*4.32*	*4.61*	*8.8*	*3.4*	*5.9*	*1.0*	*4.69*	*7.0*	*-4*

Breakout: 24% *Improve: 57%* *Collapse: 19%*

So the Expos trade Bartolo Colon for this, and Biddle goes from mediocre to terrible. They keep him around, hopefully to redeem the trade in some small sense, and this is what he gives them. Dame Fortune just kept kicking this team when it was down.

BILL BRAY **Bats: L** **Throws: L** Born: 5-Jun-1983 Age: 22

Having just said some bad things about the contributions of relief prospects, here's a good one. He's got control and good stuff, he'll be in the majors soon, and he should be a contributor. Picked in the first round in 2004 out of William & Mary, they'll let him build on the 7.1 A-ball innings for a while before he gets a shot at a big league job, unless he gets on the Chad Cordero fast track.

WILTON CHAVEZ **Bats: R** **Throws: R** Born: 13-Jun-1978 Age: 27

YEAR	TM	LG	AGE	G	GS	IP	H	BB	SO	HR	ERA	EQERA	EQH9	EQBB9	EQSO9	EQHR9	PERA	VORP	STF
2002	DAY	FSL	24	8	6	24.7	30	12	25	2	4.74	7.50	10.5	4.5	6.4	1.5	6.00	-1.1	-13
2002	WTN	SOU	24	18	18	103.0	97	39	86	7	3.76	5.14	9.4	3.4	5.7	1.2	4.95	7.0	2
2003	IOW	PCL	25	26	22	140.0	144	51	113	17	4.24	4.96	9.5	3.7	6.3	1.6	5.30	4.4	-2
2004	EDM	PCL	26	28	27	164.0	177	43	114	21	4.61	5.75	9.4	2.5	4.8	1.3	4.73	15.3	7
2005	*WAS*	*NL*	*27*	*12*	*12*	*69.3*	*68*	*25*	*49*	*10*	*4.47*	*4.78*	*8.8*	*2.8*	*5.7*	*1.3*	*4.69*	*7.2*	*6*

Breakout: 16% *Improve: 44%* *Collapse: 23%*

His win-loss record and ERA in Edmonton were pretty unimpressive, but see the hitters section of this chapter for comments on some of the sad sacks that were backing him up. Chavez could start for the team next year, eat innings in the back of the rotation, and acquit himself well. His limited repertoire curtails his upside, but he'll be useful if used correctly.

ROY CORCORAN **Bats: R** **Throws: R** Born: 11-May-1980 Age: 25

YEAR	TM	LG	AGE	G	GS	IP	H	BB	SO	HR	ERA	EQERA	EQH9	EQBB9	EQSO9	EQHR9	PERA	VORP	STF
2002	CLN	MDW	22	48	1	80.0	82	24	106	5	4.16	7.23	10.2	3.4	7.2	1.6	5.42	1.5	-15
2003	BRV	FSL	23	28	0	33.0	19	11	35	1	1.91	3.99	7.4	3.7	7.1	0.9	3.68	6.3	7
2003	HAR	EAS	23	14	0	23.7	14	7	26	0	0.38	2.49	6.6	2.9	8.3	0.4	2.49	7.5	25
2004	EDM	PCL	24	30	0	44.3	39	24	35	0	3.05	3.61	7.9	5.1	5.5	0.2	3.83	8.3	-4
2005	*WAS*	*NL*	*25*	*31*	*3*	*51.0*	*49*	*25*	*40*	*5*	*4.21*	*4.50*	*8.6*	*3.8*	*6.4*	*0.9*	*4.69*	*6.2*	*-3*

Breakout: 22% *Improve: 49%* *Collapse: 21%*

A righty reliever with a good performance record heading into 2004, but Corcoran gave up a lot of walks, snuffing out his shot at a promotion. The low home-run rates are intriguing, and PECOTA thinks he'll do fine if given a shot. Nevertheless, designated for assignment by new management.

CHAD CORDERO **Bats: R** **Throws: R** Born: 18-Mar-1982 Age: 23

YEAR	TM	LG	AGE	G	GS	IP	H	BB	SO	HR	ERA	EQERA	EQH9	EQBB9	EQSO9	EQHR9	PERA	VORP	STF
2003	BRV	FSL	21	19	0	26.3	17	10	17	1	2.05	4.63	8.1	4.2	4.2	1.2	4.24	3.5	-8
2003	MON	NL	21	12	0	11.0	4	3	12	1	1.64	1.80	5.4	2.7	9.9	0.9	1.80	4.9	39
2004	MON	NL	22	69	0	82.7	68	43	83	8	2.94	2.92	7.8	4.2	8.1	0.8	3.94	24.4	17
2005	*WAS*	*NL*	*23*	*35*	*7*	*76.3*	*69*	*36*	*68*	*10*	*4.31*	*4.61*	*8.1*	*3.7*	*7.2*	*1.2*	*4.61*	*9.7*	*2*

Breakout: 11% *Improve: 34%* *Collapse: 34%*

Wow, that's a fast track for you. Only a year removed from being drafted, Cordero claimed a regular gig in the majors and looked sweet. The Cal State Fullerton product throws a nasty fastball, striking out a batter an inning in the closer's role at age 22. If he can tweak his command a bit he could become an elite reliever pretty quickly. PECOTA thinks he'll take a step back before that consolidation season arrives.

ZACH DAY **Bats: R** **Throws: R** Born: 15-Jun-1978 Age: 27

YEAR	TM	LG	AGE	G	GS	IP	H	BB	SO	HR	ERA	EQERA	EQH9	EQBB9	EQSO9	EQHR9	PERA	VORP	STF
2002	MON	NL	24	19	2	37.3	28	15	25	3	3.62	4.33	7.6	3.3	5.6	0.8	3.57	4.4	0
2002	OTT	INT	24	17	16	90.0	77	32	68	5	3.50	4.43	8.6	3.7	6.0	0.8	4.54	9.8	9
2003	MON	NL	25	23	23	131.3	132	59	61	8	4.18	4.12	9.1	3.6	3.8	0.5	4.48	19.1	1
2004	MON	NL	26	19	19	116.7	117	45	61	13	3.93	3.87	9.3	3.1	4.3	0.9	4.67	21.7	1
2005	*WAS*	*NL*	*27*	*21*	*19*	*113.0*	*118*	*45*	*65*	*11*	*4.36*	*4.66*	*9.4*	*3.2*	*4.6*	*0.9*	*4.79*	*11.2*	*0*

Breakout: 15% *Improve: 44%* *Collapse: 25%*

Looked pretty well recovered from his rotator cuff injury, though he spent significant time on the DL with "dead arm" and then broke a finger bunting. Day's a low-strikeout guy who depends on his defense, not giving up walks, and getting a lot of groundballs to keep the ball in the stadium. Vidro and Guzman are locked in for years to come, so the Expos might do well to move Day for full value soon, before their defense starts making him look bad.

SCOTT DOWNS Bats: L Throws: L Born: 17-Mar-1976 Age: 29

YEAR	TM	LG	AGE	G	GS	IP	H	BB	SO	HR	ERA	EQERA	EQH9	EQBB9	EQSO9	EQHR9	PERA	VORP	STF
2002	OTT	INT	26	17	0	23.3	31	3	15	6	5.79	8.59	12.7	1.2	4.9	3.3	8.18	-6.3	-27
2003	EDM	PCL	27	21	21	121.7	119	39	54	13	4.29	5.54	9.2	3.3	3.5	1.5	4.67	11.7	10
2004	EDM	PCL	28	22	22	135.3	143	26	67	16	3.53	4.12	9.3	1.8	3.5	1.3	4.47	16.2	14
2004	MON	NL	28	12	12	63.0	79	23	38	9	5.14	6.21	10.4	2.9	4.8	1.2	5.49	-6.6	20
2005	*TOR*	*AL*	*29*	*17*	*17*	*94.7*	*117*	*31*	*47*	*15*	*5.55*	*5.22*	*11.0*	*2.6*	*4.1*	*1.3*	*5.26*	*6.8*	*-5*

Breakout: 16% *Improve: 42%* *Collapse: 23%*

He's 28, and there's no reason to believe that he's suddenly going to blossom into a good major league starter. At his best, he's a right-handed Zach Day with better control and fewer groundballs. Signed a minor league deal with Toronto, where he'll get consideration for the fifth spot in the rotation.

JOEY EISCHEN Bats: L Throws: L Born: 25-May-1970 Age: 35

YEAR	TM	LG	AGE	G	GS	IP	H	BB	SO	HR	ERA	EQERA	EQH9	EQBB9	EQSO9	EQHR9	PERA	VORP	STF
2002	MON	NL	32	59	0	53.7	43	18	51	1	1.34	1.90	7.3	2.6	7.6	0.2	2.77	21.1	19
2003	MON	NL	33	70	0	53.0	57	13	40	7	3.06	4.35	9.4	1.9	6.1	1.0	4.53	6.1	0
2004	MON	NL	34	21	0	18.3	16	8	17	2	3.93	4.58	8.2	3.6	7.6	1.0	4.08	1.6	4
2005	*WAS*	*NL*	*35*	*38*	*0*	*38.7*	*36*	*14*	*33*	*3*	*3.65*	*3.90*	*8.4*	*2.9*	*6.9*	*0.8*	*4.01*	*7.6*	*3*

Breakout: 24% *Improve: 43%* *Collapse: 31%*

Lost most of the season to surgery to repair two bone spurs in his elbow. Looked like Joey Eischen on his return, the normal good one and not the 2002 awesome one. Unfortunately, he's in his expensive years already, so despite the chance that all you can expect to get is another year of the normal Joey Eischen in 2005, it'll cost a pretty penny.

CLINT EVERTS Bats: R Throws: R Born: 10-Aug-1984 Age: 20

YEAR	TM	LG	AGE	G	GS	IP	H	BB	SO	HR	ERA	EQERA	EQH9	EQBB9	EQSO9	EQHR9	PERA	VORP	STF
2003	VER	NYP	18	10	10	54.0	49	35	50	4	4.17	6.36	10.8	8.1	5.2	2.5	7.52	-10.0	-7
2003	SAV	SAL	18	5	5	26.0	23	10	21	1	3.46	6.38	9.0	4.1	4.5	0.8	4.12	3.9	13
2004	SAV	SAL	19	17	17	90.3	67	21	103	3	2.49	4.00	8.0	2.5	6.5	0.4	3.13	22.9	39
2004	BRV	FSL	19	4	4	20.0	16	10	19	2	2.25	3.50	9.5	5.5	6.0	2.0	6.00	-0.8	9
2005	*WAS*	*NL*	*20*	*17*	*14*	*86.7*	*80*	*38*	*68*	*11*	*4.27*	*4.56*	*8.4*	*3.5*	*6.3*	*1.1*	*4.57*	*10.8*	*7*

Breakout: 16% *Improve: 49%* *Collapse: 18%*

Everts put up some eye-catching numbers in '04, and was looking like the best pitching prospect in the system. Then he blew out his elbow, and had to undergo Tommy John surgery. He should be back by '06, possibly earlier as new rehab techniques accelerate recovery times. If there's no other structural damage, he'll restart his climb to the majors, with a shot at a big league starting job by 2007.

LIVAN HERNANDEZ Bats: R Throws: R Born: 20-Feb-1975 Age: 30

YEAR	TM	LG	AGE	G	GS	IP	H	BB	SO	HR	ERA	EQERA	EQH9	EQBB9	EQSO9	EQHR9	PERA	VORP	STF
2002	SFG	NL	27	33	33	216.0	233	71	134	19	4.38	4.96	9.7	2.5	5.0	0.8	4.74	19.0	6
2003	MON	NL	28	33	33	233.3	225	57	178	27	3.20	3.36	8.7	2.0	6.3	1.0	4.05	55.7	17
2004	MON	NL	29	35	35	255.0	234	83	186	26	3.60	3.54	8.5	2.7	6.0	0.8	4.06	58.3	14
2005	*WAS*	*NL*	*30*	*31*	*31*	*207.3*	*206*	*66*	*151*	*23*	*3.98*	*4.26*	*9.0*	*2.5*	*5.9*	*1.0*	*4.31*	*30.7*	*12*

Breakout: 10% *Improve: 48%* *Collapse: 16%*

The turnaround continues. One of the things to love about watching Hernandez pitch is that he's not afraid to do loopy stuff, like throw a 60 mph curve to Edgar Martinez on a hitter's count. For a strike. If something's not working early, he'll come back to it later, and see if he can get it across the plate the next time. It's interesting to watch him pitch well when his stuff isn't there, and combined with what appears to be a rubber arm—check those innings pitched lines—makes you think he'll age gracefully.

SHAWN HILL Bats: R Throws: R Born: 28-Apr-1981 Age: 24

YEAR	TM	LG	AGE	G	GS	IP	H	BB	SO	HR	ERA	EQERA	EQH9	EQBB9	EQSO9	EQHR9	PERA	VORP	STF
2002	CLN	MDW	21	25	25	146.7	149	35	99	7	3.44	6.24	9.8	2.7	3.7	1.1	4.60	15.2	-2
2003	BRV	FSL	22	22	21	126.7	118	26	66	3	2.56	5.09	9.4	2.2	3.4	0.6	4.17	18.5	2
2004	HAR	EAS	23	17	17	87.7	90	20	53	4	3.39	4.39	9.2	2.1	4.1	0.5	3.96	15.3	2
2004	MON	NL	23	3	3	9.0	17	7	10	1	16.00	14.40	12.6	5.4	8.1	0.9	7.20	-10.2	-7
2005	*WAS*	*NL*	*24*	*23*	*13*	*88.0*	*97*	*32*	*51*	*8*	*4.66*	*4.98*	*10.0*	*2.8*	*4.7*	*0.8*	*4.94*	*5.9*	*-4*

Breakout: 8% *Improve: 40%* *Collapse: 26%*

A good control pitcher with lackluster strikeout rates, Hill's upside figures to be limited. Tommy John surgery will cost him a year of development time, meaning we may not see him get established as a big league starter until 2007. The Nationals have several back-of-the-rotation candidates among their prospects, but few potential aces. Although . . .

MIKE HINCKLEY Bats: R Throws: L Born: 05-Oct-1982 Age: 22

YEAR	TM	LG	AGE	G	GS	IP	H	BB	SO	HR	ERA	EQERA	EQH9	EQBB9	EQSO9	EQHR9	PERA	VORP	STF
2002	VER	NYP	19	16	16	91.7	60	30	66	4	1.37	4.35	8.7	4.3	4.0	1.4	4.58	8.9	15
2003	SAV	SAL	20	23	23	121.0	124	41	111	4	3.64	5.86	9.7	3.6	5.0	0.8	4.67	11.7	0
2003	BRV	FSL	20	4	4	25.0	14	1	23	1	0.72	2.45	7.4	0.4	6.1	1.2	2.86	6.7	36
2004	BRV	FSL	21	10	10	62.0	47	18	51	6	2.61	4.75	9.2	3.1	5.4	2.0	5.24	2.2	9
2004	HAR	EAS	21	16	16	94.0	83	23	80	5	2.87	3.74	8.4	2.3	5.8	0.6	3.54	20.4	28
2005	*WAS*	*NL*	*22*	*13*	*13*	*79.0*	*78*	*29*	*54*	*10*	*4.32*	*4.62*	*8.9*	*2.9*	*5.5*	*1.1*	*4.61*	*9.1*	*6*

Breakout: 8% *Improve: 38%* *Collapse: 21%*

. . . this guy may have the goods. Displaying great control and inducing outs easily with his fast, brutal stuff, Hinckley didn't seem to notice that he'd been advanced a level at mid-season. Heck, he even hit .385/.438/.538 to boot, so thank goodness the parent club's in the National League. His strikeout rate is about a half-notch away from making him a Top-10 pitching prospect, and he's young enough to take that next step any time.

JOE HORGAN Bats: L Throws: L Born: 07-Jun-1977 Age: 28

YEAR	TM	LG	AGE	G	GS	IP	H	BB	SO	HR	ERA	EQERA	EQH9	EQBB9	EQSO9	EQHR9	PERA	VORP	STF
2002	SHV	TXS	25	10	10	56.0	69	20	35	5	4.34	6.54	10.9	3.4	4.2	1.7	6.04	-2.6	-15
2002	FRE	PCL	25	27	4	57.7	65	21	37	8	5.93	5.56	10.0	3.4	4.6	1.5	5.73	-0.8	-22
2003	FRE	PCL	26	55	0	74.7	80	30	65	9	5.66	6.28	9.3	4.0	6.7	1.5	5.02	4.6	-9
2004	EDM	PCL	27	13	0	17.0	15	4	11	2	3.18	3.38	8.4	2.2	4.5	1.1	3.94	3.0	-5
2004	MON	NL	27	47	0	40.0	35	22	30	5	3.15	3.76	8.5	4.5	6.1	0.9	4.70	7.3	-9
2005	*WAS*	*NL*	*28*	*16*	*1*	*23.3*	*23*	*11*	*17*	*3*	*4.60*	*4.92*	*8.8*	*3.7*	*5.7*	*1.2*	*4.95*	*2.4*	*-9*

Breakout: 24% *Improve: 47%* *Collapse: 34%*

Made a nice big league debut. Horgan's control wavered at times, but he was generally effective, showing no significant split to boot. He's never had huge minor league numbers and he turns 28 this year, so league-average production at under $500,000 a year seems a decent proposition for the next two seasons.

JOSH KARP Bats: R Throws: R Born: 21-Sep-1979 Age: 25

YEAR	TM	LG	AGE	G	GS	IP	H	BB	SO	HR	ERA	EQERA	EQH9	EQBB9	EQSO9	EQHR9	PERA	VORP	STF
2002	BRV	FSL	22	7	7	45.3	31	11	43	1	1.59	3.24	7.6	2.4	6.3	0.4	3.02	12.0	23
2002	HAR	EAS	22	16	16	86.7	83	34	69	6	3.84	4.96	9.1	3.7	5.6	1.0	4.96	5.8	3
2003	HAR	EAS	23	23	23	122.7	126	49	77	12	4.99	6.00	9.9	4.0	4.7	1.6	5.92	-4.1	-14
2004	EDM	PCL	24	24	24	127.0	147	51	102	17	5.95	6.40	9.8	3.8	5.5	1.3	5.31	4.0	-7
2005	*WAS*	*NL*	*25*	*12*	*10*	*59.3*	*60*	*24*	*42*	*7*	*4.68*	*5.00*	*9.1*	*3.3*	*5.7*	*1.1*	*4.91*	*4.7*	*2*

Breakout: 17% *Improve: 42%* *Collapse: 24%*

Karp's no world-beater, but don't let the hits allowed fool you: Like other Triple-A pitchers last year, he was victimized by terrible defensive play behind him. If anything, hopefully his rough 2004 season will convince Karp to be more receptive to advice, former #1 draft pick or not. He'll need improved command to contribute at the next level, but perhaps an investment by the Nats in player instruction now that they're out of Montreal will help.

SUN-WOO KIM Bats: R Throws: R Born: 04-Sep-1977 Age: 27

YEAR	TM	LG	AGE	G	GS	IP	H	BB	SO	HR	ERA	EQERA	EQH9	EQBB9	EQSO9	EQHR9	PERA	VORP	STF
2002	PAW	INT	24	8	8	45.3	34	16	37	4	3.18	4.10	7.8	3.7	6.5	1.1	3.89	7.9	19
2002	BOS	AL	24	15	2	29.0	34	7	18	5	7.45	6.67	10.2	1.9	5.4	1.3	5.08	-4.7	1
2002	OTT	INT	24	7	7	43.7	29	16	28	2	1.24	2.97	7.6	3.9	5.3	0.7	3.89	7.5	14
2002	MON	NL	24	4	3	20.3	18	7	11	0	0.89	0.93	8.4	2.8	4.7	0.0	3.26	10.4	12
2003	EDM	PCL	25	22	22	132.3	147	53	83	18	5.03	6.23	9.9	4.1	4.9	1.8	5.59	0.1	-7
2004	MON	NL	26	43	17	135.7	145	55	87	17	4.58	4.99	9.4	3.3	5.2	1.0	4.92	6.5	0
2005	*WAS*	*NL*	*27*	*23*	*12*	*83.0*	*86*	*32*	*52*	*11*	*4.64*	*4.96*	*9.3*	*3.1*	*5.1*	*1.2*	*5.00*	*7.0*	*-5*

Breakout: 18% *Improve: 45%* *Collapse: 22%*

It's unfortunate that Kim and Ohka haven't revisited the fistfight they had when they were both in the Boston organization over which one was the better prospect. Ohka's settled the argument on the field—but at least another fight would make Kim interesting again. In this round, he's a guy floating between long relief and picking up starts from whoever strained a muscle that week, and never doing well enough to win a rotation spot, or badly enough to be demoted, borring.

LUKE LOCKWOOD Bats: L Throws: L Born: 21-Jul-1981 Age: 23

YEAR	TM	LG	AGE	G	GS	IP	H	BB	SO	HR	ERA	EQERA	EQH9	EQBB9	EQSO9	EQHR9	PERA	VORP	STF
2002	BRV	FSL	20	26	26	147.0	155	38	86	13	3.37	5.49	10.7	2.6	3.9	1.7	5.89	-4.4	-6
2003	HAR	EAS	21	26	26	144.7	175	41	64	16	5.16	6.01	11.1	2.8	3.3	1.6	6.27	-10.1	-18
2004	HAR	EAS	22	33	19	136.3	168	30	86	20	4.95	5.74	10.9	2.1	4.2	1.7	5.81	-3.1	-22
2005	*WAS*	*NL*	*23*	*13*	*5*	*37.7*	*43*	*13*	*21*	*6*	*5.10*	*5.45*	*10.2*	*2.7*	*4.5*	*1.4*	*5.55*	*1.0*	*-12*

Breakout: 9% *Improve: 34%* *Collapse: 23%*

The party just keeps rolling as we unveil this strapping southpaw, with his 3–17 record, earned with a 4.95 ERA. You want nasty stuff? His is below-average! You want control? His is decent! Everybody throw your hands in the a-yah, and wave 'em like you just don't cay-yah! Go lefty! Go lefty! It's your birthday! It's your birthday!

GARY MAJEWSKI Bats: R Throws: R Born: 26-Feb-1980 Age: 25

YEAR	TM	LG	AGE	G	GS	IP	H	BB	SO	HR	ERA	EQERA	EQH9	EQBB9	EQSO9	EQHR9	PERA	VORP	STF
2002	BIR	SOU	22	57	1	74.7	61	34	75	3	2.65	4.91	8.5	4.0	6.8	0.8	4.26	10.4	0
2003	CHR	INT	23	42	1	72.7	62	29	72	3	3.96	4.61	8.0	4.1	7.4	0.5	3.82	13.5	10
2004	CHR	INT	24	35	0	42.3	30	16	41	2	3.19	3.66	7.3	3.7	7.3	0.5	3.43	9.5	11
2004	EDM	PCL	24	15	0	16.3	18	8	17	0	3.87	4.50	9.0	4.5	7.3	0.0	4.50	2.0	-5
2004	MON	NL	24	16	0	21.0	28	5	12	2	3.86	6.00	10.7	1.7	4.3	0.9	5.14	-1.7	-14
2005	*WAS*	*NL*	*25*	*21*	*5*	*51.0*	*48*	*20*	*41*	*5*	*3.88*	*4.15*	*8.5*	*3.2*	*6.4*	*0.8*	*4.23*	*8.1*	*3*

Breakout: 22% *Improve: 44%* *Collapse: 20%*

Courtesy of his power assortment, Majewski had to bounce around a little, getting picked as a Rule 5er, returned to his team, then traded almost exactly a year later to Montreal in the Everett deal. He's one of the better mid-20s relief prospects in the system, which isn't a huge honor, but it should be good enough to earn him a regular job in the 2005 pen.

TOMOKAZU OHKA Bats: R Throws: R Born: 18-Mar-1976 Age: 29

YEAR	TM	LG	AGE	G	GS	IP	H	BB	SO	HR	ERA	EQERA	EQH9	EQBB9	EQSO9	EQHR9	PERA	VORP	STF
2002	MON	NL	26	32	31	192.7	194	45	118	19	3.18	3.84	9.0	1.8	5.0	0.9	3.93	34.8	10
2003	MON	NL	27	34	34	199.0	233	45	118	24	4.16	4.48	9.9	1.8	4.9	1.0	4.81	20.0	5
2004	MON	NL	28	15	15	84.7	98	20	38	11	3.40	3.97	10.1	1.9	3.6	1.1	4.96	14.2	-3
2005	*WAS*	*NL*	*29*	*23*	*18*	*116.0*	*122*	*27*	*64*	*13*	*3.96*	*4.23*	*9.5*	*1.9*	*4.4*	*1.0*	*4.36*	*18.7*	*1*

Breakout: 29% *Improve: 55%* *Collapse: 16%*

A line drive off of the bat of Carlos Beltran back in June fractured Ohka's forearm in particularly grisly fashion, and resulted in major surgery. With 2004 a lost year, Ohka will return as good rotation-filler, and just as we said last year, we expect him to put up a season like 2003. 180+ innings and a solid strikeout rate are reasonable expectations now that he's healthy. He's headed to arbitration, but won't be prohibitively expensive.

JOHN PATTERSON

Bats: R Throws: R Born: 30-Jan-1978 Age: 27

YEAR	TM	LG	AGE	G	GS	IP	H	BB	SO	HR	ERA	EQERA	EQH9	EQBB9	EQSO9	EQHR9	PERA	VORP	STF
2002	TUC	PCL	24	19	18	112.7	117	45	104	14	4.23	4.42	9.2	3.8	6.5	1.2	5.25	4.2	2
2002	ARI	NL	24	7	5	30.7	27	7	31	7	3.22	3.07	8.6	1.8	8.3	2.1	4.60	7.7	15
2003	TUC	PCL	25	18	18	109.3	100	43	74	6	2.63	4.01	8.3	4.0	5.2	0.7	4.01	18.2	5
2003	ARI	NL	25	16	8	55.0	61	30	43	7	6.05	5.76	9.4	4.3	6.3	1.0	5.10	-4.3	-5
2004	MON	NL	26	19	19	98.3	100	46	99	18	5.04	4.95	9.0	3.7	8.0	1.5	5.04	5.0	11
2005	*WAS*	*NL*	*27*	*22*	*18*	*114.0*	*105*	*49*	*100*	*15*	*4.38*	*4.69*	*8.3*	*3.4*	*7.1*	*1.2*	*4.60*	*13.7*	*11*

Breakout: 15% Improve: 43% Collapse: 29%

Is Patterson ever going to make progress? He shows you things that make you wonder. In 2004, it was a strikeout an inning, a walk every other inning, about half again as many home runs as you'd like, and then he missed time with a groin injury. Still, he's cheap, armed with good stuff, and might be a few adjustments away from becoming this rotation's #2 guy. PECOTA likes his profile, and we like his curveball; when that thing's really breaking, it's almost hypnotic. Breakout candidate.

DARRELL RASNER

Bats: R Throws: R Born: 13-Jan-1981 Age: 24

YEAR	TM	LG	AGE	G	GS	IP	H	BB	SO	HR	ERA	EQERA	EQH9	EQBB9	EQSO9	EQHR9	PERA	VORP	STF
2002	VER	NYP	21	10	10	43.7	44	18	49	1	4.32	7.88	10.1	5.2	5.8	0.7	5.40	0.9	-8
2003	SAV	SAL	22	22	22	105.3	106	36	90	8	4.19	6.33	10.3	3.7	4.7	1.9	5.87	-2.9	-15
2004	BRV	FSL	23	22	21	119.3	133	31	88	6	3.17	5.51	10.4	2.6	4.6	1.0	5.11	6.1	-11
2004	HAR	EAS	23	5	5	29.7	21	9	15	1	1.21	1.98	7.6	3.0	3.6	0.3	2.96	8.0	-7
2005	*WAS*	*NL*	*24*	*14*	*12*	*69.3*	*74*	*27*	*45*	*9*	*4.69*	*5.01*	*9.6*	*3.1*	*5.3*	*1.1*	*5.11*	*5.2*	*0*

Breakout: 13% Improve: 42% Collapse: 20%

As a college pitcher, you'd like to see Rasner pitching this well at a higher level, but 2004 was another solid season for him as he moves up the system. You'd like to see Rasner revisit those New York–Penn and Sally League strikeout rates, and he's got the three-pitch assortment (fastball, curve, change) that could make it possible. Added to his excellent control, it would stamp Rasner as a legit rotation threat for 2006.

JON RAUCH

Bats: R Throws: R Born: 27-Sep-1978 Age: 26

YEAR	TM	LG	AGE	G	GS	IP	H	BB	SO	HR	ERA	EQERA	EQH9	EQBB9	EQSO9	EQHR9	PERA	VORP	STF
2002	CHR	INT	23	19	19	109.3	91	42	97	14	4.28	5.35	8.5	4.0	7.0	1.5	4.81	8.9	21
2002	CWS	AL	23	8	6	28.7	28	14	19	7	6.59	7.24	9.5	4.3	5.9	2.0	5.93	-7.0	5
2003	CHR	INT	24	24	23	124.7	121	35	94	16	4.11	4.90	9.5	3.0	5.7	1.7	5.29	4.0	0
2004	CHR	INT	25	14	13	72.3	57	25	61	9	3.11	3.51	8.2	3.4	6.5	1.4	4.59	7.5	13
2004	EDM	PCL	25	3	3	18.0	17	2	13	3	4.50	4.76	9.0	1.1	5.3	1.6	4.24	2.6	16
2004	MON	NL	25	9	2	23.3	14	7	18	1	1.55	1.66	6.6	2.5	6.6	0.4	2.49	10.9	19
2005	*WAS*	*NL*	*26*	*26*	*14*	*99.0*	*93*	*38*	*74*	*15*	*4.46*	*4.77*	*8.5*	*3.1*	*6.0*	*1.3*	*4.61*	*9.9*	*1*

Breakout: 13% Improve: 39% Collapse: 17%

Rauch is still trying to come back from the labrum surgery he had in 2002. There's reason to be concerned about possible further injuries: At nearly 7′ tall, he is one tall drink of water, and getting all those moving parts going isn't an easy task. Despite the size, he's not really back to being a flamethrower. He had problems with White Sox management in 2004 before his trade, so he needs a good camp to help him bury picking up some sort of Jeff Juden bad boy rep that'll only get him Triple-A service time, cuz nobody counts that.

DANNY RUECKEL

Bats: R Throws: R Born: 25-Sep-1979 Age: 25

YEAR	TM	LG	AGE	G	GS	IP	H	BB	SO	HR	ERA	EQERA	EQH9	EQBB9	EQSO9	EQHR9	PERA	VORP	STF
2002	VER	NYP	22	10	0	17.7	12	3	23	0	1.53	6.19	7.9	2.2	6.8	0.6	3.38	3.9	9
2002	CLN	MDW	22	14	0	26.0	23	10	25	1	4.15	5.62	9.0	4.5	5.2	1.1	4.50	2.9	-10
2003	SAV	SAL	23	40	1	68.7	68	16	64	4	4.06	6.79	10.0	2.5	5.1	1.4	5.09	3.6	-13
2004	HAR	EAS	24	41	0	76.0	70	16	55	3	2.01	3.86	8.6	2.0	4.9	0.5	3.48	17.0	6
2005	*WAS*	*NL*	*25*	*14*	*4*	*35.7*	*36*	*12*	*24*	*5*	*4.34*	*4.64*	*9.2*	*2.6*	*5.4*	*1.2*	*4.68*	*4.4*	*-4*

Breakout: 24% Improve: 45% Collapse: 26%

Another relief prospect in his mid-twenties, but in this case, it's a soft-tossing lefty with a killer curve. Rueckel put up good numbers at Double-A last year, including a solid 56:17 K:BB ratio, so he might be a potential 11th arm this year or next. In cases like these, he'll need to wow Frank Robinson on the right day.

SEUNG SONG **Bats: R** **Throws: R** Born: 29-Jun-1980 Age: 25

YEAR	TM	LG	AGE	G	GS	IP	H	BB	SO	HR	ERA	EQERA	EQH9	EQBB9	EQSO9	EQHR9	PERA	VORP	STF
2002	TRN	EAS	22	21	21	108.7	106	37	116	11	4.39	5.62	8.9	3.2	7.4	1.4	4.24	15.7	11
2003	HAR	EAS	23	13	13	72.7	55	24	44	5	2.35	3.97	8.4	3.4	4.7	1.1	4.39	8.8	-1
2003	EDM	PCL	23	13	13	73.7	69	33	40	6	3.79	4.83	8.6	4.6	4.3	1.0	4.43	9.0	8
2004	EDM	PCL	24	13	13	63.3	70	29	59	7	4.27	5.11	9.3	4.2	6.4	1.0	4.96	4.4	0
2005	*TOR*	*AL*	*25*	*14*	*9*	*54.7*	*60*	*24*	*39*	*9*	*5.51*	*5.19*	*9.8*	*3.4*	*5.9*	*1.4*	*5.06*	*5.4*	*-1*

Breakout 17% *Improve 44%* *Collapse 28%*

The good news about Song was that his strikeout rate picked up—there always had been concern over why he wasn't getting the best out of a broad assortment of pitches. Still, he was giving up too many walks before he got taken out for the season by a broken forearm. The refined prospect we saw in Trenton has gone missing for more than two years now. Claimed off waivers by the Blue Jays, the birds got Seung for a song.

T. J. TUCKER **Bats: R** **Throws: R** Born: 20-Aug-1978 Age: 26

YEAR	TM	LG	AGE	G	GS	IP	H	BB	SO	HR	ERA	EQERA	EQH9	EQBB9	EQSO9	EQHR9	PERA	VORP	STF
2002	MON	NL	23	57	0	61.3	69	31	42	5	4.11	4.57	9.4	3.8	5.3	0.7	4.72	4.6	-9
2003	MON	NL	24	45	7	80.0	90	20	47	8	4.72	5.08	9.7	2.0	4.8	0.8	4.50	1.2	-1
2004	MON	NL	25	54	1	67.7	73	17	44	5	3.72	3.56	9.3	2.1	5.2	0.5	4.11	14.9	2
2005	*WAS*	*NL*	*26*	*28*	*8*	*72.3*	*78*	*22*	*45*	*8*	*4.23*	*4.52*	*9.7*	*2.4*	*5.1*	*0.9*	*4.66*	*8.6*	*-4*

Breakout: 22% *Improve: 51%* *Collapse: 19%*

Like Rauch, a big dude, but with even more mediocre stuff. Tucker's biggest asset is his ability to serve as a swingman, providing four or five passable innings on short notice when a Day or Ohka needs to sit for a week. This is not the guy you want in there when Armas misses half the season to his latest shoulder malady, though. The Expos have plenty of decent arms knocking on the door for that.

CLAUDIO VARGAS **Bats: R** **Throws: R** Born: 19-Jun-1978 Age: 27

YEAR	TM	LG	AGE	G	GS	IP	H	BB	SO	HR	ERA	EQERA	EQH9	EQBB9	EQSO9	EQHR9	PERA	VORP	STF
2002	CLG	PCL	24	17	16	76.3	88	35	61	18	6.72	6.53	10.4	4.4	5.7	2.5	6.78	-9.6	-19
2002	HAR	EAS	24	8	8	33.0	38	9	34	2	4.64	5.06	9.8	2.5	7.0	0.8	5.06	1.9	4
2003	MON	NL	25	23	20	114.0	111	41	62	16	4.34	4.39	9.2	2.9	4.6	1.2	4.80	13.1	-2
2004	MON	NL	26	45	14	118.3	120	64	89	26	5.25	5.35	9.4	4.4	6.1	1.8	5.75	0.4	-15
2005	*WAS*	*NL*	*27*	*28*	*13*	*94.3*	*93*	*45*	*72*	*15*	*5.08*	*5.44*	*8.9*	*3.8*	*6.2*	*1.4*	*5.30*	*4.6*	*-3*

Breakout: 17% *Improve: 37%* *Collapse: 28%*

That was a tough year. Vargas was converted to relief before the All-Star break, based on his two-pitch repertoire and struggles in the rotation. He sliced a run off of his ERA pitching in the pen, but still showed crummy peripherals. The Nats like his raw stuff, but it's going to take time and patience to get his fastball-slider combo cooking. The type of pitcher likely to do better with his next employer, assuming they sort out what to do with him quickly.

Anaheim Angels

For all the critical attention heaped on sports teams, owners often escape their rightful due for shaping their franchises. Managers and general managers are transient. The people who hire them and set the boundaries of their positions stay. Watching the product on the field, the public sees only the tip of the iceberg. On-field and middle-management personnel play a role in forming a team's identity, but in the final analysis all possibilities derive from ownership.

Under its three ownerships, the Angels franchise has taken widely divergent approaches to talent procurement, swinging between extremes as if it was the object of a tug-of-war between George Steinbrenner and Carl Lindner, or more appropriately, Arte Moreno and Mickey Mouse.

Under the Angels' initial ownership, headed by former singing cowboy Gene Autry, no team gave away more and received less than Anaheim. Autry was in his mid-50s when the Angels came into being, and after the team failed to reach the post-season in its first several years of existence the team went into perpetual hurry-up mode, always racing against Autry's mortality. To "win one for the Cowboy" meant doing it today; the old man might not be there tomorrow. When the Angels envisioned the championship trophy, it was always being licked by flames from Autry's funeral pyre.

An Angels announcer once explained that the team's long history of tragedies and last-minute disappointments, since dispelled by the dead-Gene World Series triumph of 2002, might be attributable to a curse—that Angels Stadium was built on an old Indian burial ground or something. Actually, just about *everything* in America was built on an old Indian *something,* so *that's* no excuse. As is often the case, the culprit is human error in the form of dumb trades and bad free-agent signings.

In the late 1970s and early 80s, at the height of "Don't-Let-the-Cowboy-Cross-the-River-Styx-Without-a-Ring" mania, the Angels had one of the most productive farm systems in baseball. But nearly every significant player it produced wound up on another team before contributing a thing to the Angels.

In a series of trades orchestrated by general manager Buzzie Bavasi from 1977 to 1982, the Angels gave away a complete starting lineup of young players. First basemen Willie Aikens and Bruce Bochte, second baseman Jerry Remy, third basemen Rance Mulliniks and Carney Lansford, shortstop Dickie Thon, catcher Brian Harper, outfielders Kenny Landreaux, Mike Easler, and Tom Brunansky, and starting pitchers Richard Dotson and Dennis Rasmussen were all dealt for veterans. To round out the team, throw in outfielder Mickey Rivers and pitcher Ed Figueroa, dealt to the Yankees in December, 1975, for the ghost of Bobby Bonds (by Bavasi's predecessor, Harry Dalton). As with the Rivers/Figueroa deal, the return on these trades was minimal. The one long-term keeper the Angels received was catcher-outfielder Brian Downing, who came in exchange for Bonds, Dotson, and outfielder Thad Bosley.

The dotage and death of Gene Autry removed the need for urgency from the Angels' dealings. The transfer of 25% ownership and status as managing general partner to the Walt Disney Company was consummated when Autry was still breathing the Melody Ranch air (May 15, 1996). Disney purchased the rest of the club shortly after Autry's death in March 1999.

Bill Stoneman took over as Angels general manager on November 1, 1999, and in matters of talent acquisition has proved to be one of the most conservative GMs in baseball. During the first five seasons of his administration, from 2000–2004, the Angels have had 10 players with the team for the entire period, tying them with the Twins for the most stable roster in baseball. Technically

ANGELS PROSPECTUS

2004 record: 92–70; First place, AL West; Lost to Red Sox in Division Series

Pythagenport record: 91–71

Runs scored per game: 5.16 (7th in AL)

Runs allowed per game: 4.53 (2nd in AL)

Team EqA: .265 (5th in AL)

2004 Batters Age: 29.2 (6th youngest in AL)

2004 Pitchers Age: 29.2 (5th oldest in AL)

Ballpark: Edison International Field; Moderate pitcher's park; Park Factor of 0.965

2004: A free-spending offseason set up an exciting campaign, giving the Angels the division by a nose.

2005: With a talented offense, workable rotation, and the league's best bullpen, the Angels will be looking for more.

the Twins have been more stable; their 10—Christian Guzman, Torii Hunter, Jacque Jones, Corey Koskie, Matt LeCroy, Doug Mientkiewicz, Brad Radke, Luis Rivas, J. C. Romero, and Johan Santana—consumed a slightly higher percentage of team plate appearances/opposition plate appearances than did the Angels' 10—Garret Anderson, Darin Erstad, Troy Glaus, Adam Kennedy, Bengie Molina, Ramon Ortiz, Troy Percival, Tim Salmon, Jarrod Washburn, and Ben Weber.

The rapid turnover engendered by the advent of free agency has been called an alienating force in modern sports, and indeed the kind of continuity enjoyed by the Angels has become rare. After the Twins, no other team had nine five-year vets, only the White Sox had eight, only the Dodgers retained seven. At the other end of the spectrum, the Milwaukee Brewers have retained just one player, Geoff Jenkins, since 2000. The constant turnover of the Autry years has been replaced by the far rarer policy of maintaining the team's core.

Stability has its benefits, but you wouldn't know it by looking at the Angels' offense. Table 1 shows the year-by-year Positional Marginal Lineup Value (or PMLV, the runs contributed by a batter beyond what an average player at the same position would hit in a team of otherwise league-average hitters) for the six position players in Stoneman's band.

As you can see, the contributions of these six players have dropped dramatically from their huge peak in 2000—continuity has sometimes been emphasized at the expense of merit. While showing loyalty to a core of players is notable in today's sped-up building and rebuilding cycles, the sextet's contributions cratered in 2004. The fragility of Anderson, Glaus, and Salmon, and Molina's erratic offense have hurt. The colossal bust that was the Erstad contract—doled out after a batting average-driven peak year in 2000 and compounded by the costly decision to move him to first base and rely on a hobbled Anderson in center—has hurt even more. The four-year, $48 million extension the team gave Anderson a tick before his 32nd birthday shows how the lesson of loyalty being dangerous hasn't sunk in. Paying players based on a cold, hard look at expected future performance, not on a university-style tenure system, is the surest way to keep hanging pennants, at the Big A or anywhere else.

TABLE 1. POSITIONAL MARGINAL LINEUP VALUE (PMLV) FOR MAGIC 10's SIX HITTERS, 2000–2004

Hitter	2000	2001	2002	2003	2004	Total
Anderson	18.0	4.0	31.7	37.6	12.6	103.9
Erstad	58.1	-11.6	-0.3	-7.1	-2.0	37.1
Glaus	64.4	33.2	23.3	14.9	14.0	149.8
Kennedy	-6.2	-4.8	24.7	11.5	11.1	36.3
B. Molina	4.3	-2.1	-11.4	13.0	4.1	7.9
Salmon	40.2	-8.5	25.4	23.0	-7.4	72.7
Total	**178.8**	**10.2**	**93.4**	**92.9**	**32.4**	**407.7**

TABLE 2. RUNS PREVENTED BY MAGIC 10's FOUR PITCHERS, 2000–2004

Pitcher	2000	2001	2002	2003	2004	Total
Ortiz	-2.3	6.1	17.1	-30.1	6.9	-2.3
Percival	2.9	13.5	18.0	3.6	8.6	46.6
Washburn	12.4	21.4	33.6	0.8	1.6	69.8
Weber	2.8	10.8	16.2	16.4	-11.8	34.4
Total	**15.8**	**51.8**	**84.9**	**-9.3**	**5.3**	**148.5**

To a lesser extent, the same is true of the pitchers in the group, as seen in table 2.

The performance of these four has also fallen off sharply, especially in the last two years, but here the problems are more subdued. The Angels resisted the urge to sign any of these four pitchers to monster long-term deals, and while Percival, given his relative contributions, was overpaid on a year-to-year basis, it wasn't crippling. Meanwhile, the Angels developed solid in-house options such as Francisco Rodriguez, John Lackey, and others, and they upgraded with free-agent signings, including what could turn into a very good deal with Kelvim Escobar.

Blame a lot of the lingering loyalty on the glow cast by the 2002 season. The hardest thing for a GM to do is to break up a championship core. It engenders violent opposition from the media and fans, and runs counter to a team's own emotions and foibles. The Angels didn't go the cold, hard route, and to an extent it's hurt them the last couple of years. Yet despite the Magic 10's gradual drop-off and general inconsistency, the Angels have done a good job of patching holes when their recognizable stars have faltered, as was the case during the team's 2004 division-winning campaign.

Stoneman's organization has shown its true creativity around the margins. On August 6, 2000, he claimed infielder David Eckstein on waivers from the Boston Red Sox. Brendan Donnelly, signed as a minor league free agent in 2001, was allowed to pitch his way to the majors in 2002 in spite of his 10 years in the minors, as was Kevin Gregg, despite a similarly protracted apprenticeship. Ben Weber was claimed on waivers from the Giants shortly after Eckstein and through 2003 gave the team 241.1 innings with a 2.80 ERA. The versatile Chone Figgins was stolen from the Rockies in exchange for Kimera Bartee.

Simultaneously, the organization promoted from within, with farmhands Robb Quinlan and Jeff DaVanon allowed to play important reserve roles. Lackey, a 1999 second-round draft choice, was permitted an accelerated tour through the minors and reached Anaheim in time to play an important role in the successful pursuit of the 2002 championship. Though the team has at times flirted with veteran roster-filler like Owens and Shane Halter, in the end the club has given preference to its own younger, more talented products, to great benefit.

The Angels team Stoneman inherited had major problems. His immediate predecessor, Bill Bavasi (January 1994–October 1999, now with the Mariners), kept the club in neutral, alternating A-for-effort showings with 90-loss seasons and allowing the farm system to become one of the worst in baseball. The 1999 club finished 70–92 with an offense that finished second to last in the league in runs scored and a pitching staff that posted a below-average ERA, second to last in strikeouts and strikeout-walk ratio. On his way out the door, Bavasi made a number of non-moves that left the team without a first baseman, second baseman, or shortstop.

Whereas most teams would have aggressively attacked these holes, Stoneman reacted with his trademark restraint. Mo Vaughn moved full-time from designated hitter to first base, the equivalent of putting a glove on a jelly donut. The Jim Edmonds trade—at the time rightly regarded as the unloading of an injury-prone malcontent in his walk year than the future Hall of Famer he's improbably become—filled second base at the expense of opening up center field; Erstad would move there for two years, before being inexplicably shunted to first base. The hapless Gary DiSarcina was reanimated and expected to play shortstop. The designated-hitter position was not filled, and a cast of thousands rotated through. A pattern was set that would last out the Disney era.

In fairness to Stoneman, these moves undoubtedly reflected the will of his corporate masters; Disney was going through a period of living off its reputation rather than investing in its product, resulting in the gutting of its famed animation division and shameful neglect of its theme parks. Despite the team's greater Los Angeles-area location, Disney would run the Angels as a mid-to-small market ball club.

With the transfer of ownership of the Angels to billboard magnate Arte Moreno in 2003, everything old has become new again. The club made an abrupt U-turn in the 2003–2004 off-season, going after free agents with a gusto not seen since Autry dismounted Champion. The first round of signings featured some top-tier talent, far from the desperate grabs at past-prime stars seen in the past. Vladimir Guerrero was the type of elite free agent every team wanted, and the Angels did well to land him. Jose Guillen, Bartolo Colon, and Escobar all provided some utility in 2004, with Escobar looking like the best deal of the bunch thus far.

The current off-season has seen the abortive pursuit of free agent center fielder Carlos Beltran, followed by the signing of aged but still effective center fielder Steve Finley and journeyman reliever Esteban Yan to two-year contracts, while unproven Cuban defector Kendry Morales was signed to a six-year major league deal. In short, the 2004 signings have a lesser likelihood of success then their 2003 counterparts.

Concomitant with these moves has come the breaking of the Magic 10. Glaus was not offered arbitration to make room for rookie Dallas McPherson, the enigmatic Ortiz was traded, Percival and Weber were allowed to leave as free agents, and Salmon's career is likely over. At best, the Angels will have a Magic Five in 2005.

Given the variability and advancing age of the 10 long-time Angels, the focus has rightly shifted to the farm system, which boasts one of the deepest talent bases anywhere: Though the Angels lack young outfielders, there are enough quality players to fill the big league club's needs at most other positions for the next couple of years. Indeed, it's been Mike Scioscia's brilliant deployment of both stars and role players from the system that have allowed the Angels to overcome injuries and remain contenders, including last year's AL West title. With players like McPherson and Casey Kotchman poised to become the Glauses and Salmons of the next generation, the Angels have an excellent shot at contending for years to come.

The balancing act will be pivotal. Focusing on top-tier free agents such as Guerrero and not overpriced middle-class signings like the Wright/Sexson/Renteria class will mitigate risk, despite the higher dollar figures. Stoneman's conservative approach will be crucial, as the team tries to resist the urge to trade its excellent prospects for marginal quick fixes out of owner-driven desperation. For the Angels it's a tightrope act—between the profligacy of the Autry period, and the insularity of the Disney years.

HITTERS

ALFREDO AMEZAGA   INF   Bats: B   Throws: R   Born: 16-Jan-1978   Age: 27

YEAR	TM	LG	AGE	AB	H	2B	3B	HR	BB	SO	SB	CS	AVG	OBP	SLG	MLVR	EQBA	EQOBP	EQSLG	EQMLVR	VORP	DEFENSE	
2002	SLC	PCL	24	518	130	25	7	6	45	100	23	14	.251	.317	.361	-.180	.213	.278	.305	-.345	-21.5	126-SS 5	
2003	SLC	PCL	25	317	110	20	5	3	20	39	14	8	.347	.391	.470	.171	.292	.337	.406	-.035	15.1	64-SS 8	10-2B 1
2003	ANA	AL	25	105	22	3	2	2	9	23	2	2	.210	.278	.333	-.259	.219	.292	.352	-.249	-1.6	22-SS 1	13-3B -2
2004	ANA	AL	26	93	15	2	0	2	3	24	3	2	.161	.212	.247	-.578	.172	.214	.247	-.575	-9.0	22-SS -1	
2004	SLC	PCL	26	135	35	5	2	2	13	18	7	0	.259	.329	.370	-.239	.206	.271	.290	-.383	-7.2	32-SS 5	
2005	*COL*	*NL*	*27*	*158*	*41*	*8*	*2*	*2*	*12*	*28*	*5*	*2*	*.262*	*.319*	*.376*	*-.125*	*.242*	*.299*	*.339*	*-.225*	*0.7*	*45-SS -1*	

Breakout: 23%   *Improve: 50%*   *Collapse: 34%*

This Utility Infielder is not suitable for everyday usage. Do not attempt to start Utility Infielder; starting will void Utility Infielder's warrantee. Utility Infielder is for external use only; if Utility Infielder is swallowed, seek medical attention immediately... Back in 2000, Amezaga was a 22-year-old Cal Leaguer who'd stolen 73 bases and took enough walks that his upside looked something like that of D'Angelo Jimenez, but with speed instead of power. Since then, the walks and stolen bases have disappeared, leaving defensive versatility as his only asset. Claimed on waivers from the Rockies, he'll back up Clint Barmes and Aaron Miles.

GARRET ANDERSON   OF   Bats: L   Throws: L   Born: 30-Jun-1972   Age: 33

YEAR	TM	LG	AGE	AB	H	2B	3B	HR	BB	SO	SB	CS	AVG	OBP	SLG	MLVR	EQBA	EQOBP	EQSLG	EQMLVR	VORP	DEFENSE	
2002	ANA	AL	30	638	195	56	3	29	30	80	6	4	.306	.332	.539	.209	.312	.343	.557	.216	50.1	132-LF 5	11-CF 2
2003	ANA	AL	31	638	201	49	4	29	31	83	6	3	.315	.345	.541	.256	.321	.357	.559	.252	57.7	139-LF 15	
2004	ANA	AL	32	442	133	20	1	14	29	75	2	1	.301	.343	.446	.058	.309	.355	.460	.090	26.1	86-CF -4	
2005	*ANA*	*AL*	*33*	*465*	*136*	*28*	*2*	*17*	*27*	*71*	*3*	*2*	*.293*	*.332*	*.473*	*.059*	*.295*	*.335*	*.485*	*.074*	*24.0*	*118-CF -6*	

Breakout: 2%   *Improve: 17%*   *Collapse: 30%*

Anderson got bumped to center field, which took a good left fielder and turned him into a sub-par defender, while stranding Darin Erstad's great centerfielder's glove at first base, while leaving DH totally vacant for most of the year (Angels' DHs hit only .240/.323/.401). Anderson was out April 22–June 10 with arthritis in his upper back, and posted his lowest slugging percentage since 1997. The words "arthritic" and "center field," not to mention "arthritic" and "full recovery," go together like blintzes and Tabasco sauce. Signing Steve Finley mercifully pushes him back to left.

ERICK AYBAR   SS   Bats: B   Throws: R   Born: 14-Jan-1984   Age: 21

YEAR	TM	LG	AGE	AB	H	2B	3B	HR	BB	SO	SB	CS	AVG	OBP	SLG	MLVR	EQBA	EQOBP	EQSLG	EQMLVR	VORP	DEFENSE
2002	PRO	PIO	18	273	89	15	6	4	21	43	15	10	.326	.395	.469	.234	.252	.291	.363	-.214	-1.7	63-SS 2
2003	CDR	MDW	19	496	153	30	10	6	17	54	32	9	.308	.346	.446	.189	.268	.295	.412	-.124	11.6	120-SS -16
2004	RCU	CLF	20	573	189	25	11	14	26	66	51	36	.330	.370	.485	.210	.273	.305	.397	-.123	13.1	132-SS 0
2005	*ANA*	*AL*	*21*	*413*	*108*	*21*	*3*	*7*	*12*	*58*	*14*	*6*	*.262*	*.298*	*.379*	*-.151*	*.264*	*.301*	*.389*	*-.141*	*6.6*	*106-SS -6*

Breakout: 12%   *Improve: 29%*   *Collapse: 45%*

Had a superficially exciting year, showing greater home run power along with his usual speed and ability to hit .300. Taken in the context of the hitter-friendly Cal League, the numbers lose some of their luster, especially with Aybar's extreme resistance to walking factored in. He will have to keep hitting well over .300 as he heads up the ladder to stay interesting. With his ability to make contact, Aybar has the tools to have an impact, but this is not the organization to teach him how to work the count. Youth is in his favor.

ALBERTO CALLASPO   2B/SS   Bats: B   Throws: R   Born: 19-Apr-1983   Age: 22

YEAR	TM	LG	AGE	AB	H	2B	3B	HR	BB	SO	SB	CS	AVG	OBP	SLG	MLVR	EQBA	EQOBP	EQSLG	EQMLVR	VORP	DEFENSE
2002	PRO	PIO	19	299	101	16	10	3	17	14	13	4	.338	.374	.488	.244	.259	.280	.376	-.211	-5.7	68-2B 3
2003	CDR	MDW	20	514	168	38	4	2	42	28	20	6	.327	.377	.428	.220	.283	.325	.391	-.087	14.2	120-2B -15
2004	ARK	TXS	21	550	156	29	2	6	47	25	15	14	.284	.338	.376	-.038	.242	.292	.325	-.273	-12.0	122-SS -11
2005	*ANA*	*AL*	*22*	*340*	*87*	*19*	*2*	*3*	*21*	*21*	*5*	*3*	*.256*	*.300*	*.347*	*-.195*	*.257*	*.303*	*.356*	*-.186*	*2.9*	*89-SS -10*

Breakout: 17%   *Improve: 33%*   *Collapse: 43%*

The Angels had kept Callaspo and Aybar closer than peanut butter and jelly, grooming them as a double-play combination. That changed when Callaspo moved up to Double-A and over to shortstop, a transition that wasn't entirely smooth defensively after he made 25 errors in 121 games. At the bat, Callaspo collapso'd. Like Aybar, Callaspo has to hit at least .300 to help. Another kid who's young enough, with enough skills, to be worth watching.

JEFF DAVANON — OF — Bats: B — Throws: R — Born: 08-Dec-1973 — Age: 31

YEAR	TM	LG	AGE	AB	H	2B	3B	HR	BB	SO	SB	CS	AVG	OBP	SLG	MLVR	EQBA	EQOBP	EQSLG	EQMLVR	VORP	DEFENSE	
2002	SLC	PCL	28	100	33	10	1	5	17	24	5	3	.330	.429	.600	.382	.276	.372	.490	.131	8.7	23-CF -3	
2003	ANA	AL	29	330	93	16	1	12	42	59	17	5	.282	.360	.445	.100	.287	.371	.462	.101	22.6	63-RF -4	26-CF 1
2004	ANA	AL	30	285	79	11	4	7	46	54	18	3	.277	.372	.418	.042	.282	.383	.432	.077	19.4	30-CF -2	12-RF 0
2005	*ANA*	*AL*	*31*	*277*	*74*	*14*	*2*	*9*	*40*	*55*	*14*	*4*	*.268*	*.361*	*.429*	*.027*	*.269*	*.365*	*.439*	*.041*	*16.7*	*78-CF -7*	

Breakout: 9% *Improve: 37%* *Collapse: 31%*

The rare student of Mickey Hatcher willing to shake hands with ball four. A member of the increasingly dominant subspecies of switch-hitters who aren't effective from both sides, DaVanon got a chance to play against righties when Garrett Anderson went down and did very well, batting .298/.393/.429 through the All-Star break, before back spasms cut his productivity and forced him out for 15 days. When he returned he wasn't quite the same player, in part because playing time was harder to come by. Still, he posted a .341 OBP after the break—DaVanon hurt reached base about as often as Darin Erstad healthy. Because he got a late start to his career, DaVanon's period of usefulness is going to be sadly brief, but for now he's a reserve who can be as good or better than the starters.

DAVID ECKSTEIN — SS — Bats: R — Throws: R — Born: 20-Jan-1975 — Age: 30

YEAR	TM	LG	AGE	AB	H	2B	3B	HR	BB	SO	SB	CS	AVG	OBP	SLG	MLVR	EQBA	EQOBP	EQSLG	EQMLVR	VORP	DEFENSE
2002	ANA	AL	27	608	178	22	6	8	45	44	21	13	.293	.363	.388	.028	.304	.373	.406	.041	37.8	139-SS 5
2003	ANA	AL	28	452	114	22	1	3	36	45	16	5	.252	.325	.325	-.153	.259	.335	.337	-.161	11.5	111-SS 8
2004	ANA	AL	29	566	156	24	1	2	42	49	16	5	.276	.339	.332	-.143	.286	.350	.345	-.103	15.7	127-SS 1
2005	*STL*	*NL*	*30*	*471*	*126*	*23*	*2*	*3*	*37*	*37*	*12*	*4*	*.267*	*.336*	*.342*	*-.136*	*.270*	*.337*	*.350*	*-.124*	*13.8*	*127-SS 0*

Breakout: 9% *Improve: 32%* *Collapse: 30%*

Back in the day, Eckstein saved the Angels from another DiSarcina sequel. That danger now past, it's time to admit that Eckstein is a seriously limited hitter without power and taking half the walks he did in the minors. As a defender, his doll-like arms would be less of a problem at second. Non-tendered and signed by the Cardinals, the Angels replaced him with four years of Orlando Cabrera. That's too bad for the several credible shortstop prospects in the system, whose paths are all now blocked.

DARIN ERSTAD — 1B/CF — Bats: L — Throws: L — Born: 04-Jun-1974 — Age: 31

YEAR	TM	LG	AGE	AB	H	2B	3B	HR	BB	SO	SB	CS	AVG	OBP	SLG	MLVR	EQBA	EQOBP	EQSLG	EQMLVR	VORP	DEFENSE
2002	ANA	AL	28	625	177	28	4	10	27	67	23	3	.283	.313	.389	-.060	.289	.323	.397	-.077	22.6	137-CF 32
2003	ANA	AL	29	258	65	7	1	4	18	40	9	1	.252	.309	.333	-.160	.258	.320	.340	-.187	3.0	64-CF 3
2004	ANA	AL	30	495	146	29	1	7	37	74	16	1	.295	.346	.400	-.009	.302	.356	.414	.019	22.7	119-1B 11
2005	*ANA*	*AL*	*31*	*445*	*120*	*22*	*3*	*7*	*29*	*60*	*11*	*4*	*.270*	*.318*	*.381*	*-.108*	*.272*	*.322*	*.390*	*-.097*	*4.0*	*114-1B 8*

Breakout: 4% *Improve: 21%* *Collapse: 34%*

The Evil Erstads of April and September batted .265/.290/.333 and .202/.263/.269 respectively. After a hamstring-inspired month-plus on the DL—a godsend for the Angels because it gave Robb Quinlan a chance to play—Erstad returned hot and stayed that way from June through August, batting.346/.405/.484. Erstad's productive half-season and some good glovework at first made his season palatable for the Angels, but just barely. Mike Scioscia insists that Erstad's defense at first is enough of a benefit that no thought has been given to moving him back to center, where his bat wouldn't stick out as badly and his range would be emphasized. Even good managers have their weak points—this one is Scioscia's. An ironclad rule of the game: There is no excuse for playing a non-hitter at first base.

CHONE FIGGINS — UT — Bats: B — Throws: R — Born: 22-Jan-1978 — Age: 27

YEAR	TM	LG	AGE	AB	H	2B	3B	HR	BB	SO	SB	CS	AVG	OBP	SLG	MLVR	EQBA	EQOBP	EQSLG	EQMLVR	VORP	DEFENSE	
2002	SLC	PCL	24	511	156	25	18	7	53	83	39	8	.305	.364	.466	.080	.262	.323	.400	-.094	12.3	117-2B -5	
2003	SLC	PCL	25	285	89	14	15	4	29	36	16	6	.312	.379	.509	.174	.262	.329	.434	-.035	11.8	34-2B -2	27-SS 0
2003	ANA	AL	25	240	71	9	4	0	20	38	13	7	.296	.345	.367	-.031	.307	.353	.374	-.040	10.1	37-CF 1	11-2B 1
2004	ANA	AL	26	577	171	22	17	5	49	94	34	13	.296	.350	.419	.020	.304	.363	.433	.061	30.3	76-3B -4	38-CF -3
2005	*ANA*	*AL*	*27*	*499*	*136*	*23*	*7*	*7*	*43*	*79*	*25*	*9*	*.272*	*.330*	*.387*	*-.076*	*.274*	*.334*	*.397*	*-.065*	*14.6*	*130-3B 1*	

Breakout: 6% *Improve: 23%* *Collapse: 42%*

The Gil McDougald of the Angels, and Scioscia's number one claim to managerial brilliance. For those not hip to Gil, McDougald played for the Yankees from 1951 to 1960. It was Casey Stengel's great insight that McDougald had the defensive chops to play second, short, or third and be a Gold Glove-quality defender at all three positions while still providing

(continued next page)

Chone Figgins *(continued)*

above-average pop for an infielder. Stengel could then realign his defense from year to year and day to day without sacrifice. Ironically, when he was traded to the Angels in the 1960, McDougald retired rather than go west.

With Figgins, Anaheim finally gets to see what it missed, though Figgins's value is concentrated more in his batting average, speed, and versatility than in any defensive excellence. In addition to third and center, he also appeared in left, right, second, and short. At the plate, he broke the franchise record for triples by a wide margin, which boosted his slugging percentage to .419. Figgins's power is his speed, and for now that's his whole game. Like most Angels, Figgins doesn't walk much. If he learns, he could be the new Tony Phillips, a player among Figgins's list of PECOTA comps and a hugely valuable player in his prime.

ANDRES GALARRAGA **1B** **Bats: R** **Throws: R** Born: 18-Jun-1961 Age: 44

YEAR	TM	LG	AGE	AB	H	2B	3B	HR	BB	SO	SB	CS	AVG	OBP	SLG	MLVR	EQBA	EQOBP	EQSLG	EQMLVR	VORP	DEFENSE
2002	MON	NL	41	292	76	12	0	9	30	81	2	2	.260	.344	.394	.015	.260	.337	.394	-.077	8.4	72-1B -5
2003	SFG	NL	42	272	82	15	0	12	19	61	1	3	.301	.352	.489	.168	.308	.350	.495	.132	18.1	57-1B 0
2004	SLC	PCL	43	102	31	3	0	4	6	24	0	0	.304	.342	.451	-.068	.235	.260	.347	-.309	-5.3	
2004	ANA	AL	43	10	3	0	0	1	0	3	0	0	.300	.364	.600	.309	.500	.266	.800	.957	1.2	
2005	*NYM*	*NL*	*44*	*129*	*30*	*6*	*0*	*3*	*11*	*35*	*0*	*0*	*.231*	*.300*	*.355*	*-.209*	*.234*	*.301*	*.366*	*-.191*	*-2.2*	*38-1B -9*

Breakout: 13% *Improve: 13%* *Collapse: 56%*

It was generous of the Angels to give That Old Cat a chance to rebound from a recurrence of his cancer and take a last shot at 400 home runs. That he failed makes his career no less notable, particularly for a longevity that was impossible to imagine in 1992, when Galarraga was 32 and had spent four years struggling at the plate. At his peak, was he the best Venezuelan export ever? Most Wins Above Replacement (WARP3) in a season by Galarraga and countrymen:

Player	Position	Year	WARP3	Player	Position	Year	WARP3
Edgardo Alfonzo	2B	2000	11.1	Dave Concepcion	SS	1974	9.3
Carlos Guillen	SS	2004	10.8	Melvin Mora	3B	2004	8.5
Bobby Abreu	OF	2004	10.2	**Galarraga**	**1B**	**1988**	**7.9**
Richard Hidalgo	OF	2001	10.1	Luis Aparicio	SS	1960	7.8
Magglio Ordonez	OF	2003	9.4	Omar Vizquel	SS	1998	7.7

We cheated a bit; if you include pitchers, Johan Santana zooms to the top at 12.1 for 2004.

TROY GLAUS **3B** **Bats: R** **Throws: R** Born: 03-Aug-1976 Age: 28

YEAR	TM	LG	AGE	AB	H	2B	3B	HR	BB	SO	SB	CS	AVG	OBP	SLG	MLVR	EQBA	EQOBP	EQSLG	EQMLVR	VORP	DEFENSE
2002	ANA	AL	25	569	142	24	1	30	88	144	10	3	.250	.352	.453	.071	.256	.362	.470	.069	42.2	147-3B 6
2003	ANA	AL	26	319	79	17	2	16	46	73	7	2	.248	.343	.464	.079	.253	.354	.478	.063	25.9	84-3B -11
2004	ANA	AL	27	207	52	11	1	18	31	52	2	3	.251	.355	.575	.206	.263	.367	.610	.272	19.7	16-3B -1
2005	*ARI*	*NL*	*28*	*345*	*97*	*19*	*2*	*26*	*61*	*87*	*4*	*2*	*.281*	*.391*	*.579*	*.274*	*.276*	*.384*	*.568*	*.241*	*39.1*	*98-3B -6*

Breakout: 45% *Improve: 75%* *Collapse: 5%*

Due to injuries incurred in the field, Glaus has played a total of 149 games in two years, which is why some teams were looking at him as a first baseman as he went into free agency. Batting .296/.387/.694 and leading the AL in home runs when he went down in May, he hit .202/.322/.444 (with seven homers) in 99 at-bats after his return. The Snakes signed Glaus with the expectation that they'll be getting a 40-homer third baseman, but it's possible they'll get a half-year DH, a bit of a problem since they play in the National League.

NICK GORNEAULT **OF** **Bats: R** **Throws: R** Born: 19-Apr-1979 Age: 26

YEAR	TM	LG	AGE	AB	H	2B	3B	HR	BB	SO	SB	CS	AVG	OBP	SLG	MLVR	EQBA	EQOBP	EQSLG	EQMLVR	VORP	DEFENSE	
2002	CDR	MDW	23	346	100	17	7	10	30	106	12	5	.289	.346	.465	.201	.244	.291	.403	-.163	-11.4	50-LF 0	46-RF -4
2003	RCU	CLF	24	374	120	36	2	14	20	82	11	6	.321	.362	.540	.294	.262	.298	.439	-.084	-3.3	68-LF 0	22-CF 0
2003	ARK	TXS	24	110	38	6	4	2	8	25	2	0	.345	.395	.527	.329	.312	.357	.495	.148	7.1	28-RF 1	
2004	ARK	TXS	25	495	139	28	4	21	45	128	7	5	.281	.341	.481	.108	.238	.292	.409	-.157	-14.3	54-RF -4	51-LF 0
2005	*ANA*	*AL*	*26*	*162*	*40*	*9*	*1*	*6*	*11*	*47*	*2*	*1*	*.246*	*.299*	*.420*	*-.105*	*.248*	*.302*	*.431*	*-.094*	*2.2*	*45-LF -2*	

Breakout: 26% *Improve: 48%* *Collapse: 31%*

Gorneault's middling status as a prospect took a blow in his return to Arkansas. He has some power, and his plate discipline improved slightly. But few hitters consistently hit .320 at any level, and regression in that area hurt Gorneault's overall production. He has a role to play, but given his age, weaknesses, and the players in front of him, he could have the opportunity to get some reading done. Gorneault could probably absorb some lessons in selectivity from Ted Williams's *My Turn At Bat* while sitting on the bench waiting for his.

VLADIMIR GUERRERO RF **Bats: R** **Throws: R** Born: 09-Feb-1976 Age: 29

YEAR	TM	LG	AGE	AB	H	2B	3B	HR	BB	SO	SB	CS	AVG	OBP	SLG	MLVR	EQBA	EQOBP	EQSLG	EQMLVR	VORP	DEFENSE
2002	MON	NL	26	614	206	37	2	39	84	70	40	20	.336	.417	.593	.456	.330	.411	.592	.393	86.6	153-RF -3
2003	MON	NL	27	394	130	20	3	25	63	53	9	5	.330	.426	.586	.362	.322	.418	.578	.374	48.7	111-RF -5
2004	ANA	AL	28	612	206	39	2	39	52	74	15	3	.337	.391	.598	.391	.349	.404	.623	.452	88.5	136-RF 2
2005	*ANA*	*AL*	*29*	*530*	*168*	*34*	*2*	*30*	*60*	*68*	*13*	*4*	*.318*	*.390*	*.559*	*.288*	*.320*	*.394*	*.572*	*.309*	*60.4*	*141-RF -2*

Breakout: 8% *Improve: 29%* *Collapse: 17%*

All you GMs out there, whip out your *South Pacific* original cast albums (we know you have them, boys) and sing along with "This Nearly Was Mine." Among many potential suitors, Guerrero's formerly herniated disks scared both New York teams so badly that the Yankees opted for Gary Sheffield while the Mets figured that platooning Shane Spencer and Karim Garcia was safer. Guerrero's back troubled him at times in the field and on the bases, but had no effect on his hitting: He set team records in batting average by a righty, hits by a righty, and runs scored. He was particularly effective in September, batting .371/.431/.733 to lead the Angels into the playoffs and claim AL MVP honors. His back may catch up with him at some point, but he's still in his 20s, so that won't happen for a while.

JOSE GUILLEN OF **Bats: R** **Throws: R** Born: 17-May-1976 Age: 29

YEAR	TM	LG	AGE	AB	H	2B	3B	HR	BB	SO	SB	CS	AVG	OBP	SLG	MLVR	EQBA	EQOBP	EQSLG	EQMLVR	VORP	DEFENSE
2002	ARI	NL	26	131	30	4	0	4	7	25	3	4	.229	.277	.351	-.203	.229	.266	.351	-.295	-5.4	28-RF -2
2002	CIN	NL	26	109	27	3	0	4	7	18	1	1	.248	.299	.385	-.112	.255	.292	.382	-.183	-1.1	19-RF 1
2003	CIN	NL	27	315	106	21	1	23	17	63	1	3	.337	.385	.629	.435	.332	.377	.630	.401	41.0	61-RF 0 17-LF -2
2003	OAK	AL	27	170	45	7	1	8	7	32	0	0	.265	.311	.459	.019	.266	.317	.467	-.007	5.6	27-RF 0
2004	ANA	AL	28	565	166	28	3	27	37	92	5	4	.294	.352	.497	.140	.305	.363	.520	.186	36.4	126-LF 6
2005	*WAS*	*NL*	*29*	*503*	*142*	*29*	*3*	*23*	*33*	*87*	*4*	*2*	*.283*	*.339*	*.489*	*.078*	*.286*	*.340*	*.501*	*.094*	*25.0*	*130-LF -2*

Breakout: 7% *Improve: 31%* *Collapse: 25%*

It takes a special guy to so aggravate his organization that despite being second on the team in home runs that it suspends him for the last week of the season in the thick of a pennant race; *and then,* when the team wins it without him, bars him from the playoffs as well. Guillen has had two good years in a row, so a career that threatened never to start has turned a corner. As a free agent after '05 he has a lot riding on being a solid, productive citizen. As he's never learned much in the way of plate judgment, he's just as likely to be cranky and post an OBP of .310. Traded to the Nationals for a younger, less disruptive Guillen clone in Juan Rivera, and a decent shortstop prospect in Maicer Izturis.

SHANE HALTER UT **Bats: R** **Throws: R** Born: 08-Nov-1969 Age: 35

YEAR	TM	LG	AGE	AB	H	2B	3B	HR	BB	SO	SB	CS	AVG	OBP	SLG	MLVR	EQBA	EQOBP	EQSLG	EQMLVR	VORP	DEFENSE
2002	DET	AL	32	410	98	22	6	10	39	92	0	4	.239	.309	.395	-.080	.249	.323	.413	-.086	11.4	79-SS -6 24-3B 2
2003	DET	AL	33	360	78	5	2	12	27	77	2	3	.217	.269	.342	-.257	.221	.281	.356	-.264	-6.4	46-3B 1 20-SS 0
2004	ANA	AL	34	114	23	5	0	4	7	30	1	1	.202	.248	.351	-.327	.212	.254	.345	-.338	-4.8	31-3B -5
2004	SLC	PCL	34	131	36	7	1	6	15	21	2	3	.275	.349	.481	-.039	.222	.295	.381	-.202	-5.3	14-RF 0
2005	*ANA*	*AL*	*35*	*144*	*32*	*6*	*1*	*4*	*13*	*36*	*1*	*1*	*.220*	*.284*	*.352*	*-.239*	*.221*	*.287*	*.361*	*-.232*	*-3.5*	*41-3B -2*

Breakout: 28% *Improve: 48%* *Collapse: 31%*

Played first, second, third, short, and Salt Lake City and didn't hit at any of them. Since a random productive season at the bat in 2001, his OBP column reads .309, .269 and .248. We predict the next three entries in the series to read "sitcom," "infomercial," "Diamondbacks managerial candidate."

HOWIE KENDRICK 2B **Bats: R** **Throws: R** Born: 12-Jul-1983 Age: 21

YEAR	TM	LG	AGE	AB	H	2B	3B	HR	BB	SO	SB	CS	AVG	OBP	SLG	MLVR	EQBA	EQOBP	EQSLG	EQMLVR	VORP	DEFENSE
2003	PRO	PIO	19	234	86	20	3	3	24	28	8	3	.368	.434	.517	.379	.263	.317	.368	-.150	3.2	60-2B -4
2004	CDR	MDW	20	313	115	24	6	10	12	41	15	6	.367	.398	.578	.447	.304	.331	.481	.075	23.4	64-2B 3
2005	*ANA*	*AL*	*21*	*400*	*107*	*23*	*2*	*9*	*16*	*61*	*8*	*4*	*.267*	*.306*	*.407*	*-.095*	*.269*	*.310*	*.417*	*-.084*	*13.7*	*103-2B -2*

Breakout: 6% *Improve: 21%* *Collapse: 52%*

(continued next page)

Howie Kendrick *(continue)*

Now has a .355/.403/.517 line in 183 minor league games. This guy can clearly knock 'em into the gaps, though—if you've read this chapter start to finish you can probably guess what comes next—Kendrick doesn't walk much. Still, +37% above league-average OPS can never be a bad thing. Kendrick will have to surpass Callaspo both with the bat and glove to become the keystone hope of the organization, but the Angels aren't in a hurry with Adam Kennedy is signed through 2006.

ADAM KENNEDY **2B** **Bats: L** **Throws: R** Born: 10-Jan-1976 Age: 29

YEAR	TM	LG	AGE	AB	H	2B	3B	HR	BB	SO	SB	CS	AVG	OBP	SLG	MLVR	EQBA	EQOBP	EQSLG	EQMLVR	VORP	DEFENSE
2002	ANA	AL	26	474	148	32	6	7	19	80	17	4	.312	.345	.449	.103	.321	.356	.465	.111	40.2	127-2B 15
2003	ANA	AL	27	449	121	17	1	13	45	73	22	9	.269	.344	.399	.006	.278	.356	.413	-.002	26.5	128-2B 18
2004	ANA	AL	28	468	130	20	5	10	41	92	15	5	.278	.351	.406	-.011	.288	.362	.424	.033	27.3	139-2B 1
2005	*ANA*	*AL*	*29*	*418*	*116*	*22*	*3*	*10*	*35*	*75*	*13*	*5*	*.279*	*.345*	*.418*	*-.004*	*.280*	*.349*	*.429*	*.009*	*24.3*	*111-2B 1*

Breakout: 7% *Improve: 31%* *Collapse: 23%*

Kennedy totaled his MCL and ACL in September, shelving him for the playoffs, spring training, and perhaps April. He was having a season roughly identical to his 2003, and a stay at this level, rather than bouncing back to that of 2002, is most likely. The loss in batting average from that season to this has been neatly offset by an increase in his walk rate. The Angel most likely to strike out, in part because he was working deeper counts than he had before (3.96 pitches per plate appearances, a career high). It will be fascinating to see if he continues to buck Hatcher's philosophies, assuming his approach survives the knee injury.

CASEY KOTCHMAN **1B** **Bats: L** **Throws: L** Born: 22-Feb-1983 Age: 22

YEAR	TM	LG	AGE	AB	H	2B	3B	HR	BB	SO	SB	CS	AVG	OBP	SLG	MLVR	EQBA	EQOBP	EQSLG	EQMLVR	VORP	DEFENSE
2002	CDR	MDW	19	288	81	30	1	5	48	37	2	1	.281	.390	.444	.225	.234	.321	.381	-.144	-5.7	72-1B 2
2003	RCU	CLF	20	206	72	12	0	8	30	16	2	0	.350	.441	.524	.415	.288	.359	.434	.041	8.2	45-1B 1
2004	ARK	TXS	21	114	42	11	0	3	10	7	0	0	.368	.438	.544	.427	.292	.337	.434	.005	3.1	25-1B 3
2004	SLC	PCL	21	199	74	22	0	5	14	25	0	0	.372	.423	.558	.292	.296	.338	.434	.010	5.3	40-1B 2
2004	ANA	AL	21	116	26	6	0	0	7	11	3	0	.224	.289	.276	-.334	.243	.285	.270	-.364	-4.4	28-1B 1
2005	*ANA*	*AL*	*22*	*399*	*110*	*24*	*1*	*11*	*35*	*48*	*3*	*1*	*.276*	*.353*	*.425*	*.016*	*.278*	*.357*	*.436*	*.029*	*21.1*	*108-1B -2*

Breakout: 31% *Improve: 52%* *Collapse: 22%*

The kind of player you'd order not to eat fish for fear he would choke on a bone. The Angels' version of Nick Johnson, Kotchman missed all but one game of July with wrist and shoulder strains. That's not going to do if the team is ever going to wean itself away from Erstadism. Though Kotchman has batted .333/.416/.510 in 222 minor league games, he's hit just 23 home runs (834 ABs). It's assumed the home runs will come, but instances of players suddenly developing new skill sets are more rare than is commonly believed. Still, as with all of Anaheim's top prospects, Kotchman has been challenged and might yet show more if he's not struck by lightning or trampled by an elephant.

JEFF MATHIS **C** **Bats: R** **Throws: R** Born: 31-Mar-1983 Age: 22

YEAR	TM	LG	AGE	AB	H	2B	3B	HR	BB	SO	SB	CS	AVG	OBP	SLG	MLVR	EQBA	EQOBP	EQSLG	EQMLVR	VORP	DEFENSE
2002	CDR	MDW	19	491	141	41	3	10	40	75	7	4	.287	.346	.444	.170	.245	.289	.388	-.187	-2.1	78-C 3
2003	ARK	TXS	20	95	27	11	0	2	12	16	1	2	.284	.364	.463	.139	.242	.306	.400	-.141	1.0	23-C -1
2003	RCU	CLF	20	378	122	28	3	11	35	74	5	3	.323	.384	.500	.269	.273	.325	.422	-.050	14.2	81-C -2
2004	ARK	TXS	21	432	98	24	3	14	49	102	2	1	.227	.310	.394	-.101	.192	.264	.336	-.342	-23.3	102-C -7
2005	*ANA*	*AL*	*22*	*274*	*66*	*15*	*1*	*8*	*22*	*62*	*1*	*1*	*.240*	*.305*	*.387*	*-.142*	*.242*	*.309*	*.397*	*-.132*	*6.5*	*74-C -9*

Breakout: 34% *Improve: 53%* *Collapse: 27%*

That loud noise you heard was Jeff Mathis's super-prospect status imploding. Mathis got off to a hot start, then crashed hard. There was no injury. His bat simply disappeared without paying its bar tab or leaving a forwarding address. Who knows the cause? The question is: Does the still-youthful Mathis re-establish himself or does he stagnate? He was extremely young for Double-A, and there's a tendency to exaggerate the effect of the most recent season on any player's record, so you can count on some rebound. It's way too early to write Mathis off since he'll get plenty of time to prove himself.

DALLAS McPHERSON 3B Bats: L Throws: R Born: 23-Jul-1980 Age: 24

YEAR	TM	LG	AGE	AB	H	2B	3B	HR	BB	SO	SB	CS	AVG	OBP	SLG	MLVR	EQBA	EQOBP	EQSLG	EQMLVR	VORP	DEFENSE
2002	CDR	MDW	21	499	138	24	3	15	78	128	30	6	.277	.381	.427	.187	.233	.316	.369	-.170	1.6	118-3B -18
2003	RCU	CLF	22	292	90	21	6	18	41	79	12	6	.308	.404	.606	.429	.247	.328	.474	.006	17.3	67-3B 1
2003	ARK	TXS	22	102	32	9	1	5	19	25	4	0	.314	.426	.569	.391	.267	.376	.495	.136	10.8	18-3B -2
2004	ARK	TXS	23	262	84	17	6	20	34	74	6	5	.321	.404	.660	.484	.270	.344	.544	.152	28.3	56-3B -7
2004	SLC	PCL	23	259	81	19	8	20	23	95	6	3	.313	.370	.680	.309	.242	.299	.508	-.003	13.4	61-3B -12
2004	ANA	AL	23	40	9	1	0	3	3	17	1	0	.225	.279	.475	-.102	.250	.271	.475	-.091	0.5	12-3B 0
2005	*ANA*	*AL*	*24*	*324*	*88*	*19*	*2*	*16*	*36*	*98*	*5*	*2*	*.272*	*.351*	*.496*	*.101*	*.274*	*.355*	*.508*	*.117*	*23.2*	*88-3B -8*

Breakout: 41% *Improve: 70%* *Collapse: 16%*

Going into this season, McPherson's defense was questionable enough that the Angels considered a move to the outfield. Having bidden Glaus adieu, McPherson is now at the hot corner by default. On offense, McPherson's strikeout rate jumped from roughly a quarter of his at-bats to a third, while his walk rate dropped from 12% of plate appearances to 10%. McPherson moved up three levels in '04 and all things considered he reacted well, keeping his batting average at .317 between two minor league levels and posting a major league-equivalent EqA in the .260s. Call the free swinging an adjustment phenomenon until he gets settled in one place. PECOTA sees star potential.

BEN MOLINA C Bats: R Throws: R Born: 20-Jul-1974 Age: 30

YEAR	TM	LG	AGE	AB	H	2B	3B	HR	BB	SO	SB	CS	AVG	OBP	SLG	MLVR	EQBA	EQOBP	EQSLG	EQMLVR	VORP	DEFENSE
2002	ANA	AL	27	428	105	18	0	5	15	34	0	0	.245	.274	.322	-.253	.254	.282	.333	-.273	-3.0	112-C 12
2003	ANA	AL	28	409	115	24	0	14	13	31	1	1	.281	.304	.443	.006	.288	.313	.451	-.017	21.2	109-C 12
2004	ANA	AL	29	337	93	13	0	10	18	35	0	1	.276	.313	.404	-.080	.285	.322	.411	-.062	10.8	84-C -3
2005	*ANA*	*AL*	*30*	*307*	*80*	*16*	*0*	*7*	*15*	*30*	*0*	*0*	*.261*	*.297*	*.383*	*-.147*	*.263*	*.301*	*.393*	*-.137*	*4.2*	*80-C 0*

Breakout: 11% *Improve: 31%* *Collapse: 47%*

Thanks to a fractured finger and a strained calf, Molina spent about as long on the shelf as the voyage of Noah's ark. (Fortunately, the Molinas had come two by two.) When ambulatory, he came within a few points of duplicating his career percentages. The difference between this year and last year's moderately productive season can be found in the lefty-mashing department, where the Love of Bengie dropped from a .544 slugging percentage to .398. The Angels would do well to find an Adam Melhuse type; Molina could be considerably more valuable and durable playing four days a week and being spared the toughest righties.

JOSE MOLINA C Bats: R Throws: R Born: 03-Jun-1975 Age: 30

YEAR	TM	LG	AGE	AB	H	2B	3B	HR	BB	SO	SB	CS	AVG	OBP	SLG	MLVR	EQBA	EQOBP	EQSLG	EQMLVR	VORP	DEFENSE
2002	SLC	PCL	27	290	89	14	2	4	12	60	0	3	.307	.341	.410	-.033	.260	.294	.347	-.226	-4.3	76-C 16
2003	ANA	AL	28	114	21	4	0	0	1	26	0	0	.184	.210	.219	-.562	.193	.204	.211	-.638	-10.5	34-C -2
2004	ANA	AL	29	203	53	10	2	3	10	52	4	1	.261	.296	.374	-.175	.264	.305	.383	-.150	2.7	59-C 10
2005	*ANA*	*AL*	*30*	*206*	*50*	*9*	*1*	*3*	*7*	*47*	*3*	*1*	*.241*	*.273*	*.334*	*-.270*	*.243*	*.276*	*.343*	*-.263*	*-2.1*	*55-C 1*

Breakout: 19% *Improve: 37%* *Collapse: 34%*

At bat, both Molinas combined weren't as productive as Gregg Zaun was by himself. That's the value of getting on base; the difference from the best defensive catcher to the worst isn't nearly as wide as the gulf created when one player uses his plate appearances effectively and the other toasts them like marshmallows. The younger Molina is a poor fit to back up his bro, given their too-similar skill sets.

RAUL MONDESI OF Bats: R Throws: R Born: 12-Mar-1971 Age: 34

YEAR	TM	LG	AGE	AB	H	2B	3B	HR	BB	SO	SB	CS	AVG	OBP	SLG	MLVR	EQBA	EQOBP	EQSLG	EQMLVR	VORP	DEFENSE
2002	TOR	AL	31	299	67	16	1	15	31	57	9	2	.224	.301	.435	-.058	.223	.304	.439	-.105	5.2	59-RF 2
2002	NYY	AL	31	270	65	18	0	11	28	46	6	4	.241	.315	.430	-.033	.253	.324	.442	-.040	4.4	53-RF -4 11-CF -1
2003	NYY	AL	32	361	93	23	3	16	38	66	17	7	.258	.330	.471	.062	.265	.343	.492	.073	16.4	97-RF 2
2003	ARI	NL	32	162	49	8	1	8	18	31	5	4	.302	.372	.512	.185	.287	.358	.500	.131	10.4	42-RF -3
2004	PIT	NL	33	99	28	8	0	2	11	27	0	2	.283	.355	.424	.079	.283	.339	.414	-.028	3.7	12-LF -1 12-RF 0
2004	ANA	AL	33	34	4	1	0	1	2	4	0	1	.118	.189	.235	-.632	.118	.162	.206	-.759	-4.8	
2005	*ATL*	*NL*	*34*	*248*	*62*	*13*	*1*	*10*	*29*	*53*	*5*	*1*	*.249*	*.330*	*.429*	*-.046*	*.251*	*.330*	*.434*	*-.040*	*7.6*	*69-RF -3*

Breakout 30% *Improve 57%* *Collapse 23%*

(continued next page)

Raul Mondesi *(continued)*

Started the year with the Pirates, though neither he nor the Pirates knew what he was doing there. Then he retired; it was too good to be true. In a moment of pure desperation, the Angels acquired him to play center field. He played eight games, tore his right quad, didn't show up for rehab work and had his contract terminated. That second half of '03 was probably the last flash of effectiveness we'll ever see from him.

KENDRY MORALES **1B/OF** **Bats: B** **Throws: R** Born: 20-Jun-1983 Age: 22

YEAR	TM	LG	AGE	AB	H	2B	3B	HR	BB	SO	SB	CS	AVG	OBP	SLG	MLVR	EQBA	EQOBP	EQSLG	EQMLVR	VORP	DEFENSE
2002	Ind	CBA	19	352	114	24	1	21	38	57	2	2	.324	.399	.577	.335	.247	.306	.438	-.084	6.8	
2003	Ind	CBA	20	202	79	13	2	9	42	24	0	1	.391	.512	.609	.614	.307	.402	.466	.179	49.3	
2004	Ind	CBA	21	123	44	12	1	2	9	13	0	0	.358	.406	.520	.324	.314	.354	.449	.077	32.9	
2005	*ANA*	*AL*	*22*	*288*	*77*	*18*	*1*	*9*	*27*	*59*	*0*	*0*	*.267*	*.338*	*.430*	*-.009*	*.269*	*.342*	*.441*	*.004*	*13.7*	*78-1B -2*

Breakout: 10% *Improve: 18%* *Collapse: 50%*

The Angels were so eager to get their hands on this young Cuban defector that they gave him a six-year *major league* contract. The Angels think Morales is ready to play now, so he'll get a chance to win an outfield job in the spring. Reputed to be a power hitter, a sketchily informed PECOTA thinks he might be a bit like Tony Horton, Mike Aubrey, Juan Tejada, Aramis Ramirez, and Garrett Atkins. Take that for what it's worth, because PECOTA is only as good as what we feed it. When it comes to Cuba, we might be better off giving it *empanadas* and *café con leche* than baseball statistics, because although we have some numbers, we're not entirely sure how to put them into context. The Cuban leagues look to have a talent level somewhere around that of short-season A-ball leagues, but that's an early, educated guess. We also don't know if we should be confident of Morales's reported age.

Teams are looking for cost/talent certainty. With domestic product we can forecast what they're going to get within a certain range, even if that player is just out of college. If it's a minor leaguer we can get close to the bull's-eye. If it's a Japanese player, we can forecast with confidence because we understand their leagues. With Cuba, we just don't know, not yet, so as a team-building exercise, spending a great deal on these players is the equivalent of taking a small fortune and placing it on red. If Morales's record accurately represents him, the Angels are probably into something good. If not, well, *caveat emptor.*

MICHAEL NAPOLI **C/1B** **Bats: R** **Throws: R** Born: 31-Oct-1981 Age: 23

YEAR	TM	LG	AGE	AB	H	2B	3B	HR	BB	SO	SB	CS	AVG	OBP	SLG	MLVR	EQBA	EQOBP	EQSLG	EQMLVR	VORP	DEFENSE
2002	CDR	MDW	20	362	91	19	1	10	62	104	6	5	.251	.362	.392	.101	.211	.300	.336	-.260	-10.2	36-C -4
2003	RCU	CLF	21	165	44	10	1	4	23	32	5	0	.267	.364	.412	.065	.229	.311	.355	-.202	-1.5	18-C 2
2004	RCU	CLF	22	482	136	29	4	29	88	166	9	5	.282	.394	.539	.275	.225	.322	.414	-.104	10.9	71-C 7 33-1B -5
2005	*ANA*	*AL*	*23*	*300*	*71*	*15*	*1*	*10*	*36*	*101*	*3*	*2*	*.236*	*.325*	*.393*	*-.103*	*.237*	*.328*	*.403*	*-.093*	*7.2*	*83-C -14*

Breakout: 29% *Improve: 57%* *Collapse: 21%*

Prior to the season, Napoli was regarded as the fifth-best backstop in the Angels organization, maybe worse. Then he found some tremendous power, and with it came the added respect from pitchers that allows a player with a 60-walk eye to have an 88-walk season. Negatives include 166 strikeouts, which cast doubt on his ability to sustain his batting average at higher levels, doubly so after accounting for Cal League inflation. At 6′5″ and 205 pounds., he'll likely shift to first base at some point, so his hitting needs to keep making big strides. Double-A will provide a good test.

JOSH PAUL **C** **Bats: R** **Throws: R** Born: 19-May-1975 Age: 30

YEAR	TM	LG	AGE	AB	H	2B	3B	HR	BB	SO	SB	CS	AVG	OBP	SLG	MLVR	EQBA	EQOBP	EQSLG	EQMLVR	VORP	DEFENSE
2002	CHR	INT	27	231	63	15	2	0	17	45	10	4	.273	.323	.355	-.059	.250	.298	.323	-.259	-6.0	59-C 0
2002	CWS	AL	27	104	25	4	0	0	9	22	2	0	.240	.302	.279	-.278	.252	.293	.272	-.340	-1.0	31-C -5
2003	CHR	INT	28	64	12	0	1	2	5	14	1	1	.188	.243	.312	-.291	.172	.224	.297	-.486	-6.2	16-C 1
2003	IOW	PCL	28	146	37	4	0	2	8	30	0	2	.253	.297	.322	-.183	.221	.256	.276	-.426	-10.9	22-C 5
2004	ANA	AL	29	70	17	3	0	2	7	17	2	1	.243	.308	.371	-.164	.261	.313	.362	-.167	1.5	19-C -2
2005	*ANA*	*AL*	*30*	*111*	*27*	*5*	*1*	*2*	*8*	*25*	*2*	*1*	*.244*	*.299*	*.349*	*-.200*	*.246*	*.303*	*.358*	*-.192*	*1.0*	*34-C -3*

Breakout: 35% *Improve: 51%* *Collapse: 26%*

Fate can be cruel: The difference between being Mike Matheny and Josh Paul is not so great as a butterfly's sneeze. If a Paul must be had, we recommend the Angels bag the third catcher concept and go with Ellis Paul, the Boston balladeer. He can't hit, but neither can Josh, and he'll keep the team mellow with gently strummed songs of life on the road.

ROBB QUINLAN — 1B/3B — Bats: R — Throws: R — Born: 17-Mar-1977 — Age: 28

YEAR	TM	LG	AGE	AB	H	2B	3B	HR	BB	SO	SB	CS	AVG	OBP	SLG	MLVR	EQBA	EQOBP	EQSLG	EQMLVR	VORP	DEFENSE	
2002	SLC	PCL	25	528	176	31	13	20	41	93	8	2	.333	.376	.555	.248	.284	.329	.473	.040	14.4	98-LF 2	
2003	SLC	PCL	26	393	122	18	4	9	25	59	10	3	.310	.352	.445	.044	.257	.302	.377	-.170	-9.7	57-1B 2	24-LF 1
2003	ANA	AL	26	94	27	4	2	0	6	16	1	2	.287	.330	.372	-.041	.301	.333	.366	-.094	1.3	19-1B 0	
2004	SLC	PCL	27	108	32	9	1	2	14	14	1	1	.296	.377	.454	-.007	.243	.322	.369	-.152	-2.3	23-1B 3	
2004	ANA	AL	27	160	55	14	0	5	14	26	3	1	.344	.401	.525	.316	.361	.407	.538	.348	19.6	23-3B -1	11-1B 1
2005	*ANA*	*AL*	*28*	*268*	*70*	*15*	*2*	*7*	*21*	*49*	*3*	*2*	*.262*	*.316*	*.406*	*-.084*	*.263*	*.320*	*.416*	*-.073*	*5.8*	*72-1B 2*	

Breakout: 8% *Improve: 18%* *Collapse: 50%*

Mike Scioscia claims he's a defense-first manager, but when confronted by a problem, he can't help being creative. The Angels tried to make Quinlan a third baseman back at Boise in 1999, but gave up after he fielded .892 in 73 games. Scioscia moved Quinlan back and he played extremely well on both sides of the ball until injuries shelved him for good in mid-August. Quinlan, Figgins, and DaVanon give the Angels a deep and versatile bench. Big City GMs take note: The Angels got there by trusting the B-level talent in the farm to fill roles.

ADAM RIGGS — INF — Bats: R — Throws: R — Born: 04-Oct-1972 — Age: 32

YEAR	TM	LG	AGE	AB	H	2B	3B	HR	BB	SO	SB	CS	AVG	OBP	SLG	MLVR	EQBA	EQOBP	EQSLG	EQMLVR	VORP	DEFENSE	
2002	SLT	MEX	29	242	80	19	1	7	23	50	10	0	.331	.391	.504	.232	.272	.328	.427	-.038	8.0		
2002	MEM	PCL	29	122	28	9	0	2	23	27	5	1	.230	.347	.352	-.052	.197	.305	.287	-.322	-11.1	11-LF 0	13-3B -1
2003	SLC	PCL	30	394	116	35	0	14	37	67	8	2	.294	.354	.490	.094	.238	.297	.408	-.149	-11.0	21-LF -1	20-1B -1
2003	ANA	AL	30	61	15	4	1	3	9	9	3	1	.246	.343	.492	.087	.262	.357	.508	.117	4.0		
2004	SLC	PCL	31	450	149	33	8	29	30	80	8	3	.331	.373	.633	.272	.265	.306	.492	.009	8.2	64-LF -3	11-1B 1
2004	ANA	AL	31	36	7	3	0	0	1	10	1	0	.194	.216	.278	-.500	.194	.170	.222	-.693	-2.7		
2005	*ANA*	*AL*	*32*	*162*	*40*	*9*	*1*	*6*	*12*	*38*	*2*	*1*	*.250*	*.306*	*.415*	*-.098*	*.251*	*.309*	*.425*	*-.087*	*3.2*	*46-LF -6*	

Breakout: 24% *Improve: 46%* *Collapse: 35%*

The Buzz Arlett of the 21st Century, Adam Riggs is an eight-year veteran of the Pacific Coast League, batting .307/.367/.511 in a minor league career that began in 1994. Versatile and armed with a bit of pop, Riggs would be a very effective reserve if only managers didn't feel obliged to carry 12 pitchers these days. He'll play in Japan with the Yakult Swallows, where he'll still be in a Pacific coast league of sorts.

SEAN RODRIGUEZ — SS — Bats: R — Throws: R — Born: 26-Apr-1985 — Age: 20

YEAR	TM	LG	AGE	AB	H	2B	3B	HR	BB	SO	SB	CS	AVG	OBP	SLG	MLVR	EQBA	EQOBP	EQSLG	EQMLVR	VORP	DEFENSE
2004	CDR	MDW	19	196	49	8	4	4	18	54	14	4	.250	.333	.393	.012	.210	.274	.330	-.320	-9.0	24-2B 1
2004	PRO	PIO	19	225	76	14	4	10	51	62	9	3	.338	.486	.569	.420	.216	.311	.330	-.243	-5.6	62-SS -5
2005	*ANA*	*AL*	*20*	*331*	*72*	*15*	*3*	*6*	*28*	*109*	*8*	*3*	*.218*	*.305*	*.331*	*-.227*	*.219*	*.309*	*.340*	*-.220*	*0.7*	*91-SS -9*

Breakout: 24% *Improve: 43%* *Collapse: 36%*

Started off in the Midwest League, where he kept himself active, before being demoted to the more age-appropriate Pioneer League at its season's start. There, he posted a .339 EqA, but for a teenager getting his feet wet, no part of the season was a disappointment. Given the sheer number of middle-infield prospects in the organization, there's thought that the Angels might shift Rodriguez (S-Rod? Not yet) to catcher.

TIM SALMON — OF/DH — Bats: R — Throws: R — Born: 24-Aug-1968 — Age: 36

YEAR	TM	LG	AGE	AB	H	2B	3B	HR	BB	SO	SB	CS	AVG	OBP	SLG	MLVR	EQBA	EQOBP	EQSLG	EQMLVR	VORP	DEFENSE
2002	ANA	AL	33	483	138	37	1	22	71	102	6	3	.286	.380	.503	.213	.293	.390	.522	.221	41.4	102-RF -1
2003	ANA	AL	34	528	145	35	4	19	77	93	3	1	.275	.374	.464	.152	.282	.383	.482	.145	41.5	66-RF -6
2004	ANA	AL	35	186	47	7	0	2	14	41	1	0	.253	.306	.323	-.215	.266	.312	.326	-.217	-1.7	

The franchise's career home-run leader is expected to undergo multiple surgeries that will shelve him for all of '05. A comeback at 37 next year seems improbable, so this is probably it. Salmon started late and finished early, so he doesn't have the career numbers to be a Hall of Famer, but at his peak he had that kind of ability.

BRANDON WOOD SS **Bats: R** **Throws: R** Born: 02-Mar-1985 Age: 20

YEAR	TM	LG	AGE	AB	H	2B	3B	HR	BB	SO	SB	CS	AVG	OBP	SLG	MLVR	EQBA	EQOBP	EQSLG	EQMLVR	VORP	DEFENSE
2003	PRO	PIO	18	162	45	13	2	5	16	48	1	1	.278	.348	.475	.098	.195	.249	.321	-.391	-16.4	33-SS -6
2004	CDR	MDW	19	478	120	30	5	11	46	117	21	5	.251	.322	.404	.010	.209	.268	.337	-.323	-18.2	124-SS -22
2005	*ANA*	*AL*	*20*	*345*	*75*	*18*	*2*	*7*	*23*	*95*	*7*	*2*	*.219*	*.274*	*.338*	*-.277*	*.220*	*.277*	*.346*	*-.270*	*-2.9*	*90-SS -12*

Breakout: 39% *Improve: 56%* *Collapse: 29%*

You a glass half-full type? Then a .269 EqA from a teenager in the Midwestern League won't depress you, even if that fellow was the club's 2003 first-round pick. Wood struck out 117 times and took 46 walks. Wood was a late-bloomer as an amateur; the same will have to be true as a pro for him to make hay. Let's hope so, because it would take just 49 home runs to displace Dick Schofield for #2 on the franchise list of career home runs by a shortstop.

PITCHERS

STEVE ANDRADE **Bats: R** **Throws: R** Born: 06-Feb-1978 Age: 27

YEAR	TM	LG	AGE	G	GS	IP	H	BB	SO	HR	ERA	EQERA	EQH9	EQBB9	EQSO9	EQHR9	PERA	VORP	STF
2002	CDR	MDW	24	46	0	54.3	30	16	93	1	1.16	3.14	7.2	3.5	9.8	0.6	3.33	12.3	22
2003	ARK	TXS	25	36	0	51.0	26	19	74	2	2.65	3.47	6.2	3.9	10.4	0.8	2.89	14.1	32
2004	ARK	TXS	26	35	0	48.0	37	12	59	4	2.44	3.63	7.9	2.6	8.1	1.2	3.43	10.8	16
2004	SLC	PCL	26	12	0	13.7	15	8	17	1	4.60	3.95	8.6	5.3	8.6	0.7	4.61	1.5	0
2005	*TOR*	*AL*	*27*	*18*	*3*	*35.3*	*32*	*16*	*32*	*4*	*4.07*	*3.83*	*8.0*	*3.5*	*7.4*	*0.9*	*3.86*	*8.6*	*7*

Breakout: 20% *Improve: 42%* *Collapse: 36%*

The movie about Angels' GM Bill Stoneman should be called *The Eternal Sunlight of the Open Mind.* Most every other team relies on scouting reports to segregate relievers into a Calvinist elect/non-elect, major league/Quadruple-A hierarchy while ignoring actual performances; the Angels are open to anyone. Drafted in the 32nd round in 2001? Bring him in. Monty Stratton? Why the heck not? Guy with no arms but can shoot laser beams from his eyes? Maybe he can get lefties! Andrade has all his limbs, and as his age and the 32nd round selection suggests, little else to boast of—except results. Andrade doesn't have great stuff but dominated the Texas League in '03. The Angels sent him back again, and he did it again. At this point there is no reason to think that Andrade can't sustain his success. Claimed off waivers by the Blue Jays in December, he's a solid candidate to make it this season.

DUSTY BERGMAN **Bats: L** **Throws: L** Born: 01-Feb-1978 Age: 27

YEAR	TM	LG	AGE	G	GS	IP	H	BB	SO	HR	ERA	EQERA	EQH9	EQBB9	EQSO9	EQHR9	PERA	VORP	STF
2002	ARK	TXS	24	35	0	56.0	48	8	38	3	2.41	4.15	8.5	1.4	4.7	0.9	3.29	13.3	5
2002	SLC	PCL	24	21	0	29.3	34	9	26	7	6.45	6.75	10.3	2.9	6.4	2.6	6.11	-1.6	-13
2003	ARK	TXS	25	50	10	109.3	116	33	82	7	3.79	4.88	9.8	3.0	5.1	1.1	5.14	5.3	-13
2004	SLC	PCL	26	45	0	72.7	82	13	54	2	2.85	3.98	8.6	1.6	5.0	0.2	2.86	22.0	7
2005	*ANA*	*AL*	*27*	*24*	*3*	*43.0*	*49*	*13*	*26*	*5*	*4.57*	*4.53*	*10.3*	*2.4*	*4.8*	*1.1*	*4.65*	*7.1*	*-8*

Breakout: 23% *Improve: 45%* *Collapse: 28%*

A tall lefty who has fumbled about the minors as a starter since 1999, Bergman shifted to the bullpen at Triple-A and posted a strong 54:13 strikeout-to-walk ratio (72.2 innings), though he allowed a goodly number of hits. He pitched two innings of trash-time relief against the Brewers, got hammered, and was sent back to Utah. As a lefty, he's likely to get other chances.

BARTOLO COLON **Bats: R** **Throws: R** Born: 24-May-1973 Age: 32

YEAR	TM	LG	AGE	G	GS	IP	H	BB	SO	HR	ERA	EQERA	EQH9	EQBB9	EQSO9	EQHR9	PERA	VORP	STF
2002	CLE	AL	29	16	16	116.3	104	31	75	11	2.55	2.73	8.0	2.2	5.6	0.8	3.05	40.3	17
2002	MON	NL	29	17	17	117.0	115	39	74	9	3.31	3.66	8.8	2.6	5.1	0.7	3.90	23.5	11
2003	CWS	AL	30	34	34	242.0	223	67	173	30	3.87	3.62	8.6	2.5	6.5	1.0	4.09	56.6	15
2004	ANA	AL	31	34	34	208.3	215	71	158	38	5.01	4.85	9.0	2.8	6.5	1.5	4.58	22.2	8
2005	*ANA*	*AL*	*32*	*29*	*28*	*168.3*	*176*	*55*	*115*	*24*	*4.49*	*4.45*	*9.5*	*2.6*	*5.5*	*1.2*	*4.49*	*25.8*	*7*

Breakout: 10% *Improve: 56%* *Collapse: 16%*

Sometimes a team makes a move that looks good on paper but in execution turns out to be a flop, or more accurately, a beached whale. The third-best run support in the major leagues (7.00) allowed Colon to post a winning record while allowing opponents to hit .265/.322/.472 with 38 home runs, second-most in the AL. Colon struggled with his command all year long. This may be the result of prior overwork, or a one-time event. Whatever the answer, the Angels will be living with it through 2007.

ERIC CYR Bats: R Throws: L Born: 11-Feb-1979 Age: 26

YEAR	TM	LG	AGE	G	GS	IP	H	BB	SO	HR	ERA	EQERA	EQH9	EQBB9	EQSO9	EQHR9	PERA	VORP	STF
2002	MOB	SOU	23	14	14	72.3	62	34	65	6	3.24	5.35	8.8	4.1	6.1	1.5	5.08	3.9	0
2002	POR	PCL	23	9	2	14.3	14	10	11	0	3.15	4.05	9.4	6.8	5.4	0.0	6.08	-0.7	-22
2003	ARK	TXS	24	20	20	103.3	91	52	78	9	4.97	5.63	9.2	5.3	5.4	1.5	5.72	-1.3	-3
2004	ARK	TXS	25	11	8	54.0	48	15	44	5	3.17	4.47	8.8	2.9	5.4	1.4	4.29	7.3	10
2005	*ANA*	*AL*	*26*	*19*	*10*	*68.7*	*67*	*35*	*45*	*11*	*5.35*	*5.30*	*8.8*	*4.0*	*5.2*	*1.5*	*5.01*	*4.4*	*-9*

Breakout: 13% *Improve: 46%* *Collapse: 27%*

Back in 2002, Montreal native Cyr pitched six innings for the Padres, and got the snot beaten out of him. He was subsequently the subject of an unproductive waiver battle between the Angels and Reds. The Angels claimed him from the Padres, the Reds claimed him from them, the Angels claimed him right back. Lots of paper moved back and forth, and the pitcher, recuperating from elbow surgery, suffered from too much love. Cyr has always had control problems but mastered them, at least momentarily, at Double-A. His teams have resisted making him a reliever. Once they give in, expect to see him in the majors, looking like Randy Choate.

DANIEL DAVIDSON Bats: L Throws: L Born: 08-Jan-1981 Age: 24

YEAR	TM	LG	AGE	G	GS	IP	H	BB	SO	HR	ERA	EQERA	EQH9	EQBB9	EQSO9	EQHR9	PERA	VORP	STF
2003	PRO	PIO	22	15	13	71.3	65	15	50	3	1.64	4.36	9.0	2.9	3.3	1.1	4.77	6.1	4
2004	RCU	CLF	23	28	28	163.3	196	41	121	15	4.57	5.83	10.6	2.8	4.3	1.5	5.83	-4.0	-14
2005	*ANA*	*AL*	*24*	*10*	*9*	*51.7*	*60*	*18*	*28*	*9*	*5.43*	*5.38*	*10.5*	*2.8*	*4.4*	*1.5*	*5.44*	*2.4*	*-7*

Breakout: 10% *Improve: 34%* *Collapse: 14%*

Finesse lefty who posted a promising 121–41 strikeout-walk ratio at Rancho Cucamonga last year, slightly less impressive if you throw in his nine hit batsmen. Then again, maybe Bobby Meacham had them hunting heads down there; teammate Steven Shell nailed 16. Meacham played for Billy Martin, and the way his own career worked out there's probably quite a lot of residual frustration that needs venting, so it's a possibility. Batters hit Davidson back for a lot of hits. It's a hitter's league, and control pitchers take a while to find themselves. There's no cause for excitement, but might as well stay tuned.

BRENDAN DONNELLY Bats: R Throws: R Born: 04-Jul-1971 Age: 33

YEAR	TM	LG	AGE	G	GS	IP	H	BB	SO	HR	ERA	EQERA	EQH9	EQBB9	EQSO9	EQHR9	PERA	VORP	STF
2002	SLC	PCL	31	25	0	33.7	27	11	42	5	3.47	3.41	8.0	3.1	9.1	1.7	4.26	4.7	15
2002	ANA	AL	31	46	0	49.7	32	19	54	2	2.17	2.30	6.7	3.3	9.8	0.4	3.06	20.0	30
2003	ANA	AL	32	63	0	74.0	55	24	79	2	1.58	1.77	6.8	2.9	9.6	0.3	2.78	36.1	35
2004	ANA	AL	33	40	0	42.0	34	15	56	5	3.00	2.81	6.9	2.8	11.2	0.9	3.02	15.3	32
2005	*ANA*	*AL*	*33*	*45*	*0*	*49.3*	*41*	*19*	*49*	*6*	*3.28*	*3.25*	*7.5*	*3.0*	*8.1*	*1.0*	*3.52*	*15.8*	*11*

Breakout: 34% *Improve: 44%* *Collapse: 34%*

Donnelly took ten years to make the majors. Having finally made it at 30, he established himself with two terrific years, only to have his nose blown off his face in a spring training ball-shagging accident. That sounds like hyperbole, but it's not; Donnelly's proboscis was broken in 20 places and required three surgeries to set it straight. Somewhat miraculously (think Bryce Florie), when Donnelly came back in June he pitched about as well as he always had. In many ways the pride of the Angels, Donnelly shares his birthday with jazz great/baseball fan Louis Armstrong. The birthday that Satchmo claimed, anyway.

SCOTT DUNN Bats: R Throws: R Born: 23-May-1978 Age: 27

YEAR	TM	LG	AGE	G	GS	IP	H	BB	SO	HR	ERA	EQERA	EQH9	EQBB9	EQSO9	EQHR9	PERA	VORP	STF
2002	CHT	SOU	24	37	12	110.3	99	54	114	10	3.92	5.45	8.9	4.2	6.9	1.6	4.93	7.7	0
2003	CHT	SOU	25	31	0	40.3	31	16	54	3	3.80	5.50	8.1	3.8	8.6	1.4	4.06	6.5	11
2003	BIR	SOU	25	8	0	10.7	8	5	14	0	1.68	2.70	7.2	4.5	8.1	0.0	2.70	3.2	13
2004	SLC	PCL	26	46	6	89.7	72	56	84	6	3.21	3.36	7.1	6.0	6.6	0.6	3.57	19.3	15
2005	*ANA*	*AL*	*27*	*31*	*3*	*51.0*	*48*	*30*	*38*	*7*	*4.98*	*4.93*	*8.5*	*4.6*	*6.0*	*1.2*	*4.86*	*6.4*	*-10*

Breakout: 21% *Improve: 41%* *Collapse: 25%*

Dunn has been traded twice, demonstrating that he's like a toy whose package is enticing but when you get the thing home you find out it doesn't do half the things the commercial implied it could. Dunn gets strikeouts but has always struggled with his control, walking five batters per nine as a minor leaguer. As he's drifted towards the bullpen the results have improved, if not his ability to avoid ball four. He's in a nurturing environment, so it wouldn't take much improvement to advance and claim a job.

KELVIM ESCOBAR Bats: R Throws: R Born: 11-Apr-1976 Age: 29

YEAR	TM	LG	AGE	G	GS	IP	H	BB	SO	HR	ERA	EQERA	EQH9	EQBB9	EQSO9	EQHR9	PERA	VORP	STF
2002	TOR	AL	26	76	0	78.0	75	44	85	10	4.27	4.06	8.1	4.6	9.3	1.0	4.40	12.8	9
2003	TOR	AL	27	41	26	180.3	189	78	159	15	4.29	4.20	8.4	3.7	7.7	0.6	3.90	27.9	18
2004	ANA	AL	28	33	33	208.3	192	76	191	21	3.93	3.69	7.9	2.9	7.8	0.8	3.56	53.2	26
2005	*ANA*	*AL*	*29*	*30*	*28*	*167.3*	*160*	*66*	*150*	*19*	*4.06*	*4.02*	*8.7*	*3.1*	*7.2*	*1.0*	*4.14*	*33.9*	*17*

Breakout: 15% *Improve: 49%* *Collapse: 18%*

Spent seven years in Toronto bouncing from bullpen to rotation , acquiring a reputation for not being the most coachable kid on the playground. In view of this, the $18.75 million contract offered by the Angels seemed overly generous. Instead, Escobar whittled his walks down to the best rate of his career, and ranked fourth in strikeouts and ninth in ERA in the AL. But for the 3.93 runs per game of support, least in the league among qualified starters, Escobar would have had a record to match those accomplishments. Questions for the future include the bounceback from a career high in innings pitched, but PECOTA expects a nice follow-up season.

KEVIN GREGG Bats: R Throws: R Born: 20-Jun-1978 Age: 27

YEAR	TM	LG	AGE	G	GS	IP	H	BB	SO	HR	ERA	EQERA	EQH9	EQBB9	EQSO9	EQHR9	PERA	VORP	STF
2002	MID	TXS	24	11	4	37.7	31	18	45	3	4.30	5.60	8.4	4.6	8.2	1.3	4.58	4.0	9
2002	SAC	PCL	24	16	8	58.7	82	23	45	7	7.51	8.34	10.6	3.5	5.2	1.2	5.31	1.9	-18
2003	ARK	TXS	25	15	11	66.3	60	19	60	2	3.53	4.48	8.7	2.9	6.4	0.6	4.04	10.8	13
2003	SLC	PCL	25	15	15	91.7	90	18	75	10	4.02	4.64	8.9	2.0	6.3	1.3	4.23	13.3	13
2003	ANA	AL	25	5	3	24.7	18	8	14	3	3.28	3.18	7.9	3.2	5.2	1.2	3.97	7.7	5
2004	ANA	AL	26	55	0	87.7	86	28	84	6	4.21	4.14	8.1	2.6	8.1	0.5	3.41	18.2	20
2005	*ANA*	*AL*	*27*	*37*	*9*	*91.7*	*89*	*33*	*76*	*12*	*4.33*	*4.29*	*8.8*	*2.9*	*6.7*	*1.1*	*4.22*	*16.2*	*4*

Breakout: 22% *Improve: 44%* *Collapse: 24%*

The Angels know the first rule of bullpen construction: As many relievers are born as made. So Gregg, who had been stuck in the minors since the A's drafted him back in '96, got the Donnelly treatment. He worked hard in the first half, pitching 52.2 innings, but then had his control vanish and got racked. The second rule of bullpen construction: Those journeymen relievers can be highly variable. More judicious usage could smooth out some rough edges in an otherwise solid pitcher.

MATT HENSLEY Bats: R Throws: R Born: 18-Aug-1978 Age: 26

YEAR	TM	LG	AGE	G	GS	IP	H	BB	SO	HR	ERA	EQERA	EQH9	EQBB9	EQSO9	EQHR9	PERA	VORP	STF
2002	RCU	CLF	23	12	2	31.7	42	11	27	3	5.39	6.68	11.3	3.5	4.4	1.5	5.81	-0.7	-24
2002	SLC	PCL	23	19	18	117.7	132	39	106	16	4.97	5.35	9.6	3.1	6.3	1.3	5.04	7.1	5
2003	SLC	PCL	24	27	27	158.3	194	49	85	16	4.89	5.74	10.2	3.1	4.0	1.2	5.39	3.6	-11
2004	SLC	PCL	25	30	0	43.0	29	12	49	6	2.93	3.12	6.7	2.7	8.3	1.3	2.90	12.1	7
2004	ANA	AL	25	16	0	27.7	32	7	30	5	4.87	4.50	9.0	1.9	9.0	1.3	4.18	4.3	12
2005	*ANA*	*AL*	*26*	*8*	*4*	*29.7*	*28*	*11*	*25*	*4*	*3.94*	*3.90*	*8.6*	*2.8*	*6.7*	*1.2*	*4.10*	*6.8*	*8*

Breakout: 30% *Improve: 54%* *Collapse: 13%*

Hensley went to spring training wearing uniform #82, which tells you what the Angels thought of him. Since being drafted in 2000, Hensley has compiled a minor league ERA of 4.75, giving up a great many hits, mostly as a starter. Finally shifted to the bullpen in '04, he posted the best results of his career. Hensley's best asset is his control, but major leaguers took advantage of his reliable strike-throwing to blast five home runs in 27.2 innings. The Angels have better men ahead of him, but he could be an effective 11th arm.

BOBBY JENKS Bats: R Throws: R Born: 14-Mar-1981 Age: 24

YEAR	TM	LG	AGE	G	GS	IP	H	BB	SO	HR	ERA	EQERA	EQH9	EQBB9	EQSO9	EQHR9	PERA	VORP	STF
2002	RCU	CLF	21	11	10	65.3	50	46	64	4	4.82	6.45	8.1	7.3	5.2	1.0	4.80	5.3	4
2002	ARK	TXS	21	10	10	58.0	49	44	58	2	4.66	5.93	8.1	7.4	6.9	0.5	4.61	6.0	11
2003	ARK	TXS	22	16	16	83.0	56	51	103	2	2.17	3.17	7.0	6.5	8.8	0.4	3.99	13.7	26
2004	SLC	PCL	23	3	3	12.3	19	6	13	1	8.05	9.00	10.4	4.2	6.9	0.7	5.54	0.1	-1
2005	*CWS*	*AL*	*24*	*16*	*15*	*84.3*	*78*	*63*	*69*	*11*	*5.57*	*5.25*	*8.4*	*5.9*	*6.6*	*1.0*	*4.99*	*7.3*	*1*

Breakout: 17% *Improve: 44%* *Collapse: 23%*

Taking up space on the 40-man roster like a car that's been booted, Jenks missed most of the season with a "stress reaction," the precursor to a stress fracture. It's the second time he's been shelved for this reason, and pins have been inserted into his elbow in hopes that these will hold it together. As in the old TMBG song, Jenks throws sapphire bullets of pure love, topping 102 mph in winter ball. Unfortunately, the speed is as untamed, as 6.2 walks per nine attest. He looked great at Double-A Arkansas in 2003, but he now has three hurdles—personality/maturity, health, and control—to jump before he can have a notable major league career. Those are long odds. Claimed on waivers by the White Sox, who haven't had a lot of success turning minor league projects into major league pitchers in recent years. The odds just got longer.

JOHN LACKEY **Bats: R** **Throws: R** Born: 23-Oct-1978 Age: 26

YEAR	TM	LG	AGE	G	GS	IP	H	BB	SO	HR	ERA	EQERA	EQH9	EQBB9	EQSO9	EQHR9	PERA	VORP	STF
2002	SLC	PCL	23	16	16	101.7	89	28	82	5	2.57	3.17	8.0	2.7	5.8	0.5	3.35	24.2	32
2002	ANA	AL	23	18	18	108.3	113	33	69	10	3.66	4.15	9.5	2.6	5.6	0.8	4.93	20.0	22
2003	ANA	AL	24	33	33	204.0	223	66	151	31	4.63	4.88	9.4	2.8	6.5	1.3	4.92	20.9	15
2004	ANA	AL	25	33	32	198.3	215	60	144	22	4.67	4.54	9.0	2.4	6.1	0.9	4.13	29.3	21
2005	*ANA*	*AL*	*26*	*27*	*25*	*150.0*	*163*	*50*	*105*	*21*	*4.85*	*4.80*	*9.9*	*2.6*	*5.7*	*1.2*	*4.73*	*16.8*	*6*

Breakout: 10% *Improve: 39%* *Collapse: 25%*

Lackey has started 83 games, 39 at home, 44 on the road. At home his ERA is 3.53, with .82 home runs per nine innings pitched. Away from Disneyland, the ERA shoots up to 5.33, the HRs per nine to 1.39. This year, Lackey's home runs allowed declined from 31 to 22, but this was due to almost eliminating home round-trippers (five in 93 innings) while only fractionally reducing the road rate. Teams with real power abused him: In four starts against the Yankees and Red Sox, Lackey went 0–4 with a 7.59 ERA and eight home runs in 21.1 innings. He's a fly-ball pitcher, but not an extreme case, so an alternative is needed, perhaps in the form of an improved off-speed pitch. Not one home run allowed in September, despite three starts on the road, was a good omen.

ABEL MORENO **Bats: R** **Throws: R** Born: 15-Jun-1983 Age: 22

YEAR	TM	LG	AGE	G	GS	IP	H	BB	SO	HR	ERA	EQERA	EQH9	EQBB9	EQSO9	EQHR9	PERA	VORP	STF
2003	PRO	PIO	20	13	10	68.0	58	10	79	3	2.38	5.03	8.9	2.0	5.3	1.0	4.45	8.0	17
2003	CDR	MDW	20	3	3	16.7	13	3	15	0	1.62	3.52	8.2	1.8	5.3	0.0	2.93	4.5	21
2004	CDR	MDW	21	25	25	142.7	141	31	120	7	3.41	5.56	9.8	2.5	4.5	0.9	4.82	11.5	5
2005	*ANA*	*AL*	*22*	*12*	*11*	*67.0*	*76*	*22*	*40*	*10*	*5.01*	*4.96*	*10.2*	*2.6*	*4.8*	*1.3*	*5.05*	*6.8*	*-1*

Breakout: 8% *Improve: 39%* *Collapse: 21%*

Good control and a deceptive delivery are Moreno's ticket to the bigs—in 226 career innings he's walked 44 and struck out 214. As with most pitchers of this type, Double-A will be a better test of whether his location and change-up can fool the more advanced hitters. Wants to grow up to be Orlando Hernandez. Stay tuned.

RAMON ORTIZ **Bats: R** **Throws: R** Born: 23-May-1973 Age: 32

YEAR	TM	LG	AGE	G	GS	IP	H	BB	SO	HR	ERA	EQERA	EQH9	EQBB9	EQSO9	EQHR9	PERA	VORP	STF
2002	ANA	AL	29	32	32	217.3	188	68	162	40	3.77	3.84	8.8	2.7	6.7	1.6	4.94	47.5	7
2003	ANA	AL	30	32	32	180.0	209	63	94	28	5.20	5.66	10.1	3.0	4.6	1.3	5.50	0.7	-6
2004	ANA	AL	31	34	14	128.0	139	38	82	18	4.43	4.15	9.2	2.4	5.4	1.1	4.44	24.9	0
2005	*CIN*	*NL*	*32*	*27*	*15*	*104.7*	*110*	*35*	*68*	*17*	*4.77*	*5.09*	*9.6*	*2.7*	*5.2*	*1.3*	*5.10*	*7.0*	*-3*

Breakout: 18% *Improve: 51%* *Collapse: 18%*

His actual first name is "Diogenes," which was the club at which Sherlock Holmes brother Mycroft hung out, and also the name of a Greek philosopher from the 4th century BCE known as "The Cynic." Diogenes's writings do not survive, and neither, hardly, does Ortiz.. He got one last shot at the rotation and booted it badly (9.28 ERA in five April starts), swinging from then on. He was far more effective coming out of the bullpen where Scioscia could keep him away from lefties, any of whom could be counted on to undress him like he was Charlie Brown pitching to Lou Gehrig. The good news was that Ortiz's strikeouts per nine rebounded after 2003's scary drop, and he posted the best walk ratio of his career. Traded to the Reds, he goes from being the last man in Anaheim to #3 in Cincinnati. Einstein was right: Everything is relative.

TROY PERCIVAL **Bats: R** **Throws: R** Born: 09-Aug-1969 Age: 35

YEAR	TM	LG	AGE	G	GS	IP	H	BB	SO	HR	ERA	EQERA	EQH9	EQBB9	EQSO9	EQHR9	PERA	VORP	STF
2002	ANA	AL	32	58	0	56.3	38	25	68	5	1.92	2.00	6.8	3.8	10.7	0.8	3.50	25.4	26
2003	ANA	AL	33	52	0	49.3	33	23	48	7	3.47	3.86	6.9	4.2	8.9	1.2	3.86	11.4	10
2004	ANA	AL	34	52	0	49.7	43	19	33	7	2.90	3.21	8.1	3.2	5.9	1.1	3.97	15.7	-5
2005	*DET*	*AL*	*35*	*47*	*0*	*42.0*	*39*	*20*	*32*	*7*	*4.44*	*4.49*	*8.3*	*3.7*	*6.2*	*1.6*	*4.74*	*8.0*	*-9*

Breakout: 16% *Improve: 45%* *Collapse: 24%*

On the British TV show *The Office,* they are too genteel to say they're going to downsize or fire people. They have "redundancies." Troy Percival has been made redundant by Francisco Rodriguez. To put a finer point on it, try this taste test:

	IP	H	HR	BB	K	ERA
Pitcher A	49.2	43	7	19	33	2.90
Pitcher B	49.0	42	5	15	34	2.76

Pitcher A is Percival. Pitcher B is the much-maligned Ramon Ortiz when used as a reliever. Sure, Percival's appearances were in high-leverage situations and Ortiz's were in garbage time, but Percival also had four saves of less than an inning, faced 10 inherited runners all year, and he allowed half of them to score. Percival has never maintained the level required of an elite closer, but he can still do this job in a way that lets him maintain a veneer of effectiveness. At his age, the likelihood of injury mounts, his strikeout rate has been plummeting like a stone, and there are always cheaper guys who can do this. The Tigers thought otherwise.

FRANCISCO RODRIGUEZ **Bats: R** **Throws: R** Born: 07-Jan-1982 Age: 23

YEAR	TM	LG	AGE	G	GS	IP	H	BB	SO	HR	ERA	EQERA	EQH9	EQBB9	EQSO9	EQHR9	PERA	VORP	STF
2002	ARK	TXS	20	23	0	41.3	32	15	61	2	1.96	3.69	7.6	3.5	10.2	0.7	3.46	9.3	34
2002	SLC	PCL	20	27	0	42.0	30	13	59	1	2.57	2.90	6.7	2.9	9.8	0.2	2.45	14.1	43
2003	ANA	AL	21	59	0	86.0	50	35	95	12	3.03	3.01	6.2	3.7	10.2	1.2	3.12	28.3	31
2004	ANA	AL	22	69	0	84.0	51	33	123	2	1.82	2.19	5.5	3.2	12.6	0.2	1.97	37.6	57
2005	*ANA*	*AL*	*23*	*37*	*7*	*85.0*	*60*	*40*	*94*	*10*	*3.27*	*3.24*	*6.4*	*3.7*	*8.9*	*1.0*	*3.28*	*27.0*	*17*

Breakout: 18% *Improve: 40%* *Collapse: 40%*

When Percival missed most of June, K-Rod closed and pitched extremely well, allowing seven hits and three runs in 15.2 innings pitched. Overall, Rodriguez allowed just six of 36 inherited runners to score, or 17%. When Percival returned Scioscia moved him right back into the closer's role, but Rodriguez was doing the heavy lifting. With Rodriguez slated to close, the only danger to the Angels is that Rodriguez will be "saved" for save situations. In 2004 he had 22 appearances of an inning-plus, and should continue to be used that way if the Angels want to get optimal use out of him.

ERVIN SANTANA **Bats: R** **Throws: R** Born: 10-Jan-1983 Age: 22

YEAR	TM	LG	AGE	G	GS	IP	H	BB	SO	HR	ERA	EQERA	EQH9	EQBB9	EQSO9	EQHR9	PERA	VORP	STF
2002	CDR	MDW	19	27	27	147.0	133	48	146	10	4.16	6.41	10.2	3.8	5.7	1.6	6.20	-8.8	2
2003	RCU	CLF	20	20	20	124.7	98	36	130	9	2.53	4.35	8.6	3.3	6.3	1.3	4.43	14.8	29
2003	ARK	TXS	20	6	6	29.7	23	12	23	4	3.94	5.13	9.2	4.4	5.8	2.1	5.81	-0.6	8
2004	ARK	TXS	21	8	8	43.7	41	18	48	3	3.30	4.57	8.7	4.1	7.2	0.9	4.35	5.7	17
2005	*ANA*	*AL*	*22*	*20*	*13*	*83.3*	*81*	*38*	*65*	*13*	*4.94*	*4.89*	*8.9*	*3.6*	*6.3*	*1.4*	*4.78*	*8.9*	*2*

Breakout: 11% *Improve: 47%* *Collapse: 23%*

The erstwhile "other" Johan Santana had something of a lost year. He reported to spring training with shoulder stiffness, made eight starts with good results, then had to be shut down for the year when the pain wouldn't go away. There was no surgery, and no diagnosis. Call it the Heebie Jeebies and be aware that Santana is both a prospect with stuff as good as almost any other pitcher in the minors, and a total mystery. He could be in the majors this season if he can keep it together or he could be Case #1029 in Dr. Andrews's scheduler.

JOE SAUNDERS **Bats: L** **Throws: L** Born: 16-Jun-1981 Age: 24

YEAR	TM	LG	AGE	G	GS	IP	H	BB	SO	HR	ERA	EQERA	EQH9	EQBB9	EQSO9	EQHR9	PERA	VORP	STF
2002	PRO	PIO	21	8	8	32.3	40	11	21	1	3.62	6.82	9.9	3.7	2.8	0.9	5.12	1.7	-15
2002	CDR	MDW	21	5	5	28.7	16	9	27	2	1.88	4.01	8.4	3.6	5.5	1.8	5.11	1.3	6
2004	RCU	CLF	23	19	19	105.7	106	23	76	13	3.41	5.09	10.1	2.5	4.3	2.1	5.83	-2.5	-4
2004	ARK	TXS	23	8	8	39.0	51	14	25	5	5.77	6.21	11.2	3.6	4.1	1.7	6.21	-2.6	-4
2005	*ANA*	*AL*	*24*	*9*	*7*	*40.7*	*45*	*16*	*23*	*7*	*5.33*	*5.27*	*10.0*	*3.1*	*4.5*	*1.5*	*5.34*	*2.4*	*-9*

Breakout: 12% *Improve: 39%* *Collapse: 17%*

Anaheim's first pick in the 2002 draft, Saunders missed all of 2003 after tearing his rotator cuff and partially tearing his labrum. He opted for rehab instead of surgery and was back on the mound for instructional league action last fall. At Rancho this year his control was shockingly good for a pitcher coming off a major layoff, but he was subsequently pounded in eight starts at Double-A. He's a change of speeds guy when healthy, and those pitchers take a while to find themselves even when in top shape. A low-ceiling prospect.

AARON SELE **Bats: R** **Throws: R** Born: 25-Jun-1970 Age: 35

YEAR	TM	LG	AGE	G	GS	IP	H	BB	SO	HR	ERA	EQERA	EQH9	EQBB9	EQSO9	EQHR9	PERA	VORP	STF
2002	ANA	AL	32	26	26	160.0	190	49	82	21	4.89	4.89	10.6	2.6	4.5	1.1	5.88	14.3	-3
2003	ANA	AL	33	25	25	121.7	135	58	53	17	5.77	5.68	10.0	4.1	3.9	1.2	5.68	0.2	-14
2004	ANA	AL	34	28	24	132.0	163	51	51	16	5.05	5.29	10.2	3.1	3.3	1.0	5.08	7.4	-11
2005	*SEA*	*AL*	*35*	*22*	*15*	*92.7*	*111*	*36*	*44*	*14*	*5.54*	*5.78*	*11.1*	*3.0*	*3.8*	*1.3*	*5.89*	*1.8*	*-14*

Breakout: 12% *Improve: 43%* *Collapse: 29%*

In 1984, *The Elementals,* an indy comic book, was incredibly hot. The first four issues cost serious bread—if you could find them. Those same issues now go for a total of 10 bucks. If you bought and flipped them, you made a bundle. If you went long, you got burned. Sele is the Angels' Elementals collection. His strikeouts per nine since 1999: 8.17, 5.83, 4.77, 4.61, 3.47. Yup, should have traded him in for a run of X-Men.

STEVEN SHELL **Bats: R** **Throws: R** Born: 10-Mar-1983 Age: 22

YEAR	TM	LG	AGE	G	GS	IP	H	BB	SO	HR	ERA	EQERA	EQH9	EQBB9	EQSO9	EQHR9	PERA	VORP	STF
2002	CDR	MDW	19	22	21	121.0	119	26	86	12	3.72	6.17	11.2	2.5	4.1	2.3	6.92	-15.8	-10
2003	RCU	CLF	20	22	21	127.3	123	26	100	13	4.24	5.62	9.9	2.4	4.7	1.7	5.38	2.9	8
2004	RCU	CLF	21	28	28	165.3	151	40	190	19	3.59	5.02	9.5	2.8	6.9	1.9	5.32	4.7	9
2005	*ANA*	*AL*	*22*	*12*	*11*	*62.0*	*64*	*22*	*47*	*10*	*4.91*	*4.86*	*9.4*	*2.9*	*6.1*	*1.5*	*4.87*	*6.6*	*5*

Breakout: 7% *Improve: 45%* *Collapse: 14%*

Returned to Rancho after some elbow tenderness slowed him last year and justified his standing as one of the best prospects in the organization, finishing 23 runs above replacement, and more importantly striking out 10.3 per nine innings while maintaining the command for which he is best known. He also held up under his heaviest professional workload. The stage is set for a rapid rise, though at higher levels his good location could work against him in the form of high batting averages. He'll need to make those adjustments as he moves along, but this one has some serious upside.

SCOT SHIELDS **Bats: R** **Throws: R** Born: 22-Jul-1975 Age: 29

YEAR	TM	LG	AGE	G	GS	IP	H	BB	SO	HR	ERA	EQERA	EQH9	EQBB9	EQSO9	EQHR9	PERA	VORP	STF
2002	SLC	PCL	26	28	1	47.0	39	6	50	5	3.06	3.43	7.9	1.2	7.7	1.2	3.22	11.8	20
2002	ANA	AL	26	29	1	49.0	31	21	30	4	2.20	2.40	7.4	3.8	5.6	0.8	4.00	19.5	1
2003	ANA	AL	27	44	13	148.3	138	38	111	12	2.85	3.27	8.4	2.3	6.7	0.7	3.71	44.4	18
2004	ANA	AL	28	60	0	105.3	97	40	109	6	3.33	3.35	7.7	3.0	8.8	0.4	3.18	31.5	29
2005	*ANA*	*AL*	*29*	*40*	*10*	*95.7*	*93*	*35*	*83*	*9*	*3.64*	*3.61*	*8.9*	*2.9*	*7.0*	*0.8*	*3.96*	*25.0*	*9*

Breakout: 24% *Improve: 48%* *Collapse: 19%*

Not to be confused with *Steve* Shields, replacement-level reliever of the 1980s, because this guy can actually pitch. The modern Shields led relievers in innings pitched, making 31 appearances of two or more innings, suggesting he might be able to get through five innings on a good day. Barring an appearance of the dreaded 100-inning rebound effect for relievers—which may or may not exist—he should be okay. Note though that the majority of Shields's good work was in the first half, with August and September fairly poor, so proceed with caution.

JARROD WASHBURN Bats: L Throws: L Born: 13-Aug-1974 Age: 30

YEAR	TM	LG	AGE	G	GS	IP	H	BB	SO	HR	ERA	EQERA	EQH9	EQBB9	EQSO9	EQHR9	PERA	VORP	STF
2002	ANA	AL	27	32	32	206.0	183	59	139	19	3.15	3.19	8.7	2.5	6.0	0.8	4.35	61.9	15
2003	ANA	AL	28	32	32	207.3	205	54	118	34	4.43	4.38	9.3	2.3	5.2	1.4	4.79	34.1	1
2004	ANA	AL	29	25	25	149.3	159	40	86	20	4.64	4.50	9.2	2.2	4.9	1.0	4.25	22.4	5
2005	*ANA*	*AL*	*30*	*25*	*22*	*132.0*	*144*	*39*	*79*	*19*	*4.68*	*4.64*	*9.9*	*2.3*	*4.8*	*1.3*	*4.71*	*18.1*	*1*

Breakout: 14% *Improve: 54%* *Collapse: 14%*

There is a threshold of strikeouts below which a pitcher cannot consistently succeed, especially one of the flyball clan such as Washburn. When this kind of pitcher lets a batter hit the ball fair, there is a good chance it is going to leave the building. Add in additional qualifiers like, "against a right-hander" and "away from his friendly home park," and you have a near certainty of disaster. Doubles also become a problem, particularly when management plays an arthritic left fielder in center. Given the money he's in line to make, the Angels should hit eject.

JAKE WOODS Bats: L Throws: L Born: 03-Sep-1981 Age: 23

YEAR	TM	LG	AGE	G	GS	IP	H	BB	SO	HR	ERA	EQERA	EQH9	EQBB9	EQSO9	EQHR9	PERA	VORP	STF
2002	CDR	MDW	20	27	27	153.3	128	54	121	12	3.05	5.73	10.1	4.2	4.6	2.0	6.47	-13.1	-6
2003	RCU	CLF	21	28	28	171.3	178	54	109	9	3.99	5.67	9.7	3.6	3.7	1.0	5.11	8.7	-1
2004	ARK	TXS	22	14	14	90.0	86	19	60	5	2.70	3.60	8.8	2.1	4.3	0.7	3.60	18.9	17
2004	SLC	PCL	22	15	14	83.0	108	42	60	13	6.07	6.18	10.0	4.7	4.9	1.2	5.42	1.7	-2
2005	*ANA*	*AL*	*23*	*12*	*11*	*64.0*	*72*	*28*	*35*	*10*	*5.48*	*5.43*	*10.2*	*3.5*	*4.4*	*1.4*	*5.48*	*2.8*	*-7*

Breakout: 11% *Improve: 42%* *Collapse: 22%*

Strong control, middling stuff, sometimes hints he can start in the bigs. His results against lefties are so much better than against righties that his future is in the bullpen regardless; once his managers get a taste of him in the LOOGY role, they'll never let him out. Bombed as a starter at Triple-A, which will only speed the conversion process.

BOB ZIMMERMANN Bats: R Throws: R Born: 17-Nov-1981 Age: 23

YEAR	TM	LG	AGE	G	GS	IP	H	BB	SO	HR	ERA	EQERA	EQH9	EQBB9	EQSO9	EQHR9	PERA	VORP	STF
2003	PRO	PIO	21	11	10	48.0	57	8	37	4	4.50	6.95	11.1	2.2	3.6	2.0	6.55	-4.8	-16
2004	CDR	MDW	22	53	0	67.7	48	21	82	3	2.26	4.13	8.3	3.7	6.6	0.9	4.28	8.9	4
2005	*ANA*	*AL*	*23*	*23*	*3*	*42.0*	*44*	*17*	*30*	*6*	*4.80*	*4.76*	*9.4*	*3.1*	*5.8*	*1.3*	*4.84*	*5.4*	*-6*

Breakout: 14% *Improve: 43%* *Collapse: 14%*

John Lennon said he didn't believe in Zimmermann, which may or may not have been a reference to minor league closers. When you've stolen Bob Dylan's name, you're going to have to answer that kind of question. Moved to the bullpen, the Tambourine Man showed hard stuff, striking out 11 guys per nine innings, with a .192 batting average against. He'll be moving up, 'cause he who's not busy being born is busy dying.

Baltimore Orioles

Along with their AL East counterparts the Blue Jays and Devil Rays, the Orioles confront two big problems in trying to put together a contending team. These problems have nothing to do with whom they sign and who gets hurt: They're the megalithic and megadollar teams put together in New York and Boston.

With the baseball playoff system structured the way it is, it an absolutely essential that you be able to beat all but perhaps one other team in your division, or else you stay home at season's end. Making yourself better than every team in the AL Central? As goals go, in this division that's worthless. You have to be either the division champion or the best second-place team in the league; a third-place team that is better than the other division champions gets to complain about the system, but that's about it.

The simple facts of the matter are that the Red Sox have decided to go toe-to-toe with the Yankees. Maybe not matching them dollar for dollar, but coming close enough to leave everybody else in the American League far behind on the salary chart. Now, we've argued in the past that money isn't everything, and we're not going to change our tune. It isn't everything, but used correctly it is an advantage. In Texas hold'em terms, we might say that the Yankees' advantage is roughly equivalent to having a pair of aces in the hole. The Red Sox are holding a suited king-queen. Both of them are going to be going in and bidding hard. The Orioles are starting with something like a 5-7 off-suit.

Of course, baseball teams don't have players randomly dealt to them; continuing the poker analogy, you get to buy your starting hand. The more you're willing to spend up front, the better your initial odds are. It helps a great deal if you have some knowledge about which cards will actually give you the best chances. The Yankees and Red Sox have demonstrated some competence in that respect, certainly more than the Orioles under previous management could claim. So the Orioles, along with the other also-rans of the AL East, have to make a decision. If they stay within their established spending limits, they are going to go into each season hoping for a scenario that would involve an unusually large number of injuries on either of the two Big Boys' rosters, in combination with several players on your team suddenly becoming a lot better than you thought.

This brings us back to an old baseball aphorism, attributed to Connie Mack: There's nothing more expensive than a second-place team. In the age of the Wild Card the statement has lost only a little of its validity. Spending the money to contend, calling, and raising your opponent when the odds are heavily against you, only to miss out on the playoff pot, costs more than simply folding and giving up early on. It's much easier on everybody, including your accountants, to effectively cede the division, tend to your own little garden, and just hope something good happens on its own.

ORIOLES PROSPECTUS

2004 record: 78–84; Third place, AL East

Pythagenport record: 82–80

Runs scored per game: 5.20 (6th in AL)

Runs allowed per game: 5.12 (9th in AL)

Team EqA: .262 (6th in AL)

2004 Batters Age: 30.9 (3rd oldest in AL)

2004 Pitchers Age: 27.6 (2nd youngest in AL)

Ballpark: Oriole Park; Slight hitter's park; Park Factor of 1.010

2004: The Birds rode an improved offense and a strong second half to their best finish in five years.

2005: The team's old but solid offense might be augmented by some of its young pitching on their Magical Quest for .500.

Compounding the Orioles' financial future is the Expos' move to Washington, D.C. The O's claim to get about 35% of their total revenue from D.C. and northern Virginia, and owner/lawyer Peter Angelos let it be known that he would sue to block the move if he had to. MLB partially placated him by essentially forcing the future owners of the Washington club to fork over all of their television revenue to Angelos, which was what Angelos considered reasonable compensation for the impending (and likely) loss of most of the Virginia market. That is a prime financial plum, but it may not be enough to make a difference in terms of contending with the division's Big Two.

A decade ago, the Orioles were one of the highest-spending teams in the game, but their targeting was poor. A year ago, they attempted to climb back towards the top by signing big-name free agents Miguel Tejada and Javy Lopez, and chasing, but losing, Vladimir Guerrero and Ivan Rodriguez. Initially this past off-season, the Orioles were talking about chasing big-name pitchers, big-name first basemen, and big-name outfielders,but when December rolled around, they found that they had badly misread the market. It was going to take more money than they were willing to offer to sign anyone, and more players than they were willing to give up to trade for anyone. As a result, nothing got done.

Oakland and Minnesota have demonstrated that a team doesn't have to spend freely to remain competitive—but both the A's and Twins are blessed with the good fortune not to be in the same division as the Yankees and Red Sox. It would be entirely reasonable for a team in the AL East not to try and match those teams financially, but to run a leaner organization that will be in position to capitalize on any stumbles the big teams make. You can argue, or at least hope, that both New York and Boston will have problems in the near future with age. Getting good players has typically meant committing to too many years on contracts, and they could easily be stuck someday with ordinary players at star prices.

To be in position to take advantage of such vulnerabilities, you have to spend some money for a few players, either to pick up some good free agents or to keep the good players you develop yourself. A team with a budget like the Expos the last few years has purchased the 2-7 hand: They have very little chance of winning a competitive division, and need a whole lot of luck. The emphasis here has to be on good free agents: Teams in this position really cannot afford the Jose Encarnacions of the world. The Orioles have Tejada and Lopez, both good starts.

At the heart of any strategy to compete on the cheap, though, is through the draft—getting cheap top-level talent is to pick it up *before* it becomes top-level talent—or good foreign scouting. It also means pumping resources into the minor league system, so that you have coaches who are good enough to ensure, as best as you can, that the talented players fulfill their potential. The A's have succeeded because their drafts produced Mark Mulder, Tim Hudson, Barry Zito, and Eric Chavez, with Miguel Tejada signed and similarly developed. During that same time, the Orioles produced Brian Roberts and Larry Bigbie, decent ballplayers both, but not the foundation of a championship team.

The Orioles appear to have done better with player development in recent years. Nick Markakis and Val Majewski both look like they will be contributing players—and perhaps even All-Stars. Still, "better" is a relative term: The Orioles front office preceding the Jim Beattie and Mike Flanagan power sharing arrangement had been so bad at player selection and development that improvement was virtually inevitable.

Unfortunately, their farm system broke down completely in 2004. The conflicts included a management team that was married to a particular psychological model of players, an owner who perhaps read a little too much of *Moneyball* with too little understanding, and a scouting staff stuck somewhere in between. The psych model the Orioles use is run for them by a guy named Dave Ritterpusch, brought in by co-GM Mike Flanagan a couple of years ago, who carries the title of Director of Baseball Information Systems.

Every team uses psychological models and tests to some extent, to decide whether players have the requisite desire and mental toughness to succeed in the majors.

The question here is how much weight the Orioles apparently give to these tests. Some ex-staffers have complained that the team's psychological model was given more say over whom to draft, or even to promote, than any given player's performance. We have a lot of experience in modeling baseball performance here at BP, and one of the biggest traps to fall into is to believe so strongly in a particular model that you start ignoring evidence to the contrary, because it doesn't "fit." Even the best models—statistical, psychological, or any other—are not 100% reliable, and you have to be flexible enough to be able to step away from a bad tool if circumstances merit.

The Orioles' 2004 draft has thus far proven to be a disaster. With the eighth overall pick, then-scouting director Tony DeMacio had apparently settled on Chris Nelson, a high-school shortstop from Georgia, as the player the team wanted. On the day of the draft, DeMacio was given an order from on high: Choose a high-school pitcher, one who would sign for slot money. Major league baseball had deemed $2.2 million as the "appropriate" amount for the eighth pick overall, and DeMacio was told they'd prefer a pick for less than that. DeMacio wound up choosing Wade Townsend, a college junior at Rice, without knowing what Townsend's salary demands would be. The Orioles made an initial offer of $1.8 million. Townsend was insulted and went back to school, and so may be lost to the Orioles. Nelson was drafted by the Rockies, who were right behind the Orioles with the ninth pick. He signed for slot money, hit .347 in his professional debut, and was named the top prospect in the Pioneer League.

In the aftermath, DeMacio and Doc Rodgers, the farm director, were tossed overboard. A number of scouts either jumped ship or were forced to walk the plank. After the purges, it'll take time to rebuild the scouting and player development staff. In the meantime, this is not a team currently in any position to build itself up through the draft and the minor leagues.

At the big league level, the Orioles look like they will enter 2005 with virtually the same team that finished fourth in 2004. In the infield, that's not such a bad thing. Lopez, Tejada, and Melvin Mora give the Orioles a strong offensive base at premium positions: Mora and Tejada led the AL in VORP at third and short last year, while Lopez was second behind the plate. Roberts made a convincing case that he was capable of playing second for an entire season, and although he's not an All-Star, he should mature into an above-average player. If he should falter, second base is the position where the Orioles have the most depth, as either outfielder-to-be Jerry Hairston could move back, or Mike Fontenot, one of their few non-pitcher prospects, could be called up. Only at first base, normally the easiest position to find a capable hitter, do the Orioles look weak, seemingly content to live with the twilight of Rafael Palmeiro's career.

The outfield is another story. The Orioles were below average at all three outfield positions in 2004, badly so in center and right. Injuries devastated the outfield a year ago, making awful players of Jay Gibbons and Luis Matos long before they landed on the DL. The patrons of Oriole Park were thus treated to such spectacles as seeing two second basemen in the outfield at the same time, or Karim Garcia in center field, or Chad Mottola, period. Bigbie in left field is the only reasonably certain position set for 2005. Center field looks like it will probably be Jerry Hairston learning on the job, with Matos a decided underdog to get his job back, especially since the status of his injured leg is still uncertain. Gibbons may move to first (pushing Palmeiro to DH), but that will only happen if the Orioles make a late free-agent signing or trade. The outfield will be topped off by B. J. Surhoff, David Newhan, and maybe rookie Val Majewski. All figure to get occasional playing time as injury-fillers.

The pitching staff was the Orioles' biggest problem in 2004, the worst symptom being the league-leading 687 walks issued by their staff. There was plenty of blame to go around. They led the leagues in walks by starters, walks by relievers, walks in the first half under ex-pitching coach Mark Wiley, and in walks in the second half under new pitching coach Ray Miller. Day games, night games, home games, away games, with runners on, bases empty, on a boat, with a goat, in a train, on a plane . . . the Orioles led the league. It is an organizational thing; Triple-A Ottawa and high-A Frederick were worst in their leagues, too, while Double-A Bowie was next to worst. All six of their farm teams were below league average in run prevention.

Wiley was fired primarily because of the walks, and because Oriole starters had a 5.81 ERA. On Miller's watch, the starters' ERA was a much-improved 4.50, but how much did he really have to do with it? Yes, de facto ace Sidney Ponson and young lefty Matt Riley pitched much better during Miller's tenure, but Eric Bedard and especially Daniel Cabrera did a lot worse. Most of the ERA reduction came from having the injured Kurt Ainsworth (9.68 ERA) and Eric DuBose (6.39) entirely on Wiley's side of the ledger, while Miller got surprisingly good fill-in efforts from Dave Borkowski (4.63) and Bruce Chen (3.22).

Nine different pitchers got at least seven starts for the Orioles last year, and they'll all be back in the spring fighting for five spots. Virtually all of them have recently flashed the talent to be the kind of starter who can put up a 3-something ERA in a season. Getting five of them to beat expectations, without getting hurt, would be a huge boost.

Throw in career years from a few hitters and lots of mishaps in New York and Boston, and the Orioles, instead of foldidng early, may draw the flush they need to catch the Yankees or Red Sox. Don't bet on it. In the meanwhile, they can hopefully rebuild the farm system, and set themselves up for a serious challenge someday.

HITTERS

LARRY BIGBIE LF **Bats: L** **Throws: L** Born: 04-Nov-1977 Age: 27

YEAR	TM	LG	AGE	AB	H	2B	3B	HR	BB	SO	SB	CS	AVG	OBP	SLG	MLVR	EQBA	EQOBP	EQSLG	EQMLVR	VORP	DEFENSE			
2002	ROC	INT	24	348	105	23	2	2	35	79	7	3	.302	.363	.397	.069	.280	.344	.376	-.075	-2.1	30-LF	-2	24-CF	0
2003	OTT	INT	25	117	41	14	4	3	14	31	0	0	.350	.421	.615	.503	.333	.405	.590	.385	15.9	20-LF	0		
2003	BAL	AL	25	287	87	15	1	9	29	60	7	1	.303	.365	.456	.141	.306	.374	.465	.128	19.7	73-LF	4		
2004	BAL	AL	26	478	134	23	1	15	45	113	8	3	.280	.341	.427	-.010	.281	.348	.431	.011	14.8	99-LF	3	29-CF	0
2005	*BAL*	*AL*	*27*	*429*	*118*	*25*	*2*	*13*	*43*	*103*	*7*	*3*	*.274*	*.340*	*.433*	*.003*	*.276*	*.345*	*.441*	*.014*	*12.8*	*113-LF*	*1*		

Breakout: 4% *Improve: 29%* *Collapse: 32%*

Bigbie returned to form, following up an over-his-head 2003 season with a more typical performance. He's a problem player: Good enough that you can't simply push him aside, but not so good that he's going to lead you to a championship. That's especially true if, as in 2004, he turns out to be your best outfielder.

JACK CUST — DH — Bats: L — Throws: R — Born: 16-Jan-1979 — Age: 26

YEAR	TM	LG	AGE	AB	H	2B	3B	HR	BB	SO	SB	CS	AVG	OBP	SLG	MLVR	EQBA	EQOBP	EQSLG	EQMLVR	VORP	DEFENSE
2002	CSP	PCL	23	359	95	24	0	23	83	121	6	3	.265	.407	.524	.175	.210	.347	.415	-.066	-1.3	49-LF -2 40-RF -4
2002	COL	NL	23	65	11	2	0	1	12	32	0	1	.169	.295	.246	-.356	.156	.268	.203	-.526	-5.1	13-LF 0
2003	OTT	INT	24	333	95	18	1	9	80	94	5	2	.285	.422	.426	.200	.260	.398	.403	.049	11.8	74-LF -2
2003	BAL	AL	24	73	19	7	0	4	10	25	0	0	.260	.357	.521	.162	.278	.358	.528	.161	6.2	
2004	OTT	INT	25	344	81	15	1	17	65	127	4	0	.235	.358	.433	.009	.212	.334	.385	-.128	-8.3	31-LF -3
2005	*OAK*	*AL*	*26*	*161*	*38*	*7*	*1*	*6*	*28*	*57*	*1*	*1*	*.235*	*.351*	*.407*	*-.040*	*.236*	*.356*	*.414*	*-.030*	*3.4*	*49-DH 4*

Breakout: 20% *Improve: 50%* *Collapse: 35%*

It was perhaps inevitable that Cust would end up in Oakland, where power and patience are cherished skills. In Baltimore, they don't seem to understand the value of walks, either drawing them and preventing them. The Orioles' top two farm teams were in the bottom three in drawing walks (as hitters), and simultaneously in the bottom three in allowing walks as pitchers. They didn't know what to do with Cust, and, frankly, they messed him up to the point where he didn't know what to do with himself, either. Sometimes you just gotta say "What the fungo," and let the guy hit his way. The A's will let him do just that.

JEFF FIORENTINO — OF — Bats: L — Throws: R — Born: 14-Apr-1983 — Age: 22

YEAR	TM	LG	AGE	AB	H	2B	3B	HR	BB	SO	SB	CS	AVG	OBP	SLG	MLVR	EQBA	EQOBP	EQSLG	EQMLVR	VORP	DEFENSE
2004	ABE	NYP	21	46	16	7	1	2	9	4	3	1	.348	.474	.674	.692	.286	.384	.571	.271	9.8	13-RF -1
2004	DEL	SAL	21	179	53	15	2	10	20	50	2	2	.296	.374	.570	.346	.250	.314	.461	-.035	6.4	40-CF -4
2005	*BAL*	*AL*	*22*	*329*	*86*	*21*	*2*	*13*	*33*	*87*	*3*	*2*	*.260*	*.339*	*.453*	*.017*	*.262*	*.343*	*.462*	*.028*	*17.8*	*90-CF -5*

Breakout: 23% *Improve: 48%* *Collapse: 27%*

After the debacle that cost them Wade Townsend, third-rounder Jeff Fiorentino became the flagship of the Orioles' 2004 draft class. A college catcher, the brass doesn't think he's got the arm to play behind the plate in the majors; he's athletic enough to play the outfield, so there you go. At any position, he can rake, and has the "smooth" label that is used as frequently to describe left-handed hitters as it is in beer commercials.

MIKE FONTENOT — 2B — Bats: L — Throws: R — Born: 09-Jun-1980 — Age: 25

YEAR	TM	LG	AGE	AB	H	2B	3B	HR	BB	SO	SB	CS	AVG	OBP	SLG	MLVR	EQBA	EQOBP	EQSLG	EQMLVR	VORP	DEFENSE
2002	FRD	CRL	22	481	127	16	4	8	42	117	13	9	.264	.333	.364	.004	.230	.287	.334	-.277	-15.4	112-2B -7
2003	BOW	EAS	23	449	146	24	5	12	50	89	16	5	.325	.399	.481	.303	.304	.370	.466	.120	42.9	112-2B 9
2004	OTT	INT	24	524	146	30	10	8	48	111	14	7	.279	.346	.420	.002	.252	.320	.380	-.135	6.4	135-2B -16
2005	*BAL*	*AL*	*25*	*173*	*44*	*9*	*1*	*4*	*14*	*40*	*4*	*2*	*.255*	*.322*	*.382*	*-.109*	*.257*	*.326*	*.389*	*-.101*	*7.2*	*49-2B -5*

Breakout: 15% *Improve: 34%* *Collapse: 42%*

Fontenot once again got off to a slow start, then turned it on after the All-Star break. This year, we don't know if another trip to the optometrist had anything to do with it. It could be that he's a warm-weather guy, or maybe he needs some time to get adjusted to a new league. Once again, his production after he got going equaled anything Roberts or Hairston did, so wondering why is of more than academic interest. Unfortunately, no one, probably not even Fontenot himself, truly knows the answer. He needs a good full season to force his way into the big league mix.

KARIM GARCIA — RF — Bats: L — Throws: L — Born: 29-Oct-1975 — Age: 29

YEAR	TM	LG	AGE	AB	H	2B	3B	HR	BB	SO	SB	CS	AVG	OBP	SLG	MLVR	EQBA	EQOBP	EQSLG	EQMLVR	VORP	DEFENSE
2002	COH	INT	26	288	78	16	3	12	20	48	1	5	.271	.316	.472	.078	.248	.298	.444	-.089	5.0	27-CF -2 17-LF -2
2002	CLE	AL	26	197	59	8	0	16	6	40	0	3	.299	.317	.584	.223	.311	.324	.602	.252	14.0	41-RF -2
2003	CLE	AL	27	93	18	1	0	5	5	20	0	0	.194	.238	.366	-.280	.196	.234	.359	-.367	-4.0	15-RF -2
2003	NYY	AL	27	151	46	5	0	6	9	32	0	2	.305	.342	.457	.109	..313	.343	.467	.084	7.0	30-RF 0 13-LF 0
2004	NYM	NL	28	192	45	7	2	7	10	35	3	0	.234	.272	.401	-.141	.234	.272	.406	-.202	0.1	43-RF -2
2004	BAL	AL	28	66	14	0	0	3	4	15	0	0	.212	.247	.348	-.337	.231	.231	.323	-.403	-2.9	
2005	*BAL*	*AL*	*29*	*252*	*64*	*12*	*1*	*10*	*16*	*53*	*2*	*1*	*.256*	*.300*	*.431*	*-.081*	*.258*	*.304*	*.439*	*-.073*	*5.4*	*67-RF -3*

Breakout: 28% *Improve: 46%* *Collapse: 27%*

In his first game after the Mike DeJean trade made him an Oriole, he hit two home runs and drove in five runs. For the rest of the month he was with the O's, he hit .197/.246/.246, a line that would embarrass Rey Ordonez. He was chased out of New York, chased out of Baltimore, and eventually chased out of the States, signing a deal to play for Orix in Japan in 2005.

JAY GIBBONS — RF/1B — Bats: L — Throws: L — Born: 02-Mar-1977 — Age: 28

YEAR	TM	LG	AGE	AB	H	2B	3B	HR	BB	SO	SB	CS	AVG	OBP	SLG	MLVR	EQBA	EQOBP	EQSLG	EQMLVR	VORP	DEFENSE	
2002	BAL	AL	25	490	121	29	1	28	45	66	1	3	.247	.311	.482	.037	.256	.324	.502	.046	17.0	87-RF 6	24-1B -2
2003	BAL	AL	26	625	173	39	2	23	49	89	0	1	.277	.330	.456	.063	.279	.338	.465	.040	26.7	144-RF -6	11-1B 0
2004	BAL	AL	27	346	85	14	1	10	29	64	1	1	.246	.303	.379	-.172	.244	.308	.379	-.165	-1.7	61-RF 0	13-1B 1
2005	*BAL*	*AL*	*28*	*371*	*96*	*20*	*1*	*14*	*34*	*63*	*0*	*1*	*.259*	*.321*	*.435*	*-.038*	*.261*	*.325*	*.443*	*-.028*	*10.2*	*98-RF -3*	

Breakout: 28% *Improve: 53%* *Collapse: 20%*

Gibbons wrecked his season in April when he hurt his back lifting weights. He tried to play through recurring back spasms for the next month, until they worsened to the point that he couldn't move. At some point, while compensating for the back, he managed to tear his hip flexor, and this apparently went unnoticed until he had come back from the DL and played extremely poorly for two weeks. There certainly seem to have been opportunities for timely intervention here. The hip flexor attaches directly to the spine at one end, and because it's almost impossible to move without using this muscle, strains here can be every bit as difficult (and lingering, and recurring) as back strains. Big and fragile isn't a great combination; he should come back from last year, but as a player in his prime with an older player's skills set, he's not a certain quantity.

GERONIMO GIL — C — Bats: R — Throws: R — Born: 07-Aug-1975 — Age: 29

YEAR	TM	LG	AGE	AB	H	2B	3B	HR	BB	SO	SB	CS	AVG	OBP	SLG	MLVR	EQBA	EQOBP	EQSLG	EQMLVR	VORP	DEFENSE
2002	BAL	AL	26	422	98	19	0	12	21	88	2	2	.232	.270	.363	-.214	.240	.281	.374	-.226	0.4	119-C 6
2003	BAL	AL	27	169	40	4	0	3	12	34	0	0	.237	.299	.314	-.229	.244	.303	.310	-.271	-1.1	52-C -3
2003	OTT	INT	27	134	47	10	0	1	7	28	0	3	.351	.386	.448	.228	.313	.346	.403	-.006	6.5	29-C 3
2004	OTT	INT	28	375	97	24	0	6	32	67	2	1	.259	.327	.371	-.113	.226	.292	.320	-.289	-13.0	95-C -7
2004	BAL	AL	28	32	9	2	0	0	3	5	0	0	.281	.343	.344	-.118	.323	.311	.387	-.085	0.8	
2005	*BAL*	*AL*	*29*	*169*	*42*	*8*	*0*	*3*	*11*	*33*	*1*	*1*	*.246*	*.299*	*.358*	*-.187*	*.248*	*.303*	*.365*	*-.180*	*1.6*	*47-C -2*

Breakout: 21% *Improve: 44%* *Collapse: 26%*

Gil had already lost his job before Javy Lopez arrived, but that signing put an end to whatever thoughts he might have had about getting it back. He can still dream about returning to Baltimore as Lopez's backup, since the closest thing to an in-house option they have is Eli Whiteside, who's never played above Double-A. But Gil has to face the facts: When a team is willing to use Keith Osik and Ken Huckaby instead of you, you inspire less confidence than an Ashlee Simpson sound check.

JERRY HAIRSTON — 2B/CF — Bats: R — Throws: R — Born: 29-May-1976 — Age: 29

YEAR	TM	LG	AGE	AB	H	2B	3B	HR	BB	SO	SB	CS	AVG	OBP	SLG	MLVR	EQBA	EQOBP	EQSLG	EQMLVR	VORP	DEFENSE	
2002	BAL	AL	26	426	114	25	3	5	34	55	21	6	.268	.329	.376	-.068	.278	.342	.393	-.056	19.8	116-2B -2	
2003	BAL	AL	27	218	59	12	2	2	23	25	14	5	.271	.353	.372	-.048	.276	.363	.382	-.033	10.1	47-2B 1	
2004	BAL	AL	28	287	87	19	1	2	29	29	13	8	.303	.378	.397	.029	.307	.383	.406	.061	13.8	27-RF 0	14-CF 0
2005	*BAL*	*AL*	*29*	*298*	*82*	*16*	*2*	*4*	*29*	*33*	*12*	*5*	*.274*	*.348*	*.376*	*-.058*	*.276*	*.352*	*.383*	*-.048*	*12.8*	*83-2B -6*	

Breakout: 9% *Improve: 28%* *Collapse: 39%*

Hairston has broken bones in his foot, ankle, and hand in the past two seasons. Between the broken finger in the spring and the broken ankle in August that ended his season, Hairston lost his second-base job to Brian Roberts and was thrown into the chaotic Oriole outfield mix. He actually did a credible job playing the outfield, and seems destined to return there in 2005. The real test will be whether he can handle center field on an extended basis, as his bat is acceptable for a center fielder.

TRIPPER JOHNSON — 3B — Bats: R — Throws: R — Born: 28-Apr-1982 — Age: 23

YEAR	TM	LG	AGE	AB	H	2B	3B	HR	BB	SO	SB	CS	AVG	OBP	SLG	MLVR	EQBA	EQOBP	EQSLG	EQMLVR	VORP	DEFENSE
2002	DEL	SAL	20	493	128	32	6	11	62	88	19	6	.260	.349	.416	.143	.228	.295	.371	-.212	-5.0	131-3B 10
2003	FRD	CRL	21	417	114	25	3	5	46	92	7	8	.273	.359	.384	.073	.248	.319	.371	-.152	4.0	116-3B 0
2004	FRD	CRL	22	465	125	19	2	21	51	93	14	5	.269	.343	.454	.103	.230	.295	.399	-.171	1.3	120-3B -14
2005	*BAL*	*AL*	*23*	*285*	*71*	*15*	*1*	*9*	*25*	*67*	*5*	*2*	*.248*	*.318*	*.405*	*-.093*	*.250*	*.321*	*.412*	*-.084*	*5.1*	*77-3B -6*

Breakout: 30% *Improve: 52%* *Collapse: 17%*

Two years at Frederick, and not much to show for it. That's a disappointment since, by expectation, Johnson should be a top performer: He's a former first-round pick, a great all-around athlete, and he works hard. His power numbers are

(continued next page)

Tripper Johnson *(continued)*

fine, with a .185 isolated slugging average (SLG-AVG) in 2004. The problem is that he doesn't do enough hitting for average, and his strike-zone judgment is on the poor side. PECOTA thinks he's young enough and skilled enough to improve.

JOSE LEON 3B/1B Bats: R Throws: R Born: 08-Dec-1976 Age: 28

YEAR	TM	LG	AGE	AB	H	2B	3B	HR	BB	SO	SB	CS	AVG	OBP	SLG	MLVR	EQBA	EQOBP	EQSLG	EQMLVR	VORP	DEFENSE
2002	ROC	INT	25	312	87	16	1	8	18	54	0	0	.279	.319	.413	.003	.255	.298	.390	-.160	1.8	79-3B 10
2002	BAL	AL	25	89	22	2	0	3	3	20	1	0	.247	.280	.371	-.164	.270	.284	.393	-.171	-0.1	15-1B -1
2003	OTT	INT	26	309	82	19	2	4	15	47	1	1	.265	.305	.379	-.064	.248	.293	.365	-.210	-2.7	65-3B 0
2003	BAL	AL	26	54	13	1	0	0	3	18	0	0	.241	.305	.259	-.291	.278	.286	.296	-.305	-1.6	
2004	OTT	INT	27	283	91	21	1	17	24	68	1	1	.322	.382	.583	.322	.287	.350	.520	.146	27.8	74-3B 2
2004	BAL	AL	27	66	12	2	0	2	2	19	0	0	.182	.203	.303	-.499	.185	.202	.262	-.573	-5.3	10-1B 1
2005	*BAL*	*AL*	*28*	*179*	*43*	*9*	*1*	*6*	*12*	*42*	*0*	*1*	*.241*	*.296*	*.394*	*-.148*	*.243*	*.300*	*.401*	*-.141*	*0.8*	*50-3B -2*

Breakout: 14% *Improve: 26%* *Collapse: 49%*

Leon has little chance of making a significant contribution to a major league team. He can play third base; he can play first base; he has reasonable power. That's the extent of his résumé, as his game is otherwise littered with weaknesses. Removed from the Orioles' 40-man roster, he'll seek a team with a Triple-A vacancy and an injury-prone third baseman.

LUIS LOPEZ INF Bats: B Throws: R Born: 04-Sep-1970 Age: 34

YEAR	TM	LG	AGE	AB	H	2B	3B	HR	BB	SO	SB	CS	AVG	OBP	SLG	MLVR	EQBA	EQOBP	EQSLG	EQMLVR	VORP	DEFENSE
2002	BAL	AL	31	109	23	6	0	2	3	20	1	0	.211	.232	.321	-.340	.222	.239	.315	-.404	-3.1	13-SS 0
2003	CSP	PCL	32	140	29	10	0	3	9	29	0	1	.207	.265	.343	-.305	.152	.204	.254	-.594	-17.4	25-2B -4
2003	OTT	INT	32	186	49	6	0	5	6	24	1	1	.263	.299	.376	-.079	.237	.269	.344	-.294	-6.3	32-2B 1 15-SS 1
2004	BAL	AL	33	88	16	5	0	1	3	20	0	0	.182	.211	.273	-.538	.184	.208	.253	-.574	-7.7	
2005	*BAL*	*AL*	*34*	*102*	*23*	*5*	*0*	*2*	*5*	*20*	*0*	*0*	*.223*	*.271*	*.340*	*-.275*	*.225*	*.275*	*.347*	*-.271*	*-2.4*	*31-2B -3*

Breakout: 54% *Improve: 64%* *Collapse: 28%*

It stands to reason that if a team has a 25-man roster, it should get 25 men to fill those spots. The Orioles used one of those spots on Luis Lopez for the entire season, which goes a long way toward undermining all of the work that Keith Woolner, Bill James, and others have done on the concept of "replacement level." At least they won't do it again, releasing him and replacing him with the comparatively Bonds-like Chris Gomez.

JAVY LOPEZ C Bats: R Throws: R Born: 05-Nov-1970 Age: 34

YEAR	TM	LG	AGE	AB	H	2B	3B	HR	BB	SO	SB	CS	AVG	OBP	SLG	MLVR	EQBA	EQOBP	EQSLG	EQMLVR	VORP	DEFENSE
2002	ATL	NL	31	347	81	15	0	11	26	63	0	1	.233	.299	.372	-.112	.238	.294	.384	-.189	6.8	94-C 7
2003	ATL	NL	32	457	150	29	3	43	33	90	0	1	.328	.378	.687	.520	.325	.375	.690	.476	78.0	114-C 2
2004	BAL	AL	33	579	183	33	3	23	47	97	0	0	.316	.370	.503	.178	.319	.376	.511	.210	56.3	122-C -3
2005	*BAL*	*AL*	*34*	*459*	*128*	*24*	*1*	*23*	*37*	*84*	*0*	*0*	*.278*	*.337*	*.485*	*.071*	*.281*	*.341*	*.494*	*.083*	*31.9*	*119-C -4*

Breakout: 1% *Improve: 18%* *Collapse: 39%*

The O's got about as much as they could reasonably expect for their $22.5 million, as Lopez retained much of the value from his 2003 breakout. That was a pleasant surprise, given how likely he was to suffer a natural regression to historical norms. He set career highs for plate appearances and games caught, though, and he made no secret of his unhappiness with playing that frequently, annoying some in the organization. If it hurt him down the stretch, it didn't show up in the box scores. The team has talked about getting him more time at DH or first base, but so far it's been just talk.

ROBERT MACHADO C Bats: R Throws: R Born: 03-Jun-1973 Age: 32

YEAR	TM	LG	AGE	AB	H	2B	3B	HR	BB	SO	SB	CS	AVG	OBP	SLG	MLVR	EQBA	EQOBP	EQSLG	EQMLVR	VORP	DEFENSE
2002	CHC	NL	29	58	16	4	0	1	5	11	0	0	.276	.333	.397	.003	.288	.319	.390	-.095	2.9	15-C 7
2002	MIL	NL	29	153	39	10	1	2	12	30	0	0	.255	.310	.373	-.085	.260	.313	.383	-.138	4.4	43-C 0
2003	OTT	INT	30	221	74	17	0	8	17	36	0	0	.335	.390	.520	.317	.305	.358	.491	.136	20.3	40-C 13
2003	BAL	AL	30	49	13	1	0	1	6	12	0	0	.265	.345	.347	-.083	.271	.333	.333	-.163	1.6	14-C 2
2004	OTT	INT	31	126	40	12	0	3	10	20	0	1	.317	.368	.484	.159	.268	.312	.407	-.100	2.8	27-C 6
2004	BAL	AL	31	73	11	3	0	1	4	18	0	0	.151	.195	.233	-.621	.153	.195	.222	-.656	-7.0	21-C 7
2005	*TEX*	*AL*	*32*	*141*	*36*	*8*	*0*	*4*	*11*	*28*	*0*	*0*	*.253*	*.308*	*.397*	*-.115*	*.243*	*.301*	*.383*	*-.163*	*0.9*	*40-C 0*

Breakout: 13% *Improve: 34%* *Collapse: 39%*

He had his chance to be the team's primary backup to Javy Lopez, and he blew it—no matter how good your defense is, you still have to hit a little bit. After the season, Machado signed with Texas, saying he would never sign with the Orioles again; apparently he felt his honor was impugned because the team played Gil ahead of him in September. It's left as a reader exercise to determine what sort of treatment he'd expect if he were to hit .351 instead of .151.

VAL MAJEWSKI — **OF** — **Bats: L** — **Throws: L** — Born: 19-Jun-1981 — Age: 24

YEAR	TM	LG	AGE	AB	H	2B	3B	HR	BB	SO	SB	CS	AVG	OBP	SLG	MLVR	EQBA	EQOBP	EQSLG	EQMLVR	VORP	DEFENSE	
2002	ABE	NYP	21	110	33	7	4	1	13	14	8	4	.300	.376	.464	.269	.248	.309	.389	-.146	0.1	26-CF 1	
2003	DEL	SAL	22	208	63	15	8	7	28	20	10	1	.303	.383	.553	.407	.270	.332	.488	.053	8.3	36-RF -4	21-CF -2
2003	FRD	CRL	22	159	46	18	1	5	7	23	0	0	.289	.321	.509	.201	.258	.286	.478	-.053	4.7	27-CF -3	
2004	BOW	EAS	23	433	133	24	5	15	33	68	14	4	.307	.359	.490	.241	.291	.336	.459	.038	12.4	51-LF -4	41-CF -2
2004	BAL	AL	23	13	2	1	0	0	0	1	0	0	.154	.154	.231	-.710	.077	042	.154	-1.094	-1.6		
2005	*BAL*	*AL*	*24*	*286*	*78*	*17*	*3*	*9*	*19*	*45*	*5*	*2*	*.273*	*.321*	*.448*	*-.009*	*.275*	*.325*	*.457*	*.001*	*12.2*	*76-CF -6*	

Breakout: 15% *Improve: 37%* *Collapse: 28%*

"Intensity" is one of the big watchwords that follow Majewski around. He's shown good power throughout his career without striking out much, usually a good indicator of future production. He managed to get to Baltimore last August, but was quickly sidelined by a labrum tear in his throwing shoulder. Hey, it happens to non-pitchers too. While he's probably scheduled for Triple-A, scenarios that put him in Baltimore right out of spring are easy to concoct.

NICK MARKAKIS — **RF** — **Bats: L** — **Throws: L** — Born: 17-Nov-1983 — Age: 21

YEAR	TM	LG	AGE	AB	H	2B	3B	HR	BB	SO	SB	CS	AVG	OBP	SLG	MLVR	EQBA	EQOBP	EQSLG	EQMLVR	VORP	DEFENSE	
2003	ABE	NYP	19	205	58	14	3	1	30	33	13	5	.283	.372	.395	.188	.262	.331	.379	-.108	-5.3	44-RF -4	11-CF -1
2004	DEL	SAL	20	355	106	22	3	11	42	66	12	3	.299	.371	.470	.209	.261	.319	.403	-.098	-3.7	62-RF -4	
2005	*BAL*	*AL*	*21*	*368*	*91*	*20*	*2*	*7*	*31*	*77*	*7*	*3*	*.248*	*.308*	*.376*	*-.146*	*.250*	*.312*	*.383*	*-.138*	*-1.5*	*97-RF -4*	

Breakout: 17% *Improve: 31%* *Collapse: 41%*

The Orioles' decision to look at him as a hitter first after he'd starred as a two-way player in high school, is looking good so far. Markakis's season ended prematurely when he went to Athens to play for the Greek Olympic team (and be their best player), although the Orioles weren't too happy that he wound up on the mound a couple of times. The Orioles decided to be extra-cautious and shut him down once the Olympics were over. His power improved nicely from 2003 to 2004, a trend that's expected to continue.

LUIS MATOS — **CF** — **Bats: R** — **Throws: R** — Born: 30-Oct-1978 — Age: 26

YEAR	TM	LG	AGE	AB	H	2B	3B	HR	BB	SO	SB	CS	AVG	OBP	SLG	MLVR	EQBA	EQOBP	EQSLG	EQMLVR	VORP	DEFENSE	
2002	BOW	EAS	23	218	60	14	2	9	32	45	14	4	.275	.370	.482	.204	.255	.339	.445	-.007	10.2	33-CF -5	14-RF 0
2003	OTT	INT	24	175	53	16	4	1	13	34	6	1	.303	.347	.457	.138	.286	.335	.440	.005	3.6	23-RF -1	21-CF 1
2003	BAL	AL	24	439	133	23	3	13	28	90	15	7	.303	.353	.458	.116	.310	.363	.472	.123	33.1	105-CF 5	
2004	BAL	AL	25	330	74	18	0	6	19	60	12	4	.224	.275	.333	-.293	.227	.276	.331	-.305	-8.1	87-CF 0	
2005	*BAL*	*AL*	*26*	*397*	*105*	*23*	*2*	*11*	*30*	*78*	*14*	*5*	*.264*	*.321*	*.417*	*-.059*	*.266*	*.325*	*.425*	*-.050*	*13.2*	*104-CF -1*	

Breakout: 26% *Improve: 51%* *Collapse: 22%*

That 2003 season was the first time in his career that he'd ever been healthy for a full year, and Matos did good things. The next year, he went back to being brittle: He developed a stress fracture in his right shin in March, and never did get on track after that. Eventually, he ran into the Green Monster and banged that same shin, and within a few days had what was reported as an "open stress fracture" in his leg, a stress fracture so severe that pieces of bone actually flake off. One surgery and a steel rod later—think he'll enjoy airports the rest of his life?—and it still isn't clear if he'll be okay in 2005. The Orioles see Hairston as a more likely center-field bet on Opening Day.

DARNELL McDONALD — **OF** — **Bats: R** — **Throws: R** — Born: 17-Nov-1978 — Age: 26

YEAR	TM	LG	AGE	AB	H	2B	3B	HR	BB	SO	SB	CS	AVG	OBP	SLG	MLVR	EQBA	EQOBP	EQSLG	EQMLVR	VORP	DEFENSE	
2002	BOW	EAS	23	144	42	9	1	4	22	27	9	3	.292	.393	.451	.213	.276	.364	.434	.040	9.1	14-CF -2	10-LF 0
2002	ROC	INT	23	332	96	21	6	6	32	78	11	3	.289	.353	.443	.104	.267	.334	.418	-.044	10.2	88-CF 2	
2003	OTT	INT	24	152	45	7	1	0	18	27	5	7	.296	.374	.355	.041	.257	.328	.296	-.233	-4.0	23-CF 0	14-RF 0
2004	OTT	INT	25	410	96	32	1	7	34	100	12	6	.234	.294	.368	-.191	.207	.269	.325	-.339	-23.5	69-CF -1	26-RF -1
2004	BAL	AL	25	32	5	1	0	0	2	6	1	0	.156	.206	.188	-.657	.129	.159	.161	-.823	-3.5		
2005	*BAL*	*AL*	*26*	*129*	*31*	*6*	*1*	*3*	*11*	*31*	*3*	*2*	*.240*	*.305*	*.368*	*-.167*	*.242*	*.309*	*.375*	*-.160*	*1.3*	*38-CF -4*	

Breakout: 25% *Improve: 47%* *Collapse: 33%*

(continued next page)

Darnell McDonald *(continued)*

McDonald was a highly-recruited running back out of high school, who the Orioles were able to talk into trying baseball. Five years later, the O's could look at some decent performances from 2002 and 2003 and think he was coming around. Six years later, after a disastrous 2004, he's off the 40-man roster, a free agent, and talking about going to college to play football.

MELVIN MORA 3B Bats: R Throws: R Born: 02-Feb-1972 Age: 33

YEAR	TM	LG	AGE	AB	H	2B	3B	HR	BB	SO	SB	CS	AVG	OBP	SLG	MLVR	EQBA	EQOBP	EQSLG	EQMLVR	VORP	DEFENSE
2002	BAL	AL	30	557	130	30	4	19	70	108	16	10	.233	.338	.404	-.030	.246	.350	.427	-.019	18.5	73-LF 3 35-SS 1
2003	BAL	AL	31	344	109	17	1	15	49	71	6	3	.317	.418	.503	.300	.325	.427	.523	.316	41.8	56-LF 5 11-RF -1
2004	BAL	AL	32	550	187	41	0	27	66	95	11	6	.340	.419	.562	.360	.346	.424	.576	.410	73.6	136-3B -14
2005	*BAL*	*AL*	*33*	*463*	*135*	*26*	*2*	*20*	*59*	*89*	*7*	*4*	*.291*	*.383*	*.484*	*.154*	*.293*	*.387*	*.493*	*.168*	*39.2*	*127-3B -4*

Breakout: 2% *Improve: 30%* *Collapse: 25%*

If you take a look at the all-time player page for Mora at www.baseballprospectus.com/dt/moreme01.shtml, you'll see that he had a career total of 54 batting runs above replacement level through his Age-30 season—i.e., everything that he did before 2003. In the past two years, at ages 31 and 32, he's had 112. The only non-abysmal hitter in history who can top that difference is Ken Williams, an outfielder for the St. Louis Browns who didn't establish himself as a regular until the age of 30, quickly becoming one of the better hitters in the league for the next three years. But even Williams didn't raise his rate statistics like Mora did; for that, the only comparables are the late-90s spikes of Sammy Sosa and Mark McGwire. Going from "scrub" to "star" at age 30 isn't supposed to happen, but it has here. Expect a pullback to just below 2003 levels. Even that would be a big boost for the Oriole offense.

DAVID NEWHAN UT Bats: L Throws: R Born: 07-Sep-1973 Age: 31

YEAR	TM	LG	AGE	AB	H	2B	3B	HR	BB	SO	SB	CS	AVG	OBP	SLG	MLVR	EQBA	EQOBP	EQSLG	EQMLVR	VORP	DEFENSE
2003	CSP	PCL	29	244	85	17	2	3	16	36	6	4	.348	.392	.471	.177	.295	.340	.409	-.023	11.0	32-2B -5 16-1B -2
2004	OKL	PCL	30	262	86	21	6	9	26	55	10	0	.328	.387	.557	.343	.297	.353	.484	.110	21.4	36-2B 1
2004	BAL	AL	30	373	116	15	7	8	27	72	11	1	.311	.361	.453	.080	.313	.367	.458	.112	24.5	18-RF 0 19-LF 0
2005	*BAL*	*AL*	*31*	*430*	*120*	*23*	*5*	*9*	*30*	*85*	*10*	*4*	*.280*	*.329*	*.421*	*-.027*	*.282*	*.333*	*.429*	*-.017*	*14.4*	*111-DH*

Breakout: 6% *Improve: 24%* *Collapse: 38%*

Healthy after missing most of 2001 and all of 2002 with shoulder trouble, Newhan was on the verge of quitting baseball, since no one wanted him as more than Triple-A insurance. His contract with Texas allowed him to turn free agent if the Rangers didn't call him up by mid-June. They didn't, so he did, and the O's picked him up. For 30-odd days after being called up, he was the hottest player in baseball, getting his batting average up as high as .430. After that he went back to hitting at his established career level, which is where we'd expect him to be next year. But for that month, that was one wild and fun ride.

RAFAEL PALMEIRO 1B Bats: L Throws: L Born: 24-Sep-1964 Age: 40

YEAR	TM	LG	AGE	AB	H	2B	3B	HR	BB	SO	SB	CS	AVG	OBP	SLG	MLVR	EQBA	EQOBP	EQSLG	EQMLVR	VORP	DEFENSE
2002	TEX	AL	37	546	149	34	0	43	104	94	2	0	.273	.391	.571	.252	.272	.391	.572	.269	59.0	89-1B 5
2003	TEX	AL	38	561	146	21	2	38	84	77	2	0	.260	.359	.508	.118	.251	.357	.499	.094	40.0	52-1B 3
2004	BAL	AL	39	550	142	29	0	23	86	61	2	1	.258	.359	.436	.020	.260	.362	.442	.034	26.4	126-1B 12
2005	*BAL*	*AL*	*40*	*437*	*111*	*22*	*1*	*22*	*66*	*62*	*0*	*0*	*.255*	*.355*	*.461*	*.050*	*.257*	*.359*	*.470*	*.061*	*21.7*	*120-1B 1*

Breakout: 25% *Improve: 53%* *Collapse: 18%*

The only player in baseball who not only used a performance-enhancing drug, but went on television to encourage others to do the same. Palmeiro hasn't hit his career batting average in five years, and his isolated power took its second 60-point drop in as many years. It's obvious that his once-solid production isn't so solid anymore. Getting another year from the Orioles is all about the 78 hits he needs for 3,000.

TIM RAINES JR. CF Bats: R Throws: R Born: 31-Aug-1979 Age: 25

YEAR	TM	LG	AGE	AB	H	2B	3B	HR	BB	SO	SB	CS	AVG	OBP	SLG	MLVR	EQBA	EQOBP	EQSLG	EQMLVR	VORP	DEFENSE
2002	BOW	EAS	22	491	128	17	4	5	34	101	33	15	.261	.310	.342	-.092	.239	.283	.318	-.302	-23.7	88-CF -12 25-LF -3
2003	BOW	EAS	23	247	76	15	4	4	21	40	28	6	.308	.371	.449	.199	.292	.347	.440	.032	14.0	49-CF -1
2003	OTT	INT	23	214	64	11	5	3	19	37	23	9	.299	.357	.439	.127	.280	.343	.425	-.007	9.0	51-CF 2
2004	OTT	INT	24	267	70	13	1	1	18	69	24	7	.262	.314	.330	-.189	.236	.289	.296	-.323	-13.9	67-CF -3
2004	BAL	AL	24	94	24	6	0	0	4	16	7	3	.255	.293	.319	-.277	.269	.283	.301	-.309	-1.7	18-CF 0
2005	*BAL*	*AL*	*25*	*212*	*53*	*11*	*1*	*3*	*13*	*45*	*10*	*3*	*.248*	*.299*	*.357*	*-.189*	*.249*	*.303*	*.363*	*-.182*	*-0.3*	*58-CF -4*

Breakout: 20% *Improve: 36%* *Collapse: 35%*

Even with injuries clearing out the Baltimore outfield so thoroughly that two career second basemen were playing there, a healthy Raines couldn't snag the job. He has never developed any control of the strike zone, nor any power. His only asset is speed, and even there he doesn't rank with players like Joey Gathright or Freddy Guzman, similarly one-dimensional outfielders. He's on the 40-man roster for now, but he's a top candidate to be designated for assignment the first time the team needs to open a spot on the roster.

BRIAN ROBERTS 2B Bats: B Throws: R Born: 09-Oct-1977 Age: 27

YEAR	TM	LG	AGE	AB	H	2B	3B	HR	BB	SO	SB	CS	AVG	OBP	SLG	MLVR	EQBA	EQOBP	EQSLG	EQMLVR	VORP	DEFENSE
2002	ROC	INT	24	313	86	9	7	3	40	46	22	4	.275	.361	.377	.021	.249	.336	.351	-.146	2.8	69-2B -9
2002	BAL	AL	24	128	29	6	0	1	15	21	9	2	.227	.308	.297	-.233	.242	.315	.305	-.255	0.4	25-2B 0
2003	OTT	INT	25	178	56	13	1	0	27	12	19	6	.315	.401	.399	.155	.279	.362	.352	-.074	5.7	36-2B -1
2003	BAL	AL	25	460	124	22	4	5	46	58	23	6	.270	.337	.367	-.059	.273	.346	.374	-.079	20.4	103-2B 5
2004	BAL	AL	26	641	175	50	2	4	71	95	29	12	.273	.344	.376	-.093	.273	.349	.379	-.066	22.2	147-2B -4
2005	*BAL*	*AL*	*27*	*530*	*142*	*28*	*4*	*6*	*59*	*72*	*25*	*9*	*.268*	*.342*	*.370*	*-.080*	*.270*	*.346*	*.377*	*-.072*	*19.4*	*141-2B -2*

Breakout: 11% *Improve: 40%* *Collapse: 20%*

Roberts has been going head-to-head with Jerry Hairston for the second base job for the last three years, and finally seems to have won it. Overall, 2004 wasn't appreciably different from any other year in his career: moderate average, takes walks, steals bases, a steady defender. One big difference? Doubles.

In 1901, the American League's first season, a first baseman for the Milwaukee Brewers named John Anderson hit 46 doubles, setting a league record for doubles by a switch-hitter that would stand for more than 100 years. Since those 100 years expired, four different players made a run at this record, each one getting a little closer. Ray Durham hit 42 in 2001; Carlos Beltran hit 44 in 2002; Bill Mueller hit 45 in 2003. It was Brian Roberts who finally broke it in 2004, hitting 50. He also became the first Oriole ever to hit 50 doubles in a season. It would be safe to expect fewer doubles, but similar overall production in 2005.

DAVID SEGUI DL Bats: B Throws: L Born: 19-Jul-1966 Age: 38

YEAR	TM	LG	AGE	AB	H	2B	3B	HR	BB	SO	SB	CS	AVG	OBP	SLG	MLVR	EQBA	EQOBP	EQSLG	EQMLVR	VORP	DEFENSE
2002	BAL	AL	35	95	25	4	0	2	11	22	0	0	.263	.336	.368	-.060	.284	.339	.379	-.077	2.0	
2003	BAL	AL	36	224	59	10	1	5	26	47	1	0	.263	.341	.384	-.036	.266	.349	.392	-.053	7.0	
2004	BAL	AL	37	59	20	3	0	1	5	13	0	1	.339	.400	.441	.160	.362	.389	.431	.159	4.3	
2005	*BAL*	*AL*	*38*	*165*	*42*	*7*	*1*	*4*	*16*	*38*	*0*	*0*	*.252*	*.323*	*.379*	*-.115*	*.254*	*.326*	*.386*	*-.107*	*0.8*	*47-DH*

Breakout: 17% *Improve: 33%* *Collapse: 42%*

We've been calling him a bad investment for years, so this might seem like piling on. But on December 21, 2000, the Orioles signed David Segui. Four years and $28 million bought the Orioles 192 hits, 35 doubles and 18 home runs, 92 runs, and 94 RBI. Last year alone, there were ten players who had at least 192 hits, 47 players with at least 35 doubles, more than 100 with 18 home runs, 57 with 92 runs, 43 with 94 RBI, and four with all of the above: Miguel Tejada, Vlad Guerrero, Albert Pujols, and Adrian Beltre. Michael Young would have made five, if he had held up at second on two of his nine triples. There were four players who had as many at-bats last season as Segui had in all four years put together.

NATE SPEARS — 2B — Bats: L — Throws: R — Born: 03-May-1985 — Age: 20

YEAR	TM	LG	AGE	AB	H	2B	3B	HR	BB	SO	SB	CS	AVG	OBP	SLG	MLVR	EQBA	EQOBP	EQSLG	EQMLVR	VORP	DEFENSE
2004	DEL	SAL	19	371	102	12	11	5	47	63	7	6	.275	.358	.407	.084	.240	.308	.349	-.209	-4.1	74-2B 4 13-SS 0
2005	*BAL*	*AL*	*20*	*360*	*82*	*14*	*5*	*4*	*29*	*67*	*3*	*3*	*.228*	*.290*	*.326*	*-.257*	*.230*	*.294*	*.332*	*-.252*	*-2.8*	*96-2B -4*

Breakout: 13% *Improve: 28%* *Collapse: 42%*

Spears was primarily a second baseman at Delmarva, but it would certainly behoove him and the organization to at least try shortstop full-time. He's got the range for it, though his arm is a little questionable. Spears profiles as a traditional #2 hitter: He's a contact guy with little power, takes pitches, but he's not fast enough for the leadoff spot. All of which could have been written about Brian Roberts around 2000.

B. J. SURHOFF — OF — Bats: L — Throws: R — Born: 04-Aug-1964 — Age: 40

YEAR	TM	LG	AGE	AB	H	2B	3B	HR	BB	SO	SB	CS	AVG	OBP	SLG	MLVR	EQBA	EQOBP	EQSLG	EQMLVR	VORP	DEFENSE
2002	ATL	NL	37	75	22	5	0	0	9	5	1	3	.293	.369	.360	.035	.329	.358	.368	-.022	0.9	
2003	BAL	AL	38	319	94	20	0	5	29	29	2	2	.295	.353	.404	.048	.301	.359	.411	.020	14.3	20-LF 0 18-1B -1
2004	BAL	AL	39	343	106	12	1	8	30	46	2	0	.309	.365	.420	.044	.312	.372	.424	.071	16.7	34-RF 0 32-LF 0
2005	*BAL*	*AL*	*40*	*240*	*65*	*12*	*1*	*4*	*24*	*30*	*1*	*1*	*.272*	*.337*	*.375*	*-.080*	*.274*	*.341*	*.382*	*-.071*	*2.4*	*66-LF -7*

Breakout: 12% *Improve: 34%* *Collapse: 46%*

Bringing back Palmeiro is easy to understand—that 3,000 thingie, after all. Surhoff's case isn't so simple, since he isn't chasing any milestones and takes up space in an already crowded outfield. He is very popular locally, and he can at least point to his numbers and say "I produced." At 40, he may not be able to say that again.

MIGUEL TEJADA — SS — Bats: R — Throws: R — Born: 25-May-1976 — Age: 29

YEAR	TM	LG	AGE	AB	H	2B	3B	HR	BB	SO	SB	CS	AVG	OBP	SLG	MLVR	EQBA	EQOBP	EQSLG	EQMLVR	VORP	DEFENSE
2002	OAK	AL	26	662	204	30	0	34	38	84	7	2	.308	.354	.508	.179	.315	.360	.517	.188	66.4	157-SS -4
2003	OAK	AL	27	636	177	42	0	27	53	65	10	0	.278	.336	.472	.101	.280	.340	.479	.064	58.1	158-SS -12
2004	BAL	AL	28	653	203	40	2	34	48	73	4	1	.311	.360	.534	.203	.315	.365	.545	.237	73.0	158-SS 19
2005	*BAL*	*AL*	*29*	*600*	*175*	*35*	*2*	*28*	*47*	*69*	*4*	*1*	*.292*	*.349*	*.496*	*.117*	*.295*	*.353*	*.505*	*.130*	*50.6*	*154-SS 2*

Breakout: 5% *Improve: 33%* *Collapse: 22%*

Tejada had the best year of his career, but even a better season than his MVP campaign couldn't carry the Birds to the playoffs. Although he's a solid enough defender, Tejada's fielding rating looks like a fluke in the system, driven by the fact that the Orioles had the best ratio in the majors between shortstop assists and infield putouts (normally a decent guide to shortstop range) by a mile.

ELI WHITESIDE — C — Bats: R — Throws: R — Born: 22-Oct-1979 — Age: 25

YEAR	TM	LG	AGE	AB	H	2B	3B	HR	BB	SO	SB	CS	AVG	OBP	SLG	MLVR	EQBA	EQOBP	EQSLG	EQMLVR	VORP	DEFENSE
2002	FRD	CRL	22	313	81	19	0	8	14	57	0	0	.259	.296	.396	-.013	.217	.246	.347	-.347	-16.4	70-C -8
2002	BOW	EAS	22	99	26	5	0	2	4	18	0	1	.263	.311	.374	-.045	.220	.250	.310	-.390	-6.5	25-C 0
2003	BOW	EAS	23	265	54	13	1	1	5	44	0	0	.204	.230	.272	-.364	.192	.214	.264	-.543	-29.0	72-C 2
2004	BOW	EAS	24	297	75	18	0	18	25	65	2	2	.253	.310	.495	.117	.231	.278	.441	-.144	2.7	83-C -6
2005	*BAL*	*AL*	*25*	*180*	*42*	*9*	*0*	*6*	*7*	*38*	*0*	*0*	*.231*	*.269*	*.377*	*-.227*	*.233*	*.272*	*.384*	*-.221*	*-0.2*	*49-C -4*

Breakout: 26% *Improve: 48%* *Collapse: 29%*

The only thing Geronimo Gil has on Eli Whiteside is that Gil has a couple of hundred major league at-bats, while Whiteside has yet to play above Double-A. He's got the defensive chops for the job, which is usually the first hurdle towards getting a shot in the majors, and he is a much better power hitter than Gil, but he's going to struggle to post even a .300 OBP. As a starter that kills a team, but you might be able to live with it in your backup, if the pop and defense are there.

WALTER YOUNG — 1B — Bats: L — Throws: R — Born: 18-Feb-1980 — Age: 25

YEAR	TM	LG	AGE	AB	H	2B	3B	HR	BB	SO	SB	CS	AVG	OBP	SLG	MLVR	EQBA	EQOBP	EQSLG	EQMLVR	VORP	DEFENSE
2002	HIC	SAL	22	492	164	34	2	25	36	102	2	6	.333	.390	.563	.382	.268	.310	.464	-.022	9.3	75-1B -11
2003	LYN	CRL	23	431	120	15	2	20	35	88	2	4	.278	.348	.462	.153	.243	.301	.427	-.111	-4.0	75-1B -2
2004	BOW	EAS	24	486	132	28	1	33	47	145	2	3	.272	.341	.537	.243	.251	.312	.489	.002	13.0	64-1B 0
2005	*BAL*	*AL*	*25*	*315*	*80*	*15*	*1*	*15*	*24*	*86*	*0*	*1*	*.253*	*.319*	*.448*	*-.030*	*.255*	*.323*	*.456*	*-.020*	*9.1*	*84-1B -5*

Breakout: 29% *Improve: 52%* *Collapse: 23%*

A big, big man. In fact, nobody in organized baseball currently lists as bigger than Walter Young's 298 pounds. The Orioles snatched him up when the Pirates tried to pass him through waivers after the 2003 season ended, and he spent much of 2004 chasing the Phillies' Ryan Howard for the Eastern League home run and RBI titles, coming up short in both. Think of him as Sam Horn, only bigger.

PITCHERS

KURT AINSWORTH — Bats: R — Throws: R — Born: 09-Sep-1978 — Age: 26

YEAR	TM	LG	AGE	G	GS	IP	H	BB	SO	HR	ERA	EQERA	EQH9	EQBB9	EQSO9	EQHR9	PERA	VORP	STF
2002	FRE	PCL	23	20	19	116.0	101	43	119	7	3.41	3.83	8.1	3.6	7.3	0.6	3.92	20.6	27
2002	SFG	NL	23	6	4	25.7	22	12	15	1	2.10	2.59	8.5	3.7	4.8	0.4	4.07	8.6	4
2003	SFG	NL	24	11	11	66.0	66	26	48	7	3.82	4.24	9.2	3.1	6.1	1.0	4.81	10.8	9
2004	BAL	AL	25	7	7	30.7	39	20	20	6	9.67	8.71	10.2	5.2	5.5	1.5	6.10	-12.8	-9
2005	*BAL*	*AL*	*26*	*20*	*12*	*75.3*	*80*	*38*	*56*	*10*	*5.34*	*5.28*	*9.7*	*3.9*	*6.0*	*1.1*	*5.10*	*4.5*	*-2*

Breakout: 14% *Improve: 39%* *Collapse: 28%*

Coming off a season where he was sidelined by a freak injury (a broken scapula), Ainsworth looked good to go while posting a 2.20 ERA in four spring starts. Spring starts are meaningless, though: In seven games that counted that he could start, he gave up more runs than innings pitched four times. He pitched one game at Ottawa before having elbow surgery, but was able to come back to make two appearances in Aberdeen before the season ended. There's a fair chance he'll return to being the solid pitcher the Orioles thought they were getting from the Giants, though at this point, PECOTA understandably has its doubts.

RICK BAUER — Bats: R — Throws: R — Born: 10-Jan-1977 — Age: 28

YEAR	TM	LG	AGE	G	GS	IP	H	BB	SO	HR	ERA	EQERA	EQH9	EQBB9	EQSO9	EQHR9	PERA	VORP	STF
2002	BAL	AL	25	56	1	83.7	84	36	45	12	3.98	4.16	9.3	3.7	4.7	1.2	5.29	14.5	-17
2003	OTT	INT	26	7	7	36.7	31	13	21	1	2.45	2.91	8.2	3.7	4.2	0.3	3.71	7.1	5
2003	BAL	AL	26	35	0	61.3	58	24	43	5	4.55	4.83	8.3	3.5	6.2	0.6	3.92	5.6	6
2004	OTT	INT	27	11	11	63.0	69	19	42	3	4.00	3.96	9.1	2.8	4.8	0.4	4.11	10.1	9
2004	BAL	AL	27	23	2	53.7	49	20	37	4	4.69	4.64	8.1	3.1	5.8	0.5	3.61	6.4	5
2005	*BAL*	*AL*	*28*	*26*	*14*	*92.3*	*101*	*37*	*56*	*10*	*4.90*	*4.86*	*10.0*	*3.2*	*4.9*	*0.9*	*4.75*	*10.1*	*-5*

Breakout: 16% *Improve: 43%* *Collapse: 27%*

Bauer was steadily tattooed in the first half of the season, piling up a 6.61 ERA before going on the DL with an inflamed nerve in his elbow. After returning, he was sent to Ottawa (and got himself in hot water with some unfortunate comments about the team's management), but at least there he got to start. Returning to the Orioles in September, he was excellent. Bauer struggles pitching from the stretch more than most pitchers, which is why his real ERA tends to run higher than his PERA. If he gets that straightened out and gets a chance to start, he could surprise.

ERIK BEDARD — Bats: L — Throws: L — Born: 06-Mar-1979 — Age: 26

YEAR	TM	LG	AGE	G	GS	IP	H	BB	SO	HR	ERA	EQERA	EQH9	EQBB9	EQSO9	EQHR9	PERA	VORP	STF
2002	BOW	EAS	23	13	12	68.7	43	30	66	0	1.97	3.25	6.5	4.2	6.9	0.3	2.54	21.7	21
2004	BAL	AL	25	27	26	137.3	149	71	121	13	4.59	4.76	8.8	4.1	7.4	0.7	4.37	12.1	15
2005	*BAL*	*AL*	*26*	*25*	*20*	*121.7*	*127*	*57*	*95*	*17*	*5.19*	*5.13*	*9.5*	*3.7*	*6.3*	*1.1*	*4.99*	*9.8*	*4*

Breakout: 16% *Improve: 36%* *Collapse: 31%*

Judging solely by how he pitched before, 2004 wasn't so good for Bedard. He was far more hittable, and wilder than normal, and consequently gave up a lot more runs. Considering that it was his first active duty since having Tommy John surgery, and that he was able to strike opposing batters out at an above-average rate, the results were actually pretty decent. Durability is still a big concern—last year's 137 innings is his professional best for a season—and he needs control to be the great pitcher that's within his realm of the possible. The Orioles did a good job of protecting him from over work, but it will be interesting to see if they let him work deeper into games this season.

DAVE BORKOWSKI **Bats: R** **Throws: R** Born: 07-Feb-1977 Age: 28

YEAR	TM	LG	AGE	G	GS	IP	H	BB	SO	HR	ERA	EQERA	EQH9	EQBB9	EQSO9	EQHR9	PERA	VORP	STF
2003	BOW	EAS	26	24	19	120.3	126	22	66	11	3.29	4.53	10.3	1.9	4.1	1.6	5.58	0.2	-5
2004	OTT	INT	27	16	16	85.3	99	26	56	6	4.85	5.27	9.5	2.8	4.7	0.8	4.41	11.1	3
2004	BAL	AL	27	17	8	56.0	65	15	45	6	5.14	5.14	9.3	2.1	6.8	0.8	4.18	1.8	11
2005	*BAL*	*AL*	*28*	*20*	*13*	*83.7*	*99*	*25*	*53*	*10*	*4.96*	*4.91*	*10.8*	*2.4*	*5.1*	*1.0*	*4.95*	*9.3*	*0*

Breakout: 18% *Improve: 47%* *Collapse: 21%*

Borkowski found himself trading places with Matt Riley after the latter had a meltdown in Philly. He made the most of it for a half-dozen starts, but the league soon figured out that he was the same guy who came in with a 6.93 career ERA. Unless the Orioles run into as many pitching injuries in 2005 as they did in 2004, he'll be back in Triple-A.

DANIEL CABRERA **Bats: R** **Throws: R** Born: 28-May-1981 Age: 24

YEAR	TM	LG	AGE	G	GS	IP	H	BB	SO	HR	ERA	EQERA	EQH9	EQBB9	EQSO9	EQHR9	PERA	VORP	STF
2002	BLU	APL	21	12	12	60.3	52	25	69	0	3.28	5.50	8.9	4.7	5.3	0.3	4.69	5.6	5
2003	DEL	SAL	22	26	26	125.3	105	78	120	6	4.24	7.27	9.2	6.9	5.4	1.2	5.51	1.1	-8
2004	BOW	EAS	23	5	5	27.3	11	12	35	1	2.64	3.96	5.4	4.3	9.0	0.4	2.16	9.6	39
2004	BAL	AL	23	28	27	147.7	145	89	76	14	5.00	4.56	8.8	4.9	4.4	0.8	4.69	17.2	0
2005	*BAL*	*AL*	*24*	*22*	*21*	*119.7*	*126*	*67*	*77*	*17*	*5.62*	*5.57*	*9.6*	*4.4*	*5.2*	*1.2*	*5.35*	*3.3*	*-4*

Breakout: 14% *Improve: 50%* *Collapse: 24%*

Cabrera earned a promotion by striking out 22 hitters in 13 innings at Bowie, then shut out the White Sox for six innings in his debut. For the year he managed a rookie-leading 12 wins and a third-place finish in the Rookie of the Year voting, but he was barely skating by for most of the season. Pitchers who walk more batters than they strike out are huge risks and whatever success they attain is usually fleeting. Just spent the winter pitching in the Dominican, working on a change-up, which might help.

BRUCE CHEN **Bats: L** **Throws: L** Born: 19-Jun-1977 Age: 28

YEAR	TM	LG	AGE	G	GS	IP	H	BB	SO	HR	ERA	EQERA	EQH9	EQBB9	EQSO9	EQHR9	PERA	VORP	STF
2002	MON	NL	25	15	5	37.3	47	23	43	9	7.00	6.63	10.2	4.5	8.8	2.1	6.39	-6.4	0
2002	CIN	NL	25	39	1	39.7	37	20	37	7	4.31	5.40	8.7	4.0	7.5	1.6	4.93	-0.3	-2
2003	HOU	NL	26	11	0	12.0	14	8	8	2	6.00	5.40	10.0	5.4	5.4	1.5	6.17	-0.5	-15
2003	PAW	INT	26	16	15	85.0	80	15	73	12	4.24	5.24	9.3	1.8	6.5	1.9	4.78	7.2	10
2003	BOS	AL	26	5	2	12.3	12	2	12	4	5.12	5.25	9.0	1.5	9.0	3.0	5.25	0.3	21
2004	OTT	INT	27	22	17	95.0	85	30	108	12	3.22	3.86	8.2	3.0	8.4	1.3	3.96	16.6	24
2004	BAL	AL	27	8	7	47.7	39	16	32	7	3.02	3.18	7.9	2.8	6.0	1.2	3.77	14.0	10
2005	*BAL*	*AL*	*28*	*41*	*5*	*75.0*	*74*	*31*	*59*	*12*	*4.73*	*4.69*	*9.0*	*3.2*	*6.3*	*1.3*	*4.64*	*10.3*	*-3*

Breakout: 13% *Improve: 44%* *Collapse: 21%*

I've pitched in
Baltimore, Boston, Pawtucket, Atlanta
New York, Houston, Reading, Philadelphia
Syracuse, Richmond, Montreal, Ottawa
Scranton Wilkes-Barre and in Cincinnati
I've pitched everywhere, man, I've pitched everywhere . . .

And that's just since 2000.

Hank Snow Memorial Award Finalists, since 2000:
Bruce Chen, 14 home teams and eight major league organizations
Hansel Izquierdo and Leo Estrella, 13 teams and seven organizations
Rudy Seanez, Al Reyes, Jimmy Osting, and Curtis Pride, 12 teams and seven organizations
Aaron Myette and Craig House, 12 teams and five organizations

DAVE CROUTHERS

Bats: R **Throws: R** Born: 18-Dec-1979 Age: 25

YEAR	TM	LG	AGE	G	GS	IP	H	BB	SO	HR	ERA	EQERA	EQH9	EQBB9	EQSO9	EQHR9	PERA	VORP	STF
2002	DEL	SAL	22	25	25	129.3	117	58	108	4	3.34	6.56	9.2	5.1	4.7	0.8	5.11	6.4	0
2003	FRD	CRL	23	18	18	92.7	83	43	82	1	3.59	5.52	8.2	4.5	5.8	0.2	3.68	18.8	15
2003	BOW	EAS	23	9	9	45.0	37	18	29	4	3.80	4.87	9.1	4.2	4.9	1.5	5.31	1.3	-4
2004	BOW	EAS	24	27	27	139.7	134	68	138	23	5.03	5.91	9.5	4.7	6.7	2.1	5.91	-4.5	-5
2005	*BAL*	*AL*	*25*	*9*	*8*	*47.7*	*47*	*24*	*35*	*8*	*5.27*	*5.22*	*9.0*	*3.9*	*6.0*	*1.4*	*5.11*	*3.7*	*1*

Breakout: 20% *Improve: 50%* *Collapse: 23%*

In terms of pure throwing ability, Crouthers is among the best in the organization. In terms of pitching, he has a way to go. His two biggest problems are leaving the ball up in the zone (where opposing hitters can really elevate it; he had a nearly 2:1 flyout/groundout ratio) and composure. The team hopes that switching to relief will help his mental state, as it once did for Arthur Rhodes; let's just hope that an untimely home run or two doesn't undo that good.

ZACH DIXON

Bats: L **Throws: L** Born: 29-Nov-1980 Age: 24

YEAR	TM	LG	AGE	G	GS	IP	H	BB	SO	HR	ERA	EQERA	EQH9	EQBB9	EQSO9	EQHR9	PERA	VORP	STF
2003	ABE	NYP	22	14	14	68.0	65	18	70	3	2.91	5.66	10.2	3.0	5.5	1.6	5.37	1.6	-3
2004	DEL	SAL	23	24	21	120.7	97	65	105	5	2.54	4.89	8.5	5.7	5.0	0.7	4.89	8.7	7
2004	FRD	CRL	23	3	3	18.0	15	4	15	0	2.50	4.24	7.9	2.1	5.3	0.0	2.65	5.6	19
2005	*BAL*	*AL*	*24*	*14*	*12*	*70.0*	*74*	*38*	*47*	*12*	*5.63*	*5.58*	*9.6*	*4.3*	*5.4*	*1.4*	*5.62*	*3.7*	*-6*

Breakout: 15% *Improve: 47%* *Collapse: 25%*

Dixon got a little bit of notice for his performance this year, based on his record (10–5) and ERA (2.53). Neither showed his true ability: His ERA hid 19 unearned runs, which is a lot even for the Sally League, and at 23 he was considerably older than his competition. Until he faces guys his own age, it's going to be hard to see whether this finesse lefty has a legitimate future.

ERIC DuBOSE

Bats: L **Throws: L** Born: 15-May-1976 Age: 29

YEAR	TM	LG	AGE	G	GS	IP	H	BB	SO	HR	ERA	EQERA	EQH9	EQBB9	EQSO9	EQHR9	PERA	VORP	STF
2002	BOW	EAS	26	41	0	64.7	46	21	66	2	2.50	3.71	7.1	3.1	7.3	0.4	2.67	19.8	23
2003	OTT	INT	27	19	19	114.0	112	34	107	7	3.39	4.32	8.9	3.1	6.9	0.8	4.24	16.4	16
2003	BAL	AL	27	17	10	73.7	60	25	44	6	3.79	3.86	7.7	3.0	5.4	0.6	3.34	16.8	6
2004	BAL	AL	28	14	14	74.7	76	44	48	12	6.39	5.77	9.0	4.8	5.5	1.2	4.91	-3.3	-6
2005	*BAL*	*AL*	*29*	*20*	*16*	*96.3*	*100*	*47*	*68*	*12*	*4.84*	*4.79*	*9.5*	*3.8*	*5.7*	*1.0*	*4.88*	*11.4*	*1*

Breakout: 25% *Improve: 53%* *Collapse: 22%*

Hopes were high for DuBose last season, and he left spring as the team's #2 starter. He got shelled in his first game out. While he sort of recovered—he held onto a respectable ERA for a couple of months—he was never entirely right, often struggling to get his fastball out of the mid-80s. That's a problem for anybody, but for a fastball/changeup pitcher like DuBose who lives on speed separation, it's death. He eventually went on the DL and under the knife to have chips taken out of his elbow. He should be fully recovered for 2005, but by now you know he's not exactly reliable.

JASON GRIMSLEY

Bats: R **Throws: R** Born: 07-Aug-1967 Age: 37

YEAR	TM	LG	AGE	G	GS	IP	H	BB	SO	HR	ERA	EQERA	EQH9	EQBB9	EQSO9	EQHR9	PERA	VORP	STF
2002	KCR	AL	34	70	0	71.3	64	37	59	4	3.91	3.49	7.9	4.4	7.1	0.4	3.75	15.3	5
2003	KCR	AL	35	76	0	75.0	88	36	58	6	5.16	4.90	9.3	4.1	6.7	0.6	4.78	3.8	-1
2004	KCR	AL	36	32	0	26.7	24	15	18	1	3.37	3.08	7.9	4.4	5.8	0.3	3.76	7.6	-6
2004	BAL	AL	36	41	0	36.3	37	20	21	3	4.21	5.30	8.8	4.5	5.0	0.8	4.54	0.4	-14
2005	*BAL*	*AL*	*37*	*58*	*0*	*48.7*	*50*	*23*	*36*	*3*	*3.76*	*3.72*	*9.4*	*3.7*	*6.0*	*0.6*	*4.43*	*11.9*	*-4*

Breakout: 41% *Improve: 66%* *Collapse: 6%*

The way Grimsley pitched in an Oriole uniform was punishment enough, but it was compounded by the fact that a panicky management gave up Denny Bautista to bring in this old patch for a struggling bullpen. He used to throw a mean sinker, but these days it's just kind of curmudgeonly. You can throw out that projection; Tommy John surgery in October will cost him most of the season, and could signal the end.

BUDDY GROOM Bats: L Throws: L Born: 10-Jul-1965 Age: 39

YEAR	TM	LG	AGE	G	GS	IP	H	BB	SO	HR	ERA	EQERA	EQH9	EQBB9	EQSO9	EQHR9	PERA	VORP	STF
2002	BAL	AL	37	70	0	62.0	44	12	48	4	1.60	1.71	7.3	1.7	7.0	0.6	2.95	30.1	13
2003	BAL	AL	38	60	0	45.3	58	14	34	7	5.36	4.93	10.1	2.6	6.5	1.2	5.12	3.7	-5
2004	BAL	AL	39	60	0	52.7	67	16	32	6	4.78	4.58	10.0	2.4	5.1	0.8	4.75	6.8	-9
2005	*BAL*	*AL*	*39*	*51*	*0*	*39.0*	*45*	*12*	*26*	*5*	*4.69*	*4.65*	*10.6*	*2.5*	*5.4*	*1.1*	*4.95*	*6.3*	*-9*

Breakout: 19% *Improve: 39%* *Collapse: 33%*

The biggest difference between the Buddy Grooms of 2003 and 2004 was that the Orioles recognized that he had lost something and moved him into lower-leverage situations, slotting him as bullpen filler instead of a go-to guy. His bullpen ace days are gone by, but he's still an option for managers that want multiple lefties in reserve.

DAVID HAEHNEL Bats: L Throws: L Born: 21-Jul-1982 Age: 22

YEAR	TM	LG	AGE	G	GS	IP	H	BB	SO	HR	ERA	EQERA	EQH9	EQBB9	EQSO9	EQHR9	PERA	VORP	STF
2004	ABE	NYP	21	28	0	36.3	23	11	58	1	1.24	3.86	7.7	3.9	8.3	0.8	3.58	7.3	15
2005	*BAL*	*AL*	*22*	*25*	*4*	*48.3*	*45*	*20*	*43*	*5*	*4.17*	*4.13*	*8.4*	*3.3*	*7.2*	*0.9*	*4.09*	*9.5*	*5*

Breakout: 14% *Improve: 51%* *Collapse: 25%*

Haehnel bounced between starting and relieving in college, but the Orioles took him in the eighth round last year thinking only about relief. They sent him to Aberdeen, made him the closer, and sat back and watched him roll over the competition. Even after three bad outings to end the season, his numbers were just sick—just keep in mind that isn't so uncommon for a college pitcher in a rookie league. His primary pitch is a low-90s fastball with a lot of natural movement, one the O's hope will get him zooming through the system.

JORGE JULIO Bats: R Throws: R Born: 03-Mar-1979 Age: 26

YEAR	TM	LG	AGE	G	GS	IP	H	BB	SO	HR	ERA	EQERA	EQH9	EQBB9	EQSO9	EQHR9	PERA	VORP	STF
2002	BAL	AL	23	67	0	68.0	55	27	55	5	1.99	2.91	7.8	3.5	7.2	0.7	3.74	23.1	6
2003	BAL	AL	24	64	0	61.7	60	34	52	10	4.38	4.92	8.5	4.8	7.5	1.3	4.92	5.8	-5
2004	BAL	AL	25	65	0	69.0	59	39	70	11	4.57	3.99	7.7	4.7	8.6	1.2	4.26	13.2	5
2005	*BAL*	*AL*	*26*	*43*	*2*	*63.7*	*60*	*30*	*56*	*9*	*4.42*	*4.38*	*8.7*	*3.7*	*7.1*	*1.2*	*4.56*	*10.7*	*0*

Breakout: 24% *Improve: 56%* *Collapse: 16%*

The walks and home runs finally started clumping together in an awful late-season stretch that temporarily cost Julio the closer's job. As always, that remains an extremely volatile situation, and some sort of co-closer arrangement with lefty B. J. Ryan looks like a reasonable guess for the coming year. He's put on about 40 pounds in the last three years based solely on the official height/weight numbers in the media guides, and the guides were being pretty generous to him last season. How he treats his body this winter will have a lot to do with how the team treats him in the spring.

ADAM LOEWEN Bats: L Throws: L Born: 09-Apr-1984 Age: 21

YEAR	TM	LG	AGE	G	GS	IP	H	BB	SO	HR	ERA	EQERA	EQH9	EQBB9	EQSO9	EQHR9	PERA	VORP	STF
2003	ABE	NYP	19	7	7	23.3	13	9	25	0	2.70	4.79	7.0	4.8	6.1	0.4	3.48	4.9	15
2004	DEL	SAL	20	20	19	85.3	77	58	82	3	4.11	5.81	9.0	7.2	5.4	0.6	5.70	-0.9	-5
2005	*BAL*	*AL*	*21*	*10*	*8*	*45.3*	*44*	*32*	*29*	*6*	*5.44*	*5.39*	*9.0*	*5.6*	*5.1*	*1.1*	*5.38*	*2.0*	*-10*

Breakout: 12% *Improve: 37%* *Collapse: 16%*

Another reason why signing draftees—no matter how good—to major league contracts is a bad idea. The Orioles took Loewen to spring training last year; in three games, he got three outs, walked seven and hit one, and gave up nine runs altogether. How much of what followed in Delmarva was injury and how much was shell-shock? He was ultimately found to have a torn labrum, and so far the team is resisting surgery, hoping that an exercise program will create enough strength to overcome the tear.

RODRIGO LOPEZ Bats: R Throws: R Born: 14-Dec-1975 Age: 29

YEAR	TM	LG	AGE	G	GS	IP	H	BB	SO	HR	ERA	EQERA	EQH9	EQBB9	EQSO9	EQHR9	PERA	VORP	STF
2002	BAL	AL	26	33	28	196.7	172	62	136	23	3.57	3.66	8.4	2.7	6.2	1.0	4.09	47.7	13
2003	BAL	AL	27	26	26	147.0	188	43	103	24	5.82	5.73	10.1	2.4	6.0	1.3	5.12	-1.6	4
2004	BAL	AL	28	37	23	170.7	164	54	121	21	3.59	3.31	8.5	2.6	6.1	1.0	3.90	47.3	10
2005	*BAL*	*AL*	*29*	*28*	*20*	*127.7*	*135*	*42*	*88*	*17*	*4.46*	*4.41*	*9.7*	*2.6*	*5.5*	*1.1*	*4.51*	*20.6*	*4*

Breakout: 20% *Improve: 46%* *Collapse: 20%*

The Orioles elected to start 2004 with a young rotation that included rookies Ainsworth, Bedard, and Riley, with Rodrigo Lopez left in the bullpen. With some grumbling, Lopez did his job, first becoming their best reliever, then stepping into the rotation when injuries hit to become their best starter. Back on the mound at the start of games, his performance was reminiscent of his almost-Rookie of the Year 2002 season. He won't have to grouse this spring; Lopez and Ponson are the only two starters who can comfortably claim to be starting in Baltimore in '05.

JOHN MAINE Bats: R Throws: R Born: 08-May-1981 Age: 24

YEAR	TM	LG	AGE	G	GS	IP	H	BB	SO	HR	ERA	EQERA	EQH9	EQBB9	EQSO9	EQHR9	PERA	VORP	STF
2002	DEL	SAL	21	6	5	33.0	21	4	39	0	1.36	4.20	7.5	1.5	6.6	0.3	2.70	9.7	28
2003	DEL	SAL	22	14	14	76.3	43	18	108	1	1.53	3.91	7.0	2.6	8.0	0.3	2.48	23.9	41
2003	FRD	CRL	22	12	12	70.3	48	20	77	5	3.07	4.50	7.9	3.0	7.6	1.4	3.80	12.8	26
2004	BOW	EAS	23	5	5	28.0	16	7	34	1	2.25	3.46	6.6	2.4	8.3	0.3	2.42	9.2	40
2004	OTT	INT	23	22	22	119.7	123	52	105	12	3.91	4.28	8.9	4.0	6.5	0.9	4.51	14.0	11
2005	*BAL*	*AL*	*24*	*14*	*13*	*76.3*	*78*	*32*	*61*	*11*	*4.82*	*4.77*	*9.3*	*3.3*	*6.4*	*1.2*	*4.81*	*10.4*	*8*

Breakout: 12% *Improve: 32%* *Collapse: 33%*

Last season was the first time that Maine had any problems in pro ball. The Orioles sent him to Triple-A after just five (admittedly dominant) starts in Double-A, and for the first two months he struggled with his control. He was back to his old self for the last two months and could be considered for a rotation spot sometime in 2005, depending on how he pitches at Ottawa. He throws four pitches, none of which is individually outstanding, but Maine does a nice job of mixing them up and using the entire strike zone. That's assuming the Orioles aren't soured on that sort after their experiences with Josh Towers and John Stephens.

JOHN PARRISH Bats: L Throws: L Born: 26-Nov-1977 Age: 27

YEAR	TM	LG	AGE	G	GS	IP	H	BB	SO	HR	ERA	EQERA	EQH9	EQBB9	EQSO9	EQHR9	PERA	VORP	STF
2003	BOW	EAS	25	49	0	76.3	58	33	85	5	2.01	3.45	8.1	4.4	8.4	1.2	4.48	8.7	9
2003	BAL	AL	25	14	0	23.7	17	8	15	2	1.90	2.42	7.3	3.2	5.6	0.8	3.22	9.0	5
2004	BAL	AL	26	56	1	78.0	68	55	71	4	3.46	3.96	7.6	5.7	7.7	0.3	3.84	15.4	10
2005	*BAL*	*AL*	*27*	*33*	*6*	*67.3*	*67*	*39*	*58*	*7*	*4.80*	*4.76*	*9.1*	*4.6*	*7.0*	*0.9*	*4.88*	*9.5*	*-1*

Breakout: 21% *Improve: 41%* *Collapse: 32%*

Parrish was a decent starting prospect a few years back, but it never really worked out. Besides the regular bias MLB teams have against sub-six-foot starters, there was the more pressing problem of what his lack of control did to his pitch counts. He's made the conversion to full-time reliever since missing all of 2002 with a knee injury, and figures to move up the bullpen pecking order into Buddy Groom's old spot. Still needs to improve his control or risk yielding a ton of runs.

HAYDEN PENN Bats: R Throws: R Born: 13-Oct-1984 Age: 20

YEAR	TM	LG	AGE	G	GS	IP	H	BB	SO	HR	ERA	EQERA	EQH9	EQBB9	EQSO9	EQHR9	PERA	VORP	STF
2003	BLU	APL	18	12	11	52.3	58	19	38	4	4.30	5.77	11.0	4.3	3.7	2.0	7.26	-8.9	-14
2004	DEL	SAL	19	13	6	43.3	30	19	41	4	3.33	4.66	8.4	4.9	5.6	1.4	5.12	2.1	9
2004	FRD	CRL	19	13	13	73.3	59	20	61	7	3.81	4.97	8.6	3.0	5.5	1.5	4.16	10.7	31
2004	BOW	EAS	19	4	4	20.3	22	9	20	0	4.88	5.85	9.0	4.1	6.3	0.0	4.05	3.4	20
2005	*BAL*	*AL*	*20*	*16*	*11*	*70.3*	*71*	*31*	*50*	*10*	*4.83*	*4.78*	*9.2*	*3.5*	*5.7*	*1.2*	*4.79*	*7.8*	*0*

Breakout: 18% *Improve: 58%* *Collapse: 7%*

Penn was primarily a basketball player in high school, meaning that his arm doesn't have as much wear as the typical 20-year-old hurler. Despite his lack of game experience, he's considered to be an exceptionally intelligent pitcher, working primarily off an okay fastball with a very good change-up and curve. Sometimes the best things fall into your lap: He opened the season in Delmarva's bullpen, and only started after Adam Loewen got hurt.

SIDNEY PONSON Bats: R Throws: R Born: 02-Nov-1976 Age: 28

YEAR	TM	LG	AGE	G	GS	IP	H	BB	SO	HR	ERA	EQERA	EQH9	EQBB9	EQSO9	EQHR9	PERA	VORP	STF
2002	BAL	AL	25	28	28	176.0	172	63	120	26	4.09	4.10	9.1	3.0	6.0	1.3	4.85	33.0	5
2003	BAL	AL	26	21	21	148.0	147	43	100	10	3.77	3.73	8.5	2.5	6.0	0.6	3.61	35.0	19
2003	SFG	NL	26	10	10	68.0	64	18	34	6	3.71	3.80	9.1	2.1	4.2	0.8	4.36	14.1	4
2004	BAL	AL	27	33	33	215.7	265	69	115	23	5.30	4.97	9.9	2.5	4.5	0.8	4.68	13.3	3
2005	*BAL*	*AL*	*28*	*28*	*28*	*170.3*	*191*	*54*	*104*	*20*	*4.66*	*4.62*	*10.3*	*2.5*	*4.9*	*1.0*	*4.64*	*21.0*	*5*

Breakout: 15% *Improve: 54%* *Collapse: 15%*

Ponson didn't waste any time trying to convince people that his 2003 season was a fluke, running up a 6.29 ERA in the first half before righting himself in the second. The Orioles wanted to pick up a front-line starter in the off-season to accompany Ponson, thinking that the "staff ace" title was an unnecessary burden, but it didn't happen. Pop psychology being what it is, whether that affected the big righty's season is a questionable theory at best. Ponson's always had a bit of a head-case reputation, and he didn't help himself with some off-season legal troubles in Aruba—assaulting a judge is wrong, even for a knight.

AARON RAKERS Bats: R Throws: R Born: 22-Jan-1977 Age: 28

YEAR	TM	LG	AGE	G	GS	IP	H	BB	SO	HR	ERA	EQERA	EQH9	EQBB9	EQSO9	EQHR9	PERA	VORP	STF
2002	BOW	EAS	25	36	0	48.0	39	12	45	3	2.06	3.18	7.9	2.4	6.6	1.0	3.18	12.2	11
2003	BOW	EAS	26	31	0	39.3	27	19	42	7	2.75	3.63	8.8	5.2	8.6	3.4	6.75	-4.4	-5
2003	OTT	INT	26	21	0	26.3	19	11	26	1	5.13	6.29	7.4	4.4	7.4	0.4	3.33	6.1	8
2004	OTT	INT	27	54	1	78.7	65	25	80	8	2.74	3.13	7.8	3.0	7.6	1.1	3.74	15.4	17
2004	BAL	AL	27	3	0	4.3	5	1	3	0	4.19	4.15	8.3	2.1	6.2	0.0	2.08	1.0	18
2005	*BAL*	*AL*	*28*	*17*	*3*	*34.7*	*32*	*15*	*29*	*5*	*4.44*	*4.39*	*8.5*	*3.4*	*6.7*	*1.2*	*4.35*	*6.5*	*1*

Breakout: 17% *Improve: 48%* *Collapse: 26%*

Rakers is a career minor league reliever who finally got a taste of the majors last season. The scouting report says that his splitter isn't major league quality, which partly is why he's had to wait so long for a chance. However, given that he's a got a career ERA of 2.53, he's got some room to disappoint and still be an effective member of a big league bullpen.

CHRIS RAY Bats: R Throws: R Born: 12-Jan-1982 Age: 23

YEAR	TM	LG	AGE	G	GS	IP	H	BB	SO	HR	ERA	EQERA	EQH9	EQBB9	EQSO9	EQHR9	PERA	VORP	STF
2003	ABE	NYP	21	9	8	38.3	32	10	44	0	2.82	5.60	8.7	3.1	6.1	0.3	3.82	7.0	12
2004	DEL	SAL	22	10	9	50.0	43	17	46	3	3.42	4.89	9.0	3.5	5.3	1.0	4.70	4.6	4
2004	FRD	CRL	22	14	14	73.3	82	20	74	6	3.81	4.73	9.9	2.8	6.4	1.3	4.86	5.8	10
2005	*BAL*	*AL*	*23*	*13*	*12*	*70.3*	*75*	*26*	*52*	*9*	*4.75*	*4.71*	*9.8*	*3.0*	*5.9*	*1.1*	*4.73*	*8.9*	*6*

Breakout: 11% *Improve: 43%* *Collapse: 25%*

Ray was both a starter and reliever at William & Mary before the Orioles nabbed him in the third round of the 2003 draft. So far they've used him as a starter, but long-term he's projected to toil out of the pen. The team is trying to pull off a delicate balancing act between trying to get him innings and experience without overtaxing his arm, since he's got a pretty rough delivery. In relief, he'd stand a good chance of improving his strikeout rate.

MATT RILEY Bats: L Throws: L Born: 02-Aug-1979 Age: 25

YEAR	TM	LG	AGE	G	GS	IP	H	BB	SO	HR	ERA	EQERA	EQH9	EQBB9	EQSO9	EQHR9	PERA	VORP	STF
2002	BOW	EAS	22	22	22	109.3	136	48	105	12	6.34	7.30	10.4	4.1	6.5	1.5	5.70	-1.2	-18
2003	BOW	EAS	23	14	14	72.3	56	23	73	4	3.11	4.18	8.1	3.2	7.7	0.9	4.05	11.5	2
2003	OTT	INT	23	13	13	70.3	70	28	77	4	3.58	4.28	8.8	4.0	8.0	0.7	4.41	8.9	14
2004	BAL	AL	24	14	13	64.0	60	44	60	11	5.62	5.26	8.2	5.5	8.0	1.3	4.83	1.3	12
2004	OTT	INT	24	10	10	42.0	26	23	51	3	1.71	2.06	6.4	5.3	9.2	0.7	3.20	10.5	29
2005	*BAL*	*AL*	*25*	*19*	*16*	*95.3*	*96*	*50*	*84*	*14*	*5.13*	*5.08*	*9.2*	*4.1*	*7.1*	*1.2*	*5.01*	*8.1*	*8*

Breakout: 15% *Improve: 41%* *Collapse: 23%*

Riley continues to tease the Orioles—and his fantasy owners—with glimpses of the ability to be a stud pitcher, although the chief impression is that of a kid who has no idea of what he's trying to do. He's still wild, both as a pitcher and as a human being, although the pitching part can at least be explained by some shoulder tendonitis. The team would love to be able to trade him, but finding a sucker... err... trading partner... has been difficult.

EDDY RODRIGUEZ **Bats: R** **Throws: R** Born: 08-Aug-1981 Age: 23

YEAR	TM	LG	AGE	G	GS	IP	H	BB	SO	HR	ERA	EQERA	EQH9	EQBB9	EQSO9	EQHR9	PERA	VORP	STF
2002	FRD	CRL	20	38	0	48.3	28	20	58	3	2.24	3.95	7.1	4.8	7.9	1.2	3.53	10.0	22
2003	BOW	EAS	21	56	0	73.0	49	35	66	3	2.34	4.07	7.5	4.9	6.9	0.7	3.93	12.3	14
2004	OTT	INT	22	28	0	31.7	34	18	31	4	5.11	4.99	9.1	5.3	7.0	1.2	5.28	1.1	-5
2004	BAL	AL	22	29	0	43.3	36	30	37	5	4.78	4.25	7.7	5.7	7.2	0.9	4.25	7.2	0
2005	*BAL*	*AL*	*23*	*19*	*5*	*46.0*	*41*	*28*	*37*	*8*	*5.23*	*5.18*	*8.1*	*4.9*	*6.4*	*1.4*	*5.12*	*4.5*	*-8*

Breakout: 14% *Improve: 44%* *Collapse: 29%*

From Memorial Day, when he was first called up, until the middle of August, Rodriguez was an active member of the Orioles bullpen, pitching every three days on average. He was sent down for about a week before rosters expended, but was a forgotten man in September. Like so many other Oriole pitchers, he gave away far too many walks. At his age and with good heat, he's got time to improve.

B. J. RYAN **Bats: L** **Throws: L** Born: 28-Dec-1975 Age: 29

YEAR	TM	LG	AGE	G	GS	IP	H	BB	SO	HR	ERA	EQERA	EQH9	EQBB9	EQSO9	EQHR9	PERA	VORP	STF
2002	BAL	AL	26	67	0	57.7	51	33	56	7	4.68	4.66	8.0	4.8	8.5	1.0	4.50	7.3	3
2003	BAL	AL	27	76	0	50.3	42	27	63	1	3.40	3.22	6.8	4.5	10.9	0.2	3.04	15.1	28
2004	BAL	AL	28	76	0	87.0	64	35	122	4	2.28	2.29	6.4	3.2	11.9	0.3	2.50	36.7	43
2005	*BAL*	*AL*	*29*	*63*	*0*	*73.0*	*59*	*37*	*89*	*7*	*3.20*	*3.17*	*7.4*	*4.0*	*9.9*	*0.8*	*3.65*	*23.2*	*20*

Breakout: 30% *Improve: 54%* *Collapse: 35%*

Developing to the point of dominance, Ryan's a rare lefty so good he could escape the situational role once and for all, a la Eddie Guardado. Over the past three seasons, Ryan's OPS against left-handed hitters has dropped from 693 to 497 to just 324 in 2004. Even against right-handers, he's trimmed 125 points off his OPS allowed, but that still leaves it twice as high as it is against lefties. Along with his increasing left-handed dominance, he possess a stratospheric strikeout rate, improved control, and has become a threat to Jorge Julio's closing role. There's a strong bias against using lopsided pitchers as closers, but Ryan is clearly the best hurler on the roster.

TODD WILLIAMS **Bats: R** **Throws: R** Born: 13-Feb-1971 Age: 34

YEAR	TM	LG	AGE	G	GS	IP	H	BB	SO	HR	ERA	EQERA	EQH9	EQBB9	EQSO9	EQHR9	PERA	VORP	STF
2002	OTT	INT	31	46	0	48.0	56	12	21	4	3.75	5.36	10.7	2.6	3.4	1.2	5.96	-1.8	-26
2003	DUR	INT	32	56	0	69.7	55	14	36	2	1.55	2.12	8.2	2.1	4.0	0.4	3.53	14.7	8
2004	OKL	PCL	33	27	0	29.7	37	7	11	2	3.03	4.97	10.2	2.2	2.5	0.6	4.66	3.0	-22
2004	OTT	INT	33	14	0	20.7	19	3	11	0	3.04	3.20	8.2	1.4	4.1	0.0	2.75	6.2	0
2004	BAL	AL	33	29	0	31.3	26	9	13	2	2.88	2.43	8.2	2.4	3.6	0.6	3.34	11.9	-7
2005	*BAL*	*AL*	*34*	*23*	*2*	*37.0*	*45*	*12*	*17*	*4*	*4.82*	*4.77*	*11.2*	*2.6*	*3.8*	*0.9*	*5.11*	*5.2*	*-16*

Breakout: 21% *Improve: 49%* *Collapse: 29%*

Last season was Williams's fifth in the majors, spread out over ten years and five teams. It was also the first time he pitched more than 20 innings or had an ERA under 4.50. As scrap-heap renovations go, it worked out pretty well, but it's the kind of ride where you say thanks, leave a generous tip, and don't tempt fate by trying it again.

Boston Red Sox

RED SOX PROSPECTUS

2004 record: 98–64; Second place, AL East; Beat Cardinals in World Series, 4–0

Pythagenport record: 97–65

Runs scored per game: 5.86 (1st in AL)

Runs allowed per game: 4.75 (4th in AL)

Team EqA: .274 (2nd in AL)

2004 Batters Age: 30.9 (3rd oldest in AL)

2004 Pitchers Age: 33.1 (2nd oldest in AL)

Ballpark: Fenway Park; Moderate hitter's park; Park Factor of 1.040

2004: Curse? I got your curse right here!

2005: With state-of-the-art offense, pitching, payroll, and management, the Red Sox will be in the thick of it again.

For an organization so clearly on the way up, it's ironic that the Red Sox have nowhere to go but down.

Victims of the most famous championship drought in sports, the team from the Hub finally rose up and conquered the post-season, handing the worst collapse in baseball history to their greatest tormentors along the way. It was a season and an October to remember, a fact not lost on any number of writers and commentators. Boston's victory has been analyzed, commercialized, and publicized enough to remove a great deal of the normal sheen that comes from winning the World Series, but given the town's long history of misery, we'll cut them a little slack, even if they've started charging a fee for membership in the club. Congratulations all around.

There's no shortage of reasons that the Red Sox won the World Series. The pitching—one of the main weaknesses of the 2003 team—was noticeably better than last year (see table 1). Moving from 8th in the AL in runs allowed to 4th, virtually all of Boston's improvement can be attributed to the bullpen.

After last season's attempt to return to a more egalitarian bullpen usage pattern, the Sox aggressively pursued and acquired former Oakland closer Keith Foulke, who did not disappoint. In 2003, the pen was a revolving door of players like Brandon Lyon, Todd Jones, and a terrible Ramiro Mendoza. In 2004, however, Foulke, Mile Timlin, and Alan Embree accounted for 48% of the relief innings, while the rest were filled by a more able supporting cast. The result was just shy of a run of improvement in runs allowed for the pen. That's not to diminish the singular impact of Foulke: Take him away, and instead of a 3.87 ERA, the pen would have allowed a 4.27 mark.

The rotation saw two new faces, but many new hairstyles. Curt Schilling and Bronson Arroyo were big additions, replacing John Burkett and Byung-Hyun Kim/Casey Fossum. But those two steps up were offset by two steps back. Pedro Martinez finally pitched over 200 innings in a season again, but did so with significantly reduced effectiveness, going from 2.51 RA to 4.11. While the Sox were happy to get the extra 30 innings from Martinez, they'd be a lot happier if those didn't come with 47 more runs allowed. Meanwhile Derek Lowe managed to make his decent 2003 season look great by comparison; he tossed more than 180 innings in '04, allowing nearly seven runs a game (28 unearned runs!) in the process. Schilling's Cy Young–worthy performance—in a Johan Santana–free universe—was good enough to keep things respectable, but the rest of the staff's decline prevented Boston from fielding what they'd hoped would be one of the league's top starting rotations.

Even without acquiring Alex Rodriguez last winter, the Sox led the majors in runs scored for the second straight year, falling a mere 12 runs short of their gaudy 2003 total. The only major turnover from 2003 was the replacement of Todd Walker in the keystone slot with Mark Bellhorn, the new 2B acquired from the Rockies for next to nothing. Bellhorn's defense and strikeout propensity drew jeers from the faithful, but it's hard to argue with his patience, power, and #2 VORP ranking among AL second basemen.

Somewhere in July, however, the Sox realized that the long-awaited return of Nomar Garciaparra wasn't going to live up to expectations. Looking to cut their losses, Boston dealt the symbol of the franchise to the Cubs in a four-team deal that netted them Orlando Cabrera and Doug Mientkiewicz. Defense was the publicly stated reason for the move, a startling turnaround for an administration that had gathered bats at the expense of defense in nearly every transaction of its history.

Fortunately for the brain trust, the team went on a conveniently timed 22–3 hot streak in mid-August, saving

TABLE 1. RED SOX PITCHING PERFORMANCES 2003–2004

Group	Year	ERA	RA	H/9	BB/9	HR/9	K/9
Relievers	2003	4.83	5.33	9.59	3.40	1.00	7.73
Relievers	2004	3.87	4.34	8.52	3.27	0.93	6.82
Starters	2003	4.30	4.78	9.05	2.79	0.91	6.63
Starters	2004	4.31	4.95	9.02	2.55	1.01	7.11

TABLE 2. HITTING PERFORMANCES PRE- AND POST-TRADE

Players	Dates	AVG	OBP	SLG
All Batters	Pre-Trade	.280	.358	.469
Cabrera/Mientkiewicz	Post-Trade	.269	.309	.418
Everyone Else	Post-Trade	.288	.373	.490

TABLE 3. PITCHING PERFORMANCES PRE- AND POST-TRADE

Players	Dates	RA	ERA	BB/9	SO/9	BABIP
Pitchers	Pre-Trade	4.86	4.12	2.98	6.96	.297
Pitchers	Post-Trade	4.61	4.28	2.42	7.13	.276

everyone from the media firestorm. Simultaneity is not causality: Absent some mystical hex lifted by Garciaparra's departure, the arrival of Cabrera and Mietkiewicz was not the spark that ignited the Red Sox (see tables 2 and 3).

Cabrera, while slightly better than Garciaparra with the glove, is no longer a plus defender at short and Mientkiewicz didn't see enough time in the field to be a significant defensive upgrade. While Boston's pitchers' BABIP improved after the trade, Cabrera (−6 FRAA) and Mientkiewicz (0) were not the reason. The Trade, for all the hand-wringing and hair-pulling, in the end did little to help the Sox reach and win the World Series.

Add it all up and the 2004 Sox appeared very similar to the 2003 version, except that one was able to win that last game against the Yanks and one wasn't. Like all champs, they were a little luckier than everyone else. But unlike some recent champs, this team truly was the best in baseball.

Having finally defeated the Yankees and won the World Series, the Red Sox will continue the transition begun with the hiring of the new administration two years ago. Under Dan Duquette, the Sox adopted the Soviet role in the New York–Boston Cold War: While the Yankees increased spending almost exponentially, Duquette futilely tried to keep up, a plan that inevitably led to poor investments sapping huge portions of the payroll and a farm system stripped of virtually all potential major league talent.

Duquette threw money at everyone. He was adept at acquiring marquee players, drafting Garciaparra, trading for Martinez and Jason Varitek, and signing Manny Ramirez. He also wasted millions, pouring money down the tubes on marginal players like Dante Bichette, Jose Offerman, and Troy O'Leary, failing to recognize free marginal talent when he saw it. Worse, over the last few seasons of his administration, Duquette emptied the farm system in a series of deals to acquire that same marginal talent in a sequence of futile pennant runs, leaving the prospect cupboard bare. Perestroika would not come under Duquette's watch; a team with one of the greatest cores of stars in the league continually collapsed under the weight of a poor supporting cast.

The new Red Sox combined a policy of short-term contracts with moderate risk—usually related to injury history—to construct the bulk of their roster. They instituted an in-house policy against guaranteed contracts longer than four years, citing the risk in signing players past any foreseeable future as well as insurance concerns and roster adaptability. Manny Ramirez and his $160 million contract was placed on irrevocable waivers, though he went unclaimed. The Sox traded for Schilling and signed him to a two-year extension, instead of escalating the bidding war with New York for Javier Vazquez.

Two years ago, Boston filled out the roster with Bill Mueller, Kevin Millar, Todd Walker, and Kim. Last winter it was Bellhorn, Pokey Reese, and even Tony Womack, eventually swapped out to World Series opponent St. Louis. All were players with major questions that led other teams to pass; the Sox turned what they could into everyday players or backups and cut the rest loose. With ample financial resources behind them, the Sox can draw virtually as many small and mid-sized cards from the deck as they like. They hunted out manageable risk, but avoided unnecessary gambles, keeping their commitments small and making sure not to sacrifice top prospects in the process.

It's a strategy that didn't come without cost. The bullpen implosion in 2003 was largely a result of injuries to pitchers who had to be replaced with more injury-prone relievers or players who just plain didn't work out. The situation was so bad that the Sox had to redo the Brandon Lyon–Jeff Suppan deal after Lyon failed a physical on arrival in Pittsburgh.

The team's position on contract length limits also had major ramifications on five core players whose contracts came due: Martinez, Lowe, Garciaparra, Varitek, and David Ortiz. Any decision on Garciaparra was avoided when he was traded and replaced with Cabrera, who was not pursued when the season ended. Lowe guaranteed his departure with a season of terrible pitching. Signing Ortiz to a two-year extension with a team option for a third last May looks like genius in light of his breakout season. At an average of under $6.5 million per season, Ortiz will be around through his peak years at a bargain-basement price considering performance projections. The Red Sox avoided committing to him further into his 30s, when players of his type typically decline, thus avoiding a potential Jason Giambi– or Mo Vaughn–sized problem.

While their policies may have netted them a gem in Ortiz, it did cost them Martinez. The Sox refused to give Martinez the guaranteed fourth year he demanded, leading to his departure to the Mets. Martinez has been declining steadily since his peak in the 2000 season (see table 4), and considering his injury risks and age, even the Sox's $40.5 million offer may end up being too much, if his arm doesn't hold up.

In Varitek's case, however, the Sox overextended themselves. Appearing unwilling to acquiesce to Scott Boras's ridiculous demands for a five-year, $55 million contract with a no-trade clause, the Red Sox offered Varitek arbitration and, with no other players on the catching free agent market, appeared headed towards a nifty solution of Varitek accepting arbitration and signing a generous one-year deal. Instead, the Red Sox signed their new captain to a four-year, $40 million behemoth of a contract for a catcher turning 33 in April. It's exactly the kind of move Duquette would have made, investing enormous capital past the foreseeable horizon in a player almost certain to decline. Did the Red Sox pay a significant premium to retain a fan favorite and keep the howling Boston media hounds at bay? Yes. Would they have been better served playing hardball with Boras or looking at other options, given how likely this contract is to be a bust? Definitely.

Again searching for the path of least resistance—and willing to spend more than was optimal thanks to the team's flowing revenue stream—the Sox spent another $40 million to land Edgar Renteria as their new shortstop through 2008. Renteria had two impressive seasons in 2002 and 2003, but his walk rate and defense both took a dive from '03 levels. Both deals are major departures for this administration.

TABLE 4. PEDRO MARTINEZ'S KEY INDICATORS 1999–2004

Year	EqSO/9	EqBB/9	EqSO/BB
1999	12.7	0.8	15.9
2000	11.6	0.5	24.0
2001	11.7	1.5	7.7
2002	10.4	1.4	7.3

As with the unwieldy contract the Dodgers have given Derek Lowe, it seems the highest-revenue teams are willing to overpay for certain players if that's the best the market has to offer. You can get away with that occasionally if you're an L.A., Boston, or New York. But even the richest teams have their budget limits. The Yankees, who passed on Carlos Beltran after claiming their budget was shot after the signings of Randy Johnson and the far more dubious Jaret Wright and Carl Pavano, are a prime example of the risks involved. By throwing a mint at two good but not great pitchers, they missed out on the plum of the free-agent market and a player much more likely to retain his value over the next several years.

The winter's other major acquisitions—Matt Clement (three years, $25.5 million), David Wells (two years, $8 million), and Wade Miller (one year, $1.5 million)—fit the new Sox's style. Signing the 30-year old Clement—a durable pitcher with great peripherals—for that amount looks like a bargain compared to the similar or larger amounts given inferior pitchers such as Russ Ortiz, Kris Benson, and Wright. Wells is over 40, but his performance record and his contract's low dollar figure bode well for the Sox. Miller's been racked with injuries in recent years, but even 15 starts at Miller's typical above-average level would easily be worth a million-and-a-half bucks.

Acquiring cheap players to replace expensive free agents can be done in one of two ways. Thus far, Boston has achieved this goal by using cast-offs from other teams, but they're working towards the point where they can do it with their own players, developed in-house. The upper levels of the farm system are still pretty thin, but a handful of promising players in the lower rungs have begun to stand out.

Several college pitchers drafted in the past two seasons are beginning to show signs of life. John Papelbon, Thomas Hottovy, and Andrew Dobies were all drafted under the new administration's watch, and Boston expects all three to move up the ladder quickly with their college-polished stuff. Combine these kids with a couple lucky leftovers from Duquette and company, and the Red Sox have the makings of a farm system, and a source of cheap, talented players.

It will be interesting to see whether the Sox take the Yankees' disposable approach toward prospects and shop them for immediate help rather than entrusting them with starting roles. Having inked Varitek and Renteria, the Sox have blocked the merely adequate but much cheaper Kelly Shoppach as well as talented shortstop prospects Hanley Ramirez and Dustin Pedroia—who will likely have to move to third and second. Clearly the Sox are not quite ready to start drawing on the thin upper ranks of the system.

With the overall off-season haul a good one and the Yankees aging as gracefully as so many boxes of Franzia, the Red Sox look like the favorites to win a division they should have won last year and return to the playoffs for the third consecutive season. Whether they can repeat as champs depends more on the inherent risks on which the team is built than anything else.

HITTERS

JEFF BAILEY 1B/C **Bats: R** **Throws: R** Born: 19-Nov-1978 Age: 26

YEAR	TM	LG	AGE	AB	H	2B	3B	HR	BB	SO	SB	CS	AVG	OBP	SLG	MLVR	EQBA	EQOBP	EQSLG	EQMLVR	VORP	DEFENSE
2002	HAR	EAS	23	309	87	17	1	13	63	78	3	3	.282	.416	.469	.232	.249	.368	.422	.010	9.6	69-1B -1 12-C 0
2003	HAR	EAS	24	362	89	18	3	13	35	74	2	1	.246	.321	.420	-.005	.214	.281	.379	-.237	-17.1	29-1B 0 26-C -5
2004	PME	EAS	25	299	88	23	3	13	46	80	2	0	.294	.404	.522	.248	.250	.348	.443	.002	16.6	59-C -16 14-LF -1
2005	*BOS*	*AL*	*26*	*170*	*43*	*10*	*1*	*6*	*21*	*46*	*1*	*1*	*.253*	*.349*	*.423*	*-.010*	*.249*	*.347*	*.426*	*-.022*	*9.5*	*50-C -16*

Breakout: 22% *Improve: 45%* *Collapse: 27%*

In his fourth year in Double-A, Bailey poked his OBP above .400 again and complemented his yearly 13 home runs with a good amount of doubles. Unfortunately, this is his third organization and, as a minor league free agent, he's likely to join his fourth next year. Everything would have to break just right for Bailey to make it as a backup in the majors, but he's doing everything he can to make it happen.

STEFAN BAILIE 1B **Bats: R** **Throws: R** Born: 16-May-1980 Age: 25

YEAR	TM	LG	AGE	AB	H	2B	3B	HR	BB	SO	SB	CS	AVG	OBP	SLG	MLVR	EQBA	EQOBP	EQSLG	EQMLVR	VORP	DEFENSE
2002	SAR	FSL	22	159	41	8	2	2	16	33	1	0	.258	.330	.371	.015	.228	.290	.346	-.256	-8.9	39-1B -4
2003	SAR	FSL	23	267	67	14	1	3	16	70	7	2	.251	.300	.345	-.035	.227	.265	.337	-.318	-21.0	52-1B -8
2004	SAR	FSL	24	222	68	23	1	11	20	40	1	0	.306	.383	.568	.379	.260	.320	.498	.037	8.6	28-1B -2
2004	PME	EAS	24	139	43	15	0	8	10	34	0	0	.309	.364	.590	.295	.254	.294	.486	-.031	2.1	26-1B 0
2005	*BOS*	*AL*	*25*	*299*	*80*	*19*	*1*	*10*	*18*	*65*	*1*	*1*	*.266*	*.318*	*.436*	*-.036*	*.262*	*.316*	*.439*	*-.048*	*7.2*	*79-1B -3*

Breakout: 30% *Improve: 51%* *Collapse: 29%*

Drafted out of Washington State in 2001, Bailie struggled through 2003, when he was fighting lower back problems and elbow issues. He had bone chips removed and finally flashed the power that's been expected since he was drafted. Bailie's certainly a bit old to be a serious prospect, but the fact that his improvement carried over two levels bodes well for the future. Another solid season and he may start drawing a little more attention.

MARK BELLHORN 2B **Bats: B** **Throws: R** Born: 23-Aug-1974 Age: 30

YEAR	TM	LG	AGE	AB	H	2B	3B	HR	BB	SO	SB	CS	AVG	OBP	SLG	MLVR	EQBA	EQOBP	EQSLG	EQMLVR	VORP	DEFENSE
2002	CHC	NL	27	445	115	24	4	27	76	144	7	5	.258	.374	.512	.210	.261	.374	.526	.169	46.8	63-2B 5 24-3B -2
2003	CHC	NL	28	139	29	7	1	2	29	46	3	3	.209	.341	.317	-.139	.209	.339	.324	-.199	0.8	38-3B -4
2003	COL	NL	28	110	26	3	0	0	21	32	2	3	.236	.368	.264	-.178	.229	.336	.248	-.295	-1.1	14-2B -2
2004	BOS	AL	29	523	138	37	3	17	88	177	6	1	.264	.373	.444	.048	.259	.374	.441	.054	37.6	113-2B -5 16-3B 1
2005	*BOS*	*AL*	*30*	*435*	*115*	*26*	*2*	*18*	*74*	*130*	*7*	*3*	*.265*	*.375*	*.458*	*.085*	*.260*	*.372*	*.461*	*.074*	*31.8*	*122-2B -5*

Breakout: 36% *Improve: 65%* *Collapse: 9%*

Bellhorn once again took pity on opposing defenders by neglecting to put the ball in play in 45% of his plate appearances. Maybe he was hoping they'd do the same and spare him the embarrassment of playing defense. Bellhorn is one of the league's more deceptively productive players, drawing constant scrutiny from the media for those strikeouts and that defense, but quieting his critics every time he hits a home run or ropes one of his copious doubles; his huge walk totals may look less impressive, but they add up to a whole lot of runs. Just keep focusing on that OBP and things will be just fine.

ORLANDO CABRERA SS Bats: R Throws: R Born: 02-Nov-1974 Age: 30

YEAR	TM	LG	AGE	AB	H	2B	3B	HR	BB	SO	SB	CS	AVG	OBP	SLG	MLVR	EQBA	EQOBP	EQSLG	EQMLVR	VORP	DEFENSE
2002	MON	NL	27	563	148	43	1	7	48	53	25	7	.263	.321	.380	-.054	.261	.317	.384	-.128	22.7	151-SS 6
2003	MON	NL	28	626	186	47	2	17	52	64	24	2	.297	.347	.460	.062	.288	.339	.450	.028	49.8	156-SS -3
2004	MON	NL	29	390	96	19	2	4	28	31	12	3	.246	.298	.336	-.164	.241	.292	.328	-.269	5.3	97-SS -2
2004	BOS	AL	29	228	67	19	1	6	11	23	4	1	.294	.320	.465	.017	.287	.318	.462	.007	14.7	53-SS -5
2005	*ANA*	*AL*	*30*	*488*	*130*	*28*	*2*	*10*	*35*	*52*	*12*	*4*	*.268*	*.318*	*.395*	*-.092*	*.269*	*.321*	*.405*	*-.080*	*17.8*	*126-SS -2*

Breakout: 12% Improve: 37% Collapse: 29%

The replacement for the Face of the Franchise, Cabrera was supposed to help compensate for the Garciaparra trade through his reportedly superior defense, thereby better equipping the club for postseason success. That's all well and good, but the problem is that Cabrera's defense has been in decline for several seasons since he hurt his back, and his bat hasn't exactly corrected for that drop-off. He had a good season in 2003, but failed to build on that, though he did play better once he arrived in Boston. With a career line of .268/.316/.409 and on the wrong side of 30, he was a risky free-agent signing. The Angels will be frowning before long after throwing four years and $32 million his way.

JOHNNY DAMON CF Bats: L Throws: L Born: 05-Nov-1973 Age: 31

YEAR	TM	LG	AGE	AB	H	2B	3B	HR	BB	SO	SB	CS	AVG	OBP	SLG	MLVR	EQBA	EQOBP	EQSLG	EQMLVR	VORP	DEFENSE
2002	BOS	AL	28	623	178	34	11	14	65	70	31	6	.286	.356	.443	.096	.290	.364	.453	.078	49.6	145-CF 12
2003	BOS	AL	29	608	166	32	6	12	68	74	30	6	.273	.345	.405	-.024	.270	.348	.404	-.035	28.4	142-CF 3
2004	BOS	AL	30	621	189	35	6	20	76	71	19	8	.304	.380	.477	.141	.302	.383	.475	.154	51.0	141-CF 10
2005	*BOS*	*AL*	*31*	*570*	*167*	*34*	*5*	*14*	*67*	*67*	*19*	*6*	*.292*	*.367*	*.446*	*.081*	*.287*	*.365*	*.450*	*.069*	*33.8*	*151-CF 2*

Breakout: 10% Improve: 50% Collapse: 14%

Though David Ortiz is more likely to be the player haunting Yankee Stadium for years to come, it was Damon's dramatic grand slam in Game Seven that finally broke New York, a fitting moment for a season in which Damon fulfilled the expectations of his $31 million contract. In his best season since 2000, Damon displayed a complete game, playing great defense in a tough park, hitting for average and power and adding a healthy dose of speed. He would be a five-tool player if the fifth tool was hair instead of arm strength. That's a small knock against a good player who had a great year and assured himself of never buying another drink in New England for the rest of his life.

BRIAN DAUBACH 1B/DH Bats: L Throws: R Born: 11-Feb-1972 Age: 33

YEAR	TM	LG	AGE	AB	H	2B	3B	HR	BB	SO	SB	CS	AVG	OBP	SLG	MLVR	EQBA	EQOBP	EQSLG	EQMLVR	VORP	DEFENSE
2002	BOS	AL	30	444	118	24	2	20	51	126	2	1	.266	.348	.464	.097	.270	.355	.474	.074	25.7	51-1B 1 27-LF -1
2003	CWS	AL	31	183	42	11	0	6	34	54	1	0	.230	.352	.388	-.044	.228	.349	.383	-.091	5.2	30-1B -1
2004	PAW	INT	32	336	92	23	0	21	71	93	0	1	.274	.403	.530	.281	.251	.374	.481	.100	19.8	74-1B -5
2004	BOS	AL	32	75	17	8	0	2	10	21	0	0	.227	.326	.413	-.102	.233	.321	.384	-.140	0.9	12-1B 0
2005	*BOS*	*AL*	*33*	*196*	*51*	*11*	*1*	*8*	*34*	*56*	*0*	*0*	*.260*	*.371*	*.452*	*.069*	*.256*	*.369*	*.456*	*.058*	*12.1*	*58-1B -4*

Breakout: 33% Improve: 63% Collapse: 20%

The Red Sox sure do a good job of collecting lots of the same kind of player, don't they? Daubach played well in Pawtucket last year, but he doesn't bring anything to the table that the Sox didn't already have in spades. As injury replacements go, he's nice to have around, but his chances of getting back to the majors with the Sox are marginal.

CHRIS DURBIN OF Bats: R Throws: R Born: 08-Sep-1981 Age: 23

YEAR	TM	LG	AGE	AB	H	2B	3B	HR	BB	SO	SB	CS	AVG	OBP	SLG	MLVR	EQBA	EQOBP	EQSLG	EQMLVR	VORP	DEFENSE
2003	AUG	SAL	21	96	22	4	0	4	9	19	1	2	.229	.300	.396	.013	.192	.235	.323	-.418	-11.4	12-RF -1
2004	SAR	FSL	22	470	131	32	6	7	39	79	8	10	.279	.344	.417	.103	.250	.303	.384	-.163	-2.3	75-CF -4 37-RF -1
2005	*BOS*	*AL*	*23*	*237*	*58*	*14*	*1*	*5*	*15*	*50*	*2*	*2*	*.246*	*.302*	*.381*	*-.153*	*.241*	*.300*	*.384*	*-.166*	*-2.3*	*64-CF -7*

Breakout: 27% Improve: 50% Collapse: 23%

A Baylor product drafted in the 10th round in 2003, Durbin posted a thoroughly mediocre season in his first full year in professional ball. But in a system thin on outfield prospects, he stands out because of his defense. If he can add a little more pop with the bat, Durbin could work out a nice career as a fifth outfielder.

MICKEY HALL OF **Bats: L** **Throws: L** Born: 20-May-1985 Age: 20

YEAR	TM	LG	AGE	AB	H	2B	3B	HR	BB	SO	SB	CS	AVG	OBP	SLG	MLVR	EQBA	EQOBP	EQSLG	EQMLVR	VORP	DEFENSE
2004	AUG	SAL	19	403	99	24	5	13	58	134	13	4	.246	.342	.427	.057	.210	.289	.355	-.257	-26.1	69-LF -9 23-CF -3
2005	*BOS*	*AL*	*20*	*339*	*76*	*17*	*3*	*6*	*34*	*112*	*7*	*3*	*.224*	*.301*	*.352*	*-.206*	*.220*	*.299*	*.355*	*-.218*	*-10.5*	*92-LF -6*

Breakout: 36% *Improve: 55%* *Collapse: 20%*

Drafted in the second round in '03 out of high school, Hall struggled a bit the first couple months of the season, but turned things around for a pretty solid year in a tough pitcher's park. He shows good patience at the plate, but so far that's resulted in both high strikeout and walk totals. He's only 19 and once he gets comfortable with the professional lifestyle, he could take off quickly.

TIM HUMMEL 3B **Bats: R** **Throws: R** Born: 18-Nov-1978 Age: 26

YEAR	TM	LG	AGE	AB	H	2B	3B	HR	BB	SO	SB	CS	AVG	OBP	SLG	MLVR	EQBA	EQOBP	EQSLG	EQMLVR	VORP	DEFENSE
2002	CHR	INT	23	523	136	33	0	4	51	95	6	5	.260	.332	.346	-.062	.236	.307	.317	-.258	-8.9	78-SS -5 53-2B 1
2003	CHR	INT	24	476	135	25	3	15	46	83	9	3	.284	.350	.443	.125	.269	.339	.433	-.012	25.1	95-3B -2 26-SS -4
2003	CIN	NL	24	84	19	5	0	2	8	13	0	0	.226	.290	.357	-.171	.226	.275	.345	-.288	0.3	15-3B 0
2004	LOU	INT	25	152	44	13	0	2	12	27	2	0	.289	.345	.414	-.013	.242	.296	.342	-.241	-2.8	16-3B -2
2004	CIN	NL	25	110	24	4	0	1	8	17	1	0	.218	.281	.282	-.293	.223	.277	.268	-.393	-4.6	22-3B 0
2005	*BOS*	*AL*	*26*	*165*	*42*	*8*	*1*	*4*	*14*	*30*	*2*	*1*	*.257*	*.321*	*.382*	*-.109*	*.253*	*.319*	*.385*	*-.122*	*2.4*	*47-3B -1*

Breakout: 25% *Improve: 44%* *Collapse: 33%*

Stuck in Cincinnati but out of the Reds' plans, Hummel was grabbed off waivers by the Sox in September, mostly on the strength of his strong 2003 in Charlotte with the White Sox. Hummel does a good job of drawing walks, but his power has been limited to that one year. He should make for a good utility infielder and injury insurance for the Sox in '05.

GABE KAPLER OF **Bats: R** **Throws: R** Born: 31-Jul-1975 Age: 29

YEAR	TM	LG	AGE	AB	H	2B	3B	HR	BB	SO	SB	CS	AVG	OBP	SLG	MLVR	EQBA	EQOBP	EQSLG	EQMLVR	VORP	DEFENSE
2002	TEX	AL	26	196	51	12	1	0	8	30	5	2	.260	.285	.332	-.262	.258	.280	.314	-.302	-6.5	26-LF -2 17-CF 0
2002	COL	NL	26	119	37	4	3	2	8	23	6	2	.311	.359	.445	.061	.297	.341	.432	.014	5.4	18-RF 1 12-LF 0
2003	COL	NL	27	67	15	2	0	0	8	18	2	0	.224	.307	.254	-.307	.227	.274	.242	-.434	3.0	
2003	BOS	AL	27	158	46	11	1	4	14	23	4	2	.291	.349	.449	.073	.284	.351	.445	.039	7.4	22-RF -1 12-LF -1
2004	BOS	AL	28	290	79	14	1	6	15	49	5	4	.272	.311	.390	-.128	.270	.313	.389	-.122	1.2	65-RF 2 10-CF 0
2005	*BOS*	*AL*	*29*	*181*	*48*	*10*	*1*	*3*	*13*	*32*	*3*	*2*	*.267*	*.318*	*.391*	*-.097*	*.263*	*.315*	*.394*	*-.109*	*2.7*	*50-RF -2*

Breakout: 18% *Improve: 37%* *Collapse: 33%*

Seeing quite a bit of playing time while Trot Nixon was busy in rehab, Kapler didn't hit as well as expected, looking overmatched against right-handed pitchers. He still hits lefties pretty well and plays a decent outfield, but elected to sign on with the Yomiuri Giants for far more money and playing time than he was likely to get stateside.

DAVE McCARTY 1B/P? **Bats: R** **Throws: L** Born: 23-Nov-1969 Age: 35

YEAR	TM	LG	AGE	AB	H	2B	3B	HR	BB	SO	SB	CS	AVG	OBP	SLG	MLVR	EQBA	EQOBP	EQSLG	EQMLVR	VORP	DEFENSE
2002	DUR	INT	32	114	37	7	1	8	14	33	0	1	.325	.398	.614	.437	.289	.362	.561	.225	10.9	25-1B -1
2003	SAC	PCL	33	352	95	23	2	15	44	71	4	1	.270	.351	.474	.138	.245	.324	.433	-.059	2.5	60-1B 4
2003	OAK	AL	33	26	7	2	0	0	1	7	0	0	.269	.286	.346	-.182	.308	.237	.346	-.301	-0.4	
2003	BOS	AL	33	27	11	3	0	1	2	7	0	0	.407	.448	.630	.626	.462	.441	.654	.739	4.8	
2004	BOS	AL	34	151	39	8	1	4	14	40	1	0	.258	.327	.404	-.079	.257	.329	.399	-.088	3.2	33-1B 0
2005	*BOS*	*AL*	*35*	*123*	*30*	*6*	*1*	*4*	*14*	*34*	*1*	*0*	*.243*	*.325*	*.408*	*-.079*	*.238*	*.322*	*.412*	*-.091*	*2.5*	*37-1B -3*

Breakout: 21% *Improve: 36%* *Collapse: 37%*

Over his spotty twelve-year career, McCarty has seen time with seven clubs, none of which have kept him aboard for very long. His Kieschnick-inspired attempt to become a two-way player for 2004 did result in a few brief appearances (3.2 IP), but ultimately the Red Sox just didn't need McCarty's increasingly limited array of skills. He'll make a bid for his eighth team this winter and it's likely someone's bench has a spot for him.

DOUG MIENTKIEWICZ 1B Bats: L Throws: R Born: 19-Jun-1974 Age: 31

YEAR	TM	LG	AGE	AB	H	2B	3B	HR	BB	SO	SB	CS	AVG	OBP	SLG	MLVR	EQBA	EQOBP	EQSLG	EQMLVR	VORP	DEFENSE
2002	MIN	AL	28	467	122	29	1	10	74	69	1	2	.261	.365	.392	.021	.263	.371	.400	-.003	17.7	131-1B 9
2003	MIN	AL	29	487	146	38	1	11	74	55	4	1	.300	.393	.450	.154	.300	.398	.454	.149	38.3	126-1B 10
2004	MIN	AL	30	284	70	18	0	5	38	38	2	2	.246	.340	.363	-.109	.247	.340	.369	-.115	3.0	73-1B -4
2004	BOS	AL	30	107	23	6	1	1	10	18	0	1	.215	.286	.318	-.304	.210	.287	.314	-.316	-4.5	30-1B 0
2005	*BOS*	*AL*	*31*	*345*	*94*	*21*	*1*	*8*	*48*	*49*	*2*	*1*	*.272*	*.364*	*.410*	*.011*	*.267*	*.361*	*.413*	*.000*	*12.7*	*96-1B 0*

Breakout: 26% *Improve: 56%* *Collapse: 12%*

The less-celebrated component of the The Trade, Mientkiewicz saw very limited playing time down the stretch and through the playoffs. Mientkiewicz does what he does: Draws walks, hits for average but not power, and fields his position well. A good platoon candidate for a team with a big ol' lefty thumper.

KEVIN MILLAR 1B Bats: R Throws: R Born: 24-Sep-1971 Age: 33

YEAR	TM	LG	AGE	AB	H	2B	3B	HR	BB	SO	SB	CS	AVG	OBP	SLG	MLVR	EQBA	EQOBP	EQSLG	EQMLVR	VORP	DEFENSE
2002	FLA	NL	30	438	134	41	0	16	40	74	0	2	.306	.366	.509	.250	.312	.366	.527	.209	36.9	75-LF 2 18-RF -1
2003	BOS	AL	31	544	150	30	1	25	60	108	3	2	.276	.348	.472	.082	.272	.350	.474	.067	28.6	95-1B 9 19-LF -1
2004	BOS	AL	32	508	151	36	0	18	57	91	1	1	.297	.383	.474	.137	.297	.381	.476	.147	37.6	56-1B 2 48-RF -1
2005	*BOS*	*AL*	*33*	*384*	*107*	*23*	*1*	*14*	*42*	*73*	*0*	*1*	*.279*	*.358*	*.455*	*.065*	*.274*	*.355*	*.459*	*.054*	*18.9*	*104-1B 0*

Breakout: 7% *Improve: 34%* *Collapse: 26%*

Millar once again signed up for the extra duties of "Media Clubhouse Symbol" and designated tag-line generator. All the while, he played a decent first base and kept hitting for moderate power, with and a high OBP. He automatically activated his option year for 2005 by reaching playing time goals, much to the delight of media members short on quotes at deadline time.

DOUG MIRABELLI C Bats: R Throws: R Born: 18-Oct-1970 Age: 34

YEAR	TM	LG	AGE	AB	H	2B	3B	HR	BB	SO	SB	CS	AVG	OBP	SLG	MLVR	EQBA	EQOBP	EQSLG	EQMLVR	VORP	DEFENSE
2002	BOS	AL	31	151	34	7	0	7	17	33	0	0	.225	.312	.411	-.067	.233	.313	.413	-.116	6.1	40-C 3
2003	BOS	AL	32	163	42	13	0	6	11	36	0	0	.258	.307	.448	-.042	.261	.305	.441	-.070	6.2	43-C -5
2004	BOS	AL	33	160	45	12	0	9	19	46	0	0	.281	.368	.525	.167	.287	.365	.522	.174	15.6	40-C -11
2005	*BOS*	*AL*	*34*	*137*	*34*	*7*	*0*	*6*	*16*	*39*	*0*	*0*	*.249*	*.331*	*.439*	*-.024*	*.244*	*.329*	*.443*	*-.035*	*8.2*	*41-C -7*

Breakout: 12% *Improve: 32%* *Collapse: 42%*

Being a backup catcher is kind of like being a long reliever, but without all the trouble of having to keep your arm in an ice bucket or the whiplash when you give up a home run. Mirabelli once again settled into the role of Wakefield's personal caddy, posting career highs in most offensive categories in the process. The Sox re-signed him pretty early with Varitek an uncertainty at the time. He'll return to being one of the better backup catchers in the game, even while his numbers figure to drop precipitously.

BRANDON MOSS OF Bats: L Throws: R Born: 16-Sep-1983 Age: 21

YEAR	TM	LG	AGE	AB	H	2B	3B	HR	BB	SO	SB	CS	AVG	OBP	SLG	MLVR	EQBA	EQOBP	EQSLG	EQMLVR	VORP	DEFENSE
2003	LOW	NYP	19	228	54	15	4	7	15	53	7	5	.237	.290	.430	.045	.189	.230	.352	-.389	-42.6	59-RF -3
2004	AUG	SAL	20	433	147	25	6	13	46	75	19	8	.339	.402	.515	.351	.294	.346	.440	.032	13.0	92-RF -2 12-LF -1
2004	SAR	FSL	20	83	35	2	1	2	7	15	2	0	.422	.462	.542	.570	.373	.412	.482	.286	9.3	21-RF -1
2005	*BOS*	*AL*	*21*	*395*	*102*	*22*	*3*	*11*	*28*	*86*	*7*	*3*	*.257*	*.311*	*.404*	*-.099*	*.253*	*.308*	*.408*	*-.111*	*0.7*	*103-RF -4*

Breakout: 12% *Improve: 29%* *Collapse: 43%*

While batting average varies more widely than most any other offensive metric from season to season, leaps like the one Moss made cannot be ignored. After blistering low-A-ball for most of the season, Moss had an even more impressive stint in high-A to finish out the year. Most of his value may be wrapped up in that batting average, but he improved his walk rate, cut his strikeouts, and maintained his power in his first year of full-season ball. Another year to back up this one and you'll be hearing a lot more about Moss.

BILL MUELLER 3B **Bats: B** **Throws: R** Born: 17-Mar-1971 Age: 34

YEAR	TM	LG	AGE	AB	H	2B	3B	HR	BB	SO	SB	CS	AVG	OBP	SLG	MLVR	EQBA	EQOBP	EQSLG	EQMLVR	VORP	DEFENSE	
2002	CHC	NL	31	353	94	19	4	7	51	41	0	0	.266	.355	.402	.043	.270	.356	.413	-.008	20.1	99-3B -2	
2003	BOS	AL	32	524	171	45	5	19	59	77	1	4	.326	.398	.540	.294	.326	.401	.547	.310	65.2	120-3B 6	
2004	BOS	AL	33	399	113	27	1	12	51	56	2	2	.283	.365	.446	.057	.279	.365	.446	.061	21.8	89-3B 8	12-2B -2
2005	*BOS*	*AL*	*34*	*392*	*110*	*24*	*2*	*11*	*49*	*55*	*1*	*1*	*.280*	*.362*	*.433*	*.046*	*.275*	*.360*	*.437*	*.034*	*18.6*	*107-3B -1*	

Breakout: 8% *Improve: 30%* *Collapse: 33%*

His "Outlier of the Year" Award secure after that 2003 season, Mueller did a good job fighting regression to the mean and managed to put up numbers better than his previous career averages at age 33. The Red Sox picked up his option for 2005, a move that allows them to shop him as a cheap option for teams in need of help at the hot corner or to keep him as Kevin Youkilis's overstudy for one more year.

TROT NIXON OF **Bats: L** **Throws: L** Born: 11-Apr-1974 Age: 31

YEAR	TM	LG	AGE	AB	H	2B	3B	HR	BB	SO	SB	CS	AVG	OBP	SLG	MLVR	EQBA	EQOBP	EQSLG	EQMLVR	VORP	DEFENSE	
2002	BOS	AL	28	532	136	36	3	24	65	109	4	2	.256	.338	.470	.076	.259	.346	.481	.058	25.0	136-RF 8	12-CF 1
2003	BOS	AL	29	441	135	24	6	28	65	96	4	2	.306	.396	.578	.326	.305	.401	.582	.334	49.6	119-RF -3	
2004	BOS	AL	30	149	47	9	1	6	15	24	0	0	.315	.377	.510	.194	.310	.377	.510	.201	13.1	32-RF 0	
2005	*BOS*	*AL*	*31*	*269*	*76*	*16*	*1*	*12*	*35*	*54*	*1*	*1*	*.280*	*.365*	*.488*	*.121*	*.276*	*.362*	*.492*	*.111*	*20.5*	*75-RF -1*	

Breakout: 11% *Improve: 27%* *Collapse: 40%*

It seemed at times that Nixon was trying to relive every past injury from his career all in one season, missing most of the first half with a disc injury and much of the second with a quad tear. In the 149 ABs he did manage, Nixon hit very well, right in line with his three previous seasons, a good sign considering the severity of those maladies. Nixon has quietly become one of the best right fielders in the AL when healthy; the Sox would greatly benefit from 450 healthy plate appearances.

DAVID ORTIZ DH **Bats: L** **Throws: L** Born: 18-Nov-1975 Age: 29

YEAR	TM	LG	AGE	AB	H	2B	3B	HR	BB	SO	SB	CS	AVG	OBP	SLG	MLVR	EQBA	EQOBP	EQSLG	EQMLVR	VORP	DEFENSE
2002	MIN	AL	26	412	112	32	1	20	43	87	1	2	.272	.339	.500	.122	.275	.347	.507	.110	28.2	12-1B 0
2003	BOS	AL	27	448	129	39	2	31	58	83	0	0	.288	.369	.592	.284	.286	.374	.593	.286	48.5	38-1B 1
2004	BOS	AL	28	582	175	47	3	41	75	133	0	0	.301	.380	.603	.306	.299	.382	.607	.333	71.3	29-1B -1
2005	*BOS*	*AL*	*29*	*501*	*143*	*33*	*2*	*32*	*70*	*108*	*0*	*0*	*.287*	*.375*	*.553*	*.226*	*.282*	*.373*	*.557*	*.216*	*46.9*	*136-DH 1*

Breakout: 12% *Improve: 38%* *Collapse: 13%*

What else can you say about Big Papi that hasn't already been said? Ortiz had one of the great postseasons of all time, officially arriving on the stage as a superstar and savior of a beleaguered Nation. He improved on virtually all his major statistical measures for the fourth year in a row and thrust himself into the middle of the wide-open MVP discussion in the AL. Though he did lose out to Vladimir Guerrero in the end, the Red Sox were prescient enough to sign him to a two-year, $12.5 million extension in May. While that move may have been questioned, considering the significant players headed for free agency at the end of the season, it looks downright psychic now, a major coup for the young Boston front office.

DUSTIN PEDROIA SS **Bats: R** **Throws: R** Born: 17-Aug-1983 Age: 21

YEAR	TM	LG	AGE	AB	H	2B	3B	HR	BB	SO	SB	CS	AVG	OBP	SLG	MLVR	EQBA	EQOBP	EQSLG	EQMLVR	VORP	DEFENSE
2004	AUG	SAL	20	50	20	5	0	1	6	3	2	0	.400	.474	.560	.578	.320	.343	.440	.050	4.0	11-SS 1
2004	SAR	FSL	20	107	36	8	3	2	13	4	0	2	.336	.417	.523	.393	.300	.367	.482	.134	11.9	30-SS -2
2005	*BOS*	*AL*	*21*	*411*	*123*	*28*	*3*	*7*	*37*	*20*	*4*	*3*	*.299*	*.368*	*.435*	*.072*	*.294*	*.366*	*.438*	*.061*	*32.0*	*111-SS -1*

Breakout: 14% *Improve: 31%* *Collapse: 43%*

The first pick by the Sox in the 2004 draft, Pedroia was a superstar at Arizona State, All-Pac-10 all three seasons, once Pac-10 player of the year, and twice National Defensive Player of the Year. He slipped to the Sox at 65th overall because he's only 5′8″, but the organization loves him. Though he won't show much power, he hits for a high average and keeps his walks up. His pro debut saw him blitz through the Sally League before performing well at high-A Sarasota. The presence of the newly signed Edgar Renteria and Hanley Ramirez plus Pedroia's size mean his future is most likely on the other side of second. He could quickly turn into the player everyone in Anaheim thought David Eckstein was.

KENNY PEREZ — SS — Bats: B — Throws: R — Born: 28-Sep-1981 — Age: 23

YEAR	TM	LG	AGE	AB	H	2B	3B	HR	BB	SO	SB	CS	AVG	OBP	SLG	MLVR	EQBA	EQOBP	EQSLG	EQMLVR	VORP	DEFENSE
2002	SAR	FSL	20	447	112	12	4	2	51	58	16	5	.251	.329	.309	-.069	.222	.289	.282	-.350	-21.7	96-SS 1
2003	SAR	FSL	21	230	64	17	4	2	15	24	11	4	.278	.319	.413	.098	.252	.285	.402	-.170	2.6	58-SS -8
2004	PME	EAS	22	400	112	31	5	5	23	59	12	4	.280	.323	.420	-.021	.244	.283	.367	-.229	-3.1	84-SS -11 14-2B -2
2005	*BOS*	*AL*	*23*	*272*	*70*	*17*	*2*	*4*	*17*	*39*	*6*	*2*	*.259*	*.304*	*.380*	*-.142*	*.254*	*.302*	*.383*	*-.154*	*6.1*	*72-SS -8*

Breakout: 31%   Improve: 46%   Collapse: 23%

How many shortstops are too many? With Edgar Renteria in place, the continued rise of Hanley Ramirez and the drafting of Pedroia, Perez's status has taken a big hit in the past year. He's more athlete than ballplayer and while the Sox do love his physical tools, he still hasn't developed the power or patience required to be a serious prospect. He's still young and held his own in Portland this year, but the Sox moved him to second when Ramirez arrived. With all the talent in front of him and young but talented players like Christian Lara and Luis Soto coming up behind him, his future is with another organization.

HANLEY RAMIREZ — SS — Bats: B — Throws: R — Born: 23-Dec-1983 — Age: 21

YEAR	TM	LG	AGE	AB	H	2B	3B	HR	BB	SO	SB	CS	AVG	OBP	SLG	MLVR	EQBA	EQOBP	EQSLG	EQMLVR	VORP	DEFENSE
2002	LOW	NYP	18	97	36	9	2	1	4	14	4	3	.371	.400	.536	.442	.306	.327	.459	.037	12.6	22-SS -5
2003	AUG	SAL	19	422	116	24	3	8	32	73	36	13	.275	.327	.403	.091	.240	.278	.363	-.247	-6.3	102-SS -17
2004	SAR	FSL	20	239	74	8	4	1	17	39	12	7	.310	.364	.389	.119	.277	.321	.360	-.143	4.5	60-SS -10
2004	PME	EAS	20	129	40	7	2	5	10	26	12	3	.310	.360	.512	.185	.268	.316	.433	-.055	5.6	32-SS -2
2005	*BOS*	*AL*	*21*	*430*	*113*	*24*	*3*	*8*	*23*	*81*	*13*	*5*	*.262*	*.304*	*.386*	*-.130*	*.257*	*.302*	*.389*	*-.143*	*8.1*	*110-SS -7*

Breakout: 16%   Improve: 40%   Collapse: 39%

It says a lot both about Ramirez and the Red Sox's farm system that he's been their best prospect for almost three seasons now. While there were some discipline concerns after a few incidents in '03, Ramirez carried himself like a professional in 2004, keeping out of trouble and progressing well on the field. He missed seven weeks with a broken wrist but played well at both Sarasota and Portland. He doesn't draw walks, but he's a heck of an athlete, plays excellent defense despite some lofty error totals, and controls the strike zone by putting the ball in play rather than taking the free pass. The Renteria signing means a position change is in his future if he's to stay with Boston.

MANNY RAMIREZ — LF — Bats: R — Throws: R — Born: 30-May-1972 — Age: 33

YEAR	TM	LG	AGE	AB	H	2B	3B	HR	BB	SO	SB	CS	AVG	OBP	SLG	MLVR	EQBA	EQOBP	EQSLG	EQMLVR	VORP	DEFENSE
2002	BOS	AL	30	436	152	31	0	33	73	85	0	0	.349	.450	.647	.575	.359	.457	.664	.597	83.3	59-LF -5
2003	BOS	AL	31	569	185	36	1	37	97	94	3	1	.325	.427	.587	.404	.324	.430	.592	.414	77.9	115-LF -7
2004	BOS	AL	32	568	175	44	0	43	82	124	2	4	.308	.397	.613	.353	.309	.399	.618	.386	68.6	121-LF -7
2005	*BOS*	*AL*	*33*	*503*	*155*	*34*	*1*	*33*	*85*	*106*	*1*	*1*	*.309*	*.412*	*.574*	*.332*	*.304*	*.409*	*.579*	*.322*	*55.5*	*141-LF -6*

Breakout: 12%   Improve: 40%   Collapse: 11%

Halfway through the guaranteed portion of Ramirez's contract, he's still putting up some of the best offensive numbers in the league, $160 million contract or not. His OBP dipped below .400 for the first time since 1998, but in a season where he whacked 43 home runs and 87 extra-base hits, that's really nitpicking. His defense is what it is, though with Fenway's limited real estate in left and Jesus in center, there's no better outfield spot in which to put a lousy defender. Expect more of the same in 2005.

POKEY REESE — 2B/SS — Bats: R — Throws: R — Born: 10-Jun-1973 — Age: 32

YEAR	TM	LG	AGE	AB	H	2B	3B	HR	BB	SO	SB	CS	AVG	OBP	SLG	MLVR	EQBA	EQOBP	EQSLG	EQMLVR	VORP	DEFENSE
2002	PIT	NL	29	421	111	25	0	4	41	81	12	1	.264	.330	.352	-.088	.267	.326	.356	-.146	14.5	114-2B 9
2003	PIT	NL	30	107	23	2	0	1	9	31	6	0	.215	.271	.262	-.338	.215	.265	.243	-.456	-3.0	33-2B 2
2004	BOS	AL	31	244	54	7	2	3	17	60	6	2	.221	.271	.303	-.360	.213	.269	.296	-.376	-7.3	61-SS 0 22-2B -1
2005	*BOS*	*AL*	*32*	*178*	*43*	*8*	*1*	*2*	*12*	*42*	*5*	*1*	*.239*	*.289*	*.332*	*-.245*	*.235*	*.287*	*.334*	*-.259*	*-0.8*	*50-SS 1*

Breakout: 22%   Improve: 44%   Collapse: 40%

One of the raging arguments in Boston all season long was who should be playing second. Reese made the situation debatable with a solid start to the season, but thumb and ribcage injuries curtailed his season. While Reese certainly still plays well in the field, his bat has become far too much of a liability to justify an everyday job, especially when pitted against a masher like Bellhorn.

DAVE ROBERTS CF Bats: L Throws: L Born: 31-May-1972 Age: 33

YEAR	TM	LG	AGE	AB	H	2B	3B	HR	BB	SO	SB	CS	AVG	OBP	SLG	MLVR	EQBA	EQOBP	EQSLG	EQMLVR	VORP	DEFENSE			
2002	LAD	NL	30	422	117	14	7	3	48	51	45	10	.277	.353	.365	.017	.292	.365	.387	-.011	25.9	106-CF	0		
2003	LAD	NL	31	388	97	6	5	2	43	39	40	14	.250	.331	.307	-.134	.260	.341	.321	-.170	4.9	99-CF	-1		
2004	LAD	NL	32	233	59	4	7	2	28	31	33	1	.253	.340	.356	-.071	.251	.337	.357	-.134	11.3	41-LF	1	16-CF	1
2004	BOS	AL	32	86	22	10	0	2	10	17	5	2	.256	.330	.442	-.038	.262	.325	.429	-.049	1.7	12-RF	0		
2005	*SDP*	*NL*	*33*	*275*	*72*	*10*	*3*	*3*	*29*	*36*	*23*	*6*	*.263*	*.337*	*.353*	*-.123*	*.272*	*.344*	*.377*	*-.075*	*8.2*	*76-CF*	*-4*		

Breakout: 14% *Improve: 37%* *Collapse: 42%*

The runner behind the most famous stolen base in Red Sox history, Roberts is still a decent hitter, but his game is built around speed with very little power involved. There's still a place for that kind of player on a well-managed NL team, especially one with right-handed power off the bench. For the center field-needy Padres, he'll be a nifty fit.

KELLY SHOPPACH C Bats: R Throws: R Born: 29-Apr-1980 Age: 25

YEAR	TM	LG	AGE	AB	H	2B	3B	HR	BB	SO	SB	CS	AVG	OBP	SLG	MLVR	EQBA	EQOBP	EQSLG	EQMLVR	VORP	DEFENSE	
2002	SAR	FSL	22	414	112	35	1	10	59	112	2	1	.271	.369	.432	.157	.236	.318	.397	-.126	6.6	92-C	-3
2003	PME	EAS	23	340	96	30	2	12	35	83	0	0	.282	.353	.488	.131	.237	.304	.427	-.111	6.6	82-C	7
2004	PAW	INT	24	399	93	25	0	22	46	138	0	0	.233	.320	.461	.015	.214	.297	.420	-.150	2.7	97-C	-2
2005	*BOS*	*AL*	*25*	*216*	*52*	*12*	*1*	*9*	*22*	*67*	*0*	*0*	*.242*	*.320*	*.421*	*-.071*	*.238*	*.318*	*.424*	*-.083*	*6.6*	*60-C*	*-5*

Breakout: 32% *Improve: 54%* *Collapse: 27%*

Shoppach's biggest assets have long been his arm and defense, the former having cast some doubt after shoulder surgery in the fall of 2002. Despite some rumors about declines in his defense, Shoppach drew raves for his quick release and arm strength from both the Sox front office and scouts. He had a rough year in terms of batting average and strikeouts, but his walks were back up and he flashed some real power for the first time. He had a little trouble adjusting to the more advanced pitchers in Triple-A, but a solid second half looked to put him in line for Boston some time in 2005—at least until the Sox re-signed both Mirabelli and Varitek. His future now lies either as a backup to Varitek in 2006 or with another organization.

EARL SNYDER 3B Bats: R Throws: R Born: 06-May-1976 Age: 29

YEAR	TM	LG	AGE	AB	H	2B	3B	HR	BB	SO	SB	CS	AVG	OBP	SLG	MLVR	EQBA	EQOBP	EQSLG	EQMLVR	VORP	DEFENSE			
2002	BUF	INT	26	400	105	29	1	19	43	96	0	2	.263	.341	.482	.132	.242	.320	.454	-.040	17.1	62-3B	-7	39-1B	-4
2003	PAW	INT	27	467	119	25	1	22	24	113	0	0	.255	.299	.454	.039	.238	.287	.439	-.124	7.8	102-3B	-6	12-1B	1
2004	PAW	INT	28	538	147	43	1	36	35	128	1	1	.273	.323	.558	.189	.245	.297	.504	-.009	26.1	91-3B	8	29-1B	-1
2005	*BOS*	*AL*	*29*	*286*	*72*	*16*	*1*	*13*	*21*	*72*	*0*	*1*	*.250*	*.307*	*.446*	*-.055*	*.246*	*.305*	*.449*	*-.067*	*5.9*	*76-3B*	*-4*		

Breakout: 24% *Improve: 44%* *Collapse: 26%*

Part of the collection of older potential injury replacements in Pawtucket, Snyder had the same season he always has, but with a few more home runs than usual. While his power is impressive, his defense has always been just this side of terrible, as is his strike zone management. That, combined with his age, keeps him in the category of Quad-A player.

CHAD SPANN 3B Bats: R Throws: R Born: 25-Oct-1983 Age: 21

YEAR	TM	LG	AGE	AB	H	2B	3B	HR	BB	SO	SB	CS	AVG	OBP	SLG	MLVR	EQBA	EQOBP	EQSLG	EQMLVR	VORP	DEFENSE	
2003	AUG	SAL	19	414	129	21	3	5	40	64	9	5	.312	.379	.413	.203	.273	.322	.372	-.127	7.5	100-3B	-1
2004	SAR	FSL	20	214	54	9	0	4	9	53	6	2	.252	.291	.350	-.083	.218	.241	.310	-.409	-15.1	51-3B	-3
2005	*BOS*	*AL*	*21*	*343*	*81*	*16*	*1*	*6*	*16*	*77*	*4*	*2*	*.237*	*.280*	*.342*	*-.250*	*.233*	*.278*	*.345*	*-.263*	*-13.5*	*89-3B*	*-5*

Breakout: 14% *Improve: 39%* *Collapse: 39%*

After an impressive 2003 in low-A ball, Spann was hitting well in Sarasota before badly injuring his knee, knocking him out for two months, an injury that bothered him even when he returned to the field. There are some concerns about him hitting too many balls on the ground, a problem that could worsen if his knee injury costs him some speed in the long run. He's still young, but how he plays when healthy in 2005 will do a lot to determining his future with the club.

JASON VARITEK — C — Bats: B — Throws: R — Born: 11-Apr-1972 — Age: 33

YEAR	TM	LG	AGE	AB	H	2B	3B	HR	BB	SO	SB	CS	AVG	OBP	SLG	MLVR	EQBA	EQOBP	EQSLG	EQMLVR	VORP	DEFENSE
2002	BOS	AL	30	467	124	27	1	10	41	95	4	3	.266	.332	.392	-.029	.269	.339	.399	-.060	22.6	122-C -2
2003	BOS	AL	31	451	123	31	1	25	51	106	3	2	.273	.351	.512	.130	.272	.354	.515	.131	38.5	118-C 2
2004	BOS	AL	32	463	137	30	1	18	62	126	10	3	.296	.390	.482	.156	.294	.391	.483	.171	46.0	121-C 4
2005	*BOS*	*AL*	*33*	*366*	*100*	*21*	*1*	*15*	*44*	*89*	*5*	*2*	*.273*	*.360*	*.458*	*.067*	*.269*	*.357*	*.462*	*.056*	*27.8*	*100-C -1*

Breakout: 11% *Improve: 37%* *Collapse: 27%*

Following up his impressive 2003 campaign with an equally productive 2004, Varitek has established himself as one of the best offensive catchers in the game. He established a new career high in OBP, continued to hit for power, and hasn't yet shown the inevitable wear and tear common among backstops. Still, the history of catchers entering their mid-30s is littered with disappointments. The Sox gave him $40 million through age 36, a political signing if ever there was one.

KEVIN YOUKILIS — 3B — Bats: R — Throws: R — Born: 15-Mar-1979 — Age: 26

YEAR	TM	LG	AGE	AB	H	2B	3B	HR	BB	SO	SB	CS	AVG	OBP	SLG	MLVR	EQBA	EQOBP	EQSLG	EQMLVR	VORP	DEFENSE
2002	SAR	FSL	23	268	79	16	0	3	49	37	0	2	.295	.422	.388	.193	.257	.355	.350	-.105	-2.1	40-1B -5 33-3B -2
2002	TRN	EAS	23	160	55	10	0	5	31	18	5	4	.344	.462	.500	.409	.302	.398	.444	.137	17.0	44-3B -1
2003	PME	EAS	24	312	102	23	1	6	86	40	7	0	.327	.487	.465	.332	.282	.428	.420	.143	36.3	92-3B 7
2003	PAW	INT	24	109	18	3	0	2	18	21	0	1	.165	.295	.248	-.281	.136	.256	.200	-.561	-13.7	29-3B -2
2004	PAW	INT	25	154	41	12	0	3	19	28	2	0	.266	.350	.403	.016	.247	.318	.370	-.156	1.1	35-3B 3
2004	BOS	AL	25	208	54	11	0	7	33	45	0	1	.260	.367	.413	-.000	.261	.365	.404	-.010	7.9	57-3B 6
2005	*BOS*	*AL*	*26*	*295*	*80*	*17*	*1*	*8*	*45*	*53*	*2*	*1*	*.271*	*.383*	*.415*	*.049*	*.266*	*.380*	*.418*	*.038*	*18.1*	*85-3B -2*

Breakout: 28% *Improve: 47%* *Collapse: 20%*

Youkilis's season was all about injuries, but not always his own. He took over at third in mid-May when Mueller had arthroscopic knee surgery and played well through mid-August. He then went on the DL with a bone bruise after a collision with Sandy Alomar. Youkilis played very well in Boston, hitting more home runs than he had at any level since college and erasing many of the fears after his flop in Pawtucket late last year. The Sox picked up Mueller's option for 2005, but with Youkilis looking ready to contribute at the major league level, look for one of these two to be moved by year's end.

PITCHERS

TERRY ADAMS — Bats: R — Throws: R — Born: 06-Mar-1973 — Age: 32

YEAR	TM	LG	AGE	G	GS	IP	H	BB	SO	HR	ERA	EQERA	EQH9	EQBB9	EQSO9	EQHR9	PERA	VORP	STF
2002	PHI	NL	29	46	19	136.7	132	58	96	9	4.35	5.19	9.0	3.3	5.7	0.6	4.24	7.1	3
2003	PHI	NL	30	66	0	68.0	68	23	51	1	2.65	3.12	8.7	2.7	6.1	0.1	3.53	20.5	6
2004	TOR	AL	31	42	0	43.0	49	22	35	4	3.98	3.53	9.1	3.9	6.9	0.6	4.78	10.0	-2
2004	BOS	AL	31	19	0	27.0	35	6	21	6	6.00	5.33	10.3	1.7	6.7	1.7	5.33	-1.2	-2
2005	*PHI*	*NL*	*32*	*40*	*3*	*66.0*	*69*	*24*	*48*	*6*	*4.03*	*4.19*	*9.5*	*2.9*	*5.9*	*0.7*	*4.42*	*10.2*	*-2*

Breakout: 24% *Improve: 47%* *Collapse: 21%*

Unlike other recent pickups, Adams cost the Red Sox a decent prospect in John Hattig, in exchange for 27 forgettable innings. While the Sox have done a good job of acquiring risky hitters, they've gone through more borderline bullpen arms than Jeanne Zalasko has hairstyles. Non-tendered, Adams is a free agent at press time.

ABE ALVAREZ — Bats: L — Throws: L — Born: 17-Oct-1982 — Age: 22

YEAR	TM	LG	AGE	G	GS	IP	H	BB	SO	HR	ERA	EQERA	EQH9	EQBB9	EQSO9	EQHR9	PERA	VORP	STF
2003	LOW	NYP	20	9	9	19.0	9	2	19	0	0.00	3.18	6.4	1.1	5.3	0.0	1.59	7.6	15
2004	PME	EAS	21	26	26	135.3	132	32	108	13	3.59	4.52	9.0	2.2	5.4	1.0	3.90	24.4	20
2005	*BOS*	*AL*	*22*	*14*	*14*	*83.0*	*90*	*27*	*51*	*12*	*4.64*	*4.37*	*9.5*	*2.6*	*5.0*	*1.3*	*4.46*	*14.4*	*4*

Breakout: 11% *Improve: 35%* *Collapse: 25%*

If you haven't heard of Alvarez before, you will, but not necessarily because he's a decent pitching prospect in the upper part of the Boston system. Rare as that is, Alvarez will gain attention if he continues to pitch well because he's legally blind in one eye. It hasn't affected his performance yet, so consider it a non-issue. As a pitcher, Alvarez is another one in a long line of soft-tossing lefties the Sox are stockpiling. His fastball maxes out in the 85–88 range, but he mixes in a variety of soft stuff, particularly a solid curveball. He had a good year in Portland and made an injury-replacement start against Baltimore, confirming only that he's not quite ready for the majors just yet. Look for him to compete for the fifth-starter role soon if he keeps it up.

BRONSON ARROYO **Bats: R** **Throws: R** Born: 24-Feb-1977 Age: 28

YEAR	TM	LG	AGE	G	GS	IP	H	BB	SO	HR	ERA	EQERA	EQH9	EQBB9	EQSO9	EQHR9	PERA	VORP	STF
2002	NAS	PCL	25	22	21	143.0	126	28	116	10	2.96	4.15	8.4	1.9	5.8	0.8	3.55	30.6	18
2002	PIT	NL	25	9	4	27.0	30	15	22	1	4.00	4.67	9.3	4.3	6.3	0.3	4.67	2.4	0
2003	PAW	INT	26	24	24	149.7	148	23	155	9	3.43	4.57	8.8	1.6	7.5	0.8	3.70	30.3	21
2003	BOS	AL	26	6	0	17.3	10	4	14	0	2.08	2.20	6.1	2.2	7.2	0.0	1.65	6.7	13
2004	BOS	AL	27	32	29	178.7	171	47	142	17	4.03	4.28	8.4	2.2	6.8	0.7	3.46	24.7	17
2005	*BOS*	*AL*	*28*	*27*	*26*	*153.7*	*158*	*42*	*116*	*17*	*4.24*	*4.00*	*9.0*	*2.1*	*6.2*	*1.0*	*3.87*	*31.4*	*15*

Breakout: 14% *Improve: 47%* *Collapse: 23%*

After bouncing back and forth between Triple-A and the majors for several years, Arroyo finally got a stable job in the rotation, where he performed admirably. He certainly had his memorable moments in 2004—notably, getting A-Rod in a fight with Varitek. then having his arm swatted away while trying to tag the Yankee third baseman in the ALCS. His on-field results were fairly solid, though, like Lowe, he yielded a raft of unearned runs. Still, if he keeps that control in check, Arroyo should be an above-average performer at a bargain price.

PEDRO ASTACIO **Bats: R** **Throws: R** Born: 28-Nov-1969 Age: 35

YEAR	TM	LG	AGE	G	GS	IP	H	BB	SO	HR	ERA	EQERA	EQH9	EQBB9	EQSO9	EQHR9	PERA	VORP	STF
2002	NYM	NL	32	31	31	191.7	192	63	152	32	4.79	5.18	9.3	2.6	6.4	1.6	4.74	11.2	6
2003	NYM	NL	33	7	7	36.7	47	18	20	8	7.36	7.18	10.9	3.7	4.5	2.0	6.44	-6.8	-14
2004	BOS	AL	34	5	1	8.7	13	5	6	2	10.34	9.00	11.0	4.0	6.0	2.0	7.00	-3.0	-18
2005	*BOS*	*AL*	*35*	*18*	*11*	*70.7*	*80*	*26*	*49*	*11*	*5.34*	*5.03*	*9.9*	*2.8*	*5.7*	*1.4*	*4.96*	*6.7*	*-1*

Breakout: 13% *Improve: 40%* *Collapse: 33%*

The Red Sox signed Astacio to a minor league contract in mid-July, hoping to shore up the shaky rotation for the stretch run with a pitcher out over a year with a torn rotator cuff and labrum. Though he did manage to pitch a few innings in September and start the penultimate game of the season to allow the Sox to set their playoff rotation, his main contribution was throwing behind Kenny Lofton in the last regular-season game against the Yankees. A long shot to contribute from here on in.

MANNY DELCARMEN **Bats: R** **Throws: R** Born: 16-Feb-1982 Age: 23

YEAR	TM	LG	AGE	G	GS	IP	H	BB	SO	HR	ERA	EQERA	EQH9	EQBB9	EQSO9	EQHR9	PERA	VORP	STF
2002	AUG	SAL	20	26	24	136.0	124	56	136	15	4.10	6.79	10.4	4.8	5.7	2.5	6.94	-18.0	-13
2003	SAR	FSL	21	4	3	23.0	16	7	16	1	3.13	4.87	8.4	3.1	4.9	1.3	4.43	2.6	7
2004	SAR	FSL	22	19	18	73.0	84	20	76	10	4.68	6.49	11.5	2.8	6.5	2.6	7.01	-10.7	-9
2005	*BOS*	*AL*	*23*	*26*	*12*	*86.0*	*89*	*35*	*64*	*14*	*5.08*	*4.78*	*9.1*	*3.2*	*6.1*	*1.5*	*4.75*	*10.4*	*-1*

Breakout: 11% *Improve: 48%* *Collapse: 15%*

Delcarmen blew out his elbow early in 2003 and took the standard year off for rehab from Tommy John surgery. The Sox were impressed with his rehab work and they think his stuff is better now than before the surgery. His 92–94 mph fastball is now reportedly reaching as high as 97 in the Arizona Fall League. Last year had its expected rough spots, but Delcarmen appears fully recovered and back on track.

LENNY DiNARDO **Bats: L** **Throws: L** Born: 19-Sep-1979 Age: 25

YEAR	TM	LG	AGE	G	GS	IP	H	BB	SO	HR	ERA	EQERA	EQH9	EQBB9	EQSO9	EQHR9	PERA	VORP	STF
2002	CMB	SAL	22	24	19	101.3	106	56	103	3	4.35	7.16	9.7	6.1	5.5	0.7	5.44	1.7	-16
2003	SLU	FSL	23	19	13	85.0	64	14	93	1	2.01	4.37	8.0	1.7	7.1	0.3	3.10	21.8	27
2003	BIN	EAS	23	7	7	40.0	35	13	36	3	3.60	4.82	8.4	3.1	6.8	1.2	3.86	7.2	14
2004	BOS	AL	24	22	0	27.7	34	12	21	1	4.22	4.82	9.6	3.5	6.4	0.3	4.50	2.3	-2
2005	*BOS*	*AL*	*25*	*7*	*3*	*24.0*	*25*	*9*	*18*	*2*	*4.44*	*4.18*	*9.3*	*3.1*	*6.1*	*0.8*	*4.26*	*4.3*	*4*

Breakout: 17% *Improve: 46%* *Collapse: 18%*

Boston's Rule 5 pick from the Mets last winter, DiNardo draws consistent comparisons to Jamie Moyer because he's left-handed and throws about as hard as a pitching coach. He's got a good change-up and a great cutter that rarely gets above 85. He managed to stick with the Sox throughout the season with some roster shenanigans because of Rule 5 rules, but it's tough to see where he'll fit in next year, despite a long history of solid performance. Signed to a minor league deal, he'll likely bounce back and forth between Boston and Pawtucket in 2005.

ANDREW DOBIES Bats: L Throws: L Born: 20-Apr-1983 Age: 22

YEAR	TM	LG	AGE	G	GS	IP	H	BB	SO	HR	ERA	EQERA	EQH9	EQBB9	EQSO9	EQHR9	PERA	VORP	STF
2004	LOW	NYP	21	14	14	26.7	17	8	36	0	2.02	4.88	7.5	3.8	7.1	0.4	3.00	6.9	12
2005	*BOS*	*AL*	*22*	*27*	*5*	*58.0*	*58*	*27*	*48*	*7*	*4.52*	*4.26*	*8.7*	*3.7*	*6.7*	*1.0*	*4.32*	*12.2*	*1*

Breakout: 13% *Improve: 42%* *Collapse: 35%*

Boston's top pitching pick in the 2004 draft did not disappoint, cutting through the New York–Penn League to the tune of 36 strikeouts and eight walks in 26.2 innings. Pretty much everything that can be said about Dobies can be said about Thomas Hottovy, except that Dobies's best pitch is his slider while Hottovy features his curveball. The selection of a run of polished college pitchers in the earlier rounds of the draft is exactly what a farm system nearly bereft of arms needed; we'll get a better read on Dobies's future once he starts full-season ball in '05.

ALAN EMBREE Bats: L Throws: L Born: 23-Jan-1970 Age: 35

YEAR	TM	LG	AGE	G	GS	IP	H	BB	SO	HR	ERA	EQERA	EQH9	EQBB9	EQSO9	EQHR9	PERA	VORP	STF
2002	SDP	NL	32	36	0	28.7	23	9	38	2	0.94	2.57	7.1	2.6	10.6	0.6	2.57	10.1	31
2002	BOS	AL	32	32	0	33.3	24	11	43	4	2.97	3.06	6.7	2.8	11.1	1.1	3.06	10.1	32
2003	BOS	AL	33	65	0	55.0	49	16	45	5	4.25	3.88	7.8	2.5	7.3	0.7	3.04	11.3	8
2004	BOS	AL	34	71	0	52.3	49	11	37	7	4.13	4.11	8.6	1.8	6.1	1.1	3.58	8.5	0
2005	*BOS*	*AL*	*35*	*51*	*0*	*48.0*	*47*	*14*	*38*	*6*	*3.95*	*3.72*	*8.5*	*2.3*	*6.5*	*1.1*	*3.71*	*12.9*	*1*

Breakout: 20% *Improve: 55%* *Collapse: 27%*

Embree hasn't ever really shown the splits indicative of a LOOGY, but his usage patterns are moving quickly in that direction. Two years ago, Boston was willing to gamble that he would find some consistency. The move paid off both for them and for Embree, who activated the 2005 year of his contract by appearing in at least 50 games. Getting 50 innings of slightly better than league-average performance for $3 million is a stretch, but considering the Red Sox's payroll and their other available options, there are worse players to have around.

KEITH FOULKE Bats: R Throws: R Born: 19-Oct-1972 Age: 32

YEAR	TM	LG	AGE	G	GS	IP	H	BB	SO	HR	ERA	EQERA	EQH9	EQBB9	EQSO9	EQHR9	PERA	VORP	STF
2002	CWS	AL	29	65	0	77.7	65	13	58	7	2.90	2.81	8.1	1.5	6.6	0.7	3.30	25.5	10
2003	OAK	AL	30	72	0	86.7	57	20	88	10	2.08	2.10	6.9	2.1	9.4	1.0	3.10	37.7	24
2004	BOS	AL	31	72	0	83.0	63	15	79	8	2.17	2.15	7.1	1.5	8.4	0.8	2.60	35.9	23
2005	*BOS*	*AL*	*32*	*50*	*1*	*69.3*	*63*	*17*	*62*	*9*	*3.32*	*3.13*	*8.0*	*1.9*	*7.4*	*1.2*	*3.39*	*23.0*	*10*

Breakout: 26% *Improve: 49%* *Collapse: 20%*

While many may argue that Mariano Rivera is the most dominant closer in the AL, Foulke is arguably the best relief pitcher. His change-up has by now replaced that of Trevor Hoffman as the game's best out of the pen and his versatility—on full display in the playoffs—is what distinguishes him from the rest of the game's firemen. If Boston does again try to return to the more sensible "ace reliever" concept born in the 60s and 70s, Foulke's ability to perform a variety of roles in a variety of situations will be a key reason for its success. He's a good bet to outperform that projection.

JEROME GAMBLE Bats: R Throws: R Born: 05-Apr-1980 Age: 25

YEAR	TM	LG	AGE	G	GS	IP	H	BB	SO	HR	ERA	EQERA	EQH9	EQBB9	EQSO9	EQHR9	PERA	VORP	STF
2002	AUG	SAL	22	14	14	49.3	34	22	42	2	1.83	4.12	8.0	5.2	4.9	1.0	4.53	5.2	0
2003	SAR	FSL	23	17	14	76.3	68	21	51	2	3.66	5.76	9.1	2.8	4.4	0.8	4.35	9.8	3
2003	PME	EAS	23	2	2	11.0	10	1	11	0	4.91	5.06	8.4	0.8	7.6	0.0	2.53	3.6	35
2004	PME	EAS	24	14	10	61.7	62	18	36	3	3.94	4.85	8.8	2.7	3.9	0.6	3.64	12.9	4
2005	*BOS*	*AL*	*25*	*20*	*11*	*76.0*	*84*	*28*	*42*	*10*	*4.96*	*4.68*	*9.7*	*2.9*	*4.6*	*1.2*	*4.78*	*10.4*	*-7*

Breakout: 16% *Improve: 47%* *Collapse: 24%*

The story is one that's been told many times before: Gamble was a huge hit with scouts until he went down with Tommy John in 2001 and has stalled after coming back. He's still got nasty stuff, but didn't stand out as a 24-year old in Double-A. At this point, Gamble's place is probably in the bullpen, but the more years removed from the surgery, the better.

BYUNG-HYUN KIM **Bats: R** **Throws: R** Born: 21-Jan-1979 Age: 26

YEAR	TM	LG	AGE	G	GS	IP	H	BB	SO	HR	ERA	EQERA	EQH9	EQBB9	EQSO9	EQHR9	PERA	VORP	STF
2002	ARI	NL	23	72	0	84.0	64	26	92	5	2.04	2.22	7.2	2.4	8.9	0.6	2.78	30.2	25
2003	ARI	NL	24	7	7	43.0	34	15	33	6	3.56	3.32	8.0	2.9	6.4	1.1	3.76	10.2	18
2003	BOS	AL	24	49	5	79.3	70	18	69	6	3.18	3.96	7.6	2.0	7.7	0.6	2.68	15.7	22
2004	BOS	AL	25	7	3	17.3	17	7	6	1	6.24	6.48	9.2	3.2	3.2	0.5	4.32	-3.0	-16
2004	PAW	INT	25	22	19	60.7	71	12	39	6	5.34	6.25	9.9	1.8	4.7	0.9	4.73	5.7	-3
2005	*BOS*	*AL*	*26*	*39*	*5*	*73.7*	*76*	*22*	*53*	*9*	*4.40*	*4.15*	*9.1*	*2.3*	*5.9*	*1.1*	*4.12*	*15.1*	*-1*

Breakout: 16% *Improve: 46%* *Collapse: 27%*

Kim's tenure in Boston isn't quite at the Bucknerian level of disaster, but it's certainly something well past frustrating. After struggling with shoulder and, uh, finger issues towards the end of last season, Kim came into 2004 looking to reclaim some of the lost luster and the fifth starter's job. He struggled early both with his performance and with injuries, eventually landing on the DL with "trip to Korea to fix leg imbalance." He apparently never completely figured that out and his time with the Red Sox is very limited. If Theo and Co. can point at those 2001–2002 seasons, they might be able to move him; it's tough to see him back in Boston next year.

CURT LESKANIC **Bats: R** **Throws: R** Born: 02-Apr-1968 Age: 37

YEAR	TM	LG	AGE	G	GS	IP	H	BB	SO	HR	ERA	EQERA	EQH9	EQBB9	EQSO9	EQHR9	PERA	VORP	STF
2003	MIL	NL	35	26	0	26.7	22	18	28	1	2.70	2.73	7.2	5.1	8.5	0.3	3.42	8.7	9
2003	KCR	AL	35	27	0	26.0	16	11	22	1	1.73	2.19	6.2	3.6	7.7	0.4	2.55	10.6	12
2004	KCR	AL	36	19	0	15.7	23	14	15	5	8.03	7.71	11.0	6.6	7.7	2.2	7.71	-5.1	-20
2004	BOS	AL	36	32	0	27.7	24	16	22	3	3.57	3.00	8.0	4.7	7.0	1.0	4.33	8.3	-3
2005	*BOS*	*AL*	*37*	*50*	*0*	*50.3*	*50*	*29*	*45*	*6*	*4.20*	*3.95*	*8.8*	*4.6*	*7.3*	*1.0*	*4.71*	*12.0*	*-2*

Breakout: 49% *Improve: 64%* *Collapse: 13%*

After finally breaking down and having his shoulder operated on, Leskanic began the year in the back of the Royals bullpen and performed about as well as everyone else on the Kansas City roster. The Sox picked him up after he was released and despite a month on the DL for that same shoulder, he was useful down the stretch, still throwing in the low-90s with a nice slider to boot. Whether or not he hangs 'em up this winter is anyone's guess, but we bet you'll see him tossing 50 innings some place next year.

JON LESTER **Bats: L** **Throws: L** Born: 07-Jan-1984 Age: 21

YEAR	TM	LG	AGE	G	GS	IP	H	BB	SO	HR	ERA	EQERA	EQH9	EQBB9	EQSO9	EQHR9	PERA	VORP	STF
2003	AUG	SAL	19	24	21	106.0	102	44	71	7	3.65	6.40	9.7	4.5	3.7	1.5	5.20	4.3	1
2004	SAR	FSL	20	21	20	90.3	82	37	97	2	4.29	5.82	8.7	4.2	6.6	0.4	4.24	12.8	16
2005	*BOS*	*AL*	*21*	*21*	*10*	*72.0*	*76*	*36*	*50*	*10*	*5.16*	*4.86*	*9.3*	*3.9*	*5.7*	*1.3*	*4.92*	*7.8*	*-5*

Breakout: 8% *Improve: 50%* *Collapse: 15%*

The last top pick before the new Red Sox regime, Lester came straight out of high school but has managed to avoid any serious injuries so far, though he did suffer from some shoulder tightness in June. The Sox feel that he developed enough physically and mentally in '04 that they can begin to push him a little harder. Armed with a new cutter, a little extra gas on his 93 mph fastball and improved breaking pitches, Lester will be in Double-A in 2005 and is still on track for the big leagues soon after that.

DEREK LOWE **Bats: R** **Throws: R** Born: 01-Jun-1973 Age: 32

YEAR	TM	LG	AGE	G	GS	IP	H	BB	SO	HR	ERA	EQERA	EQH9	EQBB9	EQSO9	EQHR9	PERA	VORP	STF
2002	BOS	AL	29	32	32	219.7	166	48	127	12	2.58	2.59	7.8	1.9	5.2	0.5	3.03	81.0	20
2003	BOS	AL	30	33	33	203.3	216	72	110	17	4.47	4.52	9.0	3.1	4.8	0.7	3.84	24.4	7
2004	BOS	AL	31	33	33	182.7	224	71	105	15	5.42	5.80	9.9	3.1	4.8	0.6	4.62	-11.5	4
2005	*LAD*	*NL*	*32*	*26*	*25*	*148*	*150*	*49*	*90*	*13*	*4.01*	*4.43*	*9.4*	*2.6*	*4.9*	*0.7*	*4.36*	*17.6*	*5*

Breakout: 13% *Improve: 53%* *Collapse: 21%*

Mmmm . . . over-rated post-season performances. Lowe has become the poster boy for overvaluing brief performances based on context. Though he has been subject to wild fluctuations in his H/BIP—most likely a result of his extreme groundball tendencies—this was the second year in a row that his control was absent; his performance looked better than it was because of a huge number of unearned runs. With the best arms all gone, the Dodgers de-Ishiified their rotation by overpaying Lowe to the tune of four years, $36 million.

MARK MALASKA **Bats: L** **Throws: L** Born: 17-Jan-1978 Age: 27

YEAR	TM	LG	AGE	G	GS	IP	H	BB	SO	HR	ERA	EQERA	EQH9	EQBB9	EQSO9	EQHR9	PERA	VORP	STF
2002	BAK	CLF	24	15	15	91.3	98	12	94	5	2.96	5.64	9.2	1.3	5.2	0.9	3.63	19.5	17
2002	ORL	SOU	24	12	11	70.7	82	28	49	4	3.69	5.56	10.3	3.4	4.6	0.9	5.43	1.3	-9
2003	ORL	SOU	25	19	0	25.0	21	4	22	2	2.16	3.13	9.0	1.6	5.9	1.6	4.30	3.3	0
2003	DUR	INT	25	15	0	23.0	24	8	22	1	4.30	4.91	9.0	3.7	7.0	0.4	4.50	2.7	4
2003	TBY	AL	25	22	0	16.0	13	12	17	0	2.81	3.45	7.5	6.3	9.2	0.0	4.02	3.8	10
2004	BOS	AL	26	19	0	20.0	21	12	12	2	4.50	4.12	9.2	5.0	5.0	0.9	5.03	3.0	-18
2004	PAW	INT	26	33	0	36.3	42	11	31	7	4.21	4.37	10.3	2.8	6.2	2.1	6.17	-2.2	-13
2005	*BOS*	*AL*	*27*	*18*	*7*	*55.0*	*60*	*22*	*37*	*7*	*4.76*	*4.48*	*9.6*	*3.2*	*5.6*	*1.2*	*4.73*	*9.7*	*-3*

Breakout: 27% *Improve: 46%* *Collapse: 30%*

Claimed off waivers from the Devil Rays in December of 2003, Malaska had been converted into a reliever by Tampa the year before and took very well to it. Boston was hoping that he could be another southpaw in the pen, but his control came back to haunt him and he was sent down to Pawtucket. There are a lot of teams that could use this guy for that lefty out of the pen.

ANASTACIO MARTINEZ **Bats: R** **Throws: R** Born: 03-Nov-1978 Age: 26

YEAR	TM	LG	AGE	G	GS	IP	H	BB	SO	HR	ERA	EQERA	EQH9	EQBB9	EQSO9	EQHR9	PERA	VORP	STF
2002	TRN	EAS	23	27	27	139.0	152	75	127	12	5.31	6.75	9.4	5.1	6.3	1.2	5.01	8.8	-1
2003	PME	EAS	24	34	0	40.0	31	24	37	3	2.25	3.41	8.0	6.1	7.1	1.2	4.86	3.0	-6
2003	PAW	INT	24	8	0	14.0	12	3	15	2	1.93	2.77	9.0	2.1	8.3	2.1	4.85	1.1	9
2004	PAW	INT	25	38	0	67.3	73	31	57	5	3.74	5.10	9.2	4.3	6.2	0.7	4.82	5.7	-4
2004	BOS	AL	25	11	0	10.7	13	6	5	2	8.41	7.59	10.1	4.2	4.2	1.7	5.91	-2.6	-26
2005	*BOS*	*AL*	*26*	*21*	*7*	*57.0*	*60*	*30*	*41*	*8*	*5.31*	*5.00*	*9.3*	*4.1*	*5.9*	*1.2*	*4.93*	*4.7*	*-6*

Breakout: 19% *Improve: 44%* *Collapse: 23%*

Briefly shipped to the Pirates before Brandon Lyon failed his physical, Martinez continued his steady rise up the ladder despite disturbingly high walk totals. He continues to strike out a good number of batters with a low-90s fastball, plus curve and a change-up. He may see time in the bullpen next year as an injury sub, but that's probably as good as things will get for Martinez.

PEDRO MARTINEZ **Bats: R** **Throws: R** Born: 25-Oct-1971 Age: 33

YEAR	TM	LG	AGE	G	GS	IP	H	BB	SO	HR	ERA	EQERA	EQH9	EQBB9	EQSO9	EQHR9	PERA	VORP	STF
2002	BOS	AL	30	30	30	199.3	144	40	239	13	2.26	2.72	6.8	1.7	10.5	0.6	2.44	70.5	53
2003	BOS	AL	31	29	29	186.7	147	47	206	7	2.22	2.41	6.7	2.2	9.7	0.3	2.11	74.2	51
2004	BOS	AL	32	33	33	217.0	193	61	227	26	3.90	3.55	7.8	2.3	9.0	0.9	3.30	51.2	35
2005	*NYM*	*NL*	*33*	*29*	*29*	*194.7*	*157*	*55*	*205*	*19*	*2.93*	*3.17*	*7.3*	*2.2*	*8.5*	*0.9*	*3.21*	*53.3*	*31*

Breakout: 22% *Improve: 48%* *Collapse: 16%*

Of the many crazy stories coming out of Boston this year, Martinez was involved in his fair share. Between Nelson de la Rosa, questions about the Yankees' place in his genealogy, and the debate about whether his haircut was more Michael Jackson Thriller or Eriq La Salle "Coming to America," Martinez kept fans entertained and mouths agape. And his pitching wasn't bad either. Despite a career-high ERA of 3.90—a fact that sums up his career greatness succinctly—Martinez managed to throw 217 quality innings, still striking out more than a batter per frame. Boston tendered him a three-year deal with an option, but Martinez jumped ship for the Mets for a guaranteed fourth year. He'll never again return to his Koufaxian peak, but Pedro will still be a good front-line starter, *if* handled correctly.

RAMIRO MENDOZA **Bats: R** **Throws: R** Born: 15-Jun-1972 Age: 33

YEAR	TM	LG	AGE	G	GS	IP	H	BB	SO	HR	ERA	EQERA	EQH9	EQBB9	EQSO9	EQHR9	PERA	VORP	STF
2002	NYY	AL	30	62	0	91.7	102	16	61	8	3.44	4.08	9.2	1.5	5.7	0.7	3.69	17.8	4
2003	BOS	AL	31	37	5	66.7	98	20	36	10	6.75	6.19	10.9	2.5	4.6	1.2	5.27	-5.9	-13
2004	BOS	AL	32	27	0	30.7	25	7	13	3	3.52	3.14	8.2	1.9	3.8	0.9	3.45	9.4	-9
2005	*BOS*	*AL*	*33*	*30*	*1*	*42.0*	*51*	*11*	*22*	*5*	*4.83*	*4.55*	*10.7*	*2.1*	*4.2*	*1.1*	*4.67*	*6.8*	*-12*

Breakout: 23% *Improve: 46%* *Collapse: 29%*

When he wasn't hurt, he was actually somewhat effective. That's a nice enough thing to say about most players, but when you spend the first half of the season sidelined with shoulder soreness, it doesn't add up to much in the end. The

Sox are finally out from under Mendoza's unfortunate contract, though with that "former Yankee" sheen and "World Champion" label, Mendoza he'll get opportunities to prove he's healthy somewhere in '05.

MIKE MYERS **Bats: L** **Throws: L** Born: 26-Jun-1969 Age: 36

YEAR	TM	LG	AGE	G	GS	IP	H	BB	SO	HR	ERA	EQERA	EQH9	EQBB9	EQSO9	EQHR9	PERA	VORP	STF
2002	ARI	NL	33	69	0	37.0	39	17	31	2	4.38	4.17	8.8	3.4	6.6	0.5	4.17	4.1	0
2003	ARI	NL	34	64	0	36.3	38	21	21	4	5.70	5.05	9.3	4.5	4.8	1.0	5.05	-0.3	-20
2004	SEA	AL	35	50	0	27.7	29	17	23	3	4.87	4.61	8.9	4.9	6.9	1.0	4.94	4.3	-7
2004	BOS	AL	35	25	0	15.0	16	6	9	2	4.20	3.68	9.2	3.1	4.9	1.2	4.91	3.5	-13
2005	*STL*	*NL*	*36*	*32*	*0*	*33.0*	*31*	*16*	*26*	*3*	*4.21*	*4.50*	*8.4*	*3.9*	*6.4*	*0.9*	*4.68*	*4.4*	*-5*

Breakout: 23% *Improve: 51%* *Collapse: 32%*

Of all the Red Sox's mid-season bullpen acquisitions, only Myers and Leskanic actually made it onto any of the various post-season rosters. Myers held southpaws to a .242/.336/.354 line in 2004 while getting killed by non-lefties to the tune of .323/.421/.538. He's the definition of LOOGY, a fact that will keep him employed until the rapture, but he's not the shut-down reliever he once was.

JON PAPELBON **Bats: R** **Throws: R** Born: 23-Nov-1980 Age: 24

YEAR	TM	LG	AGE	G	GS	IP	H	BB	SO	HR	ERA	EQERA	EQH9	EQBB9	EQSO9	EQHR9	PERA	VORP	STF
2003	LOW	NYP	22	13	6	32.7	43	9	36	2	6.33	8.22	12.3	3.2	5.6	2.1	7.34	-5.9	-25
2004	SAR	FSL	23	24	24	129.7	97	43	153	6	2.64	4.30	8.1	3.5	7.4	0.9	3.92	22.3	24
2005	*BOS*	*AL*	*24*	*16*	*14*	*85.3*	*87*	*36*	*72*	*12*	*4.83*	*4.55*	*9.0*	*3.3*	*6.9*	*1.2*	*4.51*	*13.5*	*11*

Breakout: 15% *Improve: 40%* *Collapse: 22%*

A dominating reliever at Mississippi State, Papelbon is another of the 2003 draft class doing well for himself in a thin system. His 153 strikeouts in 129.2 innings were impressive, though he was old for A-ball. He's a big boy—6′4″, 230—who was getting by with just a deceptive mid-90s fastball before he decided to mix in his new change-up and breaking ball, to great results. He held up well under the starter workload in his first full pro season after being closely watched last year and will start 2005 in the rotation in Double-A.

ANIBAL SANCHEZ **Bats: R** **Throws: R** Born: 27-Feb-1984 Age: 21

YEAR	TM	LG	AGE	G	GS	IP	H	BB	SO	HR	ERA	EQERA	EQH9	EQBB9	EQSO9	EQHR9	PERA	VORP	STF
2004	LOW	NYP	20	15	15	76.3	43	29	101	3	1.77	4.57	7.4	4.8	7.1	0.9	3.76	13.7	18
2005	*BOS*	*AL*	*21*	*20*	*13*	*83.7*	*66*	*50*	*63*	*13*	*4.58*	*4.32*	*7.0*	*4.7*	*6.2*	*1.4*	*4.25*	*15.8*	*–1*

Breakout: 20% *Improve: 52%* *Collapse: 17%*

After losing his entire 2003 season to elbow surgery, Sanchez came back throwing his excellent fastball faster than he had been before the surgery. He absolutely destroyed hitters in the NY-Penn League last year with that fastball, a good curve, and change-up. He'll only be 21 this year and, just like all the other young pitchers, if he can keep himself healthy, he's got a great shot to climb the ladder quickly.

CURT SCHILLING **Bats: R** **Throws: R** Born: 14-Nov-1966 Age: 38

YEAR	TM	LG	AGE	G	GS	IP	H	BB	SO	HR	ERA	EQERA	EQH9	EQBB9	EQSO9	EQHR9	PERA	VORP	STF
2002	ARI	NL	35	36	35	259.3	218	33	316	29	3.23	3.24	7.7	1.0	9.9	1.0	2.91	63.5	45
2003	ARI	NL	36	24	24	168.0	144	32	194	17	2.95	2.92	7.6	1.5	9.5	0.8	2.92	48.4	43
2004	BOS	AL	37	32	32	226.7	206	35	203	23	3.26	2.90	8.0	1.3	7.7	0.8	3.02	72.9	33
2005	*BOS*	*AL*	*38*	*32*	*32*	*208.3*	*209*	*40*	*186*	*26*	*3.70*	*3.49*	*8.8*	*1.5*	*7.4*	*1.1*	*3.53*	*56.0*	*25*

Breakout: 12% *Improve: 26%* *Collapse: 31%*

The Red Sox turned over seven players from the 2003 team that finished one pitch short of the World Series, but to hear some people tell it, if they'd only been able to bring in Schilling that would have been enough. Signer of one of the league's more interesting contracts, Schilling's 2005 salary jumps by $2 million and his $13 million option for 2007 was automatically vested the minute the Sox defeated the Cardinals. Signed to win the World Series, he delivered in storybook fashion. The only problem is that Boston is now stuck with the bill for a pitcher who's shown an increasing susceptibility to injuries and a declining strikeout rate through his age-40 season for a lot of money. For now, Schilling is still among the game's elite and the Sox are happy to trade the future risk for the present championship.

CHRIS SMITH Bats: R Throws: R Born: 09-Apr-1981 Age: 24

YEAR	TM	LG	AGE	G	GS	IP	H	BB	SO	HR	ERA	EQERA	EQH9	EQBB9	EQSO9	EQHR9	PERA	VORP	STF
2002	LOW	NYP	21	14	14	56.7	54	14	50	3	4.13	6.84	10.2	3.2	4.6	1.6	5.26	1.9	-7
2003	AUG	SAL	22	8	8	46.3	48	5	25	4	4.28	6.12	10.5	1.3	3.0	2.1	5.27	1.6	-5
2004	PME	EAS	23	14	14	74.3	77	21	85	10	3.76	4.40	9.4	2.6	7.5	1.5	4.65	7.6	19
2005	*BOS*	*AL*	*24*	*17*	*11*	*72.3*	*78*	*24*	*52*	*12*	*5.08*	*4.78*	*9.5*	*2.6*	*5.9*	*1.5*	*4.71*	*9.2*	*2*

Breakout: 7% *Improve: 26%* *Collapse: 18%*

The Red Sox's lone young pitcher injury for the season, Smith was having a good year in Portland before he went down for labrum surgery. The Sox hope he'll be ready for spring training, but labrums have derailed more impressive careers than his, so until further notice, chalk up another example for TINSTAAPP.

BRAD THOMAS Bats: L Throws: L Born: 12-Oct-1977 Age: 27

YEAR	TM	LG	AGE	G	GS	IP	H	BB	SO	HR	ERA	EQERA	EQH9	EQBB9	EQSO9	EQHR9	PERA	VORP	STF
2002	EDM	PCL	24	28	27	152.0	175	54	97	20	5.74	6.67	9.8	3.4	4.5	1.4	5.02	9.5	-6
2003	ROC	INT	25	15	11	58.7	68	10	50	3	3.53	3.90	9.4	1.7	6.1	0.6	3.90	10.9	16
2003	MIN	AL	25	3	0	4.7	6	3	2	1	7.66	7.71	11.6	5.8	3.9	1.9	7.71	-0.8	-32
2005	*BOS*	*AL*	*27*	*15*	*7*	*49.3*	*59*	*23*	*27*	*5*	*5.58*	*5.25*	*10.5*	*3.6*	*4.4*	*1.0*	*5.18*	*2.5*	*-11*

Breakout: 28% *Improve: 53%* *Collapse: 18%*

Picked up from the Twins in mid-April for a song, Thomas has had a history of erratic performances, a low-90s fastball losing velocity, and mild elbow injuries. The injuries caught up with him and he went down with season-ending surgery. Freed by the minor league free agency rules, Thomas's road back to the big leagues is going to be long and difficult.

MIKE TIMLIN Bats: R Throws: R Born: 10-Mar-1966 Age: 39

YEAR	TM	LG	AGE	G	GS	IP	H	BB	SO	HR	ERA	EQERA	EQH9	EQBB9	EQSO9	EQHR9	PERA	VORP	STF
2002	STL	NL	36	42	1	61.0	48	7	35	9	2.51	3.07	8.6	1.0	4.9	1.5	3.88	17.5	-4
2002	PHI	NL	36	30	0	35.7	27	7	15	6	3.78	4.18	8.6	1.7	3.6	1.7	4.18	5.3	-15
2003	BOS	AL	37	72	0	83.7	77	9	65	11	3.55	3.67	8.1	0.9	6.9	1.1	3.00	19.7	11
2004	BOS	AL	38	76	0	76.3	75	19	56	8	4.13	3.51	8.6	2.1	6.3	0.8	3.63	18.3	4
2005	*BOS*	*AL*	*39*	*50*	*0*	*52.7*	*55*	*12*	*37*	*6*	*4.26*	*4.01*	*9.2*	*1.8*	*5.8*	*1.1*	*3.84*	*11.9*	*-2*

Breakout: 21% *Improve: 33%* *Collapse: 26%*

One of the few relievers not voted off the island in 2003, Timlin managed to follow up that solid campaign with a good 2004 season as one of the three decent pitchers in the Boston pen. At 39, he's pitching as well as he has in his career, but obviously his age dramatically increases the risk of collapse at any time. His performance last year kicked in his option for 2005, where the Sox hope he'll again combine with Foulke and Embree to pick up the bulk of the relief innings, after which they'll wish him happy trails.

BEAU VAUGHAN Bats: B Throws: R Born: 04-Jun-1981 Age: 24

YEAR	TM	LG	AGE	G	GS	IP	H	BB	SO	HR	ERA	EQERA	EQH9	EQBB9	EQSO9	EQHR9	PERA	VORP	STF
2003	LOW	NYP	22	11	6	31.0	27	15	30	1	2.32	4.18	9.3	5.8	5.1	1.0	5.46	0.4	-14
2004	AUG	SAL	23	14	13	71.0	58	27	73	8	3.30	4.85	8.9	4.0	5.8	1.8	4.98	4.5	7
2005	*BOS*	*AL*	*24*	*14*	*10*	*60.3*	*60*	*32*	*44*	*9*	*5.12*	*4.82*	*8.8*	*4.1*	*6.0*	*1.4*	*4.79*	*6.6*	*-1*

Breakout: 16% *Improve: 46%* *Collapse: 8%*

Another pick from the 2003 draft, Vaughan has four quality pitches: fastball (usually in the 92–94 mph range), good change-up, decent slider, and a curveball. He's had some control issues in the past, but his strikeout-to-walk ratio of 73:27 in 71 innings at Augusta was impressive. Boston was a little miffed that he was out of shape last spring and he did shut things down in August with a sore arm, but assuming he's learned his lesson he should be good to go in '05. The Sox are insisting on using him as a starter for now, but he was a reliever in college and could return to the pen as he moves up the ladder.

TIM WAKEFIELD **Bats: R** **Throws: R** Born: 02-Aug-1966 Age: 38

YEAR	TM	LG	AGE	G	GS	IP	H	BB	SO	HR	ERA	EQERA	EQH9	EQBB9	EQSO9	EQHR9	PERA	VORP	STF
2002	BOS	AL	35	45	15	163.3	121	51	134	15	2.81	2.97	7.5	2.7	7.3	0.8	3.21	51.5	19
2003	BOS	AL	36	35	33	202.3	193	71	169	23	4.09	4.27	8.1	3.0	7.4	0.9	3.49	30.8	21
2004	BOS	AL	37	32	30	188.3	197	63	116	29	4.88	4.96	9.2	2.7	5.3	1.2	4.52	9.4	3
2005	*BOS*	*AL*	*38*	*29*	*25*	*152.0*	*156*	*54*	*102*	*19*	*4.59*	*4.32*	*9.0*	*2.8*	*5.5*	*1.1*	*4.27*	*24.4*	*5*

Breakout: 12% *Improve: 25%* *Collapse: 13%*

When talking about Wakefield, the conversation inevitably turns either to the fact that he's a knuckleballer or that one pitch from the 2003 ALCS instead of the fact that he's consistently been one of the league's top inning-eaters for a decade. Last year certainly wasn't one of Wakefield's best—his strikeouts were down, homers up—but he's established a history of being able to consistently contribute close to 200 innings of league-average pitching, a commodity not nearly as easy to find as it might seem. Signed for under $5 million for 2005, he'll be worth the dough.

SCOTT WILLIAMSON **Bats: R** **Throws: R** Born: 17-Feb-1976 Age: 29

YEAR	TM	LG	AGE	G	GS	IP	H	BB	SO	HR	ERA	EQERA	EQH9	EQBB9	EQSO9	EQHR9	PERA	VORP	STF
2002	CIN	NL	26	63	0	74.0	46	36	84	5	2.92	3.31	6.5	3.8	9.3	0.6	2.93	17.2	21
2003	CIN	NL	27	42	0	42.3	34	25	53	6	3.19	3.24	7.3	4.5	10.2	1.3	3.89	11.4	15
2003	BOS	AL	27	24	0	20.3	20	9	21	1	6.21	5.75	8.0	3.5	8.9	0.4	3.10	-1.2	15
2004	BOS	AL	28	28	0	28.7	11	18	28	0	1.25	1.69	5.1	5.4	8.8	0.3	2.36	14.0	14
2005	*CHC*	*NL*	*29*	*39*	*0*	*42.3*	*30*	*25*	*40*	*6*	*3.73*	*3.87*	*6.4*	*4.7*	*7.6*	*1.1*	*4.06*	*9.3*	*1*

Breakout: 19% *Improve: 49%* *Collapse: 29%*

It was a lost year for Williamson, who spent what seemed like the entire season on the DL with inflammation in his reconstructed elbow. He's a classic new Red Sox administration pick; when healthy, he has shown that he can be one of the best relievers in baseball, but it didn't work out this time. If he can prove his elbow isn't a major question, Williamson could return to form in 2005.

CHARLIE ZINK **Bats: R** **Throws: R** Born: 26-Aug-1979 Age: 25

YEAR	TM	LG	AGE	G	GS	IP	H	BB	SO	HR	ERA	EQERA	EQH9	EQBB9	EQSO9	EQHR9	PERA	VORP	STF
2002	AUG	SAL	22	26	0	48.3	42	16	48	1	1.68	5.04	8.7	3.6	5.4	0.4	4.03	7.8	-3
2003	SAR	FSL	23	24	19	136.0	123	64	94	10	3.90	6.07	10.1	5.0	4.6	2.1	6.58	-13.3	-15
2003	PME	EAS	23	6	6	39.3	21	14	18	1	3.44	4.11	6.7	3.6	3.6	0.5	2.83	10.8	13
2004	PME	EAS	24	18	18	93.3	101	72	50	3	5.79	6.55	9.1	7.1	3.6	0.4	5.06	5.4	-11
2004	SAR	FSL	24	3	3	14.3	22	9	3	0	5.66	9.42	11.9	6.3	1.3	0.0	6.91	-2.1	-42
2005	*BOS*	*AL*	*25*	*16*	*10*	*59.7*	*65*	*37*	*30*	*9*	*5.92*	*5.57*	*9.5*	*4.9*	*4.2*	*1.4*	*5.59*	*1.7*	*-18*

Breakout: 13% *Improve: 53%* *Collapse: 13%*

Explanations for Zink's terrible season range from "I don't know" to "That's what you get for putting him on your Top 50 Prospects List." The truth is Zink's a knuckleballer and knuckleballers are more susceptible to this kind of random performance variance than "normal" pitchers. That's one ugly PECOTA forecast; Zink could easily blow that projection away, or fare even worse.

Chicago White Sox

America loves itself for its sense of accomplishment, and reasonably so. Stuff gets done here. We've got all sorts of achievers, operators, guys on the level and guys working angles, builders of things great and small. Fortune smiles on us.

Which brings us to Kenny Williams and the question of non-achievement. Unlike some other teams that simply tank or can't contend or don't want to try, in the four years of Williams's regime, the team has gone into each season with a realistic of goal of winning. And they fail. Even more exasperating is that the Sox won the division in 2000, just before Williams took over the team.

Keep in mind, the division the Sox are trying to win isn't the AL East or West, nor are the Atlanta Braves in the division. For all the AL Central teams, playoff contention has been a realizable goal going into each of the last five seasons. Nobody in the division can really boast of any dynastic achievements, not even the Twins, who won the last three titles. In 2002–04, Minnesota won 94, 90, and 92 games, but even these modest division-winning totals exaggerate how their rivals might have perceived them at the start of and during those seasons. In 2003, the Royals were in first place at the All-Star break, and the White Sox were there on the morning of September 1. In 2004, the Sox were in first at the All-Star break. In both seasons, the Twins raced past with fast finishes.

In that kind of competitive environment, Williams has tried. He tried to win in 2001, hoping that David Wells would anchor his rotation; Wells suffered his only serious injury of the last 10 years. In a teardown that was relatively low-key compared to the White Flag deals, Williams discarded a good chunk of the team he'd inherited in 2002 with a few deadline deals. Williams reasonably thought he was running a contender going into the last two seasons, and in both years he was willing to make in-season deals he felt would improve his chances of winning. It's easy to say he suffered from a poverty of ideas when it came to stretch-drive moves: he acquired both Roberto Alomar and Carl Everett in separate deals in 2003 and 2004—but both made sense, especially Alomar in 2003.

Perhaps just as frustrating, Williams's record in dealing with his peers among the game's general managers hasn't been awful. But because of the organization's aversion to bidding up free agents in the winter, has been Williams's only real option for improving the big league club. Although the Foulke-for-Koch trade will never look good, picking up Damaso Marte, Jose Uribe, and Miguel Olivo in little deals were all clever. In particular, Olivo was promising and useful as a catcher in an organization that has needed one since Ron Karkovice faded away, and he was also valuable as a bartering chip to package in a deal for a top starting pitcher.

But see, there's where we run into a problem, because that wasn't exactly what happened. Since having to catch and release Wells, Williams has been questing for a top starter every year since, and it keeps not quite working out. In part, he's kept in check by Jerry Reinsdorf's reasonable reservations about signing free-agent pitchers to multi-year deals, but that in turn limits Williams's options in upgrading the rotation. In the absence of having a top-shelf anchor who can run with the big dogs, Williams has had to get by with single-season risks like Wells and Bartolo Colon. It's hard to count on such pitchers becoming available, let alone pitching to their potential. Hoping that the Esteban Loaizas and Scott Schoenweises of the world will solve the rest of your pitching problems has never worked out for long either. When a very good starter, Freddy Garcia, became available because of Seattle's swan dive, Williams felt he'd be adding that magic ingredient.

WHITE SOX PROSPECTUS

2004 record: 83–79; Second place, AL Central

Pythagenport record: 84–78

Runs scored per game: 5.34 (3rd in AL)

Runs allowed per game: 5.13 (10th in AL)

Team EqA: .259 (8th in AL)

2004 Batters Age: 28.9 (5th youngest in AL)

2004 Pitchers Age: 28.4 (6th youngest in AL)

Ballpark: U.S. Cellular Field; Moderate hitter's park; Park Factor of 1.029

2004: Hung around the race for a while. Again. Handed the division to the Twins in the second half. Again.

2005: Their opportunity has passed; the constant exodus of talent will relegate this team to second-tier status.

The GM paid a king's ransom to get him from the Mariners after his big first half, and Garcia pitched well for the Sox. Again, it wasn't enough. They still didn't win.

So you can understand the frustration here. Bobbing around in the 80- to 85-win neighborhood can be maddeningly frustrating. Combined with a habit of making trades to solve your latest batch of problems, frustration can even make you do things just for the sake of doing them, sometimes at great harm.

On that level, replacing Jerry Manuel with Ozzie Guillen might seem like a return to the script they used to hire a coach from Florida's previous world champs. The Sox keep thinking in terms of swapping out what they have for what they feel they lack; it hasn't helped. They felt their rotation was too shallow after 2003, so they figured they could replace Colon with Schoeneweis and the suddenly and inexplicably dominant Loaiza, and that would hold them. It didn't—Schoeneweis isn't a front-line starter, and Loaiza's 2003 looks like an all-time outlier. The Garcia trade thus became that much more a matter of epic wish fulfillment.

The relationship between a manager and a general manager, like all management relationships,, can be an asset, a handicap, or fulfill the doctor's credo to "do no harm." A manager and GM who can be on the same page when it comes to designing the roster can be a significant advantage to a team. It doesn't necessarily matter if the relationship is collaborative (like those between Al Rosen and Roger Craig, Harry Dalton and George Bamberger, or John Schuerholz and Bobby Cox), top-down (Theo Epstein and Terry Francona, or Kevin Towers and Bruce Bochy, in some respects), or if the manager has the stronger hand (Joe Torre and Brian Cashman, or Dusty Baker anywhere). As long as the strengths of each man are complementary in terms of player valuation, creating useful player usage patterns, and a shared understanding of what's going on within the organization, it's the sort of thing you want.

Again, to his credit, Williams has cultivated active, collaborative relationships with his managers. Sometimes, that's generated good results. Other times . . . not so good. When Manuel was managing the ballclub, it meant accepting some of his fixations, like taking his frustrations with Keith Foulke too seriously. Manuel could quit on a player, and had a tendency to gripe about him if the player wasn't gone soon enough to suit him. Rather than reflect on Foulke's value, Williams was something of an enabler, flipping Foulke to Oakland for the far inferior Billy Koch. It saved money and was a sop for Manuel.

But more important, it hurt the team.

As a result, 2004 was going to be interesting no matter what happened, because Guillen came in the personification of bombast and bluster, with equal measures of outspoken good cheer and blunt assertiveness. After Manuel's preachy droning, it was a needed breath of fresh air. As we documented last year, there were reasons to expect that Guillen might not be as bad at managing as his harshest critics had predicted, and in-season, Ozzie didn't disappoint.

Guillen inherited a team that was given to park-inflated power-hitting and uncertain pitching, and one in which some people played, while others were overlooked. He shook things up from the get-go, and if some of that involved some preseason cage-rattling for Frank Thomas, it also meant some proclamations about how he'd run the roster—proclamations he backed up with action.

Guillen was assertive in saying he'd give his pitchers chances to work their own way out of whatever trouble they'd get themselves into, and he backed that up in both the rotation and in the bullpen. Despite not having the advantage Manuel had the previous season of being able to call upon a Colon or an effective Loaiza (and only a half-season's worth of Freddy Garcia), Sox starters averaged 6.2 IP per start. Where many rookie managers like to look busy and ape the LaRussian gambit of micromanaging their bullpens for tactical advantages, Guillen finished second behind Mike Scioscia in the AL in fewest number of relievers put into each game. We can get caught up on cause and effect there—do Scioscia and Guillen prefer to leave their relievers out there, or do they have the guys with the stuff to do it—but it's a good way to keep your pen fit over a season's long haul.

In terms of offensive strategies, Guillen was a man of his word. He was fond of the bunt, easily leading the league in sac bunts attempted and successfully executed. An ill-considered basepath commando in his playing days, he overused the running game given the limitations of his roster, particularly by letting Uribe and Jose Valentin make a few too many mistakes on the bases. When it comes to the advantages of little ball, Ozzie's a man of convictions. On a more positive note, Guillen showed a willingness to use his entire bench, finding ways to spot-start players and keep everyone fresh. That sensibility informed his decision to lean on Ross Gload and, less successfully, Timo Perez when Magglio Ordonez broke down. Guillen was also creative in terms of finding ways to keep Uribe in the lineup while never needlessly benching any of the other infield regulars. Maybe it was the memory of former teammate Freddy Manrique's virtues, but Ozzie's not afraid to platoon in spots.

After another season that found the Sox suffering the same old disappointment, how did Williams react this time? After being thwarted on the field, Williams and Guillen have busily assembled the sort of team they'd like to have, without necessarily sorting out if it's the sort of team that will fulfill their ambitions. Charitably, you could consider the Sox's off-season as the product of a plan that keeps the best of what Williams has done in the past. But it also involves remaking the roster in Ozzie's image: Valentin's out, with Uribe taking over at short on an every-day basis. Rather than see if there was something to be worked out with Magglio Ordonez, Williams showed him up before running him off, replacing him with the notionally more athletic but less dangerous Jermaine Dye. Williams finally caught his white whale, getting presumptive staff ace Garcia to sign a multi-year extension. In a break with the past, he also got the occasionally healthy, very famous Orlando Hernandez and the healthy, occasionally useful Dustin Hermanson for two years apiece. Addressing the catching problem, Williams signed A. J. Pierzynski to a cheap, shrewd one-year deal, but only after first humiliating him with a lot of public posturing on the virtues of character.

But the real statement move of the winter was trading Carlos Lee to the Brewers. Lee was accused of being the face of the underachieving White Sox; Scott Podsednik becomes the symbol of a decision to build an offense that will cost them runs on the scoreboard. In so doing, the Sox are taking a risk—which isn't a bad thing—but the future of the team depends on wish fulfillment. There's no reason to believe that Jose Contreras will suddenly become a consistent starter, or that Uribe will hit as well this year as last, but they sure do hope so. They're hoping that Joe Crede and Jon Garland will stop disappointing them. They're hoping that Thomas ages a little more smoothly, instead of going straight to vinegar. They're hoping all of their rangy, toolsy outfield types down on the farm actually turn out to be good big league ballplayers.

Hope's all to the good, but Williams's shopping spree smacks of monorail mania. Magically deciding that speed and defense will change everything after four years of repeated failures is the sort of thing you turn to when the cause is lost, like super weapons or horoscopes or investment banking. The 1991 Braves are famous for having done it, but who remembers the same move by the 1991 Indians and their master plan to move out the fences and win with Alex Cole? Who wants to remember the Dave Collins Yankees of 1982? In some ways, picking up Podsednik—at the expense of Lee, a strong offensive player in his prime—closely resembles those moves, since in all three cases, the poster boy for the "new era" is or was a leadoff hitter of doubtful value. You've got an offense which, in one year, has Aaron Rowand going from arguably its worst-hitting outfielder to clearly its best.

The investment in pitching is defensible, but for all that, the rotation is still really two and a half pitchers deep: Garcia, Mark Buehrle, and El Duque whenever he's healthy. That won't be enough to make up for an offense ill-suited for its home park and likely to struggle to score anywhere else. The new master plan might be a bold stroke, but it's the sort of gamble that will more likely have the Sox keeping the Royals company in the basement than finally getting them back to the top of the standings.

HITTERS

ROBERTO ALOMAR 2B **Bats: B** **Throws: R** Born: 05-Feb-1968 Age: 37

YEAR	TM	LG	AGE	AB	H	2B	3B	HR	BB	SO	SB	CS	AVG	OBP	SLG	MLVR	EQBA	EQOBP	EQSLG	EQMLVR	VORP	DEFENSE
2002	NYM	NL	34	590	157	24	4	11	57	83	16	4	.266	.331	.376	-.017	.274	.338	.393	-.066	28.9	138-2B -7
2003	NYM	NL	35	263	69	17	1	2	29	40	6	0	.262	.336	.357	-.075	.264	.337	.366	-.113	9.0	65-2B -5
2003	CWS	AL	35	253	64	11	1	3	30	37	6	2	.253	.330	.340	-.147	.252	.334	.340	-.163	4.5	62-2B -1
2004	ARI	NL	36	110	34	5	2	3	12	18	0	2	.309	.382	.473	.158	.300	.373	.455	.106	8.8	22-2B -3
2004	CWS	AL	36	61	11	1	0	1	2	13	0	0	.180	.203	.246	-.593	.167	.188	.233	-.650	-5.8	11-2B 1
2005	*TBY*	*AL*	*37*	*220*	*57*	*10*	*1*	*3*	*21*	*39*	*3*	*1*	*.259*	*.324*	*.359*	*-.133*	*.259*	*.327*	*.366*	*-.128*	*5.5*	*61-2B -4*

Breakout: 19% *Improve: 43%* *Collapse: 29%*

Primary acquisition target for the stretch in Kenny Williams's contention playbook, which naysayers might note has yet to produce a winner, but no matter. After a Hall of Fame career, Alomar has withered into a possible but non-guaranteed OBP source against righties, and now, at the end, everyone can finally agree he's a defensive liability. Not exactly famed for his charm, so his all-around decline might lead to a quick, inglorious end to a superb career. Close to signing with either St. Louis or Texas (to ride the pine alongside his brother) at press time.

SANDY ALOMAR Pitchback **Bats: R** **Throws: R** Born: 18-Jun-1966 Age: 39

YEAR	TM	LG	AGE	AB	H	2B	3B	HR	BB	SO	SB	CS	AVG	OBP	SLG	MLVR	EQBA	EQOBP	EQSLG	EQMLVR	VORP	DEFENSE
2002	CWS	AL	36	167	48	10	1	7	5	14	0	0	.287	.309	.485	.050	.289	.314	.488	.040	11.3	47-C -3
2002	COL	NL	36	116	31	4	0	0	4	19	0	0	.267	.292	.302	-.260	.261	.264	.278	-.386	-1.9	32-C -1
2003	CWS	AL	37	194	52	12	0	5	4	17	0	0	.268	.281	.407	-.125	.271	.281	.401	-.164	3.9	55-C 1
2004	CWS	AL	38	146	35	4	0	2	11	13	0	0	.240	.298	.308	-.293	.243	.295	.299	-.303	-3.0	43-C 2
2005	*TEX*	*AL*	*39*	*115*	*28*	*5*	*0*	*2*	*8*	*13*	*0*	*0*	*.245*	*.293*	*.349*	*-.211*	*.236*	*.286*	*.337*	*-.256*	*-1.4*	*34-C -3*

Breakout: 31% *Improve: 32%* *Collapse: 47%*

Perhaps not the easy winner for Most Overrated Player of his generation, not when he has people like Joe Carter to compete with, but Alomar's on the list. He's settled into scoring paydays through backup work. One obvious value-add: Bilingual catchers are handy, especially when the pitching coach doesn't speak Spanish. Otherwise, he's used up: His knees won't let him play often enough to play everyday for a couple of weeks if the starter were hurt, and his bat's gone. Signed with Texas, ostensibly to give Gerald Laird a bit more seasoning in Triple-A.

BRIAN ANDERSON CF **Bats: R** **Throws: R** Born: 11-Mar-1982 Age: 23

YEAR	TM	LG	AGE	AB	H	2B	3B	HR	BB	SO	SB	CS	AVG	OBP	SLG	MLVR	EQBA	EQOBP	EQSLG	EQMLVR	VORP	DEFENSE
2003	GRF	PIO	21	49	19	2	1	2	9	10	3	1	.388	.492	.592	.647	.292	.374	.438	.077	6.5	12-CF 0
2004	WNS	CRL	22	254	81	22	4	8	29	44	10	1	.319	.394	.531	.315	.277	.344	.474	.061	16.9	63-CF -4
2004	BIR	SOU	22	185	50	9	3	4	19	30	3	2	.270	.346	.416	.084	.255	.322	.399	-.102	2.6	40-CF -4
2005	*CWS*	*AL*	*23*	*297*	*81*	*16*	*3*	*10*	*27*	*61*	*6*	*2*	*.271*	*.339*	*.443*	*.011*	*.268*	*.338*	*.435*	*-.011*	*15.5*	*80-CF -5*

Breakout: 18% *Improve: 43%* *Collapse: 31%*

Last season, we compared Anderson to Andy Van Slyke, and that still works, with the right balance between good raw tools and maturing baseball skills, and perhaps a grinding style that increases his propensity to get hurt. Van Slyke broke into the big leagues at 23, and PECOTA thinks that Anderson could hold his own this season too, though he'll wait in Charlotte until Scott Podsednik reminds everyone that he's neither particularly young nor particularly good.

JOE BORCHARD OF **Bats: B** **Throws: R** Born: 25-Nov-1978 Age: 26

YEAR	TM	LG	AGE	AB	H	2B	3B	HR	BB	SO	SB	CS	AVG	OBP	SLG	MLVR	EQBA	EQOBP	EQSLG	EQMLVR	VORP	DEFENSE
2002	CHR	INT	23	438	119	35	2	20	49	139	2	4	.272	.349	.498	.172	.249	.327	.466	-.005	19.6	108-CF 4
2003	CHR	INT	24	435	110	20	2	13	27	103	2	4	.253	.307	.398	-.029	.241	.299	.391	-.167	-2.6	108-CF -1
2004	CHR	INT	25	301	80	21	0	16	30	68	4	3	.266	.333	.495	.101	.242	.306	.446	-.077	-1.1	67-RF -2 12-CF 1
2004	CWS	AL	25	201	35	4	1	9	19	57	1	0	.174	.249	.338	-.372	.172	.254	.333	-.377	-11.0	49-RF 0
2005	*CWS*	*AL*	*26*	*296*	*75*	*16*	*1*	*14*	*29*	*80*	*2*	*1*	*.252*	*.324*	*.454*	*-.014*	*.249*	*.323*	*.446*	*-.037*	*10.4*	*80-RF 0*

Breakout: 49% *Improve: 72%* *Collapse: 14%*

Here he is, the "untradeable" commodity, the player that Kenny Williams can't give up on. Instead, Williams handed the Mariners Jeremy Reed in the Chief Garcia deal, shipping out the much better prospect in the process. The Sox claim Borchard has improved his plate discipline, but on that score, he was no better off in his third year in Charlotte than he was in his first, and his flailing got him cut from the Mexican Winter League. A few months removed from being untouchable, he's in danger of being overrun by the wave of young outfielders coming up through system.

JAMIE BURKE C **Bats: R** **Throws: R** Born: 24-Sep-1971 Age: 33

YEAR	TM	LG	AGE	AB	H	2B	3B	HR	BB	SO	SB	CS	AVG	OBP	SLG	MLVR	EQBA	EQOBP	EQSLG	EQMLVR	VORP	DEFENSE
2002	SLC	PCL	30	316	96	12	4	8	20	37	1	3	.304	.350	.443	.024	.260	.307	.383	-.149	2.2	31-C -5 31-3B -2
2003	CHR	INT	31	323	104	13	0	6	20	39	1	1	.322	.363	.418	.143	.299	.341	.395	-.038	13.2	72-C 0
2004	CHR	INT	32	134	31	6	0	2	9	15	0	0	.231	.286	.321	-.248	.201	.252	.269	-.453	-11.4	34-C 6
2004	CWS	AL	32	120	40	9	0	0	10	13	0	0	.333	.386	.408	.076	.350	.377	.402	.082	9.0	33-C 1
2005	*CWS*	*AL*	*33*	*150*	*37*	*7*	*0*	*2*	*10*	*19*	*0*	*0*	*.247*	*.301*	*.340*	*-.208*	*.244*	*.300*	*.334*	*-.229*	*-1.8*	*43-C -5*

Breakout: 6% *Improve: 24%* *Collapse: 55%*

You can't hold it against Burke that the reason he was on the team as its third catcher was that any team carrying the occasionally healthy Sandy Alomar and an irregular like Ben Davis probably needs a third catcher. His future on the roster was tied to Alomar's; when Alomar went to Texas and Williams picked up A. J. Pierzynski, Burke's outrighting off the roster came within a day. PECOTA is suspicious of an aging catcher whose primary skill is hitting for average, and while that .333 number looked good on the left-field scoreboard in September, Burke is not a great bet to resurface.

JOE CREDE 3B **Bats: R** **Throws: R** Born: 26-Apr-1978 Age: 27

YEAR	TM	LG	AGE	AB	H	2B	3B	HR	BB	SO	SB	CS	AVG	OBP	SLG	MLVR	EQBA	EQOBP	EQSLG	EQMLVR	VORP	DEFENSE
2002	CHR	INT	24	359	112	21	0	24	26	48	0	1	.312	.359	.571	.325	.282	.328	.525	.111	31.8	92-3B 3
2002	CWS	AL	24	200	57	10	0	12	8	40	0	2	.285	.311	.515	.093	.288	.310	.520	.080	12.9	48-3B 0
2003	CWS	AL	25	536	140	31	2	19	32	75	1	1	.261	.308	.433	-.039	.259	.311	.435	-.069	23.0	150-3B 2
2004	CWS	AL	26	490	117	25	0	21	34	81	1	2	.239	.299	.418	-.136	.238	.298	.416	-.136	1.2	138-3B -4
2005	*CWS*	*AL*	*27*	*432*	*115*	*23*	*1*	*20*	*31*	*71*	*0*	*1*	*.266*	*.321*	*.459*	*-.001*	*.263*	*.320*	*.451*	*-.024*	*11.0*	*113-3B -1*

Breakout: 27% *Improve: 55%* *Collapse: 21%*

As a friend puts it, .239 has to be the most depressing batting average ever—I doubt few Sox fans would disagree. After the last two years, it's hard to shake the sense that Crede has become what Gary Scott might have been if he'd been left alone: not much after all. Third basemen who hit like Aurelio Rodriguez might have been stars . . . well, around Aurelio Rodriguez's time, but these days, they don't deserve a lot of job security. This should be Crede's last year with any sort of guarantees about playing time. After that, Josh Fields should start entering the picture, and Crede will have an arbitration payday liable to terminate his career with the Sox if he doesn't resemble the guy who seized the job in 2002.

BEN DAVIS C **Bats: B** **Throws: R** Born: 10-Mar-1977 Age: 28

YEAR	TM	LG	AGE	AB	H	2B	3B	HR	BB	SO	SB	CS	AVG	OBP	SLG	MLVR	EQBA	EQOBP	EQSLG	EQMLVR	VORP	DEFENSE
2002	SEA	AL	25	228	59	10	1	7	18	58	1	1	.259	.313	.404	-.046	.272	.330	.425	-.038	10.0	62-C 7
2003	SEA	AL	26	246	58	18	0	6	18	61	0	0	.236	.284	.382	-.160	.242	.292	.393	-.177	2.8	68-C 4
2004	SEA	AL	27	33	3	0	0	0	3	9	0	0	.091	.162	.091	-.880	.091	.115	.091	-1.021	-5.6	10-C 2
2004	TAC	PCL	27	141	35	9	0	4	15	29	1	0	.248	.321	.397	-.103	.216	.274	.331	-.315	-6.2	38-C 1
2004	CWS	AL	27	160	37	9	0	6	9	40	1	1	.231	.276	.400	-.205	.234	.275	.392	-.216	0.2	49-C -4
2005	*CWS*	*AL*	*28*	*171*	*41*	*8*	*1*	*6*	*14*	*44*	*1*	*0*	*.239*	*.299*	*.404*	*-.133*	*.236*	*.298*	*.397*	*-.155*	*3.7*	*48-C -4*

Breakout: 35% *Improve: 54%* *Collapse: 26%*

Any enthusiasm for Davis after he came over as a throw-in in the Garcia deal was born out of desperation. Not ordinary, it's-Saturday-night desperation, more along the lines of for-god's-sake-somebody-has-to-perpetuate-the-species desperation. Davis has all his limbs, and he knows how to catch. He's been reduced to the backup role that suits his skill set now that Pierzynski's been added.

CARL EVERETT OF/DH **Bats: B** **Throws: R** Born: 03-Jun-1971 Age: 34

YEAR	TM	LG	AGE	AB	H	2B	3B	HR	BB	SO	SB	CS	AVG	OBP	SLG	MLVR	EQBA	EQOBP	EQSLG	EQMLVR	VORP	DEFENSE
2002	TEX	AL	31	374	100	16	0	16	33	77	2	3	.267	.333	.439	-.010	.266	.332	.436	-.023	10.2	30-RF 0 26-CF 0
2003	TEX	AL	32	270	74	13	3	18	31	48	4	1	.274	.356	.544	.164	.268	.356	.536	.159	22.7	31-LF -3 28-RF 1
2003	CWS	AL	32	256	77	14	0	10	22	36	4	3	.301	.377	.473	.167	.304	.377	.478	.149	20.5	56-CF -4
2004	MON	NL	33	127	32	10	0	2	8	19	0	0	.252	.319	.378	-.063	.252	.304	.370	-.179	1.9	14-LF -1 14-RF 2
2004	CWS	AL	33	154	41	7	1	5	8	26	1	0	.266	.320	.422	-.078	.263	.317	.428	-.065	3.4	
2005	*CWS*	*AL*	*34*	*280*	*76*	*15*	*1*	*10*	*24*	*49*	*1*	*1*	*.273*	*.338*	*.444*	*.013*	*.270*	*.338*	*.436*	*-.010*	*10.4*	*76-DH 7*

Breakout: 21% *Improve: 51%* *Collapse: 32%*

Your classic clubhouse chirper, noisily sounding off on all sorts of things that might make him a great Jerry Springer guest, yet somehow compatible with Kenny Williams's humorless hang-ups on "character." Everett eagerly exercised his player option the way a backgammon player might snatch the cube after an opponent's premature double. He has some semblance of his offensive skills intact, but automatically makes for a planning problem because he's so likely to get hurt.

JOSH FIELDS 3B **Bats: R** **Throws: R** Born: 14-Dec-1982 Age: 22

YEAR	TM	LG	AGE	AB	H	2B	3B	HR	BB	SO	SB	CS	AVG	OBP	SLG	MLVR	EQBA	EQOBP	EQSLG	EQMLVR	VORP	DEFENSE
2004	WNS	CRL	21	256	73	12	4	7	18	74	0	0	.285	.333	.445	.088	.247	.289	.404	-.163	1.4	57-3B -5
2005	*CWS*	*AL*	*22*	*388*	*90*	*18*	*3*	*12*	*23*	*127*	*1*	*1*	*.231*	*.279*	*.384*	*-.199*	*.228*	*.279*	*.377*	*-.221*	*-9.2*	*100-3B -7*

Breakout: 19% *Improve: 39%* *Collapse: 41%*

The Sox's top pick in the 2004 draft, and perhaps better known as the starting quarterback at Oklahoma State. Fields, indeed, had the sort of season you might expect from a converted quarterback. He displayed the ability to go long, lacked mobility afield and on the basepaths, and his impatient hitting approach attempted to solve too many problems all on its own. Eerily, Fields's fifth-closest PECOTA comparable is Drew Henson.

ROSS GLOAD 1B/OF Bats: L Throws: L Born: 05-Apr-1976 Age: 29

YEAR	TM	LG	AGE	AB	H	2B	3B	HR	BB	SO	SB	CS	AVG	OBP	SLG	MLVR	EQBA	EQOBP	EQSLG	EQMLVR	VORP	DEFENSE
2002	CSP	PCL	26	442	139	28	6	16	18	59	9	4	.314	.338	.514	.098	.266	.293	.436	-.094	-1.4	86-1B 1
2003	CHR	INT	27	508	160	40	6	18	29	60	6	3	.315	.349	.524	.263	.298	.339	.507	.120	31.2	102-1B -2 13-LF 0
2004	CWS	AL	28	234	75	16	0	7	20	37	0	3	.321	.375	.479	.151	.323	.374	.476	.160	17.0	25-1B -3 19-RF 0
2005	*CWS*	*AL*	*29*	*231*	*62*	*13*	*1*	*8*	*16*	*35*	*1*	*1*	*.270*	*.318*	*.435*	*-.035*	*.267*	*.317*	*.428*	*-.058*	*6.0*	*62-1B 0*

Breakout: 5% *Improve: 17%* *Collapse: 56%*

It's difficult to hit .321 while being shuffled back and forth between a pinch-hitting role and everyday work, so Gload provided a lot of value to the White Sox while earning barely more than the league minimum. PECOTA remembers his longer, more undistinguished track record and expects some pushback, especially in the batting average department, where Gload's slow wheels don't help him leg out any base hits. That might be an issue if the Sox were impressed enough to stick him the starting lineup, but he's buried beneath a beggar's banquet of dubious corner position talent.

WILLIE HARRIS 2B/CF Bats: L Throws: R Born: 22-Jun-1978 Age: 27

YEAR	TM	LG	AGE	AB	H	2B	3B	HR	BB	SO	SB	CS	AVG	OBP	SLG	MLVR	EQBA	EQOBP	EQSLG	EQMLVR	VORP	DEFENSE
2002	CHR	INT	24	360	102	16	5	5	33	61	32	14	.283	.345	.397	.043	.266	.330	.382	-.103	8.0	82-2B 4
2002	CWS	AL	24	163	38	4	0	2	9	21	8	0	.233	.270	.294	-.324	.230	.268	.286	-.383	-2.5	37-2B 0
2003	CHR	INT	25	100	38	6	1	6	17	20	9	3	.380	.470	.640	.654	.366	.458	.634	.566	24.8	17-2B 2
2003	CWS	AL	25	137	28	3	1	0	10	28	12	2	.204	.259	.241	-.435	.200	.257	.230	-.497	-7.1	35-CF -2
2004	CWS	AL	26	409	107	15	2	2	51	79	19	7	.262	.343	.323	-.174	.259	.346	.322	-.160	5.2	77-2B 3 23-CF 0
2005	*CWS*	*AL*	*27*	*313*	*82*	*13*	*3*	*5*	*33*	*58*	*16*	*5*	*.262*	*.333*	*.368*	*-.103*	*.259*	*.332*	*.362*	*-.124*	*9.1*	*85-2B -1*

Breakout: 11% *Improve: 37%* *Collapse: 31%*

Harris is almost a very valuable ballplayer. If he were able to add another 20 points to his on-base percentage, he'd instantly become one of the best leadoff hitters in the league, at least against right-handed pitching. But those extra 20 points are going to be awfully hard to come by. Harris works the count the best he can, using his short stature to reduce the size of the strike zone and seeing 3.98 pitches per plate appearance last season. The problem is that he rarely hits the ball out of the infield, so pitchers can just fire away, figuring that a base hit can't hurt much more than a walk. Players like this used to have an easier go of things, but the reintroduction of the high strike in 2001 made their jobs considerably more difficult.

PAUL KONERKO 1B Bats: R Throws: R Born: 05-Mar-1976 Age: 29

YEAR	TM	LG	AGE	AB	H	2B	3B	HR	BB	SO	SB	CS	AVG	OBP	SLG	MLVR	EQBA	EQOBP	EQSLG	EQMLVR	VORP	DEFENSE
2002	CWS	AL	26	570	173	30	0	27	44	72	0	0	.304	.359	.498	.169	.308	.363	.504	.167	43.3	135-1B -13
2003	CWS	AL	27	444	104	19	0	18	43	50	0	0	.234	.305	.399	-.107	.233	.306	.397	-.151	3.2	107-1B 0
2004	CWS	AL	28	563	156	22	0	41	69	107	1	0	.277	.359	.535	.159	.278	.361	.537	.179	48.1	132-1B -7
2005	*CWS*	*AL*	*29*	*473*	*131*	*24*	*0*	*26*	*54*	*77*	*0*	*0*	*.276*	*.353*	*.494*	*.106*	*.273*	*.352*	*.485*	*.083*	*25.9*	*126-1B -6*

Breakout: 26% *Improve: 56%* *Collapse: 11%*

Back on track. Konerko still doesn't walk enough to satisfy some statheads, and he's not going to win a Gold Glove, but he's proven more durable than Tommy Lasorda claimed he'd be. Admittedly, Lasorda said a few stupid things after doing a lot of stupid things in his brief regency at the end of the '90s, but the preference for Eric Karros over Konerko was the most transparent mistake. His value won't get any higher, but between Frank Thomas's big and little hurts and Paulie's popularity on the South Side, it's unlikely that the Sox will have the nerve to trade him.

CARLOS LEE LF Bats: R Throws: R Born: 20-Jun-1976 Age: 29

YEAR	TM	LG	AGE	AB	H	2B	3B	HR	BB	SO	SB	CS	AVG	OBP	SLG	MLVR	EQBA	EQOBP	EQSLG	EQMLVR	VORP	DEFENSE
2002	CWS	AL	26	492	130	26	2	26	75	73	1	4	.264	.359	.484	.117	.265	.366	.492	.113	28.5	113-LF 11
2003	CWS	AL	27	623	181	35	1	31	37	91	18	4	.291	.331	.499	.121	.288	.334	.502	.094	38.1	148-LF -1
2004	CWS	AL	28	591	180	37	0	31	54	86	11	5	.305	.366	.525	.185	.306	.368	.530	.210	46.8	144-LF 15
2005	*MIL*	*NL*	*29*	*529*	*152*	*31*	*2*	*25*	*55*	*78*	*9*	*3*	*.287*	*.356*	*.499*	*.121*	*.286*	*.353*	*.499*	*.115*	*25.7*	*139-LF 2*

Breakout: 10% *Improve: 48%* *Collapse: 16%*

Trading Carlos Lee wasn't such a bad idea. He's a good hitter who is sometimes mistaken for a great one, largely because his "scoreboard" stats—the BA, HR, and RBI numbers—tend to cover for the slight boost he's getting from U.S. Cellular

(continued next page)

Carlos Lee *(continued)*

Field and his once-found, twice-lost plate discipline. In other words, he's exactly the sort of player that traditionally-minded general managers are liable to overvalue. Instead, Kenny Williams went and completed a bizarre challenge trade for Luis Vizcaino and Scott Podsednik, the latter a player who is actually three months older than Lee and whose skills are even more overrated. At least White Sox fans, having been bilked by the Brewers, now know how Lithuanians felt after getting conquered by Poland. To Lee's credit, he's a better athlete and better defender than people realize, which makes up some of the difference between perceived and real value. His game should adapt well to Miller Park, where he could become a fan favorite.

PEDRO LOPEZ SS/2B **Bats: R** **Throws: R** Born: 28-Apr-1984 Age: 21

YEAR	TM	LG	AGE	AB	H	2B	3B	HR	BB	SO	SB	CS	AVG	OBP	SLG	MLVR	EQBA	EQOBP	EQSLG	EQMLVR	VORP	DEFENSE
2002	BRI	APL	18	260	83	11	0	0	20	27	22	8	.319	.370	.362	.081	.244	.263	.279	-.395	-33.9	52-2B 0
2003	KAN	SAL	19	390	103	23	0	0	26	43	24	14	.264	.314	.323	-.035	.219	.248	.266	-.457	-35.8	91-2B -13 14-SS -1
2004	WNS	CRL	20	432	126	13	0	4	23	35	12	9	.292	.331	.350	-.040	.239	.271	.289	-.367	-21.5	101-SS 6
2005	*CWS*	*AL*	*21*	*350*	*82*	*15*	*1*	*2*	*14*	*37*	*7*	*3*	*.233*	*.268*	*.298*	*-.333*	*.231*	*.267*	*.293*	*-.354*	*-12.6*	*91-SS -6*

Breakout: 14% *Improve: 29%* *Collapse: 46%*

Lopez has lost time at short to Andy Gonzalez, but now that Gonzalez's position is "to be named later," he's got another chance. Among the organization's gaggle of athletic shortstoppish infielders, Gonzalez can't play the position, and Rob Valido doesn't seem a great bet to hit, so Lopez could be the one left standing. He got a taste of Double-A at season's end, but with youth and tools being his only real assets, he's still far from becoming a prospect.

MAGGLIO ORDONEZ RF/DH? **Bats: R** **Throws: R** Born: 28-Jan-1974 Age: 31

YEAR	TM	LG	AGE	AB	H	2B	3B	HR	BB	SO	SB	CS	AVG	OBP	SLG	MLVR	EQBA	EQOBP	EQSLG	EQMLVR	VORP	DEFENSE
2002	CWS	AL	28	590	189	47	1	38	53	77	7	5	.320	.381	.597	.353	.324	.388	.606	.371	68.0	146-RF -2
2003	CWS	AL	29	606	192	46	3	29	57	73	9	5	.317	.380	.546	.291	.317	.385	.551	.280	63.3	150-RF 13
2004	CWS	AL	30	202	59	8	2	9	16	22	0	2	.292	.351	.485	.093	.288	.352	.485	.101	11.8	43-RF 1
2005	*CWS*	*AL*	*31*	*396*	*118*	*24*	*2*	*19*	*38*	*51*	*2*	*2*	*.298*	*.365*	*.515*	*.172*	*.295*	*.364*	*.506*	*.148*	*30.5*	*105-RF 0*

Breakout: 13% *Improve: 41%* *Collapse: 21%*

We don't know how well he's going to recover. Not us, not baseball executives, not his agent, not PECOTA. What's ironic is that Ordonez's injury might have provided cover for the Sox to re-sign him relatively cheaply, allaying Jerry Reinsdorf's fears of overextending his budget. Instead, Kenny Williams did everything that he could to spoil the relationship with his star player, first failing to make a good-faith effort to sign him to a contract extension, and then accusing Ordonez and his agent of covering up details of the slugger's injury and subsequent surgery. The outcry over the end of the Ordonez Era has been relatively muted in Chicago circles, in the same way that few seem to care about the NHL lockout.

TIMO PEREZ OF **Bats: L** **Throws: L** Born: 08-Apr-1975 Age: 30

YEAR	TM	LG	AGE	AB	H	2B	3B	HR	BB	SO	SB	CS	AVG	OBP	SLG	MLVR	EQBA	EQOBP	EQSLG	EQMLVR	VORP	DEFENSE
2002	NYM	NL	27	444	131	27	6	8	23	36	10	6	.295	.331	.437	.086	.302	.336	.455	.043	23.8	81-CF 1 20-LF -1
2003	NYM	NL	28	346	93	21	0	4	18	29	5	6	.269	.301	.364	-.125	.275	.303	.372	-.162	-3.1	32-LF -1 35-CF 3
2004	CWS	AL	29	293	72	12	0	5	15	29	3	1	.246	.285	.338	-.276	.246	.285	.332	-.274	-8.3	41-RF 2 19-CF 0
2005	*CWS*	*AL*	*30*	*250*	*66*	*13*	*1*	*5*	*14*	*26*	*3*	*2*	*.266*	*.307*	*.385*	*-.124*	*.263*	*.306*	*.379*	*-.146*	*0.2*	*67-RF 0*

Breakout: 20% *Improve: 35%* *Collapse: 35%*

Perez was never the player he was trumpeted to be when he was the Big Apple darling for the most stultifyingly dull World Series of recent memory, so there's something embarrassing about his turning up in America's Second City a few years after his 15 minutes were up. It's one of those bad things, like a Danny Bonaduce guest appearance, that you wish would just stop. When you're a fifth outfielder who's not plausibly better than Tom Goodwin, you probably don't deserve to be even Ross Gload's legs.

CASEY ROGOWSKI 1B/OF **Bats: L** **Throws: L** Born: 01-May-1981 Age: 24

YEAR	TM	LG	AGE	AB	H	2B	3B	HR	BB	SO	SB	CS	AVG	OBP	SLG	MLVR	EQBA	EQOBP	EQSLG	EQMLVR	VORP	DEFENSE	
2002	WNS	CRL	21	184	47	5	0	3	28	46	16	3	.255	.358	.332	.000	.218	.300	.293	-.314	-14.2	42-1B -1	
2003	WNS	CRL	22	357	88	20	1	7	53	73	18	4	.246	.354	.367	.028	.224	.315	.355	-.197	-14.3	101-1B 6	
2004	WNS	CRL	23	465	133	28	2	18	91	94	16	9	.286	.401	.471	.218	.239	.344	.404	-.066	2.8	108-1B 2	14-LF -1
2005	*CWS*	*AL*	*24*	*320*	*79*	*17*	*2*	*11*	*42*	*76*	*6*	*2*	*.247*	*.339*	*.410*	*-.049*	*.244*	*.338*	*.402*	*-.070*	*5.0*	*89-1B -1*	

Breakout: 25% *Improve: 56%* *Collapse: 19%*

We're supposed to love everyone who walks, but let's face it, if Rogowski can't play the outfield, you're left with a first baseman who finally mastered the Carolina League after three years. If he continues at that rate all the way up the chain, he could be a major league starter when he's 30. Basically, he needs to tear through Double-A, adding more power or learning to play left decently. Otherwise, he'll never make people forget Dan Pasqua.

AARON ROWAND OF **Bats: R** **Throws: R** Born: 29-Aug-1977 Age: 27

YEAR	TM	LG	AGE	AB	H	2B	3B	HR	BB	SO	SB	CS	AVG	OBP	SLG	MLVR	EQBA	EQOBP	EQSLG	EQMLVR	VORP	DEFENSE	
2002	CWS	AL	24	302	78	16	2	7	12	54	0	1	.258	.298	.394	-.125	.260	.302	.400	-.135	2.9	62-CF 0	28-LF 3
2003	CHR	INT	25	120	29	9	0	3	11	12	0	0	.242	.316	.392	-.030	.221	.288	.361	-.243	-3.6	21-CF 1	11-RF 0
2003	CWS	AL	25	157	45	8	0	6	7	21	0	0	.287	.327	.452	.042	.290	.327	.445	.001	8.6	41-CF 0	
2004	CWS	AL	26	487	151	38	2	24	30	91	17	5	.310	.361	.544	.203	.311	.364	.551	.239	50.0	119-CF 2	
2005	*CWS*	*AL*	*27*	*387*	*112*	*23*	*2*	*16*	*24*	*66*	*9*	*4*	*.290*	*.341*	*.482*	*.083*	*.287*	*.340*	*.474*	*.059*	*23.9*	*102-CF -2*	

Breakout: 8% *Improve: 28%* *Collapse: 28%*

PECOTA sees his progress as the high end of what's possible. That isn't an insult: He's become the player the Sox had hoped he'd be with the bat, and surprised everyone with how well he's adapted to playing center. He'll be an asset there for several years to come.

MIKE SPIDALE OF **Bats: R** **Throws: R** Born: 12-Mar-1982 Age: 23

YEAR	TM	LG	AGE	AB	H	2B	3B	HR	BB	SO	SB	CS	AVG	OBP	SLG	MLVR	EQBA	EQOBP	EQSLG	EQMLVR	VORP	DEFENSE	
2002	KAN	SAL	20	357	104	11	1	0	34	50	37	25	.291	.372	.328	.063	.238	.293	.266	-.356	-23.3	84-CF 2	
2003	WNS	CRL	21	393	103	21	5	1	57	76	25	7	.262	.362	.349	.027	.241	.326	.340	-.185	-5.2	101-CF 1	11-LF 0
2004	BIR	SOU	22	484	148	27	7	7	61	72	26	15	.306	.393	.434	.209	.290	.367	.412	.027	12.6	66-LF 2	51-CF -6
2005	*CWS*	*AL*	*23*	*282*	*73*	*15*	*2*	*4*	*27*	*47*	*9*	*4*	*.260*	*.338*	*.372*	*-.091*	*.257*	*.337*	*.365*	*-.112*	*3.2*	*78-CF -6*	

Breakout: 8% *Improve: 30%* *Collapse: 41%*

Gets less than zero in the props department from the organization, but a guy to root for. He's ethnic, he's a Chicagoland native, and anybody who can hit at a young age in Double-A should make the Show at some point. He's a bit too exciting on the basepaths, but that might recommend him to Ozzie.

RYAN SWEENEY RF **Bats: L** **Throws: L** Born: 20-Feb-1985 Age: 20

YEAR	TM	LG	AGE	AB	H	2B	3B	HR	BB	SO	SB	CS	AVG	OBP	SLG	MLVR	EQBA	EQOBP	EQSLG	EQMLVR	VORP	DEFENSE
2003	BRI	APL	18	67	21	3	0	2	7	10	3	0	.313	.387	.448	.289	.265	.298	.426	-.101	-1.7	11-RF -2
2004	WNS	CRL	19	515	146	22	3	7	40	65	8	6	.283	.342	.379	.011	.243	.293	.336	-.255	-30.1	126-RF -2
2005	*CWS*	*AL*	*20*	*352*	*86*	*17*	*2*	*6*	*22*	*55*	*3*	*2*	*.243*	*.295*	*.353*	*-.202*	*.240*	*.295*	*.347*	*-.224*	*-8.8*	*92-RF -3*

Breakout: 23% *Improve: 41%* *Collapse: 39%*

An organizational favorite since being picked in the second round of the draft in '03, his pretty swing made him the beneficiary of an awful lot of spring slobber from Guillen and hitting coach Greg Walker. Nevertheless, there are concerns he's got a slow bat, and being young for the level only means so much when you slug just .379. He's a right fielder for the moment because he's got the arm for it, but he'll have to develop significantly as a hitter.

FRANK THOMAS DH Bats: R Throws: R Born: 27-May-1968 Age: 37

YEAR	TM	LG	AGE	AB	H	2B	3B	HR	BB	SO	SB	CS	AVG	OBP	SLG	MLVR	EQBA	EQOBP	EQSLG	EQMLVR	VORP	DEFENSE
2002	CWS	AL	34	523	132	29	1	28	88	115	3	0	.252	.361	.472	.093	.255	.367	.479	.089	35.9	
2003	CWS	AL	35	546	146	35	0	42	100	115	0	0	.267	.390	.562	.278	.270	.392	.567	.262	66.5	24-1B -2
2004	CWS	AL	36	240	65	16	0	18	64	57	0	2	.271	.434	.562	.310	.274	.433	.568	.333	34.2	
2005	*CWS*	*AL*	*37*	*274*	*75*	*14*	*0*	*18*	*54*	*63*	*0*	*0*	*.274*	*.399*	*.529*	*.221*	*.271*	*.398*	*.520*	*.198*	*30.3*	

Breakout: 34% Improve: 59% Collapse: 23%

PECOTA has Thomas pegged as entering that Rico Carty or Larry Hisle portion of his career, when he'll be very good when he can play, but won't play very often. Frustratingly, Thomas delayed his ankle surgery until the season was over in October, calling into question whether he'll be ready to go for spring training. Even if he stays healthy, it's unlikely the Sox will pick up his $10 million option for 2006. Given his injury problems and his general surliness, it wouldn't surprise anyone if Thomas retired, which could lead to a tragically bad result in the 2010 Hall of Fame balloting.

ANDRES TORRES OF Bats: R Throws: R Born: 26-Jan-1978 Age: 27

YEAR	TM	LG	AGE	AB	H	2B	3B	HR	BB	SO	SB	CS	AVG	OBP	SLG	MLVR	EQBA	EQOBP	EQSLG	EQMLVR	VORP	DEFENSE
2002	TOL	INT	24	462	123	17	8	4	53	116	42	12	.266	.345	.364	-.022	.243	.324	.338	-.191	-6.1	115-CF -15
2002	DET	AL	24	70	14	1	1	0	6	16	2	2	.200	.266	.243	-.411	.229	.272	.271	-.396	-5.2	18-CF -2
2003	TOL	INT	25	271	69	13	3	2	18	61	27	11	.255	.301	.347	-.109	.245	.297	.341	-.238	-7.7	70-CF -5
2003	DET	AL	25	168	37	4	3	1	10	35	5	5	.220	.263	.298	-.341	.228	.278	.311	-.328	-10.5	29-CF -3 10-RF 0
2004	CHR	INT	26	322	95	11	4	8	35	74	23	7	.295	.371	.429	.100	.280	.354	.404	-.017	13.2	41-CF 2 30-LF 2
2005	*TEX*	*AL*	*27*	*213*	*55*	*10*	*2*	*4*	*19*	*47*	*11*	*4*	*.258*	*.325*	*.380*	*-.104*	*.249*	*.318*	*.367*	*-.151*	*2.7*	*60-CF -3*

Breakout: 15% Improve: 35% Collapse: 44%

Torres's value waxes and wanes with his batting average, which was at high tide in Charlotte last year. That might be enough to get him a second chance as a reserve outfielder, but players with this skill set are a dime a dozen, and the memory of his underperformance as a Tiger will linger. With Texas, he might get to stick as a fifth outfielder, but it's just as likely that he's booked for an exciting all-expense–paid tour of PCL cities for years to come.

JUAN URIBE SS/2B Bats: R Throws: R Born: 22-Jul-1979 Age: 25

YEAR	TM	LG	AGE	AB	H	2B	3B	HR	BB	SO	SB	CS	AVG	OBP	SLG	MLVR	EQBA	EQOBP	EQSLG	EQMLVR	VORP	DEFENSE
2002	COL	NL	22	566	136	25	7	6	34	120	9	2	.240	.286	.341	-.230	.227	.272	.328	-.317	-4.7	150-SS 15
2003	COL	NL	23	316	80	19	3	10	17	60	7	2	.253	.297	.427	-.091	.238	.283	.403	-.183	9.4	74-SS 4 11-2B 0
2004	CWS	AL	24	502	142	31	6	23	32	96	9	11	.283	.327	.506	.063	.283	.330	.512	.097	32.1	72-2B 4 34-SS 5
2005	*CWS*	*AL*	*25*	*459*	*123*	*25*	*4*	*16*	*29*	*81*	*8*	*5*	*.269*	*.316*	*.444*	*-.027*	*.266*	*.315*	*.436*	*-.051*	*18.5*	*119-SS 4*

Breakout: 15% Improve: 45% Collapse: 26%

The White Sox have a frustrating tendency to make good decisions in inverse proportion to the amount of money at stake. They can be counted on to bungle any move that would make front-page news; but they did well to pick up Juan Uribe from the Rockies, a player who can pick it at either middle infield position and had more upside than organizational filler Aaron Miles. Uribe's power is almost invariably described as "surprising" since he's not a big guy and doesn't have a particularly hefty swing. PECOTA is more concerned about his batting average, which is liable to decline given his lack of selectivity at the plate.

WILSON VALDEZ SS Bats: R Throws: R Born: 20-May-1978 Age: 27

YEAR	TM	LG	AGE	AB	H	2B	3B	HR	BB	SO	SB	CS	AVG	OBP	SLG	MLVR	EQBA	EQOBP	EQSLG	EQMLVR	VORP	DEFENSE
2002	PME	EAS	24	375	98	19	5	1	15	47	18	6	.261	.294	.347	-.151	.231	.260	.311	-.363	-18.4	107-SS -5
2003	CAR	SOU	25	144	45	6	2	0	15	17	16	5	.312	.373	.382	.123	.275	.320	.336	-.181	-0.3	32-2B 0
2003	ABQ	PCL	25	338	97	12	4	0	19	37	33	9	.287	.326	.346	-.172	.223	.264	.265	-.424	-21.6	79-SS 1
2004	ABQ	PCL	26	285	91	11	3	2	16	35	19	12	.319	.357	.400	-.108	.255	.296	.318	-.267	-5.1	65-SS 7
2004	CHR	INT	26	281	85	7	2	2	12	41	13	5	.302	.338	.363	-.044	.290	.325	.346	-.147	4.7	69-SS 3
2004	CWS	AL	26	43	10	1	0	1	2	5	1	2	.233	.267	.326	-.332	.238	.260	.333	-.327	-2.0	
2005	*CWS*	*AL*	*27*	*201*	*51*	*8*	*2*	*1*	*8*	*29*	*7*	*3*	*.254*	*.287*	*.330*	*-.243*	*.251*	*.286*	*.324*	*-.264*	*-1.8*	*55-SS -1*

Breakout: 15% Improve: 32% Collapse: 43%

Like some storied regiment of yore named for the King or Queen (or someone's spare Archduke) you can consider Valdez "Ozzie's Own." He made a big impression on Guillen when Ozzie was a coach for Jeff Torborg in Florida, and to the

Ozzeroo's credit, where the Fish saw a moody, uncoachable Latin, Guillen saw a ballplayer he could coax out of his shell. He's just a good defensive replacement and pinch-runner, but that can be handy.

JOSE VALENTIN 3B/SS Bats: L Throws: R Born: 12-Oct-1969 Age: 35

YEAR	TM	LG	AGE	AB	H	2B	3B	HR	BB	SO	SB	CS	AVG	OBP	SLG	MLVR	EQBA	EQOBP	EQSLG	EQMLVR	VORP	DEFENSE
2002	CWS	AL	32	474	118	26	4	25	43	99	3	3	.249	.311	.479	.012	.249	.317	.484	.002	25.7	83-3B 0 46-SS 1
2003	CWS	AL	33	503	119	26	2	28	54	114	8	3	.237	.313	.463	-.014	.234	.317	.466	-.036	30.1	136-SS 8
2004	CWS	AL	34	450	97	20	3	30	43	139	8	6	.216	.287	.473	-.101	.214	.290	.474	-.090	14.9	116-SS 11
2005	*LAD*	*NL*	*35*	*345*	*81*	*16*	*2*	*18*	*38*	*101*	*5*	*2*	*.235*	*.312*	*.445*	*-.066*	*.241*	*.316*	*.458*	*-.039*	*17.2*	*93-SS -2*

Breakout: 46% *Improve: 73%* *Collapse: 10%*

A low batting average is acceptable when you're a 30–home run shortstop with underrated range, but Valentin is pushing the lower bound as he swings through more and more breaking balls. Tabbing him to play third base at Dodger Stadium seems like a questionable fit, not only because the park isn't well-suited for him, but also because Valentin is the rare player who is a plus defender at shortstop but a minus one at third, where it's more about making the routine plays and less about vacuuming up the infield.

ROB VALIDO SS Bats: R Throws: R Born: 16-May-1985 Age: 20

YEAR	TM	LG	AGE	AB	H	2B	3B	HR	BB	SO	SB	CS	AVG	OBP	SLG	MLVR	EQBA	EQOBP	EQSLG	EQMLVR	VORP	DEFENSE
2003	BRI	APL	18	215	66	15	2	6	17	28	17	6	.307	.364	.479	.296	.264	.305	.414	-.106	14.5	58-SS -3
2004	KAN	SAL	19	458	115	25	0	4	36	59	28	13	.251	.313	.332	-.125	.208	.253	.273	-.443	-34.0	111-SS -4
2005	*CWS*	*AL*	*20*	*363*	*87*	*17*	*2*	*6*	*20*	*51*	*12*	*5*	*.240*	*.288*	*.347*	*-.226*	*.237*	*.287*	*.341*	*-.248*	*-0.5*	*95-SS -5*

Breakout: 32% *Improve: 47%* *Collapse: 28%*

The White Sox are excited about Valido because of his fielding prowess, but hitting like a latter-day John McDonald or Doug Baker down on the farm won't cut it. To be fair, we were excited about him last year as well, ignoring the umpteen lessons that short-season performances in the Appalachian League don't tell you a hell of a lot.

CHRIS YOUNG CF Bats: R Throws: R Born: 05-Sep-1983 Age: 21

YEAR	TM	LG	AGE	AB	H	2B	3B	HR	BB	SO	SB	CS	AVG	OBP	SLG	MLVR	EQBA	EQOBP	EQSLG	EQMLVR	VORP	DEFENSE
2003	BRI	APL	19	238	69	18	3	7	23	40	21	7	.290	.357	.479	.270	.250	.297	.410	-.137	1.7	60-CF -9
2004	KAN	SAL	20	467	122	31	5	24	67	146	31	9	.261	.365	.503	.190	.217	.300	.404	-.164	-2.6	133-CF -4
2005	*CWS*	*AL*	*21*	*351*	*84*	*19*	*2*	*11*	*31*	*100*	*11*	*4*	*.238*	*.312*	*.401*	*-.114*	*.235*	*.311*	*.394*	*-.135*	*2.3*	*95-CF -6*

Breakout: 29% *Improve: 50%* *Collapse: 23%*

In an organization with more gratuitous muscularity than a South Beach gym, Young looked like the runt of the bunch, but both his body and his ballgame are filling out. His power and his speed project to be plus skills, and while his strikeout rate is high, it's coming from working late into the count rather than an abundance of swings-and-misses. The White Sox are said to be pleased with his defense in center field, but that might decline as he adds muscle to his frame.

PITCHERS

JON ADKINS Bats: L Throws: R Born: 30-Aug-1977 Age: 27

YEAR	TM	LG	AGE	G	GS	IP	H	BB	SO	HR	ERA	EQERA	EQH9	EQBB9	EQSO9	EQHR9	PERA	VORP	STF
2002	SAC	PCL	24	20	20	97.0	139	33	76	9	6.03	6.84	10.6	3.1	5.2	0.9	4.93	7.3	-20
2002	CHR	INT	24	8	7	46.3	47	12	31	4	3.69	4.50	9.2	2.7	5.1	1.0	4.50	5.4	5
2003	CHR	INT	25	26	19	122.7	119	34	59	11	3.96	5.24	9.4	2.9	3.7	1.2	4.92	8.6	-29
2004	CWS	AL	26	50	0	62.0	75	20	44	13	4.65	4.38	10.1	2.6	6.0	1.6	5.55	8.3	-30
2005	*CWS*	*AL*	*27*	*29*	*5*	*57.0*	*64*	*20*	*36*	*9*	*4.79*	*4.51*	*10.1*	*2.7*	*5.2*	*1.2*	*4.80*	*9.5*	*-8*

Breakout: 33% *Improve: 59%* *Collapse: 18%*

One of Ozzie's bold declarations was that Adkins was going to be his flexible utility reliever, and Adkins gave it his best shot. It's kind of cool to have a manager trumpeting the virtues of your 11th pitcher. Adkins has no real breakout potential, but if your manager's singing your praises, that's better than committing the Charlotte flight schedule to memory.

JEFF BAJENARU **Bats: R** **Throws: R** Born: 21-Mar-1978 Age: 27

YEAR	TM	LG	AGE	G	GS	IP	H	BB	SO	HR	ERA	EQERA	EQH9	EQBB9	EQSO9	EQHR9	PERA	VORP	STF
2003	BIR	SOU	25	50	0	64.7	53	28	62	2	3.20	5.04	8.2	4.0	6.2	0.6	3.71	12.7	4
2004	BIR	SOU	26	32	0	33.7	19	11	51	3	1.34	3.23	7.0	3.2	9.7	1.2	3.23	8.1	24
2004	CHR	INT	26	16	0	20.0	12	3	16	2	1.80	3.00	7.0	1.5	6.5	1.0	3.00	5.2	12
2004	CWS	AL	26	9	0	8.3	15	6	8	0	10.84	9.00	12.0	5.0	7.0	0.0	6.00	-4.2	-2
2005	*CWS*	*AL*	*27*	*25*	*1*	*35.3*	*34*	*15*	*30*	*5*	*4.47*	*4.21*	*8.8*	*3.3*	*6.9*	*1.1*	*4.27*	*6.8*	*1*

Breakout: 21% *Improve: 44%* *Collapse: 22%*

After missing '02 with Tommy John surgery, Bajenaru showed no loss of velocity. He gets his sinker consistently into the low 90s, and he's developing a good splitter. Not that there's really such a thing as a relief "prospect," but Bajenaru looks like he will be a good reliever shortly, good enough to push past the likes of Politte or Adkins.

MARK BUEHRLE **Bats: L** **Throws: L** Born: 23-Mar-1979 Age: 26

YEAR	TM	LG	AGE	G	GS	IP	H	BB	SO	HR	ERA	EQERA	EQH9	EQBB9	EQSO9	EQHR9	PERA	VORP	STF
2002	CWS	AL	23	34	34	239.0	236	61	134	25	3.58	3.55	9.1	2.2	5.0	0.9	4.34	56.9	8
2003	CWS	AL	24	35	35	230.3	250	61	119	22	4.14	4.37	9.6	2.3	4.6	0.8	4.57	31.7	6
2004	CWS	AL	25	35	35	245.3	257	51	165	33	3.89	3.80	9.2	1.7	5.8	1.1	4.29	50.8	13
2005	*CWS*	*AL*	*26*	*31*	*31*	*198.3*	*224*	*50*	*126*	*26*	*4.47*	*4.21*	*10.2*	*2.0*	*5.1*	*1.0*	*4.34*	*35.1*	*8*

Breakout: 21% *Improve: 51%* *Collapse: 11%*

With each successive, successful season, we can say with more confidence that Buehrle is moving into the Jim Kaat/Tom Glavine class of southpaws, pitchers that thrive with below-average strikeout rates because of intelligent pitch sequencing, great command, and an ability to pace themselves. One thing that these pitchers do well is adjust to their situations, and Buehrle challenges hitters with the bases empty, while becoming more cautious—perhaps overly so—with runners on base. The concern about the 33 home runs that he gave up is misplaced; Buehrle generates plenty of groundballs, and the high HR counting number is mostly the result of pitching a ton of innings in a power-friendly ballpark.

JOSE CONTRERAS **Bats: R** **Throws: R** Born: 06-Dec-1971 Age: 33

YEAR	TM	LG	AGE	G	GS	IP	H	BB	SO	HR	ERA	EQERA	EQH9	EQBB9	EQSO9	EQHR9	PERA	VORP	STF
2003	NYY	AL	31	18	9	71.0	52	30	72	4	3.30	3.41	6.7	3.7	9.0	0.5	2.62	21.0	33
2004	NYY	AL	32	18	18	95.7	93	42	82	22	5.64	5.67	8.6	3.6	7.3	1.8	4.71	0.2	5
2004	CWS	AL	32	13	13	74.7	73	42	68	9	5.30	4.99	8.4	4.5	7.7	1.0	4.62	3.7	16
2005	*CWS*	*AL*	*33*	*25*	*22*	*129.3*	*127*	*59*	*117*	*18*	*4.91*	*4.62*	*8.9*	*3.6*	*7.3*	*1.1*	*4.44*	*17.1*	*13*

Breakout: 7% *Improve: 36%* *Collapse: 26%*

Wishcasting can lead you in so many directions. I mean, who doesn't have an active fantasy life? So when you hear some analysts saying that Contreras will be a good #3 or #4 starter, just keep in mind that he's been a bad fifth starter for two years, and he's no spring chicken. There's nothing exotic that's preventing Contreras from succeeding. He just doesn't find the strike zone that often.

NEAL COTTS **Bats: L** **Throws: L** Born: 25-Mar-1980 Age: 25

YEAR	TM	LG	AGE	G	GS	IP	H	BB	SO	HR	ERA	EQERA	EQH9	EQBB9	EQSO9	EQHR9	PERA	VORP	STF
2002	MOD	CLF	22	28	28	137.7	123	87	178	5	4.12	5.69	8.7	6.4	6.8	0.6	5.14	6.6	5
2003	BIR	SOU	23	21	21	108.3	67	56	133	2	2.16	3.75	6.8	4.8	8.0	0.4	3.13	27.6	26
2003	CWS	AL	23	4	4	13.3	15	17	10	1	8.12	7.43	9.4	10.8	6.8	0.7	6.75	-3.0	-25
2004	CWS	AL	24	56	1	65.3	61	30	58	13	5.65	5.37	8.5	3.8	7.6	1.6	4.81	0.6	-1
2005	*CWS*	*AL*	*25*	*34*	*7*	*73.7*	*75*	*38*	*62*	*9*	*4.93*	*4.64*	*9.2*	*4.0*	*6.8*	*0.9*	*4.58*	*9.5*	*1*

Breakout: 22% *Improve: 44%* *Collapse: 23%*

It wasn't like he was doing all that well, but this is an organization that confounds stubbornness with resolve, so Cotts's hot April, in which he gave up just one earned run in his first eight appearances, was enough to keep him in the big leagues the whole season. Though he managed to cut his walk rate, it came with a hefty price in terms of home runs, which leaves open the question of just how well his stuff will hold up against major league hitters. There are also concerns about the efficiency of Cotts's delivery. You can almost hear the sighs of resignation from the White Sox front office, which must recognize now that his upside will come as a reliever.

FELIX DIAZ **Bats: R** **Throws: R** Born: 27-Jul-1980 Age: 24

YEAR	TM	LG	AGE	G	GS	IP	H	BB	SO	HR	ERA	EQERA	EQH9	EQBB9	EQSO9	EQHR9	PERA	VORP	STF
2002	SHV	TXS	21	12	12	60.0	54	23	48	1	2.70	4.42	8.2	3.8	5.5	0.3	3.63	12.5	16
2002	BIR	SOU	21	7	6	31.0	25	8	30	4	3.48	5.14	9.6	2.2	6.8	2.2	5.46	0.4	12
2003	CHR	INT	22	27	18	115.7	122	33	83	12	3.97	5.12	9.7	3.0	5.3	1.2	5.12	5.8	4
2004	CHR	INT	23	19	17	115.0	95	24	96	14	2.97	3.38	8.4	2.0	6.4	1.2	4.13	17.4	28
2004	CWS	AL	23	18	7	49.3	62	16	33	13	6.75	6.06	10.5	2.6	5.7	2.0	6.06	-3.8	3
2005	*CWS*	*AL*	*24*	*19*	*15*	*93.0*	*99*	*30*	*67*	*16*	*5.22*	*4.92*	*9.7*	*2.5*	*5.8*	*1.3*	*4.60*	*10.7*	*4*

Breakout: 10% *Improve: 38%* *Collapse: 28%*

Part of the payoff of the '02 Lofton deal, Diaz has made steady if unexciting progress. He's got Dave Stewart's old problem, a mid-90s fastball with little movement, and a slider that doesn't really snap consistently. Stewart's solution was to learn to throw the splitter, but he was also a better prospect coming up through the Dodgers chain back then than Diaz is now.

FREDDY GARCIA **Bats: R** **Throws: R** Born: 10-Jun-1976 Age: 29

YEAR	TM	LG	AGE	G	GS	IP	H	BB	SO	HR	ERA	EQERA	EQH9	EQBB9	EQSO9	EQHR9	PERA	VORP	STF
2002	SEA	AL	26	34	34	223.7	227	63	181	30	4.39	4.43	9.0	2.4	7.0	1.2	4.35	38.7	17
2003	SEA	AL	27	33	33	201.3	196	71	144	31	4.52	4.73	9.2	3.1	6.5	1.3	5.20	27.1	6
2004	SEA	AL	28	15	15	107.0	96	32	82	8	3.20	3.14	8.2	2.4	6.6	0.6	3.57	35.1	23
2004	CWS	AL	28	16	16	103.0	96	32	102	14	4.46	4.01	8.2	2.5	8.5	1.1	3.92	18.3	28
2005	*CWS*	*AL*	*30*	*28*	*28*	*178.7*	*185*	*60*	*142*	*27*	*4.55*	*4.28*	*9.4*	*2.6*	*6.5*	*1.1*	*4.32*	*30.5*	*14*

Breakout: 8% *Improve: 46%* *Collapse: 13%*

Most pitchers are disposed to overthrow, but Garcia is fascinated with his changeup, to the point that he predictably tries to use it as his finishing pitch after a few fastballs. Garcia is not a bad pitcher, but he's not much better than an average one. The White Sox traded for him at the high-water mark of his value, entranced by his Safeco-enhanced ERA while ignoring peripheral numbers that hadn't improved much and an arm that has a lot of mileage on it. The $27 million extension the White Sox gave Garcia in July is looking more palatable compared to some of the signings this winter, but that's damning with faint praise.

JON GARLAND **Bats: R** **Throws: R** Born: 27-Sep-1979 Age: 25

YEAR	TM	LG	AGE	G	GS	IP	H	BB	SO	HR	ERA	EQERA	EQH9	EQBB9	EQSO9	EQHR9	PERA	VORP	STF
2002	CWS	AL	22	33	33	192.7	188	83	112	23	4.58	4.64	9.1	3.7	5.1	1.0	4.83	19.1	2
2003	CWS	AL	23	32	32	191.7	188	74	108	28	4.51	4.34	9.2	3.4	5.1	1.2	4.98	26.6	0
2004	CWS	AL	24	34	33	217.0	223	76	113	34	4.89	4.47	9.3	2.9	4.5	1.2	4.90	25.2	-2
2005	*CWS*	*AL*	*25*	*30*	*29*	*169.3*	*189*	*63*	*98*	*26*	*5.05*	*4.75*	*10.1*	*2.9*	*4.7*	*1.2*	*4.82*	*19.7*	*0*

Breakout: 21% *Improve: 53%* *Collapse: 14%*

The White Sox take pride in noting that Jon Garland is now their fifth starter, which obscures the fact that he pitches like a fifth starter. Garland is dissatisfying in the way that flat soda pop is on a hot day, doing the bare minimum to quench your thirst while teasing vaguely at bubblier delights. He has a reasonably high PECOTA breakout rate, and there's always the residual chance that a pitcher with a healthy arm and 800 non-embarrassing major league innings will master a second pitch or something. But Garland's middling minor league strikeout rates never really pegged him as a star to begin with.

GIO GONZALEZ **Bats: R** **Throws: L** Born: 19-Sep-1985 Age: 19

YEAR	TM	LG	AGE	G	GS	IP	H	BB	SO	HR	ERA	EQERA	EQH9	EQBB9	EQSO9	EQHR9	PERA	VORP	STF
2004	BRI	APL	18	7	6	24.0	17	8	36	0	2.25	4.98	8.3	3.7	7.1	0.4	3.74	4.5	25
2004	KAN	SAL	18	8	8	40.7	39	20	34	1	3.76	5.21	9.2	5.2	4.7	0.2	4.97	2.7	10
2005	*CWS*	*AL*	*19*	*18*	*11*	*71.3*	*79*	*38*	*47*	*11*	*5.59*	*5.27*	*10.0*	*4.1*	*5.3*	*1.2*	*5.23*	*4.7*	*-6*

Breakout: 7% *Improve: 38%* *Collapse: 20%*

Gio Gonzalez is neither an Hispanic-owned car dealership nor a Latin American product at all, but rather the White Sox's first-round supplemental pick in 2004 out of a Miami high school. His most noteworthy asset in the early going has been his ability to prevent home runs, but his groundball/flyball numbers were only about average, so it might have been a sample-size fluke. Gonzalez is considered to have more polish than your average 19-year-old, but he'll need to fill out and perhaps add a couple of ticks to his fastball.

JASON GRILLI **Bats: R** **Throws: R** Born: 11-Nov-1976 Age: 28

YEAR	TM	LG	AGE	G	GS	IP	H	BB	SO	HR	ERA	EQERA	EQH9	EQBB9	EQSO9	EQHR9	PERA	VORP	STF
2003	JUP	FSL	26	7	7	42.7	38	6	30	1	2.53	4.54	8.8	1.4	4.5	0.7	3.63	8.7	14
2003	ABQ	PCL	26	12	12	66.7	64	30	38	3	3.37	3.98	8.5	4.5	4.4	0.6	4.26	9.4	6
2004	CHR	INT	27	25	25	152.7	163	58	101	22	4.83	5.50	10.0	3.6	4.9	1.6	5.88	-4.5	-5
2004	CWS	AL	27	8	8	45.0	52	20	26	11	7.40	6.55	10.2	3.7	4.9	1.8	6.14	-6.8	-3
2005	*CWS*	*AL*	*28*	*17*	*17*	*97.3*	*109*	*39*	*58*	*18*	*5.68*	*5.35*	*10.2*	*3.2*	*4.8*	*1.4*	*5.23*	*5.6*	*-2*

Breakout: 9% *Improve: 42%* *Collapse: 24%*

Grilli was notionally going to get a look as the fifth starter in '05, but signing El Duque and keeping Garland pretty much killed that idea. Not as though it's any great loss: Grilli is already on his fourth major league organization and has yet to demonstrate anything that would suggest he's better than Triple-A filler, either before or after his Tommy John surgery in 2002.

KRIS HONEL **Bats: R** **Throws: R** Born: 07-Nov-1982 Age: 22

YEAR	TM	LG	AGE	G	GS	IP	H	BB	SO	HR	ERA	EQERA	EQH9	EQBB9	EQSO9	EQHR9	PERA	VORP	STF
2002	KAN	SAL	19	26	26	153.3	128	52	152	12	2.82	5.20	9.6	4.0	5.7	1.7	5.53	1.1	14
2003	WNS	CRL	20	24	24	133.0	122	42	122	7	3.11	4.54	9.4	3.1	6.2	1.0	4.98	8.5	13
2003	BIR	SOU	20	2	2	12.0	9	6	13	2	3.75	5.91	9.3	5.1	7.6	2.5	5.91	-0.4	17
2005	*CWS*	*AL*	*22*	*15*	*9*	*57.3*	*59*	*33*	*45*	*10*	*5.95*	*5.60*	*9.3*	*4.6*	*6.4*	*1.3*	*5.37*	*2.3*	*-4*

Breakout: 5% *Improve: 43%* *Collapse: 27%*

Honel pitched just seven innings between Birmingham and Bristol, not enough to register in the statistical record above. He did not undergo any kind of surgery, but began experiencing shoulder tendonitis early in the season, which turned his delivery into a mess. The Sox thought it better to let him rest, recuperate, and work in non-game situations than to push him back to the mound. Honel's velocity has never been impressive, so if it's true that power pitchers have an easier time recovering from injury than finesse guys, he could be in trouble. Still, he's more likely to satisfy Sox fans in this lifetime than Jason Stumm. Or Scott Ruffcorn, come to think of it.

DAMASO MARTE **Bats: L** **Throws: L** Born: 14-Feb-1975 Age: 30

YEAR	TM	LG	AGE	G	GS	IP	H	BB	SO	HR	ERA	EQERA	EQH9	EQBB9	EQSO9	EQHR9	PERA	VORP	STF
2002	CWS	AL	27	68	0	60.3	44	18	72	5	2.84	2.64	6.8	2.5	10.6	0.6	2.95	21.0	31
2003	CWS	AL	28	71	0	79.7	50	34	87	3	1.58	1.78	6.3	3.8	9.9	0.4	2.72	38.0	29
2004	CWS	AL	29	74	0	73.7	56	34	68	10	3.42	3.06	7.4	3.8	8.0	1.0	3.82	23.4	7
2005	*CWS*	*AL*	*30*	*56*	*0*	*65.7*	*58*	*29*	*68*	*9*	*3.99*	*3.76*	*8.0*	*3.5*	*8.4*	*1.1*	*3.98*	*16.6*	*10*

Breakout: 29% *Improve: 51%* *Collapse: 25%*

This is the downside to being dangerously wild. Marte's pitches have a lot of movement, and like a lot of relievers, he doesn't like to give up anything easily to batters, preferring instead to try and hit the corners and make unhittable pitches. That approach inherently entails a high degree of difficulty, and while Marte has always been a flyball pitcher, in '04 the result was a lot of home runs rather than a lot of warning-track shots. His ERA, if anything, understates the problem, and while Marte will still be one of the best relievers on the team, it's unlikely that he'll be one of the best relievers in the league. There's an appropriate parallel here with Felix Rodriguez, who went from being dominant to merely average in a flash.

BRANDON McCARTHY **Bats: R** **Throws: R** Born: 07-Jul-1983 Age: 21

YEAR	TM	LG	AGE	G	GS	IP	H	BB	SO	HR	ERA	EQERA	EQH9	EQBB9	EQSO9	EQHR9	PERA	VORP	STF
2003	GRF	PIO	19	16	15	101.0	105	15	125	7	3.65	6.27	10.2	2.0	5.6	1.6	5.04	5.9	12
2004	KAN	SAL	21	15	15	94.0	80	21	113	10	3.64	4.81	9.3	2.4	6.8	1.7	5.13	4.5	16
2004	WNS	CRL	21	8	8	52.0	31	3	60	3	2.08	3.26	7.1	0.6	7.9	1.0	2.49	16.2	51
2004	BIR	SOU	21	4	4	26.0	23	6	29	2	3.46	4.44	8.9	2.2	7.0	0.7	4.07	4.1	29
2005	*CWS*	*AL*	*21*	*15*	*14*	*82.3*	*85*	*25*	*66*	*15*	*4.77*	*4.49*	*9.3*	*2.4*	*6.5*	*1.4*	*4.51*	*12.7*	*12*

Breakout: 3% *Improve: 38%* *Collapse: 15%*

Ladies and gentlemen, your 2004 minor league strikeout leader. McCarthy is doing all those things scouts wish for: bulking up his 6′7″ frame, adding velocity into the low 90s as he matures physically, and perfecting a change-up to add to his curveball. Sensibly, the Sox recognized he'd proved enough this year, and held him back from the AFL. If there's a worry, it's that McCarthy's been relatively hittable, both for base hits and home runs, in spite of his astounding strikeout and walk numbers. That could be indicative of a pitcher who is getting hitters out as a result of his prodigious feel for the craft, rather than his tremendous raw stuff. McCarthy should be a good one, but he might not find the going quite as easy at Triple-A.

RYAN MEAUX Bats: R Throws: L Born: 05-Oct-1978 Age: 26

YEAR	TM	LG	AGE	G	GS	IP	H	BB	SO	HR	ERA	EQERA	EQH9	EQBB9	EQSO9	EQHR9	PERA	VORP	STF
2002	HAG	SAL	23	44	0	54.7	41	12	44	1	2.63	5.22	7.9	2.5	4.5	0.4	2.88	15.1	5
2003	WNS	CRL	24	32	0	55.0	49	3	43	2	1.15	3.38	9.1	0.5	5.3	0.7	3.91	9.5	5
2003	BIR	SOU	24	26	0	38.0	39	3	29	0	2.13	3.72	9.2	0.7	5.0	0.2	3.22	9.6	1
2004	BIR	SOU	25	29	21	140.3	163	46	103	4	4.04	5.25	10.0	3.0	4.5	0.4	4.72	13.2	-6
2005	*CWS*	*AL*	*26*	*13*	*10*	*62.0*	*71*	*20*	*35*	*8*	*4.69*	*4.42*	*10.4*	*2.5*	*4.6*	*0.9*	*4.56*	*10.7*	*-1*

Breakout: 15% Improve: 47% Collapse: 17%

The White Sox tried Meaux as a starter and watched his equivalent walk rate go up fivefold, though that isn't nearly as bad as it sounds since he walked just six hitters in all of 2003. He's got your standard issue, mid-80s lefty stuff, so perhaps he felt the need to get unnecessarily cute when facing hitters more than once a game. Meaux did retain his tendency to keep the ball down, posting a 1.45 GB:FB ratio at Birmingham. Whatever role winds up suiting him best, there are pitchers who have succeeded in the major leagues with less, and he's certainly as deserving of a trial as someone like Cotts or Adkins.

BRIAN MILLER Bats: R Throws: R Born: 18-Oct-1982 Age: 22

YEAR	TM	LG	AGE	G	GS	IP	H	BB	SO	HR	ERA	EQERA	EQH9	EQBB9	EQSO9	EQHR9	PERA	VORP	STF
2002	BRI	APL	19	13	13	60.7	57	30	63	3	4.30	6.87	10.0	5.7	4.9	1.1	6.55	-5.8	-5
2003	KAN	SAL	20	25	25	125.7	124	61	93	7	5.30	7.87	10.2	5.3	4.2	1.3	6.06	-5.8	-17
2004	KAN	SAL	21	21	21	112.0	103	54	84	6	3.86	5.40	9.2	5.1	4.3	0.8	5.31	3.3	-10
2004	WNS	CRL	21	7	7	33.7	34	16	19	5	4.81	5.93	10.7	5.0	3.9	2.7	7.12	-5.1	-21
2005	*CWS*	*AL*	*22*	*10*	*8*	*46.3*	*52*	*26*	*28*	*10*	*6.26*	*5.90*	*10.1*	*4.4*	*5.0*	*1.6*	*5.94*	*0.2*	*-11*

Breakout: 9% Improve: 44% Collapse: 22%

Owner of the organization's best change-up, which is sort of like winning Ms. Congeniality in a beauty pageant—I mean, who dislikes congeniality? Or change-ups? It probably helps if Doug Jones is on the panel of judges.

ARNIE MUNOZ Bats: L Throws: L Born: 21-Jun-1982 Age: 23

YEAR	TM	LG	AGE	G	GS	IP	H	BB	SO	HR	ERA	EQERA	EQH9	EQBB9	EQSO9	EQHR9	PERA	VORP	STF
2002	BIR	SOU	20	51	0	72.3	62	29	78	6	2.61	4.70	9.1	3.6	7.4	1.3	4.97	4.7	9
2003	CHR	INT	21	49	0	55.0	52	27	63	7	4.75	6.27	9.1	5.1	8.5	1.4	5.40	1.1	6
2004	BIR	SOU	22	13	13	74.7	52	22	68	1	2.05	3.80	7.3	2.9	5.9	0.1	3.01	19.8	30
2004	CHR	INT	22	13	13	69.7	81	29	60	11	5.68	6.04	10.3	3.9	6.3	1.3	6.04	-3.3	-1
2004	CWS	AL	22	11	1	14.3	20	12	11	4	10.07	8.59	11.0	6.8	6.1	1.8	7.36	-6.0	-25
2005	*CWS*	*AL*	*23*	*15*	*11*	*69.0*	*70*	*33*	*56*	*11*	*5.26*	*4.95*	*9.2*	*3.8*	*6.6*	*1.2*	*4.78*	*7.5*	*5*

Breakout: 10% Improve: 49% Collapse: 20%

Munoz is well along on that "crafty lefty" lifestyle gig, working pedestrian heat to set up a plus curve and a chilly change. Recognizing that they have an abundance of these guys, the Sox applied a see-what-sticks approach and converted a couple of them to starting pitching. Munoz survived the experiment well, his peripherals holding up much better than Ryan Meaux's. It now appears that the team has an abundance of starters, so back to the bullpen he goes.

CLIFF POLITTE Bats: R Throws: R Born: 27-Feb-1974 Age: 31

YEAR	TM	LG	AGE	G	GS	IP	H	BB	SO	HR	ERA	EQERA	EQH9	EQBB9	EQSO9	EQHR9	PERA	VORP	STF
2002	PHI	NL	28	13	0	16.3	19	9	15	0	3.87	5.51	9.4	4.4	7.2	0.0	4.41	-0.2	1
2002	TOR	AL	28	55	0	57.3	38	19	57	5	3.61	3.29	6.6	2.8	8.9	0.7	2.63	15.0	21
2003	TOR	AL	29	54	0	49.3	52	17	40	11	5.66	5.21	8.9	3.0	7.1	1.9	4.66	1.4	-2
2004	CWS	AL	30	54	0	51.3	52	22	48	6	4.39	3.88	8.6	3.4	7.9	0.9	4.41	9.8	6
2005	*CWS*	*AL*	*31*	*46*	*0*	*46.7*	*48*	*19*	*40*	*7*	*4.79*	*4.51*	*9.3*	*3.2*	*7.0*	*1.2*	*4.57*	*8.2*	*-1*

Breakout: 27% Improve: 56% Collapse: 28%

(continued next page)

Cliff Politte *(continued)*

Politte has been an above-average reliever in three of his four full major league seasons, but had the misfortune to pick the bad one to coincide with his trial as a closer in Toronto in 2003. The Blue Jays' decision to non-tender him was not a case of cold feet so much as a well-reasoned fear that the 12 saves he'd racked up might have inflated his price in arbitration. In any event, he's back in his customary role now, which is exactly halfway along the spectrum between chief fireman and mop-up gimp. Politte is 5′11″ in the same sense that Charles Barkley is 6′8″.

SCOTT SCHOENEWEIS **Bats: L** **Throws: L** Born: 02-Oct-1973 Age: 31

YEAR	TM	LG	AGE	G	GS	IP	H	BB	SO	HR	ERA	EQERA	EQH9	EQBB9	EQSO9	EQHR9	PERA	VORP	STF
2002	ANA	AL	28	54	15	118.0	119	49	65	17	4.88	4.90	9.7	3.6	4.9	1.2	5.71	10.4	-16
2003	ANA	AL	29	39	0	38.7	37	10	29	2	3.95	4.10	8.4	2.2	6.8	0.5	3.62	7.2	7
2003	CWS	AL	29	20	0	26.0	26	9	27	1	4.50	4.91	8.4	2.8	9.1	0.4	3.51	1.6	20
2004	CWS	AL	30	20	19	112.7	129	49	69	17	5.59	5.09	9.8	3.5	5.2	1.1	5.34	4.0	-2
2005	*TOR*	*AL*	*31*	*27*	*16*	*102.3*	*116*	*42*	*65*	*14*	*5.24*	*4.94*	*10.2*	*3.2*	*5.2*	*1.1*	*4.93*	*9.8*	*-4*

Breakout: 7% *Improve: 46%* *Collapse: 20%*

Schoeneweis entered last season with a 5.27 career ERA as a starter and a 4.38 career ERA in relief. There is a lot of research to be done on why a pitcher is best suited for a particular role, but Schoeneweis has always had a large platoon differential, which gives reason to believe that the split is a meaningful one: It's easier to manage the match-ups when a pitcher is coming out of the pen. Predictably, opposing managers stacked the lineup with righties when Schoeneweis was penciled in as the starter, such that they constituted more than 80% of his opposing plate appearances. Just as predictably, he struggled. Righties teed off for a .303/.375/.510 line against him. Non-tendered, then signed to a two-year, $5.2 million deal by the Blue Jays.

JOSH STEWART **Bats: L** **Throws: L** Born: 05-Dec-1978 Age: 26

YEAR	TM	LG	AGE	G	GS	IP	H	BB	SO	HR	ERA	EQERA	EQH9	EQBB9	EQSO9	EQHR9	PERA	VORP	STF
2002	BIR	SOU	23	26	26	150.3	145	56	92	11	3.53	4.99	9.9	3.3	4.2	1.3	5.31	4.5	-8
2003	CHR	INT	24	5	5	26.3	38	6	10	4	6.16	6.75	12.4	2.5	2.8	2.1	7.11	-4.2	-26
2003	CWS	AL	24	5	5	25.7	28	16	13	4	5.95	5.47	9.9	5.5	4.4	1.5	6.20	-0.7	-19
2004	CHR	INT	25	25	25	148.7	155	44	82	20	3.93	4.33	9.9	2.8	4.1	1.4	5.49	1.7	-11
2004	CWS	AL	25	3	2	7.7	16	3	5	3	15.19	12.96	14.0	3.2	5.4	3.2	9.72	-7.7	-31
2005	*CWS*	*AL*	*26*	*11*	*9*	*52.7*	*63*	*19*	*29*	*10*	*5.86*	*5.52*	*10.8*	*2.9*	*4.5*	*1.4*	*5.40*	*2.0*	*-6*

Breakout: 16% *Improve: 44%* *Collapse: 21%*

Stewart remained healthy after surviving a confrontation with a Jeff Conine line drive in 2003 that triggered some scary circulatory problems, later diagnosed as Reynauds Syndrome. That was the good news. He's a member of the very large class of minor league pitchers whose numbers look acceptable until you consider the home-run rates. Giving up 20 homers in 25 starts at Charlotte translates to Free Game–Used Baseball Day in the U.S. Cellular bleachers.

SHINGO TAKATSU **Bats: R** **Throws: R** Born: 25-Nov-1968 Age: 36

YEAR	TM	LG	AGE	G	GS	IP	H	BB	SO	HR	ERA	EQERA	EQH9	EQBB9	EQSO9	EQHR9	PERA	VORP	STF
2002	YKL	JCL	33	44	1	41.7	37	11	28	6	3.89	5.35	9.5	3.4	4.6	1.5	5.11	2.0	-19
2003	YKL	JCL	34	44	0	42.0	42	21	26	7	3.00	4.23	9.4	5.9	4.7	1.4	5.87	-1.1	-29
2004	CWS	AL	35	59	0	62.3	40	21	50	6	2.31	2.15	6.8	2.9	7.2	0.8	3.07	26.5	9
2005	*CWS*	*AL*	*36*	*40*	*1*	*54.7*	*54*	*23*	*40*	*10*	*4.54*	*4.27*	*9.0*	*3.4*	*6.0*	*1.4*	*4.77*	*11.1*	*-7*

Breakout: 35% *Improve: 55%* *Collapse: 18%*

The White Sox made a point to note that Takatsu is Japan's all-time saves leader, but his translated stats made him look like the washed-up Japanese version of Jeff Montgomery; his success last season surprised most everyone, except his employer. Takatsu's batting average against on balls in play was .207, the lowest figure in the American League for a pitcher who threw 50 or more innings. That would ordinarily be a bad predictive omen, since BA/BIP numbers regress strongly to the mean, which is why PECOTA expects his ERA to double. It has been documented, however, that knuckleballers maintain BA/BIPs much lower than the league average, as hitters struggle to make good contact with a pitch that comes in so slow. Takatsu does not throw a knuckler, but he does throw an underhanded change-up that clocks at 60 mph and freezes hitters like some bizarre Motral Kombat weapon, producing much the same effect. There's a legitimate question about how well he'll hold up as hitters get to see him for the second and third time, but in the meantime, he's an awful lot of fun to watch.

SEAN TRACEY **Bats: L** **Throws: R** Born: 14-Nov-1980 Age: 24

YEAR	TM	LG	AGE	G	GS	IP	H	BB	SO	HR	ERA	EQERA	EQH9	EQBB9	EQSO9	EQHR9	PERA	VORP	STF
2002	BRI	APL	21	13	12	65.7	57	19	50	4	3.01	5.95	9.8	3.4	3.7	1.4	5.64	-0.3	-4
2003	GRF	PIO	22	16	12	92.7	90	22	74	5	3.69	6.36	9.3	3.2	3.6	1.4	4.69	8.7	8
2003	KAN	SAL	22	14	9	41.7	51	46	28	4	9.50	13.14	12.2	12.2	3.8	2.4	10.27	-19.6	-71
2004	WNS	CRL	23	27	27	148.3	109	69	130	5	2.73	4.59	7.8	4.9	5.9	0.6	3.99	24.2	23
2005	*CWS*	*AL*	*24*	*15*	*14*	*79.3*	*77*	*44*	*54*	*12*	*5.25*	*4.94*	*8.8*	*4.3*	*5.6*	*1.1*	*4.93*	*7.1*	*-1*

Breakout: 10% *Improve: 42%* *Collapse: 15%*

Although there's a lot about the organization's fascination with character that's downright silly, they do get enthusiastic for appropriate reasons at times, like Tracey's aggressive willingness to take the ball. Some think he's got the best fastball in the organization, and he complements it with a nasty sinker that allowed him to post a 1.68 GB:FB ratio on the season. That package might do well at the front end of a bullpen, but the Sox will give him at least one more season to improve his command to the point that he becomes a viable starter.

TETSU YOFU **Bats: R** **Throws: R** Born: 26-Jun-1973 Age: 32

YEAR	TM	LG	AGE	G	GS	IP	H	BB	SO	HR	ERA	EQERA	EQH9	EQBB9	EQSO9	EQHR9	PERA	VORP	STF
2003	BIR	SOU	30	29	20	131.0	117	37	114	8	3.50	5.08	8.9	2.6	5.7	1.3	4.27	18.1	15
2004	BIR	SOU	31	7	7	41.0	39	9	41	4	2.63	3.76	9.4	2.1	6.3	1.4	4.70	3.8	13
2004	CHR	INT	31	21	17	113.0	107	33	111	20	4.62	5.08	9.2	2.8	7.4	2.0	5.42	2.1	12
2005	*CWS*	*AL*	*32*	*11*	*9*	*57.3*	*58*	*19*	*43*	*12*	*4.99*	*4.70*	*9.2*	*2.6*	*6.0*	*1.6*	*4.67*	*8.3*	*6*

Breakout: 17% *Improve: 42%* *Collapse: 16%*

The MVP of the 2001 Taiwan Series. To be cruel, that might inspire a joke about the Black Sox and how appropriate it is that he's here, since baseball in Taipei has been known to be played on less than the level. The main problem has been that Yofu places home runs in the bleachers about as liberally as the PRC places warships in the Taiwan Strait.

Cleveland Indians

Maybe Indians baseball can teach us something about women. Question: How should a fellow respond to a tease?

A true story, with only the names changed: When little Bobby Prospectus was in the seventh grade, 13 years old and bursting with pubescent longing for the female of the species, he shared several classes with Abby Cohen, a cute-as-a-button bespectacled blonde. Abby seemed to take an instant liking to Bobby despite his awkwardness, hanging on him before classes, joking with him, inventing affectionate pet names for him: "Doc." "Prof." "Woody." "Horace Greeley J. Wainscot." With every word that dropped from her lips, Bobby inwardly floated out of his desk and bumped up against the drop ceiling like a balloon.

This went on for months. Bobby desperately wanted to act on the attraction that obviously existed between them, but was too shy. Finally, after being unable to eat for a week, he screwed up his courage. One afternoon, after she'd spent an entire art class laughing at his jokes and calling him "Lawrence Livermore National Laboratory" in a way that made it sound synonymous with "My dearest darling," he asked her to be his girlfriend.

He said the words. He smiled and waited hopefully. She blinked. A look of terror identical to the countenance of the cat who finds herself pursued by an amorous skunk in the old "Pepe Le Pew" cartoons passed across her face. On recovering, she said, "I'll think about it. Come back tomorrow."

Bobby went home, heart soaring, thinking that this was somehow normal, to be expected. Naively, he felt that there was a chance she would consent to be his. The next day he returned to her. "I'm still thinking," she said. The pet names, the physical contact, were suddenly gone. In fact, it seemed as if she was completely avoiding him. Bobby didn't get it. On the third day, for reasons known only to herself, Abby put him out of his misery, saying firmly, finally, coldly, "No." Though they remained in school together for another five years and shared several classes, they never spoke again.

As these words are being written, the Cleveland front office is wrestling with a similar question, tease vs. the real thing. Which version of the Indians was the genuine article—the one that appeared ready to challenge the Minnesota Twins for the AL Central title, or the sad sack outfit that played at a 97-loss pace over the last quarter of the season? It's an important question, because the answer determines what to do next: Build quickly, as if the team is about to peak; or go with the original, more organic growing process.

INDIANS PROSPECTUS

2004 record: 80–82; Third place, AL Central

Pythagenport record: 81–81

Runs scored per game: 5.30 (5th in AL)

Runs allowed per game: 5.29 (13th in AL)

Team EqA: .271 (3rd in AL)

2004 Batters Age: 29.2 (6th youngest in AL)

2004 Pitchers Age: 27.4 (Youngest in AL)

Ballpark: Jacobs Field; Moderate pitcher's park; Park Factor of 0.968

2004: Thanks to some surprising individual performances, the Indians approached .500 ahead of schedule.

2005: Should see continued development overall, but beware the exceptions—even young players can have career years.

There weren't high expectations for the 2004 Indians. The previous year, a 68–94 turkey, had been used for rebuilding, as GM Mark Shapiro rid the team of the remnants of the John Hart Era. The emphasis was on developing the young talent. Unlike the division rival Tigers, the Indians declined to make any big, off-season signings, seemingly content with their strategy to muddle through the present in exchange for a bright, homegrown future.

As the year began, it looked like that future might be some time in coming. The offense and pitching staff was a slew of gambles and question marks. Some of them had high upsides. But as the curtains rose on Tribequest '04, it was no sure thing that Milton Bradley could avoid injury and incoherent rage long enough to put in a full season; that Victor Martinez, Travis Hafner, and Ben Broussard could bring some of their minor league magic to the majors; that the outfield would provide any pop whatsoever; that Ron Belliard could hit or field well enough to play second base.

The pitching staff appeared to be a lost cause. The rotation was fronted by C. C. Sabathia, a four-year veteran but still just 23 years old and very inconsistent. There was Jake Westbrook, whose lack of an out pitch made him one of baseball's most contact-friendly pitchers. In Jason Davis they had an erstwhile sinkerball pitcher whose lack of both groundouts and strikeouts made him a disaster waiting to happen. Cliff Lee, a promising but untried southpaw, offered good peripherals but a cloudy future. Bringing up the rear was Jeff D'Amico, one of America's most oft-injured, oft-battered pitchers, who, like Westbrook and Davis could only get a strikeout if the batter felt sorry for him. They couldn't strike out Adam Dunn if he came to the plate without a bat in his hands. They could make Preston Wilson look like Rod Carew. They—well, you get the picture.

The Tribe started slowly and then gradually improved. A 9–13 April was followed by a .500 May, then a 15–13 June. The weak AL Central, led by a Twins team that was having difficulty getting its act together, conspired to keep the Indians in the race. Though the Indians were only 42–45 at the All-Star break, they were just 5.5 games out of first. The rotation had a shockingly strong first half despite its lacking of brand equity, posting a 4.06 ERA before the All-Star break. The emergence of Jake Westbrook took almost everyone by surprise; he logged among the best GB:FB ratios in the game. Meanwhile Cliff Lee's first half (9–1, 3.77 ERA) suggested that Cleveland had a second homegrown lefty ace to pair with Sabathia.

Youth and maturity had intersected for some nice results at the plate, as the offense came out swinging, putting up solid numbers that were sufficient to support the strong pitching. The Indians would finish the year fifth in the AL in runs per game allowed, and much closer to third place than sixth. Only the bullpen met low pre-season expectations, struggling from the outset. Cleveland relievers would blow 28 of 60 saves, tying them with Detroit for most blown saves in the American League. When Bob Wickman came off the DL in July, he was received as if he represented the second coming of Doug Jones; in context, maybe he was.

As the trading deadline approached, Shapiro and company were presented with a difficult decision: Treat what was happening before their eyes as "real," or decide that it was an illusion, that the team didn't really have what it took to win even the weak AL Central, and bail out, much as the White Sox did when they made the infamous "White Flag" trade of July 31, 1997. This is a tough position to be in. Much as we would like to think that tactical decisions are the result of pure, undistracted thought, media and fan reactions are undeniable influences. Shapiro was in a damned-if-you-do, damned-if-you-don't situation.

As the trading deadline came and went, the front office chose to stay the course, sticking with their most marketable veterans, infielders Belliard and Omar Vizquel. By the time the Indians met division-leading Minnesota on August 13, it looked like Shapiro had made the right call. The team was just three games out of first place, riding a stretch of eight wins in 10 days, while the Twins seemed to be falling apart, losing six of their last eight.

The Indians took the first two games in dominating fashion, beating Carlos Silva and Kyle Lohse by a combined score of 15–3. At that moment, just one game out of first place, the Indians went into cardiac arrest. The third and final game of the series ended in an extra-inning loss, as the Twins took advantage of Cleveland's shaky bullpen. Reliever Rick White surrendered a game-losing, two-run homer to Corey Koskie in the top of the 10th inning. Though they didn't know it at the time, Cleveland's season essentially ended with that home run.

Cleveland lost their next eight games, including three more to Minnesota. They were on the verge of flat-lining. Playing just .405 baseball the rest of the way, the Indians limped to an 80–82 finish, 12 games back of the eventual division champion Twins. So much for the resurrected Indians.

To claim that the Indians were broken by one tough August loss smacks of sports page–style hyperbole—the team didn't have heart, and as the song goes, that's something you've gotta have. However, the actual reasons for the quick fade are more prosaic. They go back to Shapiro's dilemma—had the rebuilding program paid off early and the Indians transmogrified into real contenders, or were they just on a sustained hot streak? The correct answer was the latter. It's possible that the illusion was irrevocably shattered by Koskie's home run, but causality's a sticky subject and there is no way of knowing for sure. To paraphrase Abraham Lincoln, people who like this sort of explanation will find this the sort of explanation they like. For everyone else, we have some stats.

Virtually every Cleveland hitter was well over his head leading into August (see table 1)—so much so that a simple regression to the mean might be enough to explain the collapse that the team experienced following the series with the Twins. Call it the Wile E. Coyote Syndrome: You play in the clouds for long enough, eventually you're going to realize that there's nothing under your feet except wishful thinking.

Here, PECOTA's weighted-mean projections serve as a guide to reasonable expectations of the player's season. Call them ballpark figures, then note that most Indians were out of the ballpark: Six of the nine regulars were posting OBPs of at least 40 points greater than their projections, and eight regulars were slugging at least 60 points higher than their projections. Although we like to think of players as taking grand, sudden leaps forward to higher levels of production, most of the time they are what they are, and once established tend to stay within certain

TABLE 1. INDIANS' HITTER PRODUCTION BEFORE AND AFTER TWINS SERIES, 2004

Lineup	PECOTA OBP/SLG	OBP/SLG thru 8/14	OBP/SLG 8/15–10/3	Improve/Decline
M. Lawton	.345/.393	.366/.454	.366/.314	Significant decline
O. Vizquel	.326/.341	.368/.409	.311/.329	Significant decline
T. Hafner	.344/.436	.418/.595	.382/.538	Decline
V. Martinez	.326/.399	.367/.518	.338/.420	Significant decline
C. Blake	.307/.384	.362/.478	.333/.506	Slight decline
B. Broussard	.319/.413	.388/.471	.333/.521	Decline
R. Belliard	.313/.368	.372/.421	.272/.439	Significant decline
J. Gerut	.331/.435	.332/.395	.345/.461	Improve
C. Crisp	.321/.376	.320/.444	.380/.450	Improve

TABLE 2. INDIANS' PITCHER PRODUCTION BEFORE AND AFTER TWINS SERIES, 2004

Rotation	PECOTA ERA/Innings	ERA/Innings thru 8/14	ERA/Innings 8/15–10/3	Improve/Decline
Sabathia	4.18/172	3.77/143.1	5.24/44.2	Decline
Westbrook	4.79/103	3.61/147.0	2.88/68.2	Improve
Davis	5.10/129	6.00/102.0	1.46/12.0	Injured
Lee	4.78/90	4.69/134.1	7.66/44.2	Significant decline
D'Amico	4.70/157.1	7.63/30.2	N/A	Released

ranges. What goes up generally comes down. That's exactly what happened to the Indians. The pitching staff was not immune from Coyote Syndrome either (see table 2).

It's not clear which team is going to show up in the spring. There's an interesting parallel here with the Kansas City Royals of 2003. The Royals, who have been in one of the most sustained, desperate downward spirals of any team since the Indians of the 1970s and 1980s or the Phillies of the 1930s (if they haven't yet reached the historic lows of those teams, they have already matched them in the seeming insolubility of their plight), turned in a shocking 83–79 third-place finish under second-year manager Tony Pena—not all that different from Cleveland's unexpected 80–82 third place showing under Eric Wedge.

The Royals took their turnaround to be the real deal and rolled in the veterans. They acquired Benito Santiago, Matt Stairs, Tony Graffanino, and as the big fish, undermotivated bopper Juan Gonzalez. The pitching wasn't there, the hitters didn't hit, the Royals lost 103 games and spent more money than they had to in order to do it.

Perhaps smelling blood in the water in a soft division, Shapiro has spent some money to upgrade his ballclub as well, though not acting as injudiciously as did the Royals. Rather than re-sign aging fan favorite Vizquel, Shapiro allowed him to leave as a free agent, creating opportunities for Johnny Peralta and Brandon Phillips. At the same time, he hedged his bets by retaining Belliard and signing veteran infielder Jose Hernandez. The overrated Kevin Millwood brings the faint hope of a veteran ace; recent injuries and ineffectiveness make him an iffy bet, but the move only cost the Indians a one-year deal, a reasonable risk. Matt Lawton was dealt to the Pirates, both to unclog the crowded outfield and bring in Arthur Rhodes—a pitcher who in the short term might shore up a troubled pen and in the long term could be flipped at the deadline for something good. The Indians GM was on less certain ground when he elected to bring the injury-prone Wickman back for another tour.

The only truly uncomfortable move is the one that most quickly brings to mind the 2004 Royals—the acquisition of Juan Gonzalez. Though the name alone is sufficient to bring to mind bloated contracts buoying up an even more bloated personality, there is a method to Shapiro's madness. First, the Royals spent actual money on Gonzalez, while the Indians have given him a minor league deal and a bunch of incentives. Second, despite the many intriguing young outfielders the Indians possess, the outfield unit was weak, hitting just 53 home runs last year. If his back stays intact and he finds motivation, Gonzalez could help them do better; if not, the cost was minimal.

Shapiro has a sharp eye as a trader. Since taking over for John Hart in November 2001, he has secured strong prospects in nearly every deal he's made. He landed Phillips, Lee, and Grady Sizemore for Bartolo Colon; stole Travis

Hafner for Einar Diaz and Ryan Drese; and turned the Milton Bradley giveaway into Franklin Gutierrez and Andrew Brown, a reasonable return under the circumstances.

This is a terrific asset for the club to have, as it means the roster is continually evolving. Unlike young Bobby Prospectus, if one of his clubs turns coquettish and can't make up its mind, Shapiro can always go looking for another date. It is safe to say that Shapiro has not overreacted to 2004's tantalizing run at the division title. He'll maintain the perspective necessary to build the club back up to the point that it can *really* compete . . . instead of just teasing.

HITTERS

MIKE AUBREY 1B Bats: L Throws: L Born: 15-Apr-1982 Age: 23

YEAR	TM	LG	AGE	AB	H	2B	3B	HR	BB	SO	SB	CS	AVG	OBP	SLG	MLVR	EQBA	EQOBP	EQSLG	EQMLVR	VORP	DEFENSE
2003	LKC	SAL	21	138	48	13	0	5	14	22	0	0	.348	.409	.551	.466	.284	.321	.454	-.002	3.6	37-1B 3
2004	KIN	CRL	22	218	74	14	1	10	27	26	3	1	.339	.438	.550	.466	.309	.388	.516	.226	22.0	49-1B -5
2004	AKR	EAS	22	134	35	7	0	5	15	18	0	0	.261	.340	.425	.004	.216	.278	.351	-.280	-8.2	25-1B 0
2005	*CLE*	*AL*	*23*	*329*	*88*	*18*	*1*	*12*	*28*	*52*	*1*	*1*	*.267*	*.338*	*.437*	*-.001*	*.267*	*.340*	*.448*	*.008*	*14.1*	*89-1B -3*

Breakout: 9% *Improve: 40%* *Collapse: 38%*

Aubrey's the best hitter in the system and one of the best first-base prospects in the game. Upon reaching Double-A, there was a marked decline in both batting average and overall power, but at least some of that can be chalked up to a season-ending hamstring pull. Right now Aubrey smells a lot like Mark Grace, which is just fine as long as you know how to use him properly, which was never the case with the actual Grace—even though Grace's primary skill was reaching base, Cubs managers never could come to grips with the idea that a slow first baseman could bat leadoff or second. Let's hope the Indians know better than to let labels do their thinking for them.

JOSH BARD C Bats: B Throws: R Born: 30-Mar-1978 Age: 27

YEAR	TM	LG	AGE	AB	H	2B	3B	HR	BB	SO	SB	CS	AVG	OBP	SLG	MLVR	EQBA	EQOBP	EQSLG	EQMLVR	VORP	DEFENSE
2002	BUF	INT	24	344	102	26	2	6	20	45	0	0	.297	.332	.436	.086	.281	.322	.421	-.050	12.3	93-C 4
2003	BUF	INT	25	115	38	7	0	5	14	17	1	2	.330	.408	.522	.361	.313	.381	.522	.227	14.7	29-C 2
2003	CLE	AL	25	303	74	13	1	8	22	53	0	2	.244	.293	.373	-.143	.247	.302	.380	-.173	3.6	81-C 8
2004	BUF	INT	26	156	41	10	0	4	11	23	0	0	.263	.310	.404	-.057	.239	.279	.361	-.249	-3.4	33-C -2
2005	*CLE*	*AL*	*27*	*219*	*55*	*12*	*0*	*6*	*18*	*34*	*0*	*0*	*.252*	*.310*	*.395*	*-.117*	*.252*	*.312*	*.404*	*-.110*	*6.6*	*60-C -3*

Breakout: 21% *Improve: 40%* *Collapse: 31%*

Muscled out of the way by an emergent Victor Martinez, Bard spent the year in Buffalo as a replacement-level catcher. With a sunny personality, strong defensive reputation, and .310 major league OBP, Bard could be a backup forever.

RON BELLIARD 2B Bats: R Throws: R Born: 07-Apr-1975 Age: 30

YEAR	TM	LG	AGE	AB	H	2B	3B	HR	BB	SO	SB	CS	AVG	OBP	SLG	MLVR	EQBA	EQOBP	EQSLG	EQMLVR	VORP	DEFENSE
2002	MIL	NL	27	289	61	13	0	3	18	46	2	3	.211	.257	.287	-.318	.218	.256	.297	-.398	-11.6	40-2B -2 28-3B -4
2003	COL	NL	28	447	124	31	2	8	49	71	7	2	.277	.351	.409	.000	.260	.335	.388	-.089	21.3	104-2B -11
2004	CLE	AL	29	599	169	48	1	12	60	98	3	2	.282	.348	.426	.030	.288	.359	.438	.047	37.2	143-2B -3
2005	*CLE*	*AL*	*30*	*478*	*123*	*28*	*2*	*11*	*44*	*78*	*3*	*2*	*.258*	*.322*	*.389*	*-.099*	*.258*	*.324*	*.399*	*-.092*	*12.3*	*125-2B -4*

Breakout: 8% *Improve: 34%* *Collapse: 31%*

After years of limp performances that suggested his bat had suffered the kind of terrifying bout with impotence that blues man Robert Johnson sang about in "Stones in My Passway," Belliard got his mojo working from the get-go last season with a .417/.500/.548 April. Thereafter he alternated hot and cold streaks, finishing the season in a soft 15-for-87 slump. Belliard's glove is as inconsistent as his bat, making him an occasionally valuable, highly frustrating player. PECOTA thinks he'll hit roughly as he did in the second half, which is not quite enough to keep his job if Brandon Phillips or Jose Hernandez has an interesting spring. *I got stones in my passway, and the road seems dark at night . . . I got pains in my heart, they have taken my appetite . . .*

CASEY BLAKE — 3B/RF — Bats: R — Throws: R — Born: 23-Aug-1973 — Age: 31

YEAR	TM	LG	AGE	AB	H	2B	3B	HR	BB	SO	SB	CS	AVG	OBP	SLG	MLVR	EQBA	EQOBP	EQSLG	EQMLVR	VORP	DEFENSE	
2002	EDM	PCL	28	482	149	25	3	19	54	78	24	9	.309	.383	.492	.236	.289	.359	.454	.070	37.5	110-3B 7	
2003	CLE	AL	29	557	143	35	0	17	38	109	7	9	.257	.312	.411	-.056	.264	.319	.424	-.066	18.0	133-3B 1	15-1B 0
2004	CLE	AL	30	587	159	36	3	28	68	139	5	8	.271	.354	.486	.112	.281	.366	.507	.149	36.5	149-3B -9	
2005	*CLE*	*AL*	*31*	*513*	*137*	*29*	*2*	*20*	*53*	*114*	*7*	*4*	*.268*	*.342*	*.447*	*.020*	*.268*	*.345*	*.458*	*.030*	*21.1*	*136-3B -5*	

Breakout: 18% *Improve: 50%* *Collapse: 27%*

Blake unexpectedly peaked, exceeding his 90th-percentile PECOTA projection with room to spare. Still, his horror show defense (including 26 errors) created a need for Aaron Boone in the organization's mind, and so Blake will begin 2005 as a potential right fielder in a crowded outfield. At 31, it's likely that we've just seen the best 600 ABs of Blake's career, but he should retain enough value to be at least an average contributor. He's a lock to outperform the .245/.338/.395 Cleveland got out of right field in '04, should he fend off challenges from everyone this side of Rocky Colavito.

AARON BOONE — 3B — Bats: R — Throws: R — Born: 09-Mar-1973 — Age: 31

YEAR	TM	LG	AGE	AB	H	2B	3B	HR	BB	SO	SB	CS	AVG	OBP	SLG	MLVR	EQBA	EQOBP	EQSLG	EQMLVR	VORP	DEFENSE	
2002	CIN	NL	29	606	146	38	2	26	56	111	32	8	.241	.314	.439	-.028	.239	.310	.445	-.073	27.1	144-3B 18	13-SS -1
2003	CIN	NL	30	403	110	19	3	18	35	74	15	3	.273	.339	.469	.076	.272	.337	.472	.041	29.5	81-3B 10	19-2B 2
2003	NYY	AL	30	189	48	13	0	6	11	30	8	0	.254	.302	.418	-.071	.261	.306	.426	-.089	8.9	53-3B 4	
2005	*CLE*	*AL*	*32*	*336*	*90*	*19*	*2*	*12*	*28*	*61*	*11*	*2*	*.267*	*.330*	*.436*	*-.016*	*.267*	*.332*	*.446*	*-.007*	*15.7*	*90-3B 2*	

Breakout: 25% *Improve: 52%* *Collapse: 26%*

Signed to provide steadier defense than Casey Blake, Boone brings a strong glove and a tendency to overswing to Cleveland's hot corner. Assuming his skills have survived an idle year and two knee surgeries, the Indians will get good range at third and a bat that flirts with league average at the plate. It would be a net gain, but not a big one.

BEN BROUSSARD — 1B — Bats: L — Throws: L — Born: 24-Sep-1976 — Age: 28

YEAR	TM	LG	AGE	AB	H	2B	3B	HR	BB	SO	SB	CS	AVG	OBP	SLG	MLVR	EQBA	EQOBP	EQSLG	EQMLVR	VORP	DEFENSE	
2002	LOU	INT	25	187	51	14	1	11	31	50	4	1	.273	.396	.535	.275	.249	.366	.497	.106	11.0	43-1B -4	
2002	BUF	INT	25	153	37	8	0	5	24	30	0	0	.242	.354	.392	.022	.214	.318	.351	-.203	-7.2	18-LF 1	16-RF 0
2003	CLE	AL	26	386	96	21	3	16	32	75	5	2	.249	.312	.443	-.017	.253	.321	.454	-.029	11.8	101-1B -6	
2004	CLE	AL	27	418	115	28	5	17	52	95	4	2	.275	.370	.488	.144	.285	.381	.507	.178	33.0	114-1B 4	
2005	*CLE*	*AL*	*28*	*364*	*96*	*20*	*2*	*16*	*45*	*81*	*4*	*2*	*.263*	*.351*	*.460*	*.048*	*.263*	*.354*	*.471*	*.058*	*20.5*	*100-1B -2*	

Breakout: 18% *Improve: 38%* *Collapse: 23%*

Broussard clobbered the ball following the All-Star break (.300/.395/.595), at last fulfilling some of the expectations generated by a minor league career in which he was often mentioned in the same breath as Austin Kearns and Adam Dunn—all hail the glory of the age-27 season. Broussard should continue doing a swell Paul Sorrento impression until Aubrey arrives.

COCO CRISP — CF — Bats: B — Throws: R — Born: 01-Nov-1979 — Age: 25

YEAR	TM	LG	AGE	AB	H	2B	3B	HR	BB	SO	SB	CS	AVG	OBP	SLG	MLVR	EQBA	EQOBP	EQSLG	EQMLVR	VORP	DEFENSE	
2002	NHV	EAS	22	355	107	16	1	9	36	56	26	10	.301	.365	.428	.161	.280	.339	.403	-.046	11.2	79-CF 2	
2003	BUF	INT	23	225	81	19	6	1	26	24	20	8	.360	.434	.511	.415	.352	.425	.509	.323	33.6	51-CF 3	
2003	CLE	AL	23	414	110	15	6	3	23	51	15	9	.266	.302	.353	-.147	.271	.314	.363	-.157	-1.3	50-CF -2	39-LF 3
2004	CLE	AL	24	491	146	24	2	15	36	69	20	13	.297	.344	.446	.055	.307	.359	.462	.098	25.3	86-CF -8	37-LF 3
2005	*CLE*	*AL*	*25*	*426*	*121*	*23*	*3*	*10*	*34*	*58*	*16*	*7*	*.284*	*.338*	*.424*	*-.004*	*.285*	*.341*	*.434*	*.005*	*18.0*	*112-CF -4*	

Breakout: 8% *Improve: 30%* *Collapse: 38%*

Crisp had a decent year that looks a bit better than it actually was, adding power to his repertoire for the first time (his professional *total* in homers was 29). However, on the bases he was a hazard to himself and others. Kids: Friends don't let friends run the bases like Covelli Crisp. He's 39-for-62 in his career and should really be greeted with a permanent stop sign, if not flat out tackled by the coach as soon as he reaches first base. He showed surprisingly little instinct for center field and more aptitude for hitting lefties than righties, both of which should be clues as to how he might be better utilized in the future—rather than just knee-jerking him to center and to the top of the order because he's "speedy."

RYAN GARKO Not C Bats: R Throws: R Born: 02-Jan-1981 Age: 24

YEAR	TM	LG	AGE	AB	H	2B	3B	HR	BB	SO	SB	CS	AVG	OBP	SLG	MLVR	EQBA	EQOBP	EQSLG	EQMLVR	VORP	DEFENSE	
2003	MHV	NYP	22	165	45	8	1	4	12	19	1	1	.273	.337	.406	.096	.219	.264	.343	-.317	-13.6	35-C -9	
2004	KIN	CRL	23	238	78	17	1	16	26	34	4	1	.328	.425	.609	.515	.287	.365	.545	.206	22.1	26-1B -1	21-C 1
2004	AKR	EAS	23	172	57	15	0	6	14	28	1	0	.331	.397	.523	.279	.281	.332	.439	-.006	8.7	21-C 1	16-1B 1
2005	*CLE*	*AL*	*24*	*293*	*77*	*16*	*1*	*11*	*22*	*50*	*1*	*1*	*.262*	*.333*	*.430*	*-.022*	*.262*	*.336*	*.440*	*-.013*	*14.4*	*80-C -11*	

Breakout: 13% *Improve: 37%* *Collapse: 36%*

Garko (the kind of name that sounds like it should be followed by "the Barbarian" or "Bat-Lord of Ganymede") is more likely to have a solid position on free trade than on a baseball field. The lad can rake, so it will be tragic if the Indians let him rot in the sticks rather than make a contribution to the big league club. Hiding him at catcher, first, or DH depending on who's hurt, the opposing pitcher, and the defensive needs of Cleveland's own pitcher might be the way to get value out of him. Think Matt LeCroy.

JODY GERUT RF Bats: L Throws: L Born: 18-Sep-1977 Age: 27

YEAR	TM	LG	AGE	AB	H	2B	3B	HR	BB	SO	SB	CS	AVG	OBP	SLG	MLVR	EQBA	EQOBP	EQSLG	EQMLVR	VORP	DEFENSE	
2002	AKR	EAS	24	256	72	15	2	9	34	30	17	8	.281	.368	.461	.160	.254	.333	.418	-.056	7.3	54-CF -2	
2002	BUF	INT	24	183	59	7	2	1	23	20	3	5	.322	.401	.399	.167	.306	.386	.383	.034	10.3	28-CF 1	17-LF 1
2003	CLE	AL	25	480	134	33	2	22	35	70	4	5	.279	.336	.494	.127	.285	.345	.509	.120	28.1	63-RF 1	36-LF 1
2004	CLE	AL	26	481	121	31	5	11	54	59	13	6	.252	.334	.405	-.052	.258	.344	.422	-.027	13.1	110-RF 3	10-CF -1
2005	*CLE*	*AL*	*27*	*474*	*132*	*28*	*3*	*16*	*52*	*66*	*10*	*5*	*.278*	*.354*	*.451*	*.053*	*.278*	*.356*	*.462*	*.063*	*23.1*	*126-RF 2*	

Breakout: 27% *Improve: 56%* *Collapse: 16%*

Gerut had a good April and May by his own standards, then his bat fell asleep and dozed through most of the rest of the season. Here's what we know about him based on current evidence: Even at his peak in '03 he was not a huge plus; he doesn't hit lefties; he doesn't hit at home. Having waited far too long to bench him, the Indians have pushed him so far down their 2005 depth chart that you'd need Captain Nemo to find him. He's best used in a platoon or as a fourth outfielder.

RYAN GOLESKI 1B Bats: R Throws: R Born: 19-Mar-1982 Age: 23

YEAR	TM	LG	AGE	AB	H	2B	3B	HR	BB	SO	SB	CS	AVG	OBP	SLG	MLVR	EQBA	EQOBP	EQSLG	EQMLVR	VORP	DEFENSE
2003	MHV	NYP	21	243	72	15	2	8	21	66	3	5	.296	.358	.473	.222	.235	.284	.393	-.197	-18.7	56-RF 0
2004	LKC	SAL	22	505	150	22	5	28	55	100	6	7	.297	.372	.527	.271	.251	.310	.434	-.079	-2.1	116-RF -4
2005	*CLE*	*AL*	*23*	*356*	*87*	*17*	*2*	*12*	*27*	*85*	*2*	*2*	*.245*	*.306*	*.403*	*-.116*	*.245*	*.309*	*.412*	*-.109*	*0.7*	*94-RF -4*

Breakout: 19% *Improve: 42%* *Collapse: 26%*

Goleski was a 24th-round pick in 2003, overlooked because he had recently broken his hand. Whether the fruit of perspicacious scouting or just a fluke, he and his lively bat qualify as a real steal for the Indians. He cut his strikeout rate from once every 3.68 ABs to once every 5.05, which was something he needed to do to keep his batting average up at the higher levels. The main knock on Goleski is that he's old for his leagues; he needs to come quicker, or risk breaking in when he's 26.

FRANKLIN GUTIERREZ CF Bats: R Throws: R Born: 21-Feb-1983 Age: 22

YEAR	TM	LG	AGE	AB	H	2B	3B	HR	BB	SO	SB	CS	AVG	OBP	SLG	MLVR	EQBA	EQOBP	EQSLG	EQMLVR	VORP	DEFENSE	
2002	SGA	SAL	19	361	102	18	4	12	31	88	13	4	.283	.344	.454	.210	.253	.297	.415	-.128	2.2	58-CF -4	27-LF -1
2003	VRO	FSL	20	425	120	28	5	20	39	111	17	5	.282	.345	.513	.230	.237	.290	.457	-.094	7.6	102-CF 0	
2003	JAX	SOU	20	67	21	3	2	4	7	20	3	3	.313	.387	.597	.457	.279	.343	.544	.160	6.7	15-CF -1	
2004	AKR	EAS	21	262	79	24	2	5	23	77	6	3	.302	.372	.466	.139	.263	.324	.408	-.080	5.4	45-CF -3	
2005	*CLE*	*AL*	*22*	*337*	*84*	*18*	*1*	*12*	*25*	*96*	*5*	*2*	*.248*	*.310*	*.416*	*-.090*	*.249*	*.312*	*.426*	*-.083*	*7.1*	*90-CF -7*	

Breakout: 22% *Improve: 49%* *Collapse: 27%*

Gutierrez was the key prospect acquired in the "Who will rid us of this turbulent outfielder" Milton Bradley anti-love swap. Coming off a year in which he showed tremendous power for a 20-year-old in the Florida State League, Gutierrez struggled with the strike zone and the effects of bone chips in his left elbow. Considered a useful defender, Gutierrez may turn out to be an above-average bat for center field even if he never does learn better pitch recognition. Given his age, the ceiling could be much higher.

TRAVIS HAFNER DH Bats: L Throws: R Born: 03-Jun-1977 Age: 28

YEAR	TM	LG	AGE	AB	H	2B	3B	HR	BB	SO	SB	CS	AVG	OBP	SLG	MLVR	EQBA	EQOBP	EQSLG	EQMLVR	VORP	DEFENSE
2002	OKL	PCL	25	401	137	22	1	21	79	76	2	1	.342	.463	.559	.509	.323	.436	.525	.331	51.8	62-1B 4
2003	BUF	INT	26	100	27	4	0	2	25	26	2	1	.270	.421	.370	.140	.238	.377	.317	-.116	-1.2	24-1B -1
2003	CLE	AL	26	291	74	19	3	14	22	81	2	1	.254	.327	.485	.083	.259	.333	.503	.065	17.1	39-1B -3
2004	CLE	AL	27	482	150	41	3	28	68	111	3	2	.311	.410	.583	.374	.323	.421	.610	.424	70.9	
2005	*CLE*	*AL*	*28*	*464*	*133*	*29*	*2*	*26*	*71*	*110*	*3*	*2*	*.287*	*.392*	*.524*	*.215*	*.287*	*.395*	*.537*	*.229*	*47.8*	*130-DH*

Breakout: 13% *Improve: 39%* *Collapse: 22%*

Holy Moly, that was sweet, not that many noticed. The guy slugs nearly .600 and was one of the five most productive hitters in the American League. This nets him two points in the MVP voting, and he finishes behind Erubiel Durazo, tied with Lew Ford, Chone Figgins, and Billy Boyd, so memorable as Pippin the Hobbit in the Lord of the Rings trilogy. Hafner has his flaws. As a first baseman he's a good DH, and he doesn't have the same magic against lefties that he does against righties (though his OBP against southpaws, .364, meant that he needn't be yanked out of the game if a LOOGY reared its ugly head). That's what makes Mark Shapiro's acquisition of him so beautiful: He was there for the taking, if one was only willing to see what he could do instead of what he couldn't.

KEVIN KOUZMANOFF 3B Bats: R Throws: R Born: 25-Jul-1981 Age: 23

YEAR	TM	LG	AGE	AB	H	2B	3B	HR	BB	SO	SB	CS	AVG	OBP	SLG	MLVR	EQBA	EQOBP	EQSLG	EQMLVR	VORP	DEFENSE
2003	MHV	NYP	21	206	56	8	1	8	21	36	2	1	.272	.342	.437	.139	.213	.269	.360	-.287	-13.0	51-3B 6
2004	LKC	SAL	22	473	156	35	5	16	44	75	5	4	.330	.394	.526	.335	.283	.333	.446	.007	27.5	114-3B -4
2005	*CLE*	*AL*	*23*	*248*	*63*	*13*	*2*	*7*	*17*	*49*	*1*	*1*	*.252*	*.309*	*.403*	*-.107*	*.253*	*.311*	*.413*	*-.100*	*2.6*	*67-3B -3*

Breakout: 14% *Improve: 32%* *Collapse: 35%*

Teamed with Goleski to trash the Sally League, but Kouzmanoff is nearly a year older, so he's going to have to hustle to have any sort of career before his peak years are spilled in the minors like some Onanistic waste of precious bodily fluids. The pace screams "Casey Blake if things break right," not, "They'll keep Eric Chavez out of the Hall of Fame until this guy gets in."

MATT LAWTON OF Bats: L Throws: R Born: 03-Nov-1971 Age: 33

YEAR	TM	LG	AGE	AB	H	2B	3B	HR	BB	SO	SB	CS	AVG	OBP	SLG	MLVR	EQBA	EQOBP	EQSLG	EQMLVR	VORP	DEFENSE
2002	CLE	AL	30	416	98	19	2	15	59	34	8	9	.236	.342	.399	-.040	.242	.351	.413	-.038	3.9	85-RF -3 23-LF -1
2003	CLE	AL	31	374	93	19	0	15	47	47	10	3	.249	.343	.420	.011	.256	.350	.431	-.006	13.7	54-LF 2 11-RF 0
2004	CLE	AL	32	591	164	25	0	20	74	84	23	9	.277	.366	.421	.053	.288	.375	.438	.076	28.1	113-LF 7 17-RF 0
2005	*PIT*	*NL*	*33*	*456*	*121*	*23*	*2*	*16*	*64*	*60*	*11*	*4*	*.266*	*.363*	*.430*	*.024*	*.267*	*.362*	*.439*	*.034*	*15.4*	*125-LF -2*

Breakout: 28% *Improve: 64%* *Collapse: 8%*

At this stage of his career, Lawton is a broad-based talent who can do a lot of things—walk, hit a home run, steal a base—but he doesn't do any of them exceptionally well. He's a placeholder until something better and cheaper comes along, and he'll put up league-average numbers for the next couple years. Lawton will take over right field in Pittsburgh, pushing Craig Wilson to first base. This will at least be a net improvement, if nothing to get excited about.

RYAN LUDWICK OF Bats: R Throws: L Born: 13-Jul-1978 Age: 26

YEAR	TM	LG	AGE	AB	H	2B	3B	HR	BB	SO	SB	CS	AVG	OBP	SLG	MLVR	EQBA	EQOBP	EQSLG	EQMLVR	VORP	DEFENSE
2002	OKL	PCL	23	305	87	27	4	15	38	76	2	2	.285	.370	.548	.287	.266	.346	.502	.093	21.5	54-CF -5 22-RF -2
2002	TEX	AL	23	81	19	6	0	1	7	24	2	1	.235	.295	.346	-.227	.237	.283	.338	-.275	-1.0	14-CF 0
2003	OKL	PCL	24	317	96	24	3	17	33	71	1	1	.303	.372	.558	.349	.284	.352	.517	.142	20.0	50-RF -1
2003	CLE	AL	24	136	36	7	1	7	8	39	2	0	.265	.306	.485	.056	.267	.312	.504	.038	6.2	19-RF 1 13-LF 1
2004	BUF	INT	25	166	45	15	0	8	16	52	0	0	.271	.346	.506	.155	.241	.306	.452	-.069	-0.2	25-RF -1
2004	CLE	AL	25	50	11	2	0	2	2	14	0	0	.220	.278	.380	-.208	.240	.266	.380	-.246	-0.7	14-RF 0
2005	*CLE*	*AL*	*26*	*264*	*70*	*16*	*1*	*12*	*24*	*72*	*1*	*1*	*.265*	*.334*	*.474*	*.039*	*.266*	*.336*	*.485*	*.050*	*17.1*	*72-RF -2*

Breakout: 23% *Improve: 51%* *Collapse: 27%*

Ludwick spent most of 2004 getting his knee healthy after an off-season operation. Acquired from Texas in 2003, he's hit relatively well in the minors but failed to produce in his brief time in the majors. In part this is because playing in the PCL overstated his offensive potential a little, in part because a mid-range offensive prospect without plate judgment is like a parachutist who fills his container with chocolate pudding instead of silk.

VICTOR MARTINEZ — C — Bats: B — Throws: R — Born: 23-Dec-1978 — Age: 26

YEAR	TM	LG	AGE	AB	H	2B	3B	HR	BB	SO	SB	CS	AVG	OBP	SLG	MLVR	EQBA	EQOBP	EQSLG	EQMLVR	VORP	DEFENSE
2002	AKR	EAS	23	443	149	40	0	22	58	62	3	3	.336	.417	.576	.437	.291	.362	.507	.152	44.9	101-C 6
2003	BUF	INT	24	274	90	19	0	7	26	32	3	5	.328	.395	.474	.278	.304	.367	.449	.091	22.5	56-C -10 13-1B -1
2003	CLE	AL	24	159	46	4	0	1	13	21	1	1	.289	.345	.333	-.073	.297	.346	.335	-.117	4.9	39-C 0
2004	CLE	AL	25	520	147	38	1	23	60	69	0	1	.283	.359	.492	.142	.290	.369	.511	.168	47.1	123-C -7
2005	*CLE*	*AL*	*26*	*487*	*140*	*30*	*1*	*18*	*53*	*66*	*0*	*1*	*.287*	*.362*	*.464*	*.090*	*.287*	*.365*	*.475*	*.101*	*37.5*	*130-C -6*

Breakout: 12% *Improve: 31%* *Collapse: 30%*

If anyone is likely to sidestep the pitfalls of young catcherdom, it's Martinez. In his first year as a full-timer behind the plate in Cleveland, Martinez put his broad base of offensive skills on display, his 2004 looking like something out of the career of Yogi Berra—whose exceptional bat control he mirrors. As with Yogi, Martinez's bat is a better tool than his glove. The high Collapse number above is a nod to the rough road traveled by young catchers and the frequent regression that occurs when a player has a huge year in his first full big league season. We're going to tell PECOTA to grab a Fresca and chill out on this one.

JOHN McDONALD — INF — Bats: R — Throws: R — Born: 24-Sep-1974 — Age: 30

YEAR	TM	LG	AGE	AB	H	2B	3B	HR	BB	SO	SB	CS	AVG	OBP	SLG	MLVR	EQBA	EQOBP	EQSLG	EQMLVR	VORP	DEFENSE
2002	CLE	AL	27	264	66	11	3	1	10	50	3	0	.250	.288	.326	-.242	.255	.296	.335	-.243	-0.9	56-2B 7 16-SS 0
2003	CLE	AL	28	214	46	9	1	1	11	31	3	3	.215	.258	.280	-.364	.221	.268	.291	-.380	-9.1	27-2B 4 20-SS 0
2004	CLE	AL	29	93	19	5	1	2	4	11	0	0	.204	.237	.344	-.363	.207	.247	.359	-.335	-3.0	20-SS 0
2005	*TOR*	*AL*	*30*	*158*	*39*	*8*	*1*	*2*	*8*	*23*	*1*	*1*	*.246*	*.286*	*.354*	*-.215*	*.243*	*.285*	*.353*	*-.233*	*-0.4*	*44-SS -5*

Breakout: 33% *Improve: 54%* *Collapse: 28%*

Fell out of the glove tree and hit every branch on the way down, but was home sick the day they handed out bats. Dealt to Toronto for a PTBNL, he'll back up Russ Adams, Orlando Hudson, and the rest of the Jays' young middle infielders.

JHONNY PERALTA — SS/3B — Bats: R — Throws: R — Born: 28-May-1982 — Age: 23

YEAR	TM	LG	AGE	AB	H	2B	3B	HR	BB	SO	SB	CS	AVG	OBP	SLG	MLVR	EQBA	EQOBP	EQSLG	EQMLVR	VORP	DEFENSE
2002	AKR	EAS	20	470	132	28	5	15	45	97	4	2	.281	.343	.457	.117	.252	.308	.416	-.107	13.6	128-SS 10
2003	BUF	INT	21	237	61	12	1	1	15	45	1	3	.257	.310	.329	-.111	.245	.304	.316	-.260	-4.1	60-SS 11
2003	CLE	AL	21	242	55	10	1	4	20	65	1	3	.227	.295	.326	-.220	.233	.306	.333	-.239	-0.7	67-SS 5
2004	BUF	INT	22	556	181	44	2	15	54	126	8	4	.326	.384	.493	.254	.309	.368	.466	.122	53.1	77-SS -5 59-3B -2
2004	CLE	AL	22	25	6	1	0	0	3	6	0	1	.240	.321	.280	-.244	.280	.263	.280	-.374	-0.7	
2005	*CLE*	*AL*	*23*	*304*	*81*	*17*	*2*	*8*	*27*	*68*	*4*	*2*	*.265*	*.330*	*.410*	*-.052*	*.265*	*.332*	*.420*	*-.044*	*17.5*	*82-SS -3*

Breakout: 14% *Improve: 37%* *Collapse: 36%*

Peralta and Brandon Phillips, who may be 2006's double-play combination, have two things in common: they each bombed in their initial big league exposure in 2003, and their offensive games are way too reliant on batting average to be trusted. It was time for Cleveland to move on from Omar Vizquel, but unless Peralta's jump in BA comes to the majors and then sustains—and both those things almost never happen—he won't be an impact player. PECOTA doesn't penalize him for having an unnecessary consonant in his first name, but it should.

JOSH PHELPS — DH — Bats: R — Throws: R — Born: 12-May-1978 — Age: 27

YEAR	TM	LG	AGE	AB	H	2B	3B	HR	BB	SO	SB	CS	AVG	OBP	SLG	MLVR	EQBA	EQOBP	EQSLG	EQMLVR	VORP	DEFENSE
2002	SYR	INT	24	257	75	20	1	24	32	83	0	0	.292	.380	.658	.423	.261	.350	.595	.222	30.9	34-C -12
2002	TOR	AL	24	265	82	20	1	15	19	82	0	0	.309	.362	.562	.281	.313	.369	.569	.276	28.6	
2003	TOR	AL	25	396	106	18	1	20	39	115	1	2	.268	.358	.470	.088	.265	.357	.472	.070	23.6	
2004	TOR	AL	26	295	70	13	2	12	18	73	0	0	.237	.296	.417	-.140	.234	.294	.416	-.147	2.3	11-1B 0
2004	CLE	AL	26	76	23	6	0	5	4	20	0	0	.303	.338	.579	.244	.320	.341	.587	.267	7.5	
2005	*CLE*	*AL*	*27*	*401*	*107*	*23*	*1*	*22*	*36*	*108*	*0*	*1*	*.267*	*.339*	*.495*	*.077*	*.268*	*.342*	*.507*	*.088*	*26.3*	*107-DH*

Breakout: 27% *Improve: 55%* *Collapse: 15%*

He has more power than your local utility but has no clue what to do with it, swinging indiscriminately at pitches, relay throws from the outfield, low-hanging clouds. As his time in Toronto went on, Phelps crossed the line dividing productive aggression and diminishing returns, so this positionless player was sent south for nothing more than Eric Crozier.

(continued next page)

Josh Phelps *(continued)*

Working with Eddie Murray, he cut his strikeouts just slightly, but that sample is so small as to be nearly meaningless. Signed by Tampa, Phelps will meet Lou Piniella at the same age that the somewhat similar Jay Buhner did. Buhner blossomed at that point; Phelps will need to follow instruction a lot better than he did with the Jays to have a chance to do the same.

BRANDON PHILLIPS 2B/SS Bats: R Throws: R Born: 28-Jun-1981 Age: 24

YEAR	TM	LG	AGE	AB	H	2B	3B	HR	BB	SO	SB	CS	AVG	OBP	SLG	MLVR	EQBA	EQOBP	EQSLG	EQMLVR	VORP	DEFENSE	
2002	HAR	EAS	21	245	80	13	2	9	16	33	6	3	.327	.380	.506	.269	.291	.337	.459	.040	17.5	53-SS -3	
2002	BUF	INT	21	223	63	14	0	8	14	39	8	2	.283	.321	.453	.079	.256	.293	.417	-.130	4.7	44-SS 5	11-2B 2
2003	BUF	INT	22	154	27	7	0	3	12	22	7	3	.175	.247	.279	-.330	.161	.228	.258	-.536	-17.0	42-2B 1	
2003	CLE	AL	22	370	77	18	1	6	14	77	4	5	.208	.242	.311	-.356	.213	.253	.319	-.376	-16.0	108-2B 6	
2004	BUF	INT	23	521	158	34	4	8	44	56	14	11	.303	.363	.430	.108	.288	.347	.405	-.022	23.3	69-2B -3	65-SS -10
2004	CLE	AL	23	22	4	2	0	0	2	5	0	2	.182	.250	.273	-.426	.227	.206	.273	-.529	-2.3		
2005	*CLE*	*AL*	*24*	*265*	*68*	*14*	*1*	*6*	*19*	*38*	*5*	*3*	*.257*	*.314*	*.388*	*-.114*	*.258*	*.317*	*.397*	*-.107*	*10.1*	*72-2B -1*	

Breakout: 25% *Improve: 41%* *Collapse: 22%*

Everything that was said about Peralta, above, could be said about Phillips, except the part about the extra consonants. Phillips has clearly improved his understanding of the strike zone from where it was two years ago, making far better contact and taking a few more walks. He's still going to have to do a disproportionate amount of hitting 'em where they ain't to make an impact.

GRADY SIZEMORE OF Bats: L Throws: L Born: 02-Aug-1982 Age: 22

YEAR	TM	LG	AGE	AB	H	2B	3B	HR	BB	SO	SB	CS	AVG	OBP	SLG	MLVR	EQBA	EQOBP	EQSLG	EQMLVR	VORP	DEFENSE	
2002	BRV	FSL	19	256	66	15	4	0	36	41	9	9	.258	.351	.348	.052	.240	.313	.319	-.241	-16.4	64-LF -4	
2002	KIN	CRL	19	172	59	9	3	3	33	30	14	7	.343	.451	.483	.413	.307	.403	.449	.157	12.3	39-LF -2	
2003	AKR	EAS	20	496	151	26	11	13	46	73	10	9	.304	.373	.480	.190	.269	.329	.441	-.019	19.5	111-CF -18	11-LF 1
2004	BUF	INT	21	418	120	23	8	8	42	72	15	10	.287	.360	.438	.100	.273	.345	.412	-.028	14.8	103-CF -4	
2004	CLE	AL	21	138	34	6	2	4	14	34	2	0	.246	.333	.406	-.060	.255	.341	.423	-.034	4.9	42-CF -3	
2005	*CLE*	*AL*	*22*	*377*	*107*	*23*	*3*	*10*	*38*	*66*	*10*	*4*	*.285*	*.358*	*.447*	*.061*	*.286*	*.361*	*.458*	*.071*	*27.3*	*101-CF -7*	

Breakout: 32% *Improve: 57%* *Collapse: 18%*

It's not your Sizemore but how you use him, and that's what the Indians are struggling with right now. The ex-Expo farmhand started slowly, delaying his promotion until August. Sizemore's ability to hit for average seems reasonably certain (unlike Peralta and Phillips, mentioned earlier, he has done it for more than two minutes at a time). The other facets of his offensive game are evolving. That makes his position key. Though his defensive rep is good, the stats don't scream ace center fielder, and in an outfield corner his bat is going to be a lot less of a plus. Sizemore's only competition for best Grady in major league history is 3B Grady Hatton, whose 1947 peak he will surpass this season, at least according to PECOTA, which is having a very opinionated chapter.

COREY SMITH 3B/OF Bats: R Throws: R Born: 15-Apr-1982 Age: 23

YEAR	TM	LG	AGE	AB	H	2B	3B	HR	BB	SO	SB	CS	AVG	OBP	SLG	MLVR	EQBA	EQOBP	EQSLG	EQMLVR	VORP	DEFENSE
2002	KIN	CRL	20	505	129	29	2	13	59	141	7	2	.255	.341	.398	.081	.231	.304	.375	-.187	-1.0	130-3B -19
2003	AKR	EAS	21	473	128	27	3	9	50	99	7	2	.271	.340	.397	.001	.239	.302	.369	-.193	-1.9	122-3B -21
2004	AKR	EAS	22	454	113	14	3	19	63	106	3	2	.249	.347	.419	-.002	.216	.304	.359	-.218	-5.4	125-3B -16
2005	*CLE*	*AL*	*23*	*300*	*72*	*15*	*2*	*8*	*30*	*79*	*2*	*1*	*.239*	*.315*	*.383*	*-.131*	*.240*	*.317*	*.392*	*-.124*	*0.6*	*81-3B -13*

Breakout: 39% *Improve: 56%* *Collapse: 19%*

Smith is sometimes listed as a good prospect, and that's true if you like utility players who play poor defense and hit with occasional power. Smith's Pedro Guerrero–like defense at the hot corner has the Tribe considering a shift to an OF corner, which is a problem because the Indians have more outfielders than most organizations and he could barely hit well enough to play third, let alone right field. Basically, Corey Smith is the cube root of Cory Snyder, and that ain't good.

BRAD SNYDER CF **Bats: L** **Throws: L** Born: 25-May-1982 Age: 23

YEAR	TM	LG	AGE	AB	H	2B	3B	HR	BB	SO	SB	CS	AVG	OBP	SLG	MLVR	EQBA	EQOBP	EQSLG	EQMLVR	VORP	DEFENSE
2003	MHV	NYP	21	225	64	11	6	6	41	82	14	5	.284	.393	.467	.246	.232	.320	.391	-.134	2.0	64-CF -8
2004	LKC	SAL	22	304	85	15	5	10	48	78	11	4	.280	.382	.461	.183	.238	.322	.381	-.139	0.8	55-CF -1 16-LF -1
2004	KIN	CRL	22	110	39	7	1	6	13	28	4	2	.355	.424	.600	.536	.315	.377	.550	.263	14.6	24-CF -2
2005	*CLE*	*AL*	*23*	*356*	*90*	*19*	*3*	*10*	*41*	*108*	*8*	*3*	*.252*	*.334*	*.404*	*-.062*	*.252*	*.336*	*.414*	*-.054*	*8.2*	*96-CF -5*

Breakout: 22% *Improve: 49%* *Collapse: 22%*

A Ball State product, Snyder came to the pros equipped with a willingness to work the count and take a walk, a welcome and too-rare trait. Snyder was slowed by an eye infection early on, but got it straightened out and really took off upon promotion to High-A Kinston. Snyder's been a little old for his leagues, but he's going to Double-A this year so he's actually not that far away. If his selectivity survives the big jump in competition, he'll come quickly and will crisp Coco, or whoever's the RF du jour.

OMAR VIZQUEL SS **Bats: B** **Throws: R** Born: 24-Apr-1967 Age: 38

YEAR	TM	LG	AGE	AB	H	2B	3B	HR	BB	SO	SB	CS	AVG	OBP	SLG	MLVR	EQBA	EQOBP	EQSLG	EQMLVR	VORP	DEFENSE
2002	CLE	AL	35	582	160	31	5	14	56	64	18	10	.275	.341	.418	.001	.282	.351	.428	.013	33.9	146-SS 11
2003	CLE	AL	36	250	61	13	2	2	29	20	8	3	.244	.321	.336	-.148	.250	.332	.343	-.164	6.3	64-SS 7
2004	CLE	AL	37	567	165	28	3	7	57	62	19	6	.291	.353	.388	-.026	.299	.365	.401	.015	33.3	136-SS 3
2005	*SFG*	*NL*	*38*	*410*	*109*	*22*	*2*	*5*	*41*	*38*	*12*	*3*	*.266*	*.333*	*.366*	*-.111*	*.269*	*.334*	*.381*	*-.090*	*15.5*	*110-SS -2*

Breakout: 19% *Improve: 48%* *Collapse: 27%*

Back in the 1930s, Rabbit Maranville had such a good defensive rep at short that teams kept giving him contracts into his 40s, well after the point of diminishing returns. Brian Sabean put on his Maranville blinders before giving Vizquel a contract that will keep him on the payroll through age 40. That the glove is not the leather of Vizquel's youth and that the bat has never been that big a deal both seem to have been overlooked. It's understood that Sabean is trying to win now, but unless he's planning to work for another team by the time this and other contracts come home to roost, he's going to have a hell of a mess on his hands. Maybe we should amend that to say that he should probably *plan* to be working for another team by the time these contracts come home to roost.

PITCHERS

CLIFF BARTOSH **Bats: L** **Throws: L** Born: 05-Sep-1979 Age: 25

YEAR	TM	LG	AGE	G	GS	IP	H	BB	SO	HR	ERA	EQERA	EQH9	EQBB9	EQSO9	EQHR9	PERA	VORP	STF
2002	MOB	SOU	22	62	0	70.7	54	32	70	4	3.18	4.39	8.1	4.0	6.7	1.0	4.11	10.9	5
2003	POR	PCL	23	64	0	71.3	67	22	51	4	4.29	5.21	8.6	3.2	5.6	0.7	3.88	12.9	1
2004	BUF	INT	24	28	0	35.3	26	8	46	3	2.80	3.21	7.0	2.1	9.6	0.8	2.67	11.0	28
2004	CLE	AL	24	34	0	19.3	22	11	25	4	4.66	4.12	9.2	4.6	10.5	1.4	5.03	3.5	15
2005	*CLE*	*AL*	*25*	*7*	*0*	*9.3*	*9*	*4*	*9*	*1*	*4.00*	*3.92*	*8.5*	*3.2*	*7.9*	*1.2*	*4.16*	*2.0*	*7*

Breakout: 25% *Improve: 57%* *Collapse: 14%*

A situational-lefty, Bartosh performed decently in limited action, getting a lot of strikeouts but struggling with his control, not to mention the guys he was supposed to get out—lefties hit .286/.412/.524. The high strikeout/low home-run rates of Mobile '02 and Buffalo '04 point to better times ahead, if he gets the opportunity.

RAFAEL BETANCOURT **Bats: R** **Throws: R** Born: 29-Apr-1975 Age: 30

YEAR	TM	LG	AGE	G	GS	IP	H	BB	SO	HR	ERA	EQERA	EQH9	EQBB9	EQSO9	EQHR9	PERA	VORP	STF
2003	AKR	EAS	28	31	0	45.3	33	13	75	0	1.39	2.68	6.8	2.7	12.0	0.2	2.47	15.2	40
2003	CLE	AL	28	33	0	38.0	27	13	36	5	2.13	2.50	7.2	3.0	8.8	1.2	3.50	14.7	15
2004	CLE	AL	29	68	0	66.7	71	18	76	7	3.91	4.01	8.4	2.1	9.5	0.8	3.48	14.5	23
2005	*CLE*	*AL*	*30*	*55*	*0*	*71.7*	*67*	*24*	*71*	*9*	*3.77*	*3.69*	*8.4*	*2.7*	*8.1*	*1.2*	*3.90*	*18.4*	*10*

Breakout: 21% *Improve: 48%* *Collapse: 21%*

The year began roughly for Betancourt, who surrendered a number of poorly timed home runs, and though on the whole he had a good year, he was up and down a little too much for comfort. His esoteric journey to the majors comprised his development time, so what you see is probably what you get, but that's not all that bad.

ANDREW BROWN Bats: R Throws: R Born: 17-Feb-1981 Age: 24

YEAR	TM	LG	AGE	G	GS	IP	H	BB	SO	HR	ERA	EQERA	EQH9	EQBB9	EQSO9	EQHR9	PERA	VORP	STF
2002	VRO	FSL	21	25	24	127.0	97	62	129	13	4.11	5.24	8.9	5.0	6.9	2.0	5.71	-1.4	6
2004	JAX	SOU	23	8	8	40.3	36	14	58	5	4.02	5.92	9.0	3.3	9.0	1.7	4.97	2.7	20
2004	AKR	EAS	23	17	17	77.3	66	36	67	7	4.66	5.20	8.4	4.5	5.9	1.1	4.46	9.2	0
2005	*CLE*	*AL*	*24*	*28*	*12*	*91.7*	*87*	*44*	*73*	*16*	*5.18*	*5.08*	*8.5*	*3.7*	*6.4*	*1.6*	*4.86*	*8.4*	*-2*

Breakout: 7% *Improve: 36%* *Collapse: 25%*

The other prospect acquired by the Indians in the Milton Bradley deal, Brown needs to quell nagging injury concerns (he missed a number of starts in July because of a dead arm, and the entire 2003 campaign with an elbow injury) and wrestle down his control if he wants to make the jump to the big club. His rep is that he's not the most coachable cat in the zoo, so he's going to have to open his ears if he wants to avoid future injury and not be just another Brown stain on the road to success.

FERNANDO CABRERA Bats: R Throws: R Born: 16-Nov-1981 Age: 23

YEAR	TM	LG	AGE	G	GS	IP	H	BB	SO	HR	ERA	EQERA	EQH9	EQBB9	EQSO9	EQHR9	PERA	VORP	STF
2002	KIN	CRL	20	21	21	110.0	83	40	107	7	3.52	5.38	8.6	4.2	6.5	1.3	4.74	9.4	23
2002	AKR	EAS	20	7	4	27.0	26	12	29	1	5.33	5.96	9.1	4.2	7.4	0.4	4.91	2.0	15
2003	AKR	EAS	21	36	15	109.0	96	40	115	8	2.97	4.03	8.4	3.6	7.8	1.1	4.30	14.8	17
2004	BUF	INT	22	45	0	76.0	57	43	93	9	3.79	4.65	7.4	5.4	9.2	1.1	4.14	11.6	22
2004	CLE	AL	22	4	0	5.3	3	1	6	0	3.40	5.40	5.4	1.8	10.8	0.0	1.80	0.7	48
2005	*CLE*	*AL*	*23*	*26*	*7*	*64.7*	*57*	*34*	*57*	*9*	*4.66*	*4.57*	*8.0*	*4.1*	*7.1*	*1.2*	*4.38*	*10.2*	*2*

Breakout: 17% *Improve: 45%* *Collapse: 28%*

Cabrera's a big, imposing character often compared by scouts to Jose Mesa. A power arm who's been phased out of starting in his early-20s, Cabrera should begin the year in Cleveland. Like so many minor league relievers, improved control and continued good health are the only things keeping him from making a positive impact on the Tribe's bullpen, as soon as this season.

FAUSTO CARMONA Bats: R Throws: R Born: 07-Dec-1983 Age: 21

YEAR	TM	LG	AGE	G	GS	IP	H	BB	SO	HR	ERA	EQERA	EQH9	EQBB9	EQSO9	EQHR9	PERA	VORP	STF
2002	BNC	APL	18	13	11	76.3	89	10	42	4	3.30	6.22	10.8	1.5	2.5	1.1	5.47	1.0	-6
2003	LKC	SAL	19	24	24	148.3	117	14	83	10	2.06	4.89	9.7	1.0	3.2	1.6	5.17	6.2	18
2004	KIN	CRL	20	13	13	70.0	68	20	57	6	2.83	4.87	9.7	3.1	5.4	1.4	5.29	2.2	7
2004	AKR	EAS	20	15	15	87.0	114	21	63	3	4.76	5.48	10.2	2.2	4.7	0.3	4.34	12.2	5
2005	*CLE*	*AL*	*21*	*12*	*11*	*66.3*	*79*	*19*	*38*	*10*	*5.13*	*5.03*	*10.8*	*2.3*	*4.7*	*1.3*	*5.12*	*5.6*	*0*

Breakout: 7% *Improve: 42%* *Collapse: 18%*

Listed at 6′4″, 170 lbs., Carmona would probably have had a cool nickname like "Beanstalk," "Daddy Long Legs," or "The Cuyahoga Letter Opener" if this were the 1940s. The holder of strong K:BB ratios, he jumped all the way from A-ball to Triple-A Buffalo in '04, where he had a run of 16 scoreless innings during the postseason. An Indian since he was 16, Carmona struggled to miss bats during his turn at Akron, allowing nearly 12 hits per nine innings. He's going to Triple-A anyway, where he'll be one of the youngest starters in the league.

FRANCISCO CRUCETA Bats: R Throws: R Born: 04-Jul-1981 Age: 23

YEAR	TM	LG	AGE	G	GS	IP	H	BB	SO	HR	ERA	EQERA	EQH9	EQBB9	EQSO9	EQHR9	PERA	VORP	STF
2002	SGA	SAL	21	20	20	112.7	98	34	111	7	2.80	5.33	9.7	3.5	5.5	1.4	5.15	5.1	3
2002	KIN	CRL	21	7	7	39.7	31	25	37	2	2.49	4.58	8.7	7.4	6.4	1.0	5.60	0.0	6
2003	AKR	EAS	22	27	25	163.3	141	66	134	7	3.09	4.41	8.2	4.0	6.1	0.6	4.06	26.2	27
2004	AKR	EAS	23	15	15	88.7	89	33	45	11	5.28	5.94	9.6	3.6	3.5	1.5	5.08	4.8	-1
2004	BUF	INT	23	14	14	83.0	78	36	62	6	3.25	4.10	8.5	4.1	5.6	0.7	4.10	13.2	20
2005	*CLE*	*AL*	*23*	*13*	*12*	*68.7*	*75*	*32*	*44*	*10*	*5.36*	*5.25*	*9.9*	*3.7*	*5.2*	*1.3*	*5.16*	*4.7*	*-2*

Breakout: 12% *Improve: 45%* *Collapse: 22%*

You think you've got troubles? Try keeping Fernando Cabrera, Fausto Carmona, and Francisco Cruceta straight in your head without snapping completely and biting strangers on the ankles. This actually happened to Joe Sheehan years ago, but we managed to keep it a secret until that incident with Henry Kissinger. Cruceta's struggled at Double-A Akron, but the Indians promoted him anyway and got away with it, in part because he added a splitter to his arsenal. He'll start 2005 in the minors, but anything can happen when you're young and Scott Elarton is the only thing blocking you from making major league moolah.

JASON DAVIS **Bats: R** **Throws: R** Born: 08-May-1980 Age: 25

YEAR	TM	LG	AGE	G	GS	IP	H	BB	SO	HR	ERA	EQERA	EQH9	EQBB9	EQSO9	EQHR9	PERA	VORP	STF
2002	KIN	CRL	22	17	17	99.7	107	31	68	7	4.15	7.14	10.5	3.4	4.4	1.5	5.87	-2.8	-9
2002	AKR	EAS	22	10	10	59.0	63	16	45	2	3.51	4.63	9.7	2.6	5.3	0.5	4.95	4.1	2
2002	CLE	AL	22	3	2	14.7	12	4	11	1	1.84	1.93	7.7	2.6	6.4	0.6	2.57	6.7	12
2003	CLE	AL	23	27	27	165.3	172	47	85	25	4.68	5.13	9.6	2.5	4.7	1.3	4.90	10.8	-5
2004	CLE	AL	24	26	19	114.3	148	51	72	13	5.51	5.82	10.1	3.5	5.2	0.9	5.04	-1.8	0
2004	BUF	INT	24	9	9	54.0	53	18	39	4	3.00	4.53	8.7	3.1	5.4	0.7	3.83	10.2	11
2005	*CLE*	*AL*	*25*	*24*	*21*	*123.3*	*141*	*45*	*81*	*16*	*5.11*	*5.01*	*10.3*	*2.9*	*5.3*	*1.1*	*4.93*	*10.5*	*2*

Breakout: 15% *Improve: 48%* *Collapse: 22%*

Davis ended 2003 with shoulder soreness and began 2004 with control problems, walking nearly a batter every other inning. When you're only good for 5.5 strikeouts per nine frames, this is a recipe for professional extinction. Sure enough, Davis was sent down. Despite better numbers at Buffalo, he's earned himself a one-way ticket to the bullpen, where he can use his hard stuff for an inning or two. This yielded fair results in September's seven-inning trial (four runs, only one earned).

DAN DENHAM **Bats: R** **Throws: R** Born: 24-Dec-1982 Age: 22

YEAR	TM	LG	AGE	G	GS	IP	H	BB	SO	HR	ERA	EQERA	EQH9	EQBB9	EQSO9	EQHR9	PERA	VORP	STF
2002	CGA	SAL	19	28	28	124.7	123	65	109	7	4.76	7.13	10.0	5.9	4.8	1.2	6.02	-5.3	-5
2003	LKC	SAL	20	14	14	73.0	75	22	63	4	3.08	5.37	10.6	3.2	4.8	1.3	6.31	-5.3	-11
2003	KIN	CRL	20	14	14	72.0	82	27	39	2	4.50	6.42	10.1	3.7	3.5	0.5	5.11	3.7	-5
2004	KIN	CRL	21	13	13	71.0	73	29	62	6	4.18	5.59	10.0	4.2	5.7	1.5	5.86	-1.9	-5
2004	AKR	EAS	21	14	13	76.0	84	30	50	12	4.74	6.10	10.2	3.7	4.5	1.7	5.72	-1.0	-4
2005	*CLE*	*AL*	*22*	*9*	*8*	*47.3*	*52*	*22*	*32*	*8*	*5.53*	*5.41*	*9.9*	*3.7*	*5.4*	*1.4*	*5.45*	*2.3*	*-3*

Breakout: 10% *Improve: 47%* *Collapse: 26%*

Cleveland's first-round pick in 2001 (three picks ahead of Jeremy Sowers, Cleveland's 2004 first-rounder), Denham was smoked on first exposure to Double-A and hasn't been a notable success at his earlier stops. There's nothing remarkable about him at this point, but he's young enough that he could find success three years from now and still work in a big league career of decent length.

KYLE DENNEY **Bats: R** **Throws: R** Born: 27-Jul-1977 Age: 27

YEAR	TM	LG	AGE	G	GS	IP	H	BB	SO	HR	ERA	EQERA	EQH9	EQBB9	EQSO9	EQHR9	PERA	VORP	STF
2002	KIN	CRL	24	15	14	85.0	76	41	68	5	3.60	5.38	9.4	5.5	5.3	1.3	5.73	-1.1	-3
2002	AKR	EAS	24	6	5	34.7	23	5	32	2	1.56	2.56	7.7	1.4	6.8	0.9	3.41	7.7	28
2003	AKR	EAS	25	18	18	104.0	97	24	87	7	2.42	3.58	8.8	2.3	6.2	1.1	4.22	15.0	19
2003	BUF	INT	25	6	6	30.7	35	10	26	4	5.28	5.83	10.1	3.4	6.1	1.8	5.83	-0.7	6
2004	BUF	INT	26	24	24	134.7	134	39	113	17	4.41	5.11	9.0	2.7	6.2	1.3	4.34	18.0	13
2004	CLE	AL	26	4	4	16.0	32	8	13	3	9.56	8.66	12.7	3.6	6.1	1.5	7.13	-5.9	0
2005	*CLE*	*AL*	*27*	*11*	*11*	*63.0*	*68*	*23*	*43*	*9*	*4.89*	*4.79*	*9.7*	*2.9*	*5.6*	*1.3*	*4.79*	*7.5*	*4*

Breakout: 17% *Improve: 42%* *Collapse: 24%*

A low-upside prospect, Denney was injured in a shooting after a game in September, but avoided serious harm thanks to an ironically well-timed hazing incident in which he was forced to wear a USC cheerleading outfit. The bullet deflected off the impenetrable white sweater he was wearing, grazing the right-hander and leaving no permanent damage. If Eddie Waitkus had been dressed like that when he went to Ruth Ann Burns's room on July 15, 1949, he could have avoided a literal hole in the heart, Bernard Malamud would have never written *The Natural,* and Randy Newman wouldn't have written the greatest baseball film score. Two out of three ain't bad, and while we're glad that Denney was unhurt, it appears the culture was seriously harmed by his survival.

JAKE DITTLER — Bats: R — Throws: R — Born: 24-Nov-1982 — Age: 22

YEAR	TM	LG	AGE	G	GS	IP	H	BB	SO	HR	ERA	EQERA	EQH9	EQBB9	EQSO9	EQHR9	PERA	VORP	STF
2002	CGA	SAL	19	25	25	128.3	127	51	108	4	4.28	7.11	9.5	4.5	4.6	0.7	4.92	9.0	6
2003	LKC	SAL	20	17	17	89.0	86	20	82	4	2.63	5.84	10.1	2.4	5.2	1.1	5.51	0.8	-2
2003	KIN	CRL	20	8	8	48.7	47	11	32	2	2.40	4.37	9.3	2.2	4.4	0.8	4.37	6.2	12
2004	AKR	EAS	21	21	20	107.7	119	40	85	7	5.01	6.11	9.5	3.4	5.2	0.7	4.47	13.1	5
2005	*CLE*	*AL*	*22*	*20*	*11*	*71.3*	*83*	*31*	*44*	*8*	*5.18*	*5.08*	*10.4*	*3.4*	*5.0*	*1.1*	*5.17*	*5.7*	*-6*

Breakout: 8% *Improve: 35%* *Collapse: 26%*

"Dirk" Dittler failed to follow up his strong 2003, as minor physical problems and a vanishing change-up left him exposed to those hungry hitters in Double-A. Thirty innings for Peoria in the Arizona Fall League were marginally better, so it's back to Akron, not a big setback given his relative youthfulness. With minor refinements he'll be a serviceable starter, but as with all pitchers it's not a question of when, but if.

SCOTT ELARTON — Bats: R — Throws: R — Born: 23-Feb-1976 — Age: 29

YEAR	TM	LG	AGE	G	GS	IP	H	BB	SO	HR	ERA	EQERA	EQH9	EQBB9	EQSO9	EQHR9	PERA	VORP	STF
2003	CSP	PCL	27	20	20	118.7	146	39	92	15	5.31	5.90	10.2	3.3	5.8	1.6	5.51	1.2	-5
2003	COL	NL	27	11	10	51.7	73	20	20	13	6.27	6.97	11.3	3.0	3.1	1.9	6.45	-13.3	-28
2004	COL	NL	28	8	8	41.3	57	20	23	8	9.81	8.36	10.7	3.6	4.3	1.5	6.00	-18.5	-9
2004	BUF	INT	28	3	3	20.0	19	5	10	1	3.15	3.32	8.5	2.4	3.8	0.5	3.79	3.8	5
2004	CLE	AL	28	21	21	117.3	107	42	80	25	4.53	4.39	8.5	3.0	6.0	1.8	4.39	19.2	3
2005	*CLE*	*AL*	*29*	*23*	*22*	*128.7*	*144*	*45*	*80*	*21*	*5.31*	*5.20*	*10.1*	*2.7*	*5.0*	*1.5*	*5.12*	*9.0*	*0*

Breakout: 16% *Improve: 58%* *Collapse: 18%*

One of baseball's most extreme flyball pitchers, Elarton getting his career back on track in Colorado was about as likely as Ben Affleck winning the Academy Award for Best Actor . . . in a musical . . . of *Schindler's List.* The promise that Elarton showed as a young pitcher is a thousand miles and a million home runs ago, but he did turn a corner of sorts after the All-Star break, posting a 4.12 ERA in 91.2 innings. Given his tendencies, that's probably as good as it's going to get, barring a move to Safeco Field or a planet with heavier gravity.

MARIANO GOMEZ — Bats: L — Throws: L — Born: 12-Sep-1982 — Age: 22

YEAR	TM	LG	AGE	G	GS	IP	H	BB	SO	HR	ERA	EQERA	EQH9	EQBB9	EQSO9	EQHR9	PERA	VORP	STF
2002	CGA	SAL	19	34	13	111.3	106	40	98	3	2.75	5.33	9.3	4.0	4.8	0.5	4.46	13.0	5
2003	KIN	CRL	20	18	18	100.7	91	38	69	11	3.66	5.58	10.2	3.9	4.8	2.2	6.48	-8.8	0
2004	AKR	EAS	21	7	3	20.3	27	8	15	2	5.32	6.20	10.6	3.5	4.9	0.9	5.75	-0.3	-13
2005	*CLE*	*AL*	*22*	*16*	*7*	*51.7*	*58*	*23*	*35*	*7*	*5.49*	*5.38*	*10.1*	*3.5*	*5.4*	*1.2*	*5.16*	*3.8*	*-6*

Breakout: 14% *Improve: 48%* *Collapse: 36%*

Gomez missed most of 2004 with an injury to his throwing hand, a holdover from 2003, when he didn't pitch after July 14. When healthy, whenever that is, he has three workable pitches and is the namesake of a martyr of the Filipino struggle for independence from Spain. Non-tendered in December, he was immediately re-signed to a minor league contract and invited to spring training.

JEREMY GUTHRIE — Bats: B — Throws: R — Born: 08-Apr-1979 — Age: 26

YEAR	TM	LG	AGE	G	GS	IP	H	BB	SO	HR	ERA	EQERA	EQH9	EQBB9	EQSO9	EQHR9	PERA	VORP	STF
2003	AKR	EAS	24	10	9	62.7	44	14	35	0	1.44	2.35	7.4	2.2	4.2	0.2	2.83	17.6	27
2003	BUF	INT	24	18	18	96.7	129	30	62	15	6.51	7.35	11.5	3.2	4.6	2.0	6.77	-12.1	-33
2004	AKR	EAS	25	23	21	130.3	145	42	94	16	4.21	5.39	9.9	3.0	4.8	1.5	5.10	7.0	-1
2004	BUF	INT	25	4	4	19.3	23	18	10	0	7.93	8.53	9.5	8.5	3.8	0.5	6.16	-1.2	-22
2005	*CLE*	*AL*	*26*	*11*	*10*	*57.7*	*63*	*24*	*36*	*8*	*5.25*	*5.15*	*9.8*	*3.3*	*5.0*	*1.3*	*5.09*	*4.4*	*-3*

Breakout: 18% *Improve: 46%* *Collapse: 23%*

Guthrie had a terrific pro debut at Double-A Akron in 2003, but even then his low strikeout rate hinted that there might be trouble in the future. Indeed, promoted to Triple-A that same season, he was pounded harder than Judge Hoffman's gavel during the trial of the Chicago Seven. The return to Akron was not a triumphal one, and the second charge at the International League also crapped out. A brief trip to the majors was intriguing for its reverse split—lefties went 4-for-25, righties fired at will. A long shot at best.

BOBBY HOWRY Bats: L Throws: R Born: 04-Aug-1973 Age: 31

YEAR	TM	LG	AGE	G	GS	IP	H	BB	SO	HR	ERA	EQERA	EQH9	EQBB9	EQSO9	EQHR9	PERA	VORP	STF
2002	CWS	AL	28	47	0	50.7	45	17	31	7	3.91	3.56	8.6	2.8	5.4	1.1	4.31	11.6	-7
2002	BOS	AL	28	20	0	18.0	22	4	14	2	5.00	7.00	10.0	2.0	6.5	1.0	4.50	-3.1	1
2004	BUF	INT	30	18	0	26.0	22	6	24	3	5.19	5.47	8.0	2.2	6.9	1.5	3.65	5.4	10
2004	CLE	AL	30	37	0	42.7	37	12	39	5	2.74	2.81	7.8	2.4	7.8	0.9	3.24	15.8	17
2005	*CLE*	*AL*	*31*	*40*	*0*	*28.7*	*29*	*9*	*22*	*4*	*4.15*	*4.07*	*9.1*	*2.4*	*6.3*	*1.2*	*4.31*	*6.3*	*-2*

Breakout: 25% *Improve: 57%* *Collapse: 21%*

Costello: "How're we going to get anybody out with such a bad bullpen?"
Abbott: "Howry!"
Costello: "That's what I'm asking you. How're we?"
Abbott: "Yes."
Costello: "Well, go ahead and tell me!"
Abbott: "Howry!"
Costello: "How're we?"
Abbott: "Now, that's the first thing you've said right."
Costello: "I don't even know what I'm *talking* about!"

Howry's 2003 was mercifully brought to a close by elbow surgery after four disastrous outings. The Indians caught him on the rebound and got quite a bargain, as he was one of the few bright spots in a pen dreamed up by Dali. He completely dominated right-handed hitters, holding them to .169/.216/.301. This is the opposite of his 1998–2000 peak, when he was the rare right-hander who could lock down lefties. There is almost zero chance he will be as effective against righties again, but a successful season setting up Bob Wickman is not too much to expect.

CLIFF LEE Bats: L Throws: L Born: 30-Aug-1978 Age: 26

YEAR	TM	LG	AGE	G	GS	IP	H	BB	SO	HR	ERA	EQERA	EQH9	EQBB9	EQSO9	EQHR9	PERA	VORP	STF
2002	HAR	EAS	23	15	15	86.3	61	23	105	12	3.23	3.89	8.2	2.6	8.8	1.9	4.58	8.9	19
2002	BUF	INT	23	8	8	43.0	36	22	30	7	3.77	4.42	9.3	5.6	5.8	2.1	6.28	-2.9	-3
2003	BUF	INT	24	11	11	63.3	62	31	61	4	3.27	4.05	8.9	5.1	7.1	0.9	4.95	4.3	5
2003	CLE	AL	24	9	9	52.3	41	20	44	7	3.61	4.53	7.8	3.4	7.6	1.1	3.81	7.4	16
2004	CLE	AL	25	33	33	179.0	188	81	161	30	5.43	5.21	8.8	3.6	7.6	1.3	4.60	10.9	9
2005	*CLE*	*AL*	*26*	*26*	*25*	*147.7*	*144*	*64*	*125*	*22*	*4.76*	*4.67*	*8.8*	*3.4*	*6.9*	*1.3*	*4.59*	*19.4*	*11*

Breakout: 18% *Improve: 47%* *Collapse: 20%*

Lee, one of three Cleveland pitchers to make more than 30 starts, saw his performance—pardon the pun—fall off a cliff in the second half, going 5–7 with an ERA of 7.91 after a sterling 9–1, 3.77 ERA in the first half. His pre-All-Star performance was more in keeping with his minor league record than what came after. Part of the problem was a predilection for launching fly balls that was borrowed from either Scott Elarton or NASA. The rest was fatigue, as Lee was so successful that he threw just 30 fewer innings in the first half than he had in all of 2003. For what it's worth, he finished the year with consecutive quality starts against Kansas City and Minnesota. Perhaps, then, the nightmare is over, but the "dead arm" of the second half does merit concern.

J. D. MARTIN Bats: R Throws: R Born: 02-Jan-1983 Age: 22

YEAR	TM	LG	AGE	G	GS	IP	H	BB	SO	HR	ERA	EQERA	EQH9	EQBB9	EQSO9	EQHR9	PERA	VORP	STF
2002	CGA	SAL	19	27	26	138.3	141	46	131	12	3.90	6.64	10.6	3.8	5.3	1.9	6.21	-8.5	-5
2003	KIN	CRL	20	16	16	86.3	95	30	57	7	4.28	6.39	10.6	3.5	4.5	1.6	6.27	-6.0	-8
2004	KIN	CRL	21	25	24	147.7	139	41	98	15	4.39	5.76	9.9	2.9	4.4	1.8	5.69	-1.3	-1
2005	*CLE*	*AL*	*22*	*10*	*9*	*54.0*	*63*	*21*	*33*	*9*	*5.52*	*5.41*	*10.5*	*3.0*	*4.9*	*1.5*	*5.52*	*2.2*	*-4*

Breakout: 9% *Improve: 39%* *Collapse: 19%*

A supplemental first-round pick in 2001 (for the loss of Manny Ramirez), Martin looked like money in the bank after his first two seasons. A strained elbow ligament put a damper on the fun: Though he avoided the surgeon's knife, it sure looked like there was some hangover in 2004 as his strikeout rate failed to recover. Martin doesn't throw hard, so everything has to be in sync for him pitch effectively. It could happen, sure. "An optimist is a guy who has never had much experience."

ADAM MILLER

Bats: R **Throws: R** Born: 26-Nov-1984 Age: 20

YEAR	TM	LG	AGE	G	GS	IP	H	BB	SO	HR	ERA	EQERA	EQH9	EQBB9	EQSO9	EQHR9	PERA	VORP	STF
2003	BNC	APL	18	10	10	32.7	30	9	23	2	4.95	6.98	9.7	3.3	3.6	1.8	5.76	-0.5	-5
2004	LKC	SAL	19	19	19	91.0	79	28	106	7	3.36	4.78	8.9	3.2	6.5	1.1	4.57	9.7	23
2004	KIN	CRL	19	8	8	43.3	29	12	46	1	2.08	4.76	7.3	2.9	7.0	0.5	3.18	10.7	40
2005	*CLE*	*AL*	*20*	*16*	*13*	*79.0*	*77*	*31*	*61*	*11*	*4.54*	*4.45*	*8.7*	*3.1*	*6.3*	*1.3*	*4.46*	*12.3*	*7*

Breakout: 13% *Improve: 47%* *Collapse: 14%*

One of the top pitching prospects in the business, the Indians picked up then-prep pitcher Miller with the supplemental first-round pick they received for losing Jim Thome. It's been money well spent so far, though keep in mind that he's yet to see Double-A. There is a lot here to like, though, including good stuff, two really strong pitches and a third on the way, and a reputation for dedication and focus, which gives him a developmental advantage over thick-headed man-children who've graduated from the Jimmy Haynes School of Self-Defeatism. We're willing to go out on a limb and say he will be a better pitcher for Cleveland than Smoky Joe Wood ever was. Of course, Smoky Joe mostly played the outfield after he got to Cleveland.

MATT MILLER

Bats: R **Throws: R** Born: 23-Nov-1971 Age: 33

YEAR	TM	LG	AGE	G	GS	IP	H	BB	SO	HR	ERA	EQERA	EQH9	EQBB9	EQSO9	EQHR9	PERA	VORP	STF
2002	SAC	PCL	30	54	0	71.0	81	28	63	5	4.31	5.50	9.1	3.7	6.0	0.8	3.97	12.7	-2
2003	CSP	PCL	31	61	0	63.3	46	23	83	0	2.13	2.82	6.5	3.7	10.1	0.3	2.52	20.8	32
2004	CLE	AL	32	57	0	55.3	42	23	55	1	3.09	3.33	6.8	3.3	8.5	0.2	2.50	16.6	22
2005	*CLE*	*AL*	*33*	*43*	*1*	*57.3*	*54*	*26*	*53*	*4*	*3.78*	*3.70*	*8.4*	*3.6*	*7.4*	*0.6*	*3.97*	*14.3*	*6*

Breakout: 26% *Improve: 37%* *Collapse: 32%*

Here's a sweet story. Miller entered pro baseball as a non-draft free agent of the Rangers back in 1997. A sidearmer, he pitched effectively for most of his minor league career, but because of his limited stuff no one wanted to trust him. The Rockies, who had, have, will have nothing to lose, finally gave him a chance, then passed him onto the Indians where, glory be, he became exhibit #52,398 in the brief on *Why Minor League Statistics Are Meaningful.* Lefties are not intimidated by Miller. This is the common affliction of sidearmers, whose manner of pitching gives lefties a very good look at every pitch. As long as Miller is used as a righty specialist, he'll be fine; he held right-handed hitters to .201/.263/.266 last season. A player who toiled in the minor league underworld for so long should have his own moderately threatening theme song, something like "Matt the Knife." *Oh, the line forms . . . on the right, babe . . . Now that Matt is back in town . . .*

DAVID RISKE

Bats: R **Throws: R** Born: 23-Oct-1976 Age: 28

YEAR	TM	LG	AGE	G	GS	IP	H	BB	SO	HR	ERA	EQERA	EQH9	EQBB9	EQSO9	EQHR9	PERA	VORP	STF
2002	CLE	AL	25	51	0	51.3	49	35	65	8	5.26	5.23	7.8	5.6	10.6	1.2	4.18	2.1	13
2003	CLE	AL	26	68	0	74.7	52	20	82	9	2.29	2.54	6.8	2.4	10.0	1.0	2.92	29.6	26
2004	CLE	AL	27	72	0	77.3	69	41	78	11	3.73	3.42	7.8	4.2	8.6	1.2	4.01	22.0	7
2005	*CLE*	*AL*	*28*	*42*	*2*	*63.7*	*54*	*32*	*62*	*8*	*3.89*	*3.82*	*7.7*	*3.9*	*7.9*	*1.1*	*4.07*	*16.2*	*6*

Breakout: 27% *Improve: 55%* *Collapse: 20%*

In his three seasons as a bullpen regular, Riske has been everywhere between Bob Tewksbury and Mitch Williams on the control meter, passing 6.1, 2.4, and 4.8 batters per nine. If you're a physician and you have a pill that will solve this problem, there's likely a job waiting for you in Cleveland. The Indians have toyed with the idea of making Riske a closer at times, but because he's yet another member of their band who is prolific in the flyball department, he'll always be vulnerable to the home run—not ideal for a fellow who has to protect one-run leads (then again, we all know that closers are rarely called upon to protect one-run leads, don't we?). Keep an eye on that home-run rate, which is starting to creep into dangerous territory.

C. C. SABATHIA Bats: L Throws: L Born: 21-Jul-1980 Age: 24

YEAR	TM	LG	AGE	G	GS	IP	H	BB	SO	HR	ERA	EQERA	EQH9	EQBB9	EQSO9	EQHR9	PERA	VORP	STF
2002	CLE	AL	21	33	33	210.0	198	88	149	17	4.37	4.34	8.1	3.5	6.1	0.7	3.38	30.6	20
2003	CLE	AL	22	30	30	197.7	190	66	141	19	3.60	3.68	8.7	2.9	6.4	0.8	4.11	48.6	18
2004	CLE	AL	23	30	30	188.0	176	72	139	20	4.12	3.97	8.2	3.1	6.4	0.8	3.72	40.2	16
2005	*CLE*	*AL*	*24*	*28*	*28*	*165.7*	*174*	*63*	*121*	*19*	*4.45*	*4.36*	*9.4*	*3.0*	*5.9*	*1.0*	*4.52*	*26.8*	*9*

Breakout: 18% *Improve: 56%* *Collapse: 22%*

Sabathia's been worked hard at times, but he's made it through the bulk of the injury nexus without his arm falling off (though he did have some bicipital tendonitis early in the season). On a larger scale, that of innings pitched, the Indians have done a good job with Sabathia—he's only been over 200 innings once; by the time Dwight Gooden was Sabathia's age, he'd pitched 248 or more innings three times. Nonetheless, the Indians should note that Sabathia wasn't much fun in starts after high-pitch outings. After a 123-pitch start June 21, Sabathia left his next outing with a sore left shoulder after one inning, then spent all of July and August pitching poorly. Three of four September starts were good, but then a strained hammy ended Sabathia's season early. He's closer to a breakdown than a breakout, which should worry the Indians even more as Sabathia starts to get expensive.

JASON STANFORD Bats: L Throws: L Born: 23-Jan-1977 Age: 28

YEAR	TM	LG	AGE	G	GS	IP	H	BB	SO	HR	ERA	EQERA	EQH9	EQBB9	EQSO9	EQHR9	PERA	VORP	STF
2002	AKR	EAS	25	18	18	102.3	108	33	86	3	3.43	4.50	9.6	3.0	5.8	0.5	4.87	7.9	3
2002	BUF	INT	25	6	5	35.7	33	11	23	5	2.77	3.58	9.6	3.3	5.2	1.9	5.79	-0.7	-13
2003	BUF	INT	26	20	20	126.0	124	25	108	13	3.43	4.63	9.3	2.0	6.4	1.4	4.63	12.8	12
2003	CLE	AL	26	13	8	50.0	48	16	30	5	3.60	3.38	8.8	2.8	5.4	0.9	4.12	13.8	5
2005	*CLE*	*AL*	*28*	*13*	*9*	*58.3*	*65*	*22*	*39*	*7*	*4.55*	*4.45*	*9.9*	*3.0*	*5.4*	*1.1*	*4.83*	*9.3*	*0*

Breakout: 18% *Improve: 46%* *Collapse: 20%*

After an impressive showing the previous year, Stanford underwent Tommy John surgery in April. He'll still be recuperating when spring training rolls around. You wonder if there's a support group for the multitude of pitchers who are recovering from TJ surgery at any one time. They could talk out their anxieties, show off their scars, and TJ himself could bestow the ceremonial sling on each new initiate.

KAZ TADANO Bats: R Throws: R Born: 25-Apr-1980 Age: 25

YEAR	TM	LG	AGE	G	GS	IP	H	BB	SO	HR	ERA	EQERA	EQH9	EQBB9	EQSO9	EQHR9	PERA	VORP	STF
2003	KIN	CRL	23	7	1	19.0	13	3	28	0	1.89	3.57	7.1	1.5	10.2	0.0	2.55	6.0	36
2003	AKR	EAS	23	31	0	72.7	62	15	78	4	1.24	2.62	8.1	2.0	7.9	0.8	3.54	15.7	17
2004	BUF	INT	24	12	8	44.7	49	14	39	9	5.44	5.65	9.8	2.9	6.5	2.1	5.44	0.8	-2
2004	CLE	AL	24	14	4	50.3	55	18	39	6	4.65	4.86	9.0	2.9	6.5	0.9	4.14	5.0	8
2005	*CLE*	*AL*	*25*	*24*	*16*	*106.7*	*108*	*35*	*84*	*14*	*4.53*	*4.44*	*9.1*	*2.6*	*6.4*	*1.2*	*4.30*	*17.3*	*9*

Breakout: 15% *Improve: 48%* *Collapse: 21%*

Tadano pitched better in Cleveland than would have been expected, given his rock 'em–sock 'em results at Buffalo. A bulging disk ended his season in early September. Fortunately, that's the only part of Tadano that's publicly bulging these days.

BRIAN TALLET Bats: L Throws: L Born: 21-Sep-1977 Age: 27

YEAR	TM	LG	AGE	G	GS	IP	H	BB	SO	HR	ERA	EQERA	EQH9	EQBB9	EQSO9	EQHR9	PERA	VORP	STF
2002	AKR	EAS	24	18	16	102.3	93	32	73	9	3.08	4.29	9.3	3.1	5.2	1.3	5.34	2.7	3
2002	BUF	INT	24	8	7	44.0	47	16	25	1	3.07	4.07	9.4	3.6	4.3	0.2	4.50	5.1	-2
2003	BUF	INT	25	15	15	84.0	89	34	67	10	5.14	5.81	9.8	4.2	5.9	1.6	5.70	-0.9	-8
2004	AKR	EAS	26	14	0	22.7	26	13	23	0	5.55	6.04	9.3	5.2	6.4	0.4	4.84	1.9	-9
2005	*CLE*	*AL*	*27*	*22*	*9*	*63.7*	*71*	*29*	*44*	*7*	*4.96*	*4.86*	*10.0*	*3.7*	*5.6*	*1.0*	*5.08*	*7.5*	*-5*

Breakout: 26% *Improve: 49%* *Collapse: 22%*

Another Tommy John survivor, Tallet pitched about as well as could be expected, given that he retuned to the mound less than a year after surgery. After being TJ'd, the second year is usually better.

JAKE WESTBROOK Bats: R Throws: R Born: 29-Sep-1977 Age: 27

YEAR	TM	LG	AGE	G	GS	IP	H	BB	SO	HR	ERA	EQERA	EQH9	EQBB9	EQSO9	EQHR9	PERA	VORP	STF
2002	AKR	EAS	24	3	3	15.0	13	1	8	0	4.80	5.14	8.4	0.6	3.9	0.0	3.21	3.7	8
2002	CLE	AL	24	11	4	41.7	50	12	20	6	5.83	5.88	9.8	2.4	4.1	1.1	4.35	-2.3	-7
2003	BUF	INT	25	2	2	10.0	0	4	7	0	0.00	1.08	3.2	4.3	5.4	0.0	1.08	4.2	14
2003	CLE	AL	25	34	22	133.0	142	56	58	9	4.33	4.42	9.5	3.7	3.9	0.6	4.77	19.9	-7
2004	CLE	AL	26	33	30	215.7	208	61	116	19	3.38	3.67	8.6	2.3	4.7	0.7	3.62	54.4	9
2005	*CLE*	*AL*	*27*	*27*	*27*	*155.7*	*181*	*51*	*85*	*16*	*4.67*	*4.58*	*10.4*	*2.6*	*4.4*	*0.9*	*4.71*	*18.8*	*1*

Breakout: 9% *Improve: 45%* *Collapse: 16%*

Westbrook's 2.72 GB:FB rate was third in the major leagues, behind only Derek Lowe (2.82) and Brandon Webb (3.55). What's intriguing is that this alone cannot account for his breakthrough season; his GB:FB rate actually *declined* from 2003, when it was 3.02. Similarly, his double-play rate of .19 double plays per opportunity was slightly lower than the .222 of 2003. What is more telling is Westbrook's greatly improved strikeout-to-walk ratio—which went from roughly even to nearly two-to-one—and his strikeouts per nine, where he averaged nearly five, one more than the year before.

These adjustments, some of them small in themselves, created a positive cascade. When a pitcher puts as many balls in play as Westbrook does, then walks some more, and never strikes anyone out, he's expecting the defense to catch anything that moves and do his work for him. It doesn't work for long. When Westbrook took more of the effort onto himself, the results were revealing. Continuation depends on Westbrook's maintaining his control and the Tribe's new keystone combo.

BOB WICKMAN Bats: R Throws: R Born: 06-Feb-1969 Age: 36

YEAR	TM	LG	AGE	G	GS	IP	H	BB	SO	HR	ERA	EQERA	EQH9	EQBB9	EQSO9	EQHR9	PERA	VORP	STF
2002	CLE	AL	33	36	0	34.3	42	10	36	3	4.46	5.35	8.9	2.3	8.7	0.8	3.82	0.8	15
2004	CLE	AL	35	30	0	29.7	33	10	26	4	4.24	3.94	9.1	2.7	7.3	0.9	4.25	6.7	6
2005	*CLE*	*AL*	*36*	*28*	*0*	*37.3*	*37*	*14*	*32*	*4*	*3.91*	*3.83*	*8.9*	*3.1*	*6.9*	*0.9*	*4.10*	*8.9*	*3*

Breakout: 31% *Improve: 59%* *Collapse: 17%*

Groundball specialist Wickman missed all of 2003 and three months of 2004 recovering from reconstructive elbow surgery. Yes, kids, too many French fries will not only clog your arteries . . . they'll clog your elbow too! Old enough to have been traded for Steve Sax and in sub-optimal condition for anything smaller than a parade float, a return to 2001 form (the last time Wickman was more than mediocre) was unlikely. Wickman did not pitch all that well and saved 13 of 14 opportunities. This proves either (A) that the odds are always on the closer's side, because even the worst pitcher can usually get three outs before the opposition scores two or three runs, or (B) Wickman possesses the rare "closer's mentality" that gives him the mental strength, the guts, to close out the tough ones even if he's half the pitcher and twice the man he used to be. The Indians apparently went for door #2, because they brought him back for one more year.

Detroit Tigers

We live in a society addicted to instant gratification, made worse in some respects by media that prefer storylines providing instant gratification. People like it when closure occurs in a single news cycle. Executives exploit that, whether they're heading nations, companies, or baseball teams. Questions of pressure over time rarely excite audiences, which is why the Tigers represent a disappointment. However far they may have come back from fielding the worst baseball team since the McKinley Administration in 2003, there's not a happy ending, and perhaps more difficult to accept, there isn't about to be one.

That might seem a tough thing to say, since the Tigers improved their record by almost 30 games. But BP is a long-view outfit, and for whatever splash the Tigers made last season while regaining some measure of dignity, the team—and worse still, the organization—has more in common with those from the tail end of the Sparky Anderson era than with a franchise that's going places.

It's not hard to forget the season before last, when the Tigers managed to lose 119 games. As we documented last year, that might be enough to consider the 2003 Tigers the worst big league team since syndicate baseball passed into history (although with so many former Yankee minority stakeholders owning their own teams these days, wags might claim those days are back). When you're bad enough that people have to think before saying, "yes, they were probably better than the Cleveland Spiders," you've achieved something, but not the sort of something you want to brag about.

It's one thing for Dave Dombrowski to point out that 2003 was only his second year dealing with the worst-run franchise in the game, and that rebuilding takes time. Unfortunately, statements of fact don't sell tickets, and selling tickets has been very important to team owner Mike Ilitch. After Ilitch's bid to consolidate his debt-service with Sumitomo Bank on Comerica Park fell short in 2001, keeping the organizational wheels greased was hardly easy in 2002 and 2003. Proving yet again the lie that new stadia create revenue streams in a vacuum, the Tigers went from drawing 2.5 million in 2000—Comerica's first season—down to the 1.3 million people who paid to see the 2003 Tigers. Moreover, Comerica isn't winning any prizes as a baseball-viewing venue. It may not be the gloomy observatory that Miller Park is, but it also isn't a Camden Yards–style gem. When you're an owner and paying your own bills, losing half of your attendance not only hurts you on the ledger, it provides an easy-to-understand reminder that the audience shows up to see the product, not ride the Ferris wheel.

TIGERS PROSPECTUS

2004 record: 72–90; Fourth place, AL Central

Pythagenport record: 79–83

Runs scored per game: 5.10 (8th in AL)

Runs allowed per game: 5.21 (11th in AL)

Team EqA: .267 (4th in AL)

2004 Batters Age: 28.7 (4th youngest in AL)

2004 Pitchers Age: 27.7 (3rd youngest in AL)

Ballpark: Comerica Park; Severe pitcher's park; Park Factor of 0.958

2004: Several newly minted Tigers spurred the team to a hot start, but injuries helped derail the season.

2005: The Tigers have some holes on their roster, but filling those could make the next couple of seasons very interesting.

Charged with making some noise in the offseason to shore up a club ruined by years of bad investments in free agents and even worse choices in player development, Dombrowski kept his ambitions relatively modest. When you start off by picking up Al Levine and Mike DiFelice, nobody holds the presses. After the market started to settle, Dombrowski then picked up Jason Johnson to give the rotation a young veteran anchor, Rondell White to give the lineup a source of regular right-handed sock, and Fernando Vina to notionally lead off and do some of his acrobatics around the keystone. Although Vina and White aren't key components, they were easy upgrades, and Johnson could be expected to provide the staff with at least a symbolic ace, behind which the young trio of Jeremy Bonderman, Mike Maroth, and Nate Cornejo could line up.

Modest ambitions generally yield modest results, but where things got interesting was when Dombrowski found opportunities that only come at the end of the offseason, just before camps open. First, he took advantage of Bill

Bavasi, who apparently had no use for shortstop Carlos Guillen. After a rumored deal with the Mariners for Omar Vizquel fell through, Bavasi apparently wanted to make some deal, any deal, involving Guillen, because Rich Aurilia was his man for the job. So Dombrowski tossed him Ramon Santiago to give Bavasi a token big leaguer, as well as a promising young Venezuelan shortstop inconveniently named Juan Gonzalez.

Guillen filled a basic need for the Tigers,. Santiago and Omar Infante had done nothing to win the job at shortstop in '03, while Guillen was a useful, established regular. But he was also going into his last season before free agency, so he was supposed to be a temporary solution, and let's face it, it was a good move, but not one likely to quicken the pace of Motown baseball fans.

The bigger feat came in early February, when the Tigers signed Pudge Rodriguez, postseason hero par excellence of the world champion Marlins. The Tigers had been in the bidding from early on, but they landed Rodriguez by continuing to pursue him while the Orioles, Mariners, and Cubs all came up with reasons not to. It was the public relations coup that this team desperately needed, if not to make the Tigers a contender in the first year or two of his four-year contract, but to at least put them back on the map in their own city and their sport. Ticket sales picked up, and the deal reaped another reward when Rodriguez's Marlin teammate, closer Ugueth Urbina, also decided to sign with Detroit.

Getting a player of this caliber was something else altogether from Dombrowski's other, middlebrow moves; this was signing a star. Not a Juan Gonzalez, cranky of back and crankier of disposition, but one of the greatest defensive backstops in the game's history, who, after his October heroics, achieved the rare feat of changing his buzz factor long after he became a known quantity. Pudge is an icon, a great player who answered the bell. Not since another Pudge has the game had a catcher so famous for all the right reasons.

And just like that, the Tigers became a pretty fun ballclub. They were even better than the 29 wins they gained; their miserable 12–27 record in one-run ballgames indicates how unlucky they were, all things considered. With an improved lineup, they scored a run and a half more per game. Pudge seemed ageless. Guillen suddenly resembled an MVP-quality player. Carlos Pena finally started doing some hitting, years after everyone had expected so much from him. Pena wasn't the only former prospect who got back on track. Losing Vina to a knee injury early on opened the door for Infante to step back into the lineup. Squeezing into a utility role before claiming more and more starts at the hot corner, Inge was suddenly a worthwhile ballplayer. When Dmitri Young and Rondell White started showing signs of strain, joining Vina on the DL, the club was able to go four-for-four, turning around one-time prospects becoming useful big leaguers when Marcus Thames was called up.

The pitching staff enjoyed its own successes, but these were mostly homegrown pleasures. Johnson chewed up innings, fulfilling at least that aspect of his bargain. Mike Maroth may have been the symbol of the 2003 season for his admirable refusal to dodge a 20-loss season, but he avenged it with a season that put him tenth in the AL in BP's Support-Neutral metrics (which you can find on baseballprospectus.com). Nate Robertson took a big step forward, and might be capable of more. But the most promising of all was Bonderman, who, after a rough start, seemed to grow into a staff ace as the season progressed. On the other hand, perhaps predictably considering the team's record in one-run games, the bullpen was a goat, with Urbina doing only passably well. Esteban Yan was the only truly effective reliever.

So looking at all that, 2004 was a qualified success. It was a reminder that people in Detroit like good baseball, as attendance jumped by nearly 50%, to 1.9 million, the team's best mark since Comerica's second season. And yet, with renewed popularity, comes renewed responsibility, which is why the success of 2004 presents the Tigers with a problem:

Everyone expects more.

This isn't so bad in itself. The Tigers can't count on anything besides performance to really put people in the stands, and that's a good incentive to improve. But at its core, if the message of last season was that hope is back in town, the difficulty will be in telling the masses that it really only stayed for the weekend, and that the drab disappointments of everyday Tigerdom aren't over. In part, that's because outside of Bonderman, the key talents on this team and the sources of its improvement aren't young. Pudge is 33, and although the Dombrowski sewed up Guillen with a three-year contract extension three months into his Tiger career, he's already 29 and tore up his knee at season's end. Rehabilitating players like Pena, Infante, and Inge is nice, but only Infante looks like a decent bet to turn into a star.

To his credit, Dombrowski seems to know this. But in the face of fans' hunger for more spending and more improvement, Dombrowski has been forced to keep his winter activities to a minimum. To some extent, the money that could be spent on big league improvements was already spent last year on Pudge's four-year deal and Guillen's extension. And what little free cash there was to spend was unfortunately used on an ill-advised spending binge to acquire fading closer Troy Percival.

Moreover, that caution is even more justified when you consider the state of the farm system. The Tigers are on the short list for the game's worst organization when it comes to developing or developed talent. Although they can look forward to Curtis Granderson taking over the job in center field at some point during 2005, that's just about the extent of the system's capacity to help the big league club, at least for the foreseeable future. The Tigers harbor high hopes for young pitchers like Kyle Sleeth, Justin Verlander, and Joel Zumaya, but Verlander just got here, and Sleeth and Zumaya both suffered setbacks in '04. As we're prone to say early and often, betting on specific pitching prospects is a fool's errand.

Acting on his knowledge of that weakness, Dombrowski may finally have found the man to help him fix the problems inherited from Randy Smith. David Chadd comes over from the Red Sox with a great reputation for scouting acumen, earned on his watch as Boston's scouting director. Adding Chadd to the management team might even augur a return to Dombrowski's preferred M.O. when he was in Montreal and Florida: relying on a good group of player development people to help cultivate talent by the bushel, and then reap the benefits at the major league level through trades and breakthroughs.

After more than twenty years of Detroit's sputtering on the player development front , fixing the farm system has got to be Dombrowski's highest priority. If Tigers fans can settle in and enjoy what they get from players like Rodriguez and Guillen, and embrace Bonderman as he continues to meet expectations,, they'll hopefully thank Dombrowski and Chadd in the years to come for the work they do now building for the future.. There's no reason to expect 80 wins—indeed, some feel Dombrowski's best-case goal is contention by 2006, and even that's a reach—but at least there are some signs of a baseball organization being built where once there were only ruins.

HITTERS

DAVID ESPINOSA OF Bats: B Throws: R Born: 16-Dec-1981 Age: 23

YEAR	TM	LG	AGE	AB	H	2B	3B	HR	BB	SO	SB	CS	AVG	OBP	SLG	MLVR	EQBA	EQOBP	EQSLG	EQMLVR	VORP	DEFENSE
2002	STO	CLF	20	367	90	13	7	7	62	104	26	17	.245	.356	.376	.049	.222	.313	.334	-.231	-6.6	94-2B -4
2003	LAK	FSL	21	350	95	18	7	4	50	78	13	10	.271	.359	.397	.117	.245	.319	.384	-.136	1.4	57-CF -5 34-RF -5
2004	ERI	EAS	22	511	135	23	5	19	80	134	20	7	.264	.366	.440	.069	.229	.322	.379	-.148	-13.3	127-RF -2
2005	*DET*	*AL*	*23*	*245*	*58*	*12*	*2*	*6*	*31*	*67*	*6*	*3*	*.235*	*.323*	*.364*	*-.144*	*.238*	*.328*	*.380*	*-.122*	*2.7*	*69-RF -3*

Breakout: 21% *Improve: 47%* *Collapse: 30%*

Half of the ill-considered first-round duo handed contracts in 2001 by Jim Bowden (Dane Sardinha was the other guy). Espinosa's scatter-shot arm has forced him out of the infield, but he's athletic enough to handle an outfield corner. The question is whether he'll continue to slug well enough to win a job. Last year's power spike came out of nowhere, and Espinosa's PECOTA comparables list is as strange as it gets, with names ranging from Stan Javier to Mark Bellhorn.

TONY GIARRATANO SS Bats: B Throws: R Born: 29-Nov-1982 Age: 22

YEAR	TM	LG	AGE	AB	H	2B	3B	HR	BB	SO	SB	CS	AVG	OBP	SLG	MLVR	EQBA	EQOBP	EQSLG	EQMLVR	VORP	DEFENSE
2003	ONE	NYP	20	189	62	11	4	3	12	22	9	4	.328	.369	.476	.262	.272	.304	.414	-.101	10.8	44-SS 0
2004	WMI	MDW	21	165	47	6	1	1	25	22	11	3	.285	.383	.352	.097	.249	.333	.308	-.211	-0.4	42-SS 3
2004	LAK	FSL	21	202	76	11	0	5	16	38	14	8	.376	.423	.505	.407	.319	.352	.436	.059	18.0	52-SS 1
2005	*DET*	*AL*	*22*	*313*	*82*	*16*	*2*	*5*	*23*	*55*	*8*	*3*	*.263*	*.319*	*.378*	*-.115*	*.267*	*.324*	*.394*	*-.091*	*14.4*	*84-SS -3*

Breakout: 16% *Improve: 45%* *Collapse: 37%*

Injuries at Tulane derailed what could have been a fine college career, but they also helped the Tigers steal Giarratano in the third round of the '03 draft. The word that comes up most to describe his defense is "reliable," a judgment confirmed by Clay Davenport's ratings. The defense could make a big difference because there are a lot of shortstops with his sort of offensive profile, heavy on batting average and speed but light on power. The ones that can pick it turn into Tony Fernandez or Dave Concepcion; the ones that can't fare considerably worse. Giarratano suffered a shoulder injury that ended his season early, but he's expected to be fully recovered by training camp.

CURTIS GRANDERSON CF Bats: L Throws: R Born: 16-Mar-1981 Age: 24

YEAR	TM	LG	AGE	AB	H	2B	3B	HR	BB	SO	SB	CS	AVG	OBP	SLG	MLVR	EQBA	EQOBP	EQSLG	EQMLVR	VORP	DEFENSE	
2002	ONE	NYP	21	212	73	15	4	3	20	35	9	2	.344	.417	.495	.357	.276	.331	.419	-.041	1.6	50-LF -1	
2003	LAK	FSL	22	476	136	29	10	11	49	91	10	7	.286	.365	.458	.212	.253	.316	.433	-.068	12.7	75-CF -1	51-LF -2
2004	ERI	EAS	23	462	139	19	8	21	80	95	14	8	.301	.405	.513	.252	.258	.356	.438	.016	24.2	121-CF 9	
2004	DET	AL	23	25	6	1	1	0	3	8	0	0	.240	.321	.360	-.132	.280	.303	.400	-.117	0.3		
2005	*DET*	*AL*	*24*	*284*	*75*	*15*	*3*	*8*	*30*	*60*	*4*	*3*	*.264*	*.343*	*.425*	*-.010*	*.268*	*.349*	*.444*	*.018*	*16.3*	*78-CF 1*	

Breakout: 21% *Improve: 45%* *Collapse: 23%*

A gamer, in that the organization likes his work ethic, but also a bona-fide prospect by any reckoning, probably the best the Tigers have produced in several seasons. Reports suggest Granderson can handle center, not because of tremendous raw speed, but because he gets good reads and good jumps. Granderson has no one outstanding skill but instead a diversity of good ones. That generally translates into modest risk and perhaps modest reward, but once in a while everything works out right and the player turns into Bobby Abreu.

CARLOS GUILLEN SS Bats: B Throws: R Born: 30-Sep-1975 Age: 29

YEAR	TM	LG	AGE	AB	H	2B	3B	HR	BB	SO	SB	CS	AVG	OBP	SLG	MLVR	EQBA	EQOBP	EQSLG	EQMLVR	VORP	DEFENSE	
2002	SEA	AL	26	475	124	24	6	9	46	91	4	5	.261	.326	.394	-.031	.276	.344	.417	-.020	20.5	126-SS -20	
2003	SEA	AL	27	388	107	19	3	7	52	64	4	4	.276	.359	.394	.019	.288	.375	.412	.040	24.3	69-SS 0	32-3B -1
2004	DET	AL	28	522	166	37	10	20	52	87	12	5	.318	.379	.542	.279	.329	.394	.568	.332	70.5	131-SS 14	
2005	*DET*	*AL*	*29*	*464*	*132*	*27*	*4*	*14*	*51*	*83*	*8*	*4*	*.285*	*.356*	*.452*	*.064*	*.289*	*.362*	*.472*	*.096*	*39.2*	*124-SS 0*	

Breakout: 7% *Improve: 33%* *Collapse: 37%*

Indians GM Mark Shapiro must be cursing Omar Vizquel's balky knee, which caused the Mariners to void a trade with the Tribe and make an equally ill-advised move by shipping Carlos Guillen to the Tigers. Nobody expected the MVP-caliber season that followed, but Guillen has always had a well-rounded skill set that was underrated because he played in such a poor hitter's park. Guillen has had some injury problems of his own, of course, including a knee bang-up that ended his season three weeks early, and there's virtually no chance he's going to replicate his numbers of a year ago, either in the field or at the plate. But if he retains even half his improvement, he'll be one of the better players in his league.

JACK HANNAHAN 3B Bats: L Throws: R Born: 04-Mar-1980 Age: 25

YEAR	TM	LG	AGE	AB	H	2B	3B	HR	BB	SO	SB	CS	AVG	OBP	SLG	MLVR	EQBA	EQOBP	EQSLG	EQMLVR	VORP	DEFENSE
2002	LAK	FSL	22	246	67	11	1	6	36	44	9	3	.272	.362	.398	.102	.240	.319	.368	-.161	1.6	63-3B 9
2002	ERI	EAS	22	226	54	12	1	3	21	50	2	1	.239	.309	.341	-.151	.204	.267	.298	-.381	-14.1	64-3B 8
2003	ERI	EAS	23	471	121	18	0	9	48	78	2	0	.257	.328	.352	-.101	.216	.279	.306	-.340	-23.4	132-3B 11
2004	ERI	EAS	24	374	102	21	1	8	53	60	7	3	.273	.365	.398	.021	.233	.319	.343	-.200	-2.3	98-3B 17
2005	*DET*	*AL*	*25*	*157*	*37*	*8*	*1*	*3*	*16*	*30*	*2*	*1*	*.237*	*.310*	*.347*	*-.189*	*.240*	*.315*	*.362*	*-.168*	*-2.5*	*45-3B 5*

Breakout: 40% *Improve: 62%* *Collapse: 29%*

Hannahan's defense is Rolenesque according to both scouting reports and our translated numbers, so he'd have an excellent shot at winning the AL Gold Glove if promoted to the big leagues this year. Unfortunately, Hannahan's offensive gains have been modest at best, and he's spent more time in Western Pennsylvania than John Kerry did in October. He needs to get his on-base percentages high enough to have a shot at a sort of supercharged Rance Mulliniks career.

ANDERSON HERNANDEZ SS Bats: B Throws: R Born: 30-Oct-1982 Age: 22

YEAR	TM	LG	AGE	AB	H	2B	3B	HR	BB	SO	SB	CS	AVG	OBP	SLG	MLVR	EQBA	EQOBP	EQSLG	EQMLVR	VORP	DEFENSE
2002	LAK	FSL	19	410	106	13	7	2	33	102	16	14	.259	.310	.339	-.059	.229	.273	.308	-.342	-17.9	121-SS -1
2003	LAK	FSL	20	380	87	11	4	2	27	69	15	7	.229	.278	.295	-.149	.200	.241	.277	-.465	-32.5	98-SS 2
2004	LAK	FSL	21	97	28	3	3	0	6	19	5	0	.289	.327	.381	.029	.224	.248	.286	-.426	-7.2	26-SS 2
2004	ERI	EAS	21	394	108	19	3	5	26	89	17	6	.274	.326	.376	-.074	.237	.283	.326	-.292	-10.2	99-SS -7
2005	*DET*	*AL*	*22*	*353*	*83*	*16*	*3*	*3*	*20*	*77*	*8*	*3*	*.235*	*.277*	*.324*	*-.281*	*.238*	*.281*	*.338*	*-.263*	*-4.5*	*92-SS -5*

Breakout: 32% *Improve: 52%* *Collapse: 31%*

A speedy, glove-first shortstop prospect, Hernandez was dealt to the Mets for a backup catcher, Vance Wilson, which tells you about all you need to know. Anderson is a good first name for prematurely gray cable newscasters, but not for baseball players.

BOBBY HIGGINSON OF Bats: L Throws: R Born: 18-Aug-1970 Age: 34

YEAR	TM	LG	AGE	AB	H	2B	3B	HR	BB	SO	SB	CS	AVG	OBP	SLG	MLVR	EQBA	EQOBP	EQSLG	EQMLVR	VORP	DEFENSE
2002	DET	AL	31	444	125	24	3	10	41	45	12	5	.282	.345	.417	.056	.293	.359	.437	.050	20.7	113-LF -4
2003	DET	AL	32	469	110	13	4	14	59	73	8	8	.235	.320	.369	-.108	.242	.332	.386	-.111	-2.2	111-RF 0
2004	DET	AL	33	448	110	24	2	12	70	84	5	2	.246	.353	.388	-.038	.253	.364	.406	-.016	14.6	105-RF 5
2005	*DET*	*AL*	*34*	*325*	*85*	*16*	*2*	*9*	*46*	*55*	*4*	*2*	*.261*	*.356*	*.406*	*-.015*	*.265*	*.362*	*.423*	*.012*	*12.6*	*91-RF -3*

Breakout: 38% Improve: 61% Collapse: 16%

Is this the most disappointing career of the past two decades? OK, so the Tigers have gotten more out of Higginson than the Yankees did from Hensley Meulens, and he hasn't fallen from grace quite as quickly as Bob Horner, nor has he had the tragic backstory of Doc Gooden or Dernell Stenson. But Higginson's last really productive season was 2000. He's like the lively friend we once had that succumbed to depression, aided by neither Prozac nor therapy, graying one hair at a time. He was a great ballplayer once, really he was.

OMAR INFANTE 2B/SS Bats: R Throws: R Born: 26-Dec-1981 Age: 23

YEAR	TM	LG	AGE	AB	H	2B	3B	HR	BB	SO	SB	CS	AVG	OBP	SLG	MLVR	EQBA	EQOBP	EQSLG	EQMLVR	VORP	DEFENSE
2002	TOL	INT	20	436	117	16	8	4	28	49	19	15	.268	.309	.369	-.075	.249	.294	.350	-.229	-3.3	119-SS 7
2003	TOL	INT	21	224	50	10	0	2	22	32	22	4	.223	.299	.295	-.198	.208	.282	.279	-.375	-12.3	62-SS -6
2003	DET	AL	21	221	49	6	1	0	18	37	6	3	.222	.278	.258	-.351	.228	.287	.256	-.387	-7.1	63-SS 4
2004	DET	AL	22	503	133	27	9	16	40	112	13	7	.264	.317	.449	-.015	.273	.330	.466	.021	26.9	96-2B -1 20-SS 2
2005	*DET*	*AL*	*23*	*464*	*120*	*23*	*4*	*10*	*38*	*79*	*16*	*6*	*.259*	*.316*	*.391*	*-.106*	*.263*	*.321*	*.408*	*-.081*	*17.7*	*121-2B 1*

Breakout: 25% Improve: 49% Collapse: 18%

As we have all learned with Luis Rivas, just because you're in the major leagues at a young age doesn't make you a future star. Careers of low-power infielders in particular are frequently frittered away by the time they're 27 or 28, their speed and defense declining just as their arbitration-eligible years are exhausted. Thus it was a very good sign that Infante demonstrated such growth in the power department. It wasn't some sort of fluke. There are few cheap home runs at Comerica Park, and Infante completely changed his approach at the plate, posting a 0.84 GB:FB ratio after being at 1.44 the year before. PECOTA expects a bit of regression in the near-term, but also cites some favorable names on his comparables list, most notably Ryne Sandberg.

BRANDON INGE C/UT Bats: R Throws: R Born: 19-May-1977 Age: 28

YEAR	TM	LG	AGE	AB	H	2B	3B	HR	BB	SO	SB	CS	AVG	OBP	SLG	MLVR	EQBA	EQOBP	EQSLG	EQMLVR	VORP	DEFENSE
2002	DET	AL	25	321	65	15	3	7	24	101	1	3	.202	.266	.333	-.265	.213	.280	.350	-.279	-5.1	93-C -1
2003	TOL	INT	26	142	39	9	0	5	11	23	3	1	.275	.327	.444	.078	.246	.296	.415	-.135	1.7	35-C 9
2003	DET	AL	26	330	67	15	3	8	24	79	4	4	.203	.265	.339	-.273	.210	.278	.354	-.279	-7.2	100-C 7
2004	DET	AL	27	408	117	15	7	13	32	72	5	4	.287	.340	.453	.055	.297	.352	.475	.095	23.3	62-3B 1 33-C 7
2005	*DET*	*AL*	*28*	*302*	*74*	*15*	*2*	*9*	*25*	*65*	*3*	*3*	*.246*	*.311*	*.399*	*-.114*	*.250*	*.316*	*.416*	*-.089*	*8.7*	*82-C -1*

Breakout: 21% Improve: 38% Collapse: 33%

Inge had a fine season for the Tigers, and showed rare versatility by providing plus defense at both catcher and third base. According to Clay Davenport's ratings, he became the only player in baseball history to play 30 games at both positions in the same season, while scoring a positive defensive rating at each. Still, we ought to be at least a little bit skeptical of a breakout season that comes at age 27, particularly one that was fueled largely by batting average, with a disproportionate number of at-bats against left-handed pitchers. He'll apparently be the Tigers' regular third baseman in 2005. Unfortunately, the potential for disappointment is higher in that role than it would be at catcher or in a super-utility gig.

KODY KIRKLAND 3B Bats: R Throws: R Born: 09-Jun-1983 Age: 22

YEAR	TM	LG	AGE	AB	H	2B	3B	HR	BB	SO	SB	CS	AVG	OBP	SLG	MLVR	EQBA	EQOBP	EQSLG	EQMLVR	VORP	DEFENSE
2003	ONE	NYP	20	254	77	15	11	4	25	60	14	5	.303	.390	.496	.289	.250	.310	.420	-.099	12.0	64-3B -7
2004	WMI	MDW	21	496	117	30	11	10	15	149	6	8	.236	.276	.401	-.038	.205	.233	.348	-.379	-29.1	121-3B -10
2005	*DET*	*AL*	*22*	*348*	*77*	*17*	*3*	*7*	*14*	*107*	*3*	*2*	*.221*	*.270*	*.351*	*-.264*	*.224*	*.275*	*.366*	*-.245*	*-10.7*	*90-3B -7*

Breakout: 20% Improve: 45% Collapse: 29%

After falling a step behind Scott Moore in the organization chart at third, Kirkland had to deal with a slow start made worse by his struggles to hit anything with a little wiggle in it. His task wasn't made any easier by his awful plate discipline, which completely collapsed over the course of the year. Kirkland is a big guy with some power potential, but short of the general premise that 22 is not too young to learn how to hit, there isn't much to look at here.

NOOK LOGAN CF Bats: B Throws: R Born: 28-Nov-1979 Age: 25

YEAR	TM	LG	AGE	AB	H	2B	3B	HR	BB	SO	SB	CS	AVG	OBP	SLG	MLVR	EQBA	EQOBP	EQSLG	EQMLVR	VORP	DEFENSE	
2002	LAK	FSL	22	506	136	14	7	2	40	111	55	16	.269	.321	.336	-.040	.239	.283	.310	-.314	-26.3	121-CF 3	
2003	ERI	EAS	23	514	129	16	7	4	51	103	37	13	.251	.316	.333	-.151	.214	.276	.294	-.364	-34.6	128-CF 12	
2004	TOL	INT	24	426	112	14	9	2	23	95	38	11	.263	.303	.352	-.143	.252	.293	.334	-.252	-13.2	103-CF -6	
2004	DET	AL	24	133	37	5	2	0	13	24	8	2	.278	.340	.346	-.122	.295	.348	.341	-.106	3.2	46-CF -1	
2005	*DET*	*AL*	*25*	*281*	*69*	*12*	*2*	*2*	*20*	*60*	*15*	*5*	*.246*	*.297*	*.332*	*-.226*	*.250*	*.301*	*.347*	*-.207*	*0.4*	*75-CF 0*	

Breakout: 27% Improve: 47% Collapse: 31%

Supposedly doing better with his bunting, which is news of some sort, but at this level of the food chain, nobody's safe, and the fact that DeWayne Wise was claimed off waivers over the winter means there are no guarantees he'll stick as a pinch-runner and sixth outfielder. Logan's top PECOTA comparable is Milt Cuyler.

GILBERTO MEJIA 2B/SS Bats: B Throws: R Born: 01-Sep-1982 Age: 22

YEAR	TM	LG	AGE	AB	H	2B	3B	HR	BB	SO	SB	CS	AVG	OBP	SLG	MLVR	EQBA	EQOBP	EQSLG	EQMLVR	VORP	DEFENSE	
2002	WMI	MDW	19	69	17	4	2	2	11	23	4	2	.246	.341	.449	.167	.222	.303	.403	-.157	-0.7		
2003	WMI	MDW	20	115	23	2	1	1	8	31	0	1	.200	.252	.261	-.232	.179	.226	.248	-.546	-13.2	21-2B -2	
2004	LAK	FSL	21	354	94	13	5	7	35	76	16	10	.266	.330	.390	.029	.231	.285	.357	-.248	-5.6	34-SS 0	27-2B 0
2005	*DET*	*AL*	*22*	*303*	*70*	*15*	*2*	*5*	*23*	*77*	*6*	*3*	*.231*	*.285*	*.340*	*-.245*	*.234*	*.290*	*.355*	*-.226*	*-6.8*	*81-2B -9*	

Breakout: 47% Improve: 65% Collapse: 19%

Mejia has an intriguing potpourri of undercooked skills, the effect of which is a little bit like what happens when you unleash your culinarily-challenged Uncle Leo on the local Korean barbeque joint: What looks promising while still raw may not be so appetizing after it's been on the grill. The Tigers are deep in middle-infield prospects, and Mejia will need a big year to avoid getting lost in the system.

CRAIG MONROE OF Bats: R Throws: R Born: 27-Feb-1977 Age: 28

YEAR	TM	LG	AGE	AB	H	2B	3B	HR	BB	SO	SB	CS	AVG	OBP	SLG	MLVR	EQBA	EQOBP	EQSLG	EQMLVR	VORP	DEFENSE	
2002	TOL	INT	25	358	115	30	4	10	35	57	7	3	.321	.379	.511	.270	.297	.357	.482	.114	17.9	67-LF 2	10-CF -1
2003	DET	AL	26	425	102	18	1	23	27	89	4	2	.240	.287	.449	-.063	.246	.298	.467	-.058	4.9	69-LF -1	33-RF -1
2004	DET	AL	27	447	131	27	3	18	29	79	3	4	.293	.337	.488	.111	.303	.351	.507	.146	26.7	53-LF -6	49-RF 2
2005	*DET*	*AL*	*28*	*421*	*115*	*26*	*2*	*17*	*30*	*83*	*4*	*3*	*.273*	*.322*	*.464*	*.012*	*.276*	*.327*	*.484*	*.043*	*16.6*	*108-LF -1*	

Breakout: 4% Improve: 32% Collapse: 26%

Another Tiger hitter who had a breakout season, as is bound to happen when you tack on a collective 236 runs. Like Brandon Inge, Monroe put together about as good a season as possible for a player with his skills set. He's been a nice, cheap find for Detroit, but Monroe's plate discipline is poor, and he could quickly go from an asset to a liability as the team grows more serious about contention.

SCOTT MOORE 3B Bats: L Throws: R Born: 17-Nov-1983 Age: 21

YEAR	TM	LG	AGE	AB	H	2B	3B	HR	BB	SO	SB	CS	AVG	OBP	SLG	MLVR	EQBA	EQOBP	EQSLG	EQMLVR	VORP	DEFENSE
2003	WMI	MDW	19	372	89	16	6	6	41	110	2	4	.239	.325	.363	.030	.212	.280	.335	-.300	-14.4	95-3B -15
2004	LAK	FSL	20	391	87	13	4	14	49	125	2	4	.223	.322	.384	-.018	.192	.273	.343	-.315	-18.6	114-3B -22
2005	*DET*	*AL*	*21*	*304*	*63*	*12*	*1*	*7*	*27*	*100*	*1*	*1*	*.208*	*.290*	*.331*	*-.261*	*.211*	*.295*	*.345*	*-.243*	*-8.5*	*83-3B -12*

Breakout: 33% Improve: 56% Collapse: 22%

He beat out Kody Kirkland for the third-base job in Lakeland, but that was about all that went his way. It's being said that Moore gained confidence at the plate and in the field, which is scout-speak for not giving up during an awful season. If there's a more credible positive spin, it's that his power is ahead of his other skills.

ERIC MUNSON 3B/1B **Bats: L** **Throws: R** Born: 03-Oct-1977 Age: 27

YEAR	TM	LG	AGE	AB	H	2B	3B	HR	BB	SO	SB	CS	AVG	OBP	SLG	MLVR	EQBA	EQOBP	EQSLG	EQMLVR	VORP	DEFENSE
2002	TOL	INT	24	477	125	30	4	24	77	114	1	3	.262	.367	.493	.175	.238	.343	.453	-.003	12.1	129-1B -13
2003	DET	AL	25	313	75	9	0	18	35	61	3	0	.240	.312	.441	-.027	.245	.320	.452	-.040	16.5	81-3B -9
2004	DET	AL	26	321	68	14	2	19	29	90	1	1	.212	.289	.445	-.105	.219	.298	.467	-.081	3.8	82-3B 2
2005	*MIN*	*AL*	*27*	*341*	*86*	*17*	*1*	*19*	*41*	*85*	*1*	*1*	*.251*	*.336*	*.474*	*.030*	*.249*	*.336*	*.481*	*.029*	*15.7*	*93-3B -6*

Breakout 34% *Improve 62%* *Collapse 14%*

Munson got off to an awful start at the plate, hitting .222 in April and .196 in May, striking out about a quarter of the time, and losing his everyday job to Brandon Inge. As ugly as those numbers are to look at, they're even harder to watch every day, so it wasn't surprising that he fell out of favor with the Tigers, who non-tendered him after the season. Obscured were the improvements in his defense at third, which was never as bad as advertised to begin with, as well as the continued growth in his isolated power, which shot up 35 points on the year. Munson is perceived as a tweener, lacking the glove to be an everyday third baseman or the bat to be a regular at first. But as a cheap waiver-wire find, he represents almost pure upside.

GREG NORTON PH **Bats: B** **Throws: R** Born: 06-Jul-1972 Age: 32

YEAR	TM	LG	AGE	AB	H	2B	3B	HR	BB	SO	SB	CS	AVG	OBP	SLG	MLVR	EQBA	EQOBP	EQSLG	EQMLVR	VORP	DEFENSE
2002	COL	NL	30	168	37	8	1	7	24	52	2	3	.220	.314	.405	-.104	.205	.302	.380	-.201	1.6	18-3B -3
2003	COL	NL	31	179	47	15	0	6	16	47	2	1	.263	.325	.447	-.003	.250	.309	.415	-.108	8.5	27-3B -4
2004	TOL	INT	32	184	38	6	1	4	24	48	1	1	.207	.297	.315	-.240	.191	.280	.290	-.372	-11.2	51-3B 2
2004	DET	AL	32	86	15	1	0	2	12	21	0	0	.174	.276	.256	-.407	.188	.282	.271	-.395	-5.7	
2005	*DET*	*AL*	*32*	*111*	*25*	*5*	*1*	*3*	*13*	*30*	*1*	*0*	*.225*	*.308*	*.360*	*-.181*	*.228*	*.313*	*.376*	*-.160*	*0.7*	*34-3B -5*

Breakout: 51% *Improve: 64%* *Collapse: 24%*

White Sox public address announcer Gene Honda is one of the best in the game, introducing each Chicago hitter with a gruff and ferocious delivery that can be downright inspiring when that player is Frank Thomas or Paul Konerko. When the hitter isn't as intimidating, it comes off as superfluous and outright funny—many vocal cords at Northwestern and The University of Chicago were lost to drunken imitations of Honda's introductions of Greg Norton and Noberto Martin. Norton, two organizations later, is the same dubious hitter he's always been, and without Coors Field to boost his numbers, it may be a while before he's introduced at a major league park again.

CARLOS PENA 1B **Bats: L** **Throws: L** Born: 17-May-1978 Age: 27

YEAR	TM	LG	AGE	AB	H	2B	3B	HR	BB	SO	SB	CS	AVG	OBP	SLG	MLVR	EQBA	EQOBP	EQSLG	EQMLVR	VORP	DEFENSE
2002	SAC	PCL	24	175	42	10	1	10	24	49	3	0	.240	.340	.480	.079	.217	.312	.429	-.108	-1.3	40-1B 2
2002	OAK	AL	24	124	27	4	0	7	15	38	0	0	.218	.305	.419	-.095	.228	.307	.415	-.128	0.9	38-1B 5
2002	DET	AL	24	273	69	13	4	12	26	73	2	2	.253	.321	.462	.054	.261	.335	.482	.042	12.4	70-1B -1
2003	DET	AL	25	452	112	21	6	18	53	123	4	5	.248	.332	.440	.015	.256	.345	.459	.023	16.4	123-1B -9
2004	DET	AL	26	481	116	22	4	27	70	146	7	1	.241	.338	.472	.039	.248	.349	.493	.070	26.9	131-1B -5
2005	*DET*	*AL*	*27*	*439*	*111*	*23*	*3*	*22*	*60*	*124*	*5*	*3*	*.252*	*.347*	*.470*	*.044*	*.255*	*.352*	*.490*	*.074*	*25.1*	*120-1B -3*

Breakout: 20% *Improve: 50%* *Collapse: 15%*

Pena found himself benched and conjuring up unpleasant memories of Travis Lee before going on a tear in the season's final two months, including a 1004 OPS in August. Second-half numbers correlate better with the following season's success than first-half numbers, and Pena is relatively young at 27, so he's a good bet to provide league-average offense at first base. Still, a lot of us were expecting more. Pena's added bulk hasn't boosted his batting average, which isn't likely to get much better with that high strikeout rate. His defense has also been disappointing.

RYAN RABURN 2B/3B **Bats: R** **Throws: R** Born: 17-Apr-1981 Age: 24

YEAR	TM	LG	AGE	AB	H	2B	3B	HR	BB	SO	SB	CS	AVG	OBP	SLG	MLVR	EQBA	EQOBP	EQSLG	EQMLVR	VORP	DEFENSE
2002	WMI	MDW	21	150	33	10	1	6	16	46	0	2	.220	.306	.420	.062	.192	.255	.359	-.329	-6.9	17-3B -2
2003	LAK	FSL	22	325	72	14	3	12	45	89	2	1	.222	.332	.394	.047	.196	.285	.369	-.254	-8.3	82-3B -1
2004	ERI	EAS	23	366	110	29	4	16	47	96	3	0	.301	.390	.533	.254	.260	.341	.460	.021	22.1	95-2B -12
2004	DET	AL	23	29	4	1	0	0	2	15	1	0	.138	.194	.172	-.700	.138	.146	.138	-.881	-3.1	
2005	*DET*	*AL*	*24*	*256*	*62*	*14*	*1*	*9*	*25*	*77*	*2*	*1*	*.241*	*.321*	*.407*	*-.089*	*.244*	*.326*	*.425*	*-.064*	*11.5*	*71-2B -9*

Breakout: 22% *Improve: 51%* *Collapse: 21%*

(continued next page)

Ryan Raburn *(continued)*

Sleeper. Raburn is popular in-house because he didn't let a career-threatening dislocated hip stop him in '01. Perhaps typically, he worked his way through hitting with a broken finger in the early going, compiling an impressive .296 EqA in July and .310 EqA in August, and earning a September cup of coffee. This was Rayburn's first full professional season at second base and the results were mixed at best. The Tigers should have an opening at third base sooner than at second, and while Raburn must continue to develop, his power and plate discipline could well prove to be good enough for the position.

IVAN RODRIGUEZ — C — Bats: R — Throws: R — Born: 30-Nov-1971 — Age: 33

YEAR	TM	LG	AGE	AB	H	2B	3B	HR	BB	SO	SB	CS	AVG	OBP	SLG	MLVR	EQBA	EQOBP	EQSLG	EQMLVR	VORP	DEFENSE
2002	TEX	AL	30	408	128	32	2	19	25	71	5	4	.314	.353	.542	.196	.313	.357	.542	.217	41.1	97-C 7
2003	FLA	NL	31	511	152	36	3	16	55	92	10	6	.297	.369	.474	.189	.303	.373	.487	.154	49.1	126-C 7
2004	DET	AL	32	527	176	32	2	19	41	91	7	4	.334	.383	.510	.261	.345	.397	.534	.307	63.1	120-C -3
2005	*DET*	*AL*	*33*	*500*	*146*	*31*	*2*	*17*	*40*	*87*	*7*	*3*	*.292*	*.346*	*.464*	*.069*	*.296*	*.352*	*.484*	*.101*	*37.7*	*129-C -1*

Breakout: 2% *Improve: 25%* *Collapse: 32%*

Year One was a roaring success. Rodriguez flirted with the league batting crown for much of the season, provided plenty of extra-base power, and broke Johnny Bench's record by winning his 11th Gold Glove (his caught-stealing numbers aren't as good as they once were, but he prevents most runners from attempting to steal in the first place). More importantly, he actually seemed to enjoy playing in Detroit, actively participating in promotional and charity work, and providing some badly needed credibility to a franchise whose once-loyal fans were convinced that the organization was throwing in the towel.

But Rodriguez's was a four-year contract. I-Rod contributed 8.2 wins above replacement last season after factoring in his defense. PECOTA, which understands the long history of poor aging patterns from catchers, figures that Rodriguez will be worth 5.9 wins this year, but just 3.9 in 2006 and 2.7 in 2007. That would work out to $40 million for 20.7 wins, or about $1.93 million per, which is a pretty decent deal by today's standards, and especially compared to that bilked out of the Red Sox by Scott Boras for Jason Varitek. The trouble is that there is the usual structural problem involving escalating salaries and declining production: This could easily look like a bad deal in 2007, even if the Tigers got pretty good bang for their buck up to that point. We don't mean to take away from Rodriguez's fine season, nor from Dave Dombrowski's ballsy signing. This doesn't need to be a problem; it's just something that the Tigers need to be prepared for, rather than becoming complacent after Pudge's 2004 success.

ALEX SANCHEZ — Menace — Bats: L — Throws: L — Born: 26-Aug-1976 — Age: 28

YEAR	TM	LG	AGE	AB	H	2B	3B	HR	BB	SO	SB	CS	AVG	OBP	SLG	MLVR	EQBA	EQOBP	EQSLG	EQMLVR	VORP	DEFENSE	
2002	MIL	NL	25	394	114	10	7	1	31	62	37	14	.289	.343	.358	-.019	.294	.346	.367	-.073	14.6	86-CF 0	16-LF 1
2003	MIL	NL	26	163	46	10	3	0	7	28	8	6	.282	.316	.380	-.064	.287	.309	.372	-.141	2.2	36-CF 1	
2003	DET	AL	26	394	114	13	5	1	18	46	44	18	.289	.320	.355	-.104	.301	.335	.372	-.081	9.5	99-CF -9	
2004	DET	AL	27	332	107	9	3	2	7	50	19	13	.322	.335	.386	-.037	.333	.350	.403	.020	9.5	73-CF -7	
2005	*DET*	*AL*	*28*	*419*	*117*	*18*	*5*	*3*	*17*	*62*	*24*	*9*	*.279*	*.309*	*.363*	*-.142*	*.283*	*.314*	*.379*	*-.118*	*7.6*	*106-CF -1*	

Breakout: 4% *Improve: 22%* *Collapse: 39%*

We often talk about the perils of empty batting averages. Sanchez hit .322, but almost never draws a walk, almost never hits for power, runs his team out of rallies on the basepaths, plays a middling center field, and missed much of the season with a hamstring injury. He hits .322 and he's a reasonable if overrated player; he hits .279, as PECOTA thinks he's going to do, and he's a Big Problem. The Tigers, to their credit, threatened to non-tender him before agreeing to a cheap, one-year deal. Curtis Granderson could take over sooner than anyone thinks, perhaps even by Opening Day.

CHRIS SHELTON — 1B — Bats: R — Throws: R — Born: 26-Jun-1980 — Age: 25

YEAR	TM	LG	AGE	AB	H	2B	3B	HR	BB	SO	SB	CS	AVG	OBP	SLG	MLVR	EQBA	EQOBP	EQSLG	EQMLVR	VORP	DEFENSE	
2002	HIC	SAL	22	332	113	27	2	17	47	74	0	0	.340	.425	.587	.459	.272	.343	.475	.056	15.0	51-1B -5	24-C -6
2003	LYN	CRL	23	315	113	24	1	21	68	67	1	4	.359	.478	.641	.612	.303	.412	.569	.331	48.0	39-1B 0	28-C 0
2003	ALT	EAS	23	122	34	10	1	0	8	23	0	1	.279	.331	.377	.013	.246	.281	.336	-.276	-7.1	20-1B 1	10-C 0
2004	DET	AL	24	46	9	1	0	1	9	14	0	0	.196	.321	.283	-.260	.200	.311	.267	-.335	-1.1		
2004	TOL	INT	24	62	21	2	0	0	10	13	0	0	.339	.425	.371	.163	.295	.342	.328	-.136	-0.2		
2005	*DET*	*AL*	*25*	*226*	*61*	*12*	*1*	*8*	*30*	*51*	*0*	*1*	*.269*	*.359*	*.439*	*.039*	*.273*	*.365*	*.458*	*.068*	*19.1*	*64-1B 1*	

Breakout: 13% *Improve: 35%* *Collapse: 37%*

Rule 5 picks have awfully high injury rates, and Shelton missed about five weeks with plantar fascitis, first on the Disabled List and then on a rehab stint with Toledo, and was used sparingly in Detroit when he was around. The Tigers dispatched him to the AFL to make up for the lost playing time, and he responded by hitting a monster .404/.470/.667. The organization doesn't seem serious about using him as a backup catcher—most of his appearances in the AFL were at DH—and there's less need for an emergency backstop with Brandon Inge also on the roster, but Shelton looks like a legitimate major leaguer based on his potent bat alone.

JASON SMITH INF Bats: L Throws: R Born: 24-Jul-1977 Age: 27

YEAR	TM	LG	AGE	AB	H	2B	3B	HR	BB	SO	SB	CS	AVG	OBP	SLG	MLVR	EQBA	EQOBP	EQSLG	EQMLVR	VORP	DEFENSE	
2002	DUR	INT	24	206	57	11	2	4	10	44	5	1	.277	.312	.408	-.013	.254	.293	.380	-.185	1.1	46-SS 3	
2003	DUR	INT	25	515	147	20	14	15	11	128	14	9	.285	.304	.466	.049	.260	.288	.440	-.103	14.8	87-SS -6	26-2B -1
2004	TOL	INT	26	122	33	8	2	3	6	26	5	1	.270	.300	.443	-.015	.264	.295	.430	-.101	2.9	32-3B -2	
2004	DET	AL	26	155	37	7	4	5	8	37	1	2	.239	.280	.432	-.135	.247	.292	.448	-.095	3.1	30-2B 0	11-SS 1
2005	*DET*	*AL*	*27*	*250*	*62*	*13*	*2*	*7*	*10*	*60*	*5*	*3*	*.247*	*.279*	*.404*	*-.161*	*.251*	*.284*	*.421*	*-.137*	*7.0*	*66-2B -2*	

Breakout: 16% *Improve: 38%* *Collapse: 40%*

A cast-off from the Devil Rays organization, Smith found himself in the starting lineup in September after Carlos Guillen got hurt. The results were about what was to be expected from his minor league numbers, which projected moderate power, excellent speed, and reasonable defense, but extreme shortcomings in the plate discipline department. He wouldn't hurt the team in a backup role, but the Tigers have gone in a different direction, signing Ramon Martinez instead.

JUAN TEJEDA 1B Bats: R Throws: R Born: 26-Jan-1982 Age: 23

YEAR	TM	LG	AGE	AB	H	2B	3B	HR	BB	SO	SB	CS	AVG	OBP	SLG	MLVR	EQBA	EQOBP	EQSLG	EQMLVR	VORP	DEFENSE
2002	WMI	MDW	20	524	157	34	6	11	60	89	5	1	.300	.372	.450	.254	.265	.323	.408	-.080	0.5	134-1B -13
2003	LAK	FSL	21	461	129	28	4	10	56	68	6	3	.280	.360	.423	.157	.251	.318	.406	-.103	-3.1	109-1B -19
2004	ERI	EAS	22	457	132	29	3	23	51	102	0	0	.289	.362	.516	.181	.252	.318	.447	-.045	5.3	117-1B -7
2005	*DET*	*AL*	*23*	*323*	*82*	*18*	*1*	*11*	*29*	*68*	*1*	*1*	*.253*	*.320*	*.418*	*-.068*	*.257*	*.325*	*.436*	*-.041*	*8.2*	*87-1B -7*

Breakout: 22% *Improve: 46%* *Collapse: 28%*

Tejada is filling out into more of a slugger's profile, with both his isolated power and his strikeout rate well up at Erie. A player like this might as well go for the gusto, because he's not going to win any jobs with his defense or athleticism. Tejada's offensive game is reasonably well rounded, and he's not as far behind some more heralded first-base prospects as you might think.

MARCUS THAMES OF Bats: R Throws: R Born: 06-Mar-1977 Age: 28

YEAR	TM	LG	AGE	AB	H	2B	3B	HR	BB	SO	SB	CS	AVG	OBP	SLG	MLVR	EQBA	EQOBP	EQSLG	EQMLVR	VORP	DEFENSE	
2002	COH	INT	25	386	80	21	3	13	43	71	5	4	.207	.297	.378	-.121	.192	.282	.352	-.285	-16.5	104-CF -8	
2003	COH	INT	26	194	54	15	2	2	17	48	3	4	.278	.332	.407	.034	.263	.321	.392	-.108	2.3	39-CF -1	11-RF 0
2003	OKL	PCL	26	66	17	4	0	2	8	12	1	0	.258	.338	.409	.039	.212	.269	.333	-.325	-4.1		
2003	TEX	AL	26	73	15	2	0	1	8	18	0	1	.205	.298	.274	-.328	.208	.289	.264	-.381	-4.3	15-RF 1	
2004	TOL	INT	27	234	77	21	1	24	33	40	4	1	.329	.410	.735	.632	.300	.383	.670	.423	36.7	60-RF -8	
2004	DET	AL	27	165	42	12	0	10	16	42	0	1	.255	.326	.509	.081	.264	.332	.528	.103	8.4	38-LF -1	
2005	*DET*	*AL*	*28*	*268*	*67*	*15*	*1*	*12*	*29*	*60*	*2*	*1*	*.252*	*.328*	*.448*	*-.015*	*.255*	*.334*	*.467*	*.013*	*11.7*	*74-RF -2*	

Breakout: 13% *Improve: 39%* *Collapse: 25%*

He didn't outshine Cal Pickering, but as the other journeyman who finally slugged his way into the majors to stay, Thames did just fine. Thames isn't likely to have a long career—players who make it this late usually leave sooner than later—but he's capable of putting together a couple of useful seasons in Motown, in a Bubba Trammell sort of way.

FERNANDO VINA 2B Bats: L Throws: R Born: 16-Apr-1969 Age: 36

YEAR	TM	LG	AGE	AB	H	2B	3B	HR	BB	SO	SB	CS	AVG	OBP	SLG	MLVR	EQBA	EQOBP	EQSLG	EQMLVR	VORP	DEFENSE
2002	STL	NL	33	622	168	29	5	1	44	36	17	11	.270	.333	.338	-.068	.278	.336	.351	-.127	18.0	144-2B -9
2003	STL	NL	34	259	65	14	4	4	11	24	4	4	.251	.309	.382	-.088	.259	.310	.399	-.122	4.3	60-2B -8
2004	DET	AL	35	115	26	5	0	0	9	9	2	1	.226	.308	.270	-.304	.252	.307	.278	-.303	-2.5	29-2B 0
2005	*DET*	*AL*	*36*	*218*	*54*	*10*	*1*	*2*	*14*	*19*	*3*	*2*	*.247*	*.308*	*.327*	*-.212*	*.250*	*.313*	*.341*	*-.192*	*2.3*	*60-2B -4*

Breakout: 20% *Improve: 39%* *Collapse: 34%*

(continued next page)

Fernando Vina *(continued)*

While the Ivan Rodriguez and Rondell White signings are at least debatable both then and now, bringing in Vina for two years was one of the most inexplicable deals in recent memory. Frankly, the fact that he got hurt early on, allowing Omar Infante to work his way into the lineup, was probably the best-case scenario for the Tigers. The knee isn't healing well, so odds are he'll miss Opening Day. The only question left is whether the Tigers are willing to eat the last year of his contract and simply release him.

RONDELL WHITE LF **Bats: R** **Throws: R** Born: 23-Feb-1972 Age: 33

YEAR	TM	LG	AGE	AB	H	2B	3B	HR	BB	SO	SB	CS	AVG	OBP	SLG	MLVR	EQBA	EQOBP	EQSLG	EQMLVR	VORP	DEFENSE
2002	NYY	AL	30	455	109	21	0	14	25	86	1	2	.240	.288	.378	-.146	.249	.296	.390	-.168	-4.6	109-LF 9
2003	SDP	NL	31	413	115	17	3	18	25	71	1	4	.278	.330	.465	.112	.288	.337	.489	.081	17.8	94-LF -2
2003	KCR	AL	31	75	26	6	1	4	6	8	0	0	.347	.400	.613	.396	.338	.390	.622	.416	9.9	17-LF 0
2004	DET	AL	32	448	121	21	2	19	39	77	1	2	.270	.337	.453	.038	.279	.349	.471	.067	19.3	64-LF -4
2005	*DET*	*AL*	*33*	*406*	*108*	*20*	*1*	*15*	*29*	*72*	*1*	*1*	*.267*	*.324*	*.432*	*-.031*	*.271*	*.330*	*.451*	*-.003*	*10.9*	*106-LF -5*

Breakout: 6% *Improve: 37%* *Collapse: 26%*

The .270 batting average, decent power and intermittent injury problems were exactly what we've come to expect from White (although, actually, he hit a little bit better than PECOTA projected). The athleticism White exhibited early in his career has probably helped him to survive this long, but it's gone now, and it's more a matter of surviving this last year of his two-year deal than thriving.

DMITRI YOUNG DH **Bats: B** **Throws: R** Born: 11-Oct-1973 Age: 31

YEAR	TM	LG	AGE	AB	H	2B	3B	HR	BB	SO	SB	CS	AVG	OBP	SLG	MLVR	EQBA	EQOBP	EQSLG	EQMLVR	VORP	DEFENSE
2002	DET	AL	28	201	57	14	0	7	12	39	2	0	.284	.329	.458	.081	.299	.337	.478	.076	12.2	14-1B -1
2003	DET	AL	29	562	167	34	7	29	58	130	2	1	.297	.372	.537	.262	.305	.383	.561	.277	60.7	58-LF -1 16-3B -1
2004	DET	AL	30	389	106	23	2	18	33	71	0	1	.272	.336	.481	.074	.281	.346	.501	.106	23.7	24-1B -1
2005	*DET*	*AL*	*31*	*432*	*123*	*26*	*2*	*21*	*38*	*89*	*1*	*1*	*.285*	*.348*	*.497*	*.110*	*.289*	*.354*	*.519*	*.144*	*31.3*	*114-DH*

Breakout: 9% *Improve: 39%* *Collapse: 28%*

PECOTA nailed his year almost exactly, right down to the playing time missed to injury—though Young's broken leg came on a freak play and wasn't the chronic sort of problem you might expect a slow, 250-pound guy to have. In spite of his apparent late peak, his lack of athleticism is not likely to age very well, but Young is one of the more lovable guys in the game and we wish him the best, our forecasting system be damned.

PITCHERS

MATT ANDERSON **Bats: R** **Throws: R** Born: 17-Aug-1976 Age: 28

YEAR	TM	LG	AGE	G	GS	IP	H	BB	SO	HR	ERA	EQERA	EQH9	EQBB9	EQSO9	EQHR9	PERA	VORP	STF
2002	DET	AL	25	12	0	11.0	17	8	8	1	9.00	10.03	10.8	5.4	6.2	0.8	6.17	-5.7	-20
2003	DET	AL	26	23	0	23.3	25	9	13	5	5.41	6.04	9.7	3.2	4.8	2.0	5.64	-1.2	-25
2003	TOL	INT	26	23	5	38.0	50	8	31	4	3.79	5.79	10.8	2.2	5.8	1.4	5.54	0.2	-15
2004	TOL	INT	27	34	0	34.0	41	23	25	5	5.82	6.82	10.1	6.3	5.5	1.6	6.27	-2.5	-28
2005	*DET*	*AL*	*28*	*25*	*3*	*43.3*	*45*	*23*	*31*	*6*	*5.47*	*5.52*	*9.3*	*4.3*	*5.7*	*1.4*	*5.41*	*2.8*	*-13*

Breakout: 37% *Improve: 54%* *Collapse: 16%*

When you draft a starting pitcher first overall and he gets hurt, at least you can hope that he'll make a decent reliever one day. When you draft Matt Anderson and he gets hurt, the hope becomes that one day he'll make a decent Toledo Mudhen. There's no way a pitcher can walk this many Triple-A hitters without something being terribly wrong. The over/under on his remaining MLB innings pitched is about 35.

KENNY BAUGH **Bats: R** **Throws: R** Born: 05-Feb-1979 Age: 26

YEAR	TM	LG	AGE	G	GS	IP	H	BB	SO	HR	ERA	EQERA	EQH9	EQBB9	EQSO9	EQHR9	PERA	VORP	STF
2003	ERI	EAS	24	19	19	109.7	111	32	58	16	4.59	6.03	10.5	3.0	4.1	2.3	6.66	-11.8	-13
2004	ERI	EAS	25	24	24	142.7	154	41	107	13	3.72	4.69	9.8	2.7	5.0	1.1	5.15	6.8	1
2005	*DET*	*AL*	*26*	*11*	*10*	*57.3*	*63*	*20*	*36*	*9*	*5.12*	*5.17*	*9.9*	*2.8*	*5.0*	*1.4*	*5.07*	*3.9*	*-2*

Breakout: 17% *Improve: 44%* *Collapse: 22%*

Finally healthy after losing much of '02 and '03 to labrum surgery, Baugh seems to have retained a good amount of velocity. He came to camp throwing in the 90s, and didn't lose velocity during the year at Erie. He also showed good command of his curve and change, so he may yet reclaim some of his old prospect status.

JEREMY BONDERMAN **Bats: R** **Throws: R** Born: 28-Oct-1982 Age: 22

YEAR	TM	LG	AGE	G	GS	IP	H	BB	SO	HR	ERA	EQERA	EQH9	EQBB9	EQSO9	EQHR9	PERA	VORP	STF
2002	MOD	CLF	19	25	25	144.7	129	55	160	15	3.61	5.78	9.3	3.9	5.9	1.5	5.37	3.4	22
2003	DET	AL	20	33	28	162.0	193	58	108	23	5.56	6.11	9.7	3.0	5.8	1.2	4.87	-8.5	19
2004	DET	AL	21	33	32	184.0	168	73	168	24	4.89	4.59	8.0	3.2	7.8	1.0	3.74	26.4	35
2005	*DET*	*AL*	*22*	*28*	*27*	*160.3*	*164*	*59*	*133*	*20*	*4.70*	*4.75*	*9.3*	*2.9*	*6.7*	*1.2*	*4.50*	*18.3*	*12*

Breakout: 13% *Improve: 41%* *Collapse: 18%*

In a season of progress, Bonderman spotted his fastball-slider combination more aggressively, increasing his strikeout rate without any trade-off in terms of command. What's more, he improved dramatically as the season went on, compiling a 3.70 ERA after the All-Star break and a 2.53 ERA in September. His ERAs have been higher than his peripheral stats suggest they should be, and while that can sometimes be a sign of a pitcher who has difficulty working from the stretch, for the most part it's just plain old bad luck. Bonderman should beat that PECOTA, and might even be one of the best pitchers in his league. To the Tigers' credit, they've done what they can to contain any damage from his premature promotion, limiting their barely-legal prodigy to 90 pitches per start last season.

STEVE COLYER **Bats: L** **Throws: L** Born: 22-Feb-1979 Age: 26

YEAR	TM	LG	AGE	G	GS	IP	H	BB	SO	HR	ERA	EQERA	EQH9	EQBB9	EQSO9	EQHR9	PERA	VORP	STF
2002	JAX	SOU	23	59	0	62.7	50	40	68	6	3.44	5.18	9.3	5.8	7.5	1.7	6.44	-5.3	-15
2003	LVG	PCL	24	44	0	47.7	44	22	50	1	3.21	3.72	7.8	4.7	8.0	0.2	3.72	9.6	5
2003	LAD	NL	24	13	0	19.7	22	9	16	0	2.74	2.79	9.8	3.7	6.5	0.0	4.66	6.3	-2
2004	TOL	INT	25	25	0	25.7	26	25	23	2	4.20	4.68	8.6	9.0	6.5	0.7	5.40	0.6	-25
2004	DET	AL	25	41	0	32.0	33	24	31	8	6.47	6.19	9.0	5.9	8.2	2.0	5.62	-1.7	-12
2005	*DET*	*AL*	*26*	*22*	*1*	*29.7*	*29*	*21*	*25*	*4*	*4.96*	*5.01*	*8.8*	*5.5*	*6.8*	*1.1*	*5.42*	*3.3*	*-9*

Breakout: 29% *Improve: 42%* *Collapse: 23%*

Acquired last April for Cody Ross in a deal that involved swapping a token outfielder for a notional second lefty. If somebody came out ahead, it would take a mass spectrometer to measure how. He won't have much of a future if his command remains as bad as it's been.

NATE CORNEJO **Bats: R** **Throws: R** Born: 24-Sep-1979 Age: 25

YEAR	TM	LG	AGE	G	GS	IP	H	BB	SO	HR	ERA	EQERA	EQH9	EQBB9	EQSO9	EQHR9	PERA	VORP	STF
2002	TOL	INT	22	21	20	132.3	163	31	86	11	4.42	5.32	10.4	2.3	4.9	0.9	5.11	7.0	0
2002	DET	AL	22	9	9	50.0	63	18	23	6	5.04	5.62	10.1	2.9	4.0	1.1	4.89	0.2	-11
2003	DET	AL	23	32	32	194.7	236	58	46	18	4.67	4.84	10.3	2.6	2.1	0.8	4.79	20.6	-14
2004	DET	AL	24	5	5	25.7	42	11	12	4	8.40	8.10	12.2	3.4	3.7	1.0	6.41	-7.2	-16
2005	*DET*	*AL*	*25*	*17*	*14*	*83.3*	*105*	*28*	*42*	*8*	*5.30*	*5.35*	*11.4*	*2.7*	*4.1*	*0.9*	*5.38*	*4.6*	*-6*

Breakout: 15% *Improve: 57%* *Collapse: 22%*

Cornejo's season ended in July when it was revealed that he had a small labrum tear in his shoulder. At least now we have an explanation for his bizarre 2003, in which he put together a respectable season while posting the lowest strikeout rate in half a century. Cornejo's velocity was down in 2003 and it's likely he'd been pitching with the injury for some time. One wonders whether the injury would have been diagnosed sooner if he hadn't managed to spend a full season retiring batters with smoke and mirrors.

EULOGIO DE LA CRUZ Bats: R Throws: R Born: 12-Mar-1984 Age: 21

YEAR	TM	LG	AGE	G	GS	IP	H	BB	SO	HR	ERA	EQERA	EQH9	EQBB9	EQSO9	EQHR9	PERA	VORP	STF
2004	WMI	MDW	20	54	0	54.0	51	33	44	2	3.83	6.39	9.3	7.1	4.4	0.7	6.02	-2.3	-25
2005	*DET*	*AL*	*21*	*11*	*1*	*15.3*	*17*	*11*	*10*	*2*	*5.89*	*5.96*	*10.2*	*5.9*	*5.0*	*1.0*	*6.33*	*0.0*	*-23*

Breakout: 20% *Improve: 50%* *Collapse: 25%*

De la Cruz hits triple digits on the radar gun but otherwise has little to recommend him, as his fastball is straight, his command is poor, his build is slight, and he's yet to develop a useful secondary pitch. We haven't done a comprehensive study on how pitchers like this progress, but it's a safe guess that the success rate is pretty low. More fundamentally, it's hard to see how useful 100 mph heat can be if it can't even be leveraged into an above-average strikeout rate in the Midwest League.

CRAIG DINGMAN Bats: R Throws: R Born: 12-Mar-1974 Age: 31

YEAR	TM	LG	AGE	G	GS	IP	H	BB	SO	HR	ERA	EQERA	EQH9	EQBB9	EQSO9	EQHR9	PERA	VORP	STF
2003	YUC	MEX	29	27	0	26.3	25	9	20	1	3.08	4.40	8.2	3.1	6.9	0.6	3.77	2.9	4
2003	CCN	MEX	29	15	0	17.0	16	4	17	1	4.24	7.20	8.1	1.8	8.1	0.9	3.60	2.2	17
2003	IOW	PCL	29	11	0	18.0	14	7	12	0	2.00	2.70	7.6	4.3	5.4	0.0	3.24	4.4	-2
2004	TOL	INT	30	21	0	25.7	26	11	31	5	4.55	5.11	9.1	4.0	8.8	2.2	5.47	0.4	3
2004	DET	AL	30	24	0	29.3	33	22	16	3	6.76	6.14	9.5	5.8	4.6	0.9	5.22	-1.5	-23
2005	*DET*	*AL*	*31*	*17*	*2*	*30.7*	*30*	*17*	*24*	*4*	*5.11*	*5.17*	*8.9*	*4.4*	*6.4*	*1.3*	*5.14*	*3.0*	*-8*

Breakout: 32% *Improve: 58%* *Collapse: 26%*

It's plenty easy to make fun of millionaires, be they players or owners, quibbling over a hundred thousand here and there, but there are a lot of less-heralded ballplayers for whom a steady major league paycheck over the course of even a season or two could make a huge difference in terms of their financial future. That's why Dingman went to Mexico to pitch at the age of 29. In spite of strikeout rates that have been impressive at times, he doesn't keep the ball down or in the strike zone, so he'll need to look for another employer.

FRANKLYN GERMAN Bats: R Throws: R Born: 20-Jan-1980 Age: 25

YEAR	TM	LG	AGE	G	GS	IP	H	BB	SO	HR	ERA	EQERA	EQH9	EQBB9	EQSO9	EQHR9	PERA	VORP	STF
2002	MID	TXS	22	37	0	41.3	28	27	59	0	3.05	3.92	6.7	6.5	9.9	0.2	3.46	9.3	16
2002	TOL	INT	22	23	0	22.7	15	7	31	0	1.59	2.11	6.3	3.0	10.5	0.0	2.11	8.3	35
2003	TOL	INT	23	24	0	29.3	21	9	32	2	2.46	3.33	7.3	3.3	8.3	1.0	3.33	6.8	16
2003	DET	AL	23	45	0	44.7	47	45	41	5	6.04	6.04	8.7	8.5	7.9	1.0	5.64	-1.7	-10
2004	TOL	INT	24	49	0	49.0	46	25	60	6	4.59	4.75	8.4	4.8	8.9	1.1	4.37	6.5	3
2004	DET	AL	24	16	0	14.7	17	11	8	4	7.35	8.16	10.0	6.3	4.4	1.9	6.91	-4.8	-35
2005	*DET*	*AL*	*25*	*33*	*1*	*43.3*	*40*	*25*	*38*	*5*	*4.58*	*4.63*	*8.4*	*4.5*	*7.0*	*1.1*	*4.71*	*5.8*	*-3*

Breakout: 15% *Improve: 46%* *Collapse: 18%*

German's situation isn't quite as dire as Matt Anderson's, but he's another reminder that, whatever other skills a pitcher might bring to the table, he isn't a major leaguer until he develops at least some modicum of command. The odds of a breakout are not very high. Of the top 10 pitchers on German's PECOTA comparables list, only one, Sammy Stewart, can be described as having put together a moderately valuable major league career; the rest are folks like Ken Ryan and Lance McCullers. German pitched in Venezuela, and pitched well, but a few winter ball innings do not negate a career's worth of unacceptable walk rates.

ROB HENKEL Bats: R Throws: L Born: 03-Aug-1978 Age: 26

YEAR	TM	LG	AGE	G	GS	IP	H	BB	SO	HR	ERA	EQERA	EQH9	EQBB9	EQSO9	EQHR9	PERA	VORP	STF
2002	JUP	FSL	23	14	12	75.3	55	22	82	4	2.51	4.02	8.2	3.0	7.3	1.0	3.89	13.2	23
2002	PME	EAS	23	13	13	70.0	54	27	68	6	3.86	4.48	8.3	3.8	7.0	1.3	4.34	9.0	17
2003	ERI	EAS	24	16	16	82.7	67	27	70	7	3.37	4.04	8.6	3.3	6.4	1.3	4.76	7.1	14
2005	*DET*	*AL*	*26*	*18*	*14*	*85.7*	*87*	*40*	*57*	*12*	*4.92*	*4.98*	*9.2*	*3.7*	*5.4*	*1.3*	*4.89*	*8.7*	*-2*

Breakout: 29% *Improve: 50%* *Collapse: 21%*

Henkel had shoulder surgery to repair a torn labrum at mid-season after needing Tommy John surgery when he was pitching for UCLA, so his star is more than a little dim these days. The ordinary course of action would be to convert him to the bullpen, where the strain on his arm might be lessened, but Henkel's strength is mixing several good pitches rather than relying on one dominant one, so he doesn't fit that profile.

JASON JOHNSON Bats: R Throws: R Born: 27-Oct-1973 Age: 31

YEAR	TM	LG	AGE	G	GS	IP	H	BB	SO	HR	ERA	EQERA	EQH9	EQBB9	EQSO9	EQHR9	PERA	VORP	STF
2002	BAL	AL	28	22	22	131.3	141	41	97	19	4.59	4.43	9.4	2.6	6.4	1.2	4.92	19.3	10
2003	BAL	AL	29	32	32	189.7	216	80	118	22	4.18	4.41	9.4	3.6	5.4	1.0	4.80	28.2	4
2004	DET	AL	30	33	33	196.7	222	60	125	22	5.12	5.13	9.4	2.5	5.4	0.9	4.21	15.2	9
2005	*DET*	*AL*	*31*	*27*	*25*	*147.3*	*165*	*49*	*95*	*18*	*4.81*	*4.86*	*10.1*	*2.6*	*5.2*	*1.2*	*4.84*	*15.1*	*3*

Breakout: 8% *Improve: 41%* *Collapse: 26%*

OPS against

Year	Overall	Runners In Scoring Position
2003	774	686
2004	772	898

Is a table worth 100 words? Johnson's hit rate, strikeout rate, and home-run rate were left essentially unchanged from 2003. He gave up a few more doubles and triples, but compensated by walking one fewer hitter per appearance. And yet his ERA was up nearly a full point, simply because he gave up what he gave up at inopportune times. Johnson's true level of ability lies somewhere in between his past two seasons. The hope is that the Tigers won't need to sign third-tier free agents like this as their farm system becomes more robust.

GARY KNOTTS Bats: R Throws: R Born: 12-Feb-1977 Age: 28

YEAR	TM	LG	AGE	G	GS	IP	H	BB	SO	HR	ERA	EQERA	EQH9	EQBB9	EQSO9	EQHR9	PERA	VORP	STF
2002	CLG	PCL	25	42	0	53.0	53	32	44	4	4.25	4.59	8.8	5.8	5.8	0.7	5.12	2.7	-14
2002	FLA	NL	25	28	0	30.7	21	16	21	6	4.40	4.45	7.9	4.1	5.7	1.9	4.76	3.3	-13
2003	TOL	INT	26	13	13	79.0	98	28	63	15	5.13	6.48	11.3	3.6	5.9	2.5	7.20	-13.3	-22
2003	DET	AL	26	20	18	95.3	111	47	51	14	6.04	6.15	9.9	4.2	4.7	1.2	5.38	-5.6	-17
2004	DET	AL	27	36	19	135.3	142	58	81	20	5.25	5.10	9.2	3.5	5.1	1.2	4.56	9.9	-10
2005	*DET*	*AL*	*28*	*22*	*14*	*85.7*	*96*	*40*	*52*	*13*	*5.56*	*5.62*	*10.1*	*3.7*	*4.9*	*1.4*	*5.51*	*2.7*	*-9*

Breakout: 15% *Improve: 44%* *Collapse: 31%*

There is no truth to the rumor that the left-field bleachers at Comerica Park are nicknamed Knotts' Landing, but this is a pitcher who ranks below major league standards in every essential department. He won't be returning to the rotation; the best he can hope for is mop-up duty.

PRESTON LARRISON Bats: R Throws: R Born: 19-Nov-1980 Age: 24

YEAR	TM	LG	AGE	G	GS	IP	H	BB	SO	HR	ERA	EQERA	EQH9	EQBB9	EQSO9	EQHR9	PERA	VORP	STF
2002	LAK	FSL	21	21	19	120.3	86	45	92	6	2.39	4.07	8.5	3.9	5.2	1.0	4.57	12.4	18
2003	ERI	EAS	22	24	24	126.7	161	59	53	10	5.61	6.40	11.1	4.5	3.0	1.2	6.84	-16.7	-35
2004	ERI	EAS	23	20	20	118.0	122	36	59	12	3.05	4.46	9.8	2.9	3.4	1.2	5.27	4.1	-7
2005	*DET*	*AL*	*24*	*19*	*11*	*70.0*	*80*	*30*	*37*	*9*	*5.17*	*5.23*	*10.4*	*3.3*	*4.3*	*1.1*	*5.27*	*4.0*	*-11*

Breakout: 12% *Improve: 44%* *Collapse: 17%*

Another Tiger farmhand with mechanics that needed correcting; he apparently went through most of '03 overthrowing with alarming regularity. The new way of doing things made him more successful, but it didn't mean that his low-90s sinker was blowing people away. Then his elbow started hurting in August, and the exercise became purely academic. Out for the 2005 season after Tommy John surgery.

WIL LEDEZMA Bats: L Throws: L Born: 21-Jan-1981 Age: 24

YEAR	TM	LG	AGE	G	GS	IP	H	BB	SO	HR	ERA	EQERA	EQH9	EQBB9	EQSO9	EQHR9	PERA	VORP	STF
2002	AUG	SAL	21	5	5	23.7	23	8	38	0	3.80	5.64	9.3	3.6	8.5	0.4	4.43	2.9	25
2003	DET	AL	22	34	8	84.0	99	35	49	12	5.79	5.53	9.8	3.6	5.1	1.2	4.99	1.9	-9
2004	ERI	EAS	23	17	16	111.7	95	24	98	8	2.42	3.44	8.4	2.1	6.0	0.9	3.87	20.1	17
2004	DET	AL	23	15	8	53.3	55	18	29	3	4.39	4.47	8.8	2.8	4.6	0.5	3.78	9.0	1
2005	*DET*	*AL*	*24*	*22*	*18*	*112.0*	*120*	*40*	*76*	*16*	*4.82*	*4.87*	*9.7*	*2.8*	*5.4*	*1.3*	*4.82*	*12.4*	*2*

Breakout: 11% *Improve: 39%* *Collapse: 21%*

(continued next page)

Wil Ledezma *(continued)*

A Rule 5 pick that worked. The Tigers nabbed Ledezma after 2002, kept him active in '03, let him return to regular rotation work in '04, and now it looks like he's ready. And why not? Lefties who throw 90-plus with a good curveball don't grow on trees. PECOTA expects some near-term regression, mostly because Ledezma's history as a flyball pitcher could portend a rising home-run rate, but if he can use his developing change-up to keep hitters off-balance, he should beat that projection.

AL LEVINE Bats: L Throws: R Born: 22-May-1968 Age: 37

YEAR	TM	LG	AGE	G	GS	IP	H	BB	SO	HR	ERA	EQERA	EQH9	EQBB9	EQSO9	EQHR9	PERA	VORP	STF
2002	ANA	AL	34	52	0	63.7	61	34	40	8	4.24	4.75	9.2	4.6	5.6	1.0	5.49	7.2	-15
2003	TBY	AL	35	36	0	49.7	45	18	25	7	2.90	3.86	9.1	3.3	4.6	1.2	4.82	10.6	-15
2003	KCR	AL	35	18	0	21.3	22	11	5	2	2.54	2.21	9.3	4.4	2.2	0.9	4.87	8.5	-33
2004	DET	AL	36	65	0	70.7	83	24	32	10	4.58	4.39	9.9	2.7	3.9	1.2	4.78	12.3	-19
2005	*DET*	*AL*	*37*	*37*	*0*	*40.7*	*48*	*16*	*20*	*5*	*4.81*	*4.86*	*10.6*	*3.2*	*4.0*	*1.2*	*5.44*	*4.7*	*-20*

Breakout: 33% *Improve: 60%* *Collapse: 17%*

Levine has never been a big strikeout guy, nor has his platoon split been particularly large, so he's highly reliant on keeping the ball down. He didn't do that very well last year and may have trouble doing it in the future. The Tigers declined his option, and at his age he may have trouble hooking on elsewhere.

SHANE LOUX Bats: R Throws: R Born: 31-Aug-1979 Age: 25

YEAR	TM	LG	AGE	G	GS	IP	H	BB	SO	HR	ERA	EQERA	EQH9	EQBB9	EQSO9	EQHR9	PERA	VORP	STF
2002	TOL	INT	22	26	26	158.3	196	38	87	11	4.72	5.73	10.3	2.4	4.1	0.8	5.03	9.8	-1
2003	TOL	INT	23	21	20	128.0	129	30	58	5	3.02	4.26	9.2	2.5	3.4	0.5	4.11	19.9	12
2003	DET	AL	23	11	4	30.3	37	12	8	4	7.13	6.67	10.3	3.3	2.4	1.2	5.16	-3.5	-15
2004	TOL	INT	24	22	22	132.7	154	34	86	14	5.29	5.79	9.8	2.4	4.7	1.0	4.53	15.3	0
2005	*DET*	*AL*	*25*	*23*	*15*	*95.7*	*113*	*30*	*54*	*11*	*4.95*	*5.00*	*10.7*	*2.5*	*4.5*	*1.1*	*5.00*	*8.2*	*-4*

Breakout: 10% *Improve: 42%* *Collapse: 18%*

Loux pitched well out of the gate at Toledo, but his arm began bothering him as the season went on, sending his ERA skyward. He was placed on the minor league DL in August with a sore elbow, cutting his season short. Loux has never had overpowering raw stuff, so if the injury takes anything more from his arsenal, he could be done as a prospect.

MIKE MAROTH Bats: L Throws: L Born: 17-Aug-1977 Age: 27

YEAR	TM	LG	AGE	G	GS	IP	H	BB	SO	HR	ERA	EQERA	EQH9	EQBB9	EQSO9	EQHR9	PERA	VORP	STF
2002	TOL	INT	24	11	11	73.3	53	22	51	7	2.82	3.65	8.0	3.2	5.7	1.2	3.92	12.5	22
2002	DET	AL	24	21	21	128.7	136	36	58	7	4.48	4.52	9.0	2.4	3.9	0.4	3.52	17.5	20
2003	DET	AL	25	33	33	193.3	231	50	87	34	5.73	5.69	10.2	2.2	4.0	1.5	5.11	-0.3	0
2004	DET	AL	26	33	33	217.0	244	59	108	25	4.31	4.35	9.5	2.2	4.3	0.9	4.27	39.2	10
2005	*DET*	*AL*	*27*	*28*	*27*	*153.3*	*185*	*46*	*78*	*20*	*5.13*	*5.19*	*10.9*	*2.4*	*4.1*	*1.2*	*5.21*	*8.8*	*-4*

Breakout: 12% *Improve: 40%* *Collapse: 24%*

Maroth sometimes gets lumped in with the Mark Buerhle category of pitchers, but he doesn't change speeds as well, and gives up a goodly number of home runs, which puts him more in the class of, say, Allan Anderson or Greg Hibbard. There's a big difference between a pitcher who doesn't overpower his opponents but does pretty much everything else well, and one whose only real asset is his location. Maroth's ERA is going to rise and he's not likely to have a long career.

ROBERTO NOVOA Bats: R Throws: R Born: 15-Aug-1979 Age: 25

YEAR	TM	LG	AGE	G	GS	IP	H	BB	SO	HR	ERA	EQERA	EQH9	EQBB9	EQSO9	EQHR9	PERA	VORP	STF
2002	WPT	NYP	22	12	12	66.7	62	8	56	4	3.64	6.94	10.7	1.5	4.4	2.0	5.88	-1.9	-4
2002	HIC	SAL	22	10	10	42.7	61	15	29	2	5.48	7.62	12.0	3.7	3.5	1.1	6.75	-5.3	-31
2003	LAK	FSL	23	19	15	99.0	93	25	71	8	3.73	5.58	10.0	2.7	4.7	2.2	5.38	2.2	-2
2004	ERI	EAS	24	41	0	79.0	63	18	59	7	2.96	4.07	8.4	2.2	5.2	1.1	4.07	12.4	8
2004	DET	AL	24	16	0	21.0	25	6	15	4	5.57	6.00	9.9	2.1	6.0	1.3	4.71	-0.3	8
2005	*DET*	*AL*	*25*	*23*	*4*	*49.0*	*53*	*16*	*33*	*7*	*4.78*	*4.83*	*9.8*	*2.5*	*5.4*	*1.3*	*4.80*	*5.8*	*-6*

Breakout: 21% *Improve: 46%* *Collapse: 21%*

He's already the prize of the deal that dumped Randall Simon on the Pirates. Novoa's major league line looks ugly, but it was mostly the result of a disastrous take-one-for-the-team outing in Anaheim in which he gave up five runs in less than an inning. His translated strikeout rates have improved at each rung of the ladder, which attests to his major league-caliber stuff, and he has a good chance to be what Fernando Rodney was not—a quality set-up man coming out of the system.

NATE ROBERTSON Bats: R Throws: L Born: 03-Sep-1977 Age: 27

YEAR	TM	LG	AGE	G	GS	IP	H	BB	SO	HR	ERA	EQERA	EQH9	EQBB9	EQSO9	EQHR9	PERA	VORP	STF
2002	PME	EAS	24	27	27	163.0	156	50	109	12	3.42	4.67	9.3	3.0	4.7	1.1	4.73	14.7	6
2003	TOL	INT	25	24	23	155.0	145	47	102	14	3.14	4.13	9.1	3.2	4.9	1.2	4.82	12.5	4
2003	DET	AL	25	8	8	44.7	55	23	33	6	5.44	5.20	9.8	4.4	6.4	1.0	5.20	3.2	10
2004	DET	AL	26	34	32	196.7	210	66	155	30	4.90	4.91	9.0	2.7	6.7	1.2	4.26	20.2	16
2005	*DET*	*AL*	*27*	*26*	*25*	*145.3*	*162*	*51*	*102*	*17*	*4.68*	*4.73*	*10.1*	*2.8*	*5.7*	*1.1*	*4.81*	*16.0*	*6*

Breakout: 10% *Improve: 50%* *Collapse: 20%*

Robertson was in the midst of a breakout season before struggling mightily with home runs in the second half. He gave up two-thirds of his home runs after the All-Star break, including eight in his last five starts. He rates as a pretty strong groundball pitcher, so it may have been a matter of hitting the wall, as his previous professional high in innings pitched was 171.3, in 2002. Provided he's handled carefully, he should outpitch some of the Tigers that rank higher on the depth chart, allowing the team to reclaim something from the Mark Redman deal.

FELIX SANCHEZ Bats: R Throws: L Born: 03-Aug-1981 Age: 23

YEAR	TM	LG	AGE	G	GS	IP	H	BB	SO	HR	ERA	EQERA	EQH9	EQBB9	EQSO9	EQHR9	PERA	VORP	STF
2002	LNS	MDW	20	26	21	119.3	130	44	101	7	4.15	6.73	11.0	4.2	4.8	1.4	6.73	-13.8	-28
2003	WTN	SOU	21	30	8	64.0	57	31	55	3	3.23	5.22	8.5	4.5	5.5	0.7	4.18	9.5	2
2004	ERI	EAS	22	14	0	13.7	18	6	12	2	7.23	7.43	11.5	4.1	6.1	1.4	6.75	-1.7	-21
2005	*DET*	*AL*	*23*	*15*	*7*	*48.0*	*57*	*23*	*32*	*5*	*5.41*	*5.47*	*10.7*	*3.8*	*5.4*	*1.0*	*5.55*	*1.8*	*-7*

Breakout: 18% *Improve: 47%* *Collapse: 28%*

A middling relief prospect who was acquired from the Cubs for stathead favorite Jon Connolly, the organization's pitcher of the year in 2003, Sanchez has a live arm, but his command hasn't been good and he's yet to develop a breaking ball. It's hard to say what kind of upside the Tigers envisioned here—do you trade even a B-minus starting prospect for the future Scott Sauerbeck? Sanchez was sidelined for most of the season with the ominous sounding shoulder impingement syndrome, which can be a precursor to a rotator-cuff tear.

HUMBERTO SANCHEZ Bats: R Throws: R Born: 28-May-1983 Age: 22

YEAR	TM	LG	AGE	G	GS	IP	H	BB	SO	HR	ERA	EQERA	EQH9	EQBB9	EQSO9	EQHR9	PERA	VORP	STF
2002	ONE	NYP	19	9	9	32.3	29	21	26	1	3.62	6.99	9.8	8.6	4.4	1.0	6.99	-4.4	-20
2003	WMI	MDW	20	23	23	116.0	107	78	96	3	4.42	7.30	9.1	7.7	5.1	0.7	5.69	-1.1	-6
2004	LAK	FSL	21	19	19	105.3	103	51	115	9	5.21	6.73	9.9	5.1	6.8	1.7	6.08	-5.2	-7
2004	ERI	EAS	21	2	2	12.7	10	6	15	1	2.13	3.75	8.2	4.5	8.2	0.8	4.50	1.5	23
2005	*DET*	*AL*	*22*	*16*	*10*	*63.7*	*62*	*40*	*50*	*8*	*5.07*	*5.12*	*8.9*	*4.9*	*6.3*	*1.1*	*5.16*	*4.7*	*-2*

Breakout: 17% *Improve: 56%* *Collapse: 15%*

Another one of the organization's mechanical messes, Sanchez is a tall, chunky kid with good stuff and variable command. On the plus side, he's shown an improved commitment to conditioning to avoid that classic El Guapo figure. Sanchez throws a good sinking fastball, which leaves Carlos Zambrano out there as an absolute best-case scenario, but there's lots of work left to be done.

KYLE SLEETH Bats: R Throws: R Born: 20-Dec-1981 Age: 23

YEAR	TM	LG	AGE	G	GS	IP	H	BB	SO	HR	ERA	EQERA	EQH9	EQBB9	EQSO9	EQHR9	PERA	VORP	STF
2004	LAK	FSL	22	9	9	54.0	47	15	55	3	3.67	5.40	8.8	2.9	6.3	1.1	4.32	7.1	14
2004	ERI	EAS	22	13	13	80.0	93	34	57	14	6.30	6.51	10.8	4.0	4.7	2.0	6.75	-9.7	-18
2005	*DET*	*AL*	*23*	*12*	*12*	*66.7*	*73*	*28*	*45*	*10*	*5.10*	*5.15*	*9.8*	*3.3*	*5.5*	*1.4*	*5.24*	*4.8*	*1*

Breakout: 11% *Improve: 47%* *Collapse: 9%*

(continued next page)

Kyle Sleeth *(continued)*

The object of constant tinkering because he came into the organization throwing cross-body with little command. The Tigers are trying to teach him to use his legs while preserving the giddy-up on his mid-90s fastball. Even if you give him something of a mulligan on 2004, he illustrates the problem with getting overly excited about pitchers with a high draft pedigree but no track record in professional ball.

UGUETH URBINA **Bats: R** **Throws: R** Born: 15-Feb-1974 Age: 31

YEAR	TM	LG	AGE	G	GS	IP	H	BB	SO	HR	ERA	EQERA	EQH9	EQBB9	EQSO9	EQHR9	PERA	VORP	STF
2002	BOS	AL	28	61	0	60.0	44	20	71	8	3.00	2.97	7.0	2.8	10.5	1.1	3.12	18.8	26
2003	TEX	AL	29	39	0	38.7	33	18	41	6	4.19	3.79	7.3	4.0	9.2	1.2	3.55	7.2	14
2003	FLA	NL	29	33	0	38.3	23	13	37	2	1.41	1.75	6.2	2.8	8.2	0.5	2.25	17.9	19
2004	DET	AL	30	54	0	54.0	38	32	56	7	4.50	4.30	6.9	4.8	8.9	1.0	3.44	9.7	10
2005	*DET*	*AL*	*31*	*46*	*0*	*47.3*	*42*	*22*	*44*	*8*	*4.46*	*4.51*	*8.0*	*3.6*	*7.6*	*1.5*	*4.52*	*8.9*	*0*

Breakout: 32% *Improve: 50%* *Collapse: 29%*

While America's attention is squarely focused on the Middle East, some of the most dangerous places in the world are in our own hemisphere. There's not much to say about the kidnapping of Urbina's mother, still unresolved as of press time, other than that we wish both of them the best. Urbina returned to Venezuela over the winter and was working out with the Caracas club, but had not pitched in a game. As a pitcher, he's extremely similar to Troy Percival, the man who will be replacing him as the Tigers' closer; his strikeouts are more the result of guile than his declining raw stuff.

MATT VASQUEZ **Bats: R** **Throws: R** Born: 07-Jun-1982 Age: 23

YEAR	TM	LG	AGE	G	GS	IP	H	BB	SO	HR	ERA	EQERA	EQH9	EQBB9	EQSO9	EQHR9	PERA	VORP	STF
2003	ONE	NYP	21	11	11	53.3	76	10	35	5	6.92	8.88	13.8	2.2	3.4	3.1	8.88	-18.1	-42
2004	WMI	MDW	22	27	27	168.3	156	34	120	14	3.64	5.41	9.9	2.4	3.9	1.6	5.53	1.2	0
2005	*DET*	*AL*	*23*	*11*	*10*	*56.7*	*69*	*18*	*32*	*10*	*5.61*	*5.67*	*11.0*	*2.6*	*4.5*	*1.6*	*5.79*	*1.4*	*-6*

Breakout: 9% *Improve: 36%* *Collapse: 18%*

Vasquez was the team's eighth-round selection out of Cal-Santa Barbara in 2003, in spite of collegiate numbers that weren't much to look at. He was selected on the basis of his projectability, which thus far has projected as good command without a real plus pitch, leading to some high hit and home-run rates. Yes, the strikeout rate looks reasonable on the surface, but Midwest League pitchers averaged nearly eight strikeouts per nine innings, so it comes out decidedly lukewarm after translation.

JUSTIN VERLANDER **Bats:R** **Throws: R** Born: 20-Feb-1983 Age: 22

Verlander was the first pitcher taken in the 2004 draft and signed with the Tigers in October after a protracted negotiation. It goes without saying that he has electric stuff, but he rates as more of a project than his draft pedigree would suggest; he walked 3.5 hitters per nine innings during his three-year tenure at Old Dominion. He was not rushed to winter ball and will likely start the year at Lakeland.

JAMIE WALKER **Bats: L** **Throws: L** Born: 01-Jul-1971 Age: 34

YEAR	TM	LG	AGE	G	GS	IP	H	BB	SO	HR	ERA	EQERA	EQH9	EQBB9	EQSO9	EQHR9	PERA	VORP	STF
2002	DET	AL	31	57	0	43.7	32	9	40	9	3.71	3.70	7.4	1.7	8.3	1.7	3.27	10.0	17
2003	DET	AL	32	78	0	65.0	61	17	45	9	3.32	3.90	8.5	2.3	6.2	1.2	3.90	14.0	4
2004	DET	AL	33	70	0	64.7	69	12	53	8	3.20	3.66	8.9	1.5	6.9	1.0	3.66	17.1	14
2005	*DET*	*AL*	*33*	*45*	*1*	*63.0*	*63*	*15*	*48*	*10*	*4.15*	*4.19*	*9.1*	*1.9*	*6.2*	*1.5*	*4.31*	*13.2*	*-1*

Breakout: 30% *Improve: 49%* *Collapse: 22%*

The Tigers acquired Walker four seasons ago and pulled the plug on the Royals' intermittent attempts to turn him into a starting pitcher. He's rewarded them by quietly becoming one of the better lefty relievers in the league, limiting opposing southpaws to a nasty .205/.250/.382 line over the course of the past three seasons. The trouble is that Walker's soft stuff leaves him vulnerable to the long ball, which makes it risky to bring him in with runners on base.

ESTEBAN YAN **Bats: R** **Throws: R** Born: 22-Jun-1975 Age: 30

YEAR	TM	LG	AGE	G	GS	IP	H	BB	SO	HR	ERA	EQERA	EQH9	EQBB9	EQSO9	EQHR9	PERA	VORP	STF
2002	TBY	AL	27	55	0	69.0	70	29	53	10	4.30	4.28	8.8	3.5	6.7	1.2	4.41	10.8	-3
2003	TEX	AL	28	15	0	23.3	31	7	25	5	6.95	6.38	9.8	2.6	9.0	1.5	4.88	-3.2	12
2003	STL	NL	28	39	0	43.3	53	16	28	8	6.03	5.91	10.3	3.0	5.3	1.7	5.91	-1.9	-16
2004	DET	AL	29	69	0	87.0	92	32	69	8	3.83	4.17	8.8	2.9	6.7	0.7	3.86	17.7	4
2005	*ANA*	*AL*	*30*	*47*	*1*	*64.7*	*70*	*24*	*49*	*8*	*4.34*	*4.30*	*9.8*	*2.9*	*6.2*	*1.1*	*4.72*	*12.4*	*-3*

Breakout: 29% *Improve: 50%* *Collapse: 24%*

Yan is successful when his splitter is working, and it was top-notch for much of last season, allowing him to limit home runs against him and post a career best 1.74 groundball-to-flyball ratio. Of course Yan's splitter, has been lost and re-introduced more often than the McRib; the Angels picked up a box of Alka Seltzor and will take their chances.

JOEL ZUMAYA **Bats: R** **Throws: R** Born: 09-Nov-1984 Age: 20

YEAR	TM	LG	AGE	G	GS	IP	H	BB	SO	HR	ERA	EQERA	EQH9	EQBB9	EQSO9	EQHR9	PERA	VORP	STF
2003	WMI	MDW	18	19	19	90.3	69	38	126	3	2.79	5.36	8.3	4.8	8.6	0.8	4.26	12.3	40
2004	LAK	FSL	19	16	16	94.0	65	43	92	8	3.54	5.14	8.4	4.9	6.3	1.5	4.93	6.3	34
2004	ERI	EAS	19	4	4	20.0	19	10	29	6	6.30	8.68	10.1	4.8	10.1	2.9	6.75	-2.4	32
2005	*DET*	*AL*	*20*	*14*	*14*	*79.0*	*70*	*41*	*66*	*12*	*4.69*	*4.74*	*8.0*	*4.1*	*6.8*	*1.4*	*4.66*	*10.0*	*8*

Breakout: 19% *Improve: 45%* *Collapse: 13%*

Zumaya has suffered through some back problems caused by a high-intensity delivery, but when you throw mid-90s heat, the easy, lazy thing to do is hope he doesn't hurt himself and let him keep doing it. He deserved his late-season promotion to Erie on the basis of his track record, which made him one of just seven teenagers to throw a pitch in Double-A last season; four of the other six are on our Top 50 prospects list. Zumaya's prodigious pace, of course, underscores the fact that time is on the Tigers' side, but this is the organization that broke camp with Jeremy Bonderman on its big league roster four days before his 20th birthday.

Kansas City Royals

Every so often, a team will enjoy a season in which everything goes right. A season that vindicates all the decisions made over the winter. A season in which every free agent signed lives up to his salary and every rookie lives up to his promise.

This was not one of those seasons.

No, it was a season in which every move the Royals made, no matter how well researched or well intentioned, blew up in their face like a firecracker made by the Acme Corporation. The strange part wasn't that the Royals so colossally underperformed expectations—disappointment has been a theme for this franchise over the last decade—but that it occurred after an off-season in which the front office seemingly did everything right.

The journey from a team's first winning season in nine years to a 104-loss stinker the next typically involves complacency of the highest order: The team becomes so enamored with its modest success that it becomes reluctant to tweak its roster in the slightest. That was not the case here. On the contrary, the Royals treated a squad that held first place into late August in 2003 like the 73-win team it really was on paper.

They re-signed the starting pitcher (Brian Anderson) and closer (Curt Leskanic) they had traded for during their pennant run. They signed a new starting catcher (Benito Santiago), a new backup catcher (Kelly Stinnett), a new set-up man (Scott Sullivan), a new DH (Matt Stairs), and topped it all off with a shiny new cleanup hitter in Juan Gonzalez.

The team's biggest free-agent spending spree since the strike did not pay the expected dividends. As table 1 shows, it didn't come close.

The eleven players the Royals signed last winter—nearly half the Opening Day roster—combined for barely half as much value in 2004 as they had in 2003. Granted that some decline could have been expected as a group, the 14-win drop-off in value goes a surprisingly long way in explaining the team's nosedive last season.

The team should have seen some of this coming: Gonzalez hasn't been a paragon of health and consistency for a while now. But Anderson's complete meltdown in the first half—the team's Opening Day starter had to be pulled out of the rotation completely by the end of May—was certainly uncharacteristic. Losing both Santiago and Stinnett to season-ending injuries in a 48-hour span was a cruel touch.

ROYALS PROSPECTUS

2004 record: 58–104; Fifth place, AL Central

Pythagenport record: 63–99

Runs scored per game: 4.44 (12th in AL)

Runs allowed per game: 5.59 (14th in AL)

Team EqA: .242 (14th in AL)

2004 Batters Age: 29.5 (5th oldest in AL)

2004 Pitchers Age: 27.6 (2nd youngest in AL)

Ballpark: Royals Stadium; Moderate hitter's park; Park Factor of 1.029

2004: Hoping to hit the ground running after a surprising 2003, the Royals did a face-plant instead.

2005: Some of their young pitching will be fun to watch, but there's no reason to expect them to contend.

If there's a silver lining to this, it's that a big free-agent gamble in the winter of 2003–04 didn't carry as much risk as the same venture might have carried in 2000–01. (Or, for that matter, this winter.) The depressed player market gave the Royals an opportunity to roll the dice without making any long-term commitments. Not one of the free agents signed was guaranteed a third year, and contracts that called for over $20 million last season guarantee just half that in 2005. Even including buyouts for Gonzalez and Randa, the Royals are responsible for less than $9 million this season (plus an additional million after re-signing Stairs for another year). After a venture into free agency that was both frenzied and disastrous, that's as soft a landing as you can ask for.

The irony is that when the Royals went hunting for players with their wallets closed, they did another bang-up job of rounding up underappreciated talent. GM Allard Baird has shown an admirable willingness to mine the "free" market of talent readily available to major league teams; he's shown more than the occasional knack for using that free-talent market to acquire useful players at next to no cost.

Three transactions last year illustrate this best. In late January, with the Mets needing to clear some room off their 40-man roster, Baird offered Shawn Sedlacek—a Quadruple-A pitcher who had already been outrighted off

TABLE 1. RANKED BY SALARY, PERFORMANCE OF THE ELEVEN FREE AGENTS SIGNED IN THE WINTER OF 2003–2004

Player	2003 WARP	2004 Salary	2004 WARP
Juan Gonzalez	3.0	$4 million	0.3
Joe Randa	3.1	$3.25 million	3.4
Brian Anderson	4.9	$3.25 million	2.0
Benito Santiago	2.8	$2.15 million	0.5
Scott Sullivan	2.2	$2.1 million	1.9
Curt Leskanic	2.9	$1.5 million	−0.2*
Tony Graffanino	2.2	$1.1 million	2.7
Matt Stairs	3.6	$1 million	2.0
Jason Grimsley	2.0	$1 million	2.8
Kelly Stinnett	0.9	$500,000	0.5
Kevin Appier	1.9	$500,000	−0.3
Total	**29.5**	**$20.15 million**	**15.6**

* Before being released

TABLE 2. ROYALS' LOW-LEVEL ACQUISITIONS SINCE THE END OF THE 2003 SEASON

Date	Player Acquired	Mechanism
10/29/03	Shawn Camp	Minor league free agent
10/30/03	Dennys Reyes	Free agent signed as NRI
11/09/03	Calvin Pickering	Minor-league free agent
12/16/03	Rich Thompson	Rule 5 pick
01/26/04	Jamie Cerda	Trade for Shawn Sedlacek
04/09/04	Justin Huisman	Trade for two non-prospects
06/21/04	Denny Bautista	Trade for Jason Grimsley
06/28/04	Jose Bautista	Waiver claim
07/02/04	Ruben Mateo	Waiver claim
07/30/04	Justin Huber	Trade for Jose Bautista
07/31/04	Abraham Nunez	Trade for Rudy Seanez
08/13/04	Matt Kinney	Waiver claim

the Royals' 40-man roster—for Jamie Cerda, he of the 1.40 career minor league ERA. The Mets dumped Sedlacek by May; Cerda led the Royals' bullpen in ERA and allowed one homer all season.

At the trading deadline, Baird injected himself into trade talks between the Pirates and Mets, and for his part in facilitating the Kris Benson trade, Baird managed to turn Jose Bautista—himself claimed on waivers after being taken in the Rule 5 Draft by Baltimore—into top catching prospect Justin Huber. And while it technically does not qualify as a "free talent" acquisition, Baird's swindle of Denny Bautista from the Orioles for Jason Grimsley was a major coup.

Table 2 summarizes all of the Royals' low-level acquisitions over a 12-month span starting with the end of the 2003 season.

Like any mass talent grab, the Royals ended up with a few turkeys among the genuine finds. But at the cost of a few waiver claims and half dozen players with no tangible value to the team, the Royals acquired two top prospects in Bautista and Huber, a potential poor man's David Ortiz in Calvin Pickering, and half a bullpen worth of competent relievers making the major league minimum. They're already off to a good start for 2005, having landed the consensus prize in the Rule 5 Draft in left-hander Andy Sisco.

Chief among the turkeys last year were Ruben Mateo, who after a promising two months in Triple-A for the Pirates (.316/.391/.711) hit an impotent .206 for the Royals, and Abraham Nunez, who was plugged in as the everyday right fielder and proceeded to hit .214/.297/.319. Mateo and Nunez were only two of the contributors to a corps of outfielders flanking Carlos Beltran (and later, David DeJesus) that ranked by far the worst collection of corner outfielders in baseball.

Aaron Guiel and Gonzalez, the starting left and right fielders on Opening Day, combined to play in only 75 games before being felled by vision problems and a bad back, respectively. (When he did play, Guiel's .156 average was the lowest in baseball for anyone with 100 at-bats.) The Royals gave one-time phenom Dee Brown one final chance to redeem himself and he flubbed it. For the year, all Royals right fielders combined to hit .228 with a .301 OBP and a .380 slugging average. The OBP bested the mark of the Mets' right fielders by one point, otherwise the Royals would have swept the majors with the worst figures in all three categories. Every other team had an OPS at least 30 points higher than the Royals from the right-field position.

Even worse, the Royals right fielders towered over their left fielders, who hit—brace yourself—.216/.283/ .324. Combined, all Royal corner outfielders hit .222/.293/.353, and got thrown out in eight of 14 steal attempts. From two of the most offense-oriented positions on the field, the Royals got production that would have embarrassed a 1970s-era shortstop.

Table 3 lists the five worst corner outfields since 1972, as ranked by MLVr, which calculates how many runs per game a team would score with their players relative to an average player at that position, after accounting for league and park effects. Negative numbers indicate below-average performance. MLVr is calculated per position; since we're looking at two positions here (LF and RF), double the numbers to get the full effect. In other words, these two positions alone put the Royals in a hole of nearly half a run per game.

TABLE 3. ROYALS' FIVE WORST CORNER OUTFIELDS SINCE 1972, BY MLVR

Year	Team	AVG	OBP	SLG	MLVR
1979	Oakland	.211	.274	.302	−0.253
1995	Detroit	.216	.291	.352	−0.241
2002	Kansas City	.233	.303	.372	−0.228
2004	Kansas City	.222	.293	.353	−0.192
1981	Toronto	.229	.274	.334	−0.161

Not only did last year's Royals have one of the five worst corner outfields in a generation, it wasn't even their worst performance in the last three years! This isn't a case of the same players torpedoing both teams—only Guiel contributed to both entries. The cause is far more fundamental, and far more troubling: The Royals' farm system has been an utter embarrassment when it comes to developing quality (or even mediocre) outfielders. Since Johnny Damon and Michael Tucker debuted in 1995, only two outfielders developed by the Royals' farm system have gone on to have even 400 at-bats in a season: Beltran and Mark Quinn.

With no ready internal options to halt this trend, it's no surprise that the Royals were linked to just about every available outfielder on the trade market this winter, from Austin Kearns to Jason Michaels to Kevin Mench to Sammy Sosa. Unable to close on any of those deals, the Royals made the regrettable decision to overpay for Eli Marrero, to the tune of $2.5 million this year in return for maybe 300 plate appearances of league-average performance.

Long-term, who the Royals round up to flank DeJesus this year is less important than what they do about the underlying cause: a farm system that has simply not been productive enough to compensate for the Royals' inherent payroll restrictions. For all the rhetoric used to contrast the approach used by the two pillars of small-market success, the Twins and the A's, the reality is that the success of both teams is the result of variations on a theme: Develop Your Own Players.

Moneyball is the art of cost-effective winning, and the most cost-effective player is the one whose rights you control for six years, whose salary you control for the first three. Billy Beane's success starts with the fact that his player development system coughed up Jason Giambi, Eric Chavez, Miguel Tejada, Ramon Hernandez, and the Big Three starting pitchers in the span of about five years. While the Twins may not always make the most sensible baseball decisions—they released David Ortiz two years ago, for one—thanks to arguably the most productive farm system in baseball, they've won three straight AL Central titles anyway.

The point is that all the shrewd waiver claims and Rule 5 picks in the world won't matter if the franchise isn't churning out ballplayers of its own, year after year. For the better part of the last 15 years, the Royals' farm system has been among the least productive in the game. That fact, more than the team's small-market status, is responsible for the franchise's .434 winning percentage over the past 10 years.

On that note, the most important development for the Royals in 2004 was that the team continued to show signs of reversing a decade-long drought in the minor leagues. An approach that was heavy on tools and light on performance, one that led the Royals to use every one of their 10 first-round picks between 1997 and 2001 on pitchers (to date, Mike MacDougal and Jimmy Gobble have had the most "success"), reached its nadir with the appalling 2001 draft, which may well end up not sending a single player to the major leagues.

That draft was so utterly D.O.A. that it forced the team to re-evaluate its entire draft philosophy. There was, at least, a happy result: In the past three drafts, the Royals have used their first-round draft picks on three hitters, two polished college pitchers with excellent collegiate statistics, and Zack Greinke, the most polished high-school pitcher in years. For whatever a first impression is worth, last year's draft effort was rated third-best in the game by Baseball America. (The Twins ranked #1; the A's were #4.)

The 2004 season served to remind the Royals of something they should have known anyway: Smoke and mirrors can come through for the occasional storybook season, but they're no way to build a winning franchise. The construction of a perennial contender can't be done on the back of a hot three months, or on the basis of a single off-season. The good news is that the converse is also true; as calamitous as last season was, it has little long-term impact on the Royals' efforts to build a winner.

It will help if the Royals don't screw the pooch on the free-agent market again in the future. It will help if Baird continues to nab solid prospects for his riff-raff. It definitely helps that the Royals are bringing back Guy Hansen, their pitching coach from the staff's glory days of the early 1990s. Hansen, as the Braves' Triple-A pitching coach the last four years, has quietly reaped a big dose of credit for much of the hosannas thrown Leo Mazzone's way.

Ultimately, whether the Royals are able to contend come 2007—when virtually every significant player on their roster today will still be under contract—comes down to whether a player like Billy Butler, last year's first-round pick, develops into a quality hitter. Similarly, it will come down to whether players like David DeJesus, Ruben Gotay, and Jeremy Affeldt develop into minor stars. And it will come down to whether Zack Greinke develops into a Cy Young candidate. Plucking talent away from other teams is nice. But there's no substitute for developing talent of your own.

HITTERS

MIKE AVILES SS Bats: R Throws: R Born: 13-Mar-1981 Age: 24

YEAR	TM	LG	AGE	AB	H	2B	3B	HR	BB	SO	SB	CS	AVG	OBP	SLG	MLVR	EQBA	EQOBP	EQSLG	EQMLVR	VORP	DEFENSE
2004	WIL	CRL	23	463	139	40	4	6	39	57	2	5	.300	.352	.443	.155	.270	.316	.410	-.006	16.7	120-SS 0
2005	*KCR*	*AL*	*24*	*262*	*71*	*18*	*2*	*5*	*17*	*39*	*1*	*2*	*.270*	*.315*	*.412*	*-.071*	*.266*	*.313*	*.413*	*-.085*	*11.1*	*69-SS -1*

Breakout: 21% *Improve: 39%* *Collapse: 30%*

Aviles is a good example of how the Royals are more of a *Moneyball* team than most people realize. He was the Division II Player of the Year from tiny Concordia College in 2003 after hitting .500 with 22 homers in 45 games, yet he lasted into the seventh round before the Royals grabbed him. In his first pro season, he was named the Arizona League MVP, and in his second he was the best hitter on a Wilmington team that fell one game short of the Carolina League title. The same marginal tools that kept him from being drafted higher have kept him from rising up the prospect charts. Just keep in mind that his next slump will be his first as a pro.

ANGEL BERROA SS Bats: R Throws: R Born: 27-Jan-1978 Age: 27

YEAR	TM	LG	AGE	AB	H	2B	3B	HR	BB	SO	SB	CS	AVG	OBP	SLG	MLVR	EQBA	EQOBP	EQSLG	EQMLVR	VORP	DEFENSE
2002	OMA	PCL	24	297	64	11	4	8	15	84	6	4	.215	.277	.360	-.206	.204	.257	.338	-.346	-12.2	77-SS -4
2002	KCR	AL	24	75	17	7	1	0	7	10	3	0	.227	.301	.347	-.230	.216	.283	.297	-.344	0.6	20-SS 1
2003	KCR	AL	25	567	163	28	7	17	29	100	21	5	.287	.338	.451	.010	.282	.335	.446	.010	39.4	156-SS 0
2004	KCR	AL	26	512	134	27	6	8	23	87	14	8	.262	.308	.385	-.113	.261	.308	.387	-.141	15.7	131-SS -13
2005	*KCR*	*AL*	*27*	*459*	*122*	*24*	*4*	*11*	*22*	*81*	*12*	*5*	*.265*	*.310*	*.409*	*-.087*	*.261*	*.309*	*.410*	*-.102*	*15.2*	*118-SS -4*

Breakout: 17% *Improve: 39%* *Collapse: 24%*

Berroa had all the markers for a Rookie of the Year likely to suffer a sophomore slump—he was fairly old (25) for a RoY, and had a season that was out of sync with his minor league track record. Still, the sheer magnitude of Berroa's fall was surprising, especially on defense: He declined by nearly as many runs in the field (13) as at the plate (18). The Royals blame his struggles on trying too hard to justify his RoY status and new long-term deal. Having his season interrupted by a spinal tap to rule out meningitis didn't help. Some bounceback can be expected, but he's looking like a better version of either Alex Gonzalez.

ANDRES BLANCO SS Bats: B Throws: R Born: 11-Apr-1984 Age: 21

YEAR	TM	LG	AGE	AB	H	2B	3B	HR	BB	SO	SB	CS	AVG	OBP	SLG	MLVR	EQBA	EQOBP	EQSLG	EQMLVR	VORP	DEFENSE
2003	WIL	CRL	19	394	96	11	3	0	44	50	13	7	.244	.330	.287	-.096	.217	.286	.258	-.391	-23.6	106-SS -8
2004	WIC	TXS	20	324	80	10	2	0	18	44	7	6	.247	.299	.290	-.216	.215	.254	.245	-.477	-26.6	88-SS 5
2004	KCR	AL	20	60	19	2	2	0	5	6	1	2	.317	.379	.417	.093	.339	.369	.407	.065	4.3	19-SS 0
2005	*KCR*	*AL*	*21*	*436*	*100*	*18*	*2*	*1*	*25*	*64*	*7*	*4*	*.229*	*.283*	*.291*	*-.315*	*.226*	*.281*	*.291*	*-.331*	*-9.1*	*115-SS -5*

Breakout: 16% *Improve: 41%* *Collapse: 40%*

As we wrote last year, Blanco is about as good a prospect as you can be without any ability to actually hit. He struggled to post a .300 OBP in Double-A last year, but is still one of the players most sought after in trade talks with the Royals, for two obvious reasons: glovework and youth. As he showed in his brief big league auditions, Blanco has the agility and smoothness to be one of the game's best defensive shortstops. His inability to hit becomes less damning when you consider he was only 20 years old last season; they're hoping he's a future Cesar Izturis.

DEE BROWN OF Bats: L Throws: R Born: 27-Mar-1978 Age: 27

YEAR	TM	LG	AGE	AB	H	2B	3B	HR	BB	SO	SB	CS	AVG	OBP	SLG	MLVR	EQBA	EQOBP	EQSLG	EQMLVR	VORP	DEFENSE
2002	OMA	PCL	24	458	126	23	1	17	44	111	10	4	.275	.344	.441	.075	.254	.320	.406	-.097	-5.8	79-LF -5
2002	KCR	AL	24	51	12	3	1	1	4	20	0	0	.235	.291	.392	-.184	.220	.291	.380	-.212	-0.7	
2003	KCR	AL	25	132	30	7	0	2	8	37	1	1	.227	.280	.326	-.290	.223	.270	.308	-.351	-6.0	17-RF 2 12-LF -1
2004	WIC	TXS	26	241	73	19	2	12	24	38	1	4	.303	.367	.548	.306	.267	.322	.479	.020	5.6	41-LF -4
2004	KCR	AL	26	195	49	7	0	4	11	50	2	2	.251	.293	.349	-.193	.250	.288	.344	-.249	-4.3	45-LF 0
2005	*TBY*	*AL*	*27*	*233*	*59*	*12*	*1*	*7*	*17*	*56*	*3*	*1*	*.253*	*.309*	*.409*	*-.099*	*.253*	*.311*	*.417*	*-.093*	*1.8*	*63-LF -5*

Breakout: 31% *Improve: 50%* *Collapse: 31%*

Against all odds, he made it back to the Royals last season, but that was after no team claimed him on waivers in spring training and his bat showed signs of life for the first time in years. It was a mirage; he hit as poorly as ever after a July promotion, and now has sports a 615 OPS in nearly 900 career plate appearances. He might get another shot with another team, but realistically, he's just about through.

JOHN BUCK C Bats: R Throws: R Born: 07-Jul-1980 Age: 24

YEAR	TM	LG	AGE	AB	H	2B	3B	HR	BB	SO	SB	CS	AVG	OBP	SLG	MLVR	EQBA	EQOBP	EQSLG	EQMLVR	VORP	DEFENSE
2002	ROU	TXS	21	448	118	29	3	12	31	93	2	3	.263	.314	.422	.039	.239	.281	.397	-.194	-2.8	99-C 1
2003	NWO	PCL	22	274	70	18	2	2	14	53	1	0	.255	.301	.358	-.065	.258	.301	.364	-.189	-1.3	68-C -6
2004	NWO	PCL	24	227	68	11	0	12	21	39	0	1	.300	.368	.507	.244	.280	.335	.449	.012	12.7	55-C -6
2004	KCR	AL	24	238	56	9	0	12	15	79	1	1	.235	.280	.424	-.132	.235	.280	.415	-.174	4.8	66-C -4
2005	*KCR*	*AL*	*24*	*331*	*87*	*19*	*1*	*12*	*22*	*73*	*1*	*1*	*.263*	*.314*	*.432*	*-.051*	*.259*	*.312*	*.433*	*-.066*	*13.4*	*87-C -4*

Breakout: 20% *Improve: 52%* *Collapse: 24%*

Consider Buck a lesson in why it's best not to get too worked up over first impressions. In his first six weeks in the major leagues, Buck looked about as bad as any player has, ever, hitting .149/.222/.203 in his first 74 AB. His bat speed showed all the blazing quickness of continental drift. It turns out hitting coach Jeff Pentland was tinkering with his swing; from July 31 on, Buck hit .274/.308/.524. His K:BB ratio was troubling, especially since that ratio did not improve in concert with his power numbers. But his power is legit, and it's nearly impossible for a catcher to hit 20 homers and not have value. He's a solid second player from the Beltran trade.

BILLY BUTLER "3B" Bats: R Throws: R Born: 18-Apr-1986 Age: 19

YEAR	TM	LG	AGE	AB	H	2B	3B	HR	BB	SO	SB	CS	AVG	OBP	SLG	MLVR	EQBA	EQOBP	EQSLG	EQMLVR	VORP	DEFENSE
2004	IDA	PIO	18	260	97	22	3	10	57	63	5	0	.373	.486	.596	.467	.235	.313	.346	-.206	-4.0	47-3B -2
2005	*KCR*	*AL*	*19*	*371*	*90*	*21*	*2*	*8*	*40*	*117*	*3*	*2*	*.243*	*.324*	*.381*	*-.116*	*.239*	*.322*	*.382*	*-.130*	*1.3*	*100-3B -12*

Breakout: 39% *Improve: 57%* *Collapse: 24%*

Butler was widely considered a signability choice when the Royals took him with the 14th overall pick last summer, and he did sign for $250,000 less than slot money. In this case, you can't spell "signability" without "ability." Butler went straight from high school to the Pioneer League and won two legs of the triple crown (batting average and RBI) while finishing second in walks. His glove at third base is dubious at best, but since the Royals have Mark Teahen to play third and the majors' worst corner outfielders, all signs point towards a change of position.

SHANE COSTA OF Bats: L Throws: R Born: 12-Dec-1981 Age: 23

YEAR	TM	LG	AGE	AB	H	2B	3B	HR	BB	SO	SB	CS	AVG	OBP	SLG	MLVR	EQBA	EQOBP	EQSLG	EQMLVR	VORP	DEFENSE
2004	WIL	CRL	22	451	139	20	4	7	32	43	9	4	.308	.364	.417	.144	.275	.322	.388	-.103	-6.7	61-LF -3 40-CF -1
2005	*KCR*	*AL*	*23*	*294*	*77*	*16*	*2*	*4*	*17*	*36*	*2*	*2*	*.262*	*.318*	*.376*	*-.120*	*.257*	*.316*	*.377*	*-.135*	*-2.4*	*79-LF -3*

Breakout: 18% *Improve: 37%* *Collapse: 39%*

The Royals' second-round pick in 2003 tripped coming out of the gate, starting the season 4-for-40, then hitting .328/.386/.443 the rest of the way. Costa has yet to quell the main concern that existed when he was drafted, namely that he didn't have the power needed from a corner outfielder. He's an impressive physical specimen—his dad was a competitive body-builder—so there's hope that the power will come, especially given how tough it is to hit in Wilmington. He might be the best outfield prospect in the system.

DAVID DeJESUS CF Bats: L Throws: L Born: 20-Dec-1979 Age: 25

YEAR	TM	LG	AGE	AB	H	2B	3B	HR	BB	SO	SB	CS	AVG	OBP	SLG	MLVR	EQBA	EQOBP	EQSLG	EQMLVR	VORP	DEFENSE
2002	WIL	CRL	22	334	99	22	6	4	48	42	15	6	.296	.400	.434	.236	.272	.356	.415	-.004	15.5	74-CF 0
2003	WIC	TXS	23	71	24	4	0	2	9	8	1	3	.338	.422	.479	.342	.282	.347	.394	-.042	2.4	17-CF 0
2003	OMA	PCL	23	215	64	16	3	5	34	30	8	4	.298	.412	.470	.267	.279	.383	.443	.089	15.8	50-CF -5
2004	OMA	PCL	24	197	62	14	4	6	21	30	7	6	.315	.400	.518	.287	.289	.366	.454	.083	13.6	49-CF -4
2004	KCR	AL	24	363	104	15	3	7	33	53	8	11	.287	.360	.402	.025	.291	.365	.408	.018	15.5	83-CF 1
2005	*KCR*	*AL*	*25*	*420*	*119*	*26*	*3*	*11*	*45*	*63*	*10*	*6*	*.283*	*.367*	*.434*	*.056*	*.278*	*.365*	*.434*	*.042*	*23.5*	*115-CF -4*

Breakout: 14% Improve: 46% Collapse: 22%

DeJesus had one of the quietest strong rookie seasons in baseball last year, leading all freshmen (300+ PA) with a .360 OBP. If the Royals can give up the idea that he's a basestealing threat—he's 27-for-52 in attempted thefts the last three years—and use him just for his skill at getting on base, he'll be one of the better leadoff hitters in the game for the rest of the decade. Assuming he stays healthy, that is: Last year was his first injury-free season since college.

BYRON GETTIS OF Bats: R Throws: R Born: 13-Mar-1980 Age: 25

YEAR	TM	LG	AGE	AB	H	2B	3B	HR	BB	SO	SB	CS	AVG	OBP	SLG	MLVR	EQBA	EQOBP	EQSLG	EQMLVR	VORP	DEFENSE
2002	WIL	CRL	22	449	127	33	2	8	48	103	10	5	.283	.364	.419	.156	.256	.323	.399	-.100	-4.8	109-RF -3
2003	WIC	TXS	23	510	154	31	4	16	55	110	15	11	.302	.377	.473	.233	.278	.346	.451	.033	15.8	128-RF 5
2004	WIC	TXS	24	58	21	4	1	2	8	12	0	1	.362	.448	.569	.518	.328	.396	.517	.261	6.1	12-RF -2
2004	OMA	PCL	24	179	46	7	0	4	33	61	4	1	.257	.366	.363	-.058	.226	.322	.305	-.249	-11.2	46-LF -1
2004	KCR	AL	24	39	7	1	1	0	8	14	0	1	.179	.327	.256	-.278	.184	.312	.263	-.345	-2.1	11-LF 0
2005	*DET*	*AL*	*25*	*283*	*73*	*15*	*1*	*8*	*31*	*76*	*3*	*2*	*.257*	*.340*	*.405*	*-.047*	*.260*	*.345*	*.423*	*-.020*	*8.2*	*78-RF -1*

Breakout: 29% Improve: 46% Collapse: 30%

Gettis was the Royals' Minor League Player of the Year in 2003, but as we said last year, he's a tweener prospect with not enough bat to handle an outfield corner, and not enough glove to handle center. His awful major league audition and Triple-A struggles lowered his stock to the point that he was claimed by the Tigers off waivers. Fourth outfielderdom beckons.

JUAN GONZALEZ OF Bats: R Throws: R Born: 16-Oct-1969 Age: 35

YEAR	TM	LG	AGE	AB	H	2B	3B	HR	BB	SO	SB	CS	AVG	OBP	SLG	MLVR	EQBA	EQOBP	EQSLG	EQMLVR	VORP	DEFENSE
2002	TEX	AL	32	277	78	21	1	8	17	56	2	0	.282	.324	.451	-.004	.278	.326	.451	-.003	7.2	59-RF 3
2003	TEX	AL	33	327	96	17	1	24	14	73	1	1	.294	.329	.572	.187	.287	.328	.564	.173	24.3	50-RF 3
2004	KCR	AL	34	127	35	4	1	5	9	19	0	1	.276	.326	.441	-.003	.272	.327	.440	-.022	4.4	26-RF -2
2005	*CLE*	*AL*	*35*	*251*	*67*	*13*	*1*	*10*	*16*	*49*	*0*	*1*	*.265*	*.311*	*.447*	*-.034*	*.266*	*.313*	*.458*	*-.025*	*7.7*	*66-RF -5*

Breakout: 8% Improve: 38% Collapse: 29%

We'd describe his season as a disaster, except that term implies an event that was unforeseeable. No one was surprised when Gonzalez, who suffered a "day-to-day" back injury on May 21, was still recuperating 120 days later. Gonzalez hit 340 homers by his 30th birthday—only seven players have hit more by the same age—but only 94 in the five years since, stopping his once irresistible Hall of Fame chances dead in their tracks. Signed by Cleveland to a minor league deal, which is all the risk a team should be willing to take at this stage.

RUBEN GOTAY 2B Bats: B Throws: R Born: 25-Dec-1982 Age: 22

YEAR	TM	LG	AGE	AB	H	2B	3B	HR	BB	SO	SB	CS	AVG	OBP	SLG	MLVR	EQBA	EQOBP	EQSLG	EQMLVR	VORP	DEFENSE
2002	BUR	MDW	19	509	145	42	9	9	73	110	5	4	.285	.377	.456	.233	.246	.319	.400	-.113	10.1	115-2B 9
2003	WIL	CRL	20	502	131	31	2	9	60	97	8	1	.261	.343	.384	.059	.239	.309	.377	-.169	1.0	123-2B 2
2004	WIC	TXS	21	405	117	22	6	9	51	60	9	10	.289	.373	.440	.150	.262	.334	.402	-.070	13.6	105-2B -11
2004	KCR	AL	21	152	41	7	3	1	9	36	0	1	.270	.315	.375	-.101	.267	.315	.380	-.133	4.1	37-2B 3
2005	*KCR*	*AL*	*22*	*330*	*88*	*20*	*2*	*8*	*32*	*62*	*3*	*2*	*.266*	*.337*	*.414*	*-.035*	*.262*	*.335*	*.415*	*-.049*	*16.7*	*90-2B -4*

Breakout: 34% Improve: 51% Collapse: 21%

The very definition of a sleeper prospect, Gotay again showed exciting offensive potential for a middle infielder his age, and once again, he was completely ignored by prospect mavens. (According to *Baseball America,* he wasn't among the Top 20 Prospects in the Texas League.) Gotay's defense was reported to have improved under Frank White's tutelage in Wichita last season, but the numbers above say otherwise; one observer compares him to Todd Walker. His glove aside, 21-year-old second basemen who can hold their own offensively in the major leagues should not be nearly this unheralded.

TONY GRAFFANINO 2B Bats: R Throws: R Born: 06-Jun-1972 Age: 33

YEAR	TM	LG	AGE	AB	H	2B	3B	HR	BB	SO	SB	CS	AVG	OBP	SLG	MLVR	EQBA	EQOBP	EQSLG	EQMLVR	VORP	DEFENSE
2002	CWS	AL	30	229	60	12	4	6	22	38	2	1	.262	.329	.428	-.016	.264	.336	.432	-.023	11.5	31-3B 0 19-2B 0
2003	CWS	AL	31	250	65	15	3	7	24	37	8	0	.260	.331	.428	-.008	.259	.334	.429	-.035	16.3	27-SS 1 27-2B 0
2004	KCR	AL	32	278	73	11	0	3	27	38	10	2	.263	.332	.335	-.136	.260	.329	.330	-.182	8.1	75-2B 12
2005	*KCR*	*AL*	*33*	*252*	*67*	*12*	*2*	*5*	*25*	*38*	*5*	*2*	*.267*	*.338*	*.393*	*-.059*	*.262*	*.336*	*.394*	*-.074*	*10.3*	*70-2B 0*

Breakout: 21% *Improve: 44%* *Collapse: 32%*

As a starting second baseman, he makes a hell of a utility infielder. Graffanino and Relaford were on the active roster together for barely two months, wrecking the Royals' hopes that between them they'd have an adequate second baseman and a top utility infielder. Graffanino's season ended early when, after suffering his second knee injury of the season, he took the combo package and got an old rotator cuff injury repaired at the same time. Players get hurt; second basemen get hurt more often. Graffanino is the putative starter, but with Gotay and Murphy charging up the system, it's a job he'll hold only long enough for the Royals to find a taker for him.

AARON GUIEL OF Bats: L Throws: R Born: 05-Oct-1972 Age: 32

YEAR	TM	LG	AGE	AB	H	2B	3B	HR	BB	SO	SB	CS	AVG	OBP	SLG	MLVR	EQBA	EQOBP	EQSLG	EQMLVR	VORP	DEFENSE
2002	OMA	PCL	29	215	76	11	1	9	29	34	8	1	.353	.443	.540	.457	.335	.416	.512	.294	23.9	54-RF 3
2002	KCR	AL	29	240	56	13	0	4	19	61	1	5	.233	.296	.338	-.246	.232	.293	.325	-.277	-11.9	57-RF 0
2003	OMA	PCL	30	190	53	9	2	8	33	43	3	0	.279	.408	.474	.249	.255	.374	.432	.039	6.2	47-RF 2
2003	KCR	AL	30	354	98	30	0	15	27	63	3	5	.277	.346	.489	.069	.275	.341	.484	.068	14.6	84-RF 7
2004	KCR	AL	31	135	21	4	0	5	17	42	1	1	.156	.263	.296	-.385	.158	.259	.278	-.446	-10.3	38-LF 0
2004	OMA	PCL	31	116	36	6	0	10	21	33	0	2	.310	.438	.621	.492	.270	.371	.513	.155	7.8	25-LF 0
2005	*KCR*	*AL*	*32*	*172*	*43*	*9*	*1*	*6*	*21*	*46*	*1*	*1*	*.252*	*.350*	*.423*	*-.010*	*.248*	*.348*	*.424*	*-.023*	*5.3*	*51-RF 0*

Breakout: 32% *Improve: 49%* *Collapse: 24%*

The Royals' favorite surprise of 2003 was a complete non-factor last season, thanks to a vision problem no one could get a handle on. He required nearly six weeks to get back on the field after LASIK surgery in May, which was the first clue that something was amiss. After a successful rehab stint in Omaha, he returned to the lineup in August and struggled, before the team admitted he was still having vision troubles. Everyone claims Guiel should be fine in the spring, but neither the team nor its medical staff inspires confidence.

KEN HARVEY 1B Bats: R Throws: R Born: 01-Mar-1978 Age: 27

YEAR	TM	LG	AGE	AB	H	2B	3B	HR	BB	SO	SB	CS	AVG	OBP	SLG	MLVR	EQBA	EQOBP	EQSLG	EQMLVR	VORP	DEFENSE
2002	OMA	PCL	24	488	135	30	1	20	42	87	8	3	.277	.342	.465	.108	.255	.317	.426	-.074	1.3	109-1B -8
2003	KCR	AL	25	485	129	30	0	13	29	94	2	3	.266	.313	.408	-.097	.260	.309	.400	-.121	3.5	91-1B 10
2004	KCR	AL	26	456	131	20	1	13	28	89	1	1	.287	.338	.421	.020	.286	.340	.420	-.015	20.8	72-1B -1
2005	*KCR*	*AL*	*27*	*424*	*114*	*23*	*1*	*14*	*29*	*84*	*2*	*1*	*.268*	*.323*	*.428*	*-.038*	*.264*	*.321*	*.429*	*-.052*	*9.0*	*110-1B -2*

Breakout: 18% *Improve: 44%* *Collapse: 26%*

Perhaps one of the best things to come out of the Royals' season-long malaise was that Harvey regressed to the mean in the second half: Harvey was hitting .379 on June 3, but hit .230 the rest of the way. That may have finally opened some eyes to the reality that they have a poor defensive first baseman whose average isn't nearly high enough to compensate for few walks and little power. The team may now save millions that would have otherwise been heaped on a below-average player Call him the new Ricky Jordan, call him the new Pat Tabler, just don't call him an everyday player. With a career .306/.347/.489 line against left-handers, he would make a heck of a platoon partner for Pickering. Unfortunately, he's far more likely to make 400 outs.

JUSTIN HUBER C Bats: R Throws: R Born: 01-Jul-1982 Age: 23

YEAR	TM	LG	AGE	AB	H	2B	3B	HR	BB	SO	SB	CS	AVG	OBP	SLG	MLVR	EQBA	EQOBP	EQSLG	EQMLVR	VORP	DEFENSE
2002	CMB	SAL	20	330	96	22	2	11	45	81	1	2	.291	.408	.470	.293	.251	.333	.412	-.067	11.4	69-C -2
2002	SLU	FSL	20	100	27	2	1	3	11	18	0	0	.270	.370	.400	.121	.250	.322	.394	-.113	1.9	23-C -4
2003	SLU	FSL	21	183	52	15	0	9	17	30	1	1	.284	.370	.514	.292	.243	.302	.476	-.041	7.9	34-C -6
2003	BIN	EAS	21	193	51	13	0	6	19	54	0	2	.264	.350	.425	.061	.231	.297	.379	-.195	-1.3	39-C -3
2004	SLU	FSL	22	53	15	2	0	2	5	8	2	0	.283	.356	.434	.135	.241	.276	.389	-.214	-1.6	
2004	BIN	EAS	22	236	64	16	1	11	46	57	2	2	.271	.414	.487	.259	.249	.372	.440	.041	16.6	64-C -4
2005	*KCR*	*AL*	*22*	*338*	*89*	*19*	*1*	*14*	*37*	*80*	*1*	*1*	*.263*	*.362*	*.450*	*.053*	*.259*	*.360*	*.451*	*.039*	*25.9*	*95-C -9*

Breakout: 36% *Improve: 53%* *Collapse: 21%*

Allard Baird has a fetish for three-team deals, and this was one time where he was able to extract a nifty fee for his part as the middleman. Huber injured his knee in his last game in the Mets system and never suited up after the trade, but the dramatic improvement in plate discipline he showed earlier alleviated concerns about whether he had the bat to be moved to an offensive position. That should accelerate his shift to first or an outfield corner. If the Royals can stomach the growing pains on defense, Huber would make a better left fielder this season than any of the players being considered.

CHRIS LUBANSKI **CF** **Bats: L** **Throws: L** Born: 24-Mar-1985 Age: 20

YEAR	TM	LG	AGE	AB	H	2B	3B	HR	BB	SO	SB	CS	AVG	OBP	SLG	MLVR	EQBA	EQOBP	EQSLG	EQMLVR	VORP	DEFENSE
2004	BUR	MDW	19	483	133	26	7	9	43	104	16	11	.275	.336	.414	.108	.244	.295	.371	-.201	-8.3	117-CF -16
2005	*KCR*	*AL*	*20*	*376*	*90*	*19*	*3*	*7*	*26*	*89*	*6*	*4*	*.239*	*.292*	*.362*	*-.200*	*.235*	*.291*	*.362*	*-.215*	*-3.9*	*98-CF -8*

Breakout: 25% *Improve: 45%* *Collapse: 34%*

The fifth overall pick in the 2003 draft provided a mixed bag in his full-season debut. His batting average was marginal, he didn't make as much use of his speed as expected—he got nailed on 11 of 27 steal attempts—and his poor defensive instincts in center correlated with his terrible fielding rating. However, he did hit for more power than expected, and drew a passable number of walks for a 19-year-old. With the Royals moving their High-A affiliate to High Desert, Lubanski could create a lot of prospect buzz by hitting .330 without really improving.

MITCH MAIER **3B** **Bats: L** **Throws: R** Born: 30-Jun-1982 Age: 23

YEAR	TM	LG	AGE	AB	H	2B	3B	HR	BB	SO	SB	CS	AVG	OBP	SLG	MLVR	EQBA	EQOBP	EQSLG	EQMLVR	VORP	DEFENSE
2004	BUR	MDW	22	317	95	24	3	4	27	51	34	10	.300	.354	.432	.178	.266	.312	.384	-.134	4.7	71-3B 1
2004	WIL	CRL	22	174	46	9	2	3	15	29	10	2	.264	.326	.391	.018	.234	.289	.360	-.234	-2.9	48-3B -5
2005	*KCR*	*AL*	*23*	*330*	*84*	*19*	*4*	*5*	*21*	*65*	*14*	*5*	*.255*	*.301*	*.380*	*-.149*	*.251*	*.300*	*.381*	*-.163*	*-2.3*	*86-3B -4*

Breakout: 22% *Improve: 41%* *Collapse: 33%*

The stat of the year for the Royals was that Maier, drafted in the first round out of the University of Toledo as a catcher in 2003, stole 44 bases last season—more than Carlos Beltran. Unfortunately, the Royals weren't looking for a flash of blinding speed, but the thump of a power; on that score, he was a bit of a disappointment. Seven homers and 42 walks might be acceptable if he were still behind the plate, but his catching days are behind him, and after committing 27 errors at third base last season, his likely destination is a corner outfield spot. Unless his bat perks up significantly this season, Maier looks destined to become a tweener.

DONNIE MURPHY **2B** **Bats: R** **Throws: R** Born: 10-Mar-1983 Age: 22

YEAR	TM	LG	AGE	AB	H	2B	3B	HR	BB	SO	SB	CS	AVG	OBP	SLG	MLVR	EQBA	EQOBP	EQSLG	EQMLVR	VORP	DEFENSE
2002	SPO	NWN	19	109	33	10	2	0	6	17	0	0	.303	.356	.431	.193	.250	.265	.357	-.274	-4.2	23-SS -1
2002	BUR	MDW	19	120	27	6	3	0	11	31	0	2	.225	.300	.325	-.083	.176	.222	.248	-.555	-13.0	31-SS -5
2003	BUR	MDW	20	504	158	29	6	5	65	78	15	6	.313	.397	.425	.256	.280	.346	.401	-.036	22.5	82-2B 1 40-SS -2
2004	WIL	CRL	21	485	123	32	4	10	52	96	1	1	.254	.326	.398	.019	.227	.289	.365	-.232	-8.8	102-2B 9 15-SS 1
2004	KCR	AL	21	27	5	3	0	0	0	7	1	0	.185	.185	.296	-.528	.185	.132	.259	-.720	-1.7	
2005	*KCR*	*AL*	*22*	*346*	*90*	*23*	*2*	*8*	*27*	*70*	*3*	*2*	*.260*	*.322*	*.405*	*-.076*	*.256*	*.320*	*.406*	*-.091*	*13.6*	*92-2B 0*

Breakout: 33% *Improve: 56%* *Collapse: 26%*

Those of you who remember the legendary battle between Geronimo Pena and Luis Alicea for the Cardinals' second-base job will no doubt enjoy watching Murphy and Gotay duke it out over the next few years. Both are solid Grade B prospects, and they're less than three months apart in age. Gotay has the more developed bat, while Murphy is considered the superior defensive player. The Royals like Murphy enough that they made him the first Royals hitter since Mike Sweeney in 1995 to be promoted directly from A-ball to the majors. We say this every year, but Wilmington is the place where gaudy statistics go to die, and Murphy's OPS there was a point higher than Gotay's OPS there in 2003.

ABRAHAM NUNEZ RF Bats: B Throws: R Born: 05-Feb-1977 Age: 28

YEAR	TM	LG	AGE	AB	H	2B	3B	HR	BB	SO	SB	CS	AVG	OBP	SLG	MLVR	EQBA	EQOBP	EQSLG	EQMLVR	VORP	DEFENSE
2002	CLG	PCL	25	428	107	24	5	21	51	112	31	6	.250	.329	.477	-.025	.208	.286	.394	-.211	-8.8	118-CF 3
2003	ABQ	PCL	26	212	66	13	2	11	32	56	9	4	.311	.398	.547	.221	.248	.335	.442	-.024	2.7	32-RF -1 27-CF 1
2004	FLA	NL	27	64	11	1	1	1	9	21	1	2	.172	.274	.266	-.356	.185	.284	.292	-.364	-5.2	15-LF 1
2004	KCR	AL	27	221	50	9	0	5	25	48	0	1	.226	.304	.335	-.207	.226	.301	.327	-.262	-4.0	54-RF -2
2005	*KCR*	*AL*	*28*	*200*	*46*	*10*	*1*	*6*	*24*	*53*	*4*	*2*	*.231*	*.312*	*.388*	*-.136*	*.228*	*.310*	*.388*	*-.150*	*1.0*	*57-RF 1*

Breakout: 33% *Improve: 51%* *Collapse: 30%*

Nunez was once considered one of the best outfield prospects in the game, but that was before his birth date was moved back three years. Acquired for Rudy Seanez, the Royals saw him as a possible Mark Whiten–type, not a star, but valuable as a player who could switch-hit, draw walks, hit the occasional homer, and kill baserunners with an excellent arm. His two-month audition dashed those hopes, to the point that they had him bat exclusively right-handed in winter ball, then enrolled him with Athletes Performance in Arizona to bulk him up for this season. A career as a caddy for a mediocre left-handed hitter like Terrence Long is probably his upside.

PAUL PHILLIPS C Bats: R Throws: R Born: 15-Apr-1977 Age: 28

YEAR	TM	LG	AGE	AB	H	2B	3B	HR	BB	SO	SB	CS	AVG	OBP	SLG	MLVR	EQBA	EQOBP	EQSLG	EQMLVR	VORP	DEFENSE
2004	OMA	PCL	27	311	97	17	1	6	20	36	4	3	.312	.358	.431	.075	.286	.329	.385	-.085	7.9	76-C 2
2005	*KCR*	*AL*	*28*	*128*	*33*	*6*	*1*	*2*	*6*	*18*	*1*	*1*	*.261*	*.302*	*.360*	*-.171*	*.257*	*.300*	*.360*	*-.186*	*1.4*	*36-C −1*

Breakout: 17% *Improve: 30%* *Collapse: 44%*

Phillips was the Royals' best catching prospect in 2000, but he injured his elbow so badly that he was able to play in a grand total of 13 games over the next three years. Finally coming back, he was not only able to stay healthy for most of 2004, but also put up the best offensive numbers of his career in his first crack at Triple-A. The Royals like him a lot, having kept him on the 40-man roster throughout his ordeal, and Phillips has only NRI Alberto Castillo to beat out for the role of backup catcher.

CALVIN PICKERING DH Bats: L Throws: L Born: 29-Sep-1976 Age: 28

YEAR	TM	LG	AGE	AB	H	2B	3B	HR	BB	SO	SB	CS	AVG	OBP	SLG	MLVR	EQBA	EQOBP	EQSLG	EQMLVR	VORP	DEFENSE
2003	VAQ	MEX	26	291	94	13	0	25	75	84	1	0	.323	.465	.625	.391	.243	.370	.485	.092	27.3	
2003	LOU	INT	26	81	23	3	0	4	17	31	0	0	.284	.422	.469	.237	.232	.356	.390	-.066	0.5	12-1B -1
2004	OMA	PCL	27	299	94	12	1	35	70	85	0	1	.314	.451	.712	.645	.279	.408	.595	.333	41.7	51-1B -7
2004	KCR	AL	27	122	30	8	1	7	18	42	0	0	.246	.338	.500	.093	.244	.342	.496	.058	8.9	
2005	*KCR*	*AL*	*28*	*337*	*92*	*18*	*1*	*24*	*69*	*118*	*0*	*1*	*.272*	*.400*	*.543*	*.238*	*.268*	*.398*	*.544*	*.225*	*36.6*	*99-DH 1*

Breakout: 39% *Improve: 61%* *Collapse: 6%*

You've heard of the Ken Phelps All-Stars? Pickering isn't just a Ken Phelps All-Star, he *is* Ken Phelps. Like Phelps, Pickering has prodigious power and a tremendous batting eye. Also like Phelps, Pickering is rendered useless at the sight of two things: left-handed pitchers, and a fielding glove on his hand. Used in a Phelps-like role as a DH for 400 plate appearances, Pickering could be the best hitter on the team this year. Inexplicably, the Royals, have yet to commit to giving Pickering a spot on the roster. You'll know just how serious the Royals are about building a winning team by where Pickering is on Opening Day: in the lineup, on the bench, in Omaha . . . or in Oakland.

JOE RANDA 3B Bats: R Throws: R Born: 18-Dec-1969 Age: 35

YEAR	TM	LG	AGE	AB	H	2B	3B	HR	BB	SO	SB	CS	AVG	OBP	SLG	MLVR	EQBA	EQOBP	EQSLG	EQMLVR	VORP	DEFENSE
2002	KCR	AL	32	549	155	36	5	11	46	69	2	1	.282	.341	.426	-.018	.277	.340	.420	-.022	24.6	126-3B -3
2003	KCR	AL	33	502	146	31	1	16	41	61	1	0	.291	.348	.452	.037	.282	.345	.444	.025	32.7	123-3B -2
2004	KCR	AL	34	485	139	31	2	8	40	77	0	1	.287	.343	.408	.009	.286	.345	.408	-.023	20.1	114-3B 9
2005	*CIN*	*NL*	*35*	*381*	*102*	*21*	*2*	*9*	*33*	*55*	*0*	*0*	*.269*	*.331*	*.402*	*-.064*	*.267*	*.328*	*.398*	*-.078*	*4.0*	*101-3B -1*

Breakout: 7% *Improve: 31%* *Collapse: 28%*

After predicting Randa's imminent demise for each of the last four years, it's time to give him his props and admit that he's aged a lot better than we expected. He was arguably the most popular player on the team, but the Royals' unwillingness to guarantee that Randa would hold off Mark Teahen even for another season closed the door on his Kansas City career. In the big picture, it's a good sign for the Royals that they no longer value sentiment over winning. Randa's a good one-year risk for the Reds, if for no other reason than that it puts an end to the ridiculous Austin Kearns Third Base Experiment.

DESI RELAFORD — INF — Bats: B — Throws: R — Born: 16-Sep-1973 — Age: 31

YEAR	TM	LG	AGE	AB	H	2B	3B	HR	BB	SO	SB	CS	AVG	OBP	SLG	MLVR	EQBA	EQOBP	EQSLG	EQMLVR	VORP	DEFENSE
2002	SEA	AL	28	329	88	13	2	6	33	51	10	3	.267	.339	.374	-.035	.282	.354	.397	-.025	14.1	33-SS -4 26-3B 0
2003	KCR	AL	29	500	127	27	5	8	40	70	20	4	.254	.315	.376	-.151	.246	.312	.370	-.168	9.0	85-2B -10 27-3B 0
2004	KCR	AL	30	380	84	14	0	6	34	56	5	4	.221	.296	.305	-.275	.221	.294	.304	-.310	-10.8	37-3B 1 33-2B 3
2005	*COL*	*NL*	*31*	*325*	*86*	*16*	*3*	*5*	*31*	*45*	*7*	*2*	*.263*	*.334*	*.377*	*-.096*	*.243*	*.313*	*.341*	*-.197*	*-3.9*	*88-2B -4*

Breakout: 19% *Improve: 47%* *Collapse: 25%*

Sometimes good ideas lead to bad outcomes. The two-year contract the Royals gave Relaford after the 2002 season appeared to be a fine use of $900,000 a year; Relaford was a 29-year-old middle infielder who had hit .284 over the previous two seasons. He was hitting .288 at the All-Star Break in 2003, when he hurt his wrist, and has since hit .216 over a span of more than 600 plate appearances. Now a Rockie, he'll continue his attempt to duplicate Mark McLemore's lengthy, versatile career.

BENITO SANTIAGO — C — Bats: R — Throws: R — Born: 09-Mar-1965 — Age: 40

YEAR	TM	LG	AGE	AB	H	2B	3B	HR	BB	SO	SB	CS	AVG	OBP	SLG	MLVR	EQBA	EQOBP	EQSLG	EQMLVR	VORP	DEFENSE
2002	SFG	NL	37	478	133	24	5	16	27	73	4	2	.278	.315	.450	.072	.284	.318	.470	.016	31.9	120-C 1
2003	SFG	NL	38	401	112	21	2	11	29	69	0	1	.279	.329	.424	.024	.279	.330	.429	-.026	19.7	100-C -7
2004	KCR	AL	39	175	48	10	0	6	8	32	1	2	.274	.312	.434	-.039	.273	.309	.430	-.068	7.1	44-C -5
2005	*PIT*	*NL*	*40*	*179*	*45*	*10*	*1*	*6*	*12*	*35*	*1*	*0*	*.250*	*.301*	*.412*	*-.117*	*.252*	*.300*	*.421*	*-.108*	*5.1*	*50-C -5*

Breakout: 11% *Improve: 42%* *Collapse: 55%*

Santiago was having a pretty good season for a 39-year-old catcher when he broke a bone in his hand on June 18. Injuries of this type typically take six-to-eight weeks to heal, but the Royals' training staff is probably the worst in the majors, and Santiago wasn't able to suit up again for the rest of the season. That the Royals were able to dump him on the Pirates and only be on the hook for half his salary is a credit to them. That they also got a legitimate prospect for him in Leo Nunez is simply an embarrassment for the Pirates.

MATT STAIRS — OF/1B — Bats: L — Throws: R — Born: 27-Feb-1968 — Age: 37

YEAR	TM	LG	AGE	AB	H	2B	3B	HR	BB	SO	SB	CS	AVG	OBP	SLG	MLVR	EQBA	EQOBP	EQSLG	EQMLVR	VORP	DEFENSE
2002	MIL	NL	34	270	66	15	0	16	36	50	2	0	.244	.349	.478	.114	.246	.343	.485	.047	15.5	39-RF -1 27-LF 2
2003	PIT	NL	35	305	89	20	1	20	45	64	0	1	.292	.389	.561	.316	.289	.386	.561	.264	33.7	30-RF 0 22-1B -3
2004	KCR	AL	36	439	117	21	3	18	49	92	1	0	.267	.345	.451	.058	.265	.349	.451	.027	25.1	50-RF -3 25-1B -2
2005	*KCR*	*AL*	*37*	*311*	*83*	*16*	*1*	*15*	*41*	*66*	*0*	*0*	*.267*	*.359*	*.472*	*.079*	*.263*	*.357*	*.473*	*.065*	*16.0*	*86-RF -6*

Breakout: 29% *Improve: 57%* *Collapse: 17%*

Okay, sentiment still has its place in the organization. Stairs's slugging average dropped 110 points in his first season as a Royal, but the team loved his clubhouse influence so much that they signed him for another year before the season had even ended. He's not part of the solution, he's part of the problem, especially since he's a menace to his pitchers in left field, and at DH he's a menace to Pickering's playing time.

KELLY STINNETT — C — Bats: R — Throws: R — Born: 04-Feb-1970 — Age: 35

YEAR	TM	LG	AGE	AB	H	2B	3B	HR	BB	SO	SB	CS	AVG	OBP	SLG	MLVR	EQBA	EQOBP	EQSLG	EQMLVR	VORP	DEFENSE
2002	CIN	NL	32	93	21	5	0	3	15	25	2	0	.226	.333	.376	-.086	.226	.319	.376	-.160	3.3	29-C -2
2003	CIN	NL	33	179	41	13	0	3	13	51	0	0	.229	.294	.352	-.175	.233	.291	.344	-.254	0.2	45-C 0
2004	KCR	AL	34	59	18	0	0	3	5	16	0	0	.305	.379	.458	.130	.328	.352	.483	.139	5.7	18-C -2
2005	*ARI*	*NL*	*35*	*129*	*31*	*6*	*1*	*4*	*12*	*39*	*0*	*0*	*.239*	*.311*	*.387*	*-.141*	*.235*	*.305*	*.380*	*-.166*	*2.3*	*39-C -1*

Breakout: 17% *Improve: 27%* *Collapse: 44%*

On June 18, Benito Santiago broke a bone in his hand, but there were no worries because Stinnett, an underrated backup catcher throughout his career, had been signed precisely because he wouldn't embarrass himself if forced to start for an extended period of time. However, on June 19, Stinnett injured his right elbow so severely that he had to have Tommy John surgery. Don't be surprised if he shows up in Diamondbacks camp with his suitcase filled with horseshoes and rabbit's feet.

MIKE SWEENEY — 1B — Bats: R — Throws: R — Born: 22-Jul-1973 — Age: 31

YEAR	TM	LG	AGE	AB	H	2B	3B	HR	BB	SO	SB	CS	AVG	OBP	SLG	MLVR	EQBA	EQOBP	EQSLG	EQMLVR	VORP	DEFENSE
2002	KCR	AL	28	471	160	31	1	24	61	46	9	7	.340	.417	.563	.332	.338	.418	.561	.370	57.2	100-1B 3
2003	KCR	AL	29	392	115	18	1	16	64	56	3	2	.293	.391	.467	.137	.285	.389	.460	.128	29.8	43-1B 4
2004	KCR	AL	30	411	118	23	0	22	33	44	3	2	.287	.347	.504	.147	.288	.348	.506	.124	33.1	55-1B -2
2005	*KCR*	*AL*	*31*	*414*	*120*	*24*	*1*	*18*	*46*	*51*	*3*	*2*	*.290*	*.364*	*.478*	*.115*	*.285*	*.362*	*.479*	*.101*	*27.1*	*111-1B -3*

Breakout: 11% *Improve: 45%* *Collapse: 25%*

Back problems suck. They destroyed the career of Don Mattingly, and Sweeney, as good a hitter as he is, is no Don Mattingly. The bad news for Sweeney is that he has missed at least a month with back pain each of the last three years. The good news is that when his back is fine, like last April (.324/.373/.544) or July (.344/.392/.633), he can still rake. His erratic availability and $11 million salary have created an awkward situation: Publicly, the Royals are marketing him as the face of the club and reassuring the fans that an off-season of rest will cure what ails him. Privately, they're willing to trade Sweeney to any team that has an unhealthy tolerance for risk.

MARK TEAHEN — 3B — Bats: L — Throws: R — Born: 06-Sep-1981 — Age: 23

YEAR	TM	LG	AGE	AB	H	2B	3B	HR	BB	SO	SB	CS	AVG	OBP	SLG	MLVR	EQBA	EQOBP	EQSLG	EQMLVR	VORP	DEFENSE
2002	MOD	CLF	20	234	56	9	1	1	21	53	1	2	.239	.307	.299	-.168	.217	.270	.272	-.405	-15.4	58-3B 2
2003	MOD	CLF	21	453	128	27	4	3	66	113	4	0	.283	.377	.380	.067	.242	.322	.324	-.215	-4.7	115-3B 3
2004	MID	TXS	22	197	66	15	4	6	29	44	0	0	.335	.419	.543	.373	.289	.368	.469	.107	17.7	52-3B 5
2004	SAC	PCL	22	69	19	8	0	0	11	22	0	1	.275	.383	.391	.008	.191	.259	.250	-.470	-6.0	20-3B -2
2004	OMA	PCL	22	246	69	15	1	8	21	69	0	0	.280	.344	.447	.041	.256	.315	.393	-.123	4.2	66-3B 2
2005	*KCR*	*AL*	*23*	*344*	*86*	*19*	*2*	*7*	*34*	*93*	*1*	*1*	*.251*	*.322*	*.375*	*-.121*	*.247*	*.320*	*.376*	*-.136*	*-1.1*	*92-3B -2*

Breakout: 17% *Improve: 38%* *Collapse: 39%*

As soon as it was clear that the Mets wouldn't give up David Wright for Beltran, Baird identified Teahen as the player he wanted, scouting him personally and making him the centerpiece of the Carlos Beltran trade. Teahen justified Baird's faith in that he hit for more power after the trade (a career-high 14 homers), albeit with a career-high 135 strikeouts. The Royals think he needs another half-season in Triple-A, but given that Chris Truby is the place-holder at third base, Teahen will be given every opportunity to nab the job by June.

PITCHERS

JEREMY AFFELDT — Bats: L — Throws: L — Born: 06-Jun-1979 — Age: 26

YEAR	TM	LG	AGE	G	GS	IP	H	BB	SO	HR	ERA	EQERA	EQH9	EQBB9	EQSO9	EQHR9	PERA	VORP	STF
2002	KCR	AL	23	34	7	77.7	85	37	67	8	4.63	4.06	8.9	3.9	7.3	0.8	4.52	10.6	5
2003	KCR	AL	24	36	18	126.0	126	38	98	12	3.93	3.65	8.5	2.6	6.9	0.7	3.87	27.2	14
2004	KCR	AL	25	38	8	76.3	91	32	49	6	4.95	4.91	9.4	3.3	5.4	0.6	4.32	4.0	-2
2005	*KCR*	*AL*	*26*	*31*	*10*	*83.3*	*88*	*33*	*63*	*10*	*4.65*	*4.38*	*9.4*	*3.1*	*6.2*	*1.0*	*4.39*	*14.0*	*1*

Breakout: 21% *Improve: 48%* *Collapse: 21%*

The player who epitomizes the Royals' 2004 season, more than any other. Affeldt came into the season as one of the prime breakout candidates in baseball, a southpaw who threw 96, spun a nasty curveball, and had put up fine numbers the year before, when he wasn't hindered by a blister problem—a problem that was fixed with corrective nail surgery over the winter. But then he struggled from Opening Day, was bumped from the rotation, struggled in relief, tore an oblique muscle and missed two months, came back and pitched lights out for a month, then collapsed down the stretch. When healthy, his electric stuff was still there, and the club appears committed to him as their closer, but his upside as a 220-inning ace appears lost forever. It was rumored he was tipping his pitches.

BRIAN ANDERSON — Bats: B — Throws: L — Born: 26-Apr-1972 — Age: 33

YEAR	TM	LG	AGE	G	GS	IP	H	BB	SO	HR	ERA	EQERA	EQH9	EQBB9	EQSO9	EQHR9	PERA	VORP	STF
2002	ARI	NL	30	35	24	156.0	174	32	81	23	4.79	4.74	10.0	1.6	4.2	1.3	4.68	9.2	-5
2003	CLE	AL	31	25	24	148.0	162	32	72	21	3.71	5.00	9.8	1.9	4.4	1.2	4.81	12.0	0
2003	KCR	AL	31	7	7	49.7	50	11	15	6	3.98	3.45	9.4	1.9	2.7	1.0	4.40	11.6	-5
2004	KCR	AL	32	35	26	166.0	217	53	70	33	5.64	5.69	10.5	2.5	3.5	1.5	5.48	-8.0	-16
2005	*KCR*	*AL*	*33*	*25*	*18*	*110.0*	*139*	*32*	*48*	*20*	*5.82*	*5.48*	*11.2*	*2.3*	*3.6*	*1.6*	*5.43*	*5.7*	*-13*

Breakout: 15% *Improve: 47%* *Collapse: 28%*

Before the All-Star break: 1-8, 7.23 ERA, 80 IP, 126 H, 30 BB, 30 K, 19 HR
After the All-Star break: 5-4, 4.17 ERA, 86 IP, 91 H, 23 BB, 40 K, 14 HR

In this case, the All-Star break isn't just an arbitrary cutoff: Mike Mason, who had just replaced John Cumberland as the team's pitching coach, noticed a few mechanical flaws in Anderson's delivery and worked with him over the three days to fix them. Anderson's second-half numbers are almost perfectly in line with the rest of his career, so it does appear that his first half was the outlier. There's a lot of value in a pitcher who can give you 32 starts and an ERA of 4.50; pitchers little better than that were getting $7 million a year or more this winter, and Anderson's contract calls for only half that. Still, PECOTA is not optimistic.

DENNY BAUTISTA **Bats: R** **Throws: R** Born: 23-Aug-1980 Age: 24

YEAR	TM	LG	AGE	G	GS	IP	H	BB	SO	HR	ERA	EQERA	EQH9	EQBB9	EQSO9	EQHR9	PERA	VORP	STF
2002	JUP	FSL	21	19	15	88.3	80	40	79	6	4.99	6.59	9.3	4.5	5.9	1.3	5.27	3.0	-1
2003	JUP	FSL	22	14	14	84.0	68	35	77	2	3.21	5.12	8.4	4.3	5.9	0.7	4.19	12.1	11
2003	CAR	SOU	22	11	11	53.3	45	35	61	5	3.71	6.61	9.4	6.2	7.5	1.7	6.24	-3.5	-2
2004	BOW	EAS	23	14	13	62.7	58	33	72	5	4.74	6.00	8.7	4.9	7.7	1.0	4.65	6.3	8
2004	WIC	TXS	23	12	12	81.7	68	32	73	3	2.53	4.36	8.0	4.0	5.9	0.6	3.77	15.5	11
2004	KCR	AL	23	5	5	27.7	38	11	18	2	6.50	5.65	10.0	3.1	5.3	0.6	5.02	-0.8	2
2005	*KCR*	*AL*	*24*	*17*	*16*	*91.0*	*96*	*47*	*70*	*11*	*5.21*	*4.91*	*9.3*	*4.0*	*6.3*	*1.0*	*4.76*	*9.7*	*6*

Breakout: 12% *Improve: 45%* *Collapse: 22%*

It's still a mystery how the Royals managed to trade Jason Grimsley to the Orioles for Bautista, who immediately became the team's best pitching prospect. He's far from a finished product, but he throws very, very hard, and his curveball is very, very good. Bautista averaged nearly seven innings a start for Wichita after the trade, and was pitching (poorly) in winter ball, so in the short term he may struggle from overuse. It would be a mistake if he's in the rotation come Opening Day.

RYAN BUKVICH **Bats: R** **Throws: R** Born: 13-May-1978 Age: 27

YEAR	TM	LG	AGE	G	GS	IP	H	BB	SO	HR	ERA	EQERA	EQH9	EQBB9	EQSO9	EQHR9	PERA	VORP	STF
2002	WIC	TXS	24	23	0	34.3	17	15	47	0	1.31	3.16	6.0	4.3	9.8	0.3	2.59	10.5	26
2002	KCR	AL	24	26	0	25.0	26	19	20	2	6.12	5.76	8.6	6.1	6.8	0.7	5.04	-2.4	-7
2003	OMA	PCL	25	34	0	36.7	39	25	44	2	4.90	5.80	8.8	6.8	9.1	0.8	5.30	1.2	3
2004	OMA	PCL	26	38	0	47.3	33	30	60	4	4.38	5.04	7.1	6.0	9.1	0.8	4.03	7.8	11
2005	*SDP*	*NL*	*27*	*46*	*0*	*37.7*	*29*	*27*	*39*	*3*	*4.25*	*4.84*	*7.0*	*5.8*	*8.3*	*0.8*	*4.78*	*3.4*	*0*

Breakout: 25% *Improve: 44%* *Collapse: 33%*

Great arm, great scouting find (he was drafted as a college drop-out), but unless and until he develops some semblance of command, he'll never be a great pitcher. Bukvich was dispatched to the Padres in the Darrell May–for–Terrence Long deal as a throw-in. One of these years, a random confluence of ballpark, health, and pitching coach will propel Bukvich to a big season. The rest of the time, he'll be allowing too many baserunners.

AMBIORIX BURGOS **Bats: R** **Throws: R** Born: 19-Apr-1984 Age: 21

YEAR	TM	LG	AGE	G	GS	IP	H	BB	SO	HR	ERA	EQERA	EQH9	EQBB9	EQSO9	EQHR9	PERA	VORP	STF
2004	BUR	MDW	20	27	26	133.7	109	75	172	13	4.38	6.14	9.5	6.7	7.2	1.9	6.37	-10.2	-4
2005	*KCR*	*AL*	*21*	*8*	*7*	*40.0*	*34*	*29*	*28*	*10*	*6.03*	*5.68*	*7.5*	*5.7*	*5.6*	*2.2*	*5.50*	*0.4*	*-12*

Breakout: 13% *Improve: 41%* *Collapse: 15%*

Prospects like these are always great fun to watch, because you never quite know what they're going to do from year to year, or even from start to start. Just 20 years old, Burgos led the organization with 172 Ks in just 134 innings, prompting the Royals to add him to the 40-man roster. On the down side, he seems to take the edict to "throw strikes" as no more than a suggestion. His leading indicators are all trending upward: He had a 2.82 ERA after Flag Day, and was the talk of the Dominican League this winter. He's been everything the Royals thought Colt Griffin would be, but a little rough around the edges, so no sense in getting too excited just yet.

SHAWN CAMP Bats: R Throws: R Born: 18-Nov-1975 Age: 29

YEAR	TM	LG	AGE	G	GS	IP	H	BB	SO	HR	ERA	EQERA	EQH9	EQBB9	EQSO9	EQHR9	PERA	VORP	STF
2002	NAS	PCL	26	39	0	58.3	50	15	59	5	3.24	3.93	8.3	2.5	7.2	1.0	3.76	11.2	10
2003	ALT	EAS	27	18	0	29.0	26	11	35	2	4.34	5.27	8.6	3.6	8.9	1.3	4.61	3.0	9
2003	NAS	PCL	27	33	1	43.3	50	15	36	2	4.99	6.21	9.6	3.4	6.2	0.6	4.50	5.1	-8
2004	OMA	PCL	28	15	0	22.0	26	6	21	2	5.32	5.82	9.6	2.5	6.6	0.8	4.57	2.5	-1
2004	KCR	AL	28	42	0	66.7	74	16	51	10	3.91	4.21	9.1	1.9	6.5	1.1	4.07	9.5	1
2005	*KCR*	*AL*	*29*	*37*	*6*	*72.7*	*77*	*23*	*55*	*9*	*4.15*	*3.91*	*9.4*	*2.5*	*6.2*	*1.1*	*4.29*	*16.1*	*2*

Breakout: 28% *Improve: 50%* *Collapse: 24%*

A nifty little find as an NRI, Camp had a long and lackluster minor league career primarily because he was essentially a one-pitch pitcher. Cumberland taught him a slider in the spring, Camp mastered it, and with a new weapon to match a very good sinking fastball—voila! A fine middle reliever was born. His overall numbers were brought down by a home-run rate which was flukishly high given Camp's excellent groundball:flyball ratio of 2.16.

D. J. CARRASCO Bats: R Throws: R Born: 12-Apr-1977 Age: 28

YEAR	TM	LG	AGE	G	GS	IP	H	BB	SO	HR	ERA	EQERA	EQH9	EQBB9	EQSO9	EQHR9	PERA	VORP	STF
2002	LYN	CRL	25	55	0	72.7	52	18	83	1	1.61	3.63	7.5	2.8	7.4	0.3	3.09	18.7	19
2003	KCR	AL	26	50	2	80.3	82	40	57	8	4.82	4.23	8.7	4.3	6.3	0.8	4.58	10.4	1
2004	OMA	PCL	27	32	1	56.3	60	18	50	2	3.20	3.93	8.8	2.9	6.1	0.3	3.93	10.2	1
2004	KCR	AL	27	30	0	35.3	41	15	22	5	4.84	4.84	9.4	3.3	5.3	1.0	4.84	2.7	-13
2005	*KCR*	*AL*	*28*	*46*	*1*	*61.0*	*66*	*25*	*42*	*7*	*4.62*	*4.35*	*9.6*	*3.2*	*5.6*	*0.9*	*4.58*	*10.5*	*-7*

Breakout: 23% *Improve: 45%* *Collapse: 24%*

The Royals' Rule 5 pick after the 2002 season seems to have found his level; unfortunately it's that of a slightly-above-replacement-level reliever. Carrasco's ability to drop down against right-handed hitters laredo-style does give him some value vs. righties, but left-handed hitters have a career line of .300/.412/.440 against him, with more walks (38) than strikeouts (31). A rising G:F ratio is the only reason to hope he might have better years ahead.

JAIME CERDA Bats: L Throws: L Born: 26-Oct-1978 Age: 26

YEAR	TM	LG	AGE	G	GS	IP	H	BB	SO	HR	ERA	EQERA	EQH9	EQBB9	EQSO9	EQHR9	PERA	VORP	STF
2002	BIN	EAS	23	14	0	31.7	21	10	33	0	2.27	3.07	7.1	3.1	7.4	0.3	2.76	9.2	15
2002	NOR	INT	23	12	0	21.0	10	7	17	0	0.43	1.89	5.7	3.3	6.6	0.0	1.89	7.8	17
2002	NYM	NL	23	32	0	25.7	22	14	21	0	2.45	2.88	7.9	4.3	6.5	0.4	3.60	8.3	7
2003	NOR	INT	24	22	0	32.3	29	10	35	3	1.67	2.67	8.6	3.3	8.0	1.2	4.45	3.9	6
2003	NYM	NL	24	27	0	32.3	32	20	19	4	5.85	5.74	9.2	4.9	4.9	1.1	5.17	-0.8	-19
2004	KCR	AL	25	53	0	45.7	41	30	33	1	3.15	3.57	7.7	5.4	6.2	0.2	3.77	10.9	-4
2005	*KCR*	*AL*	*26*	*25*	*4*	*46.0*	*48*	*24*	*32*	*6*	*5.16*	*4.86*	*9.3*	*4.2*	*5.8*	*1.1*	*4.94*	*5.7*	*-9*

Breakout: 23% *Improve: 51%* *Collapse: 28%*

Stolen from the Mets in a deal for Shawn Sedlacek, Cerda throws in the upper 80s with a deceptive delivery. Against left-handed hitters, he aims for the outside corner at the knees on seemingly every pitch, a formula for success for many successful lefty specialists.

NATHAN FIELD Bats: R Throws: R Born: 11-Dec-1975 Age: 29

YEAR	TM	LG	AGE	G	GS	IP	H	BB	SO	HR	ERA	EQERA	EQH9	EQBB9	EQSO9	EQHR9	PERA	VORP	STF
2002	COH	INT	26	21	2	38.7	46	21	25	6	6.74	7.23	10.1	5.3	4.8	1.9	5.79	-0.8	-24
2003	WIC	TXS	27	15	0	20.0	20	8	20	2	3.60	4.82	9.6	4.3	7.2	1.9	6.27	-1.4	-9
2003	OMA	PCL	27	19	0	22.7	15	4	17	4	3.17	4.05	8.6	1.8	6.3	2.7	4.95	1.4	1
2003	KCR	AL	27	19	0	21.7	19	14	19	3	4.15	3.43	8.1	5.6	7.7	1.3	4.71	4.7	4
2004	KCR	AL	28	43	0	44.3	40	19	30	5	4.27	4.36	8.1	3.5	5.8	0.8	3.95	5.9	2
2005	*KCR*	*AL*	*29*	*21*	*0*	*24.7*	*25*	*11*	*17*	*4*	*4.96*	*4.67*	*9.1*	*3.6*	*5.7*	*1.4*	*4.87*	*3.9*	*-11*

Breakout: 28% *Improve: 58%* *Collapse: 17%*

The Royals have long been fans of this undrafted indy league veteran, and Field started to reward their confidence in him last season. Dialing it up to 94, Field even served as the closer for a few days when the bullpen was melting down.Sadly, his year ended two months early with a torn oblique muscle. As long as guys like this are available for the major league minimum—which is to say, forever—handing seven-figure contracts to the Jose Mesas of the world is pure folly.

CHRIS GEORGE **Bats: L** **Throws: L** Born: 16-Sep-1979 Age: 25

YEAR	TM	LG	AGE	G	GS	IP	H	BB	SO	HR	ERA	EQERA	EQH9	EQBB9	EQSO9	EQHR9	PERA	VORP	STF
2002	OMA	PCL	22	22	21	127.3	145	65	94	15	5.87	6.18	10.0	4.9	5.2	1.2	5.74	-1.9	-2
2002	KCR	AL	22	6	6	27.3	37	8	13	2	5.60	4.88	10.4	2.3	3.9	0.7	4.88	1.2	0
2003	OMA	PCL	23	10	10	54.3	71	22	28	8	7.29	8.54	11.5	4.2	4.0	1.7	7.14	-8.8	-25
2003	KCR	AL	23	18	18	93.7	120	44	39	22	7.11	6.16	10.9	4.0	3.6	1.9	6.55	-11.7	-29
2004	OMA	PCL	24	20	19	105.3	97	40	74	7	3.42	4.14	8.4	3.7	4.9	0.6	3.96	18.2	15
2004	KCR	AL	24	10	7	42.3	60	25	15	1	7.23	7.01	10.5	4.5	2.9	0.2	5.15	-9.7	-7
2005	*KCR*	*AL*	*25*	*16*	*13*	*75.7*	*92*	*35*	*41*	*12*	*6.09*	*5.73*	*10.8*	*3.6*	*4.4*	*1.4*	*5.64*	*2.0*	*-10*

Breakout: 20% *Improve: 45%* *Collapse: 27%*

The former wunderkind hit rock bottom last season after posting a strikeout-to-walk ratio that looked like a misprint (9 Ks:20 BBs) in a brief trial in the Royals rotation. With his career on life support, George returned to Omaha and found the four mph that had disappeared from his fastball in 2001. No one has any explanation for where the extra velocity came from, but it helped George go 7–1 down the stretch in Triple-A and get a September call-up. Despite struggling yet again, he was kept on the 40-man roster over the winter. Left-handers who throw 94 in relief will continue to get chances.

JIMMY GOBBLE **Bats: L** **Throws: L** Born: 19-Jul-1981 Age: 23

YEAR	TM	LG	AGE	G	GS	IP	H	BB	SO	HR	ERA	EQERA	EQH9	EQBB9	EQSO9	EQHR9	PERA	VORP	STF
2002	WIC	TXS	20	13	13	69.3	71	19	52	3	3.38	4.82	9.6	2.6	5.2	0.7	4.68	6.7	11
2003	WIC	TXS	21	22	22	132.7	128	40	100	11	3.19	4.66	9.4	3.1	5.3	1.3	5.17	5.9	11
2003	KCR	AL	21	9	9	52.7	56	15	31	8	4.61	4.76	9.4	2.5	5.3	1.2	4.76	3.6	18
2004	KCR	AL	22	25	24	148.0	157	43	49	24	5.35	4.91	9.4	2.4	2.9	1.3	4.53	8.5	-8
2005	*KCR*	*AL*	*23*	*24*	*22*	*126.0*	*151*	*43*	*65*	*22*	*5.80*	*5.46*	*10.6*	*2.7*	*4.2*	*1.5*	*5.30*	*6.4*	*-7*

Breakout: 13% *Improve: 52%* *Collapse: 29%*

Gobble made 24 starts last season, and struck out five batters in exactly one of them. He became only the third pitcher in the last decade to throw 130+ innings and strike out less than three batters per nine innings. All the moxie and control in the world won't make up for asking your defense to make 24 outs a game. His prospects for recovery are better, owing to a good curve and better control.

ZACK GREINKE **Bats: R** **Throws: R** Born: 21-Oct-1983 Age: 21

YEAR	TM	LG	AGE	G	GS	IP	H	BB	SO	HR	ERA	EQERA	EQH9	EQBB9	EQSO9	EQHR9	PERA	VORP	STF
2003	WIL	CRL	19	14	14	87.0	56	13	78	5	1.14	2.90	8.0	1.5	6.4	1.0	3.59	17.4	47
2003	WIC	TXS	19	9	9	53.0	58	5	34	5	3.23	4.14	10.3	0.9	4.5	1.3	5.04	3.1	17
2004	OMA	PCL	20	6	6	28.7	25	6	23	2	2.51	3.00	8.0	2.0	5.7	0.7	3.33	6.8	24
2004	KCR	AL	20	24	24	145.0	143	26	100	26	3.97	3.45	8.6	1.5	5.9	1.4	3.83	36.4	22
2005	*KCR*	*AL*	*21*	*24*	*24*	*152.7*	*164*	*36*	*117*	*26*	*4.24*	*3.99*	*9.5*	*1.9*	*6.3*	*1.5*	*4.43*	*33.2*	*14*

Breakout: 23% *Improve: 63%* *Collapse: 0%*

With apologies to Jon Landau, we have seen the future of pitching, and his name is Zack Greinke. There are two sets of opinions on Greinke. There's the camp that thinks all the talk about his being the most extraordinary young pitcher of his generation is overblown hype. Then there's the camp of people who have seen him pitch.

Start with his statistical record. He debuted in the majors less than two years after he was drafted out of high school. His 3.97 ERA would have ranked him in the AL's top ten if he'd qualified. Most impressively, he walked just 1.67 men per 9 innings. In the last 70 years, only three other pitchers as young as Greinke walked fewer than 2.1 men per 9 innings. Two of them were Bert Blyleven and Bret Saberhagen.

But Greinke's stats are less distinctive than his style, which may be unprecedented for a pitcher his age. A scouting report will say that he throws his fastball 93–94, but he only throws maximum velocity on maybe a quarter of his fastballs, preferring to throw 88 with precision than sacrifice some command for increased velocity. He changes speeds on all of his pitches, actually; in any given start he'll throw at least one pitch at 62, another at 94, and hit most every number in between. And that doesn't count the 50 mph floater he learned from Dave LaRoche, his Triple-A pitching coach and famed a generation ago for that pitch.

Greinke's ability to keep hitters off-balance extends beyond simply changing speeds. He struck out Ivan Rodriguez looking on a quick-pitch last summer before Pudge could plant his feet. In the minors, he was known for setting up hitters with a quick-pitch to rile them up before returning with a slow curveball that they would invariably be out in front of by a yard or two.

(continued next page)

Zack Greinke *(continued)*

He brings other assets to the table. He started pitching full-time only in his senior year of high school, keeping his arm fresh. He would have been a top-three round selection as a shortstop, and has Gold Glove potential as a pitcher. His next error will be his first as a pro. He has excellent mechanics, has never thrown 110 pitches in a game, and since he rarely throws at maximum velocity, he's about as low an injury risk as any young pitcher in the game.

His profile is so unique that trying to project his future is a fool's errand, although the fact that PECOTA projects a collapse rate of 0% is astonishing for a young pitcher. All we can say is that in the past 30 years, the pitcher Greinke best compares to as a rookie, both statistically and stylistically, is Saberhagen. As a sophomore, Saberhagen won the Cy Young Award.

COLT GRIFFIN Bats: R Throws: R Born: 29-Sep-1982 Age: 22

YEAR	TM	LG	AGE	G	GS	IP	H	BB	SO	HR	ERA	EQERA	EQH9	EQBB9	EQSO9	EQHR9	PERA	VORP	STF
2002	BUR	MDW	19	19	19	90.7	75	82	66	1	5.36	7.67	8.4	10.6	4.2	0.2	5.67	-0.6	-1
2003	BUR	MDW	20	27	27	149.7	127	97	107	7	3.91	6.66	9.5	7.7	4.6	1.3	6.60	-14.7	-11
2004	WIL	CRL	21	8	8	33.0	40	28	28	1	8.73	10.34	10.6	8.6	5.5	0.6	7.18	-5.5	-28
2004	WIC	TXS	21	26	0	31.3	29	16	26	2	4.03	4.91	8.9	5.2	5.5	0.9	4.91	2.2	-10
2005	*KCR*	*AL*	*22*	*12*	*7*	*42.0*	*43*	*30*	*28*	*6*	*5.87*	*5.53*	*9.1*	*5.6*	*5.5*	*1.3*	*5.56*	*1.8*	*-13*

Breakout: 25% *Improve: 51%* *Collapse: 22%*

As his third straight season as a starter was shaping up to be the most disappointing of them all, the Royals finally took the hint and moved Griffin and his occasionally triple-digit fastball to the bullpen. The funny thing is, they were so confident he could make the transition that they simultaneously promoted him and his 8.73 ERA to Double-A. Somehow it worked: His walks, hit batsmen, and wild pitches all dropped dramatically. He took to the bullpen so well that it was mildly surprising when no team took him in the Rule 5 Draft.

RUNELVYS HERNANDEZ Bats: R Throws: R Born: 27-Apr-1978 Age: 27

YEAR	TM	LG	AGE	G	GS	IP	H	BB	SO	HR	ERA	EQERA	EQH9	EQBB9	EQSO9	EQHR9	PERA	VORP	STF
2002	WIC	TXS	24	16	14	106.3	96	24	86	3	2.71	4.35	8.9	2.3	5.6	0.5	3.99	17.8	17
2002	KCR	AL	24	12	12	74.3	79	22	45	8	4.36	3.72	9.0	2.5	5.2	0.9	4.21	13.4	8
2003	KCR	AL	25	16	16	91.7	87	37	48	9	4.61	4.30	8.7	3.6	4.7	0.8	4.40	11.0	3
2005	*KCR*	*AL*	*27*	*17*	*17*	*95.3*	*107*	*36*	*60*	*12*	*5.01*	*4.72*	*10.0*	*3.0*	*5.2*	*1.1*	*4.77*	*12.2*	*3*

Breakout: 18% *Improve: 43%* *Collapse: 25%*

Sometimes the best thing that can happen to a pitcher is that he goes under the knife. The Royals were already frustrated with Hernandez's work ethic before he blew out his elbow, and were skeptical that he would dedicate himself to his rehab. They were pleasantly surprised that he used his Tommy John surgery as a wake-up call to take his career more seriously; his rehab went very well and he's expected back in the Royals' rotation on Opening Day. Before his elbow started to hurt, Hernandez had a 3.50 ERA in his first 17 career starts,

J. P. HOWELL Bats: L Throws: L Born: 25-Apr-1983 Age: 22

YEAR	TM	LG	AGE	G	GS	IP	H	BB	SO	HR	ERA	EQERA	EQH9	EQBB9	EQSO9	EQHR9	PERA	VORP	STF
2004	IDA	PIO	21	6	4	26.0	16	12	38	1	2.77	5.40	7.3	5.4	6.2	0.8	3.86	4.5	8
2005	*KCR*	*AL*	*22*	*21*	*12*	*77.7*	*68*	*48*	*53*	*13*	*5.01*	*4.72*	*7.7*	*4.9*	*5.6*	*1.4*	*4.68*	*10.7*	*-8*

Breakout: 17% *Improve: 44%* *Collapse: 18%*

Another example of the Royals' growing sabermetric bent, Howell throws 87 on a good day, but the Royals used a supplemental first-round pick to draft him last season based largely on his performance: a 2.26 ERA and 153 strikeouts in 124 IP during his junior season at Texas, and his being a finalist for the inaugural Roger Clemens Award for best collegiate pitcher (won by Jered Weaver). Armed with an excellent curve, Howell had no trouble in his pro debut, and along with fellow collegiate draftees Matt Campbell and Billy Buckner figures to move up the Royals chain quickly.

JUSTIN HUISMAN Bats: R Throws: R Born: 16-Apr-1979 Age: 26

YEAR	TM	LG	AGE	G	GS	IP	H	BB	SO	HR	ERA	EQERA	EQH9	EQBB9	EQSO9	EQHR9	PERA	VORP	STF
2002	SLM	CRL	23	41	0	51.7	47	14	24	0	1.57	3.40	8.9	3.0	3.0	0.2	3.97	8.6	-12
2002	CAR	SOU	23	18	0	24.3	30	12	10	4	6.67	8.74	12.3	4.4	2.8	2.8	7.94	-5.9	-41
2003	TUL	TXS	24	57	0	61.7	55	7	46	1	1.75	4.01	8.3	1.1	5.1	0.3	2.93	17.3	9
2004	OMA	PCL	25	32	0	42.3	50	18	37	3	3.62	4.97	9.5	3.9	6.0	0.6	4.75	3.9	-3
2004	KCR	AL	25	14	0	25.0	36	8	13	3	6.84	5.96	10.9	2.5	4.2	1.1	5.61	-2.6	-11
2005	*KCR*	*AL*	*26*	*30*	*0*	*27.0*	*32*	*10*	*17*	*3*	*4.80*	*4.52*	*10.4*	*2.9*	*5.1*	*0.9*	*4.74*	*4.0*	*-10*

Breakout: 23% *Improve: 50%* *Collapse: 21%*

When the Rockies let it be known that they were planning to waive Huisman off of their 40-man roster last spring, the Royals quickly acquired him for two non-prospects. He entered 2004 with a 2.31 career ERA in the minors, but his early struggles and Shawn Camp's emergence relegated him to Omaha for most of the season. He'll be back; Huisman is a groundball pitcher who throws strikes, and you really can't have too many pitchers like that on your roster.

MATT KINNEY Bats: R Throws: R Born: 16-Dec-1976 Age: 28

YEAR	TM	LG	AGE	G	GS	IP	H	BB	SO	HR	ERA	EQERA	EQH9	EQBB9	EQSO9	EQHR9	PERA	VORP	STF
2002	MIN	AL	25	14	12	66.0	78	33	45	13	4.64	4.85	10.1	4.2	5.8	1.7	6.09	4.9	-7
2003	MIL	NL	26	33	31	190.7	201	80	152	27	5.19	5.47	9.1	3.3	6.5	1.2	4.51	-0.3	9
2004	MIL	NL	27	32	6	62.3	77	23	52	8	5.78	5.63	10.0	2.9	6.5	1.0	4.91	-1.3	0
2004	KCR	AL	27	11	0	16.3	27	7	21	3	7.18	6.62	10.7	3.1	10.2	1.5	6.11	-2.6	13
2005	*SFG*	*NL*	*28*	*25*	*9*	*72.0*	*73*	*27*	*57*	*9*	*4.41*	*4.76*	*9.0*	*3.0*	*6.4*	*1.2*	*4.86*	*8.6*	*1*

Breakout: 22% *Improve: 52%* *Collapse: 24%*

The waiver claim the Royals put on Kinney in August should have worked—Kinney's struggles with Milwaukee were mostly the product of phenomenally bad luck on balls in play—but he was even worse in that department with KC. Signed with the Giants, who have the perfect ballpark for him.

DEVON LOWERY Bats: L Throws: R Born: 24-Mar-1983 Age: 22

YEAR	TM	LG	AGE	G	GS	IP	H	BB	SO	HR	ERA	EQERA	EQH9	EQBB9	EQSO9	EQHR9	PERA	VORP	STF
2003	BUR	MDW	20	26	10	96.3	78	34	74	9	3.36	5.49	10.3	4.3	4.9	2.6	6.88	-11.9	-14
2004	WIL	CRL	21	28	28	145.0	139	52	115	16	3.66	5.62	10.2	3.8	5.3	2.0	6.37	-11.2	-12
2005	*KCR*	*AL*	*22*	*8*	*7*	*41.0*	*45*	*20*	*27*	*8*	*5.77*	*5.43*	*9.7*	*3.8*	*5.4*	*1.7*	*5.38*	*2.1*	*-5*

Breakout: 12% *Improve: 42%* *Collapse: 16%*

Listed here only because the Royals chose to add him to their 40-man roster, for reasons not easily discerned from his statistical record. A 3.66 ERA in Wilmington is a reason NOT to add a pitcher to your roster. Sure, he's athletic, throws in the low 90s, and wins points for his work ethic—but none of those things were going to get him picked in the Rule 5 Draft.

MIKE MacDOUGAL Bats: B Throws: R Born: 05-Mar-1977 Age: 28

YEAR	TM	LG	AGE	G	GS	IP	H	BB	SO	HR	ERA	EQERA	EQH9	EQBB9	EQSO9	EQHR9	PERA	VORP	STF
2002	OMA	PCL	25	12	10	53.0	52	55	30	4	5.60	7.07	9.1	10.1	4.2	0.9	6.70	-6.1	-31
2003	KCR	AL	26	68	0	64.0	64	32	57	4	4.08	4.41	8.2	4.3	7.8	0.4	4.12	7.4	11
2004	KCR	AL	27	13	0	11.3	16	9	14	2	5.58	5.25	9.8	6.0	9.8	1.5	6.00	-0.1	5
2004	OMA	PCL	27	14	0	14.3	12	11	8	1	5.66	5.40	8.1	7.4	4.1	0.7	4.72	1.3	-28
2004	WIC	TXS	27	17	2	18.3	14	14	13	0	1.48	4.24	7.4	7.9	4.8	0.5	4.76	1.6	-24
2005	*KCR*	*AL*	*28*	*36*	*1*	*47.7*	*45*	*33*	*36*	*5*	*4.78*	*4.51*	*8.3*	*5.5*	*6.1*	*0.8*	*4.68*	*7.9*	*-10*

Breakout: 20% *Improve: 53%* *Collapse: 12%*

When he's on, MacDougal is a dominant reliever; he's just never on. There are his massive control problems, a string-bean body that can't keep on weight—he missed the first month of the season because a stomach virus cost him 15 pounds—and inconsistent mechanics which shut him down twice last season with elbow soreness. His talent could make him a top closer, but few think he'll ever make full use of it. He isn't worth the headache.

DARRELL MAY Bats: L Throws: L Born: 13-Jun-1972 Age: 33

YEAR	TM	LG	AGE	G	GS	IP	H	BB	SO	HR	ERA	EQERA	EQH9	EQBB9	EQSO9	EQHR9	PERA	VORP	STF
2002	KCR	AL	30	30	21	131.3	144	50	95	28	5.35	4.83	9.4	3.2	6.2	1.7	5.18	4.3	-2
2003	KCR	AL	31	35	32	210.0	197	53	115	31	3.77	3.68	8.7	2.2	5.0	1.2	4.22	44.0	6
2004	KCR	AL	32	31	31	186.0	234	55	120	38	5.61	5.35	10.0	2.4	5.4	1.5	5.16	-1.2	1
2005	*SDP*	*NL*	*33*	*27*	*22*	*138.7*	*143*	*42*	*92*	*20*	*4.51*	*5.13*	*9.4*	*2.4*	*5.3*	*1.4*	*5.04*	*8.8*	*1*

Breakout: 13% *Improve: 35%* *Collapse: 26%*

Scouting May out of the Japanese leagues was an inspired move by Baird, but it didn't work out quite as well as he would have liked. May's only serious vice is a propensity for doling out homers, which makes him appealing in his new venue in Petco Park, which reduced home runs by over 30% last season. Turn ten home runs into outs, and May's ERA drops by half a run, even before you account for the lack of DH. He's a good bet for 200 innings with an ERA close to four.

DENNYS REYES Bats: R Throws: L Born: 19-Apr-1977 Age: 28

YEAR	TM	LG	AGE	G	GS	IP	H	BB	SO	HR	ERA	EQERA	EQH9	EQBB9	EQSO9	EQHR9	PERA	VORP	STF
2002	COL	NL	25	43	0	40.3	43	24	30	1	4.24	3.79	8.9	4.5	5.8	0.2	4.24	5.1	-6
2002	TEX	AL	25	15	5	42.3	55	21	29	9	6.38	6.12	10.3	4.0	5.7	1.7	6.12	-4.9	-13
2003	TUC	PCL	26	33	0	31.7	24	22	30	0	2.84	4.55	7.0	7.3	7.3	0.3	3.94	5.5	-2
2003	PIT	NL	26	12	0	10.3	10	9	11	1	10.49	10.45	8.7	7.0	8.7	0.9	5.23	-6.5	0
2004	KCR	AL	27	40	12	108.0	114	50	91	12	4.75	4.57	8.6	3.7	7.1	0.8	4.15	11.0	10
2005	*SDP*	*NL*	*28*	*32*	*10*	*85.0*	*85*	*41*	*70*	*8*	*4.43*	*5.05*	*9.1*	*3.9*	*6.6*	*0.9*	*5.11*	*5.5*	*0*

Breakout: 18% *Improve: 40%* *Collapse: 28%*

Reyes has long been one of our favorite pitchers, and not just because he's a delightfully portly left-hander who's occasionally breaks out a screwball. We're talking about a pitcher who can handle almost any role, and he's always available for a song: The Royals picked him up as a NRI last spring, and the Padres just signed him for $550,000. He might be a minor star if he wasn't determined to prove DIPS theory wrong—he has surrendered more hits than expected in each of his ten major league seasons. His ERA last season was 4.75, and for his career it's 4.76, identical stats to those for Eric Milton, who will be making more than 15 times as much this season.

JIM SERRANO Bats: R Throws: R Born: 09-May-1976 Age: 29

YEAR	TM	LG	AGE	G	GS	IP	H	BB	SO	HR	ERA	EQERA	EQH9	EQBB9	EQSO9	EQHR9	PERA	VORP	STF
2002	NOR	INT	26	53	0	74.0	88	31	76	3	4.01	5.50	9.3	4.0	7.6	0.5	4.40	9.8	-7
2003	NOR	INT	27	27	0	49.0	38	19	47	2	2.39	3.15	7.5	4.1	7.1	0.6	3.55	10.4	12
2003	OMA	PCL	27	19	0	28.0	25	11	28	2	3.21	4.44	8.5	4.1	7.9	1.0	4.44	3.4	3
2004	WIC	TXS	28	11	11	64.3	42	18	74	6	1.96	3.53	7.5	2.9	7.7	1.5	3.84	11.5	33
2004	OMA	PCL	28	16	1	32.3	32	21	41	4	5.02	6.32	8.6	6.0	8.9	1.4	5.46	0.5	0
2004	KCR	AL	28	10	5	32.7	35	12	25	5	4.68	3.90	8.9	3.1	6.4	1.1	4.45	5.7	3
2005	*OAK*	*AL*	*29*	*20*	*9*	*69.0*	*65*	*31*	*59*	*10*	*4.39*	*4.35*	*8.5*	*3.6*	*6.9*	*1.2*	*4.49*	*12.2*	*5*

Breakout: 22% *Improve: 46%* *Collapse: 23%*

Serrano was a lifetime minor league farmhand who accomplished something both common (he gained velocity after switching roles) and highly unusual (switching from the bullpen to the rotation, not the other way around). The Royals brought him up in August, and he acquitted himself fairly well. When the Royals took him off of their roster after the season, the A's snatched him up. He has everything you want in an 11th pitcher: competence, versatility, and a willingness to work for the minimum.

MIKE STODOLKA Bats: L Throws: L Born: 24-Sep-1981 Age: 23

YEAR	TM	LG	AGE	G	GS	IP	H	BB	SO	HR	ERA	EQERA	EQH9	EQBB9	EQSO9	EQHR9	PERA	VORP	STF
2002	BUR	MDW	20	27	27	148.7	173	51	105	15	5.27	8.34	11.8	3.9	4.0	2.4	7.21	-24.3	-36
2003	WIL	CRL	21	5	5	21.0	15	9	10	0	3.00	4.74	8.1	4.3	3.3	0.5	4.26	2.8	-6
2004	WIL	CRL	22	14	14	62.3	66	18	33	5	4.33	6.12	10.5	3.0	3.5	1.4	5.97	-2.4	-12
2005	*KCR*	*AL*	*23*	*21*	*11*	*71.3*	*85*	*33*	*36*	*12*	*5.83*	*5.49*	*10.5*	*3.6*	*4.2*	*1.5*	*5.63*	*2.8*	*-16*

Breakout: 16% *Improve: 43%* *Collapse: 14%*

Not to say that Stodolka hasn't panned out quite as well as the Royals would have liked, but last spring Baseball America ranked him as the worst #4 overall pick in history. That was before Stodolka returned from Tommy John surgery, and when he returned, his fastball showed signs of regaining the velocity that he had on draft day but which had never materialized as a pro. The Royals sent him to the AFL, where he fared well. At this point the Royals will take any contribution they can get.

SCOTT SULLIVAN **Bats: R** **Throws: R** Born: 13-Mar-1971 Age: 34

YEAR	TM	LG	AGE	G	GS	IP	H	BB	SO	HR	ERA	EQERA	EQH9	EQBB9	EQSO9	EQHR9	PERA	VORP	STF
2002	CIN	NL	31	71	0	78.7	93	31	78	15	6.06	6.66	9.9	3.0	7.8	1.6	5.40	-13.0	-3
2003	CIN	NL	32	50	0	49.7	39	26	43	4	3.62	3.97	7.6	4.2	7.2	0.8	3.59	9.0	3
2003	CWS	AL	32	15	0	14.3	9	6	13	2	3.78	3.38	6.8	4.1	8.1	1.4	3.38	3.7	10
2004	KCR	AL	33	49	0	60.3	73	24	45	8	4.78	4.28	9.4	3.1	6.2	1.0	4.57	8.1	-4
2005	*KCR*	*AL*	*34*	*45*	*0*	*52.7*	*56*	*22*	*41*	*8*	*5.12*	*4.82*	*9.4*	*3.4*	*6.4*	*1.4*	*4.95*	*6.9*	*-6*

Breakout: 19% *Improve: 44%* *Collapse: 23%*

When the Royals were dreaming of another pennant run in 2004, Sullivan looked like a solid piece of bullpen depth. Now that the Royals are in the cellar, he's a luxury they'd like to jettison *tout de suite.* The reigning dean of sidearmers, he's still effective against right-handed hitters; left-handers, on the other hand, hit .355 and slugged .688 against him last year, which may explain his league-leading ten intentional walks.

DANNY TAMAYO **Bats: R** **Throws: R** Born: 03-Jun-1979 Age: 26

YEAR	TM	LG	AGE	G	GS	IP	H	BB	SO	HR	ERA	EQERA	EQH9	EQBB9	EQSO9	EQHR9	PERA	VORP	STF
2002	WIL	CRL	23	23	20	123.3	121	32	108	13	2.77	5.00	10.6	2.9	5.8	2.3	6.45	-10.5	-14
2003	WIC	TXS	24	27	26	154.0	159	56	95	16	4.56	5.61	10.1	3.8	4.4	1.8	6.25	-10.3	-10
2004	WIC	TXS	25	25	25	142.3	166	36	123	15	3.98	4.94	10.3	2.5	5.5	1.6	5.47	2.0	-6
2005	*KCR*	*AL*	*26*	*10*	*8*	*47.0*	*55*	*17*	*31*	*8*	*5.57*	*5.24*	*10.3*	*2.9*	*5.4*	*1.5*	*5.21*	*3.2*	*-2*

Breakout: 13% *Improve: 40%* *Collapse: 19%*

Hey, it's the Royals Minor League Pitcher of the Year! Tamayo won the award in part because he finished the season on fire, with a 1.88 ERA in his last 10 starts, and in part because he was the team's only actual prospect in the high minors who spent the entire year in a rotation. He lost whatever favor he had in the organization by doing his part to make 2004 the most offense-oriented year ever in the AFL (10.73 ERA in eight horrific starts). If Quadruple-A ever goes from a theoretical construct to an actual league, he's got All-Star potential.

J. J. TRUJILLO **Bats: R** **Throws: R** Born: 09-Oct-1975 Age: 29

YEAR	TM	LG	AGE	G	GS	IP	H	BB	SO	HR	ERA	EQERA	EQH9	EQBB9	EQSO9	EQHR9	PERA	VORP	STF
2002	MOB	SOU	26	31	0	41.0	25	12	49	1	0.66	1.66	6.6	2.6	8.3	0.5	2.61	12.6	24
2002	POR	PCL	26	18	1	27.0	30	8	28	2	4.33	5.19	10.0	2.8	7.3	0.7	5.19	1.2	-3
2003	MOB	SOU	27	28	0	41.3	35	12	33	1	3.70	5.12	8.4	2.8	5.1	0.5	3.72	8.1	0
2003	POR	PCL	27	27	0	32.0	32	10	22	6	5.62	6.67	10.0	3.3	5.5	2.7	6.07	-1.6	-16
2004	WIC	TXS	28	59	2	96.7	95	22	79	4	3.16	4.70	8.8	2.2	5.3	0.7	3.72	19.2	7
2005	*KCR*	*AL*	*29*	*15*	*3*	*32.0*	*36*	*11*	*21*	*4*	*4.32*	*4.07*	*9.8*	*2.7*	*5.5*	*1.0*	*4.57*	*6.9*	*-3*

Breakout: 31% *Improve: 51%* *Collapse: 24%*

Trujillo is a soft-tossing Padres refugee who compensates for decidedly below-average velocity with a funky submarine delivery that has baffled right-handed hitters from the independent leagues to Triple-A. He's a poor man's Chad Bradford, which tells you how slim the margin for error is among this subset of pitchers. Trujillo is 90% the pitcher Bradford is, but that's often the difference between a long career in big league relief and life in the minors.

JORGE VASQUEZ **Bats: R** **Throws: R** Born: 16-Jul-1978 Age: 26

YEAR	TM	LG	AGE	G	GS	IP	H	BB	SO	HR	ERA	EQERA	EQH9	EQBB9	EQSO9	EQHR9	PERA	VORP	STF
2002	BUR	MDW	23	22	0	46.0	22	15	55	3	1.57	3.63	7.5	3.9	7.0	1.8	4.08	6.7	10
2003	WIL	CRL	24	17	0	23.0	19	14	31	1	1.96	3.80	8.4	5.9	9.3	0.8	5.06	1.3	1
2003	WIC	TXS	24	36	0	51.7	39	18	52	3	1.91	3.02	7.9	3.6	7.2	0.9	3.97	8.6	7
2004	WIC	TXS	25	49	0	59.7	52	27	71	3	4.67	5.75	8.3	4.5	7.7	0.8	4.31	8.1	3
2005	*ATL*	*NL*	*26*	*22*	*1*	*30.0*	*26*	*14*	*26*	*4*	*4.17*	*4.41*	*8.0*	*3.8*	*7.0*	*1.1*	*4.41*	*4.4*	*0*

Breakout: 23% *Improve: 45%* *Collapse: 23%*

(continued next page)

Jorge Vasquez *(continued)*

Wherever he pitches, hitters have a habit of walking back to the dugout after an at-bat: Vasquez has struck out more than a batter an inning at every stop in his pro career, 312 Ks in 258 innings total, and without much trotting (15 homers allowed). He matches those solid peripherals with a good repertoire, including a low-90s fastball and good slider. There's no obvious reason why he can't be an effective reliever in the majors, especially now that he'll get to work with Leo Mazzone, after being traded to Atlanta for Eli Marrero.

LES WALROND **Bats: L** **Throws: L** Born: 07-Nov-1976 Age: 28

YEAR	TM	LG	AGE	G	GS	IP	H	BB	SO	HR	ERA	EQERA	EQH9	EQBB9	EQSO9	EQHR9	PERA	VORP	STF
2002	NHV	EAS	25	4	4	22.3	19	10	31	2	2.42	4.29	8.6	4.3	9.9	1.3	4.71	2.1	24
2002	MEM	PCL	25	28	18	123.0	127	63	111	20	4.98	5.82	9.9	5.0	6.5	1.9	6.52	-11.9	-15
2003	MEM	PCL	26	10	1	17.3	12	7	14	0	1.04	1.69	7.3	4.5	6.2	0.0	3.94	3.0	1
2003	OMA	PCL	26	18	0	25.7	19	9	20	1	2.45	3.80	7.6	3.8	6.1	0.4	3.42	5.7	3
2004	WIC	TXS	27	8	6	39.0	30	17	34	2	4.38	5.25	7.8	4.5	5.8	0.8	4.00	6.4	11
2004	OMA	PCL	27	19	19	123.7	114	41	107	12	3.06	3.75	8.4	3.2	6.1	1.1	4.13	19.2	23
2005	*KCR*	*AL*	*28*	*14*	*13*	*72.3*	*77*	*38*	*53*	*10*	*5.45*	*5.13*	*9.5*	*4.1*	*6.0*	*1.2*	*5.02*	*6.3*	*2*

Breakout: 10% *Improve: 40%* *Collapse: 30%*

The Royals claimed Walrond off waivers from the Cardinals in 2003, not only for his collegiate roots at KU but also his track record, which other than his command was impressive. Walrond made strides in that department last season, cutting his walk rate in Omaha, and winning the PCL ERA title. He's a minor league free agent at this writing, and one of the better ones out there; he's could give some team a few good years out of the bullpen.

MIKE WOOD **Bats: R** **Throws: R** Born: 26-Apr-1980 Age: 25

YEAR	TM	LG	AGE	G	GS	IP	H	BB	SO	HR	ERA	EQERA	EQH9	EQBB9	EQSO9	EQHR9	PERA	VORP	STF
2002	MOD	CLF	22	7	7	41.3	41	6	50	4	3.49	4.85	9.9	1.4	6.5	1.6	5.08	2.3	14
2002	MID	TXS	22	17	17	105.7	103	29	63	8	3.15	4.38	9.4	2.7	4.1	1.3	4.65	10.4	6
2003	SAC	PCL	23	16	16	91.3	87	23	59	5	3.06	4.08	8.9	2.6	5.0	0.6	3.98	15.5	16
2004	SAC	PCL	24	15	15	90.0	83	24	66	8	2.80	4.40	8.2	2.5	5.1	0.8	3.35	21.5	24
2004	KCR	AL	24	17	17	100.0	112	28	54	16	5.94	5.11	9.4	2.3	4.6	1.2	4.47	2.2	14
2005	*KCR*	*AL*	*25*	*23*	*22*	*127.0*	*141*	*40*	*80*	*16*	*4.85*	*4.57*	*9.8*	*2.5*	*5.2*	*1.1*	*4.44*	*16.9*	*5*

Breakout: 14% *Improve: 46%* *Collapse: 15%*

The third player in the Beltran deal is the classic third fiddle, a low-upside innings sponge who couldn't crack the A's rotation but was ready to pitch in the major leagues. Wood is the pitching equivalent of a secondary skills hitter, a pitcher who takes walks and homers off the board so he can be successful even if hitters bat .290 against him. His control came with him to Kansas City, but his sinker was lost in transition, as he surrendered a homer nearly every six innings. Wood's name rarely comes up when the Royals' projected rotation is brought up, but if his ERA had matched his PERA last season, people might see him for the league-average starter that he is.

Minnesota Twins

Another year in the Twin Cities, another fillip to GM Terry Ryan and his staff for building a low-cost contender, and another year in which the Twins didn't win the World Series, let alone a pennant. Insiders, industry wags, beat writers, and performance analysts can all generally acknowledge the Twins' 2004 as another small market triumph defined as a success, a definition made uncomplicated by not having a bestseller written about it.

Our own Keith Woolner coined the term "competitive ecology" to describe everything that might be involved with trying to win ballgames. Within the game, let's say thirty teams are trying to win the World Series. Not necessarily this year, of course; it doesn't make a lot of sense to compare the Diamondbacks, mired in their gray implosion since winning the 2001 World Series, to the Red Sox, the defending champion. (The Diamondbacks are in the middle of trying to win again, but they have unique handicaps and strengths in their pursuit of that goal.) But if, in general, everyone is after the same thing, then everyone's looking for edges, adapting to the competition, and doing what's in their power to maximize their advantages, win some ballgames, and put themselves in the best possible position to win the World Series.

In the case of the Twins, you have to ask if their actions within that environment boil down to accepting an unfortunately low threshold of "good enough." Having won the division in each of the last three seasons, the Twins have been widely congratulated for having done a tremendous job of assembling and developing homegrown talent. In part, that rush has been the product of a desire by some to prop up the Twins as an example of how baseball teams can contend without adapting to whatever competitive advantages are supposed to be the intellectual property of so-called "Moneyball" teams.

Is the contrast between these two purported archetypes a fair one? Probably not, but the same segment of the media that myopically sees scouting and performance analysis as incompatible seems a bit cranky about the idea that there might be more ways than one to skin a cat. On a more basic level, it seems a bit strange to hype the Twins beyond a certain point. Squashing the dwarfish aspirations of their rivals within the division is not a good enough standard for success.

TWINS PROSPECTUS

2004 record: 92–70; First place, AL Central; Lost to Yankees in Division Series

Pythagenport record: 87–75

Runs scored per game: 4.81 (10th in AL)

Runs allowed per game: 4.41 (1st in AL)

Team EqA: .256 (9th in AL)

2004 Batters Age: 28.3 (2nd youngest in AL)

2004 Pitchers Age: 28.7 (7th oldest in AL)

Ballpark: Metrodome; Slight hitter's park; Park Factor of 1.020

2004: Another steady campaign for the Twins, who captured their third straight Central title.

2005: Their major-league talent and enviable minor-league depth make them easy favorites to win the division again.

In some ways, the Twins' problems are similar to those the old AL West had when trying to win the World Series between Oakland's two mini-dynasties: 1976–1987, the period between when Charlie Finley's Moustache Gang passed into history, and before the rise of the Bash Brothers. In that 11-year stretch (throwing out the oddities of the strike-shortened '81 season), the winner of the AL West would have to face an AL East team that had to field a stronger team designed to win more games and contend with stronger competition. On average, it took 99 wins to capture the AL East during that stretch, versus 92 to capture the West over that same period. The higher threshold made for more sour grapes during a period without wild cards or the divisional series: In seven of those seasons, the second-place finisher in the AL East won more games than the AL West champ, and in four of those years, so did the third-place team. For the curious, 1979 and 1984 are particularly nasty in this regard. In '79, the fourth-place Yankees won one more game than the division-winning Angels, while in '84, the fifth-place Orioles were a game up on a Royals team doomed to be sacrificed in the ALCS to a seemingly unbeatable Tigers squad.

The only times an AL West team won the pennant during this period were 1980, 1985, and 1987. The 1980 Royals lost to the Phillies, while the '85 Royals and the '87

Twins are both on the short list of weakest pennant winners and World Series championship teams of all time. In some Octobers, David beats Goliath not just once, but twice, providing a useful reminder that in a short postseason series, anything can happen. But over that stretch, which is considered one of the game's finest in terms of competitiveness, the AL East usually fielded the league's pennant winner, and the lower standards for what it took to win in the AL West didn't generally provide them with the best possible competition. Since the Twins have been splattered in the playoffs by the pennant winner in each of the last three years, their predicament isn't that different.

So, let's look at one of the Twins' other current bragging rights: How rare is it to win 90 or more games, three years in a row, and not win a pennant? Since the institution of divisional play in 1969, the point at which winning the pennant got more complicated, table 1 shows a list of those teams.

Only the sequencing of what seems like an annual exercise in postseason futility in Atlanta keeps the Braves of the '90s off the list. It's interesting to note the two clusters in that table, which could be broadly labeled "The Disco Era of Futility" and "Right Now." On some level, these teams had the same problems that the Twins do now: The Pirates and Phillies of the '70s couldn't get past the Reds and Dodgers, while many of the recently frustrated have had the Yankees killing off their dreams.

For the teams of the '70s, multi-year stretches of frustration of this sort didn't mean the end of the line. Rather, these stretches usually meant there was a need to shake things up, after which they'd win a pennant and take their shot at winning the whole thing. There must have been something sort of redeeming about both the '79 and '80 World Series, since all four teams had endured their share of frustrations beforehand.

TABLE 1. THREE-YEAR OR MORE PENNANTLESS STREAKS WITH 90+ WINS

Team	Streak	Next Pennant
Baltimore Orioles	1973–1975	1979
Kansas City Royals	1975–1978	1980
Pittsburgh Pirates	1975–1977	1979
Philadelphia Phillies	1976–1978	1980
Boston Red Sox	1977–1979	1986
Pittsburgh Pirates	1990–1992	—
Cleveland Indians	1999–2001	—
Oakland Athletics	2000–2004	—
Seattle Mariners	2000–2003	—
St. Louis Cardinals	2000–2002	2004
Atlanta Braves	2002–2004	—
Minnesota Twins	2002–2004	—

The anomalies are the teams we might remember as Don Zimmer's Red Sox and Jim Leyland's Pirates. Those Red Sox are the only team on the list who didn't make the playoffs during the period in question; Boston had to wait until Roger Clemens was ready to start dominating the game before they had their shot. The Pirates infamously committed themselves to Andy Van Slyke instead of Barry Bonds, and haven't bothered anyone since.

Anyway, getting back to the "Right Now" teams, the Twins amongst them, keep in mind that there's a little more opportunity to contend in a three-division environment with a Wild Card, which encourages some teams to chase postseason berths at the same time that more teams understand the economic advantages to ditching talent at the end of July and keeping next year's possibilities in mind. That's the competitive ecology of the present, with few rewards for being somebody like the White Sox—a team always near or just above .500, rarely cracking the postseason, rarely cashing in veterans for good prospects, and usually settling for middling positions in the draft.

As we've discussed in the cases of the Cardinals and to a different extent the challenges that face the Orioles and life inside the AL East, teams have specific competitive advantages and disadvantages. Walt Jocketty has proven consistently willing to do whatever is in his power to improve his team down the stretch, and he's good at it; that's a competitive advantage. Whatever aspirations the Orioles have for reaching the playoffs have to deal with the presence of the twin ambition-squelching giants within their division, making both a title and the Wild Card exceptionally difficult goals to achieve; that's a competitive disadvantage.

Having received and deserved credit for the homegrown talent starring in Minnesota today, the question is whether that talent is good enough to win by itself, or simply represents a starting point, a base of talent that Ryan should exploit to maximize his opportunities to achieve the real goal: winning the World Series.

On that score, the Twins general manager has been able to get by and settle for less, in part because he hasn't had to build such a great team to get to the playoffs. He's put up with a middle-infield combo that hasn't put runs on the board, and he got by with a merely adequate hitter at first in Doug Mientkiewicz. When circumstances inspire gumption and Ryan has to go shopping outside of his own system to shore up the team's modest ambitions, his trades during the season have never put the Twins over the top. In his first run at relevance in 2001, he dumped his leadoff man, Matt Lawton, on the Mets to add Rick Reed, a mediocre starter at the end of his tether. Ryan did not have an adequate replacement for Lawton on hand, and the Twins finished second. In 2002, he decided to stand pat. In '03, he took his one area of significant depth, the outfield, and traded for... another outfielder. Shannon Stewart was nicer to have than Bobby Kielty, to be sure, but like Reed, he wasn't a player who was going to make the difference for the Twins against the American League's powerhouses. In '04, you could argue that Ryan made his first really significant in-season improvement, but that involved dumping Mientkiewicz to make room for Justin Morneau, something that should have been done months earlier.

This pattern of putting up with "good enough" can change, starting now. Skip the "Aw, shucks, we're just old-fashioned" themes plastered onto them; Terry Ryan can be just as bloodily market-minded as the next modern GM. You think they're going to miss Cristian Guzman, and woe to them that they can't afford him? Don't be ridiculous. Guzman wasn't worth the money, and whatever shekels Carl Pohlad grudgingly surrenders are best spent elsewhere. Signing Juan Castro might make you think Ryan has an incorrigible sweet tooth for no-hit middle infielders, but there's talent enough in-house that the Twins can improve on the production they've gotten out of the middle infield in recent years. Second baseman Luis Rivas should be in danger of losing his job. The question is whether Ryan will move as he finally did with Morneau at first, and put his best lineup on the field.

Unfortunately, on that score there are other mistakes that will similarly have to be outlasted, should Ryan fail to fix them. Jacque Jones is becoming the sort of player you don't brag about, as he starts to decline at the plate at the same time as he reaches that point in his career when arbitration-induced pay hikes make him even more of a liability. Losing top prospect Jason Kubel for the year will preserve Jones and hurt a weaker lineup. Another potential hole is at catcher. If Joe Mauer doesn't work out, sifting between Mike Redmond and Corky Miller for who should catch regularly isn't likely to produce any significant difference between the two, or provide much benefit to the lineup.

The pitching side of the equation isn't quite as settled as you might think. Behind an excellent pair in Johan Santana and the smartly re-signed Brad Radke, the remainder of the rotation will be an interesting problem in camp. Carlos Silva is both last year's success story and this year's question mark. Within the organization, lefty Francisco Liriano and righty Scott Baker have the most promise, and might be ready by season's end to step in. Before that happens, Ryan and manager Ron Gardenhire will have to sort through two of last year's suspects (Matt Guerrier and Terry Mulholland), Joe Mays if he's healthy, and perhaps minor league lefty Dave Gassner. If the Twins simply hand the last two rotation slots to Kyle Lohse and Mays, it wouldn't be surprising, but it would almost certainly mean they also haven't done their due diligence in spring training to see who's really ready to help.

This remains a team good enough to win the AL Central. But if that's the extent of their ambitions, then odds are the Twins won't join those teams from that list of 90-game winners who did go on to win a pennant. The challenge here isn't to win 90 or win a title; it's to field a team that can beat the Yankees or the Red Sox (and maybe the Angels, A's or Rangers). Armed with the game's best starter, one of its best bullpens, and a tremendous young thumper in Morneau, they've got a great initial hand. It's up to Ryan to add to it.

HITTERS

JASON BARTLETT **SS** **Bats: R** **Throws: R** Born: 30-Oct-1979 Age: 25

YEAR	TM	LG	AGE	AB	H	2B	3B	HR	BB	SO	SB	CS	AVG	OBP	SLG	MLVR	EQBA	EQOBP	EQSLG	EQMLVR	VORP	DEFENSE
2002	LEL	CLF	22	308	77	14	4	1	32	53	24	5	.250	.329	.331	-.077	.224	.286	.298	-.333	-12.0	75-SS -12
2002	FTM	FSL	22	145	38	7	0	2	17	24	11	2	.262	.341	.352	.043	.235	.291	.315	-.293	-4.3	28-SS -3
2003	NBR	EAS	23	548	162	31	8	8	58	67	41	24	.296	.380	.425	.147	.269	.342	.401	-.052	26.1	139-SS 5
2004	ROC	INT	24	269	89	15	7	3	33	37	7	3	.331	.415	.472	.237	.305	.388	.432	.105	25.1	65-SS 8
2005	*MIN*	*AL*	*25*	*237*	*63*	*12*	*2*	*3*	*22*	*34*	*8*	*2*	*.266*	*.341*	*.376*	*-.076*	*.264*	*.341*	*.381*	*-.080*	*15.7*	*66-SS 0*

Breakout: 7% *Improve: 35%* *Collapse: 44%*

A strong-armed shortstop who possesses solid lateral range and can handle plays from deep in the hole and, Bartlett is one to watch. Although he missed almost two months at mid-season with a broken wrist, he bounced back, finishing with a strong stint in the AFL. The Twins are probably going to enjoy turning him loose on the basepaths, since Cristian Guzman's happy feet have already walked out of town. Bartlett will get every opportunity to win the job at short in camp, and he'll add some OBP the Twins have been lacking from their middle infielders for years.

HENRY BLANCO C Bats: R Throws: R Born: 29-Aug-1971 Age: 33

YEAR	TM	LG	AGE	AB	H	2B	3B	HR	BB	SO	SB	CS	AVG	OBP	SLG	MLVR	EQBA	EQOBP	EQSLG	EQMLVR	VORP	DEFENSE
2002	ATL	NL	30	221	45	9	1	6	20	51	0	2	.204	.267	.335	-.240	.207	.269	.347	-.308	-3.8	61-C 4
2003	ATL	NL	31	151	30	8	0	1	10	21	0	0	.199	.252	.272	-.370	.204	.252	.263	-.460	-7.4	40-C 1
2004	MIN	AL	32	315	65	19	1	10	21	56	0	3	.206	.260	.368	-.293	.203	.262	.367	-.297	-8.0	94-C 17
2005	*CHC*	*NL*	*33*	*159*	*36*	*8*	*1*	*4*	*13*	*30*	*0*	*0*	*.226*	*.288*	*.367*	*-.216*	*.226*	*.286*	*.366*	*-.223*	*-0.6*	*46-C 1*

Breakout: 45% *Improve: 69%* *Collapse: 22%*

The Twins like to congratulate themselves on a lot of things, but signing Blanco a year ago should not have been one of the things to boast about. Offensively, he's a zero, below even the Matheny Line of usefulness. He's a great defensive replacement, and if your starting catcher was a Piazza or a LeCroy, someone you don't want to catch every inning, he'd be handy. In Chicago, Cubs fans can hope he gets dusty on the bench.

PAT BORDERS Deathless Bats: R Throws: R Born: 14-May-1963 Age: 42

YEAR	TM	LG	AGE	AB	H	2B	3B	HR	BB	SO	SB	CS	AVG	OBP	SLG	MLVR	EQBA	EQOBP	EQSLG	EQMLVR	VORP	DEFENSE
2002	TAC	PCL	39	317	84	16	1	12	11	47	3	2	.265	.289	.435	-.028	.252	.278	.408	-.174	-0.1	78-C 9
2003	TAC	PCL	40	293	92	27	1	12	20	54	1	2	.314	.362	.536	.321	.291	.339	.503	.107	24.5	66-C -2
2004	TAC	PCL	41	137	35	5	1	5	3	28	0	1	.255	.287	.416	-.137	.244	.272	.385	-.225	-2.0	35-C 3
2004	SEA	AL	41	53	10	2	0	1	1	12	1	1	.189	.204	.283	-.509	.208	.203	.283	-.530	-4.0	17-C 3
2004	MIN	AL	41	42	12	4	0	0	0	10	2	0	.286	.302	.381	-.138	.293	.256	.341	-.285	1.4	12-C 2
2005	*MIL*	*NL*	*42*	*91*	*22*	*5*	*0*	*2*	*3*	*19*	*1*	*0*	*.240*	*.270*	*.370*	*-.235*	*.240*	*.269*	*.370*	*-.241*	*0.6*	*27-C -2*

Breakout: 16% *Improve: 30%* *Collapse: 44%*

If there's one thing that Nationals fans can take some small solace in, it's that by not getting Pat Gillick as their GM, Washington will have no Borders. And who needs one? The nation's capital has some great independent bookstores, like Politics and Prose and Olsson's. Meanwhile, the next episode of "It's Pat" will be held in Milwaukee's training camp.

ROB BOWEN C Bats: B Throws: R Born: 24-Feb-1981 Age: 24

YEAR	TM	LG	AGE	AB	H	2B	3B	HR	BB	SO	SB	CS	AVG	OBP	SLG	MLVR	EQBA	EQOBP	EQSLG	EQMLVR	VORP	DEFENSE
2002	FTM	FSL	21	342	63	12	1	10	38	69	1	0	.184	.272	.313	-.159	.173	.242	.304	-.440	-29.9	83-C 7
2003	NBR	EAS	22	134	41	13	0	1	13	24	0	0	.306	.376	.425	.150	.261	.312	.366	-.163	0.4	37-C 3
2003	ROC	INT	22	105	27	7	0	6	11	25	0	0	.257	.333	.495	.115	.212	.285	.423	-.170	0.1	26-C 4
2004	NBR	EAS	23	249	49	10	0	9	31	76	3	0	.197	.292	.345	-.184	.175	.257	.303	-.410	-19.4	65-C 2
2005	*MIN*	*AL*	*24*	*268*	*59*	*13*	*1*	*8*	*25*	*73*	*1*	*1*	*.221*	*.293*	*.362*	*-.209*	*.219*	*.293*	*.367*	*-.214*	*-2.4*	*73-C -4*

Breakout: 51% *Improve: 68%* *Collapse: 15%*

He's often been labeled a prospect, but another season like 2004 and Bowen will drop behind Jose Morales faster than you can say "Brandon Marsters." OK, so Marsters never really was that much of a prospect, despite falling from sight before Bowen's erratic ascent up the chain. It's a dog-eat-dog world, but after flopping two out of the last three years, Bowen is more likely to wind up among the eaten.

MIKE CUDDYER 3B? Bats: R Throws: R Born: 27-Mar-1979 Age: 26

YEAR	TM	LG	AGE	AB	H	2B	3B	HR	BB	SO	SB	CS	AVG	OBP	SLG	MLVR	EQBA	EQOBP	EQSLG	EQMLVR	VORP	DEFENSE
2002	EDM	PCL	23	330	102	16	9	20	36	79	12	7	.309	.379	.594	.375	.284	.352	.532	.163	23.3	73-RF 0
2002	MIN	AL	23	112	29	7	0	4	8	30	2	0	.259	.311	.429	-.021	.270	.314	.423	-.071	3.5	21-RF 1
2003	ROC	INT	24	186	57	17	0	3	25	49	5	4	.306	.381	.446	.165	.274	.345	.403	-.039	1.5	26-RF 0
2003	MIN	AL	24	102	25	1	3	4	12	19	1	1	.245	.325	.431	-.028	.248	.327	.436	-.047	2.6	11-RF 0
2004	MIN	AL	25	339	89	22	1	12	37	74	5	5	.263	.339	.440	.003	.264	.345	.444	.010	14.7	34-2B 4 34-3B -5
2005	*MIN*	*AL*	*26*	*358*	*97*	*21*	*2*	*15*	*41*	*80*	*7*	*3*	*.270*	*.348*	*.467*	*.057*	*.268*	*.348*	*.474*	*.056*	*23.3*	*97-3B -4*

Breakout: 23% *Improve: 61%* *Collapse: 15%*

It took a year or two longer than he might have liked, but Cuddyer finally got his opportunity to stick, and he didn't disappoint. An underrated second baseman, Cuddyer is the player Keith Ginter wishes he was. With both starters on the left side of the infield gone, Cuddyer looks more likely to start at third, but nothing's set in stone: The Twins also have Eric Munson and Terry Tiffee around, and Luis Rivas is both a lousy hitter and a long-time incumbent and favorite of management. Regardless, Cuddyer should have a nice career, with a peak something like that of a slighter slower Phil Garner. There's still potential for much more than that, especially in terms of power (see Edmonton, 2002).

LEW FORD OF **Bats: R** **Throws: R** Born: 12-Aug-1976 Age: 28

YEAR	TM	LG	AGE	AB	H	2B	3B	HR	BB	SO	SB	CS	AVG	OBP	SLG	MLVR	EQBA	EQOBP	EQSLG	EQMLVR	VORP	DEFENSE	
2002	NBR	EAS	25	373	116	27	2	15	49	47	17	5	.311	.401	.515	.319	.284	.363	.472	.098	29.5	93-CF -7	
2002	EDM	PCL	25	193	64	11	2	5	13	21	11	1	.332	.390	.487	.265	.318	.371	.464	.133	16.1	37-CF -1	
2003	ROC	INT	26	211	64	18	2	3	10	28	4	5	.303	.357	.450	.130	.284	.338	.436	.003	9.3	27-CF -3	10-LF 0
2003	MIN	AL	26	73	24	7	1	3	8	9	2	0	.329	.402	.575	.350	.333	.413	.583	.387	9.7		
2004	MIN	AL	27	569	170	31	4	15	67	75	20	2	.299	.381	.446	.114	.299	.385	.450	.119	44.0	81-LF -2	39-CF 0
2005	*MIN*	*AL*	*28*	*513*	*152*	*32*	*3*	*15*	*51*	*69*	*12*	*5*	*.297*	*.370*	*.459*	*.105*	*.295*	*.370*	*.465*	*.104*	*30.1*	*137-LF 0*	

Breakout: 8% *Improve: 43%* *Collapse: 16%*

You might be scratching your noggin and wondering why PECOTA is so down on Ford, but let's face it, that he had a year like he did in his Age 27 season makes it unlikely he'll "break out" beyond. Take solace in the fact that PECOTA sees a strong likelihood that he's going to build on it anyway, but don't expect a long career. Edgar Martinez aside, when you can play a fourth outfielder who hits well enough he can start for any of the other three, and soak up at-bats at DH, that's a great way to exploit the role.

CRISTIAN GUZMAN SS **Bats: B** **Throws: R** Born: 21-Mar-1978 Age: 27

YEAR	TM	LG	AGE	AB	H	2B	3B	HR	BB	SO	SB	CS	AVG	OBP	SLG	MLVR	EQBA	EQOBP	EQSLG	EQMLVR	VORP	DEFENSE
2002	MIN	AL	24	623	170	31	6	9	17	79	12	13	.273	.292	.385	-.117	.277	.299	.392	-.138	11.7	142-SS -2
2003	MIN	AL	25	534	143	15	14	3	30	79	18	9	.268	.311	.365	-.139	.269	.317	.367	-.147	12.7	137-SS -5
2004	MIN	AL	26	576	158	31	4	8	30	64	10	5	.274	.309	.384	-.131	.273	.313	.384	-.127	15.5	142-SS 17
2005	*WAS*	*NL*	*27*	*509*	*134*	*25*	*4*	*6*	*27*	*59*	*11*	*4*	*.263*	*.301*	*.367*	*-.168*	*.266*	*.302*	*.376*	*-.155*	*9.7*	*129-SS 4*

Breakout: 3% *Improve: 27%* *Collapse: 31%*

One old insight into human nature is that if you know when a man was 20, you understand him. There might be something to that with Jim Bowden, because in signing Guzman, he might not have aged a day beyond 1980. Back then, guys like Ivan DeJesus or Gary Templeton were stars, and people said nice things about Dale Berra. Progress, A-Rod, Nomar, Jeter, Tejada, throw it all in a hopper, and we're in age when those sorts of sensibilities are as out of place as calling Rammstein's mosh pit a sock hop. Now that he's in D.C. and supposed to be a star, Guzman is about to become as identifiable and regretted as Pauly Shore.

TORII HUNTER CF **Bats: R** **Throws: R** Born: 18-Jul-1975 Age: 29

YEAR	TM	LG	AGE	AB	H	2B	3B	HR	BB	SO	SB	CS	AVG	OBP	SLG	MLVR	EQBA	EQOBP	EQSLG	EQMLVR	VORP	DEFENSE
2002	MIN	AL	26	561	162	37	4	29	35	118	23	8	.289	.334	.524	.169	.291	.342	.534	.157	50.8	134-CF -4
2003	MIN	AL	27	581	145	31	4	26	50	106	6	7	.250	.312	.451	-.023	.249	.316	.456	-.039	19.8	144-CF 0
2004	MIN	AL	28	520	141	37	0	23	40	101	21	7	.271	.330	.475	.042	.272	.332	.477	.039	31.2	119-CF 2
2005	*MIN*	*AL*	*29*	*497*	*137*	*31*	*2*	*23*	*41*	*99*	*14*	*5*	*.275*	*.334*	*.487*	*.065*	*.273*	*.334*	*.493*	*.064*	*27.8*	*129-CF -3*

Breakout: 29% *Improve: 52%* *Collapse: 15%*

Sort of a latter-day Chet Lemon, in that he's short of being a great player, but he's a damned good one, and one that PECOTA sees as having some upside in the near future. Hunter will continue to age gracefully for another couple of seasons, but after that, the future could be Grissom-as-Brewer grim.

JACQUE JONES OF **Bats: L** **Throws: L** Born: 25-Apr-1975 Age: 30

YEAR	TM	LG	AGE	AB	H	2B	3B	HR	BB	SO	SB	CS	AVG	OBP	SLG	MLVR	EQBA	EQOBP	EQSLG	EQMLVR	VORP	DEFENSE
2002	MIN	AL	27	577	173	37	2	27	37	129	6	7	.300	.341	.511	.170	.304	.349	.521	.164	38.5	131-LF 14
2003	MIN	AL	28	517	157	33	1	16	21	105	13	1	.304	.333	.464	.078	.302	.337	.469	.065	27.3	82-LF -1
2004	MIN	AL	29	555	141	22	1	24	40	117	13	10	.254	.315	.427	-.064	.254	.318	.433	-.063	10.5	137-RF 8
2005	*MIN*	*AL*	*30*	*448*	*122*	*26*	*2*	*17*	*31*	*96*	*8*	*4*	*.273*	*.325*	*.456*	*.007*	*.271*	*.325*	*.463*	*.005*	*14.8*	*116-RF 1*

Breakout: 11% *Improve: 42%* *Collapse: 24%*

After a miserable '04 season, Jones is moving out of the period of his career when he was a success story any thrifty-minded GM wished he had, to a period when he will be an overpriced problem. That's the nature of the career clock for arbitration: Jones has been good enough that everyone would shriek if he's non-tendered until it's a year too late, but you can hide behind the fig leaf of free agency if he leaves of his own volition. He'll be bad news for as long as he's an everyday player.

GARRETT JONES 1B **Bats: L** **Throws: L** Born: 21-Jun-1981 Age: 24

YEAR	TM	LG	AGE	AB	H	2B	3B	HR	BB	SO	SB	CS	AVG	OBP	SLG	MLVR	EQBA	EQOBP	EQSLG	EQMLVR	VORP	DEFENSE
2002	QUD	MDW	21	223	45	8	0	10	11	82	3	1	.202	.238	.372	-.147	.160	.184	.302	-.566	-33.1	39-1B -4
2003	FTM	FSL	22	404	89	12	5	18	32	98	5	4	.220	.280	.408	.026	.201	.249	.395	-.285	-26.0	108-1B 1
2004	NBR	EAS	23	450	140	33	2	30	28	98	11	4	.311	.356	.593	.348	.278	.317	.524	.087	23.9	120-1B -11
2005	*MIN*	*AL*	*24*	*341*	*82*	*17*	*1*	*14*	*20*	*89*	*4*	*1*	*.241*	*.287*	*.418*	*-.133*	*.239*	*.287*	*.424*	*-.137*	*-4.1*	*89-1B -5*

Breakout: 19% *Improve: 45%* *Collapse: 28%*

When injuries pushed Jones up to Double-A last year, he could do no wrong. Before then, Jones hadn't been taken all that seriously by the organization. Let's face it, streaky, all-or-nothing hitters who put up more nothing than all earn the right to be overlooked. It probably doesn't help that he's got that lean frame that can lead to Dave Kingman flashbacks. Anyway, he's now considered a prospect, but not one so good that Justin Morneau needs to look over his shoulder. Given his weak peripheral numbers, it's going to be hard to sustain last season's power spike.

COREY KOSKIE 3B **Bats: L** **Throws: R** Born: 28-Jun-1973 Age: 32

YEAR	TM	LG	AGE	AB	H	2B	3B	HR	BB	SO	SB	CS	AVG	OBP	SLG	MLVR	EQBA	EQOBP	EQSLG	EQMLVR	VORP	DEFENSE
2002	MIN	AL	29	490	131	37	3	15	72	127	10	11	.267	.368	.447	.104	.274	.377	.459	.096	36.6	134-3B 14
2003	MIN	AL	30	469	137	29	2	14	77	113	11	5	.292	.393	.452	.149	.292	.398	.459	.148	46.6	123-3B 11
2004	MIN	AL	31	422	106	24	2	25	49	103	9	3	.251	.342	.495	.075	.251	.345	.501	.076	26.7	113-3B -8
2005	*TOR*	*AL*	*32*	*417*	*116*	*25*	*2*	*19*	*57*	*103*	*9*	*4*	*.278*	*.373*	*.487*	*.131*	*.274*	*.371*	*.485*	*.114*	*29.9*	*115-3B -1*

Breakout: 23% *Improve: 54%* *Collapse: 14%*

Beyond signing him because he's Canadian—and they do like their own up there—Koskie's a solid citizen, and Toronto is hoping that his graying years are golden. He's relatively athletic, which encouraged PECOTA to see a lot of potential for bounceback, keeping last year's additional power while ratcheting his average back up. His propensity for injuries makes him a significant risk, though, such that $17 million may not end up all that well-spent.

JASON KUBEL DL **Bats: L** **Throws: R** Born: 25-May-1982 Age: 23

YEAR	TM	LG	AGE	AB	H	2B	3B	HR	BB	SO	SB	CS	AVG	OBP	SLG	MLVR	EQBA	EQOBP	EQSLG	EQMLVR	VORP	DEFENSE
2002	QUD	MDW	20	424	136	26	4	17	41	48	3	5	.321	.380	.521	.325	.266	.314	.438	-.053	1.6	106-RF -6
2003	FTM	FSL	21	420	125	20	4	5	48	54	4	6	.298	.361	.400	.181	.278	.332	.398	-.067	-0.3	106-RF 2
2004	NBR	EAS	22	138	52	14	4	6	19	19	0	2	.377	.453	.667	.658	.341	.409	.594	.407	21.8	35-RF 0
2004	ROC	INT	22	350	120	28	0	16	34	40	16	3	.343	.398	.560	.344	.305	.359	.497	.147	22.0	75-RF 4 10-LF 0
2004	MIN	AL	22	60	18	2	0	2	6	9	1	1	.300	.358	.433	.064	.322	.352	.458	.095	3.2	
2005	*MIN*	*AL*	*23*	*316*	*93*	*19*	*2*	*11*	*29*	*42*	*5*	*2*	*.296*	*.354*	*.471*	*.094*	*.293*	*.354*	*.477*	*.093*	*22.2*	*85-RF -1*

Breakout: 16% *Improve: 42%* *Collapse: 24%*

Kubel is a squat power hitter who doesn't exactly fit the Twins' mold where athleticism is concerned. But it's a moot point, insofar as you won't get to see him this year. He's out after a career-threatening knee injury, and it's hard to know what to expect going forward. You can throw out that projection, certainly. He played an adequate right field before blowing out his ACL; we can't know how well he'll move around once he gets back, or if he'll have to become a young DH. With his kind of power to all fields, you can be sure that the Twins are willing to wait and see.

MATT LeCROY C/1B **Bats: R** **Throws: R** Born: 13-Dec-1975 Age: 29

YEAR	TM	LG	AGE	AB	H	2B	3B	HR	BB	SO	SB	CS	AVG	OBP	SLG	MLVR	EQBA	EQOBP	EQSLG	EQMLVR	VORP	DEFENSE
2002	EDM	PCL	26	174	61	7	1	12	17	34	2	0	.351	.412	.609	.498	.329	.387	.566	.318	26.2	10-C 0
2002	MIN	AL	26	181	47	11	1	7	13	38	0	2	.260	.306	.448	-.002	.263	.316	.453	-.031	5.6	
2003	MIN	AL	27	345	99	19	0	17	25	82	0	1	.287	.342	.490	.115	.290	.345	.493	.102	22.9	17-C -3 12-1B 0
2004	MIN	AL	28	264	71	14	0	9	16	60	0	0	.269	.321	.424	-.052	.269	.318	.423	-.065	8.5	19-C -7 19-1B -2
2005	*MIN*	*AL*	*29*	*259*	*71*	*14*	*1*	*11*	*21*	*61*	*0*	*0*	*.273*	*.333*	*.460*	*.025*	*.270*	*.333*	*.466*	*.023*	*14.0*	*70-DH*

Breakout: 19% *Improve: 39%* *Collapse: 25%*

As much as it might be nice if he could reliably provide insurance for Mauer's knee, LeCroy has knee problems of his own, and with his weak arm, he's better off in a role where he doesn't catch all that often. Still, he's a championship-caliber role player, a nifty DH or spot-starter at first against all lefties. If one of the outfielders broke down for a long stretch, it would be nice to see what he could do in an extended trial in a corner, before he gets much older.

JOE MAUER C **Bats: L** **Throws: R** Born: 19-Apr-1983 Age: 22

YEAR	TM	LG	AGE	AB	H	2B	3B	HR	BB	SO	SB	CS	AVG	OBP	SLG	MLVR	EQBA	EQOBP	EQSLG	EQMLVR	VORP	DEFENSE
2002	QUD	MDW	19	411	124	23	1	4	61	42	0	0	.302	.393	.392	.161	.248	.322	.331	-.201	-3.9	81-C 11 12-1B -2
2003	FTM	FSL	20	233	78	13	1	1	24	24	3	0	.335	.395	.412	.271	.310	.361	.397	.011	14.0	39-C 11
2003	NBR	EAS	20	276	94	17	1	4	25	25	0	0	.341	.400	.453	.257	.305	.359	.422	.039	18.2	58-C 4
2004	MIN	AL	21	107	33	8	1	6	11	14	1	0	.308	.369	.570	.274	.314	.373	.581	.300	14.2	30-C 1
2005	*MIN*	*AL*	*22*	*371*	*112*	*24*	*2*	*10*	*36*	*44*	*2*	*1*	*.301*	*.367*	*.456*	*.101*	*.299*	*.367*	*.462*	*.100*	*35.0*	*100-C -2*

Breakout: 6% *Improve: 34%* *Collapse: 24%*

If Kubel's knee is Questionable Joint #1, Joe Mauer's knee isn't all that far behind as Questionable Joint #1A. The Twins are telling everyone that there's no problem, and if you smoke enough oregano, you might completely believe it. Don't listen, because their actions tell you they're worried. Why else pick up both Mike Redmond and Corky Miller this winter? Even if Mauer heals, there's still the issue of his size, since he's probably the biggest catcher in the league behind the perpetually fragile Sandy Alomar. It's time to accept that Bunyanesque catchers aren't meant for long and healthy careers. The kid can hit, so the Twins will need to make sure they don't sacrifice his bat if squatting isn't feasible. Stay tuned.

LUIS MAZA 2B **Bats: R** **Throws: R** Born: 22-Jun-1980 Age: 25

YEAR	TM	LG	AGE	AB	H	2B	3B	HR	BB	SO	SB	CS	AVG	OBP	SLG	MLVR	EQBA	EQOBP	EQSLG	EQMLVR	VORP	DEFENSE
2002	FTM	FSL	22	344	83	15	3	4	19	53	4	6	.241	.302	.337	-.049	.228	.268	.329	-.323	-12.9	66-SS -10 22-2B -4
2003	FTM	FSL	23	410	119	18	6	5	34	79	1	1	.290	.368	.400	.184	.277	.334	.412	-.045	17.1	103-2B -12
2004	NBR	EAS	24	492	153	26	8	12	28	70	5	6	.311	.365	.470	.188	.287	.331	.432	-.013	24.8	121-2B -6
2005	*MIN*	*AL*	*25*	*219*	*59*	*12*	*2*	*4*	*10*	*36*	*2*	*1*	*.270*	*.324*	*.400*	*-.072*	*.267*	*.325*	*.405*	*-.075*	*13.9*	*60-2B -7*

Breakout: 11% *Improve: 42%* *Collapse: 38%*

Despite what our performance metrics say, the organization likes Maza's glovework at second. More basically, he started to hit for considerably more power since leaving the Florida State League's damp air, having learned to cut down on his stroke and hit to all fields. You might think he's a bit old to be taken seriously in the second-base mix, but the Twins signed Juan Castro, and they take Augie Ojeda more seriously than anybody. If he makes an impression, he could knock Rivas out of the box by Opening Day '06.

JOSE MORALES C **Bats: B** **Throws: R** Born: 20-Feb-1983 Age: 22

YEAR	TM	LG	AGE	AB	H	2B	3B	HR	BB	SO	SB	CS	AVG	OBP	SLG	MLVR	EQBA	EQOBP	EQSLG	EQMLVR	VORP	DEFENSE
2003	QUD	MDW	20	170	46	10	1	2	5	32	0	1	.271	.302	.376	.009	.238	.260	.349	-.304	-6.6	26-C -4
2004	FTM	FSL	21	331	95	13	4	4	29	77	0	1	.287	.340	.387	.087	.263	.308	.364	-.172	0.1	81-C -2
2005	*MIN*	*AL*	*22*	*320*	*75*	*15*	*2*	*5*	*17*	*78*	*1*	*1*	*.235*	*.277*	*.339*	*-.260*	*.233*	*.277*	*.344*	*-.265*	*-6.4*	*83-C -7*

Breakout: 16% *Improve: 23%* *Collapse: 53%*

Before 2003, Morales was a second baseman with a great arm, but the Twins didn't see the speed to be a turf infielder in him. So they moved him behind the plate full-time, starting in 2003, and they have to like what they've seen so far.

JUSTIN MORNEAU 1B **Bats: L** **Throws: R** Born: 15-May-1981 Age: 24

YEAR	TM	LG	AGE	AB	H	2B	3B	HR	BB	SO	SB	CS	AVG	OBP	SLG	MLVR	EQBA	EQOBP	EQSLG	EQMLVR	VORP	DEFENSE
2002	NBR	EAS	21	494	147	31	4	16	42	88	7	0	.298	.356	.474	.184	.271	.322	.438	-.035	7.4	124-1B -11
2003	NBR	EAS	22	79	26	3	1	6	7	14	0	0	.329	.384	.620	.459	.295	.345	.551	.191	6.7	20-1B 1
2003	ROC	INT	22	265	71	11	1	16	28	56	0	2	.268	.344	.498	.144	.246	.325	.470	-.006	6.4	58-1B -4
2003	MIN	AL	22	106	24	4	0	4	9	30	0	0	.226	.287	.377	-.188	.229	.283	.371	-.234	-0.9	
2004	ROC	INT	23	288	88	23	0	22	32	47	1	1	.306	.377	.615	.344	.268	.336	.542	.134	18.8	68-1B -1
2004	MIN	AL	23	280	76	17	0	19	28	54	0	0	.271	.340	.536	.145	.273	.340	.538	.140	22.0	59-1B -1
2005	*MIN*	*AL*	*24*	*448*	*127*	*27*	*1*	*25*	*45*	*86*	*0*	*1*	*.282*	*.351*	*.513*	*.132*	*.280*	*.351*	*.519*	*.132*	*29.0*	*118-1B -3*

Breakout: 25% *Improve: 60%* *Collapse: 10%*

It takes a peculiar brand of genius to have "helped" Morneau take as long as he did to get here, but when you had a big league regular as loveably unpronounceable as Minky, that makes everything all right. Of course, with the threat of his leaving to bat cleanup for Team Canada in the Olympics in Greece, you could say that genius had a timetable. His glovework gets bad-mouthed, but that's exaggerated Mientkiewicz-mongering in action; Morneau has the soft hands for the job, he just needs to improve his footwork. He'll soon become one of the 20 best hitters in the league.

JOSE OFFERMAN   DH   Bats: B   Throws: R   Born: 11-Nov-1968   Age: 36

YEAR	TM	LG	AGE	AB	H	2B	3B	HR	BB	SO	SB	CS	AVG	OBP	SLG	MLVR	EQBA	EQOBP	EQSLG	EQMLVR	VORP	DEFENSE
2002	BOS	AL	33	237	55	10	0	4	33	29	8	5	.232	.325	.325	-.151	.238	.329	.328	-.198	-1.9	36-1B 3
2002	SEA	AL	33	47	11	2	1	1	4	9	1	1	.234	.294	.383	-.149	.255	.314	.404	-.110	-0.5	
2004	MIN	AL	35	172	44	14	2	2	29	31	1	1	.256	.363	.395	-.018	.250	.367	.393	-.029	7.3	
2005	*MIN*	*AL*	*36*	*124*	*30*	*6*	*1*	*2*	*20*	*23*	*1*	*1*	*.246*	*.349*	*.356*	*-.099*	*.244*	*.350*	*.361*	*-.103*	*4.5*	*38-DH*

Breakout: 26%   Improve: 37%   Collapse: 36%

As fans, there are some comebacks we root for, some we note with mild interest, and some are things that make you say "huh." As a pinch-hitter for the Twins' weak-hitting middle infielders or for Blanco, Offerman had value, but when the organization was playing him instead of calling up Morneau, that's when disinterest became concern.

AUGIE OJEDA   INF   Bats: B   Throws: R   Born: 20-Dec-1974   Age: 30

YEAR	TM	LG	AGE	AB	H	2B	3B	HR	BB	SO	SB	CS	AVG	OBP	SLG	MLVR	EQBA	EQOBP	EQSLG	EQMLVR	VORP	DEFENSE
2002	IOW	PCL	27	291	67	20	4	1	31	30	5	3	.230	.318	.337	-.156	.219	.298	.318	-.284	-7.1	68-SS -5
2002	CHC	NL	27	70	13	4	0	0	5	5	1	0	.186	.247	.243	-.413	.208	.235	.236	-.532	-4.0	13-SS 0
2003	IOW	PCL	28	283	71	10	3	2	34	25	4	0	.251	.351	.329	-.075	.231	.321	.304	-.250	-4.2	50-SS 8 25-2B -2
2004	ROC	INT	29	331	80	19	0	2	39	33	7	5	.242	.331	.317	-.182	.215	.297	.278	-.342	-13.9	62-SS 8
2004	MIN	AL	29	59	20	1	0	2	10	3	1	1	.339	.429	.458	.238	.362	.418	.483	.285	7.3	12-2B 1
2005	*MIN*	*AL*	*30*	*160*	*39*	*8*	*1*	*1*	*16*	*17*	*2*	*1*	*.245*	*.325*	*.332*	*-.175*	*.243*	*.325*	*.337*	*-.180*	*2.3*	*47-SS -2*

Breakout: 35%   Improve: 54%   Collapse: 26%

In the competition for a utility infielder's spot, Augie squashed Alex Prieto like a bug, probably the only context in which a mighty mite like Ojeda could make that claim. Ojeda's a worthy inheritor to the Cookie Newman spot on the roster, since he can pick it and bunt, and that just about taps out his list of positives.

NICK PUNTO   INF   Bats: B   Throws: R   Born: 08-Nov-1977   Age: 27

YEAR	TM	LG	AGE	AB	H	2B	3B	HR	BB	SO	SB	CS	AVG	OBP	SLG	MLVR	EQBA	EQOBP	EQSLG	EQMLVR	VORP	DEFENSE
2002	SWB	INT	24	443	120	12	5	1	76	84	42	8	.271	.378	.327	.000	.253	.358	.309	-.157	6.4	115-SS 13
2002	PHI	NL	24	6	1	0	0	0	0	3	0	0	.167	.167	.167	-.690	.143	.043	.143	-1.091	-0.8	
2003	SWB	INT	25	111	35	7	1	0	7	13	7	1	.315	.353	.396	.080	.270	.304	.324	-.233	-1.0	25-SS 3
2003	PHI	NL	25	92	20	2	0	1	7	22	2	1	.217	.273	.272	-.302	.228	.269	.272	-.401	-3.1	12-2B -1
2004	MIN	AL	26	91	23	0	0	2	12	19	6	0	.253	.340	.319	-.162	.258	.321	.326	-.204	3.3	11-2B 1
2005	*MIN*	*AL*	*27*	*237*	*61*	*9*	*2*	*3*	*27*	*44*	*12*	*3*	*.256*	*.333*	*.346*	*-.136*	*.254*	*.333*	*.351*	*-.140*	*9.1*	*66-SS -1*

Breakout: 11%   Improve: 34%   Collapse: 40%

Punto is Augie Ojeda's bigger buddy, but much more than the little guy, he's a punch-and-judy hitter whose plate judgment is his primary offensive weapon. He can also run well. Assuming he's fully healed up from the broken collarbone that kept him off of the playoff roster, he'll make the decision to sign Juan Castro for real money and multiple years look that much worse.

MIKE RESTOVICH   OF   Bats: R   Throws: R   Born: 03-Jan-1979   Age: 26

YEAR	TM	LG	AGE	AB	H	2B	3B	HR	BB	SO	SB	CS	AVG	OBP	SLG	MLVR	EQBA	EQOBP	EQSLG	EQMLVR	VORP	DEFENSE
2002	EDM	PCL	23	518	148	32	7	29	53	151	11	7	.286	.353	.542	.236	.265	.330	.492	.051	18.5	60-RF -1 61-LF -1
2003	ROC	INT	24	454	125	34	2	16	47	117	10	3	.275	.346	.465	.111	.248	.323	.436	-.055	1.5	93-RF 7 17-LF 1
2003	MIN	AL	24	53	15	3	2	0	10	12	0	0	.283	.406	.415	.129	.288	.389	.385	.029	3.5	
2004	ROC	INT	25	425	105	20	3	20	25	104	4	3	.247	.291	.449	-.076	.222	.268	.403	-.223	-19.1	58-RF 0 38-LF -2
2004	MIN	AL	25	47	12	3	0	2	4	10	0	0	.255	.314	.447	-.042	.261	.291	.435	-.104	1.2	
2005	*MIN*	*AL*	*26*	*199*	*49*	*11*	*1*	*8*	*17*	*54*	*2*	*1*	*.247*	*.308*	*.431*	*-.075*	*.245*	*.309*	*.436*	*-.078*	*2.6*	*55-RF -2*

Breakout: 25%   Improve: 47%   Collapse: 29%

Sometimes a guy goes stale after enough time spent marooned at Triple-A, but leaving the PCL radically changed Restovich's outlook as a power source, and hitting for power is practically his only offensive asset. A broken collarbone suffered during the winter (slipping on a patch of ice is a hazard up north, donchaknow) shouldn't be a problem by the time spring training rolls around. He's going to need a good camp to avoid being dealt or outrighted off the 40-man roster.

LUIS RIVAS 2B/SS? **Bats: R** **Throws: R** Born: 30-Aug-1979 Age: 25

YEAR	TM	LG	AGE	AB	H	2B	3B	HR	BB	SO	SB	CS	AVG	OBP	SLG	MLVR	EQBA	EQOBP	EQSLG	EQMLVR	VORP	DEFENSE
2002	MIN	AL	22	316	81	23	4	4	19	51	9	4	.256	.305	.392	-.097	.261	.313	.398	-.116	10.1	87-2B -7
2003	MIN	AL	23	475	123	16	9	8	30	65	17	7	.259	.308	.381	-.126	.260	.313	.383	-.138	10.0	125-2B -11
2004	MIN	AL	24	336	86	19	5	10	13	53	15	1	.256	.283	.432	-.124	.254	.285	.432	-.125	11.6	97-2B 15
2005	*MIN*	*AL*	*25*	*358*	*95*	*19*	*4*	*8*	*19*	*51*	*13*	*5*	*.266*	*.308*	*.403*	*-.099*	*.264*	*.308*	*.408*	*-.102*	*12.7*	*93-2B 1*

Breakout: 13% *Improve: 46%* *Collapse: 25%*

His defenders craft excuses for their guy, the most common being the claim that he doesn't feel challenged in the 9th spot of the order. However, the Twins have challenged him with more than 300 PA in the second slot in the order, and he hasn't hit any better there either. Not even a modest power spike can overshadow a four-year failure to develop as a hitter. Once upon a time, he was a shortstop, so it isn't inconceivable that he could get a look there if Bartlett isn't ready and the Twins notice that Juan Castro isn't good for anything. Barring major improvements, this year should be his last as a regular.

LUIS RODRIGUEZ 2B/SS **Bats: B** **Throws: R** Born: 27-Jun-1980 Age: 25

YEAR	TM	LG	AGE	AB	H	2B	3B	HR	BB	SO	SB	CS	AVG	OBP	SLG	MLVR	EQBA	EQOBP	EQSLG	EQMLVR	VORP	DEFENSE
2002	NBR	EAS	22	455	117	18	2	8	61	44	3	2	.257	.349	.358	-.014	.233	.316	.330	-.224	-3.1	119-SS 12
2003	ROC	INT	23	518	153	35	2	1	46	46	6	8	.295	.354	.376	.024	.273	.337	.356	-.121	8.5	112-2B 4 11-SS -1
2004	ROC	INT	24	486	139	33	1	5	53	49	3	3	.286	.353	.389	-.019	.258	.328	.351	-.156	2.8	110-2B -6
2005	*MIN*	*AL*	*25*	*219*	*59*	*13*	*1*	*2*	*21*	*22*	*1*	*1*	*.270*	*.335*	*.368*	*-.095*	*.268*	*.335*	*.373*	*-.098*	*7.7*	*62-2B -3*

Breakout: 27% *Improve: 51%* *Collapse: 25%*

Rodriguez is perhaps the darkest dark horse in the infield competition, since he won't overwhelm anyone with his power, speed, or glovework. But if Cuddyer goes to third and stays there, for everyone else it becomes all about beating out Rivas, and that can be done. Rodriguez has line-drive sock, and he's an accomplished bunter. Throw in his willingness to take a walk, and the Twins would do well to give him a look, especially given the competition.

MIKE RYAN OF **Bats: L** **Throws: R** Born: 06-Jul-1977 Age: 27

YEAR	TM	LG	AGE	AB	H	2B	3B	HR	BB	SO	SB	CS	AVG	OBP	SLG	MLVR	EQBA	EQOBP	EQSLG	EQMLVR	VORP	DEFENSE
2002	EDM	PCL	25	540	141	36	6	31	55	124	4	5	.261	.330	.522	.143	.239	.308	.471	-.041	2.3	60-LF -2 45-CF -4
2003	ROC	INT	26	408	92	20	4	15	38	89	6	1	.225	.289	.404	-.094	.207	.276	.382	-.247	-24.1	72-LF -6 11-CF -1
2003	MIN	AL	26	61	24	7	0	5	6	12	2	1	.393	.441	.754	.772	.417	.430	.783	.844	14.1	12-RF 1
2004	MIN	AL	27	71	17	2	1	0	4	16	1	1	.239	.280	.296	-.319	.243	.266	.271	-.401	-3.0	
2004	ROC	INT	27	175	37	7	1	6	16	38	3	4	.211	.281	.366	-.229	.190	.264	.328	-.354	-10.7	18-CF -1 17-LF -1
2005	*MIN*	*AL*	*27*	*160*	*39*	*8*	*1*	*6*	*14*	*37*	*2*	*1*	*.246*	*.309*	*.419*	*-.091*	*.244*	*.309*	*.424*	*-.094*	*4.0*	*46-LF -3*

Breakout: 44% *Improve: 62%* *Collapse: 25%*

When you're an annual contender for the Randy Bush roster spot, there's nothing worse than *careerus interruptus.* Not only is it inconveniently messy, it leaves you wondering when you'll get your next shot. Demoted after he failed to thrive in the role, Ryan's no threat to challenge the starters or Ford in the outfield, and he's been reduced to competing with the Offermans of the world for the next-to-last spot on the roster.

SHANNON STEWART OF **Bats: R** **Throws: R** Born: 25-Feb-1974 Age: 31

YEAR	TM	LG	AGE	AB	H	2B	3B	HR	BB	SO	SB	CS	AVG	OBP	SLG	MLVR	EQBA	EQOBP	EQSLG	EQMLVR	VORP	DEFENSE
2002	TOR	AL	28	577	175	38	6	10	54	60	14	2	.303	.371	.442	.126	.305	.377	.445	.104	39.7	92-LF 0
2003	TOR	AL	29	303	89	22	2	7	27	30	1	2	.294	.347	.449	.059	.289	.346	.450	.041	11.7	69-LF 6
2003	MIN	AL	29	270	87	22	0	6	25	36	3	4	.322	.384	.470	.191	.327	.387	.474	.183	19.1	44-LF 1 14-RF 0
2004	MIN	AL	30	378	115	17	2	11	47	44	6	3	.304	.380	.447	.118	.305	.385	.451	.126	24.4	62-LF -5
2005	*MIN*	*AL*	*31*	*452*	*131*	*27*	*2*	*11*	*48*	*51*	*6*	*3*	*.289*	*.360*	*.431*	*.047*	*.287*	*.361*	*.437*	*.045*	*17.0*	*120-LF -4*

Breakout: 6% *Improve: 33%* *Collapse: 28%*

It's going to be the second year since his fanciful MVP campaign, and if Stewart is still short of true stardom, he's still a hell of a leadoff man for an offense that does a great job of powering the ball to the Dome's spongy gaps and billowing outfield "wall." Such are the increasingly rare pleasures of indoor baseball. It seems the grass/turf debate was one generation's hobbyhorse; now that we're down to three turf fields in the majors, all in the AL—Minnesota's Hump Dome,

(continued next page)

Shannon Stewart *(continued)*

Tampa Bay, and Toronto. It still makes for a fun brand of baseball, and the '87 World Series was enjoyable if for no other reason than to see a home-field effect really be a home-field effect. If the Twins ever do get back to the World Series, here's hoping the Hefty Bag looms just as large as it did then.

TERRY TIFFEE 3B **Bats: B** **Throws: R** Born: 21-Apr-1979 Age: 26

YEAR	TM	LG	AGE	AB	H	2B	3B	HR	BB	SO	SB	CS	AVG	OBP	SLG	MLVR	EQBA	EQOBP	EQSLG	EQMLVR	VORP	DEFENSE
2002	FTM	FSL	23	473	133	31	0	8	25	49	0	3	.281	.316	.397	.081	.254	.278	.373	-.223	-20.6	75-1B 5 35-3B -4
2003	NBR	EAS	24	530	167	31	3	14	31	49	4	1	.315	.351	.464	.175	.290	.324	.446	-.003	28.4	126-3B 9
2004	ROC	INT	25	316	97	26	3	12	21	26	0	0	.307	.357	.522	.188	.280	.332	.473	.041	20.2	67-3B -10
2004	MIN	AL	25	44	12	4	0	2	3	3	0	0	.273	.333	.500	.087	.279	.318	.488	.037	2.7	11-3B -2
2005	*MIN*	*AL*	*26*	*273*	*74*	*16*	*1*	*8*	*15*	*29*	*0*	*0*	*.273*	*.313*	*.423*	*-.057*	*.271*	*.314*	*.429*	*-.060*	*5.6*	*72-3B -5*

Breakout: 17% *Improve: 28%* *Collapse: 44%*

Last year, Tiffee lost time to a strained hamstring at mid-season, but he healed in time to make his debut, at which point he separated his shoulder. Even without being that ill-starred and a bit of a long shot, he can be taken seriously as a potential starter. Cuddyer should wind up with the job at third, but if Tiffee (or Eric Munson) has a great camp, Cuddyer could move to second. So Tiffee's competing with Rivas and Munson, and he offers more at the plate than one, more with the glove than the other. The organization has been encouraging Tiffee to be an aggressive hitter, and he's responded, but that only gives them a switch-hitting version of Ron Coomer.

KEVIN WEST OF **Bats: R** **Throws: R** Born: 01-Jan-1980 Age: 25

YEAR	TM	LG	AGE	AB	H	2B	3B	HR	BB	SO	SB	CS	AVG	OBP	SLG	MLVR	EQBA	EQOBP	EQSLG	EQMLVR	VORP	DEFENSE
2002	FTM	FSL	22	444	122	25	4	12	46	96	7	4	.275	.351	.430	.169	.258	.317	.417	-.084	-2.7	110-RF -9
2003	NBR	EAS	23	494	138	41	1	14	27	110	3	5	.279	.318	.451	.074	.246	.282	.415	-.161	-14.2	133-RF -5
2004	NBR	EAS	24	434	127	35	1	25	41	98	2	3	.293	.359	.551	.273	.257	.316	.482	.005	9.8	62-RF -2
2004	ROC	INT	24	79	22	8	0	4	4	19	0	0	.278	.306	.532	.091	.218	.236	.423	-.257	-3.0	
2005	*MIN*	*AL*	*25*	*255*	*67*	*15*	*1*	*10*	*18*	*58*	*1*	*1*	*.262*	*.316*	*.449*	*-.027*	*.260*	*.316*	*.455*	*-.030*	*9.5*	*68-RF -5*

Breakout: 24% *Improve: 49%* *Collapse: 32%*

West was a juco product of that big northern half of California that doesn't get talked up as a hotbed of baseball talent. Just about everything broke his way last year: Not only did he see a few of those 2003 doubles turn into 2004 home runs in his repeat engagement in the Eastern League, he was also handed Kubel's spot in the AFL after the latter's knee exploded. West then hit there too—though most good ones do—and he now has to be taken at least a bit more seriously. He was Bayloresque in his inclination to put himself in front of a pitch early in his career, but he's eased up on that the last two years, which is better for his prospects.

PITCHERS

SCOTT BAKER **Bats: R** **Throws: R** Born: 19-Sep-1981 Age: 23

YEAR	TM	LG	AGE	G	GS	IP	H	BB	SO	HR	ERA	EQERA	EQH9	EQBB9	EQSO9	EQHR9	PERA	VORP	STF
2003	QUD	MDW	21	11	11	50.7	45	8	47	4	2.49	4.50	9.8	1.8	5.7	2.2	5.28	1.6	2
2004	FTM	FSL	22	7	7	45.0	40	6	37	1	2.40	4.04	8.5	1.3	5.1	0.4	2.76	13.3	18
2004	NBR	EAS	22	10	10	70.3	44	13	72	2	2.43	3.58	6.7	1.8	7.0	0.4	2.48	22.6	45
2004	ROC	INT	22	9	9	54.3	65	15	36	3	4.97	4.89	9.6	2.5	4.7	0.5	4.39	7.2	7
2005	*MIN*	*AL*	*23*	*16*	*16*	*95.0*	*103*	*26*	*63*	*15*	*4.80*	*4.61*	*9.7*	*2.2*	*5.4*	*1.4*	*4.56*	*14.0*	*6*

Breakout: 6% *Improve: 34%* *Collapse: 28%*

The organization's pitcher of the year, Baker has the full four-pitch assortment: a low 90s sinker, a change, and both the curve and slider. He'll be taken seriously in the competition for the last spot in the rotation, but you can expect him to lose and start off in Rochester. The Twins might be cautious with him beyond the obvious reasons, in that as a 2003 pick, he doesn't need to be added to the 40-man until after this season.

GRANT BALFOUR Bats: R Throws: R Born: 30-Dec-1977 Age: 27

YEAR	TM	LG	AGE	G	GS	IP	H	BB	SO	HR	ERA	EQERA	EQH9	EQBB9	EQSO9	EQHR9	PERA	VORP	STF
2002	EDM	PCL	24	58	0	71.3	60	30	88	3	4.17	4.59	7.5	4.1	8.7	0.5	3.28	17.7	16
2003	ROC	INT	25	21	11	71.0	48	16	87	6	2.41	3.14	7.0	2.3	9.1	1.1	2.86	20.1	27
2003	MIN	AL	25	17	1	26.0	23	14	30	4	4.15	3.86	7.7	4.6	10.2	1.4	4.21	5.6	16
2004	MIN	AL	26	36	0	39.3	35	21	42	4	4.35	3.69	7.6	4.4	9.0	0.7	3.69	8.4	13
2005	*MIN*	*AL*	*27*	*18*	*5*	*44.3*	*42*	*21*	*42*	*6*	*4.22*	*4.05*	*8.4*	*3.8*	*7.8*	*1.1*	*4.32*	*9.7*	*8*

Breakout: 26% *Improve: 43%* *Collapse: 29%*

There was a spot of drama in camp, as everyone wondered whether Balfour would start, relieve, or wind up being the guy who really shot J. R. For all that, trouble with a sore shoulder ruled out starting when he was healthy enough to pitch. Going into '05, it looks like he'll be left in the pen for the time being, and he has the movement on his heat to make a good living in the role.

BOOF BONSER Bats: R Throws: R Born: 14-Oct-1981 Age: 23

YEAR	TM	LG	AGE	G	GS	IP	H	BB	SO	HR	ERA	EQERA	EQH9	EQBB9	EQSO9	EQHR9	PERA	VORP	STF
2002	SJO	CLF	20	23	23	128.3	89	70	139	9	2.88	4.36	8.2	5.8	6.0	1.1	5.14	5.9	22
2002	SHV	TXS	20	5	5	24.3	30	14	23	3	5.56	6.56	11.2	5.4	6.6	1.9	7.33	-4.5	-4
2003	NRW	EAS	21	24	24	135.0	122	67	103	11	4.00	6.00	8.7	4.9	5.7	1.2	4.64	13.4	16
2003	FRE	PCL	21	4	4	23.0	17	8	28	4	3.13	5.48	7.6	3.8	9.7	1.7	4.22	3.3	39
2004	NBR	EAS	22	27	27	154.3	160	56	146	22	4.37	5.58	9.8	3.4	6.4	1.7	5.65	-0.8	-2
2005	*MIN*	*AL*	*23*	*11*	*11*	*65.0*	*68*	*31*	*47*	*11*	*5.30*	*5.09*	*9.3*	*3.8*	*5.9*	*1.5*	*5.06*	*5.8*	*3*

Breakout: 12% *Improve: 39%* *Collapse: 23%*

There's just something about that name that conjures up images of an army of moderately psyched surf dudes, drunk on the inspirations of beach blanket bushido, attacking waves with a suicidal desperation. Anyway, Bonser is still learning how to locate his fastball, but he struggles with command of all four pitches that he can occasionally throw for strikes. He got off to a slow start, but eventually put together an adequate season. He'll get a polite look at the fifth spot in the rotation, but he can use time at Triple-A to show that he's consolidated the gains he made in the second half.

TRAVIS BOWYER Bats: R Throws: R Born: 03-Aug-1981 Age: 23

YEAR	TM	LG	AGE	G	GS	IP	H	BB	SO	HR	ERA	EQERA	EQH9	EQBB9	EQSO9	EQHR9	PERA	VORP	STF
2002	QUD	MDW	20	39	9	91.7	74	46	90	2	2.16	4.55	8.7	5.7	5.5	0.5	5.10	4.6	-2
2003	FTM	FSL	21	45	0	80.0	68	56	70	1	3.83	6.69	8.5	7.3	5.6	0.4	4.99	5.0	-11
2004	FTM	FSL	22	17	0	29.7	18	17	32	0	0.30	3.33	6.7	6.0	7.0	0.3	3.00	7.8	0
2004	NBR	EAS	22	31	0	61.3	42	38	65	3	1.76	3.16	7.3	6.0	7.3	0.6	4.11	9.4	9
2005	*MIN*	*AL*	*23*	*43*	*0*	*53.0*	*46*	*37*	*40*	*6*	*5.00*	*4.80*	*7.7*	*5.4*	*6.2*	*1.1*	*4.64*	*6.9*	*-11*

Breakout: 16% *Improve: 46%* *Collapse: 22%*

Could the Twins be cloning relievers with great stuff, instead of just drafting or signing them, the way everyone else does it? In yet another credit to the organization's ability to find guys who can bring it, Bowyer can pump gas in the high 90s, and mixes in some unhittable breaking stuff now and again. He's towards the back of the line for now, but he's a dropped walk per nine away from making an impact.

JESSE CRAIN Bats: R Throws: R Born: 05-Jul-1981 Age: 23

YEAR	TM	LG	AGE	G	GS	IP	H	BB	SO	HR	ERA	EQERA	EQH9	EQBB9	EQSO9	EQHR9	PERA	VORP	STF
2003	FTM	FSL	22	10	0	19.0	10	5	25	0	2.84	4.67	6.2	2.6	8.8	0.0	2.08	6.8	29
2003	NBR	EAS	22	22	0	39.0	13	10	56	0	0.69	2.02	4.5	2.5	10.9	0.3	1.51	16.2	56
2003	ROC	INT	22	23	0	26.0	24	10	33	0	3.12	3.91	7.8	3.9	9.2	0.4	3.55	5.8	20
2004	ROC	INT	23	41	0	50.7	38	17	64	5	2.49	3.56	7.3	3.2	9.4	0.9	3.38	11.8	28
2004	MIN	AL	23	22	0	27.0	17	12	14	2	2.00	1.78	6.8	3.9	4.6	0.7	3.20	12.8	-1
2005	*MIN*	*AL*	*23*	*45*	*2*	*69.3*	*56*	*33*	*56*	*10*	*4.01*	*3.86*	*7.2*	*3.8*	*6.6*	*1.2*	*3.81*	*16.9*	*-1*

Breakout: 19% *Improve: 38%* *Collapse: 34%*

They brought Crain along a little more slowly than some might have liked, but putting him on the postseason roster reflected the Twins' regard for him. Anyone who mixes mid-90s velocity with a tremendous slider is going to earn that. There won't be any danger of his not cracking the roster on Opening Day this year; after a season or two as an apprentice, he should slip into the closer's role once Nathan prices himself out of the Twins' budget.

J. D. DURBIN Bats: R Throws: R Born: 24-Feb-1982 Age: 23

YEAR	TM	LG	AGE	G	GS	IP	H	BB	SO	HR	ERA	EQERA	EQH9	EQBB9	EQSO9	EQHR9	PERA	VORP	STF
2002	QUD	MDW	20	27	27	161.0	144	51	163	14	3.19	5.38	10.3	3.7	5.8	2.1	6.62	-16.3	-6
2003	FTM	FSL	21	14	14	87.3	73	22	69	3	3.09	5.40	8.9	2.6	5.2	0.9	4.16	12.8	15
2003	NBR	EAS	21	14	14	94.7	102	29	70	10	3.14	4.43	10.0	3.0	5.4	1.5	5.44	1.6	4
2004	NBR	EAS	22	13	13	64.3	62	22	53	4	2.52	3.67	9.0	3.2	5.6	0.7	4.40	8.2	7
2004	ROC	INT	22	7	7	35.7	49	16	38	4	4.54	6.50	10.5	4.0	7.5	1.0	5.75	-0.6	3
2004	MIN	AL	22	4	1	7.3	12	6	6	0	7.40	6.75	11.2	5.6	6.8	0.0	5.62	-0.9	-18
2005	*MIN*	*AL*	*23*	*18*	*12*	*74.3*	*80*	*31*	*56*	*10*	*4.89*	*4.69*	*9.6*	*3.3*	*6.1*	*1.1*	*4.75*	*9.5*	*3*

Breakout: 17% *Improve: 50%* *Collapse: 14%*

Surgery to repair a torn labrum and clean up his rotator cuff and biceps cost him six weeks in the first half of 2004. That doesn't sound like much considering so many different areas needed work, but Durbin's mechanics are a bit of an adventure. For now, he's got a hard slurve and high-90s heat, which sounds nice enough to start off with, but he also has a funky change he grips differently, wrapping his pinky around the bottom of the ball; the digit apparently has an unusual range of motion since being broken. He'll contend for a job at the bottom of either the rotation or the pen, but his mechanics are enough of a concern to raise a caution flag.

WILLIE EYRE Bats: R Throws: R Born: 21-Jul-1978 Age: 26

YEAR	TM	LG	AGE	G	GS	IP	H	BB	SO	HR	ERA	EQERA	EQH9	EQBB9	EQSO9	EQHR9	PERA	VORP	STF
2002	FTM	FSL	23	19	0	33.7	28	13	25	0	2.40	3.69	8.2	3.7	4.8	0.3	3.69	6.7	-4
2002	NBR	EAS	23	28	0	50.0	40	21	43	1	3.24	4.40	7.9	4.0	6.1	0.2	3.26	12.2	5
2003	NBR	EAS	24	29	10	96.3	93	38	66	6	3.46	4.67	9.0	3.9	5.1	1.0	4.76	8.5	0
2003	ROC	INT	24	6	5	24.0	30	16	23	2	6.00	6.85	9.9	6.5	6.8	1.1	6.08	-1.3	-12
2004	ROC	INT	25	36	21	136.0	131	53	91	13	3.64	3.97	8.8	3.7	5.0	1.0	4.45	16.5	-7
2005	*MIN*	*AL*	*26*	*12*	*8*	*49.7*	*53*	*22*	*31*	*6*	*4.94*	*4.75*	*9.5*	*3.5*	*5.1*	*1.1*	*4.77*	*6.2*	*-4*

Breakout: 17% *Improve: 47%* *Collapse: 20%*

Eyre tends to get overlooked amidst the cornucopia of live arms in the organization, but he's done one thing that separates a lot of talents from their destiny: He's remained healthy. Having put up a solid season at Rochester, he's earned some consideration. He's struggled with command of his fastball, but seems to have tackled the problem. He was the homegrown product in the trio of reliable starters at Rochester last year, but probably ranks behind Guerrier and Gassner internally, because of his lukewarm strikeout rates.

AARON FULTZ Bats: L Throws: L Born: 04-Sep-1973 Age: 31

YEAR	TM	LG	AGE	G	GS	IP	H	BB	SO	HR	ERA	EQERA	EQH9	EQBB9	EQSO9	EQHR9	PERA	VORP	STF
2002	FRE	PCL	28	17	0	22.7	18	11	22	1	3.17	3.38	7.6	4.6	7.2	0.4	3.80	4.3	2
2002	SFG	NL	28	43	0	41.3	47	19	31	4	4.79	5.09	10.0	3.5	6.0	0.9	5.31	2.7	-6
2003	TEX	AL	29	64	0	67.3	75	27	53	9	5.22	4.95	8.8	3.3	6.8	1.1	4.14	2.6	-2
2004	MIN	AL	30	55	0	50.0	50	23	37	5	5.04	4.38	8.6	3.6	6.2	0.7	4.20	6.9	-1
2005	*PHI*	*NL*	*31*	*35*	*1*	*47.0*	*49*	*21*	*36*	*6*	*4.70*	*4.87*	*9.3*	*3.4*	*6.1*	*1.0*	*4.90*	*4.5*	*-5*

Breakout: 19% *Improve: 44%* *Collapse: 28%*

Despite never posting an ERA under 4.50 in any of his five big league seasons, Fultz is now pretty well established on the LOOGY gravy train, which is a better thing than it sounds. Your basic moderately serviceable second lefty, he was snagged off waivers by the Phillies.

DAVE GASSNER Bats: R Throws: L Born: 14-Dec-1978 Age: 26

YEAR	TM	LG	AGE	G	GS	IP	H	BB	SO	HR	ERA	EQERA	EQH9	EQBB9	EQSO9	EQHR9	PERA	VORP	STF
2002	DUN	FSL	23	23	21	146.7	143	26	104	17	3.44	4.81	10.4	1.8	4.7	2.3	5.88	-4.2	-4
2002	TEN	SOU	23	4	4	25.3	22	7	14	1	2.49	3.86	8.9	2.3	3.9	0.8	3.86	4.5	12
2003	NHV	EAS	24	35	19	145.3	139	28	92	10	2.79	4.29	9.0	1.9	4.7	1.1	3.96	24.8	11
2004	ROC	INT	25	28	28	174.3	175	30	93	16	3.41	3.75	9.1	1.6	4.0	0.9	4.02	29.1	4
2005	*MIN*	*AL*	*26*	*24*	*13*	*89.7*	*103*	*23*	*48*	*14*	*4.95*	*4.75*	*10.3*	*2.0*	*4.4*	*1.4*	*4.76*	*12.3*	*-6*

Breakout: 19% *Improve: 43%* *Collapse: 28%*

The PTBNL from the Shannon Stewart trade, so for Bobby Kielty, the Twins got two months of Stewart in '03 (he had to be re-signed as a free agent), plus Gassner, a nifty exchange. Gassner's not overpowering, but he's a better prospect than most minor league lefty finesse guys. He's never struggled as a pro, and nothing in his peripheral stats suggests that what you see isn't what you'll get. If he has a good camp, and if Ron Gardenhire decides he has to have a second lefty in his rotation, Gassner makes a better choice than taking another spin with Terry Mulholland.

SETH GREISINGER **Bats: R** **Throws: R** Born: 29-Jul-1975 Age: 29

YEAR	TM	LG	AGE	G	GS	IP	H	BB	SO	HR	ERA	EQERA	EQH9	EQBB9	EQSO9	EQHR9	PERA	VORP	STF
2002	DET	AL	26	8	8	37.7	46	13	14	4	6.21	5.79	10.1	2.9	3.1	1.0	4.58	-1.0	-11
2003	TOL	INT	27	25	21	136.0	154	23	80	16	3.97	5.53	10.4	1.7	4.3	1.6	5.39	3.0	-5
2004	ROC	INT	28	13	13	74.3	94	19	44	10	4.97	5.08	10.4	2.4	4.3	1.4	5.33	2.2	-5
2004	MIN	AL	28	12	9	51.0	68	15	36	12	6.18	6.10	10.5	2.3	5.9	1.7	5.57	-4.7	-2
2005	*MIN*	*AL*	*29*	*19*	*14*	*85.7*	*102*	*26*	*50*	*13*	*5.28*	*5.07*	*10.6*	*2.4*	*4.7*	*1.3*	*5.10*	*8.2*	*-4*

Breakout: 17% *Improve: 42%* *Collapse: 25%*

Next on Fox: When Human Interest Stories Attack! Greisinger's recovery from Tommy John surgery was one of the longest on record, costing him 1999 through 2001, and it's hard not to have sympathy for him. Nevertheless, it's time to forget that he was the sixth overall pick of the 1996 draft, and instead recognize that he has never been a very effective pitcher, before or after the injury. It does scouting no credit as a profession when people can't let go of what might have been.

MATT GUERRIER **Bats: R** **Throws: R** Born: 02-Aug-1978 Age: 26

YEAR	TM	LG	AGE	G	GS	IP	H	BB	SO	HR	ERA	EQERA	EQH9	EQBB9	EQSO9	EQHR9	PERA	VORP	STF
2002	NAS	PCL	23	27	26	157.0	154	47	130	20	4.59	5.47	9.3	2.9	6.0	1.4	4.80	13.2	11
2003	NAS	PCL	24	20	19	105.3	108	18	78	15	4.53	5.58	10.0	1.7	5.9	1.9	5.13	5.1	-1
2004	ROC	INT	25	24	23	144.0	135	25	97	15	3.19	4.04	8.7	1.7	5.0	1.1	3.84	26.6	11
2004	MIN	AL	25	9	2	19.0	22	6	11	5	5.68	5.30	10.1	2.4	4.8	1.9	5.79	0.2	-12
2005	*MIN*	*AL*	*26*	*24*	*11*	*78.7*	*86*	*23*	*52*	*13*	*4.97*	*4.77*	*9.7*	*2.3*	*5.4*	*1.4*	*4.62*	*9.9*	*-3*

Breakout: 13% *Improve: 34%* *Collapse: 32%*

A slider-fastball guy with pedestrian heat, Guerrier was snagged off waivers from the Pirates last winter. (Guerrier had been dealt to Pittsburgh by the White Sox for Damaso Marte, not one of Dave Littlefield's finer moments.) You'd think that Travis Miller might have weaned the Twins off overhyped Kent State prospects, but a first good season in his fourth try at Triple-A was apparently enough to make him a keeper on their 40-man roster for now. He'll be considered for the fifth starter slot, and perhaps win it if Mays struggles and Gassner doesn't impress.

ADAM HARBEN **Bats: R** **Throws: R** Born: 19-Aug-1983 Age: 21

YEAR	TM	LG	AGE	G	GS	IP	H	BB	SO	HR	ERA	EQERA	EQH9	EQBB9	EQSO9	EQHR9	PERA	VORP	STF
2003	QUD	MDW	19	16	15	87.3	91	35	77	5	4.33	7.11	10.1	4.6	5.3	1.3	5.78	-1.6	1
2004	QUD	MDW	20	26	26	142.7	114	68	171	5	3.09	5.22	8.6	5.6	6.5	0.7	4.94	9.5	12
2005	*MIN*	*AL*	*21*	*14*	*13*	*71.0*	*72*	*43*	*55*	*9*	*5.24*	*5.03*	*9.0*	*4.8*	*6.3*	*1.2*	*5.10*	*6.0*	*2*

Breakout: 16% *Improve: 49%* *Collapse: 18%*

Harben is already being touted by minor league mavens as a stealth prospect, and it's easy to see why: Big guys with big fastballs that bore into hitters inspire praise. Harben also has the advantage of clean mechanics, but his ability to develop a refined breaking or off-speed pitch is going to determine his future. If he can throw one without altering his mechanics, he'll avoid hurting himself, with the added benefit of not tipping his pitches. The Midwest League rarely tells us much, so check back a year from now.

BEAU KEMP **Bats: R** **Throws: R** Born: 31-Oct-1980 Age: 24

YEAR	TM	LG	AGE	G	GS	IP	H	BB	SO	HR	ERA	EQERA	EQH9	EQBB9	EQSO9	EQHR9	PERA	VORP	STF
2002	FTM	FSL	21	59	0	68.3	49	18	49	0	0.66	3.27	7.5	2.7	4.8	0.3	2.98	18.4	12
2003	FTM	FSL	22	22	0	26.3	30	7	16	3	3.76	6.46	12.2	2.7	4.2	3.0	7.61	-5.3	-22
2003	NBR	EAS	22	36	0	52.0	63	23	38	1	3.98	6.14	9.6	4.2	5.1	0.4	4.73	5.0	-17
2004	NBR	EAS	23	18	0	29.7	27	12	24	1	2.73	3.81	8.6	3.8	5.4	0.3	3.81	5.6	-13
2004	ROC	INT	23	36	0	48.3	46	19	35	1	3.54	4.27	8.4	3.7	5.4	0.2	3.69	9.8	0
2005	*MIN*	*AL*	*24*	*31*	*2*	*48.0*	*53*	*20*	*31*	*5*	*4.63*	*4.45*	*9.8*	*3.3*	*5.2*	*0.9*	*4.65*	*7.5*	*-9*

Breakout: 20% *Improve: 49%* *Collapse: 24%*

In most organizations, a guy who can dial up 95 on his heater and complement it with a pretty vicious slider would be a prospect, but competition for bullpen spots on the Twins borders on Darwinian in its mercilessness. A bad '03 took Kemp off most people's radar, and a merely solid '04 didn't put him back on. As a six-footer, he's also considered on the short side for what most scouts want in a power reliever, so we'll have to wait a while to see if something pans out.

FRANCISCO LIRIANO **Bats: L** **Throws: L** Born: 26-Oct-1983 Age: 21

YEAR	TM	LG	AGE	G	GS	IP	H	BB	SO	HR	ERA	EQERA	EQH9	EQBB9	EQSO9	EQHR9	PERA	VORP	STF
2002	HAG	SAL	18	16	16	80.0	61	31	85	6	3.49	6.56	8.8	4.5	6.1	1.5	4.79	6.4	27
2004	FTM	FSL	20	21	21	117.0	118	43	125	6	4.00	5.69	9.5	3.7	6.5	0.9	4.55	12.9	11
2004	NBR	EAS	20	7	7	39.7	45	17	49	4	3.17	3.72	10.0	4.0	8.1	0.9	5.35	1.1	19
2005	*MIN*	*AL*	*21*	*13*	*12*	*71.3*	*77*	*34*	*57*	*9*	*4.87*	*4.68*	*9.7*	*3.7*	*6.6*	*1.1*	*4.94*	*9.3*	*8*

Breakout: 12% *Improve: 51%* *Collapse: 12%*

The hidden gem from the deal that sent A. J. Pierzynski to the Giants, Liriano missed most of 2003 to shoulder trouble. Happily, he didn't require surgery, and instead came into the Twins system and showed surprising velocity for his slight frame. He can push up into the mid 90s once in a while, but usually, he's several notches below that, while mixing in a big yakker of a curve. Letting him ease up at his age makes sense, because you don't create a staff workhorse by working him to death in Fort Myers. The most promising arm in the system, bar none.

KYLE LOHSE **Bats: R** **Throws: R** Born: 04-Oct-1978 Age: 26

YEAR	TM	LG	AGE	G	GS	IP	H	BB	SO	HR	ERA	EQERA	EQH9	EQBB9	EQSO9	EQHR9	PERA	VORP	STF
2002	MIN	AL	23	32	31	180.7	181	70	124	26	4.23	4.23	9.1	3.3	6.0	1.2	4.90	28.1	5
2003	MIN	AL	24	33	33	201.0	211	45	130	28	4.61	4.33	9.1	1.9	5.8	1.2	4.28	28.9	11
2004	MIN	AL	25	35	34	194.0	240	76	111	28	5.34	5.14	10.0	3.1	4.8	1.1	5.28	6.3	-2
2005	*MIN*	*AL*	*26*	*28*	*25*	*147.7*	*169*	*53*	*88*	*23*	*5.27*	*5.07*	*10.2*	*2.8*	*4.9*	*1.3*	*5.06*	*12.4*	*-2*

Breakout: 11% *Improve: 45%* *Collapse: 23%*

Lohse has teased us with streaks of effectiveness, which combined with his age encourages people to think he's on the cusp of turning a corner. But after watching him spend the better part of four years in the big league rotation, it's time to liken him to Jon Garland—useful, but mediocre. It's helpful that he seems to have the White Sox's number, the sort of tiebreaker that can make you stick with someone's limited horizons, and he does a good job controlling the running game and fielding his position, so he creates no attention-getting nuisances that might exasperate management.

JOE MAYS **Bats: B** **Throws: R** Born: 10-Dec-1975 Age: 29

YEAR	TM	LG	AGE	G	GS	IP	H	BB	SO	HR	ERA	EQERA	EQH9	EQBB9	EQSO9	EQHR9	PERA	VORP	STF
2002	MIN	AL	26	17	17	95.3	113	25	38	14	5.38	5.17	10.3	2.2	3.5	1.2	5.36	3.4	-5
2003	MIN	AL	27	31	21	130.0	159	39	50	21	6.30	5.74	10.4	2.6	3.4	1.3	5.53	-4.1	-13
2005	*MIN*	*AL*	*29*	*19*	*14*	*86.3*	*106*	*26*	*39*	*14*	*5.53*	*5.31*	*10.9*	*2.4*	*3.7*	*1.4*	*5.24*	*6.6*	*-10*

Breakout: 22% *Improve: 50%* *Collapse: 22%*

Mays was supposed to be back on the mound at some level last season, rehabbing his way back from Tommy John surgery. After several setbacks, it didn't happen. Even at his best, he wasn't overpowering. Officially, the Twins think he'll be at full strength in time for spring training. Even at his best, he wasn't overpowering. His performance record outside of his 2001 season isn't impressive enough for them to cut him any slack; he should have to fight for a job in the rotation, walk year of his four-year deal or no.

JASON MILLER Bats: L Throws: L Born: 20-Jul-1982 Age: 22

YEAR	TM	LG	AGE	G	GS	IP	H	BB	SO	HR	ERA	EQERA	EQH9	EQBB9	EQSO9	EQHR9	PERA	VORP	STF
2002	QUD	MDW	19	23	8	65.3	55	22	71	7	2.34	4.87	10.4	4.1	6.3	2.5	6.91	-8.3	-2
2003	QUD	MDW	20	13	12	68.7	67	21	50	4	2.36	5.00	9.9	3.4	4.4	1.6	5.29	2.2	-1
2003	FTM	FSL	20	13	10	51.0	60	21	39	3	4.24	7.12	11.1	4.1	4.9	1.5	6.38	-4.2	-15
2004	FTM	FSL	21	19	0	29.3	16	11	40	2	1.54	3.08	7.2	4.1	8.9	1.4	3.42	6.4	20
2004	NBR	EAS	21	33	1	40.0	33	21	42	2	4.28	4.74	8.1	5.0	7.1	0.5	4.03	6.6	5
2005	*MIN*	*AL*	*22*	*16*	*5*	*41.0*	*39*	*21*	*33*	*7*	*5.04*	*4.84*	*8.5*	*4.0*	*6.6*	*1.5*	*4.76*	*5.2*	*-3*

Breakout: 15% Improve: 49% Collapse: 16%

A Florida high school lefty nabbed in the fourth round of the 2000 draft, Miller scuffled as a starter, so the Twins decided to harness his live arm in the pen. In that role, he didn't merely make it; he earned a promotion to Double-A, where he was among the youngest pitchers in the Eastern League. It's going to be a lot easier for a talented lefty reliever to get the Twins' attention, given the crowd of flamethrowing right-handers in the system.

VICTOR MORENO Bats: R Throws: R Born: 10-Jun-1979 Age: 26

YEAR	TM	LG	AGE	G	GS	IP	H	BB	SO	HR	ERA	EQERA	EQH9	EQBB9	EQSO9	EQHR9	PERA	VORP	STF
2002	BAT	NYP	23	17	0	26.7	19	21	34	3	3.71	6.75	11.0	11.4	7.6	4.2	10.97	-12.7	-49
2003	FTM	FSL	24	16	0	26.7	21	14	32	1	2.02	4.81	8.5	5.5	7.8	1.1	4.81	2.1	-2
2003	NBR	EAS	24	24	0	33.7	37	22	27	5	6.94	7.67	10.5	6.5	6.0	2.3	7.39	-6.3	-31
2004	NBR	EAS	25	33	5	75.3	56	42	86	4	2.27	3.06	7.5	5.3	7.8	0.6	4.08	11.9	13
2004	ROC	INT	25	6	0	11.3	12	6	12	1	6.37	7.36	9.0	4.9	7.4	0.8	4.91	0.8	7
2005	*OAK*	*AL*	*26*	*16*	*5*	*43.3*	*38*	*26*	*37*	*8*	*5.31*	*5.25*	*8.1*	*4.8*	*6.9*	*1.5*	*5.06*	*3.4*	*-4*

Breakout: 16% Improve: 52% Collapse: 18%

Probably not Rita's lovechild by Luis Tiant, but we can always hope. Moreno is a wild Venezuelan hurler who has skipped from the Snakes to the Phillies to the Twins organization. Relief pitchers can pop up all over the place; in this case, the Twins added him in the less-heralded minor league portion of the Rule 5 Draft. His performance record was pretty slim before last year's breakthrough, which is why he was available (and taken, by Oakland), in this year's minor league Rule 5 Draft.

TERRY MULHOLLAND Bats: R Throws: L Born: 09-Mar-1963 Age: 42

YEAR	TM	LG	AGE	G	GS	IP	H	BB	SO	HR	ERA	EQERA	EQH9	EQBB9	EQSO9	EQHR9	PERA	VORP	STF
2002	LAD	NL	39	21	0	32.0	45	7	17	10	7.31	8.51	12.6	1.8	4.4	2.9	7.92	-9.9	-28
2002	CLE	AL	39	16	3	47.0	56	14	21	5	4.60	4.82	9.6	2.5	3.9	1.0	4.24	4.2	-9
2003	CLE	AL	40	45	3	99.0	117	37	42	17	4.91	5.08	10.4	3.3	3.8	1.4	5.83	7.0	-24
2004	MIN	AL	41	39	15	123.3	163	33	60	17	5.18	4.79	10.5	2.1	4.1	1.0	5.15	9.6	-10
2005	*MIN*	*AL*	*42*	*28*	*7*	*65.0*	*86*	*21*	*26*	*11*	*5.92*	*5.69*	*11.8*	*2.5*	*3.3*	*1.5*	*5.84*	*0.0*	*-21*

Breakout: 13% Improve: 24% Collapse: 40%

Now that Miguel Batista has graduated to rotation regular, somebody ought to hold the title for Mr. Utility Pitcher, so why not the rubber-armed, ageless Mulholland? Although he's been re-signed (to a minor league deal), Mulholland's role with the club is sketchy, as you might expect for a graying swingman. If nobody does well in camp, he could again be handed the last spot in the rotation. Bet on his sticking as the staff's "in case of emergency, break glass" 11th man.

JOE NATHAN Bats: R Throws: R Born: 22-Nov-1974 Age: 30

YEAR	TM	LG	AGE	G	GS	IP	H	BB	SO	HR	ERA	EQERA	EQH9	EQBB9	EQSO9	EQHR9	PERA	VORP	STF
2002	FRE	PCL	27	31	25	146.3	167	74	117	20	5.60	5.68	10.0	4.8	5.6	1.5	6.13	-8.3	-13
2003	SFG	NL	28	78	0	79.0	51	33	83	7	2.96	3.01	6.9	3.4	8.9	0.8	3.38	23.3	17
2004	MIN	AL	29	73	0	72.3	48	23	89	3	1.62	1.54	6.1	2.6	10.6	0.4	2.30	36.5	37
2005	*MIN*	*AL*	*30*	*56*	*0*	*70.3*	*64*	*30*	*70*	*9*	*4.07*	*3.91*	*8.1*	*3.3*	*8.1*	*1.1*	*4.02*	*16.7*	*8*

Breakout: 26% Improve: 48% Collapse: 23%

The name player in the booty lifted from the Giants in the Pierzynski deal, Nathan showed that his adaptation to a relief role the previous season was no fluke. A change of scenery can be just as much something to look forward to for an organization as it is for a player, and the Twins were slobbering over the prospect of putting him into the closer's role and letting him torch the league. The moving fastball and power slider are the classic Gossage-like assortment for relief dominance, and you can expect more of the same for as long as he's healthy.

BRAD RADKE Bats: R Throws: R Born: 27-Oct-1972 Age: 32

YEAR	TM	LG	AGE	G	GS	IP	H	BB	SO	HR	ERA	EQERA	EQH9	EQBB9	EQSO9	EQHR9	PERA	VORP	STF
2002	MIN	AL	29	21	21	118.3	124	20	62	12	4.72	4.42	9.3	1.4	4.6	0.9	4.26	14.7	7
2003	MIN	AL	30	33	33	212.3	242	28	120	32	4.49	4.26	9.7	1.1	5.0	1.2	4.48	32.5	7
2004	MIN	AL	31	34	34	219.7	229	26	143	23	3.48	3.31	8.8	1.0	5.6	0.8	3.65	60.1	18
2005	*MIN*	*AL*	*32*	*29*	*28*	*169.7*	*191*	*24*	*102*	*25*	*4.35*	*4.18*	*10.0*	*1.1*	*4.9*	*1.3*	*4.20*	*32.0*	*8*

Breakout: 19% *Improve: 50%* *Collapse: 17%*

For years, Radke has been sparing himself by relying more heavily on his change against righties or lefties,and saving the breaking stuff for what Christy Mathewson called "the clinches." It's produced a career's worth of reliability, but last year he was particularly impressive, as he put up the second-best year of his career, after 1999. Improving his strikeout rate and yielding fewer bleacher souvenirs bodes well for his future: Even if he regresses, it's probably only going to be down to previous levels, and there's enough here to like that he could continue to age more gracefully than that. That the Twins only needed two years, $18 million to bring him back now looks inspired, compared to the Milton-Ortiz-Pavano extravagances of the off-season.

JUAN RINCON Bats: R Throws: R Born: 23-Jan-1979 Age: 26

YEAR	TM	LG	AGE	G	GS	IP	H	BB	SO	HR	ERA	EQERA	EQH9	EQBB9	EQSO9	EQHR9	PERA	VORP	STF
2002	EDM	PCL	23	19	16	101.7	111	35	75	12	4.78	5.22	9.3	3.3	5.2	1.2	4.58	11.1	6
2002	MIN	AL	23	10	3	28.7	44	9	21	5	6.27	6.44	11.7	2.5	6.1	1.2	6.44	-4.0	1
2003	MIN	AL	24	58	0	85.7	74	38	63	5	3.68	3.70	7.8	3.9	6.6	0.4	3.70	20.0	2
2004	MIN	AL	25	77	0	82.0	52	32	106	5	2.63	2.59	6.0	3.2	11.1	0.4	2.36	30.2	34
2005	*MIN*	*AL*	*26*	*52*	*2*	*76.0*	*70*	*31*	*78*	*9*	*4.12*	*3.96*	*8.2*	*3.2*	*8.4*	*1.0*	*3.90*	*16.4*	*11*

Breakout: 25% *Improve: 47%* *Collapse: 39%*

Don't get us wrong, a good closer isn't a bad thing to have, but it really helps to have one of the best setup men in baseball. Nathan ranked sixth in the AL in *BP*'s Adjusted Runs Prevented, a measure of relief performance; Rincon finished seventh. Only the Yankees' combo of Mariano Rivera and Tom Gordon matched that, but you've probably already heard about them. PECOTA's a bit down on Rincon because the track record of short right-handers isn't replete with success stories, but he's durable enough toremain in the ranks of the game's best setup men.

JOE ROA Bats: R Throws: R Born: 11-Oct-1971 Age: 33

YEAR	TM	LG	AGE	G	GS	IP	H	BB	SO	HR	ERA	EQERA	EQH9	EQBB9	EQSO9	EQHR9	PERA	VORP	STF
2002	SWB	INT	30	17	17	111.0	83	16	74	4	1.86	2.65	7.9	1.5	5.3	0.5	3.26	26.5	41
2002	PHI	NL	30	14	11	71.3	78	13	35	11	4.04	4.39	10.2	1.5	4.0	1.5	5.05	10.5	15
2003	PHI	NL	31	6	3	19.3	28	4	16	3	6.06	5.95	11.0	1.4	6.4	1.4	5.49	-0.8	3
2003	IND	INT	31	5	4	24.7	32	3	18	3	4.74	5.62	10.9	1.1	5.2	1.9	5.62	-0.1	0
2003	SDP	NL	31	18	1	25.3	34	6	18	5	6.76	7.11	11.0	1.8	5.7	1.8	5.68	-4.2	-10
2004	MIN	AL	32	48	0	70.0	84	24	47	9	4.50	4.24	9.6	2.7	5.7	1.0	4.89	10.8	-7
2005	*PIT*	*NL*	*33*	*26*	*3*	*47.3*	*52*	*14*	*32*	*6*	*4.49*	*4.75*	*9.8*	*2.3*	*5.5*	*1.2*	*4.85*	*5.5*	*-5*

Breakout 21% *Improve 46%* *Collapse 30%*

Roa has been popping in and out of the big leagues since 1995, and if he never could really dent bread with his best stuff, he's a useful journeyman. He got a bit huffy after being left off the postseason roster, going home when he could have traveled with the team and remained eligible for the second round if the Twins made it that far. A NRI with the Bucs, Roa is as much a long shot as ever, and strictly roster filler.

J. C. ROMERO Bats: B Throws: L Born: 04-Jun-1976 Age: 29

YEAR	TM	LG	AGE	G	GS	IP	H	BB	SO	HR	ERA	EQERA	EQH9	EQBB9	EQSO9	EQHR9	PERA	VORP	STF
2002	MIN	AL	26	81	0	81.0	62	36	76	3	1.89	1.85	7.2	3.8	8.2	0.3	3.23	36.7	17
2003	MIN	AL	27	73	0	63.0	66	42	50	7	5.00	4.76	8.8	5.6	6.9	0.9	5.05	5.7	-9
2004	MIN	AL	28	74	0	74.3	61	38	69	4	3.51	3.33	7.3	4.2	7.9	0.4	3.33	19.9	14
2005	*MIN*	*AL*	*29*	*53*	*1*	*67.3*	*64*	*35*	*61*	*6*	*3.99*	*3.84*	*8.5*	*4.1*	*7.4*	*0.8*	*4.30*	*15.8*	*3*

Breakout: 26% *Improve: 52%* *Collapse: 27%*

The other half of the setup tandem that turned over so many save situations to Joe Nathan, Romero didn't mow down lefties with his usual aplomb, but the Twins realize that he's not just a situational lefty. He's a more valuable thing indeed, a rubber-armed middle reliever in the old sense of the term, ready to work in situational roles or toss two or three innings when a starter has to hit the showers early. He kills the running game, and keeps the ball on the ground, which proves particularly handy with men on base, and he can overpower hitters with his low-90s sinker. As long as he keeps that walk rate in check, he's a valuable asset. The Twins rewarded him with a two-year deal.

JOHAN SANTANA **Bats: L** **Throws: L** Born: 13-Mar-1979 Age: 26

YEAR	TM	LG	AGE	G	GS	IP	H	BB	SO	HR	ERA	EQERA	EQH9	EQBB9	EQSO9	EQHR9	PERA	VORP	STF
2002	EDM	PCL	23	11	9	48.7	37	27	75	7	3.14	4.66	7.4	5.2	11.1	1.6	4.27	6.8	29
2002	MIN	AL	23	27	14	108.3	84	49	137	7	2.99	3.22	6.9	3.8	10.9	0.5	3.22	31.0	44
2003	MIN	AL	24	45	18	158.3	127	47	169	17	3.07	2.93	7.2	2.6	9.5	0.9	3.17	51.1	33
2004	MIN	AL	25	34	34	228.0	156	54	265	24	2.61	2.45	6.5	2.0	10.1	0.8	2.54	88.8	48
2005	*MIN*	*AL*	*26*	*30*	*30*	*193.7*	*158*	*54*	*221*	*21*	*3.11*	*2.99*	*7.3*	*2.2*	*9.3*	*1.0*	*2.95*	*63.6*	*37*

Breakout: 29% *Improve: 65%* *Collapse: 14%*

The reigning best pitcher in baseball, and not by a little bit. Skip past gripes about when the Twins would let it happen: Santana's here, and this should be the beginning of a multi-year run of great work. He led all pitchers across both leagues in VORP, and the highest Expected Winning Percentage for their games of any starter in the big leagues (67.3%). But the treat? That devastating difference between his fastball and his change-up. Frank Viola fans know what we're talking about. With the division looking even weaker going into 2005, Santana could exploit the unbalanced schedule and put up numbers similar to last year's.

CARLOS SILVA **Bats: R** **Throws: R** Born: 23-Apr-1979 Age: 26

YEAR	TM	LG	AGE	G	GS	IP	H	BB	SO	HR	ERA	EQERA	EQH9	EQBB9	EQSO9	EQHR9	PERA	VORP	STF
2002	PHI	NL	23	68	0	84.0	88	22	41	4	3.21	3.90	9.5	2.0	4.0	0.4	4.02	16.2	-6
2003	PHI	NL	24	62	1	87.3	92	37	48	7	4.43	4.57	9.5	3.4	4.6	0.7	4.68	11.6	-11
2004	MIN	AL	25	33	33	203.0	255	35	76	23	4.21	3.85	10.3	1.4	3.2	0.9	4.70	40.5	-1
2005	*MIN*	*AL*	*26*	*31*	*26*	*154.7*	*188*	*39*	*73*	*19*	*4.67*	*4.48*	*10.8*	*2.0*	*3.9*	*1.1*	*4.81*	*23.6*	*-4*

Breakout: 20% *Improve: 55%* *Collapse: 14%*

Silva's success in the rotation is a tribute to Twins scouting, because during '04, he rewarded their faith in him by giving the Twins a solid #3 starter, which was the sort of thing their division rivals lacked. However, his Peripheral ERAs weren't great either of the last two years, in or out of a big league rotation, which contributes to PECOTA's pessimism about his ability to sustain last year's success. When you're counting on your defense to get 90% of the outs made while you're on the mound, you'll end up taking a lot of lumps for it.

SCOTT TYLER **Bats: R** **Throws: R** Born: 20-Aug-1982 Age: 22

YEAR	TM	LG	AGE	G	GS	IP	H	BB	SO	HR	ERA	EQERA	EQH9	EQBB9	EQSO9	EQHR9	PERA	VORP	STF
2002	ELZ	APL	19	14	13	67.7	37	46	92	5	2.92	5.43	7.9	8.2	6.7	1.7	5.74	-0.9	1
2003	QUD	MDW	20	30	20	106.3	93	82	110	7	5.50	7.42	9.5	9.1	6.6	1.7	7.04	-15.2	-18
2004	QUD	MDW	21	22	19	103.7	73	64	132	3	2.60	4.37	8.0	7.3	7.1	0.6	4.95	6.7	8
2005	*MIN*	*AL*	*22*	*25*	*9*	*69.7*	*60*	*54*	*55*	*10*	*5.52*	*5.31*	*7.7*	*6.1*	*6.4*	*1.3*	*5.08*	*5.7*	*-9*

Breakout: 22% *Improve: 50%* *Collapse: 16%*

A slow-developing high school pitcher with a classic power pitcher's frame. True to form, Tyler throws a mid-90s fastball. Everything else is a work in progress. Despite his wildness, he doesn't throw a lot of wild pitches or hit many batters; he just really can't control the strike zone. He could take a big step forward, or scrag his arm before he reaches Double-A, or collapse against more advanced competition, but until then, he's a name to remember.

New York Yankees

In some ways, the Yankees, one of baseball's great success stories since 1996, have upped their game in the last few years. In 2004 the team reached triple digits in the win column for the third consecutive year. It was a first for the Yankees, who became only the fourth team in baseball history to display this kind of concentrated dominance, joining the 1929–1931 A's, the 1942–1944 Cardinals, the 1969–1971 Orioles, and the 1997–1999 Braves. Slice it any way you want—the Yankees have been the winningest team in the game (see table 1).

During this period the Yankees have benefited from financial superiority and an unbalanced schedule that sees them play 57 games against the soft underbelly of their own division. Yet they've failed to win the World Series the last four years. In some sense, then, the team has to be classified a failure.

Looking back at a season in which the Red Sox celebrated their first championship in 86 years, it seems odd to say that the Yankees failed because they haven't won one in four. The Pirates haven't won 100 games since the Taft administration, but the Yankees do so almost casually. To call the team anything but a great success would seem unfair.

It was the Yankees, though, that set the bar where it is. The Yankees build to win the championship each year, and with their advantages, they *should* win it. Bad luck can only take so much of the blame. After that, team planning has to be taken into account.

The Yankees are not good at detail work. Every year they use their riches to buy the world's biggest cake but often forget to bring home the candles, forks, and napkins. There is nothing inherently wrong with pressing an advantage, but in loading up on luxury items, the team often misses the small, nuts-and-bolts details that win championships.

The 2004 Yankees were based on a number of faulty assumptions and ill-fitting solutions to problems:

The Yankees at first believed that Enrique Wilson could start at second base; then they believed he could play well as a substitute. Mike Lamb, acquired to play third base just before Alex Rodriquez became available to the Yankees, was off-handedly dealt to the Astros for minor league reliever Juan De Leon as soon as A-Rod was in the fold, with little attention paid to what role, if any, he might have played on the bench.

YANKEES PROSPECTUS

2004 record: 101–61; First place, AL East; Lost to Red Sox in Championship Series

Pythagenport record: 89–73

Runs scored per game: 5.54 (2nd in AL)

Runs allowed per game: 4.99 (6th in AL)

Team EqA: .276 (1st in AL)

2004 Batters Age: 32.7 (Oldest in AL)

2004 Pitchers Age: 33.3 (Oldest in AL)

Ballpark: Yankee Stadium; Moderate pitcher's park; Park Factor of 0.966

2004: The juggernaut picked up parts and kept rolling until a shocking collapse in the LCS.

2005: This year's crop of free-agent imports should be good enough to stake the Yankees to their 11th straight postseason appearance.

Then-35-year-old center fielder Bernie Williams seemed to be in a state of rapid decline, especially on defense. The team signed Kenny Lofton, 37 last year, which was a non-reaction. The Yankees led the league in triples allowed and were fourth in doubles allowed, numbers that speak to the weakness of the outfield—including left, where Hideki Matsui was a butcher after a dependable rookie year, and right, where Gary Sheffield's peregrinations looked like the choreography to "Flight of the Bumblebee."

They never seriously considered moving the defensively mediocre (at best) Derek Jeter, even after Rodriguez had been obtained, a move which would have been a boon to a pitching staff that was likely to allow opposing batters to make contact more often than any other team of the Joe Torre era (the staff missed being Torre's most contact-friendly by the thin margin of .03 strikeouts per nine innings).The absence of a good lefty in the bullpen was haltingly and inadequately addressed. The Yankees elected to sign Felix Heredia to a two-year contract despite a body of work that was mixed at best, then messed around with him all year (including a reeducation trip to the minors) rather than acquiring another reliever or attempting an internal solution.

TABLE 1. YANKEES' DOMINANCE, 2000–2004

Team	W	L	PCT
Three Years (2002–2004)			
1. Yankees	305	180	.629
2. Braves	298	186	.616
3. A's	290	196	.597
4. Cardinals	287	199	.591
5. Giants	286	198	.591
Five Years (2000–2004)			
1. Yankees	487	319	.604
2. A's	483	326	.597
3. Braves	481	327	.595
4. Cardinals	475	335	.586
5. Giants	473	335	.585

Jason Giambi had proved to be a first baseman who couldn't play first. The Yankees' thinking in regards to their designated hitter position was so muddled that they could not conceive of acquiring an everyday, productive first baseman, so journeymen Tony Clark and Travis Lee were signed. Giambi, they insisted, would play first the majority of the time. The DH would be Bernie Williams, who was to be displaced by Kenny Lofton. "Sometimes," Lewis Carroll wrote in *Alice in Wonderland,* "I've believed as many as six impossible things before breakfast."

All of these moves and non-moves were typical of the Yankees in recent years: Lack of attention to the bench and the back end of the bullpen had a direct effect on the outcome of the 2001 and 2003 World Series. But in 2004 they took on greater importance, because the 2003–2004 off-season ensured that the team would not be able to coast, as the winter had been devastating to New York's starting rotation. In losing Roger Clemens, Andy Pettitte, and David Wells, the Yankees saw better than half the value of its 2003 staff depart (as measured by VORP). The loss was roughly equivalent to deducting Dwight Gooden, Ron Darling, and Sid Fernandez from the 1986 Mets, or taking Ron Guidry and Goose Gossage away from the 1978 Yankees. With the likelihood of reassembling a dominant pitching staff in time for 2004 remote, it was more important than ever that the team be optimized elsewhere on the diamond.

The Yankees met these defections by trading for Javier Vazquez. They also dealt Jeff Weaver, a pitcher they'd come to believe did not have the psychological makeup for New York, for Kevin Brown, a great but aging and injury-prone right-hander. They hoped that Jon Lieber could approximate his 20-game winning form of 2001 after a year of rehabilitation, and prayed they could figure out what the heck was up with Cuban escapee Jose Contreras. Later, they signed the debilitated Orlando Hernandez, which would prove a season-saving gamble. A quality left-hander was not forthcoming (Brian Cashman has said the best available to them was Brian Anderson), so the Yankees did without. This hurt them very little during the regular season (not any more than the starting staff did in general) but was crushing in October.

The root of all of the actions described above, as well as winter 2004's avid pursuit of less-than-sure-thing pitchers Carl Pavano, Jaret Wright, and the marvelous but aged Randy Johnson—not to mention the predictable Tino Martinez sequel—is the team's dysfunctional relationship with its own farm system. Damaged for years by abysmally poor drafting, underfunded relative to the rest of the Yankees enterprise (with money that could have gone to upgrading the system as a whole being dispersed to a bevy of international free agents), the collapse of the system has forced the Yankees to rely solely on the free-agent market to fight the forces of entropy to which all ballclubs are subject.

The problem with being dependent on the market to staff your team is that you can only buy what the market has in stock. If you need oranges and all the market has are bananas, you have to buy bananas. If all they have are bruised bananas, you buy bruised bananas. If you need a #1 starting pitcher and all that's available are questionable #4s, you buy a #4. The best pitchers in the free-agent class of 1988 were Nolan Ryan and Bruce Hurst. Ryan didn't want to leave Texas, Hurst wanted to head west. There was a steep drop off to Andy Hawkins. The Yankees signed him. In just 66 appearances over three years he was 57.9 runs worse than the average pitcher. That same winter they signed Dave LaPoint, −24.4 runs over two seasons. Though they are unlikely to be the disasters that Hawkins and LaPoint turned out to be, Pavano and Wright represent yet another reenactment of this desperate play.

Scouting, drafting and player development, areas that are not automatically improved by throwing dollars at them, have resisted the Yankee touch for decades. Apologists for the Yankees have argued that their minor league effort has been hamstrung by the major league team's success; the Yankees win, so they're always drafting at the bottom. This is not quite true. First, the weakness of the system has been, with rare exceptions, a consistent feature of the entire Steinbrenner regime, in both winning and losing times. Second, in recent years teams such as the Reds have opted to spend their first-round picks on players who would normally be taken later and thus have lower bonus demands. That pushes top-tier talent downward towards the Yankees. The Yankees have also had the option of taking unlikely-to-sign players later in the draft and using their monetary advantage to sign them; they've largely eschewed this approach. Finally, the departure of a number of Type-A free agents over the years has allowed the

TABLE 2. YANKEES' DRAFTS, OTHER THAN LAST, SINCE 1995

Year	First Round Number	Player	Majors
1995	27.	Shea Morenz, OF	No
1996	20. (From Angels for signing Randy Velarde. Yankees donated their own pick, #24, to the Rangers for Kenny Rogers)	Eric Milton, LHP	Yes
1997	24. (From Rangers for John Wetteland; Orioles received Yankees pick, #26, for David Wells)	Tyrell Godwin, OF (DNS)	Negative
1998	24.	Andy Brown, OF	Not happening
1999	27.	David Walling, RHP	Nope
2000	28.	David Parrish, C	Nuh-uh
2001	23. (From Mariners for Jeff Nelson; Yankees traded down from #19 for Mike Mussina)	John-Ford Griffin, OF	Nah
2002	None. Pick, #24, to A's for signing Jason Giambi	A's took Nick Swisher	Not as a Yank
2003	27.	Eric Duncan, 3B	Not yet
2004	23. (From Astros for Andy Pettitte; Yankees pick at #28 went to the Dodgers for Paul Quantrill)	Phillip Hughes, RHP	Nein

Yankees to "trade up" in the draft. Thus since 1995, the Yankees have drafted at a number of positions other than dead last as shown in table 2.

Thanks to Jon Lieber's move to Philadelphia, the Yankees will have the 17th pick in the 2005 draft. It will be their highest draft position since 1993, when they selected high school right-hander/notorious flameout Matt Drews with the 13th pick.

To further demolish the myth that success has ruined New York's drafting effort, consider that some major league-quality players have been on the board each time the Yankees drafted and were subsequently taken as first-round supplemental or second-round picks. Remember, these are not eighth-round, shot-in-the-dark picks, but players who fell just short of being a first-round pick, and often turned out to be better than players taken earlier (see table 3).

Of course, had the Yankees drafted any of these players the owner may very well have refused to use them. It is worth remembering that had Tony Fernandez not suffered a season-ending injury during spring training in 1996, Derek Jeter may have become the matinee idol of Columbus, Oh.

In many ways, George M. Steinbrenner III is a fan's owner. Despite common assumptions to the contrary, the Yankees' well of cash is not infinite. What Steinbrenner does, in continually exceeding his own budgets, is cut into the team's profit margin, which means that he and his minority partners take home less money in exchange for

TABLE 3. MAJOR LEAGUE-QUALITY PICKS AVAILABLE AS FIRST-ROUND SUPPLEMENTALS OR SECOND ROUND, 1995–2001

Year	Players
1995	Jarrod Washburn, Brett Tomko, Sean Casey, Ben Petrick, Carlos Beltran, Mark Bellhorn, Marlon Anderson, Craig Wilson
1996	Jake Westbrook, Gil Meche, Eric Munson, Jacque Jones, Milton Bradley, Jimmy Rollins
1997	Jack Cust, Jim Parque, Jeff Weaver, Gookie Dawkins, Aaron Cook, Chase Utley, Matt LeCroy, Mike Restovich, Chad Harville, Randy Wolf, Rick Ankiel, Jason Grabowski
1998	Dave Kelton, Adam Dunn, Nate Cornejo, Brandon Inge, Nick Neugebauer, Brad Wilkerson, Mark Prior (drafted by the Yankees as a first-round supplemental pick but not signed), Eric Valent
1999	John Lackey, Casey Daigle, Brian Roberts, Bobby Hill, Ben Broussard, Jimmy Gobble, Brandon Phillips, Ryan Ludwick, Jerome Williams, Carl Crawford
2000	Bobby Hill, Tim Hummel, Adam Wainwright, Jason Stokes, Chad Qualls, Aaron Heilman, Xavier Nady
2001	Bobby Crosby, Jeremy Bonderman, Jeff Mathis, Dallas McPherson, J. J. Hardy, David Wright, Neal Cotts, Dan Haren, Jesse Foppert

winning. While no one should rush out with a collection bowl—Steinbrenner's diminished take-home pay is still more dough than most of us will see in a lifetime—it should be noted that most owners are more protective of their personal bottom line.

At the same time, the owner's overly skeptical posture on prospects, as old as his ownership of the franchise, *costs* him a great deal of money, as mediocre, expensive vets have taken even the reserve positions that could have been filled by inexpensive prospects and minor league veterans. Not only would the Yankees be a better team if they reversed this policy, and would fans be able to root for more home-grown players —(who are are usually more popular and, therefore, more merchandisable, than the imported variety) but also the money saved would be enough for the team to endow a college. Yankee University: The School of Being Screamed at By a Disembodied Voice From Tampa.

The organizational structure, or non-structure, imposed by the disembodied voice helps explain the team's occasionally incoherent response to its problems. In the Yankees system, both the general manager and the owner may initiate action. When the former initiates action, he must seek approval from the owner and his platoon of Tampa-bound advisors. When the owner initiates action, he is unlikely to inform the general manager of what it is he is doing. When a plan of attack is brought before the owner, he has a tendency to carp, issue threats of reprisal should the proposal prove to be mistaken, procrastinate. Decisive action is often impossible.

While it would be foolish to predict that the Yankees are in immediate danger of becoming non-contenders, the team is in a state of decline, and the day is coming when expensive imports will no longer serve to paper over the team's flaws. As bad, Giambi-style contracts pile up, the team's ability to solve problems by throwing cash at them will be curtailed—giving out long-term contracts to 30-year-olds almost guarantees that those players will have to be replaced before their contracts are up. Even the Yankees have a limit to how many backloaded contracts they can carry.

An ugly result has already sprouted out of this policy: The Yankees blew multi-millions on Pavano and Wright, then passed on young, super-talented center fielder Carlos Beltran—reportedly despite being offered a discount. Beltran would have helped solve a number of key Yankee problems: improving their terrible outfield defense, providing another much-needed big bat, and injecting youth into a geriatric roster. Instead they get to watch their outfield chase after more extra-base hits while praying Wright has some Mazzone pixie dust left and Pavano's pedestrian strikeout rate and injury history don't come back to bite them.

If the signings they make fail and budget room starts to get tight, the Yankees will have to fall back on their farm system—only to find there's nothing there. One way or another the system will have to change. The question is whether the team has the focus and the will to fix it before the inevitable breakdown.

PLAYERS

MELKY CABRERA OF Bats: B Throws: L Born: 11-Aug-1984 Age: 20

YEAR	TM	LG	AGE	AB	H	2B	3B	HR	BB	SO	SB	CS	AVG	OBP	SLG	MLVR	EQBA	EQOBP	EQSLG	EQMLVR	VORP	DEFENSE
2003	STA	NYP	18	279	79	10	2	2	23	36	13	5	.283	.345	.355	.117	.256	.302	.329	-.239	-15.0	64-CF -11
2004	BCR	MDW	19	171	57	16	3	0	15	23	7	2	.333	.383	.462	.272	.273	.309	.372	-.152	-0.2	41-CF -1
2004	TAM	FSL	19	333	96	20	3	8	23	59	3	1	.288	.341	.438	.148	.261	.304	.409	-.117	3.2	81-CF -6
2005	*NYY*	*AL*	*20*	*421*	*105*	*22*	*3*	*7*	*23*	*76*	*5*	*3*	*.250*	*.295*	*.364*	*-.185*	*.253*	*.299*	*.373*	*-.173*	*-1.9*	*108-CF -6*

Breakout: 16% *Improve: 25%* *Collapse: 42%*

A line-drive hitter out of the Dominican Republic, Cabrera will either play center field or be a borderline bat in left. Showed good extra-base power as a 19-year-old in the Florida State League last year, an encouraging sign.

MIGUEL CAIRO 2B Bats: R Throws: R Born: 04-May-1974 Age: 31

YEAR	TM	LG	AGE	AB	H	2B	3B	HR	BB	SO	SB	CS	AVG	OBP	SLG	MLVR	EQBA	EQOBP	EQSLG	EQMLVR	VORP	DEFENSE	
2002	STL	NL	28	184	46	9	2	2	13	36	1	1	.250	.307	.353	-.124	.255	.309	.372	-.165	1.3	12-2B -1	
2003	STL	NL	29	261	64	15	2	5	13	30	4	1	.245	.289	.375	-.127	.251	.290	.388	-.181	2.3	28-2B -2	14-LF 0
2004	NYY	AL	30	360	105	17	5	6	18	49	11	3	.292	.346	.417	.005	.304	.357	.435	.053	22.2	97-2B -7	
2005	*NYM*	*NL*	*31*	*269*	*70*	*14*	*2*	*5*	*15*	*39*	*5*	*2*	*.261*	*.316*	*.383*	*-.121*	*.265*	*.318*	*.396*	*-.101*	*11.4*	*73-2B -4*	

Breakout: 14% *Improve: 27%* *Collapse: 43%*

(continued next page)

Miguel Cairo *(continued)*

A year ago we wrote, "Any team that uses him as a regular isn't serious." The Yankees were even less serious than that, pretending Enrique Wilson was the starter before falling back on Cairo. That Cairo then went out and had a season lodged somewhere between his 75th and 90th percentile PECTOTA forecast was just pure, dumb luck. Expecting it to happen again would be like expecting to win the lottery twice. Cairo is a fine utility player, but that's all. Apparently the Yankees think so too, because they signed Tony Womack to play second. That doesn't make them any more serious than they were last year. Cairo signed with the Mets.

ROBINSON CANO **2B** **Bats: L** **Throws: R** Born: 22-Oct-1982 Age: 22

YEAR	TM	LG	AGE	AB	H	2B	3B	HR	BB	SO	SB	CS	AVG	OBP	SLG	MLVR	EQBA	EQOBP	EQSLG	EQMLVR	VORP	DEFENSE
2002	GRB	SAL	19	474	131	20	9	14	29	78	2	1	.276	.321	.445	.117	.232	.267	.383	-.246	-6.1	57-SS -10 54-2B -7
2002	STA	NYP	19	87	24	5	1	1	4	8	6	1	.276	.308	.391	.091	.250	.275	.364	-.245	-3.4	19-2B 1
2003	TAM	FSL	20	366	101	16	3	5	17	49	1	1	.276	.313	.377	.061	.258	.287	.382	-.190	-1.8	88-2B -6
2003	TRN	EAS	20	164	46	9	1	1	9	16	0	0	.280	.341	.366	-.019	.255	.303	.339	-.223	-2.4	43-2B -3
2004	TRN	EAS	21	292	88	20	8	7	24	40	2	4	.301	.356	.497	.204	.274	.323	.449	-.014	13.9	70-2B 0
2004	COH	INT	21	216	56	9	2	6	18	27	0	1	.259	.316	.403	-.063	.247	.304	.381	-.167	0.5	57-2B 2
2005	*NYY*	*AL*	*22*	*304*	*77*	*16*	*2*	*7*	*17*	*45*	*1*	*1*	*.255*	*.298*	*.389*	*-.142*	*.258*	*.303*	*.399*	*-.128*	*7.0*	*79-2B -6*

Breakout: 23% *Improve: 41%* *Collapse: 36%*

Cano started out strong at Double-A Trenton but struggled when the Yankees pushed him up to Columbus. The signing of Tony Womack pushes back his timetable by two years, at least on paper; when Womack reverts to his pre-2003 form (not that 2003 was anything to celebrate), his $2 million per annum contract will be but a petit four for George Steinbrenner to swallow. Not that Cano is necessarily going to be the next Willie Randolph, but sometimes it pays to take a tactical risk rather than bet on the definitively mediocre.

TONY CLARK **1B** **Bats: B** **Throws: R** Born: 15-Jun-1972 Age: 33

YEAR	TM	LG	AGE	AB	H	2B	3B	HR	BB	SO	SB	CS	AVG	OBP	SLG	MLVR	EQBA	EQOBP	EQSLG	EQMLVR	VORP	DEFENSE
2002	BOS	AL	30	275	57	12	1	3	21	57	0	0	.207	.265	.291	-.323	.209	.271	.297	-.372	-13.6	74-1B 5
2003	NYM	NL	31	254	59	13	0	16	24	73	0	0	.232	.300	.472	.000	.239	.300	.478	-.045	8.2	55-1B -5
2004	NYY	AL	32	253	56	12	0	16	26	92	0	0	.221	.297	.458	-.069	.228	.302	.472	-.060	5.7	71-1B 0
2005	*NYY*	*AL*	*33*	*184*	*41*	*9*	*0*	*9*	*20*	*62*	*0*	*0*	*.225*	*.305*	*.417*	*-.115*	*.227*	*.309*	*.427*	*-.102*	*3.1*	*52-1B -3*

Breakout: 22% *Improve: 51%* *Collapse: 26%*

Terrific guy, terrible player. Clark would be a useful platoon player/spot starter if he didn't get into funks where he is incapable of making contact with anything smaller than God's own telephone pole. He finished the season in just such a slump, then proceeded to kill the Yankees in the playoffs. After hitting lefties well for the last few years, he couldn't touch them, making it impossible to know just when to play him. The Yankees can do better, even for a backup.

BUBBA CROSBY **OF** **Bats: L** **Throws: L** Born: 11-Aug-1976 Age: 28

YEAR	TM	LG	AGE	AB	H	2B	3B	HR	BB	SO	SB	CS	AVG	OBP	SLG	MLVR	EQBA	EQOBP	EQSLG	EQMLVR	VORP	DEFENSE
2002	JAX	SOU	25	150	39	6	2	2	11	23	7	3	.260	.317	.367	-.014	.243	.285	.362	-.233	-8.2	27-LF 2
2002	LVG	PCL	25	279	73	12	1	9	19	47	3	1	.262	.312	.409	-.113	.223	.275	.350	-.283	-10.8	65-CF 1
2003	LVG	PCL	26	277	100	24	8	12	25	47	8	0	.361	.410	.635	.472	.314	.367	.557	.256	27.0	27-RF 1 24-LF 0
2004	COH	INT	27	116	32	5	2	1	14	26	3	3	.276	.365	.379	.006	.267	.352	.371	-.076	2.6	18-CF -1
2004	NYY	AL	27	53	8	2	0	2	2	13	2	0	.151	.196	.302	-.530	.170	.194	.302	-.541	-4.3	
2005	*NYY*	*AL*	*28*	*121*	*32*	*6*	*1*	*3*	*10*	*25*	*2*	*1*	*.261*	*.323*	*.412*	*-.064*	*.264*	*.328*	*.422*	*-.049*	*5.8*	*36-CF -6*

Breakout: 18% *Improve: 42%* *Collapse: 38%*

Winner of the Columbus Shuttle Frequent Flyer Award, Crosby didn't get to do much besides pinch-run, sub on defense, and fetch Joe Torre his pre-game cup of herbal tea. He's not vastly overqualified for any of those roles.

ERIC DUNCAN   3B   Bats: L   Throws: R   Born: 07-Dec-1984   Age: 20

YEAR	TM	LG	AGE	AB	H	2B	3B	HR	BB	SO	SB	CS	AVG	OBP	SLG	MLVR	EQBA	EQOBP	EQSLG	EQMLVR	VORP	DEFENSE
2003	YNK	GCL	18	180	50	12	2	2	18	33	0	2	.278	.350	.400	.000	.202	.246	.295	-.429	-442.3	
2003	STA	NYP	18	59	22	5	4	2	2	11	1	0	.373	.413	.695	.752	.328	.357	.623	.356	17.7	13-3B -1
2004	BCR	MDW	19	288	75	23	2	12	38	84	7	1	.260	.351	.479	.186	.221	.297	.405	-.166	1.4	74-3B -4
2004	TAM	FSL	19	177	45	20	2	4	31	47	0	2	.254	.364	.458	.177	.227	.319	.409	-.115	4.1	46-3B -6
2005	*NYY*	*AL*	*20*	*387*	*93*	*24*	*3*	*12*	*36*	*114*	*3*	*2*	*.241*	*.311*	*.410*	*-.102*	*.244*	*.316*	*.420*	*-.088*	*3.8*	*102-3B -6*

Breakout: 24%   *Improve: 40%*   *Collapse: 35%*

The Yankees' first-round pick in 2003, Duncan has some real positives that don't yet scream budding star, but hint at better things to come. "Stay tuned," they gently say. He has power and shows comfort with the strike zone at a young age, but his batting averages have been a bit low, the strikeouts a bit high. His defense at third is suspect, and with Alex Rodriguez blocking him a move to first may come about, raising questions about whether he'll hit enough to play there. It probably won't matter: Duncan's still very, very young, and should develop quite a bit wherever he ends up after the Yankees trade him.

JOHN FLAHERTY   C   Bats: R   Throws: R   Born: 21-Oct-1967   Age: 37

YEAR	TM	LG	AGE	AB	H	2B	3B	HR	BB	SO	SB	CS	AVG	OBP	SLG	MLVR	EQBA	EQOBP	EQSLG	EQMLVR	VORP	DEFENSE
2002	TBY	AL	34	281	73	20	0	4	15	50	2	2	.260	.296	.374	-.137	.269	.304	.380	-.153	5.6	75-C -3
2003	NYY	AL	35	105	28	8	0	4	4	19	0	0	.267	.297	.457	-.023	.276	.298	.467	-.031	4.8	28-C 1
2004	NYY	AL	36	127	32	9	0	6	5	25	0	2	.252	.286	.465	-.047	.262	.289	.476	-.047	4.1	36-C -1
2005	*NYY*	*AL*	*37*	*148*	*37*	*8*	*0*	*4*	*7*	*28*	*0*	*0*	*.250*	*.289*	*.392*	*-.157*	*.254*	*.294*	*.402*	*-.144*	*2.2*	*42-C -5*

Breakout: 10%   *Improve: 36%*   *Collapse: 36%*

Has slugged .461 as a Yankee, and that's his entire offensive contribution—he can't get on base to save his life. The Yankees went 20–15 (.571), with Flaherty starting 81–46 (.638) in other games. This dramatic fall-off makes Joe Torre's decision not to DH Posada on his days off, when the Yankees had no better DH, inexplicable. You can't replace a .400 OBP with a .286 OBP and not expect to suffer for it. But that's detail work, and the Yankees aren't about that.

JASON GIAMBI   DH/1B   Bats: L   Throws: R   Born: 08-Jan-1971   Age: 34

YEAR	TM	LG	AGE	AB	H	2B	3B	HR	BB	SO	SB	CS	AVG	OBP	SLG	MLVR	EQBA	EQOBP	EQSLG	EQMLVR	VORP	DEFENSE
2002	NYY	AL	31	560	176	34	1	41	109	112	2	2	.314	.435	.598	.448	.326	.448	.624	.486	90.0	86-1B 6
2003	NYY	AL	32	535	134	25	0	41	129	140	2	1	.250	.412	.527	.265	.261	.419	.553	.279	63.5	82-1B 0
2004	NYY	AL	33	264	55	9	0	12	47	62	0	1	.208	.342	.379	-.093	.218	.348	.391	-.089	4.6	43-1B -4
2005	*NYY*	*AL*	*34*	*307*	*76*	*14*	*0*	*18*	*62*	*73*	*0*	*0*	*.249*	*.386*	*.472*	*.109*	*.252*	*.392*	*.484*	*.128*	*26.5*	*91-1B -6*

Breakout: 20%   *Improve: 57%*   *Collapse: 17%*

Giambi's year began with questions about possible steroid use, moved on to questions about possible cancer, and ended with confirmation of his steroid use. In between he had intestinal parasites. Given how slow, how ponderous Giambi was *before* he came down with every illness this side of beriberi, it's unlikely he will return to anything like the MVP form the Yankees thought they were buying back in 2001. By definition his through-2008 contract would someday be an albatross. That bird has come home to roost (OK, so the albatross doesn't roost. Call the Analogy Police).

RUDY GUILLEN   OF   Bats: R   Throws: R   Born: 23-Nov-1983   Age: 21

YEAR	TM	LG	AGE	AB	H	2B	3B	HR	BB	SO	SB	CS	AVG	OBP	SLG	MLVR	EQBA	EQOBP	EQSLG	EQMLVR	VORP	DEFENSE
2003	BCR	MDW	19	493	128	29	4	13	32	87	13	6	.260	.311	.414	.075	.226	.265	.377	-.262	-17.7	95-CF -15 31-RF -2
2004	TAM	FSL	20	307	81	16	2	1	22	59	1	0	.264	.313	.339	-.045	.239	.280	.316	-.311	-24.4	45-RF 1 32-CF -2
2005	*NYY*	*AL*	*21*	*366*	*83*	*18*	*2*	*7*	*19*	*81*	*2*	*1*	*.228*	*.272*	*.341*	*-.271*	*.231*	*.276*	*.349*	*-.262*	*-13.0*	*94-CF -8*

Breakout: 21%   *Improve: 45%*   *Collapse: 33%*

Played all year with a sprained ankle and that damped down his numbers. Still, he's a free swinger, doesn't hit .300, doesn't have big power, isn't a big time baserunner. He has "tools," but tools are overrated; you can get a complete set at Home Depot for $25.

ESTEE HARRIS — OF — Bats: L — Throws: R — Born: 08-Jan-1985 — Age: 20

YEAR	TM	LG	AGE	AB	H	2B	3B	HR	BB	SO	SB	CS	AVG	OBP	SLG	MLVR	EQBA	EQOBP	EQSLG	EQMLVR	VORP	DEFENSE
2004	BCR	MDW	19	192	41	8	2	3	21	82	5	1	.214	.305	.323	-.114	.188	.258	.289	-.420	-22.2	16-LF -3 11-RF -2
2004	STA	NYP	19	173	42	10	2	6	18	65	9	3	.243	.327	.428	.139	.212	.278	.374	-.251	-20.0	38-LF -5
2005	*NYY*	*AL*	*20*	*289*	*59*	*13*	*2*	*6*	*23*	*119*	*6*	*3*	*.203*	*.278*	*.321*	*-.299*	*.205*	*.282*	*.329*	*-.291*	*-13.2*	*78-LF -10*

Breakout: 33% *Improve: 52%* *Collapse: 32%*

Harris was New York's second-round pick in 2003. Even if Harris, Duncan and others pan out, it's daft for the Yankees to focus on high-school players when they have the fiscal resources and strategic need for polished college players who are going to have a quicker path to the majors. Their farm system is rusty from disuse and has no clue what to do with a teenager, exacerbating the inherently risky nature of prep prospects. There are a ton of second-round 2003 class college pitchers who will make the majors before Harris (one of whom, Logan Kensing, already has). As for Harris, he has strong power and a weak strike zone. He'll have to cut the strikeouts dramatically before he can move up.

DEREK JETER — SS — Bats: R — Throws: R — Born: 26-Jun-1974 — Age: 31

YEAR	TM	LG	AGE	AB	H	2B	3B	HR	BB	SO	SB	CS	AVG	OBP	SLG	MLVR	EQBA	EQOBP	EQSLG	EQMLVR	VORP	DEFENSE
2002	NYY	AL	28	644	191	26	0	18	73	114	32	3	.297	.373	.421	.098	.307	.383	.435	.102	60.0	152-SS -16
2003	NYY	AL	29	482	156	25	3	10	43	88	11	5	.324	.393	.450	.200	.333	.405	.467	.210	53.9	112-SS -18
2004	NYY	AL	30	643	188	44	1	23	46	99	23	4	.292	.352	.471	.096	.302	.363	.490	.140	59.7	150-SS 5
2005	*NYY*	*AL*	*31*	*550*	*162*	*31*	*3*	*16*	*49*	*90*	*16*	*5*	*.294*	*.360*	*.451*	*.076*	*.298*	*.366*	*.462*	*.095*	*46.6*	*145-SS -4*

Breakout: 6% *Improve: 31%* *Collapse: 28%*

For those of us in the performance analysis biz, Jeter is a difficult problem because any realistic evaluation of his skills, no matter how flattering, seems like a slight when compared to his reputation. In the eyes of true believers, Honus Wagner and Superman combined couldn't do half the things Jeter does. In truth, he's terrific at going back on shallow pop-ups and executing the jump throw in the hole. Other aspects of the job—fielding grounders to his left for instance—elude him, and it doesn't take an MS in scouting or statistics to see it. When watching a Yankees game, *simply pay attention to the opposing shortstop. He will routinely get to balls that Jeter cannot.* As for the Gold Glove, peel back the foil on the award and you'll find there's some tasty chocolate underneath. That's about what it's worth, though at least Jeter was better this year. On offense, Jeter walked less than ever before and doubled his previous high in sac bunts, perhaps because he lost confidence after a shockingly poor April. Jeter is a Hall of Famer to be, a key player on a great team, an inspirational leader, a fine hitter... and he gives up a lot of singles with his glove. In light of the rest, why is that last part so difficult to accept?

MITCH JONES — 1B — Bats: R — Throws: R — Born: 15-Oct-1977 — Age: 27

YEAR	TM	LG	AGE	AB	H	2B	3B	HR	BB	SO	SB	CS	AVG	OBP	SLG	MLVR	EQBA	EQOBP	EQSLG	EQMLVR	VORP	DEFENSE
2002	TAM	FSL	24	229	61	19	0	13	20	71	0	0	.266	.329	.520	.254	.235	.283	.466	-.096	-1.0	25-1B 2 23-LF -1
2002	NRW	EAS	24	216	47	16	0	10	18	59	1	4	.218	.290	.431	-.031	.193	.250	.385	-.302	-12.0	
2003	TRN	EAS	25	463	112	18	0	23	58	131	5	4	.242	.338	.430	.034	.209	.291	.385	-.213	-22.0	67-RF -6 48-LF -3
2004	TRN	EAS	26	496	122	25	4	39	64	152	8	1	.246	.334	.548	.187	.216	.296	.475	-.076	-3.3	70-LF -6 46-RF -5
2005	*NYY*	*AL*	*27*	*164*	*39*	*8*	*0*	*9*	*16*	*52*	*1*	*1*	*.237*	*.314*	*.452*	*-.046*	*.240*	*.319*	*.463*	*-.030*	*5.7*	*47-LF -7*

Breakout: 45% *Improve: 56%* *Collapse: 25%*

One-dimensional slugger who led the Eastern League in home runs and strikeouts in '04. He might have a career resembling Shane Spencer's, albeit without the off-field stupidity. Even that remains a long shot, as he would be pressed to sustain a batting average above .230 in the show.

TRAVIS LEE — 1B — Bats: L — Throws: L — Born: 26-May-1975 — Age: 30

YEAR	TM	LG	AGE	AB	H	2B	3B	HR	BB	SO	SB	CS	AVG	OBP	SLG	MLVR	EQBA	EQOBP	EQSLG	EQMLVR	VORP	DEFENSE
2002	PHI	NL	27	536	142	26	2	13	54	104	5	3	.265	.331	.394	.021	.272	.335	.412	-.047	15.7	135-1B 8
2003	TBY	AL	28	542	149	37	3	19	64	97	6	2	.275	.348	.459	.079	.278	.357	.468	.076	30.8	142-1B 14
2004	NYY	AL	29	19	2	1	0	0	1	3	0	0	.105	.150	.158	-.828	.105	.100	.158	-.959	-3.1	
2005	*NYY*	*AL*	*30*	*258*	*63*	*14*	*1*	*8*	*26*	*55*	*1*	*1*	*.244*	*.311*	*.400*	*-.113*	*.246*	*.316*	*.409*	*-.099*	*3.2*	*70-1B 1*

Breakout: 16% *Improve: 38%* *Collapse: 37%*

Injured himself right off, missing all but seven games with a torn labrum. In this he was more useful than he normally is. A first baseman with a good glove and a below-average bat for the position, Lee has the markings of a bench player, and maybe after a year off he finally will be one. Ironically, the Yankees would have been better off with him once the injuries hit, but that's the whole point—he's someone you plug in *after* your first option has driven off a cliff, not before.

KENNY LOFTON OF **Bats: L** **Throws: L** Born: 31-May-1967 Age: 38

YEAR	TM	LG	AGE	AB	H	2B	3B	HR	BB	SO	SB	CS	AVG	OBP	SLG	MLVR	EQBA	EQOBP	EQSLG	EQMLVR	VORP	DEFENSE
2002	CWS	AL	35	352	91	20	6	8	49	51	22	8	.259	.348	.418	.001	.259	.354	.422	-.008	18.7	91-CF 0
2002	SFG	NL	35	180	48	10	3	3	23	22	7	3	.267	.353	.406	.066	.275	.359	.423	.015	10.5	42-CF 3
2003	PIT	NL	36	339	94	19	4	9	28	29	18	5	.277	.333	.437	.046	.274	.331	.440	-.013	18.9	79-CF 3
2003	CHC	NL	36	208	68	13	4	3	18	22	12	4	.327	.381	.471	.200	.329	.380	.481	.184	20.4	55-CF -2
2004	NYY	AL	37	276	76	10	7	3	31	27	7	3	.275	.346	.395	-.030	.283	.357	.412	.003	10.9	65-CF -1
2005	*PHI*	*NL*	*38*	*287*	*78*	*15*	*3*	*5*	*31*	*30*	*9*	*3*	*.271*	*.343*	*.398*	*-.047*	*.271*	*.341*	*.397*	*-.054*	*10.6*	*79-CF -3*

Breakout: 11% *Improve: 35%* *Collapse: 32%*

There are things you can anticipate based on human nature and history rather than stats. Under the impression center field was his job to win, Lofton sat, sulked, had two DL tours, and blamed his injuries on *not* playing. For a while the Yankees were excited by the idea of Lofton batting ninth as a "second leadoff man," but inevitably he yielded his job back to Ruben Sierra. Despite both running and hitting less than he has in the past, Still, Lofton was more valuable than Sierra, especially batting ninth, where he hit .310./.393/.430. Next year he'll try to help the Phillies win as their oldest center fielder in about 80 years.

HIDEKI MATSUI OF **Bats: L** **Throws: R** Born: 12-Jun-1974 Age: 31

YEAR	TM	LG	AGE	AB	H	2B	3B	HR	BB	SO	SB	CS	AVG	OBP	SLG	MLVR	EQBA	EQOBP	EQSLG	EQMLVR	VORP	DEFENSE
2002	YOM	JCL	28	500	167	27	1	50	114	104	3	0	.334	.463	.692	.630	.315	.405	.524	.272	72.4	
2003	NYY	AL	29	623	179	42	1	16	63	86	2	2	.287	.353	.435	.078	.293	.363	.448	.072	30.9	110-LF -8 43-CF -3
2004	NYY	AL	30	584	174	34	2	31	88	103	3	0	.298	.390	.522	.249	.308	.403	.543	.287	57.5	158-LF -8
2005	*NYY*	*AL*	*31*	*524*	*150*	*32*	*2*	*23*	*75*	*95*	*2*	*2*	*.287*	*.377*	*.484*	*.140*	*.290*	*.383*	*.496*	*.161*	*33.8*	*142-LF -6*

Breakout: 10% *Improve: 40%* *Collapse: 15%*

So maybe there was something to that "He needs to adjust" stuff that Yanks flaks were peddling after 2003. After endangering every worm, gopher, and burrow owl in the vicinity of Yankee Stadium in '03, Hideki cut his ground ball/fly ball ratio in half and hit home runs instead of double-play grounders. That was all the difference between being an overrated "RBI man" and one of the top 30 players in the game (as per VORP). After giving out way too many huge contracts, the Yankees were conservative with Hideki, and his indentures are up after this year. Since the Yankees' system hasn't produced a starting outfielder since 1991, Godzilla's possible departure should provoke something of a crisis.

DIONER NAVARRO C **Bats: B** **Throws: R** Born: 09-Feb-1984 Age: 21

YEAR	TM	LG	AGE	AB	H	2B	3B	HR	BB	SO	SB	CS	AVG	OBP	SLG	MLVR	EQBA	EQOBP	EQSLG	EQMLVR	VORP	DEFENSE
2002	GRB	SAL	18	328	78	12	2	8	39	61	1	2	.238	.326	.360	-.013	.200	.267	.310	-.367	-20.1	79-C 5
2003	TAM	FSL	19	197	59	16	4	3	17	27	1	0	.299	.364	.467	.266	.281	.331	.463	.026	13.0	50-C -1
2003	TRN	EAS	19	208	71	15	0	4	18	26	2	3	.341	.388	.471	.253	.295	.331	.420	-.023	9.7	40-C -4
2004	TRN	EAS	20	255	69	14	1	3	33	44	1	0	.271	.354	.369	.002	.246	.322	.332	-.201	-2.2	52-C 2
2004	COH	INT	20	136	34	8	2	1	14	17	1	0	.250	.316	.360	-.128	.237	.304	.333	-.241	-2.8	39-C 7
2005	*LAD*	*NL*	*21*	*348*	*85*	*19*	*2*	*7*	*30*	*56*	*1*	*1*	*.244*	*.306*	*.366*	*-.173*	*.250*	*.311*	*.377*	*-.150*	*3.9*	*93-C -4*

Breakout: 13% *Improve: 28%* *Collapse: 43%*

Very young, he burned a year with a case of bigleagueitis. His reputation rests entirely on 110 games at A-ball and Double-A in 2003, and there is the possibility that he had a minor league catcher/Daffy Duck "I can only do this trick *once*" season. His offensive game is centered entirely around batting average, so until that comes up there's really no point in getting excited. Dealt to Arizona in the Randy Johnson deal, then flipped to the Dodgers, where he'll have a much clearer path to the majors.

JOHN OLERUD 1B Bats: L Throws: L Born: 05-Aug-1968 Age: 36

YEAR	TM	LG	AGE	AB	H	2B	3B	HR	BB	SO	SB	CS	AVG	OBP	SLG	MLVR	EQBA	EQOBP	EQSLG	EQMLVR	VORP	DEFENSE
2002	SEA	AL	33	553	166	39	0	22	98	66	0	0	.300	.403	.490	.264	.318	.419	.518	.289	59.1	147-1B 4
2003	SEA	AL	34	539	145	35	0	10	84	67	0	1	.269	.372	.390	.032	.279	.383	.406	.039	23.4	144-1B 4
2004	SEA	AL	35	261	64	13	1	5	40	41	0	0	.245	.354	.360	-.067	.255	.366	.378	-.048	6.3	70-1B 5
2004	NYY	AL	35	164	46	7	0	4	21	20	0	0	.280	.367	.396	.018	.296	.373	.407	.035	7.5	43-1B 0
2005	*NYY*	*AL*	*36*	*359*	*96*	*16*	*0*	*9*	*53*	*52*	*0*	*0*	*.268*	*.364*	*.392*	*-.014*	*.271*	*.370*	*.402*	*.002*	*12.0*	*100-1B -1*

Breakout: 15%   Improve: 46%   Collapse: 25%

Although his ALCS injury opened the door to Tony Clark throwing away some critical at-bats, Olerud's only advantage was his ability to make contact. If Clark was the flood and first base the dike, really anyone's little finger could have plugged that hole. Having hit like an underfed shortstop for two years, Olerud has little left to give. It will be a shame, though, if baseball loses its only player who can be seen emerging from the clubhouse shower wearing a towel and a batting helmet.

ANDY PHILLIPS 1B/3B Bats: R Throws: R Born: 06-Apr-1977 Age: 28

YEAR	TM	LG	AGE	AB	H	2B	3B	HR	BB	SO	SB	CS	AVG	OBP	SLG	MLVR	EQBA	EQOBP	EQSLG	EQMLVR	VORP	DEFENSE
2002	COH	INT	25	205	54	11	1	9	10	46	0	1	.263	.296	.459	.023	.246	.287	.438	-.119	3.4	40-2B -1
2002	NRW	EAS	25	272	83	24	2	19	33	56	4	3	.305	.381	.618	.441	.274	.343	.551	.164	25.8	
2004	TRN	EAS	27	42	15	2	1	4	3	1	3	0	.357	.383	.738	.657	.333	.349	.643	.381	6.3	
2004	COH	INT	27	434	137	19	6	25	51	61	2	1	.316	.386	.560	.323	.296	.368	.520	.185	36.1	85-1B 4
2005	*NYY*	*AL*	*28*	*194*	*51*	*10*	*1*	*8*	*18*	*36*	*1*	*1*	*.263*	*.326*	*.456*	*.000*	*.266*	*.331*	*.467*	*.017*	*10.4*	*54-1B 1*

Breakout: 8%   Improve: 34%   Collapse: 36%

Yankees pinch-hitters couldn't touch lefties, and the bench had Enrique Wilson, who served no useful purpose once Cairo displaced him. Phillips could have solved the former problem and eliminated the latter. Phillips has always hit for decent averages with reasonable patience, his power coming late; it was the lack of a position (too many errors at third) and bone spurs that cost him most of 2003. Phillips is versatile, able to play a bit of second in a pinch. He's an ideal role player, but he may not make enough money to qualify for New York's bench.

JORGE POSADA C Bats: B Throws: R Born: 17-Aug-1971 Age: 33

YEAR	TM	LG	AGE	AB	H	2B	3B	HR	BB	SO	SB	CS	AVG	OBP	SLG	MLVR	EQBA	EQOBP	EQSLG	EQMLVR	VORP	DEFENSE
2002	NYY	AL	30	511	137	40	1	20	81	143	1	0	.268	.370	.468	.135	.276	.381	.486	.141	48.7	134-C 3
2003	NYY	AL	31	481	135	24	0	30	93	110	2	4	.281	.405	.518	.268	.293	.415	.540	.287	61.5	134-C 5
2004	NYY	AL	32	449	122	31	0	21	88	92	1	3	.272	.400	.481	.184	.284	.412	.501	.222	48.9	124-C -2
2005	*NYY*	*AL*	*33*	*368*	*99*	*21*	*1*	*18*	*71*	*87*	*0*	*1*	*.269*	*.393*	*.479*	*.144*	*.272*	*.399*	*.490*	*.164*	*39.5*	*106-C -2*

Breakout: 11%   Improve: 56%   Collapse: 17%

Early in the off-season there were rumors that Posada might be traded, a ludicrous proposition. In previous seasons, when Posada was one of one or two productive backstops in the league, he represented a huge advantage, as if the Yankees got to play two first basemen to their opponents' one. Now that there are a few more hitters at the position, he still prevents the strategic balance from shifting towards other teams. Posada had a torrid spring, a weak June, then spent the rest of the season hitting about like he always does. Given the light workload of his early career—thanks Joe Girardi!—there is no reason to think he can't keep it up at least through the '06 end of his contract. The Yankees undervalue him at their own risk.

KEVIN REESE OF Bats: L Throws: L Born: 11-Mar-1978 Age: 27

YEAR	TM	LG	AGE	AB	H	2B	3B	HR	BB	SO	SB	CS	AVG	OBP	SLG	MLVR	EQBA	EQOBP	EQSLG	EQMLVR	VORP	DEFENSE
2002	NRW	EAS	24	514	149	24	6	4	77	87	22	14	.290	.385	.383	.116	.267	.352	.356	-.096	5.1	
2003	COH	INT	25	55	12	1	0	1	6	8	1	0	.218	.295	.291	-.217	.200	.269	.273	-.414	-4.4	11-CF -1
2003	TRN	EAS	25	309	84	13	2	4	25	58	27	5	.272	.328	.366	-.046	.240	.294	.334	-.257	-10.5	81-CF -12
2004	TRN	EAS	26	329	98	37	4	6	23	48	13	5	.298	.348	.489	.179	.274	.318	.447	-.026	11.7	73-CF -9
2004	COH	INT	26	217	70	13	3	8	12	34	4	4	.323	.370	.521	.251	.300	.347	.479	.095	9.5	50-LF -1
2005	*NYY*	*AL*	*27*	*159*	*43*	*9*	*1*	*4*	*12*	*29*	*5*	*2*	*.267*	*.325*	*.405*	*-.066*	*.271*	*.330*	*.414*	*-.051*	*6.4*	*45-CF -9*

Breakout: 22%   Improve: 46%   Collapse: 30%

Acquired from the Padres for second baseman Bernie Castro, Reese was well on the way to establishing himself as a solid fourth outfielder with leadoff potential when he stalled out at Triple-A in 2003 and had to be remanded to the Eastern League, where he continued to scuffle. Although his batting average recovered, his good plate judgment did not—though he added a new wrinkle, power. He can help a major league team as a low-cost reserve.

ALEX RODRIGUEZ **3B** **Bats: R** **Throws: R** Born: 27-Jul-1975 Age: 29

YEAR	TM	LG	AGE	AB	H	2B	3B	HR	BB	SO	SB	CS	AVG	OBP	SLG	MLVR	EQBA	EQOBP	EQSLG	EQMLVR	VORP	DEFENSE
2002	TEX	AL	26	624	187	27	2	57	87	122	9	4	.300	.392	.623	.349	.299	.395	.624	.376	94.7	157-SS 13
2003	TEX	AL	27	607	181	30	6	47	87	126	17	3	.298	.396	.600	.329	.291	.393	.593	.321	96.3	154-SS 13
2004	NYY	AL	28	601	172	24	2	36	80	131	28	4	.286	.375	.512	.200	.296	.387	.534	.236	62.3	151-3B 13
2005	*NYY*	*AL*	*29*	*542*	*157*	*29*	*2*	*36*	*78*	*119*	*16*	*5*	*.289*	*.383*	*.551*	*.238*	*.292*	*.389*	*.565*	*.262*	*60.3*	*148-3B 9*

Breakout: 16% *Improve: 50%* *Collapse: 9%*

A-Rod's EqA dropped by roughly 5%, partly attributable to the difference between hitting in Arlington and in the Bronx. In neutral parks, Rodriguez was consistent with his recent past:

	Home			Away		
Year	**AVG**	**OBP**	**SLG**	**AVG**	**OBP**	**SLG**
2001	.361	.439	.677	.276	.359	.567
2002	.323	.403	.700	.277	.381	.547
2003	.314	.407	.621	.282	.384	.577
2004	.280	.365	.492	.293	.386	.534

Rodriguez was the intended cleanup hitter, but fared much better batting second or third. He also struggled with runners on base throughout the first half and acted like a complete git in the ALCS. These are transient, minor issues, much ado about small beer. Rodriguez was one of the top 25 players in baseball, made a Gold Glove-caliber adaptation to third base, and had the best season by a third baseman in the history of the franchise. He'll do it again in '05; in fact, look for a big year.

BRONSON SARDINHA **3B?** **Bats: L** **Throws: R** Born: 06-Apr-1983 Age: 22

YEAR	TM	LG	AGE	AB	H	2B	3B	HR	BB	SO	SB	CS	AVG	OBP	SLG	MLVR	EQBA	EQOBP	EQSLG	EQMLVR	VORP	DEFENSE	
2002	GRB	SAL	19	342	90	13	0	12	34	78	15	6	.263	.334	.406	.074	.216	.267	.345	-.310	-11.4	63-SS -17	12-LF -1
2002	STA	NYP	19	124	40	8	0	4	24	36	4	1	.323	.433	.484	.410	.285	.359	.446	.055	8.7	26-LF -2	
2003	BCR	MDW	20	269	74	16	0	8	40	40	5	3	.275	.374	.424	.184	.227	.304	.367	-.200	-13.2	32-LF -1	16-RF -1
2003	TAM	FSL	20	212	41	8	2	1	24	57	8	2	.193	.279	.264	-.180	.188	.255	.275	-.445	-21.5	57-CF -5	
2004	TAM	FSL	21	248	78	12	2	2	29	39	9	2	.315	.389	.403	.190	.282	.345	.369	-.081	8.3	61-3B -9	
2004	TRN	EAS	21	266	71	11	1	6	37	65	4	1	.267	.356	.383	.023	.244	.328	.346	-.171	0.8	52-3B -16	
2005	*NYY*	*AL*	*22*	*323*	*78*	*16*	*1*	*8*	*31*	*75*	*4*	*2*	*.241*	*.313*	*.372*	*-.147*	*.244*	*.318*	*.381*	*-.135*	*-1.3*	*87-3B -14*	

Breakout: 25% *Improve: 52%* *Collapse: 23%*

Sardinha should be traded while he maintains a good reputation, because he and the Yankees organization aren't doing each other any good. Drafted as a shortstop, Sardinha has also been a left fielder, center fielder, and third baseman. With the position shifts came fluctuations in offense, which obscured the issue of whether or not his bat can sustain a position outside of the middle infield. The good news is that he should hit for decent averages and is willing to take a walk. Someone with a better idea should sort this out, if it can be sorted out.

GARY SHEFFIELD **OF** **Bats: R** **Throws: R** Born: 18-Nov-1968 Age: 36

YEAR	TM	LG	AGE	AB	H	2B	3B	HR	BB	SO	SB	CS	AVG	OBP	SLG	MLVR	EQBA	EQOBP	EQSLG	EQMLVR	VORP	DEFENSE
2002	ATL	NL	33	492	151	26	0	25	72	53	12	2	.307	.404	.512	.301	.309	.400	.521	.253	52.5	117-RF 2
2003	ATL	NL	34	576	190	37	2	39	86	55	18	4	.330	.419	.604	.467	.329	.417	.610	.426	87.5	143-RF 0
2004	NYY	AL	35	573	166	30	1	36	92	83	5	6	.290	.393	.534	.264	.300	.405	.560	.305	63.4	129-RF 0
2005	*NYY*	*AL*	*36*	*512*	*149*	*28*	*1*	*28*	*80*	*72*	*7*	*2*	*.292*	*.392*	*.518*	*.212*	*.295*	*.398*	*.531*	*.234*	*49.9*	*142-RF -4*

Breakout: 13% *Improve: 42%* *Collapse: 14%*

(continued next page)

Gary Sheffield *(continued)*

His season was a huge success until you consider that George Steinbrenner reportedly passed on a signed-sealed-delivered Vlad Guerrero to grab Sheffield instead. The Iron Sheff is signed through 2007, when he'll be 38 (Guerrero will be a spry 31), and the sore shoulder that kept him from raising his left arm above his head for most of the season was a harbinger of things to come—note that Sheffield was batting .313 for September when took his last cortisone shot of the season on the 20th, then hit.171 through the remainder of the season, derailing his MVP bid. Sheffield's routes to fly balls have always been esoteric, but the injury caused him to turn his every play into a miniature voyage of Magellan, with the outfielder circumnavigating an imaginary globe before arriving at the spot where he could catch the ball without raising his glove hand above his belt. As with Magellan, there were times when Sheffield was unable to complete the trip. Sheffield loves to DH and hit very well in limited time at the position. Only the bloated remains of Jason Giambi's career prevent the Yankees from planting him there and making him even more of an asset.

RUBEN SIERRA

DH **Bats: B** **Throws: R** Born: 06-Oct-1965 Age: 39

YEAR	TM	LG	AGE	AB	H	2B	3B	HR	BB	SO	SB	CS	AVG	OBP	SLG	MLVR	EQBA	EQOBP	EQSLG	EQMLVR	VORP	DEFENSE
2002	SEA	AL	36	419	113	23	0	13	31	66	4	0	.270	.319	.418	-.003	.284	.333	.437	-.005	14.2	42-LF -2
2003	TEX	AL	37	133	35	9	0	3	14	27	1	1	.263	.333	.398	-.061	.262	.327	.377	-.118	2.3	12-LF -1
2003	NYY	AL	37	174	48	8	1	6	13	20	1	0	.276	.323	.437	.029	.279	.333	.448	.006	7.4	
2004	NYY	AL	38	307	75	12	1	17	25	55	1	0	.244	.296	.456	-.047	.251	.306	.469	-.037	9.9	18-RF -1
2005	*NYY*	*AL*	*39*	*199*	*51*	*10*	*1*	*8*	*17*	*38*	*1*	*0*	*.258*	*.315*	*.432*	*-.052*	*.261*	*.320*	*.443*	*-.037*	*5.1*	*55-DH 2*

Breakout: 21% *Improve: 49%* *Collapse: 19%*

Coming off the bench as a big-inning finisher against righties (only!), Sierra had value. Unfortunately, a fluke Player of the Week citation in early May propelled the old man into way too much playing time. Exhibit A in the brief for Brian Cashman/Joe Torre having a mental acuity off-year is their somehow never realizing that getting a .281 OBP/.456 SLG from your primary DH will kill you faster than drinking Drano. Sick joke of the year: Sierra wants to be a batting coach after he retires. "OK, lad. First set up as far to the outside of the batter's box as you can without sitting in the dugout. Then, when a pitcher throws one on the outside corner, you waive at it like it was the Love Boat pulling out of Puerto Vallarta. Dig?"

BERNIE WILLIAMS

OF **Bats: B** **Throws: R** Born: 13-Sep-1968 Age: 36

YEAR	TM	LG	AGE	AB	H	2B	3B	HR	BB	SO	SB	CS	AVG	OBP	SLG	MLVR	EQBA	EQOBP	EQSLG	EQMLVR	VORP	DEFENSE
2002	NYY	AL	33	612	204	37	2	19	83	97	8	4	.333	.415	.493	.301	.343	.428	.512	.322	75.5	147-CF -15
2003	NYY	AL	34	445	117	19	1	15	71	61	5	0	.263	.367	.411	.048	.268	.377	.424	.044	27.8	112-CF -7
2004	NYY	AL	35	561	147	29	1	22	85	96	1	5	.262	.360	.435	.048	.269	.372	.450	.071	31.0	88-CF -4
2005	*NYY*	*AL*	*36*	*447*	*122*	*23*	*1*	*16*	*68*	*76*	*2*	*2*	*.273*	*.369*	*.435*	*.054*	*.276*	*.375*	*.446*	*.072*	*27.9*	*123-CF -12*

Breakout: 24% *Improve: 51%* *Collapse: 20%*

Williams has always been a streak hitter, but as he's gotten older the lows have been lower and the highs not as high. Even so, he'd still be an above-average hitter for center field if only he had the range to play the position, which he no longer does. Off-season discussion focusing on making Williams a first baseman or DH skirts the question of whether his offense can sustain those positions. Essentially, he's become a misfit.

ENRIQUE WILSON

INF **Bats: B** **Throws: R** Born: 27-Jul-1973 Age: 31

YEAR	TM	LG	AGE	AB	H	2B	3B	HR	BB	SO	SB	CS	AVG	OBP	SLG	MLVR	EQBA	EQOBP	EQSLG	EQMLVR	VORP	DEFENSE	
2002	NYY	AL	28	105	19	2	2	2	8	22	1	1	.181	.239	.295	-.404	.183	.248	.308	-.417	-5.7	14-3B -1	
2003	NYY	AL	29	135	31	9	0	3	7	14	3	1	.230	.276	.363	-.216	.239	.283	.358	-.246	0.1	20-SS -3	12-3B 2
2004	NYY	AL	30	240	51	9	0	6	15	20	1	2	.212	.254	.325	-.340	.219	.261	.329	-.342	-8.0	63-2B -7	
2005	*NYY*	*AL*	*31*	*204*	*48*	*9*	*1*	*4*	*12*	*23*	*2*	*1*	*.237*	*.282*	*.349*	*-.236*	*.239*	*.286*	*.358*	*-.226*	*-2.2*	*56-2B -3*	

Breakout: 38% *Improve: 56%* *Collapse: 25%*

The Enrique Wilson Era lasted approximately 1,200 fewer games than the Horace Clarke Era, but still almost managed to surpass it in terms of negative value. Going into 2004, Wilson had batted .218/.266/.336 as a Yankee, and the team's belief he could start at second base was an act of blind faith inspired by a few lucky at-bats against Pedro Martinez. The Yankees' insistence on paying Wilson a premium for replacement-level abilities is yet another example of how this big-picture team often misses the little stuff. In an act of supreme hubris, Wilson bitched about his playing time during the stretch run. Some people live in a world without mirrors.

PITCHERS

ERIC ABREU

Bats: R **Throws: R** Born: 02-Jun-1983 Age: 22

YEAR	TM	LG	AGE	G	GS	IP	H	BB	SO	HR	ERA	EQERA	EQH9	EQBB9	EQSO9	EQHR9	PERA	VORP	STF
2004	STA	NYP	21	7	2	27.7	24	6	47	1	1.62	3.91	9.6	2.8	8.5	1.1	4.62	2.8	20
2004	TAM	FSL	21	3	3	17.0	7	6	15	1	1.06	2.45	6.8	3.7	6.1	1.2	3.07	4.1	19
2005	*NYY*	*AL*	*22*	*22*	*12*	*84.7*	*80*	*33*	*75*	*13*	*4.43*	*4.43*	*8.7*	*3.1*	*7.1*	*1.3*	*4.43*	*13.7*	*9*

Breakout: 9% *Improve: 37%* *Collapse: 21%*

Abreu is a Dominican starter who manifested, Lamont Cranston–like, in the Yankees system and made it all the way to high-A Tampa with an ERA for the season of 1.43. His fastball sits in the low-90s, but he knows where to put it. The Yankees supposedly do well scouting in the Dominican Republic, though you never see the results in the majors. If the Yankees had signed Vladimir Guerrero, we may never have heard of him.

COLTER BEAN

Bats: R **Throws: R** Born: 16-Jan-1977 Age: 28

YEAR	TM	LG	AGE	G	GS	IP	H	BB	SO	HR	ERA	EQERA	EQH9	EQBB9	EQSO9	EQHR9	PERA	VORP	STF
2002	TAM	FSL	25	46	0	54.7	34	21	78	2	1.97	4.09	7.1	3.9	9.4	0.7	3.20	13.5	22
2002	NRW	EAS	25	12	0	10.7	14	6	9	1	6.73	6.97	11.3	5.2	6.1	1.7	6.97	-1.6	-26
2003	COH	INT	26	50	0	69.0	53	27	70	5	2.87	4.78	7.7	4.1	7.6	1.0	3.94	11.8	11
2004	COH	INT	27	53	0	82.7	61	23	109	3	2.29	2.95	6.8	2.6	9.8	0.3	2.50	27.3	36
2005	*NYY*	*AL*	*28*	*28*	*4*	*56.7*	*47*	*22*	*61*	*7*	*3.50*	*3.50*	*7.6*	*3.0*	*8.6*	*1.1*	*3.72*	*16.2*	*15*

Breakout: 29% *Improve: 51%* *Collapse: 24%*

Randall C. Bean was Rule 5'd away from the Yankees last winter by the Red Sox. The Sox returned him in the spring, to their detriment. Although a 6′6″, 255 lb. behemoth, Bean doesn't have much giddy-up on his fastball and relies on a deceptive sidearm delivery to retire hitters. Regardless of his method, his ERA for 218 minor league games is 2.64, he's K'd 11.8 batters per nine innings, and his K:BB ratio is 3.47. Given their dearth of relievers, the Yankees owe it to themselves to give him a trial run.

KEVIN BROWN

Bats: R **Throws: R** Born: 14-Mar-1965 Age: 40

YEAR	TM	LG	AGE	G	GS	IP	H	BB	SO	HR	ERA	EQERA	EQH9	EQBB9	EQSO9	EQHR9	PERA	VORP	STF
2002	LAD	NL	37	17	10	63.7	68	23	58	9	4.80	5.40	9.8	2.8	7.3	1.3	5.25	2.7	10
2003	LAD	NL	38	32	32	211.0	184	56	185	11	2.39	3.03	8.2	2.1	7.3	0.5	3.43	66.6	32
2004	NYY	AL	39	22	22	132.0	132	35	83	14	4.09	4.13	8.7	2.2	5.4	0.8	3.64	26.4	13
2005	*NYY*	*AL*	*40*	*28*	*22*	*135.0*	*143*	*41*	*92*	*15*	*4.09*	*4.09*	*9.7*	*2.4*	*5.4*	*0.9*	*4.31*	*24.7*	*6*

Breakout: 20% *Improve: 60%* *Collapse: 3%*

Currently persona non grata around the Bronx, but as the Blues Brothers used to sing, whaddya want for nothing? The list of starting pitchers age 39 or older who did positive things for their teams numbers less than 100 all-time (including stellar elderly 2004s from Rocket Roger and the Big Unit). Factor in that Brown has the worst constitution this side of Ukraine and the personality of a menstrual hippopotamus, and that he'd be facing the DH for the first time since 1995, and what you got was the Yankees taking a gamble with long odds.

TYLER CLIPPARD

Bats: R **Throws: R** Born: 14-Feb-1985 Age: 20

YEAR	TM	LG	AGE	G	GS	IP	H	BB	SO	HR	ERA	EQERA	EQH9	EQBB9	EQSO9	EQHR9	PERA	VORP	STF
2004	BCR	MDW	19	26	25	149.0	153	32	145	12	3.44	5.74	9.9	2.4	5.2	1.4	4.83	12.0	12
2005	*NYY*	*AL*	*20*	*12*	*12*	*66.7*	*73*	*22*	*46*	*12*	*5.12*	*5.12*	*10.1*	*2.6*	*5.5*	*1.5*	*5.22*	*5.4*	*3*

Breakout: 5% *Improve: 41%* *Collapse: 16%*

A Jon Lieber wannabe, Clippard doesn't have the strongest fastball in the world but has a good curve and excellent control. His pro K:W ratio is 5.43—few walks and lots of Ks. He's fairly hittable so he'll need another pitch, and as a nonflamethrower he'll have to keep proving himself, particularly as a member of the New York Skeptics.

JORGE DePAULA

Bats: R Throws: R Born: 10-Nov-1978 Age: 26

YEAR	TM	LG	AGE	G	GS	IP	H	BB	SO	HR	ERA	EQERA	EQH9	EQBB9	EQSO9	EQHR9	PERA	VORP	STF
2002	NRW	EAS	23	27	26	175.0	141	52	152	11	3.45	4.58	8.2	2.9	6.2	0.9	3.64	35.5	15
2003	COH	INT	24	27	27	167.7	168	57	125	22	4.35	5.30	9.6	3.6	5.6	1.7	5.41	3.3	-1
2005	*NYY*	*AL*	*26*	*8*	*5*	*32.3*	*34*	*13*	*21*	*6*	*5.23*	*5.23*	*9.6*	*3.1*	*5.2*	*1.5*	*5.14*	*3.3*	*-5*

Breakout: 29% *Improve: 48%* *Collapse: 33%*

"Jorge, you came in here a chorus girl, but you're going out there a star!" Well, no. With openings aplenty on the Yankees' staff, DePaula pitched nine innings and required Tommy John surgery. Recovery time is about a year, so he'll be shaking out the cobwebs in spring training.

MATT DeSALVO

Bats: R Throws: R Born: 11-Sep-1980 Age: 24

YEAR	TM	LG	AGE	G	GS	IP	H	BB	SO	HR	ERA	EQERA	EQH9	EQBB9	EQSO9	EQHR9	PERA	VORP	STF
2003	STA	NYP	22	10	10	49.0	42	19	52	2	1.84	5.52	9.6	4.7	5.7	1.4	5.32	1.4	-2
2003	BCR	MDW	22	3	3	22.0	15	5	21	0	0.82	4.05	7.7	2.7	5.8	0.4	3.15	5.4	21
2004	TAM	FSL	23	13	13	75.3	48	30	80	1	1.43	3.82	7.2	4.2	6.7	0.3	3.42	16.5	28
2004	TRN	EAS	23	5	5	27.3	27	10	24	3	6.59	6.84	8.9	3.4	5.8	1.4	4.10	4.4	14
2005	*NYY*	*AL*	*24*	*18*	*15*	*90.0*	*90*	*44*	*71*	*11*	*4.85*	*4.85*	*9.1*	*3.8*	*6.3*	*1.0*	*4.74*	*11.0*	*5*

Breakout: 13% *Improve: 39%* *Collapse: 25%*

A little guy with a funky delivery, DeSalvo was an astute pickup by Yankees scouts who grabbed him as a non-drafted free agent in 2003. His first 26 pro starts were pure chewing satisfaction: 146.1 innings, 105 hits, 54 walks, 153 strikeouts, 1.48 ERA (2.64 runs allowed). Five late-season starts at Double-A Trenton were less successful (Double-A: Where Yankees prospects go to die). Those 27 innings, in which a bad back may have been complicit, don't erase what he did at the lower levels, but they bring up all the usual questions about whether a guy who hides a weak fastball with guile can survive against more advanced hitters. Stand by for a conversion to middle relief.

ABEL GOMEZ

Bats: L Throws: L Born: 29-Nov-1984 Age: 20

YEAR	TM	LG	AGE	G	GS	IP	H	BB	SO	HR	ERA	EQERA	EQH9	EQBB9	EQSO9	EQHR9	PERA	VORP	STF
2004	BCR	MDW	19	29	25	142.7	115	73	149	7	3.66	6.02	8.4	6.0	5.7	0.9	4.64	13.9	22
2005	*NYY*	*AL*	*20*	*13*	*12*	*67.7*	*65*	*41*	*46*	*12*	*5.39*	*5.39*	*8.8*	*4.8*	*5.5*	*1.4*	*5.38*	*4.0*	*-5*

Breakout: 18% *Improve: 47%* *Collapse: 14%*

Smallish lefty who throws hard but has trouble with his control. His story is just beginning, and he could develop into anything from a top starter to the President of the United States in a time travel–affected alternate reality in which Ulysses Grant succeeded in annexing Santa Domingo back in 1869. Your chronoshuttle to the gilded age leaving from Gate 82 . . .

TOM GORDON

Bats: R Throws: R Born: 18-Nov-1967 Age: 37

YEAR	TM	LG	AGE	G	GS	IP	H	BB	SO	HR	ERA	EQERA	EQH9	EQBB9	EQSO9	EQHR9	PERA	VORP	STF
2002	CHC	NL	34	19	0	23.7	27	10	31	1	3.42	4.81	8.9	3.0	10.0	0.4	3.70	2.1	23
2002	HOU	NL	34	15	0	19.0	15	6	17	2	3.32	3.50	7.5	2.5	7.5	1.0	3.50	4.3	10
2003	CWS	AL	35	66	0	74.0	57	31	91	4	3.16	3.24	6.8	3.6	10.8	0.5	3.11	21.1	33
2004	NYY	AL	36	80	0	89.7	56	23	96	5	2.21	2.20	6.1	2.1	9.3	0.4	1.99	39.6	33
2005	*NYY*	*AL*	*37*	*47*	*2*	*73.0*	*64*	*26*	*76*	*8*	*3.34*	*3.34*	*8.1*	*2.9*	*8.4*	*0.9*	*3.66*	*22.9*	*14*

Breakout: 20% *Improve: 38%* *Collapse: 35%*

Old Man Flash set a career high for games and innings as a reliever in '04. More than half of those innings came in the first half, and while Gordon did not break down, he added nearly a run to his ERA in the second half and appeared to be seriously gassed by the playoffs. His post-season performance suffered accordingly, which reflects less on Gordon than on Daddy Warbucks Baseball Inc., which couldn't figure out how to get Joe Torre more than one other reliever that he could trust. While Gordon didn't cross the dreaded 100-inning threshold, a fatigue reaction for '05 is a lock.

ALEX GRAMAN **Bats: L** **Throws: L** Born: 17-Nov-1977 Age: 27

YEAR	TM	LG	AGE	G	GS	IP	H	BB	SO	HR	ERA	EQERA	EQH9	EQBB9	EQSO9	EQHR9	PERA	VORP	STF
2002	NRW	EAS	24	8	8	50.0	46	13	31	2	2.88	4.21	8.6	2.5	4.4	0.6	3.64	10.2	11
2002	COH	INT	24	20	20	124.0	141	37	98	11	4.65	5.77	9.2	3.0	5.9	1.0	3.92	22.7	7
2003	COH	INT	25	26	26	142.7	135	63	110	14	4.48	5.28	9.0	4.6	5.8	1.3	5.01	8.7	-5
2004	COH	INT	26	24	22	131.0	115	53	129	12	3.37	3.96	8.1	3.8	7.3	0.9	3.89	23.8	24
2005	*NYY*	*AL*	*27*	*22*	*13*	*84.7*	*90*	*37*	*64*	*11*	*5.02*	*5.02*	*9.7*	*3.5*	*6.1*	*1.1*	*4.86*	*7.6*	*1*

Breakout: 16% *Improve: 44%* *Collapse: 28%*

He set back the cause of Yankees mid-range pitching prospects by getting bombed in two big league starts. Ownership is inclined to believe that all young pitchers look "scared" and Graman really did look overwhelmed, confirming an incredibly counterproductive prejudice. Otherwise, Graman had the best of his three seasons at Columbus, upping his strikeout rate and dropping more than a run from his ERA. Given his stuff, his future might be in middle relief—if he can just get out of here. Out of options, the Yankees will either use him or lose him.

BRAD HALSEY **Bats: L** **Throws: L** Born: 14-Feb-1981 Age: 24

YEAR	TM	LG	AGE	G	GS	IP	H	BB	SO	HR	ERA	EQERA	EQH9	EQBB9	EQSO9	EQHR9	PERA	VORP	STF
2002	STA	NYP	21	11	10	56.0	39	17	53	0	1.93	4.86	8.1	3.8	5.0	0.4	3.78	10.1	13
2003	TAM	FSL	22	14	13	84.0	96	14	56	3	3.43	5.54	10.5	1.7	4.2	0.9	4.86	6.6	8
2003	TRN	EAS	22	15	15	91.3	123	22	78	4	4.93	5.54	9.9	2.2	5.8	0.7	4.08	15.7	0
2004	COH	INT	23	24	23	144.0	128	37	109	8	2.62	3.15	8.1	2.4	5.6	0.5	3.22	36.2	32
2004	NYY	AL	23	8	7	32.0	41	14	25	4	6.47	6.61	9.9	3.3	6.3	0.8	4.68	-3.8	22
2005	*ARI*	*NL*	*24*	*23*	*13*	*88.7*	*95*	*32*	*61*	*12*	*4.83*	*4.82*	*9.4*	*2.9*	*5.7*	*1.1*	*4.68*	*9.6*	*1*

Breakout: 13% *Improve: 35%* *Collapse: 38%*

There is nothing outstanding about "Admiral" Halsey but for the arm he throws with and his good control (2.16 walks per nine). As the Yankees were dramatically short of southpaws, their refusal to try Halsey in the bullpen represents a serious failure of imagination. Halsey had good success against lefties (.143/.212/.250), and though the sample is small, the Yankees were desperate enough that the numbers merited further exploration. If God is in the details, Halsey would be in middle relief. He'll be starting for the Arizona Diamondbacks, so . . . uhh . . . there is no God?

SEAN HENN **Bats: R** **Throws: L** Born: 23-Apr-1981 Age: 24

YEAR	TM	LG	AGE	G	GS	IP	H	BB	SO	HR	ERA	EQERA	EQH9	EQBB9	EQSO9	EQHR9	PERA	VORP	STF
2003	TAM	FSL	22	16	16	72.3	69	37	52	3	3.61	5.56	9.8	5.3	4.6	1.1	5.56	0.3	-13
2004	TRN	EAS	23	27	27	163.3	173	63	118	11	4.41	5.65	8.9	3.6	4.7	0.8	3.78	32.2	4
2005	*NYY*	*AL*	*24*	*14*	*14*	*78.7*	*89*	*36*	*46*	*11*	*5.44*	*5.44*	*10.4*	*3.6*	*4.7*	*1.2*	*5.42*	*3.1*	*-4*

Breakout: 6% *Improve: 33%* *Collapse: 25%*

A real disappointment. Henn had a lively arm when he signed, causing radar guns to go "tilt." Then came the injuries, Tommy John surgery and shoulder problems erased some of that velocity and cost Henn all of 2002. He was finally able to put in a full season and while his fastball showed some rebound, the overall numbers were mediocre. He's heading for the bullpen like a runaway train.

FELIX HEREDIA **Bats: L** **Throws: L** Born: 18-Jun-1975 Age: 30

YEAR	TM	LG	AGE	G	GS	IP	H	BB	SO	HR	ERA	EQERA	EQH9	EQBB9	EQSO9	EQHR9	PERA	VORP	STF
2002	TOR	AL	27	53	0	52.3	51	26	31	5	3.61	4.44	8.7	4.3	5.2	0.7	4.44	5.7	-12
2003	CIN	NL	28	57	0	72.0	61	28	41	9	3.00	3.31	8.3	3.2	4.8	1.1	3.97	18.0	-10
2003	NYY	AL	28	12	0	15.0	13	5	4	1	1.20	3.21	8.4	3.2	2.6	0.6	3.86	5.2	-22
2004	NYY	AL	29	47	0	38.7	44	20	25	5	6.28	6.05	9.3	4.2	5.4	0.9	4.66	-1.0	-12
2005	*NYM*	*NL*	*30*	*45*	*0*	*42.3*	*44*	*18*	*29*	*4*	*4.28*	*4.62*	*9.3*	*3.5*	*5.6*	*0.9*	*4.90*	*5.0*	*-9*

Breakout: 29% *Improve: 54%* *Collapse: 19%*

After a grand total of 15 unspectacular outings, the Yankees handed Felix the Assassin a two-year contract and made him the lead lefty out of the pen. It is antithetical to common sense to think that one can use a pitcher with a career rate of 4.66 walks per nine innings for specific batter match-ups because you never know to whom he's actually going to pitch.

(continued next page)

Felix Heredia *(continued)*

David Ortiz was able to kill the Yankees in the ALCS because Torre wouldn't use Heredia. In 2004, the Yankees had no lefty starters and, effectively, no lefty relievers. It was an interesting, if inadvertent experiment, and it didn't work. Getting the Mets, whose pitching coach Rick Peterson thinks he can "fix" Heredia, to pick him up for a decayed but functional Mike Stanton was a small-scale stroke of brilliance.

ORLANDO HERNANDEZ **Bats: R** **Throws: R** Born: 11-Oct-1969 Age: 35

YEAR	TM	LG	AGE	G	GS	IP	H	BB	SO	HR	ERA	EQERA	EQH9	EQBB9	EQSO9	EQHR9	PERA	VORP	STF
2002	NYY	AL	32	24	22	146.0	131	36	113	17	3.64	3.77	8.1	2.1	6.8	1.0	3.39	34.0	21
2004	COH	INT	34	3	3	17.7	17	3	16	3	5.59	5.40	9.2	1.6	7.0	2.2	4.86	1.4	18
2004	NYY	AL	34	15	15	84.7	73	36	84	9	3.29	3.13	7.6	3.5	8.4	0.9	3.46	27.6	30
2005	*CWS*	*AL*	*35*	*23*	*18*	*113.0*	*109*	*46*	*98*	*17*	*4.35*	*4.10*	*8.8*	*3.2*	*7.0*	*1.1*	*4.33*	*24.2*	*12*

Breakout: 24% *Improve: 51%* *Collapse: 18%*

Credit the Yankees with taking a chance here, though temper your praise with the knowledge that (1) it's easy to take risks when you have cash, and (2) the Yankees are both a baseball team and an alumni club, and this organization loves its veterans. El Duque remains the same pitcher he always was. He's devastating to righties with a variety of slow, slower, slowest stuff, including a beauty of an eephus pitch. But he's also vulnerable to lefty hitters, subject to mysterious injuries, and toast at 95 pitches. In Hernandez's penultimate start of the regular season, Torre let him throw 123 pitches. Hernandez's umpteenth physical breakdown followed directly, though it could have been just a coincidence. Off to Chicago to keep Jose Contreras company.

JESSE HOOVER **Bats: R** **Throws: R** Born: 08-Jan-1982 Age: 23

YEAR	TM	LG	AGE	G	GS	IP	H	BB	SO	HR	ERA	EQERA	EQH9	EQBB9	EQSO9	EQHR9	PERA	VORP	STF
2004	STA	NYP	22	16	9	55.7	28	26	90	0	1.78	4.38	6.6	6.0	8.6	0.4	3.47	11.7	23
2005	*NYY*	*AL*	*23*	*23*	*12*	*86.0*	*52*	*64*	*73*	*13*	*4.27*	*4.27*	*5.6*	*5.9*	*6.8*	*1.2*	*4.00*	*16.9*	*-1*

Breakout: 26% *Improve: 61%* *Collapse: 17%*

New York's fifth-round pick in 2004, Hoover had great success in the New York–Penn league, striking out 14.73 batters per nine and allowing just 28 hits in 55 innings. Terrific numbers, and strikeout rate is one of the best indicators of a pitcher's future success; but why leave a college starter in a short-season league all year and have him dominate teenagers when he'd be much better suited to a higher level? Hoover is still working on off-speed stuff. If he doesn't find it, the bullpen beckons.

BEN JULIANEL **Bats: B** **Throws: L** Born: 04-Sep-1979 Age: 25

YEAR	TM	LG	AGE	G	GS	IP	H	BB	SO	HR	ERA	EQERA	EQH9	EQBB9	EQSO9	EQHR9	PERA	VORP	STF
2002	PEO	MDW	22	38	8	100.3	106	32	96	9	3.50	6.33	11.4	3.7	5.4	2.3	7.22	-16.4	-37
2003	PEO	MDW	23	51	0	51.7	41	25	78	1	1.04	3.78	8.3	5.5	9.3	0.6	4.72	4.7	2
2004	TAM	FSL	24	44	0	61.3	53	24	72	2	2.50	4.74	8.8	4.1	7.3	0.6	4.58	6.5	-1
2005	*NYY*	*AL*	*25*	*32*	*4*	*56.3*	*60*	*26*	*48*	*7*	*4.97*	*4.97*	*9.7*	*3.7*	*6.9*	*1.0*	*4.92*	*5.0*	*-1*

Breakout: 16% *Improve: 44%* *Collapse: 26%*

Stop us if you've heard this one: soft-tossing lefty reliever. Funky delivery. Too old for his level. Double-A was unkind in a short trial. Acquired for Sterling Hitchcock. Here because the Yankees have a need for guys like this. Cheaper than free agent. Can't be worse than Felix Heredia, but then neither is being kicked in the groin.

STEVE KARSAY **Bats: R** **Throws: R** Born: 24-Mar-1972 Age: 33

YEAR	TM	LG	AGE	G	GS	IP	H	BB	SO	HR	ERA	EQERA	EQH9	EQBB9	EQSO9	EQHR9	PERA	VORP	STF
2002	NYY	AL	30	78	0	88.3	87	30	65	7	3.26	3.34	8.5	2.8	6.4	0.6	3.65	25.6	4
2004	COH	INT	32	11	0	11.3	12	6	8	0	5.58	7.36	9.0	4.9	4.9	0.0	4.09	1.8	-13
2004	NYY	AL	32	7	0	6.7	5	2	4	2	2.69	4.26	8.5	2.8	5.7	2.8	5.68	1.7	-12
2005	*NYY*	*AL*	*33*	*27*	*0*	*29.3*	*33*	*13*	*19*	*3*	*4.68*	*4.68*	*10.2*	*3.5*	*5.1*	*0.9*	*4.98*	*3.9*	*-12*

Breakout: 20% *Improve: 42%* *Collapse: 28%*

In an alternate reality, Steve Karsay has won a couple of Cy Young awards. In ours, he's a talented pitcher whose arm just won't let him pitch much. Karsay missed all of 2003 and most of 2004 recovering from shoulder surgery. When he came back in September the Yankees didn't pitch him much and left him off the post-season roster, perhaps because he'd been smoked in most of his rehab appearances. He might help in '05. More likely, he'll strain something.

JON LIEBER **Bats: L** **Throws: R** Born: 02-Apr-1970 Age: 35

YEAR	TM	LG	AGE	G	GS	IP	H	BB	SO	HR	ERA	EQERA	EQH9	EQBB9	EQSO9	EQHR9	PERA	VORP	STF
2002	CHC	NL	32	21	21	141.0	153	12	87	15	3.70	4.24	9.5	0.7	5.0	1.0	3.57	22.2	14
2004	NYY	AL	34	27	27	176.7	216	18	102	20	4.33	4.51	9.8	0.8	4.9	0.9	4.00	27.3	14
2005	*PHI*	*NL*	*35*	*25*	*24*	*147.7*	*172*	*17*	*90*	*19*	*4.39*	*4.55*	*10.5*	*0.9*	*4.9*	*1.1*	*4.43*	*19.1*	*9*

Breakout: 21% *Improve: 37%* *Collapse: 25%*

It took Lieber the better part of the season to find consistency, though his control was always exemplary. In implying that Lieber was not their preferred pitcher because he doesn't "miss bats," the Yankees missed the forest for the trees. Lieber allowed a ton of hits—lefties hit .346/.358/.524 against him— but because he was effective against righties and walks no one, he was better than league average in baserunners allowed. As a roughly neutral fly ball/ground ball pitcher, presumably he suffered for the inadequacy of the outfield gloves. As a pitcher returning from Tommy John surgery, New York's giving Lieber's good September and post-season showing extra weight in their evaluations would have been wise. Instead, their gamble that they would be able to sign him to a cheap multi-year deal was upset by Omar Minaya's overgenerous Kris Benson deal that set the wacky off-season market for second-tier starters. Lieber jumped to the Phillies, where the park and the defense will work against him.

ESTEBAN LOAIZA **Bats: R** **Throws: R** Born: 31-Dec-1971 Age: 33

YEAR	TM	LG	AGE	G	GS	IP	H	BB	SO	HR	ERA	EQERA	EQH9	EQBB9	EQSO9	EQHR9	PERA	VORP	STF
2002	TOR	AL	30	25	25	151.3	192	38	87	18	5.71	5.42	10.2	2.1	4.9	1.0	4.83	-1.4	5
2003	CWS	AL	31	34	34	226.3	196	56	207	17	2.90	2.76	7.9	2.2	8.2	0.6	3.34	78.0	34
2004	CWS	AL	32	21	21	140.7	156	45	83	23	4.86	4.51	9.6	2.6	5.0	1.2	5.03	16.4	0
2004	NYY	AL	32	10	6	42.3	61	26	34	9	8.51	8.39	10.8	4.7	6.5	1.6	6.34	-13.6	-7
2005	*WAS*	*NL*	*33*	*26*	*26*	*152.3*	*155*	*50*	*107*	*18*	*4.25*	*4.55*	*9.2*	*2.6*	*5.7*	*1.1*	*4.55*	*19.1*	*8*

Breakout: 17% *Improve: 53%* *Collapse: 17%*

Life Isn't Fair, Chapter MMMCMXXIV: The addition of a splendid new cut fastball breaks your lifelong tie with mediocrity, but almost as soon as it happens your arm gives back a few mph on your fastball. Loaiza finished 2003 on a bad note, recouped slightly in April and May of '04, and then the wheels came off. Three factors suggest a recovery is possible: Loaiza's usually excellent control deserted him last year, with his walk rate with the Yankees jumping to 5.53/nine innings compared to a career rate of 2.51; he was more of a fly ball pitcher than ever; and he pitched quite well in the playoffs. If his control comes back, he won't be up in the strike zone, won't give up a career high in home runs. If, if, if, if, if.

MIKE MUSSINA **Bats: R** **Throws: R** Born: 08-Dec-1968 Age: 36

YEAR	TM	LG	AGE	G	GS	IP	H	BB	SO	HR	ERA	EQERA	EQH9	EQBB9	EQSO9	EQHR9	PERA	VORP	STF
2002	NYY	AL	33	33	33	215.7	208	48	182	27	4.05	4.16	8.4	1.9	7.3	1.1	3.51	40.3	24
2003	NYY	AL	34	31	31	214.7	192	40	195	21	3.40	3.53	7.7	1.6	8.0	0.8	2.84	59.1	34
2004	NYY	AL	35	27	27	164.7	178	40	132	22	4.59	4.63	8.9	1.9	6.8	1.0	3.91	23.0	19
2005	*NYY*	*AL*	*36*	*26*	*24*	*149.3*	*151*	*41*	*120*	*19*	*4.02*	*4.02*	*9.2*	*2.2*	*6.5*	*1.1*	*4.09*	*31.5*	*15*

Breakout: 21% *Improve: 47%* *Collapse: 18%*

On Mussina's progress towards 300 wins, consider Don Sutton, a pitcher high on the list of Moose comps. Like Mussina, Sutton had trouble reaching 20 wins in a season—he did so only once, Mussina never. Through age 35 (1980), Sutton had been credited with 230 wins. Mussina has 211. Sutton had picked up another 35 wins by his 40th birthday. To match him, Mussina would need to average 11 wins over the next five years. This says nothing about his actual ability to pitch, which remains strong despite being shelved with right elbow stiffness. After struggling with the injury all year, the real Moose showed up in September (2.14 ERA in 42 innings). A good bet to chop his ERA back to 4 or lower.

BRET PRINZ **Bats: R** **Throws: R** Born: 15-Jun-1977 Age: 28

YEAR	TM	LG	AGE	G	GS	IP	H	BB	SO	HR	ERA	EQERA	EQH9	EQBB9	EQSO9	EQHR9	PERA	VORP	STF
2002	TUC	PCL	25	37	0	39.3	42	9	34	4	2.98	3.32	9.2	2.1	6.2	0.9	4.50	4.6	0
2002	ARI	NL	25	20	0	13.3	23	10	10	1	9.47	8.79	11.9	5.0	5.7	0.6	6.91	-6.0	-21
2003	TUC	PCL	26	10	0	12.0	19	3	7	1	6.00	6.57	11.7	2.2	4.4	0.7	5.84	-0.3	-22
2003	COH	INT	26	10	0	12.3	20	1	13	2	8.05	8.53	12.1	0.7	7.1	2.1	6.39	-1.1	-5
2004	COH	INT	27	29	0	30.7	27	9	33	3	3.52	3.68	8.0	2.8	8.0	0.9	3.68	6.3	12
2004	NYY	AL	27	26	0	28.3	28	14	22	5	5.09	4.88	8.8	3.9	6.8	1.3	4.55	2.8	-3
2005	*NYY*	*AL*	*28*	*29*	*0*	*27.3*	*29*	*10*	*22*	*4*	*4.47*	*4.47*	*9.6*	*2.9*	*6.4*	*1.2*	*4.69*	*5.0*	*-4*

Breakout: 31% *Improve: 55%* *Collapse: 25%*

Every time Prinz came into a game last year, Yankees broadcasters blathered as if Goose Gossage had just taken the magic bullpen car back from retirement. It's impossible to say why. But for 2001, Prinz has never posted great numbers anywhere. He's a mediocre righty reliever. That and a cheese pizza will get you . . . a cheese pizza. The Yankees have better options.

SCOTT PROCTOR **Bats: R** **Throws: R** Born: 02-Jan-1977 Age: 28

YEAR	TM	LG	AGE	G	GS	IP	H	BB	SO	HR	ERA	EQERA	EQH9	EQBB9	EQSO9	EQHR9	PERA	VORP	STF
2002	JAX	SOU	25	26	25	133.3	111	85	131	10	3.51	5.20	9.2	5.7	6.7	1.4	6.15	-7.5	-3
2003	COH	INT	26	10	0	19.0	13	3	26	2	1.42	2.04	7.1	1.5	10.2	1.5	3.06	5.0	32
2003	JAX	SOU	26	17	0	27.0	20	7	24	0	1.00	3.24	7.6	2.5	5.8	0.4	2.88	7.6	8
2003	LVG	PCL	26	24	0	39.3	35	13	35	2	3.66	4.10	8.0	3.4	7.0	0.7	3.62	8.2	7
2004	COH	INT	27	35	0	44.0	37	18	42	4	2.86	3.24	7.8	3.9	7.1	1.1	3.67	8.9	7
2004	NYY	AL	27	26	0	25.0	29	14	21	5	5.40	6.12	9.4	4.3	7.2	1.4	5.40	-0.6	-2
2005	*NYY*	*AL*	*28*	*19*	*4*	*42.7*	*43*	*22*	*33*	*6*	*4.93*	*4.93*	*9.2*	*4.1*	*6.2*	*1.1*	*4.96*	*5.0*	*-5*

Breakout: 18% *Improve: 48%* *Collapse: 26%*

Acquired in exchange for Robin Ventura, Proctor throws in the high 90s but struggled with his control in the major leagues. He can do better if the Yankees are patient. "Ha ha!" you say, "now tell me another one!"

PAUL QUANTRILL **Bats: L** **Throws: R** Born: 03-Nov-1968 Age: 36

YEAR	TM	LG	AGE	G	GS	IP	H	BB	SO	HR	ERA	EQERA	EQH9	EQBB9	EQSO9	EQHR9	PERA	VORP	STF
2002	LAD	NL	33	86	0	76.7	80	25	53	1	2.70	3.51	9.3	2.5	5.6	0.1	4.12	18.8	2
2003	LAD	NL	34	89	0	77.3	61	15	44	2	1.75	2.38	8.0	1.6	4.9	0.2	3.12	30.3	3
2004	NYY	AL	35	86	0	95.3	124	20	37	5	4.72	4.70	10.2	1.7	3.2	0.4	4.14	12.5	-9
2005	*NYY*	*AL*	*36*	*46*	*2*	*65.0*	*77*	*17*	*32*	*6*	*4.39*	*4.39*	*10.9*	*2.1*	*3.9*	*0.8*	*4.75*	*11.3*	*-13*

Breakout: 30% *Improve: 46%* *Collapse: 12%*

Quantrill's groundball-flyball ratio was the lowest it has been since 1994, as the knee injury he suffered during the opening series in Japan altered his mechanics. He still set the club single-season record for games pitched as Joe Torre seemed to use him three times a game, despite declining effectiveness. His strikeouts dropped to an untenable 3.49 per nine innings, and unless a pitcher is an extreme groundball pitcher in the mold of Dan Kolb, allowing that many balls in play is going to result in frequent poundings. Quantrill has led his league in appearances for four consecutive seasons. It's good to be gung-ho, but everyone's durability has a limit.

RAMON RAMIREZ **Bats: R** **Throws: R** Born: 31-Aug-1981 Age: 23

YEAR	TM	LG	AGE	G	GS	IP	H	BB	SO	HR	ERA	EQERA	EQH9	EQBB9	EQSO9	EQHR9	PERA	VORP	STF
2003	TAM	FSL	21	14	14	74.3	88	20	70	7	5.21	7.43	11.9	2.7	6.0	2.5	7.04	-11.0	-23
2004	TRN	EAS	22	18	18	114.0	115	32	128	11	4.66	5.19	8.8	2.6	7.4	1.1	3.73	23.1	19
2004	COH	INT	22	4	4	18.0	25	8	17	3	8.50	9.00	11.0	4.0	6.5	1.5	6.50	-1.8	-2
2005	*NYY*	*AL*	*23*	*15*	*13*	*81.0*	*85*	*31*	*67*	*15*	*5.14*	*5.15*	*9.6*	*3.0*	*6.6*	*1.6*	*5.09*	*7.1*	*7*

Breakout: 8% *Improve: 42%* *Collapse: 21%*

Another peewee hurler; the Yankees apparently pluck 'em early, like baby carrots or new potatoes. Like potatoes, they are placed in a silo and aged a couple of years. In this case, the trick is on the potatoes, because no one ever comes to get them out of the silo. Eventually they are rescued by sympathetic beings from outer space, but often not in time to have major league careers. Ramirez has a 95 mph fastball, a good curve, and strikes out many a batter when they're not hitting line drives off him. Currently a starter, headed to middle relief.

MARIANO RIVERA Bats: R Throws: R Born: 29-Nov-1969 Age: 35

YEAR	TM	LG	AGE	G	GS	IP	H	BB	SO	HR	ERA	EQERA	EQH9	EQBB9	EQSO9	EQHR9	PERA	VORP	STF
2002	NYY	AL	32	45	0	46.0	35	11	41	3	2.74	3.07	7.2	2.0	7.8	0.6	2.66	14.5	17
2003	NYY	AL	33	64	0	70.7	61	10	63	3	1.65	1.96	7.3	1.2	8.0	0.4	2.22	32.9	25
2004	NYY	AL	34	74	0	78.7	65	20	66	3	1.94	1.89	7.3	2.1	7.3	0.4	2.59	37.9	18
2005	*NYY*	*AL*	*35*	*51*	*3*	*79.3*	*76*	*24*	*68*	*7*	*3.46*	*3.46*	*8.8*	*2.4*	*6.9*	*0.7*	*3.67*	*22.7*	*8*

Breakout: 26% *Improve: 41%* *Collapse: 40%*

A one-trick pony, and maybe the best of all-time. He just cues up that cut fastball and throws it to different spots. He's very good at changing planes on the hitter, climbing up (and in) until the hitter chases. This shtick works very well against everyone but the Red Sox, who seem to have figured out his M.O. and have sworn not to swing. When not facing the champs, Rivera yielded 1.59 unintentional walks per nine innings. Boston worked him for five unintentional passes in 10 innings, not including two more in the ALCS. Distant early warning: Since Rivera adopted the cutter in 1999, lefties haven't had a chance against him—until 2004. Year by year: .143, .207, .187, .181, .199, .234.

EDWARDO SIERRA Bats: R Throws: R Born: 15-Apr-1982 Age: 23

YEAR	TM	LG	AGE	G	GS	IP	H	BB	SO	HR	ERA	EQERA	EQH9	EQBB9	EQSO9	EQHR9	PERA	VORP	STF
2002	VAN	NWN	20	9	7	28.0	42	17	23	0	6.11	9.88	12.2	6.6	4.0	0.3	7.24	-5.0	-25
2003	KNC	MDW	21	51	0	60.3	46	24	52	2	2.09	5.30	8.4	4.6	5.3	0.8	4.64	5.8	-11
2004	TAM	FSL	22	45	0	48.7	44	45	57	2	3.33	5.40	9.0	9.6	7.4	0.8	6.40	-4.0	-22
2005	*NYY*	*AL*	*23*	*25*	*1*	*35.3*	*35*	*24*	*29*	*4*	*5.31*	*5.31*	*9.1*	*5.3*	*6.7*	*1.0*	*5.37*	*2.3*	*-9*

Breakout: 26% *Improve: 58%* *Collapse: 22%*

Relief prospect obtained from the A's for Chris Hammond, Sierra throws a fast fastball and a splitter but sometimes can't control them. While he was generally effective as Tampa's (Class A) closer, his walks per nine ballooned to 8.3. Unless the Yankees hold auditions for the Dominican Rick Vaughn, he'll wait a while.

TANYON STURTZE Bats: R Throws: R Born: 12-Oct-1970 Age: 34

YEAR	TM	LG	AGE	G	GS	IP	H	BB	SO	HR	ERA	EQERA	EQH9	EQBB9	EQSO9	EQHR9	PERA	VORP	STF
2002	TBY	AL	31	33	33	224.0	271	89	137	33	5.18	5.23	10.0	3.3	5.2	1.2	5.23	7.9	0
2003	TOR	AL	32	40	8	89.3	107	43	54	14	5.95	5.97	9.7	4.0	5.3	1.2	5.26	-6.5	-14
2004	LVG	PCL	33	6	6	36.0	26	12	32	2	2.50	2.91	6.9	3.2	6.4	0.5	2.91	10.2	28
2004	NYY	AL	33	28	3	77.3	75	33	56	9	5.47	5.23	8.4	3.4	6.2	1.0	3.93	4.9	12
2005	*NYY*	*AL*	*34*	*28*	*11*	*82.7*	*91*	*35*	*59*	*12*	*5.28*	*5.28*	*10.1*	*3.4*	*5.7*	*1.2*	*5.23*	*6.0*	*-5*

Breakout: 16% *Improve: 47%* *Collapse: 27%*

Bought sight unseen by Brian Cashman at the recommendation of a scout, which is a nice story but makes one wonder why the Yankees would sample the dregs of another organization before sampling what's floating at the bottom of their own cup. Initially, Sturtze pitched like himself, but each time he appeared the Yankees talked up how great he had been, eventually pretending him into the #3 man in the pen. Then a strange thing happened: Sturtze began to pitch well. If the Yankees invested this much faith in some of the talent in their system they would have a better, cheaper team over the next several years instead of a few out-of-character months from a sub-journeyman.

JAVIER VAZQUEZ Bats: R Throws: R Born: 25-Jul-1976 Age: 28

YEAR	TM	LG	AGE	G	GS	IP	H	BB	SO	HR	ERA	EQERA	EQH9	EQBB9	EQSO9	EQHR9	PERA	VORP	STF
2002	MON	NL	25	34	34	230.3	243	49	179	28	3.91	4.26	9.2	1.6	6.2	1.1	4.14	29.8	15
2003	MON	NL	26	34	34	230.7	198	57	241	28	3.24	3.44	7.9	2.0	8.6	1.1	3.56	53.0	32
2004	NYY	AL	27	32	32	198.0	195	60	150	33	4.91	4.79	8.7	2.5	6.5	1.4	4.05	23.1	12
2005	*ARI*	*NL*	*28*	*28*	*28*	*176.7*	*176*	*47*	*139*	*25*	*4.17*	*4.16*	*8.8*	*2.1*	*6.5*	*1.1*	*4.08*	*29.7*	*16*

Breakout: 16% *Improve: 51%* *Collapse: 15%*

Vazquez was terrific until just before Joe Torre put him on the All-Star team; he then went into a death spiral after the break with a 6.92 ERA. Always inclined to give up the long ball, he and the DH league didn't take kindly to one another. His collapse led to speculation about his mental suitability to pitching in New York, something both he and the Yankees vehemently disputed, and also questions about a possible injury, about which Vazquez disagreed and the Yankees kept an open mind. If Vazquez is neither mental nor injured, what does that leave? Incompetence? One of the goats of the season, he was shipped to Arizona in the Randy Johnson deal.

CHIEN-MING WANG Bats: R Throws: R Born: 31-Mar-1980 Age: 25

YEAR	TM	LG	AGE	G	GS	IP	H	BB	SO	HR	ERA	EQERA	EQH9	EQBB9	EQSO9	EQHR9	PERA	VORP	STF
2002	STA	NYP	22	13	13	78.3	63	14	64	2	1.72	5.12	9.1	2.3	4.4	0.9	4.35	9.8	12
2003	TRN	EAS	23	21	21	122.0	143	32	84	7	4.65	5.78	9.4	2.5	4.9	0.8	3.90	22.7	13
2004	TRN	EAS	24	18	18	109.0	112	26	90	6	4.05	4.91	8.6	2.2	5.4	0.7	3.13	29.2	22
2004	COH	INT	24	6	5	40.3	31	8	35	3	2.01	2.37	7.3	1.9	6.6	0.7	2.61	12.6	30
2005	*NYY*	*AL*	*25*	*15*	*15*	*92.3*	*104*	*27*	*59*	*11*	*4.68*	*4.68*	*10.3*	*2.3*	*5.2*	*1.1*	*4.64*	*11.4*	*6*

Breakout: 6% *Improve: 33%* *Collapse: 22%*

Taiwanese import who has lost development time to shoulder injuries. His performances have varied with health, mostly to the bad, but he finally regained some of his luster with 40 good-looking innings at Triple-A late in the year. His fastball reportedly has returned from the land of the dead, but his secondary pitches are erratic. If he continues pitching well, he'll move to the top of the emergency starter/trade bait pile.

STEVEN WHITE Bats: R Throws: R Born: 15-Jun-1981 Age: 24

YEAR	TM	LG	AGE	G	GS	IP	H	BB	SO	HR	ERA	EQERA	EQH9	EQBB9	EQSO9	EQHR9	PERA	VORP	STF
2004	BCR	MDW	23	9	9	57.7	36	26	56	4	2.65	4.59	7.6	5.5	5.5	1.4	4.41	6.7	13
2004	TAM	FSL	23	12	12	59.7	51	19	44	4	2.56	5.33	9.3	3.3	4.7	1.3	5.17	2.6	-1
2005	*NYY*	*AL*	*24*	*15*	*12*	*73.0*	*75*	*37*	*47*	*12*	*5.22*	*5.22*	*9.4*	*4.0*	*5.2*	*1.3*	*5.15*	*4.7*	*-5*

Breakout: 14% *Improve: 44%* *Collapse: 14%*

One of the starting pitchers in the system who might actually retain that job description as he climbs the ladder. White has a good fastball that's getting faster, he knows where it's going, and the off-speed pitches are coming along. A long holdout has him a year behind where he could be, and he needs to move quickly to have a shot. Prospects, remember the five Gs: **G**et the money, **G**et to the bigs, **G**et the service time, **G**o to arbitration, **G**et the last laugh.

Oakland Athletics

Genius. As a label that's been stapled to General Manager Billy Beane's lapel, however accurate it may or may not be, it's stuck there, to be acknowledged by admirers, or used to mock him by his critics. The criticism might seem strange, given Oakland's track record for success. But if 2003 was the year of the "Moneyball" phenomenon, 2004 was the year that the defensive backlash within baseball against that phenomenon became a persistent element within industry, one likely to have considerable staying power of its own. Perhaps every revolution demands counter-revolution. After last season, traditionalists could go from defensive griping to insincere pity. Because this year, the A's not only "failed to win the big one," they didn't play any big ones, at least none that weren't already on the schedule.

It's easy to dispassionately treat this year's failure as a simple matter of wins and losses, a question of what players broke down, or when the rotation went cold, or why the Big Three faltered. All due consideration can be given to when the Angels played well while asking when did the A's play badly. Theories can be posited, fingers wagged, and cautionary tales dolefully doled out. As ever, the cottage industry of analysts and commentators stands ready to digest the logistics of failure.

As exercises go, there are some causes for Oakland's absence from the playoffs, although they don't exactly rise to the level of lessons. The game on the field isn't radically different from what it was like twenty, forty, or even eighty years ago; winning games still boils down to the number of runs you score and allow. The A's didn't win enough games to retain the AL West title for several reasons. Despite their worthy faith in the virtues of OBP, the offense remained merely a middle-of-the-pack outfit, finishing ninth in runs scored. In a more advance metric like Equivalent Average, they not only finished behind expected hitting powerhouses like the Yankees, Angels, and Red Sox, but also behind non-contenders like the Orioles and Tigers. That's effectively where Oakland should have ranked: other than losing Eric Chavez for a stretch, the lineup was pretty healthy all season, and everyone played about as well or better than you could expect. Sure, Scott Hatteberg did better and Jermaine Dye did worse than you might have thought they'd do on Opening Day, 2004, but at season's end, nothing about the lineup makes you say "if only that guy had worked out." In the lineup, everything basically worked out, and it simply wasn't good enough.

ATHLETICS PROSPECTUS

2004 record: 91–71; Second place, AL West

Pythagenport record: 86–76

Runs scored per game: 4.90 (9th in AL)

Runs allowed per game: 4.58 (3rd in AL)

Team EqA: .262 (6th in AL)

2004 Batters Age: 30.1 (4th oldest in AL)

2004 Pitchers Age: 28.2 (5th youngest in AL)

Ballpark: Network Associates Coliseum; Neutral park; Park Factor of 0.999

2004: The organization's trademark in-season roster juggling fell one game short.

2005: The wholesale restructuring of the pitching staff will hurt this team a lot less than most of their fans think.

But instead of noting the aspiring mediocrity of a lineup no longer amongst the league's best, most of the finger-pointing has been directed at the pitching staff. The rotation went from famous to troubled down the stretch, with Mark Mulder going flaky, Zito staying flaky, Tim Hudson breaking down, and Mark Redman doing an excellent impression of himself. The bullpen was and remained a sore point over the full length of the season, even after the deal that brought in Octavio Dotel. The complaints here tend to be a bit overstated, letting the offense off the hook. For most of the stretch run, Mulder alternated good starts with bad, instead of being consistently terrible, but his struggles have been magnified to something akin to those of Steve Blass or Rick Ankiel.

Despite all of these failures, there's still a statistical argument to be made that the A's should have won anyway. As we explained in the Introduction, in discussing Pythagenport Win-Loss projections, by looking at a team's runs scored and allowed, you'll get a pretty good representation of how many wins a team should have. That didn't work out quite so neatly in last year's American League West as seen in table 1.

TABLE 1. EXPECTED WINS AND LOSSES IN THE AL WEST, 2004

Team	W	L	RS	RA	W1	L1	EQR	EQRA	W2	L2	AEQR	AEQRA	W3	L3
Angels	92	70	836	734	91.0	71.0	812	750	87.2	74.8	829	759	87.9	74.1
Athletics	91	71	793	742	86.1	75.9	842	747	90.2	71.8	848	751	90.4	71.6
Rangers	89	73	860	794	87.3	74.7	829	815	82.3	79.7	837	814	83.1	78.9
Mariners	63	99	698	823	68.5	93.5	741	829	72.4	89.6	769	832	74.9	87.1

A few definitions are in order. W, L, R (Runs) and RS (Runs Scored) are what happened on the field. W1 and L1 are your Pythagenports, how many wins and losses the teams should have had on the basis of their runs scored and allowed. At this point, it looks like the A's were pretty lucky to hang with the Angels.

But look a little more closely, and you find that's not entirely the case. EQR and EQRA are the teams' Equivalent Runs and Equivalent Runs Allowed, what the teams should have scored and allowed given how many hits, extra-base hits, walks, etc. they had. W2 and L2 (what Clay Davenport calls Second-Order Wins and Losses) are the expected records you get from Equivalent Runs scored and allowed. Oakland pops right back to around where they actually finished; it's the Angels who start looking like they were a bit lucky. Take the analysis a bit further, to AEQR and AEQRA (Adjusted Equivalent Runs and Runs Allowed), and you're looking at what the teams should have scored and allowed after adjusting for strength of schedule, which generates W3 and L3 (Third-Order Wins and Losses). Again, Oakland winds up around where they did actually wind up, in terms of wins; the Angels end up looking slightly lucky. (For more of this sort of thing, check out http://www.baseballprospectus.com/statistics/standings.html.)

Some of this reflects one of the things we've learned over the years. Having a strong bullpen is one of the things that helps a team outperform their projected wins and losses. The Angels had one of the best bullpens in baseball; the A's did not. But the chart basically underscores that nobody should consider the A's unfortunate, in that they did about as well as you'd think they should have, and that should have been enough to take the title. Beyond the obvious reason why the Angels can consider themselves fortunate, what with winning the division and all that, we can see them as a little lucky.

So what did Beane do? The A's lost by a hair, but that loss was exactly the margin needed to decide to retool, if not rebuild. Can you blame him? The famous (and increasingly expensive) guys didn't win and haven't won, and if the goal is to win championships and take your shot at a World Series title, why keep that team together? Beane started converting players with expensive mid-career value for inexpensive players with upside. (See table 2.)

Dismantling the rotation by tossing three-fifths of it might seem a radical solution, but keep in mind, the immediate objective is to keep a contender on the field. Eventually losing Mulder and Hudson to free agency wouldn't do that; it's a rare draft choice who is ready to help soon after being picked. Keeping Mulder and Hudson provided no guarantees that they'd win, while eating up more of Beane's financial flexibility to redesign the roster as new needs arose.

Keep in mind what he's achieved: in Haren and Meyer, he's added two big-league ready starters with the talent to be good rotation regulars. That's without accounting for his also having Joe Blanton on hand to step in, and potentially Japanese Leagues star Keiichi Yabu as well. Beane also added two relievers with some of the nastiest stuff in the game; both Cruz and Calero could make the bullpen an asset capable of going toe-to-toe with that of the Angels. Thomas and Ginter give the lineup two potential starters, at second and left field, respectively, and Ginter should be an improvement over the likes of Marco Scutaro or Mark Ellis. And then there's Kendall, who represents a massive offensive upgrade over Damian Miller. Kendall should be on-base as often as ever, creating runs

TABLE 2. THIS WINTER'S BEANE SHOPPING

Deal	Team	Get	Give Up
11/27	Pirates	C Jason Kendall	LHPs Arthur Rhodes and Mark Redman
12/15	Brewers	2B/3B Keith Ginter	RHP Justin Lehr, OF Nelson Cruz
12/16	Braves	RHP Juan Cruz, LHP Dan Meyer, OF Charles Thomas	RHP Tim Hudson
12/18	Cardinals	C-L Daric Barton, RHPs Kiko Calero and Dan Haren	LHP Mark Mulder

in a lineup that needed the help. Add in that Daric Barton's one of the best hitting talents in the minor leagues today, whatever his future position may be, and it's a superb group of deals. This should still be a 90-plus win team, with the talent to top the division for years to come.

Naturally, these moves generated some criticism, usually from people inclined to write off Oakland's good fortune in recent years to the presence of the Big Three. But they also garnered some appreciation. In this, Beane's track record for canny dealing has afforded him considerable leeway, not only with the team's owners, who trust him implicitly, but also amongst many in the chattering classes of the Fourth Estate.

Nevertheless, the A's remain baseball's black sheep. How much disdain does Oakland's farm system generate? Nobody got picked in the Rule 5 Draft. Not in the big league portion, not in the minor league portion. Several players from the now notorious "Moneyball draft" of '02 were available. A number of players from that draft were considered non-prospects by player development people throughout the game; given a chance to pick one of them up, a collective nose was turned up at the suggestion. Yet this system deserves more props than it gets from the industry as a whole. Sacramento won the Pacific Coast League again, making this the fifth time in the last nine years that Oakland's PCL affiliate has won the league's championship. Nevertheless, for all of the disgust the '02 draft generated for the attention it's been given outside of baseball circles, their '03 and '04 drafts have been relatively well-regarded, even by prospect hounds. Players like Rich Robnett, Javier Herrera, and Kurt Suzuki inspire excitement, and if they're all a few years away, they're cause for inspiration beyond the team's immediate future.

There is a desperate savagery in the hatred of Beane and everything he represents held by scouts and the flabby boomers on the beat alike. On a symbolic level, Beane represents certain judgment, the knowledge that everything will be evaluated, and that everyone will be held accountable. That represents an enormous threat to what remains an insular industry burdened with neo-feudal sensibilities. And baseball is a pretty tin-eared outfit anyway; offering criticism is a great way to earn a permanent cold shoulder.

Just as threatening is the creation of an empty office. The easy accessibility of information in today's world makes it easier to operate a major league team with a smaller staff. So instead of piling up the usual flunkies and hangers-on as extra Special Assistants to the General Manager and similar sinecures, Beane's outfit keeps light and loose. You think that doesn't frighten people throughout the industry? If Oakland's smaller overhead costs start getting noticed by other team owners, it could mean the end of hundreds of front office free lunches in an industry that coddles cronyism.

As a result, there are going to be a lot of people rooting for Oakland to fail in 2005. Given Beane's characteristically bold management of the roster, they can harbor continued hope that everything the A's have come to represent will disappear into the abyss if the high-wire act of constant retooling finally slips up. But Beane's moves are exactly the sort of thing this organization has been and will continue to be all about. The A's may have come up short last year, but the critics will have to live with the disappointment that the guys in green and gold aren't about to go away.

HITTERS

JOHN BAKER — **C** — **Bats: L** — **Throws: R** — Born: 20-Jan-1981 — Age: 24

YEAR	TM	LG	AGE	AB	H	2B	3B	HR	BB	SO	SB	CS	AVG	OBP	SLG	MLVR	EQBA	EQOBP	EQSLG	EQMLVR	VORP	DEFENSE	
2002	VAN	NWN	21	115	27	5	0	1	22	37	2	0	.235	.389	.304	.081	.200	.293	.264	-.376	-14.4	16-C -6	
2003	KNC	MDW	22	304	94	23	2	6	47	77	1	0	.309	.414	.457	.326	.277	.357	.431	.024	19.4	59-C -5	
2003	MID	TXS	22	150	36	3	0	1	14	46	0	0	.240	.316	.280	-.205	.193	.257	.220	-.514	-15.2	41-C -1	
2004	MID	TXS	23	439	123	32	5	15	37	94	0	2	.280	.355	.478	.136	.244	.305	.417	-.117	7.3	48-C -11	14-1B -1
2004	SAC	PCL	23	49	17	3	0	0	6	23	0	0	.347	.429	.408	.185	.255	.293	.277	-.331	-2.2	12-C 1	
2005	*OAK*	*AL*	*24*	*302*	*71*	*15*	*1*	*8*	*25*	*85*	*0*	*1*	*.237*	*.314*	*.373*	*-.148*	*.238*	*.318*	*.379*	*-.141*	*2.9*	*82-C -16*	

Breakout: 15% *Improve: 38%* *Collapse: 38%*

Oakland has a good group of catchers in the organization, but it remains to be seen if any of them have much star power. Baker and Brown are already in the upper levels, they had two interesting guys at full-season A-ball in John Suomi and David Castillo, and they picked two more in '04, Kurt Suzuki and Landon Powell. All of them could turn into serviceable backups, but it's most likely the last pair who might be something more.

Meanwhile, Baker and Brown have a Kendall-sized problem in front of them. Baker helped himself last year when, in having to rehab his shoulder after '03, he started taking his overall conditioning more seriously. He gets good marks within the organization for his catching skills, and backup backstops who can hit and hit lefty tend to be in demand.

JEREMY BROWN C Bats: R Throws: R Born: 25-Oct-1979 Age: 25

YEAR	TM	LG	AGE	AB	H	2B	3B	HR	BB	SO	SB	CS	AVG	OBP	SLG	MLVR	EQBA	EQOBP	EQSLG	EQMLVR	VORP	DEFENSE
2002	VAN	NWN	22	28	8	1	0	0	10	5	1	0	.286	.487	.321	.270	.161	.271	.161	-.572	-8.8	
2002	VIS	CLF	22	187	58	14	0	10	44	49	1	1	.310	.444	.545	.397	.249	.357	.429	-.001	10.7	48-C -3
2003	MID	TXS	23	233	64	10	1	5	41	38	3	0	.275	.388	.391	.080	.240	.345	.361	-.121	3.9	61-C -5
2004	MID	TXS	24	446	114	27	0	6	71	80	2	1	.256	.361	.357	-.035	.215	.306	.303	-.290	-16.4	87-C 0
2005	*OAK*	*AL*	*25*	*176*	*41*	*8*	*0*	*4*	*24*	*37*	*1*	*0*	*.234*	*.331*	*.355*	*-.140*	*.236*	*.335*	*.362*	*-.132*	*2.7*	*52-C -9*

Breakout: 27% *Improve: 50%* *Collapse: 32%*

How vindictive are some people within the game? To the point that, courtesy of *Moneyball,* you have scouts saying they hope Brown never pans out. That seems like a radical departure from professionalism: If a guy *BP* says won't work out does, we treat it as an example to learn from, to improve our modeling and fill in a potential gap in our knowledge of the game. Actively hoping Brown fails is one of those things like breaking Galileo to get your way. He's still not considered much of a physical specimen, but he's improved behind the plate; if he doesn't start adding power, though, he'll be strictly bench material.

FREDDIE BYNUM UT Bats: L Throws: R Born: 15-Mar-1980 Age: 25

YEAR	TM	LG	AGE	AB	H	2B	3B	HR	BB	SO	SB	CS	AVG	OBP	SLG	MLVR	EQBA	EQOBP	EQSLG	EQMLVR	VORP	DEFENSE
2002	VIS	CLF	22	539	165	26	5	3	64	116	41	21	.306	.385	.390	.101	.260	.323	.330	-.193	-3.0	133-2B -15
2003	MID	TXS	23	510	134	18	9	5	56	135	22	8	.263	.344	.363	-.036	.234	.309	.338	-.226	-7.8	114-2B -16
2004	MID	TXS	24	265	71	13	4	1	24	56	18	7	.268	.332	.358	-.075	.235	.293	.318	-.285	-10.8	61-CF -7
2004	SAC	PCL	24	258	74	11	3	2	19	61	21	4	.287	.343	.376	-.086	.262	.313	.332	-.209	-11.0	20-LF -1 17-SS -2
2005	*OAK*	*AL*	*25*	*207*	*51*	*10*	*2*	*2*	*16*	*49*	*8*	*3*	*.248*	*.309*	*.347*	*-.184*	*.250*	*.312*	*.354*	*-.177*	*1.1*	*58-2B -10*

Breakout: 23% *Improve: 43%* *Collapse: 34%*

Once considered a serious middle-infield prospect, Bynum is now reduced to being groomed for a utility role, flitting from second to short to center to third. Bynum might grow up to be a useful 25th man, but speed is his only real weapon, and his inexperience at the number of positions he's been asked to play shows.

ERIC BYRNES OF Bats: R Throws: R Born: 16-Feb-1976 Age: 29

YEAR	TM	LG	AGE	AB	H	2B	3B	HR	BB	SO	SB	CS	AVG	OBP	SLG	MLVR	EQBA	EQOBP	EQSLG	EQMLVR	VORP	DEFENSE
2002	SAC	PCL	26	119	31	7	0	4	7	15	5	1	.261	.302	.420	-.054	.231	.264	.359	-.286	-7.6	17-LF -1 13-CF -1
2002	OAK	AL	26	94	23	4	2	3	4	17	3	0	.245	.291	.426	-.093	.255	.297	.436	-.096	1.1	17-LF 0
2003	OAK	AL	27	414	109	27	9	12	42	71	10	2	.263	.333	.459	.064	.264	.339	.465	.028	25.1	76-CF -2 31-LF 1
2004	OAK	AL	28	569	161	39	3	20	46	111	17	1	.283	.347	.467	.071	.287	.352	.478	.090	33.1	97-LF 2 25-CF 3
2005	*OAK*	*AL*	*29*	*529*	*148*	*31*	*4*	*19*	*45*	*99*	*13*	*5*	*.279*	*.341*	*.465*	*.051*	*.282*	*.345*	*.473*	*.063*	*22.0*	*138-LF 1*

Breakout: 18% *Improve: 45%* *Collapse: 18%*

As we pegged a couple of years ago, Byrnes's power turned out pretty nicely, although keep in mind, he needs those 600 plate appearances to flirt with 40 doubles and 20 home runs. He's likely to have been dealt by the time you read this, since his scrappiness seems to feed some folks' Dykstra nostalgia. Of course, Nails would have scored the run and then shoved the catcher in '03, instead of trying to do it the other way around. Byrnes is also already 29, at the tail end of his peak, and moving into the arbitration inflation portion of his career.

ERIC CHAVEZ 3B Bats: L Throws: R Born: 07-Dec-1977 Age: 27

YEAR	TM	LG	AGE	AB	H	2B	3B	HR	BB	SO	SB	CS	AVG	OBP	SLG	MLVR	EQBA	EQOBP	EQSLG	EQMLVR	VORP	DEFENSE
2002	OAK	AL	24	585	161	31	3	34	65	119	8	3	.275	.348	.513	.144	.279	.356	.522	.151	51.4	138-3B 1
2003	OAK	AL	25	588	166	39	5	29	62	89	8	3	.282	.350	.514	.187	.284	.359	.522	.161	61.6	152-3B 20
2004	OAK	AL	26	475	131	20	0	29	95	99	6	3	.276	.397	.501	.198	.282	.404	.514	.223	45.5	125-3B 12
2005	*OAK*	*AL*	*27*	*532*	*151*	*30*	*2*	*32*	*84*	*105*	*5*	*2*	*.283*	*.381*	*.526*	*.198*	*.285*	*.386*	*.536*	*.213*	*47.9*	*146-3B 4*

Breakout: 18% *Improve: 60%* *Collapse: 10%*

If not for the injury, A's fans might have been able to remember 2004 as the year when Chavez put everything together. He's finally started hitting lefties, and his walk rate finally reached the clip Billy Beane's been predicting would eventually come. The defense remains top shelf. Chavez is on the short list of people likely to contend for the AL MVP this year.

BOBBY CROSBY SS **Bats: R** **Throws: R** Born: 12-Jan-1980 Age: 25

YEAR	TM	LG	AGE	AB	H	2B	3B	HR	BB	SO	SB	CS	AVG	OBP	SLG	MLVR	EQBA	EQOBP	EQSLG	EQMLVR	VORP	DEFENSE
2002	MOD	CLF	22	280	86	17	2	2	33	43	5	0	.307	.393	.404	.168	.275	.340	.359	-.110	7.8	70-SS 2
2002	MID	TXS	22	228	64	16	0	7	19	41	9	2	.281	.335	.443	.077	.238	.281	.388	-.208	-0.3	57-SS -1
2003	SAC	PCL	23	465	143	32	6	22	63	110	24	4	.308	.395	.544	.339	.280	.364	.495	.128	46.1	120-SS -1
2004	OAK	AL	24	545	130	34	1	22	58	141	7	3	.239	.319	.426	-.077	.242	.324	.433	-.062	23.0	148-SS 10
2005	*OAK*	*AL*	*25*	*488*	*127*	*28*	*2*	*19*	*50*	*114*	*9*	*3*	*.260*	*.338*	*.443*	*.001*	*.262*	*.342*	*.452*	*.012*	*32.5*	*131-SS 1*

Breakout: 15% *Improve: 52%* *Collapse: 12%*

There was some concern that, at 6′3″, Crosby might be too tall to comfortably handle short, but he turned out to be one of the best in the league in his Rookie of the Year campaign. He has quick hands and feet, positions himself well, and sports a strong arm that allows him to set up deeper than most. The .239 batting average was an outlier, and Crosby should continue to improve his power and plate judgment as he progresses. A championship-caliber player about to happen.

NELSON CRUZ OF **Bats: R** **Throws: R** Born: 01-Jul-1980 Age: 24

YEAR	TM	LG	AGE	AB	H	2B	3B	HR	BB	SO	SB	CS	AVG	OBP	SLG	MLVR	EQBA	EQOBP	EQSLG	EQMLVR	VORP	DEFENSE
2002	VAN	NWN	22	214	59	14	0	4	9	58	12	1	.276	.316	.397	.121	.240	.258	.353	-.300	-27.2	36-RF -6 14-LF -1
2003	KNC	MDW	23	470	112	26	2	20	29	128	10	5	.238	.292	.430	.074	.208	.248	.389	-.290	-31.4	106-RF -1 17-CF 0
2004	MOD	CLF	24	261	90	27	1	11	24	73	8	4	.345	.407	.582	.434	.282	.335	.471	.046	7.5	47-LF 3 23-RF -1
2004	MID	TXS	24	262	82	14	2	14	26	69	8	3	.313	.377	.542	.288	.271	.330	.469	.024	7.0	54-RF 1
2005	*MIL*	*NL*	*24*	*227*	*57*	*12*	*1*	*9*	*15*	*72*	*4*	*1*	*.252*	*.306*	*.441*	*-.068*	*.252*	*.305*	*.441*	*-.074*	*3.1*	*62-RF 0*

Breakout: 37% *Improve: 53%* *Collapse: 34%*

When your winter ball team cuts you from its roster eight months before the season begins, your prospect status has gotten a bit iffy. But one good season later, they took him back. Cruz came to the organization from the Mets in a deal for Jorge Velandia, and has now been flipped to the Brewers for Keith Ginter. Not a bad return on investment, although it also took Justin Lehr to make the deal happen. Cruz is a power player in every sense, trying to hammer everything at the plate while flashing a great arm in the field. He's a bit old for a guy who just cracked Double-A, but the Brewers need all the help they can get, and it might only take the next Geoff Jenkins breakdown to get him into the big leagues.

ERUBIEL DURAZO DH **Bats: L** **Throws: L** Born: 23-Jan-1974 Age: 31

YEAR	TM	LG	AGE	AB	H	2B	3B	HR	BB	SO	SB	CS	AVG	OBP	SLG	MLVR	EQBA	EQOBP	EQSLG	EQMLVR	VORP	DEFENSE
2002	ARI	NL	28	222	58	12	2	16	49	60	0	1	.261	.395	.550	.260	.253	.386	.538	.197	22.3	50-1B -4
2003	OAK	AL	29	537	139	29	0	21	100	105	1	1	.259	.374	.430	.094	.262	.379	.436	.059	35.9	31-1B -5
2004	OAK	AL	30	511	164	35	1	22	56	104	3	2	.321	.396	.523	.266	.326	.403	.537	.299	57.2	
2005	*OAK*	*AL*	*31*	*423*	*116*	*24*	*1*	*19*	*62*	*92*	*2*	*2*	*.273*	*.371*	*.472*	*.104*	*.276*	*.375*	*.481*	*.117*	*30.8*	*117-DH*

Breakout: 6% *Improve: 31%* *Collapse: 22%*

The A's DH had an outstanding '04 campaign, but he's nevertheless the subject of occasional speculation that with Dan Johnson pushing his way up, somebody making more than the minimum must go. Since nobody values Hatteberg as much as the A's do, and Durazo will make $4.7 million, that would seem to favor Durazo being the guy dealt. Given how long Beane pursued ways to acquire him, I guess we have to ask ourselves if Ahab would give up his white whale to Sea World after he'd finally caught him. PECOTA's expecting him to level off the spikes of his walk rates and power that he's enjoyed in separate seasons, but that doesn't translate to a better all-around season.

JERMAINE DYE RF **Bats: R** **Throws: R** Born: 28-Jan-1974 Age: 31

YEAR	TM	LG	AGE	AB	H	2B	3B	HR	BB	SO	SB	CS	AVG	OBP	SLG	MLVR	EQBA	EQOBP	EQSLG	EQMLVR	VORP	DEFENSE
2002	OAK	AL	28	488	123	27	1	24	52	108	2	0	.252	.333	.459	.032	.256	.340	.470	.030	18.0	101-RF -7
2003	OAK	AL	29	221	38	6	0	4	25	42	1	0	.172	.261	.253	-.402	.174	.262	.251	-.469	-17.2	53-RF 3
2004	OAK	AL	30	532	141	29	4	23	49	128	4	2	.265	.329	.464	.023	.267	.335	.471	.032	23.3	130-RF -1
2005	*CWS*	*AL*	*31*	*384*	*98*	*20*	*2*	*17*	*41*	*88*	*3*	*1*	*.256*	*.332*	*.449*	*-.004*	*.253*	*.331*	*.442*	*-.027*	*11.2*	*103-RF -5*

Breakout: 31% *Improve: 58%* *Collapse: 19%*

You might wonder if Dye's injuries helped overwrite a frank evaluation of whether or not Beane pegged his value too high. His breakout season in 2000 came around the time a career year is supposed to happen in a player's career (27, although they generally wind up in a range between 25 and 29). Dye's really a poor man's Jesse Barfield, but less athletic and significantly more fragile. If he's healthy enough to play a full season, he'll enjoy hitting on Chicago's South side, just like every other right-handed pull hitter.

MARK ELLIS 2B/SS **Bats: R** **Throws: R** Born: 06-Jun-1977 Age: 28

YEAR	TM	LG	AGE	AB	H	2B	3B	HR	BB	SO	SB	CS	AVG	OBP	SLG	MLVR	EQBA	EQOBP	EQSLG	EQMLVR	VORP	DEFENSE
2002	OAK	AL	25	345	94	16	4	6	44	54	4	2	.272	.359	.394	-.007	.278	.368	.401	.004	19.5	83-2B -9
2003	OAK	AL	26	553	137	31	5	9	48	94	6	2	.248	.313	.371	-.111	.248	.318	.376	-.147	13.9	147-2B 9
2005	*OAK*	*AL*	*28*	*316*	*83*	*17*	*2*	*6*	*32*	*52*	*5*	*2*	*.262*	*.337*	*.388*	*-.070*	*.264*	*.342*	*.395*	*-.061*	*15.6*	*87-2B -1*

Breakout: 16% *Improve: 42%* *Collapse: 32%*

Back in the day, he played a pretty good short, playing it with consistency if not flair. Since he's not likely to win the job at second back with Keith Ginter in the fold, he could turn into a quality utility infielder, perhaps starting at second to help out the groundball pitchers once in a while. The real question is whether his bat will come back from its post-All-Star Game collapse in 2003.

ESTEBAN GERMAN INF **Bats: R** **Throws: R** Born: 26-Jan-1978 Age: 27

YEAR	TM	LG	AGE	AB	H	2B	3B	HR	BB	SO	SB	CS	AVG	OBP	SLG	MLVR	EQBA	EQOBP	EQSLG	EQMLVR	VORP	DEFENSE
2002	SAC	PCL	24	458	126	16	4	2	78	66	26	14	.275	.390	.341	.011	.258	.366	.314	-.131	6.1	115-2B -13
2003	SAC	PCL	25	467	143	20	8	3	56	64	32	8	.306	.379	.403	.115	.284	.355	.377	-.049	17.4	110-2B -7
2004	SAC	PCL	26	231	76	8	4	2	19	28	18	2	.329	.380	.424	.098	.301	.346	.381	-.048	8.2	40-2B -4 13-SS -2
2004	OAK	AL	26	60	15	1	1	0	4	13	0	1	.250	.297	.300	-.282	.254	.290	.305	-.298	-1.6	11-3B 0
2005	*TEX*	*AL*	*27*	*193*	*52*	*9*	*2*	*2*	*18*	*28*	*7*	*2*	*.270*	*.337*	*.363*	*-.098*	*.260*	*.329*	*.350*	*-.145*	*6.6*	*54-2B -4*

Breakout: 11% *Improve: 27%* *Collapse: 52%*

PECOTA really doesn't cut players like German much slack, but the number of prospects who have thrived through a walks-and-singles offensive game is pretty slim, and German's repeated struggles in his brief major league trials don't offer much of a counter argument. Since he also isn't a gloveman, you're left with a utility infielder who gets the bat knocked out his hands that you don't want in the field. Signed a minor league deal with Texas, where he'll compete for a sixth infielder/pinch-runner job.

SCOTT HATTEBERG 1B **Bats: L** **Throws: R** Born: 14-Dec-1969 Age: 35

YEAR	TM	LG	AGE	AB	H	2B	3B	HR	BB	SO	SB	CS	AVG	OBP	SLG	MLVR	EQBA	EQOBP	EQSLG	EQMLVR	VORP	DEFENSE
2002	OAK	AL	32	492	138	22	4	15	68	56	0	0	.280	.374	.433	.088	.285	.382	.443	.092	28.7	83-1B 10
2003	OAK	AL	33	541	137	34	0	12	66	53	0	1	.253	.342	.383	-.031	.256	.346	.388	-.072	14.3	125-1B -10
2004	OAK	AL	34	550	156	30	0	15	72	48	0	0	.284	.367	.420	.039	.289	.372	.426	.054	28.1	138-1B -16
2005	*OAK*	*AL*	*35*	*397*	*109*	*21*	*1*	*10*	*54*	*41*	*0*	*0*	*.275*	*.365*	*.408*	*.015*	*.278*	*.370*	*.416*	*.026*	*15.9*	*110-1B -8*

Breakout: 18% *Improve: 51%* *Collapse: 15%*

One of the major disconnects among the ranks of people who do quantitative analysis is Hatteberg's defensive reputation. The A's have a defensive performance analysis tool that swears Hatteberg's one of the best in the game, and ours says he's pretty lousy. Generally, most tools that assess defense make broad agreements, and if you look at a lot of different ones, you find a lot of the same people ranking high, and a lot of the same ranking low. But Hatteberg's almost like Jeter: The numbers say he's not an asset, and yet reasonable people totally disagree. Unlike Jeter, Hatteberg looks pretty good out there, but the dilemma highlights how much more crude analysis of defensive performance is, compared to what we know about hitting or pitching stats.

The disagreement might help explain why the A's pay Hatteberg a premium. It doesn't justify it, but it helps explain it.

DAN JOHNSON 1B **Bats: L** **Throws: R** Born: 10-Aug-1979 Age: 25

YEAR	TM	LG	AGE	AB	H	2B	3B	HR	BB	SO	SB	CS	AVG	OBP	SLG	MLVR	EQBA	EQOBP	EQSLG	EQMLVR	VORP	DEFENSE
2002	MOD	CLF	22	426	125	23	1	21	57	87	4	1	.293	.371	.500	.255	.249	.315	.420	-.091	-1.0	79-1B 0
2003	MID	TXS	23	538	156	26	4	27	68	82	7	4	.290	.365	.504	.205	.252	.325	.454	-.023	10.0	107-1B 4
2004	SAC	PCL	24	535	160	29	5	29	89	93	0	1	.299	.403	.535	.272	.263	.362	.450	.048	21.0	95-1B 6 15-LF -2
2005	*OAK*	*AL*	*25*	*215*	*56*	*11*	*1*	*9*	*27*	*41*	*0*	*1*	*.259*	*.343*	*.445*	*.011*	*.261*	*.347*	*.453*	*.022*	*11.3*	*61-1B 0*

Breakout: 24% *Improve: 54%* *Collapse: 29%*

Johnson is ready to step in and take Hatteberg's job, although there's always the chance that the A's might move Durazo instead. Last season saw Johnson put in a lot of time working on his footwork around the bag, which might at least take one internal argument in Hatteberg's favor off of the table. An inner ear problem kept him from being called up in September, but he'll be in camp, ready to challenge for the job. It's just up to the A's to let him try. He'll beat that projection if he gets the playing time.

BOBBY KIELTY OF **Bats: B** **Throws: R** Born: 05-Aug-1976 Age: 28

YEAR	TM	LG	AGE	AB	H	2B	3B	HR	BB	SO	SB	CS	AVG	OBP	SLG	MLVR	EQBA	EQOBP	EQSLG	EQMLVR	VORP	DEFENSE
2002	MIN	AL	25	289	84	14	3	12	52	66	4	1	.291	.405	.484	.227	.294	.412	.497	.225	29.5	35-RF 1 25-CF -1
2003	MIN	AL	26	238	60	13	0	9	42	56	6	2	.252	.370	.420	.037	.255	.370	.421	.017	11.0	28-RF 0
2003	TOR	AL	26	189	44	13	1	4	29	36	2	1	.233	.342	.376	-.082	.226	.341	.371	-.124	2.0	51-RF -3
2004	OAK	AL	27	238	51	14	1	7	35	47	1	0	.214	.321	.370	-.157	.214	.326	.376	-.154	-1.2	40-LF 0 13-RF 0
2005	*OAK*	*AL*	*28*	*234*	*58*	*12*	*1*	*9*	*36*	*50*	*2*	*1*	*.247*	*.354*	*.420*	*-.010*	*.249*	*.358*	*.428*	*.000*	*9.9*	*68-RF -5*

Breakout: 19% *Improve: 53%* *Collapse: 25%*

When they traded Ted Lilly to the Jays, the A's felt they might be getting the new Mitch Webster. What they got was Ron Roenicke, which isn't terrible as your fourth or fifth outfielder, but it's also not the sort of thing you put on your Amazon wish list. Beane remains optimistic about finally getting Kielty v2002, but hoping that Kielty would match his 2002 production over 400 at-bats would be a bit much. It's more likely that he'll end up being a great platoon partner for Charles Thomas in left should the A's deal Byrnes, which would at least be an upgrade in Roenickes from Ron to Gary.

MARK KIGER INF **Bats: R** **Throws: R** Born: 30-May-1980 Age: 25

YEAR	TM	LG	AGE	AB	H	2B	3B	HR	BB	SO	SB	CS	AVG	OBP	SLG	MLVR	EQBA	EQOBP	EQSLG	EQMLVR	VORP	DEFENSE
2002	VAN	NWN	22	246	60	12	1	5	40	58	7	4	.244	.346	.362	.094	.215	.292	.323	-.291	-17.3	51-2B -1 12-SS -2
2003	MOD	CLF	23	526	148	38	3	8	77	106	3	0	.281	.375	.411	.104	.238	.317	.346	-.197	-3.5	77-2B -6 48-SS -4
2004	MID	TXS	24	487	128	24	3	5	78	96	12	6	.263	.369	.355	-.019	.228	.323	.311	-.238	-9.7	97-2B -5 25-SS -4
2005	*OAK*	*AL*	*25*	*194*	*46*	*10*	*1*	*3*	*21*	*43*	*3*	*1*	*.239*	*.316*	*.346*	*-.177*	*.241*	*.320*	*.352*	*-.171*	*2.1*	*55-2B -6*

Breakout: 29% *Improve: 44%* *Collapse: 32%*

If you've noticed, the A's have their share of combustible projections where PECOTA is concerned. In part, that's because it sees guys who walk without power, and the system pigeonholes them as likely flop material. If you're feeling generous, you could call Kiger the new Mark Ellis, but he's really just sort of a better version of Eric Bruntlett, praise so faint it swoons.

GRAHAM KOONCE 1B **Bats: L** **Throws: L** Born: 15-May-1975 Age: 30

YEAR	TM	LG	AGE	AB	H	2B	3B	HR	BB	SO	SB	CS	AVG	OBP	SLG	MLVR	EQBA	EQOBP	EQSLG	EQMLVR	VORP	DEFENSE
2002	MID	TXS	27	470	129	28	0	24	133	117	2	0	.274	.440	.487	.280	.227	.375	.414	-.003	13.3	116-1B -5
2003	SAC	PCL	28	480	133	23	1	34	98	119	0	0	.277	.403	.542	.315	.246	.366	.479	.079	24.8	80-1B 5
2004	SAC	PCL	29	439	106	25	0	22	77	129	0	0	.241	.362	.449	.019	.205	.313	.364	-.201	-15.6	47-1B 4
2005	*PIT*	*NL*	*30*	*123*	*29*	*6*	*0*	*5*	*22*	*40*	*0*	*0*	*.239*	*.363*	*.418*	*-.010*	*.240*	*.362*	*.427*	*-.001*	*6.9*	*39-1B -3*

Breakout: 41% *Improve: 56%* *Collapse: 30%*

Koonce is the most recent recipient of the Jarrod Patterson Kiss of Death. What's that, you say? Well, if William Gibson is right, and something starts getting major media buzz right around the time that it's jumping the shark and a good two years after it's hip, then like Patterson before him, Koonce was doomed once mags like *Sports Weekly* started giving him winter touts after his nifty '03 season. He's moved over to Pittsburgh as a minor league free agent, and might get a shot as a pinch-hitter. That's survival. Sort of.

MARK KOTSAY CF **Bats: L** **Throws: L** Born: 02-Dec-1975 Age: 29

YEAR	TM	LG	AGE	AB	H	2B	3B	HR	BB	SO	SB	CS	AVG	OBP	SLG	MLVR	EQBA	EQOBP	EQSLG	EQMLVR	VORP	DEFENSE
2002	SDP	NL	26	578	169	27	7	17	59	89	11	9	.292	.359	.452	.153	.305	.368	.479	.136	43.8	140-CF -4
2003	SDP	NL	27	482	128	28	4	7	56	82	6	3	.266	.343	.384	.010	.275	.351	.402	-.029	19.6	126-CF 11
2004	OAK	AL	28	606	190	37	3	15	55	70	8	5	.314	.370	.459	.122	.317	.377	.468	.148	45.3	137-CF 17
2005	*OAK*	*AL*	*29*	*521*	*148*	*30*	*3*	*14*	*52*	*74*	*6*	*4*	*.285*	*.350*	*.438*	*.035*	*.287*	*.354*	*.446*	*.046*	*26.7*	*137-CF 4*

Breakout: 5% *Improve: 33%* *Collapse: 25%*

PECOTA's skeptical. At an earlier point in their careers, it would have also been skeptical about Jim Edmonds or Steve Finley. Kotsay might be one of those players who winds up being better in his 30s than he was in his 20s, but that's only if the nagging hurts that have cut into his production in recent years plague him less often in the future, *and* if he develops at a different rate than most major leaguers do. If it doesn't happen, he's still a brilliant defender in center field, and the leadoff man they thought they'd be getting. That's more than they can say for Johnny Damon.

MARK McLEMORE — UT — Bats: B — Throws: R — Born: 04-Oct-1964 — Age: 40

YEAR	TM	LG	AGE	AB	H	2B	3B	HR	BB	SO	SB	CS	AVG	OBP	SLG	MLVR	EQBA	EQOBP	EQSLG	EQMLVR	VORP	DEFENSE	
2002	SEA	AL	37	337	91	17	2	7	61	63	18	10	.270	.380	.395	.072	.288	.400	.421	.098	18.1	66-LF -3	
2003	SEA	AL	38	309	72	15	2	2	38	71	5	5	.233	.318	.314	-.191	.244	.333	.329	-.185	-1.6	34-SS 2	27-3B 2
2004	OAK	AL	39	250	62	14	0	2	41	33	0	2	.248	.355	.328	-.132	.249	.358	.327	-.135	3.1	45-2B 1	22-3B 1

When he came up as the slick-fielding replacement for Bobby Grich in 1987, there was no way to expect McLemore would still be around, 17 seasons later. He came up the same year as Jerry Browne, an extremely similar player: They were both fast, switch-hitting second basemen, and they were both willing to take a walk. Both of their parent organizations soured on them in their sophomore seasons. They both wound up in Cleveland by 1990; Browne was the starter, and Carlos Baerga later doomed both of them. Browne contributed to the last hurrah of the LaRussa A's in '92 as a utility man. That same season, McLemore wound up on Baltimore's bench, where he spent a lot of time watching Billy Ripken play with his brother. McLemore got his big opportunity in '93, when injuries created an opening in the Oriole outfield, which got Mac a decade of regular playing time. Browne was out of the game by 1996. The kicker? McLemore's more than a year older than Browne. He's retired, capping a fine career.

BILLY McMILLON — OF — Bats: L — Throws: L — Born: 17-Nov-1971 — Age: 33

YEAR	TM	LG	AGE	AB	H	2B	3B	HR	BB	SO	SB	CS	AVG	OBP	SLG	MLVR	EQBA	EQOBP	EQSLG	EQMLVR	VORP	DEFENSE
2002	COH	INT	30	442	133	32	3	8	59	71	2	5	.301	.388	.441	.175	.280	.367	.418	.027	11.4	71-LF -11
2003	SAC	PCL	31	153	51	10	0	8	17	30	1	1	.333	.401	.556	.394	.303	.359	.500	.149	9.6	25-RF -4
2003	OAK	AL	31	153	41	11	0	6	19	36	0	0	.268	.354	.458	.106	.272	.354	.464	.060	9.8	29-LF 0
2004	OAK	AL	32	92	17	4	0	3	8	22	0	1	.185	.255	.326	-.358	.187	.251	.319	-.394	-5.4	13-LF 0
2005	*BOS*	*AL*	*33*	*149*	*40*	*9*	*1*	*5*	*18*	*32*	*0*	*1*	*.266*	*.349*	*.427*	*.003*	*.262*	*.346*	*.430*	*-.009*	*4.2*	*44-LF -7*

Breakout: 21% *Improve: 44%* *Collapse: 34%*

Where McLemore has managed to find new life with a zest only Ponce de Leon might appreciate, McMillon might have the weight of what could have been crushing down on him. He could have been a poor man's Bobby Abreu, adding moderate power and a ton of OBP. But getting blocked in Florida, then cycling through the Phillies and Tigers organizations at their worst moments really used up most of what should have been his best years. We could joke that he's headed to the *Moneyball* Eastern branch campus now that he's signed with Boston, but Pawtucket's just another place he'll get to call home in a career that's been wasted in the minors.

ADAM MELHUSE — C — Bats: B — Throws: R — Born: 27-Mar-1972 — Age: 33

YEAR	TM	LG	AGE	AB	H	2B	3B	HR	BB	SO	SB	CS	AVG	OBP	SLG	MLVR	EQBA	EQOBP	EQSLG	EQMLVR	VORP	DEFENSE	
2002	CSP	PCL	30	115	40	10	1	6	16	23	2	1	.348	.424	.609	.390	.288	.370	.505	.160	11.9	25-C -1	
2002	IOW	PCL	30	226	66	19	0	7	28	47	2	3	.292	.370	.469	.168	.268	.337	.420	-.035	9.6	45-C -5	11-3B 0
2003	SAC	PCL	31	147	42	9	0	3	26	32	0	1	.286	.394	.408	.133	.245	.342	.347	-.142	1.4	27-C 10	
2003	OAK	AL	31	77	23	7	0	5	9	19	0	0	.299	.372	.584	.338	.316	.374	.592	.320	11.0	20-C 1	
2004	OAK	AL	32	214	55	11	0	11	16	47	0	1	.257	.309	.463	-.025	.261	.309	.479	-.008	9.4	54-C -1	
2005	*OAK*	*AL*	*33*	*257*	*66*	*14*	*0*	*10*	*29*	*60*	*0*	*1*	*.256*	*.333*	*.427*	*-.031*	*.258*	*.337*	*.435*	*-.021*	*12.1*	*71-C -5*	

Breakout: 16% *Improve: 44%* *Collapse: 23%*

A backup catcher in the old Earl Weaver sense of the word, a guy you insert into the lineup to get some offense, and a good alternative to a catch-and-throw type who isn't hopeless at the plate. No, not Ellie Hendricks or Dave Skaggs; more like Dan Graham or Joe Nolan, as alternatives to Rick Dempsey. A handy bench player, Melhuse is unfortunately older than you might think now that he's here, and with Kendall in town, he won't be getting 257 at-bats.

DAMIAN MILLER — C — Bats: R — Throws: R — Born: 13-Oct-1969 — Age: 35

YEAR	TM	LG	AGE	AB	H	2B	3B	HR	BB	SO	SB	CS	AVG	OBP	SLG	MLVR	EQBA	EQOBP	EQSLG	EQMLVR	VORP	DEFENSE
2002	ARI	NL	32	297	74	22	0	11	38	88	0	0	.249	.340	.434	.020	.242	.329	.428	-.059	16.8	89-C 8
2003	CHC	NL	33	352	82	19	1	9	39	91	1	0	.233	.310	.369	-.121	.234	.312	.372	-.173	5.5	108-C 8
2004	OAK	AL	34	397	108	25	0	9	39	87	0	1	.272	.339	.403	-.043	.276	.343	.404	-.040	16.8	108-C 10
2005	*MIL*	*NL*	*35*	*268*	*65*	*14*	*1*	*7*	*30*	*70*	*0*	*0*	*.244*	*.320*	*.386*	*-.122*	*.243*	*.318*	*.386*	*-.128*	*5.2*	*74-C 4*

Breakout: 22% *Improve: 41%* *Collapse: 31%*

In a world predisposed to overcompensate guys like Mike Matheny or Brad Ausmus, there's something nice about seeing Miller cash in, even if it has to be with the Brewers. He's a more useful version than either one, yet still not a bargain at three years, $8.75 million guaranteed.

ADAM MORRISSEY 2B/3B Bats: R Throws: R Born: 08-Jun-1981 Age: 24

YEAR	TM	LG	AGE	AB	H	2B	3B	HR	BB	SO	SB	CS	AVG	OBP	SLG	MLVR	EQBA	EQOBP	EQSLG	EQMLVR	VORP	DEFENSE
2002	MOD	CLF	21	141	41	7	1	3	20	28	4	3	.291	.383	.418	.159	.252	.325	.357	-.157	0.8	28-2B -7
2002	MID	TXS	21	302	71	15	1	2	38	71	4	2	.235	.323	.311	-.143	.205	.280	.277	-.383	-19.5	83-2B -16
2003	MID	TXS	22	469	125	27	2	5	50	99	9	1	.267	.335	.365	-.045	.240	.305	.343	-.223	-6.0	105-3B -14 16-2B -3
2004	SAC	PCL	23	392	114	26	1	9	40	89	1	1	.291	.358	.431	.031	.255	.319	.370	-.148	2.9	72-2B -10 26-3B -3
2005	*OAK*	*AL*	*24*	*237*	*58*	*12*	*1*	*5*	*21*	*56*	*2*	*1*	*.246*	*.311*	*.365*	*-.157*	*.248*	*.314*	*.372*	*-.150*	*1.6*	*65-2B -12*

Breakout: 31% *Improve: 50%* *Collapse: 19%*

He's unfortunately statuesque when he tries to play second, and he's extremely raw at third. Since he doesn't have the offensive game that makes you want to deal with the problems he has at either position, he's certain to have to spend another year in Triple-A. A combination of youth, talent, and the relative inexperience you take for granted with Aussie imports are all reasons to hold out hope that Morrissey can improve.

JASON PERRY RF Bats: L Throws: R Born: 18-Aug-1980 Age: 24

YEAR	TM	LG	AGE	AB	H	2B	3B	HR	BB	SO	SB	CS	AVG	OBP	SLG	MLVR	EQBA	EQOBP	EQSLG	EQMLVR	VORP	DEFENSE
2003	DUN	FSL	22	135	41	11	1	1	10	32	1	0	.304	.356	.422	.165	.283	.323	.428	-.037	0.8	11-LF -2
2003	MOD	CLF	22	190	58	9	1	4	21	46	0	1	.305	.393	.426	.176	.267	.336	.377	-.098	-1.8	31-RF -5
2004	MOD	CLF	23	325	110	39	1	24	34	87	4	4	.338	.431	.686	.605	.258	.330	.515	.076	13.4	59-RF -3
2004	MID	TXS	23	81	16	5	1	1	4	23	3	1	.198	.275	.321	-.269	.159	.219	.256	-.558	-10.0	
2005	*OAK*	*AL*	*24*	*219*	*57*	*13*	*1*	*8*	*16*	*60*	*2*	*1*	*.261*	*.340*	*.446*	*.010*	*.263*	*.345*	*.454*	*.021*	*13.3*	*62-RF -4*

Breakout: 29% *Improve: 47%* *Collapse: 31%*

Having lost a good chunk of 2003 to back problems, the former Georgia Tech bopper had a nifty comeback, winning the Cal League MVP last year. Perry has to pursue an accelerated timetable that's the product of his age and the well-regarded kids coming up behind him, particularly Javier Herrera and top '04 choice Richie Robnett.

OMAR QUINTANILLA SS/2B Bats: L Throws: R Born: 24-Oct-1981 Age: 23

YEAR	TM	LG	AGE	AB	H	2B	3B	HR	BB	SO	SB	CS	AVG	OBP	SLG	MLVR	EQBA	EQOBP	EQSLG	EQMLVR	VORP	DEFENSE
2003	VAN	NWN	21	129	44	5	4	0	12	20	7	1	.341	.401	.442	.320	.282	.309	.359	-.164	2.7	29-SS -3
2004	MOD	CLF	22	451	142	32	5	11	37	54	1	3	.315	.370	.481	.195	.263	.311	.398	-.118	10.9	103-SS -9
2004	MID	TXS	22	94	33	10	0	2	10	9	2	0	.351	.419	.521	.361	.283	.333	.413	-.040	4.6	23-SS 3
2005	*OAK*	*AL*	*23*	*268*	*71*	*15*	*2*	*5*	*17*	*41*	*1*	*1*	*.266*	*.315*	*.396*	*-.095*	*.268*	*.319*	*.404*	*-.086*	*13.0*	*72-SS -4*

Breakout: 12% *Improve: 34%* *Collapse: 38%*

After a brilliant college career at Texas, Quintanilla was a 2003 supplemental first rounder, so he's supposed to move up fast. On that score, spending most of the year in A-ball was a disappointment. It's anticipated that quick hands and lack of range make him the team's second baseman of the future, but he'll have to first show continued improvement at the plate in a full season at Midland or Sacramento. His first month above A-ball at the end of the season was a good sign, but making contact in Midland is bound to make you look pretty good, and his power in the Cal League is pretty pedestrian after you make allowances for it being a high-octane hitting environment.

MIKE ROSE C Bats: B Throws: R Born: 25-Aug-1976 Age: 28

YEAR	TM	LG	AGE	AB	H	2B	3B	HR	BB	SO	SB	CS	AVG	OBP	SLG	MLVR	EQBA	EQOBP	EQSLG	EQMLVR	VORP	DEFENSE
2002	WIC	TXS	25	59	18	5	0	2	7	11	0	1	.305	.379	.492	.271	.254	.300	.407	-.133	-0.1	
2002	OMA	PCL	25	177	46	12	2	3	28	40	2	3	.260	.364	.401	.044	.249	.347	.379	-.087	4.8	42-C -10
2003	SAC	PCL	26	221	58	10	1	8	44	50	2	1	.262	.390	.425	.130	.242	.360	.399	-.040	9.3	61-C -9
2004	SAC	PCL	27	349	98	20	2	6	76	80	0	0	.281	.407	.401	.075	.251	.369	.347	-.086	9.6	83-C -10
2005	*LAD*	*NL*	*28*	*142*	*34*	*7*	*1*	*4*	*24*	*39*	*0*	*0*	*.242*	*.353*	*.383*	*-.068*	*.248*	*.358*	*.394*	*-.043*	*8.4*	*44-C -10*

Breakout: 32% *Improve: 49%* *Collapse: 33%*

After puttering around his hometown, Sacramento, for a couple of seasons, Rose will get a real opportunity to win a share of the playing time behind the plate in L.A. He might yet be the new Gregg Zaun, famed as the Practically Perfect Backup Catcher: He switch-hits, he hits well, and he can catch. He's also one of those guys that the front office new kids keep to themselves, like Tom Wilson or Jason Grabowski, getting flipped back and forth between Kansas City and L.A. and Oakland, and perhaps Toronto and Boston too when all is said and done.

MIKE ROUSE — INF — Bats: L — Throws: R — Born: 25-Apr-1980 — Age: 25

YEAR	TM	LG	AGE	AB	H	2B	3B	HR	BB	SO	SB	CS	AVG	OBP	SLG	MLVR	EQBA	EQOBP	EQSLG	EQMLVR	VORP	DEFENSE	
2002	TEN	SOU	22	231	60	11	0	9	29	47	7	6	.260	.342	.424	.056	.221	.282	.374	-.237	-2.4	57-SS -3	
2003	MID	TXS	23	457	137	33	3	3	63	83	7	2	.300	.392	.405	.122	.267	.351	.376	-.071	18.7	120-SS 10	
2004	SAC	PCL	24	323	89	11	2	10	50	68	0	4	.276	.379	.415	.034	.249	.344	.361	-.117	8.3	82-SS -4	10-2B -2
2005	*OAK*	*AL*	*25*	*172*	*43*	*9*	*1*	*4*	*19*	*36*	*1*	*1*	*.252*	*.333*	*.380*	*-.094*	*.253*	*.337*	*.387*	*-.085*	*10.1*	*51-SS -3*	

Breakout: 26% *Improve: 47%* *Collapse: 33%*

Coming over after the 2002 season, Rouse is another Blue Jay farmhand received by Oakland as payment for the Lend Lease pitching staff the organizations have conspired to put in Toronto over the last three years. Stealthily picking up steam, Rouse could end up giving this team the lefty-hitting infield reserve they'd love to have to alternate with Crosby, Ginter, and Ellis. With Omar Quintanilla coming up behind, and Rouse's seeming ability to keep getting nicked up, he might have to settle for being a bargaining chip for the A's.

MARCO SCUTARO — 2B — Bats: R — Throws: R — Born: 30-Oct-1975 — Age: 29

YEAR	TM	LG	AGE	AB	H	2B	3B	HR	BB	SO	SB	CS	AVG	OBP	SLG	MLVR	EQBA	EQOBP	EQSLG	EQMLVR	VORP	DEFENSE	
2002	NOR	INT	26	354	113	22	6	7	30	61	7	8	.319	.375	.475	.255	.311	.367	.468	.125	32.4	48-2B -6	25-SS 2
2003	NOR	INT	27	244	76	18	3	9	33	34	11	6	.311	.401	.520	.358	.303	.390	.518	.226	32.1	35-3B -1	23-2B -2
2003	NYM	NL	27	75	16	4	0	2	13	14	2	0	.213	.333	.347	-.110	.224	.321	.355	-.185	2.0	22-2B -3	
2004	OAK	AL	28	455	124	32	1	7	16	58	0	0	.273	.297	.393	-.136	.274	.303	.399	-.123	9.3	102-2B 8	13-SS 0
2005	*OAK*	*AL*	*29*	*402*	*106*	*23*	*2*	*10*	*28*	*61*	*3*	*2*	*.263*	*.314*	*.408*	*-.084*	*.265*	*.318*	*.415*	*-.075*	*14.3*	*105-2B -2*	

Breakout: 10% *Improve: 22%* *Collapse: 38%*

Scooter finally got his break, and he did do good stuff, mostly in the field, lacing 30-plus doubles. But on this team, his problems with working counts or getting on base stand out, and he has nothing like the hold over the organization that Ellis seems to command. He'll fight for a utility role, but if he loses, he'll be waiver bait, and given his price tag, experience, and performance, he won't make it through to Sacramento when he's outrighted.

BRIAN STAVISKY — LF/1B — Bats: L — Throws: R — Born: 06-Jul-1980 — Age: 24

YEAR	TM	LG	AGE	AB	H	2B	3B	HR	BB	SO	SB	CS	AVG	OBP	SLG	MLVR	EQBA	EQOBP	EQSLG	EQMLVR	VORP	DEFENSE	
2002	VAN	NWN	22	102	30	10	1	1	15	30	5	0	.294	.407	.441	.310	.264	.338	.400	-.064	-0.6	13-LF -1	
2003	KNC	MDW	23	331	88	20	2	6	62	74	4	1	.266	.396	.393	.188	.239	.341	.371	-.116	-6.7	14-LF -1	
2004	MOD	CLF	24	513	176	39	5	19	54	89	6	4	.343	.413	.550	.393	.285	.345	.450	.036	13.5	63-LF 1	32-1B -3
2005	*OAK*	*AL*	*24*	*283*	*75*	*17*	*2*	*8*	*28*	*64*	*2*	*1*	*.264*	*.343*	*.426*	*-.009*	*.266*	*.347*	*.434*	*.001*	*10.9*	*78-LF -7*	

Breakout: 19% *Improve: 46%* *Collapse: 30%*

The Domer nabbed in the sixth round of the now-famous 2002 draft, Stavisky was more of a DH than anything else when picked. He's made progress in left, learning to take better routes to balls, but his throwing arm is scattershot at best; the defensive half of every inning looks like it's always going to be something of an adventure for him. His bat's the only thing that can carry him, and making the jump to Double-A this year will tell us if he has a future.

NICK SWISHER — OF — Bats: B — Throws: L — Born: 25-Nov-1980 — Age: 24

YEAR	TM	LG	AGE	AB	H	2B	3B	HR	BB	SO	SB	CS	AVG	OBP	SLG	MLVR	EQBA	EQOBP	EQSLG	EQMLVR	VORP	DEFENSE	
2002	VIS	CLF	21	183	44	13	2	4	26	48	3	1	.240	.340	.399	-.007	.205	.285	.335	-.294	-8.2	38-CF -4	
2003	MOD	CLF	22	189	56	14	2	10	41	49	0	2	.296	.418	.550	.374	.246	.351	.440	.001	9.1	33-CF -4	
2003	MID	TXS	22	287	66	24	2	5	37	76	0	1	.230	.324	.380	-.067	.201	.287	.344	-.281	-11.8	61-CF -5	
2004	SAC	PCL	23	443	119	28	2	29	103	109	3	3	.269	.406	.537	.248	.232	.361	.438	.006	21.5	105-CF -10	11-RF -1
2004	OAK	AL	23	60	15	4	0	2	8	11	0	0	.250	.352	.417	-.019	.271	.351	.407	-.025	1.8	11-LF 0	
2005	*OAK*	*AL*	*24*	*327*	*80*	*17*	*2*	*13*	*50*	*87*	*1*	*2*	*.244*	*.351*	*.423*	*-.013*	*.246*	*.355*	*.431*	*-.003*	*14.7*	*93-CF -8*	

Breakout: 31% *Improve: 62%* *Collapse: 17%*

Poised for a big breakout, as we discuss in our Top Prospects segment later on. After recovering from a bad thumb in the early going, last year was the sort of step forward at the plate that Swisher needed to justify his prospect status. As a hitter, he learned the critical distinction between working counts to try to get his pitch and kill it, versus working counts for a walk as an end unto itself. In that sense, you can consider the A's old school: A walk isn't a bad result, but they teach their hitters that it isn't the ideal one. The optimal choice is to learn pitch identification, and know what to do with your pitch when you get it. Swisher's started doing that. There was also a concern that his gregariousness could become a nuisance, but everyone agrees that he seems to have settled down in the last year.

MATT WATSON OF **Bats: L** **Throws: R** Born: 05-Sep-1978 Age: 26

YEAR	TM	LG	AGE	AB	H	2B	3B	HR	BB	SO	SB	CS	AVG	OBP	SLG	MLVR	EQBA	EQOBP	EQSLG	EQMLVR	VORP	DEFENSE
2002	BIN	EAS	23	437	122	26	2	10	39	52	12	8	.279	.339	.416	.035	.248	.302	.376	-.177	-16.6	72-LF 1 30-RF -3
2003	NOR	INT	24	254	75	18	1	11	23	23	2	2	.295	.366	.504	.268	.287	.355	.504	.132	14.7	56-LF -2
2004	SAC	PCL	25	476	145	37	3	19	54	75	3	4	.305	.377	.515	.202	.270	.338	.440	-.004	8.4	102-RF -11 18-LF -2
2005	*OAK*	*AL*	*26*	*155*	*41*	*9*	*1*	*5*	*14*	*25*	*1*	*1*	*.264*	*.331*	*.426*	*-.030*	*.266*	*.335*	*.434*	*-.020*	*6.5*	*45-RF -5*

Breakout: 20% *Improve: 36%* *Collapse: 33%*

Waiting for his chance to be allowed to be the new Darren Bragg. Now, we know what you're saying, who wants to grow up to be that? But face it, there was some kid in your class who liked the scrubs instead of the stars, some kid who thought Margot Kidder made a cute Lois Lane, some kid who thought school lunches were tasty. There's no accounting for taste, and once you accept the basic utility of the things in question—scrubs, meals, or actresses—you can be broad-minded enough to accept Bragg 2.0. Watson has a shot at beating out Charles Thomas or Bobby Kielty for a reserve role, but it isn't a great shot, and his middling power and questionable defense are major handicaps.

PITCHERS

JOE BLANTON **Bats: R** **Throws: R** Born: 11-Dec-1980 Age: 24

YEAR	TM	LG	AGE	G	GS	IP	H	BB	SO	HR	ERA	EQERA	EQH9	EQBB9	EQSO9	EQHR9	PERA	VORP	STF
2002	VAN	NWN	21	4	2	14.3	11	2	15	0	3.15	5.54	8.3	1.4	5.5	0.0	2.77	4.1	11
2003	KNC	MDW	22	21	21	133.0	110	19	144	6	2.57	5.10	9.1	1.6	6.7	1.3	4.29	17.7	19
2003	MID	TXS	22	7	5	35.7	21	7	30	1	1.26	2.48	6.3	1.9	6.1	0.6	1.93	13.3	32
2004	SAC	PCL	23	28	26	176.3	199	34	143	13	4.19	5.17	9.0	1.8	5.5	0.7	3.47	41.2	20
2004	OAK	AL	23	3	0	8.0	6	2	6	1	5.62	4.70	7.0	2.3	7.0	1.2	3.52	0.6	14
2005	*OAK*	*AL*	*24*	*15*	*15*	*95.0*	*103*	*28*	*66*	*13*	*4.60*	*4.55*	*9.9*	*2.3*	*5.6*	*1.1*	*4.52*	*14.1*	*9*

Breakout: 8% *Improve: 32%* *Collapse: 28%*

It was almost a good year, and the problem is that at least a good year was expected of him. Blanton stayed healthy, he was mixing and matching his solid slider and curve with his low-90s heat, but he just never seemed to get into a real groove on the mound. The PCL isn't the best place for a starter to get on top of his game, but neither are the majors for a rookie. He has the command to pick his strikeout rate back up a notch and become the rotation horse that he's supposed to be, but Beane's wholesale acquisition of other people's pitching prospects this winter can't be considered an endorsement of Blanton as a sure thing.

STEVEN BONDURANT **Bats: L** **Throws: L** Born: 03-Mar-1980 Age: 25

YEAR	TM	LG	AGE	G	GS	IP	H	BB	SO	HR	ERA	EQERA	EQH9	EQBB9	EQSO9	EQHR9	PERA	VORP	STF
2003	VAN	NWN	23	14	8	58.7	51	20	54	5	3.53	6.88	10.1	4.0	4.8	2.8	6.02	-2.4	-13
2004	KNC	MDW	24	21	21	125.7	92	27	132	6	2.08	4.38	8.0	2.5	5.7	0.9	3.37	28.5	33
2004	MID	TXS	24	7	7	38.0	43	14	29	1	6.39	7.05	9.5	3.6	4.9	0.5	4.62	4.0	-1
2005	*OAK*	*AL*	*25*	*15*	*11*	*70.3*	*72*	*27*	*47*	*13*	*5.11*	*5.06*	*9.4*	*3.0*	*5.3*	*1.5*	*4.93*	*6.9*	*-2*

Breakout: 10% *Improve: 41%* *Collapse: 24%*

Picked in 2003 in the 15th round out of the University of South Carolina, Bondurant is already trekking down the crafty lefty career path, living and dying on his breaking stuff. He can get into the upper 80s, but he loses velocity early in his starts, and he's still learning where to safely spot that sort of fastball around the strike zone. As an older college product, like Blanton, he may skip the Cal League altogether. Bondurant's old enough that he needs to be pushed, otherwise he might not have any prospect status at all.

CHAD BRADFORD **Bats: R** **Throws: R** Born: 14-Sep-1974 Age: 30

YEAR	TM	LG	AGE	G	GS	IP	H	BB	SO	HR	ERA	EQERA	EQH9	EQBB9	EQSO9	EQHR9	PERA	VORP	STF
2002	OAK	AL	27	75	0	75.3	73	14	56	2	3.11	3.21	8.5	1.6	6.5	0.2	3.33	21.0	13
2003	OAK	AL	28	72	0	77.0	67	30	62	7	3.04	3.05	8.2	3.4	7.3	0.7	4.15	24.2	5
2004	OAK	AL	29	68	0	59.0	51	24	34	5	4.42	4.31	8.3	3.4	5.1	0.6	3.99	9.2	-7
2005	*OAK*	*AL*	*30*	*55*	*0*	*53.0*	*53*	*21*	*39*	*5*	*3.87*	*3.83*	*9.2*	*3.2*	*5.9*	*0.8*	*4.23*	*12.3*	*-4*

Breakout: 27% *Improve: 57%* *Collapse: 18%*

(continued next page)

Chad Bradford *(continued)*

In the way that Kent Tekulve was fun to simply watch, Bradford's an in-game delight. He's a big string bean of a guy, and on the mound there's a loopy, tentacle-like quality to his delivery. But where Teke was a bullpen workhorse, Bradford has been hidden in a situational role, becoming reliant on the intentional walk to protect him from any mildly dangerous left-handed hitter. Could he handle more? He's an extreme groundball pitcher, and that can be a good thing, but it can also be a defensive nuisance if he's constantly working with other people's runners on base, and the infielders constantly have to move around. It's worth noting that he's consistently worse than a DIPS believer would expect when it comes to allowing hits on balls in play, not surprising for an extreme groundballer. Now that Juan Cruz and Kiko Calero are A's, Bradford's reduced to a ROOGY here, or somebody else's setup man someplace else.

OCTAVIO DOTEL Bats: R Throws: R Born: 25-Nov-1973 Age: 31

YEAR	TM	LG	AGE	G	GS	IP	H	BB	SO	HR	ERA	EQERA	EQH9	EQBB9	EQSO9	EQHR9	PERA	VORP	STF
2002	HOU	NL	28	83	0	97.3	58	27	118	7	1.85	2.05	6.1	2.2	9.9	0.7	2.34	37.1	33
2003	HOU	NL	29	76	0	87.0	53	31	97	9	2.48	2.52	6.6	3.0	9.4	0.9	3.07	29.3	23
2004	HOU	NL	30	32	0	34.7	27	15	50	4	3.11	3.71	6.9	3.4	11.6	1.1	3.18	7.0	32
2004	OAK	AL	30	45	0	50.7	41	18	72	9	4.08	3.60	7.2	2.9	12.1	1.4	3.78	12.4	33
2005	*OAK*	*AL*	*31*	*57*	*1*	*80.7*	*59*	*28*	*82*	*12*	*3.21*	*3.17*	*6.6*	*2.8*	*8.1*	*1.3*	*3.21*	*27.7*	*12*

Breakout: 33% *Improve: 53%* *Collapse: 25%*

The object of the '04 Big Deal wasn't quite what he was cracked up to be. There was something intensely dissatisfying for any A's fan who has to watch that damned Kirk Gibson re-run every few days, then have to see their newfound closer's fastball get hammered. Blowing a half-dozen saves in a half-season doesn't please anybody, and there's no bragging right for vulturing wins in three of them. Dotel has the talent to dominate and become a premiere closer, but he also has to have the good sense to make adjustments.

JUSTIN DUCHSCHERER Bats: R Throws: R Born: 19-Nov-1977 Age: 27

YEAR	TM	LG	AGE	G	GS	IP	H	BB	SO	HR	ERA	EQERA	EQH9	EQBB9	EQSO9	EQHR9	PERA	VORP	STF
2002	SAC	PCL	24	14	11	63.0	73	17	52	7	5.57	6.39	9.4	2.5	5.7	1.2	4.21	9.6	2
2003	SAC	PCL	25	24	23	155.0	151	18	117	12	3.25	4.11	9.0	1.2	5.8	1.0	3.87	28.2	15
2003	OAK	AL	25	4	3	16.3	17	3	15	1	3.31	3.38	9.0	1.7	7.9	0.6	3.94	4.0	22
2004	OAK	AL	26	53	0	96.3	85	32	59	13	3.27	3.14	8.5	2.7	5.4	1.1	4.32	30.2	-6
2005	*OAK*	*AL*	*27*	*31*	*8*	*78.3*	*80*	*26*	*50*	*11*	*4.35*	*4.30*	*9.4*	*2.6*	*5.1*	*1.2*	*4.49*	*14.4*	*-5*

Breakout: 27% *Improve: 48%* *Collapse: 23%*

There were times during the season when Duchscherer seemed to be the only reliever the A's could hand a lead to. The veteran situational guys wallowed through some bad stretches, and Rhodes and Dotel were equally prone to give up that home run that would force folks to ask whether they wanted to hit the parking lot or stick around for the inevitable extra innings. So where'd Duchscherer come from? Back before people were afraid of dealing with the A's, he was a pickup from the Rangers for Luis Vizcaino. Hey, c'mon, Texas was a consenting adult. At any rate, for a modestly useful middle reliever, the A's got a more old-fashioned, more durable middle-relief animal. As a former starter, he could also step into the rotation in an emergency.

JAIRO GARCIA Bats: R Throws: R Born: 07-Mar-1983 Age: 22

YEAR	TM	LG	AGE	G	GS	IP	H	BB	SO	HR	ERA	EQERA	EQH9	EQBB9	EQSO9	EQHR9	PERA	VORP	STF
2003	KNC	MDW	20	14	9	42.3	40	19	28	0	2.55	4.85	9.2	5.1	3.9	0.2	4.62	4.2	-10
2004	KNC	MDW	21	25	0	30.0	16	6	49	0	0.30	2.30	6.6	2.3	8.9	0.3	2.30	10.0	27
2004	MID	TXS	21	13	0	18.0	10	15	32	0	1.50	2.70	6.5	8.6	11.9	0.0	3.78	3.4	23
2004	SAC	PCL	21	11	0	13.7	10	9	21	1	3.94	4.15	6.9	6.2	11.1	0.7	4.15	2.1	22
2004	OAK	AL	21	4	0	5.7	5	9	5	3	12.63	11.12	9.5	12.7	7.9	4.8	9.53	-4.0	-35
2005	*OAK*	*AL*	*22*	*22*	*5*	*49.3*	*39*	*31*	*49*	*6*	*4.48*	*4.43*	*7.2*	*4.9*	*8.0*	*1.0*	*4.29*	*8.0*	*5*

Breakout: 23% *Improve: 65%* *Collapse: 9%*

A righty with a true over-the-top delivery isn't something we see so much of these days, but it's that motion which makes it that much harder to pick up Garcia's moving mid-90s fastball. If there's a problem, it's that the heater is his only consistent offering; the breaking stuff is all in the developmental stage. Rushing him through the system was a bit of wishcasting run amok. As much as he was overpowering people, a pitcher who struggles to walk less than a man per inning above A-ball isn't ready for the big leagues. If the A's are smart they'll give him a repeat engagement in Triple-A, and the time in which to earn a longer visit to the majors this year.

CHRIS HAMMOND **Bats: L** **Throws: L** Born: 21-Jan-1966 Age: 39

YEAR	TM	LG	AGE	G	GS	IP	H	BB	SO	HR	ERA	EQERA	EQH9	EQBB9	EQSO9	EQHR9	PERA	VORP	STF
2002	ATL	NL	36	63	0	76.0	53	31	63	1	0.95	2.02	7.3	3.3	6.9	0.1	3.28	30.4	12
2003	NYY	AL	37	62	0	63.0	65	11	45	5	2.86	3.19	8.6	1.5	6.2	0.7	3.19	19.7	7
2004	OAK	AL	38	41	0	53.7	56	13	34	4	2.68	3.10	9.1	2.1	5.5	0.5	4.13	16.5	-1
2005	*SDP*	*NL*	*39*	*44*	*0*	*49.3*	*48*	*16*	*34*	*4*	*3.49*	*3.97*	*9.0*	*2.6*	*5.4*	*0.7*	*4.27*	*8.8*	*-4*

Breakout: 11% *Improve: 53%* *Collapse: 13%*

By the time the A's added Hammond on top of Rhodes and picking aspiring LOOGY Frank Brooks in the Rule 5 Draft, you had to wonder if anyone upstairs was keeping track of how many lefties the A's had in tow. If it was an attempt to get a trade offer for one of them, the offer never came, and Brooks was given back to the Pirates. They're doing a bit of it this year, picking up Tyler Johnson from the Cardinals through Rule 5, but Hammond and Rhodes have both been punted. If a team will accept that Hammond's value is as a middle reliever, and not as a situational specialist, they'll be doing themselves a favor. Step right up, Padres.

RICH HARDEN **Bats: L** **Throws: R** Born: 30-Nov-1981 Age: 23

YEAR	TM	LG	AGE	G	GS	IP	H	BB	SO	HR	ERA	EQERA	EQH9	EQBB9	EQSO9	EQHR9	PERA	VORP	STF
2002	VIS	CLF	20	12	12	67.7	49	24	85	4	2.92	4.60	7.9	3.7	6.8	0.9	3.88	12.0	30
2002	MID	TXS	20	16	16	85.3	67	52	102	2	2.95	4.35	7.5	5.9	8.3	0.3	3.79	16.2	35
2003	SAC	PCL	21	16	14	88.7	72	35	91	6	3.15	4.12	7.9	4.1	8.0	0.8	3.90	15.7	38
2003	OAK	AL	21	15	13	74.7	72	40	67	5	4.46	4.19	8.5	4.7	7.9	0.5	4.56	12.5	33
2004	OAK	AL	22	31	31	189.7	171	81	167	16	3.99	3.79	8.1	3.5	7.6	0.7	3.93	41.3	25
2005	*OAK*	*AL*	*23*	*25*	*25*	*148.3*	*143*	*65*	*124*	*19*	*4.46*	*4.41*	*8.8*	*3.5*	*6.7*	*1.0*	*4.39*	*23.8*	*13*

Breakout: 12% *Improve: 37%* *Collapse: 26%*

It was interesting to watch as the rotation started to fray down the stretch, because Harden very nearly wound up being the hero. In August, with Hudson absent, Mulder and Zito struggling and Redman giving up 11 homers in five starts, it was Harden who starred, posting a 2.97 ERA. Who knows, if Macha doesn't reshuffle the rotation in the middle of September, the Angels would have drawn Harden in the clinching 161st game, and Zito the next day, and things might have been different. Although PECOTA is being modest, in part that's a product of Harden's youth. He'll be one of the 10 best starters in the league this year.

TIM HUDSON **Bats: R** **Throws: R** Born: 14-Jul-1975 Age: 29

YEAR	TM	LG	AGE	G	GS	IP	H	BB	SO	HR	ERA	EQERA	EQH9	EQBB9	EQSO9	EQHR9	PERA	VORP	STF
2002	OAK	AL	26	34	34	238.3	237	62	152	19	2.98	3.10	8.9	2.2	5.6	0.7	4.11	71.4	15
2003	OAK	AL	27	34	34	240.0	197	61	162	15	2.70	2.98	8.1	2.3	6.2	0.5	3.54	78.2	22
2004	OAK	AL	28	27	27	188.7	194	44	103	8	3.53	3.49	9.0	1.9	4.7	0.3	3.88	48.6	16
2005	*ATL*	*NL*	*29*	*27*	*27*	*167.7*	*170*	*47*	*105*	*14*	*3.65*	*3.86*	*9.2*	*2.2*	*5.1*	*0.7*	*4.00*	*31.8*	*10*

Breakout: 22% *Improve: 60%* *Collapse: 18%*

You know people are finding reasons to complain when there's grousing that Hudson might be too athletic, too good at trying to be a fifth infielder, too likely to wear himself out doing the parts of his job beyond pitching. Still, those are qualities the Braves like in their pitchers; Maddux and Glavine were always good in every phase of the game, and Hampton does everything well (except pitch). There are whispers that Huddy's splitter won't be going with him to Atlanta due to injury, which might be a non-financial reason for the deal, and for the precipitous drop in his strikeout rate. If so, it'll make for an interesting problem for Mr. Mazzone.

BRAD KNOX **Bats: R** **Throws: R** Born: 27-May-1982 Age: 23

YEAR	TM	LG	AGE	G	GS	IP	H	BB	SO	HR	ERA	EQERA	EQH9	EQBB9	EQSO9	EQHR9	PERA	VORP	STF
2003	VAN	NWN	21	15	12	70.0	55	18	63	2	2.06	5.18	8.4	2.9	4.6	0.8	3.50	15.0	14
2004	KNC	MDW	22	26	25	156.3	141	24	174	11	2.59	4.66	9.3	1.7	6.0	1.4	4.22	22.2	15
2005	*OAK*	*AL*	*23*	*15*	*15*	*89.7*	*95*	*24*	*61*	*12*	*4.41*	*4.37*	*9.7*	*2.1*	*5.5*	*1.2*	*4.37*	*14.9*	*9*

Breakout: 9% *Improve: 45%* *Collapse: 17%*

A less famous (or infamous) pick from the '02 draft in the 14th round, Knox is a juco product who spins a nifty curve. Back trouble ended his '04 season early, but it may also have permitted a risk, as the A's left him off of their 40-man roster and nobody picked him. He completely outclassed the Midwest League, but he wasn't that young for the level, and the Cal League has a nasty habit of chewing pitchers up. Still, Knox's command merits attention; he could start moving up fast.

JUSTIN LEHR
Bats: R **Throws: R** Born: 03-Aug-1977 Age: 27

YEAR	TM	LG	AGE	G	GS	IP	H	BB	SO	HR	ERA	EQERA	EQH9	EQBB9	EQSO9	EQHR9	PERA	VORP	STF
2002	MID	TXS	24	58	0	80.0	88	31	59	7	4.05	5.09	10.1	3.8	5.1	1.5	5.57	0.3	-22
2003	SAC	PCL	25	53	0	75.0	74	27	64	3	3.72	4.77	8.7	3.6	6.5	0.5	4.02	12.6	1
2004	SAC	PCL	26	32	0	37.3	37	10	40	1	2.65	3.68	8.1	2.5	7.4	0.2	2.95	10.8	11
2004	OAK	AL	26	27	0	32.7	35	14	16	3	5.23	4.50	9.3	3.4	4.2	0.8	4.78	3.8	-16
2005	*MIL*	*NL*	*27*	*30*	*0*	*29.0*	*30*	*11*	*21*	*3*	*4.21*	*4.37*	*9.2*	*3.0*	*5.7*	*0.9*	*4.53*	*4.3*	*-6*

Breakout: 28% *Improve: 49%* *Collapse: 24%*

Another former position player turned pitcher, "Panzer" has a nifty power assortment: a mid-90s four-seam fastball, a mid-80s splitter he doesn't tip out of a sneaky delivery, and a solid curveball. Although the A's gave him a look, he never did get consistent work, so it was hard for him to settle in. He could become a much more significant asset in Milwaukee's pen than PECOTA's allowing for.

CHRIS MABEUS
Bats: R **Throws: R** Born: 11-Feb-1979 Age: 26

YEAR	TM	LG	AGE	G	GS	IP	H	BB	SO	HR	ERA	EQERA	EQH9	EQBB9	EQSO9	EQHR9	PERA	VORP	STF
2002	MOD	CLF	23	37	1	84.7	97	32	69	3	4.04	5.14	9.8	3.7	4.2	0.5	5.14	4.2	-18
2003	MOD	CLF	24	18	0	23.7	19	6	30	1	1.52	3.68	8.2	2.9	7.4	0.8	3.68	4.7	8
2003	MID	TXS	24	32	0	38.3	37	9	40	1	3.52	5.11	8.3	2.4	7.1	0.5	3.16	10.0	9
2004	MID	TXS	25	20	0	22.7	23	2	27	0	1.98	2.86	9.0	0.8	7.4	0.4	3.27	5.7	13
2004	SAC	PCL	25	38	0	51.0	45	12	61	6	3.00	3.49	7.9	2.2	8.3	1.1	3.12	13.5	12
2005	*OAK*	*AL*	*26*	*47*	*0*	*59.3*	*58*	*20*	*50*	*7*	*4.13*	*4.09*	*8.9*	*2.7*	*6.7*	*1.0*	*4.03*	*12.0*	*2*

Breakout: 22% *Improve: 44%* *Collapse: 28%*

On some level, Mabeus is still learning how to play the game, relative to other players his age: Growing up in Alaska didn't afford him a lot of long springs to get into lots of amateur competition. A relative dark horse overshadowed by fellow rookies Garcia and Street going into camp, Mabeus deserves equal consideration. He can dial it up into the mid 90s, mixes in the occasional slider and splitter, and he's got the upper-level track record for success that the other two lack.

JIM MECIR
Bats: B **Throws: R** Born: 16-May-1970 Age: 35

YEAR	TM	LG	AGE	G	GS	IP	H	BB	SO	HR	ERA	EQERA	EQH9	EQBB9	EQSO9	EQHR9	PERA	VORP	STF
2002	OAK	AL	32	61	0	67.7	68	29	53	5	4.25	4.36	8.7	3.5	6.8	0.5	4.23	8.9	2
2003	OAK	AL	33	41	0	37.0	40	16	25	4	5.59	5.50	9.5	3.8	6.0	1.0	5.25	0.1	-10
2004	OAK	AL	34	65	0	47.7	45	19	49	5	3.58	3.45	8.2	3.3	8.8	0.8	4.02	12.3	12
2005	*OAK*	*AL*	*35*	*46*	*0*	*39.0*	*39*	*16*	*32*	*4*	*4.19*	*4.15*	*9.0*	*3.3*	*6.7*	*0.9*	*4.31*	*7.7*	*-1*

Breakout: 29% *Improve: 46%* *Collapse: 24%*

Gimpy gave it his best shot again, this time turning in a season as good as someone pitching on one leg can possibly expect. He's a bit of a unique bullpen problem or asset: He isn't durable enough to be a middle reliever, and as a screwball pitcher, it takes a manager thoughtful enough to not simply press him into situational use to get what mileage there is to get out of him. As of mid-January, he's wavering between retiring and finding somebody willing to give him one last season. A's fans can remember him fondly as the reliever who was solid during last year's stretch run.

MARK MULDER
Bats: L **Throws: L** Born: 05-Aug-1977 Age: 27

YEAR	TM	LG	AGE	G	GS	IP	H	BB	SO	HR	ERA	EQERA	EQH9	EQBB9	EQSO9	EQHR9	PERA	VORP	STF
2002	OAK	AL	24	30	30	207.3	182	55	159	21	3.47	3.59	8.3	2.3	6.8	0.9	3.82	49.8	21
2003	OAK	AL	25	26	26	186.7	180	40	128	15	3.13	3.02	8.8	1.9	6.2	0.7	3.97	60.2	20
2004	OAK	AL	26	33	33	225.7	223	83	140	25	4.43	4.20	8.9	3.0	5.4	0.9	4.49	37.2	7
2005	*STL*	*NL*	*27*	*28*	*28*	*182.0*	*180*	*61*	*131*	*16*	*3.78*	*4.05*	*8.9*	*2.7*	*5.8*	*0.8*	*4.19*	*30.8*	*12*

Breakout: 16% *Improve: 49%* *Collapse: 13%*

As glorious as it was that Mulder dispelled concerns about his hip from the get-go last year, his second-half collapse was agonizing. He was 12–2, 3.21 ERA before the All-Star break, and 5–6 with a 6.13 ERA after. Nobody thinks he was hurt, and the A's are pretty careful in how they handle their rotation. Mulder has said he was putting pressure on himself after Hudson got hurt in July. It wasn't like he was consistently awful in July and August: He was alternating quality starts and rougher outings into mid-September, when he went into a ditch in his last four starts, giving up 25 runs in 15.2 IP and boosting his season ERA from 3.90 to 4.43. So let's give him, and Walt Jocketty, some benefit of the doubt.

If there's a potential source of concern, it's that Mulder was the beneficiary of the highest rate of induced double plays in double-play situations last year, and equaling that as a Cardinal with David Eckstein at shortstop seems highly doubtful. Such are the risks of being one of the game's extreme groundball pitchers. Keep in mind, even if his infield defense presents a problem and PECOTA's mild pessimism is right, he could still win 20 games with the Cardinals lineup scoring runs for him

MARK REDMAN **Bats: L** **Throws: L** Born: 05-Jan-1974 Age: 31

YEAR	TM	LG	AGE	G	GS	IP	H	BB	SO	HR	ERA	EQERA	EQH9	EQBB9	EQSO9	EQHR9	PERA	VORP	STF
2002	DET	AL	28	30	30	203.0	211	51	109	15	4.21	4.55	8.9	2.1	4.6	0.6	3.45	27.9	11
2003	FLA	NL	29	29	29	190.7	172	61	151	16	3.59	4.01	8.2	2.5	6.6	0.7	3.47	38.7	21
2004	OAK	AL	30	32	32	191.0	218	68	102	28	4.71	4.57	9.9	2.9	4.6	1.2	5.25	22.2	-2
2005	*PIT*	*NL*	*31*	*27*	*24*	*143.7*	*159*	*50*	*88*	*19*	*4.92*	*5.21*	*9.9*	*2.7*	*4.9*	*1.2*	*5.16*	*8.3*	*0*

Breakout: 10% *Improve: 39%* *Collapse: 25%*

Clubhouse Bolshevik or clubhouse lawyer, which term has the more negative connotations these days? Either way, the euphemism used when Redman was dealt was that he didn't "fit in." He's annoyed managers and organizations in the past, and we've been willing to chalk it up to things like Tom Kelly's orneriness. But there comes a point when you ask if it's something else. Redman's no more than a useful fourth starter, so why put up with him if you don't want to? A move back to the NL should make his life easier than PECOTA allows for, but the number that won't come back is that 2003 K/9 column.

JOHN RHEINECKER **Bats: L** **Throws: L** Born: 29-May-1979 Age: 26

YEAR	TM	LG	AGE	G	GS	IP	H	BB	SO	HR	ERA	EQERA	EQH9	EQBB9	EQSO9	EQHR9	PERA	VORP	STF
2002	VIS	CLF	23	9	9	50.7	41	10	62	2	2.31	3.97	8.1	2.1	6.4	0.6	3.40	11.7	23
2002	MID	TXS	23	20	20	128.0	137	24	100	7	3.38	5.21	9.5	1.8	5.3	0.9	4.18	19.4	13
2003	MID	TXS	24	23	23	142.3	186	32	89	13	4.74	6.07	10.7	2.2	4.2	1.5	5.36	3.7	-13
2003	SAC	PCL	24	6	6	38.0	47	12	26	1	3.79	5.06	9.9	3.1	5.1	0.2	4.58	4.2	0
2004	SAC	PCL	25	28	27	172.3	194	51	129	22	4.44	5.35	9.3	2.8	5.1	1.2	4.33	23.7	-1
2005	*OAK*	*AL*	*26*	*19*	*10*	*69.7*	*77*	*22*	*45*	*9*	*4.74*	*4.69*	*10.0*	*2.5*	*5.2*	*1.1*	*4.69*	*8.7*	*-1*

Breakout: 10% *Improve: 42%* *Collapse: 26%*

Rumors in the game are part of its fun, and one of its guiltier pleasures is slyly making a player appear more of a prospect than he is. Rheinecker gets mentioned as someone who won't get traded but his is not the sort of talent that breaks a deal. Perhaps it makes him seem more valuable, but he's a standard-issue organizational lefty. He's worked on diversifying his assortment, improving his slider and the movement on his cut fastball, but he's no more likely to get any big league consideration this year than he was in the last. If he is ever dealt, you can expect his employer to eventually wonder what the fuss was all about.

ARTHUR RHODES **Bats: L** **Throws: L** Born: 24-Oct-1969 Age: 35

YEAR	TM	LG	AGE	G	GS	IP	H	BB	SO	HR	ERA	EQERA	EQH9	EQBB9	EQSO9	EQHR9	PERA	VORP	STF
2002	SEA	AL	32	66	0	69.7	45	13	81	4	2.32	2.44	6.4	1.6	10.3	0.5	2.17	28.2	37
2003	SEA	AL	33	67	0	54.0	53	18	48	4	4.17	4.13	8.8	2.9	7.9	0.7	4.30	11.6	9
2004	OAK	AL	34	37	0	38.7	46	21	34	9	5.12	4.66	10.0	4.4	7.4	1.9	6.28	4.0	-9
2005	*CLE*	*AL*	*35*	*56*	*0*	*42.3*	*41*	*18*	*39*	*5*	*4.12*	*4.04*	*8.7*	*3.3*	*7.5*	*1.0*	*4.22*	*9.5*	*3*

Breakout: 29% *Improve: 55%* *Collapse: 25%*

It sure seemed like a good idea at the time, but Rhodes just didn't turn into that block of late-inning ice that Beane thought he'd get when he gave Arthur Lee a three-year, $9.2 million deal, theoretically to be a Yankee killer. Instead, he seemed to start dissolving in his new surroundings, struggling on the mound and through back trouble that seemed to sap his velocity, before he finally started popping off about people's expectations. Those on the beat will say this says something about how making "non-closers" your closer is a bad idea, but a quick gander at his performance record should remind everyone that Rhodes was struggling in 2003—without getting a full season of save opportunities. Can he get it back in Cleveland? Not to the level that got him that contract, and not when he's counting on a cut fastball to get by, but he should be a better option than Cliff Bartosh.

RICARDO RINCON

Bats: L **Throws: L** Born: 13-Apr-1970 Age: 35

YEAR	TM	LG	AGE	G	GS	IP	H	BB	SO	HR	ERA	EQERA	EQH9	EQBB9	EQSO9	EQHR9	PERA	VORP	STF
2002	CLE	AL	32	46	0	35.7	36	8	30	3	4.79	4.84	8.2	1.8	7.1	0.8	3.06	2.7	10
2002	OAK	AL	32	25	0	20.3	11	3	19	1	3.10	2.84	6.2	1.4	8.5	0.5	1.89	6.5	25
2003	OAK	AL	33	64	0	55.3	45	32	40	4	3.25	3.25	8.0	5.1	6.5	0.7	4.44	16.5	-5
2004	OAK	AL	34	67	0	44.0	45	22	40	3	3.68	3.92	8.7	3.9	7.6	0.6	4.33	8.7	4
2005	*OAK*	*AL*	*35*	*64*	*0*	*36.0*	*36*	*17*	*29*	*4*	*4.52*	*4.47*	*9.2*	*3.8*	*6.4*	*0.9*	*4.61*	*6.1*	*-6*

Breakout: 25% *Improve: 44%* *Collapse: 28%*

There comes a point in a situational lefty's career when the right-handers you're allowed to face keep clocking you, and your manager has you walking the best of them, which means you're even worse at it than your simple platoon split shows. That's the point of your career when you're withering into Oroscan irrelevance. Like Jesse, Rincon will hang around, but now that his value is against those few lefty hitters who won't get pulled with the game on the line, he's a better postseason roster asset than a player who adds a lot of value over 162 games. During the season's long haul, a guy like this encourages managers to carry seven relievers, and the tactical value basically washes out over that length of time.

KIRK SAARLOOS

Bats: R **Throws: R** Born: 23-May-1979 Age: 26

YEAR	TM	LG	AGE	G	GS	IP	H	BB	SO	HR	ERA	EQERA	EQH9	EQBB9	EQSO9	EQHR9	PERA	VORP	STF
2002	ROU	TXS	23	13	13	83.3	48	21	82	1	1.40	3.07	6.5	2.6	7.0	0.2	2.24	28.5	32
2002	HOU	NL	23	17	17	85.3	100	27	54	12	6.01	5.89	9.9	2.5	5.0	1.2	4.82	-6.8	0
2003	NWO	PCL	24	13	7	61.3	54	11	34	4	3.08	4.15	8.9	1.9	4.5	1.0	4.31	8.1	6
2003	HOU	NL	24	36	4	49.3	55	17	43	4	4.93	5.36	9.4	2.8	7.0	0.7	4.62	-0.1	9
2004	SAC	PCL	25	5	5	20.3	19	9	17	1	3.55	3.66	7.8	4.1	5.9	0.5	3.20	5.3	8
2004	OAK	AL	25	6	5	24.3	27	12	10	4	4.44	4.18	9.9	4.2	3.4	1.1	5.70	3.9	-13
2005	*OAK*	*AL*	*26*	*22*	*11*	*77.0*	*81*	*28*	*51*	*9*	*4.51*	*4.46*	*9.7*	*2.8*	*5.3*	*1.0*	*4.55*	*11.5*	*-1*

Breakout: 23% *Improve: 47%* *Collapse: 25%*

As a type, we don't really invest the "crafty righty" with any particular magic, not unless he's grizzled or colorful. But what if you're a clean-shaven guy at the start of your career, and your calling cards are throwing strikes and a nice change-up? For starters, you get dumped, as Saarloos effectively was by the Astros. When you finally do get a look from the one organization willing to look past your limitations, it probably isn't a good idea to hurt your elbow. He's a question mark after elbow surgery, so you can probably toss him into that same mental dustbin as other delightfully-monikered sometime A's, like Joe Slusarski, Will Schock, or Big Bird Birtsas.

HUSTON STREET

Bats: R **Throws: R** Born: 02-Aug-1983 Age: 21

YEAR	TM	LG	AGE	G	GS	IP	H	BB	SO	HR	ERA	EQERA	EQH9	EQBB9	EQSO9	EQHR9	PERA	VORP	STF
2004	KNC	MDW	20	9	0	10.7	9	5	14	0	1.68	3.60	8.1	5.4	7.2	0.0	3.60	2.2	4
2004	MID	TXS	20	10	0	13.3	10	3	14	0	1.35	2.19	7.3	2.2	7.3	0.0	2.92	3.7	17
2005	*OAK*	*AL*	*21*	*34*	*5*	*63.3*	*62*	*27*	*51*	*7*	*4.20*	*4.16*	*9.0*	*3.3*	*6.5*	*0.9*	*4.28*	*14.7*	*1*

Breakout: 7% *Improve: 35%* *Collapse: 27%*

A pitching prospect that both scouts and statheads might like? How unusual. Scouts love his moxie and improved velocity, and statheads are probably over-ready to sign on because he's Oakland property. The former closer for the Texas Longhorns was available with the 40th pick of last year's draft, in part because his velocity had dropped into the high 80s during the college season. But he was throwing in the low 90s again once he turned pro, and he'd never lost touch with his tremendous slider. Street will get a chance to step into the big leagues straight out of spring training; PECOTA is surprisingly optimistic, given his relative lack of pro experience.

KEIICHI YABU Bats: R Throws: R Born: 28-Sep-1968 Age: 36

YEAR	TM	LG	AGE	G	GS	IP	H	BB	SO	HR	ERA	EQERA	EQH9	EQBB9	EQSO9	EQHR9	PERA	VORP	STF
2002	HNS	JCL	33	20	15	131.7	118	30	97	14	3.14	4.34	9.2	2.8	5.1	1.1	4.56	13.7	3
2003	HNS	JCL	34	23	15	97.7	97	27	67	13	3.96	4.85	9.1	3.2	4.9	1.1	4.55	10.6	-3
2004	HNS	JCL	35	19	18	116.3	108	36	75	8	3.02	3.63	8.4	3.3	4.5	0.5	3.80	21.3	7
2005	*OAK*	*AL*	*36*	*25*	*14*	*94.0*	*102*	*37*	*54*	*12*	*4.62*	*4.57*	*9.9*	*3.1*	*4.6*	*0.1*	*4.85*	*13.1*	*-6*

Breakout: 24% *Improve: 49%* *Collapse: 13%*

What's the former Hanshin star do? The comparison Billy Beane has made is to Shigetoshi Hasegawa, which, although not awe-inspiring, at least isn't terrible. Perhaps predictably, Yabu has a broad assortment, including a splitter, with velocity that sometimes tops 90. Keep in mind, his '04 was significantly better than his previous seasons in terms of hits and home runs allowed, and he was playing in a pitcher's park. For a million bucks plus incentives, the A's were willing to see what will happen if he can win the fifth slot in the rotation; if that doesn't work out, putting him in the pen isn't the end of the world.

BARRY ZITO Bats: L Throws: L Born: 13-May-1978 Age: 27

YEAR	TM	LG	AGE	G	GS	IP	H	BB	SO	HR	ERA	EQERA	EQH9	EQBB9	EQSO9	EQHR9	PERA	VORP	STF
2002	OAK	AL	24	35	35	229.3	182	78	182	24	2.75	2.94	7.8	2.9	7.1	0.9	3.72	73.4	21
2003	OAK	AL	25	35	35	231.7	186	88	146	19	3.30	3.56	8.1	3.4	5.8	0.7	4.06	58.6	13
2004	OAK	AL	26	34	34	213.0	216	81	163	28	4.48	4.32	8.9	3.1	6.6	1.0	4.58	31.5	12
2005	*OAK*	*AL*	*27*	*30*	*30*	*177.7*	*174*	*67*	*133*	*24*	*4.37*	*4.33*	*8.9*	*3.0*	*6.0*	*1.1*	*4.32*	*30.6*	*10*

Breakout: 22% *Improve: 50%* *Collapse: 19%*

There's no point in complaining about run support—Zito simply had his worst year yet. The expected won-lost record from how he pitched would have been 11–13; he actually finished 11–11. Maybe he has too many distractions, or maybe he creates them. Maybe the league's seen his bag of tricks often enough. He'll still flash that knee-buckling bender now and again, but it's been two years since has been able to snap those off for strikes at will. Vida Blue didn't age that well either, and he had more talent than Zito. Still, PECOTA seems to like his odds of taking a step back in the right direction, probably in part because he made up lost ground in striking people out.

Seattle Mariners

The Mariners' search for a general manager to replace the legendary Pat Gillick settled on a who-dat choice: Bill Bavasi, former GM of the Angels and then a functionary with the Dodgers. Seattle fans scratched their heads—how could someone they had never heard of take over for the man regarded by some as the best in the business?

He couldn't. Surprise! Gillick hadn't retired so much as decided he wanted to control personnel decisions without the aggravation from fans and the press that accompanies being GM. The show would be run by Gillick and Mariners President Howard Lincoln. Bavasi would take the blame if things turned out badly, but Gillick, as active advisor, would get to share in the credit if things went well. It was a cowardly move by Gillick.

First on Gillick's to-do list for Bavasi: sign Raul Ibanez, identified by the team's baseball minds as the left-handed power bat the offense desperately needed—a gap hitter who could exploit the wide power alleys at Safeco. A former Mariner who'd failed to win Lou Piniella's favor, Ibanez became an average left fielder in Kansas City while earning a reputation as a great clubhouse guy and community leader—important qualifications for the M's ownership.

Before the market for average left fielders was set at one or two years for a couple million annually, the Mariners spent $13 million to sign the 31-year old Ibanez to a three-year deal, and they couldn't do it fast enough. The Royals did not intend to offer Ibanez arbitration, but the Mariners signed him early anyway, allowing the Royals to take the M's first-round pick as compensation.

Seattle management didn't care. The organization felt the cost of taking a gamble on first-round draft picks to be not worth it, that the money would be better spent on foreign amateurs outside the draft, and in pursuing players considered unsignable later in the draft by buying them out of their unsignability.

That may seem like a reasonable argument in some ways. However, other teams find ways to identify quality players in the draft. The Mariners, having experienced failure of their own making, declared the whole process stupid and gave up. In 2000, the Mariners didn't draft until the fourth round. When they couldn't get out of picking, they drafted high school pitchers and tools goofs. No draft conducted by Frank Mattox and Pat Gillick has reaped anything valuable. The last time the Mariners had a first-round pick with star potential was in 1997, when they selected Ryan Anderson, a tall, left-handed high school pitcher.

MARINERS PROSPECTUS

2004 record: 63–99; Fourth place, AL West

Pythagenport record: 68–94

Runs scored per game: 4.31 (14th in AL)

Runs allowed per game: 5.08 (7th in AL)

Team EqA: .255 (10th in AL)

2004 Batters Age: 32.1 (2nd oldest in AL)

2004 Pitchers Age: 30.9 (4th oldest in AL)

Ballpark: Safeco Field; Severe pitcher's park; Park Factor of 0.942

2004: Pinning their fortunes on old men caught up to the Mariners with a vengeance.

2005: Dropped a ton of cheddar on two corner infielders, but they'll rise or fall with the performance of a suspect pitching staff.

In stark contrast to their total failure in the draft was the team's superb Pacific Rim operation, as well as its international and independent league scouting. However, after striking it rich with Ichiro Suzuki, the M's watched as the best Japanese free agents went to other clubs, such as the White Sox and Padres. International signings elsewhere continue to pay dividends, though, with the M's producing a solid crop of players that stayed together in the system, reaching Triple-A Tacoma last year. The problem so far has been finding and developing young talent with the potential to be impact players, not just back-end starters or cheap relievers.

Which brings us back to the house Bill Bavasi bought. Raul Ibanez was the first part of a simple plan: trade defense for offense and grit. Gillick and company would purge their perceived problems by bringing in solid, unremarkable team leaders: from general manager to left fielder, all the way down to pinch-hitter. The result? Nearly every move was a disaster.

Mike Cameron, criticized for years by the team for striking out too much, despite his other offensive contributions and stellar defense, was not even offered arbitration. This was regardless of his enthusiastic desire to return and his willingness to work out a deal. Randy

Winn, who had turned in a good two-way performance in left field, moved to center, where it was thought his bat could carry his glove. He was replaced in left by Ibanez, a much worse defender who pulled himself up to an average contribution by hitting decently.

Carlos Guillen had long been regarded as too fragile due to a series of unrelated freak injuries. This in addition to a DUI stop combined with a belief that he contributed to Freddy Garcia's . . . uh . . . lifestyle choices soured management on him. He was discarded and replaced with Rich Aurilia. Aurilia hadn't hit for power since injuring his elbow years before, and there was a good chance that Guillen might still put together a healthy season at age 28. Aurilia was terrible. Guillen made a run at the MVP.

Smilin' Scott Spiezio played decent defense at the corners, but hit almost badly enough to remind fans of reputed clubhouse cancer Jeff Cirillo, who'd been exchanged for equally bad contracts from San Diego.

While many expressed their doubts about this older, grittier roster's ability to compete in the AL West, no one expected the team to be as bad as it was. Pessimistic Mariner analysts picked them to win 80 games. Instead they narrowly avoided 100 losses on the season.

Even the good went bad. Bret Boone turned into a pumpkin. Ben Davis stunk even worse than already low expectations predicted. The pitching staff disintegrated entirely. Every single pitcher who started the year on the roster of the Tacoma Rainiers was called up or injured (sometimes both) by the end of the year. John Olerud's offensive game had been whittled down to singles and walks against right-handers, and yet he was the Mariners' second-most-valuable hitter for much of the year. The team was even worse in the same boring way: unproductive singles and walks. Loss followed loss.

The front office fractured. Rumors swirled. Decisions were made, rescinded, and reinstated. You could talk to two good sources in the front office and hear two completely different ideas of what would happen to a particular player, and both would be wholly convinced they were right. Then something else entirely would happen. To reassure the fan base, they gave manager Bob Melvin a contract extension for 2005 early in the season as a show of confidence in the modestly talented manager.

When the team finally gave up hope, the season actually got interesting. Free-agent-to-be Freddy Garcia started the season strong, and his trade to the White Sox netted a bounty of goods: Jeremy Reed, who immediately became the best position prospect in the system, Miguel Olivo, who immediately became the best catcher in the system, and Michael Morse, who can hit but has issues. Olerud and Aurilia were given the heave-ho. Between injury, roster clearance, and benching bad players, the team on the field changed dramatically. They called up an array interesting players: guys who hit for power, dropped balls, or were totally overmatched; pitchers who stunk; and a really cool Native American guy with no fear and mound presence to burn. The season was lost, but it got a lot more entertaining. They had promise.

Bavasi emerged the winner in the intra-office fight. Howard Lincoln and ownership supported him over Gillick, after Gillick's moves failed in spectacular fashion. As we went to press, Gillick remained with the organization but was no longer welcome; he publicly lobbied for the Washington GM job that went to Jim Bowden, and is probably on the phone now looking for one of his old cronies who'll bring him on as a special assistant or something. Bavasi, who seems like a nice enough guy without a bad thing to say—even about Mo Vaughn, his most disastrous signing while GM of the Angels—will likely have some nice comments when Gillick officially leaves. He'll then return to his office, sit down in his chair, and sigh "What a prick." Melvin, and his new contract, were axed at season's end. Bavasi is carrying out a needed, polite purge of Gillick's people.

In compiling the '04 roster, the Mariners had obsessed over the 2001 team that won 116 games. They believed it taught them valuable lessons. They needed more singles hitters like Ichiro, and depth in pitching—and no stars, just quality veteran leadership. They spent three years trying to recapture the qualities they saw in that team, chasing a mirage.

That's over. This off-season, for the first time in team history, they went after top free agents and signed them to huge deals. They showed they were willing to pay top dollar for what they considered top talent. Now, the Mariners' record in finding top talent has, in the past, been spotty. But signing Adrian Beltre to a five-year, $64 million deal has the potential to work out well. A soon-to-be 26-year old, talented offensive player—who plays a strong third base, an important position where the Mariners have no prospects behind him—is a big improvement on some of their past expenditures.

The team followed that move by signing Richie Sexson to a four-year deal worth $50 million—great-player money for a good player. If you look at his monster 2003, Sexson's an elite hitter. However, despite a series of intense medical workups they did on him, we're not going to know if his shoulder will hold up until well into the season; in any case, chances that he'll make this deal worth the money are slim.

And yet—this is a sea change in approach from the club's pursuit of the likes of Ibanez, Spiezio, and others of last year's host of average players paid too much money for too many years. As a bonus, with Bavasi and staff ousting Gillick, they've got nowhere to go but up in their record of draft selections.

It's going to take time to get the ship righted. The Mariners may have a couple years coming up when they're going to be bad. However, they have revenue flowing in from all sides, coming out their ears; fan discontent and front-office turmoil have finally convinced ownership to spend it.

So, if the Mariners do spend wisely, they might compete sooner than a 99-loss season might lead you to believe. They have a legitimate star in Ichiro, a top-tier pitching prospect in Felix Hernandez, and a host of modest pitching talent that can fill a cheap, effective bullpen and the back-end of the rotation. Jose Lopez could take over for Boone at second in 2006 or earlier. Despite the team's constant use of local shills in the press to lower expectations and put out word of how poor and cash-strapped they are, the Mariners are estimated by outside sources to be the third-richest franchise in baseball, behind only the Red Sox and Yankees. Last season saw attendance (as "tickets sold") down 10%, with actual butts-in-seats far below that. Walk-up sales were non-existent for much of the season. Season-ticket holders with beautiful box seats stood on Occidental after work and couldn't find takers at 50% off. If they're going to start spending with the big teams, and make a run at it, this will get interesting real soon.

Much hinges on Bavasi. His career in Anaheim was undistinguished. Though he's given some credit for the World Series winning team that followed him years later, he had little to do with its composition. There's little evidence in Bavasi's career or statements that should make fans optimistic. Hired to be Gillick's marionette, he offers a nice public face but is clearly not one of the state-of-the-art GM candidates that was available.

Bavasi is not the candidate you might have hired to do the job he faces. He needs to build a good farm system through the draft, while continuing to get results from the team's international scouting. He needs to spend wisely on premium young free agents that can contribute to the next competitive team, instead of on long-term deals for older veterans who'll get in the team's way, as the 2003 signings did. As he juggles minor leaguers who might not cut it, he's going to need to adeptly handle rosters and stock quality filler from minor league free agents.

There are strong signs of hope. The team hired a full-time scout to work in Japan, increasing even further their strength there. While Bavasi's most famous move was the huge, disastrous contract to Mo Vaughn, he seems to have learned the right lessons from it and spent this off-season's money on younger, better players with knees.

Bavasi has brought in a stathead to expand the team's range of expertise. For the first time, the team has someone in the big chair who doesn't simply dismiss innovation in baseball management. Bavasi may not yet fully get it, but he understands there is something worth getting. There has been an arrogant vacuum in the Mariners front office as of late, and if the team is going to rebound from last season, humility and willingness to learn from mistakes will be as important as Gillick's reputation among his peers ever was.

HITTERS

WLADIMIR BALENTIEN OF **Bats: R** **Throws: R** Born: 02-Jul-1984 Age: 20

YEAR	TM	LG	AGE	AB	H	2B	3B	HR	BB	SO	SB	CS	AVG	OBP	SLG	MLVR	EQBA	EQOBP	EQSLG	EQMLVR	VORP	DEFENSE	
2004	WIS	MDW	20	260	72	12	3	15	12	77	10	2	.277	.315	.519	.190	.230	.264	.425	-.193	-3.6	46-CF -7	13-LF -1
2004	SBR	CLF	20	38	11	1	0	2	4	10	1	0	.289	.357	.474	.161	.243	.283	.378	-.214	-1.7	13-RF -1	
2005	*SEA*	*AL*	*20*	*346*	*76*	*15*	*1*	*11*	*17*	*116*	*5*	*2*	*.219*	*.263*	*.366*	*-.259*	*.226*	*.270*	*.384*	*-.228*	*-8.3*	*89-CF -10*	

Breakout: 17% *Improve: 33%* *Collapse: 48%*

In Wisconsin, over 40% of Balentien's hits were for extra bases; 20% went over the fences. That's crazy. But minor league hitters with massive strikeout problems can be devoured by strikeouts as they move up the system, and Balentien struck out in 30% of his at-bats at the same level. He's young and talented, so he's got lots of time.

WILLIE BLOOMQUIST INF **Bats: R** **Throws: R** Born: 27-Nov-1977 Age: 27

YEAR	TM	LG	AGE	AB	H	2B	3B	HR	BB	SO	SB	CS	AVG	OBP	SLG	MLVR	EQBA	EQOBP	EQSLG	EQMLVR	VORP	DEFENSE	
2002	TAC	PCL	24	337	91	14	3	6	29	44	20	10	.270	.331	.383	-.024	.263	.321	.370	-.139	3.8	26-2B -1	26-LF -3
2002	SEA	AL	24	33	15	4	0	0	5	2	3	1	.455	.526	.576	.767	.576	.510	.667	1.106	8.3		
2003	SEA	AL	25	196	49	7	2	1	19	39	4	1	.250	.317	.321	-.179	.262	.333	.333	-.168	1.4	28-3B 0	15-SS 0
2004	SEA	AL	26	188	46	10	0	2	10	48	13	2	.245	.283	.330	-.245	.257	.291	.332	-.255	-2.1	22-3B 2	15-SS -2
2005	*SEA*	*AL*	*27*	*217*	*55*	*10*	*1*	*3*	*16*	*45*	*9*	*3*	*.253*	*.306*	*.361*	*-.166*	*.261*	*.315*	*.379*	*-.132*	*3.8*	*59-3B -2*	

Breakout: 24% *Improve: 47%* *Collapse: 41%*

When syphilis first attacked humans, it was amazingly virulent and destructive. Pustules quickly covered the body until the poor victim's skin fell off and they died. It was too fast and too obvious. Within a generation, syphilis had evolved. It became far less destructive to the host, instead taking its time tearing up the nervous system, heart, and brain until the host was driven insane or died, the longer life of the host (and their healthier appearance) allowing the virus to spread far more widely.

Willie Bloomquist came up in 2002 and found himself in the spotlight, hitting .455/.526/.576 in a spectacular September call-up. He quickly turned to incubation, though, never taking a regular role long enough to be exposed as worthless, spreading across the field to take root at every position. This kind of infection by local white boys with scrappy personalities is often untreatable, though direct injections of new personnel into the front office does sometimes solve the problem.

It's too late for the Mariners. I would only caution other teams to take a lesson from this and work towards prevention, ensuring that their farm systems exercise protection.

HIRAM BOCACHICA

OF **Bats: R** **Throws: R** Born: 04-Mar-1976 Age: 29

YEAR	TM	LG	AGE	AB	H	2B	3B	HR	BB	SO	SB	CS	AVG	OBP	SLG	MLVR	EQBA	EQOBP	EQSLG	EQMLVR	VORP	DEFENSE	
2002	LAD	NL	26	65	14	3	0	4	5	19	1	1	.215	.271	.446	-.059	.227	.263	.500	-.091	1.5	10-LF 0	
2002	DET	AL	26	103	23	4	0	4	5	22	2	2	.223	.259	.379	-.209	.243	.265	.388	-.234	-1.9	19-CF -3	
2003	TOL	INT	27	322	78	19	3	12	24	57	11	6	.242	.313	.432	.014	.230	.301	.423	-.127	2.0	29-CF -3	20-LF 0
2004	TAC	PCL	28	136	39	5	1	10	17	36	12	3	.287	.393	.559	.309	.255	.348	.467	.039	4.4	25-RF -2	
2004	SEA	AL	28	90	22	5	0	3	12	27	5	4	.244	.337	.400	-.054	.270	.347	.416	-.021	1.8	22-CF 0	
2005	*OAK*	*AL*	*29*	*155*	*39*	*7*	*1*	*6*	*14*	*39*	*5*	*3*	*.254*	*.327*	*.433*	*-.034*	*.256*	*.331*	*.442*	*-.024*	*7.6*	*45-CF -4*	

Breakout: 32% *Improve: 56%* *Collapse: 29%*

Bocachica's probably going to be floating around the league as a spare outfielder and utility guy for years to come. He's got the range for center, but doesn't hit well enough to be anything more than a defensive sub.

BRET BOONE

2B **Bats: R** **Throws: R** Born: 06-Apr-1969 Age: 36

YEAR	TM	LG	AGE	AB	H	2B	3B	HR	BB	SO	SB	CS	AVG	OBP	SLG	MLVR	EQBA	EQOBP	EQSLG	EQMLVR	VORP	DEFENSE
2002	SEA	AL	33	608	169	34	3	24	53	102	12	5	.278	.339	.462	.098	.292	.355	.489	.115	49.3	144-2B 12
2003	SEA	AL	34	622	183	35	5	35	68	125	16	3	.294	.366	.535	.244	.306	.381	.563	.278	75.9	155-2B 12
2004	SEA	AL	35	593	149	30	0	24	56	135	10	5	.251	.317	.423	-.040	.262	.329	.442	-.024	27.1	144-2B -10
2005	*SEA*	*AL*	*36*	*491*	*128*	*25*	*2*	*21*	*49*	*109*	*8*	*3*	*.262*	*.332*	*.451*	*.003*	*.269*	*.341*	*.473*	*.045*	*31.9*	*129-2B -3*

Breakout: 17% *Improve: 45%* *Collapse: 20%*

The optimistic view is that Boone's poor season was due to a combination of the oppressive losing, aging, and personal issues. This is supported by Boone's flashing his peak skills—hitting well for stretches and displaying quick reactions and good hands—as often as he was caught napping with balls skipping by him or through his legs or off his glove. He could bounce back a little, or that might just have been the cliff. He won't be returning to MVP form, or anywhere close.

ASDRUBAL CABRERA

SS **Bats: B** **Throws: R** Born: 13-Nov-1985 Age: 19

YEAR	TM	LG	AGE	AB	H	2B	3B	HR	BB	SO	SB	CS	AVG	OBP	SLG	MLVR	EQBA	EQOBP	EQSLG	EQMLVR	VORP	DEFENSE	
2004	EVE	NWN	18	239	65	16	3	5	21	43	7	5	.272	.330	.427	.019	.199	.239	.303	-.434	-30.5	40-SS -2	17-2B -3
2005	*SEA*	*AL*	*19*	*350*	*72*	*16*	*2*	*4*	*17*	*82*	*6*	*3*	*.205*	*.248*	*.299*	*-.382*	*.212*	*.255*	*.314*	*-.358*	*-12.1*	*92-SS -7*	

Breakout: 41% *Improve: 54%* *Collapse: 27%*

The best position player the Mariners have in the low minors. He's compared to Jose Lopez, but Cabrera's showing a little more power and a somewhat better batting eye than Lopez did at the same level (at 17). He also has a much better chance to stick at short.

JOLBERT CABRERA

INF **Bats: R** **Throws: R** Born: 08-Dec-1972 Age: 32

YEAR	TM	LG	AGE	AB	H	2B	3B	HR	BB	SO	SB	CS	AVG	OBP	SLG	MLVR	EQBA	EQOBP	EQSLG	EQMLVR	VORP	DEFENSE	
2003	LAD	NL	30	347	98	32	2	6	17	62	6	4	.282	.332	.438	.065	.293	.338	.457	.041	19.8	36-2B 0	24-CF 0
2004	SEA	AL	31	359	97	19	2	6	16	70	10	3	.270	.312	.384	-.096	.283	.326	.403	-.067	7.5	33-3B 5	18-1B 1
2005	*SEA*	*AL*	*32*	*308*	*78*	*15*	*2*	*5*	*17*	*58*	*6*	*3*	*.254*	*.304*	*.366*	*-.163*	*.261*	*.312*	*.384*	*-.129*	*1.8*	*81-3B -2*	

Breakout: 7% *Improve: 26%* *Collapse: 35%*

When Spiezio injured his back, the Mariners had to trade two prospects—one interesting, LHP Ryan Ketchner, and one not, RHP Aaron Looper—to the Dodgers for this guy. Cabrera plays several positions passably and hits for some average. There are many players like him. Having to trade value for Cabrera shows a lack of preparation and foresight.

ISMAEL CASTRO 2B Bats: B Throws: R Born: 14-Aug-1983 Age: 21

YEAR	TM	LG	AGE	AB	H	2B	3B	HR	BB	SO	SB	CS	AVG	OBP	SLG	MLVR	EQBA	EQOBP	EQSLG	EQMLVR	VORP	DEFENSE	
2002	EVE	NWN	18	284	89	26	1	9	16	41	13	2	.313	.356	.507	.272	.249	.279	.415	-.165	1.6	64-2B -1	
2003	SBR	CLF	19	327	90	19	2	3	12	33	9	7	.275	.314	.373	-.043	.240	.269	.326	-.318	-13.6	57-2B -1	26-SS 1
2004	SBR	CLF	20	66	20	7	0	2	4	3	0	1	.303	.343	.500	.191	.277	.288	.446	-.079	1.9	12-2B -2	
2005	*SEA*	*AL*	*21*	*403*	*102*	*24*	*1*	*9*	*13*	*44*	*4*	*2*	*.253*	*.283*	*.384*	*-.177*	*.261*	*.291*	*.403*	*-.142*	*4.1*	*102-2B -2*	

Breakout: 25% *Improve: 52%* *Collapse: 26%*

Castro blew out his knee after only 16 games. Next year he's going to face a squeeze as the organization pushes their other infield prospects up. He'll find playing time, but it's tough to know which position it will be at in '05.

YUNG CHEN INF Bats: R Throws: R Born: 13-Jul-1983 Age: 21

YEAR	TM	LG	AGE	AB	H	2B	3B	HR	BB	SO	SB	CS	AVG	OBP	SLG	MLVR	EQBA	EQOBP	EQSLG	EQMLVR	VORP	DEFENSE	
2004	EVE	NWN	20	200	60	13	1	3	16	36	25	3	.300	.353	.420	.066	.221	.254	.307	-.386	-22.5	26-3B 0	19-2B -4
2005	*SEA*	*AL*	*21*	*376*	*80*	*17*	*2*	*4*	*14*	*91*	*17*	*6*	*.212*	*.247*	*.297*	*-.382*	*.219*	*.254*	*.312*	*-.359*	*-17.4*	*96-3B -2*	

Breakout: 23% *Improve: 42%* *Collapse: 37%*

Yung played for the Taiwanese Olympic team this year, where he wasn't all that impressive. In Everett he looked good, though at 21 you'd like to see him start sprinting up the system. He needs to get playing time, preferably at short, where the traffic jam is.

SHIN-SOO CHOO OF Bats: L Throws: L Born: 13-Jul-1982 Age: 22

YEAR	TM	LG	AGE	AB	H	2B	3B	HR	BB	SO	SB	CS	AVG	OBP	SLG	MLVR	EQBA	EQOBP	EQSLG	EQMLVR	VORP	DEFENSE	
2002	WIS	MDW	19	420	127	24	8	6	70	98	34	21	.302	.417	.440	.267	.256	.346	.382	-.080	9.7	69-CF -9	37-RF -4
2003	SBR	CLF	20	412	118	18	13	9	44	84	18	10	.286	.365	.459	.175	.246	.309	.389	-.147	-11.8	62-LF -5	33-RF 0
2004	SAN	TXS	21	517	163	17	7	15	56	97	40	8	.315	.382	.462	.282	.303	.361	.443	.071	22.7	80-RF -5	44-LF -2
2005	*SEA*	*AL*	*22*	*290*	*77*	*15*	*2*	*7*	*27*	*63*	*10*	*3*	*.265*	*.334*	*.402*	*-.056*	*.273*	*.343*	*.422*	*-.017*	*8.7*	*79-RF -5*	

Breakout: 18% *Improve: 34%* *Collapse: 31%*

Choo hasn't progressed in a while. Don't let his performance in the Arizona Batting Practice League fool you. Remember Kenny Kelly, among others. PECOTA agrees that his hopes have dimmed a bit. Needs a power spike to claim elite prospect status, and may not find one.

CASEY CRAIG LF Bats: L Throws: R Born: 12-Jan-1985 Age: 20

YEAR	TM	LG	AGE	AB	H	2B	3B	HR	BB	SO	SB	CS	AVG	OBP	SLG	MLVR	EQBA	EQOBP	EQSLG	EQMLVR	VORP	DEFENSE
2004	EVE	NWN	19	200	53	10	3	5	45	59	18	6	.265	.398	.420	.110	.186	.290	.279	-.369	-39.0	49-LF -4
2005	*SEA*	*AL*	*20*	*291*	*57*	*12*	*2*	*4*	*34*	*112*	*10*	*4*	*.197*	*.281*	*.295*	*-.330*	*.203*	*.289*	*.309*	*-.305*	*-19.3*	*80-LF -5*

Breakout: 42% *Improve: 59%* *Collapse: 27%*

Craig doesn't make enough contact yet, but he's starting to drive the balls he hits. The question is whether a hitting game can be built around his good strike zone control; a .265 average with only moderate power in the Northwest League isn't encouraging.

GREG DOBBS 3B Bats: L Throws: R Born: 02-Jul-1978 Age: 26

YEAR	TM	LG	AGE	AB	H	2B	3B	HR	BB	SO	SB	CS	AVG	OBP	SLG	MLVR	EQBA	EQOBP	EQSLG	EQMLVR	VORP	DEFENSE
2002	WIS	MDW	24	320	88	16	2	10	31	50	13	3	.275	.338	.431	.130	.231	.283	.372	-.231	-5.2	72-3B 3
2002	SAN	TXS	24	96	35	2	0	5	9	17	1	3	.365	.425	.542	.536	.347	.376	.520	.255	9.5	22-RF -2
2004	SAN	TXS	26	203	66	14	4	5	11	23	5	4	.325	.373	.507	.347	.314	.352	.490	.134	19.6	49-3B -6
2004	TAC	PCL	26	255	69	9	2	8	5	36	4	3	.271	.286	.416	-.124	.252	.268	.376	-.239	-4.3	64-3B -5
2004	SEA	AL	26	53	12	1	0	1	1	14	0	0	.226	.250	.302	-.357	.245	.243	.302	-.401	-2.5	
2005	*SEA*	*AL*	*26*	*230*	*58*	*11*	*1*	*6*	*8*	*40*	*2*	*1*	*.252*	*.282*	*.391*	*-.171*	*.260*	*.290*	*.410*	*-.136*	*-0.1*	*60-3B -3*

Breakout: 18% *Improve: 41%* *Collapse: 37%*

His promotion was a reward for the good year they thought he had in Tacoma. No, really, that's what they said. Dobbs is a defensively limited Bloomquist. Until they can look at these guys without cartoon hearts throbbing in their eyes, the organization's in trouble.

JESUS GUZMAN 3B Bats: B Throws: R Born: 14-Jun-1984 Age: 21

YEAR	TM	LG	AGE	AB	H	2B	3B	HR	BB	SO	SB	CS	AVG	OBP	SLG	MLVR	EQBA	EQOBP	EQSLG	EQMLVR	VORP	DEFENSE
2004	SBR	CLF	20	442	137	35	3	6	57	105	10	9	.310	.393	.443	.197	.267	.338	.374	-.098	11.4	108-3B -18
2005	*SEA*	*AL*	*21*	*391*	*90*	*19*	*2*	*5*	*33*	*114*	*5*	*4*	*.232*	*.297*	*.332*	*-.233*	*.238*	*.306*	*.349*	*-.203*	*-8.2*	*103-3B -6*

Breakout: 9% *Improve: 20%* *Collapse: 48%*

Those stats don't look so great in the hitter-hugging Cal League—if you don't look at the birth date. At 20, this is a promising line, and Guzman's extra-base power makes him one to watch. Still, just being young and hitting OK for a level doesn't a future star make. See: Luis Rivas, others.

RAUL IBANEZ OF/1B Bats: L Throws: R Born: 02-Jun-1972 Age: 33

YEAR	TM	LG	AGE	AB	H	2B	3B	HR	BB	SO	SB	CS	AVG	OBP	SLG	MLVR	EQBA	EQOBP	EQSLG	EQMLVR	VORP	DEFENSE
2002	KCR	AL	30	497	146	37	6	24	40	76	5	3	.294	.346	.537	.145	.288	.345	.532	.156	33.9	42-1B -1 32-LF -2
2003	KCR	AL	31	608	179	33	5	18	49	81	8	4	.294	.345	.454	.040	.287	.343	.448	.031	23.0	116-LF -3 19-1B 2
2004	SEA	AL	32	481	146	31	1	16	36	72	1	2	.304	.353	.472	.139	.314	.367	.495	.167	30.1	105-LF 3
2005	*SEA*	*AL*	*33*	*412*	*111*	*22*	*2*	*12*	*32*	*64*	*2*	*2*	*.270*	*.324*	*.420*	*-.045*	*.278*	*.333*	*.441*	*-.004*	*9.7*	*107-LF -3*

Breakout: 2% *Improve: 22%* *Collapse: 32%*

There's some weird stuff afoot here. Ibanez strained his right hamstring mid-season, and was a different hitter afterwards. Pre-hamstring-injury, .268/.330/.505, and post-hamstring-injury, .328/.369/.449.

Ibanez's overall line defied projections and is due to a fluke. Historically helpless against lefties, in '04 he hit .295/.342/.438 against them and that, as Robert Frost would say, made all the difference. There are rumors the team is thinking of playing Sexson in left, moving Ibanez to first. Ibanez would become a shadowy version of John Olerud: an aging, power-deficient lefty who needs a platoon partner . . . except Ibanez is horrible defensively, while Olerud was a picking machine.

BUCKY JACOBSEN DH Bats: R Throws: R Born: 30-Aug-1975 Age: 29

YEAR	TM	LG	AGE	AB	H	2B	3B	HR	BB	SO	SB	CS	AVG	OBP	SLG	MLVR	EQBA	EQOBP	EQSLG	EQMLVR	VORP	DEFENSE
2002	HUN	SOU	26	198	50	9	2	11	22	41	2	2	.253	.336	.485	.158	.228	.293	.450	-.106	-1.5	44-1B -5
2002	NHV	EAS	26	102	30	11	0	4	9	25	0	0	.294	.360	.520	.273	.262	.306	.466	-.031	1.6	13-1B -1
2003	TEN	SOU	27	447	133	24	1	31	56	91	3	1	.298	.388	.564	.340	.260	.339	.515	.093	25.8	109-1B -8
2004	TAC	PCL	28	292	91	22	1	26	50	88	1	1	.312	.422	.661	.536	.274	.378	.556	.228	33.8	
2004	SEA	AL	28	160	44	9	0	9	14	47	0	0	.275	.335	.500	.127	.289	.342	.535	.156	11.8	21-1B 0
2005	*SEA*	*AL*	*29*	*366*	*93*	*18*	*1*	*20*	*43*	*101*	*1*	*1*	*.254*	*.341*	*.473*	*.040*	*.261*	*.351*	*.496*	*.084*	*22.4*	*100-DH*

Breakout: 15% *Improve: 41%* *Collapse: 21%*

A long-time minor leaguer and fan favorite (buckybackers.com), Bucky came up to spell Edgar at DH and play a little at first. Until his knee took him down, his bat helped the team's offense immensely. He'll try and bash his way into the lineup next year as the starting designated hitter.

ADAM JONES SS Bats: R Throws: R Born: 01-Aug-1985 Age: 19

YEAR	TM	LG	AGE	AB	H	2B	3B	HR	BB	SO	SB	CS	AVG	OBP	SLG	MLVR	EQBA	EQOBP	EQSLG	EQMLVR	VORP	DEFENSE
2003	MRN	AZL	17	109	31	5	1	0	5	19	5	1	.284	.371	.349	.000	.174	.207	.193	-.664	-784.3	
2004	WIS	MDW	18	510	136	23	7	11	33	124	8	4	.267	.314	.404	.026	.228	.268	.348	-.296	-14.5	116-SS -19
2005	*SEA*	*AL*	*19*	*385*	*89*	*18*	*3*	*6*	*17*	*101*	*4*	*2*	*.231*	*.268*	*.339*	*-.278*	*.238*	*.276*	*.355*	*-.249*	*-3.1*	*98-SS -13*

Breakout: 19% *Improve: 46%* *Collapse: 41%*

A good season at Wisconsin at 18. His strikeouts are trouble: He's not only not making contact for hits, he's unable to make contact at all in almost a quarter of his at-bats. With the abundance of shortstops in the organization, he'll need to improve both his hitting and his defense to have a shot.

JUSTIN LEONE 3B Bats: R Throws: R Born: 09-Jul-1977 Age: 27

YEAR	TM	LG	AGE	AB	H	2B	3B	HR	BB	SO	SB	CS	AVG	OBP	SLG	MLVR	EQBA	EQOBP	EQSLG	EQMLVR	VORP	DEFENSE
2002	SBR	CLF	24	358	89	20	5	18	57	98	6	0	.249	.358	.483	.177	.214	.304	.404	-.159	2.5	96-3B -2
2003	SAN	TXS	25	455	131	38	7	21	92	104	20	6	.288	.405	.541	.408	.274	.381	.519	.184	56.2	121-3B 6
2004	TAC	PCL	26	253	68	10	5	21	26	82	5	6	.269	.344	.597	.258	.240	.309	.504	.007	14.6	45-3B -8 11-SS 0
2004	SEA	AL	26	102	22	5	0	6	9	32	1	0	.216	.298	.441	-.083	.235	.305	.451	-.077	2.2	27-3B 1
2005	*SEA*	*AL*	*27*	*322*	*80*	*17*	*1*	*16*	*38*	*96*	*6*	*3*	*.250*	*.334*	*.461*	*.010*	*.257*	*.344*	*.483*	*.053*	*18.9*	*88-3B -3*

Breakout: 26% *Improve: 56%* *Collapse: 23%*

(continued next page)

Justin Leone *(continued)*

Leone in his peak years had two seasons in the minors outperforming the team's terrible third basemen. He got nothing for it. The acquisition of Beltre makes it almost certain he'll be moved, if the team remembers him at all.

JOSE LOPEZ SS **Bats: R** **Throws: R** Born: 24-Nov-1983 Age: 21

YEAR	TM	LG	AGE	AB	H	2B	3B	HR	BB	SO	SB	CS	AVG	OBP	SLG	MLVR	EQBA	EQOBP	EQSLG	EQMLVR	VORP	DEFENSE
2002	SBR	CLF	18	522	169	39	5	8	27	45	31	13	.324	.360	.464	.226	.289	.317	.410	-.069	20.3	116-SS -20
2003	SAN	TXS	19	538	139	35	2	13	27	56	18	8	.258	.303	.403	.031	.252	.292	.408	-.148	8.7	88-SS -11 34-2B 1
2004	TAC	PCL	20	275	81	19	0	13	16	30	6	2	.295	.342	.505	.148	.262	.302	.428	-.093	8.9	42-SS -3 20-3B -3
2004	SEA	AL	20	207	48	13	0	5	8	31	0	1	.232	.263	.367	-.238	.243	.269	.383	-.234	-0.6	54-SS -8
2005	*SEA*	*AL*	*21*	*485*	*130*	*28*	*2*	*14*	*20*	*58*	*7*	*3*	*.269*	*.303*	*.422*	*-.078*	*.277*	*.312*	*.443*	*-.038*	*21.3*	*123-SS -7*

Breakout: 29% *Improve: 58%* *Collapse: 21%*

We've expressed some doubts about Lopez's age in the past, but it now seems that much more the case. He was overmatched after his promotion while the team disintegrated from injuries and inept management. Defensively, he's weak on the routine plays, booting easy grounders and throwing balls into the stands. His long term future is at second, and hey—Boone's contract runs out this year.

EDGAR MARTINEZ DH **Bats: R** **Throws: R** Born: 02-Jan-1963 Age: 42

YEAR	TM	LG	AGE	AB	H	2B	3B	HR	BB	SO	SB	CS	AVG	OBP	SLG	MLVR	EQBA	EQOBP	EQSLG	EQMLVR	VORP	DEFENSE
2002	SEA	AL	39	328	91	23	0	15	67	69	1	1	.277	.403	.485	.239	.298	.418	.514	.262	35.6	
2003	SEA	AL	40	497	146	25	0	24	92	95	0	1	.294	.406	.489	.244	.307	.418	.513	.270	54.5	
2004	SEA	AL	41	486	128	23	0	12	58	107	1	0	.263	.342	.385	-.039	.274	.354	.401	-.025	17.5	

Edgar had a distinguished and great career, filled with both personal triumph and disappointment tied to a team that went from pathetic to good to amazing to abjectly awful. He was everything you could want in both a player and a neighbor. He deserved better than this. A legitimate Hall of Fame candidate.

MICHAEL MORSE SS **Bats: R** **Throws: R** Born: 22-Mar-1982 Age: 23

YEAR	TM	LG	AGE	AB	H	2B	3B	HR	BB	SO	SB	CS	AVG	OBP	SLG	MLVR	EQBA	EQOBP	EQSLG	EQMLVR	VORP	DEFENSE
2002	KAN	SAL	20	417	107	30	4	2	25	73	7	6	.257	.310	.362	-.006	.226	.263	.332	-.330	-16.1	88-SS -8 23-3B -2
2003	WNS	CRL	21	432	106	30	2	10	25	91	4	4	.245	.296	.394	-.023	.220	.261	.371	-.282	-11.1	118-SS -14
2004	BIR	SOU	22	209	60	9	5	11	15	46	0	3	.287	.336	.536	.246	.267	.313	.495	.027	14.7	49-SS -9
2004	SAN	TXS	22	157	43	10	1	6	9	27	0	2	.274	.326	.465	.152	.258	.299	.434	-.093	5.3	40-SS 0
2005	*SEA*	*AL*	*23*	*298*	*72*	*16*	*2*	*8*	*15*	*66*	*1*	*1*	*.240*	*.286*	*.390*	*-.172*	*.247*	*.294*	*.409*	*-.138*	*8.0*	*78-SS -9*

Breakout: 26% *Improve: 39%* *Collapse: 38%*

Shortly after acquiring Morse, the team suspended him for the season, echoing a White Sox team suspension earlier in the year. No reasons have been given for either suspension. We're not concerned about his height (6′5″), but he is a bad defensive shortstop and needs to find a position to hide his glove. Like designated hitter.

MIGUEL OLIVO C **Bats: R** **Throws: R** Born: 15-Jul-1978 Age: 26

YEAR	TM	LG	AGE	AB	H	2B	3B	HR	BB	SO	SB	CS	AVG	OBP	SLG	MLVR	EQBA	EQOBP	EQSLG	EQMLVR	VORP	DEFENSE
2002	BIR	SOU	23	359	110	24	10	6	40	66	29	13	.306	.381	.479	.288	.294	.352	.474	.091	30.6	99-C 0
2003	CWS	AL	24	317	75	19	1	6	19	80	6	4	.237	.287	.360	-.201	.236	.289	.363	-.229	-0.7	101-C 9
2004	CWS	AL	25	141	38	7	2	7	10	29	5	4	.270	.316	.496	.019	.273	.324	.504	.065	7.8	38-C -2
2004	SEA	AL	25	160	32	8	2	6	10	55	2	2	.200	.260	.388	-.229	.208	.269	.415	-.214	-1.1	42-C -2
2005	*SEA*	*AL*	*26*	*307*	*76*	*17*	*2*	*10*	*23*	*77*	*7*	*3*	*.248*	*.307*	*.418*	*-.094*	*.256*	*.315*	*.438*	*-.056*	*15.4*	*82-C -1*

Breakout: 33% *Improve: 59%* *Collapse: 28%*

A couple pitches each game sail past Olivo, who watches them with a curious expression on his face, as if surprised by the flying ball. Olivo does have an arm, and a little power. At 25, he was too old to blame all his problems on bad instruction. Nonetheless, PECOTA sees better times ahead.

JEREMY REED OF Bats: L Throws: L Born: 15-Jun-1981 Age: 24

YEAR	TM	LG	AGE	AB	H	2B	3B	HR	BB	SO	SB	CS	AVG	OBP	SLG	MLVR	EQBA	EQOBP	EQSLG	EQMLVR	VORP	DEFENSE
2002	KAN	SAL	21	210	67	15	0	4	11	24	17	5	.319	.377	.448	.251	.267	.299	.387	-.154	-5.6	35-RF -4 19-CF 1
2003	WNS	CRL	22	222	74	18	1	4	41	17	27	6	.333	.431	.477	.339	.294	.383	.447	.107	13.9	44-RF -3 21-CF 1
2003	BIR	SOU	22	242	99	17	3	7	29	19	18	13	.409	.474	.591	.654	.382	.439	.574	.476	43.5	41-RF 0 21-CF -1
2004	CHR	INT	23	276	76	14	1	8	36	34	12	7	.275	.357	.420	.049	.258	.339	.393	-.076	6.3	64-CF 2
2004	TAC	PCL	23	233	71	10	5	5	23	22	14	2	.305	.366	.455	.126	.284	.340	.410	-.031	8.3	61-CF 0
2004	SEA	AL	23	58	23	4	0	0	7	4	3	1	.397	.470	.466	.400	.456	.459	.491	.481	9.1	16-CF 0
2005	*SEA*	*AL*	*24*	*350*	*100*	*19*	*2*	*8*	*33*	*38*	*12*	*5*	*.286*	*.353*	*.423*	*.021*	*.295*	*.363*	*.443*	*.064*	*24.6*	*95-CF 0*

Breakout: 11% *Improve: 29%* *Collapse: 37%*

His offensive game is driven by batting average, and so he's going to be a tremendously streaky hitter. When he's on, he'll seem invincible, especially if he keeps developing that gap power. When he's not, he'll look like the worst hitter on the team. Defensively, he could play center, though he won't be good there. He could play the corners well, but can he hit enough there? The Mariners will get him in somewhere.

RENE RIVERA C Bats: R Throws: R Born: 31-Jul-1983 Age: 21

YEAR	TM	LG	AGE	AB	H	2B	3B	HR	BB	SO	SB	CS	AVG	OBP	SLG	MLVR	EQBA	EQOBP	EQSLG	EQMLVR	VORP	DEFENSE
2002	EVE	NWN	18	227	55	18	1	1	16	38	5	2	.242	.314	.344	-.037	.200	.243	.294	-.438	-32.4	57-C 5
2003	WIS	MDW	19	407	112	19	0	9	38	81	2	2	.275	.344	.388	.085	.227	.278	.340	-.288	-14.7	107-C 14
2004	SBR	CLF	20	379	89	22	1	6	28	70	0	1	.235	.300	.346	-.171	.200	.251	.292	-.424	-28.3	106-C 13
2005	*SEA*	*AL*	*21*	*272*	*59*	*12*	*1*	*5*	*15*	*56*	*1*	*1*	*.217*	*.272*	*.326*	*-.298*	*.223*	*.279*	*.342*	*-.270*	*-4.3*	*73-C 2*

Breakout: 40% *Improve: 54%* *Collapse: 26%*

A collapse of a season, in which Rivera wore down and didn't hit at all. Figure him as a backstop with an arm—check out those defensive numbers. Mike Matheny became a rich man, so anything's possible.

RAMON SANTIAGO SS Bats: B Throws: R Born: 31-Aug-1979 Age: 25

YEAR	TM	LG	AGE	AB	H	2B	3B	HR	BB	SO	SB	CS	AVG	OBP	SLG	MLVR	EQBA	EQOBP	EQSLG	EQMLVR	VORP	DEFENSE
2002	DET	AL	22	222	54	5	5	4	13	48	8	5	.243	.306	.365	-.129	.260	.320	.390	-.115	4.7	63-SS -1
2003	DET	AL	23	444	100	18	1	2	33	66	10	4	.225	.292	.284	-.302	.235	.305	.296	-.291	-9.4	76-SS 7 50-2B 0
2004	TAC	PCL	24	243	47	7	2	1	24	31	9	6	.193	.288	.251	-.420	.178	.261	.223	-.507	-22.7	59-SS -2
2004	SEA	AL	24	39	7	1	0	0	3	3	0	0	.179	.256	.205	-.536	.205	.223	.205	-.602	-3.1	13-SS -2
2005	*SEA*	*AL*	*25*	*213*	*49*	*8*	*2*	*2*	*15*	*31*	*6*	*2*	*.232*	*.301*	*.313*	*-.253*	*.238*	*.309*	*.328*	*-.223*	*3.2*	*60-SS -2*

Breakout: 42% *Improve: 63%* *Collapse: 19%*

This is all they got for Carlos Guillen. Santiago doesn't hit, but he can play short well, so it was baffling that with Santiago on the roster, and the team in need of a shortstop, they decided to start Jose Lopez's service time clock. Isn't that situation—team dead and buried, starter hurt—what emergency backups are for?

CHRIS SNELLING OF Bats: L Throws: L Born: 03-Dec-1981 Age: 23

YEAR	TM	LG	AGE	AB	H	2B	3B	HR	BB	SO	SB	CS	AVG	OBP	SLG	MLVR	EQBA	EQOBP	EQSLG	EQMLVR	VORP	DEFENSE
2002	SAN	TXS	20	89	29	9	2	1	12	11	5	1	.326	.429	.506	.442	.333	.410	.527	.303	12.9	11-CF 0 10-LF 0
2003	SAN	TXS	21	186	62	12	2	3	8	30	1	7	.333	.371	.468	.307	.330	.362	.473	.143	11.4	15-RF -1 11-LF 1
2003	TAC	PCL	21	67	18	2	0	3	5	12	1	0	.269	.333	.433	.078	.254	.295	.418	-.127	-1.2	11-RF 1
2005	*SEA*	*AL*	*23*	*106*	*31*	*7*	*1*	*3*	*7*	*16*	*1*	*1*	*.292*	*.352*	*.463*	*.077*	*.300*	*.362*	*.485*	*.123*	*18.9*	*32-RF -1*

Breakout: 10% *Improve: 34%* *Collapse: 41%*

Because he's friendly, funny, has an accent and was into Yoda, Snelling was a novelty prospect, now forgotten. His battles with injuries, though, have honed his dedication, and he's still got potential even now as he works his way back . . . wait, no, he just injured himself again. It's been so long since he's played regularly that predictions are meaningless.

SCOTT SPIEZIO INF Bats: B Throws: R Born: 21-Sep-1972 Age: 32

YEAR	TM	LG	AGE	AB	H	2B	3B	HR	BB	SO	SB	CS	AVG	OBP	SLG	MLVR	EQBA	EQOBP	EQSLG	EQMLVR	VORP	DEFENSE
2002	ANA	AL	29	491	140	34	2	12	67	52	6	7	.285	.371	.436	.109	.293	.383	.451	.112	28.8	125-1B 0 13-3B -1
2003	ANA	AL	30	521	138	36	7	16	46	66	6	3	.265	.326	.453	.047	.271	.337	.468	.035	28.1	89-1B 1 40-3B -4
2004	SEA	AL	31	367	79	12	3	10	36	60	4	1	.215	.288	.346	-.230	.225	.301	.363	-.213	-6.7	65-3B 11 33-1B 0
2005	*SEA*	*AL*	*32*	*288*	*72*	*14*	*2*	*8*	*30*	*43*	*2*	*1*	*.249*	*.322*	*.391*	*-.102*	*.257*	*.331*	*.410*	*-.065*	*7.0*	*79-1B 4*

Breakout: 22% *Improve: 51%* *Collapse: 28%*

(continued next page)

Scott Spiezio *(continued)*

As amazing as this sounds, he was still an improvement. "Cheer up, you're better than Jeff Cirillo" should be a universal pep-talk. He'll bounce back some and be a backup corner infielder if the M's can't find a taker for his contract.

JAMAL STRONG CF Bats: R Throws: R Born: 05-Aug-1978 Age: 26

YEAR	TM	LG	AGE	AB	H	2B	3B	HR	BB	SO	SB	CS	AVG	OBP	SLG	MLVR	EQBA	EQOBP	EQSLG	EQMLVR	VORP	DEFENSE
2002	SAN	TXS	23	503	140	16	5	1	62	87	46	16	.278	.366	.336	.069	.276	.348	.338	-.123	3.9	123-CF 4
2003	TAC	PCL	24	210	64	6	1	2	25	38	26	11	.305	.390	.371	.121	.292	.372	.358	-.038	7.2	53-CF -7
2004	TAC	PCL	25	238	77	11	2	3	38	29	19	6	.324	.421	.424	.206	.305	.394	.386	.052	15.4	50-CF -3
2005	*SEA*	*AL*	*26*	*205*	*54*	*9*	*1*	*2*	*21*	*34*	*11*	*4*	*.265*	*.342*	*.346*	*-.114*	*.272*	*.352*	*.363*	*-.079*	*9.8*	*58-CF -4*

Breakout: 14% *Improve: 22%* *Collapse: 47%*

For the second year, Strong didn't play much, his time limited by injuries. Strong's got a good eye, good speed, good bat control, and no power at all. He would make a quality backup outfielder, complementing the right lineup, but with Jeremy Reed's breakout audition, it's going to take a lot of injuries to get his chance at a pension.

ICHIRO! RF Bats: L Throws: R Born: 22-Oct-1973 Age: 31

YEAR	TM	LG	AGE	AB	H	2B	3B	HR	BB	SO	SB	CS	AVG	OBP	SLG	MLVR	EQBA	EQOBP	EQSLG	EQMLVR	VORP	DEFENSE
2002	SEA	AL	28	647	208	27	8	8	68	62	31	15	.321	.388	.425	.168	.341	.409	.451	.202	44.6	146-RF 11
2003	SEA	AL	29	679	212	29	8	13	36	69	34	8	.312	.352	.436	.096	.323	.367	.455	.118	39.3	155-RF 16
2004	SEA	AL	30	704	262	24	5	8	49	63	36	11	.372	.414	.455	.287	.388	.433	.477	.330	80.9	158-RF 4
2005	*SEA*	*AL*	*31*	*651*	*202*	*30*	*6*	*9*	*42*	*57*	*23*	*8*	*.311*	*.355*	*.415*	*.034*	*.320*	*.365*	*.436*	*.079*	*30.7*	*164-RF 3*

Breakout: 0% *Improve: 7%* *Collapse: 56%*

Ichiro! Say it! Ichiro! You can't say his name without enthusiasm! Two-hundred and sixty-two hits in a season, a new record! A .414 on-base percentage in one of the most punishing pitcher's parks in baseball! Ichiro's not the most valuable player in baseball—but he is absolutely the coolest!

There was some scorn towards Ichiro's record pursuit because it relied on so many singles. But it's a long-standing record, which is part of why it got so little attention before this year. Ichiro broke it while having a great year that kept a city excited about baseball during a time as depressing as a Seattle winter come early. Ichiro is the best dead-ball player modern baseball has seen in ages, and we should celebrate that baseball is a game where players can be so good while contributing in such unique ways.

There is no player in the major leagues who respects baseball more than Ichiro, from the records he chases, to his teammates and opponents, to the gloves he wears. When he broke the hits record, he jogged to Sisler's kids and grandkids in the stands, bowed, talked briefly to them, bowed again, and returned to first. People who dislike him because his first name is on his uniform miss the larger picture.

MATT TUIASOSOPO OF? Bats: R Throws: R Born: 10-May-1986 Age: 19

YEAR	TM	LG	AGE	AB	H	2B	3B	HR	BB	SO	SB	CS	AVG	OBP	SLG	MLVR	EQBA	EQOBP	EQSLG	EQMLVR	VORP	DEFENSE
2004	EVE	NWN	18	106	27	6	1	3	11	38	4	3	.255	.350	.415	.022	.194	.252	.306	-.406	-16.6	
2005	*SEA*	*AL*	*19*	*315*	*62*	*15*	*1*	*7*	*18*	*135*	*4*	*3*	*.198*	*.282*	*.317*	*-.299*	*.204*	*.290*	*.333*	*-.272*	*-2.6*	*86-DH -2*

Breakout: 43% *Improve: 67%* *Collapse: 26%*

Even tools mavens thought this was a stretch pick, and the Mariners spent heavily to sign him—just as they did with Michael Garciaparra the year before. You could put a pitch-back screen between second and third, aim it at first, and it would have been just as effective in the field. Hitting? He's got a bat, but his performance last year in Everett . . . more pitch-back screen. At some point, he's going to move to the outfield, or at least third.

DAN WILSON C Bats: R Throws: R Born: 25-Mar-1969 Age: 36

YEAR	TM	LG	AGE	AB	H	2B	3B	HR	BB	SO	SB	CS	AVG	OBP	SLG	MLVR	EQBA	EQOBP	EQSLG	EQMLVR	VORP	DEFENSE
2002	SEA	AL	33	359	106	16	1	6	18	81	1	0	.295	.326	.396	-.010	.309	.343	.415	.003	19.5	100-C 1
2003	SEA	AL	34	316	76	15	2	4	15	52	0	0	.241	.272	.339	-.244	.248	.286	.350	-.245	-3.1	90-C 3
2004	SEA	AL	35	319	80	13	0	2	26	57	0	1	.251	.305	.310	-.236	.263	.317	.320	-.217	-2.1	92-C 2
2005	*SEA*	*AL*	*36*	*207*	*50*	*8*	*1*	*3*	*13*	*40*	*0*	*1*	*.240*	*.286*	*.323*	*-.261*	*.247*	*.294*	*.339*	*-.232*	*-2.1*	*57-C -2*

Breakout: 10% *Improve: 34%* *Collapse: 41%*

His reputation still outweighs his play. He's a nice guy who visits kids in hospitals and makes the ladies swoon. His short, relatively cheap deal won't hurt them too much, though a more aggressive team would have kicked his useless bat to the curb by now.

RANDY WINN "CF" Bats: B Throws: R Born: 09-Jun-1974 Age: 31

YEAR	TM	LG	AGE	AB	H	2B	3B	HR	BB	SO	SB	CS	AVG	OBP	SLG	MLVR	EQBA	EQOBP	EQSLG	EQMLVR	VORP	DEFENSE
2002	TBY	AL	28	607	181	39	9	14	55	109	27	8	.298	.360	.461	.128	.306	.371	.475	.137	50.5	132-CF 1
2003	SEA	AL	29	600	177	37	4	11	41	108	23	5	.295	.346	.425	.051	.306	.360	.445	.075	28.1	135-LF -2 18-CF 3
2004	SEA	AL	30	626	179	34	6	14	53	98	21	7	.286	.346	.427	.037	.299	.361	.449	.076	34.6	119-CF 3 33-LF 1
2005	*SEA*	*AL*	*31*	*552*	*153*	*31*	*5*	*13*	*45*	*94*	*16*	*5*	*.277*	*.337*	*.420*	*-.016*	*.285*	*.347*	*.441*	*.025*	*22.4*	*144-CF -3*

Breakout: 7% *Improve: 32%* *Collapse: 25%*

Early last season, Winn was terrible afield. He was slow to read hits, took crazy routes to the ball, and his arm . . . his arm is the worst. Frank Thomas went second-to-third on him in spring training, and all year long teams with good advance scouting took the extra base on even shallow fly balls. Things improved. He hit better and his defense picked up markedly. His arm's still awful. At the close of the season, his contract doesn't look so bad. A couple million dollars for a decent performance from a center fielder is a good deal.

PITCHERS

SCOTT ATCHISON Bats: R Throws: R Born: 29-Mar-1976 Age: 29

YEAR	TM	LG	AGE	G	GS	IP	H	BB	SO	HR	ERA	EQERA	EQH9	EQBB9	EQSO9	EQHR9	PERA	VORP	STF
2002	TAC	PCL	26	27	21	124.3	123	31	112	13	4.63	5.22	8.9	2.4	6.4	1.2	4.16	19.0	11
2003	TAC	PCL	27	39	7	108.7	114	37	83	8	4.31	5.40	9.4	3.5	5.9	1.0	4.96	7.3	-5
2004	TAC	PCL	28	40	1	69.3	71	26	76	8	4.16	4.84	9.0	3.5	7.7	1.2	4.70	6.7	1
2004	SEA	AL	28	25	0	30.7	29	14	36	4	3.52	3.26	8.0	3.6	10.1	1.2	4.15	9.4	18
2005	*SEA*	*AL*	*29*	*29*	*3*	*52.0*	*50*	*21*	*44*	*6*	*4.01*	*4.18*	*8.9*	*3.2*	*6.8*	*1.1*	*4.44*	*10.3*	*2*

Breakout: 24% *Improve: 45%* *Collapse: 27%*

Atchison is the new Ryan Franklin, which is nice if he's cheap. The Mariners signed Franklin to an expensive deal when they had a reasonable facsimile right there. Atchison will be in the bullpen in '05, where he's well-suited for long relief. Good peripherals.

CHA BAEK Bats: R Throws: R Born: 29-May-1980 Age: 25

YEAR	TM	LG	AGE	G	GS	IP	H	BB	SO	HR	ERA	EQERA	EQH9	EQBB9	EQSO9	EQHR9	PERA	VORP	STF
2003	SBR	CLF	23	13	10	56.7	55	9	50	3	3.65	5.43	9.5	1.9	5.3	1.0	4.58	6.0	3
2003	SAN	TXS	23	9	9	56.0	49	17	46	2	2.57	3.98	8.7	3.1	5.7	0.7	4.33	7.3	12
2004	TAC	PCL	24	14	14	72.7	85	24	56	7	4.21	5.32	9.8	3.0	5.3	0.9	4.82	6.2	-4
2004	SEA	AL	24	7	5	31.0	35	11	20	5	5.52	6.23	9.8	3.0	5.6	1.2	5.04	-1.5	-6
2005	*SEA*	*AL*	*25*	*17*	*15*	*90.0*	*96*	*30*	*61*	*13*	*4.89*	*5.10*	*9.9*	*2.7*	*5.4*	*1.2*	*4.93*	*7.9*	*3*

Breakout: 11% *Improve: 43%* *Collapse: 28%*

Baek, like many others, was thrown into service as the season spiraled out of control.

To his credit, while he was clearly not ready, he took his lumps without suffering the confidence problems that afflicted others. His season ended when his elbow started to bother him, which in this organization means he should schedule his ligament replacement early and beat the rush.

TRAVIS BLACKLEY Bats: L Throws: L Born: 04-Nov-1982 Age: 22

YEAR	TM	LG	AGE	G	GS	IP	H	BB	SO	HR	ERA	EQERA	EQH9	EQBB9	EQSO9	EQHR9	PERA	VORP	STF
2002	SBR	CLF	19	21	20	121.3	102	44	152	11	3.49	5.00	9.2	3.8	6.8	1.3	5.00	7.4	26
2003	SAN	TXS	20	27	27	162.3	125	62	144	11	2.61	4.21	8.5	4.0	6.4	1.1	4.70	14.7	31
2004	TAC	PCL	21	19	18	110.3	100	47	80	14	3.83	4.35	8.7	4.2	5.2	1.0	4.62	11.2	28
2004	SEA	AL	21	6	6	26.0	35	22	16	9	10.04	9.69	11.4	6.6	5.2	2.8	8.31	-13.0	0
2005	*SEA*	*AL*	*22*	*18*	*10*	*66.0*	*65*	*35*	*46*	*12*	*5.48*	*5.71*	*9.2*	*4.2*	*5.5*	*1.5*	*5.49*	*0.8*	*-9*

Breakout: 5% *Improve: 41%* *Collapse: 25%*

(continued next page)

Travis Blackley *(continued)*

Blackley is a handsome, charming guy who really pours on the Australian accent when it's time to talk to the ladies. He got worked over in his starts with the big team, with lousy control and nine home runs allowed in six starts. Then he was sent down and a "tender shoulder" shut him down for the season. Not a good sign.

CHRIS BUGLOVSKY Bats: L Throws: R Born: 22-Nov-1979 Age: 25

YEAR	TM	LG	AGE	G	GS	IP	H	BB	SO	HR	ERA	EQERA	EQH9	EQBB9	EQSO9	EQHR9	PERA	VORP	STF
2002	SLM	CRL	22	27	27	164.7	161	58	126	12	3.11	5.13	9.8	3.9	5.0	1.5	5.66	-1.0	-7
2003	TUL	TXS	23	28	28	158.3	204	60	75	10	4.83	6.94	10.9	3.8	3.2	1.0	5.94	-5.8	-15
2004	SAN	TXS	24	24	21	121.0	121	45	81	7	3.64	6.14	9.1	3.7	4.3	0.9	4.41	15.1	4
2005	*SEA*	*AL*	*25*	*15*	*8*	*54.7*	*60*	*24*	*31*	*7*	*4.98*	*5.20*	*10.1*	*3.4*	*4.5*	*1.2*	*5.39*	*4.3*	*-10*

Breakout: 15% Improve: 52% Collapse: 24%

An unimpressive season for the former Rockies prospect. Where'd that "heavy fastball" go? Where's the strikeout rate? His season wasn't bad, certainly, but there's nothing here to get excited about.

RYAN FRANKLIN Bats: R Throws: R Born: 05-Mar-1973 Age: 32

YEAR	TM	LG	AGE	G	GS	IP	H	BB	SO	HR	ERA	EQERA	EQH9	EQBB9	EQSO9	EQHR9	PERA	VORP	STF
2002	SEA	AL	29	41	12	118.7	117	22	65	14	4.02	4.70	9.2	1.6	4.9	1.0	4.14	16.8	0
2003	SEA	AL	30	32	32	212.0	199	61	99	34	3.57	3.92	9.5	2.6	4.3	1.4	5.28	50.3	-5
2004	SEA	AL	31	32	32	200.3	224	61	104	33	4.90	4.85	9.9	2.5	4.5	1.3	5.13	22.7	-3
2005	*SEA*	*AL*	*32*	*28*	*25*	*147.7*	*162*	*43*	*76*	*26*	*4.99*	*5.21*	*10.2*	*2.3*	*4.1*	*1.6*	*5.19*	*10.1*	*-6*

Breakout: 12% Improve: 41% Collapse: 20%

The pre-season favorite of local scribes to improve, because he had such poor run support in '03. They ignored that Franklin is a low-walk, low-strikeout flyball pitcher who depended heavily on a historically good outfield defense that had been massively degraded in the off-season. Plus, all the run support in the world doesn't make him Randy Johnson. The M's, deluded, gave Franklin a hefty two-year deal. The contracts of Franklin and Hasegawa are damning evidence the organization is unable to see the whole picture. Although Franklin nearly always goes deep into games, which is more than you get out of many fourth and fifth starters, he's still not worth what he's getting.

EDDIE GUARDADO Bats: R Throws: L Born: 02-Oct-1970 Age: 34

YEAR	TM	LG	AGE	G	GS	IP	H	BB	SO	HR	ERA	EQERA	EQH9	EQBB9	EQSO9	EQHR9	PERA	VORP	STF
2002	MIN	AL	31	68	0	67.7	53	18	70	9	2.92	2.77	7.5	2.2	9.1	1.1	3.46	22.9	19
2003	MIN	AL	32	66	0	65.3	50	14	60	7	2.89	2.89	7.2	1.9	8.4	0.9	2.89	22.3	19
2004	SEA	AL	33	41	0	45.3	31	14	45	8	2.78	2.72	7.1	2.5	8.8	1.5	3.35	17.6	15
2005	*SEA*	*AL*	*34*	*52*	*0*	*45.3*	*36*	*15*	*44*	*8*	*3.61*	*3.77*	*7.3*	*2.6*	*7.8*	*1.6*	*3.74*	*12.0*	*6*

Breakout: 17% Improve: 42% Collapse: 25%

Guardado's knee problem led to a shoulder problem, ending his season. Rehabbing a torn rotator cuff seems reasonable if it's as minor a tear as they say. If it was caused by mechanical problems resulting from another injury, it also seems reasonable that it won't recur. But once it's torn, there's no going back. We wouldn't count on him pitching regularly or even returning this year. Rotator cuff problems are particularly subject to setbacks, or worse, the heart-breaking discovery that the injury's much worse than previously suspected. Like breaking up with a hot, crazy girlfriend.

SHIGETOSHI HASEGAWA Bats: R Throws: R Born: 01-Aug-1968 Age: 36

YEAR	TM	LG	AGE	G	GS	IP	H	BB	SO	HR	ERA	EQERA	EQH9	EQBB9	EQSO9	EQHR9	PERA	VORP	STF
2002	SEA	AL	33	53	0	70.3	60	30	39	4	3.20	3.38	8.2	3.6	5.0	0.5	3.78	20.7	-6
2003	SEA	AL	34	63	0	73.0	62	18	32	5	1.48	1.60	8.8	2.3	4.1	0.7	4.26	37.5	-9
2004	SEA	AL	35	68	0	68.0	67	31	46	5	5.16	5.16	8.8	3.7	5.8	0.5	4.34	5.5	-4
2005	*SEA*	*AL*	*36*	*50*	*0*	*52.7*	*54*	*23*	*32*	*6*	*4.09*	*4.26*	*9.6*	*3.4*	*4.8*	*1.0*	*4.88*	*10.8*	*-13*

Breakout: 38% Improve: 64% Collapse: 14%

And now a word from our sponsor, the Seattle Mariners.

Fellow front offices, you're well aware of the crippling shortage of high-quality closers affecting teams today. With a plague of injuries last year, the increasing cost of international free agents, and the unfortunate trend of overly aggressive college players choosing lacrosse, finding a closer is harder today than ever. And with the tighter finances and increased oversight of today's ownership groups, you want to make sure that your closer investment is the right one.

So choose Shigetoshi Hasegawa. In 2003, he converted 16 of 17 save chances, and allowed more than one run only once—when he allowed two—in 63 appearances! Why, given a three-run lead, he would convert every save you threw at him! Our acquisition of Guardado has forced him out of the closer position, and he's struggled since. If you want a proven reliever who can immediately step back into the role, please give us a call at (206) 346-4001 and ask for Bill.

FELIX HERNANDEZ **Bats: R** **Throws: R** Born: 08-Apr-1986 Age: 19

YEAR	TM	LG	AGE	G	GS	IP	H	BB	SO	HR	ERA	EQERA	EQH9	EQBB9	EQSO9	EQHR9	PERA	VORP	STF
2003	EVE	NWN	17	11	7	55.0	43	24	73	2	2.29	4.86	8.6	5.0	6.8	0.9	4.68	5.1	27
2004	SBR	CLF	18	16	15	92.0	85	26	114	5	2.74	4.24	8.7	3.1	7.2	0.7	3.93	16.1	44
2004	SAN	TXS	18	10	10	57.3	47	21	58	3	3.30	4.70	8.0	3.7	6.5	0.7	3.69	11.4	41
2005	*SEA*	*AL*	*19*	*13*	*13*	*76.3*	*71*	*32*	*61*	*9*	*4.16*	*4.34*	*8.7*	*3.4*	*6.4*	*1.1*	*4.45*	*11.9*	*10*

Breakout: 5% *Improve: 28%* *Collapse: 18%*

All will bow before King Felix. Hernandez breezed through the California and Texas leagues. He struck out 172 batters in less than 150 innings of total work, walking just 47. Hernandez had as many wild pitches last year as home runs allowed: eight. It's not just stats, either, he's amazing to watch. And he's not even allowed to throw his slider yet! King Felix could force his way into the rotation this spring, before his nineteenth birthday. He certainly will be there for 2006 if he stays healthy.

JON HUBER **Bats: R** **Throws: R** Born: 07-Jul-1981 Age: 23

YEAR	TM	LG	AGE	G	GS	IP	H	BB	SO	HR	ERA	EQERA	EQH9	EQBB9	EQSO9	EQHR9	PERA	VORP	STF
2002	FTW	MDW	20	28	26	146.0	168	59	86	7	5.12	7.90	10.7	4.5	3.2	1.2	5.93	-5.0	-22
2003	FTW	MDW	21	7	7	38.3	31	11	34	2	3.76	5.97	9.1	3.4	5.5	1.3	4.41	4.6	-2
2003	LEL	CLF	21	12	11	57.3	69	31	43	2	5.18	7.32	9.8	5.9	4.2	0.7	5.20	2.5	-15
2004	LEL	CLF	23	20	20	107.0	107	44	100	9	3.70	5.36	9.7	4.6	5.6	1.4	5.55	0.6	-10
2004	SBR	CLF	23	7	5	32.3	42	14	38	4	6.13	7.26	11.3	4.6	6.7	2.0	6.97	-4.7	-10
2005	*SEA*	*AL*	*23*	*25*	*12*	*81.3*	*86*	*43*	*55*	*12*	*5.26*	*5.49*	*9.8*	*4.2*	*5.3*	*1.3*	*5.56*	*3.0*	*-10*

Breakout: 12% *Improve: 44%* *Collapse: 19%*

The Mariners are ex-huber-ant about the return they got for Dave Hansen. He's got heat on his fastball and throws a good curve that racked up the strikeouts, barely missing a K an inning in '04. Old for his level, he'll need to impress in the Texas League to stay in the team's good graces.

RETT JOHNSON **Bats: L** **Throws: R** Born: 06-Jul-1979 Age: 25

YEAR	TM	LG	AGE	G	GS	IP	H	BB	SO	HR	ERA	EQERA	EQH9	EQBB9	EQSO9	EQHR9	PERA	VORP	STF
2002	SBR	CLF	23	7	7	37.0	27	11	34	1	3.65	5.29	7.9	3.2	5.0	0.5	3.44	8.2	8
2002	SAN	TXS	23	21	21	117.0	107	53	104	5	3.62	6.11	9.1	4.5	6.2	0.7	4.87	8.8	3
2003	SAN	TXS	24	14	14	83.0	74	21	63	7	3.04	4.52	9.5	2.6	5.5	1.5	5.23	3.1	-4
2003	TAC	PCL	24	11	10	71.0	63	18	49	2	2.15	4.05	8.4	2.6	5.4	0.4	3.65	14.5	21
2004	SBR	CLF	25	7	7	20.3	32	14	14	0	7.98	9.30	11.5	7.1	4.0	0.4	7.08	-3.3	-40
2005	*SEA*	*AL*	*25*	*20*	*12*	*75.3*	*81*	*36*	*48*	*8*	*4.92*	*5.13*	*10.0*	*3.8*	*5.1*	*1.0*	*5.26*	*5.1*	*-6*

Breakout: 18% *Improve: 49%* *Collapse: 22%*

Johnson left the team for personal reasons, and didn't throw against live batters until the end of the year. Whether Johnson wants to work to be the major league pitcher it appeared he would become at the end of 2003 is entirely up to him. The Mariners didn't offer him a contract for '05.

BOBBY LIVINGSTON **Bats: L** **Throws: L** Born: 03-Sep-1982 Age: 22

YEAR	TM	LG	AGE	G	GS	IP	H	BB	SO	HR	ERA	EQERA	EQH9	EQBB9	EQSO9	EQHR9	PERA	VORP	STF
2002	EVE	NWN	19	15	14	80.3	80	14	76	2	3.03	5.59	9.6	1.9	4.5	0.6	4.28	11.1	9
2003	WIS	MDW	20	26	26	178.0	176	28	105	10	2.73	5.35	9.9	1.8	3.6	1.4	4.80	14.7	5
2004	SBR	CLF	21	28	27	186.7	187	30	141	15	3.57	5.37	9.3	1.8	4.4	1.3	4.30	25.4	13
2005	*SEA*	*AL*	*22*	*12*	*12*	*75.0*	*83*	*21*	*41*	*11*	*4.65*	*4.86*	*10.3*	*2.3*	*4.4*	*1.3*	*4.99*	*8.1*	*0*

Breakout: 5% *Improve: 43%* *Collapse: 20%*

King Felix and Bobby Livingston provided a great 1-2 combo for the Inland Empire 66ers much of last season. That's unfair. Livingston's got great command and as he matures his pitches are getting nastier and nastier. At this rate, when he reaches the Show, his pitches will do loop-de-loops on the way to the plate. Livingston's behind only Hernandez in the system's pitcher hierarchy.

BOBBY MADRITSCH

Bats: L Throws: L Born: 28-Feb-1976 Age: 29

YEAR	TM	LG	AGE	G	GS	IP	H	BB	SO	HR	ERA	EQERA	EQH9	EQBB9	EQSO9	EQHR9	PERA	VORP	STF
2003	SAN	TXS	27	27	27	158.7	133	67	154	11	3.63	5.38	8.8	4.4	6.9	1.4	5.25	5.7	13
2004	TAC	PCL	28	12	12	62.3	61	26	53	3	3.76	4.95	8.6	3.9	5.8	0.4	4.05	10.3	12
2004	SEA	AL	28	15	11	88.0	74	33	60	3	3.27	3.19	7.9	3.1	6.0	0.3	3.40	28.0	23
2005	*SEA*	*AL*	*29*	*22*	*17*	*106.7*	*108*	*45*	*76*	*13*	*4.49*	*4.68*	*9.4*	*3.4*	*5.7*	*1.1*	*4.87*	*13.6*	*2*

Breakout: 18% *Improve: 43%* *Collapse: 21%*

The only pitcher who is absolutely in the 2005 rotation. Madritsch is utterly unflappable. Blown calls, cheap errors, mistake pitches jumped on, none of these things affect him. His work in '04 was as good as you could have expected, and that's a solid contribution on any team. Considering that the Reds abandoned him after supposedly career-ending injuries and he then fought his way back up from the independent leagues, we take our hats off to him.

Madritsch claims he's never had health problems since getting the medicine wheel tattooed on his neck. The Mariners should consider offering it free to any player in their system. It couldn't make things worse. Even protected by that talisman, the late-season abuse was unconscionable. In meaningless games Madritsch racked up huge pitch counts. Sometimes he looked fresh, sometimes he was clearly dragging when Melvin sent him out for more punishment. For his failure to preserve his best healthy pitcher for next year, Melvin should have been fired far earlier than he was.

JULIO MATEO

Bats: R Throws: R Born: 02-Aug-1977 Age: 27

YEAR	TM	LG	AGE	G	GS	IP	H	BB	SO	HR	ERA	EQERA	EQH9	EQBB9	EQSO9	EQHR9	PERA	VORP	STF
2002	SAN	TXS	24	12	0	17.3	7	3	18	2	0.52	3.00	7.2	1.8	7.8	2.4	3.60	3.3	16
2002	TAC	PCL	24	20	0	31.0	39	7	23	2	4.06	4.70	10.0	2.1	5.0	0.6	4.40	4.1	-10
2002	SEA	AL	24	12	0	21.0	20	12	15	2	4.29	4.43	8.9	4.9	6.2	0.9	4.87	3.9	-12
2003	SEA	AL	25	50	0	85.7	69	13	71	14	3.15	3.36	8.2	1.3	7.6	1.5	4.03	26.0	5
2004	SEA	AL	26	45	0	57.7	56	16	43	11	4.68	4.37	8.9	2.3	6.5	1.6	4.69	10.2	-7
2005	*SEA*	*AL*	*27*	*31*	*3*	*54.0*	*51*	*16*	*40*	*10*	*4.33*	*4.51*	*8.7*	*2.4*	*5.8*	*1.6*	*4.54*	*9.2*	*-5*

Breakout: 21% *Improve: 51%* *Collapse: 25%*

Stop me if you've heard this one before. Twenty pitchers go into a season, and they all get badly injured. . . . Mateo suffered elbow tendonitis in '04, which took him out for much of the season, but shockingly,given the Mariners' recent history, was not a symptom of a career-threatening injury. He is a good, serviceable part of the bullpen for not much dough. The Mariners can do much worse, like Masao Kida.

GIL MECHE

Bats: R Throws: R Born: 08-Sep-1978 Age: 26

YEAR	TM	LG	AGE	G	GS	IP	H	BB	SO	HR	ERA	EQERA	EQH9	EQBB9	EQSO9	EQHR9	PERA	VORP	STF
2002	SAN	TXS	23	25	13	65.0	68	32	56	8	6.51	7.99	10.9	5.0	6.0	2.3	7.24	-10.9	-24
2003	SEA	AL	24	32	32	186.3	187	63	130	30	4.59	4.55	9.4	3.0	6.3	1.4	5.31	28.9	4
2004	TAC	PCL	25	10	10	57.0	55	27	45	8	5.05	6.00	9.0	4.5	5.7	1.5	5.17	2.6	-3
2004	SEA	AL	25	23	23	127.7	139	47	99	21	5.00	4.80	9.4	3.0	6.6	1.4	4.94	15.4	7
2005	*SEA*	*AL*	*26*	*23*	*21*	*124.0*	*126*	*50*	*91*	*19*	*4.84*	*5.05*	*9.5*	*3.2*	*5.9*	*1.3*	*4.97*	*11.0*	*4*

Breakout: 13% *Improve: 38%* *Collapse: 24%*

After struggling early, Meche was sent to Tacoma to work on his approach and his endurance. He was to work on his endurance by being forced to throw 115–126 pitches every start he made, no matter what that took. He came back a different pitcher entirely. Pre-anvil treatment, 7.06 ERA, 43.1 IP, 55 H, 6 HR, 29 BB, 41 K, and post-anvil treatment, 3.95 ERA, 84.1 IP, 84 IP, 15 IP, 18 BB, 58 K.

The walks that plagued him earlier in the season disappeared as he put more balls into play. Before, more than a third of balls in play turned into hits. After, only a quarter did. Walks and defense, that's *all* it was. Meche is getting expensive and nearing free agency, which makes the team's decision to risk breaking him in order to turn him into something useful easier to understand.

JAMIE MOYER

Bats: L **Throws: L** Born: 18-Nov-1962 Age: 42

YEAR	TM	LG	AGE	G	GS	IP	H	BB	SO	HR	ERA	EQERA	EQH9	EQBB9	EQSO9	EQHR9	PERA	VORP	STF
2002	SEA	AL	39	34	34	230.7	198	50	147	28	3.32	3.52	8.4	1.9	5.7	1.1	3.77	64.3	13
2003	SEA	AL	40	33	33	215.0	199	66	129	19	3.27	3.45	8.9	2.7	5.5	0.8	4.51	62.3	10
2004	SEA	AL	41	34	33	202.0	217	63	125	44	5.21	5.25	9.7	2.6	5.3	1.8	5.34	12.9	-4
2005	*SEA*	*AL*	*42*	*28*	*24*	*146.0*	*154*	*48*	*82*	*23*	*4.65*	*4.85*	*9.8*	*2.6*	*4.5*	*1.4*	*5.00*	*15.1*	*-3*

Breakout: 23% *Improve: 41%* *Collapse: 18%*

There may be no coming back from this. Hitters smoked him for a massive dollop of extra home runs this year. If Moyer has lost enough of his super-fine control that he can't play the location-location-location game, his career as a starter will end. Moyer is such a dedicated player and preparation freak that he's not going to go out without a struggle, but struggle may not be enough.

CLINT NAGEOTTE

Bats: R **Throws: R** Born: 25-Oct-1980 Age: 24

YEAR	TM	LG	AGE	G	GS	IP	H	BB	SO	HR	ERA	EQERA	EQH9	EQBB9	EQSO9	EQHR9	PERA	VORP	STF
2002	SBR	CLF	21	29	29	164.7	153	68	214	10	4.54	6.49	9.5	4.2	6.9	1.0	5.08	8.9	2
2003	SAN	TXS	22	27	27	154.0	127	67	157	6	3.10	4.67	8.3	4.5	7.2	0.7	4.48	17.8	15
2004	TAC	PCL	23	14	14	80.7	78	35	63	9	4.46	4.93	8.9	4.2	5.5	1.1	4.81	6.7	9
2004	SEA	AL	23	12	5	36.7	48	27	24	3	7.36	6.99	10.4	5.8	5.3	0.7	6.03	-5.5	-6
2005	*SEA*	*AL*	*24*	*22*	*13*	*86.7*	*85*	*44*	*67*	*10*	*4.79*	*5.00*	*9.1*	*4.0*	*6.1*	*1.0*	*4.89*	*8.9*	*0*

Breakout: 14% *Improve: 49%* *Collapse: 25%*

Because Melvin was a poor judge of talent, he was convinced from brief spring training exposure that Nageotte was the strike-throwing right-handed set-up man the club needed. The front office, however, didn't want to call Nageotte up to be a reliever, preferring to get him more work as a starter. They should have stuck to their guns. His ill control keeps him from being a major league success, and he's not suited for the role Melvin envisioned. Nageotte's got great stuff, but until he can throw those wicked pitches for consistent strikes, he'll rise no further.

THOMAS OLDHAM

Bats: L **Throws: L** Born: 18-May-1982 Age: 23

YEAR	TM	LG	AGE	G	GS	IP	H	BB	SO	HR	ERA	EQERA	EQH9	EQBB9	EQSO9	EQHR9	PERA	VORP	STF
2003	EVE	NWN	21	13	11	63.0	48	23	63	2	2.86	5.81	8.3	4.2	5.2	0.9	4.08	9.7	11
2004	WIS	MDW	22	19	19	116.7	108	30	132	15	2.93	5.01	10.1	3.0	6.2	2.5	5.86	-3.1	-2
2004	SBR	CLF	22	7	6	42.0	47	6	56	5	3.21	5.62	10.4	1.6	7.9	2.0	5.40	0.9	25
2005	*SEA*	*AL*	*23*	*10*	*9*	*54.7*	*52*	*21*	*42*	*9*	*4.55*	*4.74*	*8.9*	*3.0*	*6.1*	*1.4*	*4.70*	*6.5*	*6*

Breakout: 7% *Improve: 44%* *Collapse: 15%*

You wonder if the team doesn't notice him. In an organization racked with pitching injuries, you'd think they'd have moved him up, given his age and performance, and put him against some more advanced competition to see if he could even turn into a useful LOOGY. They didn't. Who knows why.

JOEL PINEIRO

Bats: R **Throws: R** Born: 25-Sep-1978 Age: 26

YEAR	TM	LG	AGE	G	GS	IP	H	BB	SO	HR	ERA	EQERA	EQH9	EQBB9	EQSO9	EQHR9	PERA	VORP	STF
2002	SEA	AL	23	37	28	194.3	189	54	136	24	3.24	3.52	8.9	2.4	6.2	1.1	4.24	54.1	11
2003	SEA	AL	24	32	32	211.7	192	76	151	19	3.78	3.93	8.7	3.2	6.5	0.8	4.51	49.1	15
2004	SEA	AL	25	21	21	140.7	144	43	111	21	4.67	4.59	9.0	2.5	6.8	1.2	4.52	20.4	13
2005	*SEA*	*AL*	*26*	*24*	*23*	*138.3*	*137*	*46*	*102*	*17*	*4.20*	*4.38*	*9.2*	*2.7*	*5.8*	*1.1*	*4.39*	*22.4*	*9*

Breakout: 14% *Improve: 48%* *Collapse: 25%*

Another pitching injury! This time, the promising young pitcher was sidelined by a strained right elbow, and didn't require surgery. That we know about. The M's are pretty bad about these things. The team anticipates he'll be back for '05, when he will, most likely, be the nominal #1 starter—until Madritsch beats him up in the clubhouse and steals the badge from him. Hopefully, the rest will do him good and Pineiro will start to combine all his talents into the star package he's been flirting with since 2001.

J. J. PUTZ | **Bats: R** | **Throws: R** | Born: 22-Feb-1977 | Age: 28

YEAR	TM	LG	AGE	G	GS	IP	H	BB	SO	HR	ERA	EQERA	EQH9	EQBB9	EQSO9	EQHR9	PERA	VORP	STF
2002	SAN	TXS	25	15	15	84.0	84	28	60	7	3.64	5.68	10.1	3.4	5.0	1.6	5.79	-1.6	-6
2002	TAC	PCL	25	9	9	54.0	51	21	39	4	3.83	4.21	8.6	3.7	5.1	0.9	4.03	8.9	6
2003	TAC	PCL	26	41	0	86.0	69	34	60	4	2.51	3.97	8.1	4.1	5.6	0.7	4.08	13.4	7
2004	SEA	AL	27	54	0	63.0	66	24	47	10	4.71	4.67	9.2	3.1	6.4	1.3	4.96	9.0	-7
2005	*SEA*	*AL*	*28*	*29*	*5*	*58.3*	*58*	*23*	*42*	*7*	*4.30*	*4.48*	*9.2*	*3.2*	*5.8*	*1.1*	*4.60*	*9.3*	*-4*

Breakout: 21% *Improve: 48%* *Collapse: 22%*

Here's a great gift for the busy general manager having trouble making that off-season blockbuster trade. A closer gift certificate from the Seattle Mariners! Available in approximated VORP denominations of 0, 5, 10, and 15, our certificates can be redeemed for whatever size and style of closer best fits a team's needs. General managers will appreciate your thoughtfulness and good taste in selecting a closer gift certificate from the Seattle Mariners. You get one Putz for a 10-VORP certificate, if you were curious.

Took over late in the season as the closer and finished strongly, which makes him an interesting sleeper pick in fantasy leagues, due to Guardado's shoulder issue.

TIM RALL | **Bats: R** | **Throws: L** | Born: 30-Sep-1979 | Age: 25

YEAR	TM	LG	AGE	G	GS	IP	H	BB	SO	HR	ERA	EQERA	EQH9	EQBB9	EQSO9	EQHR9	PERA	VORP	STF
2003	SBR	CLF	23	10	4	37.0	34	9	30	5	3.65	5.13	10.3	3.0	4.9	2.7	6.48	-3.3	-12
2004	SAN	TXS	24	56	0	65.0	62	35	78	12	4.57	5.73	10.0	5.6	8.0	3.0	6.94	-8.9	-21
2005	*SEA*	*AL*	*25*	*8*	*1*	*14.7*	*14*	*8*	*12*	*3*	*5.20*	*5.43*	*8.8*	*4.2*	*6.3*	*1.7*	*5.32*	*1.1*	*-10*

Breakout: 23% *Improve: 42%* *Collapse: 32%*

Why spend on Mike Myers when you can find left-handed guys like Tim Rall in the indy leagues? Rall's got the added benefit of being able to go more than one inning as required, so you've got a little more flexibility if you need it. Here's hoping the team notices.

RYAN ROWLAND-SMITH | **Bats: L** | **Throws: L** | Born: 26-Jan-1983 | Age: 22

YEAR	TM	LG	AGE	G	GS	IP	H	BB	SO	HR	ERA	EQERA	EQH9	EQBB9	EQSO9	EQHR9	PERA	VORP	STF
2002	EVE	NWN	19	18	6	61.7	58	22	58	2	2.77	5.21	9.5	3.9	4.6	0.8	4.89	4.5	-2
2002	WIS	MDW	19	12	8	41.3	50	19	38	7	6.76	9.82	13.5	5.4	5.4	3.9	9.82	-17.2	-30
2003	WIS	MDW	20	13	0	32.3	22	14	37	0	1.11	5.46	7.3	4.9	7.0	0.3	3.34	7.5	15
2003	SBR	CLF	20	15	0	19.7	12	8	15	0	3.20	5.09	7.1	4.6	4.6	0.5	3.57	4.0	-3
2004	SBR	CLF	21	29	12	99.7	107	30	119	10	3.70	5.53	9.9	3.3	7.0	1.6	5.34	2.7	-8
2005	*MIN*	*AL*	*22*	*29*	*7*	*69.3*	*71*	*32*	*54*	*11*	*5.27*	*5.06*	*9.1*	*3.7*	*6.4*	*1.4*	*4.95*	*6.2*	*-4*

Breakout: 8% *Improve: 40%* *Collapse: 25%*

Another Australian, and another Olympic participant (he was outstanding). Rowland-Smith's bounced between starting and relieving as he's moved up slowly through the system. He's trying to improve his delivery to make it shorter and easier, while increasing the speed on his fastball and movement on his pitches. With the kind of stuff he offers, the split role is a little baffling; you'd think they'd want to keep him starting, if only to get him the work he needs until he clearly forced the conversion issue later.

GEORGE SHERRILL | **Bats: L** | **Throws: L** | Born: 19-Apr-1977 | Age: 28

YEAR	TM	LG	AGE	G	GS	IP	H	BB	SO	HR	ERA	EQERA	EQH9	EQBB9	EQSO9	EQHR9	PERA	VORP	STF
2003	SAN	TXS	26	16	0	27.3	19	12	31	1	0.33	1.80	7.6	4.7	7.9	0.7	4.32	3.6	8
2004	TAC	PCL	27	36	0	50.3	42	9	62	4	2.33	3.00	7.9	1.7	8.6	0.9	3.19	12.9	22
2005	*SEA*	*AL*	*28*	*18*	*3*	*37.0*	*34*	*13*	*31*	*5*	*3.83*	*3.99*	*8.6*	*2.8*	*6.6*	*1.1*	*4.07*	*8.1*	*3*

Breakout: 22% *Improve: 45%* *Collapse: 25%*

Say, folks, here's another great shopping tip from our sponsor, the Seattle Mariners. Did you know that minor league closers can provide the same effectiveness as a name-brand closer at a fraction of the cost? Even if you already have a closer, if your team tends to be racked by injuries or you play so many close games one closer just won't do, you'll save money by purchasing minor league closers. Smart shoppers don't neglect quality either, which is why you should trust George Sherrill, who offers great control and gets the strikeouts you like, all with the value and versatility that comes with being left-handed. Minor league closers: an effective solution for any team! Call (206) 346-4001 and ask for Bill today!

RAFAEL SORIANO Bats: R Throws: R Born: 19-Dec-1979 Age: 25

YEAR	TM	LG	AGE	G	GS	IP	H	BB	SO	HR	ERA	EQERA	EQH9	EQBB9	EQSO9	EQHR9	PERA	VORP	STF
2002	SAN	TXS	22	10	8	46.7	32	15	52	6	2.31	3.92	8.7	3.3	8.3	2.4	5.23	1.7	15
2002	SEA	AL	22	10	8	47.3	45	16	32	8	4.57	4.80	9.0	3.0	6.0	1.4	4.60	6.5	10
2003	TAC	PCL	23	11	10	62.0	43	12	63	2	3.19	4.21	7.0	2.0	8.0	0.5	2.65	18.9	42
2003	SEA	AL	23	40	0	53.0	30	12	68	2	1.53	1.61	5.7	2.0	11.6	0.4	2.32	26.9	53
2004	SEA	AL	24	6	0	3.3	9	3	3	0	13.64	15.75	15.8	6.8	6.8	0.0	9.00	-3.7	-29
2005	*SEA*	*AL*	*25*	*19*	*7*	*59.3*	*54*	*20*	*55*	*8*	*4.07*	*4.24*	*8.5*	*2.6*	*7.3*	*1.2*	*4.09*	*10.8*	*10*

Breakout: 14% *Improve: 43%* *Collapse: 30%*

The team rushed an injured Soriano back, but he wasn't ready and went on the DL again. He ended up having his elbow ligament replaced. Through the minors, Soriano had complained of arm pain and stiffness. Hopefully, this will finally resolve his problems. He's an immensely talented pitcher, and it was a shame his arm problems didn't get solved much earlier.

AARON TAYLOR Bats: R Throws: R Born: 20-Aug-1977 Age: 27

YEAR	TM	LG	AGE	G	GS	IP	H	BB	SO	HR	ERA	EQERA	EQH9	EQBB9	EQSO9	EQHR9	PERA	VORP	STF
2002	SAN	TXS	24	61	0	77.0	51	34	93	5	2.34	4.63	7.7	4.5	8.6	1.3	4.37	9.6	10
2003	TAC	PCL	25	33	0	40.3	30	13	34	3	2.46	3.41	7.8	3.4	6.8	1.0	3.65	8.0	7
2003	SEA	AL	25	10	0	12.7	17	6	9	0	8.50	7.82	10.7	4.3	6.4	0.0	5.68	-3.4	-2
2004	SAN	TXS	26	30	0	37.3	27	14	37	2	2.90	4.19	7.6	3.9	6.6	0.8	3.41	8.3	6
2004	SEA	AL	26	5	0	3.7	5	3	4	2	9.73	9.82	12.3	7.4	9.8	4.9	9.82	-1.4	-11
2005	*COL*	*NL*	*27*	*25*	*0*	*26.0*	*29*	*13*	*22*	*4*	*5.69*	*4.97*	*9.3*	*3.8*	*7.1*	*1.2*	*4.93*	*2.7*	*-3*

Breakout: 21% *Improve: 39%* *Collapse: 37%*

Taylor came back from a "partially torn rotator cuff" to get shelled in the big leagues. He's a nice guy who's kind to kids at the ballpark, so that sucks. What sucks more is that he went through all that rehab for a chance to arm-wrestle Scott Atchison this spring for a right-handed reliever slot.

MATT THORNTON Bats: L Throws: L Born: 15-Sep-1976 Age: 28

YEAR	TM	LG	AGE	G	GS	IP	H	BB	SO	HR	ERA	EQERA	EQH9	EQBB9	EQSO9	EQHR9	PERA	VORP	STF
2002	SAN	TXS	25	12	12	62.0	52	29	44	3	3.63	5.88	8.9	4.8	5.1	1.0	5.08	3.3	1
2003	SAN	TXS	26	4	4	25.3	8	9	18	0	0.36	2.45	5.3	4.1	5.3	0.4	2.45	7.7	24
2004	SEA	AL	27	19	1	32.7	30	25	30	2	4.13	3.90	8.1	6.1	7.8	0.6	4.45	7.8	0
2004	TAC	PCL	27	16	15	83.0	86	63	74	4	5.42	6.27	8.9	7.2	6.2	0.6	5.38	2.0	-4
2005	*SEA*	*AL*	*28*	*17*	*12*	*74.0*	*70*	*47*	*57*	*8*	*5.00*	*5.21*	*8.8*	*5.1*	*6.1*	*1.0*	*5.21*	*4.9*	*-3*

Breakout: 16% *Improve: 47%* *Collapse: 16%*

Thornton's got a prospect-like aura around him that's totally unwarranted. He can't control the ball. We have no idea why he causes people to salivate so much—maybe he has rabies, and bites them? Thornton, who had Tommy John surgery that cost him his 2002 season, developed shoulder pain in '04. He probably wanted to feel included.

RON VILLONE Bats: L Throws: L Born: 16-Jan-1970 Age: 35

YEAR	TM	LG	AGE	G	GS	IP	H	BB	SO	HR	ERA	EQERA	EQH9	EQBB9	EQSO9	EQHR9	PERA	VORP	STF
2002	PIT	NL	32	45	7	93.0	95	34	55	8	5.81	5.92	9.2	2.8	4.8	0.8	4.52	-6.9	-6
2003	HOU	NL	33	19	19	106.7	91	48	91	16	4.13	4.07	8.4	3.6	7.2	1.3	4.60	16.5	15
2004	SEA	AL	34	56	10	117.0	102	64	86	12	4.08	4.62	8.2	4.5	6.4	0.9	4.38	17.4	3
2005	*SEA*	*AL*	*35*	*32*	*7*	*72.3*	*72*	*36*	*53*	*9*	*4.94*	*5.16*	*9.2*	*3.9*	*5.8*	*1.1*	*5.02*	*6.0*	*-7*

Breakout: 17% *Improve: 48%* *Collapse: 29%*

Did his versatility hold the team together through hard times? No. Villone, the starter: 5.43 ERA, 10 starts, 2–2 record, 53 IP, 31 BB, 34 K, and Villone, the reliever: 2.95 ERA, 64 IP, 33 BB, 52 K.

That he did two things and wasn't crappy at one of them doesn't mean that he's somehow that much more valuable. Plenty of people can fail at a second career. As with Raul Ibanez's persistent reputation as a clutch hitter, Villone winning the team's pitching MVP award is a demonstration of the power of media memes.

Tampa Bay Devil Rays

You could almost celebrate in Tampa Bay. For the first time in their history, they didn't finish last. For the first time in their history, they won 70 games.

We did say "almost." The fact of the matter is that the Rays finished next to last (beating only Toronto) and set a team record by winning exactly 70 games. Nevertheless, there is some cause for optimism down on the Gulf Coast.

GM Chuck LaMar has been pursuing a high-risk/high-reward draft strategy since the franchise began; 2004 was the first year that some of those risks started to pay off. It has to be this way. The franchise is financially limited, and its forays into the free-agent market have resulted mostly in bad burns, so they probably won't be looking to spend significant money on a free agent anytime soon.

Consider these scouting and development success stories:

Carl Crawford, a second-round pick out of high school in 1999, emerged as one of the American League's most exciting players, leading the junior circuit in stolen bases for the second year in a row and hitting 19 triples.

Rocco Baldelli, a first-round pick out of high school in 2000, had another solid season in center field, boosting his power in the process.

Jorge Cantu, a free agent from Mexico signed in 1998, suddenly developed into a power-hitting second baseman, knocking out 53 doubles and 25 home runs between Tampa Bay and Durham. He continued mashing in winter ball.

B. J. Upton, the second pick overall in 2002, reached the majors with less than two years of professional experience behind him, hitting all the way.

Delmon Young, the first overall pick in 2003, overcame a slow start and absolutely crushed opposing pitching during the final month of the season, establishing a legitimate claim on being the best hitter in the minors.

Of course, not that everything came up roses. Former first overall pick Josh Hamilton missed another entire season, this time due to drug problems, and 2001 first-round pick Dewon Brazelton continued to disappoint as a starting pitcher. Still, any manager has to drool over the fact that the team finished the year with players at second, short, left, and center who were at least holding their own in the majors at the age of 23 or less.

Now is the time for patience. The window of opportunity for the Rays to make the playoffs is not yet open.

DEVIL RAYS PROSPECTUS

2004 record: 70–91; Fourth place, AL East

Pythagenport record: 68–94

Runs scored per game: 4.43 (13th in AL)

Runs allowed per game: 5.23 (12th in AL)

Team EqA: .251 (12th in AL)

2004 Batters Age: 28.7 (4th youngest in AL)

2004 Pitchers Age: 28.1 (2nd youngest in AL)

Ballpark: Tropicana Field; Slight pitcher's park; Park Factor of 0.977

2004: Clawing your way out of the cellar is always sweet; having never been anywhere else must make it all the better.

2005: They've got a few interesting players, but come on—we're still talking about a team that spends nine figures less than two division rivals.

The Yankees and Red Sox are both loaded for bear this coming season, having spent the off-season trying yet again to one-up each other. In this and recently past off-seasons, New York and Boston have taken on whatever contracts, at whatever cost, they've needed to get the players they wanted. Eventually there will come a point when the objects of those contracts become too old, injured or both to perform at their expected level. That probably won't happen this year. Nevertheless, the likelihood of it occurring is going to rise in 2006, 2007, and 2008.

By 2008, the baby Rays currently on the field will be just entering their primes: Baldelli and Crawford will be 26, Cantu 25, Upton and Young still youngsters at 23 and 22. Aubrey Huff will be the grand old man at 31, still likely to be a prime year for a player with his skill set, though he probably will no longer be a Ray. That is four years with which to not only further develop the talent already in Tampa, but to sort out one or more of their strong minor league collection: Players like Wes Bankston, Elijah Dukes, Joey Gathright, and Jason Pridie all have the ability to play in the majors, if they can properly harness their talents. Four years should be enough time for at least one of them to step forward, and that also gives time for Hamilton to (one can dream) resurrect his career. Remember, this is a guy who was once considered by some the #1 prospect in all of baseball; that's a solid talent base to work from, even with a two-year interruption.

All this gives the Rays three years to develop some pitching. Since their first year of existence, when they finished fourth in ERA, Tampa Bay's pitching has not cracked the top half of the league. They were close in 2004, finishing ninth, entirely on the strength of their bullpen. Their starters, all 14 of them, were horrible. They pitched fewer innings than any staff in the majors, including Colorado's, and for good reason: Their 5.40 ERA was third-worst in the bigs.

The bullpen, by contrast, was third-best in the American League, with an ERA of 3.87. Newcomer Danys Baez got most of the acclaim with his 30 saves, but in reality he was only a middle-of-the-pack reliever. Nobody in the pen was absolutely dominant, in the way that, say, the two Franciscos, Rodriguez, and Cordero, did for Anaheim and Texas—the top two bullpens in the league. Instead, the Rays had balanced depth: Nine of the 10 pitchers who worked 15 or more innings in relief had ERAs under 4.28.

Last year saw the team make two significant moves to strengthen the rotation. The first was in the draft, where Tampa used its first-round pick to grab Jeff Niemann out of Rice. Unfortunately, they weren't able to sign him immediately; fortunately, they still have the option to do so until the 2005 draft. Niemann is a big, big guy—listed at 6′9″, 260—who's already had elbow problems. The track record on pitchers with his build isn't good, but the skills are certainly there. Niemann has an outstanding fastball and an even better curveball, and there's little doubt that he has the ability to be a front-line starter.

The second move is the one pretty much everybody regards as the best trade of 2004 (or worst, depending from which side your looking)—the heisting of Scott Kazmir from the Mets for the price of Victor Zambrano. Kazmir had a reasonable claim as the best pitcher in the minors, with a fastball that jumps on hitters and a slider that falls down a well. No one, not even the Mets, doubted his enormous talent. The doubts are all about sustainability. It is curious that a guy who was described as having a "free, easy motion, putting no strain on the arm at all" when he was a high-school prospect, could be considered just two years later as someone whose mechanics were so flawed that he was unfixable—even by purported pitching guru Rick Peterson—and would likely be either injured or relegated to relief work. If Kazmir makes it through the injury nexus, he becomes a big piece of the Rays' future pennant dreams.

To complete the picture, the Rays finally have some pitching prospects worthy of the label. James Houser, Jason Hammel, and Chris Seddon have all done more in the minors than any of the previously touted players, like Brazelton and Doug Waechter. When it comes to pitching, it frequently comes down to quantity, and having three good mid-level pitching prospects raises the odds that at least one will survive to be part of a future rotation. For the bullpen's future, they can point to Chad Orvella, who had the best stats of any pitcher in pro ball last year, with an absurd 117:10 strikeout-to-walk ratio in just 74 innings. This is a system that is about to thrust a ton of talent into the majors.

Tampa Bay is reminiscent of two teams from the 1990s that successfully developed a string of successful minor leaguers: the Cleveland Indians and the Montreal Expos. Cleveland was able to run off six division titles in seven years, with two (unsuccessful) trips to the World Series; Montreal led NL East in '94, when the strike killed the team's playoff hopes, came close a couple times, and nothing else. The difference is that the Indians spent the money they needed to keep the players they developed on the shores of Lake Erie. The Expos, meanwhile, sold their top talent away as soon as they had to start paying real salaries.

That is why it is so disturbing that upper management has sent players racing at such breakneck speed through the Tampa system. When you promote a talented prospect at the age of 20, it seems like you have a cheap asset—good player, minimum salary, woo-woo! What you are really doing is starting the player's salary clock, trading a year of the player's prime (since he now turns free agent at 27) for a year of his sub-prime.

By 2008, then:

Carl Crawford will have had five full seasons in the majors, and will be arbitration eligible for the final time before becoming a free agent. His salary will depend on his performance and the player market at the time. (That market will be affected by the end of the current Collective Bargaining Agreement after the 2006 season.) An award on the order of $8 million for that year is a reasonable guess at this juncture. That would be $7.7 million more than he made last year; even accounting for inflation, that's a huge chunk of change for a team like the Rays.

Rocco Baldelli will also be entering his walk year in 2008. While his baseball value is at least as high as Crawford's, he's not as likely to have flashy features such as stolen base titles on his resume, so the guess from 2004 is that he won't get quite as large an award. As a rough exercise, let's say $7 million, $6.7 million more than at present. Combined, that's more than $14 million above what the Rays are paying their two young outfielders now.

Cantu, Upton, and Kazmir all figure to have finished their third full year in the major leagues, making them all eligible for arbitration for the first time. Even a mediocre player stands to get about $2 million in his first arbitration year, while a very good one can get perhaps as much as $4 million. Call it $8 million for the three of them, about $7 million more than what they're owed this year. The Rays, then, need to come up with $21 million more than they're spending now. Because of Baldelli's injury, Gathright is liable to start the '05 season in Tampa. If he turns out to be a useful player—and we have our doubts that a faster Jason Tyner will be worth much more than the original—he would probably be arbitration-eligible in 2008, assuming the super-two rule remains intact.

Anyone currently in the minor leagues for the Rays will have had at most two-and-a-half years of service by Opening Day 2008, so they will remain cheap commodities. This specifically includes Niemann and Young, who figure to be important cogs of a contending Devil Ray team—assuming Niemann signs—as well as farther-off possibilities like Bankston, Hamilton and Dukes. Let us assume, for accounting purposes, that the team recognizes that they are close to contending and spends an additional $15 million for another mid-level starter, a third baseman (or shortstop, depending on where Upton ends up playing), a catcher, and a reliever. That's $36 million of new owner Stuart Sternberg's money that just got added to an existing payroll of about $30 million, for a hypothetical total of about $66 million.

The Devil Rays have never had a salary quite that high, peaking at $64.4 million in 2000, then $57 million in 2001. (On the other hand, the Athletics have never had an Opening Day salary that high during their current run, the Twins also operate on a low payroll, and obviously both have fared well.) The Rays were one of the teams who were supposed to be in extreme financial duress following those years, although Vince Naimoli—still the managing general partner, even though he is no longer the majority owner—has said that the Rays' financial limitations have been overstated. Likewise, Forbes estimated that the team had an operating profit of about $7.5 million in 2003 . . . thank you, revenue sharing. On the flip side, the franchise has finished last in AL attendance four straight years, and has no history of success to gauge how much a winning team would help the bottom line. In their debut season they drew 2.5 million fans; since then they've drawn half that per season, plus or minus a couple hundred thousand. The most optimistic forecast one can reasonably make right now is that they might match their debut attendance, which would be an increase of 1.25 million fans over 2004. Utilizing past reports from Tampa Bay, they can expect about $25 revenue per attending fan after accounting for ticket prices, concessions and parking.

In this scenario, that adds up to only $31 million. If these fairly optimistic projections come to pass, that means there could be enough money in the pot through 2008 to cover the players they already have, but probably not enough to bring in players from outside—unless the team is willing to take a loss. In 2009, they are going to face a dramatic increase in payroll to retain their core, as Baldelli and Crawford turn free agent while Upton and Kazmir get their first crack at arbitration.

The Rays can help themselves if they aggressively seek more income: Winning could generate more attendance than we've assumed, plus it could create a more lucrative media package. On the other hand, many major league teams tend to show an aversion to this sort of risk. If you spend considerably more than usual to make a championship run and fail, you may not generate the extra income you were counting on. In the case of the Rays, it's an open question as to whether ownership would be willing to supplement a potentially excellent core for a post-season drive, especially given the disastrous Greg Vaughn–type contracts of the past. The hope is that the team will only make the added commitment when the Rays are legitimately ready to contend, and that when that time comes, the new owner won't reflect on the follies of his predecessor. Of course, given that Chuck LaMar remains in the same chair he's occupied through a decade of incompetence, the onus is on the Rays to spend wisely when the time comes to open the pocketbook.

With all that said, a championship run in 2007–08 is possible. While we can't know who the Yankees will have by then, we do know that they'll owe upwards of $20 million apiece to Jason Giambi (who'll be 37—if he's still there), Derek Jeter (34), and Alex Rodriguez (32). This might restrain even Steinbrenner's check writing for a time, perhaps preventing the team from doing all it can to hoist a pennant over the Bronx (see also Johnson, Randy, 2004–05 off-season). Boston may not be quite as constrained, but will probably be overpaying at $20 million and $10 million each for 36-year-olds Manny Ramirez and Jason Varitek.

And yet, it wouldn't take much for Tampa's window of opportunity to slam shut. Baldelli and Crawford may never get any better than they are now; Niemann might never sign; Josh Hamilton may never come back; maybe just a few, even none of the prospects work out; and Scott Kazmir could prove Rick Petersen right and blow out his arm. It isn't likely that *all* of these things will happen, of course, but that's not the point. The point is that you can make some reasonable assumptions about the players currently in the system, and reasonably project a way for them to win. That is much more than this so far hopeless franchise has ever been able to claim.

HITTERS

JOSH ASANOVICH 2B Bats: R Throws: R Born: 31-Jan-1983 Age: 22

YEAR	TM	LG	AGE	AB	H	2B	3B	HR	BB	SO	SB	CS	AVG	OBP	SLG	MLVR	EQBA	EQOBP	EQSLG	EQMLVR	VORP	DEFENSE
2004	HUD	NYP	21	219	64	16	2	3	19	31	9	1	.292	.361	.425	.205	.265	.316	.398	-.107	9.0	36-2B 0 19-SS -9
2005	*TBY*	*AL*	*22*	*333*	*83*	*20*	*2*	*5*	*21*	*56*	*7*	*3*	*.250*	*.307*	*.371*	*-.153*	*.251*	*.310*	*.379*	*-.148*	*8.1*	*88-2B -4*

Breakout: 20% Improve: 36% Collapse: 40%

Asanovich was drafted by the Devil Rays out of an Arizona high school in the 21st round in 2001, but turned them down to play for Central Arizona CC and Arizona State. Going back into the draft as a junior, they took him again, this time in the 11th round. Asanovich has a good glove, playing all over the infield in college, and is a patient, contact hitter who can draw a walk

ROCCO BALDELLI CF Bats: R Throws: R Born: 25-Sep-1981 Age: 23

YEAR	TM	LG	AGE	AB	H	2B	3B	HR	BB	SO	SB	CS	AVG	OBP	SLG	MLVR	EQBA	EQOBP	EQSLG	EQMLVR	VORP	DEFENSE
2002	BAK	CLF	20	312	104	19	1	14	18	63	21	6	.333	.382	.535	.354	.288	.322	.460	.012	14.7	62-CF -9
2002	ORL	SOU	20	70	26	3	1	2	5	11	3	2	.371	.412	.529	.432	.338	.362	.493	.181	7.3	12-CF -1
2002	DUR	INT	20	96	28	6	1	3	0	23	2	5	.292	.292	.469	.052	.274	.278	.453	-.089	1.5	19-CF -1
2003	TBY	AL	21	637	184	32	8	11	30	128	27	10	.289	.326	.416	-.009	.293	.334	.427	-.010	28.4	150-CF 13
2004	TBY	AL	22	518	145	27	3	16	30	88	17	4	.280	.326	.436	.000	.287	.333	.452	.019	26.8	120-CF 4
2005	*TBY*	*AL*	*23*	*517*	*145*	*28*	*5*	*16*	*26*	*92*	*17*	*5*	*.281*	*.324*	*.448*	*.001*	*.282*	*.326*	*.457*	*.009*	*24.6*	*131-CF -1*

Breakout: 11% Improve: 36% Collapse: 34%

A change in the way *Baseball Prospectus*'s Davenport Translations were calculated led to much better minor league translations for Baldelli, creating a much better balance between his minor and major league numbers. Unfortunately, the big story in 2005 will be about his recovery from the torn ACL he sustained while playing baseball in his backyard, attempting to avoid running over his seven-year-old brother. He's not expected to be able to play until April at the earliest. Even when he does, his speed will take longer to come back, with a slight chance that it never will. Since speed is an important part of his game, this could hurt him.

WES BANKSTON 1B Bats: R Throws: R Born: 23-Nov-1983 Age: 21

YEAR	TM	LG	AGE	AB	H	2B	3B	HR	BB	SO	SB	CS	AVG	OBP	SLG	MLVR	EQBA	EQOBP	EQSLG	EQMLVR	VORP	DEFENSE
2002	PRI	APL	18	246	74	10	1	18	18	46	2	1	.301	.346	.569	.249	.211	.238	.380	-.320	-29.1	
2003	CSC	SAL	19	375	96	18	1	12	53	94	2	3	.256	.346	.405	.125	.222	.291	.361	-.237	-21.2	88-RF -13
2004	CSC	SAL	20	470	136	30	3	23	73	104	9	0	.289	.390	.513	.292	.251	.334	.432	-.038	7.0	89-1B 0
2005	*TBY*	*AL*	*21*	*344*	*82*	*18*	*1*	*11*	*32*	*82*	*2*	*1*	*.240*	*.308*	*.393*	*-.131*	*.240*	*.310*	*.401*	*-.125*	*-0.6*	*92-1B -5*

Breakout: 16% Improve: 38% Collapse: 35%

Given all the outfielders in the system (Baldelli and Crawford are both young, plus prospects like Young, Gathright, Dukes, and Pridie), somebody needed to be shifted to another position. Bankston is that guy, spending a second year at Charleston while moving to first base. He can flat-out hit, and he's been doing it with persistent tendonitis in his wrist. Off-season surgery will hopefully correct that problem once and for all.

GEOFF BLUM 3B Bats: B Throws: R Born: 26-Apr-1973 Age: 32

YEAR	TM	LG	AGE	AB	H	2B	3B	HR	BB	SO	SB	CS	AVG	OBP	SLG	MLVR	EQBA	EQOBP	EQSLG	EQMLVR	VORP	DEFENSE
2002	HOU	NL	29	368	104	20	4	10	49	70	2	0	.283	.367	.440	.107	.275	.360	.439	.039	27.0	93-3B 11
2003	HOU	NL	30	420	110	19	0	10	20	50	0	0	.262	.295	.379	-.123	.258	.289	.371	-.202	5.9	63-3B 8 15-2B 0
2004	TBY	AL	31	339	73	21	0	8	24	58	2	3	.215	.266	.348	-.284	.221	.274	.352	-.283	-10.3	45-3B -3 39-2B 0
2005	*SDP*	*NL*	*32*	*234*	*53*	*11*	*1*	*4*	*18*	*40*	*1*	*1*	*.229*	*.284*	*.342*	*-.256*	*.237*	*.290*	*.364*	*-.213*	*-3.4*	*63-3B 1*

Breakout: 15% Improve: 33% Collapse: 45%

For some strange reason, the Rays' brain trust thought that Blum could be their primary third baseman in 2004, and traded Brandon Backe for him in the 2003–04 off-season. He was supposed to supply the left-hand side of a platoon with Damian Rolls; the problem was, after two years in which he hit much better from the left side, he reversed himself and hit quite a bit better from the right. If you look at his entire career, he switch-sucks about equally from both sides of the plate. Between the switch-hitting, the multi-positional play, and the hope of catching the 2002 lightning in a 2005 bottle, he was quickly able to find a new home with the Padres after Tampa dropped him from the 40-man roster.

REID BRIGNAC SS **Bats: L** **Throws: R** Born: 16-Jan-1986 Age: 19

YEAR	TM	LG	AGE	AB	H	2B	3B	HR	BB	SO	SB	CS	AVG	OBP	SLG	MLVR	EQBA	EQOBP	EQSLG	EQMLVR	VORP	DEFENSE	
2004	PRI	APL	18	97	35	4	2	1	9	10	2	1	.361	.413	.474	.261	.263	.305	.347	-.203	0.0	24-SS -2	
2005	*TBY*	*AL*	*19*	*430*	*111*	*22*	*3*	*4*	*20*	*59*	*5*	*2*	*.259*	*.295*	*.351*	*-.196*	*.259*	*.298*	*.358*	*-.192*	*3.6*	*109-SS -7*	

Breakout: 2% *Improve: 14%* *Collapse: 48%*

As high school player from Louisiana, Brignac led his team to the state championship and was supposedly a lock to go to LSU, but the Rays managed to pry him away ($795,000 was nicely persuasive). He didn't have any trouble at the plate in his first taste of pro ball, homering in his first game, hitting .378, displaying excellent (and un-Raylike) plate discipline and exceptional bat speed. There's a question about whether he'll be able to stay at short in the long term, but it doesn't cost the team anything to try to keep him there. He's expected to have little trouble if he does move to another position.

JORGE CANTU 2B **Bats: R** **Throws: R** Born: 30-Jan-1982 Age: 23

YEAR	TM	LG	AGE	AB	H	2B	3B	HR	BB	SO	SB	CS	AVG	OBP	SLG	MLVR	EQBA	EQOBP	EQSLG	EQMLVR	VORP	DEFENSE	
2002	ORL	SOU	20	512	124	31	1	3	23	74	2	6	.242	.278	.324	-.157	.224	.246	.315	-.389	-29.5	95-SS -6	33-3B -2
2003	ORL	SOU	21	158	34	10	0	3	9	27	0	3	.215	.259	.335	-.174	.193	.225	.304	-.464	-14.0	33-3B -2	
2003	DUR	INT	21	200	59	16	1	4	8	21	2	1	.295	.319	.445	.053	.271	.303	.427	-.085	6.9	49-SS -7	
2004	DUR	INT	22	368	111	33	1	22	16	64	3	0	.302	.335	.576	.201	.263	.301	.507	.020	21.1	44-2B 3	37-SS -5
2004	TBY	AL	22	173	52	20	1	2	9	44	0	0	.301	.341	.462	.090	.310	.352	.474	.107	12.8	30-2B -1	11-3B 0
2005	*TBY*	*AL*	*23*	*360*	*94*	*22*	*1*	*11*	*16*	*63*	*1*	*1*	*.261*	*.297*	*.419*	*-.100*	*.261*	*.299*	*.427*	*-.094*	*12.0*	*92-2B -5*	

Breakout: 19% *Improve: 42%* *Collapse: 35%*

Cantu had been sneakily elevating himself as a prospect when he broke out in a big way in 2004, smashing 53 doubles and 24 home runs between Triple-A and the majors, shattering his previous season highs of 31 and 7. Trying to prove it wasn't a fluke, he was hitting for an isolated power of about .250 in winter ball at this writing. Cantu still doesn't walk, and sooner or later major league pitchers are going to figure that out and start working him out of the zone. But for the moment he's got the inside track on the 2005 second-base job.

CARL CRAWFORD LF **Bats: L** **Throws: L** Born: 05-Aug-1981 Age: 23

YEAR	TM	LG	AGE	AB	H	2B	3B	HR	BB	SO	SB	CS	AVG	OBP	SLG	MLVR	EQBA	EQOBP	EQSLG	EQMLVR	VORP	DEFENSE	
2002	DUR	INT	20	353	105	17	9	7	20	69	26	8	.297	.335	.456	.107	.279	.321	.439	-.028	12.3	45-CF -1	36-LF 1
2002	TBY	AL	20	259	67	11	6	2	9	41	9	5	.259	.290	.371	-.163	.264	.299	.384	-.160	-3.9	63-LF 4	
2003	TBY	AL	21	630	177	18	9	5	26	102	55	10	.281	.309	.362	-.120	.284	.317	.369	-.133	8.3	131-LF 11	11-CF 1
2004	TBY	AL	22	626	185	26	19	11	35	81	59	15	.296	.331	.450	.042	.303	.341	.464	.066	35.8	121-LF 7	26-CF 0
2005	*TBY*	*AL*	*23*	*542*	*153*	*26*	*7*	*10*	*28*	*76*	*41*	*12*	*.282*	*.319*	*.410*	*-.058*	*.283*	*.321*	*.418*	*-.051*	*9.6*	*136-LF 7*	

Breakout: 2% *Improve: 18%* *Collapse: 42%*

The fastest player in the American League . . . as long as Tampa management keeps Joey Gathright in Durham. Carl Crawford, despite his great speed, does not meet the first prerequisite of being a great leadoff man—getting to first base. The odds are that he never will be one. He has a translated rate of 30 walks per 650 plate appearances through his first 1,500 career plate appearances. Of the 218 players who drew walks at a (translated) rate of 30 per 650 plate appearances, or worse, only 10% ever had a single season in the rest of their career that reached as high as 60. He is still a terrific player to have, as his bat continues to improve, his defense remains top-notch, and his legs will continue to bedevil opposing pitchers, catchers and outfielders. The only negative is that, thanks to his rapid promotion to the majors, he's going to get very expensive sooner than he should have.

JOSE CRUZ RF **Bats: B** **Throws: R** Born: 19-Apr-1974 Age: 31

YEAR	TM	LG	AGE	AB	H	2B	3B	HR	BB	SO	SB	CS	AVG	OBP	SLG	MLVR	EQBA	EQOBP	EQSLG	EQMLVR	VORP	DEFENSE	
2002	TOR	AL	28	466	114	26	5	18	51	106	7	1	.245	.317	.438	-.017	.245	.322	.440	-.053	13.5	54-LF 0	46-RF 2
2003	SFG	NL	29	539	135	26	1	20	102	121	5	8	.250	.366	.414	.049	.252	.367	.420	.008	16.3	152-RF 18	
2004	TBY	AL	30	545	132	25	8	21	76	117	11	6	.242	.333	.433	-.021	.248	.343	.445	-.006	19.5	146-RF -13	
2005	*TBY*	*AL*	*31*	*478*	*122*	*25*	*3*	*20*	*69*	*104*	*8*	*5*	*.254*	*.349*	*.446*	*.019*	*.255*	*.351*	*.456*	*.028*	*18.3*	*131-RF -2*	

Breakout: 30% *Improve: 63%* *Collapse: 6%*

The fielding numbers say Cruz was an outstanding right fielder in 2003 for one primary reason: He had 18 assists, 50% more than any other right fielder in the majors not named Richard Hidalgo. He gets a −13 in 2004 because he dropped to only 10 assists (middle of the pack) and committed a league-leading 10 errors (up from two). Overall, he's an average player—signed for 2005 at a non-excessive rate—and while the Rays' benched him to look at prospects last September, he's still their best RF option for 2005.

MIDRE CUMMINGS **OF** **Bats: L** **Throws: R** Born: 14-Oct-1971 Age: 33

YEAR	TM	LG	AGE	AB	H	2B	3B	HR	BB	SO	SB	CS	AVG	OBP	SLG	MLVR	EQBA	EQOBP	EQSLG	EQMLVR	VORP	DEFENSE
2002	IND	INT	30	39	12	2	0	3	2	4	1	1	.308	.341	.590	.297	.263	.283	.553	.056	2.1	
2003	IOW	PCL	31	385	98	22	2	19	40	86	1	3	.255	.328	.470	.079	.232	.303	.427	-.116	-7.4	77-LF -6
2004	DUR	INT	32	414	118	26	3	27	86	107	13	2	.285	.408	.558	.272	.251	.375	.486	.109	23.0	21-LF 0
2004	TBY	AL	32	54	15	4	0	2	5	12	1	0	.278	.361	.463	.110	.296	.344	.481	.089	4.4	
2005	*TBY*	*AL*	*33*	*185*	*47*	*10*	*1*	*8*	*26*	*48*	*3*	*1*	*.256*	*.350*	*.452*	*.030*	*.256*	*.352*	*.461*	*.038*	*10.0*	*54-DH 1*

Breakout: 32% *Improve: 53%* *Collapse: 24%*

It's been four years since Cummings spent more time on a major league roster than on a Triple-A roster, and despite what looks like a nice little season at Durham, he's just about done. He drew 91 walks last year between Durham and Tampa Bay, more than twice as many as he's ever had in a season. Walk spikes like that, at this age, don't tend to last, so anyone who decides to pick him up for a major league job, based on this season, is taking a huge risk.

MATT DIAZ **RF** **Bats: R** **Throws: R** Born: 03-Mar-1978 Age: 27

YEAR	TM	LG	AGE	AB	H	2B	3B	HR	BB	SO	SB	CS	AVG	OBP	SLG	MLVR	EQBA	EQOBP	EQSLG	EQMLVR	VORP	DEFENSE
2002	ORL	SOU	24	449	123	28	1	10	34	72	31	9	.274	.337	.408	.068	.254	.300	.401	-.141	-12.4	78-LF -5 19-RF 0
2003	ORL	SOU	25	227	87	21	0	5	19	24	9	5	.383	.444	.542	.501	.345	.388	.509	.256	23.4	57-RF 4
2003	DUR	INT	25	253	83	18	3	8	16	45	6	2	.328	.382	.518	.273	.298	.354	.488	.118	13.9	53-RF 4 14-LF 2
2004	DUR	INT	26	503	167	47	5	21	26	96	15	4	.332	.377	.571	.290	.296	.341	.508	.123	28.1	122-RF 7
2004	TBY	AL	26	21	4	1	1	1	1	6	0	0	.190	.292	.476	-.060	.190	.279	.524	-.063	0.5	
2005	*TBY*	*AL*	*27*	*210*	*59*	*13*	*1*	*7*	*12*	*40*	*4*	*2*	*.281*	*.331*	*.458*	*.026*	*.281*	*.334*	*.467*	*.035*	*14.2*	*57-RF 2*

Breakout: 12% *Improve: 34%* *Collapse: 48%*

A late bloomer, maybe too late. Drafted out of college, Diaz wasn't seen as a top prospect (not athletic enough) and consequently moved slowly (i.e., a normal pace for any other organization) through the Rays' system. He was already 25 when he had his breakthrough season in 2003, hitting .383. Now he's facing 27, hasn't established himself in the majors, and has to look over his shoulder at a pile of athletic outfielders, the kind the team prizes, coming up behind him. If he can squeeze past Jose Cruz, he might get an opportunity to be the placeholder, and you never know what can happen if he's given a chance. More likely he ends up a Triple-A regular and occasional call-up for the next few years.

ELIJAH DUKES **LF** **Bats: B** **Throws: R** Born: 26-Jun-1984 Age: 21

YEAR	TM	LG	AGE	AB	H	2B	3B	HR	BB	SO	SB	CS	AVG	OBP	SLG	MLVR	EQBA	EQOBP	EQSLG	EQMLVR	VORP	DEFENSE
2003	CSC	SAL	19	383	94	17	4	7	45	130	33	11	.245	.338	.366	.055	.223	.290	.343	-.263	-25.8	101-LF -10
2004	CSC	SAL	20	163	47	12	2	2	18	47	14	1	.288	.368	.423	.138	.267	.327	.388	-.099	-2.3	30-LF -1
2004	BAK	CLF	20	211	70	16	2	8	26	50	16	7	.332	.416	.540	.383	.273	.344	.435	.003	3.8	31-LF 1 24-CF 0
2005	*TBY*	*AL*	*21*	*406*	*99*	*22*	*2*	*9*	*36*	*124*	*14*	*5*	*.244*	*.316*	*.378*	*-.134*	*.244*	*.318*	*.385*	*-.129*	*-2.0*	*108-LF -4*

Breakout: 17% *Improve: 47%* *Collapse: 34%*

Many times in the past, the Rays have gone after has-been players whose chief virtue was that they were from Tampa. With Dukes, they got in on the ground floor, taking this Tampa native in the third round of the draft and luring him away from a football scholarship. Dukes is a sensational athlete, a scout's fantasy combination of power and speed. He has also been, to put it charitably, a thug. Too often he's treated real-life opponents the same way he treated opposing players as a linebacker. The result is a sad record of arrests, expulsions from schools, and ejections from games, leading to team-mandated anger management counseling. As a ballplayer, his primary sins are of (surprise) overaggressiveness: swinging at pitches he can't reach, gunning for base runners he can't catch, trying to take bases where he'll be out by a mile. The tricks he needs to learn to make it in the majors, and life, are in alignment.

BROOK FORDYCE C **Bats: R** **Throws: R** Born: 07-May-1970 Age: 35

YEAR	TM	LG	AGE	AB	H	2B	3B	HR	BB	SO	SB	CS	AVG	OBP	SLG	MLVR	EQBA	EQOBP	EQSLG	EQMLVR	VORP	DEFENSE
2002	BAL	AL	32	130	30	8	0	1	9	19	1	0	.231	.301	.315	-.220	.246	.306	.323	-.245	0.4	41-C -12
2003	BAL	AL	33	348	95	12	2	6	19	44	2	3	.273	.311	.371	-.102	.278	.321	.380	-.114	7.8	97-C -7
2004	TBY	AL	34	151	31	6	0	2	9	34	0	0	.205	.259	.285	-.387	.213	.262	.280	-.412	-6.6	45-C -2
2005	*TBY*	*AL*	*35*	*128*	*30*	*6*	*0*	*2*	*8*	*25*	*0*	*0*	*.233*	*.286*	*.329*	*-.257*	*.234*	*.289*	*.336*	*-.255*	*-2.2*	*37-C -2*

Breakout: 18% *Improve: 35%* *Collapse: 44%*

Fordyce has made a living from Nichols's Law of Catcher Defense (that perceptions of a catcher's defense are inversely related to his hitting). Fordyce hasn't been a half-decent hitter since the second half of the 2000 season, but has managed to since then impress his superiors with his handling of pitchers. Never mind that he can't throw out a base runner (21% over the last four years—league average was 31%). Never mind that his catcher ERA (albeit generally a garbage stat, but somewhat illuminating here) has been worse than his team's ERA for four consecutive years. No, he makes the pitchers feel comfortable—we want him out there.

JOEY GATHRIGHT CF **Bats: L** **Throws: R** Born: 27-Apr-1981 Age: 24

YEAR	TM	LG	AGE	AB	H	2B	3B	HR	BB	SO	SB	CS	AVG	OBP	SLG	MLVR	EQBA	EQOBP	EQSLG	EQMLVR	VORP	DEFENSE
2002	CSC	SAL	21	208	55	1	0	0	21	36	22	7	.264	.360	.269	-.040	.221	.278	.230	-.445	-20.9	44-CF -2 14-LF -1
2003	BAK	CLF	22	340	110	6	3	0	41	54	57	13	.324	.406	.359	.116	.269	.333	.293	-.220	-7.8	61-CF -3
2003	ORL	SOU	22	85	32	1	0	0	5	15	12	3	.376	.419	.388	.250	.302	.306	.302	-.241	-2.5	18-CF 1
2004	MNT	SOU	23	126	43	5	1	0	11	30	10	6	.341	.399	.397	.210	.299	.341	.331	-.131	0.7	22-CF -1
2004	DUR	INT	23	236	77	9	1	0	19	46	33	13	.326	.384	.373	.024	.280	.333	.310	-.190	-3.0	58-CF -2
2004	TBY	AL	23	52	13	0	0	0	2	14	6	1	.250	.316	.250	-.300	.288	.271	.288	-.341	-0.9	
2005	*TBY*	*AL*	*24*	*338*	*85*	*12*	*3*	*1*	*23*	*67*	*23*	*7*	*.252*	*.311*	*.310*	*-.226*	*.252*	*.313*	*.317*	*-.223*	*-4.5*	*89-CF -6*

Breakout: 10% *Improve: 24%* *Collapse: 56%*

Pure speed, unadulterated by any talent—including a real ability to hit. Gathright's entire game is to get just enough of the ball to be able to outrun the throws to first; he's actually fast enough to often pull it off. In 1,047 professional at-bats, he has 22 doubles, five triples and no home runs. Playing in the heart of the dead-ball era, Roy Thomas, the standard bearer for all-time no-power hitting, hit 20 doubles, 10 triples, and one home run per 1047 at bats, giving Thomas a clear edge over Gathright. Tampa Bay loves his speed—as does every scout in the country—but to us he looks like Vince Coleman without the fireworks.

JONNY GOMES LF **Bats: R** **Throws: R** Born: 22-Nov-1980 Age: 24

YEAR	TM	LG	AGE	AB	H	2B	3B	HR	BB	SO	SB	CS	AVG	OBP	SLG	MLVR	EQBA	EQOBP	EQSLG	EQMLVR	VORP	DEFENSE
2002	BAK	CLF	21	446	124	24	9	30	91	173	15	3	.278	.432	.574	.413	.234	.356	.468	.037	13.7	108-LF -13 11-RF -1
2003	ORL	SOU	22	442	110	28	3	17	53	148	23	2	.249	.348	.441	.118	.232	.314	.428	-.095	-5.9	101-LF -14
2003	TBY	AL	22	15	2	1	0	0	0	6	0	0	.133	.188	.200	-.646	.133	.104	.133	-.979	-1.9	
2004	DUR	INT	23	389	100	27	1	26	51	136	8	5	.257	.368	.532	.151	.219	.325	.461	-.040	1.8	99-LF -4
2004	TBY	AL	23	14	1	0	0	0	1	6	0	0	.071	.133	.071	-.964	.000	.033	.000	-1.326	-2.8	
2005	*TBY*	*AL*	*24*	*272*	*72*	*15*	*2*	*14*	*34*	*88*	*5*	*2*	*.265*	*.366*	*.491*	*.113*	*.265*	*.369*	*.501*	*.124*	*20.1*	*78-LF -6*

Breakout: 45% *Improve: 68%* *Collapse: 13%*

Shall I compare thee to a summer's (Rob) Deer, or even a Jack Cust?

Player	AB	H	2B	3B	HR	BB	SO	SB	CS	AVG	OBP	SLG
Gomes	57	138	29	3	26	72	179	11	5	.239	.340	.433
Cust	555	133	27	2	21	95	183	5	4	.239	.352	.408
Deer	584	130	28	2	22	66	235	6	3	.223	.302	.394

These lines are made by taking the numbers from a player's career through age 23, and using them to forecast their future performance peaks. All are cut from the same cloth: Gomes may have a slight edge on the numbers, if you squint hard enough, but they are all essentially the same player. How do you convince traditional baseball people that the power is worth the strikeouts? Pull it off, and you can have a successful 10-year major league career like Rob Deer's. Fail, and check out airfares to Osaka.

TOBY HALL C **Bats: R** **Throws: R** Born: 21-Oct-1975 Age: 29

YEAR	TM	LG	AGE	AB	H	2B	3B	HR	BB	SO	SB	CS	AVG	OBP	SLG	MLVR	EQBA	EQOBP	EQSLG	EQMLVR	VORP	DEFENSE
2002	TBY	AL	26	330	85	19	1	6	17	27	0	1	.258	.293	.376	-.140	.262	.304	.384	-.152	6.4	83-C -3
2003	TBY	AL	27	463	117	23	0	12	23	40	0	1	.253	.295	.380	-.140	.257	.301	.386	-.159	6.8	122-C 8
2004	TBY	AL	28	404	103	21	0	8	24	41	0	2	.255	.300	.366	-.163	.261	.305	.373	-.167	4.5	115-C 1
2005	*TBY*	*AL*	*29*	*319*	*81*	*16*	*0*	*6*	*18*	*33*	*0*	*1*	*.255*	*.302*	*.366*	*-.167*	*.255*	*.304*	*.373*	*-.163*	*3.6*	*84-C -2*

Breakout: 16% *Improve: 42%* *Collapse: 34%*

Hall was having a pretty good season last year until August, when his bat got an early jump on the off-season: Hitting .302 in late July, he hit only .198 the rest of the way. Hall makes plenty of contact. He just never hits the ball with any authority, which is the difference between the Hall of today and the Hall they thought they were getting when he came out of the minors four years ago. There was some thought the Rays would not go to arbitration with him, but given the salary demands of free agent Charles Johnson and their lack of trust in Pete LaForest, they decided to live with the incumbent.

AUBREY HUFF 1B/3B/DH **Bats: L** **Throws: R** Born: 20-Dec-1976 Age: 28

YEAR	TM	LG	AGE	AB	H	2B	3B	HR	BB	SO	SB	CS	AVG	OBP	SLG	MLVR	EQBA	EQOBP	EQSLG	EQMLVR	VORP	DEFENSE
2002	DUR	INT	25	126	41	9	0	3	12	13	0	0	.325	.386	.468	.226	.288	.344	.416	-.012	2.7	25-1B -1
2002	TBY	AL	25	454	142	25	0	23	37	55	4	1	.313	.364	.520	.224	.322	.374	.532	.240	42.8	44-1B -5 14-3B 0
2003	TBY	AL	26	636	198	47	3	34	53	80	2	3	.311	.367	.555	.278	.316	.375	.571	.291	65.1	95-RF -8 19-1B 2
2004	TBY	AL	27	600	178	27	2	29	56	74	5	1	.297	.360	.493	.158	.302	.369	.508	.176	50.5	79-3B -5 33-1B 2
2005	*TBY*	*AL*	*28*	*534*	*159*	*32*	*1*	*26*	*53*	*70*	*3*	*2*	*.297*	*.363*	*.505*	*.155*	*.298*	*.366*	*.515*	*.167*	*40.0*	*140-3B -11*

Breakout: 2% *Improve: 38%* *Collapse: 22%*

There's a toy statistic we have at Baseball Prospectus that combines a player's hitting, pitching and defensive stats from different seasons into an overall career rating. According to that statistic, and only considering time spent with one franchise, Aubrey Huff is the greatest player in Tampa Bay history. If he had played for the Diamondbacks, who have been in existence just as long Tampa Bay, he would rate seventh. That's a good indication of how much more successful Arizona has been at acquiring front-line talent than Tampa Bay. Huff is a high-quality hitter with a low-quality glove, and there is just no telling what position he'll end up playing.

PETE LAFOREST C **Bats: L** **Throws: R** Born: 27-Jan-1978 Age: 27

YEAR	TM	LG	AGE	AB	H	2B	3B	HR	BB	SO	SB	CS	AVG	OBP	SLG	MLVR	EQBA	EQOBP	EQSLG	EQMLVR	VORP	DEFENSE
2002	ORL	SOU	24	359	97	18	1	20	60	94	9	6	.270	.374	.493	.231	.242	.331	.456	-.017	19.3	81-C -22
2003	ORL	SOU	25	72	18	8	0	3	16	17	0	0	.250	.385	.486	.226	.216	.321	.432	-.088	1.0	
2003	DUR	INT	25	201	54	14	2	14	36	56	2	1	.269	.382	.567	.278	.239	.353	.522	.107	18.7	45-C -2
2003	TBY	AL	25	48	8	2	0	0	1	14	0	0	.167	.196	.208	-.613	.188	.177	.229	-.671	-5.4	
2004	DUR	INT	26	275	61	19	0	7	35	64	1	1	.222	.309	.367	-.187	.191	.276	.312	-.351	-15.5	72-C -3
2005	*TBY*	*AL*	*27*	*124*	*29*	*7*	*0*	*5*	*16*	*32*	*1*	*0*	*.237*	*.324*	*.413*	*-.079*	*.237*	*.327*	*.421*	*-.072*	*5.1*	*38-C -11*

Breakout: 42% *Improve: 64%* *Collapse: 21%*

If for any reason Toby Hall can't catch, the only other credible option in the organization is LaForest, and even that is a little shaky after a forgettable year in Durham. LaForest's hitting profile is similar to the aforementioned Jonny Gomes, except with a little less of everything. As for his defense . . . he's done all right for a converted third baseman.

JULIO LUGO SS **Bats: R** **Throws: R** Born: 16-Nov-1975 Age: 29

YEAR	TM	LG	AGE	AB	H	2B	3B	HR	BB	SO	SB	CS	AVG	OBP	SLG	MLVR	EQBA	EQOBP	EQSLG	EQMLVR	VORP	DEFENSE
2002	HOU	NL	26	322	84	15	1	8	28	74	9	3	.261	.322	.388	-.057	.257	.318	.387	-.125	11.8	79-SS -11
2003	HOU	NL	27	65	16	3	0	0	9	12	2	1	.246	.338	.292	-.176	.262	.310	.277	-.293	0.5	18-SS 0
2003	TBY	AL	27	433	119	13	4	15	35	88	10	3	.275	.333	.427	-.002	.277	.341	.436	.002	27.4	115-SS 8
2004	TBY	AL	28	581	160	41	4	7	54	106	21	5	.275	.338	.396	-.042	.282	.347	.408	-.022	33.4	141-SS 1
2005	*TBY*	*AL*	*29*	*481*	*127*	*25*	*3*	*11*	*44*	*94*	*13*	*5*	*.263*	*.328*	*.397*	*-.072*	*.264*	*.331*	*.405*	*-.066*	*19.9*	*127-SS -2*

Breakout: 11% *Improve: 33%* *Collapse: 29%*

The Rays are expected to go into spring 2005 with three players whose careers have been primarily spent at shortstop: Cantu, Upton, and Lugo. Cantu will almost certainly slide to second base. The more interesting decision is what they will do about Lugo and Upton. Lugo is a solid option at short, but he's not going make All-Star games or lead a team to the playoffs. He is one of Lou Piniella's favorite players, which gives him an edge. Upton may go back to Durham to work on defense. A lineup with both Lugo and Upton in it is also possible.

TINO MARTINEZ 1B Bats: L Throws: R Born: 07-Dec-1967 Age: 37

YEAR	TM	LG	AGE	AB	H	2B	3B	HR	BB	SO	SB	CS	AVG	OBP	SLG	MLVR	EQBA	EQOBP	EQSLG	EQMLVR	VORP	DEFENSE
2002	STL	NL	34	511	134	25	1	21	58	71	3	2	.262	.337	.438	.068	.265	.338	.451	.007	21.7	136-1B 14
2003	STL	NL	35	476	130	25	2	15	53	71	1	1	.273	.352	.429	.072	.276	.352	.438	.024	21.6	117-1B 9
2004	TBY	AL	36	458	120	20	1	23	66	72	3	1	.262	.362	.461	.088	.268	.371	.478	.106	31.8	106-1B 8
2005	*NYY*	*AL*	*37*	*344*	*92*	*17*	*1*	*14*	*41*	*55*	*1*	*1*	*.267*	*.350*	*.444*	*.028*	*.271*	*.355*	*.455*	*.046*	*15.8*	*94-1B 2*

Breakout: 26% *Improve: 58%* *Collapse: 16%*

Last year's *BP* singled out the signing of Martinez as an example of how the Rays' front office was working without a plan—even if Tino defied the odds and had a great year, what difference would it make to the Devil Rays' success? Well, he had a very good year, and so we ask again, what did it get them? They still lost 90 games, and they spent a million dollars to buy out his option. How does this move them closer to respectability?

FRED McGRIFF 1B Bats: L Throws: L Born: 31-Oct-1963 Age: 41

YEAR	TM	LG	AGE	AB	H	2B	3B	HR	BB	SO	SB	CS	AVG	OBP	SLG	MLVR	EQBA	EQOBP	EQSLG	EQMLVR	VORP	DEFENSE
2002	CHC	NL	38	523	143	27	2	30	63	99	1	2	.273	.353	.505	.184	.276	.352	.517	.134	38.1	128-1B -12
2003	LAD	NL	39	297	74	14	0	13	31	66	0	0	.249	.322	.428	.010	.258	.326	.445	-.028	9.2	74-1B -11
2004	TBY	AL	40	72	13	3	0	2	9	19	0	0	.181	.272	.306	-.343	.183	.267	.296	-.395	-3.3	
2005	*TBY*	*AL*	*41*	*188*	*48*	*9*	*0*	*7*	*22*	*43*	*0*	*0*	*.253*	*.332*	*.419*	*-.045*	*.253*	*.335*	*.428*	*-.038*	*4.8*	*53-1B -4*

Breakout: 31% *Improve: 55%* *Collapse: 16%*

While he hasn't admitted it yet, at least not publicly, it's over for Big Fred. How much difference does seven home runs, over a 19-year career, really make to a player's Hall of Fame qualifications? Is the difference between 493 and 500 really any bigger than the difference between 478 and 485? Of course it isn't, not really, and it is ridiculous that people focus so intently on a single threshold. Will he get in anyway? No. The home-run bonanzas of the 90s, the surge in big-time first basemen during his heyday, and the fact that McGriff never hit 40 home runs and didn't reach the 500 total are all going to be held against him, regardless of how artificial those thresholds may be. More reasonable is that he never had that one Really Big Year that fans 30 years from now (or voters five years from now) will ooh and aah over.

EDUARDO PEREZ OF Bats: R Throws: R Born: 11-Sep-1969 Age: 35

YEAR	TM	LG	AGE	AB	H	2B	3B	HR	BB	SO	SB	CS	AVG	OBP	SLG	MLVR	EQBA	EQOBP	EQSLG	EQMLVR	VORP	DEFENSE
2002	STL	NL	32	154	31	9	0	10	17	36	0	0	.201	.290	.455	-.041	.206	.284	.471	-.112	3.2	20-RF 0
2003	STL	NL	33	253	72	16	0	11	29	53	5	2	.285	.365	.478	.165	.290	.361	.486	.120	18.0	42-RF 0
2004	TBY	AL	34	38	8	2	0	1	4	9	0	0	.211	.286	.342	-.265	.216	.277	.297	-.356	-1.1	
2005	*TBY*	*AL*	*35*	*141*	*33*	*7*	*0*	*6*	*15*	*34*	*1*	*0*	*.238*	*.317*	*.415*	*-.088*	*.238*	*.319*	*.424*	*-.082*	*2.9*	*41-RF -5*

Breakout: 18% *Improve: 35%* *Collapse: 30%*

Perez was trying to stretch a double into what would have been his first triple in nine years when he blew out his Achilles tendon, and was tagged out while lying in agony on the dirt. Fortunately, for him, he had signed a two-year deal. It is not obvious that he will recover from the injury in time to start the 2005 season; Gomes and Diaz can only hope not.

JASON PRIDIE CF Bats: L Throws: R Born: 09-Oct-1983 Age: 21

YEAR	TM	LG	AGE	AB	H	2B	3B	HR	BB	SO	SB	CS	AVG	OBP	SLG	MLVR	EQBA	EQOBP	EQSLG	EQMLVR	VORP	DEFENSE
2002	PRI	APL	18	285	105	12	9	7	19	35	13	9	.368	.410	.547	.379	.269	.293	.389	-.160	-6.0	
2003	CSC	SAL	19	530	138	28	10	7	30	113	26	17	.260	.302	.391	.047	.233	.262	.357	-.292	-23.4	121-CF -2
2004	CSC	SAL	20	515	142	27	11	17	37	114	17	6	.276	.327	.470	.127	.241	.281	.401	-.187	-6.2	120-CF -5
2005	*TBY*	*AL*	*21*	*408*	*102*	*21*	*4*	*10*	*18*	*90*	*7*	*4*	*.250*	*.287*	*.389*	*-.165*	*.250*	*.289*	*.397*	*-.161*	*-2.0*	*104-CF -7*

Breakout: 24% *Improve: 52%* *Collapse: 27%*

What looks like a nice improvement between last year and the one before is really just a dramatic month: Pridie hit .355 and slugged .605 after Aug. 1 to salvage what had been a lousy season. In the end, he had improved by just an average amount for a player going from 19 to 20. If he keeps improving at just an average rate for his age, he's not going to reach the majors as anything more than fifth outfielder.

DAMIAN ROLLS 3B/OF **Bats: R** **Throws: R** Born: 15-Sep-1977 Age: 27

YEAR	TM	LG	AGE	AB	H	2B	3B	HR	BB	SO	SB	CS	AVG	OBP	SLG	MLVR	EQBA	EQOBP	EQSLG	EQMLVR	VORP	DEFENSE
2002	DUR	INT	24	244	65	6	4	6	21	43	15	0	.266	.332	.398	-.001	.245	.312	.376	-.160	-1.0	43-CF 0 12-RF 1
2002	TBY	AL	24	89	26	6	1	0	3	16	2	5	.292	.330	.382	-.037	.315	.331	.382	-.063	-0.7	13-RF 0
2003	TBY	AL	25	373	95	20	0	7	19	84	11	3	.255	.301	.365	-.149	.259	.306	.370	-.171	3.9	73-3B 5 23-RF -2
2004	DUR	INT	26	97	27	7	0	3	7	17	2	1	.278	.346	.443	.017	.219	.272	.344	-.299	-4.5	14-CF 0
2004	TBY	AL	26	117	19	5	0	0	10	36	2	1	.162	.231	.205	-.575	.172	.227	.198	-.615	-13.3	16-3B -1
2005	*TBY*	*AL*	*27*	*166*	*41*	*9*	*1*	*4*	*12*	*37*	*3*	*1*	*.248*	*.309*	*.382*	*-.139*	*.248*	*.311*	*.389*	*-.133*	*2.5*	*47-3B -2*

Breakout: 45% *Improve: 57%* *Collapse: 24%*

The high point of Rolls's season came at the start of the year, when he won the regular third-base job by hitting .327 in the spring. Seizing the opportunity to prove the meaninglessness of springtime stats, he hit all of .111 in April. After that he got benched, got moved to second base, got run over by Jose Cruz and bruised practically every internal organ north of his appendix, got sent to Durham, hit even worse in August than he did in April (.065), and ultimately chased himself right off the 40-man roster.

REY SANCHEZ 2B **Bats: R** **Throws: R** Born: 05-Oct-1967 Age: 37

YEAR	TM	LG	AGE	AB	H	2B	3B	HR	BB	SO	SB	CS	AVG	OBP	SLG	MLVR	EQBA	EQOBP	EQSLG	EQMLVR	VORP	DEFENSE
2002	BOS	AL	34	357	102	12	3	1	17	31	2	2	.286	.318	.345	-.115	.288	.325	.350	-.142	8.5	90-2B 5
2003	NYM	NL	35	174	36	3	1	0	8	18	1	1	.207	.240	.236	-.430	.218	.244	.230	-.517	-10.4	36-SS 6
2003	SEA	AL	35	170	50	5	1	0	8	21	1	0	.294	.330	.335	-.113	.312	.339	.335	-.120	5.4	44-SS 2
2004	TBY	AL	36	285	70	14	3	2	12	28	0	1	.246	.281	.337	-.255	.252	.290	.344	-.243	-3.1	84-2B 2
2005	*TBY*	*AL*	*37*	*182*	*45*	*8*	*1*	*1*	*8*	*20*	*0*	*0*	*.244*	*.278*	*.313*	*-.287*	*.245*	*.280*	*.320*	*-.285*	*-3.4*	*50-2B 1*

Breakout: 5% *Improve: 22%* *Collapse: 51%*

Sanchez has never been much of a hitter. He always did, and continues to earn employment by using his glove. His playing time is fading away as he is seen more and more as strictly a backup option. Sanchez may have another two years to play that utility infield role before his fielding skills erode too far, and maybe one more before everyone realizes it.

JARED SANDBERG 3B **Bats: R** **Throws: R** Born: 02-Mar-1978 Age: 27

YEAR	TM	LG	AGE	AB	H	2B	3B	HR	BB	SO	SB	CS	AVG	OBP	SLG	MLVR	EQBA	EQOBP	EQSLG	EQMLVR	VORP	DEFENSE
2002	DUR	INT	24	114	32	9	0	4	14	42	1	0	.281	.369	.465	.157	.254	.331	.430	-.043	4.9	20-3B -1
2002	TBY	AL	24	358	82	21	1	18	39	139	3	2	.229	.305	.444	-.051	.233	.314	.458	-.053	12.8	96-3B 4
2003	DUR	INT	25	272	63	17	1	12	30	95	1	0	.232	.312	.434	-.021	.207	.291	.402	-.191	-0.9	59-3B 5
2003	TBY	AL	25	136	29	10	1	6	16	52	0	0	.213	.305	.434	-.086	.215	.310	.444	-.093	4.5	40-3B 1
2004	DUR	INT	26	435	100	26	1	19	29	138	1	2	.230	.281	.425	-.156	.198	.252	.371	-.314	-17.5	65-3B 4 55-1B 0
2005	*TBY*	*AL*	*27*	*202*	*47*	*10*	*1*	*9*	*19*	*70*	*1*	*1*	*.231*	*.299*	*.418*	*-.119*	*.231*	*.302*	*.427*	*-.113*	*2.6*	*56-3B -1*

Breakout: 43% *Improve: 54%* *Collapse: 27%*

Tampa made the decision in the spring that Sandberg wasn't the answer to their third-base problem, even when it was conclusively proven that Blum and Rolls weren't the answer either. Granted, he removed all temptation by having an exceptionally poor year at Durham, still plagued by colossal strikeout rates.

RANDALL SIMON 1B **Bats: L** **Throws: L** Born: 26-May-1975 Age: 30

YEAR	TM	LG	AGE	AB	H	2B	3B	HR	BB	SO	SB	CS	AVG	OBP	SLG	MLVR	EQBA	EQOBP	EQSLG	EQMLVR	VORP	DEFENSE
2002	DET	AL	27	482	145	17	1	19	13	30	0	1	.301	.320	.459	.078	.311	.333	.479	.082	25.8	58-1B -3
2003	PIT	NL	28	307	84	14	0	10	12	30	0	0	.274	.305	.417	-.027	.274	.300	.417	-.102	6.0	69-1B -5
2003	CHC	NL	28	103	29	3	0	6	4	7	0	0	.282	.318	.485	.077	.291	.310	.476	.018	4.8	23-1B 0
2004	PIT	NL	29	175	34	6	0	3	15	17	0	0	.194	.264	.280	-.334	.200	.261	.274	-.429	-9.5	41-1B -5
2004	TBY	AL	29	17	2	0	0	0	3	2	0	0	.118	.286	.118	-.559	.176	.190	.176	-.723	-2.0	
2005	*TBY*	*AL*	*30*	*223*	*58*	*10*	*1*	*6*	*13*	*25*	*0*	*0*	*.262*	*.305*	*.398*	*-.113*	*.262*	*.308*	*.406*	*-.107*	*1.3*	*60-1B -6*

Breakout: 23% *Improve: 41%* *Collapse: 25%*

Not that Simon has ever been considered an elite player, but 2004 was an especially brutal one for him. He wasn't signed by the Pirates until February, in part due to the death of his mother; add visa problems, and he was a late, out-of-shape, and (understandably) unfocused arrival in camp. He never did catch up and eventually blew out his hamstring during the first week of the season. When the Pirates released him in August, the Rays, for some unfathomable reason, signed him—only to release him three weeks and 2-for-17 later.

B. J. UPTON SS? **Bats: R** **Throws: R** Born: 21-Aug-1984 Age: 20

YEAR	TM	LG	AGE	AB	H	2B	3B	HR	BB	SO	SB	CS	AVG	OBP	SLG	MLVR	EQBA	EQOBP	EQSLG	EQMLVR	VORP	DEFENSE
2003	CSC	SAL	18	384	116	22	6	7	57	80	38	17	.302	.394	.445	.275	.268	.339	.404	-.054	19.0	94-SS -21
2003	ORL	SOU	18	105	29	8	0	1	16	25	2	4	.276	.376	.381	.102	.241	.318	.333	-.211	-0.3	27-SS -6
2004	MNT	SOU	19	104	34	7	1	2	14	28	3	0	.327	.407	.471	.311	.311	.387	.453	.138	11.9	23-SS -2
2004	DUR	INT	19	264	82	17	1	12	42	72	17	5	.311	.411	.519	.251	.273	.376	.454	.086	24.9	66-SS -11
2004	TBY	AL	19	159	41	8	2	4	15	46	4	1	.258	.324	.409	-.056	.261	.330	.414	-.062	6.3	15-SS -2
2005	*TBY*	*AL*	*20*	*477*	*130*	*26*	*4*	*15*	*51*	*119*	*15*	*6*	*.272*	*.345*	*.435*	*.013*	*.273*	*.348*	*.444*	*.021*	*28.1*	*127-SS -15*

Breakout: 30% *Improve: 51%* *Collapse: 31%*

Had he not been called up, Upton would almost certainly have been our #1 prospect this year; perhaps this means he'll escape the jinx that has seemed to follow our top picks. So far, his career looks a lot like Alex Rodriguez's. Both moved very quickly through the minors, posting exceptional numbers along the way. Upton hasn't displayed quite as much power as Rodriguez did at the same age, but makes up for it with a higher average, more speed, and more walks. His defense is sloppy, with an even 100 errors in his two-year pro career, and that may send him back to Triple-A for a little while. A very little while.

DELMON YOUNG RF **Bats: R** **Throws: R** Born: 14-Sep-1985 Age: 19

YEAR	TM	LG	AGE	AB	H	2B	3B	HR	BB	SO	SB	CS	AVG	OBP	SLG	MLVR	EQBA	EQOBP	EQSLG	EQMLVR	VORP	DEFENSE
2004	CSC	SAL	18	513	165	26	5	25	53	120	21	6	.322	.388	.538	.357	.280	.332	.456	.017	13.1	116-RF 0
2005	*TBY*	*AL*	*19*	*408*	*106*	*20*	*4*	*12*	*33*	*105*	*8*	*3*	*.259*	*.321*	*.417*	*-.063*	*.260*	*.323*	*.426*	*-.056*	*10.9*	*107-RF -7*

Breakout: 18% *Improve: 36%* *Collapse: 44%*

An absolute monster of a hitter, now and for the foreseeable future. His hitting profile actually rates a little better than Upton's, although he's (A) not playing at as high a level, and (B) not a shortstop. He got off to a slow start at Charleston, but completely obliterated Sally League pitching in the second half, especially over the final month. Upton went from Charleston to Tampa Bay in little more than a year. Dmitri's little brother could do the same, although it would certainly make more sense for the team to hold off until at least 2006, especially given future service time concerns.

PITCHERS

DANNY BAEZ **Bats: R** **Throws: R** Born: 10-Sep-1977 Age: 27

YEAR	TM	LG	AGE	G	GS	IP	H	BB	SO	HR	ERA	EQERA	EQH9	EQBB9	EQSO9	EQHR9	PERA	VORP	STF
2002	CLE	AL	24	39	26	165.3	160	82	130	14	4.41	4.25	8.2	4.1	6.7	0.7	3.64	25.9	11
2003	CLE	AL	25	73	0	75.7	65	23	66	9	3.80	3.96	7.9	2.7	7.8	1.0	3.59	15.3	10
2004	TBY	AL	26	62	0	68.0	60	29	52	6	3.57	3.70	8.2	3.6	6.6	0.7	3.84	16.5	2
2005	*TBY*	*AL*	*27*	*41*	*3*	*64.3*	*63*	*28*	*49*	*8*	*4.40*	*4.31*	*8.9*	*3.4*	*6.2*	*1.1*	*4.46*	*11.8*	*-3*

Breakout: 23% *Improve: 43%* *Collapse: 32%*

Baez was unwillingly involved in a bizarre maneuver by Cleveland to get around major league salary rules in late 2003; rather than fight a battle they almost certainly would have lost, the Indians made him a free agent. Lance Carter had done an adequate job closing for the Rays in 2003, but there is no question that Baez is the better pitcher. He's actually a better pitcher than a team like the Rays should have. Closers are a luxury item, something to acquire after you've covered the basics.

ROB BELL **Bats: R** **Throws: R** Born: 17-Jan-1977 Age: 28

YEAR	TM	LG	AGE	G	GS	IP	H	BB	SO	HR	ERA	EQERA	EQH9	EQBB9	EQSO9	EQHR9	PERA	VORP	STF
2002	OKL	PCL	25	12	11	75.3	70	25	55	10	4.06	4.69	8.7	3.2	5.2	1.5	4.31	10.2	3
2002	TEX	AL	25	17	15	94.0	113	35	70	16	6.22	5.77	9.8	3.1	6.3	1.3	5.19	-6.5	6
2003	DUR	INT	26	12	12	71.7	72	15	48	10	4.02	4.48	9.9	2.2	5.0	1.9	5.56	0.3	0
2003	TBY	AL	26	19	18	101.0	103	39	44	15	5.52	5.27	9.7	3.5	4.0	1.2	5.36	4.3	-7
2004	DUR	INT	27	7	7	37.3	28	8	35	3	1.69	1.80	7.5	2.1	7.2	0.8	3.09	9.8	29
2004	TBY	AL	27	24	19	123.0	121	41	57	16	4.46	4.68	9.3	2.8	4.1	1.1	4.68	14.2	0
2005	*TBY*	*AL*	*28*	*20*	*16*	*98.0*	*108*	*34*	*56*	*14*	*5.01*	*4.91*	*9.9*	*2.7*	*4.6*	*1.2*	*4.74*	*9.8*	*-3*

Breakout: 12% *Improve: 45%* *Collapse: 21%*

Put Bell in the category of "live arms who never developed a credible second pitch." Every once in a while, a guy like this will get introduced to a new pitch or a new coach who can get through to him, and then he'll go all Esteban Loaiza on you. Most of the time they remain comfortably anonymous in the back of the rotation, in mop-up duty, or in the minors.

DEWON BRAZELTON Bats: R Throws: R Born: 16-Jun-1980 Age: 25

YEAR	TM	LG	AGE	G	GS	IP	H	BB	SO	HR	ERA	EQERA	EQH9	EQBB9	EQSO9	EQHR9	PERA	VORP	STF
2002	ORL	SOU	22	26	26	146.0	129	67	109	7	3.33	5.14	8.8	4.0	5.1	0.9	4.48	17.0	9
2003	BAK	CLF	23	9	9	49.7	62	19	42	4	5.25	6.80	10.8	4.2	4.9	1.5	6.42	-4.3	-15
2003	DUR	INT	23	5	5	25.7	23	11	18	1	4.20	5.25	8.6	4.5	5.2	0.4	4.50	2.9	2
2003	TBY	AL	23	10	10	48.3	57	23	24	9	6.89	8.29	10.6	4.2	4.4	1.5	6.36	-16.3	-13
2004	DUR	INT	24	10	10	49.7	61	15	38	0	4.71	5.84	9.7	2.7	5.5	0.2	4.38	6.7	0
2004	TBY	AL	24	22	21	120.7	121	53	64	12	4.77	4.78	9.2	3.6	4.6	0.8	4.63	12.6	-8
2005	*TBY*	*AL*	*25*	*21*	*20*	*114.3*	*127*	*49*	*72*	*17*	*5.48*	*5.37*	*10.0*	*3.4*	*5.1*	*1.3*	*5.18*	*7.1*	*-2*

Breakout: 15% *Improve: 47%* *Collapse: 29%*

To hear some Rays fans talk, you'd think Brazelton was a world-beater just waiting to bust out. There is nothing in Brazelton's record that suggests he's ever going to be much better than he is right now: no dominance over 20 innings, no gaudy minor league numbers, nothing, except the fact that he was a first-round draft pick. He's a fastball/change-up guy who needs to get ahead in the count to make his pitch sequences work, something Brazelton's never been able to do.

LANCE CARTER Bats: R Throws: R Born: 18-Dec-1974 Age: 30

YEAR	TM	LG	AGE	G	GS	IP	H	BB	SO	HR	ERA	EQERA	EQH9	EQBB9	EQSO9	EQHR9	PERA	VORP	STF
2002	DUR	INT	27	33	18	132.0	111	12	90	15	2.80	3.53	8.5	1.0	5.4	1.5	3.90	23.1	25
2002	TBY	AL	27	8	0	20.3	15	5	14	2	1.33	1.42	7.6	2.4	6.2	0.9	3.32	10.5	35
2003	TBY	AL	28	62	0	79.0	72	19	47	12	4.33	4.12	9.0	2.2	5.4	1.3	4.60	14.5	19
2004	TBY	AL	29	56	0	80.3	77	23	36	12	3.47	3.30	9.2	2.4	4.0	1.2	4.60	24.1	10
2005	*TBY*	*AL*	*30*	*35*	*5*	*69.0*	*74*	*19*	*36*	*14*	*4.70*	*4.61*	*9.6*	*2.2*	*4.2*	*1.7*	*4.85*	*11.7*	*-15*

Breakout: 28% *Improve: 51%* *Collapse: 23%*

In one more inning than in 2003, Carter allowed five more hits and four more walks, yet allowed seven fewer runs. He was lucky. Carter's strikeout rate fell precipitously, but most of that was due to a two-month stretch in May and June when he pitched through some shoulder inflammation and only struck out five in 25 innings of work; take those two months out and you wouldn't notice the drop. It shouldn't be a danger sign for 2005, and Carter should beat that projection.

JESUS COLOME Bats: R Throws: R Born: 23-Dec-1977 Age: 27

YEAR	TM	LG	AGE	G	GS	IP	H	BB	SO	HR	ERA	EQERA	EQH9	EQBB9	EQSO9	EQHR9	PERA	VORP	STF
2002	DUR	INT	24	18	0	29.0	18	13	30	1	2.17	3.04	6.4	4.7	8.4	0.3	3.04	7.6	16
2002	TBY	AL	24	32	0	41.3	56	33	33	6	8.28	8.08	10.4	6.4	6.6	1.1	6.38	-13.6	-14
2003	TBY	AL	25	54	0	74.0	69	46	69	9	4.50	4.25	8.4	5.4	8.2	1.0	4.88	13.1	5
2004	DUR	INT	26	18	0	30.7	27	16	17	0	3.52	3.41	8.1	5.0	4.0	0.3	4.03	5.1	-12
2004	TBY	AL	26	33	0	41.3	28	18	40	4	3.27	3.20	6.9	3.7	8.5	0.7	3.20	12.8	18
2005	*TBY*	*AL*	*27*	*37*	*3*	*57.0*	*54*	*30*	*46*	*7*	*4.52*	*4.43*	*8.6*	*4.1*	*6.6*	*1.1*	*4.62*	*10.4*	*-4*

Breakout: 25% *Improve: 49%* *Collapse: 25%*

Colome had fallen so far on the team's depth chart that he was essentially consigned to Durham before spring training even began. He finally learned (see Rob Bell comment) to use his slider once in a while—keeping hitters from simply timing his fastball—which puts him in position to close if anything happens to Baez. Unfortunately, he missed the last month-plus with a shoulder injury; fortunately, it was just inflammation, nothing structural, and he should be fine in the spring.

CHAD GAUDIN — Bats: R — Throws: R — Born: 24-Mar-1983 — Age: 22

YEAR	TM	LG	AGE	G	GS	IP	H	BB	SO	HR	ERA	EQERA	EQH9	EQBB9	EQSO9	EQHR9	PERA	VORP	STF
2002	CSC	SAL	19	26	17	119.3	106	37	106	5	2.26	5.17	9.0	3.5	4.9	0.9	4.35	15.2	17
2003	BAK	CLF	20	14	14	80.3	63	23	70	2	2.13	3.86	7.7	3.3	5.2	0.4	3.38	18.4	32
2003	TBY	AL	20	15	3	40.0	37	16	23	4	3.60	3.79	8.8	3.6	5.2	0.9	4.74	9.1	5
2004	DUR	INT	21	17	7	47.7	48	17	52	8	4.72	4.70	9.0	3.3	8.0	1.4	4.70	4.6	17
2004	TBY	AL	21	26	4	42.7	59	16	30	4	4.85	5.15	10.7	2.9	5.8	0.6	5.15	2.7	2
2005	*TOR*	*AL*	*22*	*23*	*8*	*64.0*	*67*	*25*	*49*	*11*	*5.04*	*4.75*	*9.4*	*3.1*	*6.3*	*1.4*	*4.80*	*8.9*	*-1*

Breakout: 8% *Improve: 40%* *Collapse: 31%*

Gaudin did some impressive work in the low minors in '02 and '03, but in this case the Rays' rapid promotion policy (to the majors with only three games above A-ball, albeit one of the three was a perfect game) went awry. His major and minor league component statistics are very similar. The only difference is that in the minors he gave up 19 fewer hits than expected from his team rate on balls in play, while in the majors he's given up 11 more. Gaudin was traded to the Blue Jays, who intend to give him some of the Triple-A experience he's missed.

JEREMI GONZALEZ — Bats: R — Throws: R — Born: 08-Jan-1975 — Age: 30

YEAR	TM	LG	AGE	G	GS	IP	H	BB	SO	HR	ERA	EQERA	EQH9	EQBB9	EQSO9	EQHR9	PERA	VORP	STF
2002	OKL	PCL	27	46	5	92.0	86	39	93	8	3.33	4.28	8.4	4.1	7.1	1.0	4.08	14.9	8
2003	DUR	INT	28	7	6	32.0	24	6	33	2	2.53	3.64	7.6	2.1	7.9	0.9	3.64	6.5	26
2003	TBY	AL	28	25	25	156.3	131	69	97	18	3.92	3.80	8.4	4.0	5.7	1.0	4.47	34.7	8
2004	TBY	AL	29	11	8	50.3	72	20	22	9	6.98	6.75	11.5	3.2	3.7	1.4	6.39	-7.1	-6
2004	DUR	INT	29	19	8	57.7	50	19	44	7	3.90	4.00	8.3	3.2	5.8	1.3	4.33	7.6	9
2005	*TBY*	*AL*	*30*	*22*	*13*	*84.7*	*89*	*34*	*54*	*14*	*4.94*	*4.84*	*9.5*	*3.2*	*5.2*	*1.4*	*4.96*	*11.2*	*-5*

Breakout: 23% *Improve: 48%* *Collapse: 21%*

Fortune smiled on Gonzalez for a while in 2003, actually giving him a chance to pitch—without having surgery. He never threw well in 2004, at least not in Tampa. Gonzalez missed some time to go to Venezuela to finalize a divorce, which might have had something to do with his awful performances. The Rays cut him loose in December, and he'll probably wangle a spring invitation from someone.

JOHN HALAMA — Bats: L — Throws: L — Born: 22-Feb-1972 — Age: 33

YEAR	TM	LG	AGE	G	GS	IP	H	BB	SO	HR	ERA	EQERA	EQH9	EQBB9	EQSO9	EQHR9	PERA	VORP	STF
2002	SEA	AL	30	31	10	101.0	112	33	70	9	3.56	4.00	9.5	2.7	6.0	0.7	4.55	22.1	3
2003	OAK	AL	31	35	13	108.7	117	36	51	18	4.22	5.12	10.0	3.0	4.3	1.4	5.56	5.5	-18
2004	TBY	AL	32	34	14	118.7	134	27	59	17	4.70	4.62	9.9	1.9	4.3	1.2	4.85	14.4	-8
2005	*BOS*	*AL*	*33*	*26*	*11*	*82.3*	*99*	*25*	*41*	*12*	*5.27*	*4.97*	*10.6*	*2.4*	*4.1*	*1.3*	*4.93*	*8.4*	*-11*

Breakout: 11% *Improve: 43%* *Collapse: 31%*

A left-handed pitcher with home-run tendencies, moving to Fenway Park? Yikes. Halama lives and dies by how well he can spot his pitches, and while his control was better than usual last year, it isn't enough to turn him into a valuable commodity. He can chew up some innings in long relief and spot starting, which each of his last three teams has recognized.

JASON HAMMEL — Bats: R — Throws: R — Born: 02-Sep-1982 — Age: 22

YEAR	TM	LG	AGE	G	GS	IP	H	BB	SO	HR	ERA	EQERA	EQH9	EQBB9	EQSO9	EQHR9	PERA	VORP	STF
2002	HUD	NYP	19	13	10	51.7	71	14	38	0	5.22	9.29	10.5	3.2	3.5	0.4	4.38	7.0	-12
2003	CSC	SAL	20	14	12	76.7	70	27	50	2	3.40	5.70	9.0	3.8	3.5	0.6	4.31	10.2	5
2004	CSC	SAL	21	18	18	94.7	94	27	88	7	3.23	6.07	9.6	2.9	5.2	1.1	4.75	8.4	9
2004	BAK	CLF	21	11	11	71.3	52	20	65	4	1.89	3.58	7.7	3.2	5.5	1.0	3.72	13.6	27
2005	*TBY*	*AL*	*22*	*14*	*13*	*74.7*	*84*	*29*	*45*	*9*	*4.94*	*4.84*	*10.1*	*3.1*	*4.9*	*1.1*	*4.96*	*7.8*	*-1*

Breakout: 6% *Improve: 40%* *Collapse: 19%*

Tall and thin, though not excessively so, Hammel brings a mid-90s fastball and a big curve to the table. His development stalled when he missed most of 2003 with a broken wrist, but he really got into a groove late last season, holding his Bakersfield opponents to just one run on 17 hits in his final 36 innings. Don't expect that groove to become permanent—he's a fine starting prospect, but not a star.

TRAVIS HARPER **Bats: L** **Throws: R** Born: 21-May-1976 Age: 29

YEAR	TM	LG	AGE	G	GS	IP	H	BB	SO	HR	ERA	EQERA	EQH9	EQBB9	EQSO9	EQHR9	PERA	VORP	STF
2002	TBY	AL	26	37	7	85.7	101	27	60	14	5.46	5.21	9.8	2.7	6.0	1.4	5.00	2.9	-10
2003	TBY	AL	27	61	0	93.0	86	31	64	9	3.77	4.04	8.6	2.9	6.2	0.8	4.25	18.0	-4
2004	TBY	AL	28	52	0	78.7	69	23	59	8	3.89	3.81	8.2	2.4	6.5	0.8	3.69	16.9	5
2005	*TBY*	*AL*	*29*	*36*	*6*	*74.7*	*75*	*24*	*53*	*9*	*4.18*	*4.09*	*9.0*	*2.5*	*5.8*	*1.1*	*4.16*	*15.1*	*-1*

Breakout: 21% *Improve: 49%* *Collapse: 20%*

Harper's steadily improved over the last four years, the last two years establishing him as a valuable bullpen arm. He actually started his season in Durham following a poor camp, got blasted by the Orioles in his first game back to the majors, then went on to have a solid season. There's nothing particularly remarkable about any particular pitch or facet of his game; he just goes out and gets the job done.

MARK HENDRICKSON **Bats: L** **Throws: L** Born: 23-Jun-1974 Age: 31

YEAR	TM	LG	AGE	G	GS	IP	H	BB	SO	HR	ERA	EQERA	EQH9	EQBB9	EQSO9	EQHR9	PERA	VORP	STF
2002	SYR	INT	28	19	14	92.0	90	22	68	12	3.52	4.19	9.5	2.5	5.9	1.8	5.02	5.5	5
2002	TOR	AL	28	16	4	36.7	25	12	21	1	2.45	2.62	7.1	2.9	5.2	0.3	2.88	13.4	11
2003	TOR	AL	29	30	30	158.3	207	40	76	24	5.51	5.58	10.4	2.2	4.2	1.2	5.07	-4.0	-5
2004	TBY	AL	30	32	30	183.3	211	46	87	21	4.81	4.99	10.0	2.1	4.1	0.9	4.74	13.9	0
2005	*TBY*	*AL*	*31*	*26*	*24*	*142.7*	*170*	*40*	*74*	*20*	*5.22*	*5.12*	*10.8*	*2.2*	*4.2*	*1.2*	*4.94*	*10.7*	*-3*

Breakout: 9% *Improve: 40%* *Collapse: 23%*

Hendrickson is a very tall pitcher whose only resemblance to Randy Johnson is his height. He doesn't throw hard, and, perhaps due to his height, he occasionally has problems getting adjusted on the mound (eight of his 21 home runs allowed came in the first inning). Led the team in innings last year, but, when you look at the rest of the starting rotation, you realize that isn't much of an accomplishment.

JAMES HOUSER **Bats: L** **Throws: L** Born: 15-Dec-1984 Age: 20

YEAR	TM	LG	AGE	G	GS	IP	H	BB	SO	HR	ERA	EQERA	EQH9	EQBB9	EQSO9	EQHR9	PERA	VORP	STF
2003	PRI	APL	18	10	10	41.0	43	13	44	1	3.73	6.28	9.8	3.7	5.4	0.7	4.66	4.0	7
2004	CSC	SAL	19	7	7	32.7	27	13	27	1	2.20	3.86	8.3	4.2	4.7	0.3	3.56	6.9	12
2005	*TBY*	*AL*	*20*	*20*	*16*	*97.7*	*104*	*40*	*65*	*7*	*4.57*	*4.48*	*9.6*	*3.3*	*5.3*	*0.6*	*4.44*	*15.8*	*4*

Breakout: 16% *Improve: 64%* *Collapse: 12%*

Like Hammel, Houser's another tall, skinny kid, only he throws from the left side. He was pitching well for Charleston last May when he felt a twinge in his elbow. Rather than challenging him to pitch through it, the Rays showed admirable restraint by shutting him down for the season. It was diagnosed as a strained ligament and didn't require surgery, but it forces us to put a question mark on his prospect status.

SCOTT KAZMIR **Bats: L** **Throws: L** Born: 24-Jan-1984 Age: 21

YEAR	TM	LG	AGE	G	GS	IP	H	BB	SO	HR	ERA	EQERA	EQH9	EQBB9	EQSO9	EQHR9	PERA	VORP	STF
2003	CMB	SAL	19	18	18	76.3	50	28	105	6	2.36	4.95	8.6	4.1	8.0	1.7	4.95	4.9	26
2003	SLU	FSL	19	7	7	33.0	29	16	40	0	3.27	5.52	8.7	4.9	7.5	0.3	4.35	4.3	24
2004	SLU	FSL	20	11	11	50.0	49	22	51	3	3.42	4.82	9.6	4.6	6.4	1.2	5.40	1.0	5
2004	BIN	EAS	20	4	4	26.0	16	9	29	0	1.73	3.00	7.1	3.4	7.9	0.4	3.00	6.9	38
2004	MNT	SOU	20	4	4	25.0	14	11	24	0	1.44	3.57	6.4	4.4	6.4	0.4	2.38	8.1	30
2004	TBY	AL	20	8	7	33.3	33	21	41	4	5.68	5.35	8.3	5.1	10.2	0.8	4.54	2.1	41
2005	*TBY*	*AL*	*21*	*19*	*16*	*98.0*	*85*	*53*	*85*	*13*	*4.51*	*4.42*	*7.8*	*4.3*	*7.0*	*1.2*	*4.31*	*15.5*	*9*

Breakout: 11% *Improve: 41%* *Collapse: 18%*

What were the Mets thinking? It certainly strikes us as a challenge trade, Rick Petersen's expertise versus overwhelming consensus opinion. Sure, Kazmir struggled in the first couple of months—an abdominal strain is pretty tough to work around—but once healthy (and, note significantly, this was not an arm injury) it was lights out for the Florida and Southern Leagues from then on. He was called up prematurely, struggled with control in most games, but also managed a few gems. He's still only 21, so you want the team to be aware of his pitch counts, but there's a good chance that he'll be the Ray's best pitcher in 2005. Not to mention a potential All-Star for many years to come.

SETH McCLUNG Bats: R Throws: R Born: 07-Feb-1981 Age: 24

YEAR	TM	LG	AGE	G	GS	IP	H	BB	SO	HR	ERA	EQERA	EQH9	EQBB9	EQSO9	EQHR9	PERA	VORP	STF
2002	BAK	CLF	21	7	7	37.0	35	11	48	1	2.92	4.79	8.6	3.0	6.8	0.5	3.53	8.2	19
2002	ORL	SOU	21	20	19	114.0	138	53	64	12	5.37	6.65	11.2	4.0	3.7	1.7	6.48	-10.6	-22
2003	TBY	AL	22	12	5	38.7	33	25	25	6	5.35	4.95	8.7	5.7	5.9	1.2	5.45	3.2	-13
2004	MNT	SOU	23	3	3	13.3	10	4	8	3	4.74	5.40	9.3	3.1	3.9	3.1	6.17	-0.7	-13
2004	DUR	INT	23	11	0	13.7	10	7	12	0	3.28	3.55	7.1	5.0	6.4	0.0	3.55	2.9	0
2005	*TBY*	*AL*	*24*	*22*	*12*	*82.0*	*80*	*42*	*58*	*13*	*5.09*	*4.99*	*8.8*	*4.1*	*5.7*	*1.4*	*5.05*	*9.0*	*-5*

Breakout: 17% *Improve: 55%* *Collapse: 18%*

Another player who was whisked through the minors by the Rays, only to struggle in the majors, wasting valuable service time. In McClung's case, he blew out an elbow ligament and lost a year to Tommy John surgery and recuperation. Post-surgery it's as if nothing has changed: he still throws hard, still doesn't rack up the strikeouts that should come with that kind of velocity, and still throws it all over the place.

TREVER MILLER Bats: R Throws: L Born: 29-May-1973 Age: 32

YEAR	TM	LG	AGE	G	GS	IP	H	BB	SO	HR	ERA	EQERA	EQH9	EQBB9	EQSO9	EQHR9	PERA	VORP	STF
2002	LOU	INT	29	65	1	82.0	76	23	80	6	3.18	3.79	8.4	2.9	7.5	1.0	4.02	13.7	12
2003	TOR	AL	30	79	0	52.7	46	28	44	7	4.61	4.59	7.8	4.6	7.4	1.1	3.88	5.7	4
2004	TBY	AL	31	60	0	49.0	48	15	43	3	3.12	3.56	8.4	2.4	7.5	0.6	3.56	13.2	16
2005	*TBY*	*AL*	*32*	*44*	*0*	*56.7*	*56*	*20*	*46*	*6*	*4.10*	*4.01*	*8.8*	*2.8*	*6.6*	*0.9*	*4.01*	*11.7*	*1*

Breakout: 18% *Improve: 39%* *Collapse: 27%*

Miller's been good for a couple of years. Combine Miller, Baez, and Carter with real gains by Colome and Harper, let someone like Orvella step up, and this could be a really, really good bullpen. Miller's the situational lefty of the group, and while he isn't as automatic as a Ray King or B. J. Ryan, he's a fine option.

FRANKLIN NUNEZ Bats: R Throws: R Born: 18-Jan-1977 Age: 28

YEAR	TM	LG	AGE	G	GS	IP	H	BB	SO	HR	ERA	EQERA	EQH9	EQBB9	EQSO9	EQHR9	PERA	VORP	STF
2004	MNT	SOU	27	6	0	10.7	4	3	19	0	0.84	3.72	5.6	2.8	11.2	0.0	1.86	4.0	43
2004	DUR	INT	27	40	0	51.3	36	34	70	1	2.81	3.67	6.6	6.2	10.1	0.2	3.49	11.5	20
2004	TBY	AL	27	8	0	10.7	11	7	14	1	5.89	5.73	8.2	4.9	10.6	0.8	4.09	-0.6	21
2005	*TBY*	*AL*	*28*	*19*	*3*	*37.0*	*26*	*26*	*35*	*4*	*3.89*	*3.81*	*6.4*	*5.6*	*7.7*	*0.9*	*3.90*	*8.9*	*2*

Breakout: 34% *Improve: 54%* *Collapse: 26%*

Back in 2001, *Baseball America* cited Nunez as having the best fastball in the Eastern League; even after shoulder problems (labrum and rotator cuff surgery) sidelined him for most of 2002 and 2003, he's still got a good one. Those shoulder problems led the Phillies, and later the Mets, to give up on him, apparently prematurely. In 73 innings of work spread between Double-A and the majors last year, Nunez fanned 103, a better rate than he ever had before surgery. Yes, he walked too many, and he's a little on the old side. But this is yet another viable option for a bullpen that could make up for a lot of other Devil Ray weaknesses.

CHAD ORVELLA Bats: R Throws: R Born: 01-Oct-1980 Age: 24

YEAR	TM	LG	AGE	G	GS	IP	H	BB	SO	HR	ERA	EQERA	EQH9	EQBB9	EQSO9	EQHR9	PERA	VORP	STF
2003	HUD	NYP	22	10	0	12.3	6	1	15	0	0.00	2.45	6.5	0.8	6.5	0.0	1.64	4.8	18
2004	CSC	SAL	23	22	0	47.3	28	5	76	4	1.33	3.14	7.5	1.0	9.2	1.5	3.14	11.8	30
2004	BAK	CLF	23	15	0	17.7	13	4	24	2	3.05	4.50	8.4	2.8	8.4	2.2	5.06	1.0	6
2005	*TBY*	*AL*	*24*	*24*	*6*	*64.0*	*54*	*15*	*58*	*9*	*3.31*	*3.25*	*7.6*	*1.9*	*7.3*	*1.2*	*3.22*	*19.8*	*13*

Breakout: 24% *Improve: 38%* *Collapse: 39%*

Back at N.C. State, he was a shortstop who couldn't hit. The Rays drafted him in the 13th round, made him a pitcher, and the results have been phenomenal. Nearly 14 strikeouts per nine innings? A 12:1 strikeout/walk ratio? 1.46 ERA? The only crack to be seen right now is that too many of the few hits he allows (5.0 per nine innings? Yes, 5.0.) go long. Between a moving mid-90s fastball and a change-up that starts in the middle of the plate and finishes in Glavine territory, hitters haven't been able to catch up to him. If you're in a fantasy keeper league, go get this guy.

TODD RITCHIE **Bats: R** **Throws: R** Born: 07-Nov-1971 Age: 33

YEAR	TM	LG	AGE	G	GS	IP	H	BB	SO	HR	ERA	EQERA	EQH9	EQBB9	EQSO9	EQHR9	PERA	VORP	STF
2002	CWS	AL	30	26	23	133.7	176	52	77	18	6.06	6.29	10.8	3.2	4.9	1.1	5.82	-15.2	-5
2003	MIL	NL	31	5	5	28.3	36	10	15	4	5.09	5.08	10.2	2.9	4.1	1.3	5.40	0.9	-4
2004	DUR	INT	32	16	16	88.7	112	23	41	19	6.29	6.54	11.0	2.4	3.4	2.3	6.54	-8.9	-15
2004	TBY	AL	32	4	2	8.0	12	6	4	4	9.00	9.00	12.4	5.6	4.5	3.4	9.00	-3.5	-31
2005	*PIT*	*NL*	*33*	*18*	*9*	*62.7*	*75*	*22*	*32*	*11*	*5.70*	*6.03*	*10.8*	*2.8*	*4.2*	*1.5*	*6.03*	*0.3*	*-15*

Breakout: 14% *Improve: 41%* *Collapse: 32%*

Franklin Nunez has a happy story to tell of his eventual recovery from a serious shoulder injury, but it took two years after the surgery. This was Ritchie's first year back, and while the overall numbers look bad, there was steady improvement. Check out his 16 starts at Durham, in groups of four (real, not translated), especially the RA and H/9:

Start Number	W–L	IP	R	H	BB	SO	RA	H/9	BB/9	SO/9
Starts 1–4	0–2	16.0	20	27	10	5	11.25	15.2	5.6	2.8
Starts 5–8	1–2	21.2	22	32	5	11	9.14	13.3	2.1	4.6
Starts 9–12	1–1	24.1	18	32	3	8	6.66	11.8	1.1	3.0
Starts 13–16	2–1	26.0	11	21	5	17	3.81	7.3	1.7	5.9

By the end, he was pitching like a legitimate major league pitcher. Even so, Tampa Bay let him go as a free agent. A good no-risk signing by the Pirates.

BOBBY SEAY **Bats: L** **Throws: L** Born: 20-Jun-1978 Age: 27

YEAR	TM	LG	AGE	G	GS	IP	H	BB	SO	HR	ERA	EQERA	EQH9	EQBB9	EQSO9	EQHR9	PERA	VORP	STF
2002	ORL	SOU	24	15	3	35.7	31	15	24	2	3.28	4.91	9.0	3.8	4.6	1.1	4.64	3.5	-8
2002	DUR	INT	24	10	0	15.0	15	2	14	1	6.00	6.28	8.8	1.3	6.9	0.6	3.77	2.9	10
2003	DUR	INT	25	25	0	30.0	23	15	29	1	2.10	3.58	7.8	5.2	7.2	0.3	4.23	4.2	-1
2003	TBY	AL	25	12	0	9.0	7	6	5	0	3.00	3.24	7.6	6.5	5.4	0.0	4.32	3.1	-19
2004	DUR	INT	26	29	0	36.7	26	9	35	3	1.72	2.36	7.1	2.4	7.3	0.8	2.88	10.4	17
2004	TBY	AL	26	21	0	22.7	21	5	17	2	2.38	2.05	8.2	1.6	6.5	0.8	3.27	9.8	13
2005	*TBY*	*AL*	*27*	*21*	*3*	*41.0*	*38*	*15*	*31*	*5*	*3.82*	*3.74*	*8.4*	*2.9*	*6.1*	*1.1*	*4.05*	*10.3*	*0*

Breakout: 27% *Improve: 53%* *Collapse: 22%*

Seay is another candidate for the situational lefty job, if he can keep his health intact. Last season was the first time in his career that he managed to get his translated walk rates below three for a full season; if he's finally learned to do that, then he'll be yet another cog in the loaded Tampa pen.

CHRIS SEDDON **Bats: L** **Throws: L** Born: 13-Oct-1983 Age: 21

YEAR	TM	LG	AGE	G	GS	IP	H	BB	SO	HR	ERA	EQERA	EQH9	EQBB9	EQSO9	EQHR9	PERA	VORP	STF
2002	CSC	SAL	18	26	20	117.0	93	68	88	7	3.62	6.68	8.9	6.8	4.3	1.2	5.47	1.5	19
2003	BAK	CLF	19	26	26	133.3	147	54	95	12	5.00	7.06	10.2	4.6	4.2	1.4	6.05	-6.2	2
2004	BAK	CLF	20	7	7	41.3	30	8	41	0	0.65	2.35	7.3	2.1	5.9	0.2	2.58	12.9	34
2004	MNT	SOU	20	21	21	119.0	129	44	102	19	4.39	5.88	10.4	3.5	5.4	1.9	5.80	-2.5	4
2005	*TBY*	*AL*	*21*	*11*	*11*	*62.7*	*67*	*28*	*40*	*11*	*5.34*	*5.24*	*9.6*	*3.5*	*5.1*	*1.5*	*5.26*	*4.2*	*-3*

Breakout: 7% *Improve: 43%* *Collapse: 16%*

Seddon is a touted lefty. Another string bean—Chuck LaMar has a fetish for that body type in a pitcher—he comes from the fastball/slider family of hurlers. Seddon was on fire at Bakersfield, and even through his first few starts at Montgomery. As the summer went on, his ERA, walks, and home runs kept going up while his strikeouts went down. Unless he develops an off-speed pitch, that's going to happen a lot. Given his youth, he's got lots of time to make it happen.

ANDREW SONNANSTINE — Bats: L — Throws: R — Born: 18-Mar-1983 — Age: 22

YEAR	TM	LG	AGE	G	GS	IP	H	BB	SO	HR	ERA	EQERA	EQH9	EQBB9	EQSO9	EQHR9	PERA	VORP	STF
2004	HUD	NYP	21	9	2	27.0	18	3	24	0	1.00	3.33	7.8	1.5	4.4	0.4	2.96	7.1	9
2004	CSC	SAL	21	8	5	30.7	18	7	42	0	0.59	2.89	7.1	2.6	7.7	0.3	2.57	9.4	32
2005	*TBY*	*AL*	*22*	*24*	*12*	*86.3*	*85*	*29*	*64*	*12*	*4.31*	*4.23*	*8.9*	*2.6*	*6.0*	*1.2*	*4.19*	*17.5*	*4*

Breakout: 7% *Improve: 28%* *Collapse: 31%*

Sonnanstine was an outstanding pitcher at Kent State, despite a fastball that only registered around 90; it has a sink to it, and when he keeps both the fastball and slider down in the zone he's tough to hit. He makes it even harder on hitters by changing arm angles on them, varying his release point while maintaining excellent control. Sonnanstine had a very good run through the NCAA playoffs, slid to Tampa in the 13th round, and just kept rolling through the New York–Penn and Sally leagues. A tougher test awaits him in the Cal League.

JORGE SOSA — Bats: B — Throws: R — Born: 28-Apr-1977 — Age: 28

YEAR	TM	LG	AGE	G	GS	IP	H	BB	SO	HR	ERA	EQERA	EQH9	EQBB9	EQSO9	EQHR9	PERA	VORP	STF
2002	TBY	AL	25	31	14	99.3	88	54	48	16	5.53	5.27	8.7	4.7	4.3	1.3	4.88	3.0	-16
2003	TBY	AL	26	29	19	128.7	137	60	72	14	4.62	4.63	9.6	4.1	5.0	0.9	5.28	16.0	-8
2004	TBY	AL	27	43	8	99.3	100	54	94	17	5.53	5.42	8.8	4.4	8.1	1.4	5.05	2.1	-1
2005	*TBY*	*AL*	*28*	*26*	*12*	*87.3*	*86*	*42*	*73*	*13*	*4.89*	*4.79*	*8.9*	*3.8*	*6.7*	*1.3*	*4.79*	*11.1*	*2*

Breakout: 15% *Improve: 46%* *Collapse: 21%*

Sosa pitched all over the place for the Rays last year, working as a starter, a mop-up man and a set-up guy down the stretch. He's a fairly extreme platoon pitcher, being the windshield against righties and the bug against lefties. His sudden strikeout spike actually made the split look even worse.

JASON STANDRIDGE — Bats: R — Throws: R — Born: 09-Nov-1978 — Age: 26

YEAR	TM	LG	AGE	G	GS	IP	H	BB	SO	HR	ERA	EQERA	EQH9	EQBB9	EQSO9	EQHR9	PERA	VORP	STF
2002	DUR	INT	23	29	29	173.0	168	64	111	12	3.12	4.19	8.9	3.8	5.0	0.8	4.52	19.6	13
2003	DUR	INT	24	12	10	60.0	62	28	37	5	4.50	4.98	9.6	4.8	4.7	1.1	5.79	-1.2	-12
2003	TBY	AL	24	8	7	35.3	38	16	20	7	6.37	5.82	9.8	4.0	5.0	1.6	5.82	-1.1	-10
2004	DUR	INT	25	20	20	119.3	120	44	76	7	3.85	4.09	8.9	3.5	4.7	0.6	4.25	17.1	5
2004	TBY	AL	25	3	1	10.0	14	4	7	5	9.00	8.10	11.7	3.6	6.3	3.6	8.10	-3.0	-17
2005	*TEX*	*AL*	*26*	*24*	*13*	*86.0*	*100*	*39*	*53*	*13*	*5.64*	*5.02*	*10.2*	*3.6*	*5.1*	*1.2*	*4.97*	*7.1*	*-6*

Breakout: 15% *Improve: 45%* *Collapse: 22%*

Standridge had shoulder surgery in August 2003, and wasn't quite recovered by the time the season started, hence the time in Montgomery and Durham. He was recalled in late May, but after consecutive shellings he was sent back to Durham for the duration. That's a shame, since he was actually showing a semblance of control and had his best season since he was in the low minors. Released, he signed a minor league deal with Texas.

DOUG WAECHTER — Bats: R — Throws: R — Born: 28-Jan-1981 — Age: 24

YEAR	TM	LG	AGE	G	GS	IP	H	BB	SO	HR	ERA	EQERA	EQH9	EQBB9	EQSO9	EQHR9	PERA	VORP	STF
2002	CSC	SAL	21	7	7	36.3	39	16	36	2	3.47	6.68	10.2	4.8	5.3	1.3	5.61	0.0	-3
2002	BAK	CLF	21	17	17	108.3	114	29	101	9	2.66	4.66	9.4	2.7	4.8	1.3	4.49	12.9	9
2003	ORL	SOU	22	13	12	76.3	74	19	45	6	4.13	5.48	9.8	2.3	3.8	1.4	4.84	6.0	0
2003	DUR	INT	22	10	10	51.3	51	12	35	9	3.33	4.60	10.1	2.5	5.2	2.1	6.13	-2.8	2
2003	TBY	AL	22	6	5	35.3	29	15	29	4	3.31	3.21	8.0	3.7	7.5	1.1	4.28	10.9	27
2004	TBY	AL	23	14	14	70.3	68	33	36	20	6.02	6.21	9.6	3.9	4.6	2.3	6.08	-5.3	-14
2004	DUR	INT	23	8	8	29.3	33	17	22	11	6.76	6.26	10.9	5.6	5.6	3.6	8.23	-8.0	-23
2005	*TBY*	*AL*	*24*	*21*	*11*	*74.3*	*78*	*37*	*46*	*14*	*5.84*	*5.73*	*9.4*	*4.0*	*5.0*	*1.7*	*5.52*	*2.6*	*-13*

Breakout: 17% *Improve: 45%* *Collapse: 25%*

Waechter jammed the middle finger on his right hand early last June, leading to an inflamed tendon that kept him out three months. It should have kept him out longer. He was awful in his rehab starts at Triple-A, and he was still awful when he returned to Tampa in September. He's a flyball (and consequently a home run) machine who could really use a trade to Safeco, Petco or some other homer-suppressing park that ends in "co."

JOHN WEBB **Bats: R** **Throws: R** Born: 23-May-1979 Age: 26

YEAR	TM	LG	AGE	G	GS	IP	H	BB	SO	HR	ERA	EQERA	EQH9	EQBB9	EQSO9	EQHR9	PERA	VORP	STF
2002	DAY	FSL	23	10	10	57.7	43	23	65	3	3.43	4.70	7.7	4.0	7.4	1.0	3.52	12.4	24
2002	WTN	SOU	23	11	11	61.7	52	22	45	5	4.52	5.75	9.1	3.2	5.1	1.4	4.79	5.1	5
2003	WTN	SOU	24	30	22	132.0	135	52	85	11	4.50	6.01	9.7	3.6	4.1	1.5	5.28	4.4	-7
2004	MNT	SOU	25	9	3	26.3	26	8	12	3	4.11	4.81	9.6	3.0	3.0	1.5	4.81	2.1	-16
2004	DUR	INT	25	6	6	33.0	31	14	22	5	3.27	4.94	9.0	4.1	4.9	1.5	4.94	2.3	1
2004	TBY	AL	25	4	0	9.0	12	7	9	2	7.00	6.75	10.6	5.8	7.7	1.9	6.75	-0.7	-1
2005	*TBY*	*AL*	*26*	*17*	*7*	*54.3*	*55*	*23*	*35*	*8*	*4.83*	*4.74*	*9.1*	*3.4*	*5.2*	*1.3*	*4.79*	*6.7*	*-6*

Breakout: 20% *Improve: 50%* *Collapse: 18%*

Webb was a lesser prospect in the Cubs system in 2003 who broke his ankle in the 2003–04 off-season while chasing his dog. The Cubs tried to sneak him through waivers, but the Devil Rays took a flyer. Nothing has been gained so far, as Webb didn't retake the mound until June, and his control (never good) was off. He's not likely to provide any help in 2005.

Texas Rangers

It isn't poor performance that breaks hearts—it's raised hopes. And for much of the 2004 season, that's what the Rangers provided. From the very start of the season, Buck Showalter and an overachieving Texas squad had fans in Arlington convinced they could keep pace with the Angels and A's in the AL West, and possibly take the division title. Considering that most pundits had picked the Rangers to finish a distant fourth behind three good clubs, the team's first-half performance was intoxicating, but, in the end, just false advertising.

RANGERS PROSPECTUS

2004 record: 89–73; Third place, AL West

Pythagenport record: 87–75

Runs scored per game: 5.31 (4th in AL)

Runs allowed per game: 4.90 (5th in AL)

Team EqA: .254 (11th in AL)

2004 Batters Age: 28.2 (Youngest in AL)

2004 Pitchers Age: 31.1 (3rd oldest in AL)

Ballpark: Ballpark at Arlington; Severe hitter's park; Park Factor of 1.075

2004: A young offense and surprising pitching staff propelled the Rangers into the division race.

2005: The offense will be fine, but it's tough to believe that this pitching staff has another command performance in it.

The 2003–04 off-season was unkind to those same fans. Instead of focusing on the many ways that Chan Ho Park could possibly void his contract, the drama was centered around baseball's best non-Barry Bonds player, and where he'd be traded. The A-Rod saga dragged on for weeks, and sucked people and organizations into a maelstrom of ego and money. So when the Rangers played great throughout the entire first half of '04, pulling into the All-Star Break with a 49–37 record, the Ranger faithful were positively giddy. The echo chamber of columnists had a field day with "Alex Who?" columns, often picking the low-hanging fruit of "This is a team that plays together, not a gathering of individuals with their own agendas." It was good theatre, and good theatre inevitably comes to an end.

Actually, the Rangers didn't really lose the division, so much as Anaheim won it. Texas didn't play badly in the second half, despite the collapse of some of the crew that had kept them above water in the first half. They also did it without the guy who was the bounty for A-Rod. On September 16, Alfonso Soriano suffered a hamstring injury that would end up sidelining him for the balance of the year. Two days later, the Rangers began their last act of defiance, ripping off a series of five wins against Anaheim and Oakland, starting with back-to-back shutouts on the road in SoCal. But in the end, Anaheim went 7–2 over the last nine games to snuff out the hopes of the faithful in Arlington.

Still, it was a good run, and a much better performance than anyone expected. Did the Rangers just get abnormally lucky and fall into a bunch of lucky wins? Well, if they were lucky, it was in the creation and prevention of runs, not necessarily in their distribution. The entire top of the AL West was tightly bunched as shown in table 1.

Just like every year, the starting pitching wasn't particularly good, though it did show some signs of improvement under Pitching Coach Orel Hershiser. But the bullpen was strong and deep, with great work coming from Francisco Cordero, and very good work from most other relievers. Showalter managed his pen well, using guys in pretty strict roles, and even getting the most out of journeymen like Ron Mahay and Brian Shouse.

Offensively, the club had significant power packed into the lineup, with 10 players getting to double figures in home runs. The main problem with the offense was that there were a lot of guys going up to the plate and making truly enormous numbers of outs. Only two players walked more than 50 times; 1,351 out of 5,615 at-bats during the season went to players with on-base percentages below .300, a horrendously high number for an American League team. You can't realistically expect to win a pennant with bad starting pitching without drubbing your opponents repeatedly with a devastating offense. And, of course, you can't have a devastating offense if you don't get on base.

The cozy confines of Ameriquest masked the underwhelming performance of the Ranger hitters, much like Coors Field has for the Rockies. Ameriquest is an extreme hitter's park, and not everyone seems to understand that. The way we calculate park factors, a park factor of 1000 is a neutral park; pitchers and hitters in such a park are on a fair playing field, so to speak. Coors Field's park factor in '04 was 1131, the highest in baseball, but The Former Ballpark

TABLE 1. AL WEST TOP THREE FOR 2004 SEASON

Team	Run Differential	Winning Percentage
Anaheim	102	.568
Oakland	51	.562
Texas	66	.549

in Arlington was second at 1087. It's a beautiful place to see a ballgame, but it's still a pachinko machine in terms of offense, and the performances of the players need to be viewed through that lens.

The Ranger hitters, much as they were praised, weren't really that good. On the road, they hit .249/.309/.428 as a club, which is awful. At home, it was .285/.350/.486. The Rangers did not have, and still lack, a solid offensive club. Only Mark Teixeira really hit well throughout the year; fellow local media stars Hank Blalock and Michael Young had to fight through major funks. Blalock's bat disappeared in July and he struggled through most of the second half as he fought a wrist injury and a loss of control of his hitting mechanics. For Young, August was the rough patch—he hit .226 with just over a single walk and extra-base hit per week.

As we went to press, the Rangers hadn't been tremendously active in the off-season, though they did sign noted enigma Richard Hidalgo to man the outfield. Hidalgo should significantly help the offense, providing some much needed on-base skills, plus moderate power that will fill out the lineup nicely. But the real offensive problem hasn't been addressed. The Rangers' offensive squad is still laden with some offensive black holes like Rod Barajas. The signing of the clearly washed-up Sandy Alomar isn't something that should fill Ranger Nation with hope and joy.

Even the offensive nucleus of the club is flawed, at least outside of Mark Teixeira. Despite some modest improvements, Blalock still struggles to hit lefties, and he's been mediocre on the road so far. Young's a plus offensive player who'd be a lot better if he'd draw some walks. Ditto Soriano. Laynce Nix regressed. Kevin Mench's solid numbers were largely an illusion created by Arlington.

In a nutshell, despite the constant media cries of "they're great hitters, if only they had some pitching," the Rangers could just as surely use a plus-50-run bopper.

That bopper isn't coming to Texas this year, at least via free agency. Is he coming through the farm system? Maybe. The Ranger farm system doesn't stack up favorably against many others; the talent's thin and young, and the track record of the organization is mixed—though more so on the pitching side. But there's some hope. Most of it resides in the form of Ian Kinsler, a late-round SS who shredded pitching in Clinton and Frisco, and had 70 extra-base hits in just over 500 at-bats last year. Joaquin Arias is another shortstop prospect with some upside; Adrian Gonzalez is still young and could have a nice major league career; and there are a couple of arms in the system that may turn into something, like 2003 first-rounder John Danks. But overall, it's not a strong farm system right now, at least not at high-A and above.

So is there hope for the offense? Absolutely. The Rangers' nucleus is very young. Blalock will play this year at 24, for cryin' out loud, and young veterans with his upside don't come along too often. Teixeira's a hitting machine who looks like he's going to start gathering MVP votes sooner rather than later. Soriano's a dramatically overrated player, but he's fully capable of hitting the ball over the fence on a regular basis, which is exceptionally helpful, particularly if the Rangers can find a way to actually get some guys on base.

The Rangers have re-upped Hershiser, and that's probably a very wise move. Yes, the rotation still had plenty of rough spots, as is the tradition in Texas. But in fairness to Hershiser and the staff, there were significant positives. Ryan Drese harnessed his control, and dropped his ERA from the sixes down to the fours. The bullpen was outstanding from top to bottom. The Ranger pitchers threw a bunch of groundballs in front of a solid left-side defense. These are all good things, and Hershiser's received a lot of credit for them. We'll find out fairly shortly whether or not all of the credit was warranted.

Even if he can squeeze the best possible results out of the staff, this could be a time bomb. Ranger pitchers' K rates aren't particularly stellar, and their ERAs look low compared to what their peripherals would suggest. It's entirely feasible that the rotation could be worse than it was in 2004, and the bullpen's likely to suffer at least some regression. There simply isn't that much pitching talent on board right now.

The Rangers, like most clubs, have some very unfortunate contract baggage. Park's complete on-field failure has cost the Rangers immensely in terms of opportunity cost. They needed a pitcher, Scott Boras convinced them that Park was the guy, and the rest is a financial disaster on the order of your company shifting your 401(k) to Speculative Haitian Holdings, Inc. Park is still owed $29 million over the next two years. And don't forget the Alex Rodriguez Dowry Dough paid to help the strapped Yankees cover his remaining contract. That's $67 million. Soriano's flash/substance ratio is high enough that he's likely to earn a lot of cash if they can't trade him, which the Rangers have been trying to do for much of the off-season, to no avail thus far.

The Rangers outlook for '05 isn't much different than '04. Some of the gains we saw in 2004 by players like

Young are likely to slip a little, and the bullpen's not going to be as dominant as it was in '04. But a number of the young hitters are going to take steps forward. Blalock and Teixeira should both improve somewhat and the offense should also improve, at least modestly, thanks to Hidalgo taking plate appearances that once went to an overmatched Laynce Nix. If the Rangers can get yeoman's work out of Kenny Rogers for another year, and—wait for it—get some league-average pitching from Park, they might be able to hang with the single-aced A's and the suspect starting pitching-shackled Angels. But it's not going to be easy; the A's, for all the sobbing about losing Tim Hudson and Mark Mulder, did very well for themselves in the deals that sent them away. The Angels, powered by an owner who wants to invest in the club, look better than they did at the start of last year. Most likely, it's another year of coming up short in Texas.

But "most likely" are just two words once the season begins. Showalter's demonstrated he knows both how to get the most out of his players and how to work with Hershiser to weave together a pitching staff that outperforms expectations. The Rangers have some financial binds they need to get through, but that's really more a question of time.

The real danger for the Rangers is that the rest of the division is just so damn good. Even Seattle, a team that deservedly imploded in 2004, looks like a considerably better club, and has spent the off-season bringing in players who will actually help. Anaheim's put together a lethal bullpen and an increasingly scary offense, with little regard for cash considerations. Oakland's managed to shed salary and get younger without significantly damaging their overall talent base. Meanwhile, the Rangers have brought in Sandy Alomar, Manny Alexander, Greg Colbrunn, Richard Hidalgo, Robert Machado, John Wasdin, and Jason Standridge. That's probably not enough to keep pace, even if Colbrunn and Hidalgo work out.

The Rangers, at the end of last year, were ahead of the Mariners, effectively even with the A's, and behind the Angels. That's still about where they are. They simply need more talent. They haven't brought it in through free agency, and the farm system is at least a year or two from providing the help they need. The first chapter in the Rangers' pennant chronicles won't be written until 2006, or later.

HITTERS

DANNY ARDOIN — C — Bats: R — Throws: R — Born: 08-Jul-1974 — Age: 30

YEAR	TM	LG	AGE	AB	H	2B	3B	HR	BB	SO	SB	CS	AVG	OBP	SLG	MLVR	EQBA	EQOBP	EQSLG	EQMLVR	VORP	DEFENSE
2002	OKL	PCL	28	106	24	5	0	2	10	31	0	0	.226	.303	.330	-.185	.198	.262	.283	-.415	-7.3	30-C -7
2003	OKL	PCL	29	239	58	11	2	7	21	58	0	2	.243	.311	.393	-.043	.226	.293	.372	-.215	-3.0	51-C 3
2004	OKL	PCL	30	237	73	12	0	10	41	66	1	1	.308	.422	.485	.274	.281	.378	.417	.046	15.9	67-C 2
2005	*TEX*	*AL*	*30*	*115*	*28*	*5*	*0*	*4*	*13*	*34*	*0*	*0*	*.240*	*.327*	*.387*	*-.104*	*.231*	*.320*	*.373*	*-.151*	*2.1*	*35-C -3*

Breakout: 16% *Improve: 36%* *Collapse: 43%*

After not doing much during a long minor league career, Ardoin had a big season in Triple-A, the kind that makes you wonder if he'd be a better, cheaper, healthier alternative to the likes of Sandy Alomar. Having shown some ability to hit and draw walks, he might go all Junior Ortiz and have a seven-year MLB career if he gets a shot.

JOAQUIN ARIAS — SS — Bats: R — Throws: R — Born: 21-Sep-1984 — Age: 20

YEAR	TM	LG	AGE	AB	H	2B	3B	HR	BB	SO	SB	CS	AVG	OBP	SLG	MLVR	EQBA	EQOBP	EQSLG	EQMLVR	VORP	DEFENSE
2003	BCR	MDW	18	481	128	12	8	3	26	44	12	5	.266	.306	.343	-.020	.232	.265	.316	-.345	-21.2	130-SS 8
2004	STO	CLF	19	500	150	20	8	4	31	53	30	14	.300	.344	.396	.027	.258	.294	.337	-.242	-5.7	112-SS -19
2005	*TEX*	*AL*	*20*	*404*	*101*	*20*	*3*	*3*	*17*	*49*	*11*	*5*	*.249*	*.284*	*.338*	*-.240*	*.240*	*.277*	*.326*	*-.285*	*-6.2*	*103-SS -7*

Breakout: 19% *Improve: 30%* *Collapse: 38%*

Came over in the A-Rod deal, and played pretty well as a 19-year-old in the California League. Still has to develop his skills, but he flashed some great speed, the occasional outstanding defensive play, and he's young enough to have a potentially solid career. If he lights up Double-A this season, he'll start showing up on some prospect lists.

ROD BARAJAS C Bats: R Throws: R Born: 05-Sep-1975 Age: 29

YEAR	TM	LG	AGE	AB	H	2B	3B	HR	BB	SO	SB	CS	AVG	OBP	SLG	MLVR	EQBA	EQOBP	EQSLG	EQMLVR	VORP	DEFENSE
2002	ARI	NL	26	154	36	10	0	3	10	25	1	0	.234	.288	.357	-.179	.232	.272	.355	-.276	0.9	38-C 0
2003	ARI	NL	27	220	48	15	0	3	14	43	0	0	.218	.265	.327	-.285	.210	.251	.315	-.387	-6.1	66-C 8
2004	TEX	AL	28	358	89	26	1	15	13	63	0	1	.249	.276	.453	-.140	.241	.272	.443	-.144	6.4	102-C 3
2005	*TEX*	*AL*	*29*	*260*	*67*	*15*	*1*	*8*	*12*	*46*	*0*	*1*	*.259*	*.295*	*.421*	*-.102*	*.249*	*.288*	*.406*	*-.152*	*3.8*	*69-C 0*

Breakout: 25% *Improve: 55%* *Collapse: 20%*

This is a ballplayer who will keep your team out of contention. There exists no major league club that should give Barajas more than about 80 at-bats, and those should be primarily against pitchers like Lefty Grove, Eddie Cicotte, and J. T. Walsh, all of whom are dead. Barajas swings hard and occasionally hits the ball over the fence. But mostly he just plain cannot hit, a fact that has had the effect of enhancing his defensive reputation. The idea that Barajas will take even one plate appearance away from someone who might some day develop into a deserving major leaguer, is nuts. Away from Arlington, he hit .221/.262/.401. Uh, no, thank you.

HANK BLALOCK 3B Bats: L Throws: L Born: 21-Nov-1980 Age: 24

YEAR	TM	LG	AGE	AB	H	2B	3B	HR	BB	SO	SB	CS	AVG	OBP	SLG	MLVR	EQBA	EQOBP	EQSLG	EQMLVR	VORP	DEFENSE
2002	OKL	PCL	21	387	119	32	1	8	34	61	2	1	.307	.363	.457	.171	.289	.343	.430	.008	20.6	89-3B -9
2002	TEX	AL	21	147	31	8	0	3	20	43	0	0	.211	.306	.327	-.240	.207	.298	.317	-.292	-1.8	39-3B -5
2003	TEX	AL	22	567	170	33	3	29	44	97	2	3	.300	.350	.522	.156	.292	.348	.515	.141	50.8	131-3B -4
2004	TEX	AL	23	624	172	38	3	32	75	149	2	2	.276	.355	.500	.093	.269	.353	.491	.093	40.2	154-3B 9
2005	*TEX*	*AL*	*24*	*532*	*155*	*34*	*2*	*26*	*60*	*105*	*1*	*2*	*.290*	*.363*	*.508*	*.153*	*.279*	*.355*	*.490*	*.098*	*30.0*	*141-3B 0*

Breakout: 21% *Improve: 55%* *Collapse: 13%*

Hank spent the first few weeks of the season channeling Will Clark's swing, and he got a ton of press during the year as a "breakout guy." The reality is that Blalock's 2004 wasn't really all that great, and there are lots of warning signs here. The first thing that leaps out at you are his home/road splits: At home, he hit .311/.386/.540, as opposed to a mere .239/.323/.460 on the road. After the All-Star break, Blalock hit only .240 with nine home runs. He did show some progress against lefties, but really, Blalock did a bunch of damage in interleague play in June, and was pretty much controllable outside of that stretch of games and April. He'll need to make some adjustments, so don't be surprised to see a down month or two in 2005.

JASON BOTTS 1B Bats: B Throws: R Born: 26-Jul-1980 Age: 24

YEAR	TM	LG	AGE	AB	H	2B	3B	HR	BB	SO	SB	CS	AVG	OBP	SLG	MLVR	EQBA	EQOBP	EQSLG	EQMLVR	VORP	DEFENSE	
2002	PCH	FSL	21	401	102	22	5	9	75	99	7	2	.254	.387	.401	.146	.231	.340	.377	-.115	-6.6	86-RF -3	
2003	STO	CLF	22	283	89	14	2	9	45	59	12	3	.314	.409	.473	.292	.273	.355	.408	-.015	6.1	72-1B -3	
2003	FRI	TXS	22	194	51	11	1	4	21	45	6	1	.263	.341	.392	.019	.237	.309	.371	-.179	-6.9	23-RF -3	10-1B 1
2004	FRI	TXS	23	481	141	25	3	24	77	126	7	4	.293	.399	.507	.259	.254	.346	.437	-.006	11.7	126-1B -10	
2005	*TEX*	*AL*	*24*	*356*	*95*	*20*	*2*	*13*	*47*	*92*	*3*	*2*	*.268*	*.361*	*.448*	*.052*	*.257*	*.352*	*.432*	*.001*	*12.4*	*98-1B -4*	

Breakout: 23% *Improve: 60%* *Collapse: 16%*

Big slugger with a good eye. Botts is a 1B/LF/DH type, and could have a nice career as kind of a Richie Sexson Lite if he gets a clean shot at a job. He's got an enormous strike zone, but he knows the edges of it very well, and has a pretty quick swing that delivers a lot of energy and backspin to the ball. Whether he gets that shot at some playing time will depend on how the whole Hidalgo/Dellucci/Colbrunn thing works out.

JASON CONTI OF Bats: L Throws: R Born: 27-Jan-1975 Age: 30

YEAR	TM	LG	AGE	AB	H	2B	3B	HR	BB	SO	SB	CS	AVG	OBP	SLG	MLVR	EQBA	EQOBP	EQSLG	EQMLVR	VORP	DEFENSE	
2002	TBY	AL	27	222	57	15	2	3	18	55	4	2	.257	.315	.383	-.106	.262	.323	.398	-.097	1.4	26-RF -1	24-CF -1
2003	IND	INT	28	456	113	17	3	10	24	120	13	8	.248	.295	.364	-.117	.230	.281	.351	-.265	-16.2	115-CF 6	
2004	OKL	PCL	29	421	138	26	5	8	33	84	5	1	.328	.381	.470	.198	.300	.349	.416	.008	18.4	55-CF 4	48-RF 3
2004	TEX	AL	29	55	10	3	0	0	5	19	0	2	.182	.250	.236	-.481	.185	.217	.204	-.623	-5.4	18-CF 0	
2005	*TEX*	*AL*	*30*	*175*	*45*	*9*	*1*	*4*	*12*	*44*	*2*	*1*	*.259*	*.313*	*.394*	*-.107*	*.249*	*.306*	*.380*	*-.155*	*0.6*	*49-CF -1*	

Breakout: 24% *Improve: 42%* *Collapse: 40%*

(continued next page)

Jason Conti *(continued)*

Organizational soldier at this point, someone to fill the roster, pinch-run and play defense in September, and be ready to fill in for a couple of weeks in the case of an injury. Conti can't really hit enough to stick in the big leagues, so he'll spend the summer awaiting the call, playing good defense, and working on hitting line drives. Worse players have bench jobs in MLB, so he's still got a shot at the big league per diem.

DAVID DELLUCCI OF/DH **Bats: L** **Throws: L** Born: 31-Oct-1973 Age: 31

YEAR	TM	LG	AGE	AB	H	2B	3B	HR	BB	SO	SB	CS	AVG	OBP	SLG	MLVR	EQBA	EQOBP	EQSLG	EQMLVR	VORP	DEFENSE
2002	ARI	NL	28	229	56	11	2	7	28	55	2	4	.245	.326	.402	-.041	.237	.316	.399	-.127	1.1	34-RF -4 15-LF 0
2003	ARI	NL	29	165	40	11	3	2	19	45	9	0	.242	.328	.382	-.101	.232	.316	.366	-.175	2.3	38-RF -3
2003	NYY	AL	29	51	9	1	0	1	4	13	3	0	.176	.263	.255	-.408	.176	.249	.235	-.517	-2.9	14-RF 1
2004	TEX	AL	30	331	80	13	1	17	47	88	9	4	.242	.342	.441	-.039	.232	.337	.430	-.049	8.1	78-LF -1
2005	*TEX*	*AL*	*31*	*218*	*53*	*10*	*1*	*8*	*28*	*58*	*7*	*2*	*.243*	*.334*	*.404*	*-.068*	*.233*	*.326*	*.390*	*-.115*	*1.1*	*62-LF -3*

Breakout: 25% *Improve: 49%* *Collapse: 31%*

He of the great expansion draft steal and grisly arm and wrist problems had a nice little season, only hinting at what might have been had he been able to stay healthy throughout his career. He's been signed to an extension, and will likely share the DH duties with Greg Colbrunn this year in Arlington, a duo which could prove to be a nifty little bargain.

JASON FRANSZ OF **Bats: R** **Throws: R** Born: 05-Feb-1981 Age: 24

YEAR	TM	LG	AGE	AB	H	2B	3B	HR	BB	SO	SB	CS	AVG	OBP	SLG	MLVR	EQBA	EQOBP	EQSLG	EQMLVR	VORP	DEFENSE
2002	BOI	NWN	21	221	63	19	1	8	21	52	2	1	.285	.352	.489	.228	.232	.280	.404	-.191	-17.1	33-LF -2 17-RF -1
2003	LNS	MDW	22	267	70	10	1	9	23	67	4	4	.262	.328	.408	.089	.222	.272	.364	-.270	-18.7	28-LF -4 27-RF -5
2004	CLN	MDW	23	162	45	12	0	5	11	42	3	2	.278	.341	.444	.109	.226	.266	.360	-.284	-7.9	
2004	DEL	SAL	23	101	32	6	0	6	11	25	1	0	.317	.385	.554	.362	.255	.300	.431	-.098	0.9	
2005	*TEX*	*AL*	*24*	*326*	*82*	*18*	*1*	*12*	*22*	*83*	*1*	*1*	*.251*	*.311*	*.419*	*-.084*	*.241*	*.303*	*.404*	*-.133*	*-1.9*	*87-DH*

Breakout: 34% *Improve: 59%* *Collapse: 19%*

Big guy, potentially a slugger, and acquired for Doug Glanville, which means it's a no-risk proposition. Showed some power and plate discipline, and a penchant for the rally-cooling strikeout. Needs to show a power spike and some ability to make consistent contact, and at 24 he'll need to get to Double-A soon.

BRAD FULLMER DH **Bats: L** **Throws: R** Born: 17-Jan-1975 Age: 30

YEAR	TM	LG	AGE	AB	H	2B	3B	HR	BB	SO	SB	CS	AVG	OBP	SLG	MLVR	EQBA	EQOBP	EQSLG	EQMLVR	VORP	DEFENSE
2002	ANA	AL	27	429	124	35	6	19	32	44	10	3	.289	.357	.531	.220	.298	.366	.552	.229	40.9	21-1B -1
2003	ANA	AL	28	206	63	9	2	9	26	31	5	4	.306	.387	.500	.249	.314	.401	.520	.258	21.1	17-1B 1
2004	TEX	AL	29	258	60	19	1	11	27	30	1	2	.233	.310	.442	-.095	.222	.306	.429	-.116	4.5	
2005	*TEX*	*AL*	*30*	*298*	*85*	*19*	*2*	*13*	*32*	*39*	*3*	*2*	*.285*	*.362*	*.498*	*.134*	*.274*	*.353*	*.481*	*.080*	*22.1*	*82-DH 0*

Breakout: 22% *Improve: 56%* *Collapse: 23%*

Not a bad gamble by Texas. Fullmer hits righties fairly well, but a knee injury effectively ended his season, and prevented a trade to San Diego at the deadline. He's a free agent, looking for an AL club to give him 400 PA against righties. In the field, he's a fine DH.

ADRIAN GONZALEZ 1B **Bats: L** **Throws: L** Born: 08-May-1982 Age: 23

YEAR	TM	LG	AGE	AB	H	2B	3B	HR	BB	SO	SB	CS	AVG	OBP	SLG	MLVR	EQBA	EQOBP	EQSLG	EQMLVR	VORP	DEFENSE
2002	PME	EAS	20	508	135	34	1	17	54	112	6	3	.266	.344	.437	.052	.227	.297	.385	-.189	-17.5	135-1B -2
2003	CAR	SOU	21	137	42	9	1	1	14	25	1	1	.307	.368	.409	.148	.290	.345	.406	-.022	2.6	36-1B -3
2003	ABQ	PCL	21	139	30	5	1	1	14	25	1	0	.216	.286	.288	-.354	.176	.247	.243	-.510	-17.9	37-1B -1
2003	FRI	TXS	21	173	49	6	2	3	11	27	0	0	.283	.326	.393	.012	.256	.296	.372	-.189	-5.5	43-1B 2
2004	OKL	PCL	22	457	139	28	3	12	39	73	1	1	.304	.364	.457	.120	.278	.334	.403	-.057	3.4	121-1B -13
2004	TEX	AL	22	42	10	3	0	1	2	6	0	0	.238	.273	.381	-.227	.244	.250	.341	-.331	-0.7	11-1B 1
2005	*TEX*	*AL*	*23*	*360*	*95*	*20*	*2*	*10*	*27*	*66*	*1*	*1*	*.264*	*.321*	*.417*	*-.059*	*.254*	*.313*	*.402*	*-.109*	*2.2*	*95-1B -5*

Breakout: 26% *Improve: 45%* *Collapse: 35%*

Once a Grade-A Prospect in Florida, Gonzalez came to Arlington as part of the Ugueth Urbina trade and is now far from a can't-miss. He's still only 23 this season, but he's at a point where it's time to pick it up with the bat if he wants to have a career as an MLB starter. In this organization, he's probably not going to see much time as the starting 1B, so don't be surprised to see him moved to fill a hole somewhere else on the roster.

BRIAN JORDAN OF Bats: R Throws: R Born: 29-Mar-1967 Age: 38

YEAR	TM	LG	AGE	AB	H	2B	3B	HR	BB	SO	SB	CS	AVG	OBP	SLG	MLVR	EQBA	EQOBP	EQSLG	EQMLVR	VORP	DEFENSE
2002	LAD	NL	35	471	134	27	3	18	34	86	2	2	.285	.338	.469	.144	.294	.344	.495	.107	27.0	115-LF 6
2003	LAD	NL	36	224	67	9	0	6	23	30	1	1	.299	.372	.420	.133	.310	.373	.429	.078	13.2	43-LF -2 14-CF 0
2004	TEX	AL	37	212	47	13	1	5	16	35	2	2	.222	.275	.363	-.277	.213	.273	.348	-.296	-7.0	41-RF 2
2005	*TEX*	*AL*	*38*	*187*	*49*	*10*	*1*	*5*	*14*	*32*	*1*	*1*	*.265*	*.319*	*.404*	*-.078*	*.255*	*.312*	*.390*	*-.127*	*-0.7*	*52-RF -3*

Breakout: 17% *Improve: 36%* *Collapse: 40%*

The Rangers declined his $4 million option, wisely so. Jordan wants to be an everyday player somewhere, and he might get that shot, but realistically, a team using him in a key role isn't going to be good. It's got to be very hard to have that realization hit you if you're an elite athlete, which is probably why we hear so many clearly washed-up players railing against the dying of the light. As a right-handed bat off the bench or extra outfielder, he might be able to help a club for $500,000 or so. How much fun can it be to hear that from your agent?

IAN KINSLER SS Bats: R Throws: R Born: 22-Jun-1982 Age: 23

YEAR	TM	LG	AGE	AB	H	2B	3B	HR	BB	SO	SB	CS	AVG	OBP	SLG	MLVR	EQBA	EQOBP	EQSLG	EQMLVR	VORP	DEFENSE
2003	SPO	NWN	21	188	52	10	6	1	20	34	11	3	.277	.352	.410	.116	.229	.279	.344	-.280	-7.8	48-SS -5
2004	CLN	MDW	22	227	91	30	1	11	26	37	16	6	.401	.465	.687	.708	.320	.378	.548	.268	34.2	57-SS 2
2004	FRI	TXS	22	277	83	21	1	9	32	47	7	4	.300	.400	.480	.231	.258	.339	.419	-.041	13.7	71-SS -9
2005	*TEX*	*AL*	*23*	*294*	*82*	*19*	*3*	*8*	*25*	*57*	*7*	*3*	*.277*	*.348*	*.445*	*.035*	*.267*	*.340*	*.429*	*-.016*	*21.8*	*80-SS -5*

Breakout: 18% *Improve: 39%* *Collapse: 35%*

Hello! Kinsler came out of nowhere to hit .400 in A-ball, then hit some more in Double-A, before continuing to smack the ball in the AFL. He might not be able to play in MLB at shortstop, but *BP*'s defensive metrics say he wouldn't be so bad as to negate his offensive value. He'll likely start the season in Triple-A, but he could reach the majors this season in the event of an injury or a trade of Alfonso Soriano.

GERALD LAIRD C Bats: R Throws: R Born: 13-Nov-1979 Age: 25

YEAR	TM	LG	AGE	AB	H	2B	3B	HR	BB	SO	SB	CS	AVG	OBP	SLG	MLVR	EQBA	EQOBP	EQSLG	EQMLVR	VORP	DEFENSE
2002	TUL	TXS	22	442	122	21	4	11	45	95	8	6	.276	.343	.416	.094	.255	.312	.396	-.125	6.7	96-C 0
2003	OKL	PCL	23	338	88	20	5	9	37	61	9	3	.260	.344	.429	.079	.248	.327	.410	-.083	9.4	89-C 3
2004	TEX	AL	24	147	33	6	0	1	12	35	0	1	.224	.287	.286	-.365	.215	.273	.264	-.411	-6.4	44-C 7
2005	*TEX*	*AL*	*25*	*255*	*66*	*14*	*1*	*7*	*22*	*56*	*4*	*1*	*.257*	*.327*	*.408*	*-.066*	*.247*	*.319*	*.394*	*-.115*	*10.2*	*70-C -2*

Breakout: 32% *Improve: 59%* *Collapse: 24%*

Laird must think he's on some sort of reality show. He was the cognoscenti's sleeper pick for a breakout year by a rookie catcher. Then he hurt his ankle, and, upon his return, suffered a very bad and very lingering thumb injury that pretty much torpedoed his season. He's supposed to be ready for spring training, where he can rub his eyes in amazement that the Rangers would rather go into the season with Barajas and Alomar as their catching corps. It's one of those things that's beyond comprehension, like Clay Aiken or Scott Stapp having a singing career.

GARY MATTHEWS JR. OF Bats: B Throws: R Born: 25-Aug-1974 Age: 30

YEAR	TM	LG	AGE	AB	H	2B	3B	HR	BB	SO	SB	CS	AVG	OBP	SLG	MLVR	EQBA	EQOBP	EQSLG	EQMLVR	VORP	DEFENSE
2002	BAL	AL	27	344	95	25	3	7	43	69	15	5	.276	.355	.427	.057	.286	.368	.446	.072	17.3	62-RF 3 12-LF 0
2003	BAL	AL	28	162	33	12	1	2	9	29	0	3	.204	.250	.327	-.317	.205	.255	.335	-.354	-8.7	35-CF 2
2003	SDP	NL	28	306	83	19	1	4	34	66	12	5	.271	.346	.379	.016	.282	.356	.398	-.020	11.4	24-RF -1 25-CF 2
2004	OKL	PCL	29	145	47	9	4	9	23	29	4	1	.324	.409	.628	.479	.289	.370	.528	.192	14.9	17-CF 0 13-LF -1
2004	TEX	AL	29	280	77	17	1	11	33	64	5	1	.275	.350	.461	.036	.265	.347	.452	.025	15.4	53-RF 3 28-CF 1
2005	*TEX*	*AL*	*30*	*321*	*88*	*20*	*2*	*11*	*37*	*68*	*6*	*3*	*.275*	*.350*	*.452*	*.044*	*.264*	*.341*	*.436*	*-.007*	*12.1*	*87-RF 4*

Breakout: 19% *Improve: 46%* *Collapse: 24%*

(continued next page)

Gary Matthews Jr. *(continued)*

A calf injury towards the end of the year cut his season short, but Matthews snagged the best performance of his career, hitting like a league-average corner outfielder. Defensively, he played pretty well in right field, and his arm was better than advertised. He and the Rangers will do the arbitration dance. It's always fascinating to see these relationships develop: There was some mumbling about Matthews not playing through his injury, and if there's an arbitration hearing, that's always a nice way to build good feelings between club and player.

RAMON NIVAR CF **Bats: R** **Throws: R** Born: 22-Feb-1980 Age: 25

YEAR	TM	LG	AGE	AB	H	2B	3B	HR	BB	SO	SB	CS	AVG	OBP	SLG	MLVR	EQBA	EQOBP	EQSLG	EQMLVR	VORP	DEFENSE			
2002	PCH	FSL	22	472	144	21	8	3	32	44	39	15	.305	.353	.403	.135	.280	.318	.380	-.118	8.1	99-2B	9	13-SS	0
2003	FRI	TXS	23	317	110	17	4	4	20	23	9	9	.347	.387	.464	.263	.316	.356	.440	.070	23.4	54-2B	-1	17-SS	0
2004	OKL	PCL	24	462	122	21	0	10	14	43	15	15	.264	.290	.374	-.191	.238	.260	.325	-.338	-23.7	65-CF	4	42-2B	2
2005	*TEX*	*AL*	*25*	*246*	*67*	*12*	*2*	*3*	*8*	*26*	*7*	*3*	*.272*	*.300*	*.375*	*-.146*	*.262*	*.293*	*.361*	*-.193*	*1.3*	*65-CF*	*3*		

Breakout: 12% *Improve: 38%* *Collapse: 38%*

Youch. The extreme contact speedster had a nasty regression year, hitting .264 with no walks and little power in Triple-A. The shine is completely gone off Nivar as a prospect, and he'll have to completely light it up this season in order to even draw attention for playing time going forward. Don't bet on it.

MARSHALL McDOUGALL INF **Bats: R** **Throws: R** Born: 19-Dec-1978 Age: 26

YEAR	TM	LG	AGE	AB	H	2B	3B	HR	BB	SO	SB	CS	AVG	OBP	SLG	MLVR	EQBA	EQOBP	EQSLG	EQMLVR	VORP	DEFENSE			
2002	MID	TXS	23	323	98	22	5	9	38	57	7	4	.303	.374	.486	.211	.267	.331	.441	-.017	16.2	36-3B	-2	27-SS	-1
2003	FRI	TXS	24	418	108	16	3	13	43	68	18	3	.258	.328	.404	.011	.233	.298	.381	-.189	1.9	90-SS	2	16-3B	-1
2003	OKL	PCL	24	111	30	4	2	2	13	21	1	1	.270	.341	.396	.037	.252	.321	.378	-.136	2.3	13-SS	1		
2004	FRI	TXS	25	73	23	7	0	2	8	12	0	0	.315	.383	.493	.237	.264	.310	.417	-.092	0.7				
2004	OKL	PCL	25	354	100	24	0	19	35	80	2	1	.282	.349	.511	.150	.250	.309	.431	-.086	9.6	77-3B	8	15-SS	0
2005	*TEX*	*AL*	*26*	*163*	*43*	*9*	*1*	*6*	*15*	*36*	*1*	*1*	*.263*	*.324*	*.435*	*-.030*	*.252*	*.317*	*.420*	*-.080*	*5.2*	*46-3B*	*2*		

Breakout: 25% *Improve: 42%* *Collapse: 33%*

McDougall's kind of been lost in the shuffle as he's bounced around, but he can help a big league club. The Rangers picked him up in the Rule 5 Draft, and thought enough of him to send a minor league pitcher back to Cleveland for his rights. He's got some pop, can play in the infield or outfield, and has no service time. McDougall's a model for the 25th guy on the roster, and he'll eventually have a major league career.

TY MEADOWS OF **Bats: R** **Throws: R** Born: 05-Sep-1977 Age: 27

YEAR	TM	LG	AGE	AB	H	2B	3B	HR	BB	SO	SB	CS	AVG	OBP	SLG	MLVR	EQBA	EQOBP	EQSLG	EQMLVR	VORP	DEFENSE			
2002	WIL	CRL	24	339	100	19	4	11	54	83	13	3	.295	.402	.472	.287	.264	.354	.438	.018	8.0	66-LF	1		
2002	WIC	TXS	24	119	41	12	3	4	14	23	4	2	.345	.421	.597	.514	.314	.379	.554	.271	12.3	17-LF	0		
2003	WIC	TXS	25	421	122	27	4	17	41	75	14	8	.290	.368	.494	.238	.267	.337	.470	.034	11.6	63-LF	1		
2004	FRI	TXS	26	344	98	20	2	18	47	72	3	1	.285	.380	.512	.229	.247	.330	.445	-.030	3.8	25-RF	1	19-LF	0
2005	*LAD*	*NL*	*27*	*158*	*41*	*9*	*1*	*7*	*16*	*36*	*2*	*1*	*.260*	*.342*	*.454*	*.016*	*.267*	*.347*	*.467*	*.044*	*12.4*	*46-DH*			

Breakout: 25% *Improve: 47%* *Collapse: 28%*

Power and plate discipline in Frisco. Meadows hit the ball with authority, drew his walks, and played credible enough defense to draw some attention. If he can hit over the course of a full season and stay healthy, he'll have a good chance to shoehorn himself into a starting position in a major league outfield. The Dodgers alertly signed him to a minor league deal, so he'll battle Grabowski, Ledee and company for playing time.

KEVIN MENCH RF **Bats: R** **Throws: R** Born: 07-Jan-1978 Age: 27

YEAR	TM	LG	AGE	AB	H	2B	3B	HR	BB	SO	SB	CS	AVG	OBP	SLG	MLVR	EQBA	EQOBP	EQSLG	EQMLVR	VORP	DEFENSE			
2002	TEX	AL	24	366	95	20	2	15	31	83	1	1	.260	.327	.448	-.020	.257	.328	.448	-.021	7.6	48-RF	2	49-LF	-4
2003	OKL	PCL	25	105	28	8	0	4	19	15	2	0	.267	.366	.457	.162	.226	.317	.387	-.149	-2.9	16-RF	-1	12-LF	-1
2003	TEX	AL	25	125	40	12	0	2	10	17	1	1	.320	.381	.464	.145	.317	.368	.455	.113	7.8	29-LF	-3		
2004	TEX	AL	26	438	122	30	3	26	33	63	0	0	.279	.335	.539	.115	.271	.331	.533	.116	29.0	57-RF	5	40-LF	-1
2005	*TEX*	*AL*	*27*	*364*	*102*	*22*	*1*	*18*	*35*	*60*	*0*	*1*	*.281*	*.350*	*.500*	*.114*	*.270*	*.342*	*.483*	*.060*	*17.2*	*98-RF*	*-1*		

Breakout: 16% *Improve: 50%* *Collapse: 17%*

Mench spent much of 2004 delivering on the promise he showed long ago as a power prospect. There are still many questions he has to answer, like "Can he hit outside of Arlington?" Right now, the answer to that is pretty much "No, his production's largely an artifice of the AL's version of Coors Field." Mench posted a .256/.299/.502 line on the road, which is Kingmanesque, and doesn't really help a club in a corner spot. He'll get regular playing time in '05, and he could well put up a huge age-27 season.

LAYNCE NIX CF Bats: L Throws: L Born: 30-Oct-1980 Age: 24

YEAR	TM	LG	AGE	AB	H	2B	3B	HR	BB	SO	SB	CS	AVG	OBP	SLG	MLVR	EQBA	EQOBP	EQSLG	EQMLVR	VORP	DEFENSE			
2002	PCH	FSL	21	512	146	27	3	21	72	105	17	1	.285	.374	.473	.239	.256	.331	.439	-.029	19.3	79-CF	-3	28-LF	0
2003	FRI	TXS	22	335	95	23	0	15	34	68	9	2	.284	.344	.487	.170	.243	.300	.432	-.106	4.3	70-CF	-3		
2003	TEX	AL	22	184	47	10	0	8	9	53	3	0	.255	.289	.440	-.101	.249	.279	.425	-.150	2.2	30-RF	0	20-CF	-1
2004	TEX	AL	23	371	92	20	4	14	23	113	1	1	.248	.293	.437	-.125	.240	.291	.424	-.137	4.8	92-CF	2		
2005	*TEX*	*AL*	*24*	*319*	*88*	*19*	*2*	*14*	*27*	*77*	*3*	*2*	*.277*	*.335*	*.476*	*.054*	*.266*	*.327*	*.459*	*.001*	*16.4*	*85-CF*	*-2*		

Breakout: 41% *Improve: 62%* *Collapse: 22%*

Didn't perform well, and suffered a shoulder injury mid-season. Like most of the Ranger regulars, Nix's production wasn't good in the second half. Unfortunately, he was also bad in the first half. He was completely lost against lefties, hitting only .176 against them. Since the Rangers were nominally in the hunt, Nix's playing time slowly went away, as Showalter had to try a run for the pennant. Nix's future isn't certain; he's still a prospect to be a very good ballplayer, but with the acquisition of Hidalgo, there's a potentially packed outfield situation which could cut his PT dramatically.

HERB PERRY DH Bats: R Throws: R Born: 15-Sep-1969 Age: 35

YEAR	TM	LG	AGE	AB	H	2B	3B	HR	BB	SO	SB	CS	AVG	OBP	SLG	MLVR	EQBA	EQOBP	EQSLG	EQMLVR	VORP	DEFENSE	
2002	TEX	AL	32	450	124	24	1	22	34	66	4	2	.276	.333	.480	.047	.274	.335	.479	.049	26.9	106-3B	-13
2004	TEX	AL	34	134	30	2	1	5	14	19	0	0	.224	.307	.366	-.197	.214	.301	.359	-.225	-1.0	12-1B	0
2005	*TEX*	*AL*	*35*	*142*	*36*	*7*	*0*	*5*	*12*	*23*	*0*	*0*	*.256*	*.320*	*.406*	*-.080*	*.246*	*.313*	*.392*	*-.128*	*1.2*	*41-DH*	*5*

Breakout: 18% *Improve: 37%* *Collapse: 31%*

We all know and love Herb Perry, and he's no fool. When you look in one direction and see Hank Blalock, and look in the other and see Mark Teixeira, it's not too hard to make out the longhand on the clubhouse wall. He's a free agent coming off knee surgery, has a long history of nasty health issues, and he'll be hard pressed to find anything more than a minor league contract with a spring training invite.

JUAN SENREISO CF Bats: R Throws: R Born: 04-Aug-1981 Age: 23

YEAR	TM	LG	AGE	AB	H	2B	3B	HR	BB	SO	SB	CS	AVG	OBP	SLG	MLVR	EQBA	EQOBP	EQSLG	EQMLVR	VORP	DEFENSE			
2002	PUL	APL	20	241	61	12	2	8	20	61	18	3	.253	.321	.419	-.016	.186	.223	.298	-.480	-63.9	61-RF	-8		
2003	CLN	MDW	21	473	102	18	4	5	30	117	45	8	.216	.265	.302	-.184	.182	.220	.276	-.518	-67.7	81-RF	-6	46-CF	-1
2004	CLN	MDW	22	127	40	10	2	2	16	31	12	6	.315	.390	.472	.244	.273	.338	.414	-.038	1.1	15-RF	-1	13-CF	0
2004	STO	CLF	22	233	69	12	2	6	15	47	12	5	.296	.344	.442	.093	.253	.293	.371	-.198	-3.5	50-CF	-5		
2004	FRI	TXS	22	46	16	1	1	2	2	7	0	1	.348	.375	.543	.335	.311	.340	.511	.142	3.5				
2005	*TEX*	*AL*	*23*	*304*	*73*	*16*	*2*	*6*	*16*	*78*	*8*	*3*	*.241*	*.285*	*.366*	*-.207*	*.232*	*.278*	*.353*	*-.252*	*-10.8*	*79-CF*	*-10*		

Breakout: 33% *Improve: 55%* *Collapse: 30%*

Hit through three levels in '04, but it was kind of unusual in that he didn't really rip any of the leagues apart. Senreiso has good speed, some ability to hit for average, projects to develop some power and could be a decent defender. He'll likely start the season at Double-A, but could move up to Triple-A quickly, and will probably get at least a look at the majors by 2006.

VINCE SINISI LF Bats: L Throws: L Born: 07-Nov-1981 Age: 23

YEAR	TM	LG	AGE	AB	H	2B	3B	HR	BB	SO	SB	CS	AVG	OBP	SLG	MLVR	EQBA	EQOBP	EQSLG	EQMLVR	VORP	DEFENSE	
2003	STO	CLF	21	62	16	1	0	1	3	8	1	1	.258	.288	.323	-.178	.210	.215	.274	-.518	-6.9		
2004	STO	CLF	22	248	77	13	3	7	33	45	7	3	.310	.383	.472	.216	.265	.333	.396	-.078	-1.8	56-LF	-1
2005	*TEX*	*AL*	*23*	*295*	*74*	*15*	*2*	*7*	*25*	*62*	*3*	*2*	*.253*	*.310*	*.382*	*-.132*	*.243*	*.303*	*.369*	*-.179*	*-10.7*	*79-LF*	*-4*

Breakout: 19% *Improve: 40%* *Collapse: 37%*

(continued next page)

Vince Sinisi *(continued)*

Played pretty well in the California League. Didn't do much to damage his reputation, nor much to help it. Had his season cut short with a broken arm; it's expected to be healed in time to start the 2005 season. It'll be nice to see him play a full year at Double-A with a clean bill of health. Still hasn't been determined whether or not he'll be able to handle the outfield.

DUSTIN SMITH **C** **Bats: R** **Throws: R** Born: 08-May-1981 Age: 24

YEAR	TM	LG	AGE	AB	H	2B	3B	HR	BB	SO	SB	CS	AVG	OBP	SLG	MLVR	EQBA	EQOBP	EQSLG	EQMLVR	VORP	DEFENSE
2002	SAV	SAL	21	176	41	6	0	0	19	38	0	2	.233	.327	.267	-.112	.181	.240	.198	-.584	-23.0	45-C -12
2003	STO	CLF	22	129	39	9	0	1	15	21	1	1	.302	.388	.395	.137	.260	.317	.344	-.185	-0.5	38-C 0
2004	STO	CLF	23	209	69	15	1	6	18	31	1	2	.330	.407	.498	.312	.284	.341	.428	-.003	10.6	46-C -5
2004	FRI	TXS	23	37	3	0	0	0	2	11	0	0	.081	.128	.081	-.897	.054	.074	.054	-1.163	-10.6	11-C -4
2005	*TEX*	*AL*	*24*	*227*	*53*	*11*	*0*	*4*	*15*	*46*	*0*	*1*	*.234*	*.302*	*.337*	*-.218*	*.225*	*.295*	*.325*	*-.262*	*-4.2*	*63-C -9*

Breakout: 9% *Improve: 23%* *Collapse: 59%*

Hit pretty well in Stockton, and got a few games in at Frisco before season's end, where he put up a 3-for-37 stinker. Smith's defense is described as "a bit raw," and it remains to be seen whether or not he'll be able to handle the rigors of catching. If he can move up the ladder at a reasonable pace and hang onto some of his offensive ability, he's got a shot to one day make it as a big league backup.

ALFONSO SORIANO **2B** **Bats: R** **Throws: R** Born: 07-Jan-1976 Age: 29

YEAR	TM	LG	AGE	AB	H	2B	3B	HR	BB	SO	SB	CS	AVG	OBP	SLG	MLVR	EQBA	EQOBP	EQSLG	EQMLVR	VORP	DEFENSE
2002	NYY	AL	26	696	209	51	2	39	23	157	41	13	.300	.332	.547	.213	.311	.345	.570	.237	77.6	154-2B -10
2003	NYY	AL	27	682	198	36	5	38	38	130	35	8	.290	.338	.525	.182	.299	.351	.546	.198	69.9	155-2B 1
2004	TEX	AL	28	608	170	32	4	28	33	121	18	5	.280	.324	.484	.024	.272	.319	.477	.017	39.8	140-2B -10
2005	*TEX*	*AL*	*29*	*594*	*179*	*37*	*4*	*32*	*34*	*114*	*22*	*6*	*.301*	*.348*	*.538*	*.180*	*.290*	*.340*	*.519*	*.123*	*48.2*	*151-2B -4*

Breakout: 19% *Improve: 47%* *Collapse: 15%*

Probably the single most overrated player in baseball. Yes, it's interesting and exciting that he can hit a pitch two feet down and in over the fence. But what the hell is he doing swinging at it in the first place? Most of the time, he flails at that pitch and misses it, in yet another mini three-act play that has Soriano loping back to the bench. He hit .244/.291/.444 on the road. Defensively, no metric pegs him as a good defensive second baseman, and one advance scout describes him as "beyond redemption" with the glove. Why, exactly, do people think this guy is anything remotely resembling a star? Are we that starved for excitement?

MARK TEIXEIRA **1B** **Bats: B** **Throws: R** Born: 11-Apr-1980 Age: 25

YEAR	TM	LG	AGE	AB	H	2B	3B	HR	BB	SO	SB	CS	AVG	OBP	SLG	MLVR	EQBA	EQOBP	EQSLG	EQMLVR	VORP	DEFENSE
2002	PCH	FSL	22	150	48	10	2	9	21	24	2	0	.320	.411	.593	.473	.286	.360	.539	.188	17.7	36-3B -8
2002	TUL	TXS	22	171	54	11	3	10	25	36	3	2	.316	.415	.591	.468	.283	.368	.532	.189	20.6	47-3B 0
2003	TEX	AL	23	529	137	29	5	26	44	120	1	2	.259	.331	.480	.034	.253	.328	.474	.011	22.0	105-1B 4 13-3B -4
2004	TEX	AL	24	545	153	34	2	38	68	117	4	1	.281	.370	.560	.201	.273	.367	.552	.204	52.6	138-1B 8
2005	*TEX*	*AL*	*25*	*535*	*158*	*33*	*3*	*33*	*64*	*110*	*3*	*2*	*.295*	*.380*	*.553*	*.244*	*.284*	*.371*	*.534*	*.187*	*43.0*	*144-1B 2*

Breakout: 31% *Improve: 70%* *Collapse: 6%*

If the Rangers contend, Teixeira's a reasonable pick for AL MVP. They won't, so he's a reasonable bet to get a bunch of MVP votes, be more deserving than some guys who finish ahead of him, and generally do to baseballs what talk radio does to dignified restraint. Teixeira's a bomber, playing in a favorable park, with the broad base of offensive skills that portend great things. There are critics who think he's never going to defend very well. That may or may not be the case, but it's a little like criticizing Jerry Rice circa 1989 for not being a tremendous pass defender. Should we really care?

ERIC YOUNG UT **Bats: R** **Throws: R** Born: 18-May-1967 Age: 38

YEAR	TM	LG	AGE	AB	H	2B	3B	HR	BB	SO	SB	CS	AVG	OBP	SLG	MLVR	EQBA	EQOBP	EQSLG	EQMLVR	VORP	DEFENSE	
2002	MIL	NL	35	496	139	29	3	3	39	38	31	11	.280	.338	.369	-.019	.285	.339	.380	-.075	25.4	119-2B -6	
2003	MIL	NL	36	404	105	18	1	15	48	34	25	7	.260	.344	.421	.021	.259	.342	.425	-.026	24.2	94-2B -11	
2003	SFG	NL	36	71	14	2	0	0	9	10	3	5	.197	.293	.225	-.355	.225	.281	.254	-.403	-6.2	17-2B 2	
2004	TEX	AL	37	344	99	25	2	1	43	28	14	9	.288	.377	.381	-.018	.281	.374	.370	-.025	12.4	33-LF -2	18-2B -3
2005	*SDP*	*NL*	*38*	*285*	*73*	*15*	*1*	*3*	*31*	*23*	*12*	*3*	*.258*	*.336*	*.355*	*-.126*	*.267*	*.343*	*.378*	*-.079*	*8.3*	*79-2B -11*	

Breakout: 27% *Improve: 53%* *Collapse: 28%*

If Young's getting close to 400 plate appearances at this stage, that probably means Plan A went awry. Still, he's a pretty good Plan B. As he enters his late 30s, Young has matured into a high-contact hitter with a great batting eye, with some pop and even some lingering speed. As a starter he's overmatched. Off the pine, or filling in on a two-week DL stint, he's a nice snag for the Padres and their much improved bench.

MIKE YOUNG SS/2B **Bats: R** **Throws: R** Born: 19-Oct-1976 Age: 28

YEAR	TM	LG	AGE	AB	H	2B	3B	HR	BB	SO	SB	CS	AVG	OBP	SLG	MLVR	EQBA	EQOBP	EQSLG	EQMLVR	VORP	DEFENSE
2002	TEX	AL	25	573	150	26	8	9	41	112	6	7	.262	.308	.382	-.140	.258	.311	.379	-.149	8.9	142-2B 8
2003	TEX	AL	26	666	204	33	9	14	36	103	13	2	.306	.339	.446	.039	.297	.336	.438	.014	42.5	157-2B -10
2004	TEX	AL	27	690	216	33	9	22	44	89	12	3	.313	.353	.483	.102	.305	.350	.473	.097	60.1	156-SS -13
2005	*TEX*	*AL*	*28*	*605*	*176*	*32*	*5*	*15*	*40*	*87*	*10*	*4*	*.291*	*.334*	*.436*	*.011*	*.279*	*.326*	*.421*	*-.041*	*23.4*	*153-SS -7*

Breakout: 3% *Improve: 19%* *Collapse: 37%*

Young embodied the Rangers' season. Started off unbelievably hot, made a number of sportscasters derisively laugh off the loss of A-Rod, but hit 100 OPS points after the All-Star Break. The drop-off was partly due to the back injury he suffered in August; the question is whether or not that's necessarily a good thing for the future. Young's locked up on a four-year deal through 2007, with a club option for 2008. If he can hang onto some of his newfound power, play good defense, and rack up 200 hits a year, he's a big plus. But it's not a lock.

PETE ZOCCOLILLO OF **Bats: L** **Throws: R** Born: 06-Feb-1977 Age: 28

YEAR	TM	LG	AGE	AB	H	2B	3B	HR	BB	SO	SB	CS	AVG	OBP	SLG	MLVR	EQBA	EQOBP	EQSLG	EQMLVR	VORP	DEFENSE	
2002	HDS	CLF	25	161	55	10	0	8	28	24	2	1	.342	.436	.553	.349	.264	.338	.428	-.025	2.1	25-RF -2	10-LF 0
2002	HUN	SOU	25	227	67	12	1	12	40	50	6	7	.295	.399	.515	.320	.265	.355	.474	.069	9.6	32-LF -1	26-RF -1
2003	IND	INT	26	443	124	36	1	12	51	70	3	5	.280	.360	.447	.120	.255	.337	.423	-.041	3.4	85-RF -6	36-LF -1
2004	OKL	PCL	27	484	142	37	1	23	65	94	4	2	.293	.375	.517	.218	.260	.337	.440	-.014	7.4	49-RF 2	20-LF -1
2005	*TEX*	*AL*	*28*	*129*	*33*	*7*	*1*	*5*	*14*	*27*	*1*	*1*	*.256*	*.333*	*.438*	*-.017*	*.246*	*.325*	*.423*	*-.067*	*5.4*	*39-RF -4*	

Breakout: 13% *Improve: 30%* *Collapse: 42%*

Z's another example of a guy who's good enough to play in the majors for the minimum who can outperform a lot of guys making millions. He can hit for some average, has a little pop, but doesn't run well. As a pinch-hitter or extra outfielder, he's earned a shot somewhere.

PITCHERS

CARLOS ALMANZAR **Bats: R** **Throws: R** Born: 06-Nov-1973 Age: 31

YEAR	TM	LG	AGE	G	GS	IP	H	BB	SO	HR	ERA	EQERA	EQH9	EQBB9	EQSO9	EQHR9	PERA	VORP	STF
2002	LOU	INT	28	21	0	23.0	21	5	19	0	2.74	3.27	8.2	2.0	6.5	0.4	3.27	5.7	6
2003	LOU	INT	29	42	0	46.3	47	3	54	2	3.50	4.17	8.5	0.6	8.3	0.6	3.18	12.2	20
2004	TEX	AL	30	67	0	72.7	66	19	44	8	3.71	3.34	8.4	2.2	5.3	0.9	3.86	18.7	-4
2005	*TEX*	*AL*	*31*	*41*	*3*	*66.7*	*73*	*20*	*44*	*9*	*4.52*	*4.02*	*9.6*	*2.3*	*5.5*	*1.0*	*4.16*	*14.3*	*-3*

Breakout: 28% *Improve: 49%* *Collapse: 27%*

Bill James spent years arguing that minor league statistics—adjusting for park, league and other variables—could predict major league performance with nearly the same degree of certainty as can major league statistics. It's a tradition we've carried on and advanced here at *Baseball Prospectus,* and it's for this reason that we always get a kick out of seeing someone like Almanzar fare well. A career minor leaguer with only sporadic cups o' joe throughout his pro career, Almanzar

(continued next page)

Carlos Almanzar *(continued)*

parlayed his tailing fastball into a fantastic 54:3 strikeout-to-walk ratio at Triple-A in 2003. The Rangers, looking for bullpen help, took a flyer on him, despite his age. The result? The righty flashed the same effective control in 67 appearances with the big club, showing he's more than a minor league lifer destined to put up good Triple-A stats.

Almanzar's game is far from perfect: He struggled late in the year—a forearm injury making matters worse—and he doesn't strike out enough hitters to truly dominate. Still, there's a valuable lesson learned here: The Rangers struck gold for a year on a cheap, effective reliever. The minute Almanzar stops being effective, they'll search for another overlooked arm putting up good numbers and give him a shot. Tendered a contract, which means a bigger payday, muting the good tidings somewhat.

MIKE BACSIK **Bats: L** **Throws: L** Born: 11-Nov-1977 Age: 27

YEAR	TM	LG	AGE	G	GS	IP	H	BB	SO	HR	ERA	EQERA	EQH9	EQBB9	EQSO9	EQHR9	PERA	VORP	STF
2002	NOR	INT	24	25	14	108.3	134	25	75	13	3.74	4.68	10.4	2.3	5.2	1.4	5.28	3.8	-15
2002	NYM	NL	24	11	9	55.7	63	19	30	8	4.36	4.86	10.2	2.7	4.4	1.3	5.20	5.0	-16
2003	NOR	INT	25	22	21	117.7	129	34	62	13	4.97	6.02	10.0	3.0	3.9	1.5	5.37	2.8	-22
2003	NYM	NL	25	5	3	17.7	28	8	12	5	10.17	10.50	12.5	3.5	5.5	2.5	8.00	-9.8	-28
2004	OKL	PCL	26	34	9	95.0	106	23	50	16	4.55	5.68	10.1	2.3	3.7	1.8	5.48	1.2	-13
2004	TEX	AL	26	3	3	15.7	16	1	6	2	4.59	3.60	9.0	0.6	3.6	1.2	3.60	2.8	11
2005	*TEX*	*AL*	*27*	*23*	*6*	*55.0*	*69*	*18*	*29*	*10*	*5.76*	*5.13*	*10.9*	*2.6*	*4.3*	*1.5*	*5.28*	*4.8*	*-14*

Breakout: 22% *Improve: 53%* *Collapse: 23%*

Swingman/non-prospect who fits the mold of the Ranger pitcher perfectly. Did manage to keep his ERA under 5, primarily by throwing seven shutout innings against the powerful Detroit offense. Considering that was half of his major league workload, that should tell you something about how the rest of the year went. Bacsik doesn't strike people out, and he has no long-term performance record to indicate he's likely to be effective going forward.

JOAQUIN BENOIT **Bats: R** **Throws: R** Born: 26-Jul-1977 Age: 27

YEAR	TM	LG	AGE	G	GS	IP	H	BB	SO	HR	ERA	EQERA	EQH9	EQBB9	EQSO9	EQHR9	PERA	VORP	STF
2002	OKL	PCL	24	16	16	98.7	74	37	103	8	3.56	4.27	7.4	3.7	7.6	0.9	3.21	24.6	35
2002	TEX	AL	24	17	13	84.7	91	58	59	6	5.31	4.80	8.9	5.7	5.9	0.5	4.80	5.3	14
2003	OKL	PCL	25	6	6	33.0	28	11	31	3	3.82	5.23	8.1	3.5	7.3	1.2	4.06	5.3	29
2003	TEX	AL	25	25	17	105.0	99	51	87	23	5.49	4.93	8.3	4.2	7.4	1.8	4.57	4.0	12
2004	TEX	AL	26	28	15	103.0	113	31	95	19	5.68	4.82	9.0	2.4	7.8	1.4	4.65	4.5	11
2005	*TEX*	*AL*	*27*	*22*	*15*	*93.3*	*95*	*38*	*76*	*16*	*4.99*	*4.45*	*8.9*	*3.2*	*6.8*	*1.3*	*4.44*	*15.9*	*7*

Breakout: 20% *Improve: 51%* *Collapse: 25%*

Benoit has stuff that can make hitters miss, which is a rarity in this organization. His main problem is pretty easy to identify—42 HR in 208 innings over the past two seasons. That keeps his ERA around that Ameriquest standard of 5.50 or so. Phrases like "biceps tendonitis" and "rotator cuff irritation" can bring someone to worry, but Benoit appears to be healthy coming into the 2005 season. He has a live arm, and a K rate that bodes well. A good candidate for some of that Hershiser groundball mojo.

DOUG BROCAIL **Bats: L** **Throws: R** Born: 16-May-1967 Age: 38

YEAR	TM	LG	AGE	G	GS	IP	H	BB	SO	HR	ERA	EQERA	EQH9	EQBB9	EQSO9	EQHR9	PERA	VORP	STF
2004	TEX	AL	37	43	0	52.3	54	20	43	2	4.13	4.13	8.4	3.1	6.9	0.3	3.78	7.5	8
2005	*TEX*	*AL*	*38*	*35*	*2*	*55.3*	*60*	*19*	*41*	*5*	*4.08*	*3.63*	*9.4*	*2.7*	*6.2*	*0.8*	*4.03*	*13.8*	*2*

Breakout: 33% *Improve: 57%* *Collapse: 24%*

Shelved for two seasons due to elbow problems, Brocail rose from the dead to give the Rangers yet another bit of crack relieving work, leaving some to wonder if Tony Fossas could have put up a 2.88 in this pen. Kudos to Brocail for resurrecting his career in his late-30s and earning a $1 million deal for 2005. As for the fan who taunted Brocail about his stillborn child, triggering the melee in the stands in Oakland . . . here's hoping he's forced to watch "Inside Starr Jones: The Wedding Night" in a constant loop for the rest of his days on Earth.

FRANCISCO CORDERO Bats: R Throws: R Born: 11-May-1975 Age: 30

YEAR	TM	LG	AGE	G	GS	IP	H	BB	SO	HR	ERA	EQERA	EQH9	EQBB9	EQSO9	EQHR9	PERA	VORP	STF
2002	TEX	AL	27	39	0	45.3	33	13	41	2	1.79	2.28	6.9	2.5	7.9	0.4	2.70	18.1	15
2003	TEX	AL	28	73	0	82.7	70	38	90	4	2.94	3.18	6.9	4.0	9.4	0.3	2.74	23.0	22
2004	TEX	AL	29	67	0	71.7	60	32	79	1	2.13	2.03	7.1	3.5	9.4	0.1	3.04	31.0	23
2005	*TEX*	*AL*	*30*	*56*	*1*	*75.7*	*70*	*35*	*78*	*9*	*3.96*	*3.52*	*8.1*	*3.6*	*8.5*	*0.9*	*3.78*	*21.3*	*12*

Breakout: 20% *Improve: 41%* *Collapse: 26%*

Very tough all year long, sizzling stunned batters unable to catch up with his high heat. Ran out of gas down the stretch and gave up a home run on September 29; this would normally be an unremarkable event, except it was the only homer he allowed *all season*. The Rangers signed Cordero and his ridiculous slider to a two-year, $8 million deal in July, avoiding arbitration. Between Cordero, K-Rod and the A's stable of young, power arms, AL West late innings should be a pitching clinic in '05.

JOHN DANKS Bats: L Throws: L Born: 15-Apr-1985 Age: 20

YEAR	TM	LG	AGE	G	GS	IP	H	BB	SO	HR	ERA	EQERA	EQH9	EQBB9	EQSO9	EQHR9	PERA	VORP	STF
2003	SPO	NWN	18	5	5	12.7	12	7	13	0	8.50	10.03	9.3	6.2	5.4	0.0	5.40	0.3	-2
2004	CLN	MDW	19	14	8	49.7	38	14	64	4	2.17	4.43	8.9	3.2	7.1	1.4	4.84	3.8	19
2004	STO	CLF	19	13	13	55.0	62	26	48	5	5.24	6.84	10.5	5.3	5.3	1.4	6.49	-5.1	-5
2005	*TEX*	*AL*	*20*	*12*	*8*	*47.7*	*54*	*23*	*34*	*7*	*5.59*	*4.97*	*9.8*	*3.8*	*5.9*	*1.2*	*4.98*	*4.9*	*-1*

Breakout: 15% *Improve: 49%* *Collapse: 16%*

Well, the inevitable comparisons to Josh Beckett and Todd Van Poppel have already begun, and Danks has shown a little of both. He's got the arm and the stuff, and he dazzled the hitters in low-A, before getting whacked around a bit in the California League. The Rangers will keep an eye on his workload, and give him a chance to work with their best coaches. The numbers are more promising than not, but he's got a long way to go in terms of development and avoiding injury.

R. A. DICKEY Bats: R Throws: R Born: 29-Oct-1974 Age: 30

YEAR	TM	LG	AGE	G	GS	IP	H	BB	SO	HR	ERA	EQERA	EQH9	EQBB9	EQSO9	EQHR9	PERA	VORP	STF
2002	OKL	PCL	27	37	19	154.0	176	47	109	8	4.09	5.07	9.3	2.9	4.9	0.6	3.87	29.0	4
2003	TEX	AL	28	38	13	116.7	135	38	94	16	5.09	4.53	9.1	2.8	6.9	1.1	4.22	10.9	10
2004	TEX	AL	29	25	15	104.3	136	33	57	17	5.61	5.50	10.4	2.5	4.6	1.2	5.50	-4.6	-9
2005	*TEX*	*AL*	*30*	*27*	*15*	*100.7*	*123*	*34*	*63*	*16*	*5.41*	*4.82*	*10.7*	*2.6*	*5.2*	*1.3*	*4.97*	*12.5*	*-3*

Breakout: 21% *Improve: 44%* *Collapse: 21%*

Probably no more than 10% of the stories about Dickey fail to mention that he lacks an ulnar collateral ligament in his elbow (See? Did it again.). While it's fascinating and admirable that he's made the big leagues without that ligament, it doesn't change the fact that he's not been particularly effective, and hence, has fit right in among Rangers starters. A back injury slowed his 2004 season, and he'll be in the mix as a potential swingman/Quadruple-A starter for 2005.

JUAN DOMINGUEZ Bats: R Throws: R Born: 18-May-1980 Age: 25

YEAR	TM	LG	AGE	G	GS	IP	H	BB	SO	HR	ERA	EQERA	EQH9	EQBB9	EQSO9	EQHR9	PERA	VORP	STF
2002	SAV	SAL	22	16	9	66.7	50	21	70	4	2.16	5.01	8.8	3.6	5.9	1.5	4.70	5.9	5
2003	STO	CLF	23	16	9	63.3	55	16	72	3	2.84	5.06	8.7	2.9	6.8	0.9	4.14	9.5	9
2003	FRI	TXS	23	9	9	55.3	35	21	54	2	2.60	3.55	6.9	3.9	6.9	0.5	3.38	12.5	19
2003	OKL	PCL	23	3	3	18.0	15	3	14	1	3.50	4.24	7.9	1.6	5.8	0.5	3.18	4.6	22
2003	TEX	AL	23	6	3	16.3	16	12	13	5	7.18	6.75	9.0	6.2	6.8	2.2	6.19	-3.0	-9
2004	OKL	PCL	24	9	9	54.7	41	19	41	3	3.13	3.73	7.5	3.4	5.5	0.5	3.20	13.5	22
2004	TEX	AL	24	4	4	23.0	25	5	14	2	3.91	3.57	9.1	1.6	5.2	0.8	3.97	4.9	20
2005	*TEX*	*AL*	*25*	*29*	*17*	*112.3*	*117*	*42*	*82*	*15*	*4.82*	*4.29*	*9.1*	*2.9*	*6.1*	*1.1*	*4.17*	*20.2*	*4*

Breakout: 17% *Improve: 47%* *Collapse: 27%*

(continued next page)

Juan Dominguez *(continued)*

One of the best pitching prospects in the organization, Dominguez pitched well enough in nine Triple-A starts to earn a call-up, then showed good control in three starts with the big club. Back and knee problems knocked him for most of the rest of the season, save for one September start in which he again looked good. His strikeout rate eroded a bit from its gaudy 2003 level, but Dominguez's peripherals otherwise held up. Transferred from the 60-day DL to the 40-man roster in November, he should win a starting job out of spring training if healthy. Assistant GM Jon Daniels's happiest dreams involve him in the GM chair circa 2007, Danks, Dominguez and Loe anchoring a young staff, Teixeira and Blalock crushing the snot out of the ball.

RYAN DRESE **Bats: R** **Throws: R** Born: 05-Apr-1976 Age: 29

YEAR	TM	LG	AGE	G	GS	IP	H	BB	SO	HR	ERA	EQERA	EQH9	EQBB9	EQSO9	EQHR9	PERA	VORP	STF
2002	CLE	AL	26	26	26	137.3	176	62	102	15	6.55	6.24	9.7	3.6	6.2	0.9	4.63	-12.7	9
2003	OKL	PCL	27	20	20	122.0	143	39	68	8	4.65	5.80	9.8	3.2	4.2	0.9	4.88	9.4	-1
2003	TEX	AL	27	11	8	46.0	61	24	26	8	6.85	6.94	10.2	4.4	4.8	1.3	5.59	-10.9	-12
2004	TEX	AL	28	34	33	207.7	233	58	98	16	4.20	3.74	9.4	2.2	4.0	0.6	4.40	39.8	6
2005	*TEX*	*AL*	*29*	*26*	*24*	*136.3*	*168*	*47*	*76*	*17*	*5.32*	*4.74*	*10.8*	*2.7*	*4.6*	*1.0*	*4.81*	*16.1*	*0*

Breakout: 14% *Improve: 50%* *Collapse: 21%*

The Rangers' most effective pitcher in 2004. Drese pitched over 200 innings while posting a very good 4.20 ERA. Observers credited a worm-killing sinker as the key to Drese's success and another sign of Orel Hershiser's impact on some of the team's young pitchers. Sinkerballers/groundball pitchers are subject to yielding more hits on balls in play, and Drese's microscopic strikeout rate means a ton of balls get put in play off him. This type of pitcher can look great one year, then put up an ERA near 6 when things break the other way.

FRANK FRANCISCO **Bats: R** **Throws: R** Born: 11-Sep-1979 Age: 25

YEAR	TM	LG	AGE	G	GS	IP	H	BB	SO	HR	ERA	EQERA	EQH9	EQBB9	EQSO9	EQHR9	PERA	VORP	STF
2002	SAR	FSL	22	16	10	53.0	33	27	58	1	2.55	4.25	7.0	5.2	7.4	0.4	3.51	11.3	11
2002	TRN	EAS	22	9	0	16.0	10	16	18	0	5.62	7.80	6.6	9.6	7.8	0.0	3.60	3.3	-3
2002	WNS	CRL	22	6	6	25.7	31	18	25	3	8.05	9.13	11.4	8.0	6.5	2.3	8.37	-7.3	-24
2003	WNS	CRL	23	16	16	78.3	59	36	67	7	3.56	5.68	9.2	4.8	6.1	1.9	5.94	-2.6	0
2003	FRI	TXS	23	7	6	35.3	43	18	22	5	8.41	8.73	11.5	5.2	4.4	2.5	7.64	-7.5	-16
2004	FRI	TXS	24	15	0	17.7	7	10	30	1	2.54	3.94	5.6	6.2	11.2	1.1	3.38	3.9	24
2004	TEX	AL	24	45	0	51.3	36	28	60	4	3.33	2.68	6.4	4.5	10.0	0.5	3.22	16.8	25
2005	*TEX*	*AL*	*25*	*28*	*3*	*49.3*	*45*	*29*	*49*	*9*	*5.19*	*4.62*	*8.0*	*4.6*	*8.2*	*1.4*	*4.63*	*7.7*	*3*

Breakout: 17% *Improve: 55%* *Collapse: 13%*

No, the numbers above do not include his chair throwing. Vilified in the media for going over the line in Oakland, he's gotten something of a bad rap. Of course you should never throw a chair at someone, but you should also not say and do the things that those fans in Oakland did. Francisco throws hard, had a pretty big breakout year, but still has the potential to see his ERA bump up a bit due to the ill-timed walk or two. Otherwise, a pretty dependable power arm, and while he'll likely be convicted of misdemeanor assault and/or battery, it's unlikely to affect him in terms of playing time.

RICK HELLING **Bats: R** **Throws: R** Born: 15-Dec-1970 Age: 34

YEAR	TM	LG	AGE	G	GS	IP	H	BB	SO	HR	ERA	EQERA	EQH9	EQBB9	EQSO9	EQHR9	PERA	VORP	STF
2002	ARI	NL	31	30	30	175.7	180	48	120	31	4.51	4.60	9.5	2.1	5.6	1.6	4.70	13.4	3
2003	BAL	AL	32	24	24	138.7	156	40	86	30	5.71	5.39	9.7	2.5	5.5	1.8	5.25	3.7	-2
2003	FLA	NL	32	11	0	16.3	11	5	12	1	0.55	0.59	7.0	2.3	6.5	0.6	2.93	9.2	7
2004	NBR	EAS	33	5	5	31.0	30	11	21	5	4.94	5.59	9.6	3.4	4.7	2.2	5.59	0.0	0
2004	OKL	PCL	33	6	6	31.0	59	11	20	8	9.00	9.74	13.6	3.1	4.2	2.5	8.35	-9.9	-33
2005	*MIL*	*NL*	*34*	*22*	*14*	*90.7*	*101*	*30*	*56*	*17*	*5.32*	*5.52*	*10.0*	*2.6*	*5.1*	*1.6*	*5.53*	*5.5*	*-6*

Breakout: 19% *Improve: 34%* *Collapse: 37%*

Signed a mid-season minor league contract with the Rangers, went to Oklahoma, and gave up two hits and a run per inning. Signed by the Brewers, but he's likely done.

BEN KOZLOWSKI **Bats: L** **Throws: L** Born: 16-Aug-1980 Age: 24

YEAR	TM	LG	AGE	G	GS	IP	H	BB	SO	HR	ERA	EQERA	EQH9	EQBB9	EQSO9	EQHR9	PERA	VORP	STF
2002	PCH	FSL	21	21	12	79.0	63	25	76	2	2.05	4.71	8.7	3.2	6.4	0.5	4.21	11.2	10
2002	TUL	TXS	21	8	8	52.0	28	22	41	3	1.90	3.30	7.0	4.5	5.8	1.0	3.50	10.8	29
2003	FRI	TXS	22	11	10	54.7	71	27	29	4	5.43	6.66	10.9	5.0	3.6	1.2	6.66	-6.2	-28
2004	STO	CLF	23	10	8	47.0	40	19	32	1	3.83	5.40	8.3	4.6	4.2	0.4	4.36	6.0	0
2004	FRI	TXS	23	8	7	38.7	38	20	23	5	4.88	6.43	10.3	5.4	4.1	2.1	7.20	-6.2	-19
2005	*CIN*	*NL*	*24*	*24*	*11*	*74.3*	*80*	*41*	*48*	*11*	*5.49*	*5.87*	*9.8*	*4.4*	*5.2*	*1.2*	*5.86*	*-0.2*	*-12*

Breakout: 11% *Improve: 43%* *Collapse: 24%*

Claimed off waivers by the Reds in October, Kozlowski will be one of the youngest, most talented attempted reclamation projects in Don Gullett's Dr. Frankenstein career. Coming off Tommy John surgery in June 2003, Kozlowski struggled with his control both at A-ball and Double-A. But getting TJ'd carries a much higher success rate than most anything shoulder-related, and Kozlowski was a talented lefty with pretty good peripherals before the procedure. An excellent, low-risk gamble.

COLBY LEWIS **Bats: R** **Throws: R** Born: 02-Aug-1979 Age: 25

YEAR	TM	LG	AGE	G	GS	IP	H	BB	SO	HR	ERA	EQERA	EQH9	EQBB9	EQSO9	EQHR9	PERA	VORP	STF
2002	OKL	PCL	22	20	20	106.7	100	28	99	4	3.63	4.54	8.1	2.5	6.6	0.3	2.97	30.1	34
2002	TEX	AL	22	15	4	34.3	42	26	28	4	6.30	5.91	9.5	6.2	6.7	1.0	5.66	-3.2	1
2003	OKL	PCL	23	7	7	47.7	36	19	43	6	3.02	3.71	8.0	4.1	7.2	1.6	4.53	5.2	21
2003	TEX	AL	23	26	26	127.0	163	70	88	23	7.30	6.30	9.9	4.6	5.9	1.4	5.53	-18.2	0
2004	TEX	AL	24	3	3	15.3	13	13	11	1	4.12	3.60	7.8	7.2	6.0	0.6	4.80	3.6	6
2005	*DET*	*AL*	*25*	*17*	*15*	*88.0*	*88*	*49*	*71*	*11*	*5.01*	*5.06*	*9.0*	*4.4*	*6.5*	*1.1*	*5.12*	*9.3*	*4*

Breakout: 31% *Improve: 44%* *Collapse: 27%*

Shoulder injuries suck. First, it's soreness, then inflammation, then more tests, and eventually, you end up having some surgery that sucks away a year of time, and never heals back to the point where you get the life back in your fastball. Lewis was once a sleeper who could have turned out to be something like a right-handed Kenny Rogers. Now, he's recovering from shoulder surgery and will be pitching in Detroit when he does finally get better, having been waived by the Rangers and claimed by the Kitties.

KAMERON LOE **Bats: R** **Throws: R** Born: 10-Sep-1981 Age: 23

YEAR	TM	LG	AGE	G	GS	IP	H	BB	SO	HR	ERA	EQERA	EQH9	EQBB9	EQSO9	EQHR9	PERA	VORP	STF
2002	PUL	APL	20	14	11	58.3	64	17	55	3	4.48	6.99	10.1	3.3	4.2	1.1	5.53	0.4	-7
2003	CLN	MDW	21	23	11	97.0	78	19	94	3	1.95	4.82	8.4	2.2	5.9	0.8	3.71	18.8	12
2003	STO	CLF	21	9	4	37.7	26	6	31	1	0.95	3.15	7.6	1.8	5.0	0.5	2.88	10.4	18
2004	FRI	TXS	22	19	19	113.3	122	29	97	5	3.10	4.17	9.8	2.6	5.5	0.7	4.92	8.2	-1
2004	OKL	PCL	22	8	8	52.3	52	13	42	6	3.27	3.78	9.0	2.3	5.6	1.1	4.32	7.1	17
2005	*TEX*	*AL*	*23*	*15*	*14*	*79.7*	*93*	*30*	*54*	*11*	*5.21*	*4.64*	*10.2*	*2.9*	*5.6*	*1.1*	*4.72*	*10.2*	*5*

Breakout: 7% *Improve: 37%* *Collapse: 27%*

One of the few promising pitchers in the organization. Loe has good command of some reasonable pitches, and will be in the running for a rotation spot, health permitting, in spring training. He's got everything you want in a pitcher except the absolutely blazing fastball, and it's conceivable he could be the Rangers' #1 starter by August.

RON MAHAY **Bats: L** **Throws: L** Born: 28-Jun-1971 Age: 34

YEAR	TM	LG	AGE	G	GS	IP	H	BB	SO	HR	ERA	EQERA	EQH9	EQBB9	EQSO9	EQHR9	PERA	VORP	STF
2002	IOW	PCL	31	39	1	46.7	32	15	50	3	1.93	2.68	7.0	3.1	7.8	0.8	3.09	12.2	20
2002	CHC	NL	31	11	0	14.7	13	8	14	6	8.57	8.36	9.0	4.5	7.7	3.9	7.07	-5.2	-1
2003	OKL	PCL	32	26	0	42.7	36	10	51	5	4.22	5.13	8.0	2.5	9.4	1.8	4.02	7.1	20
2003	TEX	AL	32	35	0	45.3	33	20	38	3	3.18	3.30	6.8	3.9	7.6	0.6	2.89	11.7	14
2004	TEX	AL	33	60	0	67.0	60	29	54	5	2.55	2.60	7.9	3.6	6.9	0.5	3.84	23.8	9
2005	*TEX*	*AL*	*34*	*43*	*2*	*63.0*	*65*	*28*	*50*	*10*	*4.83*	*4.30*	*9.0*	*3.5*	*6.6*	*1.2*	*4.43*	*12.2*	*-2*

Breakout: 24% *Improve: 48%* *Collapse: 23%*

(continued next page)

Ron Mahay *(continued)*

After two straight seasons retiring lefties and righties alike, Mahay's hit the mother lode, netting a two-year contract extension. He's learned that patented lefty-hit-the-down-and-away corner pitch that keeps people like Ricardo Rincon employed. A lock for an ERA boost of a run or more.

CHAN HO PARK **Bats: R** **Throws: R** Born: 30-Jun-1973 Age: 32

YEAR	TM	LG	AGE	G	GS	IP	H	BB	SO	HR	ERA	EQERA	EQH9	EQBB9	EQSO9	EQHR9	PERA	VORP	STF
2002	TEX	AL	29	25	25	145.7	154	78	121	20	5.74	5.18	8.9	4.4	7.1	1.1	4.86	1.8	6
2003	TEX	AL	30	7	7	29.7	34	25	16	5	7.58	6.75	9.5	7.1	4.6	1.2	5.83	-5.9	-23
2004	TEX	AL	31	16	16	95.7	105	33	63	22	5.45	4.90	9.5	2.8	5.7	1.7	5.38	3.2	0
2005	*TEX*	*AL*	*32*	*22*	*22*	*126.0*	*139*	*52*	*84*	*22*	*5.35*	*4.76*	*9.6*	*3.2*	*5.5*	*1.4*	*4.86*	*15.5*	*3*

Breakout: 14% *Improve: 47%* *Collapse: 17%*

The real inspiration for the A-Rod trade, Park was once again copious quantities of both awful and absent. Texas has paid him $34 million thus far, and in return received this pitching line:

G	GS	IP	H	BB	K	ERA
48	48	271	293	136	200	5.91

On the bright side, his control did improve in 2004, and there are only two more years left on his deal, during which the Rangers will pay him $29 million. Deep breaths, Ranger fans. Deep breaths.

ERASMO RAMIREZ **Bats: L** **Throws: L** Born: 29-Apr-1976 Age: 29

YEAR	TM	LG	AGE	G	GS	IP	H	BB	SO	HR	ERA	EQERA	EQH9	EQBB9	EQSO9	EQHR9	PERA	VORP	STF
2002	TUL	TXS	26	34	0	54.0	51	8	34	1	3.00	4.94	8.6	1.4	4.4	0.4	3.35	12.8	3
2002	OKL	PCL	26	25	0	21.0	15	4	17	0	1.29	2.75	6.9	1.8	5.9	0.0	1.83	8.3	11
2003	OKL	PCL	27	22	0	35.3	36	2	20	0	1.53	2.91	8.7	0.5	4.2	0.3	3.18	9.1	2
2003	TEX	AL	27	34	0	49.0	46	9	28	4	3.86	3.42	8.2	1.5	5.1	0.6	3.04	12.2	4
2004	TEX	AL	28	34	0	35.7	34	7	21	5	4.29	3.93	8.7	1.6	5.2	1.0	3.93	5.9	-2
2005	*TEX*	*AL*	*29*	*31*	*1*	*42.7*	*52*	*11*	*23*	*6*	*4.96*	*4.41*	*10.6*	*2.0*	*4.4*	*1.0*	*4.56*	*8.1*	*-11*

Breakout: 20% *Improve: 43%* *Collapse: 36%*

Functional lefty with good control, yet another useful cog in a Texas bullpen that found success under every possible rock. It may seem a little repetitive to keep hearing about all these non-descript relievers who pitched well for the Rangers in '04, but it could be worse: Your team could have lepers in all three outfield spots, or a mascot who stabs fans between innings, or worst of all . . . it could be run by Jim Bowden. The horror!

NICK REGILIO **Bats: R** **Throws: R** Born: 04-Sep-1978 Age: 26

YEAR	TM	LG	AGE	G	GS	IP	H	BB	SO	HR	ERA	EQERA	EQH9	EQBB9	EQSO9	EQHR9	PERA	VORP	STF
2002	TUL	TXS	23	19	19	104.7	97	47	59	8	3.44	5.04	9.4	4.5	4.0	1.4	5.42	1.9	-15
2004	OKL	PCL	25	17	17	91.7	98	46	72	6	4.71	5.08	9.1	4.8	5.5	0.6	4.87	7.2	0
2004	TEX	AL	25	6	4	19.3	20	15	12	3	6.06	6.16	9.0	6.2	5.2	0.9	5.21	-2.6	-17
2005	*TEX*	*AL*	*26*	*16*	*12*	*69.7*	*84*	*39*	*44*	*10*	*6.13*	*5.45*	*10.5*	*4.4*	*5.2*	*1.1*	*5.47*	*3.7*	*-7*

Breakout: 16% *Improve: 44%* *Collapse: 24%*

The Texas organization has been so bereft of starting pitching for so long that Regilio was once hailed as a pretty good prospect. He never really was, and he's now suffered a very serious shoulder injury. He's got a trapped nerve in his shoulder, and he'll probably start the brutal process of bouncing around as a Quad-A guy when he's healthy again. Unlikely to ever pitch in Arlington.

RICARDO RODRIGUEZ **Bats: R** **Throws: R** Born: 21-May-1978 Age: 27

YEAR	TM	LG	AGE	G	GS	IP	H	BB	SO	HR	ERA	EQERA	EQH9	EQBB9	EQSO9	EQHR9	PERA	VORP	STF
2002	JAX	SOU	24	11	11	68.0	56	13	44	4	1.99	3.82	9.2	1.8	4.5	1.2	4.84	5.2	9
2002	BUF	INT	24	4	4	25.0	26	7	14	1	3.60	4.18	9.5	2.7	4.2	0.4	4.56	2.7	1
2002	CLE	AL	24	7	7	41.3	40	18	24	5	5.67	5.40	8.6	3.6	5.2	1.1	3.83	0.5	4
2003	CLE	AL	25	15	15	81.7	89	28	41	16	5.73	5.74	10.0	3.0	4.5	1.6	5.40	-1.8	-9
2004	OKL	PCL	26	6	6	37.0	42	12	18	5	5.11	5.60	9.9	3.1	3.3	1.3	5.09	2.0	-6
2004	TEX	AL	26	5	4	26.7	28	12	15	1	2.02	2.73	8.9	3.8	4.8	0.3	4.44	8.5	4
2005	*TEX*	*AL*	*27*	*18*	*12*	*76.0*	*90*	*30*	*41*	*12*	*5.59*	*4.97*	*10.3*	*3.1*	*4.4*	*1.2*	*4.88*	*6.8*	*-7*

Breakout: 24% *Improve: 47%* *Collapse: 21%*

Suffered a very nasty injury (badly broken elbow) when hit by a line drive in July. He's been working hard on rehab, and he'll be playing in the winter leagues to get his touch back. He'll compete for a rotation spot. Rodriguez was never a tremendous prospect, and even if he comes back fully healthy, he's more likely to be Yet Another Bad Ranger Rotation Dude (YABRRD) than he is someone who pushes a team toward a pennant. His peripheral numbers have never been particularly awe-inspiring.

KENNY ROGERS **Bats: L** **Throws: L** Born: 10-Nov-1964 Age: 40

YEAR	TM	LG	AGE	G	GS	IP	H	BB	SO	HR	ERA	EQERA	EQH9	EQBB9	EQSO9	EQHR9	PERA	VORP	STF
2002	TEX	AL	37	33	33	210.7	212	70	107	21	3.84	3.84	8.9	2.8	4.4	0.8	4.11	39.0	4
2003	MIN	AL	38	33	31	195.0	227	50	116	22	4.57	4.50	9.7	2.2	5.2	0.9	4.55	23.8	8
2004	TEX	AL	39	35	35	211.7	248	66	126	24	4.76	4.11	9.6	2.5	5.0	0.9	4.75	29.5	6
2005	*TEX*	*AL*	*40*	*30*	*29*	*165.7*	*193*	*57*	*91*	*21*	*4.76*	*4.24*	*10.2*	*2.7*	*4.5*	*1.0*	*4.56*	*28.4*	*1*

Breakout: 27% *Improve: 54%* *Collapse: 0%*

He keeps on doin' what he does. Rogers has been one of the best rotation fillers in baseball for about a decade, and once again, he did what he was supposed to do in 2004—take the mound and give his team a chance to win. Two-hundred and eleven innings of a 4.76 ERA in Arlington? Cool. That's someone who helps a club. He's in the second year of a two-year deal, and the Rangers would take a replay of the 2004 season (PECOTA coincidentally predicts that identical ERA in '05). Strangely, Rogers pitched significantly better at Arlington than on the road, to the tune of about a run a game, and yes, like everyone else on the roster, started out strong, and faded as the year went along.

BRIAN SHOUSE **Bats: L** **Throws: L** Born: 26-Sep-1968 Age: 36

YEAR	TM	LG	AGE	G	GS	IP	H	BB	SO	HR	ERA	EQERA	EQH9	EQBB9	EQSO9	EQHR9	PERA	VORP	STF
2002	KCR	AL	33	23	0	14.7	15	9	11	3	6.12	5.02	8.8	5.0	6.3	1.9	5.65	-0.3	-17
2003	TEX	AL	34	62	0	61.0	62	14	40	1	3.10	3.13	8.2	1.9	5.7	0.1	2.83	17.3	9
2004	TEX	AL	35	53	0	44.3	36	18	34	3	2.23	2.09	7.5	3.3	6.7	0.4	3.56	18.9	2
2005	*TEX*	*AL*	*36*	*50*	*0*	*49*	*50*	*21*	*35*	*4*	*3.85*	*3.43*	*8.9*	*3.4*	*5.9*	*0.7*	*4.00*	*14.3*	*-4*

Breakout: 34% *Improve: 67%* *Collapse: 15%*

Just missing the ERA title within the highly productive Rangers bullpen, Shouse dominated lefties for the second year in a row, and was used judiciously enough (0.84 IP per appearance) for Texas to get only the best Shousey goodness. Lefty relievers are used—and misused—way too often as specialists, so it's nice to see someone get it right, even if it's still not our favorite part of the game.

RYAN SNARE **Bats: L** **Throws: L** Born: 08-Feb-1979 Age: 26

YEAR	TM	LG	AGE	G	GS	IP	H	BB	SO	HR	ERA	EQERA	EQH9	EQBB9	EQSO9	EQHR9	PERA	VORP	STF
2002	PME	EAS	23	11	9	55.0	46	19	52	6	3.44	4.44	8.9	3.4	6.8	1.6	4.80	4.5	6
2002	STO	CLF	23	13	13	82.0	74	18	81	4	3.07	5.19	9.3	2.2	5.3	0.8	4.48	9.5	9
2003	CAR	SOU	24	18	18	103.0	98	37	77	4	3.67	5.04	9.3	3.4	4.9	0.7	4.76	9.0	3
2003	OKL	PCL	24	9	9	54.7	59	13	28	7	3.46	4.91	10.0	2.5	4.0	1.8	5.26	1.9	-3
2004	OKL	PCL	25	26	24	137.3	171	49	79	16	4.72	5.86	10.4	3.4	4.0	1.1	5.59	0.1	-8
2005	*TEX*	*AL*	*26*	*14*	*6*	*44.7*	*54*	*18*	*25*	*8*	*5.85*	*5.21*	*10.5*	*3.1*	*4.7*	*1.4*	*5.14*	*3.4*	*-10*

Breakout: 19% *Improve: 45%* *Collapse: 21%*

His ERA's survived as he's moved up, but his peripherals haven't. He's that lefty you know so well, without the overpowering fastball, who survives by throwing to spots, changing speeds, and hoping the spirit of Eric Gregg possesses the home plate umpire. He's been somewhat successful, but those hit rates and strikeout numbers spell future trouble more often than not.

JOHN WASDIN Bats: R Throws: R Born: 05-Aug-1972 Age: 32

YEAR	TM	LG	AGE	G	GS	IP	H	BB	SO	HR	ERA	EQERA	EQH9	EQBB9	EQSO9	EQHR9	PERA	VORP	STF
2003	NAS	PCL	30	18	18	112.3	101	24	116	4	3.05	4.53	8.1	2.2	8.0	0.5	3.27	27.8	35
2003	SYR	INT	30	10	1	20.7	28	1	21	1	5.22	6.00	10.3	0.4	6.9	0.4	4.29	3.1	8
2004	OKL	PCL	31	18	14	104.0	94	19	81	10	3.46	4.12	8.5	1.7	5.5	1.1	3.84	19.2	29
2004	TEX	AL	31	15	10	65.0	83	23	36	18	6.78	5.98	10.6	2.8	4.7	2.1	6.26	-6.9	0
2005	*TEX*	*AL*	*32*	*22*	*16*	*99.0*	*118*	*31*	*65*	*19*	*5.85*	*5.21*	*10.4*	*2.4*	*5.4*	*1.5*	*4.95*	*8.2*	*0*

Breakout: 16% *Improve: 33%* *Collapse: 31%*

He was once, long ago, "The Man" in the Oakland organization. Well, he's earned the nickname of "WayBack", which is something like being slapped with the moniker of "Stinky" in grade school. It's tough to shed stuff like that sometimes. Wasdin will bounce from organization to organization, ready to fill a rotation or long-relief spot should someone get hurt.

CHRIS YOUNG Bats: R Throws: R Born: 25-May-1979 Age: 26

YEAR	TM	LG	AGE	G	GS	IP	H	BB	SO	HR	ERA	EQERA	EQH9	EQBB9	EQSO9	EQHR9	PERA	VORP	STF
2002	HIC	SAL	23	26	26	144.7	127	34	136	11	3.11	5.19	9.8	2.7	5.3	1.8	5.68	-1.2	0
2003	BRV	FSL	24	8	8	50.0	26	5	39	3	1.62	3.32	7.9	1.0	5.4	1.9	3.74	8.9	26
2003	HAR	EAS	24	15	15	83.0	83	22	64	9	4.01	4.77	9.8	2.7	5.8	1.7	5.47	1.1	0
2004	FRI	TXS	25	18	18	88.3	94	31	75	9	4.48	5.44	10.2	3.6	5.6	1.5	6.10	-4.6	-11
2004	OKL	PCL	25	5	5	30.3	20	9	34	2	1.49	2.54	7.0	2.9	7.9	0.6	2.86	8.6	27
2004	TEX	AL	25	7	7	36.3	36	10	27	7	4.71	4.33	8.7	2.3	6.4	1.5	4.58	4.2	7
2005	*TEX*	*AL*	*26*	*19*	*16*	*97.0*	*106*	*36*	*67*	*17*	*5.48*	*4.88*	*9.6*	*2.9*	*5.7*	*1.4*	*4.70*	*10.4*	*3*

Breakout: 14% *Improve: 38%* *Collapse: 11%*

His seven-start stint at year's end pegged him as a prospect with potential to be a plus in the rotation. He's still considered very raw, and more than one scout thinks we'll see an increase in his K rate over the next two seasons—not surprising given his 6′10″ frame and the usual talk of projectability. We'll find out, as he was able to leverage a potential NBA career with the Sacramento Kings into a three-year deal. His K rates have never been great, but he's got other skills: Young has always shown good control, and there are worse developments than finding an effective finesse player who can also change clubhouse light bulbs without a stepladder.

Toronto Blue Jays

In November 2001, the Blue Jays hired A's Director of Player Development J. P. Ricciardi as their new general manager. Ricciardi had been with the A's for 15 years, starting as a scout in the '80s and joining the front office in '96. On his watch, the A's system produced the core of a team that would make the playoffs four straight seasons and gain acclaim for being successful despite modest budgets. While the spotlight shone most brightly on Billy Beane, the hires of Ricciardi and, subsequently, Paul DePodesta, were a reflection of the work all three did to build and sustain the A's.

Hiring Ricciardi was the Jays' way of breaking with their frustrating recent past. Since winning back-to-back World Series in 1992 and '93, the Jays haven't finished above third in the AL East, and all the buzz from those early years at SkyDome had dissipated. Ricciardi—young, energetic, photogenic—was in many ways the opposite of Gord Ash, who presided over the decline.

Within months of taking the job, Ricciardi hired a statistical consultant. Keith Law, (like DePodesta, a Harvard graduate) was brought in to provide the sort of performance analysis that DePodesta had given the Beane front office in Oakland. The hiring was notable because Law was best known for his work as a writer for *Baseball Prospectus*. It wasn't the first time a team had reached outside for someone to work with numbers; but it was the first time someone with as public a profile had been hired.

Since then, the Jays have been lumped in with other so-called "stathead" teams, teams that have embraced the use of performance analysis in their personnel decisions. Among these, the Red Sox are the most successful, the Cardinals the most recent, and the A's the most adherent, with the Yankees and the Padres regarded as partial proponents. Being among their number is not a requirement for success—the Braves and Twins, for instance, have been very successful without showing any inclination towards performance analysis.

There's just one problem: the Jays aren't a stathead organization. Other than hiring Law and emphasizing collegians in their drafts, the Blue Jays haven't taken on the characteristics of a team leveraging 20 years of baseball research to help them win. In fact, this past winter, they seemed to run as fast and as far from that mindset as possible, making moves that can charitably be considered questionable, and which likely set the team back a year in their development.

BLUE JAYS PROSPECTUS

2004 record: 67–94; Fifth place, AL East

Pythagenport record: 70–92

Runs scored per game: 4.47 (11th in AL)

Runs allowed per game: 5.11 (8th in AL)

Team EqA: .245 (13th in AL)

2004 Batters Age: 28.4 (3rd youngest in AL)

2004 Pitchers Age: 29.0 (6th oldest in AL)

Ballpark: Skydome; Severe hitter's park; Park Factor of 1.044

2004: A disappointing horror show from the start, the Jays couldn't overcome injuries to core players down the stretch.

2005: Expect a bounce back, but Carlos Delgado's departure and untested youth throughout the roster make contention unlikely.

The Jays' big move this winter was signing Corey Koskie to a three-year, $17-million contract to play third base. In a crazy off-season, in which it was not the longest, richest, nor silliest contract handed out, it was, however, wrong in so many ways as to be generally indicative of how the Blue Jays have gotten off track:

- **Spending money on the middle class.** For a while, the industry had gotten away from overcompensating middling players who just happened to be on the market. This was an apparent application of the sabermetric principle that most free agents are bad investments, their best work in the past and highest salaries in the future. This winter, however, teams chased the middle class with a fervor that rivaled the post-collusion era of 1988–90.

  Koskie and his contract epitomize the problem. He's 32 and increasingly injury-prone, with less playing time in every season since 2001. At his best he ranged from five-to-seven wins above replacement level, but now even the lower end of that may not be reachable. Both his strikeout-to-walk ratio and his defense fell apart last year.

He's a bad investment, essentially being paid for the work he did from 2000–03 and not for what you can expect from him in the future.

This wasn't the Jays' only questionable investment. During the season, they re-signed Frank Catalanotto—31, fragile, and nothing special as an outfield bat—to a two-year contract. They gave a two-year deal to Scott Schoeneweis, a year after making a two-year investment in Kerry Ligtenberg. These are roster spots and money spent on players who don't add that much value.

- **Not recognizing where you are relative to the competition.** Of course, spending a bit for a marginal upgrade can make sense if you're very close to a strike point such as contention or a division title. Overcommitting to Corey Koskie could be justified if the Jays were one decent third baseman away from playing deep into October, and the chance that they wouldn't get average performance for less than $5.6 million was too much risk to take.

  They're not, however, realistically in contention. Adding Koskie's 4–5 WARP might push the Jays over .500, which in the American League of 2005 will get your highlights buried at the tail end of "Baseball Tonight," wedged between the Cialis commercial and "Web Gems." The buy-in for the AL East or AL Wild Card is 92 wins, and even bounceback seasons from Vernon Wells, Roy Halladay, and Duane Ward won't get them there.

- **Blocking cheaper, younger solutions of comparable quality**. Even if the Jays were on the verge of something, they have players in house who can help them get there. Set aside Eric Hinske, who may never again hit the way he did in '02. But Aaron Hill, the Jays' #1 pick in '04, is closing in on Toronto and needs a place to play. Signing Koskie means that one of Hill, Russ Adams, or Orlando Hudson has no lineup spot, and the trio might be the team's three best infielders by year's end.

  This isn't a case of a problem being created by circumstance, a prospect developing quicker than you expected or a great player in decline but retaining a large contract. This is a proactive move that creates a $17 million problem just so Koskie can be the third baseman. Add in John Hattig, and the possibility that Hinske could find himself, and the Jays might have five infielders better than Koskie by the start of '06.

- **Throwing away draft picks.** By signing Koskie, a Type-A free agent offered arbitration by the Twins, the Jays forfeit their second-round draft pick. It would have been their #1, but they were bad enough last season to avoid that fate.

  But wait, there's more. The Blue Jays declined to offer their own free agent, Carlos Delgado, arbitration. If they had, they would have been awarded a #1 pick and a supplemental pick as compensation for losing him. Offering arbitration to your top-tier free agents, the ones who are still very good players and who are desirable in the market, is one of those litmus tests for a front office. The worst-case scenario is having a star back on a one-year contract for a lot of money. It happens, but if a team's ownership is unwilling to assume that kind of risk, it's time to get out of the business.

The last of those mistakes is the most damning. Despite constant complaints about the size of signing bonuses, choosing well at the top of the draft is the least expensive route to a winning team. The Jays have implemented an approach to the draft that emphasizes collegians, players who generally carry less risk and get to the majors more quickly. Adams and Hill are just the two most visible examples.

Not offering arbitration to Delgado and signing Koskie yields a net loss of three draft picks in the top 50. That's devastating to a team whose drafting has been the strongest part of its game, not just with this regime, but going back well before the Gord Ash era.

The Koskie signing is just the most recent, high-profile example of the Jays operating in a haphazard way. In each of the past two years, they've made in-season managerial changes, and subsequently kept the interim manager on. That leads to selecting managers who haven't been thoroughly vetted, who get the job not because they're on board with the plan but because they're on board the airplane when the decision is made.

Making the mistake with Carlos Tosca was one thing, but to make it a second time, as they have with John Gibbons, is a sign that they're not learning. It's not about the merits of the men—Tosca may have worked out given time, and Gibbons gets praise from multiple circles. Rather, it's about the process—one that should involve interviews and discussions and a thoughtful attempt to bring in the most qualified candidate. The Jays have yet to hire a manager who wasn't a coach on staff at the time of the hiring, and that's an awfully small pool to be fishing in.

While the decisions Ricciardi has made of late haven't been good ones, he's well ahead of organizations that ignore, or are hostile to, performance analysis. It was Ricciardi who signed Hinske and Wells to long-term deals in 2003, and while only one of those has panned out, the thought process there is encouraging. He has one of the better player-personnel departments in the game, headed by Tony LaCava, a savvy scout who has also embraced performance analysis. The Jays' three drafts under Ricciardi have been productive, to the extent that you can judge a draft so soon.

Right now, though, the Jays can't be grouped with the A's and Red Sox, or even teams like the Cardinals, Padres, and Mets who use performance analysis in a less prominent fashion. Just hiring a stat guy isn't enough; you have to use that knowledge to make the team better. The Jays haven't been doing that of late.

For those of us on the outside, knowing a team employs someone with a certain knowledge base shouldn't serve as a pass. A team has to do more than just pay lip service to running their team in an informed fashion. If it doesn't, that team deserves the same amount of criticism we're so eager to heap on the usual punching bags.

HITTERS

RUSS ADAMS SS **Bats: L** **Throws: R** Born: 30-Aug-1980 Age: 24

YEAR	TM	LG	AGE	AB	H	2B	3B	HR	BB	SO	SB	CS	AVG	OBP	SLG	MLVR	EQBA	EQOBP	EQSLG	EQMLVR	VORP	DEFENSE
2002	AUB	NYP	21	113	40	7	3	0	24	11	13	1	.354	.464	.469	.412	.280	.360	.373	-.048	10.7	30-SS 0
2002	DUN	FSL	21	147	34	4	2	1	18	17	5	2	.231	.321	.306	-.112	.201	.277	.275	-.394	-8.9	35-SS 0
2003	DUN	FSL	22	258	72	9	5	3	38	27	9	2	.279	.380	.388	.135	.254	.335	.384	-.099	9.0	66-SS -8
2003	NHV	EAS	22	271	75	10	4	4	30	37	8	1	.277	.349	.387	.056	.257	.322	.375	-.134	5.6	62-SS -8
2004	SYR	INT	23	483	139	37	3	5	45	62	6	2	.288	.351	.408	.008	.262	.327	.373	-.124	11.4	118-SS -13
2004	TOR	AL	23	72	22	2	1	4	5	5	1	0	.306	.359	.528	.181	.310	.362	.521	.192	7.9	18-SS -4
2005	*TOR*	*AL*	*24*	*303*	*81*	*17*	*3*	*6*	*30*	*40*	*4*	*2*	*.268*	*.338*	*.396*	*-.054*	*.264*	*.337*	*.394*	*-.070*	*14.1*	*82-SS -9*

Breakout: 23% *Improve: 40%* *Collapse: 30%*

The first draft pick of the Ricciardi Era reached the majors in August and had a strong debut. Adams has very little star potential, and the signing of Corey Koskie puts him in a head-to-head battle with Aaron Hill for a future in Toronto. He's a tweener; marginal defensively at shortstop, and without a bat that forces you to play him at another position—not that the Jays have openings. His career may hinge on his first 200 at-bats this year.

DAVE BERG UT **Bats: R** **Throws: R** Born: 03-Sep-1970 Age: 34

YEAR	TM	LG	AGE	AB	H	2B	3B	HR	BB	SO	SB	CS	AVG	OBP	SLG	MLVR	EQBA	EQOBP	EQSLG	EQMLVR	VORP	DEFENSE
2002	TOR	AL	31	374	101	26	2	4	26	57	0	2	.270	.322	.382	-.068	.270	.325	.385	-.105	10.2	43-2B -2 17-3B 0
2003	TOR	AL	32	161	41	6	1	4	11	34	0	1	.255	.301	.379	-.142	.247	.302	.373	-.182	1.4	17-2B 1 13-3B -2
2004	TOR	AL	33	154	39	4	0	3	4	27	0	1	.253	.278	.338	-.272	.250	.269	.329	-.307	-5.7	20-LF 0
2005	*TOR*	*AL*	*34*	*121*	*30*	*6*	*0*	*2*	*7*	*22*	*0*	*0*	*.247*	*.295*	*.358*	*-.195*	*.243*	*.293*	*.357*	*-.212*	*-2.9*	*35-LF 1*

Breakout: 25% *Improve: 42%* *Collapse: 42%*

Berg's awful two-year contract ended at season's close. The team's stubborn refusal to release him last year, instead using him for a while in left field, was one of the blights on a lost season. Berg may have played his last major league game. He's a good example of what happens to utility infielders who can't play shortstop.

KEVIN CASH C **Bats: R** **Throws: R** Born: 06-Dec-1977 Age: 27

YEAR	TM	LG	AGE	AB	H	2B	3B	HR	BB	SO	SB	CS	AVG	OBP	SLG	MLVR	EQBA	EQOBP	EQSLG	EQMLVR	VORP	DEFENSE
2002	TEN	SOU	24	213	59	15	1	8	36	44	5	2	.277	.381	.469	.181	.238	.328	.425	-.068	7.1	38-C 2
2002	SYR	INT	24	236	52	18	0	10	25	72	0	1	.220	.299	.424	-.059	.195	.270	.381	-.268	-6.7	57-C 12
2003	SYR	INT	25	326	88	28	2	8	29	81	1	0	.270	.331	.442	.062	.252	.316	.428	-.075	10.0	84-C 17
2003	TOR	AL	25	106	15	3	0	1	4	22	0	0	.142	.179	.198	-.684	.133	.169	.171	-.787	-12.9	28-C 2
2004	TOR	AL	26	181	35	9	0	4	10	59	0	0	.193	.249	.309	-.398	.190	.240	.302	-.438	-8.4	51-C 9
2005	*TBY*	*AL*	*27*	*226*	*52*	*12*	*1*	*7*	*19*	*62*	*0*	*1*	*.228*	*.294*	*.380*	*-.181*	*.229*	*.296*	*.387*	*-.177*	*4.1*	*62-C 0*

Breakout: 47% *Improve: 62%* *Collapse: 25%*

He can't hit, not even in the Mark Parent/Tim Laudner way that might get people like us interested. Worse for him is there are complaints about how he receives the ball, death for a guy with a career 484 OPS. There's little question, however, that he can throw: He's gunned down 38% of basestealers in parts of three seasons. Dealt to the Devil Rays in December, Cash will have a chance to back up Toby Hall for a man with a history of liking defensive catchers.

FRANK CATALANOTTO OF **Bats: L** **Throws: R** Born: 27-Apr-1974 Age: 31

YEAR	TM	LG	AGE	AB	H	2B	3B	HR	BB	SO	SB	CS	AVG	OBP	SLG	MLVR	EQBA	EQOBP	EQSLG	EQMLVR	VORP	DEFENSE
2002	TEX	AL	28	212	57	16	6	3	25	27	9	5	.269	.364	.443	.039	.267	.365	.443	.047	10.5	19-LF -2 15-2B 1
2003	TOR	AL	29	489	146	34	6	13	35	62	2	2	.299	.351	.472	.100	.295	.351	.473	.089	25.5	49-LF 3 35-RF -2
2004	TOR	AL	30	249	73	19	1	1	17	33	1	0	.293	.344	.390	-.052	.291	.346	.385	-.050	6.0	36-LF 0
2005	*TOR*	*AL*	*31*	*278*	*77*	*16*	*3*	*5*	*23*	*37*	*2*	*1*	*.275*	*.338*	*.412*	*-.027*	*.271*	*.337*	*.410*	*-.044*	*7.7*	*75-LF -4*

Breakout: 12% *Improve: 30%* *Collapse: 40%*

Now that he doesn't play the infield, is he anything special? He's certainly not a good corner outfielder, he's fragile, and he hasn't been impressive at the plate since 2001. The Jays locked him up for two years and $5.4 million, in part because he's a good guy. It's not a good use of money in a market that's punishing corner players who don't rake.

ERIC CROZIER 1B **Bats: L** **Throws: L** Born: 11-Aug-1978 Age: 26

YEAR	TM	LG	AGE	AB	H	2B	3B	HR	BB	SO	SB	CS	AVG	OBP	SLG	MLVR	EQBA	EQOBP	EQSLG	EQMLVR	VORP	DEFENSE
2002	KIN	CRL	23	258	84	16	2	9	42	57	4	3	.326	.423	.508	.394	.288	.374	.470	.118	17.2	46-1B 3
2002	AKR	EAS	23	142	42	8	1	1	21	50	1	0	.296	.398	.387	.121	.264	.352	.347	-.111	-1.2	37-1B 2
2003	AKR	EAS	24	347	85	10	3	19	51	92	5	3	.245	.344	.455	.065	.211	.303	.402	-.166	-9.2	95-1B -1
2004	BUF	INT	25	296	88	21	0	20	36	67	5	1	.297	.375	.571	.319	.272	.346	.517	.120	18.1	58-1B 2 12-LF 1
2004	SYR	INT	25	94	26	8	0	1	16	27	3	2	.277	.393	.394	.055	.226	.332	.312	-.220	-4.1	24-1B 1
2004	TOR	AL	25	33	5	2	0	2	6	19	0	0	.152	.282	.394	-.260	.156	.273	.406	-.253	-0.8	
2005	*TOR*	*AL*	*26*	*236*	*63*	*13*	*1*	*11*	*30*	*65*	*3*	*1*	*.268*	*.355*	*.470*	*.072*	*.265*	*.353*	*.468*	*.055*	*14.7*	*67-1B -1*

Breakout: 33% *Improve: 67%* *Collapse: 15%*

Boosted from the Indians in exchange for not having to sweat Josh Phelps's arbitration eligibility (he made it by a day), Crozier could end up as Carlos Delgado's replacement at first base if Eric Hinske fails to hit again. He's a marginal power source who isn't likely to get his average above .260 or his OBP above .330 in the majors. He'd have more value on an NL team, pinch-hitting for pitchers with two outs and no one on base.

CARLOS DELGADO 1B **Bats: L** **Throws: R** Born: 25-Jun-1972 Age: 33

YEAR	TM	LG	AGE	AB	H	2B	3B	HR	BB	SO	SB	CS	AVG	OBP	SLG	MLVR	EQBA	EQOBP	EQSLG	EQMLVR	VORP	DEFENSE
2002	TOR	AL	30	505	140	34	2	33	102	126	1	0	.277	.406	.549	.301	.280	.411	.558	.291	62.6	140-1B 9
2003	TOR	AL	31	570	172	38	1	42	109	137	0	0	.302	.426	.593	.384	.299	.426	.597	.386	83.3	144-1B -4
2004	TOR	AL	32	458	123	26	0	32	69	115	0	1	.269	.372	.535	.168	.268	.370	.536	.182	41.4	117-1B 11
2005	*TOR*	*AL*	*33*	*453*	*126*	*26*	*1*	*29*	*78*	*114*	*0*	*0*	*.277*	*.392*	*.532*	*.217*	*.273*	*.390*	*.530*	*.201*	*40.2*	*129-1B 1*

Breakout: 13% *Improve: 56%* *Collapse: 19%*

He's still an excellent hitter. Delgado's 2004 line was killed by his attempts to play through a rib-cage injury. He spent June on the disabled list, then came back to hit .305/.408/.625 after the All-Star break. His overall numbers and the perception that he was overpaid the last few years in Toronto have diminished the market for him. Still, with the Mets and Marlins reportedly bidding—one report had the Fish offering three years, $35 million—The Slender One may not be a bargain.

TYRELL GODWIN OF **Bats: L** **Throws: R** Born: 10-Jul-1979 Age: 25

YEAR	TM	LG	AGE	AB	H	2B	3B	HR	BB	SO	SB	CS	AVG	OBP	SLG	MLVR	EQBA	EQOBP	EQSLG	EQMLVR	VORP	DEFENSE
2002	CWV	SAL	22	185	52	8	5	0	20	23	10	2	.281	.364	.378	.098	.234	.293	.319	-.284	-13.2	29-LF -3 18-CF -1
2003	DUN	FSL	23	322	88	16	0	1	29	39	20	7	.273	.348	.332	.019	.239	.294	.305	-.299	-15.6	94-CF -2
2003	NHV	EAS	23	123	38	6	3	1	3	27	6	1	.309	.328	.431	.113	.293	.305	.423	-.068	-0.1	27-RF -5
2004	NHP	EAS	24	521	132	21	7	6	52	110	42	12	.253	.326	.355	-.071	.237	.301	.330	-.251	-32.2	82-LF 1 29-RF 1
2005	*WAS*	*NL*	*25*	*226*	*56*	*12*	*2*	*3*	*17*	*44*	*8*	*3*	*.247*	*.308*	*.354*	*-.185*	*.249*	*.309*	*.362*	*-.173*	*-3.0*	*62-LF 0*

Breakout: 28% *Improve: 51%* *Collapse: 25%*

Fast fifth-outfielder prospect, twice a first-round pick, who has never been able to get on base enough for his speed to be a weapon. In some ways, he's the classic Rule 5 pick—all tools, no performance. Enter the Nationals, who grabbed him with the third pick in the major league phase. Godwin could make a run at Endy Chavez's job with a good spring; even if he doesn't, he's likely to stay in the Washington organization, as he doesn't fit in this one.

CHRIS GOMEZ INF Bats: R Throws: R Born: 16-Jun-1971 Age: 34

YEAR	TM	LG	AGE	AB	H	2B	3B	HR	BB	SO	SB	CS	AVG	OBP	SLG	MLVR	EQBA	EQOBP	EQSLG	EQMLVR	VORP	DEFENSE
2002	TBY	AL	31	461	122	31	3	10	21	58	1	3	.265	.305	.410	-.068	.270	.314	.423	-.071	15.8	123-SS 10
2003	MIN	AL	32	175	44	9	3	1	7	13	2	1	.251	.279	.354	-.207	.249	.280	.358	-.245	0.2	20-2B -2 17-3B 2
2004	TOR	AL	33	341	96	11	1	3	28	41	3	2	.282	.337	.346	-.134	.278	.338	.341	-.137	7.2	72-SS -7 13-1B 0
2005	*BAL*	*AL*	*34*	*226*	*57*	*11*	*1*	*3*	*15*	*27*	*2*	*1*	*.254*	*.303*	*.352*	*-.184*	*.256*	*.307*	*.359*	*-.177*	*4.2*	*61-SS -4*

Breakout: 17% *Improve: 32%* *Collapse: 42%*

Gomez was the starting shortstop for most of the season, until Adams reached the majors. He's a replacement-level player on both sides of the ball, but tends to have a good season every three years that keeps him around. Gomez will go to camp with the Orioles, who have precious little need for a backup shortstop right now.

JOHN-FORD GRIFFIN OF Bats: L Throws: L Born: 19-Nov-1979 Age: 25

YEAR	TM	LG	AGE	AB	H	2B	3B	HR	BB	SO	SB	CS	AVG	OBP	SLG	MLVR	EQBA	EQOBP	EQSLG	EQMLVR	VORP	DEFENSE
2002	TAM	FSL	22	255	68	16	1	3	29	45	1	0	.267	.344	.373	.079	.252	.315	.366	-.164	-9.3	45-LF -5
2002	NRW	EAS	22	67	22	3	0	5	8	13	0	1	.328	.400	.597	.465	.284	.329	.507	.089	4.7	
2003	NHV	EAS	23	373	104	23	3	13	49	85	2	0	.279	.361	.461	.180	.259	.334	.437	-.024	3.5	61-LF 0
2004	NHP	EAS	24	467	116	28	1	22	56	128	1	1	.248	.330	.454	.064	.221	.295	.402	-.174	-17.9	23-LF 0 15-1B -3
2005	*TOR*	*AL*	*25*	*243*	*61*	*13*	*1*	*10*	*25*	*62*	*1*	*1*	*.251*	*.323*	*.433*	*-.043*	*.247*	*.322*	*.432*	*-.060*	*5.3*	*67-DH 3*

Breakout: 26% *Improve: 59%* *Collapse: 25%*

If you'd told someone in April of '03 that Griffin wouldn't have reached Triple-A by the end of '04, they would have never believed it. Injuries and a poor contact rate have stopped him in his tracks in the Eastern League. He won't move up without big hitting numbers, because he doesn't bring speed or defense to the table. To his credit, he bounced back from a hand injury and a horrible start to have a good second half. He absolutely has to build on that this year.

GABE GROSS OF Bats: L Throws: R Born: 21-Oct-1979 Age: 25

YEAR	TM	LG	AGE	AB	H	2B	3B	HR	BB	SO	SB	CS	AVG	OBP	SLG	MLVR	EQBA	EQOBP	EQSLG	EQMLVR	VORP	DEFENSE
2002	TEN	SOU	22	403	96	17	5	10	53	71	8	2	.238	.333	.380	-.029	.208	.286	.350	-.270	-25.5	101-RF -3
2003	NHV	EAS	23	310	99	23	3	7	52	53	3	2	.319	.423	.481	.336	.300	.393	.463	.152	21.6	77-RF -7
2003	SYR	INT	23	182	48	16	2	5	31	56	1	1	.264	.380	.456	.152	.246	.361	.437	.015	4.9	42-RF 0
2004	SYR	INT	24	377	111	29	2	9	53	81	4	5	.294	.381	.454	.127	.270	.359	.415	.000	6.5	24-LF 0 10-RF 0
2004	TOR	AL	24	129	27	4	0	3	19	31	2	2	.209	.311	.310	-.275	.206	.305	.294	-.309	-5.9	38-LF 2
2005	*TOR*	*AL*	*25*	*278*	*75*	*16*	*1*	*10*	*35*	*60*	*3*	*2*	*.268*	*.354*	*.440*	*.031*	*.264*	*.353*	*.438*	*.015*	*13.4*	*78-LF -3*

Breakout: 27% *Improve: 52%* *Collapse: 27%*

An elbow injury killed Gross's numbers and forced him into a DH role for much of the year. As much slack as you want to give him for the injury, he hasn't hit more than 12 homers in a season as a pro, or slugged above .500 since 2001 in the Florida State League. With minimal defensive value and a strikeout rate high enough to limit his batting average, he has to start hitting the ball off of and over fences or lose his prospect status. The first half of 2005 is going to be critical to his future.

JOHN HATTIG 3B Bats: B Throws: R Born: 27-Feb-1980 Age: 25

YEAR	TM	LG	AGE	AB	H	2B	3B	HR	BB	SO	SB	CS	AVG	OBP	SLG	MLVR	EQBA	EQOBP	EQSLG	EQMLVR	VORP	DEFENSE
2002	AUG	SAL	22	347	98	20	0	7	52	73	1	2	.282	.377	.401	.150	.234	.307	.342	-.224	-5.3	82-3B 1
2003	SAR	FSL	23	400	118	29	2	6	59	70	9	7	.295	.385	.422	.208	.266	.343	.412	-.037	20.9	97-3B 2
2004	PME	EAS	24	264	78	21	1	12	47	68	3	3	.295	.411	.519	.255	.250	.356	.439	.011	16.4	69-3B 0
2004	NHP	EAS	24	142	42	7	0	10	12	41	0	1	.296	.352	.556	.282	.259	.298	.483	-.024	6.9	34-3B 3
2005	*TOR*	*AL*	*25*	*213*	*55*	*12*	*1*	*7*	*24*	*51*	*1*	*1*	*.258*	*.338*	*.420*	*-.030*	*.254*	*.336*	*.419*	*-.047*	*6.4*	*60-3B -2*

Breakout: 23% *Improve: 47%* *Collapse: 31%*

One reason middle-of-the-pack teams sign veterans is that there are two ways they can pay off—by contributing if you manage to contend, or by being traded to another contender. The Jays flipped Terry Adams for Hattig, who's been like Mini-Youkilis coming up through the Sox system. Slugging .532 in the Eastern League is nothing to sneeze at, either. He's a year away, and the Koskie signing creates the kind of logjam that probably puts his future in another organization.

AARON HILL SS Bats: R Throws: R Born: 21-Mar-1982 Age: 23

YEAR	TM	LG	AGE	AB	H	2B	3B	HR	BB	SO	SB	CS	AVG	OBP	SLG	MLVR	EQBA	EQOBP	EQSLG	EQMLVR	VORP	DEFENSE
2003	AUB	NYP	21	122	44	4	0	4	16	20	1	1	.361	.446	.492	.435	.295	.350	.426	.020	15.7	30-SS -1
2003	DUN	FSL	21	119	34	7	0	0	11	10	1	0	.286	.343	.345	.035	.215	.248	.248	-.485	-10.8	29-SS -6
2004	NHP	EAS	22	479	134	26	2	11	63	61	3	2	.280	.369	.411	.096	.258	.337	.378	-.101	15.8	134-SS -5
2005	*TOR*	*AL*	*23*	*267*	*71*	*14*	*1*	*5*	*26*	*39*	*1*	*1*	*.266*	*.340*	*.387*	*-.064*	*.262*	*.338*	*.385*	*-.080*	*12.9*	*74-SS -6*

Breakout: 18% *Improve: 35%* *Collapse: 35%*

Hill bounced back from a slow start to win the Futures Game MVP, recording a strong second half. Don't be discouraged by his lack of advancement; the Jays had Adams in Syracuse ahead of him, and wanted to keep both at shortstop in '04. Long term, Hill is likely to move off the position. At this rate, his power should develop enough for him to be a good third baseman. With Koskie in house, however, his future is uncertain beyond 2005.

ERIC HINSKE 3B/1B Bats: L Throws: R Born: 05-Aug-1977 Age: 27

YEAR	TM	LG	AGE	AB	H	2B	3B	HR	BB	SO	SB	CS	AVG	OBP	SLG	MLVR	EQBA	EQOBP	EQSLG	EQMLVR	VORP	DEFENSE
2002	TOR	AL	24	566	158	38	2	24	77	138	13	1	.279	.365	.481	.148	.279	.370	.483	.121	55.4	142-3B -9
2003	TOR	AL	25	449	109	45	3	12	59	104	12	2	.243	.329	.437	-.025	.238	.331	.431	-.054	24.1	120-3B -15
2004	TOR	AL	26	570	140	23	3	15	54	109	12	8	.246	.312	.375	-.159	.242	.312	.372	-.168	-2.2	148-3B 7
2005	*TOR*	*AL*	*27*	*450*	*117*	*26*	*2*	*17*	*52*	*94*	*9*	*4*	*.259*	*.338*	*.442*	*-.001*	*.256*	*.336*	*.440*	*-.017*	*13.9*	*120-3B -3*

Breakout: 38% *Improve: 69%* *Collapse: 12%*

Maybe this isn't going to work out. Hinske, the 2002 AL Rookie of the Year, has hit .245/.320/.402 in the two years since. The team still has three years left on its contract commitment to him, and an attempt to trade him in the off-season was fruitless. The loss of Delgado and acquisition of Koskie means that Hinske likely gets to try first base in '05. He's under the gun; he needs to hit this year, or he may find himself without a job.

ORLANDO HUDSON 2B Bats: B Throws: R Born: 12-Dec-1977 Age: 27

YEAR	TM	LG	AGE	AB	H	2B	3B	HR	BB	SO	SB	CS	AVG	OBP	SLG	MLVR	EQBA	EQOBP	EQSLG	EQMLVR	VORP	DEFENSE
2002	SYR	INT	24	417	127	27	3	10	35	54	8	5	.305	.363	.456	.149	.282	.343	.434	.007	22.3	97-2B 6
2002	TOR	AL	24	192	53	10	5	4	11	27	0	1	.276	.319	.443	.006	.274	.323	.447	-.017	10.2	52-2B 2
2003	TOR	AL	25	474	127	21	6	9	39	87	5	4	.268	.328	.395	-.066	.266	.331	.394	-.084	15.4	131-2B 25
2004	TOR	AL	26	489	132	32	7	12	51	98	7	3	.270	.341	.438	-.011	.265	.341	.434	-.011	27.4	133-2B 14
2005	*TOR*	*AL*	*27*	*428*	*116*	*23*	*3*	*11*	*41*	*78*	*6*	*3*	*.271*	*.337*	*.416*	*-.026*	*.267*	*.336*	*.415*	*-.043*	*17.6*	*113-2B 8*

Breakout: 13% *Improve: 32%* *Collapse: 19%*

Hudson's defensive numbers are off the charts for a second baseman. He's so good with the glove that he's limited the team's options for Adams and Hill, the Jays being committed to Hudson at second base. His development as a hitter hasn't been as impressive, but he did improve across the board in 2004, and is coming into his peak years. At a .280 EqA—within reach—Hudson would be one of the 30 most valuable players in the league.

REED JOHNSON OF Bats: R Throws: R Born: 08-Dec-1976 Age: 28

YEAR	TM	LG	AGE	AB	H	2B	3B	HR	BB	SO	SB	CS	AVG	OBP	SLG	MLVR	EQBA	EQOBP	EQSLG	EQMLVR	VORP	DEFENSE	
2002	SYR	INT	25	159	37	8	3	2	12	23	1	4	.233	.317	.358	-.105	.219	.300	.344	-.244	-4.5	32-CF 0	11-LF 1
2003	SYR	INT	26	101	33	4	1	2	3	13	3	1	.327	.369	.446	.174	.307	.355	.436	.054	6.0	17-CF 0	
2003	TOR	AL	26	412	121	21	2	10	20	67	5	3	.294	.353	.427	.043	.294	.354	.429	.030	14.8	58-RF -4	40-LF 2
2004	TOR	AL	27	537	145	25	2	10	28	98	6	3	.270	.320	.380	-.127	.267	.317	.378	-.132	2.4	52-LF 2	43-RF 0
2005	*TOR*	*AL*	*28*	*425*	*113*	*22*	*2*	*9*	*22*	*74*	*4*	*3*	*.266*	*.320*	*.390*	*-.095*	*.262*	*.318*	*.389*	*-.112*	*-0.2*	*110-LF 2*	

Breakout: 11% *Improve: 29%* *Collapse: 43%*

The classic case of a fourth outfielder who plays too much on a bad team. A Catalanotto/Johnson platoon in left field might be a bit above league average—more so if this is one of Cat's .330 years—because Johnson is adequate against lefties. When Johnson and Alexis Rios flank Vernon Wells, the Jays sport a great defensive outfield.

FRANK MENECHINO INF **Bats: R** **Throws: R** Born: 07-Jan-1971 Age: 34

YEAR	TM	LG	AGE	AB	H	2B	3B	HR	BB	SO	SB	CS	AVG	OBP	SLG	MLVR	EQBA	EQOBP	EQSLG	EQMLVR	VORP	DEFENSE
2002	SAC	PCL	31	314	78	12	0	6	46	58	10	3	.248	.356	.344	-.067	.229	.324	.312	-.234	-2.9	68-SS -7
2002	OAK	AL	31	132	27	7	0	3	20	32	0	0	.205	.312	.326	-.213	.214	.314	.321	-.250	0.1	27-2B -2
2003	OAK	AL	32	83	16	0	0	2	19	16	0	0	.193	.364	.265	-.178	.207	.351	.280	-.232	0.7	13-2B 1
2004	OAK	AL	33	33	3	0	0	0	1	8	0	0	.091	.143	.091	-.919	.061	.076	.061	-1.149	-5.6	
2004	TOR	AL	33	236	71	13	4	9	36	44	0	2	.301	.400	.504	.211	.296	.401	.504	.218	25.9	24-2B 1 12-SS -2
2005	*TOR*	*AL*	*34*	*176*	*44*	*8*	*1*	*4*	*26*	*37*	*1*	*1*	*.249*	*.355*	*.372*	*-.067*	*.246*	*.354*	*.370*	*-.083*	*8.6*	*52-2B -7*

Breakout: 30% *Improve: 48%* *Collapse: 37%*

The A's preferred Mark McLemore, so they traded Menechino to the Jays in May. He had the best half-season of his life in Toronto, filling in at second base while Hudson's hamstring healed and playing some at third base and shortstop thereafter. He won't have another .300 EqA, but will provide enough OBP, especially against lefties, to be worth the roster spot. Infinitely better than Dave Berg.

GUILLERMO QUIROZ C **Bats: R** **Throws: R** Born: 29-Nov-1981 Age: 23

YEAR	TM	LG	AGE	AB	H	2B	3B	HR	BB	SO	SB	CS	AVG	OBP	SLG	MLVR	EQBA	EQOBP	EQSLG	EQMLVR	VORP	DEFENSE
2002	DUN	FSL	20	411	107	28	1	12	35	91	1	0	.260	.330	.421	.059	.221	.275	.374	-.251	-9.7	90-C 2
2003	NHV	EAS	21	369	104	27	0	20	45	83	0	0	.282	.372	.518	.276	.251	.326	.475	.007	20.5	96-C 7
2004	SYR	INT	22	255	58	19	1	8	28	54	0	0	.227	.309	.404	-.116	.206	.285	.368	-.249	-5.9	70-C -4
2004	TOR	AL	22	52	11	2	0	0	2	8	1	0	.212	.263	.250	-.447	.216	.234	.255	-.503	-2.8	13-C -1
2005	*TOR*	*AL*	*23*	*291*	*74*	*16*	*1*	*12*	*26*	*68*	*0*	*1*	*.254*	*.326*	*.441*	*-.026*	*.250*	*.325*	*.439*	*-.043*	*13.9*	*79-C -5*

Breakout: 41% *Improve: 64%* *Collapse: 19%*

Injuries marred Quiroz's progress for a second straight season. A pitched ball broke a bone in his left hand, costing him a couple of months and dampening his output when he returned. He's still regarded as a good defensive catcher, even though his caught-stealing numbers dipped. As a hitter, he'll rely on his extra-base power, putting runs on the board without reaching a .280 average. Likely to be underrated throughout his career, which will begin for real in July.

ALEXIS RIOS OF **Bats: R** **Throws: R** Born: 18-Feb-1981 Age: 24

YEAR	TM	LG	AGE	AB	H	2B	3B	HR	BB	SO	SB	CS	AVG	OBP	SLG	MLVR	EQBA	EQOBP	EQSLG	EQMLVR	VORP	DEFENSE
2002	DUN	FSL	21	456	139	22	8	3	27	55	14	8	.305	.344	.408	.094	.269	.301	.374	-.167	-13.9	88-RF -5 22-CF -1
2003	NHV	EAS	22	514	181	32	11	11	39	85	11	3	.352	.402	.521	.402	.332	.377	.510	.225	56.3	120-CF -6
2004	SYR	INT	23	185	48	10	1	3	9	30	2	1	.259	.292	.373	-.166	.236	.275	.341	-.287	-7.5	30-CF -1 16-RF -1
2004	TOR	AL	23	426	122	24	7	1	31	84	15	3	.286	.338	.383	-.074	.281	.337	.379	-.083	11.2	106-RF 2
2005	*TOR*	*AL*	*24*	*456*	*124*	*27*	*4*	*9*	*27*	*79*	*10*	*4*	*.271*	*.316*	*.405*	*-.078*	*.267*	*.314*	*.404*	*-.095*	*5.1*	*116-RF 1*

Breakout: 5% *Improve: 22%* *Collapse: 45%*

Rios, a 1998 pick out of Puerto Rico who did very little in his first four pro seasons, emerged as a prospect during a monster 2003 campaign at Double-A. He's a legitimate center fielder with an excellent arm, uses his speed well, and has shown some improvement in his command of the strike zone. However, he was rushed last year; having had a .292 OBP at Syracuse when he was promoted, and hit just four homers all year season. He isn't going to hit enough to play right field regularly, at least not in '05. He's on the cusp; he could become Devon White, or he could stagnate and end up as Juan Encarnacion.

RAUL TABLADO SS **Bats: R** **Throws: R** Born: 03-Mar-1982 Age: 23

YEAR	TM	LG	AGE	AB	H	2B	3B	HR	BB	SO	SB	CS	AVG	OBP	SLG	MLVR	EQBA	EQOBP	EQSLG	EQMLVR	VORP	DEFENSE
2002	CWV	SAL	20	361	80	23	0	2	21	98	2	1	.222	.268	.302	-.180	.181	.212	.255	-.564	-41.3	66-3B -5 19-SS -3
2003	CWV	SAL	21	226	43	10	1	6	25	69	2	1	.190	.272	.323	-.144	.164	.227	.284	-.501	-22.8	61-SS 3
2003	DUN	FSL	21	182	47	9	3	5	17	47	1	2	.258	.328	.423	.097	.227	.285	.395	-.198	0.3	25-SS -4 13-2B 2
2004	DUN	FSL	22	323	98	28	0	21	24	91	0	0	.303	.354	.585	.342	.249	.288	.492	-.038	16.7	31-SS -2 21-3B -3
2005	*TOR*	*AL*	*23*	*350*	*80*	*18*	*1*	*12*	*22*	*104*	*1*	*1*	*.230*	*.280*	*.391*	*-.189*	*.227*	*.279*	*.389*	*-.206*	*-4.9*	*91-SS -12*

Breakout: 30% *Improve: 45%* *Collapse: 26%*

A leftover from the Gillick Administration, Tablado gets into the book because it's really, really hard to slug .585 in the Florida State League. He's never shown this kind of power before, he missed a month with a pulled quad, and he won't be a shortstop much longer, but that kind of power from an infielder is worth mentioning. The Jays liked him enough to protect him from the Rule 5 draft, so they think so, too.

VERNON WELLS CF Bats: R Throws: R Born: 08-Dec-1978 Age: 26

YEAR	TM	LG	AGE	AB	H	2B	3B	HR	BB	SO	SB	CS	AVG	OBP	SLG	MLVR	EQBA	EQOBP	EQSLG	EQMLVR	VORP	DEFENSE
2002	TOR	AL	23	608	167	34	4	23	27	85	9	4	.275	.305	.457	.012	.276	.311	.460	-.018	27.7	138-CF 2 12-RF 1
2003	TOR	AL	24	678	215	49	5	33	42	80	4	1	.317	.359	.550	.245	.313	.360	.552	.237	71.0	159-CF 2
2004	TOR	AL	25	536	146	34	2	23	51	83	9	2	.272	.337	.472	.033	.267	.338	.469	.034	30.8	129-CF 5
2005	*TOR*	*AL*	*26*	*538*	*156*	*33*	*2*	*24*	*45*	*76*	*7*	*3*	*.290*	*.346*	*.492*	*.106*	*.286*	*.345*	*.490*	*.088*	*33.4*	*139-CF 0*

Breakout: 12% *Improve: 40%* *Collapse: 24%*

Lost in a generally disappointing season was that Wells continued to work on his plate discipline, with career highs in walks, walk rate and pitches seen per PA. The rest of his decline was part a fluctuation in his batting average, part a loss in power caused by hitting the ball on the ground more. Look for him to get back to his '03 swing and surpass even that year's stellar performance. His next three seasons are going to be huge.

CHRIS WOODWARD SS Bats: R Throws: R Born: 27-Jun-1976 Age: 29

YEAR	TM	LG	AGE	AB	H	2B	3B	HR	BB	SO	SB	CS	AVG	OBP	SLG	MLVR	EQBA	EQOBP	EQSLG	EQMLVR	VORP	DEFENSE
2002	TOR	AL	26	312	86	13	4	13	26	72	3	0	.276	.330	.468	.063	.278	.335	.472	.043	23.6	79-SS -1
2003	TOR	AL	27	349	91	22	2	7	28	72	1	2	.261	.316	.395	-.094	.256	.316	.392	-.123	11.4	100-SS -1
2004	TOR	AL	28	213	50	13	4	1	14	46	1	2	.235	.283	.347	-.269	.230	.284	.340	-.275	-2.6	59-SS -4
2005	*TOR*	*AL*	*29*	*236*	*59*	*12*	*2*	*5*	*19*	*50*	*2*	*1*	*.250*	*.310*	*.386*	*-.129*	*.247*	*.308*	*.385*	*-.146*	*5.8*	*64-SS -3*

Breakout: 17% *Improve: 40%* *Collapse: 35%*

Kind of the infield version of Reed Johnson, Woodward is a player who's not good enough to be a regular but who picked up a job because the team didn't have anyone else. Now the Jays do, along with a better utilityman in Menechino, so Woodward is dangerously close to handling his own luggage again. He has enough pop and glove to be a useful fifth infielder somewhere else.

GREGG ZAUN C Bats: B Throws: R Born: 14-Apr-1971 Age: 34

YEAR	TM	LG	AGE	AB	H	2B	3B	HR	BB	SO	SB	CS	AVG	OBP	SLG	MLVR	EQBA	EQOBP	EQSLG	EQMLVR	VORP	DEFENSE
2002	HOU	NL	31	185	41	7	1	3	12	36	1	0	.222	.275	.319	-.254	.220	.273	.323	-.326	-2.4	41-C -9
2003	HOU	NL	32	120	26	7	0	1	14	14	1	0	.217	.299	.300	-.249	.217	.287	.283	-.355	-1.8	23-C -3
2003	COL	NL	32	46	12	1	0	3	5	7	0	1	.261	.333	.478	.062	.267	.309	.422	-.084	2.3	13-C -2
2004	SYR	INT	33	23	7	1	0	0	2	5	1	0	.304	.346	.348	-.071	.174	.167	.174	-.776	-4.5	
2004	TOR	AL	33	338	91	24	0	6	47	61	0	2	.269	.367	.393	-.018	.267	.365	.388	-.028	16.9	90-C -4
2005	*TOR*	*AL*	*34*	*211*	*53*	*10*	*0*	*5*	*24*	*40*	*1*	*1*	*.250*	*.335*	*.371*	*-.104*	*.247*	*.333*	*.370*	*-.120*	*5.4*	*60-C -5*

Breakout: 27% *Improve: 51%* *Collapse: 26%*

It was a nice year for the Practically Perfect Backup Catcher, as he shook off an early-year release to post the most valuable season of his career. He did wear down under the heaviest workload he'd carried in a while, ending the season in a 9-for-49 tailspin. Nevertheless, he's back in Toronto in '05; his skills make him a good backup for Quiroz.

PITCHERS

JASON ARNOLD Bats: R Throws: R Born: 02-May-1979 Age: 26

YEAR	TM	LG	AGE	G	GS	IP	H	BB	SO	HR	ERA	EQERA	EQH9	EQBB9	EQSO9	EQHR9	PERA	VORP	STF
2002	TAM	FSL	23	13	13	80.0	64	22	83	2	2.48	4.32	8.0	2.8	6.8	0.5	3.24	19.7	27
2002	MID	TXS	23	10	10	58.0	42	24	53	2	2.33	4.19	7.4	4.2	6.4	0.7	3.52	12.4	18
2003	NHV	EAS	24	6	6	35.3	18	11	33	2	1.53	2.84	6.3	3.1	7.4	0.9	2.84	9.7	33
2003	SYR	INT	24	21	20	120.7	121	46	82	16	4.32	5.45	9.5	4.0	5.1	1.8	5.45	1.9	-2
2004	SYR	INT	25	7	7	37.0	40	12	15	6	3.65	4.37	10.0	3.1	3.1	1.5	5.14	1.8	-11
2004	NHP	EAS	25	4	4	20.0	17	5	14	4	3.15	4.00	10.0	2.5	5.0	2.5	6.50	-1.8	-4
2005	*TOR*	*AL*	*26*	*14*	*8*	*53.0*	*56*	*20*	*35*	*9*	*5.24*	*4.94*	*9.5*	*3.0*	*5.3*	*1.5*	*4.85*	*5.9*	*-3*

Breakout: 19% *Improve: 45%* *Collapse: 21%*

The only bold type on Arnold's résumé is that two years ago he was part of a four-team, four-player deal at the winter meetings that brought him to Toronto.His 2004 was interrupted by a torn labrum for which he eschewed surgery, rehabbing for most of the year. He was just passable at lower levels late in the year and in the AFL. He's just another guy in this organization now, and at 26, is unlikely ever to be an impact player.

JOSH BANKS Bats: R Throws: R Born: 18-Jul-1982 Age: 22

YEAR	TM	LG	AGE	G	GS	IP	H	BB	SO	HR	ERA	EQERA	EQH9	EQBB9	EQSO9	EQHR9	PERA	VORP	STF
2003	AUB	NYP	20	15	15	66.7	58	10	81	1	2.43	4.99	9.4	1.8	6.5	0.4	4.26	9.1	22
2004	DUN	FSL	21	11	11	60.0	49	8	60	4	1.80	3.90	8.6	1.5	6.3	1.3	3.90	10.4	23
2004	NHP	EAS	21	18	17	91.3	89	28	76	15	5.03	5.76	10.2	3.0	5.8	1.9	6.30	-6.6	-2
2005	*TOR*	*AL*	*22*	*11*	*10*	*60.0*	*68*	*19*	*43*	*10*	*5.16*	*4.86*	*10.1*	*2.5*	*5.8*	*1.4*	*4.79*	*7.0*	*6*

Breakout: 8% *Improve: 40%* *Collapse: 22%*

The Jays' #2 pick in '03 out of Florida International—almost all of the pitching prospects in this chapter were collegians—owned the Florida State League with his five-pitch assortment. Blister problems that hampered him in college didn't resurface last year. Like a lot of the Jays' recent draftees, Banks's success at lower levels is to be expected. It's Double-A, which treated him badly last year, that provides the real test.

MIGUEL BATISTA Bats: R Throws: R Born: 19-Feb-1971 Age: 34

YEAR	TM	LG	AGE	G	GS	IP	H	BB	SO	HR	ERA	EQERA	EQH9	EQBB9	EQSO9	EQHR9	PERA	VORP	STF
2002	ARI	NL	31	36	29	184.7	172	70	112	12	4.29	4.62	8.6	3.0	4.9	0.6	3.81	13.8	8
2003	ARI	NL	32	36	29	193.3	197	60	142	13	3.54	3.62	8.8	2.5	6.0	0.6	3.76	37.3	17
2004	TOR	AL	33	38	31	198.7	206	96	104	22	4.80	4.41	9.1	3.9	4.5	0.8	4.82	22.6	-3
2005	*TOR*	*AL*	*34*	*28*	*22*	*129.0*	*149*	*56*	*74*	*15*	*5.21*	*4.91*	*10.3*	*3.4*	*4.7*	*1.0*	*4.93*	*11.9*	*-4*

Breakout: 8% *Improve: 40%* *Collapse: 21%*

On the list of "Silly Things the Jays Are Doing," messing around with Batista as a closer is high on the list. He doesn't have the skill set of a short reliever, and he's a groundball machine in the rotation. Last year went poorly, as he lost his command early on and never quite found it. His role in 2005 will tell us a lot about what kind of organization this is. If he's on the team, but not in the rotation, they're lost.

DAVID BUSH Bats: R Throws: R Born: 09-Nov-1979 Age: 25

YEAR	TM	LG	AGE	G	GS	IP	H	BB	SO	HR	ERA	EQERA	EQH9	EQBB9	EQSO9	EQHR9	PERA	VORP	STF
2002	AUB	NYP	22	18	0	22.3	13	7	39	1	2.83	6.05	8.4	4.2	9.8	1.4	4.66	2.0	11
2002	DUN	FSL	22	7	0	13.3	10	2	9	1	2.03	3.00	9.0	1.5	4.5	1.5	4.50	1.5	-6
2003	DUN	FSL	23	14	14	77.0	64	9	75	6	2.81	4.93	9.7	1.3	6.5	2.2	5.45	1.2	8
2003	NHV	EAS	23	14	14	81.0	73	19	73	4	2.78	3.87	8.3	2.3	6.7	0.8	3.52	17.7	24
2004	SYR	INT	24	16	16	99.7	108	20	88	7	4.06	4.53	9.1	1.8	6.4	0.6	3.79	19.6	13
2004	TOR	AL	24	16	16	97.7	95	25	64	11	3.68	3.61	8.7	2.1	5.7	0.9	3.99	20.6	6
2005	*TOR*	*AL*	*25*	*23*	*22*	*133.0*	*140*	*37*	*96*	*19*	*4.64*	*4.37*	*9.4*	*2.2*	*5.9*	*1.2*	*4.26*	*22.1*	*11*

Breakout: 16% *Improve: 36%* *Collapse: 22%*

We hear a lot about converted starters who become good relievers. Bush was actually a closer at Wake Forest and became a starter in 2003, his second pro season. He has little upside, but with a healthy arm, reasonable command and four good pitches, he's ready to be a mid-rotation innings muncher for a few years, Jim Clancy to Halladay's Dave Stieb. Not pitching until college, and being a reliever until he was 23, bodes well for his health.

GUSTAVO CHACIN Bats: L Throws: L Born: 04-Dec-1980 Age: 24

YEAR	TM	LG	AGE	G	GS	IP	H	BB	SO	HR	ERA	EQERA	EQH9	EQBB9	EQSO9	EQHR9	PERA	VORP	STF
2002	TEN	SOU	21	35	13	119.7	131	59	68	12	4.66	6.07	10.5	4.3	3.8	1.6	6.23	-7.9	-19
2003	NHV	EAS	22	46	2	69.3	78	29	55	1	4.16	5.96	9.1	4.0	5.7	0.3	4.24	10.3	-9
2004	NHP	EAS	23	25	25	141.7	113	49	109	15	2.92	4.05	8.9	3.4	5.4	1.3	5.09	7.3	-6
2004	SYR	INT	23	2	2	11.7	16	3	14	0	2.31	3.00	9.8	2.2	8.2	0.0	3.75	2.5	25
2004	TOR	AL	23	2	2	14.0	8	3	6	0	2.57	2.13	7.1	2.1	4.3	0.0	2.13	5.7	7
2005	*TOR*	*AL*	*24*	*15*	*15*	*83.0*	*92*	*35*	*53*	*12*	*5.28*	*4.97*	*9.9*	*3.4*	*5.2*	*1.2*	*4.93*	*8.7*	*1*

Breakout: 13% *Improve: 40%* *Collapse: 25%*

Chacin reached Double-A in 2000, making two starts in the Southern League as a 19-year-old. That was the first of his five seasons at that level; over the next three years he drifted from prospect to suspect to organization pitcher, lacking a third pitch that would help him advance. He added that pitch—a cut fastball—last year, and proceeded to rip off a 34-inning shutout streak, go 16–2 and finally (finally!) got out of the Eastern League.

(continued next page)

Gustavo Chacin *(continued)*

It's hard to know what to make of Chacin. His performance record, even in his big year, wasn't impressive, and instead of being a fastball/change-up guy, he's now a fastball/cut fastball guy. He doesn't miss enough bats to project as a top starter, and his use of the cutter means he's not suited to be a lefty specialist. He seems suited for a role, swingman, that doesn't really exist these days. A Chacin/Chad Gaudin fifth starter tandem could be fairly effective.

CHI-HUNG CHENG **Bats: L** **Throws: L** Born: 20-Jun-1980 Age: 25

YEAR	TM	LG	AGE	G	GS	IP	H	BB	SO	HR	ERA	EQERA	EQH9	EQBB9	EQSO9	EQHR9	PERA	VORP	STF
2004	PUL	APL	24	14	14	60.7	47	35	74	4	2.82	5.47	8.8	6.8	6.0	1.3	5.96	-2.2	-6
2005	*TOR*	*AL*	*25*	*12*	*7*	*42.7*	*40*	*31*	*31*	*7*	*5.63*	*5.30*	*8.3*	*5.6*	*5.9*	*1.4*	*5.25*	*3.1*	*-10*

Breakout: 16% *Improve: 47%* *Collapse: 15%*

The Jays' first dalliance in Asia, Cheng impressed in his stateside debut with two good pitches, including a fastball that touches 90. That doesn't sound great, but he turned 19 during the season. Signed out of Taiwan for $400,000, last year wasn't Cheng's first success in America: he was on his nation's Little League World Series champion team in 1996. He's a long way from both home and the majors, but remember the name.

VINNY CHULK **Bats: R** **Throws: R** Born: 19-Dec-1978 Age: 26

YEAR	TM	LG	AGE	G	GS	IP	H	BB	SO	HR	ERA	EQERA	EQH9	EQBB9	EQSO9	EQHR9	PERA	VORP	STF
2002	TEN	SOU	23	25	24	152.0	133	53	108	12	2.96	4.10	9.1	3.1	4.9	1.3	4.87	11.4	-1
2003	SYR	INT	24	23	21	119.3	118	46	90	14	4.22	5.56	9.3	4.0	5.6	1.5	5.16	5.5	0
2004	SYR	INT	25	18	0	28.7	27	11	26	5	2.82	4.00	9.0	3.7	6.7	1.7	5.00	1.8	2
2004	TOR	AL	25	47	0	56.0	59	27	44	6	4.66	4.04	8.9	3.9	6.6	0.8	4.69	9.1	4
2005	*TOR*	*AL*	*26*	*24*	*5*	*52.0*	*55*	*23*	*38*	*8*	*5.09*	*4.80*	*9.5*	*3.5*	*6.0*	*1.3*	*4.84*	*6.6*	*-5*

Breakout: 25% *Improve: 47%* *Collapse: 21%*

Chulk has been bounced back and forth between the rotation and the pen three times in five professional seasons. He was one of the only Jays relievers to not get a crack at the closer's job last year, instead serving a the main set-up guy in June and July. He had problems with left-handed batters (905 OPS) that he needs to address, unusual for a guy whose best pitch is a sinker. Fantasy players: Here's your sleeper in this bullpen.

JASON FRASOR **Bats: R** **Throws: R** Born: 09-Aug-1977 Age: 27

YEAR	TM	LG	AGE	G	GS	IP	H	BB	SO	HR	ERA	EQERA	EQH9	EQBB9	EQSO9	EQHR9	PERA	VORP	STF
2002	LAK	FSL	24	24	24	117.0	112	46	87	10	3.54	5.13	10.3	4.0	5.0	1.8	6.31	-8.4	-15
2003	VRO	FSL	25	15	0	24.3	16	4	36	0	1.85	3.97	7.1	1.6	9.5	0.4	2.38	8.1	29
2003	JAX	SOU	25	35	0	36.7	33	14	50	2	2.94	4.67	8.8	3.6	8.8	1.0	4.41	4.6	6
2004	TOR	AL	26	63	0	68.3	64	36	54	4	4.08	3.48	8.2	4.3	6.7	0.4	4.01	16.7	3
2005	*TOR*	*AL*	*27*	*33*	*4*	*57.0*	*57*	*27*	*46*	*7*	*4.52*	*4.26*	*8.9*	*3.7*	*6.6*	*1.0*	*4.45*	*11.1*	*-1*

Breakout: 27% *Improve: 54%* *Collapse: 21%*

The best minor trade of the year brought Frasor to Toronto in exchange for Jayson Werth; Werth panned out with the Dodgers, but the Jays were likely to lose him on waivers. Frasor, a small righty with a strong arm, got a turn in the closer role thanks to pitching in good fortune for the first six weeks of his career. Like Chulk, he doesn't throw enough strikes to hold a major role, and that caught up with him down the stretch. The Jays have a lot of relief depth, so Frasor will likely either pitch well for them in 2005 or quickly be sent to Syracuse. They have the luxury of being tough evaluators.

ROY HALLADAY **Bats: R** **Throws: R** Born: 14-May-1977 Age: 28

YEAR	TM	LG	AGE	G	GS	IP	H	BB	SO	HR	ERA	EQERA	EQH9	EQBB9	EQSO9	EQHR9	PERA	VORP	STF
2002	TOR	AL	25	34	34	239.3	223	62	168	10	2.93	3.22	8.2	2.2	6.1	0.3	3.22	66.1	25
2003	TOR	AL	26	36	36	266.0	253	32	204	26	3.25	3.41	8.2	1.0	6.8	0.8	3.06	68.8	28
2004	TOR	AL	27	21	21	133.0	140	39	95	13	4.20	3.78	8.9	2.4	6.1	0.8	4.19	26.1	16
2005	*TOR*	*AL*	*28*	*25*	*25*	*162.3*	*168*	*44*	*122*	*13*	*3.94*	*3.71*	*9.2*	*2.1*	*6.1*	*0.7*	*3.62*	*36.7*	*17*

Breakout: 18% *Improve: 51%* *Collapse: 14%*

Maybe it wasn't a surprise that Halladay broke down after leading the AL in innings pitched in '02 and '03. On the other hand, it's hard to argue that he was abused in those seasons: His tremendous command kept his pitch counts down, and he doesn't show up anywhere near the top of the Pitcher Abuse Points lists in either year. He exceeded 120 pitches twice in 70 starts those two seasons, which is a very low total. The injury he suffered, a strained muscle in his right shoulder, isn't an overuse injury. It did cost him three months, and while a few starts at the end of the season were inconclusive, his outlook for 2005 is positive. With the exodus of so many top starters from the AL, he's a strong Cy Young contender—even though PECOTA's hedging its bet.

PAT HENTGEN **Bats: R** **Throws: R** Born: 13-Nov-1968 Age: 36

YEAR	TM	LG	AGE	G	GS	IP	H	BB	SO	HR	ERA	EQERA	EQH9	EQBB9	EQSO9	EQHR9	PERA	VORP	STF
2002	BAL	AL	33	4	4	22.0	31	10	11	6	7.77	7.48	12.0	3.7	4.2	2.1	7.89	-5.4	-16
2003	BAL	AL	34	28	22	160.7	150	58	100	25	4.09	3.92	8.6	3.2	5.6	1.3	4.38	34.6	4
2004	TOR	AL	35	18	16	80.3	90	42	33	16	6.95	6.32	10.0	4.3	3.6	1.5	5.86	-11.4	-20
2005	*TOR*	*AL*	*36*	*21*	*15*	*91.7*	*107*	*40*	*47*	*17*	*5.74*	*5.40*	*10.4*	*3.5*	*4.2*	*1.6*	*5.62*	*4.8*	*-12*

Breakout: 25% *Improve: 35%* *Collapse: 17%*

You worry about Halladay because of Hentgen's career path. He was never the same after throwing 530 innings in 1996 and 1997, winning the AL Cy Young Award in the first of those seasons. Hentgen never had Halladay's command, however, and worked a lot harder in those years than Doc did in 2002–03. After showing up with nothing and getting battered for three months, Hentgen retired in July. He walks away with a Cy Young, two World Series rings and a small place in the game's history.

JASON KERSHNER **Bats: L** **Throws: L** Born: 19-Dec-1976 Age: 28

YEAR	TM	LG	AGE	G	GS	IP	H	BB	SO	HR	ERA	EQERA	EQH9	EQBB9	EQSO9	EQHR9	PERA	VORP	STF
2002	POR	PCL	25	31	12	86.0	65	26	83	8	3.03	3.66	8.2	3.0	7.2	1.1	4.35	10.9	7
2002	SDP	NL	25	15	0	18.7	15	10	11	2	5.78	7.13	8.2	4.1	5.1	1.0	3.57	-2.9	-12
2003	SYR	INT	26	24	0	45.7	42	9	30	1	2.36	3.53	8.3	2.1	4.8	0.2	2.91	12.9	6
2003	TOR	AL	26	40	0	54.0	43	15	32	5	3.17	3.18	7.6	2.5	5.5	0.7	3.00	15.6	4
2004	TOR	AL	27	24	2	22.3	30	8	15	3	6.05	5.56	10.3	2.8	5.6	1.2	5.16	-0.5	-11
2004	SYR	INT	27	28	0	36.3	45	10	31	6	5.21	5.30	10.3	2.5	6.1	1.8	5.55	0.2	-11
2005	*BOS*	*AL*	*28*	*25*	*1*	*34.3*	*38*	*13*	*22*	*4*	*4.92*	*4.63*	*9.6*	*3.0*	*5.3*	*1.1*	*4.60*	*5.2*	*-9*

Breakout: 19% *Improve: 46%* *Collapse: 27%*

Carlos Tosca shares some responsibility here. After being the Jays' second-best reliever in 2003, Kershner got off to a poor start in '04, but had been pitching well for a month when he was asked to make a spot start on June 1. He did so, poorly, and then made another bad start on June 6. By June 23, he was in the minors, never to return. As much as the Jays needed a lefty reliever throughout the year, the casual handling of someone who'd been so good for them a year before was disheartening. Kershner signed a minor league deal with the Red Sox, a team with an opening for a good second lefty.

BRANDON LEAGUE **Bats: R** **Throws: R** Born: 16-Mar-1983 Age: 22

YEAR	TM	LG	AGE	G	GS	IP	H	BB	SO	HR	ERA	EQERA	EQH9	EQBB9	EQSO9	EQHR9	PERA	VORP	STF
2002	AUB	NYP	19	16	16	85.7	80	23	72	2	3.15	6.61	9.8	3.4	4.4	0.7	5.21	3.4	0
2003	CWV	SAL	20	12	12	70.7	58	18	61	1	1.91	3.88	8.4	2.8	4.8	0.3	3.60	14.4	19
2003	DUN	FSL	20	13	12	66.3	76	20	34	3	4.75	6.82	10.9	3.0	3.2	1.2	6.10	-3.4	-13
2004	NHP	EAS	21	41	10	104.0	92	41	90	3	3.38	4.44	8.8	3.8	5.9	0.4	4.44	12.5	5
2005	*TOR*	*AL*	*22*	*15*	*7*	*47.3*	*54*	*20*	*30*	*5*	*4.95*	*4.66*	*10.2*	*3.4*	*5.2*	*0.9*	*4.91*	*6.1*	*-5*

Breakout: 6% *Improve: 40%* *Collapse: 24%*

League's high-90s heat and MLB-ready slider have scouts drooling; *Baseball America* named him the Jays' #1 prospect. The Jays believed enough to push him to the majors at the end of last year, and are counting on him to be a contributor to this year's bullpen. As good as his stuff is, though, his strikeout rate and command haven't been overwhelming. His success has come as much from his location—his "heavy" fastball gets a lot of ground balls and has kept his home-run rate below sea level—as his power. With very little experience above Double-A, and some reason to worry about his control, League doesn't project as an impact pitcher this year if he opens the season in Toronto.

KERRY LIGTENBERG Bats: R Throws: R Born: 11-May-1971 Age: 34

YEAR	TM	LG	AGE	G	GS	IP	H	BB	SO	HR	ERA	EQERA	EQH9	EQBB9	EQSO9	EQHR9	PERA	VORP	STF
2002	ATL	NL	31	52	0	66.7	52	33	51	6	2.97	3.30	8.2	4.0	6.3	0.9	4.45	16.8	-3
2003	BAL	AL	32	68	0	59.3	60	14	47	9	3.34	3.26	8.7	2.0	7.0	1.2	4.03	17.2	3
2004	TOR	AL	33	57	0	55.0	73	25	49	6	6.38	5.56	10.0	3.5	7.3	0.8	5.24	-1.6	0
2005	*TOR*	*AL*	*34*	*48*	*0*	*49.7*	*55*	*20*	*38*	*8*	*4.98*	*4.69*	*9.9*	*3.2*	*6.2*	*1.3*	*5.00*	*7.6*	*-7*

Breakout: 21% *Improve: 46%* *Collapse: 25%*

With so many right-handed relievers within shouting distance of Toronto, signing Ligtenberg to a two-year deal was an unnecessary commitment, one that exploded in a hail of hits. In fairness to all parties, Ligtenberg's ERA was pushed up by an extraordinary .376 average allowed on balls in play. His non-ball-in-play numbers were largely in line with his career norms. The Jays still have a backlog of arms, so Ligtenberg may be posting an ERA in the mid-threes for your favorite team this year.

TED LILLY Bats: L Throws: L Born: 04-Jan-1976 Age: 29

YEAR	TM	LG	AGE	G	GS	IP	H	BB	SO	HR	ERA	EQERA	EQH9	EQBB9	EQSO9	EQHR9	PERA	VORP	STF
2002	NYY	AL	26	16	11	76.7	57	24	59	10	3.40	3.61	7.5	2.7	6.8	1.1	3.24	19.9	15
2002	OAK	AL	26	6	5	23.3	23	7	18	5	4.64	4.43	9.3	2.4	6.9	1.6	4.84	3.5	6
2003	OAK	AL	27	32	31	178.3	179	58	147	24	4.34	4.27	9.0	2.8	7.3	1.1	4.64	28.5	16
2004	TOR	AL	28	32	32	197.3	171	89	168	26	4.06	3.52	7.9	3.7	7.4	1.0	4.09	44.6	17
2005	*TOR*	*AL*	*29*	*27*	*23*	*138.7*	*140*	*59*	*109*	*21*	*4.82*	*4.54*	*9.0*	*3.4*	*6.4*	*1.3*	*4.57*	*20.3*	*8*

Breakout: 10% *Improve: 41%* *Collapse: 26%*

While he's had back-to-back years that are eerily similar, Lilly might have a bit more improvement in him as he gets older and becomes better at placing his breaking stuff. The mental picture doesn't work, but there are enough skill and statistical similarities to Sid Fernandez, who pitched in much better run environments, that you can get a little excited about Lilly's upside. Fernandez's body broke down right about when he was at his command peak; his last full season was at 29. Lilly is 29 this year, and with just a little improvement in his command, could lop a run off his ERA.

AQUILINO LOPEZ Bats: R Throws: R Born: 21-Apr-1975 Age: 30

YEAR	TM	LG	AGE	G	GS	IP	H	BB	SO	HR	ERA	EQERA	EQH9	EQBB9	EQSO9	EQHR9	PERA	VORP	STF
2002	TAC	PCL	27	34	11	109.3	89	27	103	6	2.39	3.22	7.8	2.4	6.8	0.7	3.14	28.2	29
2003	TOR	AL	28	72	0	73.7	58	34	64	5	3.42	3.41	7.1	4.0	7.7	0.5	3.15	18.9	24
2004	TOR	AL	29	18	0	21.0	21	13	13	5	6.00	5.31	9.3	5.3	5.3	1.8	5.75	-0.3	-23
2004	SYR	INT	29	32	0	42.7	58	10	32	8	7.17	7.02	11.1	2.1	5.3	1.9	5.95	-1.6	-18
2005	*LAD*	*NL*	*30*	*35*	*0*	*41.3*	*40*	*17*	*31*	*6*	*4.41*	*4.86*	*9.1*	*3.3*	*6.1*	*1.2*	*5.04*	*4.5*	*-7*

Breakout: 24% *Improve: 42%* *Collapse: 31%*

Just like Kershner, Lopez was a key part of the Jays' pen in '03, ineffective in April '04, and off the team for good before the All-Star break. Also like Kershner, Lopez pitched better after a hideous April, but never regained Tosca's confidence. Tosca's inability to run a bullpen was a problem for the Jays all year, and contributed to not only game losses, but the effective loss of Kershner and Lopez as contributors. We shouldn't have been surprised to see John Gibbons take the reins.

SHAUN MARCUM Bats: R Throws: R Born: 14-Dec-1981 Age: 23

YEAR	TM	LG	AGE	G	GS	IP	H	BB	SO	HR	ERA	EQERA	EQH9	EQBB9	EQSO9	EQHR9	PERA	VORP	STF
2003	AUB	NYP	21	21	0	34.0	15	7	47	1	1.32	3.68	7.1	2.5	7.7	0.9	3.38	7.2	20
2004	CWV	SAL	22	13	13	79.0	64	16	83	7	3.19	4.60	9.0	2.1	6.0	1.4	4.60	8.0	17
2004	DUN	FSL	22	12	12	69.3	74	4	72	6	3.12	5.07	10.1	0.5	6.3	1.6	4.80	5.8	21
2005	*TOR*	*AL*	*23*	*14*	*13*	*80.3*	*86*	*20*	*60*	*14*	*4.64*	*4.37*	*9.5*	*1.9*	*6.1*	*1.4*	*4.28*	*14.0*	*11*

Breakout: 9% *Improve: 42%* *Collapse: 19%*

Like Bush, Marcum was a closer in college, making the move to the rotation only this year. As you might expect from a college draftee taken for his polish, Marcum has slapped around the lower levels, and has nearly an 8-to-1 K:BB ratio as a pro. The test comes this year at New Hampshire; the Jays love him, but we'll see if Marcum's combination of decent stuff and great command fools hitters at Double-A and beyond.

DUSTIN McGOWAN Bats: R Throws: R Born: 24-Mar-1982 Age: 23

YEAR	TM	LG	AGE	G	GS	IP	H	BB	SO	HR	ERA	EQERA	EQH9	EQBB9	EQSO9	EQHR9	PERA	VORP	STF
2002	CWV	SAL	20	28	28	148.3	143	59	163	10	4.19	6.33	10.1	4.5	6.1	1.5	5.93	-5.0	-8
2003	DUN	FSL	21	14	14	75.7	62	25	66	1	2.85	4.89	8.4	3.5	5.7	0.4	3.99	12.5	16
2003	NHV	EAS	21	14	14	76.7	78	19	72	1	3.17	4.22	8.4	2.4	6.8	0.2	3.25	19.5	25
2004	NHP	EAS	22	6	6	31.0	24	15	29	4	4.06	4.76	8.9	4.8	6.7	1.6	5.72	-0.4	4
2005	*TOR*	*AL*	*23*	*20*	*15*	*92.7*	*95*	*42*	*74*	*13*	*4.95*	*4.66*	*9.2*	*3.6*	*6.5*	*1.1*	*4.59*	*12.6*	*6*

Breakout: 17% *Improve: 46%* *Collapse: 18%*

Even in an organization that is aware of the dangers of overworking young pitchers and manages them cautiously, high school draftees get hurt. McGowan, arguably the Jays' #1 prospect coming into 2004, suffered a torn right UCL in May and underwent Tommy John surgery. It's guys like McGowan who give life to the idea that there's no such thing as a pitching prospect. He's expected to be healthy this year; he'll make Toronto in September and be part of the 2006 rotation.

JUSTIN MILLER Bats: R Throws: R Born: 27-Aug-1977 Age: 27

YEAR	TM	LG	AGE	G	GS	IP	H	BB	SO	HR	ERA	EQERA	EQH9	EQBB9	EQSO9	EQHR9	PERA	VORP	STF
2002	SYR	INT	24	8	8	44.7	34	16	29	0	1.61	2.83	7.6	3.7	5.2	0.2	3.27	10.7	14
2002	TOR	AL	24	25	18	102.3	103	66	68	12	5.54	5.49	8.9	5.4	5.8	1.0	5.13	-2.0	-1
2004	TOR	AL	26	19	15	81.7	101	42	47	14	6.06	5.40	10.1	4.1	4.8	1.3	5.84	-1.4	-13
2005	*TOR*	*AL*	*27*	*19*	*13*	*80.3*	*91*	*39*	*54*	*11*	*5.40*	*5.09*	*10.1*	*3.8*	*5.5*	*1.2*	*5.26*	*7.5*	*-3*

Breakout: 18% *Improve: 37%* *Collapse: 29%*

He's gotten tattooed for years. His body, that is. Miller's beefy corpus is covered in ink, so much so that he has to wear long-sleeved undershirts when he pitches. Alas, that's the extent of his fame. Command problems have plagued him, and a hamstring pull complicated his return from shoulder surgery last summer. At his best, he's a back-end innings guy.

MICHEAL NAKAMURA Bats: R Throws: R Born: 06-Sep-1976 Age: 28

YEAR	TM	LG	AGE	G	GS	IP	H	BB	SO	HR	ERA	EQERA	EQH9	EQBB9	EQSO9	EQHR9	PERA	VORP	STF
2002	EDM	PCL	25	46	4	87.3	85	22	80	7	4.74	5.44	8.4	2.3	6.4	0.9	3.42	20.4	6
2003	ROC	INT	26	43	0	78.3	71	28	95	4	2.99	3.58	7.9	3.6	8.8	0.7	3.58	16.9	15
2004	SYR	INT	27	31	1	55.0	42	17	76	3	3.11	3.42	7.0	2.9	10.3	0.5	2.73	16.8	32
2004	TOR	AL	27	19	0	25.7	27	7	24	7	7.35	6.75	9.2	2.1	7.8	2.1	4.97	-5.1	6
2005	*TOR*	*AL*	*28*	*29*	*2*	*45.0*	*43*	*16*	*42*	*6*	*4.37*	*4.11*	*8.5*	*2.8*	*7.7*	*1.1*	*3.99*	*9.2*	*8*

Breakout: 25% *Improve: 44%* *Collapse: 25%*

The Australian Steve Reed. Well, he could be, if he ever gets an extended chance. Nakamura eats up righties with a nasty sidearm delivery and very good command. In brief major league stints, that's translated to a horrific home-run rate, as his strikes get pounded. He was caught in the Toronto bullpen's revolving door last year and signed with the Nippon Ham Fighters in Japan.

ADAM PETERSON Bats: R Throws: R Born: 18-May-1979 Age: 26

YEAR	TM	LG	AGE	G	GS	IP	H	BB	SO	HR	ERA	EQERA	EQH9	EQBB9	EQSO9	EQHR9	PERA	VORP	STF
2002	AUB	NYP	23	18	0	31.3	29	9	19	2	2.30	5.27	10.9	3.6	3.3	2.3	6.91	-4.0	-32
2003	CWV	SAL	24	10	0	24.7	15	13	19	1	2.19	4.57	7.9	5.8	4.6	1.2	4.57	2.5	-13
2003	DUN	FSL	24	9	0	12.7	5	0	13	1	0.71	2.53	6.8	0.8	7.6	2.5	3.38	2.6	16
2003	NHV	EAS	24	24	0	24.0	24	7	24	1	4.88	5.79	8.5	2.7	7.3	0.8	3.86	4.5	3
2004	NHP	EAS	25	27	0	28.3	20	10	38	1	2.54	3.42	7.5	3.4	9.2	0.3	3.42	6.4	18
2004	SYR	INT	25	19	0	21.0	38	16	19	6	12.86	11.63	13.3	6.6	6.2	2.5	9.14	-8.5	-36
2005	*ARI*	*NL*	*26*	*7*	*1*	*13.0*	*13*	*6*	*11*	*2*	*5.06*	*5.05*	*9.0*	*3.8*	*7.2*	*1.2*	*4.96*	*0.8*	*0*

Breakout: 21% *Improve: 43%* *Collapse: 18%*

The hard thrower packs a slider, change-up and career ERA of 13.70 above Double-A. Peterson pitched well in the Arizona Fall League, though, a rare feat in that hitter's haven. Traded for Shea Hillenbrand, he'll need to master Tucson before having any chance to make an impact on the Diamondbacks' bullpen, even given its sorry state.

DAVID PURCEY

Bats: L **Throws: L** Born: 22-Apr-1982 Age: 23

YEAR	TM	LG	AGE	G	GS	IP	H	BB	SO	HR	ERA	EQERA	EQH9	EQBB9	EQSO9	EQHR9	PERA	VORP	STF
2004	AUB	NYP	22	3	2	12.0	6	1	13	0	1.50	3.38	6.8	0.8	5.9	0.0	1.69	4.6	22

As they've done in all three seasons under Ricciardi, the Jays took a college player with their #1 pick. That's a reflection of the player-acquisition personnel more so than any Ricciardi directive: The draft is largely run by staff. Purcey is a big guy—6′5″, 240—out of the University of Oklahoma. He gets his fastball up as high as 95 mph, and brings it with what are described as good mechanics. We won't know anything until he gets to Double-A.

ISMAEL RAMIREZ

Bats: R **Throws: R** Born: 03-Mar-1981 Age: 24

YEAR	TM	LG	AGE	G	GS	IP	H	BB	SO	HR	ERA	EQERA	EQH9	EQBB9	EQSO9	EQHR9	PERA	VORP	STF
2002	MED	PIO	21	11	10	54.3	51	14	51	4	2.98	5.62	10.0	3.1	4.3	2.0	5.80	-1.1	-4
2003	CWV	SAL	22	24	22	119.3	110	31	70	6	3.02	5.63	9.7	2.8	3.3	1.2	4.97	7.6	-1
2004	DUN	FSL	23	28	27	165.3	151	25	131	5	2.72	4.34	8.7	1.6	4.9	0.6	3.47	36.8	22
2005	*TOR*	*AL*	*24*	*15*	*13*	*78.7*	*92*	*24*	*45*	*13*	*5.26*	*4.95*	*10.4*	*2.4*	*4.7*	*1.3*	*4.93*	*7.6*	*-2*

Breakout: 6% *Improve: 32%* *Collapse: 17%*

A holdover from the prior administration—he signed as a teenager back in 1998—Ramirez was named the most valuable pitcher in the Florida State League. That's performance; his skills haven't generated as much excitement, as he pitches in the low 90s and doesn't have great secondary stuff. He's a command guy who had not just age, but experience on most of the FSL, so '05 could be a letdown.

FRANCISCO ROSARIO

Bats: R **Throws: R** Born: 28-Sep-1980 Age: 24

YEAR	TM	LG	AGE	G	GS	IP	H	BB	SO	HR	ERA	EQERA	EQH9	EQBB9	EQSO9	EQHR9	PERA	VORP	STF
2002	CWV	SAL	21	13	13	66.7	50	14	78	5	2.56	4.85	9.1	2.4	6.7	1.7	4.70	5.9	11
2002	DUN	FSL	21	13	12	63.0	33	25	65	3	1.29	2.54	6.8	4.1	7.0	1.0	3.49	13.3	32
2004	DUN	FSL	23	6	6	17.3	16	11	16	2	4.68	7.47	9.8	6.9	5.7	2.3	6.89	-2.3	-21
2004	NHP	EAS	23	12	12	48.0	48	16	45	6	4.31	5.20	10.0	3.2	6.4	1.6	6.00	-2.0	0
2005	*TOR*	*AL*	*24*	*27*	*10*	*79.0*	*81*	*37*	*61*	*14*	*5.42*	*5.10*	*9.1*	*3.7*	*6.3*	*1.5*	*4.95*	*7.4*	*-3*

Breakout: 14% *Improve: 45%* *Collapse: 21%*

Rosario came back from Tommy John surgery and resumed his place among the Jays' top prospects, throwing in the mid-90s with a good change-up. Consistent with the path back from TJ, his command improved considerably as the year progressed, although he had a rough AFL stint. As much as scouts love him, his lack of experience above A-ball means he should be a year away.

JUSTIN SPEIER

Bats: R **Throws: R** Born: 06-Nov-1973 Age: 31

YEAR	TM	LG	AGE	G	GS	IP	H	BB	SO	HR	ERA	EQERA	EQH9	EQBB9	EQSO9	EQHR9	PERA	VORP	STF
2002	COL	NL	28	63	0	62.3	51	19	47	9	4.33	3.97	8.1	2.4	6.3	1.2	3.81	6.2	-2
2003	COL	NL	29	72	0	73.3	73	23	66	11	4.05	4.00	8.5	2.5	7.4	1.2	4.12	8.8	2
2004	TOR	AL	30	62	0	69.0	61	25	52	8	3.91	3.51	8.1	3.0	6.5	0.9	3.92	16.2	1
2005	*TOR*	*AL*	*31*	*41*	*0*	*54.0*	*56*	*18*	*41*	*9*	*4.79*	*4.51*	*9.2*	*2.6*	*6.2*	*1.4*	*4.59*	*9.1*	*-4*

Breakout: 24% *Improve: 50%* *Collapse: 27%*

By Wins Above Replacement Player, the Jays got the short end of last winter's three-pitcher/three-team deal. Speier's 3.6 WARP trailed both Joe Kennedy (5.6) and Mark Hendrickson (4.1), although he was the better pitcher on a per-inning basis. A bum elbow cut a chunk out of his year. Even when healthy, Speier is a bit too homer-prone to be a high-leverage reliever. (Fantasy alert!) Despite that, he's a good bet to lead the Jays in saves.

JOSH TOWERS Bats: R Throws: R Born: 26-Feb-1977 Age: 28

YEAR	TM	LG	AGE	G	GS	IP	H	BB	SO	HR	ERA	EQERA	EQH9	EQBB9	EQSO9	EQHR9	PERA	VORP	STF
2002	BAL	AL	25	5	3	27.3	42	5	13	11	7.91	7.33	13.0	1.7	4.0	3.3	8.33	-5.8	-19
2002	ROC	INT	25	15	13	69.0	109	14	43	16	7.57	8.52	12.7	2.0	4.6	2.8	7.34	-13.3	-24
2003	SYR	INT	26	21	20	132.7	133	20	76	10	3.32	4.16	9.1	1.6	4.2	1.0	3.88	23.9	16
2003	TOR	AL	26	14	8	64.3	67	7	42	15	4.48	4.21	9.3	1.0	5.8	1.9	4.35	9.5	18
2004	SYR	INT	27	6	5	36.0	33	7	25	5	2.50	2.94	8.8	1.9	5.3	1.6	4.28	4.9	14
2004	TOR	AL	27	21	21	116.3	148	26	51	16	5.11	4.53	10.4	1.8	3.7	1.0	5.07	10.5	1
2005	*TOR*	*AL*	*28*	*22*	*17*	*103.7*	*128*	*26*	*54*	*18*	*5.38*	*5.07*	*11.0*	*2.0*	*4.3*	*1.4*	*5.17*	*10.4*	*-5*

Breakout: 18% *Improve: 41%* *Collapse: 29%*

Towers threw fewer strikes and more ground balls last year than ever before, without seeing much change in his results. He doesn't have the stuff to get by without a microscopic walk rate. Given the Jays' outfield defense, he'd be better off going back to working in the zone and letting Vernon Wells and Alexis Rios keep his ERA down. His hold on a job is tenuous.

JAMIE VERMILYEA Bats: R Throws: R Born: 10-Feb-1982 Age: 23

YEAR	TM	LG	AGE	G	GS	IP	H	BB	SO	HR	ERA	EQERA	EQH9	EQBB9	EQSO9	EQHR9	PERA	VORP	STF
2003	AUB	NYP	21	9	2	30.3	22	5	53	0	2.38	5.20	8.8	2.0	9.4	0.3	3.90	5.2	28
2003	DUN	FSL	21	9	0	21.7	21	2	25	1	2.49	3.98	9.7	0.9	7.5	1.3	4.43	2.6	13
2004	DUN	FSL	22	18	6	55.3	54	13	37	4	3.09	4.73	9.6	2.5	4.2	1.4	4.91	3.9	-14
2004	NHP	EAS	22	21	6	58.3	43	12	39	2	2.47	3.71	8.1	2.0	4.7	0.5	3.71	11.2	9
2005	*TOR*	*AL*	*23*	*15*	*7*	*48.3*	*54*	*15*	*32*	*6*	*4.62*	*4.35*	*9.9*	*2.5*	*5.4*	*1.0*	*4.40*	*8.0*	*-1*

Breakout: 10% *Improve: 47%* *Collapse: 27%*

Another of the Jays' college draftees, Vermilyea is a sinker/slider guy who gained some fame for tossing a seven-inning perfect game for New Hampshire last summer. Like League, he's an extreme groundball pitcher, one of the most extreme in pro ball. A starter in college, he's projected as a reliever in the majors.

Station to Station: The Expensive Art of Baserunning

by James Click

Stolen bases have been tracked since baseball's early days and caught stealing statistics since around 1950, but baserunning has been excluded. Occasionally, various players will be described as good baserunners or bad baserunners, but baserunning data has not been widely available to support or dispute such arguments. With complete play-by-play data stretching back to 1972, it is now possible to objectively assess which players truly are good baserunners and which ones are not.

Baserunning is exactly like stealing bases. The runner is faced with a choice at each base: do I continue on to the next base or do I stay safe where I am? The risks and rewards are the same as stolen bases: the batter is weighing the likelihood and costs of an extra out against the likelihood and benefits of an extra base.

Like stolen bases, baserunning decisions can be evaluated both by attempt rate (extra bases attempted divided by opportunities) and success rate (extra bases successfully taken divided by extra bases attempted). Both of these measures must be considered; players who only take the basic base may appear to be superior baserunners based on success rate, but their plodding on the basepaths is likely costing their team runs by not taken an extra base when it's available. Likewise, players who always attempt the extra base but are caught often are also costing their team runs by adding outs, removing baserunners (themselves), and shortening innings.

For the purposes of this article, three basic baserunning situations will be examined as shown in table 1.

TABLE 1. BASERUNNING SITUATIONS TO BE CONSIDERED

	Runner's Starting Base	Hit Type	Basic Base	Extra Base
Situation 1	First	Single	Second	Third
Situation 2	First	Double	Third	Home
Situation 3	Second	Single	Third	Home

While there may be cases where the baserunning action does not fit neatly into this table, those instances are rare and will be considered in the nearest accurate section. For example, if a runner in Situation 3 remains at second base rather than advancing to take the basic base (third), he will be considered to have only taken the basic base. Likewise, a runner who scores from first on a single (Situation 1) will be considered to have taken the extra base. These adjustments are not entirely accurate, but are acceptable for this study because they are rare—thus unlikely to affect overall conclusions—and because they are registered in the data as representative of the baserunner's performance.

Situations will only be considered where there is no baserunner on the base immediately in front of the baserunner being examined. Another baserunner on the bases in front of the baserunner to be examined could either prevent the second baserunner from taking the extra base or making it easier for him to do so by drawing the attention of the defense. Because these situations do not remove a significant percentage of the available data and their complexity makes them significantly more difficult to analyze, they will not be considered here.

Fundamental Adjustments

Looking at raw baserunning numbers, however, doesn't truly reveal who the best baserunners in the game are or how much they affect their team's run scoring ability. There are four primary adjustments that will be considered as possible adjustments for the raw baserunning totals for inequalities in each baserunners' opportunities.

Outfield Defenders – Outfielders have a variety of arm strengths and accuracies. Much like catchers who throw out a high number of basestealers, outfielders with good reputations can cause baserunners to reconsider attempting to reach an additional base by increasing perceived risk. Likewise, certain outfielders cause more baserunners to attempt to reach the extra base when they are fielding because of a perception that they will not be able to throw the runner out. Both the baserunners' perception of the risk or opportunity posed by a particular outfielder as well as the actual risk or opportunity posed by the fielder must be accounted for.

Park – In "How Parks Affect Baserunning: Looking for the Home-Field Advantage" (http://baseballprospectus.com/article.php?articleid=3347), I examined the effects of the ballpark on baserunning numbers. While this article was originally intended to seek out possible reasons behind the inherent home field advantage in baseball, it did establish that different ballparks do have a consistent effect on baserunning numbers, both in attempt rate and success rate. Parks with more expansive outfields, Coors Field in particular, seemed to lend themselves towards increased baserunning attempts and success, a fact likely due to the extra distance the outfield must cover both in fielding the ball and in returning it to the infield.

Outs – Baserunners adhere to certain general rules while on the basepaths, most notably "Don't make the first or third out of an inning at third base." Additionally, runners run "on contact" when there are two outs since they need not confirm that the ball is a hit before deciding to attempt to reach the next base, since the risk of getting picked off at their original base is zero.

Batter – Do certain batters tend to advance runners the extra base more often than other batters? It would stand to reason that batters who put the ball in play with more power would give baserunners the opportunity to advance the extra base more often, whereas players who tend to beat out infield singles or bunt singles would advance the baserunner less often. Because the analysis will be based on what type of hit the batter registered, the batters' speed also has an effect on the baserunning. For instance, if two players hit the same exact ball, yet the fast batter reached second while the slower batter only reached first, the slower batter would appear to have advanced the baserunner the extra base while the fast batter would not. Thus, baserunners who bat in front of slower players should not be unduly credited and those in front of fast batters not unduly slighted.

Outfield Defense

As mentioned above, outfield defenders have an influence on baserunning decisions, based both on their actual performance and the baserunners' perceptions of their performance. Before preparing to make adjustments to the baserunning numbers for the quality of the outfield defense, we must confirm that outfielders do have a consistent effect on baserunning from year to year.

Considering the frequent movement of players and the constant shuffling of outfielders, doing this on a team level would likely yield little useful information. Instead, we can look at the individual fielder who fields the ball. Exactly like analysis for runners or batters, both attempt and success rates will be computed for each individual outfielder.

Unfortunately, application of this information to baserunning statistics is difficult and fails to yield significant improvement to the metric for one simple reason: it is uncommon for an outfielder to field the ball more than once in a season when a certain runner is in a position to take an extra base. Much like players stealing bases are not adjusted for the catcher behind the plate, adjusting the baserunning numbers based on the particular outfielder fielding the ball is a level of granularity far lower than is necessary to analyze.

While certain runners may face a collective group of outfielders who are better than average, the fielders they face are, on the whole, random. Thus, while an individual fielder may influence a particular decision, these instances tend to even out over the season. Much like batters are not credited for facing superior or poor pitching, the benefit of adjusting running stats based on outfielders faced is minimal and thus will not be considered when measuring baserunner performance.

Park Factors

As mentioned, analysis of park affects on baserunning was already performed in my article on the baseballprospectus.com web site, but I'll provide a brief recap here. First, I confirmed that baserunning attempt and success rates were fairly consistent from year to year when broken down by park. Therefore, it is reasonably certain that ballparks do have a consistent effect on baserunning. Second, each current major league park was observed and the effect it has on baserunning was calculated, specifically (looking at) the differences between home and visiting team performances. Because there was no evidence found confirming a consistent home team advantage with regards to baserunning, we can safely calculate one park factor for each park without having to adjust for whether a baserunner is at home or on the road.

There are a couple different ways to compute park factors. The first is to look at visiting team statistics in each park, a method that removes the quality of the home team from the equation. Another is to compare a certain team's performance at home versus its performance on the road. Initially it appeared that the first method would be inappropriate here since the quality of the outfield defense is a factor in baserunning decisions and performances. While the sample of baserunners from visiting teams would be reasonably average, they are always running against the same outfield defense. However, because individual outfielders do not face individual runners more than once or twice a season, it's acceptable to have one factor for both park and outfield, meaning this method will work well. Combining this park factor with home team's home/road performance yields a reasonable estimate for the difficulty of running in each park.

As mentioned in my baseballprospectus.com article, baserunning park factors tend to vary quite a bit from year to year, so to stabilize them, three-year samples of data will be taken. The consistency between three-year blocks of data is much more consistent than single-year park factors, more accurately reflecting the true park factor. While five-year factors are more consistent than three-year factors, quite a few changes can occur in five years (new ballparks, changes to the outfield wall configurations, and changing outfielders playing the same outfield) making three-year factors more attractive because they capture more of that variance.

The Number of Outs

The attempt and success rates of all batters in a particular season broken down by the number of outs are very consistent from year to year. There is a steady increase in extra base attempts as outs increase during each inning. Each out situation changes the risks and rewards of attempting the extra base. With no one out, an out on the basepaths can quickly stall what would have been a big inning. With two outs, the team has very few chances remaining to get the baserunners home, so attempting the extra base can be much more appealing to the baserunner.

In fact, the league average attempt rate broken down by the numbers of outs is remarkably consistent from year to year when considering attempt rate. (See table 2.) Therefore, a baserunner may appear to be more aggressive than the rest of the league simply because a higher percentage of his baserunning opportunities came with a higher number of outs in each inning. Thus, each baserunners' total will be adjusted to remove the effect of the number of outs in each inning.

TABLE 2. BASERUNNING BY OUTS, 1995–2004

Year	Overall Attempt Rate			Overall Success Rate		
	0 Outs	1 Out	2 Outs	0 Outs	1 Out	2 Outs
1995	34.8%	42.0%	55.3%	94.8%	92.6%	92.6%
1996	33.8%	40.9%	54.6%	94.5%	94.4%	93.3%
1997	32.9%	40.3%	53.3%	94.3%	94.0%	93.7%
1998	33.6%	40.7%	53.2%	95.3%	94.0%	93.3%
1999	33.9%	39.9%	55.0%	93.3%	93.8%	93.7%
2000	32.7%	40.0%	53.6%	96.3%	93.5%	94.1%
2001	31.1%	39.0%	53.7%	94.3%	93.6%	93.4%
2002	32.3%	37.9%	53.2%	94.4%	94.5%	92.2%
2003	32.1%	38.1%	51.9%	95.2%	93.4%	93.4%
2004	31.0%	36.7%	52.2%	95.3%	93.5%	93.4%

Notice, however, that success rate does not show distinct differences between the three out situations. While players tend to have somewhat more success with no one out, the effect is neither consistent nor significant and will therefore not be considered.

The Batter at the Plate

Because batters and baserunners tend to occupy regular spots in a lineup, batters come to the plate with the same players on base frequently and, likewise, baserunners are often advanced by the same small set of batters. Therefore, adjustments can be made when evaluating batters for the quality of the baserunners on base and for baserunners by the quality of the batter hitting because these situations arise often.

Before adjusting for the batter, however, we must confirm that batters show a consistent ability to advance runners from year to year. If the year-to-year difference in batter baserunning rates appears random, we must concede that the batter does not have a consistent, demonstrated affect on baserunning and, therefore, no adjustments for the batter can be made.

The first way to confirm that there is a consistent ability is to compare each batter's season to his next season. However, with the small sample size usually associated with baserunning numbers, a minimum threshold removes the vast majority of seasons from the analysis. Limiting the analysis to seasons in which the batter was involved in at least 40 baserunning situations yields over 5000 samples (in this case, a pair of two consecutive seasons). However, the coefficient of correlation between these seasons is only .1246, very close to total randomness.

However, considering the small sample size issues involved in single seasons, another approach may yield different results. Instead of using single consecutive seasons or larger groups of seasons, we'll break each batter's career into even and odd seasons, hoping to generate large enough samples to drown out most of the noise. Comparing each half of each batter's career in this way yields a coefficient of .4277, still below the threshold we'd like to see for a reasonable degree of confidence. Further, the distribution of the baserunning rates falls very neatly into the standard normal curve. Of the season, 70.0% fall within one standard deviation and 96.0% fall within two standard deviations. If the population were completely random, we would expect about 68% to fall within one standard deviation and 95% to fall within two.

With virtually no evidence that the batter has a deterministic affect on the baserunner, any adjustment to the baserunning numbers based on the batter at the plate must be removed from the analysis.

Valuation of Extra Bases

Now that two suitable adjustments have been found for the raw baserunning numbers, we can begin to assign value to the baserunners in question. While simply comparing each baserunner to the league average adjusted as above would yield valuable information about which baserunners have the highest attempt and success rates, it would leave us short of determining baserunning's importance to game outcomes.

Because baserunning involves as much decision as skill, the game situation can be applied to the valuation of the analysis. It would be ideal to map baserunning decisions to the expected win matrix, but because so many situations occur so rarely and because they can be affected equally as much by other decisions not factored into our analysis—the next batter due up, the pitcher and other available pitchers, etc.—stopping with simply predicting runs added or lost is as far as we can confidently analyze.

For each of the three baserunning situations involved in our analysis, there are three possible output situations: the baserunner takes the basic base, he takes the extra base, or he is thrown out. Mapping those situations to the expected run matrix for each season, we can estimate how many runs each extra base adds and each extra out removes.

For example, see the expected run matrix for 2004 in table 3. In our first baserunning situation, say we have a runner on first and no one out. The batter hits a single and the runner advances only to second, yielding first and second with no one out, a run expectation of 1.4669. If he advances to third, the expected runs are 1.8540. Therefore, in this particular situation, the extra base is worth .3871 runs. If the runner is out, run expectation drops to 0.5496 (a runner on first and one out). Thus, getting caught costs the team 0.9173 runs.

By then applying these valuations to the adjusted baserunning totals for each baserunner, we can now begin to place a price on baserunning.

TABLE 3. 2004 EXPECTED RUNS MATRIX

Runners	The League Average Runs Scored in the Remainder of the Inning, Given Baserunners and Outs		
	0 Outs	1 Out	2 Outs
None	0.5379	0.2866	0.1135
1st	0.9259	0.5496	0.2460
2nd	1.1596	0.7104	0.3359
1st and 2nd	1.4669	0.9577	0.4605
3rd	1.4535	0.9722	0.3623
1st and 3rd	1.854	1.2236	0.5219
2nd and 3rd	2.1343	1.4717	0.6179
Loaded	2.2548	1.5946	0.8082

Applying the Adjustments

For each baserunner, a baseline will be established using league average baserunning data for the season in question. This yields ATTr+ and SUCr+, the attempt and success rate of each batter expressed as a percentage of the league average, similar to ERA+ or OPS+. For example, a player with an ATTr+ of 110 attempts 10% more extra bases than the league average.

Next, a baseline of expected runs for each baserunner will be determined, based on the expected runs matrix, the number of outs when the baserunner was running, and the park factor. Multiplying this number by the number of baserunning decisions faced by the baserunner yields EBR, or Expected Base Runs. Similarly, PBR—Player Base Runs, with a nod to our ale-savvy comrades—is calculated using each baserunner's raw baserunning numbers instead of the adjusted league average in EBR. Subtracting EBR from PBR yields EqBR—Equivalent Base Runs—the difference between what the player did on the basepaths and what a league average runner would have done given that runner's particular park and out circumstances.

As a walk through, let's look at the best and worst of 2004 in table 4. At the top we find the surprising Matt Holliday, the new Rockies left fielder. The "Bases" column indicates that Holliday was the baserunner in 39 situations among the three we examined. His raw attempt rate (ATTr) was an impressive .667, 61% higher than the league average in 2004 as indicated by his 161 ATTr+. Given his park and outs situations, a league average baserunner would have registered 4.0 runs on the basepaths, but Holliday, by virtue of taking 61% more bases and never getting caught, accumulated 9.0 runs for a difference of 5.0, his EqBR.

The players we find at the top and bottom of the 2004 numbers are, for the most part, whom we would expect. The players at the top have reputations as either very fast or very savvy players, with the possible exception of Scott Rolen, who bolstered his already impressive season with an additional 4.5 runs on the bases. Likewise, players at the bottom of the list are mostly catchers, first basemen, or sluggers with slow reputations. The exceptions are Bill Mueller, who has had severe knee problems in the past that may be affecting his baserunning, and Marcus Giles, who also spent much of the year dealing with the repercussions from his collision with Andruw Jones.

TABLE 4. BASERUNNING NUMBERS FOR 2004

Baserunner	Year	Bases	ATTr	SUCr	ATTr+	SUCr+	EBR	PBR	EqBR
Matt Holliday	2004	39	0.667	1.000	161	107	4.0	9.0	5.0
Rafael Furcal	2004	60	0.583	1.000	141	107	5.1	10.0	4.9
Vernon Wells	2004	34	0.706	1.000	171	107	4.1	8.6	4.5
Scott Rolen	2004	52	0.596	1.000	144	107	5.0	9.6	4.5
Royce Clayton	2004	58	0.638	0.946	154	101	6.0	10.4	4.4
Edgar Renteria	2004	59	0.542	1.000	131	107	6.1	10.4	4.3
Carlos Beltran	2004	54	0.537	1.000	130	107	5.3	9.2	3.9
Aaron Rowand	2004	47	0.574	1.000	139	107	5.0	8.9	3.9
Omar Vizquel	2004	59	0.508	1.000	123	107	6.8	10.6	3.7
Johnny Damon	2004	58	0.586	0.971	142	104	5.5	9.0	3.5
Dan Wilson	2004	32	0.281	0.778	68	83	4.1	1.0	−3.1
Marcus Giles	2004	36	0.444	0.750	108	80	3.8	0.6	−3.2
Sammy Sosa	2004	31	0.323	0.700	78	75	3.1	−0.4	−3.4
Jim Thome	2004	65	0.323	0.857	78	91	6.7	3.1	−3.6
Jorge Posada	2004	49	0.306	0.800	74	85	4.7	1.0	−3.7
Rafael Palmeiro	2004	54	0.370	0.800	90	85	6.1	2.3	−3.8
Jason Michaels	2004	27	0.519	0.643	125	69	3.1	−1.0	−4.1
Bill Mueller	2004	51	0.235	0.833	57	89	6.1	2.0	−4.2
A. J. Pierzynski	2004	41	0.341	0.714	83	76	4.2	−0.2	−4.4
Mike Piazza	2004	32	0.219	0.571	53	61	3.3	−1.3	−4.7

Tables 5 through 8 show both the best and worst of baserunners over the past 33 seasons, with complete best and worst lists for 2003 and 2002 as well as any single season and career totals, based on EqBR.

TABLE 5. BASERUNNING NUMBERS FOR 2003

Baserunner	Year	Bases	ATTr	SUCr	ATTr+	SUCr+	EBR	PBR	EqBR
Raul Ibanez	2003	57	0.579	1.000	138	107	7.1	12.6	5.5
Orlando Cabrera	2003	51	0.627	1.000	150	107	6.0	11.4	5.4
Jay Payton	2003	47	0.681	0.969	163	103	5.2	10.2	5.0
Derek Jeter	2003	55	0.582	1.000	139	107	6.4	11.4	5.0
Carlos Lee	2003	52	0.596	1.000	143	107	6.7	11.6	4.9
Carlos Beltran	2003	54	0.574	1.000	137	107	6.1	11.0	4.9
Todd Helton	2003	66	0.500	1.000	120	107	8.3	13.0	4.7
Casey Blake	2003	60	0.550	1.000	132	107	6.6	11.2	4.6
Marcus Giles	2003	54	0.556	1.000	133	107	5.3	9.5	4.2
Jose Guillen	2003	33	0.697	1.000	167	107	3.5	7.7	4.1
Vance Wilson	2003	21	0.429	0.667	102	71	2.6	−0.1	−2.7
Josh Phelps	2003	31	0.419	0.769	100	82	4.2	1.5	−2.7
Ben Grieve	2003	24	0.417	0.700	100	75	2.9	0.1	−2.8
Brad Ausmus	2003	38	0.263	0.800	63	85	4.7	1.4	−3.3
Dustan Mohr	2003	27	0.333	0.667	80	71	2.9	−0.7	−3.6
Lance Berkman	2003	67	0.418	0.821	100	88	7.9	4.1	−3.8
Jim Thome	2003	54	0.333	0.833	80	89	7.7	3.7	−4.0
Roger Cedeno	2003	52	0.519	0.778	124	83	4.7	0.5	−4.2
John Olerud	2003	60	0.300	0.833	72	89	6.9	2.6	−4.3
Mike Lieberthal	2003	52	0.269	0.786	64	84	5.9	1.1	−4.8

TABLE 6. BASERUNNING NUMBERS FOR 2002

Baserunner	Year	Bases	ATTr	SUCr	ATTr+	SUCr+	EBR	PBR	EqBR
Carlos Beltran	2002	69	0.652	1.000	155	107	8.4	16.9	8.4
Alfonso Soriano	2002	68	0.691	1.000	164	107	6.7	14.9	8.2
Juan Pierre	2002	59	0.695	1.000	165	107	6.2	14.1	7.9
Ray Durham	2002	74	0.595	1.000	141	107	7.1	13.6	6.5
Jose Vidro	2002	72	0.597	0.977	142	105	7.8	13.4	5.5
Rafael Furcal	2002	61	0.590	1.000	140	107	5.3	10.6	5.3
Miguel Tejada	2002	70	0.543	1.000	129	107	8.0	13.4	5.3
Jimmy Rollins	2002	55	0.600	1.000	142	107	6.8	11.9	5.1
Larry Walker	2002	64	0.531	1.000	126	107	6.5	11.5	5.0
Tony Womack	2002	70	0.571	0.975	136	104	7.9	12.8	4.9
John Vander Wal	2002	23	0.435	0.600	103	64	2.0	−2.0	−4.1
Jeff Kent	2002	66	0.530	0.800	126	86	7.1	3.0	−4.1
John Olerud	2002	69	0.246	0.882	58	94	8.2	3.7	−4.5
Barry Bonds	2002	95	0.305	0.897	72	96	11.1	6.5	−4.5
Doug Mientkiewicz	2002	54	0.333	0.778	79	83	6.6	2.0	−4.7
David Ortiz	2002	44	0.250	0.727	59	78	5.3	0.5	−4.8
Ben Grieve	2002	59	0.271	0.813	64	87	7.1	2.3	−4.8
Mark Grace	2002	40	0.400	0.688	95	74	4.4	−0.6	−4.9
Frank Thomas	2002	66	0.242	0.813	57	87	8.0	2.3	−5.7
Ben Molina	2002	51	0.235	0.583	56	62	5.2	−2.2	−7.4

TABLE 7. BEST AND WORST BASERUNNING SEASONS 1972–2004 AS RANKED BY EQBR

Baserunner	Year	Bases	ATTr	SUCr	ATTr+	SUCr+	EBR	PBR	EqBR
Rod Carew	1977	74	0.743	0.982	156	107	10.0	19.5	9.5
Terry Pendleton	1985	64	0.781	1.000	167	107	7.8	17.2	9.3
Eddie Milner	1985	82	0.695	1.000	149	107	8.9	17.9	9.0
Robin Yount	1983	60	0.733	1.000	158	109	8.1	16.7	8.7
Julio Franco	1985	110	0.600	1.000	129	107	11.7	20.4	8.7
Dave Hollins	1993	65	0.708	1.000	159	108	8.9	17.6	8.7
Ryne Sandberg	1982	61	0.721	1.000	158	108	7.0	15.6	8.6
Carlos Beltran	2002	69	0.652	1.000	155	107	8.4	16.9	8.4
Ryne Sandberg	1985	73	0.671	1.000	144	107	8.9	17.1	8.2
Alfonso Soriano	2002	68	0.691	1.000	164	107	6.7	14.9	8.2
Rickey Henderson	1985	82	0.756	0.968	162	104	7.5	15.6	8.1
Lance Johnson	1990	56	0.750	1.000	164	107	6.8	14.9	8.0
Willie McGee	1985	98	0.602	1.000	129	107	10.2	18.1	7.9
Juan Pierre	2002	59	0.695	1.000	165	107	6.2	14.1	7.9
Bake McBride	1974	54	0.759	1.000	166	109	6.0	13.9	7.9
Tim Salmon	1996	75	0.653	1.000	148	107	8.6	16.3	7.7
Mark Whiten	1992	67	0.657	1.000	146	106	9.9	17.6	7.7
Kenny Lofton	1996	93	0.645	0.983	146	105	9.4	17.2	7.7
Willie Wilson	1980	73	0.630	1.000	136	108	8.6	16.2	7.6
Julio Franco	1990	89	0.663	0.966	145	103	12.2	19.8	7.6
Freddie Patek	1973	52	0.731	1.000	157	109	6.4	14.0	7.6
Larry Walker	1997	63	0.698	0.977	161	104	7.7	15.1	7.4
Travis Fryman	1995	64	0.641	1.000	141	108	8.5	15.8	7.3
Brian Jordan	2001	57	0.684	1.000	161	107	6.8	14.2	7.3
Harold Reynolds	1991	72	0.653	1.000	143	107	10.0	17.2	7.2
Randy Milligan	1991	67	0.284	0.789	62	84	7.7	1.5	−6.2
Mike Lavalliere	1992	27	0.185	0.200	41	21	3.3	−2.9	−6.2
Harold Reynolds	1987	41	0.561	0.696	117	74	5.6	−0.6	−6.2
Chris Sabo	1993	61	0.508	0.742	114	80	6.5	0.2	−6.3
Tony Phillips	1990	76	0.566	0.767	124	82	9.3	2.9	−6.4
Todd Zeile	2000	52	0.385	0.700	89	74	6.0	−0.5	−6.4
Ted Simmons	1974	50	0.300	0.667	65	73	6.2	−0.2	−6.4
Dave Magadan	1994	37	0.405	0.600	90	65	4.8	−1.6	−6.4
Richie Hebner	1978	41	0.512	0.619	111	68	5.3	−1.3	−6.6
Jose Oquendo	1990	62	0.387	0.750	85	80	9.3	2.7	−6.6
Orlando Cepeda	1973	34	0.176	0.333	38	36	4.1	−2.6	−6.7
Kent Hrbek	1990	56	0.321	0.722	70	77	7.7	1.0	−6.7
Javy Lopez	2001	37	0.270	0.500	64	53	3.8	−2.8	−6.7
Gregg Jefferies	1995	60	0.317	0.737	70	79	7.4	0.7	−6.7
Wade Boggs	1991	95	0.274	0.885	60	94	12.3	5.5	−6.8
Randy Milligan	1992	67	0.358	0.750	79	80	7.3	0.4	−6.8
Pedro Guerrero	1991	51	0.176	0.667	39	71	6.6	−0.3	−7.0
Carlos Delgado	1998	59	0.356	0.714	81	76	7.0	0.1	−7.0
Eric Karros	1997	66	0.379	0.720	87	77	7.6	0.3	−7.4
Ben Molina	2002	51	0.235	0.583	56	62	5.2	−2.2	−7.4
Jack Clark	1990	55	0.291	0.688	64	73	8.3	0.7	−7.6
Danny Heep	1985	25	0.440	0.273	94	29	3.2	−5.1	−8.3
Mike Piazza	1996	67	0.179	0.667	41	71	7.9	−0.6	−8.4
Carl Yastrzemski	1983	46	0.326	0.467	70	51	4.8	−4.8	−9.6
Mark McGwire	1999	87	0.207	0.722	47	77	10.2	0.5	−9.7

TABLE 8. BEST AND WORST CAREER BASERUNNING TOTALS 1972–2004 AS RANKED BY EQBR

Baserunner	Bases	ATTr	SUCr	ATTr+	SUCr+	EBR	PBR	EqBR
Robin Yount	1075	0.553	0.987	118	106	133.8	198.8	65.0
Rickey Henderson	1405	0.565	0.956	123	103	151.6	208.8	57.1
Ozzie Smith	1038	0.559	0.971	121	105	129.4	183.2	53.8
Ryne Sandberg	853	0.573	0.975	123	105	104.2	157.2	53.0
Willie Wilson	719	0.605	0.979	134	106	86.1	138.4	52.2
Willie Randolph	1018	0.540	0.971	112	104	119.8	168.6	48.8
Brett Butler	1086	0.552	0.965	122	104	121.7	168.7	47.1
Barry Larkin	917	0.525	0.988	119	106	112.4	159.3	46.8
Kenny Lofton	901	0.567	0.965	126	104	94.7	140.6	46.0
Tim Raines	1035	0.517	0.981	100	96	120.0	164.9	44.9
Rod Carew	785	0.637	0.934	136	101	94.1	138.8	44.7
George Brett	1010	0.555	0.952	114	98	128.3	172.2	43.9
Julio Franco	971	0.545	0.964	113	103	117.8	161.4	43.6
Willie McGee	779	0.591	0.961	128	102	98.3	140.9	42.6
Alan Trammell	862	0.565	0.961	120	103	107.8	149.4	41.7
Toby Harrah	676	0.593	0.958	130	104	80.3	121.2	40.9
Steve Finley	1009	0.513	0.967	114	104	115.0	151.2	36.3
Paul Molitor	1351	0.497	0.960	108	103	162.0	197.9	35.9
Davey Lopes	587	0.579	0.971	122	99	68.5	104.2	35.8
Mookie Wilson	446	0.648	0.976	135	105	53.4	89.0	35.6
Ozzie Guillen	617	0.566	0.974	123	105	75.6	111.1	35.5
Dave Hollins	442	0.631	0.975	121	98	54.6	90.1	35.4
Tom Goodwin	496	0.575	0.986	124	97	53.6	88.8	35.2
Kirby Puckett	841	0.548	0.959	117	103	107.5	140.7	33.2
Larry Walker	820	0.517	0.958	122	103	96.6	129.7	33.0
Bob Boone	568	0.428	0.877	90	89	73.8	54.8	−19.0
Greg Luzinski	544	0.327	0.921	71	98	66.4	47.4	−19.0
Terry Steinbach	584	0.390	0.904	95	96	74.4	55.3	−19.1
Cecil Fielder	517	0.271	0.950	58	95	57.7	38.4	−19.3
Kent Hrbek	646	0.362	0.932	87	101	85.1	65.8	−19.3
Mike Lavalliere	231	0.216	0.860	46	80	28.9	9.2	−19.7
Dan Wilson	452	0.323	0.897	75	90	56.9	34.9	−21.9
Javy Lopez	448	0.326	0.877	65	81	50.5	28.0	−22.5
Tim Wallach	760	0.384	0.918	79	90	95.5	72.9	−22.6
Dave Magadan	586	0.355	0.909	75	97	74.9	52.1	−22.8
Charlie Hayes	600	0.400	0.879	78	81	74.8	51.3	−23.5
Chili Davis	1023	0.479	0.882	101	89	126.1	101.9	−24.1
Alvin Davis	428	0.297	0.945	66	101	61.5	37.3	−24.2
Mark McGwire	751	0.293	0.964	71	103	95.5	69.8	−25.7
Rick Cerone	385	0.361	0.835	65	76	49.9	24.2	−25.8
Eric Karros	637	0.344	0.890	75	90	68.8	42.5	−26.3
Carlos Delgado	592	0.314	0.909	57	74	70.0	43.7	−26.3
Mo Vaughn	686	0.302	0.932	69	101	81.3	54.1	−27.2
Darrin Fletcher	352	0.224	0.861	45	92	43.1	15.0	−28.2
Tino Martinez	737	0.358	0.898	80	93	88.5	59.3	−29.2
Todd Zeile	881	0.378	0.895	81	97	105.0	74.3	−30.8
John Olerud	983	0.304	0.953	63	96	117.4	86.3	−31.1
Edgar Martinez	997	0.353	0.920	78	92	121.8	87.9	−34.0
Mike Piazza	680	0.315	0.893	80	95	84.2	50.2	−34.0
Fred McGriff	1001	0.356	0.899	71	86	122.2	81.4	−40.8

Conclusions and Outlook

In the most extreme cases, baserunning can add up to close to 10 runs per season, or about one win, not an insignificant amount when evaluating players. More frequently, however, the best and worst baserunners only add and subtract about five runs over the course of a season. Over a career, if the baserunner is consistent enough, some very impressive totals can accumulate. Carlos Beltran, one of the most complete players ever, has been among the ten best baserunners each of the last three seasons, placing first, sixth, and seventh in 2002–04, adding an extra 17.2 runs over those seasons.

There is quite a lot more analysis that can be done using these numbers. Outfield defenses can be analyzed using not only the number of baserunners they throw out, but also the number of runners who take the extra base on them. Third base coaches—who draw a great deal of criticism from fans and media alike—could be analyzed more objectively as well.

Besides adding outfield defenses and third base coaches, there are also other possible adjustments to the current EqBR model. Runners generally start running earlier if the batter is facing a full count, so if a player is in that situation more or less often than the league average, his numbers may be misleading.

Most of these adjustments would likely not dramatically alter the conclusions reached thus far. Baserunning is one of baseball's finer points, but it clearly has a cumulative effect over the course of a season. Sammy Sosa posted a VORP (Value Over Replacement Player) of 27.9 in 2004 while Holliday had 15.2, making Sosa worth about 12.7 more runs than Holliday with the bat. However, adding in EqBR closes the gap to 24.5 to 20.2. So while Sosa was clearly worth more than Holliday with the bat last year, as with many players who run the bases extremely well or extremely poorly, the difference between their complete contributions to their teams isn't quite as disparate as it might appear at first glance.

An Analytical Framework for Win Expectancy

by Keith Woolner

Introduction

The immediate strategic objective at any point during a baseball game is to win, a statement that will be blindingly obvious to most fans. Most sabermetric tools have been developed with the intent of better understanding some aspect of the game with the goal of improving a team's chances to win. One way of considering value is to assess how much more likely a win is following any particular action (or replacing a player). This value is called win expectancy.

Since wins relate directly to runs scored by each team, run expectancy is a related offshoot of win expectancy. Thorn & Palmer introduced an expected runs matrix in their landmark book *The Hidden Game of Baseball* for different situations (number of outs and runners on base) as one of the first important steps towards analyzing different strategies on the existing game state.

One limitation of that approach is that the static expected runs matrix doesn't take into account both the range of teams who play games (including stronger and weaker offenses), nor the overall change in the game itself (higher scoring since the mid 1990s., low scoring pre-1920, and in the expanded strike zone era of the 1960's. A more useful tool would be one that allows us to directly consider the effect of different run scoring environments on runs scoring, and hence win expectation in general.

In this article, I introduce an analytic framework for win expectancy. This will allows computations of expected runs in different situations , at different during a game, as well as in cases where knowledge of game state is unequal between the two teams, where the strengths of both teams are unequal. In addition, I'll show how some sabermetric tools already in use can be recast as special cases of win expectancy, and how we can use that knowledge to useful improvements such as park adjustments, comparison to replacement level, and strength of opposition adjustments as well. Furthermore, I'll show how an analytic framework for win expectancy enables us to quantify situational value, including the higher leverage applicable to relievers used in game-critical situations.

Win Expectancy Defined Conceptually

Simple defined, win expectancy is the probability of winning the current game, given some information about the teams playing and the current score, current inning, and runners on base.

To indicate who's on bass (Baserunner State) we designate an empty (unoccupied) base with a '0', and an occupied base by the number of the base (1 = first base, 2 = second base, 3 = third base). All bases are represented by a three digit string (possibly with a leading zero). E.g. '000' = bases empty;

'020' = runner on second base;
'103' = runners on first and third;
'123' = bases loaded

The **Base-Out State** refers to the Baserunner State, combined with the number of outs in the current half-inning. E.g. '2-103' indicates 2 outs with runners on first and third.

Runs Per Inning refers to the average number of runs scored per inning by a given team or lineup. Abbreviated RPI, it's a measure of the strength of a team's offense (or conversely, the strength of the opposing team's pitching staff).

Win Expectancy refers to the probability of a Team, at any given point in the game (The Starting Inning) winning the game against the Opponent, beginning from its own Starting Inning, given a Run Differential and Baserunner State.

One important thing to note here is that we do not assume that we have equal knowledge of each's teams scoring success to the same point in time. We could have a starting point of the top of the 2nd inning for the Team, and the top of the 6th inning for the Opponent. Our Run Differential would be reflective of what we know the team scored in its first inning for the Team, and the first 5 innings for the Opponent. Thus, Win Expectancy does not always directly map to an actual point in the game where this state actually existed. This is important for understanding Win Expectancy's relationship to Support Neutral pitching statistics, which will be described later on.

The foundation for computing win expectancy is to determine the frequency and patterns in which runs score. Since the bases are cleared and outs reset to zero at the end of each inning, that is the fundamental period of "time" in baseball where we begin our investigation of run scoring patterns.

Single Inning Run Scoring Distribution

In most innings, zero runs are scored. In most of the rest, 1 run is scored, with the frequency of scoring 2, 3, and more runs becoming less and less likely. This determines the "shape" of how runs are scored. We refer to this shape as a run scoring distribution.

I introduced a first formula for computing the per-inning run scoring distribution back in 2000 (http://www.base ballprospectus.com/article.php?articleid=472), and it looked like this:

$$\Pr\{A,R\} = \left(\begin{array}{l} \text{if } R>0 \text{ then } C \times c^{\left[mA + pR + n\left(\frac{R}{A}\right) + b\right]} \\ \text{if } R=0 \text{ then } 1 - C \times \sum_{r=1}^{R_{max}} e^{\left[mA + pr + n\left(\frac{r}{A}\right) + b\right]} \\ \text{Where } C = \dfrac{A}{9\sum_{r=1}^{R_{max}} r \times e^{\left[mr + pr + n\left(\frac{r}{A}\right) + b\right]}} \\ \text{and} \\ m = -0.01219 \\ n = -1.813 \\ p = -0.3865 \\ b = -1.042 \end{array} \right)$$

Fortunately, work by others has refined this initial stab at providing an analytic expression for the runs-per-inning distribution. The most concise revision I've found is due to an analyst who works under the pseudonym Tangotiger (www.tangotiger.net): and appears in a slightly rearranged form below:

Given:
R = average runs scored per inning, and empirically derived constant K = 0.761
P(r) = probability of r runs scored in an inning

$$P(0) = \frac{1}{R \times K + 1}$$

$$P(1) = P(0) \times \frac{R \times K^2}{R \times K + 1} = \frac{R \times K^2}{(R \times K + 1)^2}$$

$$P(N, N \geq 2) = P(1) \times \left(\frac{1-K}{R \times K + 1}\right)^{(N-1)} = \frac{R \times K^2 \times (R \times K - K + 1)^{N-2}}{(R \times K + 1)^{N-1}}$$

This representation, while not trivial, is still considerably cleaner than my original formulation, and marginally more accurate as well, so we'll base our win expectancy work on this model for per-inning run scoring.

Some examples of the probabilities arising from this model for various levels of offense is shown in table 1.

Multiple Inning Run Scoring Distribution

A one inning scoring distribution is an important first step, but it is only the beginning. The next step towards building our win expectancy model is to consider how

TABLE 1. EXAMPLES OF PROBABILITY OF RUNS SCORED [P(R)] FROM MODEL

Runs	Runs/Game								
	3.00	3.50	4.00	4.50	5.00	5.50	6.00	6.50	7.00
	Runs/Inning								
	0.333	0.389	0.444	0.500	0.556	0.611	0.667	0.722	0.778
	Probability								
0	79.766%	77.164%	74.726%	72.438%	70.285%	68.257%	66.342%	64.532%	62.818%
1	12.282%	13.410%	14.372%	15.194%	15.894%	16.489%	16.993%	17.418%	17.775%
2	4.827%	5.535%	6.199%	6.818%	7.393%	7.924%	8.414%	8.864%	9.277%
3	1.897%	2.285%	2.674%	3.060%	3.439%	3.808%	4.166%	4.511%	4.842%
4	0.745%	0.943%	1.153%	1.373%	1.599%	1.830%	2.063%	2.296%	2.527%
5	0.293%	0.389%	0.497%	0.616%	0.744%	0.879%	1.021%	1.168%	1.319%
6	0.115%	0.161%	0.215%	0.276%	0.346%	0.423%	0.506%	0.595%	0.689%
7	0.045%	0.066%	0.093%	0.124%	0.161%	0.203%	0.250%	0.303%	0.359%
8	0.018%	0.027%	0.040%	0.056%	0.075%	0.098%	0.124%	0.154%	0.188%
9	0.007%	0.011%	0.017%	0.025%	0.035%	0.047%	0.061%	0.078%	0.098%
10	0.003%	0.005%	0.007%	0.011%	0.016%	0.023%	0.030%	0.040%	0.051%

this single-inning run scoring distribution forms the basis of a multiple-inning run-scoring distribution.

If we want to consider that the probability that a team with a R/G of 4.50 scores zero runs over two innings, we simply need to multiply the probability of scoring zero runs in an inning by itself:

Inning 1	Inning 2	Probability of this combination (Inn 1 × Inn 2)
0 runs (79.77%)	0 runs (79.77%)	63.63%

For scoring exactly 1 run over two innings, the run could score in either inning, with zero runs in the other inning. Adding the probabilities of each combination gives the total probability of exactly 1 run scoring over 2 innings.

Inning 1	Inning 2	Probability of this combination (Inn 1 × Inn 2)
0 runs (79.77%)	1 runs (12.28%)	9.80%
1 runs (12.28%)	0 runs (79.77%)	9.80%
Total probability:		**19.6%**

For exactly 2 runs over two innings, there are 3 combinations that yield that result: 1 run in each inning, or 2 runs in either the first or second inning, and zero in the other.

Inning 1	Inning 2	Probability of this combination (Inn 1 × Inn 2)
0 runs (79.77%)	2 runs (4.83%)	3.85%
1 runs (12.28%)	1 runs (12.28%)	1.51%
2 runs (4.83%)	0 runs (79.77%)	3.85%
Total probability:		**9.2%**

If we know that the Team scored 5 runs in the game, the probability of the team winning can be determined by adding up the probability of the Opponent scoring 0, 1, 2, 3, or 4 runs over 9 innings (excluding extra innings, which we'll cover later). We can use a similar process for as many complete innings as we want, and for any run total we want as well.

Partial Inning Run Scoring Distribution

Having full inning run scoring distribution is a useful place to start, but it does not give us enough granularity to determine the probability of a win. Pitchers can leave a game in the middle of an inning, and relief pitchers often enter a game in the middle of an inning. In order to fully specify the run distribution for the rest of the game, we need to be able to characterize the likelihoods of run scoring given the base-out state within a given inning as well.

"The Hidden Game Of Baseball" (as well as other sources) introduced a matrix that shows the expected number of runs from various base-out situations, we know that there are various expected runs from different base-out situations, compiled using data from seasons from 1900 to 1977. (See table 2.)

While this is an excellent starting point, as we've seen, we need to determine the probability of scoring specific numbers of runs, rather than just the expected value. In addition, the aggregate data shown above doesn't account for how run scoring changes between high and low offense eras, or in pitchers parks vs. hitting parks. By analyzing over 30 years of play by play data (1972–2004), I've determined the actual run distributions form various intra-inning base-out states, and in different offensive environments. For example, determining what the probability of 2 runs scoring after a 1-out, runner on 2nd base situation, in a league that averaged 4.47 runs per game per team. It turns out that every base-out state has its own unique distribution shape. Furthermore, that shape also depends on the league-wide offensive.

From the actual data, I derived at least twelve parameters per base-out state. Two parameters were the results (slope and intercept) of a linear regression to determine the probability of scoring zero runs as a function of the league offensive level. The other ten parameters were a vector to indicate what portion of the remaining probability to allocate to scoring 1 run, 2 runs, 3, runs, and so on, up to 10 runs.

The full table of slopes, intercepts, and run scoring probability vectors is shown in table 3.

The actual computations are done to a higher precision than is shown in the table, and consider the rarer possibilities of scoring more than 10 runs in a partial inning as well.

This is better shown by example than by explaining it in words.

TABLE 2. EXPECTED NUMBER OF RUNS FOR BASE-OUT STATES

Outs	Baserunner State							
	000	100	020	120	003	103	023	123
0	0.454	0.783	1.068	1.380	1.277	1.639	1.946	2.254
1	0.249	0.478	0.699	0.888	0.897	1.088	1.371	1.546
2	0.095	0.209	0.348	0.457	0.382	0.494	0.661	0.798

TABLE 3. SLOPES, INTERCEPTS, AND RUN SCORING PROBABILITIES FOR BASE-OUT STATES

State	Slope	Intercept	R1	R2	R3	R4	R5	R6	R7	R8	R9	R10
0-100	-0.278	0.716	42.4%	29.9%	15.0%	7.2%	3.2%	1.3%	0.5%	0.2%	0.1%	0.0%
0-020	-0.358	0.559	56.6%	22.6%	11.4%	5.3%	2.3%	1.0%	0.4%	0.2%	0.1%	0.0%
0-120	-0.167	0.450	36.2%	25.6%	19.4%	10.4%	4.8%	2.0%	0.9%	0.4%	0.2%	0.1%
0-003	-0.370	0.355	65.4%	18.5%	8.9%	4.1%	1.8%	0.8%	0.3%	0.1%	0.1%	0.1%
0-103	-0.216	0.247	51.4%	19.4%	15.0%	7.7%	3.7%	1.7%	0.6%	0.3%	0.1%	0.1%
0-023	-0.229	0.261	31.5%	35.6%	16.8%	8.6%	4.4%	1.8%	0.7%	0.4%	0.2%	0.0%
0-123	-0.127	0.193	31.1%	24.7%	17.0%	14.4%	7.1%	3.1%	1.3%	0.8%	0.3%	0.2%
1-000	-0.296	0.988	60.0%	24.3%	9.7%	3.7%	1.4%	0.6%	0.2%	0.1%	0.0%	0.0%
1-100	-0.268	0.863	44.4%	32.6%	13.7%	5.6%	2.2%	0.9%	0.3%	0.1%	0.0%	0.0%
1-020	-0.191	0.693	59.4%	23.4%	10.4%	4.2%	1.7%	0.6%	0.3%	0.1%	0.0%	0.0%
1-120	-0.174	0.669	40.1%	25.8%	20.3%	8.3%	3.4%	1.3%	0.5%	0.2%	0.1%	0.0%
1-003	-0.270	0.477	73.7%	15.2%	6.7%	2.7%	1.1%	0.4%	0.1%	0.1%	0.0%	0.0%
1-103	-0.116	0.406	59.6%	17.6%	13.2%	5.7%	2.4%	0.9%	0.4%	0.1%	0.0%	0.0%
1-023	-0.311	0.478	41.3%	32.8%	13.8%	7.3%	2.9%	1.1%	0.5%	0.2%	0.1%	0.0%
1-123	-0.142	0.402	39.7%	24.4%	15.1%	12.3%	5.1%	2.1%	0.8%	0.3%	0.1%	0.0%
2-000	-0.163	1.014	67.3%	22.2%	7.1%	2.3%	0.7%	0.2%	0.1%	0.0%	0.0%	0.0%
2-100	-0.194	0.974	45.3%	37.4%	11.6%	3.9%	1.2%	0.5%	0.1%	0.0%	0.0%	0.0%
2-020	-0.107	0.832	68.6%	20.4%	7.3%	2.5%	0.8%	0.2%	0.1%	0.0%	0.0%	0.0%
2-120	-0.144	0.841	49.4%	23.7%	18.1%	6.0%	1.8%	0.7%	0.2%	0.1%	0.0%	0.0%
2-003	-0.047	0.763	73.2%	17.7%	6.0%	2.1%	0.7%	0.2%	0.1%	0.0%	0.0%	0.0%
2-103	-0.199	0.828	55.9%	20.6%	15.8%	5.2%	1.7%	0.5%	0.2%	0.1%	0.0%	0.0%
2-023	-0.095	0.785	18.5%	54.8%	16.9%	6.7%	2.3%	0.6%	0.2%	0.0%	0.0%	0.0%
2-123	-0.209	0.789	27.3%	35.5%	17.0%	13.8%	4.1%	1.5%	0.5%	0.1%	0.0%	0.0%

Consider a team with an offense averaging 4.77 runs per 9 innings. We want to know the distribution of runs scored in the rest of the inning, starting with 1 out, and runners on first and third.

First, we determine the average number of runs per inning:

Runs per inning = 4.77 / 9 = 0.530

Next, we estimate the probability of scoring zero runs, using the slope and intercept from the table above, and the team's offensive production. (See table 4.)

$$P(0) = \text{Slope} \times \text{RPI} + \text{Intercept} = -0.16 \times 0.53 + 0.406$$
$$= 0.345 = 34.5\% \text{ chance of 0 runs}$$

The remaining probability $[1 - \text{Prob}(0)] = 65.5\%$ is divided among the positive numbers of runs in the proportions shown in table 4 by the equation:

$$P(1) = 1 - P(0) \times R1 = 65.5\% \times 59.6\% = 39.1\% \text{ chance of scoring exactly 1 run}$$

The full distribution for this example is shown below:

Runs	Modeled	Actual
0	34.5%	35.4%
1	39.1%	36.0%
2	11.5%	11.8%
3	8.7%	9.8%
4	3.7%	4.2%
5	1.6%	2.0%
6	0.6%	0.6%
7	0.2%	0.1%
8	0.1%	0.0%
9	0.0%	0.0%
10	0.0%	0.0%

To-End-of-Game Run Scoring Distribution

To get the run scoring distribution from a point in time to the end of the game, we simply need to combine the partial-inning run scoring distribution (if the point in time is

TABLE 4. PARAMETERS FOR 1-OUT AND RUNNERS ON 1ST AND 3RD

State	Slope	Intercept	R1	R2	R3	R4	R5	R6	R7	R8	R9	R10
1-103	-0.116	0.406	59.6%	17.6%	13.2%	5.7%	2.4%	0.9%	0.4%	0.1%	0.0%	0.0%

not at the start of an inning), with the distribution representing the number of full innings that follow.

$$P(R,N)=\sum_{i=0}^{R} p_i \times P(R-i,N-1) \quad \text{for } N>0;$$
$$=1 \text{ for } N=0 \text{ and } R=0;$$
$$=0 \text{ for } N=0 \text{ and } R\,!=0$$

Where:
p_i = probability of team scoring "i" runs in a single inning (or partial inning).

A side note: The number of combinations of innings, base-out states, offensive levels, and number of runs quickly runs into the thousands, with each one requiring a large number of calculations to solve. One more practical way of representing all of this data is to precompute the results and store them in a lookup table rather than computing the answer each time from scratch.

Combining Team and Opponent Run Scoring Distributions

Both the team and its opponent have their own players, lineups, and offensive profiles, and thus their own scoring distribution. In our model, each team's average runs per inning determines this distribution. By combining the two run scoring distributions, we can determine the probability of a specific game score.

e.g., Prob (Team wins 3 − 1) = Prob (Team scores 3) × Prob (Opponent scores 1)

We can extend this further by asking what the probability is that the Team wins, given that they score 3 runs. This would be sum of the probabilities of the Opponent scoring 0, 1, or 2 runs. The total probability for this subset of events happening would be:

$$\text{Prob}\begin{pmatrix}\text{Team scores 3}\\ \text{runs and wins}\end{pmatrix} = \text{Prob(Team scores 3)} \times [\text{Prob (Opponent scores 0)} + \text{Prob(Opponent scores 1)} + \text{Prob(Opponent scores 2)}]$$

Winning in Extra Innings

To this point, we've only considered the case where one team or the other wins outright at the end of nine innings. There is a chance, of course, that the teams will be tied at that point, requiring extra innings. One inning after another is played until one team is leading at the end of the inning. Thus:

If RA > RB then A wins, and game ends.
If RA < RB than B wins, and game ends.
If RA = RB then another inning is played.

In our model, the run scoring distribution for each team doesn't change from inning to inning, so the probability that Team A wins assuming the game goes into extra innings is recursive:

Let Prob(XAB)= Probability that Team A defeats Team B if the game goes to extra innings

$$\text{Prob}(X_{AB})=\text{Prob}(R_A>R_B)+\text{Prob}(R_A=R_B) \times [\text{Prob}(R_A>R_B)+\text{Prob}(R_A=R_B)\times(\ldots)]$$

Another way to look at it is that an extra inning in which the teams score the same number of runs "doesn't count", making the only two events worth considering as RA > RB and RA < RB

$$\text{Prob}(X_{AB})=\frac{\text{Prob}(R_A>R_B)}{\text{Prob}(R_A>R_B)+\text{Prob}(R_A<R_B)}=\frac{\text{Prob}(R_A>R_B)}{1-\text{Prob}(R_A=R_B)}$$

Or, expressing it in terms of the single inning run scoring distributions for each team:

$$P(X_{AB})=\frac{\sum_{i=1}^{\infty}\left[\text{Prob}(R_A=i)\times\sum_{j=0}^{i-1}\text{Prob}(R_B=j)\right]}{1-\sum_{i=0}^{\infty}\text{Prob}(R_A=i)\times\text{Prob}(R_B=i)}$$

Win Expectancy Function

Extending this concept of combining run scoring distributions from two teams across all possible scoring combinations gives the probability of the team winning the game, and thus directly leads us to Win Expectancy.

By summing across all the possible run combinations, we can determine the probability of one team winning or losing (or ending 9 innings tied). We can now estimate the probability of a team winning given the following parameters:

1. The team's current inning, out, and baserunner state
2. The opponent's last known inning, out, and baserunner state
3. The team's offensive strength (expressed in average runs per inning)
4. The opponent's offensive strength (expressed in average runs per inning)
5. Whether to consider the probability of winning in 9 innings outright, or to include extra innings

Formula for probability of winning outright at the end of 9 innings:

$$P(W_{AB})=\sum_{i=1}^{\infty}\sum_{j=0}^{i-1}P(R_A=i)\times P(R_B=j)$$

Formula including probability of winning in extra innings:

$$P(W_{AB}) = \sum_{i=1}^{\infty} \sum_{j=0}^{i-1} P(R_A = i) \times P(R_B = j) + P(X_{AB}) \times \sum_{i=0}^{\infty} P(R_A = i) \times P(R_B = i)$$

Where:

P(WAB): probability of Team A winning against Team B

P(RA = i): probability of team A scoring i runs in the game

P(XAB): probability of team A defeating team B if the game goes to extra innings

Applications of Win Expectancy

Now that we have an imposing-looking formula for win expectancy, what can we actually do with it? The most obvious application is to be able to assess a team's chance of winning from any game situation we want to investigate. But this only scratches the surface. Win expectancy is actually an incredibly versatile tool, and we'll cover three examples of how it can be used—as a way of improving upon Support Neutral pitching statistics for pitchers, to measure relief pitcher's contributions to winning, and to quantify

Support Neutral Pitching Statistics Update

Many long-time readers will be familiar with Support Neutral pitching metrics for evaluating starting pitching. The Support Neutral Win-Loss (SNWL) measures has been an integral part of Baseball Prospectus since our inception in the mid 1990s. In fact, it goes back even further, as Michael Wolverton invented SNWL in 1993, when it was presented in a paper published by SABR's "By The Numbers" statistical newsletter.

The original concept behind Support Neutral pitching statistics is a simple one: determine what a pitcher's W/L record "should" have been, if he had gotten average performances from his teammates, adjusted for park, and looking at each start individually.

A related concept is one Michael called Support Neutral Value Added (SNVA), the likelihood that the team will win when a pitcher takes the mound by measuring how much the outing by the starter changes the team's chance of winning from what it was at the beginning of the game.

The concept of SNVA for a single start is the probability that the team wins the game behind a starting pitcher who gives that performance, assuming average bullpen support, and average run support.

SNVA as Win Expectation Special Case

Support Neutral Value turns out to be a just a special case of our win expectation formula—we know how many innings are left in the game, the base-out state, and how many runs the opposition scored thus far. So we compute the run distribution for the opponent's remainder of the game, and a full 9 innings worth of the team's own offense, to determine the probability of winning.

$$\text{SNVA(IP, RUNS,RUNNERS,LgRPI)} = \text{WINEXP(1,'000',IP + 1,RUNNERS,} - \text{RUNS,LgRPI,LgRPI}$$

Where RUNS is specifically the runs allowed while the starting pitcher was in the game, not any inherited runners who scored afterwards (the chances of those scoring are covered by the inclusion of the RUNNERS variable). The LgRPI variable is the league-wide average Runs Per Inning value, or RA/9. It is used twice in the WinExp formula to represent both the strength of run support from the pitcher's own team, and the level of offensive production expected from the opposition facing the starter's bullpen when he leaves the game.

Using the Win Expectancy framework, and we can augment SNVA in a couple of useful ways by introducing adjustments for the strength of:

- Park adjustments (a form of which were actually part of Michael's original formulation)
- The opposing hitters in the lineup faced by a pitcher.
- The bullpen supporting the pitcher
- The strength of the offense supporting the pitcher

Park Adjustments

The simplest adjustment we would want to make is a park adjustment, which is an inflation or deflation of the expected level of run scoring, based on the league average. In a park that inflates scoring, the chance of overcoming a small run differential is greater, even if the relative strengths of the two teams playing don't change.

$$\text{PkLgRA} = \text{League RA} \times \text{Park Factor}$$

Note that if we are talking about a game in a specific park, we do not need to apply the "halving" process on the park factor typically used when park adjusting a full season of stats, where half a player's games are played away from the park.

Replacement Level and SNVA

One change to SNVA is in how replacement level is calculated. In the first iteration of SNWL, replacement level was set to a .425 winning percentage. However, based on the research presented in Baseball Prospectus 2002, we now have a formula that can estimate the RA of a replacement level starter as a function of league offensive level. We refer to this as Support Neutral Value Added above Replacement (SNVAR).

$$\text{RepLvlRA} = 1.37 \times \text{League RA} - 0.66$$

$$\text{RepLvlRPI} = \frac{1.37 \times \text{League RA} - 0.66}{9}$$

Combining this with the park adjustment yields:

$$\text{Park\_RepLvl\_RPI} = \text{ParkFactor} \times \left(\frac{1.37 \times \text{League RA} - 0.66}{9} \right)$$

This parameter simply replaces one of the RPI values passed to the WinExp function shown earlier.

$$\text{SNVAR}\begin{pmatrix} \text{IP, RUNS,} \\ \text{RUNNERS,} \\ \text{LgRPI, ParkF} \end{pmatrix} = \text{WinExp}\left\{ \begin{matrix} 1,\text{'000'}, \\ \text{IP}+1,\text{RUNNERS}, \\ -\text{RUNS}, \\ \text{LgRPI} \times \text{ParkF}, \\ \text{ParkF} \times \left[\frac{(1.37 \times \text{LgRPI}) - 0.66}{9}\right] \end{matrix} \right\}$$

Lineup Adjustments

With the advent of play by play databases, it's possible to now collect precise data about exactly which batters a pitcher has faced, and adjust our expectations for a pitcher's performance accordingly. In particular, we can compute the average strength of a hitter the pitcher faced. Using MLVr is beneficial because it already is denominated in runs/game. Therefore, if a pitcher in a league that averages 4.50 runs per game is faces a series of batters who's average MLVr is +0.100, that means that the lineup he actually faced would be expected to score about 5.40 runs/game (4.50 league average + 9 players × 0.100 MLVr/player). This significantly affects our expectations about how many runs an average pitcher would allow against this series of batters, and thus should affect our assessment of how effective the pitcher actually was as well.

$$\text{SNLVAR}\begin{pmatrix} \text{IP, RUNS,} \\ \text{RUNNERS,} \\ \text{LgRPI, ParkF} \\ \text{MLVr} \end{pmatrix} = \text{WinExp}\begin{pmatrix} 1,\text{'000'}, \\ \text{IP}+1,\text{RUNNERS}, \\ -\text{RUNS}, \\ \text{LgRPI} \times \text{ParkF}, \\ \text{ParkF} \times \left\{\frac{1.37 \times [\text{LgRPI} + (9 \times \text{MLVr})] - 0.66}{9}\right\} \end{pmatrix}$$

The Win Expectation function need not be limited to SNVA-style uses, of course. If you wanted to measure the specific impact on winning from having a superior bullpen, you could deflate the opposition's RPI parameter accordingly. Or see the effect of a stronger supporting offense has by increasing the team's own RPI. The flexibility of the Win Expectation framework makes it useful for a variety of questions.

One problem we run into when using opponent's actual seasonal MLVr to determine opposition strength is when an opposing batter has very few plate appearances. As with any rate statistic, the value of MLVr can vary widely with small sample sizes, to the point where it is no longer a good estimate of the batter's actual skill. Consider a game in late September, where the team starts several recently-promoted prospects. They each may have just a few plate appearances, and several of them may have gone 0-for-their first few AB. This would mean they have MLVr's below negative one (−1). Having several of them on the team could result is the nonsensical result that the lineup the pitcher faced would be expected to score negative runs!

There are several ways we could resolve this situation. A lineup's strength could be based on more than one year's worth of data for each player. Or a player with few major league plate appearances could be rated on his translated minor league performance. Or perhaps a prediction system such as PECOTA could be used to project what his batting performance is expected to be.

Another, simpler approach would be to give less weight to a player's MLVr when he has fewer plate appearances, and only consider his full track record when he has accumulated enough plate appearances. We'll assume 500 plate appearances for our purposes. For players with fewer than 500 PA, we'll make up the difference by assuming the remaining plate appearances (up to 500) are made by a league average batter (MLVr = .000). This provides a conservative adjustment to the measurement of lineup strength. An opposing batter will only move the pitcher's quality of opposition if there is a large enough sample size of plate appearances to observe to have some confidence that we know what his true batting level is. Otherwise, we'll assume that the pitcher is facing a more or less average opposing lineup.

$$\text{Opposing Batter's Adjusted MLVr} = \frac{\text{PA} \times \text{MLVr}}{\text{Max}(\text{PA}, 500)}$$

Relievers and Game States upon Entering or Exiting

For relievers, the situation is more complicated than with starting pitchers. They do not enter the game at a known point, like the first batter of the first inning, so we must determine:

a. the inning and base-out state when they entered the game

b. the win probability at the time they entered the game

c. the number of runs they allowed while in the game (including inherited runs)
d. the inning and base-out state when they left the game
e. the team's expected run scoring distribution from the point the reliever entered the game
f. the opponent's expected run scoring distribution at the point the reliever leaves the game
g. combine all of the above to get total change in win probability due to reliever's performance

Note that it is not correct to simply look at the win prob at the start and end of his appearance, since the offense may have scored additional runs, that change the probability of winning in ways that are not dependent on the pitcher's performance. A pitcher who enters the game in a high leverage situation may continue to pitch after his team has racked up an 8 run lead, turning it into a low leverage performance. We have to assume a typical distribution of run scoring from the point the reliever entered the game to determine what the impact of his own performance, in isolation, is on the win expectancy for the game as a whole.

$$\text{WinExp}\begin{pmatrix}\text{Start\_Inn,'000',End\_Inn,}\\ \text{End\_Runners, Start\_Rundiff}\\ \text{+Inh\_Scored}\\ \text{+Runs\_Given\_Up,RPI, RPI,1}\end{pmatrix} - \text{WinExp}\begin{pmatrix}\text{Start\_Inn,'000',}\\ \text{Start\_Inn,}\\ \text{Start\_Runners,}\\ \text{Start\_Rundiff,RPI,RPI,1}\end{pmatrix}$$

Where:

Start_Inn =	inning (including outs in partial inning) when reliever entered game
End_Inn =	Inning (including outs in partial inning) when reliever exited game
Start_Runners =	baserunner state when reliever entered game
End_Runners =	baserunner state when reliever exited game
Start_Rundiff =	Run differential when reliever entered game
Inh_Scored =	Number of inherited runners reliever allowed to score during his appearance
Runs_Given_Up =	Runs charged to the reliever that scored during his appearance (does not include his own bequeathed runners who later scored)
RPI =	league average runs per inning

The first WinExp expression is the win expectancy at the time the reliever leaves the game, but assuming no knowledge of how his teammates performed on offense while he was in the game, and counts any runs that actually scored while he was on the mound. The second WinExp expression is the win expectancy when the reliever entered the game. Remember that win expectancy includes the likelihood of runners on base eventually scoring already, so any runners the reliever bequeaths to other pitchers are accounted for.

Starters Don't Equal Relievers at the Start of a Game

Another factor that may not be obvious is that a reliever who enters in the first inning with the bases empty and zero outs does not necessarily have the same win probability as a starting pitcher, even if no runs have scored. Consider the away team's starter gets hurt while taking his warm-up tosses in the bottom of the first. The reliever comes into the game, however, half an inning has already elapsed. This changes the expected run distribution for the rest of the game (since the away team has one less turn at bat). The point at which the decision is made and the pitcher committed to appearing determines the context for win probability. For a starting pitcher, it's when the lineup cards are submitted, prior to any actual baseball being played. For any reliever thereafter, some amount of baseball has been played, which necessarily changes the expected run distribution (other than an injury to the home starter before the first batter is retired). This is a minor point, and one that rarely comes into play, but it is an example that highlights the importance of the game context on win expectancy.

Leverage

We often talk about relievers, particularly closers, being used in "higher leverage" situations, meaning they have a disproportionate effect on the chance of winning that their innings pitched totals alone would suggest. Actually measuring this leverage is more difficult. However, win expectancy gives us a way to do it.

I propose defining leverage as the impact on the probability of winning the game from scoring (or allowing) one additional run relative to a run scoring at the start of the game. Dividing the change in probability in the current situation with the change in probability at the start of the game yields a number that reflects how "important" it is to score or prevent a run in the current situation. Values below one represent situations that are less leveraged than at the start of a game (when the entire outcome of all innings is unknown). Values above 1 represent situations with more leverage (a run is more important than when the game started).

We could measure leverage at each plate appearance during a reliever's stint in the game. However, the dynamics of what actually happens during the game changes the leverage. Each out recorded by the reliever lowers the leverage of the next PA. Runs scoring by either team may raise or lower leverage. Since the decision to bring in the reliever (versus the non-action of leaving him in the game) is the strategic aspect of the move, we'll rate a pitcher's leverage for an outing as the leverage when he first entered the game. We could also call this the "Initial Marginal Run Leverage", to distinguish it from other potential ways of measuring leverage, but since we'll just concern ourselves with this model now, we'll simply keep using "leverage" as our term of choice.

Measuring Leverage with Win Expectancy

To compute leverage for a given game situation, we need to determine a total of 4 different win expectancies:

1. the win expectancy at the current game state
2. the win expectancy at the current game state, if one more run had been allowed
3. the win expectancy at the very start of the game
4. the win expectancy at the very start of the game, if the opponent had been spotted a run instead of starting at a score of 0–0

The difference between 1. and 2. Determine the marginal win value of a run in the current game situation. The difference between 3. and 4. Determine the marginal win value of a run at the start of the game.

The ratio of these two differences is the leverage in the current situation. If a run now has a greater impact that a run at the start of the game, it is a higher leverage situation (leverage greater than 1.0). If a run now has a lesser impact than a run at the start of the game, it is a lower leverage situation (leverage less than 1.0)

$$\text{Leverage} = \frac{\begin{array}{c}\text{Winexp}[\text{INN}+(1-\text{HOME}), \text{'000'}, \text{INN}, \text{BASE}, \text{DIFF}, \text{RPI}, \text{RPI}, 1] \\ -\text{Winexp}[\text{INN}+(1-\text{HOME}), \text{'000'}, \text{INN}, \text{BASE}, \text{DIFF}-1, \text{RPI}, \text{RPI}, 1]\end{array}}{\begin{array}{c}\text{Winexp}(1, \text{'000'}, 1, \text{'000'} \text{ BASE}, 0, \text{RPI}, \text{RPI}, 1) \\ -\text{Winexp}(1, \text{'000'}, 1,\text{'000'},\text{BASE}, -1, \text{RPI}, \text{RPI}, 1)\end{array}}$$

Interpreting Leverage

It's important to realize that leverage is not a measure of a pitcher's actual performance, but rather a measure of how he was used. Was he brought in for game-critical situations, or was he used more for mop up when the game outcome was more or less determined? By looking at the leverage upon entering the game for each of his appearances, and taking the average over the entire season, we can determine how his manager chose to use him.

Other Applications

Although the examples shown above all relate to pitching, there is nothing that prevents win expectancy from being used with any other aspect of the game. Batters could be evaluated based on how much they increase (or decrease) their team's expected chances of winning for each plate appearance (a technique used by the Mills brothers in their book "Player Win Averages"). While not necessarily predictive, such an approach can be useful to illuminate past performance. Leverage for batters could be calculated much the same way as leverage for relievers has been (though the usefulness is not as obvious).

Analysis of in-game strategies such as sacrifices, stolen base attempts, and other one-run ploys can be further refined using win expectancy. Being able to vary the strength of both teams in analyzing these situations means such results will be more robust for making decisions in actual games.

Win expectancy could even be used to measure characteristics of games themselves. The ebb and flow of a game could be captured by the number of times a the win probability moves back and forth across 50%. Or the tightness of a game could be measured by how little the win probability changes over a large series of plate appearances. Games for a single team could be examined to see if the games get out of hand early (indicating problems with starting pitching, or lack of offense), or tended to fade late (perhaps indicating a weak bullpen, or poor end-game strategic maneuvering).

An analytic framework for win expectancy may also help us evaluate park effects in a new light. By determining how win expectancy changes when the offensive environment rises or falls, we may be able to see how the optimal mix of pitching and offensive changes. If the higher variability in scoring in a high-offense ballpark like Coors Field overwhelms differences in pitching quality when computing win expectancy, it may be more to the Rockies advantage to spend more money on offense, for example.

Future Research Directions

The framework presented here is extremely useful, but is not without room for improvements. One of the big areas not addressed here are lineup effects. We've modeled the entire team offense as a single level of production, but in reality, win expectancy is heavily influenced by who the next batter or batters is, particularly in late innings. A team with a lineup balanced top to bottom may have a different scoring profile than a "stars and scrubs" lineup of similar overall offensive quality.

Similarly, we did not consider the quality of baserunners in different situations. Having Carl Crawford on second base with two outs means a team is much more likely to score a run on a single than if David Ortiz was there instead. Adjusting the partial-inning and full-inning run-scoring distributions to account for baserunning ability may be a minor effect, but perhaps one worth investigating.

As with the original runs-per-inning distribution, there may be simpler and more accurate ways to model partial inning run scoring than the method presented here. This would not change the conceptual framework for win expectancy, but would provide more accurate results, and potentially cut down on the amount of computation necessary.

The interaction of a lineup with a given pitching staff has been largely ignored as well. We've discussed adjusting the RPI parameter based on having better hitters or pitchers, but computing the actual expected run production from a lineup who averages X runs per inning facing a pitcher who gives up runs at rate Y to plug into the formula has not been directly addressed.

The concept of leverage presented here is only one approach out of many that are possible. We defined leverage as the change in marginal win expectation from allowing 1 additional run at the start of the appearance relative to the start of the game. Other formulations of leverage could compute the average leverage across all batters a pitcher faces during an appearance. Or compute the impact on win expectation from getting an additional out, rather than scoring a run.

Conclusions

Baseball Prospectus is not the first to realize the value of win expectancy. Attempts by various researchers date back several decades, in fact. What we have done is go beyond a simple analysis of play by play data that determines a static set of win probabilities, to a analytical framework for computing win expectancy in different situations, where we can adjust different parameters, and determine the impact on the change of winning. By being able to model run scoring distributions for full and partial innings, and by being able to vary the run-scoring potential of each team separately, we've invented a flexible framework that lends itself to a greater number of uses than ever before. Park effects on win expectation can be determined. Support Neutral pitching statistics can be recast as Win Expectancy results. Relievers can be assessed based on how they changed a particular game's outcome. Lineup strength can be measured and accounted for. Replacement level concepts can be incorporated. Pitcher usage patterns can be quantified. And that is just the beginning. Many other questions can be answered using this framework, and surely will be in the years to come. The team's goal in a baseball game is to win, and these advances allow us to measure winning from any point in a game or with any state of knowledge more completely than ever before.

TABLE 5. 20 BEST AND 10 WORST STARTING PITCHER SEASON PERFORMANCES (BY SNLVAR)

Year	Name	Team	GS	IP	W	L	RA	FRA	SNVA	SNLVAR
					Best					
1985	Dwight Gooden	NYM	35	276.7	24	4	1.66	1.61	8.33	12.7
1997	Roger Clemens	TOR	34	264	21	7	2.22	2.23	7.86	12.27
2000	Pedro Martinez	BOS	29	217	18	6	1.82	1.84	7.78	11.53
1973	Tom Seaver	NYM	36	290	19	10	2.3	2.3	6.61	11.4
1972	Steve Carlton	PHI	41	346.3	27	10	2.18	2.21	7.07	11.33
1975	Andy Messersmith	LAD	40	319	19	14	2.6	2.58	5.96	10.86
1975	Jim Palmer	BAL	38	322.3	23	11	2.43	2.53	6.72	10.84
1999	Randy Johnson	ARI	35	271.7	17	9	2.85	2.87	6.38	10.75
1995	Greg Maddux	ATL	28	209.7	19	2	1.67	1.67	7.24	10.70
1978	Ron Guidry	NYY	35	273.7	25	3	2.01	2.08	7.17	10.42
1972	Gaylord Perry	CLE	40	341.7	24	16	2.08	2.08	5.99	10.41
1985	John Tudor	SLN	36	275	21	8	2.23	2.22	6.03	10.28
1986	Mike Scott	HOU	37	275.3	18	10	2.39	2.39	5.94	10.11
1996	Kevin Brown	FLO	32	233	17	11	2.32	2.33	5.98	10.08
1999	Pedro Martinez	BOS	29	208.3	22	4	2.38	2.41	6.57	10.02
1997	Greg Maddux	ATL	33	232.7	19	4	2.24	2.21	6.11	10.00
1973	Jim Palmer	BAL	37	295.3	22	9	2.62	2.57	6.3	9.98
1975	Tom Seaver	NYM	36	280.3	22	9	2.6	2.61	5.07	9.87
1977	Jim Palmer	BAL	39	319	20	11	2.99	3.01	5.61	9.81
2000	Randy Johnson	ARI	35	248.7	19	7	3.22	3.17	5.35	9.73

(continued next page)

TABLE 5. 20 BEST AND 10 WORST STARTING PITCHER SEASON PERFORMANCES (BY SNLVAR) *(continued)*

Year	Name	Team	GS	IP	W	L	RA	FRA	SNVA	SNLVAR
					Worst					
1996	Todd Van Poppel	2TM	15	63.3	2	7	11.79	11.4	−3.02	−1.23
1972	John Cumberland	2TM	7	26	0	5	11.42	10.4	−1.97	−1.23
2004	Denny Stark	COL	6	26	0	5	14.88	15.01	−2.13	−1.23
1973	Bill Stoneman	MON	17	75.7	3	8	7.85	8.01	−3.37	−1.23
1972	Steve Renko	MON	12	56.7	1	9	8.1	8.05	−2.71	−1.27
1973	Mike Kekich	2TM	10	35.7	2	5	10.85	10.44	−2.19	−1.31
1984	Mike Brown	BOS	11	54	1	8	8.83	8.75	−2.42	−1.31
1988	Steve Trout	SEA	13	54.3	4	7	8.78	8.72	−2.58	−1.33
1976	Bill Lee	BOS	14	74.3	4	7	7.14	7.26	−2.71	−1.43
1978	Dick Pole	SEA	18	95	4	10	7.2	7.31	−3.29	−1.51
1992	Ryan Bowen	HOU	9	31.7	0	7	12.22	11.92	−2.58	−1.61
1976	Jim Hughes	MIN	26	155.7	7	13	6.19	5.89	−3.89	−1.74
1973	Steve Blass	PIT	18	78	3	9	9.23	8.84	−4.22	−2.19

TABLE 6. 10 BEST AND 10 WORST STARTING PITCHER TEAM PERFORMANCES

Year	Team	GS	IP	T_W	T_L	RA	FRA	SNVA	SNLVAR
					Best				
1997	ATL	162	1096.7	95.4	66.6	3.41	3.4	14.43	33.77
1975	LAD	162	1160.3	95.8	66.2	3.07	3.09	14.79	33.69
1998	ATL	162	1074.7	94.9	67.1	3.4	3.46	14	33.48
1993	ATL	162	1083	94.3	67.7	3.43	3.41	13.76	32.7
1985	NYM	162	1091.7	93.8	68.2	3.08	3.08	12.44	30.96
1999	ATL	162	1051.7	90.2	71.8	4.08	4.17	9.16	30.23
1999	ARI	162	1056.7	90.5	71.5	4.15	4.14	9.47	30.08
1980	OAK	162	1261.3	93.5	68.5	3.62	3.66	12.43	29.97
1979	HOU	162	1115.7	91.1	70.9	3.51	3.5	10.23	29.94
1973	LAD	162	1163	90.4	71.6	3.46	3.45	9.63	29.81
					Worst				
1973	TEX	162	899	70	92	5.61	5.63	−11.12	5.38
2001	TEX	162	926.7	67.4	94.6	6.39	6.4	−13.41	5.37
1999	COL	162	935.3	65.1	96.9	6.65	6.7	−15.73	5.32
2003	TEX	162	832	67.4	94.6	6.6	6.54	−13.52	4.94
1976	MIN	162	987.3	71.5	90.5	4.92	4.84	−9.98	4.7
1995	MIN	144	813.3	59.3	84.7	6.69	6.72	−12.87	4.53
1981	BOS	108	646.3	48	60	4.73	4.78	−5.89	4.28
1993	COL	162	878.7	65.7	96.3	6.08	6.17	−15.07	4.18
1984	SFG	162	884	67.9	94.1	5.39	5.32	−13.26	3.98
1978	SEA	160	881	66.1	93.9	5.65	5.63	−14.02	2.67

TABLE 7. 20 BEST AND 10 WORST RELIEVER SEASON PERFORMANCES

Year	Name	Team	G	IP	SV	RA	FRA	ARP	WX	WXRL
					Best					
1973	John Hiller	DET	65	125.3	38	1.51	-0.48	75.8	7.75	9.64
2003	Eric Gagne	LAD	77	82.3	55	1.31	1.01	36.6	6.8	9.25
1984	Willie Hernandez	DET	80	140.3	32	1.92	1.59	49.2	7.16	9.15
1996	Troy Percival	CAL	62	74	36	2.43	1.06	39.9	6.19	8.38
1998	Trevor Hoffman	SDP	66	73	53	1.48	0.79	35.2	6.06	8.32
2002	Eric Gagne	LAD	77	82.3	52	1.97	1.27	33.4	5.73	8.25
2000	Keith Foulke	CWS	72	88	34	3.17	2.61	30.7	5.97	8.22
1980	Dan Quisenberry	KCR	75	128.3	33	3.37	1.46	51.3	6.21	8.18
2004	Brad Lidge	HOU	80	94.7	29	2	1.14	41.6	5.59	8.13
1977	Rich Gossage	PIT	72	133	26	1.83	0.88	56.4	5.33	8.12
2004	Eric Gagne	LAD	70	82.3	45	2.62	2	28.6	5.35	8
1980	Doug Corbett	MIN	73	136.3	23	2.05	0.76	64.6	6.24	7.93
1979	Aurelio Lopez	DET	61	127	21	2.62	1.89	43.8	6.01	7.93
1996	Trevor Hoffman	SDP	70	88	42	2.35	1.71	31.2	5.42	7.72
2004	Joe Nathan	MIN	73	72.3	44	1.74	1.39	29.9	5.68	7.71
1984	Bruce Sutter	SLN	71	122.7	45	1.91	1.05	45	4.88	7.71
1972	Tug McGraw	NYM	54	106	27	2.21	1	38.8	5.97	7.66
1975	Rich Gossage	CWS	62	141.7	26	2.03	1.07	57.6	5.73	7.63
1977	Bruce Sutter	CHC	62	107.3	31	1.76	1.01	46.9	5.01	7.59
1993	Rod Beck	SFG	76	79.3	48	2.27	1.6	30.6	5.43	7.47
					Worst					
1997	Norm Charlton	SEA	71	69.3	14	7.66	8.02	−20.4	−3.66	−2.26
1979	Rollie Fingers	SDP	54	83.7	13	5.06	5.58	−10.9	−3.96	−2.28
1983	Dan Spillner	CLE	59	92	8	5.28	5.13	−2.1	−3.02	−2.31
1986	Ron Davis	2TM	53	58.7	2	9.2	8.01	−19.8	−2.86	−2.34
2001	Juan Acevedo	2TM	57	60.7	0	5.19	5.34	−4.3	−3.27	−2.57
1998	Bobby Ayala	SEA	62	75.3	8	7.88	7.12	−15.6	−3.92	−2.58
1984	Pete Ladd	MIL	53	87	3	5.48	4.88	−2.2	−3.75	−2.72
1988	Rich Gossage	CHC	46	43.7	13	4.74	5.09	−3.2	−3.29	−2.77
1992	Steve Wilson	LAD	60	66.7	0	5	4.47	−4.8	−3.54	−2.81
1991	Doug Jones	CLE	32	32.3	7	7.52	8.42	−13	−3.9	−3.15

TABLE 8. 10 BEST AND 10 WORST RELIEVER TEAM PERFORMANCES

Year	Team	G	IP	SV	RA	FRA	ARP	WX	WXRL
					Best				
2003	LAD	437	472.3	58	2.61	2.47	118.3	14.19	21.45
2002	ATL	469	512	57	2.9	2.81	103.4	11.33	19.08
1997	BAL	399	477.3	59	3.6	3.29	105.1	10.92	17.89
2001	SEA	391	470.7	56	3.29	2.85	122	10.51	17.75
2003	HOU	502	581.3	50	3.42	3.23	101.9	9.19	17.73
2002	MIN	436	530	47	3.89	3.63	84.3	10.06	16.84
1995	CLE	334	421.7	50	3.52	3.2	102.7	10.54	16.29
2004	LAD	459	518	51	3.3	3.29	92	8.75	16.27
1996	SDP	411	512.7	47	3.7	3.38	85.1	9.06	16.07
1998	SDP	369	421	59	3.74	3.37	68.5	8.88	15.98
					Worst				
1979	SDP	280	448.3	25	4.06	4.27	8.5	−8.1	−2.39
1991	CLE	289	409	33	4.84	4.84	−1.2	−7.24	−2.41
1980	SLN	297	416.7	27	4.58	4.37	−8.1	−7.04	−2.59
1992	PHI	323	422.3	34	4.62	4.62	-28.4	−7.62	−2.6
1978	NYM	270	417	26	4.1	3.94	9.7	−8.14	−2.93
1974	CAL	189	294	12	4.68	4.31	5	−5.04	−2.94
1993	NYM	298	373.3	22	5.33	5.19	−22.1	−8.81	−3.36
1990	ATL	346	447.3	30	5.61	5.75	−65.7	−9.82	−4.57
1973	ATL	276	385.7	33	5.58	5.43	−46.2	−11.26	−6.54
1999	KCR	416	485.3	29	6.23	6.21	−35.5	−13.97	−7.59

TABLE 8. 10 BEST AND 10 WORST RELIEVER TEAM PERFORMANCES

Year	Team	G	IP	SV	RA	FRA	ARP	WX	WXRL
					Best				
2003	LAD	437	472.3	58	2.61	2.47	118.3	14.19	21.45
2002	ATL	469	512	57	2.9	2.81	103.4	11.33	19.08
1997	BAL	399	477.3	59	3.6	3.29	105.1	10.92	17.89
2001	SEA	391	470.7	56	3.29	2.85	122	10.51	17.75
2003	HOU	502	581.3	50	3.42	3.23	101.9	9.19	17.73
2002	MIN	436	530	47	3.89	3.63	84.3	10.06	16.84
1995	CLE	334	421.7	50	3.52	3.2	102.7	10.54	16.29
2004	LAD	459	518	51	3.3	3.29	92	8.75	16.27
1996	SDP	411	512.7	47	3.7	3.38	85.1	9.06	16.07
1998	SDP	369	421	59	3.74	3.37	68.5	8.88	15.98

Year	Team	G	IP	SV	RA	FRA	ARP	WX	WXRL
					Worst				
1979	SDP	280	448.3	25	4.06	4.27	8.5	−8.1	−2.39
1991	CLE	289	409	33	4.84	4.84	−1.2	−7.24	−2.41
1980	SLN	297	416.7	27	4.58	4.37	−8.1	−7.04	−2.59
1992	PHI	323	422.3	34	4.62	4.62	−28.4	−7.62	−2.6
1978	NYM	270	417	26	4.1	3.94	9.7	−8.14	−2.93
1974	CAL	189	294	12	4.68	4.31	5	−5.04	−2.94
1993	NYM	298	373.3	22	5.33	5.19	−22.1	−8.81	−3.36
1990	ATL	346	447.3	30	5.61	5.75	−65.7	−9.82	−4.57
1973	ATL	276	385.7	33	5.58	5.43	−46.2	−11.26	−6.54
1999	KCR	416	485.3	29	6.23	6.21	−35.5	−13.97	−7.59

TABLE 9. 10 HIGHEST AND 10 LOWEST LEVERAGE RELIEVER SEASONS (MIN 40 GAMES)

Year	Name	Team	G	IP	SV	ARP	WX	WXRL	LEVERAGE
				Highest					
2000	Troy Percival	ANA	54	50	32	-0.2	-1.05	0.61	2.59
1986	Jeff Reardon	MON	62	89	35	11.4	0.84	3.22	2.55
1985	Rich Gossage	SDN	50	79	26	19.7	3.71	5.48	2.41
1992	Lee Smith	SLN	70	75	43	3.2	0.5	2.62	2.4
2000	Trevor Hoffman	SDN	70	72.3	43	15.4	1.15	3.83	2.36
1996	Randy Myers	BAL	62	58.7	31	11.1	0.59	2.32	2.35
1996	Trevor Hoffman	SDN	70	88	42	31.2	5.42	7.72	2.33
2000	John Wetteland	TEX	62	60	34	-1.5	-0.56	1.79	2.31
1996	Roberto Hernandez	CHA	72	84.7	38	37.6	4.25	6.25	2.29
1999	Troy Percival	ANA	60	57	31	9.8	0.81	2.88	2.29
				Lowest					
1996	Rodney Myers	CHC	45	67.3	0	−8.2	−0.76	−0.28	0.5
2003	Gary Glover	2TM	42	62.7	0	0.6	−0.35	−0.09	0.49
2004	Jay Witasick	SDP	44	61.7	1	11.4	−0.4	−0.2	0.47
2001	David Lee	SDP	41	48.7	0	9.7	0.43	0.7	0.47
1976	Dave Tomlin	SDP	48	71	0	25.5	0.61	0.78	0.47
1997	Todd Ritchie	MIN	42	74.7	0	2.5	−0.81	−0.41	0.45
2004	C. J. Nitkowski	2TM	41	33	0	−8.5	−0.47	−0.41	0.43
1987	Greg Booker	SDP	44	68.3	1	10.1	−0.15	0.15	0.42
2001	Lou Pote	ANA	43	81.7	2	9	−0.13	0.3	0.41
2003	Jay Powell	TEX	51	58.7	0	−18.5	−0.11	0.03	0.31

Life, Death, and Zombies

by Derek Zumsteg

How did we get here?

A brief timeline of the current Nationals franchise:

1969—Montreal Expos born. They go 52–100. Also, man walks on the moon in one of humanity's greatest achievements.

1971—Man plays golf on the moon. The Expos go 71–90.

Then, for a long time, nothing happened.

1979–1981—team enjoys brief run of success, winning division in 1981.

Ten years pass as the team remains average with one good year. (1987)

1990s—Despite modest payrolls of $14–$20 million the team puts together a sustained run at contention.

1994—The strike ends a brilliant 74-40 season and the Expos' chance at a second playoff run.

1995–1999—Players leave. The team gets worse. Attempts to build a new stadium fail. The relationship between ownership and the city of Montreal become acrimonious.

1999—A group of Montreal investors buys the team to keep it in town. It includes New York art dealer Jeffrey Loria, who owns 24% of the team.

2000—By making a series of cash calls the other owners refuse to answer, Loria increases his stake in the team from 24 to 94%. This money is spent on Graeme Lloyd and other useless parts as the team doubles payroll and gets one game better.

November 6, 2001—Commissioner Bud Selig announces that baseball will be eliminating two teams (Expos, Twins) and paying off their owners.

2001—MLB pays Loria $120 million for the Expos, and loans him $38.5 million so that he can buy the Marlins from John Henry for $158.5 million. John Henry buys the Red Sox.

2001 to late 2004—Relocation effort is headed by Bob DuPuy ("Formerly Bud Selig's personal lawyer"). MLB announces deadlines for moving the team, extends deadlines, sets newer, more serious deadlines, repeats for four years. Key requirements for host cities include willingness to build the team a new—and free—stadium.

Which brings us to Washington, D.C. and the current situation.

Baseball spent years watching baseball in Montreal fail, and did nothing. That they spent years paralyzed between stalling to get a better deal and needing to make a move because the situation was embarrassing and teams were getting restless that paying to operate their competition is almost expected. Take Olympic Stadium. It was supposed to open in 1976. It was late because of labor problems. The roof didn't get completed until 1987, when the Expos had been there for 10 years. Five years later, it had to be permanently closed. Six years after that in 1998, the roof was removed and then later replaced by another, different roof. Then the team left for Washington, D.C.

What wasn't to like? A population of over three million, though other sports like football would compete for attention. Excellent public transportation to an existing site that had once supported baseball and also to potential new stadium sites. A history of supporting good baseball teams in the past. But enough about Montreal.

Before I move on, I want to write my piece on this. The best place for the Expos was Montreal. Baseball didn't feel a moral duty to rebuild the franchise. It seemed to think the path to making baseball more of an international sport started with abandoning a French-speaking Canadian city. They don't have to agree with me on any of points, of course. I will not deny that the Expos could not draw a million fans in recent years, but what reason did even a die-hard baseball fan have go see a bad team without an owner, without a future, and so support the very people who'd done them so wrong, for so long? The least MLB could do is confess to their role in poisoning the city and destroying relationships, creating a situation in which the team could could do little but move.

I feel better now.

To the situation at hand, It was always going to be D.C. BP's Dayn Perry wrote a piece in *The Washington Monthly* back in December of 2001 that correctly pointed out baseball would end up in D.C., no matter what happened between now and then.

It is a tremendous media market. There's money. Moving baseball to D.C. helps the often-strained relationship between the two. A sport that enjoys lying to Congress and has a unique and bizarre anti-trust exemption, and a Congress that likes to stick its big nose into places it doesn't belong if it means more camera time and appearances on shows like *Firing Squad and Bare-knuckle Punditry.* Congress' wailing-baby reaction to losing the Senators the last time turned into a long campaign of subtle arm-twisting and public Indian rubs. This year, baseball cried "uncle" and gave up.

Teams have political weight. Many people can name their President, even their Senators, some their Congressional Representative. Fewer know who represents them in the state legislature. City council, forget it. Baseball players, the manager, the GM—they all enjoy major name recognition. They get free dinners and free . . . other things. Charges against those who get an "Honorable" ahead of their name and those who wear a uniform with their name on the back tend to get dropped, lost, pled down to innocuous misdemeanors. Now, the connection can be made directly. I can guarantee you there will be extremely expensive seat licensing or charter fees for premium seats, tickets for which will have a face value just under the limit for gifts to government officials.

And baseball, in return, will be rewarded for this act. Fewer subpoenas. Embarrassing hearings and investigations cut short, executives removed from the witness lists.

That kind of political maneuvering is also available to those who opposed the move as well. Baseball in D.C. almost left town for Christmas this year, and for about a week, nobody was in the holiday spirit. It was MLB's own fault. In the last D.C. Council elections, pro-baseball council members lost ground to those who opposed it. With remarkable speed, baseball settled on a site and got down to the business of moving in.

Baseball quickly struck a bargain with the mayor of D.C., Anthony Williams, for the return of Major League Baseball. The bargain, in this sense, was more "a remarkably good deal for baseball" than it was "an agreement reached through haggling." The deal included a new, modern stadium at the Navy Yard site, to be completed by 2008, entirely funded by the businesses and residents of the District; the city would cover cost overruns, and if the stadium wasn't completed on time, it would have to pay huge penalties.

Baseball's owners voted to move the team. They held one of those silly meetings with people and announcements and uniforms and protesters.

Here's an experiment for those of you with unlimited cash on your hands. Ask three contractors for bids on some modest home improvement (a new helipad, for instance). Get preliminary estimates. Then announce you absolutely must have one of them, and that you have unlimited cash. See what their final bid comes in at.

Linda Cropp is at the center of this part of the story. As the Chairman of the City Council, she could have put off passing any stadium bill forever. She toyed with this for a while, and it appeared for a while that she would block stadium legislation if it didn't build the new ballpark on a site right next to RFK Stadium. When she did let the bill out to play, it took several amendments during a marathon session, and came out barely resembling the one that went in, entirely different in several important aspects than the one baseball had agreed to:

- 50% of the stadium financed by private interests
- Cost overruns over $50 million covered by baseball
- To be paid by tax on gross receipts, concessions, rent payments

The concerns about the cost were well-founded. Optimists, like those in the mayor's office, said the new house of baseball might only cost $440 million. Others disagree, with other more realistic estimates starting at almost a hundred million more and taking off from there. Signing on for potentially massive costs of unknown duration would be crazy.

And there's a bigger issue—MLB, by its own admission, has immense sums of money lying around. If a stadium is such a great deal, especially if it would help get the team off the largesse of revenue sharing and help all teams, and if a successful franchise in D.C. is good for baseball—and particularly considering the political benefits baseball intends to reap—why didn't baseball pony up the cash itself? How good of a deal can it be if baseball prefers to earn 2.5% on CDs instead of investing in this?

In retaliation for this cheeky display of independence, MLB pulled all business and promotional operations for the team the next day. The heated trailer outside RFK selling Nationals merchandise shut its door. The Nationals web site still advertised season ticket sales, but linked to a page refusing to take deposits. The team's page also ran a constant refund offer for those who'd already made the mistake of handing over money. MLB gave D.C. 15 days to give up their plan and approve the original deal.

MLB began meeting with the other, recently spurned suitors again. Mysterious, crazy rumors floated. Baseball was going to contract the team after one season in RFK. They'd play a year and move somewhere else. They might even return to Montreal.

The threats were empty. Baseball's better off with a team in a modern stadium, making money and contributing to the revenue sharing pool, plus the national broadcast contracts were signed for 30 teams, and there would have to be compromises struck or lawsuits settled, neither of which would come cheap.

There would be no move: the best other candidate, Northern Virginia's financing package, expired on December 31st. Getting funding passed again would be extremely difficult, made worse by baseball's commitment to D.C. Even if the legislation could get funded again, it still wouldn't resolve the basic problem posed by the Northern Virginia sites' bad location. The other sites all had severe financing problems that weren't going to be resolved quickly. Moreover, even if a stadium were built, the other options were all worse than D.C. when it came down to viably supporting a team. Another location would almost certainly make the selling price lower and, hundreds of millions of dollars into this, baseball wanted as much money as they can get in return for their years of mismanagement.

Baseball had stuck itself in D.C., and was going to have to live with it. They'd announced the move in a hurry, panicked by the last set of elections where pro-stadium council members caught fire and went down. The public did not support public funding of the stadium, and were electing people who were of a like mind. If a deal was to be struck, it had to be struck now, with the lame-duck council.

But how could a compromise be reached? Mayor Anthony Williams reportedly did not talk to council Chairman Linda Cropp for days. Baseball said they wouldn't negotiate with the city, that they would either agree to the original deal or the whole thing was off. And, in particular, if they were going to negotiate, it wouldn't be with anyone but the mayor, who'd agreed to the initial deal.

Baseball knuckled under. It only took them a week. It had to. Bob DuPuy, leader of this botched operation, called Cropp. Together with the mayor, baseball hammered out a new deal over the phone.

It's notable too how far baseball was willing to come off the original deal:

If a new stadium doesn't open by March of 2008, the City's on the hook for a year's rent at RFK Stadium, instead of maybe $20 million in the deal Williams signed. The city will continue to seek private financing for the stadium. During the week of purgatory, there was interest from companies, willing to come up with cash, Citibank being the largest and most prominent, which is hopeful.

Instead of the city picking up the cost of overruns, the District and MLB are going to share the cost of insurance for cost overruns. Given the recent history of stadium building, that insurance should be quite expensive and necessary.

The construction is to be funded with a tax on businesses and a utility tax on businesses and federal offices. Compared to some funding mechanisms like a sales tax increase, this is relative benign, though it's a fair point that taxing the federal government is self-taxation.

The new deal passed 7–6 at the next Council meeting.

Joy! Rapture! In a statement, baseball claimed it was happy with the original agreement had been upheld even though it hadn't. The venomous claims, treats, and flirtations with other attractive cities were forgotten. "We are now more confident than ever of a long and productive relationship with the city," Bud Selig's statement said. The Nationals president said he'd be contacting the 563 fans who'd asked for their season ticket deposits back to see if they still wanted their money back, or if maybe, you know, they'd like to re-consider, since everyone had calmed down. Renovations at RFK resumed.

The trailer with merchandise re-opened, and fans can see the uniforms the team was going to unveil at a ceremony they cancelled out of spite. Which, let's just be honest, was petty. The team was going to have uniforms, even if they only played in RFK for a year. Couldn't baseball, even in those hard times, have conducted itself with some grace for what, at worst, would have turned out to be temporary hosts?

Can baseball survive in Washington D.C.?

Of course it can. There are eight million people in the Washington-Baltimore metro area. About 65% of them are in the DC-MD-VA-WV primary metro area, as defined by the Census Bureau. Per capita income is above the national average, though the cost of living's also a little higher. Public transportation's good.

So why did it fail twice?

It's not because of race. Or, at least, it's not about the fact that there are not many white people in D.C.

It's true, the biggest demographic difference between the residents of D.C. and those of other cities is that D.C. residents, on average, contain significantly more skin pigment.Sixty percent of them identified themselves as "Black or African American" in 2000—compared to the national figure of about 12%. Atlanta's close, but even Atlanta's never had great success at marketing to their African-American population, and instead draws more heavily from affluent white suburbs like Marietta. I would humbly suggest that maybe doing the tomahawk chant doesn't do a lot to make black people comfortable. But what do I know? Whatever the reasons, there are not a lot of black people going "Oh, way-oh-way-oh, oh-way-oh, oh-way..." at Turner Field.

It's interesting that baseball took the Expos from a multi-cultural environment where they had seen success, complained that they could never make it work because of the language and culture gaps, and moved it to the only city to have teams leave it twice because they didn't want to figure out how to market to their market, and didn't much want black people showing up at games, anyway.

This race thing has come up twice in the stories of both franchises that left the city. During the Senators' first run, owner Clark Griffith was far from being the black people's best friend. He resisted integration while running a baseball team in a city where blacks comprised the majority of the population (D.C. was the first large black-majority city in the country). When white people fled D.C. and urban decline eroded his fan base further, Griffith packed up and moved for whiter pastures. Minnesota. He justified his move thusly: "Black people don't go to ball games, but they'll fill up a rassling ring and put up such a chant they'll scare you to death. We came [to Minnesota] because you've got good, hardworking white people here."

Hey, rassling ring, scary chants—it's Atlanta again! Sorry.

With half a century of history in Washington, instead of changing to better reflect their community, or really making any attempt to see what could be done to bring in new fans, they packed up and took off. If I knew where Clark Griffith was buried, I'd go piss on his grave.

Baseball got another try in 1961. Playing in Griffith Stadium (seriously, screw that guy), they lasted ten years before Robert Short moved them to Texas. He made race an issue too, in the same way teams to today, by talking around it. He had problems with the neighborhood.

While the team didn't move until 1971, the riots after Martin Luther King Jr's assassination in April of 1968 gave Short all the reasons he'd need to move. It's difficult to convey in a short form like this the scale of devastation the riots wrought in D.C. Before President Johnson called in the troops, entire business districts were gutted and burned. The city's economy was decimated. Decimate's a word that's lost much of its original meaning—to kill one in ten—but that's easily what happened to stores across the District.

The day after MLK was buried, the Senators played their first home game against the Twins, the city was still under curfew, and there were some fourteen thousand military men in the District enforcing order, checkpoints, and tanks at many intersections.

Like the other cities that were racked with riots in the aftermath of the assassination, many of the problems D.C. fights today can be traced back to what happened that April. Many looted and burned-out businesses never reopened. The frustrated and frightened people who'd founded them left the area. White families who'd stayed through the city's changing composition were persuaded to abandon it by the open hostility and violence they faced, the collapsing educational system, and spiraling economy.

Just as baseball abandoned a city that didn't meet its owner's racial preferences, so Robert Short used the riots and the city's dire situation to drive down attendance. When he said that the stadium wasn't safe, people believed him and stayed away. He moved the team to Texas, sold them, and made a tidy profit. This was probably his plan all along; he'd previously made a ton of money moving the Lakers to Los Angeles from Minnesota. Race and safety, the riots, and the city's other problems were all convenient pretexts to a monetary end.

Could baseball have survived? We can't say for certain. D.C. would have been an extremely difficult market over the last three decades for any owner. Especially the 70s. Also the 80s. The 1990s things would have been a little better. That of course neglects the complicated political situation in D.C. That would have been tough the whole time.

So did the racial makeup of D.C. cause two teams to leave? No, a racist owner and, later, this country's shameful history, long-standing tensions, and a white racist with a rifle played a huge role in making D.C. inhospitable to baseball. There has not been any kind of clearly demonstrated social, cultural, or racial barrier to enjoyment of the sport.

That doesn't really answer the question, though. Sure, the D.C. of today is potentially as good or better a market for a baseball team as most teams are in now. Can that potential be realized? Or, as everyone wants to ask but is afraid to: "Will black people come out to games?" And let's answer that with a question: what kind of bullshit is that? Is there something inherent in the sport that turns off people with melanin? If so, how come darker people in the Caribbean are crazy for it? Arte Moreno in Anaheim is trying to build a Latino fan base—you want to tell me that black people aren't worth the effort? Many of the arguments about why baseball can't draw black fans seem to center around some conception of black fans that reveals more about those who advance them than it does about the problem. Baseball's going to have to crack this nut one way or another if wants to survive for the long term. The nation's not getting any whiter. It's time to reach out. Good franchises know this and are working on it, investing quietly. Bad franchises don't care about finding these new fans, in the same way teams once didn't care about integrating.

I don't have easy answers about what to do to bring a diverse fan base through the gates a 162 times a year. There's no advanced formula that BP has developed that allows us to translate things like a city's love for their baseball team, and predict how a team can best construct a strategy to build that kind of deep emotional attachment.

This is the failure of my experience, and of Griffith's, and of Stone's: we lack the necessary perspective. No company that sells products to women would attempt to do it with an all-male work force, but baseball ownership and management is by and large a group of white guys who scout, sign, coach, manage non-white players and scratch their heads at why only white people come out to games.

Diversity isn't only about token hires, it's about additional views on problems, new insights born of different experiences. Washington could start by trying to build a team that reflects the city. Find a diverse group of local owners. If Frank Robinson wants to retire, there are other black managers who could use the chance. When Bowden gets fired, there are qualified candidates who aren't white retreads. Hire team marketing and operations people out of the community. As long as the team's playing in RFK, open the doors and don't price the entire middle class out of coming in, try and get fans in the door and see what you can do for them.

With luck, effort, and wisdom, maybe team can be remade and marketed, and in doing so finally work off the debt of damage and ill will baseball's accumulated in its shabby treatment of D.C. and its populace. Baseball can work in the District of Columbia, just as it works in twenty-nine other places in the country with vastly different local populations, and just as it worked, briefly, in Montreal.

Top 50 Prospects

by Rany Jazayerli and Baseball Prospectus

Hi, and welcome to our Top Prospects chapter. It was six years ago that we first decided to tweak the noses of the scouting establishment by ranking the best prospects in baseball in our own inimitable way—without spending hundreds of hours at the ballpark waiting to see if Eric Chavez bails on breaking balls from left-handers or whether Jerome Williams telegraphs his changeup; without knowing which prospect has the Good Face, which one has a thick lower body, or which one has intangibles. Armed simply with the finest analytical tools available to us, along with a smattering of input from people within the game, we blindly threw our hat into the ring against an industry that had been doing this for years with access to infinitely more information than we did.

We've done pretty well so far, considering.

But we've tried to get better every year, which is why a major part of our preparation for each year's list is to look back at lists from years past, to try to learn from our mistakes and reinforce our good judgments. It was from ranking too high guys like Jackie Rexrode that we learned that minor league players with incredible OBPs but negligible power tend to lose the ability to get on base as they face better pitchers. It was from ranking too highly guys like Pablo Ozuna and Abraham Nunez based largely on their dates of birth—which turned out to be wildly inaccurate—that we learned how easy it is to come to a wrong conclusion when your data is faulty to begin with. And it was from Ryan Anderson that we learned to never, ever, ever, EVER rank a pitcher as the #1 prospect in baseball. (Gary Huckabay may have coined the acronym TINSTAAPP, but Anderson was most assuredly its creator.)

Last year, we learned something that economists have known for years: groups of people tend to make better decisions collectively than they do individually, especially when it's a matter of estimating the value of a resource. The inefficiencies in baseball economics stem from the fact that there are only 30 buyers and a few dozen sellers on the free-agent market every winter. If there were 300 teams in the major leagues, there would be 50 GMs like Billy Beane all looking for underappreciated talent and it would be that much harder for him to exploit market inefficiencies.

Groups are also better than individuals when it comes to predicting the future. Futures markets for commodities can be surprisingly accurate at predicting the actual value of that commodity six months later. The reason is simple: the more people involved in setting a market, the more information being used to reach market equilibrium. The more information available, the more accurate the prediction.

Which brings us back to the lesson we learned last year about our Top Prospect list, which is, after all, nothing more than a minor league player futures market. Last year, for the first time, all our authors were engaged in compiling our list. As you may know if you read on our web site the exhaustive transcript of our round table discussions, the process was long, grueling, and occasionally heated. But the result was probably our best list ever. Players who generated very different opinions, like Dioner Navarro or Scott Hairston, ended up being ranked lower than their supporters, and higher than their detractors, would have liked—but in retrospect, their final ranking was probably more accurate than either camp alone would have come up with.

At the same time, the first person who whispered that they thought David Wright was worthy of a Top 5 spot wasn't laughed at, but instead, received a growing swell of support that decided, yes, Wright really was that good. The eventual unanimity of the sentiment made the decision much easier to reach as a group, given that Wright didn't have the markings of a top prospect. He hadn't reached Double-A yet and hit only .270 with 15 homers in 2003.

Wright, of course, was called up in mid-season and established himself as one of the brightest young stars in baseball, but in doing so was eliminated from this year's list. Indeed, the list was dramatically affected by the promotions of some of the best players in the minor leagues, who ended up playing just enough in the majors to lose their rookie status. Wright and Justin Morneau weren't even close, but B. J. Upton (like Wright and Morneau, a potential #1 prospect) top 10 candidates such as Grady Sizemore, and even unheralded but promising prospects such as Ruben Gotay and Jorge Cantu, became ineligible by a hair.

One player's rookie eligibility situation—not to mention his talent—is so special that he requires his own section, which is why we are proud to announce an unprecedented honor to . . .

Prospect of the Year Emeritus: Joe Mauer, C, Minnesota

Joe Mauer is an excellent illustration of why Major League Baseball's peculiar definition of rookie status actually makes some sense. Mauer arrived to great fanfare last year when he was, by general consensus, the best prospect in baseball, and became the rare catcher to start on Opening Day in his major league debut. But he injured his knee the next day, and after returning in June, re-aggravated the injury in July and missed the rest of the season, finishing with only 109 at-bats. For that reason, you will still see Mauer listed as a prospect in other publications even though he spent the entire season on the Twins' roster, exceeding the limit of 45 days (before September 1st) needed to retain his rookie status. And in reality, no one in baseball thinks of Mauer as a prospect; they think of him as an established major leaguer.

But lest his limited playing time cause him to be somewhat forgotten this year, we've created this special section for him. His knee injury may have people questioning his future behind the plate—something we questioned ourselves last year when we noted that catchers as tall as Mauer tend to develop poorly, but in barely 100 at-bats last season, he showed enough hitting prowess for us believe he can develop into a superstar, even if he never catches another game again.

Not convinced? Then consider this: Mauer became only the 18th player in major league history to:

1. come to the plate 100 or more times in a season
2. bat .300 or better
3. have an isolated power of .200 or higher
4. be 21 or younger at the conclusion of the season

This isn't some arcane set of criteria. Basically, we're talking about hitters who showed the ability to hit for both average and power at a very young age. Of the 17 hitters who came before Mauer, *fourteen* of them are either in the Hall of Fame or are headed that way. We're talking about the very best hitters of the live-ball era: Hank Aaron, Orlando Cepeda, Joe DiMaggio, Jimmie Foxx, Al Kaline, Mickey Mantle, Eddie Mathews, Willie McCovey, Mel Ott, Babe Ruth, and Ted Williams are in the Hall, while Ken Griffey Jr., Alex Rodriguez, and Albert Pujols are, shall we say, favored to win induction one day.

The other three players—the three worst players among Mauer's comparables—are Cesar Cedeno, Gregg Jefferies, and Hal Trosky. When Gregg Jefferies is the absolute worst player on your comp list, you're doing well.

Sure, it's premature to rank a player with the all-time greats based on 35 games of experience. But it's not like this would be out of the question for Mauer who, after all, was our #1 prospect last year and the #1 draft pick in 2001. And given that the one knock on him was that he hadn't developed the power everyone expected, the fact that he set a career-high with six homers in those 35 games has to be reassuring.

Maybe he won't be a catcher for the majority of his career. Maybe he won't be a catcher on May Day. But Mauer is one of the brightest young talents to hit the majors in a long, long time. At any position.

And now, our Prospect of the Year for 2005 . . .

1. Andy Marte   3B   Atlanta Braves   Age 21

	AVG	OBP	SLG	Defense
2003	.268	.343	.463	3B: −14
2004	.238	.326	.471	3B: +6

5-Year WARP Trend: 3.4, 3.6, 4.5, 5.4, 5.6

No doubt the general consensus within the scouting community is that Marte is an excellent prospect, but I suspect that our selection of Marte as the best prospect in baseball will raise more than a few eyebrows. He certainly hasn't posted the gaudy statistics that you'd expect from a top prospect—he's never hit 25 homers, or walked 70 times, or batted .300 in a season. He's considered a fine third baseman, but is not exactly a Brooks Robinson with the glove. He's still very young, but there are no fewer than 17 prospects on this list who are younger.

So what are we doing, giving our #1 ranking to a player that really doesn't do anything exceptionally well, a player that most minor league experts don't even consider the best prospect in his organization? Marte's promise can't be summed up in a single number—his potential stems from his across-the-board skills. Maybe he doesn't do anything *exceptionally* well, but he does just about *everything* well.

His .274 lifetime average isn't bad at all when you consider he has spent almost his entire career in pitchers' parks, and his career .479 slugging average is outstanding for a player who has always been among the youngest players in his league. More than any other skill, isolated power augurs very well for the player who displays it at a very young age. Marte shows unusual command of the strike zone for a young player, with 127 walks in fewer than 900 at-bats the last two seasons. His OPS has increased every year since he turned pro, even as he has faced stiffer competition each year. He was rated the best defensive third baseman in the Southern League last year. He has been very durable throughout his career; a sprained ankle that cost him a month of last season was his first significant injury. He is in an organization that for the past 15 years has done an almost eerily good job of converting top prospects into top players. His PECOTA projection forecasts him to have more value over the next five years than every other prospect in baseball save one (more on him later.) It helps that the most comparable player to Marte in our database is Miguel Cabrera.

Maybe he doesn't have the highest upside of any player on this list, although an above-average defensive third baseman who hits .300 with 30 homers and 80 walks every year sounds like a superstar to me. But upside alone doesn't make a top prospect. There's also the little matter of how likely he is to reach his upside. And with such a broad foundation of skills to build from, the time to build on that foundation, and a support system with the Braves that will help him reach his potential, Marte has that rare combination of high upside and low risk. No one else on this list has that. Which is why no one else is our #1 prospect.

2. Delmon Young OF Tampa Bay Devil Rays Age: 19

	AVG	OBP	SLG	Defense
2004	.280	.332	.456	RF: 0

5-Year WARP Trend: 1.9, 2.3, 2.5, 2.7, 2.3

Marte and Young were the only two players seriously considered for our top spot, and the competition between winner and runner-up was the closest since we went with Eric Chavez over J. D. Drew back in 1999. Both Young and Marte posted numbers last season that translated almost precisely at the major league average. In the end, we decided that Marte's many small advantages—his position, his defense, his longer track record, his proximity to the majors, and perhaps most of all, his organization—trumps Young's one big advantage. But what an advantage that is.

Young played all of last season at age 18 and is two full years younger than Marte. Two years is a significant difference when evaluating any two players, and when those two years are between ages 18 and 20, when a player typically shows the most dramatic improvement of his career, that difference can be huge. Young's performance last season, when he bludgeoned the South Atlantic League to the tune of .322/.388/.538, is exceedingly rare for a player his age. Young's translated EqA last season was .270; only two 18-year-old players in the last decade have put up a higher EqA, and one of them is Adrian Beltre.

The other, though, is Sean Burroughs, who really hasn't improved as a hitter in the last five years. Much can happen on the way from the low minors to major league stardom, which is why, even though Young has hit everywhere he's played, from high school to the Arizona Fall League, he doesn't earn our #1 spot. But he's certainly the odds-on favorite to be #1 next year. Assuming he's not already in the Devil Rays' lineup.

3. Felix Hernandez RHP Seattle Mariners Age 19

	H/9	BB/9	K/9	HR/9	ERA	DERA
2003	8.5	4.5	7.1	1.0	4.76	4.48
2004	8.4	3.3	7.0	0.7	4.41	3.84

5-Year WARP Trend: 1.9, 2.1, 2.0, 1.8, 2.0

You can argue with a lot of our decisions in this chapter, but there's one thing you can't question: Felix Hernandez is the best pitching prospect in baseball. He may be the most preternatural prospect since Dwight Gooden's comet streaked across the sky over 20 years ago. Hernandez, just 18 years old last season, was dominant in the hitter-friendly California League, and then cut through hitters in the Texas League like a knife through butter. Overall, he struck out 172 batters in 149 innings, becoming the youngest professional pitcher in at least a decade to strike out that many hitters. And—this really ought to be impossible—King Felix complemented his strikeouts with one of the highest G/F ratios of any minor league pitcher. What's more unfair: his 97 mph fastball or his jaw-dropping, knee-buckling curveball? Or maybe it's his slider, which is guarded with more secrecy than the Manhattan Project, but is reputed to be the nastiest pitch of them all? Hernandez has the greatest combination of power, precision, and precocity in a generation. Gooden's career was stunted in large part because of the huge workloads of his youth. But in our new, more enlightened era of moderate workloads for young pitchers, Hernandez is the first pitcher to come along with Gooden-caliber stuff and potential. Here's hoping he reaches all of it.

4. Dallas McPherson 3B Anaheim Angels Age 24

	AVG	OBP	SLG	Defense
2003	.253	.340	.480	3B: –1
2004	.256	.321	.523	3B: –19

5-Year WARP Trend: 3.2, 3.4, 3.4, 3.6, 3.7

He's not particularly young for a prospect. In fact, for a top prospect, he's downright old—he turns 25 in July. But McPherson is one of the best prospects in baseball anyway because he has the most polished power bat of any player in the minor leagues, and was probably ready for a third-base job in the majors two years ago. Last season, he swatted 36 doubles, 40 homers, and even 14 triples between two minor league stops. For the record, that's 90 extra-base hits—not even including the four he hit with the Angels in September. In the last decade, only two other minor leaguers (Joe Dillon last year and Adam Piatt in 1999) have hit even 85. With Troy Glaus in Arizona, the third-base job in Anaheim is McPherson's to lose. He won't.

5. Casey Kotchman 1B Anaheim Angels Age 22

	AVG	OBP	SLG	Defense
2003	.288	.364	.434	1B: +1
2004	.281	.336	.388	1B: +7

5-Year WARP Trend: 2.9, 3.6, 3.5, 4.2, 4.8

Not to say the Angels' first-round pick in 2001 is a line-drive machine, but in seven minor-league stops, he has hit at least .333 in six of them, and at least .350 in five of them. Kotchman brings more than singles to the table; he should be good for 40 doubles a year, he walks more than he strikes out, and he's a potential Gold Glover at first base. Kotchman is a better player than Darin Erstad right now in every facet of the game, other than cashing paychecks. Unlike McPherson, Kotchman doesn't have a ready job anytime soon, but talent like his will get a chance soon enough—if not in Anaheim, then elsewhere.

6. Ian Stewart 3B Colorado Rockies Age 20

	AVG	OBP	SLG	Defense
2003	.224	.291	.379	3B: −7
2004	.245	.315	.449	3B: +13

5-Year WARP Trend: 2.3, 2.7, 2.8, 3.1, 3.5

For years, the Colorado Rockies stood by a draft philosophy that said, in essence, we can't lure pitchers to our ballpark, so let's develop our own. First-round pick after first-round pick was used to procure pitching, even though Coors Field diminishes the value of even the best pitchers by limiting their innings, and even though the team's one legitimate first-round success was a hitter, Todd Helton. The team finally came to its senses in 2003 and realized that if their ballpark can make a bad hitter <COUGHvinnycastillaCOUGH> look good, imagine what it can do for legitimately good hitters, the kind you can find in the first round of the draft?

Ian Stewart is the result of this experiment, and so far he's looking good. Just 19 years old, Stewart bombarded the South Atlantic League to the tune of .319/.398/.594 with 30 homers. Not bad for a third baseman, especially one whose defensive numbers last year were outstanding. Stewart would be a top prospect in any organization; add 81 games in Coors Field and the mind boggles at the statistical barrage he could muster in a few years.

7. Joel Guzman SS Los Angeles Dodgers Age 20

	AVG	OBP	SLG	Defense
2003	.204	.229	.343	SS: −14
2004	.262	.299	.479	SS: 0

5-Year WARP Trend: 2.2, 1.5, 1.9, 1.9, 2.8

High-profile signings of amateur players from outside the U.S. have gotten a bad rep over the years, as anyone old enough to remember players like Glenn Williams and Jose Pett can attest. But recently, at least, teams that shelled out record bonuses have been pleased with their investments. The $2.25 million the Dodgers gave Guzman in 2001 was the highest signing bonus ever given to a teenager from Latin America. But like the man whose record he broke—Miguel Cabrera, who signed with the Marlins for $1.8 million in 1999—Guzman looks to be worth every penny. Guzman crushed 67 extra-base hits last year between A-ball and Double-A—not bad for a shortstop who played the whole season at age 19. He still has to work on his plate discipline, and there are many who think he'll have to change positions soon, simply because he's so damn tall—depending on the source, he's listed between 6′4″ and 6′6″. (No player listed at 6′5″ in major league history has played even 50 career games at shortstop.) But much as Cal Ripken and Alex Rodriguez changed the perception of what a shortstop could look like, Guzman might be able to raise the bar even higher. Sure, he could be the next Chad Hermansen, but he's equally likely to be the next step in the evolution of the elite major league shortstop.

8. Prince Fielder 1B Milwaukee Brewers Age 21

	AVG	OBP	SLG	Defense
2003	.258	.336	.450	1B: −14
2004	.244	.329	.431	1B: −11

5-Year WARP Trend: 1.9, 2.6, 3.6, 3.6, 4.3

After pummeling the Midwest League as a teenager in 2003, Fielder the Younger skipped a level to Double-A last season and had a season which, in some ways, was even more impressive. His average dropped from .313 to .272, but his isolated power and walk rate held steady. The son of Cecil, himself listed at 5′11″ and 280 pounds, even managed to steal 11 bases. The impressive part is that he did this even as news finally leaked out that his dad had squandered the entire family fortune on gambling and bad business deals, and that father and son were no longer on speaking terms. Long a man among boys, Prince was able to weather the storm and maintain his focus on the field. Once the Brewers figure out what to do with Lyle Overbay, Fielder will get a chance to prove that he's not only a better man than his father, he may be the better player as well.

9. Daric Barton C Oakland Athletics Age 19

	AVG	OBP	SLG	Defense
2003	.229	.327	.337	C: −5
2004	.262	.373	.425	C: −4

5-Year WARP Trend: 3.1, 2.9, 3.0, 3.6, 3.2

We're not sure he can really stay a catcher; actually, we're pretty sure he can't, or at least that he won't in the major leagues. But with a bat like his, it really doesn't matter. Barton, a third-round pick of the Cardinals in 2003, made his full-season debut last year and absolutely crushed

Midwest League pitching, hitting .313 with 36 extra-base hits and 69 walks in just 90 games. Those numbers would be impressive for anyone, let alone a player who was just 18 years old for most of the season. He single-handedly justifies the Mulder trade from the A's point of view, and very well could be one of the best hitters in baseball—at any position—by the end of the decade.

10. Jeremy Reed OF Seattle Mariners Age 24

	AVG	OBP	SLG	Defense
2003	.340	.412	.514	OF: −3
2004	.289	.359	.410	CF: +2

5-Year WARP Trend: 4.2, 3.8, 3.9, 4.3, 4.0

Okay, so maybe ranking him the #2 prospect in all the land, as we did a year ago, was a tad too optimistic. But just as Reed isn't as good as his .373 average in 2003 led us to believe, neither is he as bad as suggested by his .275 average with the White Sox in 2004—which enabled the Mariners to procure him for Freddy Garcia. While Reed's average dropped, the core skills that produced that average remained the same. He still has the same line-drive stroke, he still walked more than he struck out, and he still showed excellent speed. As if to prove that his 2004 downturn was a fluke, Reed hit .397 in a September callup with the Mariners, becoming only the fifth player in major league history to hit .390 or better, with 50 or more at-bats, in his major league debut. He's not going to hit .390 again, but he should hit over .300 with walks and gap power, sort of an Ichiro Lite. That's a heck of a ballplayer.

11. Jeff Francis LHP Colorado Rockies Age 24

	H/9	BB/9	K/9	HR/9	ERA	DERA
2003	8.4	3.2	5.6	0.8	4.71	4.23
2004	8.0	2.1	8.3	1.2	3.46	3.76

5-Year WARP Trend: 3.0, 2.0, 2.2, 1.7, 2.1

After over a decade of waiting, the irresistible force has finally met the immovable object. The team that plays in the greatest hitters' park in major league history finally has a bona fide, can't-miss, sure-thing pitching prospect. And how ironic is it that the pitcher long-awaited to challenge the unique effects on a baseball of high altitude was a physics major in college? Francis, the Rockies' #1 draft pick out of that noted baseball hotbed, the University of British Columbia, has been unhittable since the middle of the 2003 season. He finished that year with a 1.06 ERA in his last 15 starts, and was nearly as dominant through all of last season, with a 2.21 ERA and only 137 hits+ walks (against 196 strikeouts) in 155 minor league innings last year. He was the easy choice for Baseball America's Minor League Player of the Year.

Enter Coors Field. Francis made seven starts for the Rockies down the stretch On the one hand, he surrendered 42 hits and 8 homers in just 37 innings; on the other, his strikeout to walk ratio was still excellent at 32 to 13. His performance in the Proving Ground for High Altitude in Colorado Springs (7 BB, 49 K, 2.85 ERA) augurs well for his eventual adjustment. and there's no reason to think his repertoire, relying on command of his fastball and a delivery that hides the ball until the last moment, should be affected by altitude more than any other pitcher. We really have no idea what to expect when worlds collide. But we're waiting with bated breath to find out.

12. Carlos Quentin OF Arizona Diamondbacks Age 22

	AVG	OBP	SLG	Defense
2004	.251	.331	.418	RF: −2

5-Year WARP Trend: 3.8, 3.5, 4.2, 4.6, 5.3

Quentin may not be #1 on this list, but he's certainly the only player listed in this chapter who set an all-time minor-league record last season. Okay, so it was for most times hit by a pitch, but 43 free trips to first base are nothing to sneeze at. Quentin was such an accomplished hitter at Stanford that the Diamondbacks took him in the first round even though they knew he would need Tommy John surgery right after he signed. Quentin recovered in time for Opening Day last year and showed no signs of rust, hitting .332/.435/.549 between A-ball and Double-A and regaining the arm strength to quiet any concerns he might have in moving to right field. The only negative is that Lancaster and El Paso, where Quentin plied his trade last year, are both notorious hitters' parks. Then again, the BOB isn't bad itself.

13. Eric Duncan 3B New York Yankees Age 20

	AVG	OBP	SLG	Defense
2003	.234	.273	.377	3B: −1
2004	.223	.305	.406	3B: −10

5-Year WARP Trend: 1.7, 1.8, 2.4, 2.6, 3.1

The one thing we don't know about Duncan, the Yankees' first-round pick in 2003, is what uniform he will be wearing by the time he reaches the majors; he was rumored to be part of a half-dozen different deals this winter. Of course, the fact that he is such a premium prospect is why his name comes up so frequently in trade talks in the first place. Duncan battled Ian Stewart for the right to be called the best third base prospect in A-ball last season. Like Stewart, Duncan adds a patient approach to his sweet left-handed swing. Duncan's power is not nearly as developed, but 16 homers and 43 doubles is nothing to sneeze at from a teenager. Whether he's still a Yankee or not by the time you read this, the presence of a certain inner-circle Hall of Famer in the Bronx all but guarantees that Duncan will eventually be plying his trade elsewhere. It's the Yankees' loss.

14. Scott Kazmir LHP Tampa Bay Devil Rays Age 21

	H/9	BB/9	K/9	HR/9	ERA	DERA
2003	8.6	4.4	7.9	1.3	5.13	4.76
2004	8.2	4.5	7.7	0.8	4.39	4.18

5-Year WARP Trend: 2.4, 2.0, 1.6, 2.0, 1.7

Amos Rusie for Christy Mathewson. Rick Wise for Steve Carlton. Victor Zambrano for Scott Kazmir may not join the list of the most lopsided pitcher-for-pitcher trades of all time, but the mere fact that we're considering the possibility is telling. Kazmir has the best pure stuff of any left-handed pitching prospect by far, unleashing upper-90s heat (and an equally nasty slider) despite a less-than-imposing height of 6 feet even. Some people—mostly those in the Mets' front office—will point to Billy Wagner and say that Kazmir won't have the stamina to remain a starting pitcher. This argument can be refuted in two words: Ron Guidry. Kazmir has a good health record—his DL stint last year was for an abdominal strain—and the benefits of a 21st-century approach to pitcher workloads are obvious. Most important, even the Alaska Pipeline doesn't bring this much gas. Kazmir struck out 11.07 batters per nine innings with the Devil Rays last season. In major league history, only two other pitchers 20 or younger (min: 10 IP) struck out 11 batters per nine in a season. One was named Bob Feller. The other was named Dwight Gooden.

15. Yusmeiro Petit RHP New York Mets Age 20

	H/9	BB/9	K/9	HR/9	ERA	DERA
2003	8.1	1.6	5.8	0.8	4.63	3.04
2004	7.2	3.1	8.7	0.9	3.91	3.13

5-Year WARP Trend: 3.4, 2.7, 2.9, 2.2, 3.3

There are those who will tell you that they don't understand how Petit has been so dominant with a repertoire that is hardly extraordinary. There are those who will tell you that Petit will meet his comeuppance when he reaches the high minors, let alone the major leagues. But then there are those—like, say, us—who look at Petit's record, including 200 strikeouts last season in just 139 innings, and conclude that there's simply no way to produce those numbers without *some* semblance of major league talent. (And those hitters unfortunate enough to face him last year would point out that his delivery was tough to read, and his fastball had excellent late movement.) The only other pitcher in our entire database to whiff 200+ hitters in fewer than 150 innings was Josh Beckett in 2001. And as if to answer concerns about how he'll fare against more experienced hitters, he finished last season with two Double-A starts and struck out 16 hitters in 12 innings. Unless they change the rules to allow pitchers to retire hitters based on style points, Petit deserves recognition as one of the best pitching prospects in the game.

16. Jered Weaver RHP Team Boras Age 22

No, Weaver doesn't have a professional record for us to analyze. (Heck, he doesn't even have a professional contract at this writing.) And unlike Mark Prior and Mark Teixeira, who both ranked in our Top 20 before ever playing a game as a pro, there are actually some scouts out there who don't think that Weaver is destined for greatness. The hitters who have faced him, on the other hand, have shown what they think of his chances. Compare these two lines:

Mark Prior, 2001:	15-1,	1.70 ERA,	138 IP,	100 H,	18 BB,	202 K,	5 HR
Jered Weaver, 2004:	15-1,	1.63 ERA,	144 IP,	81 H,	21 BB,	213 K,	8 HR

Prior's junior season is considered one of the greatest seasons by a collegiate pitcher of all time—and Weaver matches him, scoreless inning for scoreless inning, strikeout for strikeout. And while Prior really blossomed as a junior, Weaver was nearly as dominant in his sophomore season: 1.96 ERA, 133 IP, 87 H, 20 BB, 144 K, 7 HR. Oh, and in between his sophomore and junior seasons, he recorded a 0.38 ERA for Team USA. The argument can be made that Weaver is the greatest three-year college pitcher ever. A record like that gets him on our list, no matter when—or, as long as he is represented by Scott Boras, if—he signs.

17. Michael Aubrey 1B Cleveland Indians Age 23

	AVG	OBP	SLG	Defense
2003	.284	.331	.454	1B: +3
2004	.275	.350	.454	1B: −5

5-Year WARP Trend: 2.0, 2.1, 2.7, 2.8, 3.2

The prototypical sweet-swinging first baseman, Aubrey enjoyed a banner collegiate career at Tulane—including leading the Green Wave to a College World Series championship as a freshman. He's continued to hit line drives and play terrific defense since being taken in the first round by the Indians in 2003. He projects to be about as good as a first baseman can be without hitting 40 homers a year. He has batting title potential, a .403 lifetime OBP as a pro, and should settle in around 25 homers and 40 doubles a year at his peak. The only concerns are health related; he had back problems in college and missed part of last season with a pulled hamstring. If he continues to develop as projected, he might one day evoke the memory of another Louisiana native, Will Clark.

18. Chris Burke 2B Houston Astros Age 25

	AVG	OBP	SLG	Defense
2003	.277	.348	.371	2B: +5
2004	.292	.366	.447	2B: −2

5-Year WARP Trend: 2.4, 1.6, 1.6, 1.9, 1.6

Burke has about as ideal a situation as you could ask for when you're a rookie coming to camp. He has the benefit of a great hitters' park and an excellent opportunity to win a starting job now that Jeff Kent is in L.A. Burke has more than his initials in common with the man Kent replaced at second base, Craig Biggio. Like Biggio—if on a lesser scale—Burke does nothing superbly, but he does do everything very, very well. He hits for average, supplements his average walk rate with double-digit HBP totals, steals 30 bases a year, and has added a serious power dimension to his game After homering exactly three times in each of his first three minor league seasons, Burke cranked out 16 last year while also setting a career high in doubles. He may not have the long-term upside of some of the players on this list, but if Marte starts the year in the minors, Burke may have the pole position in the battle for NL Rookie of the Year.

19. Lastings Milledge OF New York Mets Age 20

	AVG	OBP	SLG	Defense
2004	.268	.315	.458	CF: –7

5-Year WARP Trend: 2.2, 2.1, 2.2, 2.5, 3.0

While Delmon Young was considered by some to be the most dominant high school hitter since Alex Rodriguez, at least a few scouts thought that Young wasn't even the best high school hitter in his draft. Milledge's raw talent inspired the Mets to draft him 12th overall in 2003, in spite of allegations of improper sexual conduct while he was in high school, and in spite of the fact that his talent was considered, well, raw. His lack of experience notwithstanding, Milledge was the best hitter in the South Atlantic League last year other than Young and Ian Stewart, and Milledge has a significant speed edge on both. And unlike Young, Milledge is considered a plus outfielder. His one major weakness is his lack of discipline at the plate, but 26 walks in 342 at-bats isn't so bad considering his youth and inexperience. There's risk here, but there's also upside. Major upside.

20. Chad Billingsley RHP Los Angeles Dodgers Age 20

	H/9	BB/9	K/9	HR/9	ERA	DERA
2003	8.3	3.7	5.2	0.4	5.51	3.38
2004	8.0	5.5	7.4	0.8	4.31	4.52

5-Year WARP Trend: 2.1, 1.7, 1.8, 1.6, 1.9

The pitching factory in Los Angeles continues unabated. Last year, it was Edwin Jackson and Greg Miller who got all the headlines. This year, it is Billingsley, arriving in Double-A just ahead of his 20th birthday, who gets to wear the phenom tiara. Billingsley was selected 24th overall in the 2003 draft and is another data point for the case that teams are doing a much better job of selecting high school pitchers in the first round. His statistical record—10 strikeouts per nine innings at every minor league stop—backs up a scouting report that details a lethal fastball/curveball combination. Of course, the statistical record also exposes some control issues—71 walks in 134 innings last year—that need to be worked on. But the kid's only 20—we'll cut him some slack for now.

21. Ian Kinsler SS Texas Rangers Age 23

	AVG	OBP	SLG	Defense
2003	.229	.279	.344	SS: –5
2004	.286	.357	.477	SS: –7

5-Year WARP Trend: 3.3, 2.4, 3.2, 2.8, 2.9

Sometimes, a player comes out of nowhere with a fluke season. And sometimes, it's not a fluke. No one knew anything about Kinsler, a lowly 17th-round draft pick out of Missouri in 2003, before last season. By July, he was the talk of the minor leagues after hitting .401 in the Midwest League. He skipped a level to Double-A in the second half and slumped all the way to .300, with power and walks. For the season, he roped 51 doubles and 20 homers, stole 23 bases, walked 58 times, and impressed the scouts along the way. His defense at shortstop is adequate at best, but at worst he projects as a slugging second baseman. Sure, he might prove to be a one-year wonder. But if he does, it was one hell of a year.

22. Edwin Encarnacion 3B Cincinnati Reds Age 22

	AVG	OBP	SLG	Defense
2003	.264	.319	.416	3B: –12
2004	.253	.320	.406	3B: –10

5-Year WARP Trend: 1.2, 2.1, 2.2, 3.0, 3.0

Quite possibly the most underrated prospect in the game today, Encarnacion has had back-to-back seasons in which he displayed a wide range of offensive skills at a very young age But he gets scant attention for his all-around game. His second try at Double-A went considerably better than his first, and he improved his K:BB ratio two years running, an excellent prognostic indicator in a young player. His defense—or at least his defensive numbers—could use some improvement, but he still has plenty of time to work on it away from the limelight. The signing of Joe Randa offers Encarnacion a full year of Triple-A to perfect his craft.

23. Brandon McCarthy RHP Chicago White Sox Age 21

	H/9	BB/9	K/9	HR/9	ERA	DERA
2003	10.2	2.0	5.6	1.6	6.27	5.04
2004	8.6	1.8	7.2	1.3	4.29	4.18

5-Year WARP Trend: 2.1, 1.7, 1.4, 1.7, 2.0

Not every American-born pitcher on this list was a first-round draft pick. McCarthy was a 17th-round find out of junior college in 2002, the sort of pitcher who had people wondering, from his first moment in pro ball, how he dropped so low. McCarthy's claim to fame is a strikeout-to-walk ratio that borders on the unreal: in a brief stop in the Carolina League last year, his ratio was 60 to 3, and for the last two seasons as a whole, he has 327 strikeouts against 45 walks. Last season, he became the first minor league pitcher to whiff 200 or more batters with 30 or fewer walks since, um, we don't know exactly—let's just say as far back as our records take us. He doesn't have anything fancy in his tool kit; he simply knows how to throw his curveball for strikes, which keeps the walks down, and he knows how to locate his fastball within the strike zone, which keeps the strikeouts up. His August audition in Double-A went off without a hitch, and the White Sox, whose struggles with their #5 starters last year were legendary, will roll out the red carpet the minute he's ready to arrive in Chicago.

24. Hanley Ramirez SS Boston Red Sox Age 21

	AVG	OBP	SLG	Defense
2003	.240	.278	.363	SS: −17
2004	.274	.319	.385	SS: −12

5-Year WARP Trend: 1.7, 1.8, 2.4, 2.6, 3.1

Ramirez made our prospect list two years ago after his first season in the United States, then fell off last year after a season that was as disappointing on the field as it was off—he had multiple incidents of immaturity that ultimately required a suspension to address. But last season, Ramirez behaved like a grown-up all year—no small feat for a 20-year-old—and hit .310 in both the Florida State and Eastern Leagues, this despite a fracture in his wrist that caused him to miss most of May and June. Though his career high in homers is eight, he slugged .512 in Double-A last year and should top double figures regularly in the majors. He is also considered the best defensive infielder in the Red Sox system. The signing of Edgar Renteria may close off the shortstop position in Boston, but whether he requires a move to third base or to another team, Ramirez has the bat and glove to succeed anywhere.

25. Anthony Reyes RHP St. Louis Cardinals Age 23

	H/9	BB/9	K/9	HR/9	ERA	DERA
2004	8.9	1.9	8.2	0.9	4.65	4.10

5-Year WARP Trend: 3.3, 2.3, 2.9, 2.7, 2.3

While at USC, Reyes was considered one of the best collegiate pitchers in the country when healthy; the problem was that he was rarely healthy. His best ERA in college was 3.46, and the Cardinals were able to steal him in the 15th round of the 2003 draft. Last season, with his elbow problems behind him, Reyes impressed Florida State hitters with his fastball and slider before pitching even better in the Southern League—check out the 102 to 13 strikeout to walk ratio. On the other hand, although his elbow didn't bother him, he did miss six weeks with shoulder pain early in the year. He profiles as a top pitcher both from the scouting reports and the stat sheets, but there's no doubt that he's a risk to blow out his arm with every pitch. Doesn't that describe every pitcher, though?

26. Nick Swisher OF Oakland Athletics Age 25

	AVG	OBP	SLG	Defense
2003	.219	.313	.382	OF: −11
2004	.236	.363	.434	OF: −12

5-Year WARP Trend: 2.6, 2.6, 2.5, 3.1, 2.5

Someday, we will refer to players selected by the Oakland A's in the 2002 draft without using the term "Moneyball." Until then, Swisher will have to bear the torch for an entire philosophy of talent acquisition. At least he is making those of us proud who believe that college numbers matter. If you look at Swisher's minor league record, what you won't see is gaudy batting averages—only once in five stops has he hit even .270. What you will see is lots of walks—his 103 for Sacramento last year led the high minors—and developing power. Throw in solid defense on either outfield corner and the ability to hit from both sides, and you have . . . uh . . . a Moneyball player. You also have an everyday player in the A's lineup, a Rookie of the Year candidate, and a minimum wage player. Now *that's* a *Moneyball* player. And a good one.

27. Jeff Francoeur OF Atlanta Braves Age 21

	AVG	OBP	SLG	Defense
2003	.250	.281	.406	CF: −11
2004	.248	.286	.431	RF: −2

5-Year WARP Trend: 1.5, 1.8, 1.6, 2.6, 3.4

From a pure scouting perspective, Francoueur just might be the best five-tool talent in the minor leagues today. He has the speed to play center and the arm to play right, and he has the perfect swing to generate both line drives and towering moon shots. He also draws raves for his passion and drive for the game; after breaking his cheekbone last May, he was thought to be lost for the season, but returned in late July and even earned a promotion to Double-A. Having said that, from an analytical perspective we'd be a little more sanguine about his future if he had drawn one measly walk in 76 at-bats after his promotion. He's certainly young enough and talented enough to develop plate discipline; if not to draw walks, then at least to prevent pitchers from feasting on his aggressiveness. And the Braves have shown an uncanny ability to correct their prospects' biggest weaknesses over time. The Dale Murphy comparisons may be a little optimistic, but if any team can turn him into a superstar, it's Atlanta.

28. Matt Cain RHP San Francisco Giants Age 20

	H/9	BB/9	K/9	HR/9	ERA	DERA
2003	9.6	3.7	7.0	1.4	4.68	5.65
2004	8.7	3.7	6.5	0.9	4.79	4.54

5-Year WARP Trend: 2.0. 1.6, 1.7, 1.2, 1.4

The Giants have shown no ability to develop hitters over the past ten years, but pitchers are another matter. Cain, a first-round pick out of high school in 2002, was just a tick behind Felix Hernandez as the most dominant pitcher in the California League last season. Cain was promoted to Double-A ahead of Hernandez and, aside from some lapses in his control (40 walks in 86 innings), continued to impress. Both his fastball and curve rate as excellent major league pitches, and while no one is as young as King Felix, Cain was just 19 all of last season. Cain does have a history of a stress fracture in his elbow, which cost him half of the 2003 season, but the Giants have since endeavored to protect him with strict pitch counts and a close eye on his mechanics. Cain figures to team with Jerome Williams to form one of the best under-25 pitching duos in baseball by 2006.

29. Dan Meyer LHP Oakland Athletics Age 23

	H/9	BB/9	K/9	HR/9	ERA	DERA
2003	9.9	2.1	6.0	1.8	5.36	5.24
2004	8.3	2.8	7.7	0.5	3.38	3.68

5-Year WARP Trend: 2.4, 1.4, 1.5, 1.6, 1.3

What, you didn't really think that Billy Beane would trade Tim Hudson and Mark Mulder without getting something in return, did you? We should have known Meyer was special when the Braves, who take college players early in the draft about as often as they take Octobers off, used a supplemental first-round pick on Meyer even though he had the audacity to attend college at James Madison. All five of the lines on Meyer's minor league resume show an ERA in the twos, and his career K:BB ratio is 4.38. A left-hander who throws in the low 90s, doesn't beat himself with walks or homers, and strikes out over a man an inning? Hudson's going to be hard to replace, but Meyer's as good a choice as any.

30. Curtis Granderson OF Detroit Tigers Age 24

	AVG	OBP	SLG	Defense
2003	.253	.316	.433	OF: −3
2004	.259	.356	.436	CF: +9

5-Year WARP Trend: 3.4, 3.1, 3.3, 3.2, 3.0

We admit it: we have a weakness for over-achievers. Granderson, who was not blessed with outstanding tools but has hit at every step—.483 his junior year of college, .344 in his pro debut, .303 in Double-A last year—certainly qualifies. And a funny thing happens when you perform well enough, long enough: suddenly the same scouts who thought you didn't have tools start using words like "gamer" and "plays above his tools" to describe you. Granderson had a true breakout season last year, nearly doubling his walk and homer rates to complement his ability to hit for average, and the scouts actually claimed that his tools improved, something you almost never hear. (If "tools" could change that easily, why would anyone bother to measure them?) As the flagbearer for the Dombrowski administration's draft efforts in Detroit, Granderson will get every opportunity to win an outfield job, possibly even in center field, as soon as this spring.

31. Adam Miller RHP Cleveland Indians Age 20

	H/9	BB/9	K/9	HR/9	ERA	DERA
2003	9.7	3.3	3.6	1.8	6.98	5.76 (30 IP)
2004	8.4	3.1	6.7	0.9	4.78	4.13

5-Year WARP Trend: 2.1, 1.6, 1.6, 1.2, 1.7

Much like Chad Billingsley, who was taken seven selections ahead of him, Miller has gone from high school to top prospect in the span of barely 18 months. (Before you get too warm and fuzzy about drafting high school pitchers in the first round, remember that the first prep pitcher taken in 2003, Jeff Allison, is now a recovering heroin addict and simply hopes to take the mound again at some point.) Miller relies on a hard slider to complement one of the fastest of fastballs in the minors, and earns major bonus points for his mound composure and work ethic. More importantly, the numbers back up the hype: 152 Ks against just 40 walks in 134 innings last year, and Miller was even more dominant after a promotion to the Carolina League late last season. The usual caveats regarding young pitchers apply even more strongly here, seeing as how Miller has yet to even reach Double-A yet. But he comfortably ranks ahead of every other pitcher who has yet to see the high minors.

32. Brian Anderson OF Chicago White Sox Age 23

	AVG	OBP	SLG	Defense	
2003	.292	.374	.438	CF: 0	(54 AB)
2004	.268	.335	.442	CF: -8	

5-Year WARP Trend: 2.7, 2.7, 3.3, 3.1, 3.3

Anderson finished an erratic career at Arizona on a high note, hitting .366/.425/.668 as a junior and getting picked by the White Sox in the first round in 2003. Despite a propensity for injuries—an injured wrist that ended his first pro season early, a strained groin that did the same last year—he has shown a balanced attack at the plate, advancing to Double-A in his first full season while hitting for average, showing gap power, commanding the strike zone reasonably well, and playing a strong center field. In other words, like Granderson, he does everything well but nothing at an exceptional level. Anderson is a year younger than Granderson, but his defense has translated less well and makes him more likely to end up on a corner, where his bat will be less of an asset. Anderson's the kind of player where improving his all-around game even slightly may be the difference between his developing into a decent everyday regular and an All-Star caliber outfielder.

33. Gavin Floyd RHP Philadelphia Phillies Age 22

	H/9	BB/9	K/9	HR/9	ERA	DERA
2003	10.0	3.4	5.4	1.6	5.59	5.66
2004	8.4	3.7	5.5	0.6	3.90	4.12

5-Year WARP Trend: 1.7, 1.6, 1.8, 1.9, 1.7

A lesson in why, with minor leaguers, it helps to know the whole story. Floyd's numbers since he was taken with the #4 overall pick in 2001 were solid but nothing that screamed TOP PROSPECT. He has a pretty strong excuse: the Phillies strictly limited the use of his curveball, considered by some to be one of the best in the game, in order to develop his other secondary pitches. The reins came off slowly, and last year, he was finally given free rein to use all the weapons in his arsenal. Not surprisingly, his K rate spiked and he rose from Double-A to the majors, where he posted a 3.49 ERA in 28 innings. His control flagged a little last year, and an adjustment period where he learns to compensate for the fact that major leaguers are likely to lay off his big bender may mean he struggles a little in the short-term. In the long-term, you can't ask for more than a pitcher with Floyd's combination of stuff, results, and lack of injury history. If all top picks spent on high school pitchers turned out like this, we wouldn't be so adamant about not using top picks on high school pitchers.

34. Willy Aybar 2B Los Angeles Dodgers Age 22

	AVG	OBP	SLG	Defense
2003	.236	.289	.396	3B: +8
2004	.257	.321	.400	2B: +11

5-Year WARP Trend: 1.7, 2.2, 2.5, 3.3, 3.5

Aybar is an example of the dangers of outsized expectations. Before the Dodgers inked Juan Guzman to a record deal, their big bonus baby was Aybar, who was persuaded to sign with a $1.4 million bonus. Aybar's career got off to a rocky start, first when his agent Enrique Soto was accused of embezzling much of his signing bonus, and then when visa problems caused him to miss the start of the 2002 season. Indeed, even now, most observers consider his younger brother Erick to be the better prospect. But over the past two years, Aybar has quietly begun to show the talent that made him such a hot property to begin with. He has settled in as a .270 hitter with 12–15 homers and 40–50 walks a year, which isn't All-Star material, but for a 21-year-old in Double-A, who switch hits and effortlessly made the transition from third to second base last year, it's a nice foundation to build on. His broad range of offensive skills give him a number of different avenues to success. He's never going to lead the league in any category, but then that hasn't stopped Ray Durham from being one of the best second basemen in the game over the last decade.

35. Jeremy Hermida OF Florida Marlins Age 21

	AVG	OBP	SLG	Defense
2003	.244	.327	.347	RF: −17
2004	.265	.333	.412	RF: −9

5-Year WARP Trend: 1.1, 1.6, 1.9, 2.5, 2.2

The first outfielder selected in the 2002 draft, Hermida was considered one of the best pure hitters to come out of high school in years, and so far has done nothing to change that perception. We wrote last year that his strong plate discipline meant that he was a good bet to develop power in the future, and sure enough, last year he raised his slugging average 50 points and set a career high with 10 homers despite missing over a month with a hamstring pull. His defense in right field is erratic, but he has both the speed and the arm to outgrow his struggles. After being forced to watch Juan Encarnacion flail about for another season in south Florida, Marlin fans ought to be overjoyed when Hermida's more diligent approach to hitting arrives in 2006.

36. Rickie Weeks 2B Milwaukee Brewers Age 22

	AVG	OBP	SLG	Defense
2003	.287	.400	.450	2B: −3 (106 PA)
2004	.242	.332	.386	2B: −15

5-Year WARP Trend: 2.7, 2.1, 2.6, 3.5, 3.5

Let this be a lesson in the risk of evaluating a prospect on the basis of a small sample size. Weeks ranked in our Top 10 last year on the basis of his high draft position (#2 overall), an awesome resume of collegiate success (at a Division I-AA program in Southern University), and a good month in pro baseball. It took a full season in the minors for the warts to show: the power he showed in college hasn't translated to the pros, and his defense at second base will always be a concern. That said, he held his own at Double-A in his full-season debut, he knows the value of a walk (and of a hit-by-pitch; he got plunked 28 times last year), and the 35 doubles and six triples he hit suggest that his home run power may yet return. And for what it's worth, he hit .382/.520/.737 in the Arizona Fall League. The Joe Morgan comparisons look pretty silly at the moment, but if 2004 was a consolidation year for Weeks, a few All-Star appearances may still be in his future.

37. Richie Gardner RHP Cincinnati Reds Age 23

	H/9	BB/9	K/9	HR/9	ERA	DERA
2004	9.0	1.7	5.7	0.9	4.12	3.87

5-Year WARP Trend: 2.1, 1.8, 1.9, 2.0, 1.4

Gardner's promising career was almost ended before it began, when a freak beaning during his sophomore year of college—he was struck by a ball being hurled across the infield during practice—left him with a concussion so severe that he spent a week in the hospital and still has occasional lapses of concentration. But as Gardner put that incident further and further behind him, his performance got better and better. He transferred to Arizona for his junior year and was nothing special (4.49 ERA), but after he was drafted in the 6th round in 2003, he showed up in Instructional League with better stuff than expected. And then, in his pro debut last season, he showed exceptional command (26 walks in 157 IP) and an unhittable changeup, allowing him to waltz to Double-A without a hitch. His unusual backstory and sudden rise make him one of the most underrated prospects in the game. Assuming he avoids further shots to the head, his combination of stuff and polish make it likely that he'll find himself in the Reds' depleted rotation sooner rather than later, though we might suggest he check out the latest fashions in helmets to wear while on the mound. It is said that John Olerud knows a good tailor.

38. Ryan Howard 1B Philadelphia Phillies Age 25

	AVG	OBP	SLG	Defense
2003	.265	.323	.480	1B: +4
2004	.256	.335	.542	1B: −9

5-Year WARP Trend: 2.6, 2.3, 2.1, 2.0, 2.3

If there's one player on this list who is almost guaranteed to find himself in another uniform before he gets an opportunity—maybe even before you read this—it's Howard, who is blocked in Philadelphia by Jim Thome, a similar player but better in every way. That's not a knock against Howard, who led the minors with 46 homers last season. Howard stands tall (6′4″) and lives big—big homers and big, very big, strikeout totals, including 166 in just 131 minor league games last season. Let's just say Adam Dunn shouldn't get too comfortable with his new major league record. If the strikeouts don't eat him alive, Howard should be the prototypical slugging first baseman for some team—preferably one with a short right-field porch—for years to come.

39. Cole Hamels LHP Philadelphia Phillies Age 21

	H/9	BB/9	K/9	HR/9	ERA	DERA
2003	7.2	4.2	8.4	0.3	3.44	3.24
2004	7.4	2.5	9.2	0.0	2.45	2.45 (16 IP)

5-Year WARP Trend: 3.8, 3.0, 3.5, 3.6, 3.9

Inning for inning, Hamels has been arguably the most dominant starter in the minor leagues in years. He has a career ERA of 1.31, and he has yet to surrender a home run in his professional career. The problem is he's thrown just 117 innings in two seasons because a pulled triceps muscle—and some elbow pain that may or may not have been tendonitis—conspired to limit him to just four starts last season. Neither injury required surgery and he was back on the mound in instructional league. The Phillies are confident t he'll be completely healthy this year, though Hamels's injury history (he broke his humerus in a freak accident in high school) inspires anything but confidence. Still, he has one of the slickest changeups in all of baseball, and so long as he's healthy enough to pitch, he's an excellent bet to continue to pitch very, very well.

40. Jose Capellan RHP Milwaukee Brewers Age 23

	H/9	BB/9	K/9	HR/9	ERA	DERA
2003	9.4	4.4	3.8	1.0	6.28	5.44
2004	8.1	3.2	7.0	0.3	3.87	3.61

5-Year WARP Trend: 2.0, 1.8, 1.5, 1.4, 1.2

Quietly, the team that may have done the most to improve themselves this winter was the Brewers, who managed to turn a bunch of players they either didn't want or didn't need into a whole mess of talent. The most interesting player they acquired, Capellan, is a Tommy John survivor who returned in mid-2003 to flash a fastball in the upper 90s. Command usually returns after velocity following Tommy John surgery, and when Capellan's command returned last season, he shot through the Braves system, advancing from A-ball to the majors in the same year. His injury history and electric fastball have some calling for the Brewers to use him as their closer, replacing the man he was traded for, Danny Kolb. With the Brewers still missing more than a few pieces of the puzzle, they'd be well advised to give him every chance to develop into a dominant starter first.

41. Guillermo Quiroz C Toronto Blue Jays Age 23

	AVG	OBP	SLG	Defense
2003	.251	.330	.475	C: +7
2004	.207	.284	.349	C: −5

5-Year WARP Trend: 2.7, 2.3, 3.2, 3.4, 2.8

A year ago, Quiroz ranked as the second-best catching prospect of the game based on his display of tremendous secondary skills in the Eastern League and superior defense at the age of 21. But after breaking a bone in his left hand in early May, Quiroz missed nearly two months last season and struggled to hit when he returned. Nevertheless, he still ranks as our second-best catching prospect, which tells you both how highly we think of Quiroz and how weak this year's catching crop is. Quiroz's core skills—his power and ability to draw walks—suffered less than his batting average did last season, which gives us confidence that a return to full health will return Quiroz to being a sturdy all-around catcher. Major sleeper potential for all you fantasy players out there.

42. Joe Blanton RHP Oakland Athletics Age 24

	H/9	BB/9	K/9	HR/9	ERA	DERA
2003	8.5	1.7	6.5	1.1	4.55	3.79
2004	8.9	1.8	5.6	0.7	5.15	3.47

5-Year WARP Trend: 2.3, 1.9, 1.8, 1.5, 1.3

You might be tempted to look at Blanton's unimpressive ERA and hits totals from last season and conclude that his repertoire, which overpowered hitters in the low minors in 2003, doesn't fool more polished hitters. Take a closer look, though, and you'll see his core skills were still outstanding: 143 Ks, 34 walks, and just 13 homers allowed in 176 innings in a good hitters' park. Blanton doesn't have the ace potential of some of the pitchers on this list, but he's polished, durable, and a rotation slot with the A's is his to lose. With the benefit of a favorable ballpark, a good offense, and a shrewd front office, he's as good a bet as anyone on this list to win 12–15 games this season.

43. Jesse Crain RHRP Minnesota Twins Age 23

	H/9	BB/9	K/9	HR/9	ERA	DERA
2003	6.0	3.0	9.9	0.2	3.22	2.30
2004	7.1	3.4	7.7	0.9	2.95	3.31

5-Year WARP Trend: 2.4, 1.7, 1.8, 1.7, 1.6

Last year, Ryan Wagner became only the second reliever to crack our Top Prospects list. Crain, the third, actually preceded Wagner as the closer for the University of Houston before he was drafted in the 2nd round in 2002. To say that he has dominated in the pro ranks would be the understatement of the year: in a little over two minor league seasons, Crain threw 161 innings, allowed 95 hits (including just 5 homers) and 53 walks, while striking out 207. Crain was then called up last August and nearly matched his 1.79 career ERA in the minors with an even 2.00 ERA with the Twins down the stretch. In fact, some observers blame Ron Gardenhire's reluctance to use Crain in a key role in last year's ALDS showdown with the Yankees as one of the main reasons they lost. Gardenhire won't make that mistake this year; Crain figures to be one of the premier set-up men in the game in front of Joe Nathan.

44. Brian McCann C Atlanta Braves Age 21

	AVG	OBP	SLG	Defense
2003	.258	.285	.418	C: +2
2004	.251	.301	.456	C: +4

5-Year WARP Trend: 1.3, 1.7, 1.8, 2.2, 2.5

Do the Braves *ever* screw up a draft pick spent on a player from the southeast? McCann was taken in the second round out of a Georgia high school, and has justified the selection with his electric combination of left-handed power (15 homers and 35 doubles in 381 AB last year) and above-average defense behind the plate. His plate discipline still needs work, but 20 year olds who hit for power in the Carolina League—at any position—don't grow on trees. And while this may not be very scientific of us, a prospect like this has to get bonus points for picking the right organization to be drafted by. This is the same franchise, after all, that turned Johnny Estrada into a .300 hitter.

45. Edwin Jackson RHP Los Angeles Dodgers Age 21

	H/9	BB/9	K/9	HR/9	ERA	DERA
2003	8.4	3.4	7.0	0.9	4.87	4.02
2004	8.9	5.3	5.3	0.7	6.03	4.82

5-Year WARP Trend: 1.3, 1.1, 1.5, 1.6, 1.5

TINSTAAPP claims another victim. Jackson edged Zack Greinke as the top pitching prospect on our list last season, but while Greinke went on to establish himself as the best rookie pitcher in baseball, Jackson struggled with control problems and a strained right forearm and spent most of the season in Triple-A. The Dodgers expect his struggles to be only temporary—they reportedly turned down the chance to acquire Randy Johnson at last year's trading deadline when the Diamondbacks insisted on Jackson in return. His struggles notwithstanding, Jackson is still younger than the majority of pitchers on this list, and he still has the benefit of a great pitchers' park and an organization with a tremendous resume of developing their young pitching talent. Give up on him at your own risk.

46. Jason Kubel OF Minnesota Twins Age 23

	AVG	OBP	SLG	Defense
2003	.278	.332	.398	RF: +2
2004	.316	.377	.518	RF: +4

5-Year WARP Trend: —, 1.9, 1.7, 1.8, 2.1

Kubel was the frontrunner for AL Rookie of the Year honors this year and a sure Top 10 prospect on our list before his knee was injured in an outfield collision in the Arizona Fall League. Okay, "injured" is a euphemism. A more precise term would be "exploded"—he tore his ACL, his MCL, some cartilage, and a few other things in his knee that don't normally get torn. The injury is so severe it will be a miracle if he's able to take the field in 2005, and so unprecedented that the only players to have suffered a comparable sports injury were football players. So it's quite possible that Kubel's career as a top-flight hitter is simply finished. But his offensive production was so stellar before the injury that, even if we pencil 2005 in as a zero and run a PECOTA forecast (as we did above), he still figures to have as much value in the ensuing four years as the other guys at the bottom of this list. (PECOTA forecasts that he will return as nearly the same caliber hitter, but in considerably less playing time.) Check back in a year, but don't be surprised if he makes an impressive comeback in 2006.

47. Kyle Davies RHP Atlanta Braves Age 21

	H/9	BB/9	K/9	HR/9	ERA	DERA
2003	9.7	4.0	5.7	1.4	5.24	5.44
2004	7.9	4.1	8.0	1.1	4.07	4.14

5-Year WARP Trend: 1.7, 1.4, 1.2, 1.2, 1.6

Yes, the Braves have placed another pitcher on our Top Prospect list. Yes, Davies is a Georgia native. Yes, he was drafted out of high school. We don't know how the Braves do it, we just know that they do—year in and year out. Davies was considered the best pitcher in his age group in the country in his early teens, but his fastball lost velocity as he got older, and he dropped to the 4th round of the draft and struggled to get out of rookie ball for two years. But after the Braves overhauled his delivery following the 2002 season—there's that organizational bonus in play again—Davies got his fastball back into the low-to-mid 90s, complementing an excellent changeup, and it's been all roses for him since. He has enough of a track record now that his prospect status isn't solely the product of being in the Atlanta chain. Of course, we might have said that about Adam Wainwright last year.

48. Josh Willingham C/1B Florida Marlins Age 26

	AVG	OBP	SLG	Defense
2003	.249	.375	.507	C: −6
2004	.245	.397	.488	C: −2

5-Year WARP Trend: 3.6, 3.3, 3.2, 3.1, 3.0

Mickey Tettleton. Gene Tenace. Willingham may not turn out like those two players, but the fact that they're both on his comparables list tells you all you need to know about him.. Behind the plate, he shows the kind of defensive aptitude you'd expect from a player who didn't learn to catch until after his third pro season. But at the plate, he's a walks-and-trots beast; in 112 Double-A games last season, he took a free pass on a walk or hit-by-pitch 109 times—leading the high minors with a .449 OBP—and hit 24 homers in just 338 at-bats. Almost as great a challenge for Willingham as improving his defense is simply getting an opportunity to play for an organization that has never shown an interest in his skill set. But much like the last player of his ilk to pass through the minors, Craig Wilson, Willingham's bat almost guarantees that he will eventually have value in some role.

49. (tie) Mitch Einertson OF Houston Astros Age 19

	AVG	OBP	SLG	Defense
2004	.241	.312	.515	CF: −4

5-Year WARP Trend: 1.4, 2.2, 3.2, 3.1, 1.7

49. (tie) Dustin Pedroia SS Boston Red Sox Age 21

	AVG	OBP	SLG	Defense
2004	.306	.370	.469	SS: 0

5-Year WARP Trend: 4.8, 4.5, 5.1, 5.2, 5.4

The competition for our coveted slot of Mr. Irrelevant was so fierce that in the end, we had to share the honor among two players. Einertson and Pedroia both represent the Baseball Prospectus philosophy incarnate. Einertson was one of the best high school hitters in southern California last spring, but dropped to the fifth round because guys who stand 5′9″ aren't supposed to hit for power. You know, like Mel Ott or Jimmy Wynn. Anyway, all Einertson did was tie the all-time Appalachian League record for homers in his debut, with 24 in just 63 games. For an 18-year-old hitter to have a translated slugging average of .515 boggles the mind.

Pedroia, on the same hand, is a player who in the words of *Baseball America* "represents one extreme of the tools vs. performance debate." At 5′8″, with marginal speed, marginal power, and a marginal throwing arm, you can guess which extreme he represents. He'll just have to console himself with the fact that he was a two-time All-American at Arizona State, hit .393/.502/.611 his junior year, then hit .400 and .336 in his two brief minor league stops after being drafted in the 2nd round last season. You can't help but be impressed by the fact that he walked nearly three times as often (19) as he struck out (7) in his pro debut. Or that PECOTA (admittedly thrown off by the small sample size) projects Pedroia to have more value over the next five years than any other prospect in baseball. If David Eckstein can be the starting shortstop for a World Championship team, then Pedroia—a similar but better player in every way—has star potential.

Honorable Mention

Russ Adams, SS, Toronto Blue Jays: The Blue Jays' #1 pick out of UNC in 2002 is about as unspectacular as they come; he's never hit .300 or swatted ten homers in a single season. But he's also a left-handed hitting shortstop who controls the strike zone and ropes doubles (39 last year). After slugging .528 in his major league debut last season, he's ready for an everyday job in Toronto. A darkhorse Rookie of the Year contender.

Garrett Atkins, 3B, Colorado Rockies: He can't really play third base, he's old for a prospect, and wouldn't put up particularly noteworthy numbers at sea level. But he hit .366/.434/.578 in Colorado Springs last year, and as much as Coors Field has done to educate the masses on the importance of park effects, that won't stop people from calling Atkins a budding star if he hits .320 with 20 homers this year. If you have any doubt that people are not fully immune to the cognitive dissonance of Coors Field, just ask people in Denver how they remember Dante Bichette.

Josh Barfield, 2B, San Diego Padres: Much like Rickie Weeks, Barfield struggled a little in Double-A last year after entering the season with so much promise. Also like Weeks, Barfield's stature as a prospect is highly dependent on whether he can actually play second base in the major leagues. Another player with a similar profile, Scott Hairston, struggled to establish himself as the Diamondbacks' second baseman last year. But keep in mind that Barfield is two years younger, and is a more skilled defensive player, than Hairston was a year ago.

Zach Duke, LHP, Pittsburgh Pirates: The quintessential projectable left-hander, Duke was a 20th-round pick out of high school in 2001, who last year dominated the Carolina League after his fastball suddenly bumped into the low 90s, making his excellent curveball that much more effective. With just 30 walks and 5 homers surrendered in 148 innings last year, Duke makes fewer mistakes than just about any other pitcher in this chapter. And unlike fellow Pirate Sean Burnett, who made our list last year, Duke also puts hitters away, averaging nearly a whiff an inning last season.

Jonny Gomes, OF, Tampa Bay Devil Rays: The Devil Rays have been producing outfielders by the bushelful, which may explain why Gomes has gotten little attention as he has worked his way up the chain—other than for the minor heart attack he suffered (really) just before Christmas in 2002.—Over the last three years, he has averaged 24 homers, 66 walks, 24 HBPs, and even 15 steals a year. Despite his unimpressive career .265 average, his combination of speed, power, and plate discipline at a reasonably young age has PECOTA salivating. If he ends up in another organization, he could wind up being a tremendous steal.

Angel Guzman, RHP, Chicago Cubs: The Cubs' one-time top prospect returned last summer after missing a year with a "mild" labrum tear—one of the worst injuries a pitcher can suffer. Upon his return, he did his best to prove that there might actually be such a thing as a mild labrum tear. In seven starts in the Florida State League, he put up a nifty strikeout to walk ratio of forty to nothing. Of course, he then got shut down after four starts in Double-A with "shoulder fatigue." If he's healthy, he could re-establish himself as a top prospect very quickly. Caveat emptor.

J. J. Hardy, SS, Milwaukee Brewers: After ranking in our Top 20 last season, Hardy started off 2004 by proving that his offensive breakthrough the year before was no fluke, hitting .277/.330/.495, before suffering a subluxation of his non-throwing shoulder, an injury similar to what Richie Sexson endured last year. He also tore his labrum at the same time, but the Brewers are so confident of his recovery that they've pencilled him in as their starting shortstop this year, even though he has yet to make his major league debut. He's likely to struggle initially, as he continues to develop with the bat and recover from his injury, but long-term, he still has a chance to develop into an All-Star shortstop.

Conor Jackson, OF, Arizona Diamondbacks: Like Carlos Quentin, Jackson was taken by the Diamondbacks in the 1st round in 2003, and teamed with Quentin and 2003 2nd-rounder Jamie D'Antona to form a formidable trio at Lancaster last season. The trio was then promoted to Double-A, where Quentin separated himself from the pack. Jackson has hit everywhere he's played, but as a corner outfielder who's played in hitters' parks at every stop, his .323/.407/.520 numbers as a pro are less impressive than they look. He'll have to keep hitting to establish himself as a top prospect, and just might.

Josh Kroeger, OF, Arizona Diamondbacks: Unlike fellow Baby Backs Quentin and Jackson, Kroeger has gotten very little attention to date. But Kroeger played at a higher level than either of his more celebrated teammates, finishing in the majors last season, and he led organized baseball with 54 doubles. Drafted out of high school in 2000, he's actually the youngest of the three. His questionable plate discipline relegates him to HM status, but if these rankings were adjusted for reputation, he'd be Top 20 for sure.

Kendry Morales, 1B, Anaheim Angels: Morales represents one of the most interesting challenges to sabermetric analysis to come around in a long time. Perhaps the youngest top prospect to defect from Cuba since Livan Hernandez, Morales was given a six-year contract by the Angels virtually sight unseen. We wouldn't rank him here solely on his scouting reports, but now that the World Wide Web's insidious tentacles have even infiltrated their way into the Communist heart of Havana —Cuban League statistics are available online—Clay Davenport was able to run a rough approximation of Morales' performance before his defection. Even adjusting Cuban baseball to the talent level of the New York–Penn League—which is what the track record of other Cuban defectors after coming stateside would have us believe—Morales' performance in Cuba isn't dramatically different than that of Michael Aubrey's. Our translation of Cuban statistics may prove to be as trustworthy as a Cuban ballplayer's date of birth, but there's enough evidence that Morales can hit that we'd be remiss not to mention him somehow.

Dioner Navarro, C, Los Angeles Dodgers: At least, he's a Dodger for the moment. Navarro wasn't as good as his .341 average in Double-A in 2003 had us believe, but neither is he as bad as his .263 average and 4 homers last year would have you think. Switch-hitting catchers who can hold their own in the high minors at age 20 have significant growth potential, if for no other reason than they're switch-hitting catchers who can hold their own in the high minors at age 20. Put it this way: the Dodgers wanted him for a reason.

Chad Orvella, RHRP, Tampa Bay Devil Rays: Yes, the Devil Rays are actually doing a pretty good job of finding young talent. Orvella was a shortstop in college, but showed enough in a few appearances on the mound that the Rays took him in the 13th round as a pitcher. His career numbers since then look like a misprint: 86 innings, 48 hits, 11 walks, 131 strikeouts, 1.47 ERA. He started last season in the South Atlantic League and finished in Triple-A. He throws three above-average pitches (fastball, slider, changeup). The usual disclaimers about the Devil Rays apply, but my goodness.

Omar Quintanilla, SS, Oakland Athletics: A left-handed hitting shortstop with a .329 average as a pro? Tasty. Quintanilla isn't the most dextrous shortstop, and his contact-hitting approach is quite the anomaly in this organization. But much like Russ Adams, a very similar player, he's the kind of player of whom scouts say "he plays above his tools." He won't knock Bobby Crosby off of shortstop in Oakland, but he could easily move across the diamond and produce a number of solidly average seasons in a Mark Loretta-ish sort of way. That's a lot more valuable than the Tony Womacks of the world, for sure.

Jason Stokes, 1B, Florida Marlins: Stokes made the big mistake of peaking as a 19-year-old in 2002, when he hit .341/.421/.645 in the Midwest League and created outsized expectations for himself. As a result, he's been somewhat forgotten the last two years, which is unfair given that few 22-year-olds can slug .513 in Double-A. Much like Ryan Howard, he's a bit of a one-trick pony, and if he only hit half as many homers as Howard last year, at least he has more than two years on the big Phillie. As much as we love Jeff Conine, he represents less a roadblock to Stokes than a speed bump.

Huston Street, RHRP, Oakland Athletics: Michael Lewis picked the wrong year to follow Billy Beane around. The A's 2002 draft, while it did produce two of the players on our Top 50 list, is shaping up to be not nearly as good as Lewis made it look in *Moneyball.* Last year, on the other hand, all the stars lined up for Beane to snag collegiate talent with promising scouting reports to go along with their tremendous numbers. Remember the names of Landon Powell, Richie Robnett, Danny Putnam, Huston Street, Michael Rogers, Kurt Suzuki, and Jason Windsor—even the scouts concede the A's did well with their first seven picks, and at least two or three of these guys ought to make our list next year. Street, a tremendous collegiate closer at the University of Texas, reached Triple-A within two months of signing and many observers thought the A's might have made the playoffs had they promoted Street to Oakland in September. He then posted a 0.98 ERA in the Arizona Fall League. Consider this: counting three college seasons, three different minor league levels last season, and his AFL experience, Street's *highest* ERA is 1.69. He dominates with a sinking fastball and a sweeping slider, but with a record like that, does it even matter what Street throws?

Team Name Key and Park Factors

by Clay Davenport

"Park factors", as presented here, are a misnomer; they are actually adjustments for teams, based on their own mix of home and road parks. Still, teams that play in hitter's parks will have adjustments greater than 1000 (the decimal point at 1.000 has been dropped for readability) and teams that play in pitcher's parks will have a rating below 1000. All park factors are relative to the league, not an absolute scale across the country; what rates as a pitcher's park in the Pacific Coast League could easily be a hitter's park in the International League. The factors used are five-year averages of one-year park factors, centered on and double-counting the given year; the rating for 2004 is found by taking the 2002 one-year factor, plus the 2003 one-year factor, plus twice the 2004 factor, divided by 4. The 2003 factor is using data from 2001–04, the 2002 factor uses data from 2000–04. We haven't been able to get park factors for Mexican and Japanese leagues every year, which is why they have the same rating across the time period.

TEAM NAME KEY AND PARK FACTORS

Abbrev	Name	League	Organization	Nickname	PF2002	PF2003	PF2004
ABE	Aberdeen	New York-Penn	Orioles	IronBirds	985	957	964
ABQ	Albuquerque	Pacific Coast	Marlins	Isotopes	—	1133	1115
AGU	Aguascalientes	Mexican	—	Railroadmen	—	—	1000
AKR	Akron	Eastern	Indians	Aeros	999	1025	1053
ALT	Altoona	Eastern	Pirates	Curve	960	950	960
ANA	Anaheim	American	Angels	Angels	990	971	965
ARI	Arizona	National	Diamondbacks	Diamondbacks	1049	1057	1051
ARK	Arkansas	Texas	Angels	Travelers	1020	1028	1020
ASH	Asheville	South Atlantic	Rockies	Tourists	1124	1123	1113
ATL	Atlanta	National	Braves	Braves	986	982	982
AUB	Auburn	New York-Penn	BlueJays	Doubledays	1005	998	1016
AUG	Augusta	South Atlantic	RedSox	GreenJackets	992	990	982
BAK	Bakersfield	California	DevilRays	Blaze	968	964	959
BAL	Baltimore	American	Orioles	Orioles	972	985	1010
BAT	Batavia	New York-Penn	Phillies	Muckdogs	1032	1003	959
BCR	Battle Creek	Midwest	Yankees	Yankees	—	991	984
BIL	Billings	Pioneer	Reds	Mustangs	949	955	967
BIN	Binghamton	Eastern	Mets	Mets	1028	1006	978
BIR	Birmingham	Southern	WhiteSox	Barons	953	977	976
BLT	Beloit	Midwest	Brewers	Snappers	1036	1033	1029
BLU	Bluefield	Appalachian	Orioles	Orioles	1088	1088	1073
BNC	Burlington (NC)	Appalachian	Indians	Indians	972	989	1007
BOI	Boise	Northwest	Cubs	Hawks	1037	1044	1049
BOS	Boston	American	RedSox	RedSox	1012	1026	1040
BOW	Bowie	Eastern	Orioles	BaySox	973	957	942
BRI	Bristol	Appalachian	WhiteSox	WhiteSox	943	926	912
BRO	Brooklyn	New York-Penn	Mets	Cyclones	984	990	977
BRV	Brevard County	Florida	Expos	Manatees	951	951	957
BUF	Buffalo	International	Indians	Bisons	992	980	968
BUR	Burlington (IA)	Midwest	Royals	Bees	985	972	959
CAR	Carolina	Southern	Marlins	Mudcats	1012	1001	995

554

Abbrev	Name	League	Organization	Nickname	PF2002	PF2003	PF2004
CAS	Casper	Pioneer	Rockies	Rockies	1039	1026	1000
CCN	Cancun	Mexican	—	Lobstermen	940	940	940
CDB	Cordoba	Mexican	—	—	1089	1089	1089
CDR	Cedar Rapids	Midwest	Angels	Kernels	996	1012	1035
CGA	Columbus (GA)	South Atlantic	Dodgers	Catfish	993	—	975
CHB	Chiba	Japanese Pacific	—	Lotte Marines	1005	1005	1005
CHC	Chicago Cubs	National	Cubs	Cubs	975	991	1003
CHR	Charlotte	International	WhiteSox	Knights	993	983	985
CHT	Chattanooga	Southern	Reds	Lookouts	1010	1016	1017
CHU	Chunichi	Japanese Central	—	Dragons	927	927	927
CIN	Cincinnati	National	Reds	Reds	1016	995	973
CLE	Cleveland	American	Indians	Indians	1000	979	968
CLG	Calgary	Pacific Coast	—	Cannons	1096	—	—
CLN	Clinton	Midwest	Rangers	LumberKings	1027	1040	1033
CLR	Clearwater	Florida	Phillies	Threshers	1001	994	988
CMB	Capitol City	South Atlantic	Mets	Bombers	980	987	993
CMP	Campeche	Mexican	—	Pirates	912	912	912
COH	Columbus (OH)	International	Yankees	Clippers	1005	997	989
COL	Colorado	National	Rockies	Rockies	1123	1112	1116
CSC	Charleston (SC)	South Atlantic	DevilRays	RiverDogs	966	961	966
CSP	Colorado Springs	Pacific Coast	Rockies	SkySox	1094	1089	1086
CWS	Chicago White Sox	American	WhiteSox	WhiteSox	1028	1022	1029
CWV	Charleston (WV)	South Atlantic	BlueJays	AlleyCats	998	994	999
DAY	Daytona	Florida	Cubs	Cubs	1029	1039	1057
DEL	Delmarva	South Atlantic	Orioles	Shorebirds	946	956	976
DET	Detroit	American	Tigers	Tigers	964	960	958
DNV	Danville	Appalachian	Braves	Braves	954	936	920
DOS	Dos Laredos	Mexican	—	—	926	926	—
DUN	Dunedin	Florida	BlueJays	BlueJays	1049	1026	1027
DUR	Durham	International	DevilRays	Bulls	1009	1037	1051
DYT	Dayton	Midwest	Reds	Dragons	1039	1053	1074
EDM	Edmonton	Pacific Coast	Expos	Trappers	961	946	935
ELP	El Paso	Texas	Diamondbacks	Diablos	1098	1102	1109
ELZ	Elizabethton	Appalachian	Twins	Twins	953	950	940
ERI	Erie	Eastern	Tigers	SeaWolves	1049	1050	1049
EUG	Eugene	Northwest	Padres	Emeralds	991	977	983
EVE	Everett	Northwest	Mariners	AquaSox	1052	1054	1057
FKU	Fukuoka	Japanese Pacific	—	Daiei Hawks	965	965	965
FLA	Florida	National	Marlins	Marlins	954	947	941
FRD	Frederick	Carolina	Orioles	Keys	1015	1017	1031
FRE	Fresno	Pacific Coast	Giants	Grizzlies	1021	1005	1004
FRI	Frisco	Texas	Rangers	RoughRiders	—	986	999
FTM	Ft. Myers	Florida	Twins	Miracle	954	956	960
FTW	Ft. Wayne	Midwest	Padres	Wizards	963	960	954
GRB	Greensboro	South Atlantic	Marlins	Bats	1007	993	979
GRF	Great Falls	Pioneer	WhiteSox	WhiteSox	959	950	944
GRN	Greenville	Southern	Braves	Braves	1011	1007	1012
GRV	Greeneville	Appalachian	Astros	Astros	—	—	939
HAG	Hagerstown	South Atlantic	Giants	Suns	1018	1018	1021
HAR	Harrisburg	Eastern	Expos	Senators	1014	1006	1005
HDS	High Desert	California	Brewers	Mavericks	1106	1106	1103
HEL	Helena	Pioneer	Brewers	Brewers	—	932	922
HIC	Hickory	South Atlantic	Pirates	Crawdads	1050	1043	1032
HNS	Hanshin	Japanese Central	—	Tigers	987	987	987
HOU	Houston	National	Astros	Astros	1035	1026	1015
HRO	Hiroshima	Japanese Central	—	Carp	1058	1058	1058
HUD	HudsonValley	New York-Penn	DevilRays	Renegades	971	952	942
HUN	Huntsville	Southern	Brewers	Stars	991	999	1000
IDA	Idaho Falls	Pioneer	Royals	Chukars	1019	1058	1077
IND	Indianapolis	International	Brewers	Indians	1024	1016	1021
IOW	Iowa	Pacific Coast	Cubs	Cubs	960	965	958
JAM	Jamestown	New York-Penn	Marlins	Jammers	1044	1064	1084
JAX	Jacksonville	Southern	Dodgers	Suns	977	966	973

(continued next page)

TEAM NAME KEY AND PARK FACTORS *(continued)*

Abbrev	Name	League	Organization	Nickname	PF2002	PF2003	PF2004
JCY	Johnson City	Appalachian	Cardinals	Cardinals	992	1005	1015
JUP	Jupiter	Florida	Marlins	Hammerheads	955	967	971
KAN	Kannapolis	South Atlantic	WhiteSox	Intimidators	977	982	1002
KCR	Kansas City	American	Royals	Royals	1080	1064	1029
KIN	Kinston	Carolina	Indians	Indians	970	970	974
KNC	Kane County	Midwest	Athletics	Cougars	964	958	976
KNG	Kingsport	Appalachian	Mets	Mets	973	973	979
LAD	Los Angeles	National	Dodgers	Dodgers	922	935	950
LAK	Lakeland	Florida	Tigers	Tigers	1019	1019	1013
LEL	Lake Elsinore	California	Padres	Storm	950	959	963
LEX	Lexington	South Atlantic	Astros	Legends	1025	1037	1052
LKC	Lake County	South Atlantic	Indians	Captains	—	977	994
LNC	Lancaster	California	Diamondbacks	JetHawks	1099	1092	1089
LNS	Lansing	Midwest	Cubs	Lugnuts	1005	997	985
LOU	Louisville	International	Reds	Bats	1013	1028	1049
LOW	Lowell	New York-Penn	RedSox	Spinners	1013	1041	1038
LVG	Las Vegas	Pacific Coast	Dodgers	51s	1063	1054	1063
LWD	Lakewood	South Atlantic	Phillies	BlueClaws	947	940	936
LYN	Lynchburg	Carolina	Pirates	Hillcats	1039	1032	1012
MAR	Martinsville	Appalachian	—	Astros	984	983	—
MCD	Mexico City	Mexican	—	Red Devils	1190	1190	1190
MCL	Monclova	Mexican	—	Steelers	980	980	980
MCN	Macon	South Atlantic	—	Braves	995	—	—
MCT	Angelopolis	Mexican	—	Tigers	1132	1132	1132
MED	Medicine Hat	Pioneer	—	BlueJays	990	—	—
MEM	Memphis	Pacific Coast	Cardinals	Redbirds	919	924	927
MHV	Mahoning Valley	New York-Penn	Indians	Scrappers	1065	1049	1012
MIC	Michigan	Midwest	—	BattleCats	1007	—	—
MID	Midland	Texas	A's	Rockhounds	1034	1021	1007
MIL	Milwaukee	National	Brewers	Brewers	989	999	1002
MIN	Minnesota	American	Twins	Twins	1018	1014	1020
MNT	Montgomery	Southern	DevilRays	Biscuits	—	—	959
MOB	Mobile	Southern	Padres	BayBears	1021	1013	1002
MOD	Modesto	California	A's	A's	956	961	974
MON	Montreal	National	Expos	Expos	1024	1034	1013
MSO	Missoula	Pioneer	Diamondbacks	Osprey	993	980	973
MTR	Monterrey	Mexican	—	Sultans	976	976	976
MYR	Myrtle Beach	Carolina	Braves	Pelicans	921	921	915
NAS	Nashville	Pacific Coast	Pirates	Sounds	908	906	920
NBR	New Britain	Eastern	Twins	RockCats	984	986	988
NHP	New Hampshire	Eastern	BlueJays	FisherCats	—	—	978
NHV	New Haven	Eastern	—	Ravens	954	950	—
NIP	Nippon Ham	Japanese Pacific	—	Fighters	1026	1026	1026
NOR	Norfolk	International	Mets	Tides	953	946	935
NRW	Norwich	Eastern	Giants	Navigators	964	964	968
NWJ	New Jersey	New York-Penn	Cardinals	Cardinals	963	996	1008
NWO	New Orleans	Pacific Coast	Astros	Zephyrs	880	880	882
NYM	NY Mets	National	Mets	Mets	948	961	968
NYY	NY Yankees	American	Yankees	Yankees	982	969	966
OAK	Oakland	American	A's	A's	1011	1000	999
OAX	Oaxaca	Mexican	—	Warriors	1078	1078	1078
OGD	Ogden	Pioneer	Dodgers	Raptors	1035	1040	1046
OKL	Oklahoma	Pacific Coast	Rangers	Redhawks	940	931	930
OMA	Omaha	Pacific Coast	Royals	Royals	950	948	932
ONE	Oneonta	New York-Penn	Tigers	Tigers	1042	1055	1070
ORL	Orlando	Southern	—	Rays	998	999	—
ORX	Orix	Japanese Pacific	—	Blue Wave	1034	1034	1034
OSA	Osaka	Japanese Pacific	—	Kintetsu Buffal	978	978	978
OTT	Ottawa	International	Orioles	Lynx	987	1008	1028
PAW	Pawtucket	International	RedSox	RedSox	980	976	970
PCH	Pt Charlotte	Florida	—	Rangers	991	—	—
PEO	Peoria	Midwest	Cardinals	Chiefs	969	974	983

Abbrev	Name	League	Organization	Nickname	PF2002	PF2003	PF2004
PHI	Philadelphia	National	Phillies	Phillies	950	954	971
PIT	Pittsburgh	National	Pirates	Pirates	1005	995	982
PMB	Palm Beach	Florida	Cardinals	Cardinals	—	973	962
PME	Portland (ME)	Eastern	RedSox	SeaDogs	1040	1057	1059
POR	Portland (OR)	Pacific Coast	Padres	Beavers	924	938	946
POT	Potomac	Carolina	Reds	Cannons	1049	1041	1021
PRI	Princeton	Appalachian	DevilRays	DevilRays	1051	1068	1088
PRO	Provo	Pioneer	Angels	Angels	1005	1016	1039
PUE	Puebla	Mexican	—	Parrots	1103	1103	—
PUL	Pulaski	Appalachian	BlueJays	BlueJays	1013	1013	1022
QUD	Quad Cities	Midwest	Twins	Swing	1024	1013	991
RCU	Rancho Cucamonga	California	Angels	Quakes	978	978	981
REA	Reading	Eastern	Phillies	Phillies	1019	1023	1034
REY	Reynosa	Mexican	—	—	937	937	—
RIC	Richmond	International	Braves	Braves	982	971	966
ROC	Rochester	International	Twins	RedWings	1018	1027	1022
ROM	Rome	South Atlantic	Braves	Braves	—	949	945
ROU	Round Rock	Texas	Astros	Express	978	979	975
SAC	Sacramento	Pacific Coast	A's	RiverCats	966	964	960
SAN	San Antonio	Texas	Mariners	Missions	898	897	893
SAR	Sarasota	Florida	RedSox	RedSox	1011	1006	998
SAV	Savannah	South Atlantic	Expos	SandGnats	970	984	967
SBN	South Bend	Midwest	Diamondbacks	SilverHawks	997	979	972
SBR	Inland Empire (San B	California	Mariners	66ers	947	940	945
SDP	San Diego	National	Padres	Padres	917	919	919
SEA	Seattle	American	Mariners	Mariners	943	947	942
SEI	Seibu	Japanese Pacific	—	Lions	1011	1011	1011
SFG	San Francisco	National	Giants	Giants	948	978	1006
SGA	South Georgia	South Atlantic	—	Waves	940	986	—
SHV	Shreveport	Texas	—	SwampDragons	957	—	—
SJO	San Jose	California	Giants	Giants	938	934	924
SLC	Salt Lake	Pacific Coast	Angels	Stingers	1073	1091	1104
SLM	Salem (VA)	Carolina	Astros	Avalanche	992	983	979
SLO	Salem-Keizer	Northwest	Giants	Volcanoes	1037	1020	1014
SLT	Saltillo	Mexican	—	Sarapemakers	1024	1024	1024
SLU	St. Lucie	Florida	Mets	Mets	1005	1011	1015
SPO	Spokane	Northwest	Rangers	Indians	1006	1005	1010
STA	Staten Island	New York-Penn	Yankees	Yankees	945	929	917
STL	St. Louis	National	Cardinals	Cardinals	972	965	959
STO	Stockton	California	Rangers	Ports	921	942	953
SWB	Scranton/W-B	International	Phillies	RedBarons	992	1001	1001
SYR	Syracuse	International	BlueJays	SkyChiefs	1019	1012	1018
TAB	Tabasco	Mexican	—	Cattlemen	830	830	830
TAC	Tacoma	Pacific Coast	Mariners	Rainiers	935	925	924
TAM	Tampa	Florida	Yankees	Yankees	951	970	979
TBY	Tampa Bay	American	DevilRays	DevilRays	994	987	977
TCV	Tri-City	New York-Penn	Astros	ValleyCats	1014	1009	1019
TEN	Tennessee	Southern	Cardinals	Smokies	1050	1041	1038
TEX	Texas	American	Rangers	Rangers	1059	1067	1075
TIJ	Tijuana	Mexican	—	Bulls	—	—	1000
TOL	Toledo	International	Tigers	MudHens	1008	988	971
TOR	Toronto	American	BlueJays	BlueJays	1032	1038	1044
TRI	Tri-City	Northwest	Rockies	DustDevils	905	913	922
TRN	Trenton	Eastern	Yankees	Thunder	993	1002	986
TUC	Tucson	Pacific Coast	Diamondbacks	Sidewinders	1080	1102	1102
TUL	Tulsa	Texas	Rockies	Drillers	966	965	966
VAN	Vancouver	Northwest	A's	Canadians	932	946	940
VAQ	Vaqueros	Mexican	—	—	1149	1149	—
VER	Vermont	New York-Penn	Expos	Expos	968	973	976
VIS	Visalia	California	Rockies	Oaks	1004	1005	1005
VRC	Veracruz	Mexican	—	Red Eagles	915	915	915
VRO	Vero Beach	Florida	Dodgers	Dodgers	1063	1059	1041
WIC	Wichita	Texas	Royals	Wranglers	972	965	964

(continued next page)

TEAM NAME KEY AND PARK FACTORS *(continued)*

Abbrev	Name	League	Organization	Nickname	PF2002	PF2003	PF2004
WIL	Wilmington	Carolina	Royals	BlueRocks	979	988	989
WIS	Wisconsin	Midwest	Mariners	TimberRattler	1003	1012	1003
WMI	Western Michigan	Midwest	Tigers	Whitecaps	952	966	972
WNS	WinstonSalem	Carolina	WhiteSox	Warthogs	1007	1016	1036
WPT	Williamsport	New York-Penn	Pirates	Crosscutters	937	936	965
WTN	West Tennessee	Southern	Cubs	DiamondJaxx	972	980	996
YAK	Yakima	Northwest	Diamondbacks	Bears	990	1007	1007
YKL	Yakult	Japanese Central	—	Swallows	956	956	956
YKO	Yokohama	Japanese Central	—	BayStars	1030	1030	1030
YOM	Yomiuri	Japanese Central	—	Giants	1014	1014	1014
YUC	Yucatan	Mexican	—	Lions	879	879	879

Index

The following is an alphabetical index of the players in *Baseball Prospectus 2005.* Players not listed here can be found at http://www.baseballprospectus.com.

A

Aardsma, David 244
Abbott, Paul 175
Abreu, Bob 168
Abreu, Eric 419
Acevedo, Jose 68
Adams, Mike 143
Adams, Russ 497
Adams, Terry 314
Adkins, Jon 331
Affeldt, Jeremy 382
Aguila, Chris 93
Aguilar, Ray 32
Ainsworth, Kurt 297
Alfaro, Jason 106
Alfonseca, Antonio 32
Alfonzo, Edgardo 237
Allison, Jeff 99
Almanzar, Carlos 487
Alomar, Roberto 324
Alomar, Sandy 325
Alou, Moises 41
Alvarez, Abe 314
Alvarez, Tony 185
Alvarez, Wilson 128
Ambres, Chip 93
Amezaga, Alfredo 272
Anderson, Brian (CWS) 325
Anderson, Brian (KCR) 382
Anderson, Garret 272
Anderson, Josh 107
Anderson, Marlon 205
Anderson, Matt 364
Andrade, Steve 280
Ankiel, Rick 212
Aquino, Greg 16
Ardoin, Danny 480
Arias, Joaquin 480
Armas, Tony 260
Arnold, Jason 502
Arroyo, Bronson 315
Asanovich, Josh 463
Astacio, Ezequiel 112
Astacio, Pedro 315
Atchison, Scott 453
Atkins, Garrett 78
Aubrey, Mike 341
Aurilia, Rich 220
Ausmus, Brad 107
Aviles, Mike 375
Avlas, Phil 9
Ayala, Luis 261
Aybar, Erick 272
Aybar, Willy 122

B

Backe, Brandon 113
Bacsik, Mike 488
Baek, Cha 453
Baerga, Carlos 9
Baez, Danny 470
Bagwell, Jeff 107
Bailey, Homer 68
Bailey, Jeff 307
Bailie, Stefan 307
Bajenaru, Jeff 332
Baker, Brad 229
Baker, Jeff 78
Baker, John 429
Baker, Scott 400
Bako, Paul 41
Baldelli, Rocco 463
Baldiris, Aarom 153
Balentien, Wladimir 446
Balfour, Grant 401
Banks, Josh 503
Bankston, Wes 463
Bannister, Brian 159
Barajas, Rod 481
Bard, Josh 341
Barden, Brian 10
Barfield, Josh 220
Barmes, Clint 79
Barrett, Michael 42
Bartlett, Jason 393
Barton, Daric 205
Bartosh, Cliff 347
Bass, Adam 17
Batista, Miguel 503
Batista, Tony 254
Bauer, Rick 297
Baugh, Kenny 365
Bautista, Danny 10
Bautista, Denny 383
Bautista, Jose 186
Bay, Jason 186
Bazardo, Yorman 99
Bean, Colter 419
Beckett, Josh 99
Bedard, Erik 297
Belisle, Matt 69
Bell, David 169
Bell, Heath 159
Bell, Rob 470
Bellhorn, Mark 307
Belliard, Ron 341
Beltran, Carlos 107
Beltran, Francis 261
Beltre, Adrian 122
Benitez, Armando 99
Bennett, Gary 136
Bennett, Jeff 144
Benoit, Joaquin 488
Benson, Kris 160
Bentz, Chad 261
Berg, Dave 497
Bergman, Dusty 280
Berkman, Lance 108
Bernadina, Rogearvin 254
Bernero, Adam 84
Berroa, Angel 375
Betancourt, Rafael 347
Betemit, Wilson 25
Bevis, P. J. 160
Biddle, Rocky 261
Bigbie, Larry 289
Biggio, Craig 108
Billingsley, Chad 128
Blackley, Travis 453
Bladergroen, Ian 153
Blake, Casey 342
Blalock, Hank 481
Blalock, Jake 169
Blanco, Andres 375
Blanco, Gregor 25
Blanco, Henry 394
Blanco, Tony 59
Blanton, Joe 437
Blasko, Chadd 49
Bloomquist, Willie 446
Blum, Geoff 463
Bocachica, Hiram 447
Boehringer, Brian 193
Boeve, Adam 186
Bonderman, Jeremy 365
Bonds, Barry 237
Bondurant, Steven 437
Bong, Jung 69
Bonser, Boof 401
Boone, Aaron 342
Boone, Bret 447
Borchard, Joe 325
Borders, Pat 394
Borkowski, Dave 298
Borowski, Joe 49
Bostick, Adam 100
Bottalico, Ricky 160
Botts, Jason 481
Bourn, Michael 169
Bowen, Rob 394
Bowyer, Travis 401
Boyd, Shaun 205
Boyer, Blaine 32
Bozied, Tagg 221
Bradford, Chad 437
Bradley, Bobby 194
Bradley, Milton 122
Bragg, Darren 59
Branyan, Russ 137
Bray, Bill 261
Brazell, Craig 153
Brazelton, Dewon 471
Brazoban, Yhency 129
Brignac, Reid 464
Brito, Juan 10
Broadway, Larry 254
Brocail, Doug 488
Brooks, Frank 194
Broussard, Ben 342
Brower, Jim 244

Brown, Andrew 348
Brown, Dee 376
Brown, Jeremy 430
Brown, Kevin 419
Brownlie, Bobby 50
Broxton, Jonathan 129
Bruney, Brian 17
Bruntlett, Eric 108
Buchanan, Brian 153
Buchholz, Taylor 113
Buck, John 376
Bucktrot, Keith 175
Buehrle, Mark 332
Buglovsky, Chris 454
Bukvich, Ryan 383
Bullington, Bryan 194
Bump, Nate 100
Burba, Dave 245
Burgos, Ambiorix 383
Burke, Chris 108
Burke, Jamie 325
Burnett, A. J. 100
Burnett, Sean 194
Burnitz, Jeromy 79
Burrell, Pat 169
Burres, Brian 245
Burroughs, Sean 221
Bush, David 503
Butler, Billy 376
Bynum, Freddie 430
Byrd, Marlon 170
Byrd, Paul 33
Byrnes, Eric 430

C

Cabrera, Asdrubal 447
Cabrera, Daniel 298
Cabrera, Fernando 348
Cabrera, Jolbert 447
Cabrera, Melky 411
Cabrera, Miguel 93
Cabrera, Orlando 308
Cain, Matt 245
Cairo, Miguel 411
Calero, Kiko 212
Cali, Carmen 212
Callaspo, Alberto 272
Calloway, Ron 254
Cameron, Mike 154
Camp, Shawn 384
Cano, Robinson 412
Cantu, Jorge 464
Capellan, Jose 33
Capuano, Chris 144
Carmona, Fausto 348
Carpenter, Chris 212
Carrara, Giovanni 129
Carrasco, D. J. 384
Carroll, Jamey 255
Carter, Lance 471
Carvajal, Marcos 129
Casey, Sean 59
Cash, Kevin 497
Castellano, John 170
Castilla, Vinny 79
Castillo, Jose 186
Castillo, Luis 94
Castro, Ismael 448
Castro, Juan 60
Castro, Ramon 94
Catalanotto, Frank 498
Cedeno, Roger 205
Cedeno, Ronny 42
Cepicky, Matt 255
Cerda, Jaime 384
Cervenak, Mike 238
Chacin, Gustavo 503
Chacon, Shawn 85
Chavez, Endy 255
Chavez, Eric 430
Chavez, Raul 109
Chavez, Wilton 262
Chen, Bruce 298
Chen, Yung 448
Cheng, Chi-Hung 504
Chick, Travis 229
Chico, Matt 17
Choate, Randy 17
Choi, Hee 122
Choo, Shin-Soo 448
Christiansen, Jason 245
Chulk, Vinny 504
Church, Ryan 255
Cintron, Alex 10
Cirillo, Jeff 221
Clark, Brady 137
Clark, Jermaine 60
Clark, Tony 412
Claussen, Brandon 69
Clayton, Royce 79
Clemens, Roger 113
Clement, Matt 50
Clippard, Tyler 419
Closser, J. D. 80
Coffey, Todd 69
Coggin, Dave 175
Colbrunn, Greg 11
Collier, Lou 170
Collins, Kevin 42
Colome, Jesus 471
Colon, Bartolo 280
Colon, Roman 33
Colyer, Steve 365
Concepcion, Ambiorix 154
Conine, Jeff 94
Connolly, Jon 50
Connolly, Mike 195
Conrad, Brooks 109
Conti, Jason 481
Contreras, Jose 332
Cook, Aaron 85
Cora, Alex 123
Corcoran, Roy 262
Cordero, Chad 262
Cordero, Francisco 489
Cordero, Wil 94
Cormier, Lance 18
Cormier, Rheal 176
Cornejo, Nate 365
Correia, Kevin 246
Cortes, Jorge 187
Costa, Shane 376
Cota, Humberto 187
Cotts, Neal 332
Counsell, Craig 137
Crabbe, Callix 137
Craig, Casey 448
Craig, Matt 42
Crain, Jesse 401
Crawford, Carl 464
Crede, Joe 326
Crisp, Coco 342
Crosby, Bobby 431
Crosby, Bubba 412
Crouthers, Dave 299
Crozier, Eric 498
Cruceta, Francisco 348
Cruz, Deivi 238
Cruz, Enrique 138
Cruz, Jacob 60
Cruz, Jose 464
Cruz, Juan 33
Cruz, Nelson 431
Cuddyer, Mike 394
Cummings, Midre 465
Curtis, Daniel 34
Cust, Jack 290
Cyr, Eric 281

D

Daigle, Casey 18
Dallimore, Brian 238
Damon, Johnny 308
Danks, John 489
Daubach, Brian 308
DaVanon, Jeff 273
Davidson, Daniel 281
Davies, Kyle 34
Davis, Ben 326
Davis, Doug 144
Davis, J. J. 187
Davis, Jason 349
Davis, Rajai 187
Day, Zach 262
De la Cruz, Eulogio 366
De la Rosa, Jorge 145
DeJaynes, Brandon 213
DeJean, Mike 160
DeJesus, David 377
Delcarmen, Manny 315
Delgado, Carlos 498
Delgado, Wilson 154
Dellucci, David 482
Dempster, Ryan 51
Denham, Dan 349
Denney, Kyle 349
DePaula, Jorge 420
DeRosa, Mark 26
DeSalvo, Matt 420
Dessens, Elmer 130
DeVore, Doug 11
Diaz, Einar 256
Diaz, Felix 333
Diaz, Matt 465
Diaz, Victor 154
Dickerson, Chris 61
Dickey, R. A. 489
Dillon, Joe 95
DiNardo, Lenny 315
Dingman, Craig 366
Dittler, Jake 350
Dixon, Zach 299
Dobbs, Greg 448
Dobies, Andrew 316
Dominguez, Juan 489
Donnelly, Brendan 281
Dopirak, Brian 43
Dotel, Octavio 438
Doumit, Ryan 188
Downs, Scott 263
Dreifort, Darren 130
Drese, Ryan 490
Drew, J. D. 26
Drew, Stephen 11
Drew, Tim 34
Dubois, Jason 43
DuBose, Eric 299
Duchscherer, Justin 438
Duckworth, Brandon 113
Duffy, Chris 188

Duke, Zach 195
Dukes, Elijah 465
Duncan, Chris 206
Duncan, Eric 413
Dunlap, Cory 123
Dunn, Adam 61
Dunn, Scott 281
Durazo, Erubiel 431
Durbin, Chris 308
Durbin, J. D. 402
Durham, Ray 238
Dye, Jermaine 431

E

Easley, Damion 95
Eaton, Adam 229
Eckstein, David 273
Edmonds, Jim 206
Einertson, Mitch 109
Eischen, Joey 263
Elarton, Scott 350
Eldred, Brad 188
Eldred, Cal 213
Ellis, Mark 432
Ellison, Jason 239
Embree, Alan 316
Encarnacion, Edwin 61
Encarnacion, Juan 95
Ensberg, Morgan 109
Erickson, Matt 138
Erstad, Darin 273
Escobar, Kelvim 282
Escobar, Rodrigo 114
Espinosa, David 357
Esposito, Mike 85
Esquivel, Matt 26
Estes, Shawn 85
Estrada, Johnny 26
Etherton, Seth 70
Eveland, Dana 145
Everett, Adam 110
Everett, Carl 326
Everts, Clint 263
Eyre, Scott 246
Eyre, Willie 402

F

Farnsworth, Kyle 51
Feliciano, Pedro 161
Feliz, Pedro 239
Fick, Robert 222
Field, Nathan 384
Fielder, Prince 138
Fields, Josh 326
Figgins, Chone 273
Figueroa, Nelson 195
Finley, Steve 123
Fiorentino, Jeff 290
Flaherty, John 413
Floyd, Cliff 155
Floyd, Gavin 176
Fogg, Josh 195
Fontenot, Mike 290
Foppert, Jesse 246
Ford, Ben 145
Ford, Lew 395
Fordyce, Brook 466
Fortunato, Bartolome 161
Fossum, Casey 18
Foulke, Keith 316
Fox, Chad 100
Francis, Jeff 86
Francisco, Frank 490
Franco, John 161
Franco, Julio 27
Francouer, Jeff 27
Franklin, Ryan 454
Franklin, Wayne 246
Fransz, Jason 482
Frasor, Jason 504
Freel, Ryan 61
Freeman, Choo 80
Fuentes, Brian 86
Fullmer, Brad 482
Fultz, Aaron 402
Furcal, Rafael 27
Furmaniak, J. J. 222

G

Gagne, Eric 130
Galarraga, Andres 274
Gallo, Mike 114
Gamble, Jerome 316
Garcia, Danny 155
Garcia, Freddy 333
Garcia, Jairo 438
Garcia, James 247
Garcia, Jesse 28
Garcia, Karim 290
Garciaparra, Nomar 43
Gardner, Richie 70
Garko, Ryan 343
Garland, Jon 333
Gassner, Dave 402
Gathright, Joey 466
Gaudin, Chad 472
Gautreau, Jake 222
Geary, Geoff 176
George, Chris 385
German, Esteban 432
German, Franklyn 366
Germano, Justin 230
Gerut, Jody 343
Gettis, Byron 377
Giambi, Jason 413
Giarratano, Tony 357
Gibbons, Jay 291
Giese, Dan 177
Gil, Geronimo 291
Gil, Jerry 11
Giles, Brian 222
Giles, Marcus 28
Ginter, Keith 139
Ginter, Matt 161
Gissell, Chris 86
Glanville, Doug 171
Glaus, Troy 274
Glavine, Tom 162
Gload, Ross 327
Gobble, Jimmy 385
Godwin, Tyrell 498
Goleski, Ryan 343
Golson, Greg 171
Gomes, Johnny 466
Gomez, Abel 420
Gomez, Chris 499
Gomez, Mariano 350
Gonzalez, Adrian 482
Gonzalez, Alex (SDP) 223
Gonzalez, Alex (FLA) 95
Gonzalez, Edgar 18
Gonzalez, Gio 333
Gonzalez, Jeremi 472
Gonzalez, Juan 377
Gonzalez, Luis 11
Gonzalez, Luis 80
Gonzalez, Mike 196
Good, Andrew 19
Goodwin, Tom 44
Gordon, Tom 420
Gorecki, Reid 206
Gorneault, Nick 274
Gorzelanny 196
Gosling, Mike 19
Gotay, Ruben 377
Gothreaux, Jared 114
Grabow, John 196
Grabowski, Jason 123
Graffanino, Tony 378
Graman, Alex 421
Granderson, Curtis 358
Graves, Danny 70
Green, Andy 12
Green, Nick 28
Green, Shawn 124
Greene, Khalil 223
Greene, Todd 80
Gregg, Kevin 282
Greinke, Zack 385
Greisinger, Seth 403
Grieve, Ben 44
Griffey Jr., Ken 62
Griffin, Colt 386
Griffin, John-Ford 499
Griffiths, Jeremy 114
Grilli, Jason 334
Grimsley, Jason 299
Grissom, Marquis 239
Groom, Buddy 300
Gross, Gabe 499
Grudzielanek, Mark 44
Gryboski, Kevin 34
Guardado, Eddie 454
Guerrero, Vladimir 275
Guerrier, Matt 403
Guevara, Carlos 71
Guiel, Aaron 378
Guillen, Carlos 358
Guillen, Jose 275
Guillen, Rudy 413
Guthrie, Jeremy 350
Gutierrez, Franklin 343
Gutierrez, Jesse 62
Guzman, Angel 51
Guzman, Freddy 223
Guzman, Javier 188
Guzman, Jesus 449
Guzman, Joel 124
Gwynn, Anthony 139

H

Habel, Josh 247
Haehnel, David 300
Haerther, Cody 207
Hafner, Travis 344
Hagerty, Luke 51
Hairston, Jerry 291
Hairston, Scott 12
Halama, John 472
Hall, Bill 139
Hall, Josh 71
Hall, Mickey 309
Hall, Toby 467
Halladay, Roy 504
Halsey, Brad 421
Halter, Shane 275
Hamels, Cole 177
Hammel, Jason 472
Hammock, Rob 12
Hammond, Chris 439

Hammonds, Jeffrey 239
Hampton, Mike 35
Hancock, Josh 71
Hannahan, Jack 358
Hanrahan, Joel 130
Hansen, Dave 224
Harang, Aaron 71
Harben, Adam 403
Harden, Rich 439
Hardy, J. J. 139
Haren, Danny 213
Harikkala,Tim 87
Harper, Travis 473
Harris, Brendan 256
Harris, Estee 414
Harris, Lenny 96
Harris, Willie 327
Hart, Corey 140
Harvey, Ken 378
Harvey, Ryan 44
Harville, Chad 115
Hasegawa, Shigetoshi 454
Hatteberg, Scott 432
Hattig, John 499
Hawkins, LaTroy 52
Hawksworth, Blake 213
Hawpe, Brad 81
Haynes, Dee 207
Heilman, Aaron 162
Helling, Rick 490
Helms, Wes 140
Helton, Todd 81
Hendrickson, Ben 146
Hendrickson, Mark 473
Henkel, Rob 366
Henn, Sean 421
Hennessey, Brad 247
Hensley, Matt 282
Hentgen, Pat 505
Heredia, Felix 421
Herges, Matt 247
Hermanson, Dustin 248
Hermida, Jeremy 96
Hernandez, Anderson 358
Hernandez, Carlos 115
Hernandez, Felix 455
Hernandez, Jose 124
Hernandez, Livan 263
Hernandez, Michel 171
Hernandez, Orlando 422
Hernandez, Ramon 224
Hernandez, Runelvys 386
Hessman, Mike 28
Hidalgo, Richard 155
Higginson, Bobby 359
Hill, Aaron 500
Hill, Bobby 189
Hill, Koyie 13
Hill, Shawn 264
Hillenbrand, Shea 13
Hinckley, Mike 264
Hinske, Eric 500
Hitchcox, Brian 171
Hoffman, Trevor 230
Hollandsworth, Todd 45
Holliday, Matt 81
Holt, J. C. 29
Honel, Kris 334
Hoover, Jesse 422
Horgan, Joe 264
Houlton, D. J. 115
House, J. R. 189
Houser, James 473
Housman, Jeff 146
Howard, Ben 101
Howard, Ryan 172
Howell, J. P. 386
Howry, Bobby 351
Hu, Chin-Lung 124
Huber, Jon 455
Huber, Justin 378
Hudson, Luke 72
Hudson, Orlando 500
Hudson, Tim 439
Huff, Aubrey 467
Huisman, Justin 387
Hummel, Tim 309
Hunter, Torii 395
Hutchinson, Trevor 101

I

Ibanez, Raul 449
Infante, Omar 359
Inge, Brandon 359
Iribarren, Hernan 140
Ishii, Kazuhisa 131
Ishikawa, Travis 240
Isringhausen, Jason 214
Izturis, Cesar 125
Izturis, Maicer 256

J

Jackson, Conor 13
Jackson, Edwin 131
Jacobs, Mike 155
Jacobsen, Bucky 449
James, Chuck 35
Jenkins, Geoff 140
Jenks, Bobby 282
Jennings, Jason 87
Jensen, Ryan 248
Jeter, Derek 414
Jimenez, D'Angelo 62
Jimerson, Charlton 110
Johnson, Ben 224
Johnson, Charles 81
Johnson, Dan 432
Johnson, Jason 367
Johnson, Kelly 29
Johnson, Mark 141
Johnson, Mike 224
Johnson, Nick 257
Johnson, Randy 19
Johnson, Reed 500
Johnson, Rett 455
Johnson, Tripper 291
Johnson, Tyler 214
Johnston, Mike 196
Jones, Adam 449
Jones, Andruw 29
Jones, Chipper 29
Jones, Garrett 396
Jones, Jacque 395
Jones, Mike 146
Jones, Mitch 414
Jones, Todd 178
Jordan, Brian 483
Journell, Jimmy 214
Julianel, Ben 422
Julio, Jorge 300

K

Kapler, Gabe 309
Karp, Josh 264
Karsay, Steve 422
Kata, Matt 13
Kazmir, Scott 473
Kearns, Austin 62
Kelly, Kenny 63
Kelly, Steve 72
Kelton, Dave 45
Kemp, Beau 404
Kemp, Matt 125
Kendall, Jason 189
Kendrick, Howie 275
Kennedy, Adam 276
Kennedy, Joe 87
Kensing, Logan 101
Kent, Jeff 110
Keppel, Bob 162
Keppinger, Jeff 156
Kershner, Jason 505
Kielty, Bobby 433
Kieschnick, Brooks 147
Kiger, Mark 433
Kim, Byung-Hyun 317
Kim, Sun-Woo 265
King, Ray 214
Kinney, Matt 387
Kinsler, Ian 483
Kirkland, Kody 359
Klesko, Ryan 225
Kline, Steve 215
Knoedler, Justin 240
Knott, Jon 225
Knotts, Gary 367
Knox, Brad 439
Koch, Billy 101
Kolb, Dan 147
Kolkhorst, Christopher 225
Konerko, Paul 327
Koonce, Graham 433
Koplove, Mike 19
Koskie, Corey 396
Kotchman, Casey 276
Kotsay, Mark 433
Kottaras, George 225
Kouzmanoff, Kevin 344
Kozlowski, Ben 491
Kroeger, Josh 14
Krynzel, David 141
Kubel, Jason 396

L

Labandeira, Josh 257
Lackey, John 283
LaForest, Pete 467
Laird, Gerald 483
Lamb, Mike 110
Lane, Jason 111
Langerhans, Ryan 30
Lankford, Ray 207
Larkin, Barry 63
LaRoche, Adam 30
LaRoche, Andy 125
Larrison, Preston 367
Larson, Brandon 63
LaRue, Jason 64
Lawrence, Brian 230
Lawton, Matt 344
League, Brandon 505
LeCroy, Matt 396
Ledee, Ricky 240
Ledezma, Wil 367
Lee, Carlos 327
Lee, Cliff 351

Lee, Derrek 45
Lee, Travis 414
Lehr, Justin 440
Leicester, Jon 52
Leiter, Al 162
Leon, Jose 292
Leone, Justin 449
Lerew, Anthony 35
Leskanic, Curt 317
Lester, Jon 317
Levine, Al 368
Lewis, Colby 491
Lewis, Fred 240
Lewis, Richard 45
Lidge, Brad 115
Lidle, Cory 178
Lieber, Jon 423
Lieberthal, Mike 172
Ligtenberg, Kerry 506
Lilly, Ted 506
Lima, Jose 131
Linden, Todd 241
Linebrink, Scott 230
Liriano, Francisco 404
Liriano, Pedro 147
Livingston, Bobby 455
Loaiza, Esteban 423
Lockwood, Luke 265
LoDuca, Paul 96
Loe, Kameron 491
Loewen, Adam 300
Lofton, Kenny 415
Logan, Nook 360
Lohse, Kyle 404
Loney, James 125
Long, Terrence 226
Looper, Aaron 163
Lopez, Aquilino 506
Lopez, Felipe 64
Lopez, Javier 87
Lopez, Javy 292
Lopez, Jose 450
Lopez, Luis 292
Lopez, Pedro 328
Lopez, Rodrigo 301
Loretta, Mark 226
Loux, Shane 368
Lowe, Derek 317
Lowell, Mike 96
Lowery, Devon 387
Lowry, Noah 248
Lubanski, Chris 379
Ludwick, Ryan 344
Lugo, Julio 467
Luna, Hector 207
Lyon, Brandon 20

M

Mabeus, Chris 440
Mabry, John 208
MacDougal, Mike 387
Machado, Alejandro 257
Machado, Andy 64
Machado, Robert 292
Macias, Jose 46
Mackowiak, Rob 189
Maddux, Greg 53
Madritsch, Bobby 456
Madson, Ryan 178
Magruder, Chris 141
Mahay, Ron 491
Maholm, Paul 197
Maier, Mitch 379
Maine, John 301
Majewski, Gary 265
Majewski, Val 293
Malaska, Mark 318
Mantei, Matt 20
Marcum, Shaun 506
Markakis, Nick 293
Maroth, Mike 368
Marquis, Jason 215
Marrero, Eli 30
Marte, Andy 30
Marte, Damaso 334
Martin, J. D. 351
Martin, Russell 126
Martin, Tom 35
Martinez, Anastacio 318
Martinez, Edgar 450
Martinez, Luis 88
Martinez, Pedro 318
Martinez, Ramon 46
Martinez, Tino 468
Martinez, Victor 345
Martinez-Esteve, Eddy 241
Mateo, Henry 258
Mateo, Julio 456
Mateo, Natanael 231
Matheny, Mike 208
Mathieson, Scott 178
Mathis, Jeff 276
Matos, Luis 293
Matsui, Hideki 415
Matsui, Kazuo 156
Matthews Jr., Gary 483
Mauer, Joe 397
May, Darrell 388
Mayne, Brent 126
Mays, Joe 404
Maza, Luis 397
McAnulty, Paul 226
McCann, Brian 31
McCarthy, Bill 31
McCarthy, Brandon 334
McCarty, Dave 309
McClung, Seth 474
McCracken, Quinton 14
McDonald, Darnell 293
McDonald, John 345
McDougall, Marshall 484
McEwing, Joe 156
McGowan, Dustin 507
McGriff, Fred 468
McKay, Cody 208
McLemore, Mark 434
McLouth, Nate 190
McMillon, Billy 434
McPherson, Dallas 277
Meadows, Brian 197
Meadows, Ty 484
Meaux, Ryan 335
Meche, Gil 456
Mecir, Jim 440
Megrew, Mike 131
Mejia, Gilberto 360
Melhuse, Adam 434
Mench, Kevin 484
Mendoza, Ramiro 318
Menechino, Frank 501
Mercker, Kent 53
Mesa, Jose 197
Meyer, Dan 36
Miceli, Dan 116
Michaels, Jason 172
Mientkiewicz, Doug 310
Miles, Aaron 82
Millar, Kevin 310
Milledge, Lastings 156
Miller, Adam 352
Miller, Brian 335
Miller, Corky 65
Miller, Damian 434
Miller, Greg 132
Miller, Jason 405
Miller, Jeff 197
Miller, Jim 88
Miller, Justin 507
Miller, Matt 352
Miller, Tony 82
Miller, Trever 474
Miller, Wade 116
Millwood, Kevin 179
Milton, Eric 179
Minor, Damon 241
Mirabelli, Doug 310
Misch, Pat 248
Mitre, Sergio 53
Moeller, Chad 141
Mohr, Dustan 241
Molina, Ben 277
Molina, Jose 277
Molina, Yadier 208
Mondesi, Raul 277
Monroe, Craig 360
Moore, Scott 360
Mora, Melvin 294
Morales, Jose 397
Morales, Kendry 278
Moran, Javon 65
Moreno, Abel 283
Moreno, Orber 163
Moreno, Victor 405
Morneau, Justin 397
Morris, Matt 215
Morrissey, Adam 435
Morse, Michael 450
Moseley, Dustin 72
Moss, Brandon 310
Mota, Guillermo 102
Moyer, Jamie 457
Mueller, Bill 311
Mulder, Mark 440
Mulholland, Terry 405
Munoz, Arnie 335
Munro, Peter 116
Munson, Eric 361
Murphy, Donnie 379
Murton, Matt 46
Mussina, Mike 423
Myers, Brett 180
Myers, Mike 319

N

Nady, Xavier 226
Nageotte, Clint 457
Nakamura, Micheal 507
Nance, Shane 20
Napoli, Michael 278
Narveson, Chris 88
Nathan, Joe 405
Navarro, Dioner 415
Neal, Blaine 231
Nelson, Brad 142
Nelson, John 209
Nen, Robb 249

Nevin, Phil 227
Newhan, David 294
Nichols, Kyle 14
Niekro, Lance 242
Nieve, Fernando 116
Nippert, Dustin 20
Nivar, Ramon 484
Nix, Jayson 82
Nix, Laynce 485
Nixon, Trot 311
Nolasco, Ricky 53
Norris, Shawn 258
Norton, Greg 361
Norton, Phil 73
Novoa, Roberto 368
Nunez, Abraham (KCR) 380
Nunez, Abraham (PIT) 190
Nunez, Franklin 474
Nunez, Leo 198
Nunez, Vladimir 88

O

Obermueller, Wes 148
Offerman, Jose 398
Ohka, Tomokazu 265
Ohman, Will 54
Ojeda, Augie 398
Ojeda, Miguel 227
Oldham, Thomas 457
Olerud, John 416
Oliver, Darren 117
Olivo, Miguel 450
Olmedo, Rainer 65
Olsen, Scott 102
Olson, Tim 14
Ordonez, Magglio 328
Ordonez, Rey 46
Ortiz, David 311
Ortiz, Ramon 283
Ortiz, Russ 36
Ortmeier, Dan 242
Orvella, Chad 474
Osuna, Antonio 231
Oswalt, Roy 117
Otsuka, Akinori 231
Overbay, Lyle 142
Owens, Jerry 258
Oxspring, Chris 232

P

Padilla, Vicente 180
Palmeiro, Orlando 111
Palmeiro, Rafael 294
Palmisano, Lou 142
Papelbon, Jon 319
Park, Chan Ho 492
Parra, Manny 148
Parrish, John 301
Pascucci, Val 258
Patterson, Corey 47
Patterson, John 266
Paul, Josh 278
Paulino, Ronny 190
Pauly, Thomas 73
Pavano, Carl 102
Payton, Jay 227
Peavy, Jake 232
Pedroia, Dustin 311
Pellow, Kit 82
Pena, Carlos 361
Pena, Luis 148
Pena, Wily Mo 65
Penn, Hayden 301
Penny, Brad 132
Peralta, Jhonny 345
Percival, Troy 284
Perez, Antonio 126
Perez, Eddie 31
Perez, Eduardo 468
Perez, Kenny 312
Perez, Miguel 66
Perez, Neifi 47
Perez, Odalis 132
Perez, Oliver 198
Perez, Timo 328
Perez, Tomas 172
Perisho, Matt 102
Perry, Herb 485
Perry, Jason 435
Peterson, Adam 507
Peterson, Matt 198
Petit, Yusmeiro 163
Pettitte, Andy 117
Phelps, Josh 345
Phelps, Tommy 103
Phillips, Andy 416
Phillips, Brandon 346
Phillips, Jason 157
Phillips, Paul 380
Piazza, Mike 157
Pickering, Cal 380
Pie, Felix 47
Piedra, Jorge 83
Pierre, Juan 97
Pierzynski, A. J. 242
Pimentel, Julio 132
Pineiro, Joel 457
Pinto, Renyel 54
Podsednik, Scott 143
Polanco, Placido 173
Politte, Cliff 335
Pomeranz, Stuart 215
Ponson, Sidney 302
Posada, Jorge 416
Powell, Brian 180
Pratt, Todd 173
Pridie, Jason 468
Prinz, Bret 424
Prior, Mark 54
Proctor, Scott 424
Pujols, Albert 209
Punto, Nick 398
Purcey, David 508
Putz, J. J. 458

Q

Qualls, Chad 117
Quantrill, Paul 424
Quentin, Carlos 15
Quinlan, Robb 279
Quintanilla, Omar 435
Quintero, Humberto 228
Quiroz, Guillermo 501

R

Raburn, Ryan 361
Radke, Brad 406
Raines Jr., Tim 295
Rakers, Aaron 302
Rall, Tim 458
Ramirez, Aramis 48
Ramirez, Erasmo 492
Ramirez, Hanley 312
Ramirez, Horacio 36
Ramirez, Ismael 508
Ramirez, Manny 312
Ramirez, Ramon 424
Randa, Joe 380
Randolph, Stephen 21
Ransom, Cody 242
Rasner, Darrell 266
Rauch, Jon 266
Ray, Chris 302
Redding, Tim 118
Redman, Mark 441
Redman, Prentice 157
Redman, Tike 190
Redmond, Mike 97
Reed, Eric 97
Reed, Jeremy 451
Reed, Steve 89
Reese, Kevin 416
Reese, Pokey 312
Regilio, Nick 492
Reichert, Dan 148
Reitsma, Chris 36
Relaford, Desi 381
Remlinger, Mike 55
Renteria, Edgar 209
Restovich, Mike 398
Reyes, Al 216
Reyes, Anthony 216
Reyes, Dennys 388
Reyes, Jose 157
Rheinecker, John 441
Rhodes, Arthur 441
Riedling, John 73
Riggs, Adam 279
Riley, Matt 302
Rincon, Juan 406
Rincon, Ricardo 442
Rios, Alexis 501
Riske, David 352
Ritchie, Todd 475
Rivas, Luis 399
Rivera, Carlos 191
Rivera, Juan 259
Rivera, Mariano 425
Rivera, Rene 451
Roa, Joe 406
Roberson, Chris 173
Roberts, Brian 295
Roberts, Dave 313
Robertson, Nate 369
Robinson, Kerry 228
Rodriguez, Alex 417
Rodriguez, Eddy 303
Rodriguez, Felix 180
Rodriguez, Francisco 284
Rodriguez, Ivan 362
Rodriguez, Luis 399
Rodriguez, Ricardo 493
Rodriguez, Sean 279
Rogers, Kenny 493
Rogers, Mark 149
Rogowski, Casey 329
Rolen, Scott 209
Rollins, Jimmy 173
Rolls, Damian 469
Romano, Jason 66
Romero, J. C. 406
Rosario, Francisco 508
Rose, Brian 73
Rose, Mike 435
Ross, Dave 126
Rouse, Mike 436
Rowand, Aaron 329
Rowland-Smith, Ryan 458
Rueckel, Danny 266
Rueter, Kirk 249

Ruiz, Carlos 174
Rusch, Glendon 55
Ryan, B. J. 303
Ryan, Brendan 210
Ryan, Mike 399

S

Saarloos, Kirk 442
Sabathia, C. C. 353
Sadler, Ray 191
Saenz, Olmedo 127
Sain, Greg 228
Salazar, Jeff 83
Salmon, Tim 279
Sanchez, Alex 362
Sanchez, Anibal 319
Sanchez, Duaner 133
Sanchez, Felix 369
Sanchez, Freddy 191
Sanchez, Humberto 369
Sanchez, Rey 469
Sandberg, Jared 469
Sanders, Reggie 210
Santana, Ervin 284
Santana, Johan 407
Santiago, Benito 381
Santiago, Ramon 451
Santos, Sergio 15
Santos, Victor 149
Sardinha, Bronson 417
Sardinha, Dane 66
Sarfate, Dennis 149
Saunders, Joe 285
Schierholtz, Nate 243
Schilling, Curt 319
Schmidt, Jason 249
Schneider, Brian 259
Schoeneweis, Scott 336
Schumaker, Skip 210
Scott, Luke 111
Scutaro, Marco 436
Seabol, Scott 210
Seanez, Rudy 103
Seay, Bobby 475
Seddon, Chris 475
Segui, David 295
Sele, Aaron 285
Self, Todd 111
Senreiso, Juan 485
Seo, Jae 163
Serrano, Jim 388
Service, Scott 21
Sexson, Richie 15
Shackelford, Brian 74
Shealy, Ryan 83
Sheets, Ben 149
Sheffield, Gary 417
Shell, Steven 285
Shelton, Chris 362
Sherrill, George 458
Shields, Scot 285
Shoppach, Kelly 313
Shouse, Brian 493
Sierra, Edwardo 425
Sierra, Ruben 418
Silva, Carlos 407
Silva, Jesus 21
Simon, Alfredo 249
Simon, Randall 469
Simontacchi, Jason 216
Simpson, Allan 89
Sing, Brandon 48
Sinisi, Vince 485
Sisco, Andy 55
Sizemore, Grady 346
Sledge, Terrmel 259
Sleeth, Kyle 369
Smith, Bud 181
Smith, Chris 320
Smith, Corey 346
Smith, Dustin 486
Smith, Jason 363
Smoltz, John 37
Snare, Ryan 493
Snell, Ian 198
Snelling, Chris 451
Snow, J. T. 243
Snyder, Brad 347
Snyder, Chris 15
Snyder, Earl 313
Song, Seung 267
Sonnastine, Andrew 476
Soriano, Alfonso 486
Soriano, Rafael 459
Sosa, Jorge 476
Sosa, Sammy 48
Sota, Geovany 49
Spann, Chad 313
Sparks, Steve 21
Spears, Nate 296
Speier, Justin 508
Speier, Ryan 89
Spencer, Shane 158
Spidale, Mike 329
Spiezio, Scott 451
Spivey, Junior 143
Stairs, Matt 381
Standridge, Jason 476
Stanford, Jason 353
Stanton, Mike 164
Stark, Denny 89
Stauffer, Tim 232
Stavisky, Brian 436
Stevens, Jake 37
Stewart, Cory 199
Stewart, Ian 83
Stewart, Josh 336
Stewart, Shannon 399
Stinnett, Kelly 381
Stodolka, Mike 388
Stokes, Jason 97
Stone, Ricky 232
Stratton, Rob 67
Street, Huston 442
Strong, Jamal 452
Sturtze, Tanyon 425
Stynes, Chris 191
Sullivan, Scott 389
Suppan, Jeff 216
Surhoff, B. J. 296
Sutton, Larry 98
Suzuki, Ichiro 452
Sweeney, Brian 233
Sweeney, Mark 84
Sweeney, Mike 382
Sweeney, Ryan 329
Swisher, Nick 436

T

Tablado, Raul 501
Tadano, Kaz 353
Taguchi, So 211
Takatsu, Shingo 336
Tallet, Brian 353
Tamayo, Danny 389
Tankersley, Dennis 233
Tankersley, Taylor 103
Tavarez, Julian 217
Taveras, Willy 112
Taylor, Aaron 459
Teahen, Mark 382
Teixeira, Mark 486
Tejada, Miguel 296
Tejeda, Juan 363
Telemaco, Amaury 181
Terrero, Luis 16
Thames, Marcus 363
Thayer, Dale 233
Thomas, Brad 320
Thomas, Charles 31
Thomas, Frank 330
Thome, Jim 174
Thompson, Brad 217
Thompson, Rich 192
Thompson, Sean 233
Thomson, John 37
Thornton, Matt 459
Thurston, Joe 127
Tiffany, Chuck 133
Tiffee, Terry 400
Timlin, Mike 320
Tomko, Brett 250
Torcato, Tony 243
Torrealba, Yorvit 243
Torres, Andres 330
Torres, Salomon 199
Towers, Josh 509
Tracey, Sean 337
Trachsel, Steve 164
Tracy, Andy 84
Tracy, Chad 16
Truby, Chris 192
Trujillo, J. J. 389
Tsao, Chin-Hui 90
Tucker, Michael 244
Tucker, T. J. 267
Tuiasosopo, Matt 452
Tyler, Scott 407

U

Upton, B. J. 470
Urbina, Ugueth 370
Uribe, Juan 330
Utley, Chase 174

V

Valdez, Ismael 103
Valdez, Merkin 250
Valdez, Wilson 330
Valent, Eric 158
Valentin, Javier 67
Valentin, Jose 331
Valentine, Joe 74
Valido, Rob 331
Valverde, Jose 22
Van Poppel, Todd 74
VanBenschoten, John 199
Vander Wal, John 67
Vargas, Claudio 267
Varitek, Jason 314
Vasquez, Jorge 389
Vasquez, Matt 370
Vaughan, Beau 320
Vazquez, Javier 425
Vazquez, Ramon 228
Velander, Justin 370
Venafro, Mike 133
Ventura, Robin 127
Vericker, Brad 244
Vermilyea, Jamie 509

Vidro, Jose 259
Villafuerte, Brandon 22
Villareal, Oscar 22
Villone, Ron 459
Vina, Fernando 363
Vizcaino, Jose 112
Vizcaino, Luis 150
Vizquel, Omar 347
Vogelsong, Ryan 200
Votto, Joey 68

W

Waechter, Doug 476
Wagner, Billy 181
Wagner, Ryan 74
Wainwright, Adam 217
Wakefield, Tim 321
Walker, Jamie 370
Walker, Kevin 250
Walker, Larry 211
Walker, Todd 49
Walker, Tyler 250
Walrond, Les 390
Wang, Chien-Ming 426
Ward, Daryle 192
Wasdin, John 494
Washburn, Jarrod 286
Wathan, Derek 98
Watkins, Steve 234
Watson, Brandon 260
Watson, Matt 437
Wayne, Justin 104
Weathers, Dave 104
Weaver, Jeff 133
Webb, Brandon 22
Webb, John 477
Weeks, Rickie 143
Wellemeyer, Todd 55
Wells, David 234
Wells, Kip 200
Wells, Vernon 502
Werth, Jayson 127
West, Kevin 400
Westbrook, Jake 354
Wheeler, Dan 118
Whitaker, Craig 251
White, Gabe 75
White, Rondell 364
White, Steven 426
Whiteman, Tommy 112
Whiteside, Eli 296
Wickman, Bob 354
Wigginton, Ty 192
Wilkerson, Brad 260
Williams, Bernie 418
Williams, Dave 200
Williams, Gerald 158
Williams, Jerome 251
Williams, Todd 303
Williams, Woody 217
Williamson, Scott 321
Willingham, Josh 98
Willis, Dontrelle 104
Wilson, Craig 193
Wilson, Dan 452
Wilson, Enrique 418
Wilson, Jack 193
Wilson, Josh 98
Wilson, Paul 75
Wilson, Preston 84
Wilson, Tom 128
Wilson, Vance 158
Winn, Randy 453
Wise, DeWayne 32
Wise, Matt 150
Witasick, Jay 234
Wolf, Randy 182
Womack, Tony 211
Wood, Brandon 280
Wood, Kerry 56
Wood, Mike 390
Woods, Jake 286
Woodward, Chris 502
Woolard, Glenn 150
Wooten, Shawn 175
Worrell, Tim 182
Wright, David 159
Wright, Jamey 90
Wright, Jaret 37
Wuertz, Mike 56

Y

Yabu, Keiichi 443
Yan, Esteban 371
Yarnall, Ed 182
Yates, Tyler 164
Yofu, Tetsu 337
Youkilis, Kevin 314
Young, Chris 331
Young, Chris 494
Young, Delmon 470
Young, Delwyn 128
Young, Dmitri 364
Young, Eric 487
Young, Jason 90
Young, Mike 487
Young, Walter 296

Z

Zambrano, Carlos 56
Zambrano, Victor 164
Zaun, Gregg 502
Zeile, Todd 159
Zeringue, Jonathan 16
Zimmerman, Bob 286
Zink, Charlie 321
Zito, Barry 443
Zoccolillo, Pete 487
Zumaya, Joel 371

Biographies

David Cameron resides in High Point, North Carolina. He spends his days working as a cost accountant, which is even less exciting than it sounds. At night, he can usually be found at one of the multitude of minor league ballparks in the area.

Will Carroll had a pretty big year in 2004. He published his first solo book, *Saving The Pitcher.* He wrote 150 articles for BP and was published in *Slate,* the *New York Times,* and *YES.* He discovered the joys of XM Radio. He still considers himself the luckiest boy in the whole world, though several other BP authors try to claim the title for themselves. He's seeking treatment for his Cubs addiction while writing his second book.

James Click spends most days thanking his girlfriend, Ace, for convincing him to come to California and follow the A's rather than stick with the Mets. His history degree from Yale has little practical application to either his day job as a tech consultant or his work at BP, but he manages to fake it well enough so far. Suckers.

Clay Davenport is a meteorologist living in Bowie, Maryland, with his wife, Susan. Outside of the day job and baseball, he picks up a ridiculous amount of trivial knowledge from God knows where and tosses it back out in bars. Or at least he used to.

Steven Goldman is the host of the long-running Pinstriped Bible column (currently appearing at www.yesnetwork.com), the author of *Forging Genius: The Making of Casey Stengel,* now available at a bookstore near you, and the editor of the as-yet-unnamed Baseball Prospectus book on the 2004 Boston Red Sox. He is very 'umble about all of these things. In his spare time, Steven writes things that aren't about baseball yet somehow always have a little baseball in them, watches pre-code flicks from the 1930s, and spends as many hours as he can with his daughter, Sarah, and wife, Stefanie.

Gary Huckabay is the founder of Baseball Prospectus, and now works as a consultant for the Oakland Athletics. He lives in Clayton, California with his wife, Kathy, and son, Charlie, whose only complaint is that dad ties his right arm behind his back in an attempt to make him a lefty.

A founding writer for Baseball Prospectus, **Rany Jazayerli** is a dermatologist who recently opened his own medical practice in St. Charles, Illinois. He has taken to life in the Chicago suburbs, where he lives with wife, Belsam, and daughter, Cedra. Just past her second birthday, Cedra has learned that the correct answer to the question "Who's the best pitcher in the world?" is something that sounds a lot like "Zakreinke."

Having moved from California to Chicago to the Washington, D.C. metro area, **Chris Kahrl** obviously didn't have Horace Greeley around to ask for directions. A University of Chicago grad, publishing professional, and founding member of Baseball Prospectus, she's ventured into unscripted territory in more ways than one. Although she feels badly for Jonah about the Nationals, she's really looking forward to that rare sighting of a healthy Nick Johnson.

Jonah Keri is a Los Angeles-based journalist, covering the stock market for a major daily newspaper. He interviews baseball's best and brightest in his series of Prospectus Q&A's, and will launch a new column, Prospectus Game of the Week, in 2005. Any time you see a random Expos reference in this book or on the BP Web site, that's a slam-dunk Jonah edit. With his beloved team now gone, he plans to tour the country with his amazing wife, Angèle, while having heated long-distance debates with Derek Zumsteg about The Transformers.

Dave Pease lives in San Diego and works for a wireless communications company. He enjoys hot weather, power tools, the Mars Volta, genuine Honda engineering, and looking back wistfully on the last decade, when the Dodgers were committed to spending lots of cash on mediocrity.

Dayn Perry is a writer for FoxSports.com. He lives with the World's Greatest Dog (TM) on Chicago's North Side, where he roots unabashedly for the Cardinals. He hails from Mississippi, which is famous for ranking last in everything having anything to do with education and cognitive achievement. This means that once you correct for "home park" Dayn has the highest adjusted IQ of anyone in the Prospectus family . . . or not.

Joe Sheehan is still a displaced New Yorker living outside of Los Angeles with his wife, Sophia, and their two cats. In addition to his work on the book, he writes a column for BP's Web site and makes regular appearances on ESPNews's HotList.

Nate Silver attended the University of Chicago, home of the first atomic bomb and the first Heisman Trophy winner, and has been stuck in the Second City ever since. A lifelong Tiger and Cub fan, Nate consoles himself by playing poker, watching *Law & Order* reruns, and visting the city's innumerable restaurants and watering holes. Nate is the Executive Vice President of BP's parent company, Prospectus Entertainment Ventures, LLC.

Keith Woolner holds a Master's Degree from Stanford University in Decision Analysis, and Bachelor's degrees from M.I.T., in Mathematics, Computer Science, and Management Science. He lives and works in Cary, North Carolina. He's convinced that it was his personal support as a fan that carried the Red Sox to victory in the World Series, though he concedes that Curt Schilling, David Ortiz, and Theo Epstein might have had a little something to do with it, too.

Derek Zumsteg is one of the internet's most trusted baseball columnists and a Baseball Prospectus writer since 1999. He invented the "run" statistic and as a Padres outfield prospect set a still-standing minor league record for consecutive games ejected for arguing strike calls (18). His ground-breaking guitar work presaged the "angular fuzz" movement of early 2001. Most importantly, he actively encourages readers not to take any part of author bios too seriously.

Author Dedications

Chris Kahrl: To Gary Huckabay, for starting the whole thing and inviting me in; to Jason Karegeannes, for being the world's best intern; and to the memory of Doug Pappas, a friend gifted with insight, integrity, and unerring sense of what's right. My writing and my life is better for having worked with all three of them.

Jonah Keri: This book is dedicated to my grandmothers, Irene Keri and Gertrude Levine, two of the kindest souls to ever walk the Earth.